Writing Resources in *Backpack Literature*

Chapters 1 to 26
"Writing Effectively" Feature

Each major chapter in Fiction, Poetry, and Drama includes a new feature, **"Writing Effectively,"** with material on writing specially focused on the chapter's topic.

Each chapter contains:
- **Writing Advice**   focused, practical advice on writing
- **Writing Checklist**   easy-to-use summaries of key points
- **Writing Assignment**   paper topic related to chapter theme or selections
- **More Topics for Writing**   additional paper topics related to chapter contents

Chapter 28
Writing About Literature

Reading Actively
Thinking About What You Have Read
Planning Your Essay
Prewriting: Discovering Ideas
Developing a Literary Argument
- Purpose
- Audience
- Topic
- Thesis
- Argument
- Organization

Writing a Rough Draft
Revising
Common Approaches to Writing About Literature
- Explication
- Analysis
- Comparison and Contrast
Format of Finished Paper

Chapter 29
Writing a Research Paper

Choosing a Topic
Finding Research Sources: Print & Online
Evaluating Sources
Using Visual Images
Organizing Your Research

Organizing Your Paper
Guarding Academic Integrity
Acknowledging Sources
Documenting Sources Using MLA Style

Reference Guide for MLA Citations, pages 1172–1178

Handy "how to" guide for works cited list

Sample Student Writing

Works in progress and finished essays show how to move from discovering ideas to a completed paper.

6 Student Papers
Drafts and Works in Progress

Brainstorming Techniques:
   On Frost's "Nothing Gold Can Stay," p. 1096

Rough Paper Draft:
   On Frost's "Nothing Gold Can Stay," p. 1105

Analysis Paper:
   On Bishop's "The Fish," p. 1128
   On Shakespeare's *Othello*, p. 1134

Argument Paper:
   On Frost's "Nothing Gold Can Stay," p. 1114

Comparison and Contrast Paper:
   On Faulkner's "A Rose for Emily" and
   Mansfield's "Miss Brill," p. 1142

Explication Papers:
   On Poe's "The Tell-Tale Heart," p. 1119
   On Frost's "Design," p. 1123

About the Authors

X. J. KENNEDY, after graduation from Seton Hall and Columbia, became a journalist second class in the Navy ("Actually, I was pretty eighth class"). His poems, some published in the *New Yorker*, were first collected in *Nude Descending a Staircase* (1961). Since then he has published seven more collections, including a volume of new and selected poems in 2007, several widely adopted literature and writing textbooks, and seventeen books for children, including two novels. He has taught at Michigan, North Carolina (Greensboro), California (Irvine), Wellesley, Tufts, and Leeds. Cited in *Bartlett's Familiar Quotations* and reprinted in some 200 anthologies, his verse has brought him a Guggenheim fellowship, a Lamont Award, a *Los Angeles Times* Book Prize, an award from the American Academy and Institute of Arts and Letters, an Aiken-Taylor prize, and the Award for Poetry for Children from the National Council of Teachers of English. He now lives in Lexington, Massachusetts, where he and his wife, Dorothy, have collaborated on five books and five children.

DANA GIOIA is a poet, critic, and teacher. Born in Los Angeles of Italian and Mexican ancestry, he attended Stanford and Harvard before taking a detour into business. ("Not many poets have a Stanford M.B.A., thank goodness!") After years of writing and reading late in the evenings after work, he quit a vice presidency to write and teach. He has published three collections of poetry, *Daily Horoscope* (1986), *The Gods of Winter* (1991), and *Interrogations at Noon* (2001), which won the American Book Award; an opera libretto, *Nosferatu* (2001); and three critical volumes including *Can Poetry Matter?* (1992), an influential study of poetry's place in contemporary America. Gioia has taught at Johns Hopkins, Sarah Lawrence, Wesleyan (Connecticut), Mercer, and Colorado College. He is also the co-founder of the summer poetry conference at West Chester University in Pennsylvania. In 2003 he became Chairman of the National Endowment for the Arts. He currently lives in Washington, D.C., with his wife, Mary, their two sons, and an uncontrollable cat.

(The surname Gioia is pronounced JOY-A. As some of you may have already guessed, *gioia* is the Italian word for joy.)

SECOND EDITION

Backpack
LITERATURE

An Introduction to Fiction, Poetry, Drama, and Writing

X. J. Kennedy
Dana Gioia

PEARSON

Longman

New York   Boston   San Francisco
London   Toronto   Sydney   Tokyo   Singapore   Madrid
Mexico City   Munich   Paris   Cape Town   Hong Kong   Montreal

Vice President and Editor in Chief: Joseph Terry
Senior Development Editor: Katharine Glynn
Executive Marketing Manager: Joyce Nilsen
Senior Supplements Editor: Donna Campion
Production Manager: Savoula Amanatidis
Project Coordination, Text Design, and Electronic Page Makeup: Nesbitt Graphics, Inc.
Cover Design Manager: John Callahan
Cover Image: "AWOL" © Ben Watson III
Photo Research: Linda Sykes
Senior Manufacturing Buyer: Roy L. Pickering, Jr.
Printer and Binder: Courier Corporation—Westford
Cover Printer: Coral Graphics Services, Inc.

Library of Congress Cataloging-in-Publication Data

Backpack literature : an introduction to fiction, poetry, drama, and writing / [edited by]
X.J. Kennedy, Dana Gioia. — 2nd ed.
    p. cm.
    Includes bibliographical references and index.
    ISBN-13: 978-0-205-55103-3 (alk. paper)
    ISBN-10: 0-205-55103-3 (alk. paper)
    1. Literature—Collections. I. Kennedy, X. J. II. Gioia, Dana.
    PN6014.B26 2008   2007036041
    808—dc22

Please visit us at http://www.ablongman.com/kennedy

ISBN-13: 978-0-205-55103-3
ISBN-10:   0-205-55103-3

    4 5 6 7 8 9 10—CRW—10 09

Contents

FICTION

1 Reading a Story 3

4 Setting 79

5 Tone and Style 115

Irony 139

WRITING EFFECTIVELY

6 Theme 158

7 Symbol   174

8 Stories for Further Reading 211

POETRY

9 Reading a Poem 311

10 Listening to a Voice 327

11 Words 352

14 Figures of Speech 399

Why Speak Figuratively? 399

18 Open Form 465

Prose Poetry 473

Seeing the Logic of Open Form Verse 474

WRITING EFFECTIVELY

19 Symbol 479

20 What Is Poetry?   491

21 Poems for Further Reading   493

DRAMA

29 Writing a Research Paper 1152

Preface

This is the second edition of *Backpack Literature*, a specially condensed version of *Literature: An Introduction to Fiction, Poetry, Drama, and Writing*. The primary aim of the book is to introduce college students to the appreciation and experience of literature in its major forms. The book also seeks to develop students' abilities to think critically and to communicate effectively through writing.

Both editors of this volume are writers. We believe that textbooks should not only be informative and accurate but also lively, accessible, and engaging. Our intent has always been to write a book that students will read eagerly and enjoy.

Backpack Literature offers selections and apparatus especially suited for instructors teaching a one-quarter or one-semester introductory class. It includes the core selections of our larger *Literature* books and much of the pedagogical material, particularly in the area of student writing. The book offers an alternative to the more extensive selections and critical coverage in the larger editions of *Literature*. Our purpose is to provide the introductory student a smaller, more portable, less expensive book.

Backpack Literature tries to help readers develop sensitivity to language, culture, and identity to lead them beyond the boundaries of their own selves and see the world through the eyes of others. This book is built on our conviction that great literature can enrich and enlarge the lives it touches. The edition's features are detailed below:

Quality Selections

- **37 Stories**—a roster of well-loved classics by authors such as Nathaniel Hawthorne, Edgar Allan Poe, and Flannery O'Connor, as well as accessible contemporary works by authors such as Margaret Atwood, T. Coraghessan Boyle, Sandra Cisneros, and Ha Jin.
- **237 Poems**—a mix of classic favorites with exciting contemporary work, including multiple poems by Shakespeare, Keats, Dickinson, Whitman, Frost, Plath, Hughes, and Bishop, to name a few, as well as works from contemporary masters such as Billy Collins, Rita Dove, Adrienne Rich, and Derek Walcott. Students will also have the chance to read exciting work from newer writers, such as Rhina Espaillat and Natasha Trethewey.
- **11 Plays**—classical tragedy by Sophocles (in Dudley Fitts and Robert Fitzgerald's beloved translation), Shakespeare's *Othello*, as well as the

essential modern dramatists such as Arthur Miller (*Death of a Salesman*) and August Wilson (*Fences*), supplemented with experimental theater by exciting new voices such as Milcha Sanchez-Scott.

Complete Writing Coverage

- **Writing Coverage in Every Major Chapter**—comprehensive introduction to composition and critical thinking, including easy-to-use checklists, exercises, and practical advice.
- **Topics for Writing in Every Major Chapter**—provide a rich source of ideas for writing papers.
- **Dedicated Chapters on Composition Process and Research Process**— concise, step-by-step coverage of the writing and research processes, amply illustrated with student writing examples.
- **Reference Guide for MLA Citations**—handy "how to" guide for works cited list.
- **Student Writing**—6 papers by real students with annotations, plus prewriting exercises and rough drafts provide credible examples of how to write about literature. Includes examples of argument, explication, analysis, and comparison/contrast.

What's New in the Second Edition

- **6 New Stories**—including works by Eudora Welty, O. Henry, Katherine Mansfield, Kurt Vonnegut, Jr., and Octavio Paz.
- **Over 50 New Poems**—including well-loved favorites by poets such as Gwendolyn Brooks, E. E. Cummings, Emily Dickinson, Walt Whitman, Robert Frost, A. E. Housman, Anne Sexton, and William Carlos Williams, as well as exciting new works by contemporary poets such as Rita Dove, Gina Valdés, newly appointed U.S. Poet Laureate Charles Simic, Marisa de los Santos, and Suji Kwock Kim.
- **3 New Plays**—including August Wilson's masterful *Fences*, as well as a scene from Christopher Marlowe's *Doctor Faustus*, and David Ives's hilarious one act play *Sure Thing*.
- **New "Illustrated Shakespeare"**—over a dozen attractive production photos illustrating *Othello*'s major scenes and characters help to visualize the action of the play and make it more accessible and engaging to today's students.
- **Newly Revised Chapter on Writing, Literary Argument, and Critical Thinking**—including step-by-step discussion of the writing process and developing a literary argument, illustrated by student papers and writing excerpts.

- **Updated Chapter on Writing a Research Paper**—including critical coverage of finding and evaluating print and online sources, as well as acknowledging and documenting sources.
- **New Design**—features a new typeface with more headings and checklists for easier reference.

Texts and Dates

Every effort has been made to supply each selection in its most accurate text and (where necessary) in a lively, faithful translation. For the reader who wishes to know when a work was written, at the right of each title appears the date of its first publication in book form. If a work was composed much earlier than its first book publication, parentheses have been added around its date.

Resources for Students and Instructors

For Students

MyLiteratureLab.com

MyLiteratureLab.com is a Web-based state-of-the-art interactive learning system designed to accompany the Kennedy/Gioia *Literature* series and help students in their literature course. It adds a new dimension to the study of literature with Longman Lectures—evocative, richly illustrated audio readings along with advice on how to read, interpret, and write about literary works from our roster of Longman authors (including X. J. Kennedy). This powerful program also features Diagnostic Tests, Interactive Readings with clickable prompts, film clips of selections in *Literature*, sample student papers, Literature Timelines, Avoiding Plagiarism, Research Navigator™ research tools, and Exchange, an electronic instructor/peer feedback tool. *MyLiteratureLab.com* can be delivered within Course Compass, Web CT, or Blackboard course management systems, enabling instructors to administer their entire course online.

For Instructors

Instructor's Manual

A separate *Instructor's Manual* is available to instructors. We actually write the manual ourselves, and we work hard to make it as interesting, lively, and informed as the parent text. It offers commentary and teaching ideas for every selection in the book. It also contains additional commentary, debate, qualifications and information—including scores of classroom ideas—from over one hundred teachers and authors. As you will see, our *Instructor's Manual* is no ordinary book.

Teaching Composition with Literature

For instructors who either use *Backpack Literature* in expository writing courses or have a special emphasis on writing in their literature courses, there is an invaluable supplement, *Teaching Composition with Literature: 101 Writing Assignments from College Instructors*. Edited by Dana Gioia and Patricia Wagner, *Teaching Composition with Literature* collects proven writing assignments and classroom exercises from scores of instructors across North America. Each assignment or exercise uses one or more selections included in the larger *Literature* book as its departure point, but a number of the exercises focus on works in this smaller backpack edition. A great many instructors have enthusiastically shared their best writing assignments for *Teaching Composition with Literature*. We encourage you to ask your sales representative for this book.

Other Supplements Available to Instructors

Penguin Discount Novel Program

Longman is proud to offer a variety of Penguin paperbacks to students at a significant discount when packaged with any Longman title. Titles include authors as diverse as Toni Morrison, Mary Shelley, or Shakespeare. To review the complete list of titles, visit our Web site: *http://www.ablongman.com/penguin*.

Video Program

An impressive selection of videotapes is available to qualified adopters, including selections from Shakespeare, Plath, Pound, and Walker.

Contact Us

For examination copies of any of these books, CDs, videos, and programs, please contact your Allyn & Bacon/Longman sales representative, or write to Literature Marketing Manager, Longman Publishers, 51 Madison Avenue, New York, NY 10010. For examination copies only, go to our Web site at *http://www.ablongman.com*, e-mail us at *exam.copies@ablongman.com*, or call (800) 922-0579.

Thanks

The collaboration necessary to create this book goes far beyond the partnership of its two editors. *Backpack Literature* has been shaped by wisdom and advice from instructors who teach shorter introductory literature courses.

Deep thanks to the instructors who reviewed and commented on the preliminary plans for this book, including: M. P. Cavanaugh, Saginaw Valley

State University; Linda DeFelice, Gloucester Community College; Linda Fretterd Earls, Chesapeake College; Laurie Fitzgerald, Madison Area Technical College; Nate Gordon, Kishwaukee College; Patricia C. Knight, Amarillo College; Walter Lowe, Green River Community College; Elaine Osio, California State University at Los Angeles; Dee Seligman, Cañada College; and Patricia Jo Teel, Victor Valley College.

We would like to thank our publisher's editorial and sales team, particularly Joseph Terry, Katharine H. Glynn, and Joyce Nilsen, who directed the creation and development of this new edition. Savoula Amanatidis and Lois Lombardo managed the complex job of production of the book from manuscript to the final printed form. We deeply appreciate their professionalism and grace working under tight deadlines with changing copy. Virginia Creeden handled the tasking job of permissions.

Mary Gioia managed the editing and execution of *Backpack Literature*. We are grateful for her capable hand and careful eye. Past debts that will never be repaid are outstanding to hundreds of instructors named in prefaces past and to Dorothy M. Kennedy for their work over the years in shaping the *Literature* anthology.

X. J. K. AND D. G.

FICTION

Ernest Hemingway at his desk in Sun Valley, Idaho, c. 1940

Here is a story, one of the shortest ever written and one of the most difficult to forget:

> A woman is sitting in her old, shuttered house. She knows that she is alone in the whole world; every other thing is dead.
>
> The doorbell rings.

In a brief space this small tale of terror, credited to Thomas Bailey Aldrich, makes itself memorable. It sets a promising scene—is this a haunted house?—introduces a character, and places her in a strange and intriguing situation. Although in reading a story that is over so quickly we don't come to know the character well, for a moment we enter her thoughts and begin to share her feelings. Then something amazing happens. The story leaves us to wonder: who or what rang that bell?

Like many richer, longer, more complicated stories, this one, in its few words, engages the imagination. Evidently, how much a story contains and suggests doesn't depend on its size. In the opening chapter of this book, we will look first at other brief stories—examples of three ancient kinds of fiction, a fable, a parable, and a tale—then at a contemporary short story. We will consider the elements of fiction one after another. By seeing a few short stories broken into their parts, you will come to a keener sense of how a story is put together. Not all stories are short, of course; later in the book, you will find a chapter on reading long stories and novels.

All in all, here are thirty-seven stories. Among them, may you find at least a few you'll enjoy and care to remember.

1
Reading a Story

After the shipwreck that marooned him on his desert island, Robinson Crusoe, in the novel by Daniel Defoe, stood gazing over the water where pieces of cargo from his ship were floating by. Along came "two shoes, not mates." It is the qualification *not mates* that makes the detail memorable. We could well believe that a thing so striking and odd must have been seen, and not invented. But in truth Defoe, like other masters of the art of fiction, had the power to make us believe his imaginings. Borne along by the art of the storyteller, we trust what we are told, even though the story may be sheer fantasy.

Fiction (from the Latin *fictio*, "a shaping, a counterfeiting") is a name for stories not entirely factual, but at least partially shaped, made up, imagined. It is true that in some fiction, such as a historical novel, a writer draws on factual information in presenting scenes, events, and characters. But the factual information in a historical novel, unlike that in a history book, is of secondary importance. Many firsthand accounts of the American Civil War were written by men who had fought in it, but few eyewitnesses give us so keen a sense of actual life on the battlefront as the author of *The Red Badge of Courage*, Stephen Crane, born after the war was over. In fiction, the "facts" may or may not be true, and a story is none the worse for their being entirely imaginary. We expect from fiction a sense of how people act, not an authentic chronicle of how, at some past time, a few people acted.

As children, we used to read (if we were lucky and formed the habit) to steep ourselves in romance, mystery, and adventure. As adults, we still do: at an airport, while waiting for a flight, we pass the time with some newsstand paperback full of fast action and brisk dialogue. Certain fiction, of course, calls for closer attention. To read a novel by the Russian master Dostoevsky instead of a James Bond thriller is somewhat like playing chess instead of a game of tic-tac-toe. Not that a great novel does not provide entertainment. In fact, it may offer more deeply satisfying entertainment than a novel of violence and soft-core pornography, in which stick figures connive, go to bed, and kill one another in accord with some market-tested formula. Reading literary fiction (as distinguished from fiction as a commercial product—the formula kind of spy, detective, Western, romance, or science fiction story), we are not necessarily led on by the promise of thrills; we do not keep reading mainly to find out what happens next. Indeed, a literary story might even disclose in its opening lines everything that happened, then spend the rest of its length revealing what that happening meant. Reading literary fiction is no merely passive activity, but one that demands both attention and insight-lending participation. In return, it offers rewards. In some works of literary fiction we see more deeply into the minds and hearts of the characters than we ever see into those of our family, our close friends, our lovers—or even ourselves.

Fable, Parable, and Tale

Modern literary fiction in English has been dominated by two forms: the novel and the short story. The two have many elements in common. Perhaps we will be able to define the short story more meaningfully—for it has traits more essential than just a particular length—if first, for comparison, we consider some related varieties of fiction: the fable and the tale. Ancient forms whose origins date back to the time of word-of-mouth storytelling, the fable and the tale are relatively simple in structure; in them we can plainly see elements also found in the short story (and in the novel). To begin, here is a **fable**: a brief story that sets forth some pointed statement of truth. The writer, W. Somerset Maugham (1874–1965), an English novelist and playwright, is retelling an Arabian folk story. (Samarra, by the way, is a city sixty miles from Baghdad.)

W. Somerset Maugham

The Appointment in Samarra   1933

Death speaks: There was a merchant in Baghdad who sent his servant to market to buy provisions and in a little while the servant came back, white and trembling, and said, Master, just now when I was in the marketplace I was jostled by a woman in the crowd and when I turned I saw it was Death that jostled me. She looked at me and made a threatening gesture; now, lend me your horse, and I will ride away from this city and avoid my fate. I will go to Samarra and there Death will not find me. The merchant lent him his horse, and the servant mounted it, and he dug his spurs in its flanks and as fast as the horse could gallop he went. Then the merchant went down to the marketplace and he saw me standing in the crowd and he came to me and said, Why did you make a threatening gesture to my servant when you saw him this morning? That was not a threatening gesture, I said, it was only a start of surprise. I was astonished to see him in Baghdad, for I had an appointment with him tonight in Samarra.

This brief story seems practically all skin and bones; that is, it contains little decoration. For in a fable everything leads directly to the **moral**, or message, sometimes stated at the end (moral: "Haste makes waste"). In "The Appointment in Samarra" the moral isn't stated outright, it is merely implied. How would you state it in your own words?

You are probably acquainted with some of the fables credited to the Greek slave Aesop (about 620–560 B.C.), whose stories seem designed to teach lessons about human life. Such is the fable of "The Goose That Laid the Golden Eggs," in which the owner of this marvelous creature slaughters her to get at the great treasure that he thinks is inside her, but finds nothing (implied moral: "Be content with what you have"). Another is the fable of "The Tortoise and the Hare" (implied moral: "Slow, steady plodding wins the race"). The characters in a fable may be talking animals (as in many of Aesop's fables), inanimate objects, or people and supernatural beings (as in "The Appointment in Samarra"). Whoever they may be, these characters are merely sketched, not greatly developed. Evidently, it would not have helped Maugham's fable to put across its point if he had portrayed the merchant, the servant, and Death in fuller detail. A more elaborate description of the marketplace would not have improved the story. Probably, such a description would strike us as unnecessary and distracting. By its very bareness and simplicity, a fable fixes itself—and its message—in memory.

Aesop

The North Wind and the Sun

6th century B.C.

TRANSLATED BY V. S. VERNON JONES

Very little is known with certainty about the man called Aesop (sixth century B.C.), but several accounts and many traditions survive from antiquity. According to the Greek historian Herodotus, Aesop was a slave on the island of Samos. He gained great fame from his fables, but he somehow met his death at the hands of the people of Delphi. The later historian Plutarch claims the Delphians hurled the author to his death from a cliff as a punishment for sacrilege. According to a less reliable tradition, Aesop was an ugly and misshapen man who charmed and amused people with his stories. No one knows if Aesop himself wrote down any of his fables, but they circulated widely in ancient Greece and were praised by Plato, Aristotle, and numerous other authors. His short and witty tales with their incisive morals influenced innumerable later writers. For two-and-a-half millennia, Aesop's fables have maintained constant popularity.

A dispute arose between the North Wind and the Sun, each claiming that he was stronger than the other. At last they agreed to try their powers upon a traveler, to see which could soonest strip him of his cloak. The North Wind had the first try; and, gathering up all his force for the attack, he came whirling furiously down upon the man, and caught up his cloak as though he would wrest it from him by one single effort: but the harder he blew, the more closely the man wrapped it round himself. Then came the turn of the Sun. At first he beamed gently upon the traveler, who soon unclasped his cloak and walked on with it hanging loosely about his shoulders: then he shone forth in his full strength, and the man, before he had gone many steps, was glad to throw his cloak right off and complete his journey more lightly clad.

Moral: Persuasion is better than force.

QUESTIONS

1. Describe the different personalities of the North Wind and the Sun.
2. What was ineffective about the North Wind's method for attempting to strip the man of his cloak?
3. Why was the Sun successful in his attempts? What did he do differently than the North Wind?
4. What purpose does the human serve in this dispute?
5. Explain the closing moral in terms of the fable.

We are so accustomed to the phrase *Aesop's fables* that we might almost start to think the two words inseparable, but in fact there have been fabulists (creators or writers of fables) in virtually every culture throughout recorded history. Here is another fable from many centuries ago, this time from India.

Bidpai

The Camel and His Friends   c. 4th century

RETOLD IN ENGLISH BY ARUNDHATI KHANWALKAR

The Panchatantra (Pañca-tantra), a collection of beast fables from India, is attributed to its narrator, a sage named Bidpai, who is a legendary figure about whom almost nothing is known for certain. The Panchatantra, which means the Five Chapters in Sanskrit, is based on earlier oral folklore. The collection was composed some time between 100 B.C. and 500 A.D. in a Sanskrit original now lost, and is primarily known through an Arabic version of the eighth century and a twelfth-century Hebrew translation, which is the source of most Western versions of the tales. Other translations spread the fables as far as central Europe, Asia, and Indonesia.

Like many collections of fables, The Panchatantra is a frame tale, with an introduction containing verse and aphorisms spoken by an eighty-year-old Brahmin teacher named Vishnusharman, who tells the stories over a period of six months for the edification of three foolish princes named Rich-Power, Fierce-Power, and Endless-Power. The stories are didactic, teaching niti, the wise conduct of life, and artha, practical wisdom that stresses cleverness and self-reliance above more altruistic virtues.

Once a merchant was leading a caravan of heavily-laden camels through a jungle when one of them, overcome by fatigue, collapsed. The merchant decided to leave the camel in the jungle and go on his way. Later, when the camel recovered his strength, he realized that he was alone in a strange jungle. Fortunately there was plenty of grass, and he survived.

One day the king of the jungle, a lion, arrived along with his three friends—a leopard, a fox, and a crow. The king lion wondered what the camel was doing in the jungle! He came near the camel and asked how he, a creature of the desert, had ended up in the hostile jungle. The camel tearfully explained what happened. The lion took pity on him and said, "You have nothing to fear now. Henceforth, you are under my protection and can stay with us." The camel began to live happily in the jungle.

Then one day the lion was wounded in a fight with an elephant. He retired to his cave and stayed there for several days. His friends came to offer their sympathy. They tried to catch prey for the hungry lion but failed. The camel had no problem as he lived on grass while the others were starving.

The fox came up with a plan. He secretly went to the lion and suggested that the camel be sacrificed for the good of the others. The lion got furious, "I can never kill an animal who is under my protection."

The fox humbly said, "But Lord, you have provided us food all the time. If any one of us voluntarily offered himself to save your life, I hope you won't mind!" The hungry lion did not object to that and agreed to take the offer.

The fox went back to his companions and said, "Friends, our king is dying of starvation. Let us go and beg him to eat one of us. It is the least we can do for such a noble soul."

So they went to the king and the crow offered his life. The fox interrupted, and said, "You are a small creature, the master's hunger will hardly be appeased by eating you. May I humbly offer my life to satisfy my master's hunger."

The leopard stepped forward and said, "You are no bigger than the crow, it is me whom our master should eat."

The foolish camel thought, "Everyone has offered to lay down their lives for the king, but he has not hurt any one. It is now my turn to offer myself." So he stepped forward and said, "Stand aside friend leopard, the king and you have close family ties. It is me whom the master must eat."

An ominous silence greeted the camel's offer. Then the king gladly said, "I accept your offer, O noble camel." And in no time he was killed by the three rogues, the false friends.

Moral: Be careful in choosing your friends.

Another traditional form of storytelling is the **parable**. Like the fable, a parable is a brief narrative that teaches a moral; but unlike the fable, its plot is plausibly realistic, and the main characters are human rather than anthropomorphized animals or natural forces. The other key difference is that parables usually possess a more mysterious and suggestive tone. A fable customarily ends by explicitly stating its moral, but parables often present their morals implicitly, and their meanings can be open to several interpretations.

In the Western tradition, the literary conventions of the parable are largely based on the brief stories told by Jesus in his preaching. The forty-three parables recounted in the four gospels reveal how frequently he used the form to teach. Jesus designed his parables to have two levels of meaning—a literal story that could immediately be understood by the crowds he addressed and a deeper meaning fully comprehended only by his disciples, an inner circle who understood the nature of his ministry. (You can see the richness of interpretations suggested by Jesus' parables by reading and analyzing "The Parable of the Prodigal Son" from St. Luke's gospel, which appears in Chapter 6.) The parable was also widely used by Eastern philosophers. The Taoist sage Chuang Tzu often portrayed the principles of Tao—which he called the "Way of Nature"—in witty parables like the following one, traditionally titled "Independence."

Chuang Tzu

Independence   Chou Dynasty (4th century B.C.)

TRANSLATED BY HERBERT GILES

Chuang Chou, usually known as Chuang Tzu (approximately 390–365 B.C.), was one of the great philosophers of the Chou period in China. He was born in the Sung feudal state and received an excellent education. Unlike most educated men, however, Chuang Tzu did not seek public office or political power. Influenced by Taoist philosophy, he believed that individuals should transcend their desire for success and wealth, as well as their fear of failure and poverty. True freedom, he maintained, came from escaping the distractions of worldly affairs. Chuang Tzu's writings have been particularly praised for their combination of humor and wisdom. His parables and stories are classics of Chinese literature.

Chuang Tzu was one day fishing, when the Prince of Ch'u sent two high officials to interview him, saying that his Highness would be glad of Chuang Tzu's assistance in the administration of his government. The latter quietly fished on, and without looking round, replied, "I have heard that in the State of Ch'u there is a sacred tortoise, which has been dead three thousand years, and which the prince keeps packed up in a box on the altar in his ancestral shrine. Now do you think that tortoise would rather be dead and have its remains thus honoured, or be alive and wagging its tail in the mud?" The two officials answered that no doubt it would rather be alive and wagging its tail in the mud; whereupon Chuang Tzu cried out "Begone! I too elect to remain wagging my tail in the mud."

QUESTIONS

1. What part of this story is the exposition? How many sentences does Chuang Tzu use to set up the dramatic situation?
2. Why does the protagonist change the subject and mention the sacred tortoise? Why doesn't he answer the request directly and immediately? Does it serve any purpose that Chuang Tzu makes the officials answer a question to which he knows the answer?
3. What does this story tell us about the protagonist Chuang Tzu's personality?

The name *tale* (from the Old English *talu,* "speech") is sometimes applied to any story, whether short or long, true or fictitious. *Tale* being a more evocative name than *story,* writers sometimes call their stories "tales" as if to imply something handed down from the past. But defined in a more limited sense, a **tale** is a story, usually short, that sets forth strange and wonderful events in more or less bare summary, without detailed character-drawing. "Tale" is pretty much synonymous with "yarn," for it implies a story in which the goal is revelation of the marvelous rather than revelation of character. In the English folktale "Jack and the Beanstalk," we take away a more vivid impression of the miraculous beanstalk and the giant who dwells at its top than of Jack's mind or personality. Because such venerable stories were told aloud before someone set them down in writing, the story-tellers had to limit themselves to brief descriptions. Probably spoken around a fire or hearth, such a tale tends to be less complicated and less closely detailed than a story written for the printed page, whose reader can linger over it. Still, such tales *can* be complicated. It is not merely greater length that makes a short story different from a tale or a fable: a mark of a short story is a fully delineated character.

Even modern tales favor supernatural or fantastic events: for instance, the **tall tale**, that variety of folk story which recounts the deeds of a superhero (Paul Bunyan, John Henry, Sally Ann Thunder) or of the storyteller. If the storyteller is telling about his or her own imaginary experience, the bragging yarn is usually told with a straight face to listeners who take pleasure in scoffing at it. Although the **fairy tale**, set in a world of magic and enchantment, is sometimes the work of a modern author (notably Hans Christian Andersen), well-known examples are those German folktales that probably originated in the Middle Ages, collected by the brothers Grimm. The label *fairy tale* is something of an English misnomer, for in the Grimm stories, though witches and goblins abound, fairies are a minority.

Jakob and Wilhelm Grimm

Godfather Death
1812 (from oral tradition)

TRANSLATED BY DANA GIOIA

Jakob Grimm (1785–1863) and Wilhelm Grimm (1786–1859), brothers and scholars, were born near Frankfurt am Main, Germany. For most of their lives they worked together—lived together, too, even when in 1825 Wilhelm married. In 1838, as librarians, they began toiling on their Deutsch Wörterbuch, or German dictionary, a vast project that was to outlive them by a century. (It was completed only in 1960.) In 1840 King Friedrich Wilhelm IV appointed both brothers to the Royal Academy of Sciences, and both taught at the University of Berlin for the rest of their days. Although

JAKOB AND WILHELM GRIMM

Jakob had a side career as a diplomat, wrote a great Deutsche Grammatik, or German grammar (1819–37), and propounded Grimm's Law (an explanation of shifts in consonant sounds, of interest to students of linguistics), the name Grimm is best known to us for that splendid collection of ancient German folk stories we call Grimm's Fairy Tales—in German, Kinder- und Hausmärchen ("Childhood and Household Tales," 1812–15). This classic work spread German children's stories around the world. Many tales we hear early in life were collected by the Grimms: "Hansel and Gretel," "Snow White and the Seven Dwarfs," "Rapunzel," "Tom Thumb," "Little Red Riding Hood," "Rumpelstiltskin." Versions of some of these tales had been written down as early as the sixteenth century, but mainly the brothers relied on the memories of Hessian peasants who recited the stories aloud for them.

A poor man had twelve children and had to work day and night just to give them bread. Now when the thirteenth came into the world, he did not know what to do, so he ran out onto the main highway intending to ask the first one he met to be the child's godfather.

The first person he met was the good Lord God, who knew very well what was weighing on the man's heart. And He said to him, "Poor man, I am sorry for you. I will hold your child at the baptismal font. I will take care of him and fill his days with happiness."

The man asked, "Who are you?"

"I am the good Lord."

"Then I don't want you as godfather. You give to the rich and let the poor starve." 5

The man spoke thus because he did not know how wisely God portions out wealth and poverty. So he turned away from the Lord and went on.

Then the Devil came up to him and said, "What are you looking for? If you take me as your child's sponsor, I will give him gold heaped high and wide and all the joys of this world."

The man asked, "Who are you?"

"I am the Devil."

"Then I don't want you as godfather," said the man. "You trick men   10 and lead them astray."

He went on, and bone-thin Death strode up to him and said, "Choose me as godfather."

The man asked, "Who are you?"

"I am Death, who makes all men equal."

Then the man said, "You are the right one. You take the rich and the poor without distinction. You will be the godfather."

Death answered, "I will make your child rich and famous. Whoever   15 has me as a friend shall lack for nothing."

The man said, "The baptism is next Sunday. Be there on time."

Death appeared just as he had promised and stood there as a proper godfather.

When the boy had grown up, his godfather walked in one day and said to come along with him. Death led him out into the woods, showed him an herb, and said, "Now you are going to get your christening present. I am making you a famous doctor. When you are called to a patient, I will always appear to you. If I stand next to the sick person's head, you may speak boldly that you will make him healthy again. Give him some of this herb, and he will recover. But if you see me standing by the sick person's feet, then he is mine. You must say that nothing can be done and that no doctor in the world can save him. But beware of using the herb against my will, or it will turn out badly for you."

It was not long before the young man was the most famous doctor in the whole world. "He needs only to look at the sick person," everyone said, "and then he knows how things stand—whether the patient will get well again or whether he must die." People came from far and wide to bring their sick and gave him so much gold that he quickly became quite rich.

Now it soon happened that the king grew ill, and the doctor was sum-   20 moned to say whether a recovery was possible. But when he came to the bed, Death was standing at the sick man's feet, and now no herb grown could save him.

"If I cheat Death this one time," thought the doctor, "he will be angry, but since I am his godson, he will turn a blind eye, so I will risk it." He took up the sick man and turned him around so that his head was now where Death stood. Then he gave the king some of the herb. The king recovered and grew healthy again.

But Death then came to the doctor with a dark and angry face and threatened him with his finger. "You have hoodwinked me this time," he said. "And I will forgive you once because you are my godson. But if you try such a thing again, it will be your neck, and I will take you away with me."

Not long after, the king's daughter fell into a serious illness. She was his only child, and he wept day and night until his eyes went blind. He let it be known that whoever saved her from death would become her husband and inherit the crown.

When the doctor came to the sick girl's bed, he saw Death standing at her feet. He should have remembered his godfather's warning, but the princess's great beauty and the happy prospect of becoming her husband so infatuated him that he flung all caution to the wind. He didn't notice that Death stared at him angrily or that he raised his hand and shook his bony fist. The doctor picked up the sick girl and turned her around to place her head where her feet had been. He gave her the herb, and right away her cheeks grew rosy and she stirred again with life.

When Death saw that he had been cheated out of his property a second time, he strode with long steps up to the doctor and said, "It is all over for you. Now it's your turn." Death seized him so firmly with his ice-cold hand that the doctor could not resist. He led him into an underground cavern. There the doctor saw thousands and thousands of candles burning in endless rows. Some were tall, others medium-sized, and others quite small. Every moment some went out and others lit up, so that the tiny flames seemed to jump to and fro in perpetual motion. 25

"Look," said Death, "these are the life lights of mankind. The tall ones belong to children, the middle-size ones to married people in the prime of life, and the short ones to the very old. But sometimes even children and young people have only a short candle."

"Show me my life light," said the doctor, assuming it would be very tall.

Death pointed to a small stub that seemed about to flicker out.

"Oh, dear godfather!" cried the terrified doctor. "Light a new candle for me. If you love me, do it, so that I may enjoy my life, become king, and marry the beautiful princess."

"That I cannot do," Death replied. "One candle must first go out before a new one is lighted." 30

"Then put my old one on top of a new candle that will keep burning when the old one goes out," begged the doctor.

Death acted as if he were going to grant the wish and picked up a tall new candle. But because he wanted revenge, he deliberately fumbled in placing the new candle, and the stub toppled over and went out. The doctor immediately dropped to the ground and fell into the hands of Death.

Plot

Like a fable, the Grimm brothers' tale seems stark in its lack of detail and in the swiftness of its telling. Compared with the fully portrayed characters of many modern stories, the characters of father, son, king, princess, and even Death himself seem hardly more than stick figures. It may have been that to draw ample characters would not have contributed to the storytellers' design; that, indeed, to have done so would have been inartistic. Yet "Godfather Death" is a compelling story. By what methods does it arouse and sustain our interest?

From the opening sentence of the tale, we watch the unfolding of a **dramatic situation**: a person is involved in some conflict. First, this character is a poor man with children to feed, in conflict with the world; very soon, we find him in conflict with God and with the Devil besides. Drama in fiction occurs in any clash of wills, desires, or powers—whether it be a conflict of character against character, character against society, character against some natural force, or, as in "Godfather Death," character against some supernatural entity.

Like any shapely tale, "Godfather Death" has a beginning, a middle, and an end. In fact, it is unusual to find a story so clearly displaying the elements of structure that critics have found in many classic works of fiction and drama. The tale begins with an **exposition**: the opening portion that sets the scene (if any), introduces the main characters, tells us what happened before the story opened, and provides any other background information that we need in order to understand and care about the events to follow. In "Godfather Death," the exposition is brief—all in the opening paragraph. The middle section of the story begins with Death's giving the herb to the boy and his warning not to defy him. This moment introduces a new conflict (a **complication**), and by this time it is clear that the son and not the father is to be the central human character of the story. Death's godson is the principal person who strives: the **protagonist** (a better term than **hero**, for it may apply equally well to a central character who is not especially brave or virtuous).

The **suspense**, the pleasurable anxiety we feel that heightens our attention to the story, inheres in our wondering how it will all turn out. Will the doctor triumph over Death? Even though we suspect, early in the story, that the doctor stands no chance against such a superhuman **antagonist**, we want to see for ourselves the outcome of his defiance. A storyteller can try to incite our anticipation by giving us some **foreshadowing** or indication of events to come. In "Godfather Death" the foreshadowings are apparent in Death's warnings ("But if you try such a thing again, it will be your neck"). When the doctor defies his godfather for the first time—when he saves the king—we have a **crisis**, a moment of high tension. The tension is momentarily resolved when Death lets him off. Then an even greater crisis—the turning point in the action—occurs with the doctor's second defiance in restoring the princess to life. In the last section of the story, with the doctor in the underworld, events come to a **climax**, the moment of greatest tension at which the outcome is to be decided, when the terrified doctor begs for a new candle. Will Death grant him one? Will he live, become king, and marry the princess? The outcome or **conclusion**—also called the **resolution** or **dénouement** ("the untying of the knot")—quickly follows as Death allows the little candle to go out.

Such a structure of events arising out of a conflict may be called the plot of the story. Like many terms used in literary discussion, *plot* is blessed with several meanings. Sometimes it refers simply to the events in a story. In this book, **plot** will mean the artistic arrangement of those events. Different arrangements of the same material are possible. A writer might decide to tell of the events in chronological order, beginning with the earliest; or he or she might open the story with the last event, then tell what led up to it. Sometimes a writer chooses to skip rapidly over the exposition and begin *in medias res* (Latin, "in the midst of things"), first presenting some exciting or significant moment, then filling in what happened earlier. This method is by no means a modern invention: Homer begins the *Odyssey* with his hero mysteriously late in returning from war and his son searching for him; John Milton's *Paradise Lost* opens with Satan already defeated in his revolt against the Lord. A device useful to writers for filling in what happened earlier is the **flashback** (or **retrospect**), a scene relived in a character's memory.

To have a plot, a story does not need an intense, sustained conflict such as we find in "Godfather Death," a tale especially economical in its structure of crisis, climax, and conclusion. Although a highly dramatic story may tend to assume such a clearly recognizable structure, many contemporary writers avoid it, considering it too contrived and arbitrary. In commercial fiction, in which exciting conflict is everything and in which the writer has to manufacture all possible suspense, such a structure is often obvious. In popular detective, Western, and adventure novels; in juvenile fiction (the perennial Hardy Boys and Nancy Drew books); and in popular series on television (soap operas, police and hospital dramas, mysteries), it is often easy to recognize crisis, climax, and conclusion. The presence of these elements does not necessarily indicate inferior literature (as "Godfather Death" shows); yet when they are reduced to parts of a formula, the result may seem stale and contrived.

The Short Story

The teller of a tale relies heavily on the method of **summary**: terse, general narration as in "Godfather Death" ("It was not long before the young man was the most famous doctor in the whole world"). But in a **short story**, a form more realistic than the tale and of modern origin, the writer usually presents the main events in greater fullness. Fine writers of short stories, although they may use summary at times (often to give some portion of a story less emphasis), are skilled in rendering a **scene**: a vivid or dramatic moment described in enough detail to create the illusion that the reader is practically there. Avoiding long summary, they try to *show* rather than simply to *tell*, as if following Mark Twain's advice to authors: "Don't say, 'The old lady screamed.' Bring her on and let her scream."

A short story is more than just a sequence of happenings. A finely wrought short story has the richness and conciseness of an excellent lyric poem. Spontaneous and natural as the finished story may seem, the writer has crafted it so artfully that there is meaning in even seemingly casual speeches and apparently trivial details. If we skim it hastily, skipping the descriptive passages, we miss significant parts. Some literary short stories, unlike commercial fiction in which the main interest is in physical action or conflict, tell of an **epiphany**: some moment of insight, discovery, or revelation by which a character's life, or view of life, is greatly altered. (For such moments in fiction, see the stories in this book by James Joyce, John Steinbeck, and Joyce Carol Oates.) Other short stories tell of a character initiated into experience or maturity: one such **story of initiation** is William Faulkner's "Barn Burning" (Chapter 5), in which a boy finds it necessary to defy his father and suddenly to grow into manhood. Less obviously dramatic, perhaps, than "Godfather Death," such a story may be no less powerful.

The fable and the tale are ancient forms; the short story is of more recent origin. In the nineteenth century, writers of fiction were encouraged by a large, literate audience of middle-class readers who wanted to see their lives reflected in faithful mirrors. Skillfully representing ordinary life, many writers perfected the art of the short story: in Russia, Anton Chekhov; in France, Honoré de Balzac, Gustave Flaubert, and Guy de Maupassant; and in America, Nathaniel Hawthorne and Edgar Allan Poe (although the Americans seem less fond of everyday life than of dream and fantasy). It would be false to claim that, in passing from the fable and the tale to the short story, fiction has made a triumphant progress; or to claim that, because short stories are modern, they are superior to fables and tales. Fable, tale, and short story are distinct forms, each achieving its own effects. (Incidentally, fable and tale are far from being extinct today: you can find many recent examples.) In the hands of Jorge Luis Borges, Joyce Carol Oates, Gabriel García Márquez, and other innovative writers, the conventions of the short story underwent great changes in the second half of the twentieth century; and, at present, stories of epiphany and initiation are not as prevalent as they once were.

But let us begin with a contemporary short story whose protagonist *does* undergo an initiation into maturity. To notice the difference between a short story and a tale, you may find it helpful to compare John Updike's "A & P" with "Godfather Death." Although Updike's short story is centuries distant from the Grimm tale in its method of telling and in its setting, you may be reminded of "Godfather Death" in the main character's dramatic situation. To defend a young woman, a young man has to defy his mentor—here, the boss of a supermarket! In so doing, he places himself in jeopardy. Updike has the protagonist tell his own story, amply and with humor. How does it differ from a tale?

John Updike

A & P   1961

John Updike, born in Pennsylvania in 1932, received his B.A. from Harvard, then went to Oxford to study drawing and fine art. In the mid-1950s he worked on the staff of the New Yorker, *at times doing errands for the aged James Thurber. Although he left the magazine to become a full-time writer, Updike has continued to supply it with memorable stories, witty light verse, and searching reviews. A famously prolific writer, he has published more than fifty books.*

JOHN UPDIKE

Updike is best known as a hardworking, versatile, highly productive writer of fiction. For his novel The Centaur *(1963) he received a National Book Award, and for* Rabbit Is Rich *(1982) a Pulitzer Prize and an American Book Award. The fourth and last Rabbit Angstrom novel,* Rabbit at Rest *(1990), won him a second Pulitzer.* Licks of Love *(2000), a collection of stories, contains a long footnote to the tetralogy, a novella called "Rabbit Remembered," in which Rabbit Angstrom's friends reminisce about him after his death.*

Updike is one of the few Americans ever to be awarded both the National Medal of Arts (1989) and the National Humanities Medal (2003)—the nation's highest honors in each respective field. His many other novels include The Witches of Eastwick *(1984), made into a successful film starring Jack Nicholson;* S. *(1988), partly inspired by Nathaniel Hawthorne's* The Scarlet Letter; Gertrude and Claudius *(2000), derived from Shakespeare's* Hamlet; *and* Terrorist *(2006), Updike's twenty-second novel. Compilations of his work include* Collected Poems *(1993),* The Complete Henry Bech *(2001),* The Early Stories, 1953–1975 *(2003, PEN/Faulkner Award for Fiction), and* Still Looking: Essays on American Art *(2005).*

Almost unique among living American writers, Updike has moved back and forth successfully among a variety of literary genres: light verse, serious poetry, drama, criticism, children's books, novels, and short stories. But it is perhaps in short fiction that he has done his finest work. Updike has been quietly innovative in expanding the forms of short fiction, especially in his volumes of interlocked stories built around recurrent characters, as in the Maple family stories in Too Far to Go *(1979) and his three collections that depict the ups and downs of fictional writer Henry Bech. Despite Updike's achievements as a novelist, some critics such as* Washington Post *writer Jonathan Yardley believe that "It is in his short stories that we find Updike's most assured work, and no doubt it is upon the best of them that his reputation ultimately will rest."*

In walks three girls in nothing but bathing suits. I'm in the third check-out slot, with my back to the door, so I don't see them until they're over by the bread. The one that caught my eye first was the one in the plaid green two-piece. She was a chunky kid, with a good tan and a sweet broad soft-looking can with those two crescents of white just under it, where the sun never seems to hit, at the top of the backs of her legs. I stood there with my hand on a box of HiHo crackers trying to remember if I rang it up or not. I ring it up again and the customer starts giving me hell. She's one of these cash-register-watchers, a witch about fifty with rouge on her cheekbones and no eyebrows, and I know it made her day to trip me up. She'd been watching cash registers for fifty years and probably never seen a mistake before.

By the time I got her feathers smoothed and her goodies into a bag— she gives me a little snort in passing, if she'd been born at the right time they would have burned her over in Salem—by the time I get her on her way the girls had circled around the bread and were coming back, without a pushcart, back my way along the counters, in the aisle between the check-outs and the Special bins. They didn't even have shoes on. There was this chunky one, with the two-piece—it was bright green and the seams on the bra were still sharp and her belly was still pretty pale so I guessed she just got it (the suit)—there was this one, with one of those chubby berry-faces, the lips all bunched together under her nose, this one, and a tall one, with black hair that hadn't quite frizzed right, and one of these sunburns right across under the eyes, and a chin that was too long—you know, the kind of girl other girls think is very "striking" and "attractive" but never quite makes it, as they very well know, which is why they like her so much—and then the third one, that wasn't quite so tall. She was the queen. She kind of led them, the other two peeking around and making their shoulders round. She didn't look around, not this queen, she just walked straight on slowly, on these long white prima-donna legs. She came down a little hard on her heels, as if she didn't walk in her bare feet that much, putting down her heels and then letting the weight move along to her toes as if she was testing the floor with every step, putting a little deliberate extra action into it. You never know for sure how girls' minds work (do you really think it's a mind in there or just a little buzz like a bee in a glass jar?) but you got the idea she had talked the other two into coming in here with her, and now she was showing them how to do it, walk slow and hold yourself straight.

She had on a kind of dirty-pink—beige maybe, I don't know— bathing suit with a little nubble all over it and, what got me, the straps were down. They were off her shoulders looped loose around the cool tops of her arms, and I guess as a result the suit had slipped a little on her, so all around the top of the cloth there was this shining rim. If it hadn't been there you wouldn't have known there could have been anything whiter than those shoulders. With the straps pushed off, there was nothing between the top of the suit and the top of her head except just *her*, this clean bare plane of the top of her chest down from the shoulder bones like a dented sheet of metal tilted in the light. I mean, it was more than pretty.

She had sort of oaky hair that the sun and salt had bleached, done up in a bun that was unraveling, and a kind of prim face. Walking into the A & P with your straps down, I suppose it's the only kind of face you *can* have. She held her head so high her neck, coming up out of those white shoulders, looked kind of stretched, but I didn't mind. The longer her neck was, the more of her there was.

She must have felt in the corner of her eye me and over my shoulder Stokesie in the second slot watching, but she didn't tip. Not this queen. She kept her eyes moving across the racks, and stopped, and turned so slow it made my stomach rub the inside of my apron, and buzzed to the other two, who kind of huddled against her for relief, and they all three of them went up the cat-and-dog-food-breakfast-cereal-macaroni-rice-raisins-seasonings-spreads-spaghetti-soft-drinks-crackers-and-cookies aisle. From the third slot I look straight up this aisle to the meat counter, and I watched them all the way. The fat one with the tan sort of fumbled with the cookies, but on second thought she put the packages back. The sheep pushing their carts down the aisle—the girls were walking against the usual traffic (not that we have one-way signs or anything)—were pretty hilarious. You could see them, when Queenie's white shoulders dawned on them, kind of jerk, or hop, or hiccup, but their eyes snapped back to their own baskets and on they pushed. I bet you could set off dynamite in an A & P and the people would by and large keep reaching and checking oatmeal off their lists and muttering "Let me see, there was a third thing, began with A, asparagus, no, ah, yes, applesauce!" or whatever it is they do mutter. But there was no doubt, this jiggled them. A few houseslaves in pin curlers even looked around after pushing their carts past to make sure what they had seen was correct.

You know, it's one thing to have a girl in a bathing suit down on the beach, where what with the glare nobody can look at each other much anyway, and another thing in the cool of the A & P, under the fluorescent lights, against all those stacked packages, with her feet padding along naked over our checkerboard green-and-cream rubber-tile floor.

"Oh Daddy," Stokesie said beside me. "I feel so faint."

"Darling," I said. "Hold me tight." Stokesie's married, with two babies chalked up on his fuselage already, but as far as I can tell that's the only difference. He's twenty-two, and I was nineteen this April.

"Is it done?" he asks, the responsible married man finding his voice. I forgot to say he thinks he's going to be manager some sunny day, maybe in 1990 when it's called the Great Alexandrov and Petrooshki Tea Company or something.

What he meant was, our town is five miles from a beach, with a big   10
summer colony out on the Point, but we're right in the middle of town, and the women generally put on a shirt or shorts or something before they get out of the car into the street. And anyway these are usually women with six children and varicose veins mapping their legs and nobody, including them, could care less. As I say, we're right in the middle of town, and if you stand at our front doors you can see two banks and the Congregational church and the newspaper store and three real-estate offices and about twenty-seven old freeloaders tearing up Central Street because the sewer broke again. It's not as if we're on the Cape; we're north of Boston and there's people in this town haven't seen the ocean for twenty years. The girls had reached the meat counter and were asking McMahon something. He pointed, they pointed, and they shuffled out of sight behind a pyramid of Diet Delight peaches. All that was left for us to see was old McMahon patting his mouth and looking after them sizing up their joints. Poor kids, I began to feel sorry for them, they couldn't help it.

Now here comes the sad part of the story, at least my family says it's sad but I don't think it's sad myself. The store's pretty empty, it being Thursday afternoon, so there was nothing much to do except lean on the register and wait for the girls to show up again. The whole store was like a pinball machine and I didn't know which tunnel they'd come out of. After a while they come around out of the far aisle, around the light bulbs, records at discount of the Caribbean Six or Tony Martin Sings or some such gunk you wonder they waste the wax on, six-packs of candy bars, and plastic toys done up in cellophane that fall apart when a kid looks at them anyway. Around they come, Queenie still leading the way, and holding a little gray jar in her hand. Slots Three through Seven are unmanned and I could see her wondering between Stokes and me, but Stokesie with his usual luck draws an old party in baggy gray pants who stumbles up with four giant cans of pineapple juice (what do these bums *do* with all that pineapple juice? I've often asked myself) so the girls come to me. Queenie puts down the jar and I take it into my fingers icy cold. Kingfish Fancy Herring Snacks in Pure Sour Cream: 49¢. Now her hands are empty, not a ring or a bracelet, bare as God made them, and I wonder where the money's coming from. Still with that prim look she lifts a folded dollar bill out of the hollow at the center of her nubbled pink top. The jar went heavy in my hand. Really, I thought that was so cute.

Then everybody's luck begins to run out. Lengel comes in from haggling with a truck full of cabbages on the lot and is about to scuttle into that door marked MANAGER behind which he hides all day when the girls touch his eye. Lengel's pretty dreary, teaches Sunday school and the rest, but he doesn't miss that much. He comes over and says, "Girls, this isn't the beach."

Queenie blushes, though maybe it's just a brush of sunburn I was noticing for the first time, now that she was so close. "My mother asked me to pick up a jar of herring snacks." Her voice kind of startled me, the way voices do when you see the people first, coming out so flat and dumb yet kind of tony, too, the way it ticked over "pick up" and "snacks." All of a sudden I slid right down her voice into her living room. Her father and the other men were standing around in ice-cream coats and bow ties and the women were in sandals picking up herring snacks on toothpicks off a big plate and they were all holding drinks the color of water with olives and sprigs of mint in them. When my parents have somebody over they get lemonade and if it's a real racy affair Schlitz in tall glasses with "They'll Do It Every Time" cartoons stencilled on.

"That's all right," Lengel said. "But this isn't the beach." His repeating this struck me as funny, as if it had just occurred to him, and he had been thinking all these years the A & P was a great big dune and he was the head lifeguard. He didn't like my smiling—as I say he doesn't miss much—but he concentrates on giving the girls that sad Sunday-school-superintendent stare.

Queenie's blush is no sunburn now, and the plump one in plaid, that 15 I liked better from the back—a really sweet can—pipes up, "We weren't doing any shopping. We just came in for the one thing."

"That makes no difference," Lengel tells her, and I could see from the way his eyes went that he hadn't noticed she was wearing a two-piece before. "We want you decently dressed when you come in here."

"We *are* decent," Queenie says suddenly, her lower lip pushing, getting sore now that she remembers her place, a place from which the crowd that runs the A & P must look pretty crummy. Fancy Herring Snacks flashed in her very blue eyes.

"Girls, I don't want to argue with you. After this come in here with your shoulders covered. It's our policy." He turns his back. That's policy for you. Policy is what the kingpins want. What the others want is juvenile delinquency.

All this while, the customers had been showing up with their carts but, you know, sheep, seeing a scene, they had all bunched up on Stokesie, who shook open a paper bag as gently as peeling a peach, not wanting to miss a word. I could feel in the silence everybody getting nervous, most of all Lengel, who asks me, "Sammy, have you rung up this purchase?"

I thought and said "No" but it wasn't about that I was thinking. I go through the punches, 4, 9, GROC, TOT—it's more complicated than you think, and after you do it often enough, it begins to make a little song, that you hear words to, in my case "Hello (*bing*) there, you (*gung*) hap-py *pee*-pul (*splat*)!"—the *splat* being the drawer flying out. I uncrease the bill, tenderly as you may imagine, it just having come from between the two smoothest scoops of vanilla I had ever known were there, and pass a half and a penny into her narrow pink palm, and nestle the herrings in a bag and twist its neck and hand it over, all the time thinking. 20

The girls, and who'd blame them, are in a hurry to get out, so I say "I quit" to Lengel quick enough for them to hear, hoping they'll stop and watch me, their unsuspected hero. They keep right on going, into the electric eye; the door flies open and they flicker across the lot to their car, Queenie and Plaid and Big Tall Goony-Goony (not that as raw material she was so bad), leaving me with Lengel and a kink in his eyebrow.

"Did you say something, Sammy?"

"I said I quit."

"I thought you did."

"You didn't have to embarrass them." 25

"It was they who were embarrassing us."

I started to say something that came out "Fiddle-de-doo." It's a saying of my grandmother's, and I know she would have been pleased.

"I don't think you know what you're saying," Lengel said.

"I know you don't," I said. "But I do." I pull the bow at the back of my apron and start shrugging it off my shoulders. A couple customers that had been heading for my slot begin to knock against each other, like scared pigs in a chute.

Lengel sighs and begins to look very patient and old and gray. He's been a friend of my parents for years. "Sammy, you don't want to do this to your Mom and Dad," he tells me. It's true, I don't. But it seems to me that once you begin a gesture it's fatal not to go through with it. I fold the apron, "Sammy" stitched in red on the pocket, and put it on the counter, and drop the bow tie on top of it. The bow tie is theirs, if you've ever wondered. "You'll feel this for the rest of your life," Lengel says, and I know that's true, too, but remembering how he made that pretty girl blush makes me so scrunchy inside I punch the No Sale tab and the machine whirs "pee-pul" and the drawer splats out. One advantage to 30 this scene taking place in summer, I can follow this up with a clean exit, there's no fumbling around getting your coat and galoshes, I just saunter into the electric eye in my white shirt that my mother ironed the night before, and the door heaves itself open, and outside the sunshine is skating around on the asphalt.

I look around for my girls, but they're gone, of course. There wasn't anybody but some young married screaming with her children about some candy they didn't get by the door of a powder-blue Falcon station wagon. Looking back in the big windows, over the bags of peat moss and aluminum lawn furniture stacked on the pavement, I could see Lengel in my place in the slot, checking the sheep through. His face was dark gray and his back stiff, as if he'd just had an injection of iron, and my stomach kind of fell as I felt how hard the world was going to be to me hereafter.

QUESTIONS

1. Notice how artfully Updike arranges details to set the story in a perfectly ordinary supermarket. What details stand out for you as particularly true to life? What does this close attention to detail contribute to the story?

2. How fully does Updike draw the character of Sammy? What traits (admirable or otherwise) does Sammy show? Is he any less a hero for wanting the girls to notice his heroism? To what extent is he more thoroughly and fully portrayed than the doctor in "Godfather Death"?

3. What part of the story seems to be the exposition? (See the definition of *exposition* in the discussion of plot earlier in the chapter.) Of what value to the story is the carefully detailed portrait of Queenie, the leader of the three girls?

4. As the story develops, do you detect any change in Sammy's feelings toward the girls?

5. Where in "A & P" does the dramatic conflict become apparent? What moment in the story brings the crisis? What is the climax of the story?

6. Why, exactly, does Sammy quit his job?

7. Does anything lead you to *expect* Sammy to make some gesture of sympathy for the three girls? What incident earlier in the story (before Sammy quits) seems a foreshadowing?

8. What do you understand from the conclusion of the story? What does Sammy mean when he acknowledges "how hard the world was going to be . . . hereafter"?

9. What comment does Updike—through Sammy—make on supermarket society?

WRITING EFFECTIVELY

WRITING ABOUT PLOT

Paying Attention to Plot

A day without conflict is pleasant, but a story without conflict is boring. The plot of every short story, novel, or movie gets its energy from conflict. A character desperately wants something he or she can't have, or is frantic to avoid an unpleasant (or deadly) event. In most stories, conflict is established and tension builds, leading to a crisis and, finally, a resolution of some sort.

The things that happen within a story—the story's plot—all relate somehow to the central conflict. How they relate is a key question we ponder when we write about plot.

When analyzing a story, be sure to remember:

- In most short stories, plot depends less on large external events than on small occurrences that set off large internal changes in the main character.
- Stories often show how the main character comes to a personal turning point, or how his or her character is tested or revealed by events.
- Good stories are a lot like life: the true nature of a character is usually revealed not just by what the character says but also by what he or she does.
- Plot is more than just a sequence of events ("First A happens, and then B, and then C . . . "). Plot is about cause and effect. The actions, events, and situations described in most stories are related to each other by more than just accident ("First A happens, which causes B to happen, which makes C all the more surprising, or inevitable, or ironic . . . ").

If a friend asks you, "What was the story you just read about?" you will probably reply by summarizing the plot. The plot of a short story is the element most readers notice first and remember longest. Plotting is such an obvious aspect of fiction that, in analyzing a short story, it is easy to overlook its importance.

Although plot might seem like the most obvious and superficial part of a story, it is an important expressive device. Plot combines with the other elements of fiction—imagery, style and symbolism, for example—to create an emotional response in the reader: suspense, humor, sadness, excitement, terror.

When you write about a short story, be sure to address its surface narrative. You may make important—even profound—discoveries by paying attention to plot.

CHECKLIST
Analyzing Plot

✓ What is the story's central conflict?
✓ Who is the protagonist? What does he or she want?
✓ What is at stake for the protagonist in the conflict?
✓ What stands in the way of the protagonist's easily achieving his or her goal?
✓ What are the main events that take place in the story? How does each event relate to the protagonist's struggle?
✓ Where do you find the story's climax, or crisis?
✓ How is the conflict resolved?
✓ Does the protagonist succeed in obtaining his or her goals?
✓ What is the impact of success, failure, or a surprising outcome on the protagonist?

WRITING ASSIGNMENT ON PLOT

Choose and read a story from this collection, and write a brief description of its plot and main characters. Then write at length about how the protagonist is changed or tested by the story's events. What do the main character's actions reveal about his or her personality? Some possible story choices are "A & P," "Everyday Use," and "Greasy Lake."

MORE TOPICS FOR WRITING

1. Briefly list the events described in "A & P." Now write several paragraphs about the ways in which the story adds up to more than the sum of its events. Why should the reader care about Sammy's thoughts and decisions?
2. How do Sammy's actions in "A & P" reveal his character? In what ways are his thoughts and actions at odds with each other?
3. Write a brief fable modeled on either "The Appointment in Samarra," "The North Wind and the Sun," or "The Camel and His Friends." Begin with a familiar proverb—"A penny saved is a penny earned" or "Too many cooks spoil the broth"—and invent a story to make the moral convincing.
4. With "Godfather Death" in mind, write a fairy tale set in the present, in a town or city much like your own. After you've completed your fairy tale, write a paragraph explaining what aspects of the fairy tale by the Brothers Grimm you hoped to capture in your story.
5. The Brothers Grimm collected and wrote down many of our best-known fairy tales—"Cinderella," "Snow White and the Seven Dwarfs," and "Little Red Riding Hood," for example. If you have strong childhood recollections of one of these stories—perhaps based on picture books or on the animated Disney versions—find and read the Brothers Grimm version. Are you surprised by the difference? Write a brief essay contrasting the original with your remembered version. What does the original offer that the adaptation does not?

2
Point of View

In the opening lines of *The Adventures of Huckleberry Finn,* Mark Twain takes care to separate himself from the leading character, who is to tell his own story:

> You don't know about me, without you have read a book by the name of *The Adventures of Tom Sawyer,* but that ain't no matter. That book was made by Mr. Mark Twain, and he told the truth, mainly.

Twain wrote the novel, but the **narrator** or speaker is Huck Finn, the one from whose perspective the story is told. Obviously, in *Huckleberry Finn,* the narrator of the story is not the same person as the "real-life" author, the one given the byline. In employing Huck as his narrator, Twain selects a special angle of vision: not his own, exactly, but that of a resourceful boy moving through the thick of events, with a mind at times shrewd, at other times innocent. Through Huck's eyes, Twain takes in certain scenes, actions, and characters and—as only Huck's angle of vision could have enabled Twain to do so well—records them memorably.

Not every narrator in fiction is, like Huck Finn, a main character, one in the thick of events. Some narrators play only minor parts in the stories they tell; others take no active part at all. In the tale of "Godfather Death," we have a narrator who does not participate in the events he recounts. He is not a character in the story but is someone not even named, who stands at some distance from the action, recording what the main characters say and do; recording also, at times, what they think, feel, or desire. He seems to have un-limited knowledge: he even knows the mind of Death, who "because he wanted revenge" let the doctor's candle go out. More humanly restricted in their knowledge, other narrators can see into the mind of only one character. They may be less willing to express opinions than the narrator of "Godfather Death" ("He ought to have remembered his godfather's warning"). A story may even be told by a narrator who seems so impartial and aloof that he lim-its himself to reporting only overheard conversation and to describing, with-out comment or opinion, the appearances of things. Evidently, narrators greatly differ in kind; however, because stories usually are told by someone, almost every story has some kind of narrator. It is rare in modern fiction for the "real-life" author to try to step out from behind the typewriter and tell the story. Real persons can tell stories, but when such a story is *written*, the result is usually *nonfiction*: a memoir, an account of travels, an autobiography.

To identify the narrator of a story, describing any part he or she plays in the events and any limits placed on his or her knowledge, is to identify the story's **point of view**. In a short story, it is usual for the writer to maintain one point of view from beginning to end, but there is nothing to stop him or her from introducing other points of view as well. In his long, panoramic novel *War and Peace*, encompassing the vast drama of Napoleon's invasion of Russia, Leo Tolstoy freely shifts the point of view in and out of the minds of many characters, among them Napoleon himself.

Theoretically, a great many points of view are possible. A narrator who says "I" might conceivably be involved in events to a much greater or a much lesser degree: as the protagonist, as some other major character, as some minor character, as a mere passive spectator, or even as a character who arrives late upon the scene and then tries to piece together what happened. Evidently, too, a narrator's knowledge might vary in gradations from total omniscience to almost total ignorance. But in reading fiction, again and again we encounter familiar and recognizable points of view. Here is a list of them—admittedly just a rough abstraction—that may provide a few terms with which to discuss the stories that you read and to describe their points of view:

Narrator a Participant (Writing in the First Person):
1. a major character
2. a minor character

Narrator a Nonparticipant (Writing in the Third Person):
3. all-knowing (seeing into any of the characters)
4. seeing into one major character
5. seeing into one minor character
6. objective (not seeing into any characters)

When the narrator is cast as a **participant** in the events of the story, he or she is a dramatized character who says "I." Such a narrator may be the protagonist (Huck Finn) or may be an **observer**, a minor character standing a little to one side, watching a story unfold that mainly involves someone else.

A narrator who remains a **nonparticipant** does not appear in the story as a character. Viewing the characters, perhaps seeing into the minds of one or more of them, such a narrator refers to them as "he," "she," or "they." When **all-knowing** (or **omniscient**), the narrator sees into the minds of all (or some) characters, moving when necessary from one to another. This is the point of view in "Godfather Death," in which the narrator knows the feelings and motives of the father, of the doctor, and even of Death himself. In that he adds an occasional comment or opinion, this narrator may be said also to show **editorial omniscience** (as we can tell from his disapproving remark that the doctor "ought to have remembered" and his observation that the father did not understand "how wisely God shares out wealth and poverty"). A narrator who shows **impartial omniscience** presents the thoughts and actions of the characters, but does not judge them or comment on them.

When a nonparticipating narrator sees events through the eyes of a single character, whether a major character or a minor one, the resulting point of view is sometimes called **limited omniscience** or **selective omniscience**. The author, of course, selects which character to see through; the omniscience is his and not the narrator's. In William Faulkner's "Barn Burning" (Chapter 5), the narrator is almost entirely confined to knowing the thoughts and perceptions of a boy, the central character. Here is another example. Early in his novel *Madame Bovary*, Gustave Flaubert tells of the first time a young country doctor, Charles Bovary, meets Emma, the woman later to become his wife. The doctor has been summoned late at night to set the broken leg of a farmer, Emma's father.

A young woman wearing a blue merino dress with three flounces came to the door of the house to greet Monsieur Bovary, and she ushered him into the kitchen, where a big open fire was blazing. Around its edges the farm hands' breakfast was bubbling in small pots of assorted sizes. Damp clothes were drying inside the vast chimney-opening. The fire shovel, the tongs, and the nose of the bellows, all of colossal proportions, shone like polished steel; and along the walls hung a lavish array of kitchen utensils, glimmering in the bright light of the fire and in the first rays of the sun that were now beginning to come in through the window-panes.

Charles went upstairs to see the patient. He found him in bed, sweating under blankets, his nightcap lying where he had flung it. He was a stocky little man of fifty, fair-skinned, blue-eyed, bald in front and wearing earrings. On a chair beside him was a big decanter of brandy: he had been pouring himself drinks to keep up his courage. But as soon as he saw the doctor he dropped his bluster, and instead of cursing as he had been doing for the past twelve hours he began to groan weakly.

The fracture was a simple one, without complications of any kind. Charles couldn't have wished for anything easier. Then he recalled his teachers' bedside manner in accident cases, and proceeded to cheer up his patient with all kinds of facetious remarks—a truly surgical attention, like the oiling of a scalpel. For splints, they sent someone to bring a bundle of laths from the carriage shed. Charles selected one, cut it into lengths and smoothed it down with a piece of broken window glass, while the maidservant tore sheets for bandages and Mademoiselle Emma tried to sew some pads. She was a long time finding her workbox, and her father showed his impatience. She made no reply; but as she sewed she kept pricking her fingers and raising them to her mouth to suck.

Charles was surprised by the whiteness of her fingernails. They were almond-shaped, tapering, as polished and shining as Dieppe ivories. Her hands, however, were not pretty—not pale enough, perhaps, a little rough at the knuckles; and they were too long, without softness of line. The finest thing about her was her eyes. They were brown, but seemed black under the long eyelashes; and she had an open gaze that met yours with fearless candor.[1]

In this famous scene, Charles Bovary is beholding people and objects in a natural sequence. On first meeting Emma, he notices only her dress, as though less interested in the woman who opens the door than in passing through to the warm fire. Needing pads for his patient's splint, the doctor observes just the hands of the woman sewing them. Obliged to wait for the splints, he then has the leisure to notice her face, her remarkable eyes. (By the way, notice the effect of the word *yours* in the last sentence of the passage. It is as if the reader, seeing through the doctor's eyes, suddenly became one with him.) Who is the narrator? Not Charles Bovary, nor Gustave Flaubert, but someone able to enter the minds of others—here limited to knowing the thoughts and perceptions of one character.

In the **objective point of view**, the narrator does not enter the mind of any character but describes events from the outside. Telling us what people say and how their faces look, he or she leaves us to infer their thoughts and feelings. So inconspicuous is the narrator that this point of view has been called "the fly on the wall." This metaphor assumes the existence of a fly with a highly discriminating gaze, who knows which details to look for to communicate the deepest meaning. Some critics would say that in the objective point of view, the narrator disappears altogether. Consider this passage by a writer famous for remaining objective, Dashiell Hammett, in his mystery novel *The Maltese Falcon*, describing his private detective Sam Spade:

Spade's thick fingers made a cigarette with deliberate care, sifting a measured quantity of tan flakes down into curved paper, spreading the flakes so that they lay equal at the ends with a slight depression in the middle, thumbs rolling the paper's inner edge down and up under the outer edge as forefingers pressed it over, thumb and fingers sliding to the paper cylinder's ends to hold it even while tongue licked the flap, left forefinger and thumb pinching their ends while right forefinger and thumb smoothed the damp seam, right forefinger and thumb twisting their end and lifting the other to Spade's mouth.[2]

In Hammett's novel, this sentence comes at a moment of crisis: just after Spade has been roused from bed in the middle of the night by a phone call telling him that his partner has been murdered. Even in times of stress (we infer) Spade is

[1]*Madame Bovary*, translated by Francis Steegmuller (New York: Random, 1957) 16–17.
[2]Chapter 2, "Death in the Fog," *The Maltese Falcon* (New York: Knopf, 1929).

deliberate, cool, efficient, and painstaking. Hammett refrains from applying all those adjectives to Spade; to do so would be to exercise editorial omniscience and to destroy the objective point of view.

Besides the common points of view just listed, uncommon points of view are possible. In *Flush,* a fictional biography of Elizabeth Barrett Browning, Virginia Woolf employs an unusual observer as narrator: the poet's pet cocker spaniel. In "The Circular Valley," a short story by Paul Bowles, a man and a woman are watched by a sinister spirit trying to take possession of them, and we see the human characters through the spirit's vague consciousness.

Also possible, but unusual, is a story written in the second person, *you.* This point of view results in an attention-getting directness, as in Jay McInerney's novel *Bright Lights, Big City* (1985), which begins:

> You are not the kind of guy who would be at a place like this at this time of the morning. But here you are, and you cannot say that the terrain is entirely unfamiliar, although the details are *fuzzy.* You are at a nightclub talking to a girl with a shaved head.

The attitudes and opinions of a narrator aren't necessarily those of the author; in fact, we may notice a lively conflict between what we are told and what, apparently, we are meant to believe. A story may be told by an **innocent narrator** or a **naive narrator,** a character who fails to understand all the implications of the story. One such innocent narrator (despite his sometimes shrewd perceptions) is Huckleberry Finn. Because Huck accepts without question the morality and lawfulness of slavery, he feels guilty about helping Jim, a runaway slave. But, far from condemning Huck for his defiance of the law—"All right, then, I'll go to hell," Huck tells himself, deciding against returning Jim to captivity—the author, and the reader along with him, silently applaud. Naive in the extreme is the narrator of one part of William Faulkner's novel *The Sound and the Fury,* the idiot Benjy, a grown man with the intellect of a child. In a story told by an **unreliable narrator,** the point of view is that of a person who, we perceive, is deceptive, self-deceptive, deluded, or deranged. As though seeking ways to be faithful to uncertainty, contemporary writers have been particularly fond of unreliable narrators.

Virginia Woolf compared life to "a luminous halo, a semi-transparent envelope surrounding us from the beginning of consciousness to the end."[3] To capture such a reality, modern writers of fiction have employed many strategies. One is the method of writing called **stream of consciousness,** from a phrase coined by psychologist William James to describe the procession of thoughts passing through the mind. In fiction, the stream of consciousness is a kind of selective omniscience: the presentation of thoughts and sense impressions in a lifelike fashion—not in a sequence arranged by logic, but mingled

---

[3]"Modern Fiction," *Collected Essays* (New York: Harcourt, 1967).

randomly. When in his novel *Ulysses* James Joyce takes us into the mind of Leopold Bloom, an ordinary Dublin mind well-stocked with trivia and fragments of odd learning, the reader may have an impression not of a smoothly flowing stream but of an ocean of miscellaneous things, all crowded and jostling.

> As he set foot on O'Connell bridge a puffball of smoke plumed up from the parapet. Brewery barge with export stout. England. Sea air sours it, I heard. Be interesting some day to get a pass through Hancock to see the brewery. Regular world in itself. Vats of porter, wonderful. Rats get in too. Drink themselves bloated as big as a collie floating.[4]

Perceptions—such as the smoke from the brewery barge—trigger Bloom's reflections. A moment later, as he casts a crumpled paper ball off the bridge, he recalls a bit of science he learned in school, the rate of speed of a falling body: "thirty-two feet per sec."

Stream-of-consciousness writing usually occurs in relatively short passages, but in *Ulysses* Joyce employs it extensively. Similar in method, an **interior monologue** is an extended presentation of a character's thoughts, not in the seemingly helter-skelter order of a stream of consciousness, but in an arrangement as if the character were speaking out loud to himself, for us to overhear. A famous interior monologue comes at the end of *Ulysses* when Joyce gives us the rambling memories and reflections of earth-mother Molly Bloom.

Every point of view has limitations. Even **total omniscience**, a knowledge of the minds of all the characters, has its disadvantages. Such a point of view requires high skill to manage, without the storyteller's losing his way in a multitude of perspectives. In fact, there are evident advantages in having a narrator not know everything. We are accustomed to seeing the world through one pair of eyes, to having truths gradually occur to us. Henry James, whose theory and practice of fiction have been influential, held that an excellent way to tell a story was through the fine but bewildered mind of an observer. "It seems probable," James wrote, "that if we were never bewildered there would never be a story to tell about us; we should partake of the superior nature of the all-knowing immortals whose annals are dreadfully dull so long as flurried humans are not, for the positive relief of bored Olympians, mixed up with them."[5]

By using a particular point of view, an author may artfully withhold information, if need be, rather than immediately present it to us. If, for instance, the suspense in a story depends on our not knowing until the end that the protagonist is a spy, the author would be ill-advised to tell the story from the protagonist's point of view. If a character acts as the narrator, the author

---

[4]*Ulysses* (New York: Random, 1934) 150.

[5]Preface, *The Princess Casamassima*, reprinted in *The Art of the Novel*, ed. R. P. Blackmur (New York: Scribner's, 1934).

must make sure that the character possesses (or can obtain) enough information to tell the story adequately. Clearly, the author makes a fundamental decision in selecting, from many possibilities, a story's point of view. What we readers admire, if the story is effective, is not only skill in execution, but also judicious choice.

Here is a short story memorable for many reasons, among them its point of view.

William Faulkner

A Rose for Emily   1931

WILLIAM FAULKNER

William Faulkner (1897–1962) spent most of his days in Oxford, Mississippi, where he attended the University of Mississippi and where he served as postmaster until angry townspeople ejected him because they had failed to receive mail. During World War I he served with the Royal Canadian Air Force and afterward worked as a feature writer for the New Orleans Times-Picayune. Faulkner's private life was a long struggle to stay solvent: even after fame came to him, he had to write Hollywood scripts and teach at the University of Virginia to support himself. His violent comic novel Sanctuary *(1931) caused a stir and turned a profit, but critics tend most to admire* The Sound and the Fury *(1929), a tale partially told through the eyes of an idiot;* As I Lay Dying *(1930);* Light in August *(1932);* Absalom, Absalom *(1936); and* The Hamlet *(1940). Beginning with* Sartoris *(1929), Faulkner in his fiction imagines a Mississippi county named Yoknapatawpha and traces the fortunes of several of its families, including the aristocratic Compsons and Sartorises and the white-trash, dollar-grabbing Snopeses, from the Civil War to modern times. His influence on his fellow Southern writers (and others) has been profound. In 1950 he received the Nobel Prize for Literature. Although we think of Faulkner primarily as a novelist, he wrote nearly a hundred short stories. Forty-two of the best are available in his* Collected Stories *(1950; 1995).*

I

When Miss Emily Grierson died, our whole town went to her funeral: the men through a sort of respectful affection for a fallen monument, the women mostly out of curiosity to see the inside of her house, which no one save an old manservant—a combined gardener and cook—had seen in at least ten years.

It was a big, squarish frame house that had once been white, decorated with cupolas and spires and scrolled balconies in the heavily lightsome style of the seventies, set on what had once been our most select street. But garages and cotton gins had encroached and obliterated even the august names of that neighborhood; only Miss Emily's house was left, lifting its stubborn and coquettish decay above the cotton wagons and the gasoline pumps—an eyesore among eyesores. And now Miss Emily had gone to join the representatives of those august names where they lay in the cedar-bemused cemetery among the ranked and anonymous graves of Union and Confederate soldiers who fell at the battle of Jefferson.

Alive, Miss Emily had been a tradition, a duty, and a care; a sort of hereditary obligation upon the town, dating from that day in 1894 when Colonel Sartoris, the mayor—he who fathered the edict that no Negro woman should appear on the streets without an apron—remitted her taxes, the dispensation dating from the death of her father on into perpetuity. Not that Miss Emily would have accepted charity. Colonel Sartoris invented an involved tale to the effect that Miss Emily's father had loaned money to the town, which the town, as a matter of business, preferred this way of repaying. Only a man of Colonel Sartoris' generation and thought could have invented it, and only a woman could have believed it.

When the next generation, with its more modern ideas, became mayors and aldermen, this arrangement created some little dissatisfaction. On the first of the year they mailed her a tax notice. February came, and there was no reply. They wrote her a formal letter, asking her to call at the sheriff's office at her convenience. A week later the mayor wrote her himself, offering to call or to send his car for her, and received in reply a note on paper of an archaic shape, in a thin, flowing calligraphy in faded ink, to the effect that she no longer went out at all. The tax notice was also enclosed, without comment.

They called a special meeting of the Board of Aldermen. A deputa- 5 tion waited upon her, knocked at the door through which no visitor had passed since she ceased giving china-painting lessons eight or ten years earlier. They were admitted by the old Negro into a dim hall from which a stairway mounted into still more shadow. It smelled of dust and disuse— a close, dank smell. The Negro led them into the parlor. It was furnished in heavy, leather-covered furniture. When the Negro opened the blinds of one window, they could see that the leather was cracked; and when they sat down, a faint dust rose sluggishly about their thighs, spinning with slow motes in the single sun-ray. On a tarnished gilt easel before the fireplace stood a crayon portrait of Miss Emily's father.

They rose when she entered—a small, fat woman in black, with a thin gold chain descending to her waist and vanishing into her belt, leaning on an ebony cane with a tarnished gold head. Her skeleton was small and spare; perhaps that was why what would have been merely plumpness in another was obesity in her. She looked bloated, like a body long submerged in motionless water, and of that pallid hue. Her eyes, lost in the fatty ridges of her face, looked like two small pieces of coal pressed into a lump of dough as they moved from one face to another while the visitors stated their errand.

She did not ask them to sit. She just stood in the door and listened quietly until the spokesman came to a stumbling halt. Then they could hear the invisible watch ticking at the end of the gold chain.

Her voice was dry and cold. "I have no taxes in Jefferson. Colonel Sartoris explained it to me. Perhaps one of you can gain access to the city records and satisfy yourselves."

"But we have. We are the city authorities, Miss Emily. Didn't you get a notice from the sheriff, signed by him?"

"I received a paper, yes," Miss Emily said. "Perhaps he considers   10
himself the sheriff . . . I have no taxes in Jefferson."

"But there is nothing on the books to show that, you see. We must go by the—"

"See Colonel Sartoris. I have no taxes in Jefferson."

"But, Miss Emily—"

"See Colonel Sartoris." (Colonel Sartoris had been dead almost ten years.) "I have no taxes in Jefferson. Tobe!" The Negro appeared. "Show these gentlemen out."

II

So she vanquished them, horse and foot, just as she had vanquished   15
their fathers thirty years before about the smell. That was two years after her father's death and a short time after her sweetheart—the one we believed would marry her—had deserted her. After her father's death she went out very little; after her sweetheart went away, people hardly saw her at all. A few of the ladies had the temerity to call, but were not received, and the only sign of life about the place was the Negro man—a young man then—going in and out with a market basket.

"Just as if a man—any man—could keep a kitchen properly," the ladies said; so they were not surprised when the smell developed. It was another link between the gross, teeming world and the high and mighty Griersons.

A neighbor, a woman, complained to the mayor, Judge Stevens, eighty years old.

"But what will you have me do about it, madam?" he said.

"Why, send her word to stop it," the woman said. "Isn't there a law?"

"I'm sure that won't be necessary," Judge Stevens said. "It's probably   20
just a snake or a rat that nigger of hers killed in the yard. I'll speak to him about it."

The next day he received two more complaints, one from a man who came in diffident deprecation. "We really must do something about it, Judge. I'd be the last one in the world to bother Miss Emily, but we've got to do something." That night the Board of Aldermen met—three gray-beards and one younger man, a member of the rising generation.

"It's simple enough," he said. "Send her word to have her place cleaned up. Give her a certain time to do it in, and if she don't . . ."

"Dammit, sir," Judge Stevens said, "will you accuse a lady to her face of smelling bad?"

So the next night, after midnight, four men crossed Miss Emily's lawn and slunk about the house like burglars, sniffing along the base of the brickwork and at the cellar openings while one of them performed a regular sowing motion with his hand out of a sack slung from his shoulder. They broke open the cellar door and sprinkled lime there, and in all the outbuildings. As they recrossed the lawn, a window that had been dark was lighted and Miss Emily sat in it, the light behind her, and her upright torso motionless as that of an idol. They crept quietly across the lawn and into the shadow of the locusts that lined the street. After a week or two the smell went away.

That was when people had begun to feel really sorry for her. People in our town, remembering how old lady Wyatt, her great-aunt, had gone completely crazy at last, believed that the Griersons held themselves a little too high for what they really were. None of the young men were quite good enough for Miss Emily and such. We had long thought of them as a tableau, Miss Emily a slender figure in white in the background, her father a spraddled silhouette in the foreground, his back to her and clutching a horsewhip, the two of them framed by the back-flung front door. So when she got to be thirty and was still single, we were not pleased exactly, but vindicated; even with insanity in the family she wouldn't have turned down all of her chances if they had really materialized.

When her father died, it got about that the house was all that was left to her; and in a way, people were glad. At last they could pity Miss Emily. Being left alone, and a pauper, she had become humanized. Now she too would know the old thrill and the old despair of a penny more or less.

The day after his death all the ladies prepared to call at the house and offer condolence and aid, as is our custom. Miss Emily met them at the door, dressed as usual and with no trace of grief on her face. She told them that her father was not dead. She did that for three days, with the ministers calling on her, and the doctors, trying to persuade her to let them dispose of the body. Just as they were about to resort to law and force, she broke down, and they buried her father quickly.

We did not say she was crazy then. We believed she had to do that. We remembered all the young men her father had driven away, and we

25

knew that with nothing left, she would have to cling to that which had robbed her, as people will.

III

She was sick for a long time. When we saw her again, her hair was cut short, making her look like a girl, with a vague resemblance to those angels in colored church windows—sort of tragic and serene.

The town had just let the contracts for paving the sidewalks, and in the summer after her father's death they began the work. The construction company came with niggers and mules and machinery, and a foreman named Homer Barron, a Yankee—a big, dark, ready man, with a big voice and eyes lighter than his face. The little boys would follow in groups to hear him cuss the niggers, and the niggers singing in time to the rise and fall of picks. Pretty soon he knew everybody in town. Whenever you heard a lot of laughing anywhere about the square, Homer Barron would be in the center of the group. Presently we began to see him and Miss Emily on Sunday afternoons driving in the yellow-wheeled buggy and the matched team of bays from the livery stable.

At first we were glad that Miss Emily would have an interest, because the ladies all said, "Of course a Grierson would not think seriously of a Northerner, a day laborer." But there were still others, older people, who said that even grief could not cause a real lady to forget *noblesse oblige°*—without calling it *noblesse oblige*. They just said, "Poor Emily. Her kinsfolk should come to her." She had some kin in Alabama; but years ago her father had fallen out with them over the estate of old lady Wyatt, the crazy woman, and there was no communication between the two families. They had not even been represented at the funeral.

And as soon as the old people said, "Poor Emily," the whispering began. "Do you suppose it's really so?" they said to one another. "Of course it is. What else could . . ." This behind their hands; rustling of craned silk and satin behind jalousies closed upon the sun of Sunday afternoon as the thin, swift clop-clop-clop of the matched team passed: "Poor Emily."

She carried her head high enough—even when we believed that she was fallen. It was as if she demanded more than ever the recognition of her dignity as the last Grierson; as if it had wanted that touch of earthiness to reaffirm her imperviousness. Like when she bought the rat poison, the arsenic. That was over a year after they had begun to say "Poor Emily," and while the two female cousins were visiting her.

"I want some poison," she said to the druggist. She was over thirty then, still a slight woman, though thinner than usual, with cold, haughty black eyes in a face the flesh of which was strained across the temples and

30

noblesse oblige: the obligation of a member of the nobility to behave with honor and dignity.

about the eye-sockets as you imagine a lighthouse-keeper's face ought to
look. "I want some poison," she said.

"Yes, Miss Emily. What kind? For rats and such? I'd recom—"   35

"I want the best you have. I don't care what kind."

The druggist named several. "They'll kill anything up to an elephant. But what you want is—"

"Arsenic," Miss Emily said. "Is that a good one?"

"Is . . . arsenic? Yes, ma'am. But what you want—"

"I want arsenic."   40

The druggist looked down at her. She looked back at him, erect, her
face like a strained flag. "Why, of course," the druggist said. "If that's what
you want. But the law requires you to tell what you are going to use it for."

Miss Emily just stared at him, her head tilted back in order to look
him eye for eye, until he looked away and went and got the arsenic and
wrapped it up. The Negro delivery boy brought her the package; the
druggist didn't come back. When she opened the package at home there
was written on the box, under the skull and bones: "For rats."

IV

So the next day we all said, "She will kill herself"; and we said it
would be the best thing. When she had first begun to be seen with Homer
Barron, we had said, "She will marry him." Then we said, "She will persuade him yet," because Homer himself had remarked—he liked men, and
it was known that he drank with the younger men in the Elks' Club—that
he was not a marrying man. Later we said, "Poor Emily," behind the
jalousies as they passed on Sunday afternoon in the glittering buggy, Miss
Emily with her head high and Homer Barron with his hat cocked and a
cigar in his teeth, reins and whip in a yellow glove.

Then some of the ladies began to say that it was a disgrace to the
town and a bad example to the young people. The men did not want to
interfere, but at last the ladies forced the Baptist minister—Miss Emily's
people were Episcopal—to call upon her. He would never divulge what
happened during that interview, but he refused to go back again. The
next Sunday they again drove about the streets, and the following day
the minister's wife wrote to Miss Emily's relations in Alabama.

So she had blood-kin under her roof again and we sat back to watch   45
developments. At first nothing happened. Then we were sure that they
were to be married. We learned that Miss Emily had been to the jeweler's
and ordered a man's toilet set in silver, with the letters H.B. on each
piece. Two days later we learned that she had bought a complete outfit of
men's clothing, including a nightshirt, and we said, "They are married."
We were really glad. We were glad because the two female cousins were
even more Grierson than Miss Emily had ever been.

So we were not surprised when Homer Barron—the streets had been finished some time since—was gone. We were a little disappointed that there was not a public blowing-off, but we believed that he had gone on to prepare for Miss Emily's coming, or to give her a chance to get rid of the cousins. (By that time it was a cabal, and we were all Miss Emily's allies to help circumvent the cousins.) Sure enough, after another week they departed. And, as we had expected all along, within three days Homer Barron was back in town. A neighbor saw the Negro man admit him at the kitchen door at dusk one evening.

And that was the last we saw of Homer Barron. And of Miss Emily for some time. The Negro man went in and out with the market basket, but the front door remained closed. Now and then we would see her at a window for a moment, as the men did that night when they sprinkled the lime, but for almost six months she did not appear on the streets. Then we knew that this was to be expected too; as if that quality of her father which had thwarted her woman's life so many times had been too virulent and too furious to die.

When we next saw Miss Emily, she had grown fat and her hair was turning gray. During the next few years it grew grayer and grayer until it attained an even pepper-and-salt iron-gray, when it ceased turning. Up to the day of her death at seventy-four it was still that vigorous iron-gray, like the hair of an active man.

From that time on her front door remained closed, save for a period of six or seven years, when she was about forty, during which she gave lessons in china-painting. She fitted up a studio in one of the downstairs rooms, where the daughters and granddaughters of Colonel Sartoris' contemporaries were sent to her with the same regularity and in the same spirit that they were sent to church on Sundays with a twenty-five-cent piece for the collection plate. Meanwhile her taxes had been remitted.

Then the newer generation became the backbone and the spirit of the town, and the painting pupils grew up and fell away and did not send their children to her with boxes of color and tedious brushes and pictures cut from the ladies' magazines. The front door closed upon the last one and remained closed for good. When the town got free postal delivery, Miss Emily alone refused to let them fasten the metal numbers above her door and attach a mailbox to it. She would not listen to them.

Daily, monthly, yearly we watched the Negro grow grayer and more stooped, going in and out with the market basket. Each December we sent her a tax notice, which would be returned by the post office a week later, unclaimed. Now and then we would see her in one of the downstairs windows—she had evidently shut up the top floor of the house— like the carven torso of an idol in a niche, looking or not looking at us, we could never tell which. Thus she passed from generation to generation— dear, inescapable, impervious, tranquil, and perverse.

And so she died. Fell ill in the house filled with dust and shadows, with only a doddering Negro man to wait on her. We did not even know she was sick; we had long since given up trying to get any information from the Negro. He talked to no one, probably not even to her, for his voice had grown harsh and rusty, as if from disuse.

She died in one of the downstairs rooms, in a heavy walnut bed with a curtain, her gray head propped on a pillow yellow and moldy with age and lack of sunlight.

V

The Negro met the first of the ladies at the front door and let them in, with their hushed, sibilant voices and their quick, curious glances, and then he disappeared. He walked right through the house and out the back and was not seen again.

The two female cousins came at once. They held the funeral on the second day, with the town coming to look at Miss Emily beneath a mass of bought flowers, with the crayon face of her father musing profoundly above the bier and the ladies sibilant and macabre; and the very old men—some in their brushed Confederate uniforms—on the porch and the lawn, talking of Miss Emily as if she had been a contemporary of theirs, believing that they had danced with her and courted her perhaps, confusing time with its mathematical progression, as the old do, to whom all the past is not a diminishing road but, instead, a huge meadow which no winter ever quite touches, divided from them now by the narrow bottleneck of the most recent decade of years.

Already we knew that there was one room in that region above stairs which no one had seen in forty years, and which would have to be forced. They waited until Miss Emily was decently in the ground before they opened it.

The violence of breaking down the door seemed to fill this room with pervading dust. A thin, acrid pall as of the tomb seemed to lie everywhere upon this room decked and furnished as for a bridal: upon the valance curtains of faded rose color, upon the rose-shaded lights, upon the dressing table, upon the delicate array of crystal and the man's toilet things backed with tarnished silver, silver so tarnished that the monogram was obscured. Among them lay collar and tie, as if they had just been removed, which, lifted, left upon the surface a pale crescent in the dust. Upon a chair hung the suit, carefully folded; beneath it the two mute shoes and the discarded socks.

The man himself lay in the bed.

For a long while we just stood there, looking down at the profound and fleshless grin. The body had apparently once lain in the attitude of an embrace, but now the long sleep that outlasts love, that conquers even the grimace of love, had cuckolded him. What was left of him, rotted

55

beneath what was left of the nightshirt, had become inextricable from the bed in which he lay; and upon him and upon the pillow beside him lay that even coating of the patient and biding dust.

Then we noticed that in the second pillow was the indentation of a head. One of us lifted something from it, and leaning forward, that faint and invisible dust dry and acrid in the nostrils, we saw a long strand of iron-gray hair. 60

QUESTIONS

1. What is meaningful in the final detail that the strand of hair on the second pillow is *iron-gray*?

2. Who is the unnamed narrator? For whom does he profess to be speaking?

3. Why does "A Rose for Emily" seem better told from his point of view than if it were told (like John Updike's "A & P") from the point of view of the main character?

4. What foreshadowings of the discovery of the body of Homer Barron are we given earlier in the story? Share your experience in reading "A Rose for Emily": did the foreshadowings give away the ending for you? Did they heighten your interest?

5. What contrasts does the narrator draw between changing reality and Emily's refusal or inability to recognize change?

6. How do the character and background of Emily Grierson differ from those of Homer Barron? What general observations about the society that Faulkner depicts can be made from his portraits of these two characters and from his account of life in this one Mississippi town?

7. Does the story seem to you totally grim, or do you find any humor in it?

8. What do you infer to be the author's attitude toward Emily Grierson? Is she simply a murderous madwoman? Why do you suppose Faulkner calls his story "A Rose . . ."?

Edgar Allan Poe

The Tell-Tale Heart
(1843) 1850

Edgar Poe was born in Boston in January 1809, the second son of actors Eliza and David Poe. Edgar inherited his family's legacy of artistic talent, financial instability, and social inferiority (actors were not considered respectable people in the nineteenth century). Although Poe later demonstrated both his mother's expressive gifts and his father's problems with alcohol, he never really knew his parents. His father abandoned the family after the birth of Edgar's little sister, Rosalie, and his mother died of tuberculosis in a Richmond, Virginia, boarding house before Edgar turned three.

EDGAR ALLAN POE

Eliza Poe's brilliance on stage had earned her many fans and their compassion saved her children. Edgar was taken in by the wealthy John and Frances Allan of Richmond, whose name he added to his own. John Allan educated his foster son at first-rate schools, where the boy excelled in all subjects. Edgar, however, grew from a precocious and charming child into a moody adolescent, and his relationship with his foster father deteriorated. His first year at the University of Virginia was marked by scholastic success as well as alcoholic binges and gambling debts. Disgraced, Poe fled to Boston, where he joined the army under the name Edgar Perry. He performed well as an enlisted man and published his first collection of poetry, Tamerlane and Other Poems, at the age of eighteen.

After an abortive stint at West Point led to a final break with his foster father, Edgar Allan Poe became a full-time writer and editor. Morbidly sensitive to criticism at anytime, and paranoid and belligerent when drunk, Poe left or was fired from every post he held. Nevertheless, he was a respected literary critic and editor and sharply improved both the content and circulation of every magazine with which he was associated. Unfortunately, he was never paid well for his work, either as an editor or a freelance writer. Works such as "The Fall of the House of Usher" and "The Raven," both of which made him famous, earned him almost nothing in his lifetime.

After the break with his foster family, Poe rediscovered his own. From 1831 on, Poe lived with his father's widowed sister, Maria Clemm, and her daughter Virginia. In 1836 Poe married this thirteen-year-old first cousin, and these women provided Poe with much-needed emotional stability. However, like his mother, Virginia died of tuberculosis at age twenty-four, her demise doubtless hastened by poverty.

Poe's life came apart after his wife's death; his drinking intensified, as did his self-destructive tendencies. In October 1849 Edgar Allan Poe died in mysterious circumstances, a few days after being found sick and incoherent on a Baltimore street.

True!—nervous—very, very dreadfully nervous I had been and am; but why *will* you say that I am mad? The disease had sharpened my senses—not destroyed—not dulled them. Above all was the sense of hearing acute. I heard all things in the heaven and in the earth. I heard many things in hell. How, then, am I mad? Hearken! and observe how healthily—how calmly, I can tell you the whole story.

It is impossible to say how first the idea entered my brain; but once conceived, it haunted me day and night. Object there was none. Passion there was none. I loved the old man. He had never wronged me. He had never given me insult. For his gold I had no desire. I think it was his eye! yes, it was this! One of his eyes resembled that of a vulture—a pale blue eye, with a film over it. Whenever it fell upon me, my blood ran cold; and so by degrees—very gradually—I made up my mind to take the life of the old man, and thus rid myself of the eye forever.

Now this is the point. You fancy me mad. Madmen know nothing. But you should have seen *me*. You should have seen how wisely I proceeded— with what caution—with what foresight—with what dissimulation I went to work! I was never kinder to the old man than during the whole week before I killed him. And every night, about midnight, I turned the latch of his door and opened it—oh, so gently! And then, when I had made an opening sufficient for my head, I put in a dark lantern, all closed, closed, so that no light shone out, and then I thrust in my head. Oh, you would have laughed to see how cunningly I thrust it in! I moved it slowly—very, very slowly, so that I might not disturb the old man's sleep. It took me an hour to place my whole head within the opening so far that I could see him as he lay upon his bed. Ha!—would a madman have been so wise as this? And then, when my head was well in the room, I undid the lantern cautiously—oh, so cautiously—cautiously (for the hinges creaked)—I undid it just so much that a single thin ray fell upon the vulture eye. And this I did for seven long nights—every night just at midnight—but I found the eye always closed; and so it was impossible to do the work; for it was not the old man who vexed me, but his Evil Eye. And every morning, when the day broke, I went boldly into the chamber, and spoke courageously to him, calling him by name in a hearty tone, and inquiring how he had passed the night. So you see he would have been a very profound old man, indeed, to suspect that every night, just at twelve, I looked in upon him while he slept.

Upon the eighth night I was more than usually cautious in opening the door. A watch's minute hand moves more quickly than did mine. Never before that night had I *felt* the extent of my own powers—of my sagacity. I could scarcely contain my feelings of triumph. To think that there I was, opening the door, little by little, and he not even to dream of my secret deeds or thoughts. I fairly chuckled at the idea; and perhaps he heard me; for he moved on the bed suddenly, as if startled. Now you may think that I drew back—but no. His room was as black as pitch with the thick darkness (for the shutters were close fastened, through fear of robbers), and so I knew that he could not see the opening of the door, and I kept pushing it on steadily, steadily.

I had my head in, and was about to open the lantern, when my thumb slipped upon the tin fastening, and the old man sprang up in the bed, crying out— "Who's there?"   5

I kept quite still and said nothing. For a whole hour I did not move a muscle, and in the meantime I did not hear him lie down. He was still sitting up in the bed, listening;—just as I have done, night after night, hearkening to the death watches° in the wall.

Presently I heard a slight groan, and I knew it was the groan of mortal terror. It was not a groan of pain or of grief—oh, no!—it was the low stifled sound that arises from the bottom of the soul when overcharged with awe.

---

death watches: beetles that infest timbers. Their clicking sound was thought to be an omen of death.

I knew the sound very well. Many a night, just at midnight, when all the world slept, it has welled up from my own bosom, deepening, with its dreadful echo, the terrors that distracted me. I say I knew it well. I knew what the old man felt, and pitied him, although I chuckled at heart. I knew that he had been lying awake ever since the first slight noise, when he had turned in the bed. His fears had been ever since growing upon him. He had been trying to fancy them causeless, but could not. He had been saying to himself— "It is nothing but the wind in the chimney—it is only a mouse crossing the floor," or "it is merely a cricket which has made a single chirp." Yes, he had been trying to comfort himself with these suppositions; but he had found all in vain. *All in vain*; because Death, in approaching him, had stalked with his black shadow before him, and enveloped the victim. And it was the mournful influence of the unperceived shadow that caused him to feel—although he neither saw nor heard—to *feel* the presence of my head within the room.

When I had waited a long time, very patiently, without hearing him lie down, I resolved to open a little—a very, very little crevice in the lantern. So I opened it—you cannot imagine how stealthily, stealthily—until, at length, a single dim ray, like the thread of the spider, shot from out of the crevice and fell upon the vulture eye.

It was open—wide, wide open—and I grew furious as I gazed upon it. I saw it with perfect distinctness—all a dull blue, with a hideous veil over it that chilled the very marrow in my bones; but I could see nothing else of the old man's face or person: for I had directed the ray as if by instinct, precisely upon the damned spot.

And now have I not told you that what you mistake for madness is 10 but over-acuteness of the senses?—now, I say, there came to my ears a low, dull, quick sound, such as a watch makes when enveloped in cotton. I knew *that* sound well, too. It was the beating of the old man's heart. It increased my fury, as the beating of a drum stimulates the soldier into courage.

But even yet I refrained and kept still. I scarcely breathed. I held the lantern motionless. I tried how steadily I could maintain the ray upon the eye. Meantime the hellish tattoo of the heart increased. It grew quicker and quicker, and louder and louder every instant. The old man's terror *must* have been extreme! It grew louder, I say, louder every moment!— do you mark me well? I have told you that I am nervous: so I am. And now at the dead hour of the night, amid the dreadful silence of that old house, so strange a noise as this excited me to uncontrollable terror. Yet, for some minutes longer I refrained and stood still. But the beating grew louder, louder! I thought the heart must burst. And now a new anxiety seized me—the sound would be heard by a neighbor! The old man's hour had come! With a loud yell, I threw open the lantern and leaped into the room. He shrieked once—once only. In an instant I dragged him to the floor, and pulled the heavy bed over him. I then smiled gaily, to find the deed so far done. But, for many minutes, the heart beat on with a muffled sound. This, however, did not vex me; it would not be heard through the wall. At length it ceased. The old man was dead. I removed the bed and examined the corpse. Yes, he was stone, stone dead. I placed my hand upon the heart and held it there many minutes.

If still you think me mad, you will think so no longer when I describe the wise precautions I took for the concealment of the body. The night waned, and I worked hastily, but in silence. First of all I dismembered the corpse. I cut off the head and the arms and the legs.

I then took up three planks from the flooring of the chamber, and deposited all between the scantlings. I then replaced the boards so cleverly, so cunningly, that no human eye—not even *his*—could have detected anything wrong. There was nothing to wash out—no stain of any kind—no blood-spot whatever. I had been too wary for that. A tub had caught all—ha! ha!

When I had made an end of these labors, it was four o'clock—still dark as midnight. As the bell sounded the hour, there came a knocking at the street door. I went down to open it with a light heart,—for what had I *now* to fear? There entered three men, who introduced themselves, with perfect suavity, as officers of the police. A shriek had been heard by a neighbor during the night; suspicion of foul play had been aroused, information had been lodged at the police office, and they (the officers) had been deputed to search the premises.

I smiled,—for *what* had I to fear? I bade the gentlemen welcome. The shriek, I said, was my own in a dream. The old man, I mentioned, was absent in the country. I took my visitors all over the house. I bade them search—search *well*. I led them, at length, to *his* chamber. I showed them his treasures, secure, undisturbed. In the enthusiasm of my confidence, I brought chairs into the room, and desired them *here* to rest from their fatigues, while I myself, in the wild audacity of my perfect triumph, placed my own seat upon the very spot beneath which reposed the corpse of the victim.

The officers were satisfied. My *manner* had convinced them. I was singularly at ease. They sat, and while I answered cheerily, they chatted of familiar things. But, ere long, I felt myself getting pale and wished them gone. My head ached, and I fancied a ringing in my ears: but still they sat and still chatted. The ringing became more distinct:—it continued and became more distinct: I talked more freely to get rid of the feeling: but it continued and gained definitiveness—until, at length, I found that the noise was *not* within my ears.

No doubt I now grew *very* pale:—but I talked more fluently, and with a heightened voice. Yet the sound increased—and what could I do? It was a *low, dull, quick sound—much such a sound as a watch makes when*

15

enveloped in cotton. I gasped for breath—and yet the officers heard it not. I talked more quickly—more vehemently; but the noise steadily increased. I arose and argued about trifles, in a high key and with violent gesticulations; but the noise steadily increased. Why *would* they not be gone? I paced the floor to and fro with heavy strides, as if excited to fury by the observations of the men—but the noise steadily increased. Oh God! what *could* I do? I foamed—I raved—I swore! I swung the chair upon which I had been sitting, and grated it upon the boards, but the noise arose over all and continually increased. It grew louder—louder—*louder!* And still the men chatted pleasantly, and smiled. Was it possible they heard not? Almighty God!—no, no! They heard!—they suspected!—they *knew!*—they were making a mockery of my horror!—this I thought, and this I think. But anything was better than this agony! Anything was more tolerable than this derision! I could bear those hypocritical smiles no longer! I felt that I must scream or die!—and now—again!—hark! louder! louder! louder! *louder!*—

"Villains!" I shrieked, "dissemble no more! I admit the deed!—tear up the planks!—here, here!—it is the beating of his hideous heart!"

QUESTIONS

1. From what point of view is Poe's story told? Why is this point of view particularly effective for "The Tell-Tale Heart"?
2. Point to details in the story that identify its speaker as an unreliable narrator.
3. What do we know about the old man in the story? What motivates the narrator to kill him?
4. In spite of all his precautions, the narrator does not commit the perfect crime. What trips him up?
5. How do you account for the police officers' chatting calmly with the murderer instead of reacting to the sound that stirs the murderer into a frenzy?

WRITING EFFECTIVELY

WRITING ABOUT POINT OF VIEW

How Point of View Shapes a Story

When we hear an outlandish piece of news, something that doesn't quite add up, we're well advised, as the saying goes, to consider the source. The same is true when we read a narrative. Who is telling us the story? And why is he or she telling it?

A story's point of view determines how much confidence a reader should have in the events related. A story told from a third-person omniscient point of view generally provides a sense of authority and stability that makes the narrative seem reliable.

The use of a first-person narrator, on the other hand, often suggests a certain bias, especially when the narrator relates events in which he or she has played a part. In such cases the narrator sometimes has an obvious interest in the audience's accepting his or her particular version of the story as truth.

Understanding the limits and rewards of a narrator's point of view is key to interpreting what a story says.

CHECKLIST

Understanding Point of View

✓ How is the story narrated? Is it told in the first or the third person?

✓ If the story is told in the third person, is the point of view omniscient, or does it stick closely to what is perceived by a particular character?

✓ What is gained by this choice?

✓ If the story is told by a first-person narrator, what is the speaker's main reason for telling the story?

✓ Does the narrator have something at stake in presenting the events? What does the narrator have to gain by making us believe his or her account?

✓ Does the first-person narrator fully understand his or her own motivations? Is there some important aspect of the narrator's character or situation that is being overlooked?

✓ If the story is told in the first person, is there anything peculiar about the narrator? Does this peculiarity create any suspicions about the narrator's accuracy or reliability?

✓ What does the speaker's perspective add? Would the story seem as memorable if related from another narrative angle?

WRITING ASSIGNMENT ON POINT OF VIEW

Choose a story from this book and analyze how point of view contributes to the story's overall meaning. Come up with a thesis sentence, and back up your argument with specific observations about the text. Incorporate at least three quotations, and document them, as explained in the writing chapters at the end of the book. Two stories that lend themselves well to this assignment are "Cathedral" and "The Tell-Tale Heart."

MORE TOPICS FOR WRITING

1. Retell the events in "A & P" from the point of view of one of the story's minor characters: Lengel, or Stokesie, or one of the girls. How does the story's emphasis change?

2. Here is another writing exercise to help you sense what a difference a point of view makes. Write a short statement from the point of view of William Faulkner's Homer Barron (on "My Affair with Miss Emily").

3. Imagine a story such as "A & P" or "A Rose for Emily" told by an omniscient third-person narrator. Write several paragraphs about what would be lost (or gained) by such a change.

4. Choose any tale from "Stories for Further Reading," and, in a paragraph or two, describe how point of view colors the general meaning. If you like, you may argue that the story might be told more effectively from an alternate point of view.

5. Think back to a confrontation in your own life, and describe that event from a point of view contrary to your own. Try to imagine yourself inside your speaker's personality, and present the facts as that person would, as convincingly as you can.

6. Tell the story of a confrontation—biographical or fictional—from the point of view of a minor character peripheral to the central action. You could, for instance, tell the story of a disastrous first date from the point of view of the unlucky waitress who serves the couple dinner.

3
Character

From popular fiction and drama, both classic and contemporary, we are acquainted with many stereotyped characters. Called **stock characters**, they are often known by some outstanding trait or traits: the *bragging* soldier of Greek and Roman comedy, the Prince *Charming* of fairy tales, the *mad* scientist of horror movies, the *fearlessly reckless* police detective of urban action films, the *greedy* explorer of Tarzan films, the *brilliant but alcoholic* brain surgeon of medical thrillers on television. Stock characters are especially convenient for writers of commercial fiction: they require little detailed portraiture, for we already know them well. Most writers of the literary story, however, attempt to create characters who strike us not as stereotypes but as unique individuals. Although stock characters tend to have single dominant virtues and vices, characters in the finest contemporary short stories tend to have many facets, like people we meet.

A **character**, then, is presumably an imagined person who inhabits a story—although that simple definition may admit to a few exceptions. In George Stewart's novel *Storm*, the protagonist is the wind; in Richard Adams's *Watership Down*, the main characters are rabbits. But usually we recognize, in the main characters of a story, human personalities that become familiar to us. If the story seems "true to life," we generally find that its characters act in a reasonably consistent manner and that the author has provided them with **motivation**: sufficient reason to behave as they do. Should a character behave in a sudden and unexpected way, seeming to deny what we have been told about his or her nature or personality, we trust that there was a reason for this behavior and that sooner or later we will discover it. This is not to claim that *all* authors insist that their characters behave with absolute consistency, for (as we shall see later in this chapter) some contemporary stories feature characters who sometimes act without apparent reason. Nor can we say that, in good fiction, characters never change or develop. In *A Christmas Carol*, Charles Dickens tells how Ebenezer Scrooge, a tightfisted miser, reforms overnight, suddenly gives to the poor, and endeavors to assist his clerk's struggling family. But Dickens amply demonstrates why Scrooge had such a change of heart: four ghostly visitors, stirring kind memories the old miser had forgotten and also warning him of the probable consequences of his habits, provide the character (and hence the story) with adequate motivation.

To borrow the useful terms of the English novelist E. M. Forster, characters may seem **flat** or **round**, depending on whether a writer sketches or sculpts them.

A flat character has only one outstanding trait or feature, or at most a few distinguishing marks: for example, the familiar stock character of the mad scientist, with his lust for absolute power and his crazily gleaming eyes. Flat characters, however, need not be stock characters: in all of literature there is probably only one Tiny Tim, though his functions in A *Christmas Carol* are mainly to invoke blessings and to remind others of their Christian duties. Some writers, notably Balzac, who peopled his many novels with hosts of characters, try to distinguish the flat ones by giving each a single odd physical feature or mannerism—a nervous twitch, a piercing gaze, an obsessive fondness for oysters. Round characters, however, present us with more facets— that is, their authors portray them in greater depth and in more generous detail. Such a round character may appear to us only as he appears to the other characters in the story. If their views of him differ, we will see him from more than one side. In other stories, we enter a character's mind and come to know him through his own thoughts, feelings, and perceptions.

Flat characters tend to stay the same throughout a story, but round characters often change—learn or become enlightened, grow or deteriorate. In William Faulkner's "Barn Burning" (Chapter 5), the boy Sarty Snopes, driven to defy his proud and violent father, becomes at the story's end more knowing and more mature. (Some critics call a fixed character **static**; a changing one, **dynamic**.) This is not to damn a flat character as an inferior work of art. In most fiction—even the greatest—minor characters tend to be flat instead of round. Why? Rounding them would cost time and space; and so enlarged, they might only distract us from the main characters.

"A character, first of all, is the noise of his name," according to novelist William Gass.[1] Names, chosen artfully, can indicate natures. A simple illustration is the completely virtuous Squire Allworthy, the foster father in *Tom Jones* by Henry Fielding. Subtler, perhaps, is the custom of giving a character a name that makes an **allusion**: a reference to some famous person, place, or thing in history, in other fiction, or in actuality. For his central characters in *Moby-Dick*, Herman Melville chose names from the Old Testament, calling his tragic and domineering Ahab after a biblical tyrant who came to a bad end, and his wandering narrator Ishmael after a biblical outcast. Whether or not it includes an allusion, a good name often reveals the character of the character. Charles Dickens, a vigorous and richly suggestive christener, named a charming confidence man Mr. Jingle (suggesting something jingly, light, and superficially pleasant), named a couple of shyster lawyers Dodgson and Fogg (suggesting dodging evasiveness and foglike obfuscation), and named two heartless educators, who grimly drill their schoolchildren in "hard facts," Gradgind and M'Choakumchild. Henry James, who so loved names that he

---

[1]"The Concept of Character in Fiction," *Fiction and the Figures of Life* (New York: Knopf, 1970).

kept lists of them for characters he might someday conceive, chose for a sensitive, cultured gentleman the name of Lambert Strether; for a down-to-earth, benevolent individual, the name of Mrs. Bread.

Instead of a hero, many a recent novel has featured an **antihero**: a protagonist conspicuously lacking in one or more of the usual attributes of a traditional hero (bravery, skill, idealism, sense of purpose). The antihero is an ordinary, unglorious citizen of the modern world, usually drawn (according to Sean O'Faolain) as someone "groping, puzzled, cross, mocking, frustrated, and isolated."[2] If epic poets once drew their heroes as decisive leaders of their people, embodying their people's highest ideals, antiheroes tend to be loners, without perfections, just barely able to survive. Antiheroes lack "character," as defined by psychologist Anthony Quinton to mean a person's conduct or "persistence and consistency in seeking to realize his long-term aims."[3] A gulf separates Leopold Bloom, antihero of James Joyce's novel *Ulysses*, from the hero of the Greek *Odyssey*. In Homer's epic, Ulysses wanders the Mediterranean, battling monsters and overcoming enchantments. In Joyce's novel, Bloom wanders the littered streets of Dublin, peddling advertising space. Meursault, the title character of Albert Camus's novel *The Stranger*, is so alienated from his own life that he is unmoved at the news of his mother's death.

Evidently, not only fashions in heroes but also attitudes toward human nature have undergone change. In the eighteenth century, Scottish philosopher David Hume argued that the nature of an individual is relatively fixed and unalterable. Hume mentioned, however, a few exceptions: "A person of an obliging disposition gives a peevish answer; but he has the toothache or has not dined. A stupid fellow discovers an obvious alacrity in his carriage; but he has met with a sudden piece of good fortune." For a long time after Hume, novelists and short-story writers seem to have assumed that characters nearly always behave in a predictable fashion and that their actions ought to be consistent with their personalities. Now and again, a writer differed: Jane Austen in *Pride and Prejudice* has her protagonist Elizabeth Bennet remark to the citified Mr. Darcy, who fears that life in the country cannot be amusing, "But people themselves alter so much, that there is something to be observed in them forever."

Many contemporary writers of fiction would deny even that people have definite selves to alter. Following Sigmund Freud and other modern psychologists, they assume that a large part of human behavior is shaped in the unconscious— that, for instance, a person might fear horses, not because of a basically timid nature, but because of unconscious memories of having been nearly trampled by a horse when a child. To some writers it now appears that what Hume

[2]*The Vanishing Hero* (Boston: Little, 1957).
[3]"The Continuity of Persons," *Times Literary Supplement*, 27 July 1973.

called a "disposition" (what we call a "personality") is more vulnerable to change from such causes as age, disease, neurosis, psychic shock, or brainwashing than was once believed. Hence, some characters in modern fiction appear to be shifting bundles of impulses. "You mustn't look in my novel for the old stable ego of character," wrote D. H. Lawrence to a friend about *The Rainbow*; and in that novel and others Lawrence demonstrated his view of individuals as bits of one vast Life Force, spurred to act by incomprehensible passions and urges—the "dark gods" in them. The idea of the **gratuitous act**, a deed without cause or motive, is explored in André Gide's novel *Lafcadio's Adventures*, in which an ordinary young man without homicidal tendencies abruptly and for no reason pushes a stranger from a speeding train. The usual limits of character are playfully violated by Virginia Woolf in *Orlando*, a novel whose protagonist, defying time, lives right on from Elizabethan days into the present, changing in midstory from a man into a woman. Characterization, as practiced by nineteenth-century novelists, almost entirely disappears in Franz Kafka's *The Castle*, whose protagonist has no home, no family, no definite appearance— not even a name, just the initial K. Characters are things of the past, insists the contemporary French novelist Alain Robbe-Grillet. Still, many writers of fiction go on portraying them.

Katherine Mansfield

Miss Brill 1922

Katherine Mansfield Beauchamp (1888–1923), who short-ened her byline, was born into a sedate Victorian family in New Zealand, daughter of a successful businessman. At fifteen, she emigrated to England to attend school and did not ever permanently return Down Under. In 1918, after a time of wild-oat sowing in bohemian London, she married the journalist and critic John Middleton Murry. All at once, Mansfield found herself struggling to define her sexual identity, to earn a living by her pen, to endure World War I (in which her brother was killed in action), and to survive the ravages of tuberculosis. She died at thirty-four, in France,

KATHERINE MANSFIELD

at a spiritualist commune where she had sought to regain her health. Mansfield wrote no novels, but during her brief career concentrated on the short story, in which form of art she has few peers. Bliss (1920) and The Garden-Party and Other Stories (1922) were greeted with an acclaim that has continued; her collected short stories were published in 1937. Some of her stories celebrate life, others wryly poke fun at it. Many reveal, in ordinary lives, small incidents that open like doorways into significances.

Although it was so brilliantly fine—the blue sky powdered with gold and great spots of light like white wine splashed over the Jardins Publiques—Miss Brill was glad that she had decided on her fur. The air was motionless, but when you opened your mouth there was just a faint chill, like a chill from a glass of iced water before you sip, and now and again a leaf came drifting—from nowhere, from the sky. Miss Brill put up her hand and touched her fur. Dear little thing! It was nice to feel it again. She had taken it out of its box that afternoon, shaken out the moth-powder, given it a good brush, and rubbed the life back into the dim little eyes. "What has been happening to me?" said the sad little eyes. Oh, how sweet it was to see them snap at her again from the red eider-down! . . . But the nose, which was of some black composition, wasn't at all firm. It must have had a knock, somehow. Never mind—a little dab of black sealing-wax when the time came—when it was absolutely necessary. . . . Little rogue! Yes, she really felt like that about it. Little rogue biting its tail just by her left ear. She could have taken it off and laid it on her lap and stroked it. She felt a tingling in her hands and arms, but that came from walking, she supposed. And when she breathed, something light and sad—no, not sad, exactly—something gentle seemed to move in her bosom.

There were a number of people out this afternoon, far more than last Sunday. And the band sounded louder and gayer. That was because the Season had begun. For although the band played all year round on Sundays, out of season it was never the same. It was like some one playing with only the family to listen; it didn't care how it played if there weren't any strangers present. Wasn't the conductor wearing a new coat, too? She was sure it was new. He scraped with his foot and flapped his arms like a rooster about to crow, and the bandsmen sitting in the green rotunda blew out their cheeks and glared at the music. Now there came a little "flutey" bit—very pretty!—a little chain of bright drops. She was sure it would be repeated. It was; she lifted her head and smiled.

Only two people shared her "special" seat: a fine old man in a velvet coat, his hands clasped over a huge carved walking-stick, and a big old woman, sitting upright, with a roll of knitting on her embroidered apron. They did not speak. This was disappointing, for Miss Brill always looked forward to the conversation. She had become really quite expert, she thought, at listening as though she didn't listen, at sitting in other people's lives just for a minute while they talked round her.

She glanced, sideways, at the old couple. Perhaps they would go soon. Last Sunday, too, hadn't been as interesting as usual. An Englishman and his wife, he wearing a dreadful Panama hat and she button boots. And she'd gone on the whole time about how she ought to wear spectacles; she knew she needed them; but that it was no good getting any; they'd be sure to break and they'd never keep on. And he'd been so patient. He'd suggested everything—gold rims, the kind that curved round your ears, little pads inside the bridge. No, nothing would please her. "They'll always be sliding down my nose!" Miss Brill wanted to shake her.

The old people sat on the bench, still as statues. Never mind, there   5 was always the crowd to watch. To and fro, in front of the flower-beds and the band rotunda, the couples and groups paraded, stopped to talk, to greet, to buy a handful of flowers from the old beggar who had his tray fixed to the railings. Little children ran among them, swooping and laughing; little boys with big white silk bows under their chins, little girls, little French dolls, dressed up in velvet and lace. And sometimes a tiny staggerer came suddenly rocking into the open from under the trees, stopped, stared, as suddenly sat down "flop," until its small high-stepping mother, like a young hen, rushed scolding to its rescue. Other people sat on the benches and green chairs, but they were nearly always the same, Sunday after Sunday, and—Miss Brill had often noticed—there was something funny about nearly all of them. They were odd, silent, nearly all old, and from the way they stared they looked as though they'd just come from dark little rooms or even—even cupboards!

Behind the rotunda the slender trees with yellow leaves down drooping, and through them just a line of sea, and beyond the blue sky with gold-veined clouds.

Tum-tum-tum tiddle-um! tiddle-um! tum tiddley-um tum ta! blew the band.

Two young girls in red came by and two young soldiers in blue met them, and they laughed and paired and went off arm-in-arm. Two peasant women with funny straw hats passed, gravely, leading beautiful smoke-colored donkeys. A cold, pale nun hurried by. A beautiful woman came along and dropped her bunch of violets, and a little boy ran after to hand them to her, and she took them and threw them away as if they'd been poisoned. Dear me! Miss Brill didn't know whether to admire that or not! And now an ermine toque and a gentleman in grey met just in front of her. He was tall, stiff, dignified, and she was wearing the ermine toque she'd bought when her hair was yellow. Now everything, her hair, her face, even her eyes, was the same color as the shabby ermine, and her hand, in its cleaned glove, lifted to dab her lips, was a tiny yellowish paw. Oh, she was so pleased to see him—delighted! She rather thought they were going to meet that afternoon. She described where she'd been— everywhere, here, there, along by the sea. The day was so charming— didn't he agree? And wouldn't he, perhaps? . . . But he shook his head, lighted a cigarette, slowly breathed a great deep puff into her face, and, even while she was still talking and laughing, flicked the match away and walked on. The ermine toque was alone; she smiled more brightly than ever. But even the band seemed to know what she was feeling and played more softly, played tenderly, and the drum beat, "The Brute! The Brute!" over and over. What would she do? What was going to happen now? But as Miss Brill wondered, the ermine toque turned, raised her hand as though she'd seen some one else, much nicer, just over there, and pattered away. And the band changed again and played more quickly, more gaily than ever, and the old couple on Miss Brill's seat got up and marched away, and such a funny old man with long whiskers hobbled along in time to the music and was nearly knocked over by four girls walking abreast.

Oh, how fascinating it was! How she enjoyed it! How she loved sitting here, watching it all! It was like a play. It was exactly like a play. Who could believe the sky at the back wasn't painted? But it wasn't till a little brown dog trotted on solemn and then slowly trotted off, like a little "theatre" dog, a little dog that had been drugged, that Miss Brill discovered what it was that made it so exciting. They were all on the stage. They weren't only the audience, not only looking on; they were acting. Even she had a part and came every Sunday. No doubt somebody would have noticed if she hadn't been there; she was part of the performance after all. How strange she'd never thought of it like that before! And yet it explained why she made such a point of starting from home at just the same time each week—so as not to be late for the performance—and it also explained why she had quite a queer, shy feeling at telling her English pupils how she spent her Sunday afternoons. No wonder! Miss Brill nearly laughed out loud. She was on the stage. She thought of the old invalid gentleman to whom she read the newspaper four afternoons a week while he slept in the garden. She had got quite used to the frail head on the cotton pillow, the hollowed eyes, the open mouth and the high pinched nose. If he'd been dead she mightn't have noticed for weeks; she wouldn't have minded. But suddenly he knew he was having the paper read to him by an actress! "An actress!" The old head lifted; two points of light quivered in the old eyes. "An actress—are ye?" And Miss Brill smoothed the newspaper as though it were the manuscript of her part and said gently: "Yes, I have been an actress for a long time."

The band had been having a rest. Now they started again. And what they played was warm, sunny, yet there was just a faint chill—a something, what was it?—not sadness—no, not sadness—a something that made you want to sing. The tune lifted, lifted, the light shone; and it seemed to Miss Brill that in another moment all of them, all the whole company, would begin singing. The young ones, the laughing ones who were moving together, they would begin, and the men's voices, very resolute and brave, would join them. And then she too, she too, and the others on the benches—they would come in with a kind of accompaniment—something low, that scarcely rose or fell, something so beautiful—moving . . . And Miss Brill's eyes filled with tears and she looked

10

smiling at all the other members of the company. Yes, we understand, we understand, she thought—though what they understood she didn't know.

Just at that moment a boy and a girl came and sat down where the old couple had been. They were beautifully dressed; they were in love. The hero and heroine, of course, just arrived from his father's yacht. And still soundlessly singing, still with that trembling smile, Miss Brill prepared to listen.

"No, not now," said the girl. "Not here, I can't."

"But why? Because of that stupid old thing at the end there?" asked the boy. "Why does she come here at all—who wants her? Why doesn't she keep her silly old mug at home?"

"It's her fu-fur which is so funny," giggled the girl. "It's exactly like a fried whiting."

"Ah, be off with you!" said the boy in an angry whisper. Then: "Tell   15
me, my petite chérie—"

"No, not here," said the girl. "Not *yet*."

On her way home she usually bought a slice of honeycake at the baker's. It was her Sunday treat. Sometimes there was an almond in her slice, sometimes not. It made a great difference. If there was an almond it was like carrying home a tiny present—a surprise—something that might very well not have been there. She hurried on the almond Sundays and struck the match for the kettle in quite a dashing way.

But today she passed the baker's boy, climbed the stairs, went into the little dark room—her room like a cupboard—and sat down on the red eiderdown. She sat there for a long time. The box that the fur came out of was on the bed. She unclasped the necklet quickly; quickly, without looking, laid it inside. But when she put the lid on she thought she heard something crying.

QUESTIONS

1. What details provide insight into Miss Brill's character and lifestyle?
2. What point of view is used in "Miss Brill"? How does this method improve the story?
3. Where and in what season does the story take place? Would the effect be the same if the story were set, say, in a remote Alaskan village in the winter?
4. What draws Miss Brill to the park every Sunday? What is the nature of the startling revelation that delights her on the day the story takes place?
5. Miss Brill's sense of herself is at least partly based on her attitudes toward others. Give instances of this tendency, showing also how it is connected with her drastic change of mood.
6. What explanations might there be for Miss Brill's thinking, in the last line of the story, that she "heard something crying"?

Raymond Carver

Cathedral

1983

Born in Clatskanie, Oregon, Raymond Carver (1938–1988) moved at three with his parents to Yakima, Washington, where his father found employment as a sawmill worker. In his early years Carver worked briefly at a lumber mill and at other unskilled jobs, including a stint as a tulip-picker. Married with two children before he was twenty, he experienced blue-collar desperation on terms more intimate than have most American writers, though he once quipped that, until he read critics' reactions to his works, he

RAYMOND CARVER

never realized that the characters in his stories "were so bad off." Carver attended several universities, including Chico State College, where he studied with novelist John Gardner, and Humboldt State College (now California State University, Humboldt), where he earned a degree in 1963. He briefly attended the Writers' Workshop of the University of Iowa, but pressured by the need to support his family, he returned to California, working for three years as a hospital custodian before finding a job editing textbooks. In 1967 he met Gordon Lish, the influential editor who would publish several of his stories in Esquire, and had one of his early stories selected for publication in The Best American Short Stories of 1967. *Under Lish's demanding tutelage, Carver learned to strip his fiction of everything but the essentials. Through the early 1970s, though plagued with bankruptcies, increasing dependency on alcohol, and marital problems, Carver began teaching in various one-year appointments at several universities.*

Carver's publishing career began with a collection of poems, Near Klamath *(1968). His collections of short stories include* Will You Please Be Quiet, Please? *(1977),* What We Talk About When We Talk About Love *(1981),* Cathedral *(1983), and* Where I'm Calling From *(1988), which contained new and selected work. The compression of language he learned as a poet may in part account for the lean quality of his prose, what has been termed "minimalist," a term Carver himself did not like, complaining that the term "smacks of smallness of vision and execution." In his last decade Carver taught creative writing at Syracuse University, living with the poet Tess Gallagher, whom he married in 1988. His receipt of the Mildred and Harold Strauss Living Award in 1983 finally allowed him to devote his full time to writing. He divided his remaining years between Syracuse and Port Angeles, Washington. Carver's personal victory in 1977 over decades of alcoholism underscored the many professional triumphs of his final decade. He once said, "If you want the truth, I'm prouder of that, that I quit drinking, than I am of anything in my life." His reputation as a master craftsman of the contemporary short story was still growing at the end of his life, which ended prematurely after a struggle with lung cancer.*

This blind man, an old friend of my wife's, he was on his way to spend the night. His wife had died. So he was visiting the dead wife's relatives in Connecticut. He called my wife from his in-laws'. Arrangements were made. He would come by train, a five-hour trip, and my wife would meet him at the station. She hadn't seen him since she worked for him one summer in Seattle ten years ago. But she and the blind man had kept in touch. They made tapes and mailed them back and forth. I wasn't enthusiastic about his visit. He was no one I knew. And his being blind bothered me. My idea of blindness came from the movies. In the movies, the blind moved slowly and never laughed. Sometimes they were led by seeing-eye dogs. A blind man in my house was not something I looked forward to.

That summer in Seattle she had needed a job. She didn't have any money. The man she was going to marry at the end of the summer was in officers' training school. He didn't have any money, either. But she was in love with the guy, and he was in love with her, etc. She'd seen something in the paper: HELP WANTED—*Reading to Blind Man*, and a telephone number. She phoned and went over, was hired on the spot. She'd worked with this blind man all summer. She read stuff to him, case studies, reports, that sort of thing. She helped him organize his little office in the county social-service department. They'd become good friends, my wife and the blind man. How do I know these things? She told me. And she told me something else. On her last day in the office, the blind man asked if he could touch her face. She agreed to this. She told me he touched his fingers to every part of her face, her nose—even her neck! She never forgot it. She even tried to write a poem about it. She was always trying to write a poem. She wrote a poem or two every year, usually after something really important had happened to her.

When we first started going out together, she showed me the poem. In the poem, she recalled his fingers and the way they had moved around over her face. In the poem, she talked about what she had felt at the time, about what went through her mind when the blind man touched her nose and lips. I can remember I didn't think much of the poem. Of course, I didn't tell her that. Maybe I just don't understand poetry. I admit it's not the first thing I reach for when I pick up something to read.

Anyway, this man who'd first enjoyed her favors, the officer-to-be, he'd been her childhood sweetheart. So okay. I'm saying that at the end of the summer she let the blind man run his hands over her face, said good-bye to him, married her childhood etc., who was now a commissioned officer, and she moved away from Seattle. But they'd kept in touch, she and the blind man. She made the first contact after a year or so. She called him up one night from an Air Force base in Alabama. She wanted to talk. They talked. He asked her to send a tape and tell him about her life. She did this. She sent the tape. On the tape, she told the blind man about her husband and about their life together in the military. She told the blind man she loved her husband but she didn't like it where they lived and she didn't like it that he was part of the military-industrial thing. She told the blind man she'd written a poem and he was in it. She told him that she was writing a poem about what it was like to be an Air Force officer's wife. The poem wasn't finished yet. She was still writing it. The blind man made a tape. He sent her the tape. She made a tape. This went on for years. My wife's officer was posted to one base and then another. She sent tapes from Moody AFB, McGuire, McConnell, and finally Travis, near Sacramento, where one night she got to feeling lonely and cut off from people she kept losing in that moving-around life. She got to feeling she couldn't go it another step. She went in and swallowed all the pills and capsules in the medicine chest and washed them down with a bottle of gin. Then she got into a hot bath and passed out.

But instead of dying, she got sick. She threw up. Her officer—why should he have a name? he was the childhood sweetheart, and what more does he want?—came home from somewhere, found her, and called the ambulance. In time, she put it all on a tape and sent the tape to the blind man. Over the years, she put all kinds of stuff on tapes and sent the tapes off lickety-split. Next to writing a poem every year, I think it was her chief means of recreation. On one tape, she told the blind man she'd decided to live away from her officer for a time. On another tape, she told him about her divorce. She and I began going out, and of course she told her blind man about it. She told him everything, or so it seemed to me. Once she asked me if I'd like to hear the latest tape from the blind man. This was a year ago. I was on the tape, she said. So I said okay, I'd listen to it. I got us drinks and we settled down in the living room. We made ready to listen. First she inserted the tape into the player and adjusted a couple of dials. Then she pushed a lever. The tape squeaked and someone began to talk in this loud voice. She lowered the volume. After a few minutes of harmless chitchat, I heard my own name in the mouth of this stranger, this blind man I didn't even know! And then this: "From all you've said about him, I can only conclude—" But we were interrupted, a knock at the door, something, and we didn't ever get back to the tape. Maybe it was just as well. I'd heard all I wanted to.

Now this same blind man was coming to sleep in my house.

"Maybe I could take him bowling," I said to my wife. She was at the draining board doing scalloped potatoes. She put down the knife she was using and turned around.

"If you love me," she said, "you can do this for me. If you don't love me, okay. But if you had a friend, any friend, and the friend came to visit, I'd make him feel comfortable." She wiped her hands with the dish towel.

"I don't have any blind friends," I said.

"You don't have *any* friends," she said. "Period. Besides," she said,   10
"goddamn it, his wife's just died! Don't you understand that? The man's
lost his wife!"

I didn't answer. She'd told me a little about the blind man's wife.
Her name was Beulah. Beulah! That's a name for a colored woman.

"Was his wife a Negro?" I asked.

"Are you crazy?" my wife said. "Have you just flipped or something?"
She picked up a potato. I saw it hit the floor, then roll under the stove.
"What's wrong with you?" she said. "Are you drunk?"

"I'm just asking," I said.

Right then my wife filled me in with more detail than I cared to   15
know. I made a drink and sat at the kitchen table to listen. Pieces of the
story began to fall into place.

Beulah had gone to work for the blind man the summer after my wife
had stopped working for him. Pretty soon Beulah and the blind man had
themselves a church wedding. It was a little wedding—who'd want to go
to such a wedding in the first place?—just the two of them, plus the minister and the minister's wife. But it was a church wedding just the same. It
was what Beulah had wanted, he'd said. But even then Beulah must have
been carrying the cancer in her glands. After they had been inseparable
for eight years—my wife's word, *inseparable*—Beulah's health went into a
rapid decline. She died in a Seattle hospital room, the blind man sitting
beside the bed and holding on to her hand. They'd married, lived and
worked together, slept together—had sex, sure—and then the blind man
had to bury her. All this without his having ever seen what the god-
damned woman looked like. It was beyond my understanding. Hearing
this, I felt sorry for the blind man for a little bit. And then I found myself
thinking what a pitiful life this woman must have led. Imagine a woman
who could never see herself as she was seen in the eyes of her loved one.
A woman who could go on day after day and never receive the smallest
compliment from her beloved. A woman whose husband could never
read the expression on her face, be it misery or something better. Someone who could wear makeup or not—what difference to him? She could,
if she wanted, wear green eye-shadow around one eye, a straight pin in
her nostril, yellow slacks, and purple shoes, no matter. And then to slip
off into death, the blind man's hand on her hand, his blind eyes streaming tears—I'm imagining now—her last thought maybe this: that he
never even knew what she looked like, and she on an express to the
grave. Robert was left with a small insurance policy and a half of a
twenty-peso Mexican coin. The other half of the coin went into the box
with her. Pathetic.

So when the time rolled around, my wife went to the depot to pick
him up. With nothing to do but wait—sure, I blamed him for that—I was

having a drink and watching the TV when I heard the car pull into the drive. I got up from the sofa with my drink and went to the window to have a look.

I saw my wife laughing as she parked the car. I saw her get out of the car and shut the door. She was still wearing a smile. Just amazing. She went around to the other side of the car to where the blind man was already starting to get out. This blind man, feature this, he was wearing a full beard! A beard on a blind man! Too much, I say. The blind man reached into the backseat and dragged out a suitcase. My wife took his arm, shut the car door, and, talking all the way, moved him down the drive and then up the steps to the front porch. I turned off the TV. I finished my drink, rinsed the glass, dried my hands. Then I went to the door.

My wife said, "I want you to meet Robert. Robert, this is my husband. I've told you all about him." She was beaming. She had this blind man by his coat sleeve.

The blind man let go of his suitcase and up came his hand. 　　　20

I took it. He squeezed hard, held my hand, and then he let it go.

"I feel like we've already met," he boomed.

"Likewise," I said. I didn't know what else to say. Then I said, "Welcome. I've heard a lot about you." We began to move then, a little group, from the porch into the living room, my wife guiding him by the arm. The blind man was carrying his suitcase in his other hand. My wife said things like, "To your left here, Robert. That's right. Now watch it, there's a chair. That's it. Sit down right here. This is the sofa. We just bought this sofa two weeks ago."

I started to say something about the old sofa. I'd liked that old sofa. But I didn't say anything. Then I wanted to say something else, small-talk, about the scenic ride along the Hudson. How going *to* New York, you should sit on the right-hand side of the train, and coming *from* New York, the left-hand side.

"Did you have a good train ride?" I said. "Which side of the train did 　　25 you sit on, by the way?"

"What a question, which side!" my wife said. "What's it matter which side?" she said.

"I just asked," I said.

"Right side," the blind man said. "I hadn't been on a train in nearly forty years. Not since I was a kid. With my folks. That's been a long time. I'd nearly forgotten the sensation. I have winter in my beard now," he said. "So I've been told, anyway. Do I look distinguished, my dear?" the blind man said to my wife.

"You look distinguished, Robert," she said. "Robert," she said. "Robert, it's just so good to see you."

My wife finally took her eyes off the blind man and looked at me. I 　　30 had the feeling she didn't like what she saw. I shrugged.

I've never met, or personally known, anyone who was blind. This blind man was late forties, a heavy-set, balding man with stooped shoulders, as if he carried a great weight there. He wore brown slacks, brown shoes, a light-brown shirt, a tie, a sports coat. Spiffy. He also had this full beard. But he didn't use a cane and he didn't wear dark glasses. I'd always thought dark glasses were a must for the blind. Fact was, I wished he had a pair. At first glance, his eyes looked like anyone else's eyes. But if you looked close, there was something different about them. Too much white in the iris, for one thing, and the pupils seemed to move around in the sockets without his knowing it or being able to stop it. Creepy. As I stared at his face, I saw the left pupil turn in toward his nose while the other made an effort to keep in one place. But it was only an effort, for that eye was on the roam without his knowing it or wanting it to be.

I said, "Let me get you a drink. What's your pleasure? We have a little of everything. It's one of our pastimes."

"Bub, I'm a Scotch man myself," he said fast enough in this big voice.

"Right," I said. Bub! "Sure you are. I knew it."

He let his fingers touch his suitcase, which was sitting alongside the 35 sofa. He was taking his bearings. I didn't blame him for that.

"I'll move that up to your room," my wife said.

"No, that's fine," the blind man said loudly. "It can go up when I go up."

"A little water with the Scotch?" I said.

"Very little," he said.

"I knew it," I said. 40

He said, "Just a tad. The Irish actor, Barry Fitzgerald? I'm like that fellow. When I drink water, Fitzgerald said, I drink water. When I drink whiskey, I drink whiskey." My wife laughed. The blind man brought his hand up under his beard. He lifted his beard slowly and let it drop.

I did the drinks, three big glasses of Scotch with a splash of water in each. Then we made ourselves comfortable and talked about Robert's travels. First the long flight from the West Coast to Connecticut, we covered that. Then from Connecticut up here by train. We had another drink concerning that leg of the trip.

I remembered having read somewhere that the blind didn't smoke because, as speculation had it, they couldn't see the smoke they exhaled. I thought I knew that much and that much only about blind people. But this blind man smoked his cigarette down to the nubbin and then lit another one. This blind man filled his ashtray and my wife emptied it.

When we sat down at the table for dinner, we had another drink. My wife heaped Robert's plate with cube steak, scalloped potatoes, green beans. I buttered him up two slices of bread. I said, "Here's bread and butter for you." I swallowed some of my drink. "Now let us pray," I said, and the blind man lowered his head. My wife looked at me, her mouth agape. "Pray the phone won't ring and the food doesn't get cold," I said.

We dug in. We ate everything there was to eat on the table. We ate 45 like there was no tomorrow. We didn't talk. We ate. We scarfed. We grazed that table. We were into serious eating. The blind man had right away located his foods, he knew just where everything was on his plate. I watched with admiration as he used his knife and fork on the meat. He'd cut two pieces of meat, fork the meat into his mouth, and then go all out for the scalloped potatoes, the beans next, and then he'd tear off a hunk of buttered bread and eat that. He'd follow this up with a big drink of milk. It didn't seem to bother him to use his fingers once in a while, either.

We finished everything, including half a strawberry pie. For a few moments, we sat as if stunned. Sweat beaded on our faces. Finally, we got up from the table and left the dirty plates. We didn't look back. We took ourselves into the living room and sank into our places again. Robert and my wife sat on the sofa. I took the big chair. We had us two or three more drinks while they talked about the major things that had come to pass for them in the past ten years. For the most part, I just listened. Now and then I joined in. I didn't want him to think I'd left the room, and I didn't want her to think I was feeling left out. They talked of things that had happened to them—to them!—these past ten years. I waited in vain to hear my name on my wife's sweet lips: "And then my dear husband came into my life"—something like that. But I heard nothing of the sort. More talk of Robert. Robert had done a little of everything, it seemed, a regular blind jack-of-all-trades. But most recently he and his wife had had an Amway distributorship, from which, I gathered, they'd earned their living, such as it was. The blind man was also a ham radio operator. He talked in his loud voice about conversations he'd had with fellow operators in Guam, in the Philippines, in Alaska, and even in Tahiti. He said he'd have a lot of friends there if he ever wanted to go visit those places. From time to time, he'd turn his blind face toward me, put his hand under his beard, ask me something. How long had I been in my present position? (Three years.) Did I like my work? (I didn't.) Was I going to stay with it? (What were the options?) Finally, when I thought he was beginning to run down, I got up and turned on the TV.

My wife looked at me with irritation. She was heading toward a boil. Then she looked at the blind man and said, "Robert, do you have a TV?"

The blind man said, "My dear, I have two TVs. I have a color set and a black-and-white thing, an old relic. It's funny, but if I turn the TV on, and I'm always turning it on, I turn on the color set. It's funny, don't you think?"

I didn't know what to say to that. I had absolutely nothing to say to that. No opinion. So I watched the news program and tried to listen to what the announcer was saying.

"This is a color TV," the blind man said. "Don't ask me how, but I 50 can tell."

"We traded up a while ago," I said.

The blind man had another taste of this drink. He lifted his beard, sniffed it, and let it fall. He leaned forward on the sofa. He positioned his ashtray on the coffee table, then put the lighter to his cigarette. He leaned back on the sofa and crossed his legs at the ankles.

My wife covered her mouth, and then she yawned. She stretched. She said, "I think I'll go upstairs and put on my robe. I think I'll change into something else. Robert, you make yourself comfortable," she said.

"I'm comfortable," the blind man said.

"I want you to feel comfortable in this house," she said. 55

"I am comfortable," the blind man said.

After she'd left the room, he and I listened to the weather report and then to the sports roundup. By that time, she'd been gone so long I didn't know if she was going to come back. I thought she might have gone to bed. I wished she'd come back downstairs. I didn't want to be left alone with a blind man. I asked him if he wanted another drink, and he said sure. Then I asked if he wanted to smoke some dope with me. I said I'd just rolled a number. I hadn't, but I planned to do so in about two shakes.

"I'll try some with you," he said.

"Damm right," I said. "That's the stuff."

"I got our drinks and sat down on the sofa with him. Then I rolled us 60 two fat numbers. I lit one and passed it. I brought it to his fingers. He took it and inhaled.

"Hold it as long as you can," I said. I could tell he didn't know the first thing.

My wife came back downstairs wearing her pink robe and her pink slippers.

"What do I smell?" she said.

"We thought we'd have us some cannabis," I said.

My wife gave me a savage look. Then she looked at the blind man 65 and said, "Robert, I didn't know you smoked."

He said, "I do now, my dear. There's a first time for everything. But I don't feel anything yet."

"This stuff is pretty mellow," I said. "This stuff is mild. It's dope you can reason with," I said. "It doesn't mess you up."

"Not much it doesn't, bub," he said, and laughed.

My wife sat on the sofa between the blind man and me. I passed her the number. She took it and toked and then passed it back to me. "Which way is this going?" she said. Then she said, "I shouldn't be smoking this. I can hardly keep my eyes open as it is. That dinner did me in. I shouldn't have eaten so much."

"It was the strawberry pie," the blind man said. "That's what did it," he said, and he laughed his big laugh. Then he shook his head. 70

"There's more strawberry pie," I said.

"Do you want some more, Robert?" my wife said.

"Maybe in a little while," he said.

We gave our attention to the TV. My wife yawned again. She said, "Your bed is made up when you feel like going to bed, Robert. I know you must have had a long day. When you're ready to go to bed, say so." She pulled his arm. "Robert?"

He came to and said, "I've had a real nice time. This beats tapes, doesn't it?" 75

I said, "Coming at you," and I put the number between his fingers. He inhaled, held the smoke, and then let it go. It was like he'd been doing it since he was nine years old.

"Thanks, bub," he said. "But I think this is all for me. I think I'm beginning to feel it," he said. He held the burning roach out for my wife.

"Same here," she said. "Ditto. Me, too." She took the roach and passed it to me. "I may just sit here for a while between you two guys with my eyes closed. But don't let me bother you, okay? Either one of you. If it bothers you, say so. Otherwise, I may just sit here with my eyes closed until you're ready to go to bed," she said. "Your bed's made up, Robert, when you're ready. It's right next to our room at the top of the stairs. We'll show you up when you're ready. You wake me up now, you guys, if I fall asleep." She said that and then she closed her eyes and went to sleep.

The news program ended. I got up and changed the channel. I sat back down on the sofa. I wished my wife hadn't pooped out. Her head lay across the back of the sofa, her mouth open. She'd turned so that her robe slipped away from her legs, exposing a juicy thigh. I reached to draw her robe back over her, and it was then that I glanced at the blind man. What the hell! I flipped the robe open again.

"You say when you want some strawberry pie," I said.

"I will," he said. 80

I said, "Are you tired? Do you want me to take you up to your bed? Are you ready to hit the hay?"

"Not yet," he said. "No, I'll stay up with you, bub. If that's all right. I'll stay up until you're ready to turn in. We haven't had a chance to talk. Know what I mean? I feel like me and her monopolized the evening." He lifted his beard and he let it fall. He picked up his cigarettes and his lighter.

"That's all right," I said. Then I said, "I'm glad for the company."

And I guess I was. Every night I smoked dope and stayed up as long as I could before I fell asleep. My wife and I hardly ever went to bed at 85 the same time. When I did go to sleep, I had these dreams. Sometimes I'd wake up from one of them, my heart going crazy.

Something about the church and the Middle Ages was on the TV. Not your run-of-the-mill TV fare. I wanted to watch something else. I turned to the other channels. But there was nothing on them, either. So I turned back to the first channel and apologized.

"Bub, it's all right," the blind man said. "It's fine with me. Whatever you want to watch is okay. I'm always learning something. Learning never ends. It won't hurt me to learn something tonight. I got ears," he said.

We didn't say anything for a time. He was leaning forward with his head turned at me, his right ear aimed in the direction of the set. Very disconcerting. Now and then his eyelids drooped and then they snapped open again. Now and then he put his fingers into his beard and tugged, like he was thinking about something he was hearing on the television.

On the screen, a group of men wearing cowls was being set upon and tormented by men dressed in skeleton costumes and men dressed as devils. The men dressed as devils wore devil masks, horns, and long tails. This pageant was part of a procession. The Englishman who was narrating the thing said it took place in Spain once a year. I tried to explain to the blind man what was happening.

"Skeletons," he said. "I know about skeletons," he said, and he nodded. 90

The TV showed this one cathedral. Then there was a long, slow look at another one. Finally, the picture switched to the famous one in Paris, with its flying buttresses and its spires reaching up to the clouds. The camera pulled away to show the whole of the cathedral rising above the skyline.

There were times when the Englishman who was telling the thing would shut up, would simply let the camera move around the cathedrals. Or else the camera would tour the countryside, men in fields walking behind oxen. I waited as long as I could. Then I felt I had to say something. I said, "They're showing the outside of this cathedral now. Gargoyles. Little statues carved to look like monsters. Now I guess they're in Italy. Yeah, they're in Italy. There's paintings on the walls of this one church."

"Are those fresco paintings, bub?" he asked, and he sipped from his drink.

I reached for my glass. But it was empty. I tried to remember what I could remember. "You're asking me are those frescoes?" I said. "That's a good question. I don't know."

The camera moved to a cathedral outside Lisbon. The differences in 95 the Portuguese cathedral compared with the French and Italian were not that great. But they were there. Mostly the interior stuff. Then something occurred to me, and I said, "Something has occurred to me. Do you have any idea what a cathedral is? What they look like, that is? Do you follow me? If somebody says cathedral to you, do you have any notion what they're talking about? Do you know the difference between that and a Baptist church, say?"

He let the smoke dribble from his mouth. "I know they took hundreds of workers fifty or a hundred years to build," he said. "I just heard the man say that, of course. I know generations of the same families worked on a cathedral. I heard him say that, too. The men who began their life's work on them, they never lived to see the completion of their work. In that wise, bub, they're no different from the rest of us, right?" He laughed. Then his eyelids drooped again. His head nodded. He seemed to be snoozing. Maybe he was imagining himself in Portugal. The TV was showing another cathedral now. This one was in Germany. The Englishman's voice droned on. "Cathedrals," the blind man said. He sat up and rolled his head back and forth. "If you want the truth, bub, that's about all I know. What I just said. What I heard him say. But maybe you could describe one to me? I wish you'd do it. I'd like that. If you want to know, I really don't have a good idea."

I stared hard at the shot of the cathedral on the TV. How could I even begin to describe it? But say my life depended on it. Say my life was being threatened by an insane guy who said I had to do it or else.

I stared some more at the cathedral before the picture flipped off into the countryside. There was no use. I turned to the blind man and said, "To begin with, they're very tall." I was looking around the room for clues. "They reach way up. Up and up. Toward the sky. They're so big, some of them, they have to have these supports. To help hold them up, so to speak. These supports are called buttresses. They remind me of viaducts, for some reason. But maybe you don't know viaducts, either? Sometimes the cathedrals have devils and such carved into the front. Sometimes lords and ladies. Don't ask me why this is," I said.

He was nodding. The whole upper part of his body seemed to be moving back and forth.

"I'm not doing so good, am I?" I said.

He stopped nodding and leaned forward on the edge of the sofa. As he listened to me, he was running his fingers through his beard. I wasn't getting through to him, I could see that. But he waited for me to go on just the same. He nodded, like he was trying to encourage me. I tried to think what else to say. "They're really big," I said. "They're massive. They're built of stone. Marble, too, sometimes. In those olden days, when they built cathedrals, men wanted to be close to God. In those olden days, God was an important part of everyone's life. You could tell this from their cathedral-building. I'm sorry," I said, "but it looks like that's the best I can do for you. I'm just no good at it."

100

"That's all right, bub," the blind man said. "Hey, listen. I hope you don't mind my asking you. Can I ask you something? Let me ask you a simple question, yes or no. I'm just curious and there's no offense. You're my host. But let me ask if you are in any way religious? You don't mind my asking?"

I shook my head. He couldn't see that, though. A wink is the same as a nod to a blind man. "I guess I don't believe in it. In anything. Sometimes it's hard. You know what I'm saying?"

"Sure, I do," he said.

"Right," I said.   105

The Englishman was still holding forth. My wife sighed in her sleep. She drew a long breath and went on with her sleeping.

"You'll have to forgive me," I said. "But I can't tell you what a cathedral looks like. It just isn't in me to do it. I can't do any more than I've done."

The blind man sat very still, his head down, as he listened to me.

I said, "The truth is, cathedrals don't mean anything special to me. Nothing. Cathedrals. They're something to look at on late-night TV. That's all they are."

It was then that the blind man cleared his throat. He brought some-   110
thing up. He took a handkerchief from his back pocket. Then he said, "I get it, bub. It's okay. It happens. Don't worry about it," he said. "Hey, listen to me. Will you do me a favor? I got an idea. Why don't you find us some heavy paper? And a pen. We'll do something. We'll draw one together. Get us a pen and some heavy paper. Go on, bub, get the stuff," he said.

So I went upstairs. My legs felt like they didn't have any strength in them. They felt like they did after I'd done some running. In my wife's room I looked around. I found some ballpoints in a little basket on her table. And then I tried to think where to look for the kind of paper he was talking about.

Downstairs, in the kitchen, I found a shopping bag with onion skins in the bottom of the bag. I emptied the bag and shook it. I brought it into the living room and sat down with it near his legs. I moved some things, smoothed the wrinkles from the bag, spread it out on the coffee table.

The blind man got down from the sofa and sat next to me on the carpet.

He ran his fingers over the paper. He went up and down the sides of the paper. The edges, even the edges. He fingered the corners.

"All right," he said. "All right, let's do her."   115

He found my hand, the hand with the pen. He closed his hand over my hand. "Go ahead, bub, draw," he said. "Draw. You'll see. I'll follow along with you. It'll be okay. Just begin now like I'm telling you. You'll see. Draw," the blind man said.

So I began. First I drew a box that looked like a house. It could have been the house I lived in. Then I put a roof on it. At either end of the roof, I drew spires. Crazy.

"Swell," he said. "Terrific. You're doing fine," he said. "Never thought anything like this could happen in your lifetime, did you, bub? Well, it's a strange life, we all know that. Go on now. Keep it up."

I put in windows with arches. I drew flying buttresses. I hung great doors. I couldn't stop. The TV station went off the air. I put down the pen and closed and opened my fingers. The blind man felt around over the paper. He moved the tips of his fingers over the paper, all over what I had drawn, and he nodded.

"Doing fine," the blind man said.   120

I took up the pen again, and he found my hand. I kept at it. I'm no artist. But I kept drawing just the same.

My wife opened up her eyes and gazed at us. She sat up on the sofa, her robe hanging open. She said, "What are you doing? Tell me, I want to know."

I didn't answer her.

The blind man said, "We're drawing a cathedral. Me and him are working on it. Press hard," he said to me. "That's right. That's good," he said. "Sure. You got it, bub, I can tell. You didn't think you could. But you can, can't you? You're cooking with gas now. You know what I'm saying? We're going to really have us something here in a minute. How's the old arm?" he said. "Put some people in there now. What's a cathedral without people?"

My wife said, "What's going on? Robert, what are you doing? What's   125
going on?"

"It's all right," he said to her. "Close your eyes now," the blind man said to me.

I did it. I closed them just like he said.

"Are they closed?" he said. "Don't fudge."

"They're closed," I said.

"Keep them that way," he said. He said, "Don't stop now. Draw."   130

So we kept on with it. His fingers rode my fingers as my hand went over the paper. It was like nothing else in my life up to now.

Then he said, "I think that's it. I think you got it," he said. "Take a look. What do you think?"

But I had my eyes closed. I thought I'd keep them that way for a little longer. I thought it was something I ought to do.

"Well?" he said. "Are you looking?"

My eyes were still closed. I was in my house. I knew that. But I didn't   135
feel like I was inside anything.

"It's really something," I said.

QUESTIONS

1. What details in "Cathedral" make clear the narrator's initial attitude toward blind people? What hints does the author give about the reasons for this attitude? At what point in the story do the narrator's preconceptions about blind people start to change?
2. For what reason does the wife keep asking Robert if he'd like to go to bed (paragraphs 74–78)? What motivates the narrator to make the same suggestion in paragraph 82? What effect does Robert's reply have on the narrator?
3. What makes the narrator start explaining what he's seeing on television?
4. How does the point of view contribute to the effectiveness of the story?
5. At the end, the narrator has an epiphany. How would you describe it?
6. Would you describe the narrator as an antihero? Use specific details from the story to back up your response.
7. Is the wife a flat or a round character? What about Robert? Support your conclusion about each of them.
8. In a good story, a character doesn't suddenly become a completely different sort of person. Find details early in the story that show the narrator's more sensitive side and thus help to make his development credible and persuasive.

Alice Walker

Everyday Use   1973

Alice Walker, a leading black writer and social activist, was born in 1944 in Eatonton, Georgia, the youngest of eight children. Her father, a sharecropper and dairy farmer, usually earned about $300 a year; her mother helped by working as a maid. Both entertained their children by telling stories. When Alice Walker was eight, she was accidentally struck by a pellet from a brother's BB gun. She lost the sight of one eye because the Walkers had no car to rush her to the hospital. Later she attended Spelman College in Atlanta and finished college at Sarah Lawrence College on a scholarship. While working for the civil

ALICE WALKER

rights movement in Mississippi, she met a young lawyer, Melvyn Leventhal. In 1967 they settled in Jackson, Mississippi, the first legally married interracial couple in town. They returned to New York in 1974 and were later divorced. First known as a poet, Walker has published seven books of her verse. She also has edited a collection of the work of the then-neglected black writer Zora Neale Hurston, and has written a study of Langston Hughes. In a collection of essays, In Search of Our Mothers' Gardens: Womanist Prose *(1983), she recalls her mother and addresses her own daughter. (By womanist she means "black feminist.") But the largest part*

of Walker's reading audience knows her fiction: three story collections, In Love
and Trouble *(1973), from which "Everyday Use" is taken,* You Can't Keep a
Good Woman Down *(1981), and* The Way Forward Is with a Broken Heart
(2000); and her novels, The Third Life of Grange Copeland *(1970) and* Meridian
(1976). Her best-known novel, The Color Purple *(1982), won a Pulitzer Prize
and was made into a film by Steven Spielberg in 1985. Her recent novels include*
The Temple of My Familiar *(1989),* Possessing the Secret of Joy *(1992),* By
the Light of My Father's Smile *(1998), and* Now Is the Time to Open Your
Heart *(2004). Walker now lives in Northern California.*

FOR YOUR GRANDMAMA

I will wait for her in the yard that Maggie and I made so clean and
wavy yesterday afternoon. A yard like this is more comfortable than most
people know. It is not just a yard. It is like an extended living room.
When the hard clay is swept clean as a floor and the fine sand around
the edges lined with tiny, irregular grooves anyone can come and sit and
look up into the elm tree and wait for the breezes that never come inside
the house.

Maggie will be nervous until after her sister goes: she will stand
hopelessly in corners, homely and ashamed of the burn scars down her
arms and legs, eyeing her sister with a mixture of envy and awe. She
thinks her sister has held life always in the palm of one hand, that
"no" is a word the world never learned to say to her.

You've no doubt seen those TV shows where the child who has
"made it" is confronted, as a surprise, by her own mother and father, tot-
tering in weakly from backstage. (A pleasant surprise, of course: What
would they do if parent and child came on the show only to curse out and
insult each other?) On TV mother and child embrace and smile into
each other's faces. Sometimes the mother and father weep, the child wraps
them in her arms and leans across the table to tell how she would not
have made it without their help. I have seen these programs.°

Sometimes I dream a dream in which Dee and I are suddenly brought
together on a TV program of this sort. Out of a dark and soft-seated
limousine I am ushered into a bright room filled with many people.
There I meet a smiling, gray, sporty man like Johnny Carson who shakes
my hand and tells me what a fine girl I have. Then we are on the stage
and Dee is embracing me with tears in her eyes. She pins on my dress a
large orchid, even though she has told me once that she thinks orchids
are tacky flowers.

---

these programs: On the NBC television show *This Is Your Life,* people were publicly and
often tearfully reunited with friends, relatives, and teachers they had not seen in years.

In real life I am a large, big-boned woman with rough, man-working 5 hands. In the winter I wear flannel nightgowns to bed and overalls during the day. I can kill and clean a hog as mercilessly as a man. My fat keeps me hot in zero weather. I can work outside all day, breaking ice to get water for washing. I can eat pork liver cooked over the open fire minutes after it comes steaming from the hog. One winter I knocked a bull calf straight in the brain between the eyes with a sledge hammer and had the meat hung up to chill before nightfall. But of course all this does not show on television. I am the way my daughter would want me to be: a hundred pounds lighter, my skin like an uncooked barley pancake. My hair glistens in the hot bright lights. Johnny Carson has much to do to keep up with my quick and witty tongue.

But that is a mistake. I know even before I wake up. Who ever knew a Johnson with a quick tongue? Who can even imagine me looking a strange white man in the eye? It seems to me I have talked to them always with one foot raised in flight, with my head turned in whichever way is farthest from them. Dee, though. She would always look anyone in the eye. Hesitation was no part of her nature.

"How do I look, Mama?" Maggie says, showing just enough of her thin body enveloped in pink skirt and red blouse for me to know she's there, almost hidden by the door.

"Come out into the yard," I say.

Have you ever seen a lame animal, perhaps a dog run over by some careless person rich enough to own a car, sidle up to someone who is ignorant enough to be kind to him? That is the way my Maggie walks. She has been like this, chin on chest, eyes on ground, feet in shuffle, ever since the fire that burned the other house to the ground.

Dee is lighter than Maggie, with nicer hair and a fuller figure. She's a 10 woman now, though sometimes I forget. How long ago was it that the other house burned? Ten, twelve years? Sometimes I can still hear the flames and feel Maggie's arms sticking to me, her hair smoking and her dress falling off her in little black papery flakes. Her eyes seemed stretched open, blazed open by the flames reflected in them. And Dee. I see her standing off under the sweet gum tree she used to dig gum out of; a look of concentration on her face as she watched the last dingy gray board of the house fall in toward the red-hot brick chimney. Why don't you do a dance around the ashes? I'd wanted to ask her. She had hated the house that much.

I used to think she hated Maggie, too. But that was before we raised the money, the church and me, to send her to Augusta to school. She used to read to us without pity; forcing words, lies, other folks' habits, whole lives upon us two, sitting trapped and ignorant underneath her voice. She washed us in a river of make-believe, burned us with a lot of knowledge we didn't necessarily need to know. Pressed us to her with the serious way she read, to shove us away at just the moment, like dimwits, we seemed about to understand.

Dee wanted nice things. A yellow organdy dress to wear to her graduation from high school; black pumps to match a green suit she'd made from an old suit somebody gave me. She was determined to stare down any disaster in her efforts. Her eyelids would not flicker for minutes at a time. Often I fought off the temptation to shake her. At sixteen she had a style of her own: and knew what style was.

I never had an education myself. After second grade the school was closed down. Don't ask me why: in 1927 colored asked fewer questions than they do now. Sometimes Maggie reads to me. She stumbles along good-naturedly but can't see well. She knows she is not bright. Like good looks and money, quickness passed her by. She will marry John Thomas (who has mossy teeth in an earnest face) and then I'll be free to sit here and I guess just sing church songs to myself. Although I never was a good singer. Never could carry a tune. I was always better at a man's job. I used to love to milk till I was hoofed in the side in '49. Cows are soothing and slow and don't bother you, unless you try to milk them the wrong way.

I have deliberately turned my back on the house. It is three rooms, just like the one that burned, except the roof is tin; they don't make shingle roofs any more. There are no real windows, just some holes cut in the sides, like the portholes in a ship, but not round and not square, with rawhide holding the shutters up on the outside. This house is in a pasture, too, like the other one. No doubt when Dee sees it she will want to tear it down. She wrote me once that no matter where we "choose" to live, she will manage to come see us. But she will never bring her friends. Maggie and I thought about this and Maggie asked me, "Mama, when did Dee ever *have* any friends?"

She had a few. Furtive boys in pink shirts hanging about on washday after school. Nervous girls who never laughed. Impressed with her they worshiped the well-turned phrase, the cute shape, the scalding humor that erupted like bubbles in lye. She read to them.

When she was courting Jimmy T she didn't have much time to pay to us, but turned all her faultfinding power on him. He *flew* to marry a cheap city girl from a family of ignorant flashy people. She hardly had time to recompose herself.

When she comes I will meet—but there they are!

Maggie attempts to make a dash for the house, in her shuffling way, but I stay her with my hand. "Come back here," I say. And she stops and tries to dig a well in the sand with her toe.

It is hard to see them clearly through the strong sun. But even the first glimpse of leg out of the car tells me it is Dee. Her feet were always neat-looking, as if God himself had shaped them with a certain style. From the other side of the car comes a short, stocky man. Hair is all over his head a foot long and hanging from his chin like a kinky mule tail. I hear Maggie suck in her breath. "Uhnnnh," is what it sounds like. Like when you see the wriggling end of a snake just in front of your foot on the road. "Uhnnnh."

Dee next. A dress down to the ground, in this hot weather. A dress so 20 loud it hurts my eyes. There are yellows and oranges enough to throw back the light of the sun. I feel my whole face warming from the heat waves it throws out. Earrings, too, gold and hanging down to her shoulders. Bracelets dangling and making noises when she moves her arm up to shake the folds of the dress out of her armpits. The dress is loose and flows, and as she walks closer, I like it. I hear Maggie go "Uhnnnh" again. It is her sister's hair. It stands straight up like the wool on a sheep. It is black as night and around the edges are two long pigtails that rope about like small lizards disappearing behind her ears.

"Wa-su-zo-Tean-o!"° she says, coming on in that gliding way the dress makes her move. The short stocky fellow with the hair to his navel is all grinning and he follows up with "Asalamalakim,° my mother and sister!" He moves to hug Maggie but she falls back, right up against the back of my chair. I feel her trembling there and when I look up I see the perspiration falling off her chin.

"Don't get up," says Dee. Since I am stout it takes something of a push. You can see me trying to move a second or two before I make it. She turns, showing white heels through her sandals, and goes back to the car. Out she peeks next with a Polaroid. She stoops down quickly and lines up picture after picture of me sitting there in front of the house with Maggie cowering behind me. She never takes a shot without making sure the house is included. When a cow comes nibbling around the edge of the yard she snaps it and me and Maggie *and* the house. Then she puts the Polaroid in the back seat of the car, and comes up and kisses me on the forehead.

Meanwhile Asalamalakim is going through the motions with Maggie's hand. Maggie's hand is as limp as a fish, and probably as cold, despite the sweat, and she keeps trying to pull it back. It looks like Asalamalakim wants to shake hands but wants to do it fancy. Or maybe he don't know how people shake hands. Anyhow, he soon gives up on Maggie.

"Well," I say. "Dee."

"No, Mama," she says. "Not 'Dee,' Wangero Leewanika Kemanjo!" 25

"What happened to 'Dee'?" I wanted to know.

Wa-su-zo-Tean-o!: salutation in Swahili, an African language. Notice that Dee has to sound it out, syllable by syllable.   *Asalamalakim*: salutation in Arabic: "Peace be upon you."

"She's dead," Wangero said. "I couldn't bear it any longer, being named after the people who oppress me."

"You know as well as me you was named after your aunt Dicie," I said. Dicie is my sister. She named Dee. We called her "Big Dee" after Dee was born.

"But who was *she* named after?" asked Wangero.

"I guess after Grandma Dee," I said.   30

"And who was she named after?" asked Wangero.

"Her mother," I said, and saw Wangero was getting tired. "That's about as far back as I can trace it," I said. Though, in fact, I probably could have carried it back beyond the Civil War through the branches.

"Well," said Asalamalakim, "there you are."

"Uhnnnh," I heard Maggie say.

"There I was not," I said, "before 'Dicie' cropped up in our family, so   35
why should I try to trace it that far back?"

He just stood there grinning, looking down on me like somebody in-specting a Model A car.° Every once in a while he and Wangero sent eye signals over my head.

"How do you pronounce this name?" I asked.

"You don't have to call me by it if you don't want to," said Wangero.

"Why shouldn't I?" I asked. "If that's what you want us to call you, we'll call you."

"I know it might sound awkward at first," said Wangero.   40

"I'll get used to it," I said. "Ream it out again."

Well, soon we got the name out of the way. Asalamalakim had a name twice as long and three times as hard. After I tripped over it two or three times he told me to just call him Hakim-a-barber. I wanted to ask him was he a barber, but I didn't really think he was, so I didn't ask.

"You must belong to those beef-cattle peoples down the road," I said. They said "Asalamalakim" when they met you, too, but they didn't shake hands. Always too busy: feeding the cattle, fixing the fences, putting up salt-lick shelters, throwing down hay. When the white folks poisoned some of the herd the men stayed up all night with rifles in their hands. I walked a mile and a half just to see the sight.

Hakim-a-barber said, "I accept some of their doctrines, but farming and raising cattle is not my style." (They didn't tell me, and I didn't ask, whether Wangero (Dee) had really gone and married him.)

We sat down to eat and right away he said he didn't eat collards and   45
pork was unclean. Wangero, though, went on through the chitlins and corn bread, the greens and everything else. She talked a blue streak over the sweet potatoes. Everything delighted her. Even the fact that we still

---

Model A car: popular low-priced automobile introduced by the Ford Motor Company in 1927.

used the benches her daddy made for the table when we couldn't afford
to buy chairs.

"Oh, Mama!" she cried. Then turned to Hakim-a-barber. "I never
knew how lovely these benches are. You can feel the rump prints," she
said, running her hands underneath her and along the bench. Then she
gave a sigh and her hand closed over Grandma Dee's butter dish. "That's
it!" she said. "I knew there was something I wanted to ask you if I could
have." She jumped up from the table and went over in the corner where
the churn stood, the milk in it clabber° by now. She looked at the churn
and looked at it.

"This churn top is what I need," she said. "Didn't Uncle Buddy whittle
it out of a tree you all used to have?"

"Yes," I said.

"Uh huh," she said happily. "And I want the dasher, too."

"Uncle Buddy whittle that, too?" asked the barber.   50

Dee (Wangero) looked up at me.

"Aunt Dee's first husband whittled the dash," said Maggie so low you
almost couldn't hear her. "His name was Henry, but they called him Stash."

"Maggie's brain is like an elephant's," Wangero said, laughing. "I can use
the churn top as a centerpiece for the alcove table," she said, sliding a plate
over the churn, "and I'll think of something artistic to do with the dasher."

When she finished wrapping the dasher the handle stuck out. I took it
for a moment in my hands. You didn't even have to look close to see where
hands pushing the dasher up and down to make butter had left a kind of
sink in the wood. In fact, there were a lot of small sinks; you could see where
thumbs and fingers had sunk into the wood. It was beautiful light yellow
wood, from a tree that grew in the yard where Big Dee and Stash had lived.

After dinner Dee (Wangero) went to the trunk at the foot of my bed   55
and started rifling through it. Maggie hung back in the kitchen over the
dishpan. Out came Wangero with two quilts. They had been pieced by
Grandma Dee and then Big Dee and me had hung them on the quilt
frames on the front porch and quilted them. One was in the Lone Star
pattern. The other was Walk Around the Mountain. In both of them
were scraps of dresses Grandma Dee had worn fifty and more years ago.
Bits and pieces of Grandpa Jarrell's paisley shirts. And one teeny faded
blue piece, about the piece of a penny matchbox, that was from Great
Grandpa Ezra's uniform that he wore in the Civil War.

"Mama," Wangero said sweet as a bird. "Can I have these old quilts?"

I heard something fall in the kitchen, and a minute later the kitchen
door slammed.

"Why don't you take one or two of the others?" I asked. "These old
things was just done by me and Big Dee from some tops your grandma
pieced before she died."

clabber: sour milk or buttermilk.

"No," said Wangero. "I don't want those. They are stitched around the borders by machine."

"That'll make them last better," I said.   60

"That's not the point," said Wangero. "These are all pieces of dresses Grandma used to wear. She did all this stitching by hand. Imagine!" She held the quilts securely in her arms, stroking them.

"Some of the pieces, like those lavender ones, come from old clothes her mother handed down to her," I said, moving up to touch the quilts. Dee (Wangero) moved back just enough so that I couldn't reach the quilts. They already belonged to her.

"Imagine!" she breathed again, clutching them closely to her bosom.

"The truth is," I said, "I promised to give them quilts to Maggie, for when she marries John Thomas."

She gasped like a bee had stung her.   65

"Maggie can't appreciate these quilts!" she said. "She'd probably be backward enough to put them to everyday use."

"I reckon she would," I said. "God knows I been saving 'em for long enough with nobody using 'em. I hope she will!" I didn't want to bring up how I had offered Dee (Wangero) a quilt when she went away to college. Then she had told me they were old-fashioned, out of style.

"But they're *priceless!*" she was saying now, furiously; for she has a temper. "Maggie would put them on the bed and in five years they'd be in rags. Less than that!"

"She can always make some more," I said. "Maggie knows how to quilt."

Dee (Wangero) looked at me with hatred. "You just will not under-   70
stand. The point is these quilts, *these* quilts!"

"Well," I said, stumped. "What would *you* do with them?"

"Hang them," she said. As if that was the only thing you *could* do with quilts.

Maggie by now was standing in the door. I could almost hear the sound her feet made as they scraped over each other.

"She can have them, Mama," she said, like somebody used to never winning anything, or having anything reserved for her. "I can 'member Grandma Dee without the quilts."

I looked at her hard. She had filled her bottom lip with checkerberry   75
snuff and it gave her face a kind of dopey, hangdog look. It was Grandma Dee and Big Dee who taught her how to quilt herself. She stood there with her scarred hands hidden in the folds of her skirt. She looked at her sister with something like fear but she wasn't mad at her. This was Maggie's portion. This was the way she knew God to work.

When I looked at her like that something hit me in the top of my head and ran down to the soles of my feet. Just like when I'm in church and the spirit of God touches me and I get happy and shout. I did something I never had done before: hugged Maggie to me, then dragged her on into the room, snatched the quilts out of Miss Wangero's hands and dumped them into Maggie's lap. Maggie just sat there on my bed with her mouth open.

"Take one or two of the others," I said to Dee.

But she turned without a word and went out to Hakim-a-barber.

"You just don't understand," she said, as Maggie and I came out to the car.

"What don't I understand?" I wanted to know.

80

"Your heritage," she said. And then she turned to Maggie, kissed her, and said, "You ought to try to make something of yourself, too, Maggie. It's really a new day for us. But from the way you and Mama still live you'd never know it."

She put on some sunglasses that hid everything above the tip of her nose and her chin.

Maggie smiled; maybe at the sunglasses. But a real smile, not scared. After we watched the car dust settle I asked Maggie to bring me a dip of snuff. And then the two of us sat there just enjoying, until it was time to go in the house and go to bed.

QUESTIONS

1. What is the basic conflict in "Everyday Use"?
2. What is the tone of Walker's story? By what means does the author communicate it?
3. From whose point of view is "Everyday Use" told? What does the story gain from this point of view—instead of, say, from the point of view of Dee (Wangero)?
4. What does the narrator of the story feel toward Dee? What seems to be Dee's present attitude toward her mother and sister?
5. What do you take to be the author's attitude toward each of her characters? How does she convey it?
6. What levels of meaning do you find in the story's title?
7. Contrast Dee's attitude toward her heritage with the attitudes of her mother and sister. How much truth is there in Dee's accusation that her mother and sister don't understand their heritage?
8. Does the knowledge that "Everyday Use" was written by a black writer in any way influence your reactions to it? Explain.

WRITING ABOUT CHARACTER

How Character Creates Action

Although readers usually consider plot the central element of fiction, writers usually remark that stories begin with characters. They imagine a person in loving detail and then wait to see what that character will do. "By the time I write a story," said Katherine Anne Porter, "my people are up and alive and walking around and taking things into their own hands." A story's action usually grows out of the personality of its protagonist and the situation he or she faces. As critic Phyllis Bottome observed, "If a writer is true to his characters, they will give him his plot."

Not all characters are created equal. A sure sign of a skilled writer is the ability to create memorable characters. A great writer like Jane Austen or Charles Dickens can create characters so vivid and compelling that readers almost have the illusion the figures are real people.

In writing about the protagonist (or any other figure) in a story, begin by studying his or her personality. What makes this individual different from the other characters in the story? Note that the way characters speak can immediately reveal important things about their personalities, beliefs, and behavior. A single line of dialogue can tell the audience a great deal, as in an old film in which the comedian W. C. Fields confides, "A woman drove me to drink and I never even had the courtesy to thank her."

CHECKLIST

Writing About Character

✓ Who is the main character or protagonist of the story?

✓ Make a quick list of the character's physical, mental, moral, or behavioral traits. Which of these characteristics seem especially significant to the action of the story?

✓ Does the main character have an antagonist in the story? How do they differ?

✓ Does the way the protagonist speaks reveal anything about his or her character?

✓ If the story is told in the first person, what is revealed about how the protagonist views his or her surroundings?

✓ What is the character's primary motivation? Does this motivation seem as reasonable to you as it does to the protagonist? If not, what is suggested by this unreasonableness?

✓ Does the protagonist fully understand his or her motivations?

✓ In what ways is the protagonist changed or tested by the events of the story?

WRITING ASSIGNMENT ON CHARACTER

Choose a story with a dynamic protagonist. (See the beginning of this chapter for a discussion of dynamic characters.) Write an essay exploring how that character evolves over the course of the story, providing evidence from the story to back up your argument.

MORE TOPICS FOR WRITING

1. Using a story from this book, write a short essay that explains why a protagonist takes a crucial life-changing action. What motivates this character to do something that seems bold or surprising? You might consider:

   • What motivates the narrator to overcome his instinctive antipathy to the blind man in "Cathedral"?

   • Why doesn't Miss Brill buy her usual slice of honeycake on her way home at the end of "Miss Brill"?

2. Choose a minor character from any of the stories in this book, and write briefly on what the story reveals about that person, reading closely for even the smallest of details. Is he or she a stock character? Why or why not? (See the beginning of this chapter for a discussion of stock characters.)

3. Choose a story in which the main character has an obvious antagonist, such as "Cathedral." What role does this second character play in bringing the protagonist to a new awareness of life?

4. Choose a favorite character from a television show you watch regularly. What details are provided (either in the show's dialogue or in its visuals) to communicate the personality of this character? Would you say this person is a stock character or a rounded one? Write a brief essay making a case for your position.

5. Browse through magazines and newspapers to find a picture of a person you can't identify. Cut out the picture. Create a character based on the picture. As many writers do, make a list of characteristics, from the large (her life's ambition) to the small (his favorite breakfast cereal). As you build your list, make sure your details add up to a rounded character. (See the beginning of this chapter for a discussion of rounded versus flat characters.)

6. Choose a stock character from one of the stories you have read from this book, and write your own short story with that character as a protagonist. Turn your stock character into a rounded one by imagining the details of his or her life more fully. (Again, be sure to look at the beginning of this chapter for a description of what makes a character rounded or flat.)

4
Setting

By the **setting** of a story, we mean its time and place. The word might remind you of the metal that holds a diamond in a ring, or of a *set* used in a play—perhaps a bare chair in front of a slab of painted canvas. But often, in an effective short story, setting may figure as more than mere background or underpinning. It can make things happen. It can prompt characters to act, bring them to realizations, or cause them to reveal their inmost natures.

To be sure, the idea of setting includes the physical environment of a story: a house, a street, a city, a landscape, a region. (*Where* a story takes place is sometimes called its **locale**.) Physical places mattered so greatly to French novelist Honoré de Balzac that sometimes, before writing a story set in a particular town, he would visit that town, select a few houses, and describe them in detail, down to their very smells. "The place in which an event occurred," Henry James admiringly said of him, "was in his view of equal moment with the event itself . . . it had a part to play; it needed to be made as definite as anything else."

But besides place, setting may crucially involve the *time* of the story—hour, year, or century. It might matter greatly that a story takes place at dawn, or on the day of the first moon landing. When we begin to read a historical novel, we are soon made aware that we aren't reading about life in the twenty-first century. In *The Scarlet Letter*, nineteenth-century author Nathaniel Hawthorne, by a long introduction and a vivid opening scene at a prison door, prepares us to witness events in the Puritan community of Boston in the earlier seventeenth century. This setting, together with scenes of Puritan times we recall from high school history, helps us understand what happens in the novel. We can appreciate the shocked agitation in town when a woman is accused of adultery: she has given illegitimate birth. Such an event might seem common today, but in the stern, God-fearing New England Puritan community, it was a flagrant defiance of church and state, which were all-powerful (and were all one). A reader who ignores the setting will make no sense of *The Scarlet Letter*—if to ignore the setting is even possible, given how much attention Hawthorne pays to it.

That Hawthorne's novel takes place in a time remote from our own leads us to expect different customs and different attitudes. Some critics and teachers regard the setting of a story as its whole society, including the beliefs and assumptions of its characters. Still, we suggest that for now you keep your working definition of *setting* simple. Call it time and place. If later you should feel that your definition needs widening and deepening, you can always expand it.

Besides time and place, setting may also include the weather, which in some stories may be crucial. Climate seems as substantial as any character in William Faulkner's "Dry September." After sixty-two rainless days, a long unbroken spell of late-summer heat has frayed every nerve in a small town and caused the main character, a hotheaded white supremacist, to feel more and more irritation. The weather, someone remarks, is "enough to make a man do anything." When a false report circulates that a white woman has been raped by a black man, the rumor, like a match flung into a dry field, ignites rage and provokes a lynching. Evidently, to understand the story we have to recognize its locale, a small town in Mississippi in the 1930s during an infernal heat wave. Fully to take in the meaning of Faulkner's story, we have to take in the setting in its entirety.

Physical place, by the way, is especially vital to a **regional writer**, who usually sets stories (or other work) in one geographic area. Such a writer, often a native of the place, tries to bring it alive to readers who live elsewhere. William Faulkner, a distinguished regional writer, almost always sets his novels and stories in his native Mississippi. Though born in St. Louis, Kate Chopin became known as a regional writer for writing about Louisiana in many of her short stories and in her novel *The Awakening.* Willa Cather, for her novels of frontier Nebraska, often is regarded as another outstanding regionalist (though she also set fiction in Quebec, the Southwest, and in Pittsburgh and New York). There is often something arbitrary, however, about calling an author a regional writer. The label often has a political tinge; it means that the author describes an area outside the political and economic centers of a society. In a sense, we might think of James Joyce as a regional writer, in that all his fiction takes place in the city of Dublin, but instead we usually call him an Irish one.

Setting and character will often reveal each other. Recall how Faulkner, at the start of "A Rose for Emily," depicts Emily Grierson's house, once hand-some but now "an eyesore among eyesores" surrounded by gas stations. Still standing, refusing to yield its old-time horse-and-buggy splendor to the age of the automobile, the house in "its stubborn and coquettish decay" embodies the character of its owner. In some fiction, setting is closely bound with theme (what the story is saying)—as you will find in John Steinbeck's "The Chrysanthemums" (Chapter 7), a story beginning with a fog that has sealed off a valley from the rest of the world—a fog like the lid on a pot. In *The Scarlet Letter,* even small details contain powerful hints. At the beginning of his novel, Hawthorne remarks of a colonial jailhouse:

> Before this ugly edifice, and between it and the wheel-track of the street, was a grass-plot, much overgrown with burdock, pigweed, apple-peru, and such unsightly vegetation, which evidently found something congenial in the soil that had so early borne the black flower of civilized society, a prison. But, on one side of the portal, and rooted almost at the

threshold, was a wild rose-bush, covered, in this month of June, with its delicate gems, which might be imagined to offer their fragrance and fragile beauty to the prisoner as he went in, and to the condemned criminal as he came forth to his doom, in token that the deep heart of Nature could pity and be kind to him.

Apparently, Hawthorne wishes to show us that Puritan Boston, a town of rutted streets and an ugly jail with a tangled grass-plot, may be rough but has beauty in it. As the story unfolds, he will further suggest (among other things) that secret sin and a beautiful child may go together like pigweed and wild roses. In his artfully crafted novel, setting is one with—not separate from—characters, theme, and symbols.

In some stories, a writer will seem to draw a setting mainly to evoke atmosphere. In such a story, setting starts us feeling whatever the storyteller would have us feel. In "The Tell-Tale Heart," Poe's setting the action in an old, dark, lantern-lit house greatly contributes to our sense of unease—and so helps the story's effectiveness.

But be warned: you'll meet stories in which setting appears hardly to matter. In W. Somerset Maugham's fable, "The Appointment in Samarra," all we need to be told about the setting is that it is a marketplace in Baghdad. In that brief fable, the inevitability of death is the point, not an exotic setting. In this chapter, though, you will meet three fine stories in which setting, for one reason or another, counts greatly. Without it, none of these stories could happen.

Kate Chopin

The Storm   1898

Kate Chopin (1851–1904) was born Katherine O'Flaherty in St. Louis, daughter of an Irish immigrant grown wealthy in retailing. On his death, young Kate was raised by her mother's family: aristocratic Creoles, descendants of the French and Spaniards who had colonized Louisiana. Young Kate received a convent schooling, and at nineteen married Oscar Chopin, a Creole cotton broker from New Orleans. Later, the Chopins lived on a plantation near Cloutierville, Louisiana, a region whose varied people—Creoles, Cajuns, blacks—Kate Chopin was later to write about with loving care in Bayou Folk *(1894) and A*

KATE CHOPIN

Night in Arcadia *(1897). The shock of her husband's sudden death in 1883, which left her with the raising of six children, seems to have plunged Kate Chopin into writing. She read and admired fine woman writers of her day, such as the Maine realist Sarah Orne Jewett. She also read Maupassant, Zola, and other new (and scandalous) French naturalist writers. She began to bring into American fiction some of their hard-eyed observation and their passion for telling unpleasant truths. Determined, in defiance of her times, frankly to show the sexual feelings of her characters, Chopin suffered from neglect and censorship. When her major novel,* The Awakening, *appeared in 1899, critics were outraged by her candid portrait of a woman who seeks sexual and professional independence. After causing such a literary scandal, Chopin was unable to get her later work published, and wrote little more before she died.* The Awakening *and many of her stories had to wait seven decades for a sympathetic audience.*

I

The leaves were so still that even Bibi thought it was going to rain. Bobinôt, who was accustomed to converse on terms of perfect equality with his little son, called the child's attention to certain somber clouds that were rolling with sinister intention from the west, accompanied by a sullen, threatening roar. They were at Friedheimer's store and decided to remain there till the storm had passed. They sat within the door on two empty kegs. Bibi was four years old and looked very wise.

"Mama'll be 'fraid, yes," he suggested with blinking eyes.

"She'll shut the house. Maybe she got Sylvie helpin' her this evenin'," Bobinôt responded reassuringly.

"No; she ent got Sylvie. Sylvie was helpin' her yistiday," piped Bibi.

Bobinôt arose and going across to the counter purchased a can of shrimps, of which Calixta was very fond. Then he returned to his perch on the keg and sat stolidly holding the can of shrimps while the storm burst. It shook the wooden store and seemed to be ripping great furrows in the distant field. Bibi laid his little hand on his father's knee and was not afraid.

II

Calixta, at home, felt no uneasiness for their safety. She sat at a side window sewing furiously on a sewing machine. She was greatly occupied and did not notice the approaching storm. But she felt very warm and often stopped to mop her face on which the perspiration gathered in beads. She unfastened her white sacque at the throat. It began to grow dark, and suddenly realizing the situation she got up hurriedly and went about closing windows and doors.

Out on the small front gallery she had hung Bobinôt's Sunday clothes to air and she hastened out to gather them before the rain fell. As she stepped outside, Alcée Laballière rode in at the gate. She had not seen him very often since her marriage, and never alone. She stood there with Bobinôt's coat in her hands, and the big rain drops began to fall. Alcée rode his horse under the shelter of a side projection where the chickens had huddled and there were plows and a harrow piled up in the corner.

"May I come and wait on your gallery till the storm is over, Calixta?" he asked.

"Come 'long in, M'sieur Alcée."

His voice and her own startled her as if from a trance, and she seized Bobinôt's vest. Alcée, mounting to the porch, grabbed the trousers and snatched Bibi's braided jacket that was about to be carried away by a sudden gust of wind. He expressed an intention to remain outside, but it was soon apparent that he might as well have been out in the open: the water beat in upon the boards in driving sheets, and he went inside, closing the door after him. It was even necessary to put something beneath the door to keep the water out.

"My! what a rain! It's good two years since it rain like that," exclaimed Calixta as she rolled up a piece of bagging and Alcée helped her to thrust it beneath the crack.

She was a little fuller of figure than five years before when she married; but she had lost nothing of her vivacity. Her blue eyes still retained their melting quality; and her yellow hair, dishevelled by the wind and rain, kinked more stubbornly than ever about her ears and temples.

The rain beat upon the low, shingled roof with a force and clatter that threatened to break an entrance and deluge them there. They were in the dining room—the sitting room—the general utility room. Adjoining was her bed room, with Bibi's couch along side her own. The door stood open, and the room with its white, monumental bed, its closed shutters, looked dim and mysterious.

Alcée flung himself into a rocker and Calixta nervously began to gather up from the floor the lengths of a cotton sheet which she had been sewing.

"If this keeps up, *Dieu sait*° if the levees goin' to stan' it!" she exclaimed.

"What have you got to do with the levees?"

"I got enough to do! An' there's Bobinôt with Bibi out in that storm—if he only didn' left Friedheimer's!"

"Let us hope, Calixta, that Bobinôt's got sense enough to come in out of a cyclone."

She went and stood at the window with a greatly disturbed look on her face. She wiped the frame that was clouded with moisture. It was stiflingly hot. Alcée got up and joined her at the window, looking over her shoulder. The rain was coming down in sheets obscuring the view of far-off cabins and enveloping the distant wood in a gray mist. The playing of the lightning was incessant. A bolt struck a tall chinaberry tree

Dieu sait: God only knows.

at the edge of the field. It filled all visible space with a blinding glare and the crash seemed to invade the very boards they stood upon.

Calixta put her hands to her eyes, and with a cry, staggered backward. 20 Alcée's arm encircled her, and for an instant he drew her close and spasmodically to him.

"*Bonté!*"° she cried, releasing herself from his encircling arm and retreating from the window, "the house'll go next! If I only knew w'ere Bibi was!" She would not compose herself; she would not be seated. Alcée clasped her shoulders and looked into her face. The contact of her warm, palpitating body when he had unthinkingly drawn her into his arms, had aroused all the old-time infatuation and desire for her flesh.

"Calixta," he said, "don't be frightened. Nothing can happen. The house is too low to be struck, with so many tall trees standing about. There! aren't you going to be quiet? say, aren't you?" He pushed her hair back from her face that was warm and steaming. Her lips were as red and moist as pomegranate seed. Her white neck and a glimpse of her full, firm bosom disturbed him powerfully. As she glanced up at him the fear in her liquid blue eyes had given place to a drowsy gleam that unconsciously betrayed a sensuous desire. He looked down into her eyes and there was nothing for him to do but gather her lips in a kiss. It reminded him of Assumption.°

"Do you remember—in Assumption, Calixta?" he asked in a low voice broken by passion. Oh! she remembered; for in Assumption he had kissed her and kissed and kissed her; until his senses would well nigh fail, and to save her he would resort to a desperate flight. If she was not an immaculate dove in those days, she was still inviolate; a passionate creature whose very defenselessness had made her defense, against which his honor forbade him to prevail. Now—well, now—her lips seemed in a manner free to be tasted, as well as her round, white throat and her whiter breasts.

They did not heed the crashing torrents, and the roar of the elements made her laugh as she lay in his arms. She was a revelation in that dim, mysterious chamber; as white as the couch she lay upon. Her firm, elastic flesh that was knowing for the first time its birthright, was like a creamy lily that the sun invites to contribute its breath and perfume to the undying life of the world.

The generous abundance of her passion, without guile or trickery, 25 was like a white flame which penetrated and found response in depths of his own sensuous nature that had never yet been reached.

When he touched her breasts they gave themselves up in quivering ecstasy, inviting his lips. Her mouth was a fountain of delight. And when he possessed her, they seemed to swoon together at the very borderland of life's mystery.

Bonté!: Heavens!   *Assumption:* a parish west of New Orleans.

He stayed cushioned upon her, breathless, dazed, enervated, with his heart beating like a hammer upon her. With one hand she clasped his head, her lips lightly touching his forehead. The other hand stroked with a soothing rhythm his muscular shoulders.

The growl of the thunder was distant and passing away. The rain beat softly upon the shingles, inviting them to drowsiness and sleep. But they dared not yield.

The rain was over; and the sun was turning the glistening green world into a palace of gems. Calixta, on the gallery, watched Alcée ride away. He turned and smiled at her with a beaming face; and she lifted her pretty chin in the air and laughed aloud.

III

Bobinôt and Bibi, trudging home, stopped without at the cistern to make themselves presentable. 30

"My! Bibi, w'at will yo' mama say! You ought to be ashame'. You oughtn' put on those good pants. Look at 'em! An' that mud on yo' collar! How you got that mud on yo' collar, Bibi? I never saw such a boy!" Bibi was the picture of pathetic resignation. Bobinôt was the embodiment of serious solicitude as he strove to remove from his own person and his son's the signs of their tramp over heavy roads and through wet fields. He scraped the mud off Bibi's bare legs and feet with a stick and carefully removed all traces from his heavy brogans. Then, prepared for the worst—the meeting with an overscrupulous housewife, they entered cautiously at the back door.

Calixta was preparing supper. She had set the table and was dripping coffee at the hearth. She sprang up as they came in.

"Oh, Bobinôt! You back! My! but I was uneasy. W'ere you been during the rain? An' Bibi? he ain't wet? he ain't hurt?" She had clasped Bibi and was kissing him effusively. Bobinôt's explanations and apologies which he had been composing all along the way, died on his lips as Calixta felt him to see if he were dry, and seemed to express nothing but satisfaction at their safe return.

"I brought you some shrimps, Calixta," offered Bobinôt, hauling the can from his ample side pocket and laying it on the table.

"Shrimps! Oh, Bobinôt! you too good fo' anything!" and she gave 35 him a smacking kiss on the cheek that resounded. "*J'vous réponds*,° we'll have feas' to night! umph-umph!"

Bobinôt and Bibi began to relax and enjoy themselves, and when the three seated themselves at table they laughed much and so loud that anyone might have heard them as far away as Laballière's.

J'vous réponds: Let me tell you.

IV

Alcée Laballière wrote to his wife, Clarisse, that night. It was a loving letter, full of tender solicitude. He told her not to hurry back, but if she and the babies liked it at Biloxi, to stay a month longer. He was getting on nicely; and though he missed them, he was willing to bear the separation a while longer—realizing that their health and pleasure were the first things to be considered.

V

As for Clarisse, she was charmed upon receiving her husband's letter. She and the babies were doing well. The society was agreeable; many of her old friends and acquaintances were at the bay. And the first free breath since her marriage seemed to restore the pleasant liberty of her maiden days. Devoted as she was to her husband, their intimate conjugal life was something which she was more than willing to forego for a while.

So the storm passed and everyone was happy.

QUESTIONS

1. Exactly where does Chopin's story take place? How can you tell?
2. What circumstances introduced in Part I turn out to have a profound effect on events in the story?
3. What details in "The Storm" emphasize the fact that Bobinôt loves his wife? What details reveal how imperfectly he comprehends her nature?
4. What general attitudes toward sex, love, and marriage does Chopin imply? Cite evidence to support your answer.
5. What meanings do you find in the title "The Storm"?
6. In the story as a whole, how do setting and plot reinforce each other?

T. Coraghessan Boyle

Greasy Lake — 1985

T. Coraghessan Boyle (the T. stands for Tom) was born in 1948 in Peekskill, New York, the son of Irish immigrants. He grew up, he recalls, "as a sort of pampered punk" who did not read a book until he was eighteen. After a brief period as a high school teacher, he studied in the University of Iowa Writers' Workshop, submitting a collection of stories for his Ph.D. He now teaches writing at the University of Southern California and sometimes plays saxophone in a rockabilly band. His stories in Esquire, Paris

T. CORAGHESSAN BOYLE

Review, *the* Atlantic, *and other magazines quickly won him notice for their outrageous macabre humor and bizarre inventiveness. Boyle has published seven volumes of short stories, including* Greasy Lake *(1985),* T.C. Boyle Stories *(1998), and* Tooth and Claw *(2005). He has also published nine novels that are quite unlike anything else in contemporary American fiction. The subjects of some Boyle novels reveal his wide-ranging and idiosyncratic interests.* Water Music *(1982) concerns an eighteenth-century expedition to Africa.* Budding Prospects *(1984) is a picaresque romp among adventurous marijuana growers.* East Is East *(1990) is a half-serious, half-comic story of a Japanese fugitive in an American writers' colony.* The Road to Wellville *(1993), which was made into a film with Anthony Hopkins and Matthew Broderick, takes place in 1907 in a sanitarium run by Dr. John Harvey Kellogg of corn flakes fame, with cameo appearances by Henry Ford, Thomas Edison, and Harvey Firestone.* The Inner Circle *(2004) concerns 1940s sex researcher Alfred Kinsey and his circle of intimates. Boyle's most recent novel is* Talk Talk *(2006). He lives in Southern California.*

It's about a mile down on the dark side of Route 88.
                                                    —Bruce Springsteen

There was a time when courtesy and winning ways went out of style, when it was good to be bad, when you cultivated decadence like a taste. We were all dangerous characters then. We wore torn-up leather jackets, slouched around with toothpicks in our mouths, sniffed glue and ether and what somebody claimed was cocaine. When we wheeled our parents' whining station wagons out onto the street we left a patch of rubber half a block long. We drank gin and grape juice, Tango, Thunderbird, and Bali Hai. We were nineteen. We were bad. We read André Gide° and struck elaborate poses to show that we didn't give a shit about anything. At night, we went up to Greasy Lake.

Through the center of town, up the strip, past the housing developments and shopping malls, street lights giving way to the thin streaming illumination of the headlights, trees crowding the asphalt in a black unbroken wall: that was the way out to Greasy Lake. The Indians had called it Wakan, a reference to the clarity of its waters. Now it was fetid and murky, the mud banks glittering with broken glass and strewn with beer cans and the charred remains of bonfires. There was a single ravaged island a hundred yards from shore, so stripped of vegetation it looked as if the air force had strafed it. We went up to the lake because everyone went there, because we wanted to snuff the rich scent of possibility on

André Gide: controversial French writer (1869–1951) whose novels, including *The Counterfeiters* and *Lafcadio's Adventures,* often show individuals in conflict with accepted morality.

the breeze, watch a girl take off her clothes and plunge into the festering murk, drink beer, smoke pot, howl at the stars, savor the incongruous full-throated roar of rock and roll against the primeval susurrus of frogs and crickets. This was nature.

I was there one night, late, in the company of two dangerous characters. Digby wore a gold star in his right ear and allowed his father to pay his tuition at Cornell; Jeff was thinking of quitting school to become a painter/musician/head-shop proprietor. They were both expert in the social graces, quick with a sneer, able to manage a Ford with lousy shocks over a rutted and gutted blacktop road at eighty-five while rolling a joint as compact as a Tootsie Roll Pop stick. They could lounge against a bank of booming speakers and trade "man"s with the best of them or roll out across the dance floor as if their joints worked on bearings. They were slick and quick and they wore their mirror shades at breakfast and dinner, in the shower, in closets and caves. In short, they were bad.

I drove. Digby pounded the dashboard and shouted along with Toots & the Maytals while Jeff hung his head out the window and streaked the side of my mother's Bel Air with vomit. It was early June, the air soft as a hand on your cheek, the third night of summer vacation. The first two nights we'd been out till dawn, looking for something we never found. On this, the third night, we'd cruised the strip sixty-seven times, been in and out of every bar and club we could think of in a twenty-mile radius, stopped twice for bucket chicken and forty-cent hamburgers, debated going to a party at the house of a girl Jeff's sister knew, and chucked two dozen raw eggs at mailboxes and hitchhikers. It was 2:00 A.M.; the bars were closing. There was nothing to do but take a bottle of lemon-flavored gin up to Greasy Lake.

The taillights of a single car winked at us as we swung into the dirt lot 5 with its tufts of weed and washboard corrugations; '57 Chevy, mint, metallic blue. On the far side of the lot, like the exoskeleton of some gaunt chrome insect, a chopper leaned against its kickstand. And that was it for excitement: some junkie halfwit biker and a car freak pumping his girlfriend. Whatever it was we were looking for, we weren't about to find it at Greasy Lake. Not that night.

But then all of a sudden Digby was fighting for the wheel. "Hey, that's Tony Lovett's car! Hey!" he shouted, while I stabbed at the brake pedal and the Bel Air nosed up to the gleaming bumper of the parked Chevy. Digby leaned on the horn, laughing, and instructed me to put my brights on. I flicked on the brights. This was hilarious. A joke. Tony would experience premature withdrawal and expect to be confronted by grim-looking state troopers with flashlights. We hit the horn, strobed the lights, and then jumped out of the car to press our witty faces to Tony's windows; for all we knew we might even catch a glimpse of some little fox's tit, and then we could slap backs with red-faced Tony, roughhouse a little, and go on to new heights of adventure and daring.

The first mistake, the one that opened the whole floodgate, was losing my grip on the keys. In the excitement, leaping from the car with the gin in one hand and a roach clip in the other, I spilled them in the grass—in the dark, rank, mysterious nighttime grass of Greasy Lake. This was a tactical error, as damaging and irreversible in its way as Westmoreland's decision to dig in at Khe Sanh.° I felt it like a jab of intuition, and I stopped there by the open door, peering vaguely into the night that puddled up round my feet.

The second mistake—and this was inextricably bound up with the first—was identifying the car as Tony Lovett's. Even before the very bad character in greasy jeans and engineer boots ripped out of the driver's door, I began to realize that this chrome blue was much lighter than the robin's-egg of Tony's car, and that Tony's car didn't have rear-mounted speakers. Judging from their expressions, Digby and Jeff were privately groping toward the same inevitable and unsettling conclusion as I was.

In any case, there was no reasoning with this bad greasy character— clearly he was a man of action. The first lusty Rockette° kick of his steel-toed boot caught me under the chin, chipped my favorite tooth, and left me sprawled in the dirt. Like a fool, I'd gone down on one knee to comb the stiff hacked grass for the keys, my mind making connections in the most dragged-out, testudineous way, knowing that things had gone wrong, that I was in a lot of trouble, and that the lost ignition key was my grail and my salvation. The three or four succeeding blows were mainly absorbed by my right buttock and the tough piece of bone at the base of my spine.

Meanwhile, Digby vaulted the kissing bumpers and delivered a savage kung-fu blow to the greasy character's collarbone. Digby had just finished a course in martial arts for phys-ed credit and had spent the better part of the past two nights telling us apocryphal tales of Bruce Lee types and of the raw power invested in lightning blows shot from coiled wrists, ankles, and elbows. The greasy character was unimpressed. He merely backed off a step, his face like a Toltec mask, and laid Digby out with a single whistling roundhouse blow . . . but by now Jeff had got into the act, and I was beginning to extricate myself from the dirt, a tinny compound of shock, rage, and impotence wadded in my throat.

Jeff was on the guy's back, biting at his ear. Digby was on the ground, cursing. I went for the tire iron I kept under the driver's seat. I kept it

10

Westmoreland's decision . . . Khe Sanh: General William C. Westmoreland commanded U.S. troops in Vietnam (1964–68). In late 1967 the North Vietnamese and Viet Cong forces attacked Khe Sanh (or Khesanh) with a show of strength, causing Westmoreland to expend great effort to defend a plateau of relatively little tactical importance. *Rockette:* member of a dance troupe in the stage show at Radio City Music Hall, New York, famous for its ability to kick fast and high with wonderful coordination.

there because bad characters always keep tire irons under the driver's seat, for just such an occasion as this. Never mind that I hadn't been involved in a fight since sixth grade, when a kid with a sleepy eye and two streams of mucus depending from his nostrils hit me in the knee with a Louisville slugger,° never mind that I'd touched the tire iron exactly twice before, to change tires: it was there. And I went for it.

I was terrified. Blood was beating in my ears, my hands were shaking, my heart turning over like a dirtbike in the wrong gear. My antagonist was shirtless, and a single cord of muscle flashed across his chest as he bent forward to peel Jeff from his back like a wet overcoat. "Motherfucker," he spat, over and over, and I was aware in that instant that all four of us—Digby, Jeff, and myself included—were chanting "motherfucker, motherfucker," as if it were a battle cry. (What happened next? the detective asks the murderer from beneath the turned-down brim of his porkpie hat. I don't know, the murderer says, something came over me. Exactly.)

Digby poked the flat of his hand in the bad character's face and I came at him like a kamikaze, mindless, raging, stung with humiliation—the whole thing, from the initial boot in the chin to this murderous primal instant involving no more than sixty hyperventilating, gland-flooding seconds—I came at him and brought the tire iron down across his ear. The effect was instantaneous, astonishing. He was a stunt man and this was Hollywood, he was a big grimacing toothy balloon and I was a man with a straight pin. He collapsed. Wet his pants. Went loose in his boots.

A single second, big as a zeppelin, floated by. We were standing over him in a circle, gritting our teeth, jerking our necks, our limbs and hands and feet twitching with glandular discharges. No one said anything. We just stared down at the guy, the car freak, the lover, the bad greasy character laid low. Digby looked at me; so did Jeff. I was still holding the tire iron, a tuft of hair clinging to the crook like dandelion fluff, like down. Rattled, I dropped it in the dirt, already envisioning the headlines, the pitted faces of the police inquisitors, the gleam of handcuffs, clank of bars, the big black shadows rising from the back of the cell . . . when suddenly a raw torn shriek cut through me like all the juice in all the electric chairs in the country.

It was the fox. She was short, barefoot, dressed in panties and a man's shirt. "Animals!" she screamed, running at us with her fists clenched and wisps of blow-dried hair in her face. There was a silver chain round her ankle, and her toenails flashed in the glare of the headlights. I think it was the toenails that did it. Sure, the gin and the cannabis and even the Kentucky Fried may have had a hand in it, but it was the sight of those flaming toes that set us off—the toad emerging from the loaf in *Virgin Spring*,° lipstick smeared on a child; she was already

15

Louisville slugger: a brand of baseball bat. *Virgin Spring*: film by Swedish director Ingmar Bergman (1960).

tainted. We were on her like Bergman's deranged brothers—see no evil, hear none, speak none—panting, wheezing, tearing at her clothes, grabbing for flesh. We were bad characters, and we were scared and hot and three steps over the line—anything could have happened.

It didn't.

Before we could pin her to the hood of the car, our eyes masked with lust and greed and the purest primal badness, a pair of headlights swung into the lot. There we were, dirty, bloody, guilty, dissociated from humanity and civilization, the first of the Ur-crimes behind us, the second in progress, shreds of nylon panty and spandex brassiere dangling from our fingers, our flies open, lips licked—there we were, caught in the spotlight. Nailed.

We bolted. First for the car, and then, realizing we had no way of starting it, for the woods. I thought nothing. I thought escape. The headlights came at me like accusing fingers. I was gone.

Ram-bam-bam, across the parking lot, past the chopper and into the feculent undergrowth at the lake's edge, insects flying up in my face, weeds whipping, frogs and snakes and red-eyed turtles splashing off into the night: I was already ankle-deep in muck and tepid water and still going strong. Behind me, the girl's screams rose in intensity, disconsolate, incriminating, the screams of the Sabine women,° the Christian martyrs, Anne Frank° dragged from the garret. I kept going, pursued by those cries, imagining cops and bloodhounds. The water was up to my knees when I realized what I was doing: I was going to swim for it. Swim the breadth of Greasy Lake and hide myself in the thick clot of woods on the far side. They'd never find me there.

I was breathing in sobs, in gasps. The water lapped at my waist as I 20 looked out over the moon-burnished ripples, the mats of algae that clung to the surface like scabs. Digby and Jeff had vanished. I paused. Listened. The girl was quieter now, screams tapering to sobs, but there were male voices, angry, excited, and the high-pitched ticking of the second car's engine. I waded deeper, stealthy, hunted, the ooze sucking at my sneakers. As I was about to take the plunge—at the very instant I dropped my shoulder for the first slashing stroke—I blundered into something. Something unspeakable, obscene, something soft, wet, moss-grown. A patch of weed? A log? When I reached out to touch it, it gave like a rubber duck, it gave like flesh.

Sabine women: members of an ancient tribe in Italy, according to legend, forcibly carried off by the early Romans under Romulus to be their wives. The incident is depicted in a famous painting, "The Rape of the Sabine Women," by seventeenth-century French artist Nicolas Poussin. *Anne Frank:* German Jewish girl (1929–1945) whose diary written during the Nazi occupation of the Netherlands later became world-famous. She hid with her family in a secret attic in Amsterdam, but was caught by the Gestapo and sent to the concentration camp at Belsen, where she died.

In one of those nasty little epiphanies for which we are prepared by films and TV and childhood visits to the funeral home to ponder the shrunken painted forms of dead grandparents, I understood what it was that bobbed there so inadmissibly in the dark. Understood, and stumbled back in horror and revulsion, my mind yanked in six different directions (I was nineteen, a mere child, an infant, and here in the space of five minutes I'd struck down one greasy character and blundered into the waterlogged carcass of a second), thinking, The keys, the keys, why did I have to go and lose the keys? I stumbled back, but the muck took hold of my feet—a sneaker snagged, balance lost—and suddenly I was pitching face forward into the buoyant black mass, throwing out my hands in desperation while simultaneously conjuring the image of reeking frogs and muskrats revolving in slicks of their own deliquescing juices. AAAAArrrgh! I shot from the water like a torpedo, the dead man rotating to expose a mossy beard and eyes cold as the moon. I must have shouted out, thrashing around in the weeds, because the voices behind me suddenly became animated.

"What was that?"

"It's them, it's them: they tried to, tried to . . . *rape* me!" Sobs.

A man's voice, flat Midwestern accent. "You sons a bitches, we'll kill you!"

Frogs, crickets.

Then another voice, harsh, *r*-less, Lower East Side: "Motherfucker!" I recognized the verbal virtuosity of the bad greasy character in the engineer boots. Tooth chipped, sneakers gone, coated in mud and slime and worse, crouching breathless in the weeds waiting to have my ass thoroughly and definitively kicked and fresh from the hideous stinking embrace of a three-days-dead-corpse, I suddenly felt a rush of joy and vindication: the son of a bitch was alive! Just as quickly, my bowels turned to ice. "Come on out of there, you pansy mothers!" the bad greasy character was screaming. He shouted curses till he was out of breath.

The crickets started up again, then the frogs. I held my breath. All at once was a sound in the reeds, a swishing, a splash: thunk-a-thunk. They were throwing rocks. The frogs fell silent. I cradled my head. Swish, swish, thunk-a-thunk. A wedge of feldspar the size of a cue ball glanced off my knee. I bit my finger.

It was then that they turned to the car. I heard a door slam, a curse, and then the sound of the headlights shattering—almost a good-natured sound, celebratory, like corks popping from the necks of bottles. This was succeeded by the dull booming of the fenders, metal on metal, and then the icy crash of the windshield. I inched forward, elbows and knees, my belly pressed to the muck, thinking of guerrillas and commandos and *The Naked and the Dead*.° I parted the weeds and squinted the length of the parking lot.

The Naked and the Dead: novel (1948) by Norman Mailer, about U.S. Army life in World War II.

25

The second car—it was a Trans-Am—was still running, its high beams washing the scene in a lurid stagy light. Tire iron flailing, the greasy bad character was laying into the side of my mother's Bel Air like an avenging demon, his shadow riding up the trunks of the trees. Whomp. Whomp. Whomp-whomp. The other two guys—blond types, in fraternity jackets—were helping out with tree branches and skull-sized boulders. One of them was gathering up bottles, rocks, muck, candy wrappers, used condoms, poptops, and other refuse and pitching it through the window on the driver's side. I could see the fox, a white bulb behind the windshield of the '57 Chevy. "Bobbie," she whined over the thumping, "come on." The greasy character paused a moment, took one good swipe at the left taillight, and then heaved the tire iron halfway across the lake. Then he fired up the '57 and was gone.

Blond head nodded at blond head. One said something to the other, too low for me to catch. They were no doubt thinking that in helping to annihilate my mother's car they'd committed a fairly rash act, and thinking too that there were three bad characters connected with that very car watching them from the woods. Perhaps other possibilities occurred to them as well—police, jail cells, justices of the peace, reparations, lawyers, irate parents, fraternal censure. Whatever they were thinking, they suddenly dropped branches, bottles, and rocks and sprang for their car in unison, as if they'd choreographed it. Five seconds. That's all it took. The engine shrieked, the tires squealed, a cloud of dust rose from the rutted lot and then settled back on darkness.

I don't know how long I lay there, the bad breath of decay all around me, my jacket heavy as a bear, the primordial ooze subtly reconstituting itself to accommodate my upper thighs and testicles. My jaws ached, my knee throbbed, my coccyx was on fire. I contemplated suicide, wondered if I'd need bridgework, scraped the recesses of my brain for some sort of excuse to give my parents—a tree had fallen on the car, I was blinded by a bread truck, hit and run, vandals had got to it while we were playing chess at Digby's. Then I thought of the dead man. He was probably the only person on the planet worse off than I was. I thought about him, fog on the lake, insects chirring eerily, and felt the tug of fear, felt the darkness opening up inside me like a set of jaws. Who was he, I wondered, this victim of time and circumstance bobbing sorrowfully in the lake at my back. The owner of the chopper, no doubt, a bad older character come to this. Shot during a murky drug deal, drowned while drunkenly frolicking in the lake. Another headline. My car was wrecked; he was dead.

When the eastern half of the sky went from black to cobalt and the trees began to separate themselves from the shadows, I pushed myself up from the mud and stepped out into the open. By now the birds had begun to take over for the crickets, and dew lay slick on the leaves. There was a smell in the air, raw and sweet at the same time, the smell of the sun

30

firing buds and opening blossoms. I contemplated the car. It lay there like a wreck along the highway, like a steel sculpture left over from a vanished civilization. Everything was still. This was nature.

I was circling the car, as dazed and bedraggled as the sole survivor of an air blitz, when Digby and Jeff emerged from the trees behind me. Digby's face was crosshatched with smears of dirt; Jeff's jacket was gone and his shirt was torn across the shoulder. They slouched across the lot, looking sheepish, and silently came up beside me to gape at the ravaged automobile. No one said a word. After a while Jeff swung open the driver's door and began to scoop the broken glass and garbage off the seat. I looked at Digby. He shrugged. "At least they didn't slash the tires," he said.

It was true: the tires were intact. There was no windshield, the headlights were staved in, and the body looked as if it had been sledge-hammered for a quarter a shot at the county fair, but the tires were inflated to regulation pressure. The car was drivable. In silence, all three of us bent to scrape the mud and shattered glass from the interior. I said nothing about the biker. When we were finished, I reached in my pocket for the keys, experienced a nasty stab of recollection, cursed myself, and turned to search the grass. I spotted them almost immediately, no more than five feet from the open door, glinting like jewels in the first tapering shaft of sunlight. There was no reason to get philosophical about it: I eased into the seat and turned the engine over.

It was at that precise moment that the silver Mustang with the flame decals rumbled into the lot. All three of us froze; then Digby and Jeff slid into the car and slammed the door. We watched as the Mustang rocked and bobbed across the ruts and finally jerked to a halt beside the forlorn chopper at the far end of the lot. "Let's go," Digby said. I hesitated, the Bel Air wheezing beneath me. 35

Two girls emerged from the Mustang. Tight jeans, stiletto heels, hair like frozen fur. They bent over the motorcycle, paced back and forth aimlessly, glanced once or twice at us, and then ambled over to where the reeds sprang up in a green fence round the perimeter of the lake. One of them cupped her hands to her mouth. "Al," she called. "Hey, Al!"

"Come on," Digby hissed. "Let's get out of here."

But it was too late. The second girl was picking her way across the lot, unsteady on her heels, looking up at us and then away. She was older—twenty-five or -six—and as she came closer we could see there was something wrong with her: she was stoned or drunk, lurching now and waving her arms for balance. I gripped the steering wheel as if it were the ejection lever of a flaming jet, and Digby spat out my name, twice, terse and impatient.

"Hi," the girl said.

We looked at her like zombies, like war veterans, like deaf-and-dumb   40
pencil peddlers.

She smiled, her lips cracked and dry. "Listen," she said, bending from
the waist to look in the window, "you guys seen Al?" Her pupils were pin-
points, her eyes glass. She jerked her neck. "That's his bike over there—
Al's. You seen him?"

Al. I didn't know what to say. I wanted to get out of the car and
retch, I wanted to go home to my parents' house and crawl into bed.
Digby poked me in the ribs. "We haven't seen anybody," I said.

The girl seemed to consider this, reaching out a slim veiny arm to
brace herself against the car. "No matter," she said, slurring the t's, "he'll
turn up." And then, as if she'd just taken stock of the whole scene—the
ravaged car and our battered faces, the desolation of the place—she said:
"Hey, you guys look like some pretty bad characters—been fightin',
huh?" We stared straight ahead, rigid as catatonics. She was fumbling in
her pocket and muttering something. Finally she held out a handful of
tablets in glassine wrappers: "Hey, you want to party, you want to do
some of these with me and Sarah?"

I just looked at her. I thought I was going to cry. Digby broke the
silence. "No, thanks," he said, leaning over me. "Some other time."

I put the car in gear and it inched forward with a groan, shaking off   45
pellets of glass like an old dog shedding water after a bath, heaving over
the ruts on its worn springs, creeping toward the highway. There was a
sheen of sun on the lake. I looked back. The girl was still standing there,
watching us, her shoulders slumped, hand outstretched.

QUESTIONS

1. Around what year, would you say, was it that "courtesy and winning ways went
   out of style, when it was good to be bad, when you cultivated decadence like a
   taste"?

2. What is it about Digby and Jeff that inspires the narrator to call them "bad"?

3. Twice in "Greasy Lake"—in paragraphs 2 and 32—appear the words, "This was
   nature." What contrasts do you find between the "nature" of the narrator's earlier
   and later views?

4. What makes the narrator and his friends run off into the woods?

5. How does the heroes' encounter with the two girls at the end of the story differ
   from their earlier encounter with the girl from the blue Chevy? How do you
   account for the difference? When at the end of the story the girl offers to party
   with the three friends, what makes the narrator say, "I thought I was going to
   cry"?

6. How important to what happens in this story is Greasy Lake itself? What details
   about the lake and its shores strike you as particularly memorable (whether
   funny, disgusting, or both)?

Amy Tan

A Pair of Tickets 1989

Amy Tan was born in Oakland, California, in 1952. Both of her parents were recent Chinese immigrants. Her father was an electrical engineer (as well as a Baptist minister); her mother was a vocational nurse. When her father and older brother both died of brain tumors, the fifteen-year-old Tan moved with her mother and younger brother to Switzerland, where she attended high school. On their return to the United States Tan attended Linfield College, a Baptist school in Oregon, but she eventually transferred to California State University at San Jose. At this

AMY TAN

time Tan and her mother argued about her future. The mother insisted her daughter pursue premedical studies in preparation for becoming a neurosurgeon, but Tan wanted to do something else. For six months the two did not speak to one another. Tan worked for IBM writing computer manuals and also wrote freelance business articles under a pseudonym. In 1987 she and her mother visited China together. This experience, which is reflected in "A Pair of Tickets," deepened Tan's sense of her Chinese American identity. "As soon as my feet touched China," she wrote, "I became Chinese." Soon after, she began writing her first novel, The Joy Luck Club (1989), which consists of sixteen interrelated stories about a group of Chinese American mothers and their daughters. (The club of the title is a woman's social group.) The Joy Luck Club became both a critical success and a best-seller, and was made into a movie in 1993. In 1991 Tan published her second novel, The Kitchen God's Wife. Her later novels include The Hundred Secret Senses (1995), The Bonesetter's Daughter (2001), and Saving Fish from Drowning (2005). She has also published two books for children, The Moon Lady (1992) and The Chinese Siamese Cat (1994). In 2003, she published The Opposite of Fate: A Book of Musings, a collection of autobiographical writings. Tan performs with a "vintage garage" band called the Rock Bottom Remainders, which also includes, among others, Stephen King, Dave Barry, and Scott Turow. She lives outside San Francisco with her husband.

The minute our train leaves the Hong Kong border and enters Shenzhen, China, I feel different. I can feel the skin on my forehead tingling, my blood rushing through a new course, my bones aching with a familiar old pain. And I think, My mother was right. I am becoming Chinese.

"Cannot be helped," my mother said when I was fifteen and had vigorously denied that I had any Chinese whatsoever below my skin. I was a sophomore at Galileo High in San Francisco, and all my Caucasian friends agreed: I was about as Chinese as they were. But my mother had studied at a famous nursing school in Shanghai, and she said she knew all about genetics. So there was no doubt in her mind, whether I agreed or not: Once you are born Chinese, you cannot help but feel and think Chinese.

"Someday you will see," said my mother. "It is in your blood, waiting to be let go."

And when she said this, I saw myself transforming like a werewolf, a mutant tag of DNA suddenly triggered, replicating itself insidiously into a *syndrome*,° a cluster of telltale Chinese behaviors, all those things my mother did to embarrass me—haggling with store owners, pecking her mouth with a toothpick in public, being color-blind to the fact that lemon yellow and pale pink are not good combinations for winter clothes.

But today I realize I've never really known what it means to be   5
Chinese. I am thirty-six years old. My mother is dead and I am on a train, carrying with me her dreams of coming home. I am going to China.

We are first going to Guangzhou, my seventy-two-year-old father, Canning Woo, and I, where we will visit his aunt, whom he has not seen since he was ten years old. And I don't know whether it's the prospect of seeing his aunt or if it's because he's back in China, but now he looks like he's a young boy, so innocent and happy I want to button his sweater and pat his head. We are sitting across from each other, separated by a little table with two cold cups of tea. For the first time I can ever remember, my father has tears in his eyes, and all he is seeing out the train window is a sectioned field of yellow, green, and brown, a narrow canal flanking the tracks, low rising hills, and three people in blue jackets riding an ox-driven cart on this early October morning. And I can't help myself. I also have misty eyes, as if I had seen this a long, long time ago, and had almost forgotten.

In less than three hours, we will be in Guangzhou, which my guide-book tells me is how one properly refers to Canton these days. It seems all the cities I have heard of, except Shanghai, have changed their spellings. I think they are saying China has changed in other ways as well. Chungking is Chongqing. And Kweilin is Guilin. I have looked these names up, because after we see my father's aunt in Guangzhou, we will catch a plane to Shanghai, where I will meet my two half-sisters for the first time.

They are my mother's twin daughters from her first marriage, little babies she was forced to abandon on a road as she was fleeing Kweilin for Chungking in 1944. That was all my mother had told me about these

---

syndrome: a group of symptoms that occur together as the sign of a particular disease or abnormality.

daughters, so they had remained babies in my mind, all these years, sitting on the side of a road, listening to bombs whistling in the distance while sucking their patient red thumbs.

And it was only this year that someone found them and wrote with this joyful news. A letter came from Shanghai, addressed to my mother. When I first heard about this, that they were alive, I imagined my identical sisters transforming from little babies into six-year-old girls. In my mind, they were seated next to each other at a table, taking turns with the fountain pen. One would write a neat row of characters: *Dearest Mama. We are alive.* She would brush back her wispy bangs and hand the other sister the pen, and she would write: *Come get us. Please hurry.*

Of course they could not know that my mother had died three months before, suddenly, when a blood vessel in her brain burst. One minute she was talking to my father, complaining about the tenants upstairs, scheming how to evict them under the pretense that relatives from China were moving in. The next minute she was holding her head, her eyes squeezed shut, groping for the sofa, and then crumpling softly to the floor with fluttering hands. 10

So my father had been the first one to open the letter, a long letter it turned out. And they did call her Mama. They said they always revered her as their true mother. They kept a framed picture of her. They told her about their life, from the time my mother last saw them on the road leaving Kweilin to when they were finally found.

And the letter had broken my father's heart so much—these daughters calling my mother from another life he never knew—that he gave the letter to my mother's old friend Auntie Lindo and asked her to write back and tell my sisters, in the gentlest way possible, that my mother was dead.

But instead Auntie Lindo took the letter to the Joy Luck Club and discussed with Auntie Ying and Auntie An-mei what should be done, because they had known for many years about my mother's search for her twin daughters, her endless hope. Auntie Lindo and the others cried over this double tragedy, of losing my mother three months before, and now again. And so they couldn't help but think of some miracle, some possible way of reviving her from the dead, so my mother could fulfill her dream.

So this is what they wrote to my sisters in Shanghai: "Dearest Daughters, I too have never forgotten you in my memory or in my heart. I never gave up hope that we would see each other again in a joyous reunion. I am only sorry it has been too long. I want to tell you everything about my life since I last saw you. I want to tell you this when our family comes to see you in China. . . ." They signed it with my mother's name.

It wasn't until all this had been done that they first told me about my sisters, the letter they received, the one they wrote back. 15

"They'll think she's coming, then," I murmured. And I had imagined my sisters now being ten or eleven, jumping up and down, holding hands, their pigtails bouncing, excited that their mother—*their* mother—was coming, whereas my mother was dead.

"How can you say she is not coming in a letter?" said Auntie Lindo. "She is their mother. She is your mother. You must be the one to tell them. All these years, they have been dreaming of her." And I thought she was right.

But then I started dreaming, too, of my mother and my sisters and how it would be if I arrived in Shanghai. All these years, while they waited to be found, I had lived with my mother and then had lost her. I imagined seeing my sisters at the airport. They would be standing on their tip-toes, looking anxiously, scanning from one dark head to another as we got off the plane. And I would recognize them instantly, their faces with the identical worried look.

"*Jyejye, Jyejye.* Sister, Sister. We are here," I saw myself saying in my poor version of Chinese.

"Where is Mama?" they would say, and look around, still smiling, two flushed and eager faces. "Is she hiding?" And this would have been like my mother, to stand behind just a bit, to tease a little and make people's patience pull a little on their hearts. I would shake my head and tell my sisters she was not hiding. 20

"Oh, that must be Mama, no?" one of my sisters would whisper excitedly, pointing to another small woman completely engulfed in a tower of presents. And that, too, would have been like my mother, to bring mountains of gifts, food, and toys for children—all bought on sale— shunning thanks, saying the gifts were nothing, and later turning the labels over to show my sisters, "Calvin Klein, 100% wool."

I imagined myself starting to say, "Sisters, I am sorry, I have come alone . . ." and before I could tell them—they could see it in my face— they were wailing, pulling their hair, their lips twisted in pain, as they ran away from me. And then I saw myself getting back on the plane and coming home.

After I had dreamed this scene many times—watching their despair turn from horror into anger—I begged Auntie Lindo to write another letter. And at first she refused.

"How can I say she is dead? I cannot write this," said Auntie Lindo with a stubborn look.

"But it's cruel to have them believe she's coming on the plane," I said. "When they see it's just me, they'll hate me." 25

"Hate you? Cannot be." She was scowling. "You are their own sister, their only family."

"You don't understand," I protested.

"What I don't understand?" she said.

And I whispered, "They'll think I'm responsible, that she died because I didn't appreciate her."

And Auntie Lindo looked satisfied and sad at the same time, as if 30 this were true and I had finally realized it. She sat down for an hour, and when she stood up she handed me a two-page letter. She had tears in her eyes. I realized that the very thing I had feared, she had done. So even if she had written the news of my mother's death in English, I wouldn't have had the heart to read it.

"Thank you," I whispered.

The landscape has become gray, filled with low flat cement buildings, old factories, and then tracks and more tracks filled with trains like ours passing by in the opposite direction. I see platforms crowded with people wearing drab Western clothes, with spots of bright colors: little children wearing pink and yellow, red and peach. And there are soldiers in olive green and red, and old ladies in gray tops and pants that stop mid-calf. We are in Guangzhou.

Before the train even comes to a stop, people are bringing down their belongings from above their seats. For a moment there is a dangerous shower of heavy suitcases laden with gifts to relatives, half-broken boxes wrapped in miles of string to keep the contents from spilling out, plastic bags filled with yarn and vegetables and packages of dried mushrooms, and camera cases. And then we are caught in a stream of people rushing, shoving, pushing us along, until we find ourselves in one of a dozen lines waiting to go through customs. I feel as if I were getting on the number 30 Stockton bus in San Francisco. I am in China, I remind myself. And somehow the crowds don't bother me. It feels right. I start pushing too.

I take out the declaration forms and my passport. "Woo," it says at the top, and below that, "June May," who was born in "California, U.S.A.," in 1951. I wonder if the customs people will question whether I'm the same person in the passport photo. In this picture, my chin-length hair is swept back and artfully styled. I am wearing false eyelashes, eye shadow, and lip liner. My cheeks are hollowed out by bronze blusher. But I had not expected the heat in October. And now my hair hangs limp with the humidity. I wear no makeup; in Hong Kong my mascara had melted into dark circles and everything else had felt like layers of grease. So today my face is plain, unadorned except for a thin mist of shiny sweat on my forehead and nose.

Even without makeup, I could never pass for true Chinese. I stand 35 five-foot-six, and my head pokes above the crowd so that I am eye level only with other tourists. My mother once told me my height came from my grandfather, who was a northerner, and may have even had some Mongol blood. "This is what your grandmother once told me," explained my mother. "But now it is too late to ask her. They are all dead, your grandparents, your uncles, and their wives and children, all killed in the war, when a bomb fell on our house. So many generations in one instant."

She had said this so matter-of-factly that I thought she had long since gotten over any grief she had. And then I wondered how she knew they were all dead.

"Maybe they left the house before the bomb fell," I suggested.

"No," said my mother. "Our whole family is gone. It is just you and I."

"But how do you know? Some of them could have escaped."

"Cannot be," said my mother, this time almost angrily. And then   40
her frown was washed over by a puzzled blank look, and she began to talk as if she were trying to remember where she had misplaced something. "I went back to that house. I kept looking up to where the house used to be. And it wasn't a house, just the sky. And below, underneath my feet, were four stories of burnt bricks and wood, all the life of our house. Then off to the side I saw things blown into the yard, nothing valuable. There was a bed someone used to sleep in, really just a metal frame twisted up at one corner. And a book, I don't know what kind, because every page had turned black. And I saw a teacup which was unbroken but filled with ashes. And then I found my doll, with her hands and legs broken, her hair burned off. . . . When I was a little girl, I had cried for that doll, seeing it all alone in the store window, and my mother had bought it for me. It was an American doll with yellow hair. It could turn its legs and arms. The eyes moved up and down. And when I married and left my family home, I gave the doll to my youngest niece, because she was like me. She cried if that doll was not with her always. Do you see? If she was in the house with that doll, her parents were there, and so everybody was there, waiting together, because that's how our family was."

The woman in the customs booth stares at my documents, then glances at me briefly, and with two quick movements stamps everything and sternly nods me along. And soon my father and I find ourselves in a large area filled with thousands of people and suitcases. I feel lost and my father looks helpless.

"Excuse me," I say to a man who looks like an American. "Can you tell me where I can get a taxi?" He mumbles something that sounds Swedish or Dutch.

"Syau Yen! Syau Yen!" I hear a piercing voice shout from behind me. An old woman in a yellow knit beret is holding up a pink plastic bag filled with wrapped trinkets. I guess she is trying to sell us something. But my father is staring down at this tiny sparrow of a woman, squinting into her eyes. And then his eyes widen, his face opens up and he smiles like a pleased little boy.

"*Aiyi! Aiyi!*" —Auntie Auntie!—he says softly.

"*Syau Yen!*" coos my great-aunt. I think it's funny she has just called   45
my father "Little Wild Goose." It must be his baby milk name, the name
used to discourage ghosts from stealing children.

They clasp each other's hands—they do not hug—and hold on like
this, taking turns saying, "Look at you! You are so old. Look how old
you've become!" They are both crying openly, laughing at the same time,
and I bite my lip, trying not to cry. I'm afraid to feel their joy. Because I
am thinking how different our arrival in Shanghai will be tomorrow, how
awkward it will feel.

Now Aiyi beams and points to a Polaroid picture of my father. My
father had wisely sent pictures when he wrote and said we were coming.
See how smart she was, she seems to intone as she compares the picture
to my father. In the letter, my father had said we would call her from the
hotel once we arrived, so this is a surprise, that they've come to meet us.
I wonder if my sisters will be at the airport.

It is only then that I remember the camera. I had meant to take a
picture of my father and his aunt the moment they met. It's not too late.

"Here, stand together over here," I say, holding up the Polaroid.
The camera flashes and I hand them the snapshot. Aiyi and my father
still stand close together, each of them holding a corner of the picture,
watching as their images begin to form. They are almost reverentially
quiet. Aiyi is only five years older than my father, which makes her
around seventy-seven. But she looks ancient, shrunken, a mummified
relic. Her thin hair is pure white, her teeth are brown with decay. So
much for stories of Chinese women looking young forever, I think to
myself.

Now Aiyi is crooning to me: "*Jandale.*" So big already. She looks up   50
at me, at my full height, and then peers into her pink plastic bag—her
gifts to us, I have figured out—as if she is wondering what she will give to
me, now that I am so old and big. And then she grabs my elbow with her
sharp pincerlike grasp and turns me around. A man and woman in their
fifties are shaking hands with my father, everybody smiling and saying,
"Ah! Ah!" They are Aiyi's oldest son and his wife, and standing next to
them are four other people, around my age, and a little girl who's around
ten. The introductions go by so fast, all I know is that one of them is
Aiyi's grandson, with his wife, and the other is her granddaughter, with
her husband. And the little girl is Lili, Aiyi's great-granddaughter.

Aiyi and my father speak the Mandarin dialect from their childhood, but the rest of the family speaks only the Cantonese of their village. I understand only Mandarin but can't speak it that well. So Aiyi
and my father gossip unrestrained in Mandarin, exchanging news about
people from their old village. And they stop only occasionally to talk to
the rest of us, sometimes in Cantonese, sometimes in English.

"Oh, it is as I suspected," says my father, turning to me. "He died last summer." And I already understood this. I just don't know who this person, Li Gong, is. I feel as if I were in the United Nations and the translators had run amok.

"Hello," I say to the little girl. "My name is Jing-mei." But the little girl squirms to look away, causing her parents to laugh with embarrassment. I try to think of Cantonese words I can say to her, stuff I learned from friends in Chinatown, but all I can think of are swear words, terms for bodily functions, and short phrases like "tastes good," "tastes like garbage," and "she's really ugly." And then I have another plan: I hold up the Polaroid camera, beckoning Lili with my finger. She immediately jumps forward, places one hand on her hip in the manner of a fashion model, juts out her chest, and flashes me a toothy smile. As soon as I take the picture she is standing next to me, jumping and giggling every few seconds as she watches herself appear on the greenish film.

By the time we hail taxis for the ride to the hotel, Lili is holding tight onto my hand, pulling me along.

In the taxi, Aiyi talks nonstop, so I have no chance to ask her about the different sights we are passing by. 55

"You wrote and said you would come only for one day," says Aiyi to my father in an agitated tone. "One day! How can you see your family in one day! Toishan is many hours' drive from Guangzhou. And this idea to call us when you arrive. This is nonsense. We have no telephone."

My heart races a little. I wonder if Auntie Lindo told my sisters we would call from the hotel in Shanghai?

Aiyi continues to scold my father. "I was so beside myself, ask my son, almost turned heaven and earth upside down trying to think of a way! So we decided the best was for us to take the bus from Toishan and come into Guangzhou—meet you right from the start."

And now I am holding my breath as the taxi driver dodges between trucks and buses, honking his horn constantly. We seem to be on some sort of long freeway overpass, like a bridge above the city. I can see row after row of apartments, each floor cluttered with laundry hanging out to dry on the balcony. We pass a public bus, with people jammed in so tight their faces are nearly wedged against the window. Then I see the skyline of what must be downtown Guangzhou. From a distance, it looks like a major American city, with high rises and construction going on everywhere. As we slow down in the more congested part of the city, I see scores of little shops, dark inside, lined with counters and shelves. And then there is a building, its front laced with scaffolding made of bamboo poles held together with plastic strips. Men and women are standing on narrow platforms, scraping the sides, working without safety straps or helmets. Oh, would OSHA° have a field day here, I think.

Aiyi's shrill voice rises up again: "So it is a shame you can't see our 60 village, our house. My sons have been quite successful, selling our vegetables in the free market. We had enough these last few years to build a big house, three stories, all of new brick, big enough for our whole family and then some. And every year, the money is even better. You Americans aren't the only ones who know how to get rich!"

The taxi stops and I assume we've arrived, but then I peer out at what looks like a grander version of the Hyatt Regency. "This is communist China?" I wonder out loud. And then I shake my head toward my father. "This must be the wrong hotel." I quickly pull out our itinerary, travel tickets, and reservations. I had explicitly instructed my travel agent to choose something inexpensive, in the thirty-to-forty-dollar range. I'm sure of this. And there it says on our itinerary: Garden Hotel, Huanshi Dong Lu. Well, our travel agent had better be prepared to eat the extra, that's all I have to say.

The hotel is magnificent. A bellboy complete with uniform and sharp-creased cap jumps forward and begins to carry our bags into the lobby. Inside, the hotel looks like an orgy of shopping arcades and restaurants all encased in granite and glass. And rather than be impressed, I am worried about the expense, as well as the appearance it must give Aiyi, that we rich Americans cannot be without our luxuries even for one night.

But when I step up to the reservation desk, ready to haggle over this booking mistake, it is confirmed. Our rooms are prepaid, thirty-four dollars each. I feel sheepish, and Aiyi and the others seem delighted by our temporary surroundings. Lili is looking wide-eyed at an arcade filled with video games.

Our whole family crowds into one elevator, and the bellboy waves, saying he will meet us on the eighteenth floor. As soon as the elevator door shuts, everybody becomes very quiet, and when the door finally opens again, everybody talks at once in what sounds like relieved voices. I have the feeling Aiyi and the others have never been on such a long elevator ride.

Our rooms are next to each other and are identical. The rugs, drapes, 65 bedspreads are all in shades of taupe. There's a color television with remote-control panels built into the lamp table between the two twin beds. The bathroom has marble walls and floors. I find a built-in wet bar with a small refrigerator stocked with Heineken beer, Coke Classic, and Seven-Up, mini-bottles of Johnnie Walker Red, Bacardi rum, and Smirnoff vodka,

OSHA: Occupational Safety and Health Administration, a federal agency that regulates and monitors workplace safety conditions.

and packets of M & M's, honey-roasted cashews, and Cadbury chocolate bars. And again I say out loud, "This is communist China?"

My father comes into my room. "They decided we should just stay here and visit," he says, shrugging his shoulders. "They say, Less trouble that way. More time to talk."

"What about dinner?" I ask. I have been envisioning my first real Chinese feast for many days already, a big banquet with one of those soups steaming out of a carved winter melon, chicken wrapped in clay, Peking duck, the works.

My father walks over and picks up a room service book next to a *Travel & Leisure* magazine. He flips through the pages quickly and then points to the menu. "This is what they want," says my father.

So it's decided. We are going to dine tonight in our rooms, with our family, sharing hamburgers, french fries, and apple pie à la mode.

Aiyi and her family are browsing the shops while we clean up. After a hot ride on the train, I'm eager for a shower and cooler clothes. 70

The hotel has provided little packets of shampoo which, upon opening, I discover is the consistency and color of hoisin sauce. This is more like it, I think. This is China. And I rub some in my damp hair.

Standing in the shower, I realize this is the first time I've been by myself in what seems like days. But instead of feeling relieved, I feel forlorn. I think about what my mother said, about activating my genes and becoming Chinese. And I wonder what she meant.

Right after my mother died, I asked myself a lot of things, things that couldn't be answered, to force myself to grieve more. It seemed as if I wanted to sustain my grief, to assure myself that I had cared deeply enough.

But now I ask the questions mostly because I want to know the answers. What was that pork stuff she used to make that had the texture of sawdust? What were the names of the uncles who died in Shanghai? What had she dreamt all these years about her other daughters? All the times when she got mad at me, was she really thinking about them? Did she wish I were they? Did she regret that I wasn't?

At one o'clock in the morning, I awake to tapping sounds on the window. I must have dozed off and now I feel my body uncramping itself. I'm sitting on the floor, leaning against one of the twin beds. Lili is lying next to me. The others are asleep, too, sprawled out on the beds and floor. Aiyi is seated at a little table, looking very sleepy. And my father is staring out the window, tapping his fingers on the glass. The last time I listened my father was telling Aiyi about his life since he last saw her. How he had gone to Yenching University, later got a post with a newspaper in Chungking, met my mother there, a young widow. How they later fled 75 together to Shanghai to try to find my mother's family house, but there was nothing there. And then they traveled eventually to Canton and then to Hong Kong, then Haiphong and finally to San Francisco. . . .

"Suyuan didn't tell me she was trying all these years to find her daughters," he is now saying in a quiet voice. "Naturally, I did not discuss her daughters with her. I thought she was ashamed she had left them behind."

"Where did she leave them?" asks Aiyi. "How were they found?"

I am wide awake now. Although I have heard parts of this story from my mother's friends.

"It happened when the Japanese took over Kweilin," says my father.

"Japanese in Kweilin?" says Aiyi. "That was never the case. Couldn't be. The Japanese never came to Kweilin." 80

"Yes, that is what the newspapers reported. I know this because I was working for the news bureau at the time. The Kuomintang often told us what we could say and could not say. But we knew the Japanese had come into Kwangsi Province. We had sources who told us how they had captured the Wuchang-Canton railway. How they were coming overland, making very fast progress, marching toward the provincial capital."

Aiyi looks astonished. "If people did not know this, how could Suyuan know the Japanese were coming?"

"An officer of the Kuomintang secretly warned her," explains my father. "Suyuan's husband also was an officer and everybody knew that officers and their families would be the first to be killed. So she gathered a few possessions and, in the middle of the night, she picked up her daughters and fled on foot. The babies were not even one year old."

"How could she give up those babies!" sighs Aiyi. "Twin girls. We have never had such luck in our family." And then she yawns again.

"What were they named?" she asks. I listen carefully. I had been 85 planning on using just the familiar "Sister" to address them both. But now I want to know how to pronounce their names.

"They have their father's surname, Wang," says my father. "And their given names are Chwun Yu and Chwun Hwa."

"What do the names mean?" I ask.

"Ah." My father draws imaginary characters on the window. "One means 'Spring Rain,' the other 'Spring Flower,' " he explains in English, "because they born in the spring, and of course rain come before flower, same order these girls are born. Your mother like a poet, don't you think?"

I nod my head. I see Aiyi nod her head forward, too. But it falls forward and stays there. She is breathing deeply, noisily. She is asleep.

"And what does Ma's name mean?" I whisper. 90

"'Suyuan,'" he says, writing more invisible characters on the glass. "The way she write it in Chinese, it mean 'Long-Cherished Wish.' Quite a fancy name, not so ordinary like flower name. See this first character, it mean something like 'Forever Never Forgotten.' But there is another way to write 'Suyuan.' Sound exactly the same, but the meaning is opposite." His finger creates the brushstrokes of another character. "The first part look the same: 'Never Forgotten.' But the last part add to first part make the whole word mean 'Long-Held Grudge.' Your mother get angry with me, I tell her her name should be Grudge."

My father is looking at me, moist-eyed. "See, I pretty clever, too, hah?"

I nod, wishing I could find some way to comfort him. "And what about my name," I ask, "what does 'Jing-mei' mean?"

"Your name also special," he says. I wonder if any name in Chinese is not something special. " 'Jing' like excellent *jing*. Not just good, it's something pure, essential, the best quality. *Jing* is good leftover stuff when you take impurities out of something like gold, or rice, or salt. So what is left—just pure essence. And 'Mei,' this is common *mei*, as in *meimei*, 'younger sister.'"

I think about this. My mother's long-cherished wish. Me, the younger   95
sister who was supposed to be the essence of the others. I feed myself with the old grief, wondering how disappointed my mother must have been. Tiny Aiyi stirs suddenly, her head rolls and then falls back, her mouth opens as if to answer my question. She grunts in her sleep, tucking her body more closely into the chair.

"So why did she abandon those babies on the road?" I need to know, because now I feel abandoned too.

"Long time I wondered this myself," says my father. "But then I read that letter from her daughters in Shanghai now, and I talk to Auntie Lindo, all the others. And then I knew. No shame in what she done. None."

"What happened?"

"Your mother running away—" begins my father.

"No, tell me in Chinese," I interrupt. "Really, I can understand."   100
He begins to talk, still standing at the window, looking into the night.

After fleeing Kweilin, your mother walked for several days trying to find a main road. Her thought was to catch a ride on a truck or wagon, to catch enough rides until she reached Chungking, where her husband was stationed.

She had sewn money and jewelry into the lining of her dress, enough, she thought, to barter rides all the way. If I am lucky, she thought, I will not have to trade the heavy gold bracelet and jade ring. These were things from her mother, your grandmother.

By the third day, she had traded nothing. The roads were filled with people, everybody running and begging for rides from passing trucks. The trucks rushed by, afraid to stop. So your mother found no rides, only the start of dysentery pains in her stomach.

Her shoulders ached from the two babies swinging from scarf slings. 105 Blisters grew on her palms from holding two leather suitcases. And then the blisters burst and began to bleed. After a while, she left the suitcases behind, keeping only the food and a few clothes. And later she also dropped the bags of wheat flour and rice and kept walking like this for many miles, singing songs to her little girls, until she was delirious with pain and fever.

Finally, there was not one more step left in her body. She didn't have the strength to carry those babies any farther. She slumped to the ground. She knew she would die of her sickness, or perhaps from thirst, from starvation, or from the Japanese, who she was sure were marching right behind her.

She took the babies out of the slings and sat them on the side of the road, then lay down next to them. You babies are so good, she said, so quiet. They smiled back, reaching their chubby hands for her, wanting to be picked up again. And then she knew she could not bear to watch her babies die with her.

She saw a family with three young children in a cart going by. "Take my babies, I beg you," she cried to them. But they stared back with empty eyes and never stopped.

She saw another person pass and called out again. This time a man turned around, and he had such a terrible expression—your mother said it looked like death itself—she shivered and looked away.

When the road grew quiet, she tore open the lining of her dress, and 110 stuffed jewelry under the shirt of one baby and money under the other. She reached into her pocket and drew out the photos of her family, the picture of her father and mother, the picture of herself and her husband on their wedding day. And she wrote on the back of each the names of the babies and this same message: "Please care for these babies with the money and valuables provided. When it is safe to come, if you bring them to Shanghai, 9 Weichang Lu, the Li family will be glad to give you a generous reward. Li Suyuan and Wang Fuchi."

And then she touched each baby's cheek and told her not to cry. She would go down the road to find them some food and would be back. And without looking back, she walked down the road, stumbling and crying, thinking only of this one last hope, that her daughters would be found by a kindhearted person who would care for them. She would not allow herself to imagine anything else.

She did not remember how far she walked, which direction she went, when she fainted, or how she was found. When she awoke, she was in the back of a bouncing truck with several other sick people, all moaning. And she began to scream, thinking she was now on a journey to Buddhist hell. But the face of an American missionary lady bent over her and smiled, talking to her in a soothing language she did not understand. And yet she could somehow understand. She had been saved for no good reason, and it was now too late to go back and save her babies.

When she arrived in Chungking, she learned her husband had died two weeks before. She told me later she laughed when the officers told her this news, she was so delirious with madness and disease. To come so far, to lose so much and to find nothing.

I met her in a hospital. She was lying on a cot, hardly able to move, her dysentery had drained her so thin. I had come in for my foot, my missing toe, which was cut off by a piece of falling rubble. She was talking to herself, mumbling.

"Look at these clothes," she said, and I saw she had on a rather unusual dress for wartime. It was silk satin, quite dirty, but there was no doubt it was a beautiful dress. 115

"Look at this face," she said, and I saw her dusty face and hollow cheeks, her eyes shining back. "Do you see my foolish hope?"

"I thought I had lost everything, except these two things," she murmured. "And I wondered which I would lose next. Clothes or hope? Hope or clothes?"

"But now, see here, look what is happening," she said, laughing, as if all her prayers had been answered. And she was pulling hair out of her head as easily as one lifts new wheat from wet soil.

It was an old peasant woman who found them. "How could I resist?" the peasant woman later told your sisters when they were older. They were still sitting obediently near where your mother had left them, looking like little fairy queens waiting for their sedan to arrive.

The woman, Mei Ching, and her husband, Mei Han, lived in a stone cave. There were thousands of hidden caves like that in and around Kweilin so secret that the people remained hidden even after the war ended. The Meis would come out of their cave every few days and forage for food supplies left on the road, and sometimes they would see something that they both agreed was a tragedy to leave behind. So one day they took back to their cave a delicately painted set of rice bowls, another day a little footstool with a velvet cushion and two new wedding blankets. And once, it was your sisters. 120

They were pious people, Muslims, who believed the twin babies were a sign of double luck, and they were sure of this when, later in the evening, they discovered how valuable the babies were. She and her husband had never seen rings and bracelets like those. And while they admired the pictures, knowing the babies came from a good family, neither of them could read or write. It was not until many months later that Mei Ching found someone who could read the writing on the back. By then, she loved these baby girls like her own.

In 1952 Mei Han, the husband, died. The twins were already eight years old, and Mei Ching now decided it was time to find your sisters' true family.

She showed the girls the picture of their mother and told them they had been born into a great family and she would take them back to see their true mother and grandparents. Mei Ching told them about the reward, but she swore she would refuse it. She loved these girls so much, she only wanted them to have what they were entitled to—a better life, a fine house, educated ways. Maybe the family would let her stay on as the girls' amah. Yes, she was certain they would insist.

Of course, when she found the place at 9 Weichang Lu, in the old French Concession, it was something completely different. It was the site of a factory building, recently constructed, and none of the workers knew what had become of the family whose house had burned down on that spot.

Mei Ching could not have known, of course, that your mother and I, 125 her new husband, had already returned to that same place in 1945 in hopes of finding both her family and her daughters.

Your mother and I stayed in China until 1947. We went to many different cities—back to Kweilin, to Changsha, as far south as Kunming. She was always looking out of one corner of her eye for twin babies, then little girls. Later we went to Hong Kong, and when we finally left in 1949 for the United States, I think she was even looking for them on the boat. But when we arrived, she no longer talked about them. I thought, At last, they have died in her heart.

When letters could be openly exchanged between China and the United States, she wrote immediately to old friends in Shanghai and Kweilin. I did not know she did this. Auntie Lindo told me. But of course, by then, all the street names had changed. Some people had died, others had moved away. So it took many years to find a contact. And when she did find an old schoolmate's address and wrote asking her to look for her daughters, her friend wrote back and said this was impossible, like looking for a needle on the bottom of the ocean. How did she know her daughters were in Shanghai and not somewhere else in China? The friend, of course, did not ask, How do you know your daughters are still alive?

So her schoolmate did not look. Finding babies lost during the war was a matter of foolish imagination, and she had no time for that.

But every year, your mother wrote to different people. And this last year, I think she got a big idea in her head, to go to China and find them herself. I remember she told me, "Canning, we should go, before it is too late, before we are too old." And I told her we were already too old, it was already too late.

I just thought she wanted to be a tourist! I didn't know she wanted 130 to go and look for her daughters. So when I said it was too late, that must have put a terrible thought in her head that her daughters might be dead. And I think this possibility grew bigger and bigger in her head, until it killed her.

Maybe it was your mother's dead spirit who guided her Shanghai schoolmate to find her daughters. Because after your mother died, the schoolmate saw your sisters, by chance, while shopping for shoes at the Number One Department Store on Nanjing Dong Road. She said it was like a dream, seeing these two women who looked so much alike, moving down the stairs together. There was something about their facial expressions that reminded the schoolmate of your mother.

She quickly walked over to them and called their names, which of course, they did not recognize at first, because Mei Ching had changed their names. But your mother's friend was so sure, she persisted. "Are you not Wang Chwun Yu and Wang Chwun Hwa?" she asked them. And then these double-image women became very excited, because they remembered the names written on the back of an old photo, a photo of a young man and woman they still honored, as their much-loved first parents, who had died and become spirit ghosts still roaming the earth looking for them.

At the airport, I am exhausted. I could not sleep last night. Aiyi had followed me into my room at three in the morning, and she instantly fell asleep on one of the twin beds, snoring with the might of a lumberjack. I lay awake thinking about my mother's story, realizing how much I have never known about her, grieving that my sisters and I had both lost her.

And now at the airport, after shaking hands with everybody, waving good-bye, I think about all the different ways we leave people in this world. Cheerily waving good-bye to some at airports, knowing we'll never see each other again. Leaving others on the side of the road, hoping that we will. Finding my mother in my father's story and saying good-bye before I have a chance to know her better.

Aiyi smiles at me as we wait for our gate to be called. She is so old. I put one arm around her and one around Lili. They are the same size, it seems. And then it's time. As we wave good-bye one more time and enter the waiting area, I get the sense I am going from one funeral to another. In my hand I'm clutching a pair of tickets to Shanghai. In two hours we'll be there.

The plane takes off. I close my eyes. How can I describe to them in my broken Chinese about our mother's life? Where should I begin?

"Wake up, we're here," says my father. And I awake with my heart pounding in my throat. I look out the window and we're already on the runway. It's gray outside.

And now I'm walking down the steps of the plane, onto the tarmac and toward the building. If only, I think, if only my mother had lived long enough to be the one walking toward them. I am so nervous I cannot even feel my feet. I am just moving somehow.

Somebody shouts, "She's arrived!" And then I see her. Her short hair. Her small body. And that same look on her face. She has the back of her hand pressed hard against her mouth. She is crying as though she had gone through a terrible ordeal and were happy it is over.

And I know it's not my mother, yet it is the same look she had when I was five and had disappeared all afternoon, for such a long time, that she was convinced I was dead. And when I miraculously appeared, sleepy-eyed, crawling from underneath my bed, she wept and laughed, biting the back of her hand to make sure it was true. 140

And now I see her again, two of her, waving, and in one hand there is a photo, the Polaroid I sent them. As soon as I get beyond the gate, we run toward each other, all three of us embracing, all hesitations and expectations forgotten.

"Mama, Mama," we all murmur, as if she is among us.

My sisters look at me, proudly. *"Meimei jandale,"* says one sister proudly to the other. "Little Sister has grown up." I look at their faces again and I see no trace of my mother in them. Yet they still look familiar. And now I also see what part of me is Chinese. It is so obvious. It is my family. It is in our blood. After all these years, it can finally be let go.

My sisters and I stand, arms around each other, laughing and wiping the tears from each other's eyes. The flash of the Polaroid goes off and my father hands me the snapshot. My sisters and I watch quietly together, eager to see what develops.

The gray-green surface changes to the bright colors of our three images, sharpening and deepening all at once. And although we don't speak, I know we all see it: Together we look like our mother. Her same eyes, her same mouth, open in surprise to see, at last, her long-cherished wish. 145

QUESTIONS

1. How is the external setting of "A Pair of Tickets" essential to what happens internally to the narrator in the course of this story?

2. How does the narrator's view of her father change by seeing him in a different setting?

3. In what ways does the narrator feel at home in China? In what ways does she feel foreign?

4. What do the narrator and her half-sisters have in common? How does this factor relate to the theme of the story?

5. In what ways does the story explore specifically Chinese American experiences? In what other ways is the story grounded in universal family issues?

WRITING EFFECTIVELY

The Importance of Setting

The time and place in which a story is set serve as more than mere backdrop. A particular setting can create a mood or provide clues to a protagonist's nature. Setting can play as large a role as plot and characters do by prompting a protagonist into an action he or she might not otherwise undertake.

A story's setting constitutes the external reality that surrounds the internal reality of the protagonist's personality. The external pressure of the setting is often the key factor that compels or invites the protagonist into action. To write about a story's setting, therefore, invites you to study not only the time and place but also their relation to the protagonist.

When preparing to write about a story, be sure to consider where and when it is set, and what role the setting plays.

CHECKLIST

Analyzing Setting

✔ Where does the story take place?

✔ What does the setting suggest about the characters' lives?

✔ Are there significant differences in the settings for different characters? What does this suggest about each person?

✔ When does the story take place? Is the time of year or time of day significant?

✔ Does the weather play a meaningful role in the story's action?

✔ What is the protagonist's relationship to the setting? Does it create a strongly positive or negative reaction?

✔ Does the setting of the story in some way compel the protagonist into action?

✔ Does the story's time or place suggest something about the character of the protagonist?

✔ Does a change in setting during the story suggest some internal change in the protagonist?

WRITING ASSIGNMENT ON SETTING

Choose a story from this chapter, and explore how character and setting are interrelated. A possible topic would be to describe the significance of setting to the protagonist in "A Pair of Tickets" or "Greasy Lake." How does the setting of the climax in the story contribute to a change in the character's personal perspective?

MORE TOPICS FOR WRITING

1. "Greasy Lake" takes its title and epigraph from Bruce Springsteen's song "Spirit in the Night," about a carefree night at a lakeside party. If you're not familiar with the song, you can find the lyrics on the Internet or download the song to get the full effect. Contrast the role setting plays in the story and in the song. What do you make of the fact that Boyle's story is so much darker than the song to which it refers?

2. Think of a place—on campus or beyond—to which you often return. If possible, go there. Make a list of every physical detail you can think of to describe that place. Then look the list over and write a paragraph on what sort of mood is suggested by it. If you were to describe your emotional connection to the place, which three details would you choose? Why?

3. Choose any story in this book, and pay careful attention to setting as you read it. Write several paragraphs reflecting on the following questions: What details in the story suggest the time and place in which it is set? Is setting central to the story? If the action were transplanted to some other place and time, how would the story change?

5
Tone and Style

In many Victorian novels it was customary for some commentator, presumably the author, to interrupt the story from time to time, remarking on the action, offering philosophical asides, or explaining the procedures to be followed in telling the story.

> Two hours later, Dorothea was seated in an inner room or boudoir of a handsome apartment in the Via Sistina. I am sorry to add that she was sobbing bitterly. . . .
> —George Eliot in *Middlemarch* (1873)

> But let the gentle-hearted reader be under no apprehension whatsoever. It is not destined that Eleanor shall marry Mr. Slope or Bertie Stanhope.
> —Anthony Trollope in *Barchester Towers* (1857)

Of course, the voice of this commentator was not identical with that of the "real-life" author—the one toiling over an inkpot, worrying about publication deadlines and whether the rent would be paid. At times the living author might have been far different in personality from that usually wise and cheerful intruder who kept addressing the reader of the book. Much of the time, to be sure, the author probably agreed with whatever attitudes this alter ego expressed. But, in effect, the author created the character of a commentator to speak for him or her and throughout the novel artfully sustained that character's voice.

Such intrusions, although sometimes useful to the "real" author and enjoyable to the reader, are today rare. Modern storytellers, carefully keeping out of sight, seldom comment on their plots and characters. Apparently they agree with Anton Chekhov that a writer should not judge the characters but should serve as their "impartial witness." And yet, no less definitely than Victorian novelists who introduced commentators, writers of effective stories no doubt have feelings toward their characters and events. The authors presumably care about these imaginary people and, in order for the story to grasp and sustain our interest, have to make us see these people in such a way that we, too, will care about them. When at the beginning of the short story "In Exile" Chekhov introduces us to a character, he does so with a description that arouses sympathy:

> The Tartar was worn out and ill, and wrapping himself in his rags, he talked about how good it was in the province of Simbirsk, and what

a beautiful and clever wife he had left at home. He was not more than twenty-five, and in the firelight his pale, sickly face and woebegone expression made him seem like a boy.

Other than the comparison of the Tartar to a child, the details in this passage seem mostly factual: the young man's illness, ragged clothes, facial expression, and topics of conversation. But these details form a portrait that stirs pity. By his selection of these imaginary details out of countless others that he might have included, Chekhov firmly directs our feelings about the Tartar, so miserable and pathetic in his sickness and his homesickness. We cannot know, of course, exactly what the living Chekhov felt; but at least we can be sure that we are supposed to share the compassion and tenderness of the narrator—Chekhov's impartial (but human) witness.

Not only the author's choice of details may lead us to infer his or her attitude, but also choice of characters, events, and situations, and choice of words. When the narrator of Joseph Conrad's *Heart of Darkness* comes upon an African outpost littered with abandoned machines and notices "a boiler wallowing in the grass," the exact word *wallowing* conveys an attitude: that there is something swinish about this scene of careless waste. Whatever leads us to infer the author's attitude is commonly called **tone.** Like a tone of voice, the tone of a story may communicate amusement, anger, affection, sorrow, contempt. It implies the feelings of the author, so far as we can sense them. Those feelings may be similar to feelings expressed by the narrator of the story (or by any character), but sometimes they may be dissimilar, even sharply opposed. The characters in a story may regard an event as sad, but we sense that the author regards it as funny. To understand the tone of a story, then, is to understand some attitude more fundamental to the story than whatever attitude the characters explicitly declare.

The tone of a story, like a tone of voice, may convey not simply one attitude, but a medley. Reading "A & P" (Chapter 1), we have mingled feelings about Sammy: delight in his wicked comments about other people and his skewering of hypocrisy; irritation at his smugness and condescension; admiration for his readiness to take a stand; sympathy for the pain of his disillusionment. Often the tone of a literary story will be too rich and complicated to sum up in one or two words. But to try to describe the tone of such a story may be a useful way to penetrate to its center and to grasp the whole of it.

One of the clearest indications of the tone of a story is the **style** in which it is written. In general, style refers to the individual traits or characteristics of a piece of writing: to a writer's particular ways of managing words that we come to recognize as habitual or customary. A distinctive style marks the work of a fine writer: we can tell his or her work from that of anyone else. From one story to another, however, the writer may fittingly change style; and in some stories, style may be altered meaningfully as the story goes along. In his novel *As I Lay Dying*, William Faulkner changes narrators with every chapter, and he distinguishes the narrators one from another by giving each an individual style or manner of speaking. Though each narrator has his or her own style, the book as a whole demonstrates Faulkner's style as well. For instance, one chapter is written from the point of view of a small boy, Vardaman Bundren, member of a family of poor Mississippi tenant farmers, whose view of a horse in a barn reads like this:

> It is as though the dark were resolving him out of his integrity, into an unrelated scattering of components—snuffings and stampings; smells of cooling flesh and ammoniac hair; an illusion of a co-ordinated whole of splotched hide and strong bones within which, detached and secret and familiar, an *is* different from my *is*.[1]

How can a small boy unaccustomed to libraries use words like *integrity, components, illusion,* and *coordinated?* Elsewhere in the story, Vardaman says aloud, with no trace of literacy, "Hit was a-laying right there on the ground." Apparently, in the passage it is not the voice of the boy that we are hearing, but something resembling the voice of William Faulkner, elevated and passionate, expressing the boy's thoughts in a style that admits Faulknerian words.

Usually, *style* indicates a mode of expression: the language a writer uses. In this sense, the notion of style includes such traits as the length and complexity of sentences, and **diction**, or choice of words: abstract or concrete, bookish ("unrelated scattering of components") or close to speech ("Hit was a-laying right there on the ground"). Involved in the idea of style, too, is any habitual use of imagery, patterns of sound, figures of speech, or other devices.

More recently, several writers of realistic fiction, called **minimalists**—Ann Beattie, Raymond Carver, Bobbie Ann Mason—have written with a flat, laid-back, unemotional tone, in an appropriately bare, unadorned style. Minimalists seem to give nothing but facts drawn from ordinary life, sometimes in picayune detail. Here is a sample passage, from Raymond Carver's story "A Small, Good Thing":

> She pulled into the driveway and cut the engine. She closed her eyes and leaned her head against the wheel for a minute. She listened to the ticking sounds the engine made as it began to cool. Then she got out of the car. She could hear the dog barking inside the house. She went to the front door, which was unlocked. She went inside and turned on lights and put on a kettle of water for tea. She opened some dog food and fed Slug on the back porch. The dog ate in hungry little smacks. It kept running into the kitchen to see that she was going to stay.

Explicit feeling and showy language are kept at a minimum here. Taken out of context, this description may strike you as banal, as if the writer himself

---

[1] Modern Library edition (New York: Random, 1930) 379.

were bored; but it works effectively as a part of Carver's entire story. As in all good writing, the style here seems a faithful mirror of what is said in it. At its best, such writing achieves "a hard-won reduction, a painful stripping away of richness, a baring of bone."[2]

To see what style means, compare the stories in this chapter by William Faulkner ("Barn Burning") and by Ernest Hemingway ("A Clean, Well-Lighted Place"). Faulkner frequently falls into a style in which a statement, as soon as uttered, is followed by another statement expressing the idea in a more emphatic way. Sentences are interrupted with parenthetical elements (asides, like this) thrust into them unexpectedly. At times, Faulkner writes of seemingly ordinary matters as if giving a speech in a towering passion. Here, from "Barn Burning," is a description of how a boy's father delivers a rug:

> "Don't you want me to help?" he whispered. His father did not answer and now he heard again that stiff foot striking the hollow portico with that wooden and clocklike deliberation, that outrageous overstatement of the weight it carried. The rug, hunched, not flung (the boy could tell that even in the darkness) from his father's shoulder struck the angle of wall and floor with a sound unbelievably loud, thunderous, then the foot again, unhurried and enormous; a light came on in the house and the boy sat, tense, breathing steadily and quietly and just a little fast, though the foot itself did not increase its beat at all, descending the steps now; now the boy could see him.

Faulkner is not merely indulging in language for its own sake. As you will find when you read the whole story, this rug delivery is vital to the story, and so too is the father's profound defiance—indicated by his walk. By devices of style—by *metaphor* and *simile* ("wooden and clocklike"), by exact qualification ("not flung"), by emphatic adjectives ("loud, thunderous")—Faulkner is carefully placing his emphases. By the words he selects to describe the father's stride, Faulkner directs how we feel toward the man and perhaps also indicates his own wondering but skeptical attitude toward a character whose very footfall is "outrageous" and "enormous." (Fond of long sentences like the last one in the quoted passage, Faulkner remarked that there are sentences that need to be written in the way a circus acrobat pedals a bicycle on a high wire: rapidly, so as not to fall off.)

Hemingway's famous style includes both short sentences and long, but when the sentences are long, they tend to be relatively simple in construction. Hemingway likes long compound sentences (clause plus clause plus clause), sometimes joined with "and"s. He interrupts such a sentence with a dependent clause or a parenthetical element much less frequently than Faulkner does. The effect is like listening to speech:

---

[2]Letter in the *New York Times Book Review,* 5 June 1988.

In the day time the street was dusty, but at night the dew settled the dust and the old man liked to sit late because he was deaf and now at night it was quiet and he felt the difference.

Hemingway is a master of swift, terse dialogue, and often casts whole scenes in the form of conversation. As if he were a closemouthed speaker unwilling to let his feelings loose, the narrator of a Hemingway story often addresses us in understatement, implying greater depths of feeling than he puts into words. Read the following story and you will see that its style and tone cannot be separated.

Ernest Hemingway

A Clean, Well-Lighted Place

1933

Ernest Hemingway (1899–1961), born in Oak Park, Illinois, bypassed college to be a cub reporter. In World War I, as an eighteen-year-old volunteer ambulance driver in Italy, he was wounded in action. In 1922 he settled in Paris, then aswarm with writers; he later recalled that time in A Moveable Feast *(1964). Hemingway won swift acclaim for his early stories,* In Our Time *(1925), and for his first, perhaps finest, novel,* The Sun Also Rises *(1926), portraying a "lost generation" of postwar American drifters in France and Spain.* For Whom the Bell Tolls

ERNEST HEMINGWAY

(1940) depicts life during the Spanish Civil War. Hemingway became a celebrity, often photographed as a marlin fisherman or a lion hunter. A fan of bullfighting, he wrote two nonfiction books on the subject: Death in the Afternoon *(1932) and* The Dangerous Summer *(1985). After World War II, with his fourth wife, journalist Mary Welsh, he made his home in Cuba, where he wrote* The Old Man and the Sea *(1952). The Nobel Prize for Literature came his way in 1954. In 1961, mentally distressed and physically ailing, he shot himself. Hemingway brought a hard-bitten realism to American fiction. His heroes live dangerously, by personal codes of honor, courage, and endurance. Hemingway's distinctively crisp, unadorned style left American literature permanently changed.*

It was late and every one had left the café except an old man who sat in the shadow the leaves of the tree made against the electric light. In the day time the street was dusty, but at night the dew settled the dust and the old man liked to sit late because he was deaf and now at night it was quiet and he felt the difference. The two waiters inside the café knew that the old man was a little drunk, and while he was a good client they

knew that if he became too drunk he would leave without paying, so they
kept watch on him.

"Last week he tried to commit suicide," one waiter said.

"Why?"

"He was in despair."

"What about?"   5

"Nothing."

"How do you know it was nothing?"

"He has plenty of money."

They sat together at a table that was close against the wall near the
door of the café and looked at the terrace where the tables were all empty
except where the old man sat in the shadow of the leaves of the tree that
moved slightly in the wind. A girl and a soldier went by in the street.
The street light shone on the brass number on his collar. The girl wore
no head covering and hurried beside him.

"The guard will pick him up," one waiter said.   10

"What does it matter if he gets what he's after?"

"He had better get off the street now. The guard will get him. They
went by five minutes ago."

The old man sitting in the shadow rapped on his saucer with his
glass. The younger waiter went over to him.

"What do you want?"

The old man looked at him. "Another brandy," he said.   15

"You'll be drunk," the waiter said. The old man looked at him. The
waiter went away.

"He'll stay all night," he said to his colleague. "I'm sleepy now. I
never get into bed before three o'clock. He should have killed himself
last week."

The waiter took the brandy bottle and another saucer from the
counter inside the café and marched out to the old man's table. He put
down the saucer and poured the glass full of brandy.

"You should have killed yourself last week," he said to the deaf man.
The old man motioned with his finger. "A little more," he said. The
waiter poured on into the glass so that the brandy slopped over and ran
down the stem into the top saucer of the pile. "Thank you," the old man
said. The waiter took the bottle back inside the café. He sat down at the
table with his colleague again.

"He's drunk now," he said.   20

"He's drunk every night."°

"He's drunk now," he said. "He's drunk every night": The younger waiter perhaps says
both these lines. A device of Hemingway's style is sometimes to have a character
pause, then speak again—as often happens in actual speech.

"What did he want to kill himself for?"

"How should I know?"

"How did he do it?"

"He hung himself with a rope."

"Who cut him down?"

"His niece."

"Why did they do it?"

"Fear for his soul."

"How much money has he got?"

"He's got plenty."

"He must be eighty years old."

"Anyway I should say he was eighty."°

"I wish he would go home. I never get to bed before three o'clock. What kind of hour is that to go to bed?"

"He stays up because he likes it."

"He's lonely. I'm not lonely. I have a wife waiting in bed for me."

"He had a wife once too."

"A wife would be no good to him now."

"You can't tell. He might be better with a wife."

"His niece looks after him."

"I know. You said she cut him down."

"I wouldn't want to be that old. An old man is a nasty thing."

"Not always. This old man is clean. He drinks without spilling. Even now, drunk. Look at him."

"I don't want to look at him. I wish he would go home. He has no regard for those who must work."

The old man looked from his glass across the square, then over at the waiters.

"Another brandy," he said, pointing to his glass. The waiter who was in a hurry came over.

"Finished," he said, speaking with that omission of syntax stupid people employ when talking to drunken people or foreigners. "No more tonight. Close now."

"Another," said the old man.

"No. Finished." The waiter wiped the edge of the table with a towel and shook his head.

The old man stood up, slowly counted the saucers, took a leather coin purse from his pocket and paid for the drinks, leaving half a peseta tip.

"He must be eighty years old." "Anyway I should say he was eighty": Is this another instance of the same character's speaking twice? Clearly, it is the younger waiter who says the next line, "I wish he would go home."

The waiter watched him go down the street, a very old man walking unsteadily but with dignity.

"Why didn't you let him stay and drink?" the unhurried waiter asked. They were putting up the shutters. "It is not half-past two."

"I want to go home to bed."

"What is an hour?"

"More to me than to him." 55

"An hour is the same."

"You talk like an old man yourself. He can buy a bottle and drink at home."

"It's not the same."

"No, it is not," agreed the waiter with a wife. He did not wish to be unjust. He was only in a hurry.

"And you? You have no fear of going home before the usual hour?" 60

"Are you trying to insult me?"

"No, hombre, only to make a joke."

"No," the waiter who was in a hurry said, rising from pulling down the metal shutters. "I have confidence. I am all confidence."

"You have youth, confidence, and a job," the older waiter said. "You have everything."

"And what do you lack?" 65

"Everything but work."

"You have everything I have."

"No. I have never had confidence and I am not young."

"Come on. Stop talking nonsense and lock up."

"I am of those who like to stay late at the café," the older waiter said. 70 "With all those who do not want to go to bed. With all those who need a light for the night."

"I want to go home and into bed."

"We are of two different kinds," the older waiter said. He was not dressed to go home. "It is not only a question of youth and confidence although those things are very beautiful. Each night I am reluctant to close up because there may be some one who needs the café."

"Hombre, there are bodegas° open all night long."

"You do not understand. This is a clean and pleasant café. It is well lighted. The light is very good and also, now, there are shadows of the leaves."

"Good night," said the younger waiter. 75

"Good night," the other said. Turning off the electric light he continued the conversation with himself. It is the light of course but it is necessary that the place be clean and pleasant. You do not want music.

---

bodegas: wineshops.

Certainly you do not want music. Nor can you stand before a bar with dignity although that is all that is provided for these hours. What did he fear? It was not fear or dread. It was a nothing that he knew too well. It was all a nothing and a man was nothing too. It was only that and light was all it needed and a certain cleanness and order. Some lived in it and never felt it but he knew it all was nada y pues nada y nada y pues nada.° Our nada who art in nada, nada be thy name thy kingdom nada thy will be nada in nada as it is in nada. Give us this nada our daily nada and nada us our nada as we nada our nadas and nada us not into nada but deliver us from nada; pues nada. Hail nothing full of nothing, nothing is with thee. He smiled and stood before a bar with a shining steam pressure coffee machine.

"What's yours?" asked the barman.

"Nada."

"Otro loco más,"° said the barman and turned away.

"A little cup," said the waiter.

The barman poured it for him.   80

"The light is very bright and pleasant but the bar is unpolished," the waiter said.

The barman looked at him but did not answer. It was too late at night for conversation.

"You want another copita?"° the barman asked.

"No, thank you," said the waiter and went out. He disliked bars and   85
bodegas. A clean, well-lighted café was a very different thing. Now, without thinking further, he would go home to his room. He would lie in the bed and finally, with daylight, he would go to sleep. After all, he said to himself, it is probably only insomnia. Many must have it.

QUESTIONS

1. What besides insomnia makes the older waiter reluctant to go to bed? Comment especially on his meditation with its *nada* refrain. Why does he so well understand the old man's need for a café? What does the café represent for the two of them?

2. Compare the younger waiter and the older waiter in their attitudes toward the old man. Whose attitude do you take to be closer to that of the author? Even though Hemingway does not editorially state his own feelings, how does he make them clear to us?

3. Point to sentences that establish the style of the story. What is distinctive in them? What repetitions of words or phrases seem particularly effective? Does Hemingway seem to favor a simple or an erudite vocabulary?

4. What is the story's point of view? Discuss its appropriateness.

nada y pues . . . . nada: nothing and then nothing and nothing and then nothing.   *Otro loco más:* another lunatic.   *copita:* little cup.

William Faulkner

Barn Burning

1939

William Faulkner (1897–1962) receives a capsule biography in Chapter 2, page 31, along with his story "A Rose for Emily." His "Barn Burning" is among his many contributions to the history of Yoknapatawpha, an imaginary Mississippi county in which the Sartorises and the de Spains are landed aristocrats living by a code of honor, and the Snopeses—most of them—are shiftless ne'er-do-wells.

The store in which the Justice of the Peace's court was sitting smelled of cheese. The boy, crouched on his nail keg at the back of the crowded room, knew he smelled cheese, and more: from where he sat he could see the ranked shelves close-packed with the solid, squat, dynamic shapes of tin cans whose labels his stomach read, not from the lettering which meant nothing to his mind but from the scarlet devils and the silver curve of fish—this, the cheese which he knew he smelled and the hermetic meat which his intestines believed he smelled coming in intermittent gusts momentary and brief between the other constant one, the smell and sense just a little of fear because mostly of despair and grief, the old fierce pull of blood. He could not see the table where the Justice sat and before which his father and his father's enemy (*our enemy* he thought in that despair: *ourn! mine and hisn both! He's my father!*) stood, but he could hear them, the two of them that is, because his father had said no word yet:

"But what proof have you, Mr. Harris?"

"I told you. The hog got into my corn. I caught it up and sent it back to him. He had no fence that would hold it. I told him so, warned him. The next time I put the hog in my pen. When he came to get it I gave him enough wire to patch up his pen. The next time I put the hog up and kept it. I rode down to his house and saw the wire I gave him still rolled on to the spool in his yard. I told him he could have the hog when he paid me a dollar pound fee. That evening a nigger came with the dollar and got the hog. He was a strange nigger. He said, 'He say to tell you wood and hay kin burn.' I said, 'What?' 'That whut he say to tell you,' the nigger said. 'Wood and hay kin burn.' That night my barn burned. I got the stock out but I lost the barn."

"Where's the nigger? Have you got him?"

"He was a strange nigger, I tell you. I don't know what became of him." 5

"But that's not proof. Don't you see that's not proof?"

"Get that boy up here. He knows." For a moment the boy thought too that the man meant his older brother until Harris said, "Not him. The little one. The boy," and, crouching, small for his age, small and wiry like his father, in patched and faded jeans even too small for him, with straight, uncombed, brown hair and eyes gray and wild as storm scud, he saw the men between himself and the table part and become a lane of grim faces, at the end of which he saw the Justice, a shabby, collarless, graying man in spectacles, beckoning him. He felt no floor under his bare feet; he seemed to walk beneath the palpable weight of the grim turning faces. His father, still in his black Sunday coat donned not for the trial but for the moving, did not even look at him. *He aims for me to lie,* he thought, again with that frantic grief and despair. *And I will have to do hit.*

"What's your name, boy?" the Justice said.

"Colonel Sartoris Snopes," the boy whispered.

"Hey?" the Justice said. "Talk louder. Colonel Sartoris? I reckon 10 anybody named for Colonel Sartoris in this country can't help but tell the truth, can they?" The boy said nothing. *Enemy! Enemy!* he thought; for a moment he could not even see, could not see that the Justice's face was kindly nor discern that his voice was troubled when he spoke to the man named Harris: "Do you want me to question this boy?" But he could hear, and during those subsequent long seconds while there was absolutely no sound in the crowded little room save that of quiet and intent breathing it was as if he had swung outward at the end of a grape vine, over a ravine, and at the top of the swing had been caught in a prolonged instant of mesmerized gravity, weightless in time.

"No!" Harris said violently, explosively. "Damnation! Send him out of here!" Now time, the fluid world, rushed beneath him again, the voices coming to him again through the smell of cheese and sealed meat, the fear and despair and the old grief of blood:

"This case is closed. I can't find against you, Snopes, but I can give you advice. Leave this country and don't come back to it."

His father spoke for the first time, his voice cold and harsh, level, without emphasis: "I aim to. I don't figure to stay in a country among people who . . ." he said something unprintable and vile, addressed to no one.

"That'll do," the Justice said. "Take your wagon and get out of this country before dark. Case dismissed."

His father turned, and he followed the stiff black coat, the wiry figure 15 walking a little stiffly from where a Confederate provost's man's musket ball had taken him in the heel on a stolen horse thirty years ago, followed the two backs now, since his older brother had appeared from somewhere in the crowd, no taller than the father but thicker, chewing tobacco steadily, between the two lines of grim-faced men and out of the store and across the worn gallery and down the sagging steps and among the dogs and half-grown boys in the mild May dust, where as he passed a voice hissed:

"Barn burner!"

Again he could not see, whirling; there was a face in a red haze, moonlike, bigger than the full moon, the owner of it half again his size, he leaping in the red haze toward the face, feeling no blow, feeling no shock when his head struck the earth, scrabbling up and leaping again, feeling no blow this time either and tasting no blood, scrabbling up to see the other boy in full flight and himself already leaping into pursuit as his father's hand jerked him back, the harsh, cold voice speaking above him: "Go get in the wagon."

It stood in a grove of locusts and mulberries across the road. His two hulking sisters in their Sunday dresses and his mother and her sister in calico and sunbonnets were already in it, sitting on and among the sorry residue of the dozen and more movings which even the boy could remember—the battered stove, the broken beds and chairs, the clock inlaid with mother-of-pearl, which would not run, stopped at some fourteen minutes past two o'clock of a dead and forgotten day and time, which had been his mother's dowry. She was crying, though when she saw him she drew her sleeve across her face and began to descend from the wagon. "Get back," the father said.

"He's hurt. I got to get some water and wash his . . ."

"Get back in the wagon," his father said. He got in too, over the tail-   20
gate. His father mounted to the seat where the older brother already sat and struck the gaunt mules two savage blows with the peeled willow, but without heat. It was not even sadistic; it was exactly that same quality which in later years would cause his descendants to over-run the engine before putting a motor car into motion, striking and reining back in the same movement. The wagon went on, the store with its quiet crowd of grimly watching men dropped behind; a curve in the road hid it. *Forever* he thought. *Maybe he's done satisfied now, now that he has . . .* stopping himself, not to say it aloud even to himself. His mother's hand touched his shoulder.

"Does hit hurt?" she said.

"Naw," he said. "Hit don't hurt. Lemme be."

"Can't you wipe some of the blood off before hit dries?"

"I'll wash to-night," he said. "Lemme be, I tell you."

The wagon went on. He did not know where they were going. None   25
of them ever did or ever asked, because it was always somewhere, always a house of sorts waiting for them a day or two days or even three days away. Likely his father had already arranged to make a crop on another farm be- fore he . . . Again he had to stop himself. He (the father) always did. There was something about his wolflike independence and even courage when the advantage was at least neutral which impressed strangers, as if they got from his latent ravening ferocity not so much a sense of depend- ability as a feeling that his ferocious conviction in the rightness of his own actions would be of advantage to all whose interest lay with his.

That night they camped, in a grove of oaks and beeches where a spring ran. The nights were still cool and they had a fire against it, of a rail lifted from a nearby fence and cut into lengths—a small fire, neat, niggard almost, a shrewd fire; such fires were his father's habit and custom always, even in freezing weather. Older, the boy might have remarked this and wondered why not a big one; why should not a man who had not only seen the waste and extravagance of war, but who had in his blood an inherent voracious prodigality with material not his own, have burned everything in sight? Then he might have gone a step farther and thought that that was the reason: that niggard blaze was the living fruit of nights passed during those four years in the woods hiding from all men, blue and gray, with his strings of horses (captured horses, he called them). And older still, he might have divined the true reason: that the element of fire spoke to some deep mainspring of his father's being, as the element of steel or of powder spoke to other men, as the one weapon for the preservation of integrity, else breath were not worth the breathing, and hence to be regarded with respect and used with discretion.

But he did not think this now and he had seen those same niggard blazes all his life. He merely ate his supper beside it and was already half asleep over his iron plate when his father called him, and once more he followed the stiff back, the stiff and ruthless limp, up the slope and on to the starlit road where, turning, he could see his father against the stars but without face or depth—a shape black, flat, and bloodless as though cut from tin in the iron folds of the frockcoat which had not been made for him, the voice harsh like tin and without heat like tin:

"You were fixing to tell them. You would have told him."

He didn't answer. His father struck him with the flat of his hand on the side of the head, hard but without heat, exactly as he had struck the two mules at the store, exactly as he would strike either of them with any stick in order to kill a horse fly, his voice without heat or anger: "You're getting to be a man. You got to learn. You got to learn to stick to your own blood or you ain't going to have any blood to stick to you. Do you think either of them, any man there this morning, would? Don't you know all they wanted was a chance to get at me because they knew I had them beat? Eh?" Later, twenty years later, he was to tell himself, "If I had said they wanted only truth, justice, he would have hit me again." But now he said nothing. He was not crying. He just stood there. "Answer me," his father said.

"Yes," he whispered. His father turned.

"Get on to bed. We'll be there tomorrow."

Tomorrow they were there. In the early afternoon the wagon stopped before a paintless two-room house identical almost with the dozen others it had stopped before even in the boy's ten years, and again, as on the other dozen occasions, his mother and aunt got down and began to

30

unload the wagon, although his two sisters and his father and brother had not moved.

"Likely hit ain't fitten for hawgs," one of the sisters said.

"Nevertheless, fit it will and you'll hog it and like it," his father said. "Get out of them chairs and help your Ma unload."

The two sisters got down, big, bovine, in a flutter of cheap ribbons; 35 one of them drew from the jumbled wagon bed a battered lantern, the other a worn broom. His father handed the reins to the older son and began to climb stiffly over the wheel. "When they get unloaded, take the team to the barn and feed them." Then he said, and at first the boy thought he was still speaking to his brother: "Come with me."

"Me?" he said.

"Yes," his father said. "You."

"Abner," his mother said. His father paused and looked back—the harsh level stare beneath the shaggy, graying, irascible brows.

"I reckon I'll have a word with the man that aims to begin tomorrow owning me body and soul for the next eight months."

They went back up the road. A week ago—or before last night, that 40 is—he would have asked where they were going, but not now. His father had struck him before last night but never before had he paused afterward to explain why; it was as if the blow and the following calm, outrageous voice still rang, repercussed, divulging nothing to him save the terrible handicap of being young, the light weight of his few years, just heavy enough to prevent his soaring free of the world as it seemed to be ordered but not heavy enough to keep him footed solid in it, to resist it and try to change the course of its events.

Presently he could see the grove of oaks and cedars and the other flowering trees and shrubs where the house would be, though not the house yet. They walked beside a fence massed with honeysuckle and Cherokee roses and came to a gate swinging open between two brick pillars, and now, beyond a sweep of drive, he saw the house for the first time and at that instant he forgot his father and the terror and despair both, and even when he remembered his father again (who had not stopped) the terror and despair did not return. Because, for all the twelve movings, they had sojourned until now in a poor country, a land of small farms and fields and houses, and he had never seen a house like this before. *Hit's big as a courthouse* he thought quietly, with a surge of peace and joy whose reason he could not have thought into words, being too young for that: *They are safe from him. People whose lives are a part of this peace and dignity are beyond his touch, he no more to them than a buzzing wasp: capable of stinging for a little moment but that's all; the spell of this peace and dignity rendering even the barns and stable and cribs which belong to it impervious to the puny flames he might contrive* . . . this, the peace and joy, ebbing for an instant as he looked again at the stiff black back, the stiff and implacable limp of the figure which was not dwarfed by the house, for the reason that it had never looked big anywhere and which now, against the serene columned backdrop, had more than ever that impervious quality of something cut ruthlessly from tin, depthless, as though, sidewise to the sun, it would cast no shadow. Watching him, the boy remarked the absolutely undeviating course which his father held and saw the stiff foot come squarely down in a pile of fresh droppings where a horse had stood in the drive and which his father could have avoided by a simple change of stride. But it ebbed only a moment, though he could not have thought this into words either, walking on in the spell of the house, which he could even want but without envy, without sorrow, certainly never with that ravening and jealous rage which unknown to him walked in the ironlike black coat before him: *Maybe he will feel it too. Maybe it will even change him now from what maybe he couldn't help but be.*

They crossed the portico. Now he could hear his father's stiff foot as it came down on the boards with clocklike finality, a sound out of all proportion to the displacement of the body it bore and which was not dwarfed either by the white door before it, as though it had attained to a sort of vicious and ravening minimum not to be dwarfed by anything— the flat, wide, black hat, the formal coat of broadcloth which had once been black but which had now that friction-glazed greenish cast of the bodies of old house flies, the lifted sleeve which was too large, the lifted hand like a curled claw. The door opened so promptly that the boy knew the Negro must have been watching them all the time, an old man with neat grizzled hair, in a linen jacket, who stood barring the door with his body, saying, "Wipe yo foots, white man, fo you come in here. Major ain't home nohow."

"Get out of my way, nigger," his father said, without heat too, flinging the door back and the Negro also and entering, his hat still on his head. And now the boy saw the prints of the stiff foot on the doorjamb and saw them appear on the pale rug behind the machinelike deliberation of the foot which seemed to bear (or transmit) twice the weight which the body compassed. The Negro was shouting "Miss Lula! Miss Lula!" somewhere behind them, then the boy, deluged as though by a warm wave by a suave turn of the carpeted stair and a pendant glitter of chandeliers and a mute gleam of gold frames, heard the swift feet and saw her too, a lady—perhaps he had never seen her like before either—in a gray, smooth gown with lace at the throat and an apron tied at the waist and the sleeves turned back, wiping cake or biscuit dough from her hands with a towel as she came up the hall, looking not at his father at all but at the tracks on the blond rug with an expression of incredulous amazement.

"I tried," the Negro cried. "I tole him to . . ."

"Will you please go away?" she said in a shaking voice. "Major de Spain is not at home. Will you please go away?"   45

His father had not spoken again. He did not speak again. He did not even look at her. He just stood stiff in the center of the rug, in his hat, the shaggy iron-gray brows twitching slightly above the pebble-colored eyes as he appeared to examine the house with brief deliberation. Then with the same deliberation he turned; the boy watched him pivot on the good leg and saw the stiff foot drag around the arc of the turning, leaving a final long and fading smear. His father never looked at it, he never once looked down at the rug. The Negro held the door. It closed behind them, upon the hysteric and indistinguishable woman-wail. His father stopped at the top of the steps and scraped his boot clean on the edge of it. At the gate he stopped again. He stood for a moment, planted stiffly on the stiff foot, looking back at the house. "Pretty and white, ain't it?" he said. "That's sweat. Nigger sweat. Maybe it ain't white enough yet to suit him. Maybe he wants to mix some white sweat with it."

Two hours later the boy was chopping wood behind the house within which his mother and aunt and the two sisters (the mother and aunt, not the two girls, he knew that; even at this distance and muffled by walls the flat loud voices of the two girls emanated an incorrigible idle inertia) were setting up the stove to prepare a meal, when he heard the hooves and saw the linen-clad man on a fine sorrel mare, whom he recognized even before he saw the rolled rug in front of the Negro youth following on a fat bay carriage horse—a suffused, angry face vanishing, still at full gallop, beyond the corner of the house where his father and brother were sitting in the two tilted chairs; and a moment later, almost before he could have put the axe down, he heard the hooves again and watched the sorrel mare go back out of the yard, already galloping again. Then his father began to shout one of the sisters' names, who presently emerged backward from the kitchen door dragging the rolled rug along the ground by one end while the other sister walked behind it.

"If you ain't going to tote, go on and set up the wash pot," the first said.

"You, Sarty!" the second shouted. "Set up the wash pot!" His father appeared at the door, framed against that shabbiness, as he had been against that other bland perfection, impervious to either, the mother's anxious face at his shoulder.

"Go on," the father said. "Pick it up." The two sisters stooped, broad, lethargic; stooping, they presented an incredible expanse of pale cloth and a flutter of tawdry ribbons. 50

"If I thought enough of a rug to have to git hit all the way from France I wouldn't keep hit where folks coming in would have to tromp on hit," the first said. They raised the rug.

"Abner," the mother said. "Let me do it."

"You go back and git dinner," his father said. "I'll tend to this."

From the woodpile through the rest of the afternoon the boy watched them, the rug spread flat in the dust beside the bubbling wash pot, the two sisters stooping over it with that profound and lethargic reluctance, while the father stood over them in turn, implacable and grim, driving them though never raising his voice again. He could smell the harsh homemade lye they were using; he saw his mother come to the door once and look toward them with an expression not anxious now but very like despair; he saw his father turn, and he fell to with the axe and saw from the corner of his eye his father raise from the ground a flattish fragment of field stone and examine it and return to the pot, and this time his mother actually spoke: "Abner. Abner. Please don't. Please, Abner."

Then he was done too. It was dusk; the whippoorwills had already   55
begun. He could smell coffee from the room where they would presently eat the cold food remaining from the mid-afternoon meal, though when he entered the house he realized they were having coffee again probably because there was a fire on the hearth, before which the rug now lay spread over the backs of the two chairs. The tracks of his father's foot were gone. Where they had been were now long, water-cloudy scoriations resembling the sporadic course of a lilliputian mowing machine.

It still hung there while they ate the cold food and then went to bed, scattered without order or claim up and down the two rooms, his mother in one bed, where his father would later lie, the older brother in the other, himself, the aunt, and the two sisters on pallets on the floor. But his father was not in bed yet. The last thing the boy remembered was the depthless, harsh silhouette of the hat and coat bending over the rug and it seemed to him that he had not even closed his eyes when the silhouette was standing over him, the fire almost dead behind it, the stiff foot prodding him awake. "Catch up the mule," his father said.

When he returned with the mule his father was standing in the back door, the rolled rug over his shoulder. "Ain't you going to ride?" he said.

"No. Give me your foot."

He bent his knee into his father's hand, the wiry, surprising power flowed smoothly, rising, he rising with it, on to the mule's bare back (they had owned a saddle once; the boy could remember it though not when or where) and with the same effortlessness his father swung the rug up in front of him. Now in the starlight they retraced the afternoon's path, up the dusty road rife with honeysuckle, through the gate and up the black tunnel of the drive to the lightless house, where he sat on the mule and felt the rough warp of the rug drag across his thighs and vanish.

"Don't you want me to help?" he whispered. His father did not an-   60
swer and now he heard again that stiff foot striking the hollow portico

with that wooden and clocklike deliberation, that outrageous overstatement of the weight it carried. The rug, hunched, not flung (the boy
could tell that even in the darkness) from his father's shoulder struck
the angle of wall and floor with a sound unbelievably loud, thunderous,
then the foot again, unhurried and enormous; a light came on in the
house and the boy sat, tense, breathing steadily and quietly and just a
little fast, though the foot itself did not increase its beat at all, descending the steps now; now the boy could see him.

"Don't you want to ride now?" he whispered. "We kin both ride
now," the light within the house altering now, flaring up and sinking.
He's coming down the stairs now, he thought. He had already ridden the
mule up beside the horse block; presently his father was up behind him
and he doubled the reins over and slashed the mule across the neck, but
before the animal could begin to trot the hard, thin arm came around
him, the hard, knotted hand jerking the mule back to a walk.

In the first red rays of the sun they were in the lot, putting plow
gear on the mules. This time the sorrel mare was in the lot before he
heard it at all, the rider collarless and even bareheaded, trembling,
speaking in a shaking voice as the woman in the house had done, his
father merely looking up once before stooping again to the hame he
was buckling, so that the man on the mare spoke to his stooping back:

"You must realize you have ruined that rug. Wasn't there anybody
here, any of your women . . ." he ceased, shaking, the boy watching him,
the older brother leaning now in the stable door, chewing, blinking
slowly and steadily at nothing apparently. "It cost a hundred dollars. But
you never had a hundred dollars. You never will. So I'm going to charge
you twenty bushels of corn against your crop. I'll add it in your contract
and when you come to the commissary you can sign it. That won't keep
Mrs. de Spain quiet but maybe it will teach you to wipe your feet off
before you enter her house again."

Then he was gone. The boy looked at his father, who still had not
spoken or even looked up again, who was now adjusting the logger-head
in the hame.

"Pap," he said. His father looked at him—the inscrutable face, the   65
shaggy brows beneath where the gray eyes glinted coldly. Suddenly the
boy went toward him, fast, stopping as suddenly. "You done the best you
could!" he cried. "If he wanted hit done different why didn't he wait and
tell you how? He won't git no twenty bushels! He won't git none! We'll
gather hit and hide hit! I kin watch . . ."

"Did you put the cutter back in that straight stock like I told you?"

"No, sir," he said.

"Then go do it."

That was Wednesday. During the rest of that week he worked
steadily, at what was within his scope and some which was beyond it,

with an industry that did not need to be driven nor even commanded twice; he had this from his mother, with the difference that some at least of what he did he liked to do, such as splitting wood with the half-size axe which his mother and aunt had earned, or saved money some-how, to present him with at Christmas. In company with the two older women (and on one afternoon, even one of the sisters), he built pens for the shoat and the cow which were a part of his father's contract with the landlord, and one afternoon, his father being absent, gone somewhere on one of the mules, he went to the field.

They were running a middle buster now, his brother holding the   70 plow straight while he handled the reins, and walking beside the strain-ing mule, the rich black soil shearing cool and damp against his bare an-kles, he thought *Maybe this is the end of it. Maybe even that twenty bushels that seems hard to have to pay for just a rug will be a cheap price for him to stop forever and always from being what he used to be;* thinking, dreaming now, so that his brother had to speak sharply to him to mind the mule: *Maybe he even won't collect the twenty bushels. Maybe it will all add up and balance and vanish—corn, rug, fire; the terror and grief; the being pulled two ways like between two teams of horses—gone, done with for ever and ever.*

Then it was Saturday; he looked up from beneath the mule he was harnessing and saw his father in the black coat and hat. "Not that," his father said. "The wagon gear." And then, two hours later, sitting in the wagon bed behind his father and brother on the seat, the wagon accom-plished a final curve, and he saw the weathered paintless store with its tattered tobacco- and patent-medicine posters and the tethered wagons and saddle animals below the gallery. He mounted the gnawed steps be-hind his father and brother, and there again was the lane of quiet, watch-ing faces for the three of them to walk through. He saw the man in spec-tacles sitting at the plank table and he did not need to be told this was a Justice of the Peace; he sent one glare of fierce, exultant, partisan defi-ance at the man in collar and cravat now, whom he had seen but twice before in his life, and that on a galloping horse, who now wore on his face an expression not of rage but of amazed unbelief which the boy could not have known was at the incredible circumstance of being sued by one of his own tenants, and came and stood against his father and cried at the Justice: "He ain't done it! He ain't burnt . . ."

"Go back to the wagon," his father said.

"Burnt?" the Justice said. "Do I understand this rug was burned too?"

"Does anybody here claim it was?" his father said. "Go back to the wagon." But he did not, he merely retreated to the rear of the room, crowded as that other had been, but not to sit down this time, instead, to stand pressing among the motionless bodies, listening to the voices:

"And you claim twenty bushels of corn is too high for the damage   75 you did to the rug?"

"He brought the rug to me and said he wanted the tracks washed out of it. I washed the tracks out and took the rug back to him."

"But you didn't carry the rug back to him in the same condition it was in before you made the tracks on it."

His father did not answer, and now for perhaps half a minute there was no sound at all save that of breathing, the faint, steady suspiration of complete and intent listening.

"You decline to answer that, Mr. Snopes?" Again his father did not answer. "I'm going to find against you, Mr. Snopes. I'm going to find that you were responsible for the injury to Major de Spain's rug and hold you liable for it. But twenty bushels of corn seems a little high for a man in your circumstances to have to pay. Major de Spain claims it cost a hundred dollars. October corn will be worth about fifty cents. I figure that if Major de Spain can stand a ninety-five dollar loss on something he paid cash for, you can stand a five-dollar loss you haven't earned yet. I hold you in damages to Major de Spain to the amount of ten bushels of corn over and above your contract with him, to be paid to him out of your crop at gathering time. Court adjourned."

It had taken no time hardly, the morning was but half begun. He thought they would return home and perhaps back to the field, since they were late, far behind all other farmers. But instead his father passed on behind the wagon, merely indicating with his hand for the older brother to follow with it, and crossed the road toward the blacksmith shop opposite, pressing on after his father, overtaking him, speaking, whispering up at the harsh, calm face beneath the weathered hat: "He won't git no ten bushels either. He won't git one. We'll . . ." until his father glanced for an instant down at him, the face absolutely calm, the grizzled eyebrows tangled above the cold eyes, the voice almost pleasant, almost gentle:

"You think so? Well, we'll wait till October anyway."

The matter of the wagon—the setting of a spoke or two and the tightening of the tires—did not take long either, the business of the tires accomplished by driving the wagon into the spring branch behind the shop and letting it stand there, the mules nuzzling into the water from time to time, and the boy on the seat with the idle reins, looking up the slope and through the sooty tunnel of the shed where the slow hammer rang and where his father sat on an upended cypress bolt, easily, either talking or listening, still sitting there when the boy brought the dripping wagon up out of the branch and halted it before the door.

"Take them on to the shade and hitch," his father said. He did so and returned. His father and the smith and a third man squatting on his heels inside the door were talking, about crops and animals; the boy, squatting too in the ammoniac dust and hoof-parings and scales of rust, heard his father tell a long and unhurried story out of the time before

80

the birth of the older brother even when he had been a professional horsetrader. And then his father came up beside him where he stood before a tattered last year's circus poster on the other side of the store, gazing rapt and quiet at the scarlet horses, the incredible poisings and convulsions of tulle and tights and the painted leers of comedians, and said, "It's time to eat."

But not at home. Squatting beside his brother against the front wall, he watched his father emerge from the store and produce from a paper sack a segment of cheese and divide it carefully and deliberately into three with his pocket knife and produce crackers from the same sack. They all three squatted on the gallery and ate, slowly, without talking; then in the store again, they drank from a tin dipper tepid water smelling of the cedar bucket and of living beech trees. And still they did not go home. It was a horse lot this time, a tall rail fence upon and along which men stood and sat and out of which one by one horses were led, to be walked and trotted and then cantered back and forth along the road while the slow swapping and buying went on and the sun began to slant westward, they—the three of them—watching and listening, the older brother with his muddy eyes and his steady, inevitable tobacco, the father commenting now and then on certain of the animals, to no one in particular.

It was after sundown when they reached home. They ate supper by 85 lamplight, then, sitting on the doorstep, the boy watched the night fully accomplish, listening to the whippoorwills and the frogs, when he heard his mother's voice: "Abner! No! No! Oh, God. Oh, God. Abner!" and he rose, whirled, and saw the altered light through the door where a candle stub now burned in a bottle neck on the table and his father, still in the hat and coat, at once formal and burlesque as though dressed carefully for some shabby and ceremonial violence, emptying the reservoir of the lamp back into the five-gallon kerosene can from which it had been filled, while the mother tugged at his arm until he shifted the lamp to the other hand and flung her back, not savagely or viciously, just hard, into the wall, her hands flung out against the wall for balance, her mouth open and in her face the same quality of hopeless despair as had been in her voice. Then his father saw him standing in the door.

"Go to the barn and get that can of oil we were oiling the wagon with," he said. The boy did not move. Then he could speak.

"What . . ." he cried. "What are you . . ."

"Go get that oil," his father said. "Go."

Then he was moving, running, outside the house, toward the stable: this the old habit, the old blood which he had not been permitted to choose for himself, which had been bequeathed him willy nilly and which had run for so long (and who knew where, battening on what of outrage and savagery and lust) before it came to him. *I could keep on*, he thought. *I could run on and on and never look back, never need to see his face again. Only I can't.* I can't, the rusted can in his hand now, the liquid sploshing in it as he ran back to the house and into it, into the sound of his mother's weeping in the next room, and handed the can to his father.

"Ain't you going to even send a nigger?" he cried. "At least you sent   90
a nigger before!"

This time his father didn't strike him. The hand came even faster than the blow had, the same hand which had set the can on the table with almost excruciating care flashing from the can toward him too quick for him to follow it, gripping him by the back of his shirt and on to tiptoe before he had seen it quit the can, the face stooping at him in breathless and frozen ferocity, the cold, dead voice speaking over him to the older brother who leaned against the table, chewing with that steady, curious, sidewise motion of cows:

"Empty the can into the big one and go on. I'll catch up with you."

"Better tie him up to the bedpost," the brother said.

"Do like I told you," the father said. Then the boy was moving, his bunched shirt and the hard, bony hand between his shoulder-blades, his toes just touching the floor, across the room and into the other one, past the sisters sitting with spread heavy thighs in the two chairs over the cold hearth, and to where his mother and aunt sat side by side on the bed, the aunt's arm about his mother's shoulders.

"Hold him," the father said. The aunt made a startled movement.   95
"Not you," the father said. "Lennie. Take hold of him. I want to see you do it." His mother took him by the wrist. "You'll hold him better than that. If he gets loose don't you know what he is going to do? He will go up yonder." He jerked his head toward the road. "Maybe I'd better tie him."

"I'll hold him," his mother whispered.

"See you do then." Then his father was gone, the stiff foot heavy and measured upon the boards, ceasing at last.

Then he began to struggle. His mother caught him in both arms, he jerking and wrenching at them. He would be stronger in the end, he knew that. But he had no time to wait for it. "Lemme go!" he cried. "I don't want to have to hit you!"

"Let him go!" the aunt said. "If he don't go, before God, I am going up there myself!"

"Don't you see I can't?" his mother cried. "Sarty! Sarty! No! No!   100
Help me, Lizzie!"

Then he was free. His aunt grasped at him but it was too late. He whirled, running, his mother stumbled forward on to her knees behind him, crying to the nearer sister: "Catch him, Net! Catch him!" But that was too late too, the sister (the sisters were twins, born at the same time, yet either of them now gave the impression of being, encompassing as much living meat and volume and weight as any other two of the family) not yet having begun to rise from the chair, her head, face, alone merely turned, presenting to him in the flying instant an astonishing expanse of young female features untroubled by any surprise even, wearing only an expression of bovine interest. Then he was out of the room, out of the house, in the mild dust of the starlit road and the heavy rifeness of honeysuckle, the pale ribbon unspooling with terrific slowness under his running feet, reaching the gate at last and turning in, running, his heart and lungs drumming, on up the drive toward the lighted house, the lighted door. He did not knock, he burst in, sobbing for breath, incapable for the moment of speech; he saw the astonished face of the Negro in the linen jacket without knowing when the Negro had appeared.

"De Spain!" he cried, panted. "Where's . . ." then he saw the white man too emerging from a white door down the hall. "Barn!" he cried. "Barn!"

"What?" the white man said. "Barn?"

"Yes!" the boy cried. "Barn!"

"Catch him!" the white man shouted.   105

But it was too late this time too. The Negro grasped his shirt, but the entire sleeve, rotten with washing, carried away, and he was out that door too and in the drive again, and had actually never ceased to run even while he was screaming into the white man's face.

Behind him the white man was shouting, "My horse! Fetch my horse!" and he thought for an instant of cutting across the park and climbing the fence into the road, but he did not know the park nor how the vine-massed fence might be and he dared not risk it. So he ran on down the drive, blood and breath roaring; presently he was in the road again though he could not see it. He could not hear either: the galloping mare was almost upon him before he heard her, and even then he held his course, as if the very urgency of his wild grief and need must in a moment more find him wings, waiting until the ultimate instant to hurl himself aside and into the weed-choked roadside ditch as the horse thundered past and on, for an instant in furious silhouette against the stars, the tranquil early summer night sky which, even before the shape of the horse and rider vanished, stained abruptly and violently upward: a long, swirling roar incredible and soundless, blotting the stars, and he springing up and into the road again, running again, knowing it was too late yet still running even after he heard the shot and an instant later, two shots, pausing now without knowing he had ceased to run, crying, "Pap! Pap!", running again before he knew he had begun to run, stumbling, tripping over something and scrabbling up again without ceasing to run, looking backward over his shoulder at the glare as he got up, running on among the invisible trees, panting, sobbing, "Father! Father!"

At midnight he was sitting on the crest of a hill. He did not know it was midnight and he did not know how far he had come. But there was no glare behind him now and he sat now, his back toward what he had called home for four days anyhow, his face toward the dark woods which he would enter when breath was strong again, small, shaking steadily in the chill darkness, hugging himself into the remainder of his thin, rotten shirt, the grief and despair now no longer terror and fear but just grief and despair. *Father. My father*, he thought. "He was brave!" he cried suddenly, aloud but not loud, no more than a whisper. "He was! He was in the war! He was in Colonel Sartoris' cav'ry!" not knowing that his father had gone to that war a private in the fine old European sense, wearing no uniform, admitting the authority of and giving fidelity to no man or army or flag, going to war as Malbrouck° himself did: for booty—it meant nothing and less than nothing to him if it were enemy booty or his own.

The slow constellations wheeled on. It would be dawn and then sun-up after a while and he would be hungry. But that would be tomorrow and now he was only cold, and walking would cure that. His breathing was easier now and he decided to get up and go on, and then he found that he had been asleep because he knew it was almost dawn, the night almost over. He could tell that from the whippoorwills. They were everywhere now among the dark trees below him, constant and inflectioned and ceaseless, so that, as the instant for giving over to the day birds drew nearer and nearer, there was no interval at all between them. He got up. He was a little stiff, but walking would cure that too as it would the cold, and soon there would be the sun. He went on down the hill, toward the dark woods within which the liquid silver voices of the birds called unceasing—the rapid and urgent beating of the urgent and quiring heart of the late spring night. He did not look back.

QUESTIONS

1. After delivering his warning to Major de Spain, the boy Snopes does not actually witness what happens to his father and brother, nor what happens to the Major's barn. But what do you assume happens? What evidence is given in the story?
2. What do you understand to be Faulkner's opinion of Abner Snopes? Make a guess, indicating details in the story that convey attitudes.
3. Which adjectives best describe the general tone of the story: *calm, amused, disinterested, scornful, marveling, excited, impassioned*? Point out passages that may

---

Malbrouck: John Churchill, Duke of Marlborough (1650–1722), English general victorious in the Battle of Blenheim (1704), which triumph drove the French army out of Germany. The French called him Malbrouck, a name they found easier to pronounce.

be so described. What do you notice about the style in which these passages are written?

4. In tone and style, how does "Barn Burning" compare with Faulkner's story "A Rose for Emily" (Chapter 2)? To what do you attribute any differences?

5. Suppose that, instead of "Barn Burning," Faulkner had written another story told by Abner Snopes in the first person. Why would such a story need a style different from that of "Barn Burning"? (Suggestion: Notice Faulkner's descriptions of Abner Snopes's voice.)

6. Although "Barn Burning" takes place some thirty years after the Civil War, how does the war figure in it?

Irony

If a friend declares, "Oh, sure, I just *love* to have four papers due on the same day," you detect that the statement contains **irony**. This is **verbal irony**, the most familiar kind, in which we understand the speaker's meaning to be far from the usual meaning of the words—in this case, quite the opposite. (When the irony is found, as here, in a somewhat sour statement tinged with mockery, it is called **sarcasm**.)

Irony, of course, occurs in writing as well as in conversation. When in a comic moment in Isaac Bashevis Singer's "Gimpel the Fool" the sexton announces, "The wealthy Reb Gimpel invites the congregation to a feast in honor of the birth of a son," the people at the synagogue burst into laughter. They know that Gimpel, in contrast to the sexton's words, is not a wealthy man but a humble baker; that the son is not his own but his wife's lover's; and that the birth brings no honor to anybody. Verbal irony, then, implies a contrast or discrepancy between what is *said* and what is *meant*. There are also times when the speaker, unlike the reader, does not realize the ironic dimension of his or her words; such instances are known as **dramatic irony**. The most famous example occurs in Sophocles' tragic drama *Oedipus the King*, when Oedipus vows to find and punish the murderer of King Laius, unaware that he himself is the man he seeks, and adds: "if by any chance / he proves to be an intimate of our house, / here at my hearth, with my full knowledge, / may the curse I just called down on him strike me!" Dramatic irony may also be used, of course, for lighter purposes: for example, the mother in Anne Tyler's "Teenage Wasteland" shifts attitudes and moods constantly according to what others tell her, yet she responds to the idea that *she* should be less strict with her son by saying, "But see, he's still so suggestible." Stories often contain other kinds of irony besides such verbal irony. A situation, for example, can be ironic if it contains some wry contrast or incongruity. In Jack London's "To Build a Fire," for example, it is ironic that a freezing man, desperately trying to strike a match to light a fire and save himself, accidentally ignites all his remaining matches.

An entire story may be told from an **ironic point of view**. Whenever we sense a sharp distinction between the narrator of a story and the author, irony is likely to occur—especially when the narrator is telling us something that we are clearly expected to doubt or to interpret very differently. In "A & P," Sammy (who tells his own story) makes many smug and cruel observations about the people around him; but the author makes clear to us that much of his superiority is based on immaturity and lack of self-knowledge. (This irony, by the way, does not negate the fact that Sammy makes some very telling comments about society's superficial values and rigid and judgmental attitudes, comments that Updike seems to endorse and wants us to endorse as well.) And when we read Hemingway's "A Clean, Well-Lighted Place," surely we feel that most of the time the older waiter speaks for the author. Though the waiter gives us a respectful, compassionate view of a lonely old man, and we don't doubt that the view is Hemingway's, still, in the closing lines of the story we are reminded that author and waiter are not identical. Musing on the sleepless night ahead of him, the waiter tries to shrug off his problem— "After all, it is probably only insomnia"—but the reader, who recalls the waiter's bleak view of *nada*, nothingness, knows that it certainly isn't mere insomnia that keeps him awake but a dread of solitude and death. At that crucial moment, Hemingway and the older waiter part company, and we perceive an ironic point of view, and also a verbal irony, "After all, it is probably only insomnia."

Storytellers are sometimes fond of ironic twists of fate—developments that reveal a terrible distance between what people deserve and what they get, between what is and what ought to be. In the novels of Thomas Hardy, some hostile fate keeps playing tricks to thwart the main characters. In *Tess of the D'Urbervilles*, an all-important letter, thrust under a door, by chance slides beneath a carpet and is not received. Such an irony is sometimes called an **irony of fate** or a **cosmic irony**, for it suggests that some malicious fate (or other spirit in the universe) is deliberately frustrating human efforts. Evidently, there is an irony of fate in the servant's futile attempt to escape Death in the fable "The Appointment in Samarra." To notice an irony gives pleasure. It may move us to laughter, make us feel wonder, or arouse our sympathy. By so involving us, irony—whether in a statement, a situation, an unexpected event, or a point of view—can render a story more likely to strike us, to affect us, and to be remembered.

An obvious prank of fate occurs in O. Henry's short story "The Cop and the Anthem," in which a hobo, wanting to spend the winter housed and fed at the city's expense, repeatedly tries and fails to get himself arrested, until the music he hears from a nearby church makes him decide to mend his ways and find a job—at which point he is run in for vagrancy and sentenced to three months! An even more famous example of O. Henry's irony is the following story, perhaps the best-known and most-loved of his many tales.

O. Henry (William Sydney Porter)

The Gift of the Magi   1906

O. HENRY

William Sydney Porter, known to the world as O. Henry (1862–1910), was born in Greensboro, North Carolina. He began writing in his mid-twenties, contributing humorous sketches to various periodicals, including his own magazine the Rolling Stone *(whose title may have been an allusion to his employment history, which included work in a drugstore, on a ranch, and in a bank, among other places). In 1896 he was indicted for embezzlement from the First National Bank of Austin, Texas; he fled to Honduras before his trial, but returned when he found that his wife was terminally ill. He was convicted, and served three years of a five-year sentence; his guilt or innocence has never been definitively established. Released in 1901, he moved to New York the following year. Already a well-known writer, for the next three years he produced a story every week for the* New York World *while also contributing tales and sketches to magazines. Beginning with* Cabbages and Kings *in 1904, his stories were published in nine highly successful collections in the few remaining years of his life, as well as in three posthumously issued volumes. Financial extravagance and alcoholism darkened his last days, culminating in his death from tuberculosis at the age of forty-seven. New York, his "Baghdad on the Hudson," is the locale of more than half of his stories, but his own experiences provided settings—such as Texas, the South, Central America, and even prisons—for many others, as well as underscoring his sympathy with the poor, the downtrodden, and the outcast. The title of his 1906 collection* The Four Million *was an allusion to the population of New York City at that time and a sarcastic play on "The Four Hundred," a phrase used to describe the upper crust of Manhattan high society. Ranked during his lifetime with Hawthorne and Poe, O. Henry is more likely now to be invoked in negative terms, for his sentimentality and especially for his reliance on frequently forced trick endings, but the most prestigious annual volume of the best American short fiction is still called* The O. Henry Prize Stories, *and the best of his own work is loved by millions of readers.*

One dollar and eighty-seven cents. That was all. And sixty cents of it was in pennies. Pennies saved one and two at a time by bulldozing the grocer and the vegetable man and the butcher until one's cheeks burned with the silent imputation of parsimony that such close dealing implied. Three times Della counted it. One dollar and eighty-seven cents. And the next day would be Christmas.

There was clearly nothing to do but flop down on the shabby little couch and howl. So Della did it. Which instigates the moral reflection that life is made up of sobs, sniffles, and smiles, with sniffles predominating.

While the mistress of the home is gradually subsiding from the first stage to the second, take a look at the home. A furnished flat at $8 per week. It did not exactly beggar description, but it certainly had that word on the lookout for the mendicancy squad.

In the vestibule below was a letter-box into which no letter would go, and an electric button from which no mortal finger could coax a ring. Also appertaining thereunto was a card bearing the name "Mr. James Dillingham Young."

The "Dillingham" had been flung to the breeze during a former period   5
of prosperity when its possessor was being paid $30 per week. Now, when the income was shrunk to $20, the letters of "Dillingham" looked blurred, as though they were thinking seriously of contracting to a modest and unassuming D. But whenever Mr. James Dillingham Young came home and reached his flat above he was called "Jim" and greatly hugged by Mrs. James Dillingham Young, already introduced to you as Della. Which is all very good.

Della finished her cry and attended to her cheeks with the powder rag. She stood by the window and looked out dully at a grey cat walking a grey fence in a grey backyard. Tomorrow would be Christmas Day, and she had only $1.87 with which to buy Jim a present. She had been saving every penny she could for months, with this result. Twenty dollars a week doesn't go far. Expenses had been greater than she had calculated. They always are. Only $1.87 to buy a present for Jim. Her Jim. Many a happy hour she had spent planning for something nice for him. Something fine and rare and sterling—something just a little bit near to being worthy of the honor of being owned by Jim.

There was a pier-glass between the windows of the room. Perhaps you have seen a pier-glass in an $8 flat. A very thin and very agile person may, by observing his reflection in a rapid sequence of longitudinal strips, obtain a fairly accurate conception of his looks. Della, being slender, had mastered the art.

Suddenly she whirled from the window and stood before the glass. Her eyes were shining brilliantly, but her face had lost its color within twenty seconds. Rapidly she pulled down her hair and let it fall to its full length.

Now, there were two possessions of the James Dillingham Youngs in which they both took a mighty pride. One was Jim's gold watch that had been his father's and his grandfather's. The other was Della's hair. Had the Queen of Sheba lived in the flat across the airshaft, Della would have let her hair hang out the window some day to dry just to depreciate Her Majesty's jewels and gifts. Had King Solomon been the janitor, with all his treasures piled up in the basement, Jim would have pulled out his watch every time he passed, just to see him pluck at his beard from envy.

So now Della's beautiful hair fell about her, rippling and shining like a cascade of brown waters. It reached below her knee and made itself almost a garment for her. And then she did it up again nervously and quickly. Once she faltered for a minute and stood still while a tear or two splashed on the worn red carpet.

On went her old brown jacket; on went her old brown hat. With a whirl of skirts and with the brilliant sparkle still in her eyes, she fluttered out the door and down the stairs to the street.

Where she stopped the sign read: "Mme. Sofronie. Hair Goods of All Kinds." One flight up Della ran, and collected herself, panting. Madame, large, too white, chilly, hardly looked the "Sofronie."

"Will you buy my hair?" asked Della.

"I buy hair," said Madame. "Take yer hat off and let's have a sight at the looks of it."

Down rippled the brown cascade.

"Twenty dollars," said Madame, lifting the mass with a practiced hand.

"Give it to me quick," said Della.

Oh, and the next two hours tripped by on rosy wings. Forget the hashed metaphor. She was ransacking the stores for Jim's present.

She found it at last. It surely had been made for Jim and no one else. There was no other like it in any of the stores, and she had turned all of them inside out. It was a platinum fob chain simple and chaste in design, properly proclaiming its value by substance alone and not by meretricious ornamentation—as all good things should do. It was even worthy of The Watch. As soon as she saw it she knew that it must be Jim's. It was like him. Quietness and value—the description applied to both. Twenty-one dollars they took from her for it, and she hurried home with the 87 cents. With that chain on his watch Jim might be properly anxious about the time in any company. Grand as the watch was, he sometimes looked at it on the sly on account of the old leather strap that he used in place of a chain.

When Della reached home her intoxication gave way a little to prudence and reason. She got out her curling irons and lighted the gas and went to work repairing the ravages made by generosity added to love. Which is always a tremendous task, dear friends—a mammoth task.

Within forty minutes her head was covered with tiny, close-lying curls that made her look wonderfully like a truant schoolboy. She looked at her reflection in the mirror long, carefully, and critically.

"If Jim doesn't kill me," she said to herself, "before he takes a second look at me, he'll say I look like a Coney Island chorus girl. But what could I do—oh! What could I do with a dollar and eighty-seven cents?"

At 7 o'clock the coffee was made and the frying-pan was on the back of the stove hot and ready to cook the chops.

Jim was never late. Della doubled the fob chain in her hand and sat on the corner of the table near the door that he always entered. Then she heard his step on the stair away down on the first flight, and she turned white for just a moment. She had a habit of saying little silent prayers about the simplest everyday things, and now she whispered: "Please God, make him think I am still pretty."

The door opened and Jim stepped in and closed it. He looked thin and   25 very serious. Poor fellow, he was only twenty-two—and to be burdened with a family! He needed a new overcoat and he was without gloves.

Jim stopped inside the door, as immovable as a setter at the scent of quail. His eyes were fixed upon Della, and there was an expression in them that she could not read, and it terrified her. It was not anger, nor surprise, nor disapproval, nor horror, nor any of the sentiments that she had been prepared for. He simply stared at her fixedly with that peculiar expression on his face.

Della wriggled off the table and went for him.

"Jim, darling," she cried, "don't look at me that way. I had my hair cut off and sold because I couldn't have lived through Christmas without giving you a present. It'll grow out again—you won't mind, will you? I just had to do it. My hair grows awfully fast. Say 'Merry Christmas!' Jim, and let's be happy. You don't know what a nice—what a beautiful, nice gift I've got for you."

"You've cut off your hair?" asked Jim, laboriously, as if he had not arrived at that patent fact yet even after the hardest mental labor.

"Cut it off and sold it," said Della. "Don't you like me just as well,   30 anyhow? I'm me without my hair, ain't I?"

Jim looked about the room curiously.

"You say your hair is gone?" he said, with an air almost of idiocy.

"You needn't look for it," said Della. "It's sold, I tell you—sold and gone, too. It's Christmas Eve, boy. Be good to me, for it went for you. Maybe the hairs of my head were numbered," she went on with a sudden serious sweetness, "but nobody could ever count my love for you. Shall I put the chops on, Jim?"

Out of his trance Jim seemed quickly to wake. He enfolded his Della. For ten seconds let us regard with discreet scrutiny some inconsequential object in the other direction. Eight dollars a week or a million a year—what is the difference? A mathematician or a wit would give you the wrong answer. The magi brought valuable gifts, but that was not among them. This dark assertion will be illuminated later on.

Jim drew a package from his overcoat pocket and threw it upon the   35 table.

"Don't make any mistake, Dell," he said, "about me. I don't think there's anything in the way of a haircut or a shave or a shampoo that could make me like my girl any less. But if you'll unwrap that package you may see why you had me going a while at first."

White fingers and nimble tore at the string and paper. And then an ecstatic scream of joy; and then, alas! a quick feminine change to hysterical tears and wails, necessitating the immediate employment of all the comforting powers of the lord of the flat.

For there lay The Combs—the set of combs, side and back, that Della had worshipped for long in a Broadway window. Beautiful combs, pure tortoise shell, with jeweled rims—just the shade to wear in the beautiful vanished hair. They were expensive combs, she knew, and her heart had simply craved and yearned over them without the least hope of possession. And now, they were hers, but the tresses that should have adorned the coveted adornments were gone.

But she hugged them to her bosom, and at length she was able to look up with dim eyes and a smile and say: "My hair grows so fast, Jim!"

And then Della leaped up like a little singed cat and cried, "Oh, oh!"   40

Jim had not yet seen his beautiful present. She held it out to him eagerly upon her open palm. The dull precious metal seemed to flash with a reflection of her bright and ardent spirit.

"Isn't it a dandy, Jim? I hunted all over town to find it. You'll have to look at the time a hundred times a day now. Give me your watch. I want to see how it looks on it."

Instead of obeying, Jim tumbled down on the couch and put his hands under the back of his head and smiled.

"Dell," said he, "let's put our Christmas presents away and keep 'em a while. They're too nice to use just at present. I sold the watch to get the money to buy your combs. And now suppose you put the chops on."

The magi, as you know, were wise men—wonderfully wise men—   45
who brought gifts to the Babe in the manger. They invented the art of giving Christmas presents. Being wise, their gifts were no doubt wise ones, possibly bearing the privilege of exchange in case of duplication. And here I have lamely related to you the uneventful chronicle of two foolish children in a flat who most unwisely sacrificed for each other the greatest treasures of their house. But in a last word to the wise of these days let it be said that of all who give gifts these two were the wisest. Of all who give and receive gifts, such as they are wisest. Everywhere they are wisest. They are the magi.

QUESTIONS

1. How would you describe the style of this story? Does the author's tone tell you anything about his attitude toward the characters and events of the narrative?
2. What do the details in paragraph 7 tell you about Della and Jim's financial situation?

3. O. Henry tells us that Jim "needed a new overcoat and he was without gloves" (paragraph 25). Why do you think Della didn't buy him these things for Christmas instead of a watch chain?

4. "Eight dollars a week or a million a year—what is the difference? A mathematician or a wit would give you the wrong answer" (paragraph 34). What, in your view, is "the wrong answer," and why is it wrong? What might the right answer be?

5. What is ironic about the story's ending? Is this plot twist the most important element of the conclusion? If not, what is?

Ha Jin

Saboteur   2000

Ha Jin is the pen name of Xuefei Jin, who was born in Liaoning, China, in 1956. The son of a military officer and a worker, Jin grew up during the turbulent Cultural Revolution, a ten-year upheaval initiated by the Communist Party in 1966 to transform China into a Marxist workers' society by destroying all remnants of the nation's ancient past. During this period many schools and universities were closed and intellectuals were required to work in proletarian jobs. At fourteen, Jin joined the People's Liberation Army, where he remained for nearly six years, and later worked as a telegraph operator for a railroad

HA JIN

company. He then attended Heilongjiang University, where in 1981 he received a B.A. in English. After earning an M.A. in American literature from Shangdong University in 1984, Jin traveled to the United States to work on a Ph.D. at Brandeis University. He intended to return to China, but the Communist Party's violent suppression of the student movement in 1989 made him decide to stay in the United States and write only in English. "It's such a brutal government," he commented, "I was very angry, and I decided not to return to China." "Writing in English became my means of survival," he remarked, "of spending or wasting my life, of retrieving losses, mine, and those of others." He completed his Ph.D. in 1993.

Jin has published three books of poetry—Between Silences (1990), Facing Shadows (1996), and Wreckage (2001)—and four novels—In the Pond (1998), Waiting (1999, National Book Award), The Crazed (2002), and War Trash (2004, PEN/Faulkner Award). His first volume of short fiction, Ocean of Words (1996), drawn from his experience in the People's Liberation Army, won the PEN/Hemingway Award. His subsequent collections of stories are Under the Red Flag (1997, Flannery O'Connor Award) and The Bridegroom (2000, Asian American Literary Award). He is a professor of English at Boston University.

Mr. Chiu and his bride were having lunch in the square before Muji Train Station. On the table between them were two bottles of soda spewing out brown foam and two paper boxes of rice and sautéed cucumber and pork. "Let's eat," he said to her, and broke the connected ends of the chopsticks. He picked up a slice of streaky pork and put it into his mouth. As he was chewing, a few crinkles appeared on his thin jaw.

To his right, at another table, two railroad policemen were drinking tea and laughing; it seemed that the stout, middle-aged man was telling a joke to his young comrade, who was tall and of athletic build. Now and again they would steal a glance at Mr. Chiu's table.

The air smelled of rotten melon. A few flies kept buzzing above the couple's lunch. Hundreds of people were rushing around to get on the platform or to catch buses to downtown. Food and fruit vendors were crying for customers in lazy voices. About a dozen young women, representing the local hotels, held up placards which displayed the daily prices and words as large as a palm, like FREE MEALS, AIR-CONDITIONING, and ON THE RIVER. In the center of the square stood a concrete statue of Chairman Mao, at whose feet peasants were napping, their backs on the warm granite and their faces toward the sunny sky. A flock of pigeons perched on the Chairman's raised hand and forearm.

The rice and cucumber tasted good, and Mr. Chiu was eating unhurriedly. His sallow face showed exhaustion. He was glad that the honeymoon was finally over and that he and his bride were heading back for Harbin. During the two weeks' vacation, he had been worried about his liver, because three months ago he had suffered from acute hepatitis; he was afraid he might have a relapse. But he had had no severe symptoms, despite his liver being still big and tender. On the whole he was pleased with his health, which could endure even the strain of a honeymoon; indeed, he was on the course of recovery. He looked at his bride, who took off her wire glasses, kneading the root of her nose with her fingertips. Beads of sweat coated her pale cheeks.

"Are you all right, sweetheart?" he asked.   5

"I have a headache. I didn't sleep well last night."

"Take an aspirin, will you?"

"It's not that serious. Tomorrow is Sunday and I can sleep in. Don't worry."

As they were talking, the stout policeman at the next table stood up and threw a bowl of tea in their direction. Both Mr. Chiu's and his bride's sandals were wet instantly.

"Hooligan!" she said in a low voice.   10

Mr. Chiu got to his feet and said out loud, "Comrade Policeman, why did you do this?" He stretched out his right foot to show the wet sandal.

"Do what?" the stout man asked huskily, glaring at Mr. Chiu while the young fellow was whistling.

"See, you dumped tea on our feet."

"You're lying. You wet your shoes yourself."

"Comrade Policemen, your duty is to keep order, but you purposely   15
tortured us common citizens. Why violate the law you are supposed to
enforce?" As Mr. Chiu was speaking, dozens of people began gathering
around.

With a wave of his hand, the man said to the young fellow, "Let's get
hold of him!"

They grabbed Mr. Chiu and clamped handcuffs around his wrists. He
cried, "You can't do this to me. This is utterly unreasonable."

"Shut up!" The man pulled out his pistol. "You can use your tongue
at our headquarters."

The young fellow added, "You're a saboteur, you know that? You're
disrupting public order."

The bride was too petrified to say anything coherent. She was a re-   20
cent college graduate, had majored in fine arts, and had never seen the
police make an arrest. All she could say was, "Oh, please, please!"

The policemen were pulling Mr. Chiu, but he refused to go with
them, holding the corner of the table and shouting, "We have a train to
catch. We already bought the tickets."

The stout man punched him in the chest. "Shut up. Let your ticket
expire." With the pistol butt he chopped Mr. Chiu's hands, which at
once released the table. Together the two men were dragging him away
to the police station.

Realizing he had to go with them, Mr. Chiu turned his head and
shouted to his bride, "Don't wait for me here. Take the train. If I'm not
back by tomorrow morning, send someone over to get me out."

She nodded, covering her sobbing mouth with her palm.

After removing his belt, they locked Mr. Chiu into a cell in the   25
back of the Railroad Police Station. The single window in the room was
blocked by six steel bars; it faced a spacious yard, in which stood a few
pines. Beyond the trees, two swings hung from an iron frame, swaying
gently in the breeze. Somewhere in the building a cleaver was chopping
rhythmically. There must be a kitchen upstairs, Mr. Chiu thought.

He was too exhausted to worry about what they would do to him, so
he lay down on the narrow bed and shut his eyes. He wasn't afraid. The
Cultural Revolution was over already, and recently the Party had been
propagating the idea that all citizens were equal before the law. The police ought to be a law-abiding model for common people. As long as he
remained coolheaded and reasoned with them, they probably wouldn't
harm him.

Late in the afternoon he was taken to the Interrogation Bureau on the
second floor. On his way there, in the stairwell, he ran into the middle-aged

policeman who had manhandled him. The man grinned, rolling his bulgy eyes and pointing his fingers at him as if firing a pistol. Egg of a tortoise! Mr. Chiu cursed mentally.

The moment he sat down in the office, he burped, his palm shielding his mouth. In front of him, across a long desk, sat the chief of the bureau and a donkey-faced man. On the glass desktop was a folder containing information on his case. He felt it bizarre that in just a matter of hours they had accumulated a small pile of writing about him. On second thought he began to wonder whether they had kept a file on him all the time. How could this have happened? He lived and worked in Harbin, more than three hundred miles away, and this was his first time in Muji City.

The chief of the bureau was a thin, bald man who looked serene and intelligent. His slim hands handled the written pages in the folder in the manner of a lecturing scholar. To Mr. Chiu's left sat a young scribe, with a clipboard on his knee and a black fountain pen in his hand.

"Your name?" the chief asked, apparently reading out the question   30
from a form.

"Chiu Maguang."

"Age?"

"Thirty-four."

"Profession?"

"Lecturer."   35

"Work unit?"

"Harbin University."

"Political status?"

"Communist Party member."

The chief put down the paper and began to speak. "Your crime is   40
sabotage, although it hasn't induced serious consequences yet. Because you are a Party member, you should be punished more. You have failed to be a model for the masses and you—"

"Excuse me, sir," Mr. Chiu cut him off.

"What?"

"I didn't do anything. Your men are the saboteurs of our social order. They threw hot tea on my feet and on my wife's feet. Logically speaking, you should criticize them, if not punish them."

"That statement is groundless. You have no witness. Why should I believe you?" the chief said matter-of-factly.

"This is my evidence." He raised his right hand. "Your man hit my   45
fingers with a pistol."

"That doesn't prove how your feet got wet. Besides, you could have hurt your fingers yourself."

"But I am telling the truth!" Anger flared up in Mr. Chiu. "Your police station owes me an apology. My train ticket has expired, my new leather sandals are ruined, and I am late for a conference in the provincial capital. You must compensate me for the damage and losses. Don't mistake me for a common citizen who would tremble when you sneeze. I'm a scholar, a philosopher, and an expert in dialectical materialism. If necessary, we will argue about this in *The Northeastern Daily*, or we will go to the highest People's Court in Beijing. Tell me, what's your name?" He got carried away with his harangue, which was by no means trivial and had worked to his advantage on numerous occasions.

"Stop bluffing us," the donkey-faced man broke in. "We have seen a lot of your kind. We can easily prove you are guilty. Here are some of the statements given by eyewitnesses." He pushed a few sheets of paper toward Mr. Chiu.

Mr. Chiu was dazed to see the different handwritings, which all stated that he had shouted in the square to attract attention and refused to obey the police. One of the witnesses had identified herself as a purchasing agent from a shipyard in Shanghai. Something stirred in Mr. Chiu's stomach, a pain rising to his rib. He gave out a faint moan.

"Now you have to admit you are guilty," the chief said. "Although 50 it's a serious crime, we won't punish you severely, provided you write out a self-criticism and promise that you won't disrupt the public order again. In other words, your release will depend on your attitude toward this crime."

"You're daydreaming," Mr. Chiu cried. "I won't write a word, because I'm innocent. I demand that you provide me with a letter of apology so I can explain to my university why I'm late."

Both the interrogators smiled contemptuously. "Well, we've never done that," said the chief, taking a puff of his cigarette.

"Then make this a precedent."

"That's unnecessary. We are pretty certain that you will comply with our wishes." The chief blew a column of smoke toward Mr. Chiu's face.

At the tilt of the chief's head, two guards stepped forward and grabbed 55 the criminal by the arms. Mr. Chiu meanwhile went on saying, "I shall report you to the Provincial Administration. You'll have to pay for this! You are worse than the Japanese military police."

They dragged him out of the room.

After dinner, which consisted of a bowl of millet porridge, a corn bun, and a piece of pickled turnip, Mr. Chiu began to have a fever, shaking with a chill and sweating profusely. He knew that the fire of anger had gotten into his liver and that he was probably having a relapse. No medicine was available, because his briefcase had been left with his bride. At home it would have been time for him to sit in front of their color TV, drinking jasmine tea and watching the evening news. It was so lonesome in here. The orange bulb above the single bed was the only source of light, which enabled the guards to keep him under surveillance at night. A moment ago he had asked them for a newspaper or a magazine to read, but they turned him down.

Through the small opening on the door noises came in. It seemed that the police on duty were playing cards or chess in a nearby office; shouts and laughter could be heard now and then. Meanwhile, an accordion kept coughing from a remote corner in the building. Looking at the ballpoint and the letter paper left for him by the guards when they took him back from the Interrogation Bureau, Mr. Chiu remembered the old saying, "When a scholar runs into soldiers, the more he argues, the muddier his point becomes." How ridiculous this whole thing was. He ruffled his thick hair with his fingers.

He felt miserable, massaging his stomach continually. To tell the truth, he was more upset than frightened, because he would have to catch up with his work once he was back home—a paper that was due at the printers next week, and two dozen books he ought to read for the courses he was going to teach in the fall.

A human shadow flitted across the opening. Mr. Chiu rushed to the door and shouted through the hole, "Comrade Guard, Comrade Guard!" 60

"What do you want?" a voice rasped.

"I want you to inform your leaders that I'm very sick. I have heart disease and hepatitis. I may die here if you keep me like this without medication."

"No leader is on duty on the weekend. You have to wait till Monday."

"What? You mean I'll stay in here tomorrow?"

"Yes." 65

"Your station will be held responsible if anything happens to me."

"We know that. Take it easy, you won't die."

It seemed illogical that Mr. Chiu slept quite well that night, though the light above his head had been on all the time and the straw mattress was hard and infested with fleas. He was afraid of ticks, mosquitoes, cockroaches—any kind of insect but fleas and bedbugs. Once, in the countryside, where his school's faculty and staff had helped the peasants harvest crops for a week, his colleagues had joked about his flesh, which they said must have tasted nonhuman to fleas. Except for him, they were all afflicted with hundreds of bites.

More amazing now, he didn't miss his bride a lot. He even enjoyed sleeping alone, perhaps because the honeymoon had tired him out and he needed more rest.

The backyard was quiet on Sunday morning. Pale sunlight streamed 70 through the pine branches. A few sparrows were jumping on the ground, catching caterpillars and ladybugs. Holding the steel bars, Mr. Chiu inhaled the morning air, which smelled meaty. There must have been an eatery or a cooked-meat stand nearby. He reminded himself that he should take this detention with ease. A sentence that Chairman Mao had written to a hospitalized friend rose in his mind: "Since you are already in here, you may as well stay and make the best of it."

His desire for peace of mind originated in his fear that his hepatitis might get worse. He tried to remain unperturbed. However, he was sure that his liver was swelling up, since the fever still persisted. For a whole day he lay in bed, thinking about his paper on the nature of contradictions. Time and again he was overwhelmed by anger, cursing aloud, "A bunch of thugs!" He swore that once he was out, he would write an article about this experience. He had better find out some of the policemen's names.

It turned out to be a restful day for the most part; he was certain that his university would send somebody to his rescue. All he should do now was remain calm and wait patiently. Sooner or later the police would have to release him, although they had no idea that he might refuse to leave unless they wrote him an apology. Damn those hoodlums, they had ordered more than they could eat!

When he woke up on Monday morning, it was already light. Somewhere a man was moaning; the sound came from the backyard. After a long yawn, and kicking off the tattered blanket, Mr. Chiu climbed out of bed and went to the window. In the middle of the yard, a young man was fastened to a pine, his wrists handcuffed around the trunk from behind. He was wriggling and swearing loudly, but there was no sight of anyone else in the yard. He looked familiar to Mr. Chiu.

Mr. Chiu squinted his eyes to see who it was. To his astonishment, he recognized the man, who was Fenjin, a recent graduate from the Law Department at Harbin University. Two years ago Mr. Chiu had taught a course in Marxist materialism, in which Fenjin had enrolled. Now, how on earth had this young devil landed here?

Then it dawned on him that Fenjin must have been sent over by   75
his bride. What a stupid woman! A bookworm, who only knew how to read foreign novels! He had expected that she would contact the school's Security Section, which would for sure send a cadre here. Fenjin held no official position; he merely worked in a private law firm that had just two lawyers; in fact, they had little business except for some detective work for men and women who suspected their spouses of having extramarital affairs. Mr. Chiu was overcome with a wave of nausea.

Should he call out to let his student know he was nearby? He decided not to, because he didn't know what had happened. Fenjin must have quarreled with the police to incur such a punishment. Yet this could never have occurred if Fenjin hadn't come to his rescue. So no matter what, Mr. Chiu had to do something. But what could he do?

It was going to be a scorcher. He could see purple steam shimmering and rising from the ground among the pines. Poor devil, he thought, as he raised a bowl of corn glue to his mouth, sipped, and took a bite of a piece of salted celery.

When a guard came to collect the bowl and the chopsticks, Mr. Chiu asked him what had happened to the man in the backyard. "He called our boss 'bandit,'" the guard said. "He claimed he was a lawyer or something. An arrogant son of a rabbit."

Now it was obvious to Mr. Chiu that he had to do something to help his rescuer. Before he could figure out a way, a scream broke out in the backyard. He rushed to the window and saw a tall policeman standing before Fenjin, an iron bucket on the ground. It was the same young fellow who had arrested Mr. Chiu in the square two days before. The man pinched Fenjin's nose, then raised his hand, which stayed in the air for a few seconds, then slapped the lawyer across the face. As Fenjin was groaning, the man lifted up the bucket and poured water on his head.

"This will keep you from getting sunstroke, boy. I'll give you some more every hour," the man said loudly. 80

Fenjin kept his eyes shut, yet his wry face showed that he was struggling to hold back from cursing the policeman, or, more likely, that he was sobbing in silence. He sneezed, then raised his face and shouted, "Let me go take a piss."

"Oh, yeah?" the man bawled. "Pee in your pants."

Still Mr. Chiu didn't make any noise, gripping the steel bars with both hands, his fingers white. The policeman turned and glanced at the cell's window; his pistol, partly holstered, glittered in the sun. With a snort he spat his cigarette butt to the ground and stamped it into the dust.

Then the door opened and the guards motioned Mr. Chiu to come out. Again they took him upstairs to the Interrogation Bureau.

The same men were in the office, though this time the scribe was sitting there empty-handed. At the sight of Mr. Chiu the chief said, "Ah, here you are. Please be seated." 85

After Mr. Chiu sat down, the chief waved a white silk fan and said to him, "You may have seen your lawyer. He's a young man without manners, so our director had him taught a crash course in the backyard."

"It's illegal to do that. Aren't you afraid to appear in a newspaper?"

"No, we are not, not even on TV. What else can you do? We are not afraid of any story you make up. We call it fiction. What we do care about is that you cooperate with us. That is to say, you must admit your crime."

"What if I refuse to cooperate?"

"Then your lawyer will continue his education in the sunshine." 90

A swoon swayed Mr. Chiu, and he held the arms of the chair to steady himself. A numb pain stung him in the upper stomach and nauseated him, and his head was throbbing. He was sure that the hepatitis was finally attacking him. Anger was flaming up in his chest; his throat was tight and clogged.

The chief resumed, "As a matter of fact, you don't even have to write out your self-criticism. We have your crime described clearly here. All we need is your signature."

Holding back his rage, Mr. Chiu said, "Let me look at that."

With a smirk the donkey-faced man handed him a sheet which carried these words:

I hereby admit that on July 13 I disrupted public order at Muji Train Station, and that I refused to listen to reason when the railroad police issued their warning. Thus I myself am responsible for my arrest. After two days' detention, I have realized the reactionary nature of my crime. From now on, I shall continue to educate myself with all my effort and shall never commit this kind of crime again.

A voice started screaming in Mr. Chiu's ears, "Lie, lie!" But he 95 shook his head and forced the voice away. He asked the chief, "If I sign this, will you release both my lawyer and me?"

"Of course, we'll do that." The chief was drumming his fingers on the blue folder—their file on him.

Mr. Chiu signed his name and put his thumbprint under his signature.

"Now you are free to go," the chief said with a smile, and handed him a piece of paper to wipe his thumb with.

Mr. Chiu was so sick that he couldn't stand up from the chair at first try. Then he doubled his effort and rose to his feet. He staggered out of the building to meet his lawyer in the backyard, having forgotten to ask for his belt back. In his chest he felt as though there were a bomb. If he were able to, he would have razed the entire police station and eliminated all their families. Though he knew he could do nothing like that, he made up his mind to do something.

"I'm sorry about this torture, Fenjin," Mr. Chiu said when they met. 100

"It doesn't matter. They are savages." The lawyer brushed a patch of dirt off his jacket with trembling fingers. Water was still dribbling from the bottoms of his trouser legs.

"Let's go now," the teacher said.

The moment they came out of the police station, Mr. Chiu caught sight of a tea stand. He grabbed Fenjin's arm and walked over to the old woman at the table. "Two bowls of black tea," he said and handed her a one-yuan note.

After the first bowl, they each had another one. Then they set out for the train station. But before they walked fifty yards, Mr. Chiu insisted on eating a bowl of tree-ear soup at a food stand. Fenjin agreed. He told his teacher, "You mustn't treat me like a guest."

"No, I want to eat something myself."

As if dying of hunger, Mr. Chiu dragged his lawyer from restaurant to restaurant near the police station, but at each place he ordered no more than two bowls of food. Fenjin wondered why his teacher wouldn't stay at one place and eat his fill.

Mr. Chiu bought noodles, wonton, eight-grain porridge, and chicken soup, respectively, at four restaurants. While eating, he kept saying through his teeth, "If only I could kill all the bastards!" At the last place he merely took a few sips of the soup without tasting the chicken cubes and mushrooms.

Fenjin was baffled by his teacher, who looked ferocious and muttered to himself mysteriously, and whose jaundiced face was covered with dark puckers. For the first time Fenjin thought of Mr. Chiu as an ugly man.

Within a month over eight hundred people contracted acute hepatitis in Muji. Six died of the disease, including two children. Nobody knew how the epidemic had started.

QUESTIONS

1. Why is Mr. Chiu in Muji?
2. In the story's second paragraph, two railroad policemen are sitting next to Mr. Chiu and his wife. Why do you think they are laughing and looking at the newly wed couple?
3. With what specific crime is Mr. Chiu charged? Is he guilty?
4. What is Mr. Chiu's initial reaction to his arrest?
5. Why does Mr. Chiu initially refuse to sign a confession? Why does he eventually decide to sign it?
6. What is ironic about Mr. Chiu's arrest? What is ironic about his ultimate confession?
7. When does Mr. Chiu decide to revenge himself on the police?
8. Is Mr. Chiu's revenge justified? Are the effects of his revenge proportionate to his own suffering?
9. What is ironic about the story's title? Who is the saboteur?

WRITING EFFECTIVELY

WRITING ABOUT TONE AND STYLE

Be Style-Conscious

If you look around a crowded classroom, you will notice—consciously or not—the styles of your fellow students. The way they dress, talk, and even sit conveys information about their attitudes. A haircut, a T-shirt, a tattoo, a piece of jewelry all silently say something. Similarly, a writer's style—his or her own distinct voice—can give the reader crucial extra information.

Style goes beyond the surface. Just as a person's gestures and vocal inflections give the listener clues to the meaning of his or her words, literary style helps to create meaning. To analyze a writer's style, think about how he or she handles the following four elements:

- *Diction: Consider the flavor of words chosen by the author for a particular story.* In "A Clean, Well-Lighted Place," for example, Hemingway favors simple, unemotional, and descriptive language, whereas in "The Storm," Chopin uses extravagant and emotionally charged diction. Each choice reveals something important about the story.
- *Sentence structure: Look for patterns in a story's sentence structure.* Hemingway is famous for his short, clipped sentences, which often repeat certain key words. Faulkner, however, favors long, elaborate syntax that immerses the reader in the emotion of the narrative.
- *Tone: Try to determine the writer's attitude toward the story he or she is telling.* Tan's "A Pair of Tickets" creates a tone of hushed excitement and direct emotional involvement. Other stories may create a sense of dispassionate objectivity.
- *Organization: Examine the order in which information is presented.* Many stories are told in a straightforward, chronological manner, which make it possible for us to appreciate complex undercurrents. Other stories (for example, Atwood's "Happy Endings" in "Stories for Further Reading") present the narrative's events in more complicated and surprising ways.

CHECKLIST

Thinking About Tone and Style

✓ Does the writer use word choice in a distinctive way?
✓ Does the author tend toward long or short—even fragmented—sentences?

✓ How would you characterize the writer's voice? Is it formal or casual? Distant or intimate? Impassioned or restrained?

✓ Can the narrator's words be taken at face value? Is there anything ironic about the narrator's voice?

✓ How does the writer arrange the material? Is information delivered chronologically, or is the organization more complex?

✓ What is the writer's attitude toward the material? How can you tell?

WRITING ASSIGNMENT ON TONE AND STYLE

Examine a short story with a style you admire. Write an essay in which you analyze the author's approach toward diction, sentence structure, tone, and organization. How do these elements work together to create a certain mood? How does that mood contribute to the story's meaning? If your chosen story has a first-person narrator, how do stylistic choices help to create a sense of that particular character?

MORE TOPICS FOR WRITING

1. Write a brief analysis of irony in either "Saboteur" or "The Gift of the Magi." What sorts of irony does your story employ? (See the section on irony earlier in this chapter for a list of the different types.)

2. Consider a short story in which the narrator is the central character, perhaps "A & P," "Greasy Lake," "Araby," or "Cathedral." In a brief essay, show how the character of the narrator determines the style of the story. Examine language in particular—words or phrases, slang expressions, figures of speech, local or regional usage.

3. Write a page in which you describe eating a meal in the company of others, either at the dining hall, or in a favorite restaurant, or at home with family. Using sensory details, convey a sense of the setting, the quality of the food, and the presence of your dining companions. Now rewrite your paragraph as Ernest Hemingway. Finally, rewrite it as William Faulkner.

4. After you have completed the previous exercise, write about the experience. What did you learn, through imitation, about the styles of Hemingway and Faulkner?

5. In a paragraph, describe a city street as seen through the eyes of a college graduate who has just moved to the city to start a new career. Now describe that same street in the voice of an old woman walking home from the hospital where her husband has just died. Finally, describe the street in the voice of a teenage runaway. In each paragraph, refrain from identifying your character or saying anything about his or her circumstances. Simply present the street as each character would perceive it.

6
Theme

The **theme** of a story is whatever general idea or insight the entire story reveals. In some stories the theme is unmistakable. At the end of Aesop's fable about the council of the mice that can't decide who will bell the cat, the theme is stated in the moral: *It is easier to propose a thing than to carry it out.* In a work of commercial fiction, too, the theme (if any) is usually obvious. Consider a typical detective thriller in which, say, a rookie police officer trained in scientific methods of crime detection sets out to solve a mystery sooner than his or her rival, a veteran sleuth whose only laboratory is carried under his hat. Perhaps the veteran solves the case, leading to the conclusion (and the theme), "The old ways are the best ways after all." Another story by the same writer might dramatize the same rivalry but reverse the outcome, having the rookie win, thereby reversing the theme: "The times are changing! Let's shake loose from old-fashioned ways." In such commercial entertainments, a theme is like a length of rope with which the writer, patently and mechanically, trusses the story neatly (usually too neatly) into meaningful shape.

In literary fiction, a theme is seldom so obvious. That is, a theme need not be a moral or a message; it may be what the happenings add up to, what the story is about. When we come to the end of a finely wrought short story such as Ernest Hemingway's "A Clean, Well-Lighted Place" (Chapter 5), it may be easy to sum up the plot—to say what happens—but it is more difficult to sum up the story's main idea. Evidently, Hemingway relates events—how a younger waiter gets rid of an old man and how an older waiter then goes to a coffee bar—but in themselves these events seem relatively slight, though the story as a whole seems large (for its size) and full of meaning. For the meaning, we must look to other elements in the story besides what happens in it. And it is clear that Hemingway is most deeply interested in the thoughts and feelings of the older waiter, the character who has more and more to say as the story progresses, until at the end the story is entirely confined to his thoughts and perceptions. What is meaningful in these thoughts and perceptions? The older waiter understands the old man and sympathizes with his need for a clean, well-lighted place. If we say that, we are still talking about what happens in the story, though we have gone beyond merely recording its external events. But a theme is usually stated in *general* words. Another try: "Solitary people who cannot sleep need a cheerful, orderly place where they can drink with dignity." That's a little better. We have indicated, at least, that Hemingway's story is about more than just an old man and a couple of waiters. But what about the older waiter's meditation on *nada*, nothingness? Coming near the end of the story, it takes great emphasis, and probably no good statement of Hemingway's theme can leave it out. Still another try at a statement: "Solitary people need a place of refuge from their terrible awareness that their lives (or, perhaps, human lives) are essentially meaningless." Neither this nor any other statement of the story's theme is unarguably right, but at least the sentence helps the reader to bring into focus one primary idea that Hemingway seems to be driving at. When we finish reading "A Clean, Well-Lighted Place," we feel that there is such a theme, a unifying vision, even though we cannot reduce it absolutely to a tag. Like some freshwater lake alive with creatures, Hemingway's story is a broad expanse, reflecting in many directions. No wonder that many readers will view it in different ways.

Moral inferences may be drawn from the story, no doubt, for Hemingway is indirectly giving us advice for properly regarding and sympathizing with the lonely, the uncertain, and the old. But the story doesn't set forth a lesson that we are supposed to put into practice. One could argue that "A Clean, Well-Lighted Place" contains *several* themes, and other statements could be made to take in Hemingway's views of love, of communication between people, of dignity. Great short stories, like great symphonies, frequently have more than one theme.

In many a fine short story, theme is the center, the moving force, the principle of unity. Clearly, such a theme is something other than the characters and events of its story. To say of James Joyce's "Araby" (Chapter 8) that it is about a boy who goes to a bazaar to buy a gift for a young woman, only to arrive too late, is to summarize plot, not theme. (The theme *might* be put, "The illusions of a romantic child are vulnerable," or it might be put in any of a few hundred other ways.) Although the title of Shirley Jackson's "The Lottery" (Chapter 7), with its hint of the lure of easy riches, may arouse pleasant expectations, which the neutral tone of the narrative does nothing to dispel, the theme—the larger realization that the story leaves us with—has to do with the ways in which cruel and insensitive attitudes can come to seem like normal and natural ones.

Sometimes you will hear it said that the theme of a story (say, Faulkner's "Barn Burning") is "loss of innocence" or "initiation into maturity," or that the theme of some other story (Hurston's "Sweat," for instance) is "the revolt of the downtrodden." This is to use *theme* in a larger and more abstract sense than we use it here. Although such general descriptions of theme can be useful—as in sorting a large number of stories into rough categories—we suggest that, in the beginning, you look for whatever truth or insight you think the writer of a story reveals. Try to sum it up *in a sentence.* By doing so, you will find yourself looking closely at the story, trying to define its principal meaning. You may find it helpful, in making your sentence-statement of theme, to consider these points:

1. Look back once more at the title of the story. From what you have read, what does it indicate?
2. Does the main character in any way change in the story? Does this character arrive at any eventual realization or understanding? Are you left with any realization or understanding you did not have before?

3. Does the author make any general observations about life or human nature? Do the characters make any? (Caution: Characters now and again will utter opinions with which the reader is not necessarily supposed to agree.)
4. Does the story contain any especially curious objects, mysterious flat characters, significant animals, repeated names, song titles, or whatever, that hint at meanings larger than such things ordinarily have? In literary stories, such symbols may point to central themes. (For a short discussion of symbolism and a few illustrations, see Chapter 7.)
5. When you have worded your statement of theme, have you cast your statement into general language, not just given a plot summary?
6. Does your statement hold true for the story as a whole, not for just part of it?

In distilling a statement of theme from a rich and complicated story, we have, of course, no more encompassed the whole story than a paleontologist taking a plaster mold of a petrified footprint has captured a living brontosaurus. A writer (other than a fabulist) does not usually set out with theme in hand, determined to make every detail in the story work to demonstrate it. Well then, the skeptical reader may ask, if only *some* stories have themes, if those themes may be hard to sum up, and if readers will probably disagree in their summations, why bother to state themes? Isn't it too much trouble? Surely it is, unless the effort to state a theme ends in pleasure and profit. Trying to sum up the point of a story in our own words is merely one way to make ourselves better aware of whatever we may have understood vaguely and tentatively. Attempted with loving care, such statements may bring into focus our scattered impressions of a rewarding story, may help to clarify and hold fast whatever wisdom the storyteller has offered us.

Chinua Achebe

Dead Men's Path (1953) 1972

Chinua Achebe was born in Ogidi, a village in eastern Nigeria, in 1930. His father was a missionary schoolteacher, and Achebe had a devout Christian upbringing. A member of the Ibo tribe, the future writer grew up speaking Igbo, but at the age of eight, he began learning English. He went abroad to study at London University but returned to Africa to complete his B.A. at the University College of Ibadan in 1953. Achebe worked for years in Nigerian radio. Shortly after Nigeria's independence from Great Britain

CHINUA ACHEBE

in 1963, civil war broke out, and the new nation split in two. Achebe left his job to join the Ministry of Information for Biafra, the new country created from eastern Nigeria. It was not until 1970 that the bloody civil war ended. Approximately one million Ibos lay dead from war, disease, and starvation as the defeated Biafrans reunited with Nigeria. Achebe is often considered Africa's premier novelist. His novels include Things Fall Apart (1958), No Longer at Ease (1962), A Man of the People (1966), and Anthills of the Savannah (1987). His short stories have been collected in Girls At War (1972). He has also published poetry, children's stories, and several volumes of essays, the most recent of which is Home and Exile (2000). In 1990 Achebe suffered massive injuries in a car accident outside Lagos that left him paralyzed from the waist down. He currently teaches at Bard College in upstate New York. In 1999 he visited Nigeria again after a deliberate nine-year absence to protest government dictatorship, and his homecoming became a national event.

Michael Obi's hopes were fulfilled much earlier than he had expected. He was appointed headmaster of Ndume Central School in January 1949. It had always been an unprogressive school, so the Mission authorities decided to send a young and energetic man to run it. Obi accepted this responsibility with enthusiasm. He had many wonderful ideas and this was an opportunity to put them into practice. He had had sound secondary school education which designated him a "pivotal teacher" in the official records and set him apart from the other headmasters in the mission field. He was outspoken in his condemnation of the narrow views of these older and often less-educated ones.

"We shall make a good job of it, shan't we?" he asked his young wife when they first heard the joyful news of his promotion.

"We shall do our best," she replied. "We shall have such beautiful gardens and everything will be just *modern* and delightful . . ." In their two years of married life she had become completely infected by his passion for "modern methods" and his denigration of "these old and superannuated people in the teaching field who would be better employed as traders in the Onitsha market." She began to see herself already as the admired wife of the young headmaster, the queen of the school.

The wives of the other teachers would envy her position. She would set the fashion in everything . . . Then, suddenly, it occurred to her that there might not be other wives. Wavering between hope and fear, she asked her husband, looking anxiously at him.

"All our colleagues are young and unmarried," he said with enthusiasm which for once she did not share. "Which is a good thing," he continued.

"Why?"

"Why? They will give all their time and energy to the school."

5

Nancy was downcast. For a few minutes she became skeptical about the new school; but it was only for a few minutes. Her little personal misfortune could not blind her to her husband's happy prospects. She looked at him as he sat folded up in a chair. He was stoop-shouldered and looked frail. But he sometimes surprised people with sudden bursts of physical energy. In his present posture, however, all his bodily strength seemed to have retired behind his deep-set eyes, giving them an extraordinary power of penetration. He was only twenty-six, but looked thirty or more. On the whole, he was not unhandsome.

"A penny for your thoughts, Mike," said Nancy after a while, imitating the woman's magazine she read.

"I was thinking what a grand opportunity we've got at last to show   10
these people how a school should be run."

Ndume School was backward in every sense of the word. Mr. Obi put his whole life into the work, and his wife hers too. He had two aims. A high standard of teaching was insisted upon, and the school compound was to be turned into a place of beauty. Nancy's dream-gardens came to life with the coming of the rains, and blossomed. Beautiful hibiscus and allamanda hedges in brilliant red and yellow marked out the carefully tended school compound from the rank neighborhood bushes.

One evening as Obi was admiring his work he was scandalized to see an old woman from the village hobble right across the compound, through a marigold flower-bed and the hedges. On going up there he found faint signs of an almost disused path from the village across the school compound to the bush on the other side.

"It amazes me," said Obi to one of his teachers who had been three years in the school, "that you people allowed the villagers to make use of this footpath. It is simply incredible." He shook his head.

"The path," said the teacher apologetically, "appears to be very important to them. Although it is hardly used, it connects the village shrine with their place of burial."

"And what has that got to do with the school?" asked the headmaster.   15

"Well, I don't know," replied the other with a shrug of the shoulders. "But I remember there was a big row some time ago when we attempted to close it."

"That was some time ago. But it will not be used now," said Obi as he walked away. "What will the Government Education Officer think of this when he comes to inspect the school next week? The villagers might, for all I know, decide to use the schoolroom for pagan ritual during the inspection."

Heavy sticks were planted closely across the path at the two places where it entered and left the school premises. These were further strengthened with barbed wire.

*

Three days later the village priest of Ani called on the headmaster. He was an old man and walked with a slight stoop. He carried a stout walking-stick which he usually tapped on the floor, by way of emphasis, each time he made a new point in his argument.

"I have heard," he said after the usual exchange of cordialities, "that our ancestral footpath has recently been closed . . ." 20

"Yes," replied Mr. Obi. "We cannot allow people to make a highway of our school compound."

"Look here, my son," said the priest bringing down his walking-stick, "this path was here before you were born and before your father was born. The whole life of this village depends on it. Our dead relatives depart by it and our ancestors visit us by it. But most important, it is the path of children coming in to be born . . ."

Mr. Obi listened with a satisfied smile on his face.

"The whole purpose of our school," he said finally, "is to eradicate just such beliefs as that. Dead men do not require footpaths. The whole idea is just fantastic. Our duty is to teach your children to laugh at such ideas."

"What you say may be true," replied the priest, "but we follow the 25 practices of our fathers. If you reopen the path we shall have nothing to quarrel about. What I always say is: let the hawk perch and let the eagle perch." He rose to go.

"I am sorry," said the young headmaster. "But the school compound cannot be a thoroughfare. It is against our regulations. I would suggest your constructing another path, skirting our premises. We can even get our boys to help in building it. I don't suppose the ancestors will find the little detour too burdensome."

"I have no more words to say," said the old priest, already outside.

Two days later a young woman in the village died in childbed. A diviner was immediately consulted and he prescribed heavy sacrifices to propitiate ancestors insulted by the fence.

Obi woke up next morning among the ruins of his work. The beautiful hedges were torn up not just near the path but right round the school, the flowers trampled to death and one of the school buildings pulled down . . . That day, the white Supervisor came to inspect the school and wrote a nasty report on the state of the premises but more seriously about the "tribal-war situation developing between the school and the village, arising in part from the misguided zeal of the new headmaster."

QUESTIONS

1. How would you describe the personalities of the main characters Michael Obi and the village priest?

2. What are the new headmaster's motivations for wanting to improve the school?

3. Why does the village priest visit the school? What choice does he offer the head-master?
4. What significance do you see in the story's title, "Dead Men's Path"?
5. What ironies do you see in the story?
6. What theme in the story seems most important to you? Is it stated anywhere in the story?

Luke 15:11–32

The Parable of the Prodigal Son (Authorized or King James Version, 1611)

And he said, A certain man had two sons: And the younger of them said to his father, Father, give me the portion of goods that falleth to me. And he divided unto them his living. And not many days after the younger son gathered all together, and took his journey into a far country, and there wasted his substance with riotous living. And when he had spent all, there arose a mighty famine in that land; and he began to be in want. And he went and joined himself to a citizen of that country; and he sent him into his fields to feed swine. And he would fain have filled his belly with the husks that the swine did eat: and no man gave unto him. And when he came to himself, he said, How many hired servants of my father's have bread enough and to spare, and I perish with hunger! I will arise and go to my father, and will say unto him, Father I have sinned against heaven, and before thee, and am no more worthy to be called thy son; make me as one of thy hired servants. And he arose, and came to his father. But when he was yet a great way off, his father saw him, and had compassion, and ran, and fell on his neck, and kissed him. And the son said unto him, Father I have sinned against heaven, and in thy sight, and am no more worthy to be called thy son. But the father said to his servants, Bring forth the best robe, and put it on him; and put a ring on his hand, and shoes on his feet: And bring hither the fatted calf, and kill it; and let us eat, and be merry: For this my son was dead, and is alive again; he was lost, and is found. And they began to be merry. Now his elder son was in the field: and he came and drew nigh to the house, he heard music and dancing. And he called one of the servants, and asked what these things meant. And he said unto him, Thy brother is come; and thy father hath killed the fatted calf, because he hath received him safe and sound. And he was angry, and would not go in: therefore came his father out, and entreated him. And he answering said to his father, Lo, these many years do I serve thee, neither transgressed I at any time thy commandment; and yet thou never gavest me a kid, that I might make merry with my friends: But as soon as this thy son was come, which hath devoured thy living with harlots, thou hast killed for him the fatted calf. And he said unto him, Son thou art ever with me, and all that I have is thine. It was meet that we should make merry, and be glad: for this thy brother was dead, and is alive again; and was lost, and is found.

QUESTIONS

1. This story has traditionally been called "The Parable of the Prodigal Son." What does *prodigal* mean? Which of the two brothers is prodigal?
2. What position does the younger son expect when he returns to his father's house? What does the father give him?
3. When the older brother sees the celebration for his younger brother's return, he gets angry. He makes a very reasonable set of complaints to his father. He has indeed been a loyal and moral son, but what virtue does the older brother lack?
4. Is the father fair to the elder son? Explain your answer.
5. Theologians have discussed this parable's religious significance for two thousand years. What, in your own words, is the human theme of the story?

Kurt Vonnegut, Jr.

Harrison Bergeron   1961

Kurt Vonnegut, Jr. (1922–2007) was born in Indianapolis. During the Depression his father, a well-to-do architect, had virtually no work, and the family lived in reduced circumstances. Vonnegut attended Cornell University, where he studied sciences but also became managing editor of the daily student newspaper. In 1943 he enlisted in the U.S. Army. During the Battle of the Bulge he was captured by German troops and interned as a prisoner of war in Dresden, where he survived the massive Allied firebombing, which killed over 130,000 people, mostly civilians. (The firebombing of Dresden became the central incident in Vonnegut's best-selling 1969

KURT VONNEGUT, JR.

novel, Slaughterhouse Five.*) After the war Vonnegut worked as a reporter and later as a public relations man for General Electric in Schenectady, New York. After publishing several science fiction stories in national magazines, he quit his job in 1951 to write full-time. His first novel,* Player Piano, *appeared in 1952, followed by* Sirens of Titan *(1959), and his first best-seller,* Cat's Cradle *(1963)—all now considered classics of literary science fiction. Among his many later books are* Jailbird *(1979),* Bluebeard *(1987),* Hocus Pocus *(1990),* Timequake *(1997),* God Bless You, Dr. Kevorkian *(2000), and* A Man Without a Country *(2005). His short fiction is collected in* Welcome to the Monkey House *(1968) and* Bagombo

Snuff Box (1999). He was named New York State Author for the period 2001–2003. Vonnegut is a singular figure in modern American fiction. An ingenious comic writer, he has combined the popular genre of science fiction with the literary tradition of dark satire—a combination splendidly realized in "Harrison Bergeron."

The year was 2081, and everybody was finally equal. They weren't only equal before God and the law. They were equal every which way. Nobody was smarter than anybody else. Nobody was better looking than anybody else. Nobody was stronger or quicker than anybody else. All this equality was due to the 211th, 212th, and 213th Amendments to the Constitution, and to the unceasing vigilance of agents of the United States Handicapper General.

Some things about living still weren't quite right, though. April, for instance, still drove people crazy by not being springtime. And it was in that clammy month that the H-G men took George and Hazel Bergeron's fourteen-year-old son, Harrison, away.

It was tragic, all right, but George and Hazel couldn't think about it very hard. Hazel had a perfectly average intelligence, which meant she couldn't think about anything except in short bursts. And George, while his intelligence was way above normal, had a little mental handicap radio in his ear. He was required by law to wear it at all times. It was tuned to a government transmitter. Every twenty seconds or so, the transmitter would send out some sharp noise to keep people like George from taking unfair advantage of their brains.

George and Hazel were watching television. There were tears on Hazel's cheeks, but she'd forgotten for the moment what they were about.

On the television screen were ballerinas.   5

A buzzer sounded in George's head. His thoughts fled in panic, like bandits from a burglar alarm.

"That was a real pretty dance, that dance they just did," said Hazel.

"Huh?" said George.

"That dance—it was nice," said Hazel.

"Yup," said George. He tried to think a little about the ballerinas.   10
They weren't really very good—no better than anybody else would have been, anyway. They were burdened with sashweights and bags of bird-shot, and their faces were masked, so that no one, seeing a free and graceful gesture or a pretty face, would feel like something the cat drug in. George was toying with the vague notion that maybe dancers shouldn't be handicapped. But he didn't get very far with it before another noise in his ear radio scattered his thoughts.

George winced. So did two out of the eight ballerinas.

Hazel saw him wince. Having no mental handicap herself, she had to ask George what the latest sound had been.

"Sounded like somebody hitting a milk bottle with a ball peen hammer," said George.

"I'd think it would be real interesting, hearing all the different sounds," said Hazel, a little envious. "All the things they think up."

"Um," said George.

15

"Only, if I was Handicapper General, you know what I would do?" said Hazel. Hazel, as a matter of fact, bore a strong resemblance to the Handicapper General, a woman named Diana Moon Glampers. "If I was Diana Moon Glampers," said Hazel, "I'd have chimes on Sunday—just chimes. Kind of in honor of religion."

"I could think, if it was just chimes," said George.

"Well—maybe make 'em real loud," said Hazel. "I think I'd make a good Handicapper General."

"Good as anybody else," said George.

"Who knows better'n I do what normal is?" said Hazel.

20

"Right," said George. He began to think glimmeringly about his abnormal son who was now in jail, about Harrison, but a twenty-one-gun salute in his head stopped that.

"Boy!" said Hazel, "that was a doozy, wasn't it?"

It was such a doozy that George was white and trembling, and tears stood on the rims of his red eyes. Two of the eight ballerinas had collapsed to the studio floor, were holding their temples.

"All of a sudden you look so tired," said Hazel. "Why don't you stretch out on the sofa, so's you can rest your handicap bag on the pillows, honeybunch." She was referring to the forty-seven pounds of birdshot in a canvas bag, which was padlocked around George's neck. "Go on and rest the bag for a little while," she said. "I don't care if you're not equal to me for a while."

George weighed the bag with his hands. "I don't mind it," he said. "I don't notice it any more. It's just a part of me."

25

"You been so tired lately—kind of wore out," said Hazel. "If there was just some way we could make a little hole in the bottom of the bag, and just take out a few of them lead balls. Just a few."

"Two years in prison and two thousand dollars fine for every ball I took out," said George. "I don't call that a bargain."

"If you could just take a few out when you came home from work," said Hazel. "I mean—you don't compete with anybody around here. You just set around."

"If I tried to get away with it," said George, "then other people'd get away with it—and pretty soon we'd be right back to the dark ages again, with everybody competing against everybody else. You wouldn't like that, would you?"

"I'd hate it," said Hazel.

30

"There you are," said George. "The minute people start cheating on laws, what do you think happens to society?"

If Hazel hadn't been able to come up with an answer to this question, George couldn't have supplied one. A siren was going off in his head.

"Reckon it'd fall all apart," said Hazel.

"What would?" said George blankly.

"Society," said Hazel uncertainly. "Wasn't that what you just said?"   35

"Who knows?" said George.

The television program was suddenly interrupted for a news bulletin. It wasn't clear at first as to what the bulletin was about, since the announcer, like all announcers, had a serious speech impediment. For about half a minute, and in a state of high excitement, the announcer tried to say, "Ladies and gentlemen—"

He finally gave up, handed the bulletin to a ballerina to read.

"That's all right—" Hazel said of the announcer, "he tried. That's the big thing. He tried to do the best he could with what God gave him. He should get a nice raise for trying so hard."

"Ladies and gentlemen—" said the ballerina, reading the bulletin.   40 She must have been extraordinarily beautiful, because the mask she wore was hideous. And it was easy to see that she was the strongest and most graceful of all the dancers, for her handicap bags were as big as those worn by two-hundred-pound men.

And she had to apologize at once for her voice, which was a very unfair voice for a woman to use. Her voice was a warm, luminous, timeless melody. "Excuse me—" she said, and she began again, making her voice absolutely uncompetitive.

"Harrison Bergeron, age fourteen," she said in a grackle squawk, "has just escaped from jail, where he was held on suspicion of plotting to overthrow the government. He is a genius and an athlete, is under-handicapped, and should be regarded as extremely dangerous."

A police photograph of Harrison Bergeron was flashed on the screen upside down, then sideways, upside down again, then right side up. The picture showed the full length of Harrison against a background calibrated in feet and inches. He was exactly seven feet tall.

The rest of Harrison's appearance was Halloween and hardware. Nobody had ever borne heavier handicaps. He had outgrown hindrances faster than the H-G men could think them up. Instead of a little ear radio for a mental handicap, he wore a tremendous pair of earphones, and spectacles with thick wavy lenses. The spectacles were intended to make him not only half blind, but to give him whanging headaches besides.

Scrap metal was hung all over him. Ordinarily, there was a certain   45 symmetry, a military neatness to the handicaps issued to strong people, but Harrison looked like a walking junkyard. In the race of life, Harrison carried three hundred pounds.

And to offset his good looks, the H-G men required that he wear at all times a red rubber ball for a nose, keep his eyebrows shaved off, and cover his even white teeth with black caps at snaggle-tooth random.

"If you see this boy," said the ballerina, "do not—I repeat, do not— try to reason with him."

There was the shriek of a door being torn from its hinges.

Screams and barking cries of consternation came from the television set. The photograph of Harrison Bergeron on the screen jumped again and again, as though dancing to the tune of an earthquake.

George Bergeron correctly identified the earthquake, and well he   50
might have—for many was the time his own home had danced to the same crashing tune. "My God—" said George, "that must be Harrison!"

The realization was blasted from his mind instantly by the sound of an automobile collision in his head.

When George could open his eyes again, the photograph of Harrison was gone. A living, breathing Harrison filled the screen.

Clanking, clownish, and huge, Harrison stood in the center of the studio. The knob of the uprooted studio door was still in his hand. Ballerinas, technicians, musicians, and announcers cowered on their knees before him, expecting to die.

"I am the Emperor!" cried Harrison. "Do you hear? I am the Emperor! Everybody must do what I say at once!" He stamped his foot and the studio shook.

"Even as I stand here—" he bellowed, "crippled, hobbled, sickened—I   55
am a greater ruler than any man who ever lived! Now watch me become what I *can* become!"

Harrison tore the straps of his handicap harness like wet tissue paper, tore straps guaranteed to support five thousand pounds.

Harrison's scrap-iron handicaps crashed to the floor.

Harrison thrust his thumbs under the bar of the padlock that secured his head harness. The bar snapped like celery. Harrison smashed his headphones and spectacles against the wall.

He flung away his rubber-ball nose, revealed a man that would have awed Thor, the god of thunder.

"I shall now select my Empress!" he said, looking down on the cow-   60
ering people. "Let the first woman who dares rise to her feet claim her mate and her throne!"

A moment passed, and then a ballerina arose, swaying like a willow.

Harrison plucked the mental handicap from her ear, snapped off her physical handicaps with marvelous delicacy. Last of all, he removed her mask.

She was blindingly beautiful.

"Now—" said Harrison, taking her hand, "shall we show the people the meaning of the word dance? Music!" he commanded.

The musicians scrambled back into their chairs, and Harrison stripped them of their handicaps, too. "Play your best," he told them, "and I'll make you barons and dukes and earls." 65

The music began. It was normal at first—cheap, silly, false. But Harrison snatched two musicians from their chairs, waved them like batons as he sang the music as he wanted it played. He slammed them back into their chairs.

The music began again and was much improved.

Harrison and his Empress merely listened to the music for a while— listened gravely, as though synchronizing their heartbeats with it.

They shifted their weights to their toes.

Harrison placed his big hands on the girl's tiny waist, letting her sense the weightlessness that would soon be hers. 70

And then, in an explosion of joy and grace, into the air they sprang!

Not only were the laws of the land abandoned, but the law of gravity and the laws of motion as well.

They reeled, whirled, swiveled, flounced, capered, gamboled, and spun.

They leaped like deer on the moon.

The studio ceiling was thirty feet high, but each leap brought the dancers nearer to it. 75

It became their obvious intention to kiss the ceiling.

They kissed it.

And then, neutralizing gravity with love and pure will, they remained suspended in air inches below the ceiling, and they kissed each other for a long, long time.

It was then that Diana Moon Glampers, the Handicapper General, came into the studio with a double-barreled ten-gauge shotgun. She fired twice, and the Emperor and the Empress were dead before they hit the floor.

Diana Moon Glampers loaded the gun again. She aimed it at the musicians and told them they had ten seconds to get their handicaps back on. 80

It was then that the Bergerons' television tube burned out.

Hazel turned to comment about the blackout to George. But George had gone out into the kitchen for a can of beer.

George came back in with the beer, paused while a handicap signal shook him up. And then he sat down again. "You been crying?" he said to Hazel.

"Yup," she said.

"What about?" he said.

"I forget," she said. "Something real sad on television." 85

"What was it?" he said.

"It's all kind of mixed up in my mind," said Hazel.

"Forget sad things," said George.

"I always do," said Hazel.

"That's my girl," said George. He winced. There was the sound of a rivetting gun in his head. 90

"Gee—I could tell that one was a doozy," said Hazel.

"You can say that again," said George.

"Gee—" said Hazel, "I could tell that one was a doozy."

QUESTIONS

1. What tendencies in present-day American society is Vonnegut satirizing? Does the story argue *for* anything? How would you sum up its theme?

2. Is Diana Moon Glampers a "flat" or a "round" character? (If you need to review these terms, see the discussion of character in Chapter 3.) Would you call Vonnegut's characterization of her "realistic"? If not, why doesn't it need to be?

3. From what point of view is the story told? Why is it more effective than if Harrison Bergeron had told his own story in the first person?

4. Two sympathetic critics of Vonnegut's work, Karen and Charles Wood, have said of his stories: "Vonnegut proves repeatedly . . . that men and women remain fundamentally the same, no matter what technology surrounds them." Try applying this comment to "Harrison Bergeron." Do you agree?

5. Stanislaw Lem, Polish author of *Solaris* and other novels, once made this thoughtful criticism of many of his contemporaries among science fiction writers:

   The revolt against the machine and against civilization, the praise of the "aesthetic" nature of catastrophe, the dead-end course of human civilization—these are their foremost problems, the intellectual content of their works. Such SF is as it were *a priori* vitiated by pessimism, in the sense that anything that may happen will be for the worse. ("The Time-Travel Story and Related Matters of SF Structuring," *Science Fiction Studies* 1 [1974], 143–54.)

   How might Lem's objection be raised against "Harrison Bergeron"? In your opinion, does it negate the value of Vonnegut's story?

WRITING ABOUT THEME

Stating the Theme

A clear, precise statement about a story's theme can serve as a promising thesis sentence. After you read a short story, you will probably have some vague sense of its theme—the central unifying idea, or the point of the story. How do you hone that vague sense of theme into a sharp and intriguing thesis?

Start by making a list of all the story's possible themes. If you are discussing Chinua Achebe's "Dead Men's Path," your list might say:

Old ways vs. new
Tradition vs. progress
Resistance to change
Intellectual arrogance
Warning: pride goes before a fall
Insensitivity to others' feelings
Live and let live

From there, determine which points are most important, and formulate a single sentence in which you touch on each one. For Achebe, you might have circled: "tradition vs. progress," "pride goes before a fall," and "insensitivity to others' feelings," and your summary might be: "The central theme of 'Dead Men's Path' is that progress is best made in a spirit of compromise, not by insensitivity to the feelings of those who follow the old ways."

Remember, your goal is to transcend a mere one-sentence plot summary. Try to capture the story's essence, its deeper meaning.

To flesh out your statement into an essay, relate details of the story to the theme you have spelled out. Like all thesis sentences, yours must stand up in the face of the evidence. If you encounter elements of the story that seem to contradict your thesis, you may need to do some fine-tuning. Your thesis, or statement of theme, should apply to everything in the story. If it doesn't, reevaluate. You may have missed some crucial detail, or you may be overlooking the story's central preoccupation, focusing instead on a peripheral one. If this is the case, you will need to start from scratch. This happens to the best of writers; recognizing your own mistakes is an important step in critical thinking.

CHECKLIST

Determining a Story's Theme

- ✓ List as many possible themes as you can.
- ✓ Circle the two or three most important points and try to combine them into a sentence. This sentence is your preliminary thesis.
- ✓ Relate particular details of the story to the theme you have spelled out. Consider plot details, dialogue, setting, point of view, title—any elements that seem especially pertinent.
- ✓ Check whether all the elements of the story fit your thesis. If not, reevaluate your thesis.
- ✓ Have you missed an important aspect of the story? Or, have you chosen to focus on a secondary idea, overlooking the central one?
- ✓ If necessary, rework your thesis until it applies to every element in the story.

WRITING ASSIGNMENT ON THEME

Choose a story that catches your attention, and go through the steps outlined above to develop a strong thesis sentence about the story's theme. Then flesh out your argument into an essay, supporting your thesis with evidence from the text, including quotations. Some good story choices might be "A Clean, Well-Lighted Place," "The Chrysanthemums," "A Good Man Is Hard to Find," and "The Lottery."

MORE TOPICS FOR WRITING

1. Define the central theme of "Harrison Bergeron." Is Vonnegut's early 1960s vision of the future still relevant today? Why or why not?

2. Think of a social trend that worries you. With "Harrison Bergeron" in mind, write a brief science fiction parable to warn against this danger to society. Try to pick a less familiar or surprising trend instead of one of the hot-button social issues that immediately pop into your mind.

3. In 500 words or more, discuss Achebe's views on the modernization of tribal Africa and its effects as demonstrated in "Dead Men's Path."

4. A recent *Time* magazine article describes a young California woman who distanced herself from her Chinese heritage until reading *The Joy Luck Club* "turned her into a 'born-again Asian.' It gave her new insights into why her mom was so hard on her and why the ways she showed love—say, through food—were different from those of the families [she] saw on TV, who seemed to say 'I love you' all day long." Have you ever had a similar experience, in which something you read gave you a better understanding of a loved one, or even yourself?

7
Symbol

In F. Scott Fitzgerald's novel *The Great Gatsby*, a huge pair of bespectacled eyes stares across a wilderness of ash heaps, from a billboard advertising the services of an oculist. Repeatedly entering into the story, the advertisement comes to mean more than simply the availability of eye examinations. Fitzgerald has a character liken it to the eyes of God; he hints that some sad, compassionate spirit is brooding as it watches the passing procession of humanity. Such an object is a **symbol**: in literature, a thing that suggests more than its literal meaning. Symbols generally do not "stand for" any one meaning, nor for anything absolutely definite; they point, they hint, or, as Henry James put it, they cast long shadows. To take a large example: in Herman Melville's *Moby-Dick*, the great white whale of the book's title apparently means more than the literal dictionary-definition meaning of an aquatic mammal. He also suggests more than the devil, to whom some of the characters liken him. The great whale, as the story unfolds, comes to imply an amplitude of meanings, among them the forces of nature and the whole created universe.

This indefinite multiplicity of meanings is characteristic of a symbolic story and distinguishes it from an **allegory**, a story in which persons, places, and things form a system of clearly labeled equivalents. In a simple allegory, characters and other elements often stand for other definite meanings, which are often abstractions. You will meet such a character in another story in this book, Nathaniel Hawthorne's "Young Goodman Brown." This tale's main female character, Faith, represents the religious virtue suggested by her name. Supreme allegories are found in some biblical parables ("The Kingdom of Heaven is like a man who sowed good seed in his field . . . ," Matthew 13:24–30). A classic allegory is the medieval play *Everyman*, whose hero represents us all, and who, deserted by false friends called Kindred and Goods, faces the judgment of God accompanied only by a faithful friend called Good Deeds. In John Bunyan's seventeenth-century allegory *Pilgrim's Progress*, the protagonist, Christian, struggles along the difficult road toward salvation, meeting along the way persons such as Mr. Worldly Wiseman, who directs him into a more comfortable path (a wrong turn), and the residents of a town called Fair Speech, among them a hypocrite named Mr. Facing-both-ways. Not all allegories are simple: Dante's *Divine Comedy*, written in the Middle Ages, continues to reveal new meanings to careful readers. Allegory was much beloved in the Middle Ages, but in contemporary fiction it is rare. One modern instance is George Orwell's long fable *Animal Farm*, in which (among its double meanings) barnyard animals stand for human victims and totalitarian oppressors.

Symbols in fiction are not generally abstract terms such as *love* or *truth*, but are likely to be perceptible objects (or worded descriptions that cause us to imagine them). In William Faulkner's "A Rose for Emily" (Chapter 2), Miss Emily's invisible watch ticking at the end of a golden chain not only indicates the passage of time, but also suggests that time passes without even being noticed by the watch's owner, and the golden chain carries suggestions of wealth and authority. Often the symbols we meet in fiction are inanimate objects, but other things also may function symbolically. In James Joyce's "Araby" (Chapter 8), the very name of the bazaar, Araby—the poetic name for Arabia—suggests magic, romance, and *The Arabian Nights*; its syllables (the narrator tells us) "cast an Eastern enchantment over me." Even a locale, or a feature of physical topography, can provide rich suggestions. Recall Ernest Hemingway's "A Clean, Well-Lighted Place" (Chapter 5), in which the café is not merely a café, but an island of refuge from night, chaos, loneliness, old age, and impending death.

In some novels and stories, symbolic characters make brief cameo appearances. Such characters often are not well-rounded and fully known, but are seen fleetingly and remain slightly mysterious. In *Heart of Darkness*, a short novel by Joseph Conrad, a steamship company that hires men to work in the Congo maintains in its waiting room two women who knit black wool—like the classical Fates. Usually such a symbolic character is more a portrait than a person—or somewhat portraitlike, as Faulkner's Miss Emily, who twice appears at a window of her house "like the carven torso of an idol in a niche." Though Faulkner invests Miss Emily with life and vigor, he also clothes her in symbolic hints: she seems almost to personify the vanishing aristocracy of the antebellum South, still maintaining a black servant and being ruthlessly betrayed by a moneymaking Yankee. Sometimes a part of a character's body or an attribute may convey symbolic meaning: a baleful eye, as in Edgar Allan Poe's "The Tell-Tale Heart" (Chapter 2).

Much as a symbolic whale holds more meaning than an ordinary whale, a **symbolic act** is a gesture with larger significance than usual. For the boy's father in Faulkner's "Barn Burning" (Chapter 5), the act of destroying a barn is no mere act of spite, but an expression of his profound hatred for anything not belonging to him. Faulkner adds that burning a barn reflects the father's memories of the "waste and extravagance of war," and further adds that "the element of fire spoke to some deep mainspring" in his being. A symbolic act, however, doesn't have to be a gesture as large as starting a conflagration. Before setting out in pursuit of the great white whale, Melville's Captain Ahab in *Moby-Dick* deliberately snaps his tobacco pipe and throws it away, as if to suggest (among other things) that he will let no pleasure or pastime distract him from his vengeance.

Why do writers have to symbolize—why don't they tell us outright? One advantage of a symbol is that it is so compact, and yet so fully laden. Both starkly concrete and slightly mysterious, like Miss Emily's invisible ticking watch, it may impress us with all the force of something beheld in a dream or in a nightmare. The watch suggests, among other things, the slow and invisible passage of time. What this symbol says, it says more fully and more memorably than could be said, perhaps, in a long essay on the subject.

To some extent (it may be claimed), all stories are symbolic. Merely by holding up for our inspection these characters and their actions, the writer lends them *some* special significance. But this is to think of *symbol* in an extremely broad and inclusive way. For the usual purposes of reading a story and understanding it, there is probably little point in looking for symbolism in every word, in every stick or stone, in every striking of a match, in every minor character. Still, to be on the alert for symbols when reading fiction is perhaps wiser than to ignore them. Not to admit that symbolic meanings may be present, or to refuse to think about them, would be another way to misread a story—or to read no further than its outer edges.

How, then, do you recognize a symbol in fiction when you meet it? Fortunately, the storyteller often gives the symbol particular emphasis. It may be mentioned repeatedly throughout the story; it may even supply the story with a title ("Barn Burning," "A Clean, Well-Lighted Place," "Araby"). At times, a crucial symbol will open a story or end it. Unless an object, act, or character is given some such special emphasis and importance, we may generally feel safe in taking it at face value. Probably it isn't a symbol if it points clearly and unmistakably toward some one meaning, like a whistle in a factory, whose blast at noon means lunch. But an object, an act, or a character is surely symbolic (and almost as surely displays high literary art) if, when we finish the story, we realize that it was that item—those gigantic eyes; that clean, well-lighted café; that burning of a barn—which led us to the author's theme, the essential meaning.

John Steinbeck

The Chrysanthemums   1938

John Steinbeck (1902–1968) was born in Salinas, California, in the fertile valley he remembers in "The Chrysanthemums." Off and on, he attended Stanford University, then sojourned in New York as a reporter and a bricklayer. After years of struggle to earn his living by fiction, Steinbeck reached a large audience with Tortilla Flat *(1935), a loosely woven novel portraying Mexican Americans in Monterey with fondness and sympathy. Great acclaim greeted* The Grapes of Wrath *(1939), the story of a family of Oklahoma farmers who, ruined by dust storms in the 1930s,*

JOHN STEINBECK

join a mass migration to California. Like Ernest Hemingway and Stephen Crane, Steinbeck prided himself on his journalism: in World War II, he filed dispatches from battlefronts in Italy and Africa, and in 1966 he wrote a column from South Vietnam. Known widely behind the Iron Curtain, Steinbeck accepted an invitation to visit the Soviet Union, and reported on his trip in A Russian Journal *(1948). In 1962 he became the seventh American to win the Nobel Prize for Literature, but critics have never placed Steinbeck on the same high shelf with Faulkner and Hemingway. He wrote much, not all good, and yet his best work adds to an impressive total. Besides* The Grapes of Wrath, *it includes* In Dubious Battle *(1936), a novel of an apple-pickers' strike;* Of Mice and Men *(1937), a powerful short novel (also a play) of comradeship between a hobo and a retarded man;* The Log *from the Sea of Cortez (1951), a nonfiction account of a marine biological expedition; and the short stories in* The Long Valley *(1938). Throughout the fiction he wrote in his prime, Steinbeck maintains an appealing sympathy for the poor and downtrodden, the lonely and dispossessed.*

The high grey-flannel fog of winter closed off the Salinas Valley° from the sky and from all the rest of the world. On every side it sat like a lid on the mountains and made of the great valley a closed pot. On the broad, level land floor the gang plows bit deep and left the black earth shining like metal where the shares had cut. On the foothill ranches across the Salinas River, the yellow stubble fields seemed to be bathed in pale cold sunshine, but there was no sunshine in the valley now in December. The thick willow scrub along the river flamed with sharp and positive yellow leaves.

It was a time of quiet and of waiting. The air was cold and tender. A light wind blew up from the southwest so that the farmers were mildly hopeful of a good rain before long; but fog and rain do not go together.

Across the river, on Henry Allen's foothill ranch there was little work to be done, for the hay was cut and stored and the orchards were plowed up to receive the rain deeply when it should come. The cattle on the higher slopes were becoming shaggy and rough-coated.

Elisa Allen, working in her flower garden, looked down across the yard and saw Henry, her husband, talking to two men in business suits. The three of them stood by the tractor shed, each man with one foot on the side of the little Fordson. They smoked cigarettes and studied the machine as they talked.

Elisa watched them for a moment and then went back to her work. 5 She was thirty-five. Her face was lean and strong and her eyes were as clear as water. Her figure looked blocked and heavy in her gardening costume, a man's black hat pulled low down over her eyes, clod-hopper shoes,

Salinas Valley: south of San Francisco in the Coast Ranges region of California.

a figured print dress almost completely covered by a big corduroy apron with four big pockets to hold the snips, the trowel and scratcher, the seeds and the knife she worked with. She wore heavy leather gloves to protect her hands while she worked.

She was cutting down the old year's chrysanthemum stalks with a pair of short and powerful scissors. She looked down toward the men by the tractor shed now and then. Her face was eager and mature and handsome; even her work with the scissors was over-eager, over-powerful. The chrysanthemum stems seemed too small and easy for her energy.

She brushed a cloud of hair out of her eyes with the back of her glove, and left a smudge of earth on her cheek in doing it. Behind her stood the neat white farm house with red geraniums close-banked around it as high as the windows. It was a hard-swept looking little house with hard-polished windows, and a clean mud-mat on the front steps.

Elisa cast another glance toward the tractor shed. The strangers were getting into their Ford coupe. She took off a glove and put her strong fingers down into the forest of new green chrysanthemum sprouts that were growing around the old roots. She spread the leaves and looked down among the close-growing stems. No aphids were there, no sowbugs or snails or cutworms. Her terrier fingers destroyed such pests before they could get started.

Elisa started at the sound of her husband's voice. He had come near quietly, and he leaned over the wire fence that protected her flower garden from cattle and dogs and chickens.

"At it again," he said. "You've got a strong new crop coming." 10

Elisa straightened her back and pulled on the gardening glove again. "Yes. They'll be strong this coming year." In her tone and on her face there was a little smugness.

"You've got a gift with things," Henry observed. "Some of those yellow chrysanthemums you had this year were ten inches across. I wish you'd work out in the orchard and raise some apples that big."

Her eyes sharpened. "Maybe I could do it, too. I've a gift with things, all right. My mother had it. She could stick anything in the ground and make it grow. She said it was having planters' hands that knew how to do it."

"Well, it sure works with flowers," he said.

"Henry, who were those men you were talking to?" 15

"Why, sure, that's what I came to tell you. They were from the Western Meat Company. I sold those thirty head of three-year-old steers. Got nearly my own price, too."

"Good," she said. "Good for you."

"And I thought," he continued, "I thought how it's Saturday afternoon, and we might go into Salinas for dinner at a restaurant, and then to a picture show—to celebrate, you see."

"Good," she repeated. "Oh, yes. That will be good."

Henry put on his joking tone. "There's fights tonight. How'd you like   20
to go to the fights?"

"Oh, no," she said breathlessly. "No, I wouldn't like fights."

"Just fooling, Elisa. We'll go to a movie. Let's see. It's two now. I'm
going to take Scotty and bring down those steers from the hill. It'll take
us maybe two hours. We'll go in town about five and have dinner at the
Cominos Hotel. Like that?"

"Of course I'll like it. It's good to eat away from home."

"All right, then. I'll go get up a couple of horses."

She said, "I'll have plenty of time to transplant some of these sets, I   25
guess."

She heard her husband calling Scotty down by the barn. And a little
later she saw the two men ride up the pale yellow hillside in search of the
steers.

There was a little square sandy bed kept for rooting the chrysanthemums. With her trowel she turned the soil over and over, and smoothed
it and patted it firm. Then she dug ten parallel trenches to receive the
sets. Back at the chrysanthemum bed she pulled out the little crisp
shoots, trimmed off the leaves of each one with her scissors and laid it on
a small orderly pile.

A squeak of wheels and plod of hoofs came from the road. Elisa
looked up. The country road ran along the dense bank of willows and
cottonwoods that bordered the river, and up this road came a curious
vehicle, curiously drawn. It was an old spring-wagon, with a round canvas
top on it like the cover of a prairie schooner. It was drawn by an old bay
horse and a little grey-and-white burro. A big stubble-bearded man sat
between the cover flaps and drove the crawling team. Underneath the
wagon, between the hind wheels, a lean and rangy mongrel dog walked
sedately. Words were painted on the canvas, in clumsy, crooked letters.
"Pots, pans, knives, sisors, lawn mores, Fixed." Two rows of articles, and
the triumphantly definitive "Fixed" below. The black paint had run
down in little sharp points beneath each letter.

Elisa, squatting on the ground, watched to see the crazy, loose-jointed
wagon pass by. But it didn't pass. It turned into the farm road in front of
her house, crooked old wheels skirling and squeaking. The rangy dog
darted from between the wheels and ran ahead. Instantly the two ranch
shepherds flew out at him. Then all three stopped, and with stiff and quivering tails, with taut straight legs, with ambassadorial dignity, they slowly
circled, sniffing daintily. The caravan pulled up to Elisa's wire fence and
stopped. Now the newcomer dog, feeling out-numbered, lowered his tail
and retired under the wagon with raised hackles and bared teeth.

The man on the wagon seat called out, "That's a bad dog in a fight   30
when he gets started."

Elisa laughed. "I see he is. How soon does he generally get started?"

The man caught up her laughter and echoed it heartily. "Sometimes not for weeks and weeks," he said. He climbed stiffly down, over the wheel. The horse and the donkey drooped like unwatered flowers.

Elisa saw that he was a very big man. Although his hair and beard were greying, he did not look old. His worn black suit was wrinkled and spotted with grease. The laughter had disappeared from his face and eyes the moment his laughing voice ceased. His eyes were dark, and they were full of the brooding that gets in the eyes of teamsters and of sailors. The calloused hands he rested on the wire fence were cracked, and every crack was a black line. He took off his battered hat.

"I'm off my general road, ma'am," he said. "Does this dirt road cut over across the river to the Los Angeles highway?"

Elisa stood up and shoved the thick scissors in her apron pocket. 35 "Well, yes, it does, but it winds around and then fords the river. I don't think your team could pull through the sand."

He replied with some asperity. "It might surprise you what them beasts can pull through."

"When they get started?" she asked.

He smiled for a second. "Yes. When they get started."

"Well," said Elisa, "I think you'll save time if you go back to the Salinas road and pick up the highway there."

He drew a big finger down the chicken wire and made it sing. "I ain't in 40 any hurry, ma'am. I go from Seattle to San Diego and back every year. Takes all my time. About six months each way. I aim to follow nice weather."

Elisa took off her gloves and stuffed them in the apron pocket with the scissors. She touched the under edge of her man's hat, searching for fugitive hairs. "That sounds like a nice kind of a way to live," she said.

He leaned confidentially over the fence. "Maybe you noticed the writing on my wagon. I mend pots and sharpen knives and scissors. You got any of them things to do?"

"Oh, no," she said quickly. "Nothing like that." Her eyes hardened with resistance.

"Scissors is the worst thing," he explained. "Most people just ruin scissors trying to sharpen 'em, but I know how. I got a special tool. It's a little bobbit kind of thing, and patented. But it sure does the trick."

"No. My scissors are all sharp." 45

"All right, then. Take a pot," he continued earnestly, "a bent pot, or a pot with a hole. I can make it like new so you don't have to buy no new ones. That's a saving for you."

"No," she said shortly. "I tell you I have nothing like that for you to do."

His face fell to an exaggerated sadness. His voice took on a whining undertone. "I ain't had a thing to do today. Maybe I won't have no supper tonight. You see I'm off my regular road. I know folks on the highway clear from Seattle to San Diego. They save their things for me to sharpen up because they know I do it so good and save them money."

"I'm sorry," Elisa said irritably. "I haven't anything for you to do."

His eyes left her face and fell to searching the ground. They roamed   50
about until they came to the chrysanthemum bed where she had been working. "What's them plants, ma'am?"

The irritation and resistance melted from Elisa's face. "Oh, those are chrysanthemums, giant whites and yellows. I raise them every year, bigger than anybody around here."

"Kind of a long-stemmed flower? Looks like a quick puff of colored smoke?" he asked.

"That's it. What a nice way to describe them."

"They smell kind of nasty till you get used to them," he said.

"It's a good bitter smell," she retorted, "not nasty at all."   55

He changed his tone quickly. "I like the smell myself."

"I had ten-inch blooms this year," she said.

The man leaned farther over the fence. "Look. I know a lady down the road a piece, has got the nicest garden you ever seen. Got nearly every kind of flower but no chrysanthemums. Last time I was mending a copper-bottom washtub for her (that's a hard job but I do it good), she said to me, 'If you ever run acrost some nice chrysanthemums I wish you'd try to get me a few seeds.' That's what she told me."

Elisa's eyes grew alert and eager. "She couldn't have known much about chrysanthemums. You *can* raise them from seed, but it's much easier to root the little sprouts you see there."

"Oh," he said. "I s'pose I can't take none to her, then."   60

"Why yes you can," Elisa cried. "I can put some in damp sand, and you can carry them right along with you. They'll take root in the pot if you keep them damp. And then she can transplant them."

"She'd sure like to have some, ma'am. You say they're nice ones?"

"Beautiful," she said. "Oh, beautiful." Her eyes shone. She tore off the battered hat and shook out her dark pretty hair. "I'll put them in a flower pot, and you can take them right with you. Come into the yard."

While the man came through the picket gate Elisa ran excitedly along the geranium-bordered path to the back of the house. And she returned carrying a big red flower pot. The gloves were forgotten now. She kneeled on the ground by the starting bed and dug up the sandy soil with her fingers and scooped it into the bright new flower pot. Then she picked up the little pile of shoots she had prepared. With her strong fingers she pressed them in the sand and tamped around them with her knuckles. The man stood over her. "I'll tell you what to do," she said. "You remember so you can tell the lady."

"Yes, I'll try to remember."   65

"Well, look. These will take root in about a month. Then she must set them out, about a foot apart in good rich earth like this, see?" She lifted a handful of dark soil for him to look at. "They'll grow fast and tall. Now remember this: In July tell her to cut them down, about eight inches from the ground."

"Before they bloom?" he asked.

"Yes, before they bloom." Her face was tight with eagerness. "They'll grow right up again. About the last of September the buds will start."

She stopped and seemed perplexed. "It's the budding that takes the most care," she said hesitantly. "I don't know how to tell you." She looked deep into his eyes, searchingly. Her mouth opened a little, and she seemed to be listening. "I'll try to tell you," she said. "Did you ever hear of planting hands?"

"Can't say I have, ma'am." 70

"Well, I can only tell you what it feels like. It's when you're picking off the buds you don't want. Everything goes right down into your fingertips. You watch your fingers work. They do it themselves. You can feel how it is. They pick and pick the buds. They never make a mistake. They're with the plant. Do you see? Your fingers and the plant. You can feel that, right up your arm. They know. They never make a mistake. You can feel it. When you're like that you can't do anything wrong. Do you see that? Can you understand that?"

She was kneeling on the ground looking up at him. Her breast swelled passionately.

The man's eyes narrowed. He looked away self-consciously. "Maybe I know," he said. "Sometimes in the night in the wagon there—"

Elisa's voice grew husky. She broke in on him, "I've never lived as you do, but I know what you mean. When the night is dark—why, the stars are sharp-pointed, and there's quiet. Why, you rise up and up! Every pointed star gets driven into your body. It's like that. Hot and sharp and—lovely."

Kneeling there, her hand went out toward his legs in the greasy 75 black trousers. Her hesitant fingers almost touched the cloth. Then her hand dropped to the ground. She crouched low like a fawning dog.

He said, "It's nice, just like you say. Only when you don't have no dinner, it ain't."

She stood up then, very straight, and her face was ashamed. She held the flower pot out to him and placed it gently in his arms. "Here. Put it in your wagon, on the seat, where you can watch it. Maybe I can find something for you to do."

At the back of the house she dug in the can pile and found two old and battered aluminum saucepans. She carried them back and gave them to him. "Here, maybe you can fix these."

His manner changed. He became professional. "Good as new I can fix them." At the back of his wagon he set a little anvil, and out of an oily tool box dug a small machine hammer. Elisa came through the gate to watch him while he pounded out the dents in the kettles. His mouth grew sure and knowing. At a difficult part of the work he sucked his under-lip.

"You sleep right in the wagon?" Elisa asked. 80

"Right in the wagon, ma'am. Rain or shine I'm dry as a cow in there."

"It must be nice," she said. "It must be very nice. I wish women could do such things."

"It ain't the right kind of a life for a woman."

Her upper lip raised a little, showing her teeth. "How do you know? How can you tell?" she said.

"I don't know, ma'am," he protested. "Of course I don't know. Now 85 here's your kettles, done. You don't have to buy no new ones."

"How much?"

"Oh, fifty cents'll do. I keep my prices down and my work good. That's why I have all them satisfied customers up and down the highway."

Elisa brought him a fifty-cent piece from the house and dropped it in his hand. "You might be surprised to have a rival some time. I can sharpen scissors, too. And I can beat the dents out of little pots. I could show you what a woman might do."

He put his hammer back in the oily box and shoved the little anvil out of sight. "It would be a lonely life for a woman, ma'am, and a scarey life, too, with animals creeping under the wagon all night." He climbed over the singletree, steadying himself with a hand on the burro's white rump. He settled himself in the seat, picked up the lines. "Thank you kindly, ma'am," he said. "I'll do like you told me; I'll go back and catch the Salinas road."

"Mind," she called, "if you're long in getting there, keep the sand damp." 90

"Sand, ma'am? . . . Sand? Oh, sure. You mean around the chrysanthemums. Sure I will." He clucked his tongue. The beasts leaned luxuriously into their collars. The mongrel dog took his place between the back wheels. The wagon turned and crawled out the entrance road and back the way it had come, along the river.

Elisa stood in front of her wire fence watching the slow progress of the caravan. Her shoulders were straight, her head thrown back, her eyes half-closed, so that the scene came vaguely into them. Her lips moved silently, forming the words "Good-bye—good-bye." Then she whispered, "That's a bright direction. There's a glowing there." The sound of her whisper startled her. She shook herself free and looked about to see whether anyone had been listening. Only the dogs had heard. They lifted their heads toward her from their sleeping in the dust, and then stretched out their chins and settled asleep again. Elisa turned and ran hurriedly into the house.

In the kitchen she reached behind the stove and felt the water tank. It was full of hot water from the noonday cooking. In the bathroom she tore off her soiled clothes and flung them into the corner. And then she scrubbed herself with a little block of pumice, legs and thighs, loins and chest and arms, until her skin was scratched and red. When she had dried herself she stood in front of a mirror in her bedroom and looked at her body. She tightened her stomach and threw out her chest. She turned and looked over her shoulder at her back.

After a while she began to dress, slowly. She put on her newest underclothing and her nicest stockings and the dress which was the symbol of her prettiness. She worked carefully on her hair, penciled her eyebrows and rouged her lips.

Before she was finished she heard the little thunder of hoofs and the 95 shouts of Henry and his helper as they drove the red steers into the corral. She heard the gate bang shut and set herself for Henry's arrival.

His step sounded on the porch. He entered the house calling, "Elisa, where are you?"

"In my room, dressing. I'm not ready. There's hot water for your bath. Hurry up. It's getting late."

When she heard him splashing in the tub, Elisa laid his dark suit on the bed, and shirt and socks and tie beside it. She stood his polished shoes on the floor beside the bed. Then she went to the porch and sat primly and stiffly down. She looked toward the river road where the willow-line was still yellow with frosted leaves so that under the high grey fog they seemed a thin band of sunshine. This was the only color in the grey afternoon. She sat unmoving for a long time. Her eyes blinked rarely.

Henry came banging out of the door, shoving his tie inside his vest as he came. Elisa stiffened and her face grew tight. Henry stopped short and looked at her. "Why—why, Elisa. You look so nice!"

"Nice? You think I look nice? What do you mean by 'nice'?" 100

Henry blundered on. "I don't know. I mean you look different, strong and happy."

"I am strong? Yes, strong. What do you mean 'strong'?"

He looked bewildered. "You're playing some kind of a game," he said helplessly. "It's a kind of a play. You look strong enough to break a calf over your knee, happy enough to eat it like a watermelon."

For a second she lost her rigidity. "Henry! Don't talk like that. You didn't know what you said." She grew complete again. "I'm strong," she boasted. "I never knew before how strong."

Henry looked down toward the tractor shed, and when he brought 105 his eyes back to her, they were his own again. "I'll get out the car. You can put on your coat while I'm starting."

Elisa went into the house. She heard him drive to the gate and idle down his motor, and then she took a long time to put on her hat. She pulled it here and pressed it there. When Henry turned the motor off she slipped into her coat and went out.

The little roadster bounced along on the dirt road by the river, raising the birds and driving the rabbits into the brush. Two cranes flapped heavily over the willow-line and dropped into the river-bed.

Far ahead on the road Elisa saw a dark speck. She knew.

She tried not to look as they passed it, but her eyes would not obey. She whispered to herself sadly, "He might have thrown them off the road. That wouldn't have been much trouble, not very much. But he kept the pot," she explained. "He had to keep the pot. That's why he couldn't get them off the road."

The roadster turned a bend and she saw the caravan ahead. She swung   110
full around toward her husband so she could not see the little covered wagon and the mismatched team as the car passed them.

In a moment it was over. The thing was done. She did not look back.

She said loudly, to be heard above the motor, "It will be good, tonight, a good dinner."

"Now you're changed again," Henry complained. He took one hand from the wheel and patted her knee. "I ought to take you in to dinner oftener. It would be good for both of us. We get so heavy out on the ranch."

"Henry," she asked, "could we have wine at dinner?"

"Sure we could. Say! That will be fine."   115

She was silent for a while; then she said, "Henry, at those prize fights, do the men hurt each other very much?"

"Sometimes a little, not often. Why?"

"Well, I've read how they break noses, and blood runs down their chests. I've read how the fighting gloves get heavy and soggy with blood."

He looked around at her. "What's the matter, Elisa? I didn't know you read things like that." He brought the car to a stop, then turned to the right over the Salinas River bridge.

"Do any women ever go to the fights?" she asked.   120

"Oh, sure, some. What's the matter, Elisa? Do you want to go? I don't think you'd like it, but I'll take you if you really want to go."

She relaxed limply in the seat. "Oh, no. No. I don't want to go. I'm sure I don't." Her face was turned away from him. "It will be enough if we can have wine. It will be plenty." She turned up her coat collar so he could not see that she was crying weakly—like an old woman.

QUESTIONS

1. When we first meet Elisa Allen in her garden, with what details does Steinbeck delineate her character for us?

2. Elisa works inside a "wire fence that protected her flower garden from cattle and dogs and chickens" (paragraph 9). What does this wire fence suggest?

3. How would you describe Henry and Elisa's marriage? Cite details from the story.

4. For what motive does the traveling salesman take an interest in Elisa's chrysanthemums? What immediate effect does his interest have on Elisa?

5. For what possible purpose does Steinbeck give us such a detailed account of Elisa's preparations for her evening out? Notice her tearing off her soiled clothes, her scrubbing her body with pumice (paragraphs 93–94).

6. Of what significance to Elisa is the sight of the contents of the flower pot discarded in the road? Notice that, as her husband's car overtakes the covered wagon, Elisa averts her eyes; and then Steinbeck adds, "In a moment it was over. The thing was done. She did not look back" (paragraph 111). Explain this passage.

7. How do you interpret Elisa's asking for wine with dinner? How do you account for her new interest in prizefights?

8. In a sentence, try to state this short story's theme.

9. Why are Elisa Allen's chrysanthemums so important to this story? Sum up what you understand them to mean.

Shirley Jackson

The Lottery

1948

*Shirley Jackson (1919–1965), a native of San Francisco, moved in her teens to Rochester, New York. She started college at the University of Rochester, but had to drop out, stricken by severe depression, a problem that was to recur at intervals throughout her life. Later she graduated from Syracuse University. With her husband, Stanley Edgar Hyman, a literary critic, she settled in Bennington, Vermont, in a sprawling house built in the nineteenth century. There Jackson conscientiously set herself to produce a fixed number of words each day. She wrote novels—*The Road Through the Wall *(1948)—and three psychological thrillers—*Hangsaman *(1951),* The Haunting*

SHIRLEY JACKSON

*of Hill House *(1959), and* We Have Always Lived in the Castle *(1962). She wrote light, witty articles for* Good Housekeeping *and other popular magazines about the horrors of housekeeping and rearing four children, collected in* Life Among the Savages *(1953) and* Raising Demons *(1957); but she claimed to have written these only for money. When "The Lottery" appeared in the* New Yorker *in 1948, that issue of the magazine quickly sold out. Her purpose in writing the story, Jackson declared, had been "to shock the story's readers with a graphic demonstration of the pointless violence and general inhumanity in their own lives."*

The morning of June 27th was clear and sunny, with the fresh warmth of a full-summer day; the flowers were blossoming profusely and the grass was richly green. The people of the village began to gather in the square, between the post office and the bank, around ten o'clock; in some towns there were so many people that the lottery took two days and had to be started on June 26th, but in this village, where there were only about three hundred people, the whole lottery took less than two hours, so it could begin at ten o'clock in the morning and still be through in time to allow the villagers to get home for noon dinner.

The children assembled first, of course. School was recently over for the summer, and the feeling of liberty sat uneasily on most of them; they tended to gather together quietly for a while before they broke into boisterous play, and their talk was still of the classroom and the teacher, of books and reprimands. Bobby Martin had already stuffed his pockets full of stones, and the other boys soon followed his example, selecting the smoothest and roundest stones; Bobby and Harry Jones and Dickie Delacroix—the villagers pronounced this name "Dellacroy"—eventually made a great pile of stones in one corner of the square and guarded it against the raids of the other boys. The girls stood aside, talking among themselves, looking over their shoulders at the boys, and the very small children rolled in the dust or clung to the hands of their older brothers or sisters.

Soon the men began to gather, surveying their own children, speaking of planting and rain, tractors and taxes. They stood together, away from the pile of stones in the corner, and their jokes were quiet and they smiled rather than laughed. The women, wearing faded house dresses and sweaters, came shortly after their menfolk. They greeted one another and exchanged bits of gossip as they went to join their husbands. Soon the women, standing by their husbands, began to call to their children, and the children came reluctantly, having to be called four or five times. Bobby Martin ducked under his mother's grasping hand and ran, laughing, back to the pile of stones. His father spoke up sharply, and Bobby came quickly and took his place between his father and his oldest brother.

The lottery was conducted—as were the square dances, the teenage club, the Halloween program—by Mr. Summers, who had time and energy to devote to civic activities. He was a roundfaced, jovial man and he ran the coal business, and people were sorry for him, because he had no children and his wife was a scold. When he arrived in the square, carrying the black wooden box, there was a murmur of conversation among the villagers and he waved and called, "Little late today, folks." The postmaster, Mr. Graves, followed him, carrying a three-legged stool, and the stool was put in the center of the square and Mr. Summers set the black box down on it. The villagers kept their distance, leaving a space between themselves and the stool, and when Mr. Summers said, "Some of you fellows want to give me a hand?" there was a hesitation before two men, Mr. Martin and his oldest son, Baxter, came forward to hold the box steady on the stool while Mr. Summers stirred up the papers inside it.

The original paraphernalia for the lottery had been lost long ago, and the black box now resting on the stool had been put into use even before Old Man Warner, the oldest man in town, was born. Mr. Summers spoke frequently to the villagers about making a new box, but no one liked to upset even as much tradition as was represented by the black box. There was a story that the present box had been made with some pieces of the box that had preceded it, the one that had been constructed when the first people settled down to make a village here. Every year, after the lottery, Mr. Summers began talking again about a new box, but every year the subject was allowed to fade off without anything's being done. The black box grew shabbier each year; by now it was no longer completely black but splintered badly along one side to show the original wood color, and in some places faded or stained.

Mr. Martin and his oldest son, Baxter, held the black box securely on the stool until Mr. Summers had stirred the papers thoroughly with his hand. Because so much of the ritual had been forgotten or discarded, Mr. Summers had been successful in having slips of paper substituted for the chips of wood that had been used for generations. Chips of wood, Mr. Summers had argued, had been all very well when the village was tiny, but now that the population was more than three hundred and likely to keep on growing, it was necessary to use something that would fit more easily into the black box. The night before the lottery, Mr. Summers and Mr. Graves made up the slips of paper and put them in the box, and it was then taken to the safe of Mr. Summers's coal company and locked up until Mr. Summers was ready to take it to the square next morning. The rest of the year, the box was put away, sometimes one place, sometimes another; it had spent one year in Mr. Graves's barn and another year underfoot in the post office, and sometimes it was set on a shelf in the Martin grocery and left there.

There was a great deal of fussing to be done before Mr. Summers declared the lottery open. There were lists to make up—of heads of families, heads of households in each family, members of each household in each family. There was the proper swearing-in of Mr. Summers by the postmaster, as the official of the lottery; at one time, some people remembered, there had been a recital of some sort, performed by the official of the lottery, a perfunctory, tuneless chant that had been rattled off duly each year; some people believed that the official of the lottery used to stand just so when he said or sang it, others believed that he was supposed to walk among the people, but years and years ago this part of the ritual had been allowed to lapse. There had been, also, a ritual salute, which the official of the lottery had had to use in addressing each person who came up to draw from the box, but this also had changed with time, until now it was felt necessary only for the official to speak to each person approaching. Mr. Summers was very good at all this; in his clean white shirt and blue jeans, with one hand resting carelessly on the black box, he seemed very proper and important as he talked interminably to Mr. Graves and the Martins.

Just as Mr. Summers finally left off talking and turned to the assembled villagers, Mrs. Hutchinson came hurriedly along the path to the square, her sweater thrown over her shoulders, and slid into place in the back of the crowd. "Clean forgot what day it was," she said to Mrs. Delacroix, who stood next to her, and they both laughed softly. "Thought my old man was out back stacking wood," Mrs. Hutchinson went on, "and then I looked out the window and the kids were gone, and then I remembered it was the twenty-seventh and came a-running." She dried her hands on her apron, and Mrs. Delacroix said, "You're in time, though. They're still talking away up there."

Mrs. Hutchinson craned her neck to see through the crowd and found her husband and children standing near the front. She tapped Mrs. Delacroix on the arm as a farewell and began to make her way through the crowd. The people separated good-humoredly to let her through; two or three people said, in voices just loud enough to be heard across the crowd, "Here comes your Missus, Hutchinson," and "Bill, she made it after all." Mrs. Hutchinson reached her husband, and Mr. Summers, who had been waiting, said cheerfully, "Thought we were going to have to get on without you, Tessie." Mrs. Hutchinson said, grinning, "Wouldn't have me leave m'dishes in the sink, now would you, Joe?" and soft laughter ran through the crowd as the people stirred back into position after Mrs. Hutchinson's arrival.

"Well, now," Mr. Summers said soberly, "guess we better get started, get this over with, so's we can go back to work. Anybody ain't here?"   10

"Dunbar," several people said. "Dunbar, Dunbar."

Mr. Summers consulted his list. "Clyde Dunbar," he said. "That's right. He's broke his leg, hasn't he? Who's drawing for him?"

"Me, I guess," a woman said, and Mr. Summers turned to look at her. "Wife draws for her husband," Mr. Summers said. "Don't you have a grown boy to do it for you, Janey?" Although Mr. Summers and everyone else in the village knew the answer perfectly well, it was the business of the official of the lottery to ask such questions formally. Mr. Summers waited with an expression of polite interest while Mrs. Dunbar answered.

"Horace's not but sixteen yet," Mrs. Dunbar said regretfully. "Guess I gotta fill in for the old man this year."

"Right," Mr. Summers said. He made a note on the list he was holding.   15
Then he asked, "Watson boy drawing this year?"

A tall boy in the crowd raised his hand. "Here," he said. "I'm draw-ing for m'mother and me." He blinked his eyes nervously and ducked his head as several voices in the crowd said things like "Good fellow, Jack," and "Glad to see your mother's got a man to do it."

"Well," Mr. Summers said, "guess that's everyone. Old Man Warner make it?"

"Here," a voice said, and Mr. Summers nodded.

A sudden hush fell on the crowd as Mr. Summers cleared his throat and looked at the list. "All ready?" he called. "Now, I'll read the names—heads of families first—and the men come up and take a paper out of the box. Keep the paper folded in your hand without looking at it until everyone has had a turn. Everything clear?"

The people had done it so many times that they only half listened to 20 the directions; most of them were quiet, wetting their lips, not looking around. Then Mr. Summers raised one hand high and said, "Adams." A man disengaged himself from the crowd and came forward. "Hi, Steve," Mr. Summers said, and Mr. Adams said, "Hi, Joe." They grinned at one another humorlessly and nervously. Then Mr. Adams reached into the black box and took out a folded paper. He held it firmly by one corner as he turned and went hastily back to his place in the crowd, where he stood a little apart from his family, not looking down at his hand.

"Allen," Mr. Summers said. "Anderson. . . . Bentham."

"Seems like there's no time at all between lotteries any more," Mrs. Delacroix said to Mrs. Graves in the back row. "Seems like we got through with the last one only last week."

"Time sure goes fast," Mrs. Graves said.

"Clark. . . . Delacroix."

"There goes my old man," Mrs. Delacroix said. She held her breath 25 while her husband went forward.

"Dunbar," Mr. Summers said, and Mrs. Dunbar went steadily to the box while one of the women said, "Go on, Janey," and another said, "There she goes."

"We're next," Mrs. Graves said. She watched while Mr. Graves came around from the side of the box, greeted Mr. Summers gravely, and se-lected a slip of paper from the box. By now, all through the crowd there were men holding the small folded papers in their large hands, turning them over and over nervously. Mrs. Dunbar and her two sons stood to-gether, Mrs. Dunbar holding the slip of paper.

"Harburt. . . . Hutchinson."

"Get up there, Bill," Mrs. Hutchinson said, and the people near her laughed.

"Jones." 30

"They do say," Mr. Adams said to Old Man Warner, who stood next to him, "that over in the north village they're talking of giving up the lottery."

Old Man Warner snorted. "Pack of crazy fools," he said. "Listening to the young folks, nothing's good enough for *them*. Next thing you know, they'll be wanting to go back to living in caves, nobody work any more, live *that* way for a while. Used to be a saying about 'Lottery in June, corn be heavy soon.' First thing you know, we'd all be eating stewed chickweed and acorns. There's *always* been a lottery," he added petulantly. "Bad enough to see young Joe Summers up there joking with everybody."

"Some places have already quit lotteries," Mrs. Adams said.

"Nothing but trouble in *that*," Old Man Warner said stoutly. "Pack of young fools."

"Martin." And Bobby Martin watched his father go forward.   35
"Overdyke. . . . Percy."

"I wish they'd hurry," Mrs. Dunbar said to her older son. "I wish they'd hurry."

"They're almost through," her son said.

"You get ready to run tell Dad," Mrs. Dunbar said.

Mr. Summers called his own name and then stepped forward precisely and selected a slip from the box. Then he called, "Warner."

"Seventy-seventh year I been in the lottery," Old Man Warner said   40
as he went through the crowd. "Seventy-seventh time."

"Watson." The tall boy came awkwardly through the crowd. Someone said, "Don't be nervous, Jack," and Mr. Summers said, "Take your time, son."

"Zanini."

After that, there was a long pause, a breathless pause, until Mr. Summers, holding his slip of paper in the air, said, "All right, fellows." For a minute, no one moved, and then all the slips of paper were opened. Suddenly, all women began to speak at once, saying, "Who is it?" "Who's got it?" "Is it the Dunbars?" "Is it the Watsons?" Then the voices began to say, "It's Hutchinson. It's Bill." "Bill Hutchinson's got it."

"Go tell your father," Mrs. Dunbar said to her older son.

People began to look around to see the Hutchinsons. Bill Hutchinson   45
was standing quiet, staring down at the paper in his hand. Suddenly, Tessie Hutchinson shouted to Mr. Summers, "You didn't give him time enough to take any paper he wanted. I saw you. It wasn't fair!"

"Be a good sport, Tessie," Mrs. Delacroix called, and Mrs. Graves said, "All of us took the same chance."

"Shut up, Tessie," Bill Hutchinson said.

"Well, everyone," Mr. Summers said, "that was done pretty fast, and now we've got to be hurrying a little more to get done in time." He consulted his next list. "Bill," he said, "you draw for the Hutchinson family. You got any other households in the Hutchinsons?"

"There's Don and Eva," Mrs. Hutchinson yelled. "Make them take their chance!"

"Daughters draw with their husbands' families, Tessie," Mr. Summers   50
said gently. "You know that as well as anyone else."

"It wasn't fair," Tessie said.

"I guess not, Joe," Bill Hutchinson said regretfully. "My daughter draws with her husband's family, that's only fair. And I've got no other family except the kids."

"Then, as far as drawing for families is concerned, it's you," Mr. Summers said in explanation, "and as far as drawing for households is concerned, that's you, too. Right?"

"Right," Bill Hutchinson said.

"How many kids, Bill?" Mr. Summers asked formally.   55

"Three," Bill Hutchinson said. "There's Bill, Jr., and Nancy, and little Dave. And Tessie and me."

"All right, then," Mr. Summers said. "Harry, you got their tickets back?"

Mr. Graves nodded and held up the slips of paper. "Put them in the box, then," Mr. Summers directed. "Take Bill's and put it in."

"I think we ought to start over," Mrs. Hutchinson said, as quietly as she could. "I tell you it wasn't *fair*. You didn't give him time enough to choose. *Everybody* saw that."

Mr. Graves had selected the five slips and put them in the box, and he   60
dropped all the papers but those onto the ground, where the breeze caught them and lifted them off.

"Listen, everybody," Mrs. Hutchinson was saying to the people around her.

"Ready, Bill?" Mr. Summers asked, and Bill Hutchinson, with one quick glance around at his wife and children, nodded.

"Remember," Mr. Summers said, "take the slips and keep them folded until each person has taken one. Harry, you help little Dave." Mr. Graves took the hand of the little boy, who came willingly with him up to the box. "Take a paper out of the box, Davy," Mr. Summers said. Davy put his hand into the box and laughed. "Take just *one* paper," Mr. Summers said. "Harry, you hold it for him." Mr. Graves took the child's hand and removed the folded paper from the tight fist and held it while little Dave stood next to him and looked up at him wonderingly.

"Nancy next," Mr. Summers said. Nancy was twelve, and her school friends breathed heavily as she went forward, switching her skirt, and took a slip daintily from the box. "Bill, Jr.," Mr. Summers said, and Billy, his face red and his feet over-large, nearly knocked the box over as he got a paper out. "Tessie," Mr. Summers said. She hesitated for a minute, looking around defiantly, and then set her lips and went up to the box. She snatched a paper out and held it behind her.

"Bill," Mr. Summers said, and Bill Hutchinson reached into the 65
box and felt around, bringing his hand out at last with the slip of paper
in it.

The crowd was quiet. A girl whispered, "I hope it's not Nancy," and
the sound of the whisper reached the edges of the crowd.

"It's not the way it used to be," Old Man Warner said clearly. "People
ain't the way they used to be."

"All right," Mr. Summers said. "Open the papers. Harry, you open
little Dave's."

Mr. Graves opened the slip of paper and there was a general sigh
through the crowd as he held it up and everyone could see that it was
blank. Nancy and Bill, Jr., opened theirs at the same time, and both
beamed and laughed, turning around to the crowd and holding their slips
of paper above their heads.

"Tessie," Mr. Summers said. There was a pause, and then Mr. Summers 70
looked at Bill Hutchinson, and Bill unfolded his paper and showed it. It was
blank.

"It's Tessie," Mr. Summers said, and his voice was hushed. "Show us her
paper, Bill."

Bill Hutchinson went over to his wife and forced the slip of paper out
of her hand. It had a black spot on it, the black spot Mr. Summers had
made the night before with the heavy pencil in the coal-company office.
Bill Hutchinson held it up, and there was a stir in the crowd.

"All right, folks," Mr. Summers said, "let's finish quickly."

Although the villagers had forgotten the ritual and lost the original
black box, they still remembered to use stones. The pile of stones the
boys had made earlier was ready; there were stones on the ground with
the blowing scraps of paper that had come out of the box. Mrs. Delacroix
selected a stone so large she had to pick it up with both hands and turned
to Mrs. Dunbar. "Come on," she said. "Hurry up."

Mrs. Dunbar had small stones in both hands, and she said, gasping 75
for breath, "I can't run at all. You'll have to go ahead and I'll catch up
with you."

The children had stones already, and someone gave little Davy
Hutchinson a few pebbles.

Tessie Hutchinson was in the center of a cleared space by now, and
she held her hands out desperately as the villagers moved in on her. "It
isn't fair," she said. A stone hit her on the side of the head.

Old Man Warner was saying, "Come on, come on, everyone." Steve
Adams was in the front of the crowd of villagers, with Mrs. Graves beside
him.

"It isn't fair, it isn't right," Mrs. Hutchinson screamed, and then they
were upon her.

QUESTIONS

1. Where do you think "The Lottery" takes place? What purpose do you suppose the writer has in making this setting appear so familiar and ordinary?
2. In paragraphs 2 and 3, what details foreshadow the ending of the story?
3. Take a close look at Jackson's description of the black wooden box (paragraph 5) and of the black spot on the fatal slip of paper (paragraph 72). What do these objects suggest to you? Are there any other symbols in the story?
4. What do you understand to be the writer's own attitude toward the lottery and the stoning? Exactly what in the story makes her attitude clear to us?
5. What do you make of Old Man Warner's saying, "Lottery in June, corn be heavy soon" (paragraph 32)?
6. What do you think Shirley Jackson is driving at? Consider each of the following interpretations and, looking at the story, see if you can find any evidence for it:

> Jackson takes a primitive fertility rite and playfully transfers it to a small town in North America.
>
> Jackson, writing her story soon after World War II, indirectly expresses her horror at the Holocaust. She assumes that the massacre of the Jews was carried out by unwitting, obedient people, like these villagers.
>
> Jackson is satirizing our own society, in which men are selected for the army by lottery.
>
> Jackson is just writing a memorable story that signifies nothing at all.

Charlotte Perkins Gilman

The Yellow Wallpaper   1892

Charlotte Perkins Gilman (1860–1935) was born in Hartford, Connecticut. Her father was the writer Frederick Beecher Perkins (a nephew of reformer-novelist Harriet Beecher Stowe, author of Uncle Tom's Cabin, *and abolitionist minister Henry Ward Beecher), but he abandoned the family shortly after his daughter's birth. Raised in meager surroundings, the young Gilman adopted her intellectual Beecher aunts as role models. Because she and her mother moved from one relation to another, Gilman's early education was neglected—at fifteen, she had had only four years of schooling. In 1878 she studied commercial art at the Rhode Island School of Design. In 1884 she married Walter Stetson, an artist. After the birth of her one*

CHARLOTTE PERKINS GILMAN

daughter, she experienced a severe depression. The rest cure her doctor prescribed became the basis of her most famous story, "The Yellow Wallpaper." This tale combines standard elements of Gothic fiction (the isolated country mansion, the brooding atmosphere of the room, the aloof but dominating husband) with the fresh clarity of Gilman's feminist perspective. Gilman's first marriage ended in an amicable divorce. A celebrated essayist and public speaker, she became an important early figure in American feminism. Her study Women and Economics *(1898) stressed the importance of both sexes having a place in the working world. Her feminist-Utopian novel* Herland *(1915) describes a thriving nation of women without men. In 1900 Gilman married a second time—this time, more happily—to her cousin George Houghton Gilman. Following his sudden death in 1934, Gilman discovered she had inoperable breast cancer. After finishing her autobiography, she killed herself with chloroform in Pasadena, California.*

It is very seldom that mere ordinary people like John and myself secure ancestral halls for the summer.

A colonial mansion, a hereditary estate, I would say a haunted house and reach the height of romantic felicity—but that would be asking too much of fate!

Still I will proudly declare that there is something queer about it.

Else, why should it be let so cheaply? And why have stood so long untenanted?

John laughs at me, of course, but one expects that.   5

John is practical in the extreme. He has no patience with faith, an intense horror of superstition, and he scoffs openly at any talk of things not to be felt and seen and put down in figures.

John is a physician, and *perhaps*—(I would not say it to a living soul, of course, but this is dead paper and a great relief to my mind)—*perhaps* that is one reason I do not get well faster.

You see, he does not believe I am sick! And what can one do?

If a physician of high standing, and one's own husband, assures friends and relatives that there is really nothing the matter with one but temporary nervous depression—a slight hysterical tendency—what is one to do?

My brother is also a physician, and also of high standing, and he says   10
the same thing.

So I take phosphates or phosphites—whichever it is—and tonics, and air and exercise, and journeys, and am absolutely forbidden to "work" until I am well again.

Personally, I disagree with their ideas.

Personally, I believe that congenial work, with excitement and change, would do me good.

But what is one to do?

I did write for a while in spite of them; but it *does* exhaust me a good   15
deal—having to be so sly about it, or else meet with heavy opposition.

I sometimes fancy that in my condition, if I had less opposition and more society and stimulus—but John says the very worst thing I can do is to think about my condition, and I confess it always makes me feel bad.

So I will let it alone and talk about the house.

The most beautiful place! It is quite alone, standing well back from the road, quite three miles from the village. It makes me think of English places that you read about, for there are hedges and walls and gates that lock, and lots of separate little houses for the gardeners and people.

There is a *delicious* garden! I never saw such a garden—large and shady, full of box-bordered paths, and lined with long grape-covered arbors with seats under them.

There were greenhouses, but they are all broken now.   20

There was some legal trouble, I believe, something about the heirs and co-heirs; anyhow, the place has been empty for years.

That spoils my ghostliness, I am afraid, but I don't care—there is something strange about the house—I can feel it.

I even said so to John one moonlight evening, but he said what I felt was a *draught,* and shut the window.

I get unreasonably angry with John sometimes. I'm sure I never used to be so sensitive. I think it is due to this nervous condition.

But John says if I feel so I shall neglect proper self-control; so I take   25
pains to control myself—before him, at least, and that makes me very tired.

I don't like our room a bit. I wanted one downstairs that opened onto the piazza and had roses all over the window, and such pretty old-fashioned chintz hangings! But John would not hear of it.

He said there was only one window and not room for two beds, and no near room for him if he took another.

He is very careful and loving, and hardly lets me stir without special direction.

I have a schedule prescription for each hour in the day; he takes all care from me, and so I feel basely ungrateful not to value it more.

He said he came here solely on my account, that I was to have per-   30
fect rest and all the air I could get. "Your exercise depends on your strength, my dear," said he, "and your food somewhat on your appetite; but air you can absorb all the time." So we took the nursery at the top of the house.

It is a big, airy room, the whole floor nearly, with windows that look all ways, and air and sunshine galore. It was a nursery first, and then play-room and gymnasium, I should judge, for the windows are barred for little children, and there are rings and things in the walls.

The paint and paper look as if a boys' school had used it. It is stripped off—the paper—in great patches all around the head of my bed, about as far as I can reach, and in a great place on the other side of the room low down. I never saw a worse paper in my life. One of those sprawling, flamboyant patterns committing every artistic sin.

It is dull enough to confuse the eye in following, pronounced enough constantly to irritate and provoke study, and when you follow the lame uncertain curves for a little distance they suddenly commit suicide—plunge off at outrageous angles, destroy themselves in unheard-of contradictions.

The color is repellent, almost revolting: a smouldering unclean yellow, strangely faded by the slow-turning sunlight. It is a dull yet lurid orange in some places, a sickly sulphur tint in others.

No wonder the children hated it! I should hate it myself if I had to   35
live in this room long.

There comes John, and I must put this away—he hates to have me write a word.

We have been here two weeks, and I haven't felt like writing before, since that first day.

I am sitting by the window now, up in this atrocious nursery, and there is nothing to hinder my writing as much as I please, save lack of strength.

John is away all day, and even some nights when his cases are serious.

I am glad my case is not serious!   40

But these nervous troubles are dreadfully depressing.

John does not know how much I really suffer. He knows there is no *reason* to suffer, and that satisfies him.

Of course it is only nervousness. It does weigh on me so not to do my duty in any way!

I meant to be such a help to John, such a real rest and comfort, and here I am a comparative burden already!

Nobody would believe what an effort it is to do what little I am   45
able—to dress and entertain, and order things.

It is fortunate Mary is so good with the baby. Such a dear baby!

And yet I *cannot* be with him, it makes me so nervous.

I suppose John never was nervous in his life. He laughs at me so about this wallpaper!

At first he meant to repaper the room, but afterward he said that I was letting it get the better of me, and that nothing was worse for a nervous patient than to give way to such fancies.

He said that after the wallpaper was changed it would be the heavy   50
bedstead, and then the barred windows, and then that gate at the head of the stairs, and so on.

"You know the place is doing you good," he said, "and really, dear, I don't care to renovate the house just for a three months' rental."

"Then do let us go downstairs," I said. "There are such pretty rooms there."

Then he took me in his arms and called me a blessed little goose, and said he would go down to the cellar, if I wished, and have it whitewashed into the bargain.

But he is right enough about the beds and windows and things.

It is as airy and comfortable a room as anyone need wish, and, of course, I would not be so silly as to make him uncomfortable just for a whim.   55

I'm really getting quite fond of the big room, all but that horrid paper.

Out of one window I can see the garden—those mysterious deep-shaded arbors, the riotous old-fashioned flowers, and bushes and gnarly trees.

Out of another I get a lovely view of the bay and a little private wharf belonging to the estate. There is a beautiful shaded lane that runs down there from the house. I always fancy I see people walking in these numerous paths and arbors, but John has cautioned me not to give way to fancy in the least. He says that with my imaginative power and habit of storymaking, a nervous weakness like mine is sure to lead to all manner of excited fancies, and that I ought to use my will and good sense to check the tendency. So I try.

I think sometimes that if I were only well enough to write a little it would relieve the press of ideas and rest me.

But I find I get pretty tired when I try.   60

It is so discouraging not to have any advice and companionship about my work. When I get really well, John says we will ask Cousin Henry and Julia down for a long visit; but he says he would as soon put fireworks in my pillow-case as to let me have those stimulating people about now.

I wish I could get well faster.

But I must not think about that. This paper looks to me as if it *knew* what a vicious influence it had!

There is a recurrent spot where the pattern lolls like a broken neck and two bulbous eyes stare at you upside down.

I get positively angry with the impertinence of it and the everlasting-   65
ness. Up and down and sideways they crawl, and those absurd unblinking eyes are everywhere. There is one place where two breadths didn't match, and the eyes go all up and down the line, one a little higher than the other.

I never saw so much expression in an inanimate thing before, and we all know how much expression they have! I used to lie awake as a child and get more entertainment and terror out of blank walls and plain furniture than most children could find in a toy-store.

I remember what a kindly wink the knobs of our big old bureau used to have, and there was one chair that always seemed like a strong friend.

I used to feel that if any of the other things looked too fierce I could always hop into that chair and be safe.

The furniture in this room is no worse than inharmonious, however, for we had to bring it all from downstairs. I suppose when this was used as a playroom they had to take the nursery things out, and no wonder! I never saw such ravages as the children have made here.

The wallpaper, as I said before, is torn off in spots, and it sticketh closer than a brother—they must have had perseverance as well as hatred. 70

Then the floor is scratched and gouged and splintered, the plaster itself is dug out here and there, and this great heavy bed, which is all we found in the room, looks as if it had been through the wars.

But I don't mind it a bit—only the paper.

There comes John's sister. Such a dear girl as she is, and so careful of me! I must not let her find me writing.

She is a perfect and enthusiastic housekeeper, and hopes for no better profession. I verily believe she thinks it is the writing which made me sick!

But I can write when she is out, and see her a long way off from these windows. 75

There is one that commands the road, a lovely shaded winding road, and one that just looks off over the country. A lovely country, too, full of great elms and velvet meadows.

This wallpaper has a kind of subpattern in a different shade, a particularly irritating one, for you can only see it in certain lights, and not clearly then.

But in the places where it isn't faded and where the sun is just so—I can see a strange, provoking, formless sort of figure that seems to skulk about behind that silly and conspicuous front design.

There's sister on the stairs!

Well, the Fourth of July is over! The people are all gone, and I am tired out. John thought it might do me good to see a little company, so we just had Mother and Nellie and the children down for a week. 80

Of course I didn't do a thing. Jennie sees to everything now.

But it tired me all the same.

John says if I don't pick up faster he shall send me to Weir Mitchell° in the fall.

But I don't want to go there at all. I had a friend who was in his hands once, and she says he is just like John and my brother, only more so!

Besides, it is such an undertaking to go so far. 85

I don't feel as if it was worthwhile to turn my hand over for anything, and I'm getting dreadfully fretful and querulous.

I cry at nothing, and cry most of the time.

Weir Mitchell (1829–1914): famed nerve specialist who actually treated the author, Charlotte Perkins Gilman, for nervous prostration with his well-known "rest cure." (The cure was not successful.) Also the author of *Diseases of the Nervous System, Especially of Women* (1881).

Of course I don't when John is here, or anybody else, but when I am alone.

And I am alone a good deal just now. John is kept in town very often by serious cases, and Jennie is good and lets me alone when I want her to.

So I walk a little in the garden or down that lovely lane, sit on the   90
porch under the roses, and lie down up here a good deal.

I'm getting really fond of the room in spite of the wallpaper. Perhaps *because* of the wallpaper.

It dwells in my mind so!

I lie here on this great immovable bed—it is nailed down, I believe—and follow that pattern about by the hour. It is as good as gymnastics, I assure you. I start, we'll say, at the bottom, down in the corner over there where it has not been touched, and I determine for the thousandth time that I *will* follow that pointless pattern to some sort of a conclusion.

I know a little of the principle of design, and I know this thing was not arranged on any laws of radiation,° or alternation, or repetition, or symmetry, or anything else that I ever heard of.

It is repeated, of course, by the breadths, but not otherwise.   95

Looked at in one way, each breadth stands alone; the bloated curves and flourishes—a kind of "debased Romanesque" with *delirium tremens*— go waddling up and down in isolated columns of fatuity.

But, on the other hand, they connect diagonally, and the sprawling outlines run off in great slanting waves of optic horror, like a lot of wallowing sea-weeds in full chase.

The whole thing goes horizontally, too, at least it seems so, and I exhaust myself trying to distinguish the order of its going in that direction.

They have used a horizontal breadth for a frieze, and that adds wonderfully to the confusion.

There is one end of the room where it is almost intact, and there,   100
when the crosslights fade and the low sun shines directly upon it, I can almost fancy radiation after all—the interminable grotesque seems to form around a common center and rush off in headlong plunges of equal distraction.

It makes me tired to follow it. I will take a nap, I guess.

I don't know why I should write this.

I don't want to.

I don't feel able.

And I know John would think it absurd. But I *must* say what I feel   105
and think in some way—it is such a relief!

---

laws of radiation: a principle of design in which all elements are arranged in some circular
pattern around a center.

*

But the effort is getting to be greater than the relief.

Half the time now I am awfully lazy, and lie down ever so much. John says I mustn't lose my strength, and has me take cod liver oil and lots of tonics and things, to say nothing of ale and wines and rare meat.

Dear John! He loves me very dearly, and hates to have me sick. I tried to have a real earnest reasonable talk with him the other day, and tell him how I wish he would let me go and make a visit to Cousin Henry and Julia.

But he said I wasn't able to go, nor able to stand it after I got there; and I did not make out a very good case for myself, for I was crying before I had finished.

It is getting to be a great effort for me to think straight. Just this nervous weakness, I suppose.

And dear John gathered me up in his arms, and just carried me upstairs and laid me on the bed, and sat by me and read to me till it tired my head.

He said I was his darling and his comfort and all he had, and that I must take care of myself for his sake, and keep well.

He says no one but myself can help me out of it, that I must use my will and self-control and not let any silly fancies run away with me.

There's one comfort—the baby is well and happy, and does not have to occupy this nursery with the horrid wallpaper.

If we had not used it, that blessed child would have! What a fortunate escape! Why, I wouldn't have a child of mine, an impressionable little thing, live in such a room for worlds.

I never thought of it before, but it is lucky that John kept me here after all; I can stand it so much easier than a baby, you see.

Of course I never mention it to them any more—I am too wise—but I keep watch for it all the same.

There are things in the wallpaper that nobody knows about but me, or ever will.

Behind that outside pattern the dim shapes get clearer every day.

It is always the same shape, only very numerous.

And it is like a woman stooping down and creeping about behind that pattern. I don't like it a bit. I wonder—I begin to think—I wish John would take me away from here!

It is so hard to talk with John about my case, because he is so wise, and because he loves me so.

But I tried it last night.

It was moonlight. The moon shines in all around just as the sun does.

I hate to see it sometimes, it creeps so slowly, and always comes in by one window or another.

John was asleep and I hated to waken him, so I kept still and watched the moonlight on that undulating wallpaper till I felt creepy.

The faint figure behind seemed to shake the pattern, just as if she wanted to get out.

I got up softly and went to feel and see if the paper *did* move, and when I came back John was awake.

"What is it, little girl?" he said. "Don't go walking about like that— you'll get cold."

I thought it was a good time to talk, so I told him that I really was not gaining here, and that I wished he would take me away.

"Why, darling!" said he. "Our lease will be up in three weeks, and I can't see how to leave before.

"The repairs are not done at home, and I cannot possibly leave town just now. Of course, if you were in any danger, I could and would, but you really are better, dear, whether you can see it or not. I am a doctor, dear, and I know. You are gaining flesh and color, your appetite is better, I feel really much easier about you."

"I don't weigh a bit more," said I, "nor as much; and my appetite may be better in the evening when you are here but it is worse in the morning when you are away!"

"Bless her little heart!" said he with a big hug. "She shall be as sick as she pleases! But now let's improve the shining hours by going to sleep, and talk about it in the morning!"

"And you won't go away?" I asked gloomily.

"Why, how can I, dear? It is only three weeks more and then we will take a nice little trip for a few days while Jennie is getting the house ready. Really, dear, you are better!"

"Better in body perhaps—" I began, and stopped short, for he sat up straight and looked at me with such a stern, reproachful look that I could not say another word.

"My darling," said he, "I beg you, for my sake and for our child's sake, as well as for your own, that you will never for one instant let that idea enter your mind! There is nothing so dangerous, so fascinating, to a temperament like yours. It is a false and foolish fancy. Can you trust me as a physician when I tell you so?"

So of course I said no more on that score, and we went to sleep before long. He thought I was asleep first, but I wasn't, and lay there for hours trying to decide whether that front pattern and the back pattern really did move together or separately.

On a pattern like this, by daylight, there is a lack of sequence, a defiance of law, that is a constant irritant to a normal mind.

The color is hideous enough, and unreliable enough, and infuriating enough, but the pattern is torturing.

You think you have mastered it, but just as you get well under way in following, it turns a back-somersault and there you are. It slaps you in the face, knocks you down, and tramples upon you. It is like a bad dream.

130

135

140

The outside pattern is a florid arabesque,° reminding one of a fungus. If you can imagine a toadstool in joints, an interminable string of toadstools, budding and sprouting in endless convolutions—why, that is something like it.

That is, sometimes!

There is one marked peculiarity about this paper, a thing nobody   145
seems to notice but myself, and that is that it changes as the light changes.

When the sun shoots in through the east window—I always watch for that first long, straight ray—it changes so quickly that I never can quite believe it.

That is why I watch it always.

By moonlight—the moon shines in all night when there is a moon—I wouldn't know it was the same paper.

At night in any kind of light, in twilight, candlelight, lamplight, and worst of all by moonlight, it becomes bars! The outside pattern, I mean, and the woman behind it is as plain as can be.

I didn't realize for a long time what the thing was that showed behind,   150
that dim subpattern, but now I am quite sure it is a woman.

By daylight she is subdued, quiet. I fancy it is the pattern that keeps her so still. It is so puzzling. It keeps me quiet by the hour.

I lie down ever so much now. John says it is good for me, and to sleep all I can.

Indeed he started the habit by making me lie down for an hour after each meal.

It is a very bad habit, I am convinced, for you see, I don't sleep.

And that cultivates deceit, for I don't tell them I'm awake—oh, no!   155

The fact is I am getting a little afraid of John.

He seems very queer sometimes, and even Jennie has an inexplicable look.

It strikes me occasionally, just as a scientific hypothesis, that perhaps it is the paper!

I have watched John when he did not know I was looking, and come into the room suddenly on the most innocent excuses, and I've caught him several times *looking at the paper!* And Jennie too. I caught Jennie with her hand on it once.

She didn't know I was in the room, and when I asked her in a   160
quiet, a very quiet voice, with the most restrained manner possible, what she was doing with the paper, she turned around as if she had been caught stealing, and looked quite angry—asked me why I should frighten her so!

---

arabesque: a type of ornamental style (Arabic in origin) that uses flowers, foliage, fruit, or other figures to create an intricate pattern of interlocking shapes and lines.

Then she said that the paper stained everything it touched, that she had found yellow smooches° on all my clothes and John's and she wished we would be more careful!

Did not that sound innocent? But I know she was studying that pattern, and I am determined that nobody shall find it out but myself!

Life is very much more exciting now than it used to be. You see, I have something more to expect, to look forward to, to watch. I really do eat better, and am more quiet than I was.

John is so pleased to see me improve! He laughed a little the other day, and said I seemed to be flourishing in spite of my wallpaper.

I turned it off with a laugh. I had no intention of telling him it was   165
because of the wallpaper—he would make fun of me. He might even want to take me away.

I don't want to leave now until I have found it out. There is a week more, and I think that will be enough.

I'm feeling so much better!

I don't sleep much at night, for it is so interesting to watch developments; but I sleep a good deal during the daytime.

In the daytime it is tiresome and perplexing.

There are always new shoots on the fungus, and new shades of yellow all   170
over it. I cannot keep count of them, though I have tried conscientiously.

It is the strangest yellow, that wallpaper! It makes me think of all the yellow things I ever saw—not beautiful ones like buttercups, but old, foul, bad yellow things.

But there is something else about that paper—the smell! I noticed it the moment we came into the room, but with so much air and sun it was not bad. Now we have had a week of fog and rain, and whether the windows are open or not, the smell is here.

It creeps all over the house.

I find it hovering in the dining-room, skulking in the parlor, hiding in the hall, lying in wait for me on the stairs.

It gets into my hair.   175

Even when I go to ride, if I turn my head suddenly and surprise it— there is that smell!

Such a peculiar odor, too! I have spent hours in trying to analyze it, to find what it smelled like.

It is not bad—at first—and very gentle, but quite the subtlest, most enduring odor I ever met.

In this damp weather it is awful. I wake up in the night and find it hanging over me.

smooches: smudges or smears.

It used to disturb me at first. I thought seriously of burning the 180
house—to reach the smell.

But now I am used to it. The only thing I can think of that it is like
is the *color* of the paper! A yellow smell.

There is a very funny mark on this wall, low down, near the mop-
board. A streak that runs round the room. It goes behind every piece of
furniture, except the bed, a long, straight, even *smooch*, as if it had been
rubbed over and over.

I wonder how it was done and who did it, and what they did it for.
Round and round and round—round and round and round—it makes me
dizzy!

I really have discovered something at last.

Through watching so much at night, when it changes so, I have 185
finally found out.

The front pattern *does* move—and no wonder! The woman behind
shakes it!

Sometimes I think there are a great many women behind, and sometimes only one, and she crawls around fast, and her crawling shakes it all
over.

Then in the very bright spots she keeps still, and in the very shady spots
she just takes hold of the bars and shakes them hard.

And she is all the time trying to climb through. But nobody could climb
through that pattern—it strangles so; I think that is why it has so many
heads.

They get through and then the pattern strangles them off and turns 190
them upside down, and makes their eyes white!

If those heads were covered or taken off it would not be half so bad.

I think that woman gets out in the daytime!

And I'll tell you why—privately—I've seen her!

I can see her out of every one of my windows!

It is the same woman, I know, for she is always creeping, and most 195
women do not creep by daylight.

I see her in that long shaded lane, creeping up and down. I see her in
those dark grape arbors, creeping all round the garden.

I see her on that long road under the trees, creeping along, and when
a carriage comes she hides under the blackberry vines.

I don't blame her a bit. It must be very humiliating to be caught
creeping by daylight!

I always lock the door when I creep by daylight. I can't do it at night,
for I know John would suspect something at once.

And John is so queer now that I don't want to irritate him. I wish 200
he would take another room! Besides, I don't want anybody to get that
woman out at night but myself.

I often wonder if I could see her out of all the windows at once.

But, turn as fast as I can, I can only see out of one at one time.

And though I always see her, she *may* be able to creep faster than I can turn! I have watched her sometimes away off in the open country, creeping as fast as a cloud shadow in a wind.

If only that top pattern could be gotten off from the under one! I mean to try it, little by little.

I have found out another funny thing, but I shan't tell it this time! It does not do to trust people too much.

There are only two more days to get this paper off, and I believe John is beginning to notice. I don't like the look in his eyes.

And I heard him ask Jennie a lot of professional questions about me. She had a very good report to give.

She said I slept a good deal in the daytime.

John knows I don't sleep very well at night, for all I'm so quiet!

He asked me all sorts of questions too, and pretended to be very loving and kind.

As if I couldn't see through him!

Still, I don't wonder he acts so, sleeping under this paper for three months.

It only interests me, but I feel sure John and Jennie are affected by it.

Hurrah! This is the last day, but it is enough. John is to stay in town over night, and won't be out until this evening.

Jennie wanted to sleep with me—the sly thing; but I told her I should undoubtedly rest better for a night all alone.

That was clever, for really I wasn't alone a bit! As soon as it was moonlight and that poor thing began to crawl and shake the pattern, I got up and ran to help her.

I pulled and she shook. I shook and she pulled, and before morning we had peeled off yards of that paper.

A strip about as high as my head and half around the room.

And then when the sun came and that awful pattern began to laugh at me, I declared I would finish it today!

We go away tomorrow, and they are moving all my furniture down again to leave things as they were before.

Jennie looked at the wall in amazement, but I told her merrily that I did it out of pure spite at the vicious thing.

She laughed and said she wouldn't mind doing it herself, but I must not get tired.

How she betrayed herself that time!

But I am here, and no person touches this paper but Me—not *alive!*

She tried to get me out of the room—it was too patent! But I said it was so quiet and empty and clean now that I believed I would lie down again and sleep all I could, and not to wake me even for dinner—I would call when I woke.

So now she is gone, and the servants are gone, and the things are gone, and there is nothing left but that great bedstead nailed down, with the canvas mattress we found on it.

We shall sleep downstairs tonight, and take the boat home tomorrow.

I quite enjoy the room, now it is bare again.

How those children did tear about here!

This bedstead is fairly gnawed!   230

But I must get to work.

I have locked the door and thrown the key down into the front path.

I don't want to go out, and I don't want to have anybody come in, till John comes.

I want to astonish him.

I've got a rope up here that even Jennie did not find. If that woman   235 does get out, and tries to get away, I can tie her!

But I forgot I could not reach far without anything to stand on!

This bed will *not* move!

I tried to lift and push it until I was lame, and then I got so angry I bit off a little piece at one corner—but it hurt my teeth.

Then I peeled off all the paper I could reach standing on the floor. It sticks horribly and the pattern just enjoys it! All those strangled heads and bulbous eyes and waddling fungus growths just shriek with derision!

I am getting angry enough to do something desperate. To jump out   240 of the window would be admirable exercise, but the bars are too strong even to try.

Besides I wouldn't do it. Of course not. I know well enough that a step like that is improper and might be misconstrued.

I don't like to *look* out of the windows even—there are so many of those creeping women, and they creep so fast.

I wonder if they all come out of that wallpaper as I did!

But I am securely fastened now by my well-hidden rope—you don't get *me* out in the road there!

I suppose I shall have to get back behind the pattern when it comes   245 night, and that is hard!

It is so pleasant to be out in this great room and creep around as I please!

I don't want to go outside. I won't, even if Jennie asks me to.

For outside you have to creep on the ground, and everything is green instead of yellow.

But here I can creep smoothly on the floor, and my shoulder just fits in that long smooch around the wall, so I cannot lose my way.

Why, there's John at the door!   250

It is no use, young man, you can't open it!

How he does call and pound!

Now he's crying to Jennie for an axe.

It would be a shame to break down that beautiful door!

"John, dear!" said I in the gentlest voice. "The key is down by the   255
front steps, under a plantain leaf!"

That silenced him for a few moments.

Then he said, very quietly indeed, "Open the door, my darling!"

"I can't," said I. "The key is down by the front door under a plantain
leaf!" And then I said it again, several times, very gently and slowly, and
said it so often that he had to go and see, and he got it of course, and
came in. He stopped short by the door.

"What is the matter?" he cried. "For God's sake, what are you doing!"

I kept on creeping just the same, but I looked at him over my   260
shoulder.

"I've got out at last," said I, "in spite of you and Jane. And I've pulled
off most of the paper, so you can't put me back!"

Now why should that man have fainted? But he did, and right
across my path by the wall, so that I had to creep over him every
time!

QUESTIONS

1. Several times at the beginning of the story, the narrator says such things as
   "What is one to do?" and "What can one do?" What do these comments refer to?
   What, if anything, do they suggest about women's roles at the time the story was
   written?

2. The narrator says, "I get unreasonably angry with John sometimes" (paragraph
   24). How unreasonable is her anger at him? What does the fact that she feels it is
   unreasonable say about her?

3. What do her changing feelings about the wallpaper tell us about the changes in
   her condition?

4. "It is so hard to talk with John about my case, because he is so wise, and because he loves me so" (paragraph 122). His wisdom is, to say the least, open
   to question, but what about his love? Do you think he suffers merely from a
   failure of perception, or is there a failure of affection as well? Explain your
   response.

5. Where precisely in the story do you think it becomes clear that she has begun to
   hallucinate?

6. What does the woman behind the wallpaper represent? Why does the narrator
   come to identify with her?

7. How ill does the narrator seem at the beginning of the story? How ill does she
   seem at the end? How do you account for the change in her condition?

WRITING EFFECTIVELY

Recognizing Symbols

One danger in analyzing a story's symbolism is the temptation to read symbolic meaning into *everything*. Writers don't simply assign arbitrary meanings to items in their stories; generally, a horse is a horse, and a hammer is just a hammer. Sometimes, though, an object means something more to a character. Think of the flowers in "The Chrysanthemums." An image acquires symbolic resonance because it is organically important to the actions and emotions of the story.

To "read" a symbol, ask yourself what it means to the protagonist of your story. Consider a symbolic object's relevance to the plot. What events, characters, and ideas are associated with it? It also helps to remember that some symbols arrive with cultural baggage. Any great white whale that swims into a work of contemporary fiction will inevitably summon up the symbolic associations of Melville's fish Moby Dick.

When you write about symbols, remember: in literature, few symbols are hidden. Don't go on a symbol hunt. As you read or reread a story, any real symbol will usually find you. If an object appears time and again, or is tied inextricably to the story's events, it's likely to suggest something beyond itself. When an object, an action, or a place has emotional or intellectual power beyond its literal importance, then it is a genuine symbol.

CHECKLIST

Thinking About Symbols

- ✓ Which objects, actions, or places seem unusually significant?
- ✓ List the specific objects, people, and ideas with which a particular symbol is associated.
- ✓ Locate the exact place in the story where the symbol links itself to the other thing.
- ✓ Ask whether each symbol comes with ready-made cultural associations. If so, what are these?
- ✓ Avoid far-fetched interpretations. Focus first on the literal things, places, and actions in the story.
- ✓ Don't make a symbol mean too much or too little; don't limit it to one narrow association or claim it summons up many different things.
- ✓ Be specific. Identify the exact place in the story where a symbol takes on a deeper meaning.

WRITING ASSIGNMENT ON SYMBOLS

From the stories in this book, choose one with a strong central symbol. Explain how the symbol helps to communicate the story's meaning, citing specific moments in the text.

MORE TOPICS FOR WRITING

1. Choose a story from this chapter. Describe your experience of reading that story, and of encountering its symbols. At what point did the main symbol's meaning become clear? What in the story indicated the larger importance of that symbol?

2. From any story in this book, select an object, or place, or action that seems clearly symbolic. How do you know? Now select an object, place, or action from the same story that clearly seems to signify no more than itself. How can you tell?

3. Analyze the symbolism in a story from another chapter of this book. Some good choices might be "Dead Men's Path," "The Story of an Hour," and "Where Are You Going, Where Have You Been?" Choose a symbol that recurs over the course of the story, and look closely at each appearance it makes. How does the story's use of the symbol evolve?

8

Stories for Further Reading

Margaret Atwood

Happy Endings

MARGARET ATWOOD

1983

Born in Ottawa, Ontario, in 1939, Margaret Eleanor Atwood was the daughter of an entomologist and spent her childhood summers in the forests of northern Quebec, where her father carried out research. Atwood began writing at the age of five and had already seriously entertained thoughts of becoming a professional writer before she finished high school. She graduated from the University of Toronto in 1961, and later did graduate work at Radcliffe and Harvard. Atwood first gained prominence as a poet. Her first full-length collection of poems, The Circle Game *(1966), was awarded a Governor General's Award, Canada's most prestigious literary honor, and she has published nearly twenty volumes of verse. Atwood also began to write fiction seriously in graduate school, and her short stories were first collected in* Dancing Girls *(1977), followed by* Bluebeard's Egg *(1983),* Murder in the Dark *(1983),* Wilderness Tips *(1991),* Good Bones *(1992), and* Moral Disorder *(2006). Among her other influential books is* Survival: A Thematic Guide to Canadian Literature *(1972), in which she argued that Canadian writers should turn from British and American models to a fuller utilization of their own cultural heritage.*

A dedicated feminist, Atwood chose the title of Dancing Girls *with care, alluding to women who are forced to move in patterns determined by a patriarchal society. In her later works of fiction she has continued to explore the complex relations between the sexes, most incisively in* The Handmaid's Tale *(1986), a futuristic novel about a world in which gender roles are ruthlessly enforced by a society based on religious fundamentalism. In the same year that* The Handmaid's Tale *appeared, Atwood was named Woman of the Year by* Ms. *magazine. Subsequent novels include* Cat's Eye *(1988),* The Robber Bride *(1993),* The Blind Assassin *(2000),* Oryx and Crake *(2003), and* The Penelopiad *(2005). Atwood has served as writer-in-residence at universities in Canada, the United States, and Europe, and she has been widely in demand for appearances at symposia devoted to literature and women's issues.* Negotiating with the Dead: A Writer on Writing *(2002) and* Writing with Intent: Essays, Reviews, Personal Prose 1983–2005 *(2005) are recent collections of her nonfiction.*

John and Mary meet.
What happens next?
If you want a happy ending, try A.

A

John and Mary fall in love and get married. They both have worthwhile and remunerative jobs which they find stimulating and challenging. They buy a charming house. Real estate values go up. Eventually, when they can afford live-in help, they have two children, to whom they are devoted. The children turn out well. John and Mary have a stimulating and challenging sex life and worthwhile friends. They go on fun vacations together. They retire. They both have hobbies which they find stimulating and challenging. Eventually they die. This is the end of the story.

B

Mary falls in love with John but John doesn't fall in love with Mary. He merely uses her body for selfish pleasure and ego gratification of a tepid kind. He comes to her apartment twice a week and she cooks him dinner, you'll notice that he doesn't even consider her worth the price of a dinner out, and after he's eaten the dinner he fucks her and after that he falls asleep, while she does the dishes so he won't think she's untidy, having all those dirty dishes lying around, and puts on fresh lipstick so she'll look good when he wakes up, but when he wakes up he doesn't even notice, he puts on his socks and his shorts and his pants and his shirt and his tie and his shoes, the reverse order from the one in which he took them off. He doesn't take off Mary's clothes, she takes them off herself, she acts as if she's dying for it every time, not because she likes sex exactly, she doesn't, but she wants John to think she does because if they do it often enough surely he'll get used to her, he'll come to depend on her and they will get married, but John goes out the door with hardly so much as a good-night and three days later he turns up at six o'clock and they do the whole thing over again.

Mary gets run-down. Crying is bad for your face, everyone knows that and so does Mary but she can't stop. People at work notice. Her friends tell her John is a rat, a pig, a dog, he isn't good enough for her, but she can't believe it. Inside John, she thinks, is another John, who is much nicer. This other John will emerge like a butterfly from a cocoon, a Jack from a box, a pit from a prune, if the first John is only squeezed enough.

One evening John complains about the food. He has never complained   5 about the food before. Mary is hurt.

Her friends tell her they've seen him in a restaurant with another woman, whose name is Madge. It's not even Madge that finally gets to Mary; it's the restaurant. John has never taken Mary to a restaurant. Mary collects all the sleeping pills and aspirins she can find, and takes them and a half a bottle of sherry. You can see what kind of a woman she is by the fact that it's not even whiskey. She leaves a note for John. She hopes he'll discover her and get her to the hospital in time and repent and then they can get married, but this fails to happen and she dies.

John marries Madge and everything continues as in A.

C

John, who is an older man, falls in love with Mary, and Mary, who is only twenty-two, feels sorry for him because he's worried about his hair falling out. She sleeps with him even though she's not in love with him. She met him at work. She's in love with someone called James, who is twenty-two also and not yet ready to settle down.

John on the contrary settled down long ago: this is what is bothering him. John has a steady, respectable job and is getting ahead in his field, but Mary isn't impressed by him, she's impressed by James, who has a motorcycle and a fabulous record collection. But James is often away on his motorcycle, being free. Freedom isn't the same for girls, so in the meantime Mary spends Thursday evenings with John. Thursdays are the only days John can get away.

John is married to a woman called Madge and they have two children,   10 a charming house which they bought just before the real estate values went up, and hobbies which they find stimulating and challenging, when they have the time. John tells Mary how important she is to him, but of course, he can't leave his wife because a commitment is a commitment. He goes on about this more than is necessary and Mary finds it boring, but older men can keep it up longer so on the whole she has a fairly good time.

One day James breezes in on his motorcycle with some top-grade California hybrid and James and Mary get higher than you'd believe possible and they climb into bed. Everything becomes very underwater, but along comes John, who has a key to Mary's apartment. He finds them stoned and entwined. He's hardly in any position to be jealous, considering Madge, but nevertheless he's overcome with despair. Finally he's middle-aged, in two years he'll be bald as an egg and he can't stand it. He purchases a handgun, saying he needs it for target practice—this is the thin part of the plot, but it can be dealt with later—and shoots the two of them and himself.

Madge, after a suitable period of mourning, marries an understanding man called Fred and everything continues as in A, but under different names.

D

Fred and Madge have no problems. They get along exceptionally well and are good at working out any little difficulties that may arise. But their charming house is by the seashore and one day a giant tidal wave approaches. Real estate values go down. The rest of the story is about what caused the tidal wave and how they escape from it. They do, though thousands drown, but Fred and Madge are virtuous and lucky. Finally on high ground they clasp each other, wet and dripping and grateful, and continue as in A.

E

Yes, but Fred has a bad heart. The rest of the story is about how kind and understanding they both are until Fred dies. Then Madge devotes herself to charity work until the end of A. If you like, it can be "Madge," "cancer," "guilty and confused," and "bird watching."

F

If you think this is all too bourgeois, make John a revolutionary and   15
Mary a counterespionage agent and see how far that gets you. Remember, this is Canada. You'll still end up with A, though in between you may get a lustful brawling saga of passionate involvement, a chronicle of our times, sort of.

You'll have to face it, the endings are the same however you slice it. Don't be deluded by any other endings, they're all fake, either deliberately fake, with malicious intent to deceive, or just motivated by excessive optimism if not by downright sentimentality.

The only authentic ending is the one provided here:
John and Mary die. John and Mary die. John and Mary die.

So much for endings. Beginnings are almost more fun. True connoisseurs, however, are known to favor the stretch in between, since it's the hardest to do anything with.

That's about all that can be said for plots, which anyway are just one   20
thing after another, a what and a what and a what.

Now try How and Why.

Kate Chopin

The Story of an Hour

1894

Kate Chopin (1851–1904) demonstrates again, as in "The Storm" in Chapter 4, her ability to write short stories of compressed intensity. For a brief biography and a portrait see page 81.

Knowing that Mrs. Mallard was afflicted with a heart trouble, great care was taken to break to her as gently as possible the news of her husband's death.

It was her sister Josephine who told her, in broken sentences, veiled hints that revealed in half concealing. Her husband's friend Richards was there, too, near her. It was he who had been in the newspaper office when intelligence of the railroad disaster was received, with Brently Mallard's name leading the list of "killed." He had only taken the time to assure himself of its truth by a second telegram, and had hastened to forestall any less careful, less tender friend in bearing the sad message.

She did not hear the story as many women have heard the same, with a paralyzed inability to accept its significance. She wept at once, with sudden, wild abandonment, in her sister's arms. When the storm of grief had spent itself she went away to her room alone. She would have no one follow her.

There stood, facing the open window, a comfortable, roomy armchair. Into this she sank, pressed down by a physical exhaustion that haunted her body and seemed to reach into her soul.

She could see in the open square before her house the tops of trees that were all aquiver with the new spring life. The delicious breath of rain was in the air. In the street below a peddler was crying his wares. The notes of a distant song which some one was singing reached her faintly, and countless sparrows were twittering in the eaves.

There were patches of blue sky showing here and there through the clouds that had met and piled one above the other in the west facing her window.

She sat with her head thrown back upon the cushion of the chair, quite motionless, except when a sob came up into her throat and shook her, as a child who has cried itself to sleep continues to sob in its dreams.

She was young, with a fair, calm face, whose lines bespoke repression and even a certain strength. But now there was a dull stare in her eyes, whose gaze was fixed away off yonder on one of those patches of blue sky. It was not a glance of reflection, but rather indicated a suspension of intelligent thought.

There was something coming to her and she was waiting for it, fearfully. What was it? She did not know; it was too subtle and elusive to name. But she felt it, creeping out of the sky, reaching toward her through the sounds, the scents, the color that filled the air.

Now her bosom rose and fell tumultuously. She was beginning to 10 recognize this thing that was approaching to possess her, and she was striving to beat it back with her will—as powerless as her two white slender hands would have been.

When she abandoned herself a little whispered word escaped her slightly parted lips. She said it over and over under her breath: "Free, free, free!" The vacant stare and the look of terror that had followed it went from her eyes. They stayed keen and bright. Her pulses beat fast, and the coursing blood warmed and relaxed every inch of her body.

She did not stop to ask if it were not a monstrous joy that held her. A clear and exalted perception enabled her to dismiss the suggestion as trivial.

She knew that she would weep again when she saw the kind, tender hands folded in death; the face that had never looked save with love upon her, fixed and gray and dead. But she saw beyond that bitter moment a long procession of years to come that would belong to her absolutely. And she opened and spread her arms out to them in welcome.

There would be no one to live for during those coming years; she would live for herself. There would be no powerful will bending her in that blind persistence with which men and women believe they have a right to impose a private will upon a fellow creature. A kind intention or a cruel intention made the act seem no less a crime as she looked upon it in that brief moment of illumination.

And yet she had loved him—sometimes. Often she had not. What 15 did it matter! What could love, the unsolved mystery, count for in face of this possession of self-assertion which she suddenly recognized as the strongest impulse of her being.

"Free! Body and soul free!" she kept whispering.

Josephine was kneeling before the closed door with her lips to the keyhole, imploring for admission. "Louise, open the door! I beg; open the door—you will make yourself ill. What are you doing, Louise? For heaven's sake open the door."

"Go away. I am not making myself ill." No; she was drinking in a very elixir of life through that open window.

Her fancy was running riot along those days ahead of her. Spring days, and summer days, and all sorts of days that would be her own. She breathed a quick prayer that life might be long. It was only yesterday she had thought with a shudder that life might be long.

She arose at length and opened the door to her sister's importuni- 20 ties. There was a feverish triumph in her eyes, and she carried herself unwittingly like a goddess of Victory. She clasped her sister's waist, and together they descended the stairs. Richards stood waiting for them at the bottom.

Some one was opening the front door with a latchkey. It was Brently Mallard who entered, a little travel-stained, composedly carrying his gripsack and umbrella. He had been far from the scene of the accident, and did not even know there had been one. He stood amazed at Josephine's piercing cry; at Richards' quick motion to screen him from the view of his wife.

But Richards was too late.

When the doctors came they said she had died of heart disease—of joy that kills.

Sandra Cisneros

The House on Mango Street   1984

Sandra Cisneros was born in Chicago in 1954. The child of a Mexican father and a Mexican American mother, she was the only daughter in a family of seven children. She attended Loyola University of Chicago and then received a master's degree from the University of Iowa Writers' Workshop. She has instructed high-school dropouts, but more recently she has taught as a visiting writer at numerous universities, including the University of California at Irvine and at Berkeley, and the University of Michigan. Her honors include fellowships from the National Endowment for the Arts and the MacArthur Foundation. Cisneros's first published work was poetry: Bad Boys *(1980),* My Wicked Wicked Ways *(1987), and* Loose Woman *(1994). Her fiction collections,* The House on Mango Street *(1984) and* Women Hollering Creek *(1991), however, earned her a broader audience. She has also published a bilingual children's book,* Hairs: Pelitos *(1994), and a novel,* Caramelo *(2002). Cisneros currently lives in San Antonio, Texas.*

SANDRA CISNEROS

We didn't always live on Mango Street. Before that we lived on Loomis on the third floor, and before that we lived on Keeler. Before Keeler it was Paulina, and before that I can't remember. But what I remember most is moving a lot. Each time it seemed there'd be one more of us. By the time we got to Mango Street we were six—Mama, Papa, Carlos, Kiki, my sister Nenny, and me.

The house on Mango Street is ours, and we don't have to pay rent to anybody, or share the yard with the people downstairs, or be careful not to make too much noise, and there isn't a landlord banging on the ceiling with a broom. But even so, it's not the house we'd thought we'd get.

We had to leave the flat on Loomis quick. The water pipes broke and the landlord wouldn't fix them because the house was too old. We had to leave fast. We were using the washroom next door and carrying water over in empty milk gallons. That's why Mama and Papa looked for a house, and that's why we moved into the house on Mango Street, far away, on the other side of town.

They always told us that one day we would move into a house, a real house that would be ours for always so we wouldn't have to move each year. And our house would have running water and pipes that worked. And inside it would have real stairs, not hallway stairs, but stairs inside like the houses on T.V. And we'd have a basement and at least three washrooms so when we took a bath we wouldn't have to tell everybody. Our house would be white with trees around it, a great big yard and grass growing without a fence. This was the house Papa talked about when he held a lottery ticket and this was the house Mama dreamed up in the stories she told us before we went to bed.

But the house on Mango Street is not the way they told it at all. It's   5 small and red with tight steps in front and windows so small you'd think they were holding their breath. Bricks are crumbling in places, and the front door is so swollen you have to push hard to get in. There is no front yard, only four little elms the city planted by the curb. Out back is a small garage for the car we don't own yet and a small yard that looks smaller between the two buildings on either side. There are stairs in our house, but they're ordinary hallway stairs, and the house has only one washroom. Everybody has to share a bedroom—Mama and Papa, Carlos and Kiki, me and Nenny.

Once when we were living on Loomis, a nun from my school passed by and saw me playing out front. The laundromat downstairs had been boarded up because it had been robbed two days before and the owner had painted on the wood YES WE'RE OPEN so as not to lose business.

Where do you live? she asked.

There, I said pointing up to the third floor.

You live *there?*

There. I had to look to where she pointed—the third floor, the paint   10 peeling, wooden bars Papa had nailed on the windows so we wouldn't fall out. You live *there?* The way she said it made me feel like nothing. *There.* I lived *there.* I nodded.

I knew then I had to have a house. A real house. One I could point to. But this isn't it. The house on Mango Street isn't it. For the time being, Mama says. Temporary, says Papa. But I know how those things go.

Nathaniel Hawthorne

Young Goodman Brown   (1829–35)

Nathaniel Hawthorne (1804–1864) was born in the clipper-ship seaport of Salem, Massachusetts, son of a merchant captain and grandson of a judge at the notorious Salem witchcraft trials. Hawthorne takes a keen interest in New England's sin-and-brimstone Puritan past in this and many other of his stories and in The Scarlet Letter (1850), that enduring novel of a woman taken in adultery. After college, Hawthorne lived at home and trained to be a writer. Only when his first collection, Twice-Told Tales (1837), made money, did he feel secure enough to marry Sophia Peabody and settle in the

NATHANIEL HAWTHORNE

Old Manse in Concord, Massachusetts. Three more novels followed The Scarlet Letter—The House of the Seven Gables (1851, a story tinged with nightmarish humor), The Blithedale Romance (1852, drawn from his short, irritating stay at a Utopian commune, Brook Farm), and The Marble Faun (1860, inspired by a stay in Italy). Hawthorne wrote for children, too, retelling classic legends in A Wonder Book (1851) and Tanglewood Tales (1853). At Bowdoin College, he had been a classmate of Franklin Pierce; later, when Pierce ran for president of the United States, Hawthorne wrote his campaign biography. The victorious Pierce appointed his old friend American consul at Liverpool, England. With his contemporary Edgar Allan Poe, Hawthorne sped the transformation of the American short story from popular magazine filler into a form of art.

Young Goodman° Brown came forth, at sunset, into the street of Salem village,° but put his head back, after crossing the threshold, to exchange a parting kiss with his young wife. And Faith, as the wife was aptly named, thrust her own pretty head into the street, letting the wind play with the pink ribbons of her cap, while she called to Goodman Brown.

"Dearest heart," whispered she, softly and rather sadly, when her lips were close to his ear, "pray thee, put off your journey until sunrise, and sleep in your own bed to-night. A lone woman is troubled with such dreams and such thoughts, that she's afraid of herself, sometimes. Pray, tarry with me this night, dear husband, of all nights in the year!"

"My love and my Faith," replied young Goodman Brown, "of all nights in the year, this one night must I tarry away from thee. My journey, as thou

---

Goodman: title given by Puritans to a male head of a household; a farmer or other ordinary citizen. *Salem village:* in England's Massachusetts Bay Colony.

callest it, forth and back again, must needs be done 'twixt now and sunrise. What, my sweet, pretty wife, dost thou doubt me already, and we but three months married!"

"Then, God bless you!" said Faith, with the pink ribbons, "and may you find all well, when you come back."

"Amen!" cried Goodman Brown. "Say thy prayers, dear Faith, and 5 go to bed at dusk, and no harm will come to thee."

So they parted; and the young man pursued his way, until, being about to turn the corner by the meeting-house, he looked back, and saw the head of Faith still peeping after him, with a melancholy air, in spite of her pink ribbons.

"Poor little Faith!" thought he, for his heart smote him. "What a wretch am I, to leave her on such an errand! She talks of dreams, too. Methought, as she spoke, there was trouble in her face, as if a dream had warned her what work is to be done to-night. But, no, no! 'twould kill her to think it. Well; she's a blessed angel on earth; and after this one night, I'll cling to her skirts and follow her to Heaven."

With this excellent resolve for the future, Goodman Brown felt himself justified in making more haste on his present evil purpose. He had taken a dreary road, darkened by all the gloomiest trees of the forest, which barely stood aside to let the narrow path creep through, and closed immediately behind. It was all as lonely as could be; and there is this peculiarity in such a solitude, that the traveller knows not who may be concealed by the innumerable trunks and the thick boughs overhead; so that, with lonely footsteps, he may yet be passing through an unseen multitude.

"There may be a devilish Indian behind every tree," said Goodman Brown, to himself; and he glanced fearfully behind him, as he added, "What if the devil himself should be at my very elbow!"

His head being turned back, he passed a crook of the road, and looking 10 forward again, beheld the figure of a man, in grave and decent attire, seated at the foot of an old tree. He arose, at Goodman Brown's approach, and walked onward, side by side with him.

"You are late, Goodman Brown," said he. "The clock of the Old South was striking as I came through Boston; and that is full fifteen minutes agone."°

"Faith kept me back awhile," replied the young man, with a tremor in his voice, caused by the sudden appearance of his companion, though not wholly unexpected.

---

full fifteen minutes agone: Apparently this mystery man has traveled in a flash from Boston's Old South Church all the way to the woods beyond Salem—as the crow flies, a good sixteen miles.

It was now deep dusk in the forest, and deepest in that part of it where these two were journeying. As nearly as could be discerned, the second traveller was about fifty years old, apparently in the same rank of life as Goodman Brown, and bearing a considerable resemblance to him, though perhaps more in expression than features. Still, they might have been taken for father and son. And yet, though the elder person was as simply clad as the younger, and as simple in manner too, he had an indescribable air of one who knew the world, and would not have felt abashed at the governor's dinner-table, or in King William's court,° were it possible that his affairs should call him thither. But the only thing about him, that could be fixed upon as remarkable, was his staff, which bore the likeness of a great black snake, so curiously wrought, that it might almost be seen to twist and wriggle itself, like a living serpent. This, of course, must have been an ocular deception, assisted by the uncertain light.

"Come, Goodman Brown!" cried his fellow-traveller, "this is dull pace for the beginning of a journey. Take my staff, if you are so soon weary."

"Friend," said the other, exchanging his slow pace for a full stop,   15 "having kept covenant by meeting thee here, it is my purpose now to return whence I came. I have scruples, touching the matter thou wot'st° of."

"Sayest thou so?" replied he of the serpent, smiling apart. "Let us walk on, nevertheless, reasoning as we go, and if I convince thee not, thou shalt turn back. We are but a little way in the forest, yet."

"Too far, too far!" exclaimed the goodman, unconsciously resuming his walk. "My father never went into the woods on such an errand, nor his father before him. We have been a race of honest men and good Christians, since the days of the martyrs.° And shall I be the first of the name of Brown, that ever took this path, and kept—"

"Such company, thou wouldst say," observed the elder person, interpreting his pause. "Well said, Goodman Brown! I have been as well acquainted with your family as with ever a one among the Puritans; and that's no trifle to say. I helped your grandfather, the constable, when he lashed the Quaker woman so smartly through the streets of Salem. And it was I that brought your father a pitch-pine knot, kindled at my own

---

King William's court: back in England, where William III reigned from 1689 to 1702. *wot'st:* know. *days of the martyrs:* a time when many forebears of the New England Puritans had given their lives for religious convictions—when Mary I (Mary Tudor, nicknamed "Bloody Mary"), queen of England from 1553 to 1558, briefly reestablished the Roman Catholic Church in England and launched a campaign of persecution against Protestants.

hearth, to set fire to an Indian village, in King Philip's war.° They were my good friends, both; and many a pleasant walk have we had along this path, and returned merrily after midnight. I would fain be friends with you, for their sake."

"If it be as thou sayest," replied Goodman Brown, "I marvel they never spoke of these matters. Or, verily, I marvel not, seeing that the least rumor of the sort would have driven them from New England. We are a people of prayer, and good works, to boot, and abide no such wickedness."

"Wickedness or not," said the traveller with the twisted staff, "I have   20 a very general acquaintance here in New England. The deacons of many a church have drunk the communion wine with me; the selectmen, of divers towns, make me their chairman; and a majority of the Great and General Court are firm supporters of my interest. The governor and I, too—but these are state-secrets."

"Can this be so!" cried Goodman Brown, with a stare of amazement at his undisturbed companion. "Howbeit, I have nothing to do with the governor and council; they have their own ways, and are no rule for a simple husbandman, like me. But, were I to go on with thee, how should I meet the eye of that good old man, our minister, at Salem village? Oh, his voice would make me tremble, both Sabbath-day and lecture-day!"°

Thus far, the elder traveller had listened with due gravity, but now burst into a fit of irrepressible mirth, shaking himself so violently, that his snake-like staff actually seemed to wriggle in sympathy.

"Ha! ha! ha!" shouted he, again and again; then composing himself, "Well, go on, Goodman Brown, go on; but pray thee, don't kill me with laughing!"

"Well, then, to end the matter at once," said Goodman Brown, considerably nettled, "there is my wife, Faith. It would break her dear little heart; and I'd rather break my own!"

"Nay, if that be the case," answered the other, "e'en go thy ways,   25 Goodman Brown. I would not, for twenty old women like the one hobbling before us, that Faith should come to any harm."

As he spoke, he pointed his staff at a female figure on the path, in whom Goodman Brown recognized a very pious and exemplary dame, who had taught him his catechism, in youth, and was still his moral and spiritual adviser, jointly with the minister and Deacon Gookin.

King Philip's war: Metacomet, or King Philip (as the English called him), chief of the Wampanoag Indians, had led a bitter, widespread uprising of several New England tribes (1675–78). Metacomet died in the war, as did one out of every ten white male colonists. *lecture-day:* a weekday when everyone had to go to church to hear a sermon or Bible-reading.

"A marvel, truly, that Goody° Cloyse should be so far in the wilderness, at night-fall!" said he. "But, with your leave, friend, I shall take a cut through the woods, until we have left this Christian woman behind. Being a stranger to you, she might ask whom I was consorting with, and whither I was going."

"Be it so," said his fellow-traveller. "Betake you to the woods, and let me keep the path."

Accordingly, the young man turned aside, but took care to watch his companion, who advanced softly along the road, until he had come within a staff's length of the old dame. She, meanwhile, was making the best of her way, with singular speed for so aged a woman, and mumbling some indistinct words, a prayer, doubtless, as she went. The traveller put forth his staff, and touched her withered neck with what seemed the serpent's tail.

"The devil!" screamed the pious old lady.   30

"Then Goody Cloyse knows her old friend?" observed the traveller, confronting her, and leaning on his writhing stick.

"Ah, forsooth, and is it your worship, indeed?" cried the good dame. "Yea, truly is it, and in the very image of my old gossip,° Goodman Brown, the grandfather of the silly fellow that now is. But—would your worship believe it?—my broomstick hath strangely disappeared, stolen, as I suspect, by that unhanged witch, Goody Cory, and that, too, when I was all anointed with the juice of smallage and cinquefoil and wolf's bane—"°

"Mingled with fine wheat and the fat of a new-born babe," said the shape of old Goodman Brown.

"Ah, your worship knows the receipt,"° cried the old lady, cackling aloud. "So, as I was saying, being all ready for the meeting, and no horse to ride on, I made up my mind to foot it; for they tell me, there is a nice young man to be taken into communion to-night. But now your good worship will lend me your arm, and we shall be there in a twinkling."

"That can hardly be," answered her friend. "I may not spare you my   35
arm, Goody Cloyse, but here is my staff, if you will."

So saying, he threw it down at her feet, where, perhaps, it assumed life, being one of the rods which its owner had formerly lent to the Egyptian Magi.° Of this fact, however, Goodman Brown could not take cognizance.

Goody: short for Goodwife, title for a married woman of ordinary station. In his story, Hawthorne borrows from history the names of two "Goodys"—Goody Cloyse and Goody Cory—and one unmarried woman, Martha Carrier. In 1692 Hawthorne's great-grandfather, John Hawthorne, a judge in the Salem witchcraft trials, had condemned all three to be hanged. *gossip:* friend or kinsman. *smallage and cinquefoil and wolf's bane:* wild plants—here, ingredients for a witch's brew. *receipt:* recipe. *Egyptian Magi:* In the Bible, Pharaoh's wise men and sorcerers who by their magical powers changed their rods into live serpents. (This incident, part of the story of Moses and Aaron, is related in Exodus 7:8–12.)

He had cast up his eyes in astonishment, and looking down again, beheld neither Goody Cloyse nor the serpentine staff, but his fellow-traveller alone, who waited for him as calmly as if nothing had happened.

"That old woman taught me my catechism!" said the young man; and there was a world of meaning in this simple comment.

They continued to walk onward, while the elder traveller exhorted his companion to make good speed and persevere in the path, discoursing so aptly, that his arguments seemed rather to spring up in the bosom of his auditor, than to be suggested by himself. As they went, he plucked a branch of maple, to serve for a walking-stick, and began to strip it of the twigs and little boughs, which were wet with evening dew. The moment his fingers touched them, they became strangely withered and dried up, as with a week's sunshine. Thus the pair proceeded, at a good free pace, until suddenly, in a gloomy hollow of the road, Goodman Brown sat himself down on the stump of a tree, and refused to go any farther.

"Friend," said he, stubbornly, "my mind is made up. Not another step will I budge on this errand. What if a wretched old woman do choose to go to the devil, when I thought she was going to Heaven! Is that any reason why I should quit my dear Faith, and go after her?"

"You will think better of this, by-and-by," said his acquaintance, 40 composedly. "Sit here and rest yourself awhile; and when you feel like moving again, there is my staff to help you along."

Without more words, he threw his companion the maple stick, and was as speedily out of sight, as if he had vanished into the deepening gloom. The young man sat a few moments, by the road-side, applauding himself greatly, and thinking with how clear a conscience he should meet the minister, in his morning-walk, nor shrink from the eye of good old Deacon Gookin. And what calm sleep would be his, that very night, which was to have been spent so wickedly, but purely and sweetly now, in the arms of Faith! Amidst these pleasant and praiseworthy meditations, Goodman Brown heard the tramp of horses along the road, and deemed it advisable to conceal himself within the verge of the forest, conscious of the guilty purpose that had brought him thither, though now so happily turned from it.

On came the hoof-tramps and the voices of the riders, two grave old voices, conversing soberly as they drew near. These mingled sounds appeared to pass along the road, within a few yards of the young man's hiding-place; but owing, doubtless, to the depth of the gloom, at that particular spot, neither the travellers nor their steeds were visible. Though their figures brushed the small boughs by the way-side, it could not be seen that they intercepted, even for a moment, the faint gleam from the strip of bright sky, athwart which they must have passed. Goodman Brown alternately crouched and stood on tip-toe, pulling aside the branches, and thrusting forth his head as far as he durst, without discerning so much as a shadow. It vexed him the more, because he could have sworn, were such a thing possible, that he recognized the voices of the minister and Deacon Gookin, jogging along quietly, as they were wont to do, when bound to some ordination or ecclesiastical council. While yet within hearing, one of the riders stopped to pluck a switch.

"Of the two, reverend Sir," said the voice like the deacon's, "I had rather miss an ordination-dinner than to-night's meeting. They tell me that some of our community are to be here from Falmouth and beyond, and others from Connecticut and Rhode Island; besides several of the Indian powows,° who, after their fashion, know almost as much deviltry as the best of us. Moreover, there is a goodly young woman to be taken into communion."

"Mighty well, Deacon Gookin!" replied the solemn old tones of the minister. "Spur up, or we shall be late. Nothing can be done, you know, until I get on the ground."

The hoofs clattered again, and the voices, talking so strangely in the empty air, passed on through the forest, where no church had ever been gathered, nor solitary Christian prayed. Whither, then, could these holy men be journeying, so deep into the heathen wilderness? Young Goodman Brown caught hold of a tree, for support, being ready to sink down on the ground, faint and overburdened with the heavy sickness of his heart. He looked up to the sky, doubting whether there really was a Heaven above him. Yet, there was the blue arch, and the stars brightening in it.

"With Heaven above, and Faith below, I will yet stand firm against the devil!" cried Goodman Brown.

While he still gazed upward, into the deep arch of the firmament, and had lifted his hands to pray, a cloud, though no wind was stirring, hurried across the zenith, and hid the brightening stars. The blue sky was still visible, except directly overhead, where this black mass of cloud was sweeping swiftly northward. Aloft in the air, as if from the depths of the cloud, came a confused and doubtful sound of voices. Once, the listener fancied that he could distinguish the accents of town's-people of his own, men and women, both pious and ungodly, many of whom he had met at the communion-table, and had seen others rioting at the tavern. The next moment, so indistinct were the sounds, he doubted whether he had heard aught but the murmur of the old forest, whispering without a wind. Then came a stronger swell of those familiar tones, heard daily in the sunshine, at Salem village, but never, until now, from a cloud of night. There was one

45

powows: Indian priests or medicine men.

voice, of a young woman, uttering lamentations, yet with an uncertain sorrow, and entreating for some favor, which, perhaps, it would grieve her to obtain. And all the unseen multitude, both saints and sinners, seemed to encourage her onward.

"Faith!" shouted Goodman Brown, in a voice of agony and desperation; and the echoes of the forest mocked him, crying—"Faith! Faith!" as if bewildered wretches were seeking her, all through the wilderness.

The cry of grief, rage, and terror, was yet piercing the night, when the unhappy husband held his breath for a response. There was a scream, drowned immediately in a louder murmur of voices, fading into far-off laughter, as the dark cloud swept away, leaving the clear and silent sky above Goodman Brown. But something fluttered lightly down through the air, and caught on the branch of a tree. The young man seized it, and beheld a pink ribbon.

"My Faith is gone!" cried he, after one stupefied moment. "There is no good on earth; and sin is but a name. Come, devil! for to thee is this world given." 50

And maddened with despair, so that he laughed loud and long, did Goodman Brown grasp his staff and set forth again, at such a rate, that he seemed to fly along the forest-path, rather than to walk or run. The road grew wilder and drearier, and more faintly traced, and vanished at length, leaving him in the heart of the dark wilderness, still rushing onward, with the instinct that guides mortal man to evil. The whole forest was peopled with frightful sounds; the creaking of the trees, the howling of wild beasts, and the yell of Indians; while, sometimes, the wind tolled like a distant church-bell, and sometimes gave a broad roar around the traveller, as if all Nature were laughing him to scorn. But he was himself the chief horror of the scene, and shrank not from its other horrors.

"Ha! ha! ha!" roared Goodman Brown, when the wind laughed at him. "Let us hear which will laugh loudest! Think not to frighten me with your deviltry! Come witch, come wizard, come Indian powow, come devil himself! and here comes Goodman Brown. You may as well fear him as he fear you!"

In truth, all through the haunted forest, there could be nothing more frightful than the figure of Goodman Brown. On he flew, among the black pines, brandishing his staff with frenzied gestures, now giving vent to an inspiration of horrid blasphemy, and now shouting forth such laughter, as set all the echoes of the forest laughing like demons around him. The fiend in his own shape is less hideous, than when he rages in the breast of man. Thus sped the demoniac on his course, until, quivering among the trees, he saw a red light before him, as when the felled trunks and branches of a clearing have been set on fire, and throw up their lurid blaze against the sky, at the hour of midnight. He paused, in a lull of the tempest that had driven him onward, and heard the swell of what seemed a hymn, rolling solemnly from a distance, with the weight of many voices. He knew the tune; it was a familiar one in the choir of the village meeting-house. The verse died heavily away, and was lengthened by a chorus, not of human voices, but of all the sounds of the benighted wilderness, pealing in awful harmony together. Goodman Brown cried out; and his cry was lost to his own ear, by its unison with the cry of the desert.

In the interval of silence, he stole forward, until the light glared full upon his eyes. At one extremity of an open space, hemmed in by the dark wall of the forest, arose a rock, bearing some rude, natural resemblance either to an altar or a pulpit, and surrounded by four blazing pines, their tops aflame, their stems untouched, like candles at an evening meeting. The mass of foliage, that had overgrown the summit of the rock, was all on fire, blazing high into the night, and fitfully illuminating the whole field. Each pendent twig and leafy festoon was in a blaze. As the red light arose and fell, a numerous congregation alternately shone forth, then disappeared in shadow, and again grew, as it were, out of the darkness, peopling the heart of the solitary woods at once.

"A grave and dark-clad company!" quoth Goodman Brown.   55

In truth, they were such. Among them, quivering to-and-fro, between gloom and splendor, appeared faces that would be seen, next day, at the council-board of the province, and others which, Sabbath after Sabbath, looked devoutly heavenward, and benignantly over the crowded pews, from the holiest pulpits in the land. Some affirm that the lady of the governor was there. At least, there were high dames well known to her, and wives of honored husbands, and widows, a great multitude, and ancient maidens, all of excellent repute, and fair young girls, who trembled, lest their mothers should espy them. Either the sudden gleams of light, flashing over the obscure field, bedazzled Goodman Brown, or he recognized a score of the church-members of Salem village, famous for their especial sanctity. Good old Deacon Gookin had arrived, and waited at the skirts of that venerable saint, his revered pastor. But, irreverently consorting with these grave, reputable, and pious people, these elders of the church, these chaste dames and dewy virgins, there were men of dissolute lives and women of spotted fame, wretches given over to all mean and filthy vice, and suspected even of horrid crimes. It was strange to see, that the good shrank not from the wicked, nor were the sinners abashed by the saints. Scattered, also, among their pale-faced enemies, were the Indian priests, or powows, who had often scared their native forest with more hideous incantations than any known to English witchcraft.

"But, where is Faith?" thought Goodman Brown; and, as hope came into his heart, he trembled.

Another verse of the hymn arose, a slow and mournful strain, such as the pious love, but joined to words which expressed all that our nature can conceive of sin, and darkly hinted at far more. Unfathomable to mere mortals is the lore of fiends. Verse after verse was sung, and still the chorus of the desert swelled between, like the deepest tone of a mighty organ. And, with the final peal of that dreadful anthem, there came a sound, as if the roaring wind, the rushing streams, the howling beasts, and every other voice of the unconverted wilderness, were mingling and according with the voice of guilty man, in homage to the prince of all. The four blazing pines threw up a loftier flame, and obscurely discovered shapes and visages of horror on the smoke-wreaths, above the impious assembly. At the same moment, the fire on the rock shot redly forth, and formed a glowing arch above its base, where now appeared a figure. With reverence be it spoken, the figure bore no slight similitude, both in garb and manner, to some grave divine of the New England churches.

"Bring forth the converts!" cried a voice, that echoed through the field and rolled into the forest.

At the word, Goodman Brown stepped forth from the shadow of the 60 trees, and approached the congregation, with whom he felt a loathful brotherhood, by the sympathy of all that was wicked in his heart. He could have well nigh sworn, that the shape of his own dead father beckoned him to advance, looking downward from a smoke-wreath, while a woman, with dim features of despair, threw out her hand to warn him back. Was it his mother? But he had no power to retreat one step, nor to resist, even in thought, when the minister and good old Deacon Gookin seized his arms, and led him to the blazing rock. Thither came also the slender form of a veiled female, led between Goody Cloyse, that pious teacher of the catechism, and Martha Carrier, who had received the devil's promise to be queen of hell. A rampant hag was she! And there stood the proselytes,° beneath the canopy of fire.

"Welcome, my children," said the dark figure, "to the communion of your race! Ye have found, thus young, your nature and your destiny. My children, look behind you!"

They turned; and flashing forth, as it were, in a sheet of flame, the fiend-worshippers were seen; the smile of welcome gleamed darkly on every visage.

"There," resumed the sable form, "are all whom ye have reverenced from youth. Ye deemed them holier than yourselves, and shrank from your own sin, contrasting it with their lives of righteousness, and prayerful

proselytes: new converts.

aspirations heavenward. Yet, here are they all, in my worshipping assembly! This night it shall be granted you to know their secret deeds; how hoary-bearded elders of the church have whispered wanton words to the young maids of their households; how many a woman, eager for widow's weeds, has given her husband a drink at bedtime, and let him sleep his last sleep in her bosom; how beardless youths have made haste to inherit their fathers' wealth; and how fair damsels—blush not, sweet ones!—have dug little graves in the garden, and bidden me, the sole guest, to an infant's funeral. By the sympathy of your human hearts for sin, ye shall scent out all the places—whether in church, bed-chamber, street, field, or forest—where crime has been committed, and shall exult to behold the whole earth one stain of guilt, one mighty bloodspot. Far more than this! It shall be yours to penetrate, in every bosom, the deep mystery of sin, the fountain of all wicked arts, and which inexhaustibly supplies more evil impulses than human power—than my power, at its utmost!—can make manifest in deeds. And now, my children, look upon each other."

They did so; and, by the blaze of the hell-kindled torches, the wretched man beheld his Faith, and the wife her husband, trembling before that unhallowed altar.

"Lo! there ye stand, my children," said the figure, in a deep and solemn tone, almost sad, with its despairing awfulness, as if his once angelic nature could yet mourn for our miserable race. "Depending upon one another's hearts, ye had still hoped, that virtue were not all a dream. Now are ye undeceived! Evil is the nature of mankind. Evil must be your only happiness. Welcome, again, my children, to the communion of your race!"

65

"Welcome!" repeated the fiend-worshippers, in one cry of despair and triumph.

And there they stood, the only pair, as it seemed, who were yet hesitating on the verge of wickedness, in this dark world. A basin was hollowed, naturally, in the rock. Did it contain water, reddened by the lurid light? or was it blood? or, perchance, a liquid flame? Herein did the Shape of Evil dip his hand, and prepare to lay the mark of baptism upon their foreheads, that they might be partakers of the mystery of sin, more conscious of the secret guilt of others, both in deed and thought, than they could now be of their own. The husband cast one look at his pale wife, and Faith at him. What polluted wretches would the next glance show them to each other, shuddering alike at what they disclosed and what they saw!

"Faith! Faith!" cried the husband. "Look up to Heaven, and resist the Wicked one!"

Whether Faith obeyed, he knew not. Hardly had he spoken, when he found himself amid calm night and solitude, listening to a roar of the wind, which died heavily away through the forest. He staggered against the rock and felt it chill and damp, while a hanging twig, that had been all on fire, besprinkled his cheek with the coldest dew.

The next morning, young Goodman Brown came slowly into the 70 street of Salem village, staring around him like a bewildered man. The good old minister was taking a walk along the grave-yard, to get an appetite for breakfast and meditate his sermon, and bestowed a blessing, as he passed, on Goodman Brown. He shrank from the venerable saint, as if to avoid an anathema.° Old Deacon Goodkin was at domestic worship, and the holy words of his prayer were heard through the open window. "What God doth the wizard pray to?" quoth Goodman Brown. Goody Cloyse, that excellent old Christian, stood in the early sunshine, at her own lattice, catechizing a little girl, who had brought her a pint of morning's milk. Goodman Brown snatched away the child, as from the grasp of the fiend himself. Turning the corner by the meeting-house, he spied the head of Faith, with the pink ribbons, gazing anxiously forth, and bursting into such joy at sight of him, that she skipt along the street, and almost kissed her husband before the whole village. But, Goodman Brown looked sternly and sadly into her face, and passed on without a greeting.

Had Goodman Brown fallen asleep in the forest, and only dreamed a wild dream of a witch-meeting?

Be it so, if you will. But, alas! it was a dream of evil omen for young Goodman Brown. A stern, a sad, a darkly meditative, a distrustful, if not a desperate man, did he become, from the night of that fearful dream. On the Sabbath-day, when the congregation were singing a holy psalm, he could not listen, because an anthem of sin rushed loudly upon his ear, and drowned all the blessed strain. When the minister spoke from the pulpit, with power and fervid eloquence, and, with his hand on the open Bible, of the sacred truths of our religion, and of saint-like lives and triumphant deaths, and of future bliss or misery unutterable, then did Goodman Brown turn pale, dreading, lest the roof should thunder down upon the gray blasphemer and his hearers. Often, awakening suddenly at midnight, he shrank from the bosom of Faith, and at morning or eventide, when the family knelt down at prayer, he scowled, and muttered to himself, and gazed sternly at his wife, and turned away. And when he had lived long, and was borne to his grave, a hoary corpse, followed by Faith, an aged woman, and children and grandchildren, a goodly procession, besides neighbors, not a few, they carved no hopeful verse upon his tombstone; for his dying hour was gloom.

---

anathema: an official curse, a decree that casts one out of a church and bans him from receiving the sacraments.

Zora Neale Hurston

Sweat

1926

Zora Neale Hurston (1901?–1960) was born in Eatonville, Florida, but no record of her actual date of birth exists (best guesses range from 1891 to 1901). Hurston was one of eight children. Her father, a carpenter and Baptist preacher, was also the three-term mayor of Eatonville, the first all-black town incorporated in the United States. When Hurston's mother died in 1912, the father moved the children from one relative to another. Consequently, Hurston never finished grammar school, although in 1918 she began taking classes at Howard University,

ZORA NEALE HURSTON

paying her way through school by working as a manicurist and maid. While at Howard, she published her first story. In early 1925 she moved to New York, arriving with "$1.50, no job, no friends, and a lot of hope." She soon became an important member of the Harlem Renaissance, a group of young black artists (including Langston Hughes, Countee Cullen, Jean Toomer, and Claude McKay) who sought "spiritual emancipation" for African Americans by exploring black heritage and identity in the arts. Hurston eventually became, according to critic Laura Zaidman, "the most prolific black American woman writer of her time." In 1925 she became the first black student at Barnard College, where she completed a B.A. in anthropology. Hurston's most famous story, "Sweat," appeared in the only issue of Fire!!, a 1926 avant-garde Harlem Renaissance magazine edited by Hurston, Hughes, and Wallace Thurman. This powerful story of an unhappy marriage turned murderous was particularly noteworthy for having the characters speak in the black country dialect of Hurston's native Florida. Hurston achieved only modest success during her lifetime, despite the publication of her memorable novel Their Eyes Were Watching God (1937) and her many contributions to the study of African American folklore. She died, poor and neglected, in a Florida welfare home and was buried in an unmarked grave. In 1973 novelist Alice Walker erected a gravestone for her carved with the words:

Zora Neale Hurston
"A Genius of the South"
1901–1960
Novelist, Folklorist
Anthropologist

I

It was eleven o'clock of a Spring night in Florida. It was Sunday. Any other night, Delia Jones would have been in bed for two hours by this time. But she was a washwoman, and Monday morning meant a great deal to her. So she collected the soiled clothes on Saturday when she returned the clean things. Sunday night after church, she sorted and put the white things to soak. It saved her almost a half-day's start. A great hamper in the bedroom held the clothes that she brought home. It was so much neater than a number of bundles lying around.

She squatted on the kitchen floor beside the great pile of clothes, sorting them into small heaps according to color, and humming a song in a mournful key, but wondering through it all where Sykes, her husband, had gone with her horse and buckboard.°

Just then something long, round, limp, and black fell upon her shoulders and slithered to the floor beside her. A great terror took hold of her. It softened her knees and dried her mouth so that it was a full minute before she could cry out or move. Then she saw that it was the big bull whip her husband liked to carry when he drove.

She lifted her eyes to the door and saw him standing there bent over with laughter at her fright. She screamed at him.

"Sykes, what you throw dat whip on me like dat? You know it would   5 skeer me—looks just like a snake, an' you knows how skeered Ah is of snakes."

"Course Ah knowed it! That's how come Ah done it." He slapped his leg with his hand and almost rolled on the ground in his mirth. "If you such a big fool dat you got to have a fit over a earth worm or a string, Ah don't keer how bad Ah skeer you."

"You ain't got no business doing it. Gawd knows it's a sin. Some day Ah'm gointuh drop dead from some of yo' foolishness. 'Nother thing, where you been wid mah rig? Ah feeds dat pony. He ain't fuh you to be drivin' wid no bull whip."

"You sho' is one aggravatin' nigger woman!" he declared and stepped into the room. She resumed her work and did not answer him at once. "Ah done tole you time and again to keep them white folks' clothes outa dis house."

He picked up the whip and glared at her. Delia went on with her work. She went out into the yard and returned with a galvanized tub and set it on the wash-bench. She saw that Sykes had kicked all of the clothes together again, and now stood in her way truculently, his whole manner hoping, *praying*, for an argument. But she walked calmly around him and commenced to re-sort the things.

---

buckboard: a four-wheeled open carriage with the seat resting on a spring platform.

"Next time, Ah'm gointer kick 'em outdoors," he threatened as he struck a match along the leg of his corduroy breeches.

Delia never looked up from her work, and her thin, stooped shoulders sagged further.

"Ah ain't for no fuss t'night Sykes. Ah just come from taking sacrament at the church house."

He snorted scornfully. "Yeah, you just come from de church house on a Sunday night, but heah you is gone to work on them clothes. You ain't nothing but a hypocrite. One of them amen-corner Christians— sing, whoop, and shout, then come home and wash white folks' clothes on the Sabbath."

He stepped roughly upon the whitest pile of things, kicking them helter-skelter as he crossed the room. His wife gave a little scream of dismay, and quickly gathered them together again.

"Sykes, you quit grindin' dirt into these clothes! How can Ah git through by Sat'day if Ah don't start on Sunday?"

"Ah don't keer if you never git through. Anyhow, Ah done promised Gawd and a couple of other men, Ah ain't gointer have it in mah house. Don't gimme no lip neither, else Ah'll throw 'em out and put mah fist up side yo' head to boot."

Delia's habitual meekness seemed to slip from her shoulders like a blown scarf. She was on her feet; her poor little body, her bare knuckly hands bravely defying the strapping hulk before her.

"Looka heah, Sykes, you done gone too fur. Ah been married to you fur fifteen years, and Ah been takin' in washin' fur fifteen years. Sweat, sweat, sweat! Work and sweat, cry and sweat, pray and sweat!"

"What's that got to do with me?" he asked brutally.

"What's it got to do with you, Sykes? Mah tub of suds is filled yo' belly with vittles more times than yo' hands is filled it. Mah sweat is done paid for this house and Ah reckon Ah kin keep on sweatin' in it."

She seized the iron skillet from the stove and struck a defensive pose, which act surprised him greatly, coming from her. It cowed him and he did not strike her as he usually did.

"Naw you won't," she panted, "that ole snaggle-toothed black woman you runnin' with ain't comin' heah to pile up on *mah* sweat and blood. You ain't paid for nothin' on this place, and Ah'm gointer stay right heah till Ah'm toted out foot foremost."

"Well, you better quit gittin' me riled up, else they'll be totin' you out sooner than you expect. Ah'm so tired of you Ah don't know whut to do. Gawd! How Ah hates skinny wimmen!"

A little awed by this new Delia, he sidled out of the door and slammed the back gate after him. He did not say where he had gone, but she knew too well. She knew very well that he would not return until nearly daybreak also. Her work over, she went on to bed but not to sleep at once. Things had come to a pretty pass!

She lay awake, gazing upon the debris that cluttered their matrimo- 25
nial trail. Not an image left standing along the way. Anything like flowers had long ago been drowned in the salty stream that had been pressed
from her heart. Her tears, her sweat, her blood. She had brought love to
the union and he had brought a longing after the flesh. Two months after
the wedding, he had given her the first brutal beating. She had the memory of his numerous trips to Orlando with all of his wages when he had
returned to her penniless, even before the first year had passed. She was
young and soft then, but now she thought of her knotty, muscled limbs,
her harsh knuckly hands, and drew herself up into an unhappy little ball
in the middle of the big feather bed. Too late now to hope for love, even
if it were not Bertha it would be someone else. This case differed from the
others only in that she was bolder than the others. Too late for everything except her little home. She had built it for her old days, and
planted one by one the trees and flowers there. It was lovely to her,
lovely.

Somehow, before sleep came, she found herself saying aloud: "Oh
well, whatever goes over the Devil's back, is got to come under his belly.
Sometime or ruther, Sykes, like everybody else, is gointer reap his sowing." After that she was able to build a spiritual earthworks° against her
husband. His shells could no longer reach her. AMEN. She went to sleep
and slept until he announced his presence in bed by kicking her feet and
rudely snatching the covers away.

"Gimme some kivah heah, an' git yo' damn foots over on yo' own
side! Ah oughter mash you in yo' mouf fuh drawing dat skillet on me."

Delia went clear to the rail without answering him. A triumphant
indifference to all that he was or did.

II

The week was full of work for Delia as all other weeks, and Saturday
found her behind her little pony, collecting and delivering clothes.

It was a hot, hot day near the end of July. The village men on Joe 30
Clarke's porch even chewed cane listlessly. They did not hurl the cane-
knots as usual. They let them dribble over the edge of the porch. Even
conversation had collapsed under the heat.

"Heah come Delia Jones," Jim Merchant said, as the shaggy pony
came 'round the bend of the road toward them. The rusty buckboard was
heaped with baskets of crisp, clean laundry.

"Yep," Joe Lindsay agreed. "Hot or col', rain or shine, jes'ez reg'lar ez
de weeks rool roun' Delia carries 'em an' fetches 'em on Sat'day."

---

spiritual earthworks: earthworks are military fortifications made of earth; here Hurston
uses it metaphorically to mean Delia's emotional defenses.

"She better if she wanter eat," said Moss. "Syke Jones ain't wuth de shot an' powder hit would tek tuh kill 'im. Not to *huh* he ain't."

"He sho' ain't," Walter Thomas chimed in. "It's too bad, too, cause she wuz a right pretty li'l trick when he got huh. Ah'd uh mah'ied huh mahself if he hadnter beat me to it."

Delia nodded briefly at the men as she drove past.   35

"Too much knockin' will ruin *any* 'oman. He done beat huh 'nough tuh kill three women, let 'lone change they looks," said Elijah Moseley. "How Syke kin stommuck dat big black greasy Mogul he's layin' roun' wid, gits me. Ah swear dat eight-rock couldn't kiss a sardine can Ah done thowed out de back do' 'way las' yeah."

"Aw, she's fat, thass how come. He's allus been crazy 'bout fat women," put in Merchant. "He'd a' been tied up wid one long time ago if he could a' found one tuh have him. Did Ah tell yuh 'bout him come sidlin' roun' *mah* wife—bringin' her a basket uh peecans outa his yard fuh a present? Yessir, mah wife! She tol' him tuh take 'em right straight back home, 'cause Delia works so hard ovah dat washtub she reckon everything on de place taste lak sweat an' soapsuds. Ah jus' wisht Ah'd a' caught 'im 'roun' dere! Ah'd a' made his hips ketch on fiah down dat shell road."

"Ah know he done it, too. Ah sees 'im grinnin' at every 'oman dat passes," Walter Thomas said. "But even so, he useter eat some mighty big hunks uh humble pie tuh git dat li'l 'oman he got. She wuz ez pretty ez a speckled pup! Dat wuz fifteen years ago. He useter be so skeered uh losin' huh, she could make him do some parts of a husband's duty. Dey never wuz de same in de mind."

"There oughter be a law about him," said Lindsay. "He ain't fit tuh carry guts tuh a bear."

Clarke spoke for the first time. "Tain't no law on earth dat kin make   40
a man be decent if it ain't in 'im. There's plenty men dat takes a wife lak dey do a joint uh sugar-cane. It's round, juicy, an' sweet when dey gits it. But dey squeeze an' grind, squeeze an' grind an' wring tell dey wring every drop uh pleasure dat's in 'em out. When dey's satisfied dat dey is wrung dry, dey treats 'em jes' lak dey do a cane-chew. Dey thows 'em away. Dey knows whut dey is doin' while dey is at it, an' hates theirselves fuh it but they keeps on hangin' after huh tell she's empty. Den dey hates huh fuh bein' a cane-chew an' in de way."

"We oughter take Syke an' dat stray 'oman uh his'n down in Lake Howell swamp an' lay on de rawhide till they cain't say Lawd a' mussy. He allus wuz uh ovahbearin niggah, but since dat white 'oman from up north done teached 'im how to run a automobile, he done got too beggety to live—an' we oughter kill 'im," Old Man Anderson advised.

A grunt of approval went around the porch. But the heat was melting their civic virtue and Elijah Moseley began to bait Joe Clarke.

"Come on, Joe, git a melon outa dere an' slice it up for yo' customers. We'se all sufferin' wid de heat. De bear's done got *me!*"

"Thass right, Joe, a watermelon is jes' whut Ah needs tuh cure de eppizu-dicks," Walter Thomas joined forces with Moseley. "Come on dere, Joe. We all is steady customers an' you ain't set us up in a long time. Ah chooses dat long, bowlegged Floridy favorite."

"A god, an' be dough. You all gimme twenty cents and slice away," Clarke retorted. "Ah needs a col' slice m'self. Heah, everybody chip in. Ah'll lend y'all mah meat knife." 45

The money was all quickly subscribed and the huge melon brought forth. At that moment, Sykes and Bertha arrived. A determined silence fell on the porch and the melon was put away again.

Merchant snapped down the blade of his jackknife and moved toward the store door.

"Come on in, Joe, an' gimme a slab uh sow belly an' uh pound uh coffee—almost fuhgot 'twas Sat'day. Got to git on home." Most of the men left also.

Just then Delia drove past on her way home, as Sykes was ordering magnificently for Bertha. It pleased him for Delia to see.

"Git whutsoever yo' heart desires, Honey. Wait a minute, Joe. Give huh two bottles uh strawberry soda-water, uh quart parched ground-peas, an' a block uh chewin' gum." 50

With all this they left the store, with Sykes reminding Bertha that this was his town and she could have it if she wanted it.

The men returned soon after they left, and held their watermelon feast.

"Where did Syke Jones git da 'oman from nohow?" Lindsay asked.

"Ovah Apopka. Guess dey musta been cleanin' out de town when she lef'. She don't look lak a thing but a hunk uh liver wid hair on it."

"Well, she sho' kin squall," Dave Carter contributed. "When she gits ready tuh laff, she jes' opens huh mouf an' latches it back tuh de las' notch. No ole granpa alligator down in Lake Bell ain't got nothin' on huh." 55

III

Bertha had been in town three months now. Sykes was still paying her room-rent at Della Lewis'—the only house in town that would have taken her in. Sykes took her frequently to Winter Park to "stomps." He still assured her that he was the swellest man in the state.

"Sho' you kin have dat li'l ole house soon's Ah git dat 'oman out-adere. Everything b'longs tuh me an' you sho' kin have it. Ah sho' 'bominates uh skinny 'oman. Lawdy, you sho' is got one portly shape on you! You kin git *anything* you wants. Dis is *mah* town an' you sho' kin have it."

Delia's work-worn knees crawled over the earth in Gethsemane° and up the rocks of Calvary° many, many times during these months. She avoided the villagers and meeting places in her efforts to be blind and deaf. But Bertha nullified this to a degree, by coming to Delia's house to call Sykes out to her at the gate.

Delia and Sykes fought all the time now with no peaceful interludes. They slept and ate in silence. Two or three times Delia had attempted a timid friendliness, but she was repulsed each time. It was plain that the breaches must remain agape.

The sun had burned July to August. The heat streamed down like a 60 million hot arrows, smiting all things living upon the earth. Grass withered, leaves browned, snakes went blind in shedding, and men and dogs went mad. Dog days!

Delia came home one day and found Sykes there before her. She wondered, but started to go on into the house without speaking, even though he was standing in the kitchen door and she must either stoop under his arm or ask him to move. He made no room for her. She noticed a soap box beside the steps, but paid no particular attention to it, knowing that he must have brought it there. As she was stooping to pass under his outstretched arm, he suddenly pushed her backward, laughingly.

"Look in de box dere, Delia, Ah done brung yuh somethin'!"

She nearly fell upon the box in her stumbling, and when she saw what it held, she all but fainted outright.

"Syke! Syke, mah Gawd! You take dat rattlesnake 'way from heah! You *gottuh*. Oh, Jesus, have mussy!"

"Ah ain't got tuh do nuthin' uh de kin'—fact is Ah ain't got tuh do 65 nothin' but die. Tain't no use uh you puttin' on airs makin' out lak you skeered uh dat snake—he's gointer stay right heah tell he die. He wouldn't bite me cause Ah knows how tuh handle 'im. Nohow he wouldn't risk breakin' out his fangs 'gin yo skinny laigs."

"Naw, now Syke, don't keep dat thing 'round tryin' tuh skeer me tuh death. You knows Ah'm even feared uh earth worms. Thass de biggest snake Ah evah did see. Kill 'im, Syke, please."

"Doan ast me tuh do nothin' fuh yuh. Goin' 'round tryin' tuh be so damn asterperious.° Naw, Ah ain't gonna kill it. Ah think uh damn sight mo' uh him dan you! Dat's a nice snake an' anybody doan lak 'im kin jes' hit de grit."

The village soon heard that Sykes had the snake, and came to see and ask questions.

"How de hen-fire did you ketch dat six-foot rattler, Syke?" Thomas asked.

Gethsemane: the garden outside Jerusalem that was the scene of Jesus' agony and arrest (see Matthew 26:36–57); hence, a scene of great suffering. *Calvary:* the hill outside Jerusalem where Jesus was crucified. *asterperious:* haughty.

"He's full uh frogs so he cain't hardly move, thass how Ah eased up   70
on 'im. But Ah'm a snake charmer an' knows how tuh handle 'em. Shux,
dat ain't nothin'. Ah could ketch one eve'y day if Ah so wanted tuh."

"Whut he needs is a heavy hick'ry club leaned real heavy on his
head. Dat's de bes' way tuh charm a rattlesnake."

"Naw, Walt, y'all jes' don't understand dese diamon' backs lak Ah
do," said Sykes in a superior tone of voice.

The village agreed with Walter, but the snake stayed on. His box remained by the kitchen door with its screen wire covering. Two or three days
later it had digested its meal of frogs and literally came to life. It rattled at
every movement in the kitchen or the yard. One day as Delia came down
the kitchen steps she saw his chalky-white fangs curved like scimitars hung
in the wire meshes. This time she did not run away with averted eyes as
usual. She stood for a long time in the doorway in a red fury that grew blood-
ier for every second that she regarded the creature that was her torment.

That night she broached the subject as soon as Sykes sat down to the
table.

"Syke, Ah wants you tuh take dat snake 'way fum heah. You done   75
starved me an' Ah put up widcher, you done beat me an Ah took dat, but
you done kilt all mah insides bringin' dat varmint heah."

Sykes poured out a saucer full of coffee and drank it deliberately
before he answered her.

"A whole lot Ah keer 'bout how you feels inside uh out. Dat snake
ain't goin' no damn wheah till Ah gits ready fuh 'im tuh go. So fur as
beatin' is concerned, yuh ain't took near all dat you gointer take ef yuh
stay 'round *me*."

Delia pushed back her plate and got up from the table. "Ah hates
you, Sykes," she said calmly. "Ah hates you tuh de same degree dat Ah
useter love yuh. Ah done took an' took till mah belly is full up tuh mah
neck. Dat's de reason Ah got mah letter fum de church an' moved mah
membership tuh Woodbridge—so Ah don't haftuh take no sacrament
wid yuh. Ah don't wantuh see yuh 'round me atall. Lay 'round wid dat
'oman all yuh wants tuh, but gwan 'way fum me an' mah house. Ah hates
yuh lak uh suck-egg dog."

Sykes almost let the huge wad of corn bread and collard greens he
was chewing fall out of his mouth in amazement. He had a hard time
whipping himself up to the proper fury to try to answer Delia.

"Well, Ah'm glad you does hate me. Ah'm sho' tiahed uh you   80
hangin' ontuh me. Ah don't want yuh. Look at yuh stringey ole neck!
Yo' rawbony laigs an' arms is enough tuh cut uh man tuh death. You
looks jes' lak de devvul's doll-baby tuh *me*. You cain't hate me no worse
dan Ah hates you. Ah been hatin' *you* fuh years."

"Yo' ole black hide don't look lak nothin' tuh me, but uh passle uh
wrinkled up rubber, wid yo' big ole yeahs flappin' on each side lak uh paih
uh buzzard wings. Don't think Ah'm gointuh be run 'way fum mah house

neither. Ah'm goin' tuh de white folks 'bout *you*, mah young man, de very nex' time you lay yo' han's on me. Mah cup is done run ovah." Delia said this with no signs of fear and Sykes departed from the house, threatening her, but made not the slightest move to carry out any of them.

That night he did not return at all, and the next day being Sunday, Delia was glad she did not have to quarrel before she hitched up her pony and drove the four miles to Woodbridge.

She stayed to the night service—"love feast"—which was very warm and full of spirit. In the emotional winds her domestic trials were borne far and wide so that she sang as she drove homeward,

> *Jurden water,° black an' col*
> *Chills de body, not de soul*
> *An' Ah wantah cross Jurden in uh calm time.*

She came from the barn to the kitchen door and stopped.

"Whut's de mattah, ol' Satan, you ain't kickin' up yo' racket?" She addressed the snake's box. Complete silence. She went on into the house with a new hope in its birth struggles. Perhaps her threat to go to the white folks had frightened Sykes! Perhaps he was sorry! Fifteen years of misery and suppression had brought Delia to the place where she would hope *anything* that looked towards a way over or through her wall of inhibitions.

She felt in the match-safe behind the stove at once for a match. There was only one there.   85

"Dat niggah wouldn't fetch nothin' heah tuh save his rotten neck, but he kin run thew whut Ah brings quick enough. Now he done toted off nigh on tuh haff uh box uh matches. He done had dat 'oman heah in mah house, too."

Nobody but a woman could tell how she knew this even before she struck the match. But she did and it put her into a new fury.

Presently she brought in the tubs to put the white things to soak. This time she decided she need not bring the hamper out of the bedroom; she would go in there and do the sorting. She picked up the pot-bellied lamp and went in. The room was small and the hamper stood hard by the foot of the white iron bed. She could sit and reach through the bedposts—resting as she worked.

"Ah wantah cross Jurden in uh calm time." She was singing again. The mood of the "love feast" had returned. She threw back the lid of the basket almost gaily. Then, moved by both horror and terror, she sprang back toward the door. *There lay the snake in the basket!* He moved sluggishly at first, but even as she turned round and round, jumped up and down in an insanity of fear, he began to stir vigorously. She saw him pouring his awful beauty from the basket upon the bed, then she seized the lamp and ran as

Jurden water: black Southern dialect for the River Jordan, which represents the last boundary before entering heaven. It comes from the Old Testament, when the Jews had to cross the River Jordan to reach the Promised Land.

fast as she could to the kitchen. The wind from the open door blew out the light and the darkness added to her terror. She sped to the darkness of the yard, slamming the door after her before she thought to set down the lamp. She did not feel safe even on the ground, so she climbed up in the hay barn.

There for an hour or more she lay sprawled upon the hay a gibbering 90 wreck.

Finally she grew quiet, and after that came coherent thought. With this stalked through her a cold, bloody rage. Hours of this. A period of introspection, a space of retrospection, then a mixture of both. Out of this an awful calm.

"Well, Ah done de bes' Ah could. If things ain't right, Gawd knows tain't mah fault."

She went to sleep—a twitch sleep—and woke up to a faint gray sky. There was a loud hollow sound below. She peered out. Sykes was at the wood-pile, demolishing a wire-covered box.

He hurried to the kitchen door, but hung outside there some minutes before he entered, and stood some minutes more inside before he closed it after him.

The gray in the sky was spreading. Delia descended without fear now, 95 and crouched beneath the low bedroom window. The drawn shade shut out the dawn, shut in the night. But the thin walls held back no sound.

"Dat ol' scratch° is woke up now!" She mused at the tremendous whirr inside, which every woodsman knows, is one of the sound illusions. The rattler is a ventriloquist. His whirr sounds to the right, to the left, straight ahead, behind, close under foot—everywhere but where it is. Woe to him who guesses wrong unless he is prepared to hold up his end of the argument! Sometimes he strikes without rattling at all.

Inside, Sykes heard nothing until he knocked a pot lid off the stove while trying to reach the match-safe in the dark. He had emptied his pockets at Bertha's.

The snake seemed to wake up under the stove and Sykes made a quick leap into the bedroom. In spite of the gin he had had, his head was clearing now.

"Mah Gawd!" he chattered, "ef Ah could on'y strack uh light!"

The rattling ceased for a moment as he stood paralyzed. He waited. 100 It seemed that the snake waited also.

"Oh, fuh de light! Ah thought he'd be too sick"—Sykes was muttering to himself when the whirr began again, closer, right underfoot this time. Long before this, Sykes' ability to think had been flattened down to primitive instinct and he leaped—onto the bed.

Outside Delia heard a cry that might have come from a maddened chimpanzee, a stricken gorilla. All the terror, all the horror, all the rage that man possibly could express, without a recognizable human sound.

---

scratch: a folk expression for the devil.

A tremendous stir inside there, another series of animal screams, the intermittent whirr of the reptile. The shade torn violently down from the window, letting in the red dawn, a huge brown hand seizing the window stick, great dull blows upon the wooden floor punctuating the gibberish of sound long after the rattle of the snake had abruptly subsided. All this Delia could see and hear from her place beneath the window, and it made her ill. She crept over to the four o'clocks and stretched herself on the cool earth to recover.

She lay there. "Delia, Delia!" She could hear Sykes calling in a most despairing tone as one who expected no answer. The sun crept on up, and he called. Delia could not move—her legs had gone flabby. She never moved, he called, and the sun kept rising.

"Mah Gawd!" She heard him moan, "Mah Gawd fum Heben!" She 105 heard him stumbling about and got up from her flower-bed. The sun was growing warm. As she approached the door she heard him call out hopefully, "Delia, is dat you Ah heah?"

She saw him on his hands and knees as soon as she reached the door. He crept an inch or two toward her—all that he was able, and she saw his horribly swollen neck and his one open eye shining with hope. A surge of pity too strong to support bore her away from that eye that must, could not, fail to see the tubs. He would see the lamp. Orlando with its doctors was too far. She could scarcely reach the chinaberry tree, where she waited in the growing heat while inside she knew the cold river was creeping up and up to extinguish that eye which must know by now that she knew.

James Joyce

Araby 1914

James Joyce (1882–1941) quit Ireland at twenty to spend his mature life in voluntary exile on the continent, writing of nothing but Dublin, where he was born. In Trieste, Zurich, and Paris, he supported his family with difficulty, sometimes teaching in Berlitz language schools, until his writing won him fame and wealthy patrons. At first Joyce met difficulty in getting his work printed and circulated. Publication of Dubliners *(1914), the collection of stories that includes "Araby," was delayed seven years because its prospective Irish publisher feared libel suits. (The book*

JAMES JOYCE

depicts local citizens, some of them recognizable, and views Dubliners *mostly as a thwarted, self-deceived lot.)* A Portrait of the Artist as a Young Man *(1916), a novel of thinly veiled autobiography, recounts a young intellectual's breaking away from country, church, and home. Joyce's immense comic novel* Ulysses *(1922), a parody of the* Odyssey, *spans eighteen hours in the life of a wandering Jew, a Dublin seller of advertising. Frank about sex but untitillating, the book was banned at one time by the U.S. Post Office. Joyce's later work stepped up its demands on readers. The challenging* Finnegans Wake *(1939), if read aloud, sounds as though a learned comic poet were sleep-talking, jumbling several languages. Joyce was an innovator whose bold experiments showed many other writers possibilities in fiction that had not earlier been imagined.*

North Richmond Street, being blind,° was a quiet street except at the hour when the Christian Brothers' School set the boys free. An uninhabited house of two stories stood at the blind end, detached from its neighbors in a square ground. The other houses of the street, conscious of decent lives within them, gazed at one another with brown imperturbable faces.

The former tenant of our house, a priest, had died in the back drawing-room. Air, musty from having long been enclosed, hung in all the rooms, and the waste room behind the kitchen was littered with old useless papers. Among these I found a few paper-covered books, the pages of which were curled and damp: *The Abbot*, by Walter Scott, *The Devout Communicant* and *The Memoirs of Vidocq*.° I liked the last best because its leaves were yellow. The wild garden behind the house contained a central apple-tree and a few straggling bushes under one of which I found the late tenant's rusty bicycle-pump. He had been a very charitable priest: in his will he had left all his money to institutions and the furniture of his house to his sister.

When the short days of winter came dusk fell before we had well eaten our dinners. When we met in the street the houses had grown somber. The space of sky above us was the color of ever-changing violet and towards it the lamps of the street lifted their feeble lanterns. The cold air stung us and we played till our bodies glowed. Our shouts echoed in the silent street. The career of our play brought us through the dark muddy lanes behind the houses where we ran the gantlet of the rough tribes from the cottages, to the back doors of the dark dripping gardens where odors arose from the ashpits, to the dark odorous stables where a coachman smoothed and combed the horse or shook music from the buckled harness. When we returned to the street light from the kitchen windows had filled the areas. If my uncle was seen turning the corner we hid in the shadow until we had seen him safely housed. Or if

being blind: being a dead-end street. *The Abbot . . . Vidocq:* a popular historical romance (1820); a book of pious meditations by an eighteenth-century English Franciscan, Pacificus Baker; and the autobiography of François-Jules Vidocq (1775–1857), a criminal who later turned detective.

Mangan's sister° came out on the doorstep to call her brother in to his tea we watched her from our shadow peer up and down the street. We waited to see whether she would remain or go in and, if she remained, we left our shadow and walked up to Mangan's steps resignedly. She was waiting for us, her figure defined by the light from the half-opened door. Her brother always teased her before he obeyed and I stood by the railings looking at her. Her dress swung as she moved her body and the soft rope of her hair tossed from side to side.

Every morning I lay on the floor in the front parlor watching her door. The blind was pulled down within an inch of the sash so that I could not be seen. When she came out on the doorstep my heart leaped. I ran to the hall, seized my books and followed her. I kept her brown figure always in my eye and, when we came near the point at which our ways diverged, I quickened my pace and passed her. This happened morning after morning. I had never spoken to her, except for a few casual words, and yet her name was like a summons to all my foolish blood.

Her image accompanied me even in places the most hostile to romance. On Saturday evenings when my aunt went marketing I had to go to carry some of the parcels. We walked through the flaring streets, jostled by drunken men and bargaining women, amid the curses of laborers, the shrill litanies of shopboys who stood on guard by the barrels of pigs' cheeks, the nasal chanting of street singers, who sang a *come-all-you* about O'Donovan Rossa,° or a ballad about the troubles in our native land. These noises converged in a single sensation of life for me: I imagined that I bore my chalice safely through the throng of foes. Her name sprang to my lips at moments in strange prayers and praises which I myself did not understand. My eyes were often full of tears (I could not tell why) and at times a flood from my heart seemed to pour itself out into my bosom. I thought little of the future. I did not know whether I would ever speak to her or not or, if I spoke to her, how I could tell her of my confused adoration. But my body was like a harp and her words and gestures were like fingers running upon the wires.

One evening I went into the back drawing-room in which the priest had died. It was a dark rainy evening and there was no sound in the house. Through one of the broken panes I heard the rain impinge upon the earth, the fine incessant needles of water playing in the sodden beds. Some distant lamp or lighted window gleamed below me. I was thankful

5

Mangan's sister: an actual young woman in this story, but the phrase recalls Irish poet James Clarence Mangan (1803–1849) and his best-known poem, "Dark Rosaleen," which personifies Ireland as a beautiful woman for whom the poet yearns. *come-all-you about O'Donovan Rossa:* the street singers earned their living by singing timely songs that usually began, "Come all you gallant Irishmen / And listen to my song." Their subject, also called Dynamite Rossa, was a popular hero jailed by the British for advocating violent rebellion.

that I could see so little. All my senses seemed to desire to veil themselves and, feeling that I was about to slip from them, I pressed the palms
of my hands together until they trembled, murmuring: O love! O love!
many times.

At last she spoke to me. When she addressed the first words to me I was
so confused that I did not know what to answer. She asked me was I going
to Araby. I forget whether I answered yes or no. It would be a splendid
bazaar, she said; she would love to go.

—And why can't you? I asked.

While she spoke she turned a silver bracelet round and round her
wrist. She could not go, she said, because there would be a retreat that
week in her convent.° Her brother and two other boys were fighting for
their caps and I was alone at the railings. She held one of the spikes,
bowing her head towards me. The light from the lamp opposite our door
caught the white curve of her neck, lit up her hair that rested there and,
falling, lit up the hand upon the railing. It fell over one side of her dress
and caught the white border of a petticoat, just visible as she stood at ease.

—It's well for you, she said.   10

—If I go, I said, I will bring you something.

What innumerable follies laid waste my waking and sleeping thoughts
after that evening! I wished to annihilate the tedious intervening days. I
chafed against the work of school. At night in my bedroom and by day in
the classroom her image came between me and the page I strove to read.
The syllables of the word Araby were called to me through the silence in
which my soul luxuriated and cast an Eastern enchantment over me. I
asked for leave to go to the bazaar on Saturday night. My aunt was surprised
and hoped it was not some Freemason° affair. I answered few questions in
class. I watched my master's face pass from amiability to sternness; he hoped
I was not beginning to idle. I could not call my wandering thoughts together.
I had hardly any patience with the serious work of life which, now that it
stood between me and my desire, seemed to me child's play, ugly monotonous child's play.

On Saturday morning I reminded my uncle that I wished to go to the
bazaar in the evening. He was fussing at the hall-stand, looking for the
hatbrush, and answered me curtly:

—Yes, boy, I know.

As he was in the hall I could not go into the front parlor and lie at   15
the window. I left the house in bad humor and walked slowly towards the
school. The air was pitilessly raw and already my heart misgave me.

---

a retreat . . . in her convent: a week devoted to religious observances more intense than
usual, at the convent school Miss Mangan attends; probably she will have to listen to a
number of hellfire sermons. *Freemason:* Catholics in Ireland viewed the Masonic
order as a Protestant conspiracy against them.

When I came home to dinner my uncle had not yet been home. Still it was early. I sat staring at the clock for some time and, when its ticking began to irritate me, I left the room. I mounted the staircase and gained the upper part of the house. The high cold empty gloomy rooms liberated me and I went from room to room singing. From the front window I saw my companions playing below in the street. Their cries reached me weakened and indistinct and, leaning my forehead against the cool glass, I looked over at the dark house where she lived. I may have stood there for an hour, seeing nothing but the brown-clad figure cast by my imagination, touched discreetly by the lamplight at the curved neck, at the hand upon the railings and at the border below the dress.

When I came downstairs again I found Mrs. Mercer sitting at the fire. She was an old garrulous woman, a pawnbroker's widow, who collected used stamps for some pious purpose. I had to endure the gossip of the tea-table. The meal was prolonged beyond an hour and still my uncle did not come. Mrs. Mercer stood up to go: she was sorry she couldn't wait any longer, but it was after eight o'clock and she did not like to be out late, as the night air was bad for her. When she had gone I began to walk up and down the room, clenching my fists. My aunt said:

—I'm afraid you may put off your bazaar for this night of Our Lord.

At nine o'clock I heard my uncle's latchkey in the halldoor. I heard him talking to himself and heard the hall-stand rocking when it had received the weight of his overcoat. I could interpret these signs. When he was midway through his dinner I asked him to give me the money to go to the bazaar. He had forgotten.

—The people are in bed and after their first sleep now, he said.

I did not smile. My aunt said to him energetically:

—Can't you give him the money and let him go? You've kept him late enough as it is.

My uncle said he was very sorry he had forgotten. He said he believed in the old saying: *All work and no play makes Jack a dull boy.* He asked me where I was going and, when I had told him a second time he asked me did I know *The Arab's Farewell to His Steed.*° When I left the kitchen he was about to recite the opening lines of the piece to my aunt.

I held a florin tightly in my hands as I strode down Buckingham Street towards the station. The sight of the streets thronged with buyers and glaring with gas recalled to me the purpose of my journey. I took my seat in a third-class carriage of a deserted train. After an intolerable delay the train moved out of the station slowly. It crept onward among ruinous

20

The Arab's Farewell to His Steed: This sentimental ballad by a popular poet, Caroline Norton (1808–1877), tells the story of a nomad of the desert who, in a fit of greed, sells his beloved horse, then regrets the loss, flings away the gold he had received, and takes back his horse. Notice the echo of "Araby" in the song title.

houses and over the twinkling river. At Westland Row Station a crowd of people pressed to the carriage doors; but the porters moved them back, saying that it was a special train for the bazaar. I remained alone in the bare carriage. In a few minutes the train drew up beside an improvised wooden platform. I passed out on to the road and saw by the lighted dial of a clock that it was ten minutes to ten. In front of me was a large building which displayed the magical name.

I could not find any sixpenny entrance and, fearing that the bazaar   25
would be closed, I passed in quickly through a turnstile, handing a shilling to a weary-looking man. I found myself in a big hall girdled at half its height by a gallery. Nearly all the stalls were closed and the greater part of the hall was in darkness. I recognized a silence like that which pervades a church after a service. I walked into the center of the bazaar timidly. A few people were gathered about the stalls which were still open. Before a curtain, over which the words *Café Chantant*° were written in colored lamps, two men were counting money on a salver.° I listened to the fall of the coins.

Remembering with difficulty why I had come I went over to one of the stalls and examined porcelain vases and flowered tea-sets. At the door of the stall a young lady was talking and laughing with two young gentlemen. I remarked their English accents and listened vaguely to their conversation.

—O, I never said such a thing!

—O, but you did!

—O, but I didn't!

—Didn't she say that?   30

—Yes. I heard her.

—O, there's a . . . fib!

Observing me the young lady came over and asked me did I wish to buy anything. The tone of her voice was not encouraging; she seemed to have spoken to me out of a sense of duty. I looked humbly at the great jars that stood like eastern guards at either side of the dark entrance to the stall and murmured:

—No, thank you.

The young lady changed the position of one of the vases and went   35
back to the two young men. They began to talk of the same subject. Once or twice the young lady glanced at me over her shoulder.

I lingered before her stall, though I knew my stay was useless, to make my interest in her wares seem the more real. Then I turned away slowly and walked down the middle of the bazaar. I allowed the two pennies

---

Café Chantant: name for a Paris nightspot featuring topical songs. *salver:* a tray like that used in serving Holy Communion.

to fall against the six-pence in my pocket. I heard a voice call from one end of the gallery that the light was out. The upper part of the hall was now completely dark.

Gazing up into the darkness I saw myself as a creature driven and derided by vanity; and my eyes burned with anguish and anger.

Franz Kafka

Before the Law

1919

TRANSLATED BY JOHN SISCOE

Franz Kafka (1883–1924) was born into a German-speaking Jewish family in Prague, Czechoslovakia (then part of the Austro-Hungarian empire). He was the only surviving son of a domineering, successful father. After earning a law degree, Kafka worked as a claims investigator for the state accident insurance company. He worked on his stories at night, especially during his frequent bouts of insomnia. He never married, and lived mostly with his parents. Kafka was such a careful and self-conscious writer that he found it difficult to finish his work and send it out for publication. During his lifetime he published only a few thin volumes of short fiction, most notably The*

FRANZ KAFKA

Metamorphosis (1915) and* In the Penal Colony *(1919). He never finished to his own satisfaction any of his three novels (all published posthumously):* Amerika *(1927),* The Trial *(1925), and* The Castle *(1926). As Kafka was dying of tuberculosis, he begged his friend and literary executor, Max Brod, to burn his uncompleted manuscripts. Brod pondered this request but didn't obey. Kafka's two major novels,* The Trial *and* The Castle, *both depict huge, remote, bumbling, irresponsible bureaucracies in whose power the individual feels helpless and blind. Kafka's works appear startlingly prophetic to readers looking back on them in the later light of Stalinism, World War II, and the Holocaust. His haunting vision of an alienated modern world led the poet W. H. Auden to remark at mid-century, "Had one to name the author who comes nearest to bearing the same kind of relation to our age as Dante, Shakespeare, and Goethe bore to theirs, Kafka is the first one would think of."*

Before the Law stands a doorkeeper. To this doorkeeper comes a man from the country who asks to be admitted to the Law. But the doorkeeper says that he can't let the man in just now. The man thinks this over and then asks if he will be allowed to enter later. "It's possible," answers the doorkeeper, "but not just now." Since the door to the Law stands open as usual and the doorkeeper steps aside, the man bends down to look through the doorway into the interior. Seeing this, the door-keeper laughs and says: "If you find it so compelling, then try to enter despite my prohibition. But bear in mind that I am powerful. And I am only the lowest doorkeeper. In hall after hall, keepers stand at every door. The mere sight of the third one is more than even I can bear." These are difficulties which the man from the country has not expected; the Law, he thinks, should be always available to everyone. But when he looks more closely at the doorkeeper in his furred robe, with his large pointed nose and his long, thin, black Tartar beard, he decides that it would be better to wait until he receives permission to enter. The doorkeeper gives him a stool and allows him to sit down beside the door. There he sits for days and years. He makes many attempts to be let in, and wearies the door-keeper with his pleas. The doorkeeper often questions him casually about his home and many other matters, but the questions are asked with indifference, the way important men might ask them, and always conclude with the statement the man can't be admitted at this time. The man, who has equipped himself with many things for his journey, spends all that he has, regardless of value, in order to bribe the doorkeeper. The doorkeeper accepts it all, though saying each time as he does so, "I'm taking this only so that you won't feel that you haven't tried everything." During these long years the man watches the doorkeeper almost continuously. He forgets about the other doorkeepers, and imagines that this first one is the sole obstacle barring his way to the Law. In the early years he loudly bewails his misfortune; later, as he grows old, he merely grumbles to himself. He becomes childish, and since during his long study of the doorkeeper he has gotten to know even the fleas in the fur collar, he begs these fleas to help him change the doorkeeper's mind. At last his eyesight grows dim and he cannot tell whether it is really growing darker or whether his eyes are simply deceiving him. Yet in the darkness he can now perceive that radiance that streams inextinguishably from the door of the Law. Now his life is nearing its end. Before he dies, all his experiences during this long time coalesce in his mind into a single question, one which he has never yet asked the doorkeeper. He beckons to the door-keeper, for he can no longer raise his stiffening body. The doorkeeper has to bend low to hear him, since the difference in size between them has increased very much to the man's disadvantage. "What do you want to know now?" asks the doorkeeper, "you are insatiable." "Surely everyone strives to reach the Law," says the man, "why then is it that in all these years no one has come seeking admittance but me?" The doorkeeper realizes that the man has reached his end and that his hearing is failing so he yells in his ear: "No one but you could have been admitted here, since this entrance was meant for you alone. Now I am going to shut it."

Jamaica Kincaid

Girl   1983

JAMAICA KINCAID

Jamaica Kincaid was born Elaine Potter Richardson in 1949 in St. John's, capital of the West Indian island nation of Antigua (she adopted the name Jamaica Kincaid in 1973 because of her family's disapproval of her writing). In 1965 she was sent to Westchester County, New York, to work as an au pair (or "servant," as she prefers to describe it). She attended Franconia College in New Hampshire, but did not complete a degree. Kincaid worked as a staff writer for the New Yorker *for nearly twenty years;* Talk Stories *(2001) is a collection of seventy-seven short pieces that she wrote for the magazine. She won wide attention for* At the Bottom of the River (1983), the volume of her stories that includes "Girl." In 1985 she published* Annie John, *an interlocking cycle of short stories about growing up in Antigua.* Lucy *(1990) was her first novel; it was followed by* The Autobiography of My Mother *(1996) and* Mr. Potter *(2002), novels inspired by the lives of her parents. Kincaid is also the author of* A Small Place *(1988), a memoir of her homeland and meditation on the destructiveness of colonialism, and* My Brother *(1997), a reminiscence of her brother Devon, who died of AIDS at thirty-three. Her most recent works are* Among Flowers: A Walk in the Himalaya *(2005), a travel book, and* My Favorite Tool *(2006), a novel. A naturalized U.S. citizen, Kincaid has said of her adopted country: "It's given me a place to be myself—but myself as I was formed somewhere else." She lives in Vermont.*

Wash the white clothes on Monday and put them on the stone heap; wash the color clothes on Tuesday and put them on the clothesline to dry; don't walk barehead in the hot sun; cook pumpkin fritters in very hot sweet oil; soak your little cloths right after you take them off; when buying cotton to make yourself a nice blouse, be sure that it doesn't have gum on it, because that way it won't hold up well after a wash; soak salt fish overnight before you cook it; is it true that you sing benna° in Sunday school?; always eat your food in such a way that it

---

benna: Kincaid defined this word, for two editors who inquired, as meaning "songs of the sort your parents didn't want you to sing, at first calypso and later rock and roll" (quoted by Sylvan Barnet and Marcia Stubbs, *The Little Brown Reader*, 2nd ed. [Boston: Little, 1980] 74).

won't turn someone else's stomach; on Sundays try to walk like a lady and not like the slut you are so bent on becoming; don't sing benna in Sunday school; you mustn't speak to wharf-rat boys, not even to give directions; don't eat fruits on the street—flies will follow you; *but I don't sing benna on Sundays at all and never in Sunday school;* this is how to sew on a button; this is how to make a buttonhole for the button you have just sewed on; this is how to hem a dress when you see the hem coming down and so to prevent yourself from looking like the slut I know you are so bent on becoming; this is how you iron your father's khaki shirt so that it doesn't have a crease; this is how you iron your father's khaki pants so that they don't have a crease; this is how you grow okra—far from the house, because okra tree harbors red ants; when you are growing dasheen, make sure it gets plenty of water or else it makes your throat itch when you are eating it; this is how you sweep a corner; this is how you sweep a whole house; this is how you sweep a yard; this is how you smile to someone you don't like too much; this is how you smile to someone you don't like at all; this is how you smile to someone you like completely; this is how you set a table for tea; this is how you set a table for dinner; this is how you set a table for dinner with an important guest; this is how you set a table for lunch; this is how you set a table for breakfast; this is how to behave in the presence of men who don't know you very well, and this way they won't recognize immediately the slut I have warned you against becoming; be sure to wash every day, even if it is with your own spit; don't squat down to play marbles—you are not a boy, you know; don't pick people's flowers—you might catch something; don't throw stones at blackbirds, because it might not be a blackbird at all; this is how to make a bread pudding; this is how to make doukona; this is how to make pepper pot; this is how to make a good medicine for a cold; this is how to make a good medicine to throw away a child before it even becomes a child; this is how to catch a fish; this is how to throw back a fish you don't like, and that way something bad won't fall on you; this is how to bully a man; this is how a man bullies you; this is how to love a man, and if this doesn't work there are other ways, and if they don't work don't feel too bad about giving up; this is how to spit up in the air if you feel like it, and this is how to move quick so that it doesn't fall on you; this is how to make ends meet; always squeeze bread to make sure it's fresh; *but what if the baker won't let me feel the bread?;* you mean to say that after all you are really going to be the kind of woman who the baker won't let near the bread?

Joyce Carol Oates

Where Are You Going, Where Have You Been? 1970

Joyce Carol Oates was born in 1938 into a blue-collar, Catholic family in Lockport, New York. As an undergraduate at Syracuse University, she won a Mademoiselle magazine award for fiction. After graduating with top honors, she took a master's degree in English at the University of Wisconsin and went on to teach at several universities: Detroit, Windsor, and Princeton. She now lives in Princeton, New Jersey, where, together with her husband, Raymond Smith, she directs the Ontario Review Press, a small literary publisher. A remarkably pro-lific writer, Oates has produced more than twenty-five collections of stories, including High Lonesome: Stories 1966–2006, *and forty novels, including them, winner of a National Book Award in 1970,* Because It Is Bitter, and Because It Is My Heart *(1990), and more recently,* Middle Age: A Romance *(2001),* The Tattooed Girl *(2003), and* Missing Mom *(2005). She also writes poetry, plays, and literary criticism.* Woman Writer: Occasions & Opportunities *(1988),* The Faith of a Writer: Life, Craft, Art *(2003), and* Uncensored: Views and (Re)views *(2005) are books of varied essays;* On Boxing *(1987) is a nonfiction memoir and study of fighters and fighting.* Foxfire *(1993), her twenty-second novel, is the story of a girl gang in upstate New York. Her 1996 Gothic novella,* First Love, *is a bizarre tale of terror and torture. Violence and the macabre may inhabit her best stories, but Oates has insisted that these elements in her work are never gratuitous. The 1985 film* Smooth Talk, *directed by Joyce Chopra, was based on "Where Are You Going, Where Have You Been?"*

JOYCE CAROL OATES
(© Jill Krementz, Inc.)

FOR BOB DYLAN

Her name was Connie. She was fifteen and she had a quick nervous giggling habit of craning her neck to glance into mirrors, or checking other people's faces to make sure her own was all right. Her mother, who noticed everything and knew everything and who hadn't much reason any longer to look at her own face, always scolded Connie about it. "Stop gawking at yourself, who are you? You think you're so pretty?" she would say. Connie would raise her eyebrows at these familiar complaints and look right through her mother, into a shadowy vision of herself as she was right at that moment: she knew she was pretty and that was everything. Her mother had been pretty once too, if you could believe those old snapshots in the album, but now her looks were gone and that was why she was always after Connie.

"Why don't you keep your room clean like your sister? How've you got your hair fixed—what the hell stinks? Hair spray? You don't see your sister using that junk."

Her sister June was twenty-four and still lived at home. She was a secretary in the high school Connie attended, and if that wasn't bad enough—with her in the same building—she was so plain and chunky and steady that Connie had to hear her praised all the time by her mother and her mother's sisters. June did this, June did that, she saved money and helped clean the house and cooked and Connie couldn't do a thing, her mind was all filled with trashy daydreams. Their father was away at work most of the time and when he came home he wanted supper and he read the newspaper at supper and after supper he went to bed. He didn't bother talking much to them, but around his bent head Connie's mother kept picking at her until Connie wished her mother was dead and she herself was dead and it was all over. "She makes me want to throw up sometimes," she complained to her friends. She had a high, breathless, amused voice which made everything she said sound a little forced, whether it was sincere or not.

There was one good thing: June went places with girl friends of hers, girls who were just as plain and steady as she, and so when Connie wanted to do that her mother had no objections. The father of Connie's best girl friend drove the girls the three miles to town and left them off at a shopping plaza, so that they could walk through the stores or go to a movie, and when he came to pick them up again at eleven he never bothered to ask what they had done.

They must have been familiar sights, walking around that shopping plaza in their shorts and flat ballerina slippers that always scuffed the sidewalk, with charm bracelets jingling on their thin wrists; they would lean together to whisper and laugh secretly if someone passed by who amused or interested them. Connie had long dark blond hair that drew anyone's eye to it, and she wore part of it pulled up on her head and puffed out and the rest of it she let fall down her back. She wore a pullover jersey blouse that looked one way when she was at home and another way when she was away from home. Everything about her had two sides to it, one for home and one for anywhere that was not home: her walk that could be childlike and bobbing, or languid enough to make anyone think she was hearing music in her head, her mouth which was pale and smirking most of the time, but bright and pink on these evenings out, her laugh which was cynical and drawling at home—"Ha, ha, very funny"— but high-pitched and nervous anywhere else, like the jingling of the charms on her bracelet.

Sometimes they did go shopping or to a movie, but sometimes they went across the highway, ducking fast across the busy road, to a drive-in restaurant where older kids hung out. The restaurant was shaped like a big bottle, though squatter than a real bottle, and on its cap was a revolving figure of a grinning boy who held a hamburger aloft. One night in mid-summer they ran across, breathless with daring, and right away someone leaned out a car window and invited them over, but it was just a boy from high school they didn't like. It made them feel good to be able to ignore him. They went up through the maze of parked and cruising cars to the bright-lit, fly-infested restaurant, their faces pleased and expectant as if they were entering a sacred building that loomed out of the night to give them what haven and what blessing they yearned for. They sat at the counter and crossed their legs at the ankles, their thin shoulders rigid with excitement, and listened to the music that made everything so good: the music was always in the background like music at a church service, it was something to depend upon.

A boy named Eddie came in to talk with them. He sat backwards on his stool, turning himself jerkily around in semi-circles and then stopping and turning again, and after a while he asked Connie if she would like something to eat. She said she did and so she tapped her friend's arm on her way out—her friend pulled her face up into a brave droll look—and Connie said she would meet her at eleven, across the way. "I just hate to leave her like that," Connie said earnestly, but the boy said that she wouldn't be alone for long. So they went out to his car and on the way Connie couldn't help but let her eyes wander over the windshields and faces all around her, her face gleaming with a joy that had nothing to do with Eddie or even this place; it might have been the music. She drew her shoulders up and sucked in her breath with the pure pleasure of being alive, and just at that moment she happened to glance at a face just a few feet from hers. It was a boy with shaggy black hair, in a convertible jalopy painted gold. He stared at her and then his lips widened into a grin. Con-nie slit her eyes at him and turned away, but she couldn't help glancing back and there he was still watching her. He wagged a finger and laughed and said, "Gonna get you, baby," and Connie turned away again without Eddie noticing anything.

She spent three hours with him, at the restaurant where they ate hamburgers and drank Cokes in wax cups that were always sweating, and then down an alley a mile or so away, and when he left her off at five to eleven only the movie house was still open at the plaza. Her girl friend was there, talking with a boy. When Connie came up the two girls smiled at each other and Connie said, "How was the movie?" and the girl said, "*You* should know." They rode off with the girl's father, sleepy and pleased, and Connie couldn't help but look at the darkened shopping plaza with its big empty parking lot and its signs that were faded and ghostly now, and over at the drive-in restaurant where cars were still circling tirelessly. She couldn't hear the music at this distance.

Next morning June asked her how the movie was and Connie said, "So-so."

She and that girl and occasionally another girl went out several 10 times a week that way, and the rest of the time Connie spent around the house—it was summer vacation—getting in her mother's way and thinking, dreaming, about the boys she met. But all the boys fell back and dissolved into a single face that was not even a face, but an idea, a feeling, mixed up with the urgent insistent pounding of the music and the humid night air of July. Connie's mother kept dragging her back to the daylight by finding things for her to do or saying, suddenly, "What's this about the Pettinger girl?"

And Connie would say nervously, "Oh, her. That dope." She always drew thick clear lines between herself and such girls, and her mother was simple and kindly enough to believe her. Her mother was so simple, Connie thought, that it was maybe cruel to fool her so much. Her mother went scuffling around the house in old bedroom slippers and complained over the telephone to one sister about the other, then the other called up and the two of them complained about the third one. If June's name was mentioned her mother's tone was approving, and if Connie's name was mentioned it was disapproving. This did not really mean she disliked Connie and actually Connie thought that her mother preferred her to June because she was prettier, but the two of them kept up a pretense of exasperation, a sense that they were tugging and struggling over something of little value to either of them. Sometimes, over coffee, they were almost friends, but something would come up—some vexation that was like a fly buzzing suddenly around their heads—and their faces went hard with contempt.

One Sunday Connie got up at eleven—none of them bothered with church—and washed her hair so that it could dry all day long, in the sun. Her parents and sister were going to a barbecue at an aunt's house and Connie said no, she wasn't interested, rolling her eyes to let her mother know just what she thought of it. "Stay home alone then," her mother said sharply. Connie sat out back in a lawn chair and watched them drive away, her father quiet and bald, hunched around so that he could back the car out, her mother with a look that was still angry and not at all softened through the windshield, and in the back seat poor old June all dressed up as if she didn't know what a barbecue was, with all the running yelling kids and the flies. Connie sat with her eyes closed in the sun, dreaming and dazed with the warmth about her as if this were a kind of love, the caresses of love, and her mind slipped over onto thoughts of the boy she had been with the night before and how nice he had been, how sweet it always was, not the way someone like June would suppose but sweet, gentle, the way it was in movies and promised in songs; and when she opened her eyes she hardly knew where she was, the back yard ran off into weeds and a fence-line of trees and behind it the sky was perfectly blue and still. The asbestos "ranch house" that was now three years old startled her—it looked small. She shook her head as if to get awake.

It was too hot. She went inside the house and turned on the radio to drown out the quiet. She sat on the edge of her bed, barefoot, and listened for an hour and a half to a program called XYZ Sunday Jamboree, record after record of hard, fast, shrieking songs she sang along with, interspersed by exclamations from "Bobby King": "An' look here you girls at Napoleon's—Son and Charley want you to pay real close attention to this song coming up!"

And Connie paid close attention herself, bathed in a glow of slow-pulsed joy that seemed to rise mysteriously out of the music itself and lay languidly about the airless little room, breathed in and breathed out with each gentle rise and fall of her chest.

After a while she heard a car coming up the drive. She sat up at once, startled, because it couldn't be her father so soon. The gravel kept crunching all the way in from the road—the driveway was long—and Connie ran to the window. It was a car she didn't know. It was an open jalopy, painted a bright gold that caught the sunlight opaquely. Her heart began to pound and her fingers snatched at her hair, checking it, and she whispered "Christ, Christ," wondering how bad she looked. The car came to a stop at the side door and the horn sounded four short taps as if this were a signal Connie knew.

She went into the kitchen and approached the door slowly, then hung out the screen door, her bare toes curling down off the step. There were two boys in the car and now she recognized the driver: he had shaggy, shabby black hair that looked crazy as a wig and he was grinning at her.

"I ain't late, am I?" he said.

"Who the hell do you think you are?" Connie said.

"Toldja I'd be out, didn't I?"

"I don't even know who you are."

She spoke sullenly, careful to show no interest or pleasure, and he spoke in a fast bright monotone. Connie looked past him to the other boy, taking her time. He had fair brown hair, with a lock that fell onto his forehead. His sideburns gave him a fierce, embarrassed look, but so far he hadn't even bothered to glance at her. Both boys wore sunglasses. The driver's glasses were metallic and mirrored everything in miniature.

"You wanta come for a ride?" he said.

Connie smirked and let her hair fall loose over one shoulder.

"Don'tcha like my car? New paint job," he said. "Hey."

"What?"

15

20

25

"You're cute."

She pretended to fidget, chasing flies away from the door.

"Don'tcha believe me, or what?" he said.

"Look, I don't even know who you are," Connie said in disgust.

"Hey, Ellie's got a radio, see. Mine's broke down." He lifted his   30
friend's arm and showed her the little transistor the boy was holding, and
now Connie began to hear the music. It was the same program that was
playing inside the house.

"Bobby King?" she said.

"I listen to him all the time. I think he's great."

"He's kind of great," Connie said reluctantly.

"Listen, that guy's *great*. He knows where the action is."

Connie blushed a little, because the glasses made it impossible for   35
her to see just what this boy was looking at. She couldn't decide if she
liked him or if he was just a jerk, and so she dawdled in the doorway and
wouldn't come down or go back inside. She said, "What's all that stuff
painted on your car?"

"Can'tcha read it?" He opened the door very carefully, as if he was
afraid it might fall off. He slid out just as carefully, planting his feet firmly
on the ground, the tiny metallic world in his glasses slowing down like
gelatine hardening and in the midst of it Connie's bright green blouse.
"This here is my name, to begin with," he said. ARNOLD FRIEND was written in tarlike black letters on the side, with a drawing of a round grinning
face that reminded Connie of a pumpkin, except it wore sunglasses. "I
wanta introduce myself, I'm Arnold Friend and that's my real name and
I'm gonna be your friend, honey, and inside the car's Ellie Oscar, he's
kinda shy." Ellie brought his transistor radio up to his shoulder and balanced it there. "Now these numbers are a secret code, honey," Arnold
Friend explained. He read off the numbers 33, 19, 17 and raised his eyebrows at her to see what she thought of that, but she didn't think much
of it. The left rear fender had been smashed and around it was written, on
the gleaming gold background: DONE BY CRAZY WOMAN DRIVER. Connie
had to laugh at that. Arnold Friend was pleased at her laughter and
looked up at her. "Around the other side's a lot more—you wanta come
and see them?"

"No."

"Why not?"

"Why should I?"

"Don'tcha wanta see what's on the car? Don'tcha wanta go for a   40
ride?"

"I don't know."

"Why not?"

"I got things to do."

"Like what?"

"Things."

He laughed as if she had said something funny. He slapped his thighs. He was standing in a strange way, leaning back against the car as if he were balancing himself. He wasn't tall, only an inch or so taller than she would be if she came down to him. Connie liked the way he was dressed, which was the way all of them dressed: tight faded jeans stuffed into black, scuffed boots, a belt that pulled his waist in and showed how lean he was, and a white pull-over shirt that was a little soiled and showed the hard small muscles of his arms and shoulders. He looked as if he probably did hard work, lifting and carrying things. Even his neck looked muscular. And his face was a familiar face, some-how: the jaw and chin and cheeks slightly darkened, because he hadn't shaved for a day or two, and the nose long and hawk-like, sniffing as if she were a treat he was going to gobble up and it was all a joke.

"Connie, you ain't telling the truth. This is your day set aside for a ride with me and you know it," he said, still laughing. The way he straightened and recovered from his fit of laughing showed that it had been all fake.

"How do you know what my name is?" she said suspiciously.

"It's Connie."

"Maybe and maybe not."

"I know my Connie," he said, wagging his finger. Now she remem-bered him even better, back at the restaurant, and her cheeks warmed at the thought of how she sucked in her breath just at the moment she passed him—how she must have looked to him. And he had remembered her. "Ellie and I come out here especially for you," he said. "Ellie can sit in back. How about it?"

"Where?"

"Where what?"

"Where're we going?"

He looked at her. He took off the sunglasses and she saw how pale the skin around his eyes was, like holes that were not in shadow but in-stead in light. His eyes were chips of broken glass that catch the light in an amiable way. He smiled. It was as if the idea of going for a ride some-where, to some place, was a new idea to him.

"Just for a ride, Connie sweetheart."

"I never said my name was Connie," she said.

"But I know what it is. I know your name and all about you, lots of things," Arnold Friend said. He had not moved yet but stood still leaning back against the side of his jalopy. "I took a special interest in you, such a pretty girl, and found out all about you like I know your parents and sister are gone somewheres and I know where and how long they're going to be gone, and I know who you were with last night, and your best girl friend's name is Betty. Right?"

45

50

55

He spoke in a simple lilting voice, exactly as if he were reciting the words to a song. His smile assured her that everything was fine. In the car Ellie turned up the volume on his radio and did not bother to look around at them.

"Ellie can sit in the back seat," Arnold Friend said. He indicated his 60 friend with a casual jerk of his chin, as if Ellie did not count and she should not bother with him.

"How'd you find out all that stuff?" Connie said.

"Listen: Betty Schultz and Tony Fitch and Jimmy Pettinger and Nancy Pettinger," he said, in a chant. "Raymond Stanley and Bob Hutter—"

"Do you know all those kids?"

"I know everybody."

"Look, you're kidding. You're not from around here." 65

"Sure."

"But—how come we never saw you before?"

"Sure you saw me before," he said. He looked down at his boots, as if he were a little offended. "You just don't remember."

"I guess I'd remember you," Connie said.

"Yeah?" He looked up at this, beaming. He was pleased. He began to 70 mark time with the music from Ellie's radio, tapping his fists lightly together. Connie looked away from his smile to the car, which was painted so bright it almost hurt her eyes to look at it. She looked at that name, ARNOLD FRIEND. And up at the front fender was an expression that was familiar—MAN THE FLYING SAUCERS. It was an expression kids had used the year before, but didn't use this year. She looked at it for a while as if the words meant something to her that she did not yet know.

"What're you thinking about? Huh?" Arnold Friend demanded. "Not worried about your hair blowing around in the car, are you?"

"No."

"Think I maybe can't drive good?"

"How do I know?"

"You're a hard girl to handle. How come?" he said. "Don't you know 75 I'm your friend? Didn't you see me put my sign in the air when you walked by?"

"What sign?"

"My sign." And he drew an X in the air, leaning out toward her. They were maybe ten feet apart. After his hand fell back to his side the X was still in the air, almost visible. Connie let the screen door close and stood perfectly still inside it, listening to the music from her radio and the boy's blend together. She stared at Arnold Friend. He stood there so stiffly relaxed, pretending to be relaxed, with one hand idly on the door handle as if he were keeping himself up that way and had no intention of ever moving again. She recognized most things about him, the tight jeans that showed his thighs and buttocks and the greasy leather boots and the tight shirt, and even that slippery friendly smile of his, that sleepy dreamy smile that all the boys used to get across ideas they didn't want to put into words. She recognized all this and also the singsong way he talked, slightly mocking, kidding, but serious and a little melancholy, and she recognized the way he tapped one fist against the other in homage to the perpetual music behind him. But all these things did not come together.

She said suddenly, "Hey, how old are you?"

His smile faded. She could see then that he wasn't a kid, he was much older—thirty, maybe more. At this knowledge her heart began to pound faster.

"That's a crazy thing to ask. Can'tcha see I'm your own age?" 80

"Like hell you are."

"Or maybe a coupla years older, I'm eighteen."

"Eighteen?" she said doubtfully.

He grinned to reassure her and lines appeared at the corners of his mouth. His teeth were big and white. He grinned so broadly his eyes became slits and she saw how thick the lashes were, thick and black as if painted with a black tarlike material. Then he seemed to become embarrassed, abruptly, and looked over his shoulder at Ellie. "*Him*, he's crazy," he said. "Ain't he a riot, he's a nut, a real character." Ellie was still listening to the music. His sunglasses told nothing about what he was thinking. He wore a bright orange shirt unbuttoned halfway to show his chest, which was a pale, bluish chest and not muscular like Arnold Friend's. His shirt collar was turned up all around and the very tips of the collar pointed out past his chin as if they were protecting him. He was pressing the transistor radio up against his ear and sat there in a kind of daze, right in the sun.

"He's kinda strange," Connie said. 85

"Hey, she says you're kinda strange! Kinda strange!" Arnold Friend cried. He pounded on the car to get Ellie's attention. Ellie turned for the first time and Connie saw with shock that he wasn't a kid either—he had a fair, hairless face, cheeks reddened slightly as if the veins grew too close to the surface of his skin, the face of a forty-year-old baby. Connie felt a wave of dizziness rise in her at this sight and she stared at him as if waiting for something to change the shock of the moment, make it all right again. Ellie's lips kept shaping words, mumbling along, with the words blasting in his ear.

"Maybe you two better go away," Connie said faintly.

"What? How come?" Arnold Friend cried. "We come out here to take you for a ride. It's Sunday." He had the voice of the man on the radio now. It was the same voice, Connie thought. "Don'tcha know it's Sunday all day and honey, no matter who you were with last night today you're with Arnold Friend and don't you forget it!—Maybe you better

step out here," he said, and this last was in a different voice. It was a little
flatter, as if the heat was finally getting to him.

"No. I got things to do."

"Hey."

"You two better leave."

"We ain't leaving until you come with us."

"Like hell I am—"

"Connie, don't fool around with me. I mean, I mean, don't fool
around," he said, shaking his head. He laughed incredulously. He placed
his sunglasses on top of his head, carefully, as if he were indeed wearing a
wig, and brought the stems down behind his ears. Connie stared at him,
another wave of dizziness and fear rising in her so that for a moment he
wasn't even in focus but was just a blur, standing there against his gold
car, and she had the idea that he had driven up the driveway all right but
had come from nowhere before that and belonged nowhere and that
everything about him and even about the music that was so familiar to
her was only half real.

"If my father comes and sees you—"

"He ain't coming. He's at the barbecue."

"How do you know that?"

"Aunt Tillie's. Right now they're—uh—they're drinking. Sitting
around," he said vaguely, squinting as if he were staring all the way to
town and over to Aunt Tillie's backyard. Then the vision seemed to get
clear and he nodded energetically. "Yeah. Sitting around. There's your
sister in a blue dress, huh? And high heels, the poor sad bitch—nothing
like you, sweetheart! And your mother's helping some fat woman with
the corn, they're cleaning the corn—husking the corn—"

"What fat woman?" Connie cried.

"How do I know what fat woman. I don't know every goddam fat
woman in the world!" Arnold Friend laughed.

"Oh, that's Mrs. Hornby. . . . Who invited her?" Connie said. She
felt a little light-headed. Her breath was coming quickly.

"She's too fat. I don't like them fat. I like them the way you are,
honey," he said, smiling sleepily at her. They stared at each other for a
while, through the screen door. He said softly, "Now what you're going to
do is this: you're going to come out that door. You're going to sit up front
with me and Ellie's going to sit in the back, the hell with Ellie, right?
This isn't Ellie's date. You're my date. I'm your lover, honey."

"What? You're crazy—"

"Yes, I'm your lover. You don't know what that is but you will," he
said. "I know that too. I know all about you. But look: it's real nice and
you couldn't ask for nobody better than me, or more polite. I always keep
my word. I'll tell you how it is, I'm always nice at first, the first time. I'll
hold you so tight you won't think you have to try to get away or pretend

anything because you'll know you can't. And I'll come inside you where it's all secret and you'll give in to me and you'll love me—"

"Shut up! You're crazy!" Connie said. She backed away from the door. 105 She put her hands against her ears as if she'd heard something terrible, something not meant for her. "People don't talk like that, you're crazy," she muttered. Her heart was almost too big now for her chest and its pumping made sweat break out all over her. She looked out to see Arnold Friend pause and then take a step toward the porch lurching. He almost fell. But, like a clever drunken man, he managed to catch his balance. He wobbled in his high boots and grabbed hold of one of the porch posts.

"Honey?" he said. "You still listening?"

"Get the hell out of here!"

"Be nice, honey. Listen."

"I'm going to call the police—"

He wobbled again and out of the side of his mouth came a fast spat 110 curse, an aside not meant for her to hear. But even this "Christ!" sounded forced. Then he began to smile again. She watched this smile come, awkward as if he were smiling from inside a mask. His whole face was a mask, she thought wildly, tanned down onto his throat but then running out as if he had plastered makeup on his face but had forgotten about his throat.

"Honey—? Listen, here's how it is. I always tell the truth and I promise you this: I ain't coming in that house after you."

"You better not! I'm going to call the police if you—if you don't—"

"Honey," he said, talking right through her voice, "honey, I'm not coming in there but you are coming out here. You know why?"

She was panting. The kitchen looked like a place she had never seen before, some room she had run inside but which wasn't good enough, wasn't going to help her. The kitchen window had never had a curtain, after three years, and there were dishes in the sink for her to do—probably—and if you ran your hand across the table you'd probably feel something sticky there.

"You listening, honey? Hey?" 115

"—going to call the police—"

"Soon as you touch the phone I don't need to keep my promise and can come inside. You won't want that."

She rushed forward and tried to lock the door. Her fingers were shaking. "But why lock it," Arnold Friend said gently, talking right into her face. "It's just a screen door. It's just nothing." One of his boots was at a strange angle, as if his foot wasn't in it. It pointed out to the left, bent at the ankle. "I mean, anybody can break through a screen door and glass and wood and iron or anything else if he needs to, anybody at all and specially Arnold Friend. If the place got lit up with a fire honey you'd come running out into my arms, right into my arms and safe at home—like you knew I was your lover and'd stopped fooling around. I don't mind a nice shy girl but I don't like no fooling around." Part of those words were spoken with a slight rhythmic lilt, and Connie somehow recognized them—the echo of a song from last year, about a girl rushing into her boyfriend's arms and coming home again—

Connie stood barefoot on the linoleum floor, staring at him. "What do you want?" she whispered.

"I want you," he said.   120

"What?"

"Seen you that night and thought, that's the one, yes sir. I never needed to look any more."

"But my father's coming back. He's coming to get me. I had to wash my hair first—" She spoke in a dry, rapid voice, hardly raising it for him to hear.

"No, your daddy is not coming and yes, you had to wash your hair and you washed it for me. It's nice and shining and all for me, I thank you, sweetheart," he said, with a mock bow, but again he almost lost his balance. He had to bend and adjust his boots. Evidently his feet did not go all the way down; the boots must have been stuffed with something so that he would seem taller. Connie stared out at him and behind him Ellie in the car, who seemed to be looking off toward Connie's right, into nothing. This Ellie said, pulling the words out of the air one after another as if he were just discovering them, "You want me to pull out the phone?"

"Shut your mouth and keep it shut," Arnold Friend said, his face red   125 from bending over or maybe from embarrassment because Connie had seen his boots. "This ain't none of your business."

"What—what are you doing? What do you want?" Connie said. "If I call the police they'll get you, they'll arrest you—"

"Promise was not to come in unless you touch that phone, and I'll keep that promise," he said. He resumed his erect position and tried to force his shoulders back. He sounded like a hero in a movie, declaring something important. He spoke too loudly and it was as if he were speaking to someone behind Connie. "I ain't made plans for coming in that house where I don't belong but just for you to come out to me, the way you should. Don't you know who I am?"

"You're crazy," she whispered. She backed away from the door but did not want to go into another part of the house, as if this would give him permission to come through the door. "What do you . . . You're crazy, you . . ."

"Huh? What're you saying, honey?"

Her eyes darted everywhere in the kitchen. She could not remember   130 what it was, this room.

"This is how it is, honey: you come out and we'll drive away, have a nice ride. But if you don't come out we're gonna wait till your people come home and then they're all going to get it."

"You want that telephone pulled out?" Ellie said. He held the radio away from his ear and grimaced, as if without the radio the air was too much for him.

"I toldja shut up, Ellie," Arnold Friend said, "you're deaf, get a hearing aid, right? Fix yourself up. This little girl's no trouble and's gonna be nice to me, so Ellie keep to yourself, this ain't your date— right? Don't hem in on me. Don't hog. Don't crush. Don't bird dog. Don't trail me," he said in a rapid meaningless voice, as if he were running through all the expressions he'd learned but was no longer sure which one of them was in style, then rushing on to new ones, making them up with his eyes closed, "Don't crawl under my fence, don't squeeze in my chipmunk hole, don't sniff my glue, suck my popsicle, keep your own greasy fingers on yourself!" He shaded his eyes and peered in at Connie, who was backed against the kitchen table. "Don't mind him honey he's just a creep. He's a dope. Right? I'm the boy for you and like I said you come out here nice like a lady and give me your hand, and nobody else gets hurt, I mean, your nice old bald-headed daddy and your mummy and your sister in her high heels. Because listen: why bring them in this?"

"Leave me alone," Connie whispered.

"Hey, you know that old woman down the road, the one with the   135
chickens and stuff—you know her?"

"She's dead!"

"Dead? What? You know her?" Arnold Friend said.

"She's dead—"

"Don't you like her?"

"She's dead—she's—she isn't here any more—"   140

"But don't you like her, I mean, you got something against her? Some grudge or something?" Then his voice dipped as if he were conscious of a rudeness. He touched the sunglasses perched on top of his head as if to make sure they were still there. "Now you be a good girl."

"What are you going to do?"

"Just two things, or maybe three," Arnold Friend said. "But I promise it won't last long and you'll like me that way you get to like people you're close to. You will. It's all over for you here, so come on out. You don't want your people in any trouble, do you?"

She turned and bumped against a chair or something, hurting her leg, but she ran into the back room and picked up the telephone. Something roared in her ear, a tiny roaring, and she was so sick with fear that she could do nothing but listen to it—the telephone was clammy and very heavy and her fingers groped down to the dial but were too weak to touch it. She began to scream into the phone, into the roaring. She cried out, she cried for her mother, she felt her breath start jerking back and forth in her lungs as if it were something Arnold Friend were stabbing her with again and again with no tenderness. A noisy sorrowful wailing rose all about her and she was locked inside it the way she was locked inside the house.

After a while she could hear again. She was sitting on the floor with her wet back against the wall. 145

Arnold Friend was saying from the door, "That's a good girl. Put the phone back."

She kicked the phone away from her.

"No, honey. Pick it up. Put it back right."

She picked it up and put it back. The dial tone stopped.

"That's a good girl. Now come outside." 150

She was hollow with what had been fear, but what was now just an emptiness. All that screaming had blasted it out of her. She sat, one leg cramped under her, and deep inside her brain was something like a pinpoint of light that kept going and would not let her relax. She thought, I'm not going to see my mother again. She thought, I'm not going to sleep in my bed again. Her bright green blouse was all wet.

Arnold Friend said, in a gentle-loud voice that was like a stage voice, "The place where you came from ain't there any more, and where you had in mind to go is cancelled out. This place you are now—inside your daddy's house—is nothing but a cardboard box I can knock down any time. You know that and always did know it. You hear me?"

She thought, I have got to think. I have to know what to do.

"We'll go out to a nice field, out in the country here where it smells so nice and it's sunny," Arnold Friend said. "I'll have my arms around you so you won't need to try to get away and I'll show you what love is like, what it does. The hell with this house! It looks solid all right," he said. He ran a fingernail down the screen and the noise did not make Connie shiver, as it would have the day before. "Now put your hand on your heart, honey. Feel that? That feels solid too but we know better, be nice to me, be sweet like you can because what else is there for a girl like you but to be sweet and pretty and give in?—and get away before her people come back?"

She felt her pounding heart. Her hand seemed to enclose it. She thought for the first time in her life that it was nothing that was hers, that belonged to her, but just a pounding, living thing inside this body that wasn't really hers either. 155

"You don't want them to get hurt," Arnold Friend went on. "Now get up, honey. Get up all by yourself."

She stood up.

"Now turn this way. That's right. Come over here to me—Ellie, put that away, didn't I tell you? You dope. You miserable creepy dope," Arnold Friend said. His words were not angry but only part of an incantation. The incantation was kindly. "Now come out through the kitchen to me honey and let's see a smile, try it, you're a brave sweet little girl and now they're eating corn and hotdogs cooked to bursting over an outdoor fire, and they don't know one thing about you and never did and honey you're better than them because not a one of them would have done this for you."

Connie felt the linoleum under her feet; it was cool. She brushed her hair back out of her eyes. Arnold Friend let go of the post tentatively and opened his arms for her, his elbows pointing in toward each other and his wrists limp, to show that this was an embarrassed embrace and a little mocking, he didn't want to make her self-conscious.

She put out her hand against the screen. She watched herself push 160 the door slowly open as if she were safe back somewhere in the other doorway, watching this body and this head of long hair moving out into the sunlight where Arnold Friend waited.

"My sweet little blue-eyed girl," he said, in a half-sung sigh that had nothing to do with her brown eyes but was taken up just the same by the vast sunlit reaches of the land behind him and on all sides of him, so much land that Connie had never seen before and did not recognize except to know that she was going to it.

Tim O'Brien

The Things They Carried 1990

Tim O'Brien was born in 1946 in Austin, Minnesota. Immediately after graduating summa cum laude from Macalester College in 1968, he was drafted into the U.S. Army. Serving as an infantryman in Vietnam, O'Brien attained the rank of sergeant and won a Purple Heart after being wounded by shrapnel. Upon his discharge in 1970, he began graduate work at Harvard. In 1973 he published If I Die in a Combat Zone, Box Me Up and Ship Me Home, *a mixture of memoir and fiction about his wartime experi-*

TIM O'BRIEN

ences. His 1978 novel Going After Cacciato *won the National Book Award, and is considered by some critics to be the best book of American fiction about the Vietnam War. "The Things They Carried" was first published in* Esquire *in 1986, and later became the title piece in a book of interlocking short stories published in 1990. His other novels include* The Nuclear Age *(1985),* In the Lake of the Woods *(1994),* Tomcat in Love *(1998) and* July, July *(2002). O'Brien currently teaches at Texas State University–San Marcos.*

First Lieutenant Jimmy Cross carried letters from a girl named Martha, a junior at Mount Sebastian College in New Jersey. They were not love letters, but Lieutenant Cross was hoping, so he kept them folded in plastic at the bottom of his rucksack. In the late afternoon, after a day's march, he would dig his foxhole, wash his hands under a canteen, unwrap the letters, hold them with the tips of his fingers, and spend the last hour of light pretending. He would imagine romantic camping trips into the White Mountains in New Hampshire. He would sometimes taste the envelope flaps, knowing her tongue had been there. More than anything, he wanted Martha to love him as he loved her, but the letters were mostly chatty, elusive on the matter of love. She was a virgin, he was almost sure. She was an English major at Mount Sebastian, and she wrote beautifully about her professors and roommates and midterm exams, about her respect for Chaucer and her great affection for Virginia Woolf. She often quoted lines of poetry; she never mentioned the war, except to say, Jimmy, take care of yourself. The letters weighed 10 ounces. They were signed Love, Martha, but Lieutenant Cross understood that Love was only a way of signing and did not mean what he sometimes pretended it meant. At dusk, he would carefully return the letters to his rucksack. Slowly, a bit distracted, he would get up and move among his men, checking the perimeter; then at full dark he would return to his hold and watch the night and wonder if Martha was a virgin.

The things they carried were largely determined by necessity. Among the necessities or near-necessities were P-38 can openers, pocket knives, heat tabs, wristwatches, dog tags, mosquito repellent, chewing gum, candy, cigarettes, salt tablets, packets of Kool-Aid, lighters, matches, sewing kits, Military Payment Certificates, C rations, and two or three canteens of water. Together, these items weighed between 15 and 20 pounds, depending upon a man's habits or rate of metabolism. Henry Dobbins, who was a big man, carried extra rations; he was especially fond of canned peaches in heavy syrup over pound cake. Dave Jensen, who practiced field hygiene, carried a toothbrush, dental floss, and several hotel-sized bars of soap he'd stolen on R&R° in Sydney, Australia. Ted Lavender, who was scared, carried tranquilizers until he was shot in the head outside the village of Than Khe in mid-April. By necessity, and because it was SOP,° they all carried steel helmets that weighed 5 pounds including the liner and camouflage cover. They carried the standard fatigue jackets and trousers. Very few carried underwear. On their feet they carried jungle boots—2.1 pounds—and Dave Jensen carried three pairs of socks and a can of Dr. Scholl's foot powder as a precaution against trench foot. Until

---

R&R: the military abbreviation for "rest and rehabilitation," a brief vacation from active service. *SOP*: standard operating procedure.

he was shot, Ted Lavender carried six or seven ounces of premium dope, which for him was a necessity. Mitchell Sanders, the RTO,° carried condoms. Norman Bowker carried a diary. Rat Kiley carried comic books. Kiowa, a devout Baptist, carried an illustrated New Testament that had been presented to him by his father, who taught Sunday school in Oklahoma City, Oklahoma. As a hedge against bad times, however, Kiowa also carried his grandmother's distrust of the white man, his grandfather's old hunting hatchet. Necessity dictated. Because the land was mined and booby-trapped, it was SOP for each man to carry a steel-centered, nylon-covered flak jacket, which weighed 6.7 pounds, but which on hot days seemed much heavier. Because you could die so quickly, each man carried at least one large compress bandage, usually in the helmet band for easy access. Because the nights were cold, and because the monsoons were wet, each carried a green plastic poncho that could be used as a raincoat or groundsheet or makeshift tent. With its quilted liner, the poncho weighed almost two pounds, but it was worth every ounce. In April, for instance, when Ted Lavender was shot, they used his poncho to wrap him up, then to carry him across the paddy, then to lift him into the chopper that took him away.

They were called legs or grunts.

To carry something was to hump it, as when Lieutenant Jimmy Cross humped his love for Martha up the hills and through the swamps. In its intransitive form, to hump meant to walk, or to march, but it implied burdens far beyond the intransitive.

Almost everyone humped photographs. In his wallet, Lieutenant   5
Cross carried two photographs of Martha. The first was a Kodacolor snapshot signed Love, though he knew better. She stood against a brick wall. Her eyes were gray and neutral, her lips slightly open as she stared straight-on at the camera. At night, sometimes, Lieutenant Cross wondered who had taken the picture, because he knew she had boyfriends, because he loved her so much, and because he could see the shadow of the picture-taker spreading out against the brick wall. The second photograph had been clipped from the 1968 Mount Sebastian yearbook. It was an action shot—women's volleyball—and Martha was bent horizontal to the floor, reaching, the palms of her hands in sharp focus, the tongue taut, the expression frank and competitive. There was no visible sweat. She wore white gym shorts. Her legs, he thought, were almost certainly the legs of a virgin, dry and without hair, the left knee cocked and carrying her entire weight, which was just over one hundred pounds. Lieutenant Cross remembered touching that left knee. A dark theater, he remembered, and the movie was *Bonnie and Clyde,* and Martha wore a

RTO: Radio and Telephone Operator.

tweed skirt, and during the final scene, when he touched her knee, she turned and looked at him in a sad, sober way that made him pull his hand back, but he would always remember the feel of the tweed skirt and the knee beneath it and the sound of the gunfire that killed Bonnie and Clyde, how embarrassing it was, how slow and oppressive. He remembered kissing her good night at the dorm door. Right then, he thought, he should've done something brave. He should've carried her up the stairs to her room and tied her to the bed and touched that left knee all night long. He should've risked it. Whenever he looked at the photographs, he thought of new things he should've done.

What they carried was partly a function of rank, partly of field specialty.

As a first lieutenant and platoon leader, Jimmy Cross carried a compass, maps, code books, binoculars, and a .45-caliber pistol that weighed 2.9 pounds fully loaded. He carried a strobe light and the responsibility for the lives of his men.

As an RTO, Mitchell Sanders carried the PRC-25 radio, a killer, 26 pounds with its battery.

As a medic, Rat Kiley carried a canvas satchel filled with morphine and plasma and malaria tablets and surgical tape and comic books and all the things a medic must carry, including M&M's° for especially bad wounds, for a total weight of nearly 20 pounds.

As a big man, therefore a machine gunner, Henry Dobbins carried   10 the M-60, which weighed 23 pounds unloaded, but which was almost always loaded. In addition, Dobbins carried between 10 and 15 pounds of ammunition draped in belts across his chest and shoulders.

As PFCs or Spec 4s, most of them were common grunts and carried the standard M-16 gas-operated assault rifle. The weapon weighed 7.5 pounds unloaded, 8.2 pounds with its full 20-round magazine. Depending on numerous factors, such as topography and psychology, the riflemen carried anywhere from 12 to 20 magazines, usually in cloth bandoliers, adding on another 8.4 pounds at minimum, 14 pounds at maximum. When it was available, they also carried M-16 maintenance gear—rods and steel brushes and swabs and tubes of LSA oil—all of which weighed about a pound. Among the grunts, some carried the M-79 grenade launcher, 5.9 pounds unloaded, a reasonably light weapon except for the ammunition, which was heavy. A single round weighed 10 ounces. The typical load was 25 rounds. But Ted Lavender, who was scared, carried 34 rounds when he was shot and killed outside Than Khe, and he went down under an exceptional burden, more than 20 pounds of ammunition, plus the flak jacket and helmet and rations and water and

_M&M's:_ comic slang for medical supplies.

toilet paper and tranquilizers and all the rest, plus the unweighed fear. He was dead weight. There was no twitching or flopping. Kiowa, who saw it happen, said it was like watching a rock fall, or a big sandbag or something—just boom, then down—not like the movies where the dead guy rolls around and does fancy spins and goes ass over teakettle—not like that, Kiowa said, the poor bastard just flat-fuck fell. Boom. Down. Nothing else. It was a bright morning in mid-April. Lieutenant Cross felt the pain. He blamed himself. They stripped off Lavender's canteens and ammo, all the heavy things, and Rat Kiley said the obvious, the guy's dead, and Mitchell Sanders used his radio to report one U.S. KIA° and to request a chopper. Then they wrapped Lavender in his poncho. They carried him out to a dry paddy, established security, and sat smoking the dead man's dope until the chopper came. Lieutenant Cross kept to himself. He pictured Martha's smooth young face, thinking he loved her more than anything, more than his men, and now Ted Lavender was dead because he loved her so much and could not stop thinking about her. When the dustoff arrived, they carried Lavender aboard. Afterward they burned Than Khe. They marched until dusk, then dug their holes, and that night Kiowa kept explaining how you had to be there, how fast it was, how the poor guy just dropped like so much concrete. Boom-down, he said. Like cement.

In addition to the three standard weapons—the M-60, M-16, and M-79—they carried whatever presented itself, or whatever seemed appropriate as a means of killing or staying alive. They carried catch-as-catch-can. At various times, in various situations, they carried M-14s and CAR-15s and Swedish Ks and grease guns and captured AK-47s and Chi-Coms and RPGs and Simonov carbines and black market Uzis and .38-caliber Smith & Wesson handguns and 66 mm LAWs and shotguns and silencers and blackjacks and bayonets and C-4 plastic explosives. Lee Strunk carried a slingshot; a weapon of last resort, he called it. Mitchell Sanders carried brass knuckles. Kiowa carried his grandfather's feathered hatchet. Every third or fourth man carried a Claymore antipersonnel mine—3.5 pounds with its firing device. They all carried fragmentation grenades—14 ounces each. They all carried at least one M-18 colored smoke grenade—24 ounces. Some carried CS or tear gas grenades. Some carried white phosphorus grenades. They carried all they could bear, and then some, including a silent awe for the terrible power of the things they carried.

In the first week of April, before Lavender died, Lieutenant Jimmy Cross received a good-luck charm from Martha. It was a simple pebble, an ounce at most. Smooth to the touch, it was a milky white color with flecks

KIA: killed in action.

of orange and violet, oval-shaped, like a miniature egg. In the accompanying letter, Martha wrote that she had found the pebble on the Jersey shoreline, precisely where the land touched water at high tide, where things came together but also separated. It was this separate-but-together quality, she wrote, that had inspired her to pick up the pebble and to carry it in her breast pocket for several days, where it seemed weightless, and then to send it through the mail, by air, as a token of her truest feelings for him. Lieutenant Cross found this romantic. But he wondered what her truest feelings were, exactly, and what she meant by separate-but-together. He wondered how the tides and waves had come into play on that afternoon along the Jersey shoreline when Martha saw the pebble and bent down to rescue it from geology. He imagined bare feet. Martha was a poet, with the poet's sensibilities, and her feet would be brown and bare, the toenails unpainted, the eyes chilly and somber like the ocean in March, and though it was painful, he wondered who had been with her that afternoon. He imagined a pair of shadows moving along the strip of sand where things came together but also separated. It was phantom jealousy, he knew, but he couldn't help himself. He loved her so much. On the march, through the hot days of early April, he carried the pebble in his mouth, turning it with his tongue, tasting sea salt and moisture. His mind wandered. He had difficulty keeping his attention on the war. On occasion he would yell at his men to spread out the column, to keep their eyes open, but then he would slip away into daydreams, just pretending, walking barefoot along the Jersey shore, with Martha, carrying nothing. He would feel himself rising. Sun and waves and gentle winds, all love and lightness.

What they carried varied by mission.

When a mission took them to the mountains, they carried mosquito netting, machetes, canvas tarps, and extra bug juice.   15

If a mission seemed especially hazardous, or if it involved a place they knew to be bad, they carried everything they could. In certain heavily mined AOs,° where the land was dense with Toe Poppers and Bouncing Betties, they took turns humping a 28-pound mine detector. With its headphones and big sensing plate, the equipment was a stress on the lower back and shoulders, awkward to handle, often useless because of the shrapnel in the earth, but they carried it anyway, partly for safety, partly for the illusion of safety.

On ambush, or other night missions, they carried peculiar little odds and ends. Kiowa always took along his New Testament and a pair of moccasins for silence. Dave Jensen carried night-sight vitamins high in carotene. Lee Strunk carried his slingshot; ammo, he claimed, would never

---

AOs: areas of operation.

be a problem. Rat Kiley carried brandy and M&M's candy. Until he was shot, Ted Lavender carried the starlight scope, which weighed 6.3 pounds with its aluminum carrying case. Henry Dobbins carried his girlfriend's pantyhose wrapped around his neck as a comforter. They all carried ghosts. When dark came, they would move out single file across the meadows and paddies to their ambush coordinates, where they would quietly set up the Claymores and lie down and spend the night waiting.

Other missions were more complicated and required special equipment. In mid-April, it was their mission to search out and destroy the elaborate tunnel complexes in the Than Khe area south of Chu Lai. To blow the tunnels, they carried one-pound blocks of pentrite high explosives, four blocks to a man, 68 pounds in all. They carried wiring, detonators, and battery-powered clackers. Dave Jensen carried earplugs. Most often, before blowing the tunnels, they were ordered by higher command to search them, which was considered bad news, but by and large they just shrugged and carried out orders. Because he was a big man, Henry Dobbins was excused from tunnel duty. The others would draw numbers. Before Lavender died there were 17 men in the platoon, and whoever drew the number 17 would strip off his gear and crawl in headfirst with a flashlight and Lieutenant Cross's .45-caliber pistol. The rest of them would fan out as security. They would sit down or kneel, not facing the hole, listening to the ground beneath them, imagining cobwebs and ghosts, whatever was down there—the tunnel walls squeezing in—how the flashlight seemed impossibly heavy in the hand and how it was tunnel vision in the very strictest sense, compression in all ways, even time, and how you had to wiggle in—ass and elbows—a swallowed-up feeling—and how you found yourself worrying about odd things: Will your flashlight go dead? Do rats carry rabies? If you screamed, how far would the sound carry? Would your buddies hear it? Would they have the courage to drag you out? In some respects, though not many, the waiting was worse than the tunnel itself. Imagination was a killer.

On April 16, when Lee Strunk drew the number 17, he laughed and muttered something and went down quickly. The morning was hot and very still. Not good, Kiowa said. He looked at the tunnel opening, then out across a dry paddy toward the village of Than Khe. Nothing moved. No clouds or birds or people. As they waited, the men smoked and drank Kool-Aid, not talking much, feeling sympathy for Lee Strunk but also feeling the luck of the draw. You win some, you lose some, said Mitchell Sanders, and sometimes you settle for a rain check. It was a tired line and no one laughed.

Henry Dobbins ate a tropical chocolate bar. Ted Lavender popped a tranquilizer and went off to pee. 20

After five minutes, Lieutenant Jimmy Cross moved to the tunnel, leaned down, and examined the darkness. Trouble, he thought—a cave-in maybe. And then suddenly, without willing it, he was thinking about Martha. The stresses and fractures, the quick collapse, the two of them buried alive under all that weight. Dense, crushing love. Kneeling, watching the hole, he tried to concentrate on Lee Strunk and the war, all the dangers, but his love was too much for him, he felt paralyzed, he wanted to sleep inside her lungs and breathe her blood and be smothered. He wanted her to be a virgin and not a virgin, all at once. He wanted to know her. Intimate secrets: Why poetry? Why so sad? Why that grayness in her eyes? Why so alone? Not lonely, just alone—riding her bike across campus or sitting off by herself in the cafeteria—even dancing, she danced alone—and it was the aloneness that filled him with love. He remembered telling her that one evening. How she nodded and looked away. And how, later, when he kissed her, she received the kiss without returning it, her eyes wide open, not afraid, not a virgin's eyes, just flat and uninvolved.

Lieutenant Cross gazed at the tunnel. But he was not there. He was buried with Martha under the white sand at the Jersey shore. They were pressed together, and the pebble in his mouth was her tongue. He was smiling. Vaguely, he was aware of how quiet the day was, the sullen paddies, yet he could not bring himself to worry about matters of security. He was beyond that. He was just a kid at war, in love. He was twenty-four years old. He couldn't help it.

A few moments later Lee Strunk crawled out of the tunnel. He came up grinning, filthy but alive. Lieutenant Cross nodded and closed his eyes while the others clapped Strunk on the back and made jokes about rising from the dead.

Worms, Rat Kiley said. Right out of the grave. Fuckin' zombie.

The men laughed. They all felt great relief.   25

Spook city, said Mitchell Sanders.

Lee Strunk made a funny ghost sound, a kind of moaning, yet very happy, and right then, when Strunk made that high happy moaning sound, when he went *Ahhooooo*, right then Ted Lavender was shot in the head on his way back from peeing. He lay with his mouth open. The teeth were broken. There was a swollen black bruise under his left eye. The cheekbone was gone. Oh shit, Rat Kiley said, the guy's dead. The guy's dead, he kept saying, which seemed profound—the guy's dead. I mean really.

The things they carried were determined to some extent by superstition. Lieutenant Cross carried his good-luck pebble. Dave Jensen carried a rabbit's foot. Norman Bowker, otherwise a very gentle person, carried a thumb that had been presented to him as a gift by Mitchell Sanders. The thumb was dark brown, rubbery to the touch, and weighed four ounces at most. It had been cut from a VC corpse, a boy of fifteen or sixteen.

They'd found him at the bottom of an irrigation ditch, badly burned, flies in his mouth and eyes. The boy wore black shorts and sandals. At the time of his death he had been carrying a pouch of rice, a rifle, and three magazines of ammunition.

You want my opinion, Mitchell Sanders said, there's a definite moral here.

He put his hand on the dead boy's wrist. He was quiet for a time, as if counting a pulse, then he patted the stomach, almost affectionately, and used Kiowa's hunting hatchet to remove the thumb. 30

Henry Dobbins asked what the moral was.

Moral?

You know. *Moral.*

Sanders wrapped the thumb in toilet paper and handed it across to Norman Bowker. There was no blood. Smiling, he kicked the boy's head, watched the flies scatter, and said, It's like with that old TV show—Paladin. Have gun, will travel.

Henry Dobbins thought about it. 35

Yeah, well, he finally said. I don't see no moral.

There it *is*, man.

Fuck off.

They carried USO stationery and pencils and pens. They carried Sterno, safety pins, trip flares, signal flares, spools of wire, razor blades, chewing tobacco, liberated joss sticks and statuettes of the smiling Buddha, candles, grease pencils, *The Stars and Stripes*, fingernail clippers, Psy Ops leaflets, bush hats, bolos, and much more. Twice a week, when the resupply choppers came in, they carried hot chow in green mermite cans and large canvas bags filled with iced beer and soda pop. They carried plastic water containers, each with a two-gallon capacity. Mitchell Sanders carried a set of starched tiger fatigues for special occasions. Henry Dobbins carried Black Flag insecticide. Dave Jensen carried empty sandbags that could be filled at night for added protection. Lee Strunk carried tanning lotion. Some things they carried in common. Taking turns, they carried the big PRC-77 scrambler radio, which weighed 30 pounds with its battery. They shared the weight of memory. They took up what others could no longer bear. Often, they carried each other, the wounded or weak. They carried infections. They carried chess sets, basketballs, Vietnamese-English dictionaries, insignia of rank, Bronze Stars and Purple Hearts, plastic cards imprinted with the Code of Conduct. They carried diseases, among them malaria and dysentery. They carried lice and ringworm and leeches and paddy algae and various rots and molds. They carried the land itself—Vietnam, the place, the soil—a powdery orange-red dust that covered their boots and fatigues and faces. They carried the sky. The whole atmosphere, they carried it, the humidity, the monsoons, the stink of fungus and decay, all of it, they carried gravity. They moved like mules. By daylight they took sniper fire, at night they were mortared, but it was not battle, it was just the endless march, village to village, without purpose, nothing won or lost. They marched for the sake of the march. They plodded along slowly, dumbly, leaning forward against the heat, unthinking, all blood and bone, simple grunts, soldiering with their legs, toiling up the hills and down into the paddies and across the rivers and up again and down, just humping, one step and then the next and then another, but no volition, no will, because it was automatic, it was anatomy, and the war was entirely a matter of posture and carriage, the hump was everything, a kind of inertia, a kind of emptiness, a dullness of desire and intellect and conscience and hope and human sensibility. Their principles were in their feet. Their calculations were biological. They had no sense of strategy or mission. They searched the villages without knowing what to look for, not caring, kicking over jars of rice, frisking children and old men, blowing tunnels, sometimes setting fires and sometimes not, then forming up and moving on to the next village, then other villages, where it would always be the same. They carried their own lives. The pressures were enormous. In the heat of early afternoon, they would remove their helmets and flak jackets, walking bare, which was dangerous but which helped ease the strain. They would often discard things along the route of march. Purely for comfort, they would throw away rations, blow their Claymores and grenades, no matter, because by nightfall the resupply choppers would arrive with more of the same, then a day or two later still more, fresh watermelons and crates of ammunition and sunglasses and woolen sweaters—the resources were stunning—sparklers for the Fourth of July, colored eggs for Easter—it was the great American war chest—the fruits of science, the smokestacks, the canneries, the arsenals at Hartford, the Minnesota forests, the machine shops, the vast fields of corn and wheat—they carried like freight trains; they carried it on their backs and shoulders—and for all the ambiguities of Vietnam, all the mysteries and unknowns, there was at least the single abiding certainty that they would never be at a loss for things to carry.

After the chopper took Lavender away, Lieutenant Jimmy Cross led   40 his men into the village of Than Khe. They burned everything. They shot chickens and dogs, they trashed the village well, they called in artillery and watched the wreckage, then they marched for several hours through the hot afternoon, and then at dusk, while Kiowa explained how Lavender died, Lieutenant Cross found himself trembling.

He tried not to cry. With his entrenching tool, which weighed five pounds, he began digging a hole in the earth.

He felt shame. He hated himself. He had loved Martha more than his men, and as a consequence Lavender was now dead, and this was something he would have to carry like a stone in his stomach for the rest of the war.

All he could do was dig. He used his entrenching tool like an ax, slashing, feeling both love and hate, and then later, when it was full dark, he sat at the bottom of his foxhole and wept. It went on for a long while. In part, he was grieving for Ted Lavender, but mostly it was for Martha, and for himself, because she belonged to another world, which was not quite real, and because she was a junior at Mount Sebastian College in New Jersey, a poet and a virgin and uninvolved, and because he realized she did not love him and never would.

Like cement, Kiowa whispered in the dark. I swear to God—boom, down. Not a word.

I've heard this, said Norman Bowker.   45

A pisser, you know? Still zipping himself up. Zapped while zipping.

All right, fine. That's enough.

Yeah, but you had to see it, the guy just—

I *heard*, man. Cement. So why not shut the fuck *up?*

Kiowa shook his head sadly and glanced over at the hole where Lieu-   50
tenant Jimmy Cross sat watching the night. The air was thick and wet. A warm dense fog had settled over the paddies and there was the stillness that precedes rain.

After a time Kiowa sighed.

One thing for sure, he said. The lieutenant's in some deep hurt. I mean that crying jag—the way he was carrying on—it wasn't fake or anything, it was real heavy-duty hurt. The man cares.

Sure, Norman Bowker said.

Say what you want, the man does care.

We all got problems.   55

Not Lavender.

No, I guess not, Bowker said. Do me a favor, though.

Shut up?

That's a smart Indian. Shut up.

Shrugging, Kiowa pulled off his boots. He wanted to say more, just to   60
lighten up his sleep, but instead he opened his New Testament and arranged it beneath his head as a pillow. The fog made things seem hollow and unattached. He tried not to think about Ted Lavender, but then he was thinking how fast it was, no drama, down and dead, and how it was hard to feel anything except surprise. It seemed unchristian. He wished he could find some great sadness, or even anger, but the emotion wasn't there and he couldn't make it happen. Mostly he felt pleased to be alive. He liked the smell of the New Testament under his cheek, the leather and ink and paper and glue, whatever the chemicals were. He

liked hearing the sounds of night. Even his fatigue, it felt fine, the stiff muscles and the prickly awareness of his own body, a floating feeling. He enjoyed not being dead. Lying there, Kiowa admired Lieutenant Jimmy Cross's capacity for grief. He wanted to share the man's pain, he wanted to care as Jimmy Cross cared. And yet when he closed his eyes, all he could think was Boom-down, and all he could feel was the pleasure of having his boots off and the fog curling in around him and the damp soil and the Bible smells and the plush comfort of night.

After a moment Norman Bowker sat up in the dark.

What the hell, he said. You want to talk, *talk*. Tell it to me.

Forget it.

No, man, go on. One thing I hate, it's a silent Indian.

For the most part they carried themselves with poise, a kind of dig- 65 nity. Now and then, however, there were times of panic, when they squealed or wanted to squeal but couldn't, when they twitched and made moaning sounds and covered their heads and said Dear Jesus and flopped around on the earth and fired their weapons blindly and cringed and sobbed and begged for the noise to stop and went wild and made stupid promises to themselves and to God and to their mothers and fathers, hoping not to die. In different ways, it happened to all of them. Afterward, when the firing ended, they would blink and peek up. They would touch their bodies, feeling shame, then quickly hiding it. They would force themselves to stand. As if in slow motion, frame by frame, the world would take on the old logic—absolute silence, then the wind, then sunlight, then voices. It was the burden of being alive. Awkwardly, the men would reassemble themselves, first in private, then in groups, becoming soldiers again. They would repair the leaks in their eyes. They would check for casualties, call in dustoffs, light cigarettes, try to smile, clear their throats and spit and begin cleaning their weapons. After a time someone would shake his head and say, No lie, I almost shit my pants, and someone else would laugh, which meant it was bad, yes, but the guy had obviously not shit his pants, it wasn't that bad, and in any case nobody would ever do such a thing and then go ahead and talk about it. They would squint into the dense, oppressive sunlight. For a few moments, perhaps, they would fall silent, lighting a joint and tracking its passage from man to man, inhaling, holding in the humiliation. Scary stuff, one of them might say. But then someone else would grin or flick his eyebrows and say, Roger-dodger, almost cut me a new asshole, *almost*.

There were numerous such poses. Some carried themselves with a sort of wistful resignation, others with pride or stiff soldierly discipline or good humor or macho zeal. They were afraid of dying but they were even more afraid to show it.

They found jokes to tell.

They used a hard vocabulary to contain the terrible softness. *Greased* they'd say. *Offed, lit up, zapped while zipping.* It wasn't cruelty, just stage presence. They were actors. When someone died, it wasn't quite dying, because in a curious way it seemed scripted, and because they had their lines mostly memorized, irony mixed with tragedy, and because they called it by other names, as if to encyst and destroy the reality of death itself. They kicked corpses. They cut off thumbs. They talked grunt lingo. They told stories about Ted Lavender's supply of tranquilizers, how the poor guy didn't feel a thing, how incredibly tranquil he was.

There's a moral here, said Mitchell Sanders.

They were waiting for Lavender's chopper, smoking the dead man's dope. 70

The moral's pretty obvious, Sanders said, and winked. Stay away from drugs. No joke, they'll ruin your day every time.

Cute, said Henry Dobbins.

Mind blower, get it? Talk about wiggy. Nothing left, just blood and brains.

They made themselves laugh.

There it is, they'd say. Over and over—there it is, my friend, there it 75 is—as if the repetition itself were an act of poise, a balance between crazy and almost crazy, knowing without going, there it is, which meant be cool, let it ride, because Oh yeah, man, you can't change what can't be changed, there it is, there it absolutely and positively and fucking well *is*.

They were tough.

They carried all the emotional baggage of men who might die. Grief, terror, love, longing—these were intangibles, but the intangibles had their own mass and specific gravity, they had tangible weight. They carried shameful memories. They carried the common secret of cowardice barely restrained, the instinct to run or freeze or hide, and in many respects this was the heaviest burden of all, for it could never be put down, it required perfect balance and perfect posture. They carried their reputations. They carried the soldier's greatest fear, which was the fear of blushing. Men killed, and died, because they were embarrassed not to. It was what had brought them to the war in the first place, nothing positive, no dreams of glory or honor, just to avoid the blush of dishonor. They died so as not to die of embarrassment. They crawled into tunnels and walked point and advanced under fire. Each morning, despite the unknowns, they made their legs move. They endured. They kept humping. They did not submit to the obvious alternative, which was simply to close the eyes and fall. So easy, really. Go limp and tumble to the ground and let the muscles unwind and not speak and not budge until your buddies picked you up and lifted you into the chopper that would roar and dip its nose and carry you off to the world. A mere matter of falling, yet no one ever fell. It was not courage, exactly; the object was not valor. Rather, they were too frightened to be cowards.

By and large they carried these things inside, maintaining the masks of composure. They sneered at sick call. They spoke bitterly about guys who had found release by shooting off their own toes or fingers. Pussies, they'd say. Candy-asses. It was fierce, mocking talk, with only a trace of envy or awe, but even so the image played itself out behind their eyes.

They imagined the muzzle against flesh. So easy: squeeze the trigger and blow away a toe. They imagined it. They imagined the quick, sweet pain, then the evacuation to Japan, then a hospital with warm beds and cute geisha nurses.

And they dreamed of freedom birds.

At night, on guard, staring into the dark, they were carried away by jumbo jets. They felt the rush of takeoff. *Gone!* they yelled. And then velocity—wings and engines—a smiling stewardess—but it was more than a plane, it was a real bird, a big sleek silver bird with feathers and talons and high screeching. They were flying. The weights fell off; there was nothing to bear. They laughed and held on tight, feeling the cold slap of wind and altitude, soaring, thinking *It's over, I'm gone!* —they were naked, they were light and free—it was all lightness, bright and fast and buoyant, light as light, a helium buzz in the brain, a giddy bubbling in the lungs as they were taken up over the clouds and the war, beyond duty, beyond gravity and mortification and global entanglements—*Sin loi!*° they yelled. *I'm sorry, mother-fuckers, but I'm out of it, I'm goofed, I'm on a space cruise, I'm gone!* —and it was a restful, unencumbered sensation, just riding the light waves, sailing that big silver freedom bird over the mountains and oceans, over America, over the farms and great sleeping cities and cemeteries and highways and the golden arches of McDonald's, it was flight, a kind of fleeing, a kind of falling, falling higher and higher, spinning off the edge of the earth and beyond the sun and through the vast, silent vacuum where there were no burdens and where everything weighed exactly nothing—*Gone!* they screamed. *I'm sorry but I'm gone!*—and so at night, not quite dreaming, they gave themselves over to lightness, they were carried, they were purely borne.

On the morning after Ted Lavender died, First Lieutenant Jimmy Cross crouched at the bottom of his foxhole and burned Martha's letters. Then he burned the two photographs. There was a steady rain falling, which made it difficult, but he used heat tabs and Sterno to build a small fire, screening it with his body, holding the photographs over the tight blue flame with the tips of his fingers.

80

Sin loi: Vietnamese for sorry.

He realized it was only a gesture. Stupid, he thought. Sentimental, too, but mostly just stupid.

Lavender was dead. You couldn't burn the blame.

Besides, the letters were in his head. And even now, without photographs, Lieutenant Cross could see Martha playing volleyball in her white gym shorts and yellow T-shirt. He could see her moving in the rain.

When the fire died out, Lieutenant Cross pulled his poncho over his shoulders and ate breakfast from a can.

There was no great mystery, he decided.

In those burned letters Martha had never mentioned the war, except to say, Jimmy, take care of yourself. She wasn't involved. She signed the letters Love, but it wasn't love, and all the fine lines and technicalities did not matter. Virginity was no longer an issue. He hated her. Yes, he did. He hated her. Love, too, but it was a hard, hating kind of love.

The morning came up wet and blurry. Everything seemed part of everything else, the fog and Martha and the deepening rain.

He was a soldier, after all.

Half smiling, Lieutenant Jimmy Cross took out his maps. He shook his head hard, as if to clear it, then bent forward and began planning the day's march. In ten minutes, or maybe twenty, he would rouse the men and they would pack up and head west, where the maps showed the country to be green and inviting. They would do what they had always done. The rain might add some weight, but otherwise it would be one more day layered upon all the other days.

He was realistic about it. There was that new hardness in his stomach. He loved her but he hated her.

No more fantasies, he told himself.

Henceforth, when he thought about Martha, it would be only to think that she belonged elsewhere. He would shut down the daydreams. This was not Mount Sebastian, it was another world, where there were no pretty poems or midterm exams, a place where men died because of carelessness and gross stupidity. Kiowa was right. Boom-down, and you were dead, never partly dead.

Briefly, in the rain, Lieutenant Cross saw Martha's gray eyes gazing back at him.

He understood.

It was very sad, he thought. The things men carried inside. The things men did or felt they had to do.

He almost nodded at her, but didn't.

Instead he went back to his maps. He was now determined to perform his duties firmly and without negligence. It wouldn't help Lavender, he knew that, but from this point on he would comport himself as an officer. He would dispose of his good-luck pebble. Swallow it, maybe, or use

Lee Strunk's slingshot, or just drop it along the trail. On the march he would impose strict field discipline. He would be careful to send out flank security, to prevent straggling or bunching up, to keep his troops moving at the proper pace and at the proper interval. He would insist on clean weapons. He would confiscate the remainder of Lavender's dope. Later in the day, perhaps, he would call the men together and speak to them plainly. He would accept the blame for what had happened to Ted Lavender. He would be a man about it. He would look them in the eyes, keeping his chin level, and he would issue the new SOPs in a calm, impersonal tone of voice, a lieutenant's voice, leaving no room for argument or discussion. Commencing immediately, he'd tell them, they would no longer abandon equipment along the route of march. They would police up their acts. They would get their shit together, and keep it together, and maintain it neatly and in good working order.

He would not tolerate laxity. He would show strength, distancing   100
himself.

Among the men there would be grumbling, of course, and maybe worse, because their days would seem longer and their loads heavier, but Lieutenant Jimmy Cross reminded himself that his obligation was not to be loved but to lead. He would dispense with love; it was not now a factor. And if anyone quarreled or complained, he would simply tighten his lips and arrange his shoulders in the correct command posture. He might give a curt little nod. Or he might not. He might just shrug and say, Carry on, then they would saddle up and form into a column and move out toward the villages west of Than Khe.

Flannery O'Connor

A Good Man Is Hard to Find   1955

Mary Flannery O'Connor (1925–1964) was born in Savannah, Georgia, but spent most of her life in the small town of Milledgeville. While attending Georgia State College for Women, she won a local reputation for her fledgling stories and satiric cartoons. After graduating in 1945, she went on to study at the University of Iowa, where she earned an M.F.A. in 1947. Diagnosed in 1950 with disseminated lupus, the same incurable illness that had killed her father, O'Connor returned home and spent the last decade of her life living with her mother in Milledgeville. Back on the family dairy farm, she wrote, maintained an extensive literary correspondence, raised peacocks, and underwent medical treatment. When her illness occasionally went into a period of remission, she made trips to lecture and read

FLANNERY O'CONNOR

her stories to college audiences. Her health declined rapidly after surgery early in 1964 for an unrelated complaint. She died at thirty-nine.

O'Connor is unusual among modern American writers in the depth of her Christian vision. A devout Roman Catholic, she attended mass daily while growing up and living in the largely Protestant South. As a latter-day satirist in the manner of Jonathan Swift, O'Connor levels the eye of an uncompromising moralist on the violence and spiritual disorder of the modern world, focusing on what she calls "the action of grace in territory held largely by the devil." She is sometimes called a "Southern Gothic" writer because of her fascination with grotesque incidents and characters. Throughout her career she depicted the South as a troubled region in which the social, racial, and religious status quo that had existed since before the Civil War was coming to a violent end. Despite the inherent seriousness of her religious and social themes, O'Connor's mordant and frequently outrageous humor is everywhere apparent. Her combination of profound vision and dark comedy is the distinguishing characteristic of her literary sensibilities.

O'Connor's published work includes two short novels, Wise Blood (1952) and The Violent Bear It Away (1960), and two collections of short stories, A Good Man Is Hard to Find (1955) and Everything That Rises Must Converge, published posthumously in 1965. A collection of essays and miscellaneous prose, Mystery and Manners (1969), and her selected letters, The Habit of Being (1979), reveal an innate cheerfulness and engaging personal warmth that are not always apparent in her fiction. The Complete Stories of Flannery O'Connor was posthumously awarded the National Book Award in 1971.

The grandmother didn't want to go to Florida. She wanted to visit some of her connections in east Tennessee and she was seizing at every chance to change Bailey's mind. Bailey was the son she lived with, her only boy. He was sitting on the edge of his chair at the table, bent over the orange sports section of the *Journal.* "Now look here, Bailey," she said, "see here, read this," and she stood with one hand on her thin hip and the other rattling the newspaper at his bald head. "Here this fellow that calls himself The Misfit is aloose from the Federal Pen and headed toward Florida and you read here what it says he did to these people. Just you read it. I wouldn't take my children in any direction with a criminal like that aloose in it. I couldn't answer to my conscience if I did."

Bailey didn't look up from his reading so she wheeled around then and faced the children's mother, a young woman in slacks, whose face was as broad and innocent as a cabbage and was tied around with a green head-kerchief that had two points on the top like rabbit's ears. She was sitting on the sofa, feeding the baby his apricots out of a jar. "The children have been to Florida before," the old lady said. "You all ought to take them somewhere else for a change so they would see different parts of the world and be broad. They never have been to east Tennessee."

The children's mother didn't seem to hear her but the eight-year-old boy, John Wesley, a stocky child with glasses, said, "If you don't want to go to Florida, why dontcha stay at home?" He and the little girl, June Star, were reading the funny papers on the floor.

"She wouldn't stay at home to be queen for a day," June Star said without raising her yellow head.

"Yes and what would you do if this fellow, The Misfit, caught you?" the grandmother said.   5

"I'd smack his face," John Wesley said.

"She wouldn't stay at home for a million bucks," June Star said. "Afraid she'd miss something. She has to go everywhere we go."

"All right, Miss," the grandmother said. "Just remember that the next time you want me to curl your hair."

June Star said her hair was naturally curly.

The next morning the grandmother was the first one in the car, ready to go. She had her big black valise that looked like the head of a hippopotamus in one corner, and underneath it she was hiding a basket with Pitty Sing, the cat, in it. She didn't intend for the cat to be left alone in the house for three days because he would miss her too much and she was afraid he might brush against one of the gas burners and accidentally asphyxiate himself. Her son, Bailey, didn't like to arrive at a motel with a cat.   10

She sat in the middle of the back seat with John Wesley and June Star on either side of her. Bailey and the children's mother and the baby sat in front and they left Atlanta at eight forty-five with the mileage on the car at 55890. The grandmother wrote this down because she thought it would be interesting to say how many miles they had been when they got back. It took them twenty minutes to reach the outskirts of the city.

The old lady settled herself comfortably, removing her white cotton gloves and putting them up with her purse on the shelf in front of the back window. The children's mother still had on slacks and still had her hair tied up in a green kerchief, but the grandmother had on a navy blue straw sailor hat with a bunch of white violets on the brim and a navy blue dress with a small white dot in the print. Her collars and cuffs were white organdy trimmed with lace and at her neckline she had pinned a purple spray of cloth violets containing a sachet. In case of an accident, anyone seeing her dead on the highway would know at once that she was a lady.

She said she thought it was going to be a good day for driving, neither too hot nor too cold, and she cautioned Bailey that the speed limit was fifty-five miles an hour and that the patrolmen hid themselves behind billboards and small clumps of trees and sped out after you before you had a chance to slow down. She pointed out interesting details of the scenery: Stone Mountain; the blue granite that in some places came up to both sides of the highway; the brilliant red clay banks slightly streaked with purple; and the various crops that made rows of green lace-work on the ground. The trees were full of silver-white sunlight and the meanest of them sparkled. The children were reading comic magazines and their mother had gone back to sleep.

"Let's go through Georgia fast so we won't have to look at it much," John Wesley said.

"If I were a little boy," said the grandmother, "I wouldn't talk about my native state that way. Tennessee has the mountains and Georgia has the hills." 15

"Tennessee is just a hillbilly dumping ground," John Wesley said, "and Georgia is a lousy state too."

"You said it," June Star said.

"In my time," said the grandmother, folding her thin veined fingers, "children were more respectful of their native states and their parents and everything else. People did right then. Oh look at the cute little pickaninny!" she said and pointed to a Negro child standing in the door of a shack. "Wouldn't that make a picture, now?" she asked and they all turned and looked at the little Negro out of the back window. He waved.

"He didn't have any britches on," June Star said.

"He probably didn't have any," the grandmother explained. "Little niggers in the country don't have things like we do. If I could paint, I'd paint that picture," she said. 20

The children exchanged comic books.

The grandmother offered to hold the baby and the children's mother passed him over the front seat to her. She set him on her knee and bounced him and told him about the things they were passing. She rolled her eyes and screwed up her mouth and stuck her leathery thin face into his smooth bland one. Occasionally he gave her a faraway smile. They passed a large cotton field with five or six graves fenced in the middle of it, like a small island. "Look at the graveyard!" the grandmother said, pointing it out. "That was the old family burying ground. That belonged to the plantation."

"Where's the plantation?" John Wesley asked.

"Gone With the Wind," said the grandmother. "Ha. Ha."

When the children finished all the comic books they had brought, they opened the lunch and ate it. The grandmother ate a peanut butter sandwich and an olive and would not let the children throw the box and the paper napkins out the window. When there was nothing else to do they played a game by choosing a cloud and making the other two guess what shape it suggested. John Wesley took one the shape of a cow and June Star guessed a cow and John Wesley said, no, an automobile, and June Star said he didn't play fair, and they began to slap each other over the grandmother. 25

The grandmother said she would tell them a story if they would keep quiet. When she told a story, she rolled her eyes and waved her head and was very dramatic. She said once when she was a maiden lady she had been courted by a Mr. Edgar Atkins Teagarden from Jasper, Georgia. She said he was a very good-looking man and a gentleman and that he brought her a watermelon every Saturday afternoon with his initials cut in it, E. A. T. Well, one Saturday, she said, Mr. Teagarden brought the watermelon and there was nobody at home and he left it on the front porch and returned in his buggy to Jasper, but she never got the watermelon, she said, because a nigger boy ate it when he saw the initials, E. A. T.!

This story tickled John Wesley's funny bone and he giggled and giggled but June Star didn't think it was any good. She said she wouldn't marry a man that just brought her a watermelon on Saturday. The grandmother said she would have done well to marry Mr. Teagarden because he was a gentleman and had bought Coca-Cola stock when it first came out and that he had died only a few years ago, a very wealthy man.

They stopped at The Tower for barbecued sandwiches. The Tower was a part stucco and part wood filling station and dance hall set in a clearing outside of Timothy. A fat man named Red Sammy Butts ran it and there were signs stuck here and there on the building and for miles up and down the highway saying, TRY RED SAMMY'S FAMOUS BARBECUE. NONE LIKE FAMOUS RED SAMMY'S! RED SAM! THE FAT BOY WITH THE HAPPY LAUGH. A VETERAN! RED SAMMY'S YOUR MAN!

Red Sammy was lying on the bare ground outside The Tower with his head under a truck while a gray monkey about a foot high, chained to a small chinaberry tree, chattered nearby. The monkey sprang back into the tree and got on the highest limb as soon as he saw the children jump out of the car and run toward him.

Inside, The Tower was a long dark room with a counter at one end   30 and tables at the other and dancing space in the middle. They all sat down at a board table next to the nickelodeon and Red Sam's wife, a tall burnt-brown woman with hair and eyes lighter than her skin, came and took their order. The children's mother put a dime in the machine and played "The Tennessee Waltz," and the grandmother said that tune always made her want to dance. She asked Bailey if he would like to dance but he only glared at her. He didn't have a naturally sunny disposition like she did and trips made him nervous. The grandmother's brown eyes were very bright. She swayed her head from side to side and pretended she was dancing in her chair. June Star said play something she could tap to so the children's mother put in another dime and played a fast number and June Star stepped out onto the dance floor and did her tap routine.

"Ain't she cute?" Red Sam's wife said, leaning over the counter. "Would you like to come be my little girl?"

"No I certainly wouldn't," June Star said. "I wouldn't live in a broken-down place like this for a million bucks!" and she ran back to the table.

"Ain't she cute?" the woman repeated, stretching her mouth politely.

"Arn't you ashamed?" hissed the grandmother.

Red Sam came in and told his wife to quit lounging on the counter   35
and hurry up with these people's order. His khaki trousers reached just to
his hip bones and his stomach hung over them like a sack of meal
swaying under his shirt. He came over and sat down at a table nearby and
let out a combination sigh and yodel. "You can't win," he said. "You can't
win," and he wiped his sweating red face off with a gray handkerchief.
"These days you don't know who to trust," he said. "Ain't that the truth?"

"People are certainly not nice like they used to be," said the grandmother.

"Two fellers come in here last week," Red Sammy said, "driving a
Chrysler. It was a old beat-up car but it was a good one and these boys
looked all right to me. Said they worked at the mill and you know I let
them fellers charge the gas they bought? Now why did I do that?"

"Because you're a good man!" the grandmother said at once.

"Yes'm, I suppose so," Red Sam said as if he were struck with this answer.

His wife brought the orders, carrying the five plates all at once   40
without a tray, two in each hand and one balanced on her arm. "It isn't
a soul in this green world of God's that you can trust," she said. "And I
don't count nobody out of that, not nobody," she repeated, looking at
Red Sammy.

"Did you read about that criminal, The Misfit, that's escaped?" asked
the grandmother.

"I wouldn't be a bit surprised if he didn't attact this place right here,"
said the woman. "If he hears about it being here, I wouldn't be none surprised to see him. If he hears it's two cent in the cash register, I wouldn't
be a-tall surprised if he . . ."

"That'll do," Red Sam said. "Go bring these people their Co'-Colas,"
and the woman went off to get the rest of the order.

"A good man is hard to find," Red Sammy said. "Everything is getting terrible. I remember the day you could go off and leave your screen
door unlatched. Not no more."

He and the grandmother discussed better times. The old lady said   45
that in her opinion Europe was entirely to blame for the way things were
now. She said the way Europe acted you would think we were made of
money and Red Sam said it was no use talking about it, she was exactly
right. The children ran outside into the white sunlight and looked at the
monkey in the lacy chinaberry tree. He was busy catching fleas on himself
and biting each one carefully between his teeth as if it were a delicacy.

They drove off again into the hot afternoon. The grandmother took
cat naps and woke up every five minutes with her own snoring. Outside of

Toombsboro she woke up and recalled an old plantation that she had visited in this neighborhood once when she was a young lady. She said the house had six white columns across the front and that there was an avenue of oaks leading up to it and two little wooden trellis arbors on either side in front where you sat down with your suitor after a stroll in the garden. She recalled exactly which road to turn off to get to it. She knew that Bailey would not be willing to lose any time looking at an old house, but the more she talked about it, the more she wanted to see it once again and find out if the little twin arbors were still standing. "There was a secret panel in this house," she said craftily, not telling the truth but wishing that she were, "and the story went that all the family silver was hidden in it when Sherman° came through but it was never found . . ."

"Hey!" John Wesley said. "Let's go see it! We'll find it! We'll poke all the woodwork and find it! Who lives there? Where do you turn off at? Hey, Pop, can't we turn off there?"

"We never have seen a house with a secret panel!" June Star shrieked. "Let's go to the house with the secret panel! Hey Pop, can't we go see the house with the secret panel!"

"It's not far from here, I know," the grandmother said. "It wouldn't take over twenty minutes."

Bailey was looking straight ahead. His jaw was as rigid as a horseshoe. 50 "No," he said.

The children began to yell and scream that they wanted to see the house with the secret panel. John Wesley kicked the back of the front seat and June Star hung over her mother's shoulder and whined desperately into her ear that they never had any fun even on their vacation, that they could never do what THEY wanted to do. The baby began to scream and John Wesley kicked the back of the seat so hard that his father could feel the blows in his kidney.

"All right!" he shouted and drew the car to a stop at the side of the road. "Will you all shut up? Will you all just shut up for one second? If you don't shut up, we won't go anywhere."

"It would be very educational for them," the grandmother murmured.

"All right," Bailey said, "but get this: this is the only time we're going to stop for anything like this. This is the one and only time."

"The dirt road that you have to turn down is about a mile back," the 55 grandmother directed. "I marked it when we passed."

"A dirt road," Bailey groaned.

After they had turned around and were headed toward the dirt road, the grandmother recalled other points about the house, the beautiful glass

---

Sherman: General William Tecumseh Sherman, Union commander, whose troops burned Atlanta in 1864, then made a devastating march to the sea.

over the front doorway and the candle-lamp in the hall. John Wesley
said that the secret panel was probably in the fireplace.

"You can't go inside this house," Bailey said. "You don't know who
lives there."

"While you all talk to the people in front, I'll run around behind and
get in a window," John Wesley suggested.

"We'll all stay in the car," his mother said. 60

They turned onto the dirt road and the car raced roughly along in a
swirl of pink dust. The grandmother recalled the times when there were
no paved roads and thirty miles was a day's journey. The dirt road was
hilly and there were sudden washes in it and sharp curves on dangerous
embankments. All at once they would be on a hill, looking down over
the blue tops of trees for miles around, then the next minute, they would
be in a red depression with the dust-coated trees looking down on them.

"This place had better turn up in a minute," Bailey said, "or I'm going
to turn around."

The road looked as if no one had traveled on it for months.

"It's not much farther," the grandmother said and just as she said it,
a horrible thought came to her. The thought was so embarrassing that
she turned red in the face and her eyes dilated and her feet jumped up,
upsetting her valise in the corner. The instant the valise moved, the
newspaper top she had over the basket under it rose with a snarl and
Pitty Sing, the cat, sprang onto Bailey's shoulder.

The children were thrown to the floor and their mother, clutching 65
the baby, was thrown out the door onto the ground; the old lady was
thrown into the front seat. The car turned over once and landed right-
side-up in a gulch off the side of the road. Bailey remained in the driver's
seat with the cat—gray-striped with a broad white face and an orange
nose—clinging to his neck like a caterpillar.

As soon as the children saw they could move their arms and legs, they
scrambled out of the car, shouting, "We've had an ACCIDENT!" The grandmother was curled up under the dashboard, hoping she was injured so that
Bailey's wrath would not come down on her all at once. The horrible
thought she had had before the accident was that the house she had
remembered so vividly was not in Georgia but in Tennessee.

Bailey removed the cat from his neck with both hands and flung it
out the window against the side of a pine tree. Then he got out of the car
and started looking for the children's mother. She was sitting against the
side of the red gutted ditch, holding the screaming baby, but she only had
a cut down her face and a broken shoulder. "We've had an ACCIDENT!"
the children screamed in a frenzy of delight.

"But nobody's killed," June Star said with disappointment as the grandmother limped out of the car, her hat still pinned to her head but the
broken front brim standing up at a jaunty angle and the violet spray hanging

off the side. They all sat down in the ditch, except the children, to recover from the shock. They were all shaking.

"Maybe a car will come along," said the children's mother hoarsely.

"I believe I have injured an organ," said the grandmother, pressing 70 her side, but no one answered her. Bailey's teeth were clattering. He had on a yellow sport shirt with bright blue parrots designed in it and his face was as yellow as the shirt. The grandmother decided that she would not mention that the house was in Tennessee.

The road was about ten feet above and they could see only the tops of the trees on the other side of it. Behind the ditch they were sitting in there were more woods, tall and dark and deep. In a few minutes they saw a car some distance away on top of a hill, coming slowly as if the occupants were watching them. The grandmother stood up and waved both her arms dramatically to attract their attention. The car continued to come on slowly, disappeared around a bend and appeared again, moving even slower, on top of the hill they had gone over. It was a big black battered hearse-like automobile. There were three men in it.

It came to a stop just over them and for some minutes, the driver looked down with a steady expressionless gaze to where they were sitting, and didn't speak. Then he turned his head and muttered something to the other two and they got out. One was a fat boy in black trousers and a red sweat shirt with a silver stallion embossed on the front of it. He moved around on the right side of them and stood staring, his mouth partly open in a kind of loose grin. The other had on khaki pants and a blue striped coat and a gray hat pulled down very low, hiding most of his face. He came around slowly on the left side. Neither spoke.

The driver got out of the car and stood by the side of it, looking down at them. He was an older man than the other two. His hair was just beginning to gray and he wore silver-rimmed spectacles that gave him a scholarly look. He had a long creased face and didn't have on any shirt or undershirt. He had on blue jeans that were too tight for him and was holding a black hat and a gun. The two boys also had guns.

"We've had an ACCIDENT!" the children screamed.

The grandmother had the peculiar feeling that the bespectacled man 75 was someone she knew. His face was as familiar to her as if she had known him all her life but she could not recall who he was. He moved away from the car and began to come down the embankment, placing his feet carefully so that he wouldn't slip. He had on tan and white shoes and no socks, and his ankles were red and thin. "Good afternoon," he said. "I see you all had you a little spill."

"We turned over twice!" said the grandmother.

"Oncet," he corrected. "We seen it happen. Try their car and see will it run, Hiram," he said quietly to the boy with the gray hat.

"What you got that gun for?" John Wesley asked. "Whatcha gonna do with that gun?"

"Lady," the man said to the children's mother, "would you mind calling them children to sit down by you? Children make me nervous. I want all you all to sit down right together there where you're at."

"What are you telling US what to do for?" June Star asked.

Behind them the line of woods gaped like a dark open mouth. "Come here," said their mother.

"Look here now," Bailey began suddenly, "we're in a predicament! We're in . . ."

The grandmother shrieked. She scrambled to her feet and stood staring. "You're The Misfit!" she said. "I recognized you at once!"

"Yes'm," the man said, smiling slightly as if he were pleased in spite of himself to be known, "but it would have been better for all of you, lady, if you hadn't of reckernized me."

Bailey turned his head sharply and said something to his mother that shocked even the children. The old lady began to cry and The Misfit reddened.

"Lady," he said, "don't you get upset. Sometimes a man says things he don't mean. I don't reckon he meant to talk to you thataway."

"You wouldn't shoot a lady, would you?" the grandmother said and removed a clean handkerchief from her cuff and began to slap at her eyes with it.

The Misfit pointed the toe of his shoe into the ground and made a little hole and then covered it up again. "I would hate to have to," he said.

"Listen," the grandmother almost screamed, "I know you're a good man. You don't look a bit like you have common blood. I know you must come from nice people!"

"Yes mam," he said, "finest people in the world." When he smiled he showed a row of strong white teeth. "God never made a finer woman than my mother and my daddy's heart was pure gold," he said. The boy with the red sweat shirt had come around behind them and was standing with his gun at his hip. The Misfit squatted down on the ground. "Watch them children, Bobby Lee," he said. "You know they make me nervous." He looked at the six of them huddled together in front of him and he seemed to be embarrassed as if he couldn't think of anything to say. "Ain't a cloud in the sky," he remarked, looking up at it. "Don't see no sun but don't see no cloud neither."

"Yes, it's a beautiful day," said the grandmother. "Listen," she said, "you shouldn't call yourself The Misfit because I know you're a good man at heart. I can just look at you and tell."

"Hush!" Bailey yelled. "Hush! Everybody shut up and let me handle this!" He was squatting in the position of a runner about to sprint forward but he didn't move.

80

85

90

"I pre-chate that, lady," The Misfit said and drew a little circle in the ground with the butt of his gun.

"It'll take a half a hour to fix this here car," Hiram called, looking over the raised hood of it.

"Well, first you and Bobby Lee get him and that little boy to step over yonder with you," The Misfit said, pointing to Bailey and John Wesley. "The boys want to ast you something," he said to Bailey. "Would you mind stepping back in them woods there with them?" 95

"Listen," Bailey began, "we're in a terrible predicament! Nobody realizes what this is," and his voice cracked. His eyes were as blue and intense as the parrots in his shirt and he remained perfectly still.

The grandmother reached up to adjust her hat brim as if she were going to the woods with him but it came off in her hand. She stood staring at it and after a second she let it fall on the ground. Hiram pulled Bailey up by the arm as if he were assisting an old man. John Wesley caught hold of his father's hand and Bobby Lee followed. They went off toward the woods and just as they reached the dark edge, Bailey turned and supporting himself against a gray naked pine trunk, he shouted, "I'll be back in a minute, Mamma, wait on me!"

"Come back this instant!" his mother shrilled but they all disappeared into the woods.

"Bailey Boy!" the grandmother called in a tragic voice but she found she was looking at The Misfit squatting on the ground in front of her. "I just know you're a good man," she said desperately. "You're not a bit common!"

"Nome, I ain't a good man," The Misfit said after a second as if he had considered her statement carefully, "but I ain't the worst in the world neither. My daddy said I was a different breed of dog from my brothers and sisters. 'You know,' Daddy said, 'it's some that can live their whole life out without asking about it and it's others has to know why it is, and this boy is one of the latters. He's going to be into everything!'" He put on his black hat and looked up suddenly and then away deep into the woods as if he were embarrassed again. "I'm sorry I don't have on a shirt before you ladies," he said, hunching his shoulders slightly. "We buried our clothes that we had on when we escaped and we're just making do until we can get better. We borrowed these from some folks we met," he explained. 100

"That's perfectly all right," the grandmother said. "Maybe Bailey has an extra shirt in his suitcase."

"I'll look and see terrectly," The Misfit said.

"Where are they taking him?" the children's mother screamed.

"Daddy was a card himself," The Misfit said. "You couldn't put anything over on him. He never got in trouble with the Authorities though. Just had the knack of handling them."

"You could be honest too if you'd only try," said the grandmother.   105
"Think how wonderful it would be to settle down and live a comfortable
life and not have to think about somebody chasing you all the time."

The Misfit kept scratching in the ground with the butt of his gun as
if he were thinking about it. "Yes'm, somebody is always after you," he
murmured.

The grandmother noticed how thin his shoulder blades were just
behind his hat because she was standing up looking down on him. "Do
you ever pray?" she asked.

He shook his head. All she saw was the black hat wiggle between his
shoulder blades. "Nome," he said.

There was a pistol shot from the woods, followed closely by another.
Then silence. The old lady's head jerked around. She could hear the wind
move through the tree tops like a long satisfied insuck of breath. "Bailey
Boy!" she called.

"I was a gospel singer for a while," The Misfit said. "I been most   110
everything. Been in the arm service, both land and sea, at home and
abroad, been twict married, been an undertaker, been with the railroads,
plowed Mother Earth, been in a tornado, seen a man burnt alive oncet,"
and he looked up at the children's mother and the little girl who were sitting close together, their faces white and their eyes glassy; "I even seen a
woman flogged," he said.

"Pray, pray," the grandmother began, "pray, pray . . ."

"I never was a bad boy that I remember of," The Misfit said in an almost dreamy voice, "but somewheres along the line I done something
wrong and got sent to the penitentiary. I was buried alive," and he looked
up and held her attention to him by a steady stare.

"That's when you should have started to pray," she said. "What did
you do to get sent to the penitentiary that first time?"

"Turn to the right, it was a wall," The Misfit said, looking up again
at the cloudless sky. "Turn to the left, it was a wall. Look up it was a
ceiling, look down it was a floor. I forget what I done, lady. I set there and
set there, trying to remember what it was I done and I ain't recalled it to
this day. Oncet in a while, I would think it was coming to me, but it never
come."

"Maybe they put you in by mistake," the old lady said vaguely.   115

"Nome," he said. "It wasn't no mistake. They had the papers on me."

"You must have stolen something," she said.

The Misfit sneered slightly. "Nobody had nothing I wanted," he said.
"It was a head-doctor at the penitentiary said what I had done was kill
my daddy but I known that for a lie. My daddy died in nineteen ought
nineteen of the epidemic flu and I never had a thing to do with it. He was
buried in the Mount Hopewell Baptist churchyard and you can go there
and see for yourself."

"If you would pray," the old lady said, "Jesus would help you."

"That's right," The Misfit said.   120

"Well then, why don't you pray?" she asked trembling with delight suddenly.

"I don't want no hep," he said. "I'm doing all right by myself."

Bobby Lee and Hiram came ambling back from the woods. Bobby Lee was dragging a yellow shirt with bright blue parrots in it.

"Thow me that shirt, Bobby Lee," The Misfit said. The shirt came flying at him and landed on his shoulder and he put it on. The grandmother couldn't name what the shirt reminded her of. "No, lady," The Misfit said while he was buttoning it up, "I found out the crime don't matter. You can do one thing or you can do another, kill a man or take a tire off his car, because sooner or later you're going to forget what it was you done and just be punished for it."

The children's mother had begun to make heaving noises as if she   125 couldn't get her breath. "Lady," he asked, "would you and that little girl like to step off yonder with Bobby Lee and Hiram and join your husband?"

"Yes, thank you," the mother said faintly. Her left arm dangled helplessly and she was holding the baby, who had gone to sleep, in the other. "Hep that lady up, Hiram," The Misfit said as she struggled to climb out of the ditch, "and Bobby Lee, you hold onto that little girl's hand."

"I don't want to hold hands with him," June Star said. "He reminds me of a pig."

The fat boy blushed and laughed and caught her by the arm and pulled her off into the woods after Hiram and her mother.

Alone with The Misfit, the grandmother found that she had lost her voice. There was not a cloud in the sky nor any sun. There was nothing around her but woods. She wanted to tell him that he must pray. She opened and closed her mouth several times before anything came out. Finally she found herself saying, "Jesus. Jesus," meaning, Jesus will help you, but the way she was saying it, it sounded as if she might be cursing.

"Yes'm," The Misfit said as if he agreed. "Jesus thrown everything off   130 balance. It was the same case with Him as with me except He hadn't committed any crime and they could prove I had committed one because they had the papers on me. Of course," he said, "they never shown me my papers. That's why I sign myself now. I said long ago, you get you a signature and sign everything you do and keep a copy of it. Then you'll know what you done and you can hold up the crime to the punishment and see do they match and in the end you'll have something to prove you ain't been treated right. I call myself The Misfit," he said, "because I can't make what all I done wrong fit what all I gone through in punishment."

There was a piercing scream from the woods, followed closely by a pistol report. "Does it seem right to you, lady, that one is punished a heap and another ain't punished at all?"

"Jesus!" the old lady cried. "You've got good blood! I know you wouldn't shoot a lady! I know you come from nice people! Pray! Jesus, you ought not to shoot a lady. I'll give you all the money I've got!"

"Lady," The Misfit said, looking beyond her far into the woods, "there never was a body that give the undertaker a tip."

There were two more pistol reports and the grandmother raised her head like a parched old turkey hen crying for water and called, "Bailey Boy, Bailey Boy!" as if her heart would break.

"Jesus was the only One that ever raised the dead," The Misfit con-   135 tinued, "and He shouldn't have done it. He thown everything off balance. If He did what He said, then it's nothing for you to do but thow away everything and follow Him, and if He didn't, then it's nothing for you to do but enjoy the few minutes you got left the best way you can—by killing somebody or burning down his house or doing some other meanness to him. No pleasure but meanness," he said and his voice had become almost a snarl.

"Maybe He didn't raise the dead," the old lady mumbled, not knowing what she was saying and feeling so dizzy that she sank down in the ditch with her legs twisted under her.

"I wasn't there so I can't say He didn't," The Misfit said. "I wisht I had of been there," he said, hitting the ground with his fist. "It ain't right I wasn't there because if I had of been there I would of known. Listen lady," he said in a high voice, "if I had of been there I would of known and I wouldn't be like I am now." His voice seemed about to crack and the grandmother's head cleared for an instant. She saw the man's face twisted close to her own as if he were going to cry and she murmured, "Why you're one of my babies. You're one of my own children!" She reached out and touched him on the shoulder. The Misfit sprang back as if a snake had bitten him and shot her three times through the chest. Then he put his gun down on the ground and took off his glasses and began to clean them.

Hiram and Bobby Lee returned from the woods and stood over the ditch, looking down at the grandmother who half sat and half lay in a puddle of blood with her legs crossed under her like a child's and her face smiling up at the cloudless sky.

Without his glasses, The Misfit's eyes were red-rimmed and pale and defenseless-looking. "Take her off and thow her where you thown the others," he said, picking up the cat that was rubbing itself against his leg.

"She was a talker, wasn't she?" Bobby Lee said, sliding down the ditch   140 with a yodel.

"She would of been a good woman," The Misfit said, "if it had been somebody there to shoot her every minute of her life."

"Some fun!" Bobby Lee said.

"Shut up, Bobby Lee," The Misfit said. "It's no real pleasure in life."

Octavio Paz

My Life with the Wave   1951

TRANSLATED BY ELIOT WEINBERGER

OCTAVIO PAZ

*Octavio Paz (1914–1998) was born in Mexico City.
His grandfather, a journalist and novelist, had fought
alongside Benito Juarez in resistance to the French occupation of Mexico in the 1860s. His father, a lawyer,
had fought for the revolution and had been the private
secretary of peasant guerrilla leader Emiliano Zapata.
Paz grew up in his grandfather's large but decaying
house, and spent much of his time in its library of more
than 6,000 volumes. He went to Spain in 1937,
intending to fight on the Loyalist side in the Spanish
Civil War, but found his leftist ideals severely tested
by what he witnessed there, and he gradually adopted a centrist political position that rejected both extremes of right-wing dictatorship and Marxist revolution; his intellectual
honesty would later bring him many enemies when he became an early critic of the
Castro regime in Cuba. Paz joined the Mexican foreign service in 1945; over the
course of his diplomatic career, he held postings in San Francisco, New York, Tokyo,
Geneva, and Delhi, but in 1968, after six years as Mexico's ambassador to India, he
resigned in protest over his government's brutal suppression of student demonstrations.
He then supported himself by teaching at Cambridge, Harvard, the University of
Texas, and elsewhere.*

*Beginning in 1933 and continuing steadily thereafter, Paz published the many
volumes of poetry that are the cornerstone of his achievement and the basis of his
worldwide reputation. His work, which has been translated by such eminent poets
as Elizabeth Bishop, Denise Levertov, John Frederick Nims, and Charles Tomlinson,
has its fullest representation in English in* The Collected Poems of Octavio Paz
1957–1987. *While immersed in his own culture and national ethos, as demonstrated in* The Labyrinth of Solitude *(1950), Paz was a profound internationalist
as well:* The Bow and the Lyre *(1956), a study of the poetic process, and Con-
vergences:* Essays on Art and Literature *(1987) range impressively from ancient
to modern times, from the old world to the new. In 1990, Paz was awarded the
Nobel Prize for Literature, becoming the only Mexican-born writer to have attained
that honor.*

When I left that sea, a wave moved ahead of the others. She was tall
and light. In spite of the shouts of the others who grabbed her by her
floating clothes, she clutched my arm and went off with me leaping. I
didn't want to say anything to her, because it hurt me to shame her in
front of her friends. Besides, the furious stares of the elders paralyzed me.
When we got to town, I explained to her that it was impossible, that life

in the city was not what she had been able to imagine with the ingenuity of a wave that had never left the sea. She watched me gravely. "No, your decision is made. You can't go back." I tried sweetness, hardness, irony. She cried, screamed, hugged, threatened. I had to apologize.

The next day my troubles began. How could we get on the train without being seen by the conductor, the passengers, the police? Certainly the rules say nothing in respect to the transport of waves on the railroad, but this same reserve was an indication of the severity with which our act would be judged. After much thought I arrived at the station an hour before departure, took my seat, and, when no one was looking, emptied the water tank for the passengers; then, carefully, poured in my friend.

The first incident came about when the children of a nearby couple declared their noisy thirst. I stopped them and promised them refreshments and lemonade. They were at the point of accepting when another thirsty passenger approached. I was about to invite her also, but the stare of her companion stopped me. The lady took a paper cup, approached the tank, and turned the faucet. Her cup was barely half full when I leaped between the woman and my friend. She looked at me astonished. While I apologized, one of the children turned the faucet again. I closed it violently. The lady brought the cup to her lips:

"Agh, this water is salty."

The boy echoed her. Various passengers rose. The husband called the conductor: 5

"This man put salt in the water."

The conductor called the Inspector:

"So you put substances in the water?"

The Inspector in turn called the police:

"So you poisoned the water?" 10

The police in turn called the Captain:

"So you're the poisoner?"

The captain called three agents. The agents took me to an empty car amid the stares and whispers of the passengers. At the next station they took me off and pushed and dragged me to the jail. For days no one spoke to me, except during the long interrogations. When I explained my story no one believed me, not even the jailer, who shook his head, saying: "The case is grave, truly grave. You didn't want to poison the children?" One day they brought me before the Magistrate.

"Your case is difficult," he repeated. "I will assign you to the Penal Judge."

A year passed. Finally they judged me. As there were no victims, my 15 sentence was light. After a short time, my day of liberty arrived.

The Chief of the Prison called me in:

"Well, now you're free. You were lucky. Lucky there were no victims. But don't do it again, because the next time won't be so short . . ."

And he stared at me with the same grave stare with which everyone watched me.

The same afternoon I took the train and after hours of uncomfortable traveling arrived in Mexico City. I took a cab home. At the door of my apartment I heard laughter and singing. I felt a pain in my chest, like the smack of a wave of surprise when surprise smacks us across the chest: my friend was there, singing and laughing as always.

"How did you get back?"

20

"Simple: in the train. Someone, after making sure that I was only salt water, poured me in the engine. It was a rough trip: soon I was a white plume of vapor, soon I fell in a fine rain on the machine. I thinned out a lot. I lost many drops."

Her presence changed my life. The house of dark corridors and dusty furniture was filled with air, with sun, with sounds and green and blue reflections, a numerous and happy populace of reverberations and echoes. How many waves is one wave, and how it can make a beach or a rock or jetty out of a wall, a chest, a forehead that it crowns with foam! Even the abandoned corners, the abject corners of dust and debris were touched by her light hands. Everything began to laugh and everywhere shined with teeth. The sun entered the old rooms with pleasure and stayed in my house for hours, abandoning the other houses, the district, the city, the country. And some nights, very late, the scandalized stars watched it sneak from my house.

Love was a game, a perpetual creation. All was beach, sand, a bed of sheets that were always fresh. If I embraced her, she swelled with pride, incredibly tall, like the liquid stalk of a poplar; and soon that thinness flowered into a fountain of white feathers, into a plume of smiles that fell over my head and back and covered me with whiteness. Or she stretched out in front of me, infinite as the horizon, until I too became horizon and silence. Full and sinuous, it enveloped me like music or some giant lips. Her present was a going and coming of caresses, of murmurs, of kisses. Entered in her waters, I was drenched to the socks and in a wink of an eye I found myself up above, at the height of vertigo, mysteriously suspended, to fall like a stone and feel myself gently deposited on the dryness, like a feather. Nothing is comparable to sleeping in those waters, to wake pounded by a thousand happy light lashes, by a thousand assaults that withdrew laughing.

But never did I reach the center of her being. Never did I touch the nakedness of pain and of death. Perhaps it does not exist in waves, that secret site that renders a woman vulnerable and mortal, that electric button where all interlocks, twitches, and straightens out to then swoon. Her sensibility, like that of women, spread in ripples, only they weren't concentric ripples, but rather eccentric, spreading each time farther, until they touched other galaxies. To love her was to extend to remote contacts, to vibrate with far-off stars we never suspected. But her center . . . no, she had no center, just an emptiness as in a whirlwind, that sucked me in and smothered me.

Stretched out side by side, we exchanged confidences, whispers, 25 smiles. Curled up, she fell on my chest and there unfolded like a vegetation of murmurs. She sang in my ear, a little snail. She became humble and transparent, clutching my feet like a small animal, calm water. She was so clear I could read all of her thoughts. Certain nights her skin was covered with phosphorescence and to embrace her was to embrace a piece of night tattooed with fire. But she also became black and bitter. At unexpected hours she roared, moaned, twisted. Her groans woke the neighbors. Upon hearing her, the sea wind would scratch at the door of the house or rave in a loud voice on the roof. Cloudy days irritated her; she broke furniture, said bad words, covered me with insults and green and gray foam. She spit, cried, swore, prophesied. Subject to the moon, to the stars, to the influence of the light of other worlds, she changed her moods and appearance in a way that I thought fantastic, but it was as fatal as the tide.

She began to miss solitude. The house was full of snails and conches, of small sailboats that in her fury she had shipwrecked (together with the others, laden with images, that each night left my forehead and sank in her ferocious or pleasant whirlwinds). How many little treasures were lost in that time! But my boats and the silent song of the snails was not enough. I had to install in the house a colony of fish. I confess that it was not without jealousy that I watched them swimming in my friend, caressing her breasts, sleeping between her legs, adorning her hair with light flashes of color.

Among all those fish there were a few particularly repulsive and ferocious ones, little tigers from the aquarium, the large fixed eyes and jagged and bloodthirsty mouths. I don't know by what aberration my friend delighted in playing with them, shamelessly showing them a preference whose significance I preferred to ignore. She passed long hours confined with those horrible creatures. One day I couldn't stand it any more; I threw open the door and launched after them. Agile and ghostly they escaped my hands while she laughed and pounded me until I fell. I thought I was drowning. And when I was at the point of death, and purple, she deposited me on the bank and began to kiss me, saying I don't know what things. I felt very weak, fatigued, and humiliated. And at the same time her voluptuousness made me close my eyes, because her voice was sweet and she spoke to me of the delicious death of the drowned. When I recovered, I began to fear and hate her.

I had neglected my affairs. Now I began to visit friends and renew old and dear relations. I met an old girlfriend. Making her swear to keep my secret, I told her of my life with the wave. Nothing moves women so much as the possibility of saving a man. My redeemer employed all of her arts, but what could a woman, master of a limited number of souls and bodies, do in front of my friend who was always changing—and always identical to herself in her incessant metamorphoses.

Winter came. The sky turned gray. Fog fell on the city. Frozen drizzle rained. My friend cried every night. During the day she isolated herself, quiet and sinister, stuttering a single syllable, like an old woman who grumbles in a corner. She became cold; to sleep with her was to shiver all night and to feel freeze, little by little, the blood, the bones, the thoughts. She turned deep, impenetrable, restless. I left frequently and my absences were each time more prolonged. She, in her corner, howled loudly. With teeth like steel and a corrosive tongue she gnawed the walls, crumbled them. She passed the nights in mourning, reproaching me. She had nightmares, deliriums of the sun, of warm beaches. She dreamt of the pole and of changing into a great block of ice, sailing beneath black skies in nights long as months. She insulted me. She cursed and laughed; filled the house with guffaws and phantoms. She called up the monsters of the depths, blind ones, quick ones, blunt. Charged with electricity, she carbonized all she touched; full of acid, she dissolved whatever she brushed against. Her sweet embraces became knotty cords that strangled me. And her body, greenish and elastic, was an implacable whip that lashed, lashed, lashed. I fled. The horrible fish laughed with ferocious smiles.

There in the mountains, among the tall pines and precipices, I 30 breathed the cold thin air like a thought of liberty. At the end of a month I returned. I had decided. It had been so cold that over the marble of the chimney, next to the extinct fire, I found a statue of ice. I was unmoved by her weary beauty. I put her in a big canvas sack and went out to the streets with the sleeper on my shoulders. In a restaurant in the outskirts I sold her to a waiter friend who immediately began to chop her into little pieces, which he carefully deposited in the buckets where bottles are chilled.

Eudora Welty

A Worn Path   1941

Eudora Welty (1909–2001) was born in Jackson, Mississippi, daughter of an insurance company president. Like William Faulkner, another Mississippi writer, she stayed close to her roots for practically all her life, except for short sojourns at the University of Wisconsin, where she took her B.A., and in New York City, where she studied advertising. She lived most of her life in her childhood home in Jackson, within a stone's throw of the state capitol. Although Welty was a novelist distinguished for The Robber Bridegroom *(1942),* Delta Wedding *(1946),* The

EUDORA WELTY

Ponder Heart (1954), Losing Battles (1970), and The Optimist's Daughter (1972), many critics think her finest work was in the short-story form. The Col-lected Stories of Eudora Welty (1980) gathers the work of more than forty years. Welty's other books include a memoir, One Writer's Beginnings (1984), and The Eye of the Story (1977), a book of sympathetic criticism on the fiction of other writers, including Willa Cather, Virginia Woolf, Katherine Anne Porter, and Isak Dinesen. One Time, One Place, a book of photographs of everyday life that Welty took in Mississippi during the Depression, was republished in a revised edition in 1996.

It was December—a bright frozen day in the early morning. Far out in the country there was an old Negro woman with her head tied in a red rag, coming along a path through the pinewoods. Her name was Phoenix Jackson. She was very old and small and she walked slowly in the dark pine shadows, moving a little from side to side in her steps, with the balanced heaviness and lightness of a pendulum in a grandfather clock. She carried a thin, small cane made from an umbrella, and with this she kept tapping the frozen earth in front of her. This made a grave and persistent noise in the still air, that seemed meditative like the chirping of a solitary little bird.

She wore a dark striped dress reaching down to her shoe tops, and an equally long apron of bleached sugar sacks, with a full pocket: all neat and tidy, but every time she took a step she might have fallen over her shoelaces, which dragged from her unlaced shoes. She looked straight ahead. Her eyes were blue with age. Her skin had a pattern all its own of numberless branching wrinkles and as though a whole little tree stood in the middle of her forehead, but a golden color ran underneath, and the two knobs of her cheeks were illumined by a yellow burning under the dark. Under the red rag her hair came down on her neck in the frailest of ringlets, still black, and with an odor like copper.

Now and then there was a quivering in the thicket. Old Phoenix said, "Out of my way, all you foxes, owls, beetles, jack rabbits, coons and wild animals! . . . Keep out from under these feet, little bob-whites. . . . Keep the big wild hogs out of my path. Don't let none of those come run-ning my direction. I got a long way." Under her small black-freckled hand her cane, limber as a buggy whip, would switch at the brush as if to rouse up any hiding things.

On she went. The woods were deep and still. The sun made the pine needles almost too bright to look at, up where the wind rocked. The cones dropped as light as feathers. Down in the hollow was the mourning dove—it was not too late for him.

The path ran up a hill. "Seem like there is chains about my feet, time I get this far," she said, in the voice of argument old people keep to use with themselves. "Something always take a hold of me on this hill— pleads I should stay." 5

After she got to the top she turned and gave a full, severe look behind her where she had come. "Up through pines," she said at length. "Now down through oaks."

Her eyes opened their widest, and she started down gently. But before she got to the bottom of the hill a bush caught her dress.

Her fingers were busy and intent, but her skirts were full and long, so that before she could pull them free in one place they were caught in another. It was not possible to allow the dress to tear. "I in the thorny bush," she said. "Thorns, you doing your appointed work. Never want to let folks pass, no sir. Old eyes thought you was a pretty little *green* bush."

Finally, trembling all over, she stood free, and after a moment dared to stoop for her cane.

"Sun so high!" she cried, leaning back and looking, while the thick   10
tears went over her eyes. "The time getting all gone here."

At the foot of this hill was a place where a log was laid across the creek.

"Now comes the trial," said Phoenix.

Putting her right foot out, she mounted the log and shut her eyes. Lifting her skirt, leveling her cane fiercely before her, like a festival figure in some parade, she began to march across. Then she opened her eyes and she was safe on the other side.

"I wasn't as old as I thought," she said.

But she sat down to rest. She spread her skirts on the bank around   15
her and folded her hands over her knees. Up above her was a tree in a pearly cloud of mistletoe. She did not dare to close her eyes, and when a little boy brought her a plate with a slice of marble-cake on it she spoke to him. "That would be acceptable," she said. But when she went to take it there was just her own hand in the air.

So she left that tree, and had to go through a barbed-wire fence. There she had to creep and crawl, spreading her knees and stretching her fingers like a baby trying to climb the steps. But she talked loudly to herself: she could not let her dress be torn now, so late in the day, and she could not pay for having her arm or her leg sawed off if she got caught fast where she was.

At last she was safe through the fence and risen up out in the clearing. Big dead trees, like black men with one arm, were standing in the purple stalks of the withered cotton field. There sat a buzzard.

"Who you watching?"

In the furrow she made her way along.

"Glad this not the season for bulls," she said, looking sideways, "and   20
the good Lord made his snakes to curl up and sleep in the winter. A pleasure I don't see no two-headed snake coming around that tree, where it come once. It took a while to get by him, back in the summer."

She passed through the old cotton and went into a field of dead corn. It whispered and shook and was taller than her head. "Through the maze now," she said, for there was no path.

Then there was something tall, black, and skinny there, moving before her.

At first she took it for a man. It could have been a man dancing in the field. But she stood still and listened, and it did not make a sound. It was as silent as a ghost.

"Ghost," she said sharply, "who be you the ghost of? For I have heard of nary death close by."

But there was no answer—only the ragged dancing in the wind.   25

She shut her eyes, reached out her hand, and touched a sleeve. She found a coat and inside that an emptiness, cold as ice.

"You scarecrow," she said. Her face lighted. "I ought to be shut up for good," she said with laughter. "My senses is gone. I too old. I the oldest people I ever know. Dance, old scarecrow," she said, "while I dancing with you."

She kicked her foot over the furrow, and with mouth drawn down, shook her head once or twice in a little strutting way. Some husks blew down and whirled in streamers about her skirts.

Then she went on, parting her way from side to side with the cane, through the whispering field. At last she came to the end, to a wagon track where the silver grass blew between the red ruts. The quail were walking around like pullets, seeming all dainty and unseen.

"Walk pretty," she said. "This the easy place. This the easy going."   30

She followed the track, swaying through the quiet bare fields, through the little strings of trees silver in their dead leaves, past cabins silver from weather, with the doors and windows boarded shut, all like old women under a spell sitting there. "I walking in their sleep," she said, nodding her head vigorously.

In a ravine she went where a spring was silently flowing through a hollow log. Old Phoenix bent and drank. "Sweet-gum makes the water sweet," she said, and drank more. "Nobody know who made this well, for it was here when I was born."

The track crossed a swampy part where the moss hung as white as lace from every limb. "Sleep on, alligators, and blow your bubbles." Then the track went into the road.

Deep, deep the road went down between the high green-colored banks. Overhead the live-oaks met, and it was as dark as a cave.

A black dog with a lolling tongue came up out of the weeds by the   35
ditch. She was meditating, and not ready, and when he came at her she only hit him a little with her cane. Over she went in the ditch, like a little puff of milkweed.

Down there, her senses drifted away. A dream visited her, and she reached her hand up, but nothing reached down and gave her a pull. So she lay there and presently went to talking. "Old woman," she said to herself, "that black dog come up out of the weeds to stall you off, and now there he sitting on his fine tail, smiling at you."

A white man finally came along and found her—a hunter, a young man, with his dog on a chain.

"Well, Granny!" he laughed. "What are you doing there?"

"Lying on my back like a June-bug waiting to be turned over, mister," she said, reaching up her hand.

He lifted her up, gave her a swing in the air, and set her down.   40
"Anything broken, Granny?"

"No sir, them old dead weeds is springy enough," said Phoenix, when she had got her breath. "I thank you for your trouble."

"Where do you live, Granny?" he asked, while the two dogs were growling at each other.

"Away back yonder, sir, behind the ridge. You can't even see it from here."

"On your way home?"

"No sir, I going to town."   45

"Why, that's too far! That's as far as I walk when I come out myself, and I get something for my trouble." He patted the stuffed bag he carried, and there hung down a little closed claw. It was one of the bob-whites, with its beak hooked bitterly to show it was dead. "Now you go on home, Granny!"

"I bound to go to town, mister," said Phoenix. "The time come around."

He gave another laugh, filling the whole landscape. "I know you old colored people! Wouldn't miss going to town to see Santa Claus!"

But something held old Phoenix very still. The deep lines in her face went into a fierce and different radiation. Without warning, she had seen with her own eyes a flashing nickel fall out of the man's pocket onto the ground.

"How old are you, Granny?" he was saying.   50

"There is no telling, mister," she said, "no telling."

Then she gave a little cry and clapped her hands and said, "Git on away from here, dog! Look! Look at that dog!" She laughed as if in admiration. "He ain't scared of nobody. He a big black dog." She whispered, "Sic him!"

"Watch me get rid of that cur," said the man. "Sic him, Pete! Sic him!"

Phoenix heard the dogs fighting, and heard the man running and throwing sticks. She even heard a gunshot. But she was slowly bending forward by that time, further and further forward, the lids stretched down over her eyes, as if she were doing this in her sleep. Her chin was lowered almost to her knees. The yellow palm of her hand came out from the fold of her apron. Her fingers slid down and along the ground under the piece of money with the grace and care they would have in lifting an egg from under a setting hen. Then she slowly straightened up, she stood erect, and the nickel was in her apron pocket. A bird flew by. Her lips moved. "God watching me the whole time. I come to stealing."

The man came back, and his own dog panted about them. "Well, I scared him off that time," he said, and then he laughed and lifted his gun and pointed it at Phoenix.   55

She stood straight and faced him.

"Doesn't the gun scare you?" he said, still pointing it.

"No, sir, I seen plenty go off closer by, in my day, and for less than what I done," she said, holding utterly still.

He smiled, and shouldered the gun. "Well, Granny," he said, "you must be a hundred years old, and scared of nothing. I'd give you a dime if I had any money with me. But you take my advice and stay home, and nothing will happen to you."

"I bound to go on my way, mister," said Phoenix. She inclined her head in the red rag. Then they went in different directions, but she could hear the gun shooting again and again over the hill.   60

She walked on. The shadows hung from the oak trees to the road like curtains. Then she smelled wood-smoke, and smelled the river, and she saw a steeple and the cabins on their steep steps. Dozens of little black children whirled around her. There ahead was Natchez shining. Bells were ringing. She walked on.

In the paved city it was Christmas time. There were red and green electric lights strung and crisscrossed everywhere, and all turned on in the daytime. Old Phoenix would have been lost if she had not distrusted her eyesight and depended on her feet to know where to take her.

She paused quietly on the sidewalk where people were passing by. A lady came along in the crowd, carrying an armful of red-, green- and silver-wrapped presents; she gave off perfume like the red roses in hot summer, and Phoenix stopped her.

"Please, missy, will you lace up my shoe?" She held up her foot.

"What do you want, Grandma?"   65

"See my shoe," said Phoenix. "Do all right for out in the country, but wouldn't look right to go in a big building."

"Stand still then, Grandma," said the lady. She put her packages down on the sidewalk beside her and laced and tied both shoes tightly.

"Can't lace 'em with a cane," said Phoenix, "Thank you, missy. I doesn't mind asking a nice lady to tie up my shoe, when I gets out on the street."

Moving slowly and from side to side, she went into the big building, and into a tower of steps, where she walked up and around and around until her feet knew to stop.

She entered a door, and there she saw nailed up on the wall the doc- 70
ument that had been stamped with the gold seal and framed in the gold
frame, which matched the dream that was hung up in her head.

"Here I be," she said. There was a fixed and ceremonial stiffness over
her body.

"A charity case, I suppose," said an attendant who sat at the desk before her.

But Phoenix only looked above her head. There was sweat on her
face, the wrinkles in her skin shone like a bright net.

"Speak up, Grandma," the woman said. "What's your name? We
must have your history, you know. Have you been here before? What
seems to be the trouble with you?"

Old Phoenix only gave a twitch to her face as if a fly were bothering 75
her.

"Are you deaf?" cried the attendant.

But then the nurse came in.

"Oh, that's just old Aunt Phoenix," she said. "She doesn't come for
himself—she has a little grandson. She makes these trips just as regular as
clockwork. She lives away back off the Old Natchez Trace." She bent
down. "Well, Aunt Phoenix, why don't you just take a seat? We won't
keep you standing after your long trip." She pointed.

The old woman sat down, bolt upright in the chair.

"Now, how is the boy?" asked the nurse. 80

Old Phoenix did not speak.

"I said, how is the boy?"

But Phoenix only waited and stared straight ahead, her face very
solemn and withdrawn into rigidity.

"Is his throat any better?" asked the nurse. "Aunt Phoenix, don't you
hear me? Is your grandson's throat any better since the last time you
came for the medicine?"

With her hands on her knees, the old woman waited, silent, erect 85
and motionless, just as if she were in armor.

"You mustn't take up our time this way, Aunt Phoenix," the nurse said.
"Tell us quickly about your grandson, and get it over. He isn't dead, is he?"

At last there came a flicker and then a flame of comprehension
across her face, and she spoke.

"My grandson. It was my memory had left me. There I sat and forgot
why I made my long trip."

"Forgot?" The nurse frowned. "After you came so far?"

Then Phoenix was like an old woman begging a dignified forgive- 90
ness for waking up frightened in the night. "I never did go to school, I
was too old at the Surrender," she said in a soft voice. "I'm an old
woman without an education. It was my memory fail me. My little
grandson, he is just the same, and I forgot it in the coming."

"Throat never heals, does it?" said the nurse, speaking in a loud, sure voice to old Phoenix. By now she had a card with something written on it, a little list. "Yes. Swallowed lye. When was it?—January—two-three years ago—"

Phoenix spoke unasked now. "No, missy, he not dead, he just the same. Every little while his throat begin to close up again, and he not able to swallow. He not get his breath. He not able to help himself. So the time come around, and I go on another trip for the soothing medicine."

"All right. The doctor said as long as you came to get it, you could have it," said the nurse. "But it's an obstinate case."

"My little grandson, he sit up there in the house all wrapped up, waiting by himself," Phoenix went on. "We is the only two left in the world. He suffer and it don't seem to put him back at all. He got a sweet look. He going to last. He wear a little patch quilt and peep out holding his mouth open like a little bird. I remembers so plain now. I not going to forget him again, no, the whole enduring time. I could tell him from all the others in creation."

"All right." The nurse was trying to hush her now. She brought her a bottle of medicine. "Charity," she said, making a check mark in a book.   95

Old Phoenix held the bottle close to her eyes, and then carefully put it into her pocket.

"I thank you," she said.

"It's Christmas time, Grandma," said the attendant. "Could I give you a few pennies out of my purse?"

"Five pennies is a nickel," said Phoenix stiffly.

"Here's a nickel," said the attendant.   100

Phoenix rose carefully and held out her hand. She received the nickel and then fished the other nickel out of her pocket and laid it beside the new one. She stared at her palm closely, with her head on one side.

Then she gave a tap with her cane on the floor.

"This is what come to me to do," she said. "I going to the store and buy my child a little windmill they sells, made out of paper. He going to find it hard to believe there such a thing in the world. I'll march myself back where he waiting, holding it straight up in this hand."

She lifted her free hand, gave a little nod, turned around, and walked out of the doctor's office. Then her slow step began on the stairs, going down.

POETRY

Gwendolyn Brooks c. 1950, the year she won the Pulitzer Prize

To the Muse

Give me leave, Muse, in plain view to array
Your shift and bodice by the light of day.
I would have brought an epic. Be not vexed
Instead to grace a niggling schoolroom text;
Let down your sanction, help me to oblige
Those who would lead fresh devots to your liege,
And at your altar, grant that in a flash
Readers and I know incense from dead ash.
　　　　　　　　　　　　　　　　—X. J. K.

What is poetry? Pressed for an answer, Robert Frost made a classic reply: "Poetry is the kind of thing poets write." In all likelihood, Frost was trying not merely to evade the question but to chide his questioner into thinking for himself. A trouble with definitions is that they may stop thought. If Frost had said, "Poetry is a rhythmical composition of words expressing an attitude, designed to surprise and delight, and to arouse an emotional response," the questioner might have settled back in his chair, content to have learned the truth about poetry. He would have learned nothing, or not so much as he might learn by continuing to wonder.

The nature of poetry eludes simple definitions. (In this respect it is rather like jazz. Asked after one of his concerts, "What is jazz?" Louis Armstrong replied, "Man, if you gotta ask, you'll never know.") Definitions will be of little help at first, if we are to know poetry and respond to it. We have to go to it willing to see and hear. For this reason, you are asked in reading this book not to be in any hurry to decide what poetry is, but instead to study poems and to let them grow in your mind. At the end of our discussions of poetry, the problem of definition will be taken up again (for those who may wish to pursue it).

Confronted with a formal introduction to poetry, you may be wondering, "Who needs it?" and you may well be right. It's unlikely that you have avoided meeting poetry before; and perhaps you already have a friendship, or at least a fair acquaintance, with some of the greatest English-speaking poets of all time. What this book provides is an introduction to the *study* of poetry. It tries to help you look at a poem closely, to offer you a wider and more accurate vocabulary with which to express what poems say to you. It will suggest ways to judge for yourself the poems you read. It may set forth some poems new to you.

A frequent objection is that poetry ought not to be studied at all. In this view, a poem is either a series of gorgeous noises to be funneled into one ear and out the other without being allowed to trouble the mind, or an experience so holy that to analyze it in a classroom is as cruel and mechanical as dissecting a hummingbird. To the first view, it might be countered that a good poem has something to say that is well worth listening to. To the second view, it might be argued that poems are much less perishable than humming-birds, and luckily, we can study them in flight. The risk of a poem's dying from observation is not nearly so great as the risk of not really seeing it at all. It is doubtful that any excellent poem has ever vanished from human memory because people have read it too closely.

That poetry matters to the people who write it has been shown unmis-takably by the ordeal of Soviet poet Irina Ratushinskaya. Sentenced to prison for three and a half years, she was given paper and pencil only twice a month to write letters to her husband and her parents and was not allowed to write anything else. Nevertheless, Ratushinskaya composed more than two hun-dred poems in her cell, engraving them with a burnt match in a bar of soap, then memorizing the lines. "I would read the poem and read it," she said, "until it was committed to memory—then with one washing of my hands, it would be gone."

Good poetry is something that readers can care about. In fact, an ancient persuasion of humankind is that the hearing of a poem, as well as the making of a poem, can be a religious act. Poetry, in speech and song, was part of classic Greek drama, which for playwright, actor, and spectator alike was a holy-day ceremony. The Greeks' belief that a poet writes a poem only by supernatural assistance is clear from the invocations to the Muse that begin the *Iliad* and the *Odyssey* and from the opinion of Socrates (in Plato's *Ion*) that a poet has no powers of invention until divinely inspired. Among the ancient Celts, poets were regarded as magicians and priests, and whoever insulted one of them might expect to receive a curse in rime potent enough to afflict him with boils and to curdle the milk of his cows. Such identifications between the poet and the magician are less common these days, although we know that poetry is involved in the primitive white magic of children, who bring themselves good luck in a game with the charm "Roll, roll, Tootsie-roll!/Roll the marble in the hole!" and who warn against a hex while jumping along a sidewalk: "Step on a crack,/Break your mother's back." To read a poem, we have to be willing to offer it responses *besides* a logical understanding. Whether we attribute the effect of a poem to a divine spirit or to the reactions of our glands and cortexes, we have to take the reading of poetry seriously (not solemnly), if only because—as some of the poems in this book may demonstrate—few other efforts can repay us so generously, both in wisdom and in joy.

If, as we hope you will do, you sometimes browse in the book for fun, you may be annoyed to see so many questions following the poems. Should you feel this way, try reading with a slip of paper to cover up the questions. You will then—if the Muse should inspire you—have paper in hand to write a poem.

9
Reading a Poem

How do you read a poem? The literal-minded might say, "Just let your eye light on it"; but there is more to poetry than meets the eye. What Shakespeare called "the mind's eye" also plays a part. Many a reader who has no trouble understanding and enjoying prose finds poetry difficult. This is to be expected. At first glance, a poem usually will make some sense and give some pleasure, but it may not yield everything at once. Sometimes it only hints at meaning still to come if we will keep after it. Poetry is not to be galloped over like the daily news: a poem differs from most prose in that it is to be read slowly, carefully, and attentively. Not all poems are difficult, of course, and some can be understood and enjoyed on first encounter. But good poems yield more if read twice; and the best poems—after ten, twenty, or a hundred readings—still go on yielding.

Approaching a thing written in lines and surrounded with white space, we need not expect it to be a poem just because it is **verse**. (Any composition in lines of more or less regular rhythm, usually ending in rimes, is verse.) Here, for instance, is a specimen of verse that few will call poetry:

Thirty days hath September,
April, June, and November;
All the rest have thirty-one
Excepting February alone,
To which we twenty-eight assign
Till leap year makes it twenty-nine.

To a higher degree than that classic memory-tickler, poetry appeals to the mind and arouses feelings. Poetry may state facts, but, more important, it makes imaginative statements that we may value even if its facts are incorrect. Coleridge's error in placing a star within the horns of the crescent moon in "The Rime of the Ancient Mariner" does not stop the passage from being good poetry, though it is faulty astronomy. According to one poet, Gerard Manley Hopkins, poetry is "to be heard for its own sake and interest even over and above its interest of meaning." There are other elements in a poem besides plain prose sense: sounds, images, rhythms, figures of speech. These may strike us and please us even before we ask, "But what does it all mean?"

This is a truth not readily grasped by anyone who regards a poem as a kind of puzzle written in secret code with a message slyly concealed. The effect of a poem (one's whole mental and emotional response to it) consists of much more than simply a message. By its musical qualities, by its suggestions, it can work on the reader's unconscious. T. S. Eliot put it well when he said in *The Use of Poetry and the Use of Criticism* that the prose sense of a poem is chiefly useful in keeping the reader's mind "diverted and quiet, while the poem does its work upon him." Eliot went on to liken the meaning of a poem to the bit of meat a burglar brings along to throw to the family dog. What is the work of a poem? To touch us, to stir us, to make us glad, and possibly even to tell us something.

How to set about reading a poem? Here are a few suggestions.

To begin with, read the poem once straight through, with no particular expectations; read open-mindedly. Let yourself experience whatever you find, without worrying just yet about the large general and important ideas the poem contains (if indeed it contains any). Don't dwell on a troublesome word or difficult passage—just push on. Some of the difficulties may seem smaller when you read the poem for a second time; at least, they will have become parts of a whole for you.

On the second reading, read for the exact sense of all the words; if there are words you don't understand, look them up in a dictionary. Dwell on any difficult parts as long as you need to.

If you read the poem silently, sound its words in your mind. (This is a technique that will get you nowhere in a speed-reading course, but it may help the poem to do its work on you.) Better still, read the poem aloud, or hear someone else read it. You may discover meanings you didn't perceive in it before. Even if you are no actor, to decide how to speak a poem can be an excellent method of getting to understand it. Some poems, like bells, seem heavy till heard. Listen while reading the following lines from Alexander Pope's *Dunciad*. Attacking the minor poet James Ralph, who had sung the praises of a mistress named Cynthia, Pope makes the goddess of Dullness exclaim:

> "Silence, ye wolves! while Ralph to Cynthia howls,
> And makes night hideous—answer him, ye owls!"

When *ye owls* slide together and become *yowls*, poor Ralph's serenade is turned into the nightly outcry of a cat.

Try to **paraphrase** the poem as a whole, or perhaps just the more difficult lines. In paraphrasing, we put into our own words what we understand the poem to say, restating ideas that seem essential, coming out and stating what the poem may only suggest. This may sound like a heartless thing to do to a poem, but good poems can stand it. In fact, to compare a poem to its paraphrase is a good way to see the distance between poetry and prose. In making a paraphrase, we generally work through a poem or a passage line by line. The statement that results may take as many words as the original, if not more. A paraphrase, then, is ampler than a **summary**, a brief condensation of gist, main idea, or story. (Summary of a horror film in *TV Guide:* "Demented biologist, coveting power over New York, swells sewer rats to hippopotamus-size.") Here is a poem worth considering line by line. The poet writes of an island in a lake in the west of Ireland, in a region where he spent many summers as a boy.

William Butler Yeats (1865–1939)

The Lake Isle of Innisfree   1892

I will arise and go now, and go to Innisfree,
And a small cabin build there, of clay and wattles made:
Nine bean-rows will I have there, a hive for the honey-bee,
And live alone in the bee-loud glade.

And I shall have some peace there, for peace comes dropping slow,   5
Dropping from the veils of the morning to where the cricket sings;
There midnight's all a glimmer, and noon a purple glow,
And evening full of the linnet's wings.

I will arise and go now, for always night and day
I hear lake water lapping with low sounds by the shore;   10
While I stand on the roadway, or on the pavements gray,
I hear it in the deep heart's core.

Though relatively simple, this poem is far from simple-minded. We need to absorb it slowly and thoughtfully. At the start, for most of us, it raises problems: what are *wattles,* from which the speaker's dream-cabin is to be made? We might guess, but in this case it will help to consult a dictionary: they are "poles interwoven with sticks or branches, formerly used in building as frameworks to support walls or roofs." Evidently, this getaway house will be built in an old-fashioned way: it won't be a prefabricated log cabin or A-frame house, nothing modern or citified. The phrase *bee-loud glade* certainly isn't commonplace language of the sort we find on a cornflakes package, but right away, we can understand it, at least partially: it's a place loud with bees. What is a *glade?* Experience might tell us that it is an open space in woods, but if that word stops us, we can look it up. Although the *linnet* doesn't live in North America, it is a creature with wings—a songbird of the finch family, adds the dictionary. But even if we don't make a special trip to the dictionary to find *linnet,* we probably recognize that the word means "bird," and the line makes sense to us.

A paraphrase of the whole poem might go something like this (in language easier to forget than that of the original): "I'm going to get up now, go to Innisfree, build a cabin, plant beans, keep bees, and live peacefully by myself amid nature and beautiful light. I want to because I can't forget the sound of that lake water. When I'm in the city, a gray and dingy place, I seem to hear it deep inside me."

These dull remarks, roughly faithful to what Yeats is saying, seem a long way from poetry. Nevertheless, they make certain things clear. For one, they spell out what the poet merely hints at in his choice of the word *gray:* that he finds the city dull and depressing. He stresses the word; instead of saying *gray pavements,* in the usual word order, he turns the phrase around and makes *gray* stand at the end of the line, where it rimes with *day* and so takes extra emphasis. The grayness of the city therefore seems important to the poem, and the paraphrase tries to make its meaning obvious.

Whenever you paraphrase, you stick your neck out. You affirm what the poem gives you to understand. And making a paraphrase can help you see the central thought of the poem, its **theme.** Theme isn't the same as **subject,** the main topic, whatever the poem is "about." In Yeats's poem, the subject is the lake isle of Innisfree, or a wish to retreat to it. But the theme is, "I yearn for an ideal place where I will find perfect peace and happiness." Themes can be stated variously, depending on what you believe matters most in the poem. Taking a different view of the poem, placing more weight on the speaker's wish to escape the city, you might instead state the theme: "This city is getting me down—I want to get back to nature." But after taking a second look at that statement, you might want to sharpen it. After all, this Innisfree seems a special, particular place, where the natural world means more to the poet than just any old trees and birds he might see in a park. Perhaps a stronger statement of theme, one closer to what matters most in the poem, might be: "I want to quit the city for my heaven on earth." That, of course, is saying in an obvious way what Yeats says more subtly, more memorably.

Not all poems clearly assert a proposition, but many do; some even declare their themes in their opening lines: "Gather ye rose-buds while ye may!"—that is, enjoy love before it's too late. This theme, stated in that famous first line of Robert Herrick's "To the Virgins, to Make Much of Time" (page 521), is so familiar that we give it a name: *carpe diem,* Latin for "seize the day." Seizing the joys of the present moment is a favorite argument of poets. You will meet it in more than these two poems in this book.

A paraphrase, of course, never tells *all* that a poem contains, nor will every reader agree that a particular paraphrase is accurate. We all make our own interpretations, and sometimes the total meaning of a poem evades even the poet who wrote it. Asked to explain a passage in one of his poems, Robert Browning replied that when he had written the poem, only God and he knew what it meant; but "Now, only God knows." Still, to analyze a poem *as if* we could be certain of its meaning is, in general, more fruitful than to proceed as if no certainty could ever be had. The latter approach is likely to end in complete subjectivity, the attitude of the reader who says, "Yeats's 'Lake Isle of Innisfree' is really about the lost island of Atlantis. It is because I think it is.

How can you prove me wrong?" Interpretations can't be proven "wrong." A more fruitful question might be, "What can we understand from the poem's very words?"

All of us bring personal associations to the poems we read. "The Lake Isle of Innisfree" might give you special pleasure if you have ever vacationed on a small island or on the shore of a lake. Such associations are inevitable, even to be welcomed, as long as they don't interfere with our reading the words on the page. We need to distinguish irrelevant responses from those the poem calls for. The reader who can't stand "The Lake Isle of Innisfree" because she is afraid of bees isn't reading a poem by Yeats, but one of her own invention.

Now and again we meet a poem—perhaps startling and memorable—into which the method of paraphrase won't take us far. Some portion of any deep poem resists explanation, but certain poems resist it almost entirely. Many poems by religious mystics seem closer to dream than waking. So do poems that purport to record drug experiences, such as Coleridge's "Kubla Khan" (page 501), as well as poems that embody some private system of beliefs, such as Blake's lines from *Jerusalem*

> For a Tear is an Intellectual thing,
> And a Sigh is the Sword of an Angel King.

So do nonsense poems, translations of primitive folk songs, and surreal poems.[1] Such poetry may move us and give pleasure (although not, perhaps, the pleasure of intellectual understanding). We do it no harm by trying to paraphrase it, though we may fail. Whether logically clear or strangely opaque, good poems appeal to the intelligence and do not shrink from it.

So far, we have taken for granted that poetry differs from prose; yet all our strategies for reading poetry—plowing straight on through and then going back, isolating difficulties, trying to paraphrase, reading aloud, using a dictionary—are no different from those we might employ in unraveling a complicated piece of prose. Poetry, after all, is similar to prose in most respects. At the very least, it is written in the same language. Like prose, poetry shares knowledge with us. It tells us, for instance, of a beautiful island in Lake Gill, County Sligo, Ireland, and of how one man feels toward it. Maybe the poet knows no more about Innisfree than a writer of a travel guidebook knows. And yet Yeats's poem indicates a kind of knowledge that tourist guidebooks do not ordinarily reveal: that the human heart can yearn for peace and happiness, that the lake isle of Innisfree with its "low sounds by the shore" can echo and reecho in memory forever.

---

[1]The French poet André Breton, founder of **Surrealism**, a movement in art and writing, declared that a higher reality exists, which to mortal eyes looks absurd. To mirror that reality, surrealist poets are fond of bizarre and dreamlike objects such as soluble fish and white-haired revolvers.

Lyric Poetry

Originally, as its Greek name suggests, a *lyric* was a poem sung to the music of a lyre. This earlier meaning—a poem made for singing—is still current today, when we use *lyrics* to mean the words of a popular song. But the kind of printed poem we now call a *lyric* is usually something else, for over the past five hundred years the nature of lyric poetry has changed greatly. Ever since the invention of the printing press in the fifteenth century, poets have written less often for singers, more often for readers. In general, this tendency has made lyric poems contain less word-music and (since they can be pondered on a page) more thought—and perhaps more complicated feelings.

Here is a rough definition of a **lyric** as it is written today: a short poem expressing the thoughts and feelings of a single speaker. Often a poet will write a lyric in the first person ("I will arise and go now, and go to Innisfree"), but not always. Instead, a lyric might describe an object or recall an experience without the speaker's ever bringing himself or herself into it. (For an example of such a lyric, one in which the poet refrains from saying "I," see William Carlos Williams's "The Red Wheelbarrow" on page 341, Theodore Roethke's "Root Cellar" on page 386, or Gerard Manley Hopkins's "Pied Beauty" on page 391.)

Perhaps because, rightly or wrongly, some people still think of lyrics as lyre-strummings, they expect a lyric to be an outburst of feeling, somewhat resembling a song, at least containing musical elements such as rime, rhythm, or sound effects. Such expectations are fulfilled in "The Lake Isle of Innisfree," that impassioned lyric full of language rich in sound (as you will hear if you'll read it aloud). Many contemporary poets, however, write short poems in which they voice opinions or complicated feelings—poems that no reader would dream of trying to sing. Most people would call such poems lyrics, too; one commentator has argued that a lyric may contain an argument.

But in the sense in which we use it, *lyric* will usually apply to a kind of poem you can easily recognize. Here, for instance, are two lyrics. They differ sharply in subject and theme, but they have traits in common: both are short, and (as you will find) both set forth one speaker's definite, unmistakable feelings.

D. H. Lawrence (1885–1930)

Piano   1918

Softly, in the dusk, a woman is singing to me;
Taking me back down the vista of years, till I see
A child sitting under the piano, in the boom of the tingling strings
And pressing the small, poised feet of a mother who smiles as she sings.

In spite of myself, the insidious mastery of song   5
Betrays me back, till the heart of me weeps to belong
To the old Sunday evenings at home, with winter outside
And hymns in the cozy parlor, the tinkling piano our guide.

So now it is vain for the singer to burst into clamour
With the great black piano appassionato. The glamour   10
Of childish days is upon me, my manhood is cast
Down in the flood of remembrance, I weep like a child for the past.

QUESTIONS

1. Jot down a brief paraphrase of this poem. In your paraphrase, clearly show what the speaker says is happening at present and also what he finds himself remembering. Make clear which seems the more powerful in its effect on him.
2. What are the speaker's various feelings? What do you understand from the words *insidious* and *betrays*?
3. With what specific details does the poem make the past seem real?
4. What is the subject of Lawrence's poem? How would you state its theme?

Adrienne Rich (b. 1929)

Aunt Jennifer's Tigers   1951

Aunt Jennifer's tigers prance across a screen,
Bright topaz denizens of a world of green.
They do not fear the men beneath the tree;
They pace in sleek chivalric certainty.

Aunt Jennifer's fingers fluttering through her wool   5
Find even the ivory needle hard to pull.
The massive weight of Uncle's wedding band
Sits heavily upon Aunt Jennifer's hand.

When Aunt is dead, her terrified hands will lie
Still ringed with ordeals she was mastered by.   10
The tigers in the panel that she made
Will go on prancing, proud and unafraid.

Narrative Poetry

Although a lyric sometimes relates an incident, or like "Piano" draws a scene, it does not usually relate a series of events. That happens in a **narrative poem**, one whose main purpose is to tell a story.

In Western literature, narrative poetry dates back to the Babylonian *Epic of Gilgamesh* (composed before 2000 B.C.) and Homer's epics the *Iliad* and the *Odyssey* (composed before 700 B.C.). It may well have originated much earlier. In England and Scotland, storytelling poems have long been popular; in the late Middle Ages, ballads—or storytelling songs—circulated widely. Some, such as "Sir Patrick Spence" and "Bonny Barbara Allan," survive in our day, and folksingers sometimes perform them.

Evidently the art of narrative poetry invites the skills of a writer of fiction: the ability to draw characters and settings briefly, to engage attention, to shape a plot. Needless to say, it calls for all the skills of a poet as well. Here are two narrative poems: one medieval, one modern. How would you paraphrase the stories they tell? How do they hold your attention on their stories?

Anonymous (traditional Scottish ballad)

Sir Patrick Spence

The king sits in Dumferling toune,
    Drinking the blude-reid wine:
"O whar will I get guid sailor
    To sail this schip of mine?"

Up and spak an eldern knicht,°   *knight*   5
    Sat at the kings richt kne:
"Sir Patrick Spence is the best sailor
    That sails upon the se."

The king has written a braid° letter,
    And signed it wi' his hand,   10
And sent it to Sir Patrick Spence,
    Was walking on the sand.

The first line that Sir Patrick red,
    A loud lauch lauchèd he;
The next line that Sir Patrick red,   15
    The teir blinded his ee.

"O wha° is this has don this deid,   *who*
    This ill deid don to me,
To send me out this time o' the yeir,
    To sail upon the se!   20

"Mak haste, mak haste, my mirry men all,
    Our guid schip sails the morne."

"O say na sae,° my master deir,so
  For I feir a deadlie storme.

"Late late yestreen I saw the new moone,25
  Wi' the auld moone in hir arme,
And I feir, I feir, my deir master,
  That we will cum to harme."

O our Scots nobles wer richt laith°loath
  To weet° their cork-heild schoone,°wet; shoes   30
Bot lang owre° a' the play wer playd,long before
  Their hats they swam aboone.°above (their heads)

O lang, lang may their ladies sit,
  Wi' their fans into their hand,
Or ere° they se Sir Patrick Spencebefore   35
  Cum sailing to the land.

O lang, lang may the ladies stand,
  Wi' their gold kems° in their hair,combs
Waiting for their ain° deir lords,own
  For they'll se thame na mair.40

Haf owre,° haf owre to Aberdour,halfway over
  It's fiftie fadom deip,
And thair lies guid Sir Patrick Spence,
  Wi' the Scots lords at his feit.

SIR PATRICK SPENCE. *9 braid:* Broad, but broad in what sense? Among guesses are *plain-spoken, official,* and *on wide paper.*

QUESTIONS

1. That the king drinks "blude-reid wine" (line 2)—what meaning do you find in that detail? What does it hint, or foreshadow?

2. What do you make of this king and his motives for sending Spence and the Scots lords into an impending storm? Is he a fool, is he cruel and inconsiderate, is he deliberately trying to drown Sir Patrick and his crew, or is it impossible for us to know? Let your answer depend on the poem alone, not on anything you read into it.

3. Comment on this ballad's methods of storytelling. Is the story told too briefly for us to care what happens to Spence and his men, or are there any means by which the poet makes us feel compassion for them? Do you resent the lack of a detailed account of the shipwreck?

4. Lines 25–28—the new moon with the old moon in her arm—have been much admired as poetry. What does this stanza contribute to the story as well?

Robert Frost (1874–1963)

"Out, Out—" 1916

The buzz-saw snarled and rattled in the yard
And made dust and dropped stove-length sticks of wood,
Sweet-scented stuff when the breeze drew across it.
And from there those that lifted eyes could count
Five mountain ranges one behind the other 5
Under the sunset far into Vermont.
And the saw snarled and rattled, snarled and rattled,
As it ran light, or had to bear a load.
And nothing happened: day was all but done.
Call it a day, I wish they might have said 10
To please the boy by giving him the half hour
That a boy counts so much when saved from work.
His sister stood beside them in her apron
To tell them "Supper." At the word, the saw,
As if to prove saws knew what supper meant, 15
Leaped out at the boy's hand, or seemed to leap—
He must have given the hand. However it was,
Neither refused the meeting. But the hand!
The boy's first outcry was a rueful laugh,
As he swung toward them holding up the hand 20
Half in appeal, but half as if to keep
The life from spilling. Then the boy saw all—
Since he was old enough to know, big boy
Doing a man's work, though a child at heart—
He saw all spoiled. "Don't let him cut my hand off— 25
The doctor, when he comes. Don't let him, sister!"
So. But the hand was gone already.
The doctor put him in the dark of ether.
He lay and puffed his lips out with his breath.
And then—the watcher at his pulse took fright. 30
No one believed. They listened at his heart.
Little—less—nothing!—and that ended it.
No more to build on there. And they, since they
Were not the one dead, turned to their affairs.

"OUT, OUT—" The title of this poem echoes the words of Shakespeare's *Macbeth* on receiving news that his queen is dead: "Out, out, brief candle! / Life's but a walking shadow, a poor player / That struts and frets his hour upon the stage / And then is heard no more. It is a tale / Told by an idiot, full of sound and fury, / Signifying nothing" (*Macbeth* 5. 5. 23–28).

QUESTIONS

1. How does Frost make the buzz-saw appear sinister? How does he make it seem, in another way, like a friend?
2. What do you make of the people who surround the boy—the "they" of the poem? Who might they be? Do they seem to you concerned and compassionate, cruel, indifferent, or what?
3. What does Frost's reference to *Macbeth* contribute to your understanding of "'Out, Out—'"? How would you state the theme of Frost's poem?
4. Set this poem side by side with "Sir Patrick Spence." How does "'Out, Out—'" resemble that medieval folk ballad in subject, or differ from it? How is Frost's poem similar or different in its way of telling a story?

Dramatic Poetry

A third kind of poetry is **dramatic poetry**, which presents the voice of an imaginary character (or characters) speaking directly, without any additional narration by the author. A dramatic poem, according to T. S. Eliot, does not consist of "what the poet would say in his own person, but only what he can say within the limits of one imaginary character addressing another imaginary character." Strictly speaking, the term *dramatic poetry* describes any verse written for the stage (and until a few centuries ago most playwrights, like Shakespeare and Molière, wrote their plays mainly in verse). But the term most often refers to the **dramatic monologue**, a poem written as a speech made by a character (other than the author) at some decisive moment. A dramatic monologue is usually addressed by the speaker to some other character who remains silent. If the listener replies, the poem becomes a dialogue (such as Thomas Hardy's "The Ruined Maid" on page 364) in which the story unfolds in the conversation between two speakers.

The Victorian poet Robert Browning, who developed the form of the dramatic monologue, liked to put words in the mouths of characters who were conspicuously nasty, weak, reckless, or crazy. The dramatic monologue has been a popular form among American poets, including Edwin Arlington Robinson, Robert Frost, Ezra Pound, Randall Jarrell, and Sylvia Plath. The most famous dramatic monologue ever written is probably Browning's "My Last Duchess," in which the poet creates a Renaissance Italian Duke whose words reveal more about himself than the aristocratic speaker intends.

Robert Browning (1812–1889)

My Last Duchess   1842

Ferrara

That's my last Duchess painted on the wall,
Looking as if she were alive. I call

That piece a wonder, now; Frà Pandolf's hands
Worked busily a day, and there she stands.
Will't please you sit and look at her? I said 5
"Frà Pandolf" by design, for never read
Strangers like you that pictured countenance,
The depth and passion of its earnest glance,
But to myself they turned (since none puts by
The curtain I have drawn for you, but I) 10
And seemed as they would ask me, if they durst,
How such a glance came there; so, not the first
Are you to turn and ask thus. Sir, 'twas not
Her husband's presence only, called that spot
Of joy into the Duchess' cheek; perhaps 15
Frà Pandolf chanced to say, "Her mantle laps
Over my lady's wrist too much," or "Paint
Must never hope to reproduce the faint
Half-flush that dies along her throat." Such stuff
Was courtesy, she thought, and cause enough 20
For calling up that spot of joy. She had
A heart—how shall I say?—too soon made glad,
Too easily impressed; she liked whate'er
She looked on, and her looks went everywhere.
Sir, 'twas all one! My favor at her breast, 25
The dropping of the daylight in the West,
The bough of cherries some officious fool
Broke in the orchard for her, the white mule
She rode with round the terrace—all and each
Would draw from her alike the approving speech, 30
Or blush, at least. She thanked men,—good! but thanked
Somehow—I know not how—as if she ranked
My gift of a nine-hundred-years-old name
With anybody's gift. Who'd stoop to blame
This sort of trifling? Even had you skill 35
In speech—which I have not—to make your will
Quite clear to such an one, and say "Just this
Or that in you disgusts me; here you miss,
Or there exceed the mark"—and if she let
Herself be lessoned so, nor plainly set 40
Her wits to yours, forsooth, and made excuse—
E'en then would be some stooping; and I choose
Never to stoop. Oh, sir, she smiled, no doubt,
Whene'er I passed her; but who passed without
Much the same smile? This grew; I gave commands; 45
Then all smiles stopped together. There she stands

As if alive. Will't please you rise? We'll meet
The company below, then. I repeat,
The Count your master's known munificence
Is ample warrant that no just pretense   50
Of mine for dowry will be disallowed;
Though his fair daughter's self, as I avowed
At starting, is my object. Nay, we'll go
Together down, sir. Notice Neptune, though,
Taming a sea-horse, thought a rarity,   55
Which Claus of Innsbruck cast in bronze for me!

MY LAST DUCHESS. Ferrara, a city in northern Italy, is the scene. Browning may have modeled his speaker after Alonzo, Duke of Ferrara (1533–1598). 3 *Frà Pandolf* and 56 *Claus of Innsbruck*: fictitious names of artists.

QUESTIONS

1. Who is the Duke addressing? What is this person's business in Ferrara?
2. What is the Duke's opinion of his last Duchess's personality? Do we see her character differently?
3. If the Duke was unhappy with the Duchess's behavior, why didn't he make his displeasure known? Cite a specific passage to explain his reticence.
4. How much do we know about the fate of the last Duchess? Would it help our understanding of the poem to know more?
5. Does Browning imply any connection between the Duke's art collection and his attitude toward his wife?

Today, lyrics in the English language seem more plentiful than other kinds of poetry. Although there has recently been a revival of interest in writing narrative poems, they have a far smaller audience today than long verse narratives, such as Henry Wadsworth Longfellow's *Evangeline* and Alfred, Lord Tennyson's *Idylls of the King,* enjoyed in the nineteenth century.

Also more fashionable in former times was a fourth variety of poetry, **didactic poetry**: a poem apparently written to state a message or teach a body of knowledge. In a lyric, a speaker may express sadness; in a didactic poem, he or she may explain that sadness is inherent in life. Poems that impart a body of knowledge, such as Ovid's *Art of Love* and Lucretius's *On the Nature of Things*, are didactic. Such instructive poetry was favored especially by classical Latin poets and by English poets of the eighteenth century. In *The Fleece* (1757), John Dyer celebrated the British woolen industry and included practical advice on raising sheep:

In cold stiff soils the bleaters oft complain
Of gouty ails, by shepherds termed the halt:
Those let the neighboring fold or ready crook

Detain, and pour into their cloven feet
Corrosive drugs, deep-searching arsenic,
Dry alum, verdegris, or vitriol keen.

One might agree with Dr. Johnson's comment on Dyer's effort: "The subject, Sir, cannot be made poetical." But it may be argued that the subject of didactic poetry does not make it any less poetical. Good poems, it seems, can be written about anything under the sun. Like Dyer, John Milton described sick sheep in "Lycidas," a poem few readers have thought unpoetic:

The hungry sheep look up, and are not fed,
But, swoll'n with wind and the rank mist they draw,
Rot inwardly, and foul contagion spread . . .

What makes Milton's lines better poetry than Dyer's is, among other things, a difference in attitude. Sick sheep to Dyer mean the loss of a few shillings and pence; to Milton, whose sheep stand for English Christendom, they mean a moral catastrophe.

WRITING EFFECTIVELY

WRITING A PARAPHRASE

Can a Poem Be Paraphrased?

A poet takes pains to choose each word of a poem for both its sound and its exact shade of meaning. Since a poem's full effect is so completely wedded to its exact wording, some would say that no poem can be truly paraphrased. But even though it represents an imperfect approximation of the real thing, a paraphrase can be useful to write and read. It can clearly map out a poem's key images, actions, and ideas. A map is no substitute for a landscape, but a good map often helps us find our way through the landscape without getting lost.

William Stafford (1914–1993)

Ask Me	1975

Some time when the river is ice ask me
mistakes I have made. Ask me whether
what I have done is my life. Others
have come in their slow way into
my thought, and some have tried to help   5

or to hurt—ask me what difference
their strongest love or hate has made.

I will listen to what you say.
You and I can turn and look
at the silent river and wait. We know   10
the current is there, hidden; and there
are comings and goings from miles away
that hold the stillness exactly before us.
What the river says, that is what I say.

William Stafford (1914–1993)

A Paraphrase of "Ask Me"   1977

I think my poem can be paraphrased—and that any poem can be paraphrased. But every pass through the material, using other words, would have
to be achieved at certain costs, either in momentum, or nuance, or dangerously explicit (and therefore misleading in tone) adjustments. I'll try one such
pass through the poem:

> When it's quiet and cold and we have some chance to interchange
> without hurry, confront me if you like with a challenge about
> whether I think I have made mistakes in my life—and ask me, if
> you want to, whether to me my life is actually the sequence of
> events or exploits others would see. Well, those others tag along in
> my living, and some of them in fact have played significant roles in
> the narrative run of my world; they have intended either helping or
> hurting (but by implication in the way I am saying this you will
> know that neither effort is conclusive). So—ask me how important
> their good or bad intentions have been (both intentions get a drastic
> *leveling* judgment from this cool stating of it all). You, too, will be
> entering that realm of maybe-help-maybe-hurt, by entering that far
> into my life by asking this serious question—so: I will stay still and
> consider. Out there will be the world confronting us both; we will
> both know we are surrounded by mystery, tremendous things that
> do not reveal themselves to us. That river, that world—and our
> lives—all share the depth and stillness of much more significance
> than our talk, or intentions. There is a steadiness and somehow a
> solace in knowing that what is around us so greatly surpasses our
> human concerns.

From "Ask Me"

CHECKLIST

Paraphrasing a Poem

✓ Read the poem closely—more than once.

✓ Go through it line by line. Don't skip lines or sentences or any key details. In your own words, what does each line say?

✓ Write your paraphrase as ordinary prose. Don't worry about line and stanza breaks.

✓ Describe the literal meaning of the poem. Don't worry about any deeper meanings.

✓ After you have described what literally happens in the poem, go over your paraphrase and see if you have captured the overall significance of the poem along with the details.

WRITING ASSIGNMENT ON PARAPHRASING

Paraphrase any short poem from the chapter "Poems for Further Reading." Be sure to do a careful line-by-line reading. Include the most vital points and details, and state the poem's main thought or theme without quoting any original passage.

MORE TOPICS FOR WRITING

1. In a paragraph, contrast William Stafford's poem with his paraphrase. What does the poem offer that the paraphrase does not? What, then, is the value of the paraphrase?

2. Write a two-page paraphrase of the events described in "'Out, Out—.'" Then take your paraphrase even further: if you had to summarize the poem's message in a single sentence, what would it be?

3. In two pages, describe the voice of the speaker of "My Last Duchess." What aspects of his personality does the speaker inadvertently reveal?

10
Listening to a Voice

Tone

In old Western movies, when one hombre taunts another, it is customary for the second to drawl, "Smile when you say that, pardner" or "Mister, I don't like your tone of voice." Sometimes in reading a poem, although we can neither see a face nor hear a voice, we can infer the poet's attitude from other evidence.

Like tone of voice, **tone** in literature often conveys an attitude toward the person addressed. Like the manner of a person, the manner of a poem may be friendly or belligerent toward its reader, condescending or respectful. Again like tone of voice, the tone of a poem may tell us how the speaker feels about himself or herself: cocksure or humble, sad or glad. But usually when we ask, "What is the tone of a poem?" we mean, "What attitude does the poet take toward a theme or a subject?" Is the poet being affectionate, hostile, earnest, playful, sarcastic, or what? We may never be able to know, of course, the poet's personal feelings. All we need know is how to feel when we read the poem.

Strictly speaking, tone isn't an attitude; it is whatever in the poem makes an attitude clear to us: the choice of certain words instead of others, the picking out of certain details. In A. E. Housman's "Loveliest of trees," for example, the poet communicates his admiration for a cherry tree's beauty by singling out for attention its white blossoms; had he wanted to show his dislike for the tree, he might have concentrated on its broken branches, birdlime, or snails. To perceive the tone of a poem rightly, we need to read the poem carefully, paying attention to whatever suggestions we find in it.

Theodore Roethke (1908–1963)

My Papa's Waltz   1948

The whiskey on your breath
Could make a small boy dizzy;
But I hung on like death:
Such waltzing was not easy.

We romped until the pans   5
Slid from the kitchen shelf;
My mother's countenance
Could not unfrown itself.

The hand that held my wrist
Was battered on one knuckle;   10
At every step you missed
My right ear scraped a buckle.

You beat time on my head
With a palm caked hard by dirt,
Then waltzed me off to bed   15
Still clinging to your shirt.

What is the tone of this poem? Most readers find the speaker's attitude toward his father critical, but nonetheless affectionate. They take this recollection of childhood to be an odd but happy one. Other readers, however, concentrate on other details, such as the father's rough manners and drunkenness. One reader has written that "Roethke expresses his resentment for his father, a drunken brute with dirty hands and whiskey breath who carelessly hurt the child's ear and manhandled him." Although this reader accurately noticed some of the events in the poem and perceived that there was something desperate in the son's hanging onto the father "like death," he simplifies the tone of the poem and so misses its humorous side.

While "My Papa's Waltz" contains the dark elements of manhandling and drunkenness, the tone remains grotesquely comic. The rollicking rhythms of the poem underscore Roethke's complex humor—half loving and half censuring of the unwashed, intoxicated father. The humor is further reinforced by playful rimes such as *dizzy* and *easy*, *knuckle* and *buckle*, as well as the joyful suggestions of the words *waltz*, *waltzing*, and *romped*. The scene itself is comic, with kitchen pans falling due to the father's roughhousing while the mother looks on unamused. However much the speaker satirizes the overly rambunctious father, he does not have the boy identify with the soberly disapproving mother. Not all comedy is comfortable and reassuring. This small boy's family life has its frightening side, but the last line suggests the boy is *still clinging* to his father with persistent if also complicated love.

Such a poem, though it includes lifelike details that aren't pretty, has a tone relatively easy to recognize. So does **satiric poetry**, a kind of comic poetry that generally conveys a message. Usually its tone is one of detached amusement, withering contempt, and implied superiority. In a satiric poem, the poet ridicules some person or persons (or perhaps some kind of human behavior), examining the victim by the light of certain principles and implying that the reader, too, ought to feel contempt for the victim.

Countee Cullen (1903–1946)

For a Lady I Know   1925

She even thinks that up in heaven
  Her class lies late and snores,
While poor black cherubs rise at seven
  To do celestial chores.

QUESTIONS

1. What is Cullen's message?
2. How would you characterize the tone of this poem? Wrathful? Amused?

In some poems the poet's attitude may be plain enough; while in other poems attitudes may be so mingled that it is hard to describe them tersely without doing injustice to the poem. Does Andrew Marvell in "To His Coy Mistress" (page 535) take a serious or playful attitude toward the fact that he and his lady are destined to be food for worms? No one-word answer will suffice. And what of T. S. Eliot's "The Love Song of J. Alfred Prufrock" (page 509)? In his attitude toward his redemption-seeking hero who wades with trousers rolled, Eliot is seriously funny. Such a mingled tone may be seen in the following poem by the wife of a governor of the Massachusetts Bay Colony and the earliest American poet of note. Anne Bradstreet's first book, *The Tenth Muse Lately Sprung Up in America* (1650), had been published in England without her consent. She wrote these lines to preface a second edition:

Anne Bradstreet (1612?–1672)

The Author to Her Book   1678

Thou ill-formed offspring of my feeble brain,
Who after birth did'st by my side remain,
Till snatched from thence by friends, less wise than true,
Who thee abroad exposed to public view;
Made thee in rags, halting, to the press to trudge,   5
Where errors were not lessened, all may judge.
At thy return my blushing was not small,
My rambling brat (in print) should mother call;
I cast thee by as one unfit for light,
Thy visage was so irksome in my sight;   10
Yet being mine own, at length affection would
Thy blemishes amend, if so I could:

I washed thy face, but more defects I saw,
And rubbing off a spot, still made a flaw.
I stretched thy joints to make thee even feet,   15
Yet still thou run'st more hobbling than is meet;
In better dress to trim thee was my mind,
But nought save homespun cloth in the house I find.
In this array, 'mongst vulgars may'st thou roam;
In critics' hands beware thou dost not come;   20
And take thy way where yet thou are not known.
If for thy Father asked, say thou had'st none;
And for thy Mother, she alas is poor,
Which caused her thus to send thee out of door.

In the author's comparison of her book to an illegitimate ragamuffin, we may
be struck by the details of scrubbing and dressing a child: details that might
well occur to a mother who had scrubbed and dressed many. As she might feel
toward such a child, so she feels toward her book. She starts by deploring it
but, as the poem goes on, cannot deny it her affection. Humor enters (as in
the pun in line 15). She must dress the creature in *homespun cloth*, something
both crude and serviceable. By the end of her poem, Bradstreet seems to regard
her book-child with tenderness, amusement, and a certain indulgent awareness
of its faults. To read this poem is to sense its mingling of several attitudes.
A poet can be merry and in earnest at the same time.

Walt Whitman (1819–1892)

To a Locomotive in Winter   1881

Thee for my recitative,
Thee in the driving storm even as now, the snow, the
       winter-day declining,
Thee in thy panoply,° thy measur'd dual throbbing and thy   *suit of armor*
       beat convulsive,
Thy black cylindric body, golden brass and silvery steel,
Thy ponderous side-bars, parallel and connecting rods, gyrating,
       shuttling at thy sides,   5
Thy metrical, now swelling pant and roar, now tapering in the
       distance,
Thy great protruding head-light fix'd in front,
Thy long, pale, floating vapor-pennants, tinged with delicate
       purple,
The dense and murky clouds out-belching from thy smoke-stack,

Thy knitted frame, thy springs and valves, the tremulous twinkle of
    thy wheels, 10
Thy train of cars behind, obedient, merrily following,
Through gale or calm, now swift, now slack, yet steadily careering;
Type of the modern—emblem of motion and power—pulse of the
    continent,
For once come serve the Muse and merge in verse, even as here I
    see thee,
With storm and buffeting gusts of wind and falling snow, 15
By day thy warning ringing bell to sound its notes,
By night thy silent signal lamps to swing.
Fierce-throated beauty!
Roll through my chant with all thy lawless music, thy swinging lamps
    at night,
Thy madly-whistled laughter, echoing, rumbling like an earthquake,
    rousing all, 20
Law of thyself complete, thine own track firmly holding,
(No sweetness debonair of tearful harp or glib piano thine,)
Thy trills of shrieks by rocks and hills return'd,
Launch'd o'er the prairies wide, across the lakes,
To the free skies unpent and glad and strong. 25

Emily Dickinson (1830–1886)

I like to see it lap the Miles (about 1862)[1]

I like to see it lap the Miles –
And lick the Valleys up –
And stop to feed itself at Tanks –
And then – prodigious step

Around a Pile of Mountains – 5
And supercilious peer
In Shanties – by the sides of Roads –
And then a Quarry pare

To fit its Ribs
And crawl between
Complaining all the while 10
In horrid – hooting stanza –
Then chase itself down Hill –

[1]Parentheses around a date that follows a poem title indicate the poem's date of composition,
when it was composed much earlier than its first publication date.

And neigh like Boanerges –
Then – punctual as a Star   15
Stop – docile and omnipotent
At its own stable door–

QUESTIONS

1. What differences in tone do you find between Whitman's and Dickinson's poems? Point out in each poem whatever contributes to these differences.

2. *Boanerges* in Dickinson's last stanza means "sons of thunder," a name given by Jesus to the disciples John and James (see Mark 3:17). How far should the reader work out the particulars of this comparison? Does it make the tone of the poem serious?

3. In Whitman's opening line, what is a *recitative?* What other specialized terms from the vocabulary of music and poetry does each poem contain? How do they help underscore Whitman's theme?

4. Poets and songwriters probably have regarded the locomotive with more affection than they have shown most other machines. Why do you suppose this is so? Can you think of any other poems or songs as examples?

5. What do these two poems tell you about locomotives that you would not be likely to find in a technical book on railroading?

6. Are the subjects of the two poems identical? Discuss.

Benjamin Alire Sáenz (b. 1954)

To the Desert   1995

I came to you one rainless August night.
You taught me how to live without the rain.
You are thirst and thirst is all I know.
You are sand, wind, sun, and burning sky,
The hottest blue. You blow a breeze and brand   5
Your breath into my mouth. You reach—then *bend
Your force, to break, blow, burn, and make me new.*
You wrap your name tight around my ribs
And keep me warm. I was born for you.
Above, below, by you, by you surrounded.   10
I wake to you at dawn. Never break your
Knot. Reach, rise, blow, *Sálvame, mi dios,
Trágame, mi tierra. Salva, traga,* Break me,
I am bread. I will be the water for your thirst.

TO THE DESERT. 6–7 *bend . . . make me new:* quoted from John Donne's "Batter my heart" (page 356). 12–13 *Sálvame, mi dios . . . traga:* Spanish for "Save me, my god, / Take me, my land. Save me, take me." (*Trágame* literally means "swallow me.")

QUESTIONS

1. How does the speaker feel about the land being described? What words in the poem suggest or convey those feelings?
2. What effect does the speaker's sudden switch into Spanish create? What is the tone of the Spanish?
3. Of what kind of language do the last few lines of the poem remind you?

Weldon Kees (1914–1955)

For My Daughter   1940

Looking into my daughter's eyes I read
Beneath the innocence of morning flesh
Concealed, hintings of death she does not heed.
Coldest of winds have blown this hair, and mesh
Of seaweed snarled these miniatures of hands;   5
The night's slow poison, tolerant and bland,
Has moved her blood. Parched years that I have seen
That may be hers appear: foul, lingering
Death in certain war, the slim legs green.
Or, fed on hate, she relishes the sting   10
Of others' agony; perhaps the cruel
Bride of a syphilitic or a fool.
These speculations sour in the sun.
I have no daughter. I desire none.

QUESTIONS

1. How does the last line of this sonnet affect the meaning of the poem?
2. "For My Daughter" was first published in 1940. What considerations might a potential American parent have felt at that time? Are these historical concerns mirrored in the poem?
3. Donald Justice has said that "Kees is one of the bitterest poets in history." Is bitterness the only attitude the speaker reveals in this poem?

The Person in the Poem

The tone of a poem, we said, is like tone of voice in that both communicate feelings. Still, this comparison raises a question: when we read a poem, whose "voice" speaks to us?

"The poet's" is one possible answer; and in the case of many a poem that answer may be right. Reading Anne Bradstreet's "The Author to Her Book," we can be reasonably sure that the poet speaks of her very own book, and of her own experiences. In order to read a poem, we seldom need to read a poet's biography; but in truth there are certain poems whose full effect depends upon our knowing at least a fact or two of the poet's life. Here is one such poem.

Natasha Trethewey (b. 1966)

White Lies   2000

The lies I could tell,
when I was growing up
light-bright, near-white,
high-yellow, red-boned
in a black place,   5
were just white lies.

I could easily tell the white folks
that we lived uptown,
not in that pink and green
shanty-fied shotgun section   10
along the tracks. I could act
like my homemade dresses
came straight out the window
of Maison Blanche. I could even
keep quiet, quiet as kept,   15
like the time a white girl said
(squeezing my hand), *Now
we have three of us in this class.*

But I paid for it every time
Mama found out.   20
She laid her hands on me,
then washed out my mouth
with Ivory soap. *This
is to purify,* she said,
and cleanse your lying tongue.   25
Believing her, I swallowed suds
thinking they'd work
from the inside out.

Through its pattern of vivid color imagery, Trethewey's poem tells of a black child light enough to "pass for white" in a society that was still extremely race-sensitive. But knowing the author's family background gives us a deeper insight into the levels of meaning in the poem. Trethewey was born in Mississippi in 1966, at a time when her parents' interracial marriage was a criminal act in that state. On her birth certificate, her mother's race was given as "colored"; in the box intended to record the race of her father—who was white and had been born in Nova Scotia—appeared the word "Canadian" (although her parents divorced before she began grade school, she remained extremely close to both of them). Trethewey has said of her birth certificate: "Something is left out of the official record that way. The irony isn't lost on me. Even in documenting myself as a person there is a little fiction." "White Lies" succeeds admirably on its own, but these biographical details allow us to read it as an even more complex meditation on issues of racial definition and personal identity in America.

Most of us can tell the difference between a person we meet in life and a person we meet in a work of art—unlike the moviegoer in the Philippines who, watching a villain in an exciting film, pulled out a revolver and peppered the screen. And yet, in reading poems, we are liable to temptation.

When the poet says "I," we may want to assume that he or she is making a personal statement. But reflect: do all poems have to be personal? Here is a brief poem inscribed on the tombstone of an infant in Burial Hill Cemetery, Plymouth, Massachusetts:

> Since I have been so quickly done for,
> I wonder what I was begun for.

We do not know who wrote those lines, but it is clear that the poet was not a short-lived infant writing from personal experience. In other poems, the speaker is obviously a **persona**, or fictitious character: not the poet, but the poet's creation. As a grown man, William Blake, a skilled professional engraver, wrote a poem in the voice of a boy, an illiterate chimney sweeper.

Let's consider a poem spoken not by a poet, but by a persona—in this case a mysterious one. Edwin Arlington Robinson's "Luke Havergal" is a dramatic monologue, but the identity of the speaker is never clearly stated. Upon first reading the poem in Robinson's *The Children of the Night* (1897), President Theodore Roosevelt was so moved that he wrote a review of the book that made the author famous. Roosevelt, however, admitted that he found the musically seductive poem difficult. "I am not sure I understand 'Luke Havergal,'" he wrote, "but I am entirely sure I like it." Possibly what most puzzled our twenty-sixth president was who was speaking in the poem. How much does Robinson let us know about the voice and the person it addresses?

Edwin Arlington Robinson (1869–1935)

Luke Havergal   1897

Go to the western gate, Luke Havergal,
There where the vines cling crimson on the wall,
And in the twilight wait for what will come.
The leaves will whisper there of her, and some,

Like flying words, will strike you as they fall;   5
But go, and if you listen she will call.
Go to the western gate, Luke Havergal—
Luke Havergal.

No, there is not a dawn in eastern skies
To rift the fiery night that's in your eyes;   10
But there, where western glooms are gathering,
The dark will end the dark, if anything:
God slays Himself with every leaf that flies,
And hell is more than half of paradise.
No, there is not a dawn in eastern skies—   15
In eastern skies.

Out of a grave I come to tell you this,
Out of a grave I come to quench the kiss
That flames upon your forehead with a glow
That blinds you to the way that you must go.   20
Yes, there is yet one way to where she is,
Bitter, but one that faith may never miss.
Out of a grave I come to tell you this—
To tell you this.

There is the western gate, Luke Havergal,   25
There are the crimson leaves upon the wall.
Go, for the winds are tearing them away,—
Nor think to riddle the dead words they say,
Nor any more to feel them as they fall;
But go, and if you trust her she will call.   30
There is the western gate, Luke Havergal—
Luke Havergal.

QUESTIONS

1. Who is the speaker of the poem? What specific details does the author reveal
   about the speaker?
2. What does the speaker ask Luke Havergal to do?
3. What do you understand "the western gate" to be?
4. Would you advise Luke Havergal to follow the speaker's advice? Why or why
   not?

No literary law decrees that the speaker in a poem even has to be human.
Good poems have been uttered by clouds, pebbles, clocks, and cats. Here is a
poem spoken by a hawk, a dramatic monologue that expresses the animal's

thoughts and attitudes in a way consciously designed to emphasize how different its worldview is from a human perspective.

Ted Hughes (1930–1998)

Hawk Roosting   1960

I sit in the top of the wood, my eyes closed.
Inaction, no falsifying dream
Between my hooked head and hooked feet:
Or in sleep rehearse perfect kills and eat.

The convenience of the high trees!   5
The air's buoyancy and the sun's ray
Are of advantage to me;
And the earth's face upward for my inspection.

My feet are locked upon the rough bark.
It took the whole of Creation   10
To produce my foot, my each feather:
Now I hold Creation in my foot

Or fly up, and revolve it all slowly—
I kill where I please because it is all mine.
There is no sophistry in my body: 15
My manners are tearing off heads—

The allotment of death.
For the one path of my flight is direct
Through the bones of the living.
No arguments assert my right: 20

The sun is behind me.
Nothing has changed since I began.
My eye has permitted no change.
I am going to keep things like this.

QUESTIONS

1. Find three observations the hawk makes about its world that a human would probably not make. What do these remarks tell us about the bird's character?

2. In what ways does Ted Hughes create an unrealistic portrayal of the hawk's true mental powers? What statements in the poem would an actual hawk be unlikely to make? Do these passages add anything to the poem's impact? What would be lost if they were omitted?

Here is a poem in which the speaker is something even more remote from humanity, something we ordinarily assume to have no thoughts or attitudes at all, but whose monologue offers an even more pointed contrast with human values.

Suji Kwock Kim (b. 1968)

Monologue for an Onion   2003

I don't mean to make you cry.
I mean nothing, but this has not kept you
From peeling away my body, layer by layer,

The tears clouding your eyes as the table fills
With husks, cut flesh, all the debris of pursuit.   5
Poor deluded human: you seek my heart.

Hunt all you want. Beneath each skin of mine
Lies another skin: I am pure onion—pure union
Of outside and in, surface and secret core.

Look at you, chopping and weeping. Idiot.   10
Is this the way you go through life, your mind
A stopless knife, driven by your fantasy of truth,

Of lasting union—slashing away skin after skin
From things, ruin and tears your only signs
Of progress? Enough is enough.   15

You must not grieve that the world is glimpsed
Through veils. How else can it be seen?
How will you rip away the veil of the eye, the veil

That you are, you who want to grasp the heart
Of things, hungry to know where meaning   20
Lies. Taste what you hold in your hands: onion-juice,

Yellow peels, my stinging shreds. You are the one
In pieces. Whatever you meant to love, in meaning to
You changed yourself: you are not who you are,

Your soul cut moment to moment by a blade   25
Of fresh desire, the ground sown with abandoned skins.
And at your inmost circle, what? A core that is

Not one. Poor fool, you are divided at the heart,
Lost in its maze of chambers, blood, and love,
A heart that will one day beat you to death.   30

QUESTIONS

1. How would you characterize the speaker's tone in this poem? What attitudes and judgments lie behind that tone?
2. "I mean nothing" (line 2) might be seen as a play on two senses of *mean*—"intend" and "signify." Is the statement true in both senses?
3. Suppose someone said to you, "The whole point of the poem is that vegetables have rights and feelings too, and humanity is being rebuked for its arrogance and insensitivity toward other species." How would you argue against that view?
4. The speaker is obviously one tough onion, cutting humanity little or no slack. To what degree do you think the speaker represents the author's views—totally, somewhat, or not at all? Explain your response.

We need not deny that a poet's experience can contribute to a poem nor that the emotion in the poem can indeed be the poet's. Still, to write a good poem one has to do more than live and feel. It seems a pity that, as Randall Jarrell has said, a cardinal may write verses worse than his youngest choirboy's. But writing poetry takes skill and imagination—qualities that extensive travel and wide experience do not necessarily give. For much of her life, Emily Dickinson seldom strayed from her family's house and grounds in Amherst, Massachusetts; yet her rimed life studies of a snake, a bee, and a hummingbird contain more poetry than we find in any firsthand description (so far) of the surface of the moon.

Langston Hughes (1902–1967)

Theme for English B   1951

The instructor said,

> Go home and write
> a page tonight.
> And let that page come out of you—
> Then, it will be true.   5

I wonder if it's that simple?
I am twenty-two, colored, born in Winston-Salem.
I went to school there, then Durham, then here
to this college on the hill above Harlem.
I am the only colored student in my class.   10
The steps from the hill lead down into Harlem,
through a park, then I cross St. Nicholas,
Eighth Avenue, Seventh, and I come to the Y,
the Harlem Branch Y, where I take the elevator
up to my room, sit down, and write this page: 15

It's not easy to know what is true for you and me
at twenty-two, my age. But I guess I'm what
I feel and see and hear, Harlem, I hear you:
hear you, hear me—we two—you, me, talk on this page.
(I hear New York, too.) Me—who?   20
Well, I like to eat, sleep, drink, and be in love.
I like to work, read, learn, and understand life.
I like a pipe for a Christmas present,
or records—Bessie, bop, or Bach.
I guess being colored doesn't make me *not* like   25
the same things other folks like who are other races.
So will my page be colored that I write?
Being me, it will not be white.

But it will be
a part of you, instructor.   30
You are white—
yet a part of me, as I am a part of you.
That's American.
Sometimes perhaps you don't want to be a part of me.
Nor do I often want to be a part of you.   35
But we are, that's true!
As I learn from you,
I guess you learn from me—
although you're older—and white—
and somewhat more free.   40

This is my page for English B.

THEME FOR ENGLISH B. 9 *College on the hill above Harlem:* Columbia University, where
Hughes was briefly a student. (Note, however, that this poem is not autobiographical. The
young speaker is a character invented by the middle-aged author.) 24 *Bessie:* Bessie Smith
(1898?–1937) was a popular blues singer often called the "Empress of the Blues."

Anne Sexton (1928–1974)

Her Kind   1960

I have gone out, a possessed witch,
haunting the black air, braver at night;
dreaming evil, I have done my hitch
over the plain houses, light by light:
lonely thing, twelve-fingered, out of mind.   5
A woman like that is not a woman, quite.
I have been her kind.

I have found the warm caves in the woods,
filled them with skillets, carvings, shelves,
closets, silks, innumerable goods; 10
fixed the suppers for the worms and the elves:
whining, rearranging the disaligned.
A woman like that is misunderstood.
I have been her kind.

I have ridden in your cart, driver,
waved my nude arms at villages going by, 15
learning the last bright routes, survivor
where your flames still bite my thigh
and my ribs crack where your wheels wind.
A woman like that is not ashamed to die. 20
I have been her kind.

QUESTIONS

1. Who is the speaker of this poem? What do we know about her?
2. What does the speaker mean by ending each stanza with the statement, "I have been her kind?"
3. Who are the figures with whom the speaker identifies? What do these figures tell us about the speaker's state of mind?

EXPERIMENT: Reading with and without Biography

Read the following poem by William Carlos Williams and state what you understand from it. Then consider the circumstances in which it probably came to be written. (Some information is offered in the first topic for writing on page 351.) Does the meaning of the poem change? To what extent does an appreciation of the poem need the support of biography?

William Carlos Williams (1883–1963)

The Red Wheelbarrow   1923

so much depends
upon

a red wheel
barrow

glazed with rain
water 5

beside the white
chickens.

Irony

To see a distinction between the poet and the words of a fictitious character—between Robert Browning and "My Last Duchess"—is to be aware of **irony**: a manner of speaking that implies a discrepancy. If the mask says one thing and we sense that the writer is in fact saying something else, the writer has adopted an **ironic point of view**. No finer illustration exists in English than Jonathan Swift's "A Modest Proposal," an essay in which Swift speaks as an earnest, humorless citizen who sets forth his reasonable plan to aid the Irish poor. The plan is so monstrous no sane reader can assent to it: the poor are to sell their children as meat for the tables of their landlords. From behind his false face, Swift is actually recommending not cannibalism but love and Christian charity.

A poem is often made complicated and more interesting by another kind of irony. **Verbal irony** occurs whenever words say one thing but mean something else, usually the opposite. The word *love* means *hate* here: "I just *love* to stay home and do my hair on a Saturday night!" If the verbal irony is conspicuously bitter, heavy-handed, and mocking, it is **sarcasm**: "Oh, he's the biggest spender in the world, all right!" (The sarcasm, if that statement were spoken, would be underscored by the speaker's tone of voice.) A famous instance of sarcasm is Mark Antony's line in his oration over the body of slain Julius Caesar: "Brutus is an honorable man." Antony repeats this line until the enraged populace begins shouting exactly what he means to call Brutus and the other conspirators: traitors, villains, murderers. We had best be alert for irony on the printed page, for if we miss it, our interpretations of a poem may go wild.

Robert Creeley (1926–2005)

Oh No   1959

If you wander far enough
you will come to it
and when you get there
they will give you a place to sit

for yourself only, in a nice chair,   5
and all your friends will be there
with smiles on their faces
and they will likewise all have places.

This poem is rich in verbal irony. The title helps point out that between the speaker's words and attitude lie deep differences. In line 2, what is *it?* Old age? The wandering suggests a conventional metaphor: the journey of life. Is *it* literally a rest home for "senior citizens," or perhaps some naïve popular concept of heaven (such as we meet in comic strips: harps, angels with hoops for halos) in which the saved all sit around in a ring, smugly congratulating one another? We can't be sure, but the speaker's attitude toward this final sitting-place is definite. It is a place for the selfish, as we infer from the phrase *for yourself only*. And *smiles on their faces* may hint that the smiles are unchanging and forced. There is a difference between saying "They had smiles on their faces" and "They smiled": the latter suggests that the smiles came from within. The word *nice* is to be regarded with distrust. If we see through this speaker, as Creeley implies we can do, we realize that, while pretending to be sweet-talking us into a seat, actually he is revealing the horror of a little hell. And the title is the poet's reaction to it (or the speaker's unironic, straightforward one): "Oh no! Not *that*!"

Dramatic irony, like verbal irony, contains an element of contrast, but it usually refers to a situation in a play wherein a character whose knowledge is limited says, does, or encounters something of greater significance than he or she knows. We, the spectators, realize the meaning of this speech or action, for the playwright has afforded us superior knowledge. In Sophocles' *King Oedipus*, when Oedipus vows to punish whomever has brought down a plague upon the city of Thebes, we know—as he does not—that the man he would punish is himself. (Referring to such a situation that precedes the downfall of a hero in a tragedy, some critics speak of **tragic irony** instead of dramatic irony.) Superior knowledge can be enjoyed not only by spectators in a theater but by readers of poetry as well. In *Paradise Lost*, we know in advance that Adam will fall into temptation, and we recognize his overconfidence when he neglects a warning. The situation of Oedipus also contains **cosmic irony**, or **irony of fate**: some Fate with a grim sense of humor seems cruelly to trick a human being. Cosmic irony clearly exists in poems in which fate or the Fates are personified and seen as hostile, as in Thomas Hardy's "The Convergence of the Twain" (page 517).

To sum up: the effect of irony depends on the reader's noticing some incongruity or discrepancy between two things. In *verbal irony*, there is a contrast between the speaker's words and meaning; in an *ironic point of view*, between the writer's attitude and what is spoken by a fictitious character; in *dramatic irony*, between the limited knowledge of a character and the fuller knowledge of the reader or spectator; in *cosmic irony*, between a character's aspiration and the treatment he or she receives at the hands of Fate. Although, in the work of an inept poet, irony can be crude and obvious sarcasm, it is invaluable to a poet of more complicated mind, who imagines more than one perspective.

W. H. Auden (1907–1973)

The Unknown Citizen   1940

(To JS/07/M/378
This Marble Monument Is Erected by the State)

He was found by the Bureau of Statistics to be
One against whom there was no official complaint,
And all the reports on his conduct agree
That, in the modern sense of an old-fashioned word, he was a saint,
For in everything he did he served the Greater Community.   5
Except for the War till the day he retired
He worked in a factory and never got fired,
But satisfied his employers, Fudge Motors Inc.
Yet he wasn't a scab or odd in his views,
For his Union reports that he paid his dues,   10
(Our report on his Union shows it was sound)
And our Social Psychology workers found
That he was popular with his mates and liked a drink.
The Press are convinced that he bought a paper every day
And that his reactions to advertisements were normal in every way. 15
Policies taken out in his name prove that he was fully insured,
And his Health-card shows he was once in hospital but left it cured.
Both Producers Research and High-Grade Living declare
He was fully sensible to the advantages of the Installment Plan
And had everything necessary to the Modern Man,   20
A phonograph, a radio, a car and a frigidaire.
Our researchers into Public Opinion are content
That he held the proper opinions for the time of year;
When there was peace, he was for peace; when there was war, he went.
He was married and added five children to the population,   25
Which our Eugenist says was the right number for a parent of his
    generation,
And our teachers report that he never interfered with their
    education.
Was he free? Was he happy? The question is absurd:
Had anything been wrong, we should certainly have heard.

QUESTIONS

1. Read the two-line epitaph at the beginning of the poem as carefully as you read
   what follows. How does the epitaph help establish the voice by which the rest
   of the poem is spoken?

2. Who is speaking?

3. What ironic discrepancies do you find between the speaker's attitude toward the subject and that of the poet himself? By what is the poet's attitude made clear?

4. In the phrase "The Unknown Soldier" (of which "The Unknown Citizen" reminds us), what does the word *unknown* mean? What does it mean in the title of Auden's poem?

5. What tendencies in our civilization does Auden satirize?

6. How would you expect the speaker to define a Modern Man, if a CD player, a radio, a car, and a refrigerator are "everything" a Modern Man needs?

Sarah N. Cleghorn (1876–1959)

The Golf Links   1917

The golf links lie so near the mill
    That almost every day
The laboring children can look out
    And see the men at play.

QUESTIONS

1. Is this brief poem satiric? Does it contain any verbal irony or is the poet making a matter-of-fact statement in words that mean just what they say?

2. What other kind of irony is present in the poem?

3. Sarah N. Cleghorn's poem dates from before the enactment of legislation against child labor. Is it still a good poem, or is it hopelessly dated?

4. How would you state its theme?

5. Would you call this poem lyric, narrative, or didactic?

Edna St. Vincent Millay (1892–1950)

Second Fig   1920

Safe upon the solid rock the ugly houses stand:
Come and see my shining palace built upon the sand!

QUESTIONS

1. What is ironic about "Second Fig"?

2. Do you think the author is making fun of the speaker's attitude or agreeing with it?

Thomas Hardy (1840–1928)

The Workbox 1914

"See, here's the workbox, little wife,
    That I made of polished oak."
He was a joiner,° of village life;   *carpenter*
    She came of borough folk.

He holds the present up to her   5
    As with a smile she nears
And answers to the profferer,
    "'Twill last all my sewing years!"

"I warrant it will. And longer too.
    'Tis a scantling that I got   10
Off poor John Wayward's coffin, who
    Died of they knew not what.

"The shingled pattern that seems to cease
    Against your box's rim
Continues right on in the piece   15
    That's underground with him.

"And while I worked it made me think
    Of timber's varied doom:
One inch where people eat and drink,
    The next inch in a tomb.   20

"But why do you look so white, my dear,
    And turn aside your face?
You knew not that good lad, I fear,
    Though he came from your native place?"

"How could I know that good young man,   25
    Though he came from my native town,
When he must have left far earlier than
    I was a woman grown?"

"Ah, no. I should have understood!
    It shocked you that I gave   30
To you one end of a piece of wood
    Whose other is in a grave?"

"Don't, dear, despise my intellect,
　Mere accidental things
Of that sort never have effect
　On my imaginings."   35

Yet still her lips were limp and wan,
　Her face still held aside,
As if she had known not only John,
　But known of what he died.   40

QUESTION

Point out the kinds of irony that occur in "The Workbox."

For Review and Further Study

Francisco X. Alarcón (b. 1954)

The X in My Name   1993

the poor
signature
of my illiterate
and peasant
self   5
giving away
all rights
in a deceiving
contract for life

QUESTION

What does the speaker imply the X in his name signifies?

EXERCISE: Telling Tone

Here are two radically different poems on a similar subject. Try stating the theme of each poem in your own words. How is tone (the speaker's attitude) different in the two poems?

Richard Lovelace (1618–1658)

To Lucasta   1649

> *On Going to the Wars*

Tell me not, Sweet, I am unkind
    That from the nunnery
Of thy chaste breast and quiet mind,
    To war and arms I fly.

True, a new mistress now I chase,   5
    The first foe in the field;
And with a stronger faith embrace
    A sword, a horse, a shield.

Yet this inconstancy is such
    As you too shall adore;   10
I could not love thee, Dear, so much,
    Loved I not Honor more.

Wilfred Owen (1893–1918)

Dulce et Decorum Est   1920

Bent double, like old beggars under sacks,
Knock-kneed, coughing like hags, we cursed through sludge,
Till on the haunting flares we turned our backs
And towards our distant rest began to trudge.
Men marched asleep. Many had lost their boots   5
But limped on, blood-shod. All went lame; all blind;
Drunk with fatigue; deaf even to the hoots
Of tired, outstripped Five-Nines that dropped behind.

Gas! Gas! Quick, boys!—An ecstasy of fumbling,
Fitting the clumsy helmets just in time;   10
But someone still was yelling out and stumbling
And flound'ring like a man in fire or lime . . .
Dim, through the misty panes and thick green light,
As under a green sea, I saw him drowning.

In all my dreams, before my helpless sight,   15
He plunges at me, guttering, choking, drowning.

If in some smothering dreams you too could pace
Behind the wagon that we flung him in,
And watch the white eyes writhing in his face,
His hanging face, like a devil's sick of sin;   20
If you could hear, at every jolt, the blood
Come gargling from the froth-corrupted lungs,
Obscene as cancer, bitter as the cud
Of vile, incurable sores on innocent tongues,—
My friend, you would not tell with such high zest   25
To children ardent for some desperate glory,
The old Lie: Dulce et decorum est
Pro patria mori.

DULCE ET DECORUM EST. 8 *Five-Nines:* German howitzers often used to shoot poison gas
shells.   17 *you too:* Some manuscript versions of this poem carry the dedication "To Jessie
Pope" (a writer of patriotic verse) or "To a certain Poetess."   27–28 *Dulce et . . . mori:* a
quotation from the Latin poet Horace, "It is sweet and fitting to die for one's country."

WRITING EFFECTIVELY

WRITING ABOUT VOICE

Listening to Tone

If tone is a speaker's attitude toward his or her material, then to understand
the tone of a poem, we need mostly just to listen—as we might listen to a real
conversation. The key is to hear not only *what* is being said but also *how* it is
being said. Does the speaker sound noticeably surprised, angry, nostalgic, tender, or expectant?

To pin down a poem's tone, begin with an obvious but often overlooked
question: who is speaking? Inexperienced readers of poetry often suppose
that every poem is spoken by its author, and in fact the speaker often is a
heightened version of someone very much like the poet. At other times,
though, a poem is spoken by someone far removed in place, time, and situation from the poet—for example, a fictional character, a historical figure, or
a celebrity.

- *Look for the ways—large and small—in which the speaker reveals aspects of his or her character.* Attitudes or emotions may be revealed directly or indirectly. D. H. Lawrence ends his poem "Piano" by saying, "I weep like a child for the past," making his nostalgic and tender tone explicit. More often, emotions must be intuited. The details a poet chooses to convey can reveal much about a speaker's stance toward his or her subject matter.

- *Consider also how the speaker addresses the listener.* In John Betjeman's "In Westminster Abbey," for example, the speaker addresses God with astonishing egocentricity and snooty nonchalance.

- *You might also look for an obvious difference between the speaker's attitude and your own honest reaction toward what is happening in the poem.* If the gap between the two responses is wide (as it is likely to be in Robert Browning's "My Last Duchess"), the poem may be taken as ironic.

In coming to a conclusion about a poem's tone, it helps to remember that many poets strive toward understatement, writing matter-of-factly about matters of intense sorrow, horror, or joy. In poems, as in conversation, understatement can be a powerful tool, more convincing—and often more moving—than hyperbole. For an example of understatement (and irony) in action, see Sarah N. Cleghorn's "The Golf Links."

CHECKLIST

Analyzing Tone

✓ Who is speaking the poem?

✓ Is the narrator's voice close to the poet's or is it the voice of a fictional or nonfictional character?

✓ How does the speaker address the listener?

✓ Does the poem directly reveal an emotion or attitude? Can you specifically identify an emotion such as anger, fear, joy, uncertainty?

✓ Does it indirectly reveal any attitudes or emotions?

✓ What sort of attitudes toward the subject matter do the poem's details suggest?

✓ Does your reaction to what is happening in the poem differ widely from that of the speaker? If so, what does that difference suggest? Is the poem in some way ironic?

✓ Is the poem passionate, or understated, or does it possess a degree of intensity somewhere in between?

✓ What adjectives would best describe the poem's tone?

WRITING ASSIGNMENT ON TONE

Choose a poem from this chapter, and analyze its speaker's attitude toward the poem's main subject. Examine the author's choice of specific words and images to create the particular tone used to convey the speaker's attitudes. (Possible subjects include Wilfred Owen's attitude toward war in "Dulce et Decorum Est," the tone and imagery of Weldon Kees's "For My Daughter," Ted Hughes's view of the workings of nature in "Hawk Roosting," and Anne Bradstreet's attitude toward her own poetry in "The Author to Her Book.")

MORE TOPICS FOR WRITING

1. **INFORMATION FOR EXPERIMENT: Reading with and without Biography**
   Write a paragraph summing up your initial reactions to William Carlos Williams's poem "The Red Wheelbarrow."

   Now write a second paragraph with the benefit of this snippet of biographical information: inspiration for this poem apparently came to Dr. Williams as he was gazing from the window of a house where one of his patients, a small girl, lay suspended between life and death. How does this information affect your reading of the poem? (This account, from the director of the public library in Williams's native Rutherford, New Jersey, is given by Geri M. Rhodes in "The Paterson Metaphor in William Carlos Williams's *Paterson*," master's essay, Tufts University, 1965.)

2. Describe the tone of W. H. Auden's "The Unknown Citizen," quoting as necessary to back up your argument. How does the poem's tone contribute to its meaning?

3. Write an analysis of Thomas Hardy's "The Workbox," focusing on what the poem leaves unsaid.

4. In an essay of 250 to 500 words, compare and contrast the tone of two poems on a similar subject. You might examine how Walt Whitman and Emily Dickinson treat the subject of locomotives, or how Richard Lovelace and Wilfred Owen write about war. (For advice on writing about poetry by the method of comparison and contrast, see the chapter "Writing About Literature.")

11
Words

Literal Meaning: What a Poem Says First

Although successful as a painter, Edgar Degas found poetry discouragingly hard to write. To his friend, the poet Stéphane Mallarmé, he complained, "What a business! My whole day gone on a blasted sonnet, without getting an inch further . . . and it isn't ideas I'm short of . . . I'm full of them, I've got too many . . . "

"But Degas," said Mallarmé, "you can't make a poem with ideas—you make it with *words!*"[1]

Like the celebrated painter, some people assume that all it takes to make a poem is a bright idea. Poems state ideas, to be sure, and sometimes the ideas are invaluable; and yet the most impressive idea in the world will not make a poem, unless its words are selected and arranged with loving art. Some poets take great pains to find the right word. Unable to fill a two-syllable gap in an unfinished line that went, "The seal's wide____gaze toward Paradise," Hart Crane paged through an unabridged dictionary. When he reached S, he found the object of his quest in *spindrift*: "spray skimmed from the sea by a strong wind." The word is exact and memorable. Any word can be the right word, however, if artfully chosen and placed. It may be a word as ordinary as *from*. Consider the difference between "The sedge is withered *on* the lake" (a misquotation of a line by Keats) and "The sedge is withered *from* the lake" (what Keats in fact wrote). Keats's original line suggests, as the altered line doesn't, that because the sedge (a growth of grasslike plants) has withered *from* the lake, it has withdrawn mysteriously.

In reading a poem, some people assume that its words can be skipped over rapidly, and they try to leap at once to the poem's general theme. It is as if they fear being thought clods unless they can find huge ideas in the poem (whether or not there are any). Such readers often ignore the literal meanings of words: the ordinary, matter-of-fact sense to be found in a dictionary. (As you will see in the next chapter, "Saying and Suggesting," words possess not only dictionary meanings—denotations—but also many associations and suggestions—connotations.) Consider the following poem and see what you make of it.

---

[1] Paul Valéry, *Degas . . . Manet . . . Morisot*, translated by David Paul (New York: Pantheon, 1960) 62.

William Carlos Williams (1883–1963)

This Is Just to Say 1934

I have eaten
the plums
that were in
the icebox

and which 5
you were probably
saving
for breakfast

Forgive me
they were delicious 10
so sweet
and so cold

Some readers distrust a poem so simple and candid. They think, "What's wrong with me? There has to be more to it than this!" But poems seldom are puzzles in need of solutions. We can begin by accepting the poet's statements, without suspecting the poet of trying to hoodwink us. On later reflection, of course, we might possibly decide that the poet is playfully teasing or being ironic; but Williams gives us no reason to think that. There seems no need to look beyond the literal sense of his words, no profit in speculating that the plums symbolize worldly joys and that the icebox stands for the universe. Clearly, a reader who held such a grand theory would have overlooked (in eagerness to find a significant idea) the plain truth that the poet makes clear to us: that ice-cold plums are a joy to taste.

To be sure, Williams's small poem is simpler than most poems are; and yet in reading any poem, no matter how complicated, you will do well to reach slowly and reluctantly for a theory to explain it by. To find the general theme of a poem, you first need to pay attention to its words. Recall Yeats's "The Lake Isle of Innisfree" (page 313), a poem that makes a statement—crudely summed up, "I yearn to leave the city and retreat to a place of ideal peace and happiness." And yet before we can realize this theme, we have to notice details: nine bean rows, a glade loud with bees, "lake water lapping with low sounds by the shore," the gray of a pavement. These details and not some abstract remark make clear what the poem is saying: that the city is drab, while the island hideaway is sublimely beautiful.

If a poem says *daffodils* instead of *plant life*, *diaper years* instead of *infancy*, we call its **diction**, or choice of words, **concrete** rather than **abstract**. Concrete words refer to what we can immediately perceive with our senses: *dog, actor, chemical,* or particular individuals who belong to those general classes: *Bonzo the fox terrier,*

Clint Eastwood, hydrogen sulfate. Abstract words express ideas or concepts: *love, time, truth*. In abstracting, we leave out some characteristics found in each individual, and instead observe a quality common to many. The word *beauty*, for instance, denotes what may be observed in numerous persons, places, and things.

Ezra Pound gave a famous piece of advice to his fellow poets: "Go in fear of abstractions." This is not to say that a poet cannot employ abstract words, nor that all poems have to be about physical things. Much of T. S. Eliot's *Four Quartets* is concerned with time, eternity, history, language, reality, and other things that cannot be physically handled. But Eliot, however high he may soar for a larger view, keeps returning to earth. He makes us aware of *things*.

Marianne Moore (1887–1972)

Silence

1924

My father used to say,
"Superior people never make long visits,
have to be shown Longfellow's grave
or the glass flowers at Harvard.
Self-reliant like the cat—   5
that takes its prey to privacy,
the mouse's limp tail hanging like a shoelace from its mouth—
they sometimes enjoy solitude,
and can be robbed of speech
by speech which has delighted them.   10
The deepest feeling always shows itself in silence;
not in silence, but restraint."
Nor was he insincere in saying, "Make my house your inn."
Inns are not residences.

QUESTIONS

1. Almost all of "Silence" consists of quotation. What are some possible reasons why the speaker prefers using another person's words?
2. What are the words the father uses to describe people he admires?
3. The poem makes an important distinction between two similar words (lines 13–14). Explain the distinction Moore implies.
4. Why is "Silence" an appropriate title for this poem?

Robert Graves (1895–1985)

Down, Wanton, Down!   1933

Down, wanton, down! Have you no shame
That at the whisper of Love's name,
Or Beauty's, presto! up you raise
Your angry head and stand at gaze?

Poor bombard-captain, sworn to reach   5
The ravelin and effect a breach—
Indifferent what you storm or why,
So be that in the breach you die!

Love may be blind, but Love at least
Knows what is man and what mere beast;   10
Or Beauty wayward, but requires
More delicacy from her squires.

Tell me, my witless, whose one boast
Could be your staunchness at the post,
When were you made a man of parts   15
To think fine and profess the arts?

Will many-gifted Beauty come
Bowing to your bald rule of thumb,
Or Love swear loyalty to your crown?
Be gone, have done! Down, wanton, down!   20

DOWN, WANTON, DOWN! 5 *bombard-captain:* officer in charge of a bombard, an early type
of cannon that hurled stones. 6 *ravelin:* fortification with two faces that meet in a protruding angle. *effect a breach:* break an opening through (a fortification). 15 *man of parts:* man of
talent or ability.

QUESTIONS

1. How do you define a *wanton?*
2. What wanton does the poet address?
3. Explain the comparison drawn in the second stanza.
4. In line 14, how many meanings do you find in *staunchness at the post?*
5. Explain any other puns you find in lines 15–19.
6. Do you take this to be a cynical poem making fun of Love and Beauty, or is
   Graves making fun of stupid, animal lust?

John Donne (1572–1631)

Batter my heart, three-personed God, for You

(about 1610)

Batter my heart, three-personed God, for You
As yet but knock, breathe, shine, and seek to mend.
That I may rise and stand, o'erthrow me, and bend
Your force to break, blow, burn, and make me new.
I, like an usurped town to another due,   5
Labor to admit You, but Oh! to no end.
Reason, Your viceroy in me, me should defend,
But is captived, and proves weak or untrue.
Yet dearly I love You, and would be lovèd fain,
But am betrothed unto Your enemy;   10
Divorce me, untie or break that knot again;
Take me to You, imprison me, for I,
Except You enthrall me, never shall be free,
Nor ever chaste, except You ravish me.

QUESTIONS

1. In the last line of this sonnet, to what does Donne compare the onslaught of God's love? Do you think the poem is weakened by the poet's comparing a spiritual experience to something so grossly carnal? Discuss.

2. Explain the seeming contradiction in the last line: in what sense can a ravished person be *chaste*? Explain the seeming contradictions in lines 3–4 and 12–13: how can a person thrown down and destroyed be enabled to *rise and stand*; an imprisoned person be *free*?

3. Sum up in your own words the message of Donne's poem. In stating its theme, did you have to read the poem for literal meanings, figurative comparisons, or both?

The Value of a Dictionary

Use the dictionary. It's better than the critics.

—ELIZABETH BISHOP TO HER STUDENTS

If a poet troubles to seek out the best words available, the least we can do is to find out what the words mean. The dictionary is a firm ally in reading poems; if the poems are more than a century old, it is indispensable. Meanings change. When the Elizabethan poet George Gascoigne wrote, "O Abraham's brats, O brood of blessed seed," the word *brats* implied neither irritation nor contempt. When in the seventeenth century Andrew Marvell imagined two lovers' "vegetable love," he referred to a vegetative or growing love, not one resembling a lettuce. And when Queen Anne, in a famous anecdote, called the just-completed Saint Paul's

Cathedral "awful, artificial, and amusing," its architect, Sir Christopher Wren, was overwhelmed with joy and gratitude, for what she had told him was that it was awe-inspiring, artful, and stimulating to contemplate (or *muse* upon).

In reading poetry, there is nothing to be done about the inevitable tendency of language to change except to watch out for it. If you suspect that a word has shifted in meaning over the years, most standard desk dictionaries will be helpful, an unabridged dictionary more helpful still, and most helpful of all the *Oxford English Dictionary (OED)*, which gives, for each definition, successive examples of the word's written use through the past thousand years. You need not feel a grim obligation to keep interrupting a poem in order to rummage in the dictionary; but if the poem is worth reading very closely, you may wish any aid you can find.

One of the valuable services of poetry is to recall for us the concrete, physical sense that certain words once had, but since have lost. As the English critic H. Coombes has remarked in *Literature and Criticism*,

> We use a word like *powerful* without feeling that it is really "powerfull." We do not seem today to taste the full flavor of words as we feel that Falstaff (and Shakespeare, and probably his audience) tasted them when he was applauding the virtues of "good sherris-sack," which makes the brain "apprehensive, quick, forgetive, full of nimble, fiery, and delectable shapes." And being less aware of the life and substantiality of words, we are probably less aware of the things . . . that these words stand for.

"Every word which is used to express a moral or intellectual fact," said Emerson in his study *Nature*, "if traced to its root, is found to be borrowed from some material appearance. *Right* means straight; *wrong* means twisted. *Spirit* primarily means wind; *transgression*, the crossing of a line; *supercilious*, the raising of an eyebrow." Browse in a dictionary and you will discover such original concretenesses. These are revealed in your dictionary's etymologies, or brief notes on the derivation of words, given in most dictionaries near the beginning of an entry on a word; in some dictionaries, at the end of the entry. Look up *squirrel*, for instance, and you will find it comes from two Greek words meaning "shadow-tail." For another example of a common word that originally contained a poetic metaphor, look up the origin of *daisy*.

EXPERIMENT: Using the Dictionary

The following short poem seems very simple and straightforward, but much of its total effect depends on the reader knowing the literal meanings of several words. The most crucial word is in the title—*aftermath*. Most readers today will assume that they know what that word means, but in this poem Longfellow uses it in both its current sense and its original, more literal meaning. Read the poem twice—first without a dictionary, then a second time after looking up the meanings of *aftermath*, *fledged*, *rowen*, and *mead*. How does knowing the exact meanings of these words add to both your literal and critical reading of the poem?

Henry Wadsworth Longfellow (1807–1882)

Aftermath   1873

When the summer fields are mown,
When the birds are fledged and flown,
   And the dry leaves strew the path;
With the falling of the snow,
With the cawing of the crow,   5
Once again the fields we mow
   And gather in the aftermath.

Not the sweet, new grass with flowers
In this harvesting of ours;
   Not the upland clover bloom;   10
But the rowen mixed with weeds,
Tangled tufts from marsh and meads,
Where the poppy drops its seeds
   In the silence and the gloom.

QUESTIONS

1. How do the etymology and meaning of *aftermath* help explain this poem? (Look the word up in your dictionary.)
2. What is the meaning of *fledged* (line 2) and *rowen* (line 11)?
3. Once you understand the literal meaning of the poem, do you think that Longfellow intended any further significance to it?

An **allusion** is an indirect reference to any person, place, or thing—fictitious, historical, or actual. Sometimes, to understand an allusion in a poem, we have to find out something we didn't know before. But usually the poet asks of us only common knowledge. When, in his poem "To Helen," Edgar Allan Poe refers to "the glory that was Greece / And the grandeur that was Rome," he assumes that we have heard of those places. He also expects that we will understand his allusion to the cultural achievements of those ancient nations and perhaps even catch the subtle contrast between those two similar words *glory* and *grandeur*, with its suggestion that, for all its merits, Roman civilization was also more pompous than Greek.

Allusions not only enrich the meaning of a poem, they also save space. In "The Love Song of J. Alfred Prufrock" (page 509), T. S. Eliot, by giving a brief introductory quotation from the speech of a damned soul in Dante's *Inferno*, is able to suggest that his poem will be the confession of a soul in torment, who sees no chance of escape and who feels the need to confide in someone but trusts that his secrets will be kept safe.

Often in reading a poem, you will meet a name you don't recognize, on which the meaning of a line (or perhaps a whole poem) seems to depend. In this book, most such unfamiliar references and allusions are glossed or foot-noted, but when you venture out on your own in reading poems, you may find yourself needlessly perplexed unless you look up such names, the way you look up any other words. Unless the name is one that the poet made up, you will probably find it in one of the larger desk dictionaries, such as *Merriam-Webster's Collegiate Dictionary* or the *American Heritage Dictionary*. If you don't solve your problem there, try an encyclopedia, a world atlas, *The Houghton Mifflin Dictionary of Biography*, or *Brewer's Dictionary of Phrase & Fable*.

EXERCISE: Catching Allusions

From your knowledge, supplemented by a dictionary or other reference work if need be, explain the allusions in the following poems.

J. V. Cunningham (1911–1985)

Friend, on this scaffold Thomas More lies dead

1960

Friend, on this scaffold Thomas More lies dead
Who would not cut the Body from the Head.

Carl Sandburg (1878–1967)

Grass

1918

Pile the bodies high at Austerlitz and Waterloo.
Shovel them under and let me work—
    I am the grass; I cover all.

And pile them high at Gettsyburg
And pile them high at Ypres and Verdun.
Shovel them under and let me work.   5

Two years, ten years, and passengers ask the conductor:
    What place is this?
    Where are we now?

    I am the grass.
    Let me work.   10

QUESTIONS

1. What do the five proper nouns in Sandburg's poem have in common?
2. How much does the reader need to understand about the allusions in "Grass" to appreciate their importance to the literal meaning of the poem?

Word Choice and Word Order

Even if Samuel Johnson's famous *Dictionary* of 1755 had been as thick as Webster's unabridged, an eighteenth-century poet searching through it for words to use would have had a narrower choice. For in English literature of the **neoclassical period** or **Augustan age**—that period from about 1660 into the late eighteenth century—many poets subscribed to a belief in **poetic diction**: "A system of words," said Dr. Johnson, "refined from the grossness of domestic use." The system admitted into a serious poem only certain words and subjects, excluding others as violations of **decorum** (propriety). Accordingly, such common words as *rat, cheese, big, sneeze,* and *elbow,* although admissible to satire, were thought inconsistent with the loftiness of tragedy, epic, ode, and elegy. Dr. Johnson's biographer, James Boswell, tells how a poet writing an epic reconsidered the word "rats" and instead wrote "the whiskered vermin race." Johnson himself objected to Lady Macbeth's allusion to her "keen knife," saying that "we do not immediately conceive that any crime of importance is to be committed with a knife; or who does not, at last, from the long habit of connecting a knife with sordid offices, feel aversion rather than terror?" Probably Johnson was here the victim of his age, and Shakespeare was right, but Johnson in one of his assumptions was right too: there are inappropriate words as well as appropriate ones.

Neoclassical poets chose their classical models more often from Roman writers than from Greek, as their diction suggests by the frequency of Latin derivatives. For example, a *net,* according to Dr. Johnson's dictionary, is "any thing reticulated or decussated, at equal distances, with interstices between the intersections." In company with Latinate words often appeared fixed combinations of adjective and noun ("finny prey" for "fish"), poetic names (a song to a lady named Molly might rechristen her Parthenia), and allusions to classical mythology. Neoclassical poetic diction was evidently being abused when, instead of saying "uncork the bottle," a poet could write

Apply thine engine to the spongy door,
Set *Bacchus* from his glassy prison free,

in some bad lines ridiculed by Alexander Pope in *Peri Bathous, or The Art of Sinking in Poetry.*

Not all poetic diction is excess baggage. To a reader who knew firsthand both living sheep and the pastoral poems of Virgil—as most readers nowadays do not—such a fixed phrase as "the fleecy care," which seems stilted to us, conveyed pleasurable associations. But "fleecy care" was more than a highfalutin way of saying "sheep"; as one scholar has pointed out, "when they wished, our poets could say 'sheep' as clearly and as often as anybody else. In the first place, 'fleecy' drew attention to wool, and demanded the appropriate visual image of sheep; for aural imagery the poets would refer to 'the bleating kind'; it all depended upon what was happening in the poem."[2]

Other poets have found some special kind of poetic language valuable: Old English poets, with their standard figures of speech ("whale-road" for the sea, "ring-giver" for a ruler); makers of folk ballads who, no less than neoclassicists, love fixed epithet-noun combinations ("milk-white steed," "blood-red wine," "steel-driving man"); and Edmund Spenser, whose example made popular the adjective ending in *-y* (*fleecy, grassy, milky*).

When Wordsworth, in his Preface to *Lyrical Ballads,* asserted that "the language really spoken by men," especially by humble rustics, is plainer and more emphatic, and conveys "elementary feelings . . . in a state of greater simplicity," he was, in effect, advocating a new poetic diction. Wordsworth's ideas invited freshness into English poetry and, by admitting words that neoclassical poets would have called "low" ("His poor old *ankles* swell"), helped rid poets of the fear of being thought foolish for mentioning a commonplace.

This theory of the superiority of rural diction was, as Coleridge pointed out, hard to adhere to, and, in practice, Wordsworth was occasionally to write a language as Latinate and citified as these lines on yew trees:

Huge trunks!—and each particular trunk a growth
Of intertwisted fibers serpentine
Up-coiling, and inveterately convolved . . .

Language so Latinate sounds pedantic to us, especially the phrase *inveterately convolved.* In fact, some poets, notably Gerard Manley Hopkins, have subscribed to the view that English words derived from Anglo-Saxon (Old English) have more force and flavor than their Latin equivalents. *Kingly,* one may feel, has more power than *regal.* One argument for this view is that so many words of Old English origin—*man, wife, child, house, eat, drink, sleep*—are basic to our living speech. It may be true that a language closer to Old English is particularly fit for rendering abstract notions concretely—as does the memorable title of a medieval work of piety, the *Ayenbite of Inwit* ("again-bite of inner wisdom" or "remorse of conscience"). And yet this view, if accepted at all, must be accepted with reservations. Some words of Latin origin carry meanings both precise and physical. In the King James Bible is the admonition, "See then that ye walk circumspectly, not as fools, but as wise" (Ephesians 5:15). To be *circumspect* (a word from two Latin roots meaning "to look" and "around") is to be watchful on all sides—a meaning altogether lost in a modernized wording of the passage once printed on a subway poster for a Bible society: "Be careful how you live, not thoughtlessly but thoughtfully."

---

[2]Bonamy Dobrée, *English Literature in the Early Eighteenth Century, 1700–1740* (New York: Oxford UP, 1959) 161.

When E. E. Cummings begins a poem, "mr youse needn't be so spry / concernin questions arty," we recognize another kind of diction available to poetry: **vulgate** (speech not much affected by schooling). Handbooks of grammar sometimes distinguish various **levels of diction**. A sort of ladder is imagined, on whose rungs words, phrases, and sentences may be ranked in an ascending order of formality, from the curses of an illiterate thug to the commencement-day address of a doctor of divinity. These levels range from vulgate through **colloquial** (the casual conversation or informal writing of literate people) and **general English** (most literate speech and writing, more studied than colloquial but not pretentious), up to **formal English** (the impersonal language of educated persons, usually only written, possibly spoken on dignified occasions). Recently, however, lexicographers have been shunning such labels. The designation *colloquial* was expelled from *Webster's Third New International Dictionary* on the grounds that "it is impossible to know whether a word out of context is colloquial or not" and that the diction of Americans nowadays is more fluid than the labels suggest. Aware that we are being unscientific, we may find the labels useful. They may help roughly to describe what happens when, as in the following poem, a poet shifts from one level of usage to another.

Robert Herrick (1591–1674)

Upon Julia's Clothes   1648

Whenas in silks my Julia goes,
Then, then, methinks, how sweetly flows
That liquefaction of her clothes.

Next, when I cast mine eyes and see
That brave vibration each way free,   5
O how that glittering taketh me!

Even in so short a poem as "Upon Julia's Clothes," we see how a sudden shift in the level of diction can produce a surprising and memorable effect. One word in each stanza—*liquefaction* in the first, *vibration* in the second—stands out from the standard, but not extravagant, language that surrounds it. Try to imagine the entire poem being written in such formal English, in mostly unfamiliar words of several syllables each: the result, in all likelihood, would be merely an oddity, and a turgid one at that. But by using such terms sparingly, Herrick allows them to take on a greater strength and significance through their contrast with the words that surround it. It is *liquefaction* in particular that strikes the reader: like a great catch by an outfielder, it impresses both for its appropriateness in the situation and for its sheer beauty as a demonstration of superior skill. Once we have read the poem, we realize that the effect would be severely compromised, if not ruined, by the substitution of any other word in its place.

At present, most poetry in English avoids elaborate literary expressions such as "fleecy care" in favor of more colloquial language. In many English-speaking areas, such as Scotland, there has even been a movement to write poems in regional dialects. (A **dialect** is a particular variety of language spoken by an identifiable regional group or social class of persons.) Dialect poets frequently try to capture the freshness and authenticity of the language spoken in their immediate locale.

Most Americans know at least part of one Scottish dialect poem by heart—"Auld Lang Syne," the song commonly sung as the clock strikes twelve on New Year's Eve. Although Robert Burns wrote most of the song's stanzas, the poet claimed to have copied down the famous opening stanza (following) from an old man he heard singing. *Auld* is the Scots word for "old"; *lang syne* means "long since." How different the lines would seem if they were standard English.

Should auld acquaintance be forgot,
And never brought to mind?
Should auld acquaintance be forgot
And days of auld lang syne?
And days of auld lang syne, my dear,
And days of auld lang syne,
Should auld acquaintance be forgot,
And days of auld lang syne?

Among languages, English is by no means the most flexible. English words must be used in fairly definite and inviolable patterns, and whoever departs too far from them will not be understood. In the sentence "Cain slew Abel," if you change the word order, you change the meaning: "Abel slew Cain." Such inflexibility was not true of Latin, in which a poet could lay down words in almost any sequence and, because their endings (inflections) showed what parts of speech they were, could trust that no reader would mistake a subject for an object or a noun for an adjective. (E. E. Cummings has striven, in certain of his poems, for the freedom of Latin. One such poem, "anyone lived in a pretty how town," appears on page 367.)

The rigidity of English word order invites the poet to defy it and to achieve unusual effects by inverting it. It is customary in English to place adjective in front of noun (*a blue mantle, new pastures*). But an unusual emphasis is achieved when Milton ends "Lycidas" by reversing the pattern:

At last he rose, and twitched his mantle blue:
Tomorrow to fresh woods, and pastures new.

Perhaps the inversion in *mantle blue* gives more prominence to the color associated with heaven (and in "Lycidas," heaven is of prime importance). Perhaps the inversion in *pastures new*, stressing the *new*, heightens the sense of a rebirth.

Coleridge offered two "homely definitions of prose and poetry; that is, *prose:* words in their best order; *poetry:* the best words in the best order." If all goes well, a poet may fasten the right word into the right place, and the result may be—as T. S. Eliot said in "Little Gidding"—a "complete consort dancing together."

Kay Ryan (b. 1945)

Blandeur	2000

If it please God,
let less happen.
Even out Earth's
rondure, flatten
Eiger, blanden   5
the Grand Canyon.
Make valleys
slightly higher,
widen fissures
to arable land,   10
remand your
terrible glaciers
and silence
their calving,
halving or doubling   15
all geographical features
toward the mean.
Unlean against our hearts.
Withdraw your grandeur
from these parts.   20

BLANDEUR. 5 *Eiger:* a mountain in the Alps.

QUESTIONS

1. The title of Ryan's poem is a word that she invented. What do you think it means? Explain the reasoning behind your theory.
2. Where else does Ryan use a different form of this new word?
3. What other unusual but real words does the author use?

Thomas Hardy (1840–1928)

The Ruined Maid	1901

"O 'Melia, my dear, this does everything crown!
Who could have supposed I should meet you in Town?
And whence such fair garments, such prosperi-ty?"—
"O didn't you know I'd been ruined?" said she.

—"You left us in tatters, without shoes or socks,   5
Tired of digging potatoes, and spudding up docks;°   *spading up dockweed*
And now you've gay bracelets and bright feathers three!"—
"Yes: that's how we dress when we're ruined," said she.

—"At home in the barton° you said 'thee' and 'thou,'   *farmyard*
And 'thik oon,' and 'theäs oon,' and 't'other'; but now   10
Your talking quite fits 'ee for high compa-ny!"—
"Some polish is gained with one's ruin," said she.

—"Your hands were like paws then, your face blue and bleak
But now I'm bewitched by your delicate cheek,
And your little gloves fit as on any la-dy!"—   15
"We never do work when we're ruined," said she.

—"You used to call home-life a hag-ridden dream,
And you'd sigh, and you'd sock;° but at present you seem   *groan*
To know not of megrims° or melancho-ly!"—   *blues*
"True. One's pretty lively when ruined," said she.   20

—"I wish I had feathers, a fine sweeping gown,
And a delicate face, and could strut about Town!"—
"My dear—a raw country girl, such as you be,
Cannot quite expect that. You ain't ruined," said she.

QUESTIONS

1. Where does this dialogue take place? Who are the two speakers?
2. Comment on Hardy's use of the word *ruined*. What is the conventional meaning of the word when applied to a woman? As 'Melia applies it to herself, what is its meaning?
3. Sum up the attitude of each speaker toward the other. What details of the new 'Melia does the first speaker most dwell on? Would you expect Hardy to be so impressed by all these details, or is there, between his view of the characters and their view of themselves, any hint of an ironic discrepancy?
4. In losing her country dialect (*thik oon* and *theäs oon* for *this one* and *that one*), 'Melia is presumed to have gained in sophistication. What does Hardy suggest by her *ain't* in the last line?

Richard Eberhart (1904–2005)

The Fury of Aerial Bombardment   1947

You would think the fury of aerial bombardment
Would rouse God to relent; the infinite spaces
Are still silent. He looks on shock-pried faces.
History, even, does not know what is meant.

You would feel that after so many centuries   5
God would give man to repent; yet he can kill
As Cain could, but with multitudinous will,
No farther advanced than in his ancient furies.

Was man made stupid to see his own stupidity?
Is God by definition indifferent, beyond us all?   10
Is the eternal truth man's fighting soul
Wherein the Beast ravens in its own avidity?

Of Van Wettering I speak, and Averill,
Names on a list, whose faces I do not recall
But they are gone to early death, who late in school   15
Distinguished the belt feed lever from the belt holding pawl.

QUESTIONS

1. As a naval officer during World War II, Richard Eberhart was assigned for a time as an instructor in a gunnery school. How has this experience apparently contributed to the diction of his poem?

2. In his *Life of John Dryden,* complaining about a description of a sea fight Dryden had filled with nautical language, Samuel Johnson argued that technical terms should be excluded from poetry. Is this criticism applicable to Eberhart's last line? Can a word succeed for us in a poem, even though we may not be able to define it?

3. Some readers have found a contrast in tone between the first three stanzas of this poem and the last stanza. How would you describe this contrast? What does diction contribute to it?

Wendy Cope (b. 1945)

Lonely Hearts   1986

Can someone make my simple wish come true?
Male biker seeks female for touring fun.
Do you live in North London? Is it you?

Gay vegetarian whose friends are few,
I'm into music, Shakespeare and the sun,   5
Can someone make my simple wish come true?

Executive in search of something new—
Perhaps bisexual woman, arty, young.
Do you live in North London? Is it you?

Successful, straight and solvent? I am too— 10
Attractive Jewish lady with a son.
Can someone make my simple wish come true?

I'm Libran, inexperienced and blue—
Need slim non-smoker, under twenty-one.
Do you live in North London? Is it you? 15

Please write (with photo) to Box 152.
Who knows where it may lead once we've begun?
Can someone make my simple wish come true?
Do you live in North London? Is it you?

LONELY HEARTS. This poem has a double form: the rhetorical, a series of "lonely heart" personal ads from a newspaper, and metrical, a **villanelle**, a fixed form developed by French courtly poets in imitation of Italian folk song. For other villanelles, see Elizabeth Bishop's "One Art" (page 497) and Dylan Thomas's "Do not go gentle into that good night" (page 460). In the villanelle, the first and the third lines are repeated in a set pattern throughout the poem.

QUESTIONS

1. What sort of language does Wendy Cope borrow for this poem?
2. The form of the villanelle requires that the poet end each stanza with one of two repeating lines. What special use does the author make of these mandatory repetitions?
3. How many speakers are there in the poem? Does the author's voice ever enter or is the entire poem spoken by individuals in personal ads?
4. The poem seems to begin satirically. Does the poem ever move beyond the critical, mocking tone typical of satire?

For Review and Further Study

E. E. Cummings (1894–1962)

anyone lived in a pretty how town   1940

anyone lived in a pretty how town
(with up so floating many bells down)
spring summer autumn winter
he sang his didn't he danced his did.

Women and men(both little and small)   5
cared for anyone not at all
they sowed their isn't they reaped their same
sun moon stars rain

children guessed(but only a few
and down they forgot as up they grew   10
autumn winter spring summer)
that noone loved him more by more

when by now and tree by leaf
she laughed his joy she cried his grief
bird by snow and stir by still   15
anyone's any was all to her

someones married their everyones
laughed their cryings and did their dance
(sleep wake hope and then)they
said their nevers they slept their dream   20

stars rain sun moon
(and only the snow can begin to explain
how children are apt to forget to remember
with up so floating many bells down)

one day anyone died i guess   25
(and noone stooped to kiss his face)
busy folk buried them side by side
little by little and was by was

all by all and deep by deep
and more by more they dream their sleep   30
noone and anyone earth by april
wish by spirit and if by yes.

Women and men(both dong and ding)
summer autumn winter spring
reaped their sowing and went their came   35
sun moon stars rain

QUESTIONS

1. Summarize the story told in this poem. Who are the characters?
2. Rearrange the words in the two opening lines into the order you would expect them usually to follow. What effect does Cummings obtain by his unconventional word order?
3. Another of Cummings's strategies is to use one part of speech as if it were another; for instance, in line 4, *didn't* and *did* ordinarily are verbs, but here they are used as nouns. What other words in the poem perform functions other than their expected ones?

EXERCISE: Different Kinds of English

Read the following poems and see what kinds of diction and word order you find in them. Is there any use of vulgate English? Any dialect? What does each poem achieve that its own kind of English makes possible?

Anonymous (American oral verse)

Carnation Milk (about 1900?)

Carnation Milk is the best in the land;
Here I sit with a can in my hand—
No tits to pull, no hay to pitch,
You just punch a hole in the son of a bitch.

CARNATION MILK. "This quatrain is imagined as the caption under a picture of a rugged-looking cowboy seated upon a bale of hay," notes William Harmon in his *Oxford Book of American Light Verse* (New York: Oxford UP, 1979). Possibly the first to print this work was David Ogilvy (1911–1999), who quotes it in his *Confessions of an Advertising Man* (New York: Atheneum, 1963).

Gina Valdés (b. 1943)

English con Salsa 1993

Welcome to ESL 100, English Surely Latinized,
inglés con chile y cilantro, English as American
as Benito Juárez. Welcome, muchachos from Xochicalco,
learn the language of dólares and Dolores, of kings
and queens, of Donald Duck and Batman. Holy Toluca!   5
In four months you'll be speaking like George Washington,
in four weeks you can ask, More coffee? In two months
you can say, May I take your order? In one year you
can ask for a raise, cool as the Tuxpan River.

Welcome, muchachas from Teocaltiche, in this class   10
we speak English refrito, English con sal y limón,
English thick as mango juice, English poured from
a clay jug, English tuned like a requinto from Uruapan,
English lighted by Oaxacan dawns, English spiked
with mezcal from Mitla, English with a red cactus   15
flower blooming in its heart.

Welcome, welcome, amigos del sur, bring your Zapotec
tongues, your Nahuatl tones, your patience of pyramids,
your red suns and golden moons, your guardian angels,

your duendes, your patron saints, Santa Tristeza,   20
Santa Alegría, Santo Todolopuede. We will sprinkle
holy water on pronouns, make the sign of the cross
on past participles, jump like fish from Lake Pátzcuaro
on gerunds, pour tequila from Jalisco on future perfects,
say shoes and shit, grab a cool verb and a pollo loco   25
and dance on the walls like chapulines.

When a teacher from La Jolla or a cowboy from Santee
asks you, Do you speak English? You'll answer, Sí,
yes, simón, of course, I love English!
                              And you'll hum
A Mixtec chant that touches la tierra and the heavens.   30

ENGLISH CON SALSA. *3 Benito Juárez:* Mexican statesman (1806–1872), president of Mexico
in the 1860s and 1870s.

Lewis Carroll
[Charles Lutwidge Dodgson] (1832–1898)

Jabberwocky   1871

'Twas brillig, and the slithy toves
   Did gyre and gimble in the wabe:
All mimsy were the borogoves,
   And the mome raths outgrabe.

"Beware the Jabberwock, my son!   5
   The jaws that bite, the claws that catch!
Beware the Jubjub bird, and shun
   The frumious Bandersnatch!"

He took his vorpal sword in hand;
   Long time the manxome foe he sought—
So rested he by the Tumtum tree   10
   And stood awhile in thought.

And, as in uffish thought he stood,
   The Jabberwock, with eyes of flame,
Came whiffling through the tulgey wood,   15
   And burbled as it came!

One, two! One, two! And through and through
   The vorpal blade went snicker-snack!
He left it dead, and with its head
   He went galumphing back.   20

"And hast thou slain the Jabberwock?
  Come to my arms, my beamish boy!
O frabjous day! Callooh, Callay!"
  He chortled in his joy.

'Twas brillig, and the slithy toves   25
  Did gyre and gimble in the wabe:
All mimsy were the borogoves,
  And the mome raths outgrabe.

JABBERWOCKY. Fussy about pronunciation, Carroll in his preface to *The Hunting of the Snark*
declares: "The first 'o' in 'borogoves' is pronounced like the 'o' in 'borrow.' I have heard
people try to give it the sound of the 'o' in 'worry.' Such is Human Perversity." *Toves,* he
adds, rimes with *groves.*

QUESTIONS

1. Look up *chortled* (line 24) in your dictionary and find out its definition and origin.
2. In *Through the Looking Glass,* Alice seeks the aid of Humpty Dumpty to decipher
    the meaning of this nonsense poem. *"Brillig,"* he explains, "means four o'clock in
    the afternoon—the time when you begin *broiling* things for dinner." Does *brillig*
    sound like any other familiar word?
3. *"Slithy,"* the explanation goes on, "means 'lithe and slimy.' 'Lithe' is the same as 'ac-
    tive.' You see it's like a portmanteau—there are two meanings packed up into one
    word." *Mimsy* is supposed to pack together both "flimsy" and "miserable." In the rest
    of the poem, what other portmanteau—or packed suitcase—words can you find?

WRITING EFFECTIVELY

WRITING ABOUT DICTION

Every Word Counts

Although a poem may contain images and ideas, it is made up of words. Language is the medium of poetry, and a poem's diction—its exact wording—is
the chief source of its power. Writers labor mightily to shape each word and
phrase to create particular expressive effects. Changing a single word sometimes ruins a poem's effect, just as changing one number in a combination
lock's sequence makes all the other numbers useless.

Poets choose words for their meanings, their associations, and even their
sounds. As you prepare to write about a poem, ask yourself if some particular
word or combination of words gives you particular pleasure or especially intrigues you. Don't worry yet about why the word or words impress you. Don't
even worry about the meaning. Just underline the word or phrase in your book.

Then let your analytical powers go to work. Try to determine what about the word or phrase commanded your attention. Maybe a word strikes you as being unexpected but just right. A phrase might seem especially musical or it might call forth a vivid picture in your imagination. Your favorite language in a poem might be concrete (denoting objects and actions) or abstract (signifying ideas or emotions). You might prefer the force of single-syllable words or the elegance of polysyllabic ones.

Next, consider your underlined words and phrases in the context of the poem. How does each relate to the words around it? What does it add to the poem as a whole?

Think, also, about the poem as a whole. In general, what sort of language does it rely on? Many poems favor the plain, straightforward language people use in everyday conversation, but others reach for more high-toned diction. Choices such as these contribute to the poem's distinctive flavor, as well as to its ultimate meaning.

A word or phrase can be your key into a poem. Often by understanding how a single word operates in the context of a poem, you gain a better sense of what the whole poem means.

CHECKLIST

Thinking About Word Choice

- ✓ As you read, underline words or phrases that appeal to you or seem especially significant.
- ✓ When you reach the end of the poem, go back and look closely at each underlined word or phrase.
- ✓ What is it about each underlined word or phrase that appeals to you?
- ✓ How does the word or phrase relate to the other lines? What does it contribute to the poem's effect?
- ✓ How does the sound of a word you've chosen add to the poem's mood?
- ✓ What would be lost if synonyms were substituted for your favorite words?
- ✓ What sort of diction does the poem use? Conversational? Lofty? Monosyllabic? Polysyllabic? Concrete? Abstract?
- ✓ How does diction contribute to the poem's flavor and meaning?

WRITING ASSIGNMENT ON WORD CHOICE

Find two poems in this book that use very different sorts of diction to address similar subjects. You might choose one with formal and elegant language and another with very down-to-earth or slangy word choices. Some good choices include John Milton's "When I consider how my light is spent" and Seamus Heaney's "Digging"; and William Shakespeare's "When, in disgrace with Fortune and men's eyes" and Jane Kenyon's "The Suitor." In a short essay (750 to 1000 words), discuss how the difference in diction affects the tones of the two poems.

MORE TOPICS FOR WRITING

1. Browse through the chapter "Poems for Further Reading," for a poem that catches your interest. Within that poem, find a word or phrase that particularly intrigues you. Write a paragraph on what the word or phrase adds to the poem, how it shades the meaning and contributes to the overall effect.

2. Choose a brief poem from this chapter. A good choice might be Kay Ryan's "Blandeur." Type the poem out, substituting synonyms for each of its nouns and verbs, using a thesaurus if necessary. Next, write a one-page analysis of the difference in feel and meaning between the original and your creation.

3. Choose a poem that strikes you as particularly inventive or unusual in its language, such as E. E. Cummings's "anyone lived in a pretty how town," Gerard Manley Hopkins's "The Windhover," or Wendy Cope's "Lonely Hearts," and write a brief analysis of it. Concentrate on the diction of the poem and word order. For what possible purposes does the poet depart from standard English or incorporate unusual vocabulary?

4. Writers are notorious word junkies who often jot down interesting words they stumble across in daily life. Over the course of a day, keep a list of any intriguing words you run across in your reading, music listening, or television viewing. Even street signs and advertisements can supply surprising words. After twenty-four hours of list-keeping, choose your five favorites. Write a five line poem, incorporating your five words, letting them take you where they will. Then write a page-long description of the process. What appealed to you in the words you chose? What did you learn about the process of composing a poem?

12
Saying and Suggesting

To write so clearly that they might bring "all things as near the mathematical plainness" as possible—that was the goal of scientists, according to Bishop Thomas Sprat, who lived in the seventeenth century. Such an effort would seem bound to fail, because words, unlike numbers, are ambiguous indicators. Although it may have troubled Bishop Sprat, the tendency of a word to have multiplicity of meaning rather than mathematical plainness opens broad avenues to poetry.

Every word has at least one **denotation**: a meaning as defined in a dictionary. But the English language has many a common word with so many denotations that a reader may need to think twice to see what it means in a specific context. The noun *field*, for instance, can denote a piece of ground, a sports arena, the scene of a battle, part of a flag, a profession, and a number system in mathematics. Further, the word can be used as a verb ("he fielded a grounder") or an adjective ("field trip," "field glasses").

A word also has **connotations**: overtones or suggestions of additional meaning that it gains from all the contexts in which we have met it in the past. The word *skeleton*, according to a dictionary, denotes "the bony framework of a human being or other vertebrate animal, which supports the flesh and protects the organs." But by its associations, the word can rouse thoughts of war, of disease and death, or (possibly) of one's plans to go to medical school. That some words denote the same thing but have sharply different connotations is pointed out in this anonymous Victorian jingle:

Here's a little ditty that you really ought to know:
Horses "sweat" and men "perspire," but ladies only "glow."

Poets aren't the only people who care about the connotations of language. Advertisers know that connotations make money. Nowadays many automobile dealers advertise their secondhand cars not as "used" but as "pre-owned," as if fearing that "used car" would connote an old heap with soiled upholstery and mysterious engine troubles. "Pre-owned," however, suggests that the previous owner has taken the trouble of breaking in the car for you.

In imaginative writing, connotations are as crucial as they are in advertising. Consider this sentence: "A new brand of journalism is being born, or spawned" (Dwight Macdonald writing in the *New York Review of Books*). The last word, by its associations with fish and crustaceans, suggests that this new journalism is scarcely the product of human beings. And what do we make of Romeo's assertion that Juliet "is the sun"? Surely even a lovesick boy cannot mean that his sweetheart is "the incandescent body of gases about which the earth and other planets revolve" (a dictionary definition). He means, of course, that he thrives in her sight, that he feels warm in her presence or even at the thought of her, that she illumines his world and is the center of his universe. Because in the mind of the hearer these and other suggestions are brought into play, Romeo's statement, literally absurd, makes excellent sense.

Here is a famous poem that groups together things with similar connotations: certain ships and their cargoes. (A *quinquireme,* by the way, was an ancient Assyrian vessel propelled by sails and oars.)

John Masefield (1878–1967)

Cargoes
1902

Quinquireme of Nineveh from distant Ophir,
Rowing home to haven in sunny Palestine,
With a cargo of ivory,
And apes and peacocks,
Sandalwood, cedarwood, and sweet white wine.　　　　　　　　　　5

Stately Spanish galleon coming from the Isthmus,
Dipping through the Tropics by the palm-green shores,
With a cargo of diamonds,
Emeralds, amethysts,
Topazes, and cinnamon, and gold moidores.°　　　*Portuguese coins*　10

Dirty British coaster with a salt-caked smoke stack,
Butting through the Channel in the mad March days,
With a cargo of Tyne coal,
Road-rails, pig-lead,
Firewood, iron-ware, and cheap tin trays.　　　　　　　　　　15

To us, as well as to the poet's original readers, the place-names in the first two stanzas suggest the exotic and faraway. Ophir, a vanished place, may have been in Arabia; according to the Bible, King Solomon sent expeditions there for its celebrated pure gold, also for ivory, apes, peacocks, and other luxury items. (See I Kings 9–10.) In his final stanza, Masefield groups commonplace things (mostly heavy and metallic), whose suggestions of crudeness, cheapness, and ugliness he deliberately contrasts with those of the precious stuffs he has listed earlier. For British readers, the Tyne is a stodgy and familiar river; the English Channel in March, choppy and likely to upset a stomach. The quinquireme is *rowing,* the galleon is *dipping,* but the dirty British freighter is *butting,* aggressively pushing. Conceivably, the poet could have described firewood and even coal as beautiful, but evidently he wants them to convey sharply different suggestions here, to go along with the rest of the coaster's cargo. In drawing such a sharp contrast between past and present, Masefield does more than merely draw up bills-of-lading. Perhaps he even implies a wry and unfavorable comment on life in the present day. His meaning lies not so much in the dictionary definitions of his words ("*moidores*: Portuguese gold coins formerly worth approximately five pounds sterling") as in their rich and vivid connotations.

William Blake (1757–1827)

London   1794

I wander through each chartered street,
Near where the chartered Thames does flow,
And mark in every face I meet
Marks of weakness, marks of woe.

In every cry of every man,   5
In every infant's cry of fear,
In every voice, in every ban,
The mind-forged manacles I hear.

How the chimney-sweeper's cry
Every black'ning church appalls   10
And the hapless soldier's sigh
Runs in blood down palace walls.

But most through midnight streets I hear
How the youthful harlot's curse
Blasts the new born infant's tear   15
And blights with plagues the marriage hearse.

Here are only a few of the possible meanings of three of Blake's words:

• *chartered* (lines 1, 2)

  Denotations: Established by a charter (a written grant or a certificate of
    incorporation); leased or hired.
  Connotations: Defined, limited, restricted, channeled, mapped, bound by
    law; bought and sold (like a slave or an inanimate object); Magna Carta;
    charters given to crown colonies by the King.
  Other words in the poem with similar connotations: Ban, which can denote (1) a
    legal prohibition; (2) a churchman's curse or malediction; (3) in medieval
    times, an order summoning a king's vassals to fight for him. *Manacles,* or
    shackles, restrain movement. *Chimney-sweeper, soldier,* and *harlot* are all
    hirelings.

Interpretation of the lines: The street has had mapped out for it the direction in which it must go; the Thames has had laid down to it the course it must follow. Street and river are channeled, imprisoned, enslaved (like every inhabitant of London).

- *black'ning* (line 10)

Denotation: Becoming black.

Connotations: The darkening of something once light, the defilement of something once clean, the deepening of guilt, the gathering of darkness at the approach of night.

Other words in the poem with similar connotations: Objects becoming marked or smudged (*marks of weakness, marks of woe* in the faces of passers-by; bloodied walls of a palace; marriage blighted with plagues); the word *appalls* (denoting not only "to overcome with horror" but "to make pale" and also "to cast a pall or shroud over"); *midnight streets.*

Interpretation of the line: Literally, every London church grows black from soot and hires a chimney-sweeper (a small boy) to help clean it. But Blake suggests too that by profiting from the suffering of the child laborer, the church is soiling its original purity.

- *Blasts, blights* (lines 15, 16)

Denotations: Both *blast* and *blight* mean "to cause to wither" or "to ruin and destroy." Both are terms from horticulture. Frost *blasts* a bud and kills it; disease *blights* a growing plant.

Connotations: Sickness and death; gardens shriveled and dying; gusts of wind and the ravages of insects; things blown to pieces or rotted and warped.

Other words in the poem with similar connotations: Faces marked with weakness and woe; the child becomes a chimney-sweep; the soldier killed by war; blackening church and bloodied palace; young girl turned harlot; wedding carriage transformed into a hearse.

Interpretation of the lines: Literally, the harlot spreads the plague of syphilis, which, carried into marriage, can cause a baby to be born blind. In a larger and more meaningful sense, Blake sees the prostitution of even one young girl corrupting the entire institution of matrimony and endangering every child.

Some of these connotations are more to the point than others; the reader of a poem nearly always has the problem of distinguishing relevant associations from irrelevant ones. We need to read a poem in its entirety and, when a word leaves us in doubt, look for other things in the poem to corroborate or refute what we think it means. Relatively simple and direct in its statement, Blake's account of his stroll through the city at night becomes an indictment of a whole social and religious order. The indictment could hardly be this effective if it were "mathematically plain," its every word restricted to one denotation clearly spelled out.

Wallace Stevens (1879–1955)

Disillusionment of Ten O'Clock   1923

The houses are haunted
By white night-gowns.
None are green,
Or purple with green rings,
Or green with yellow rings,   5
Or yellow with blue rings.
None of them are strange,
With socks of lace
And beaded ceintures.
People are not going   10
To dream of baboons and periwinkles.
Only, here and there, an old sailor,
Drunk and asleep in his boots,
Catches tigers
In red weather.   15

QUESTIONS

1. What are *beaded ceintures?* What does the phrase suggest?
2. What contrast does Stevens draw between the people who live in these houses and the old sailor? What do the connotations of *white night-gowns* and *sailor* add to this contrast?
3. What is lacking in these people who wear white night-gowns? Why should the poet's view of them be a "disillusionment"?

Gwendolyn Brooks (1917–2000)

Southeast Corner   1945

The School of Beauty's a tavern now.
The Madam is underground.
Out at Lincoln, among the graves
Her own is early found.
Where the thickest, tallest monument   5
Cuts grandly into the air
The Madam lies, contentedly.
Her fortune, too, lies there,
Converted into cool hard steel
And right red velvet lining;   10
While over her tan impassivity
Shot silk is shining.

SOUTHEAST CORNER. *3 Lincoln:* cemetery in Chicago where a number of prominent African Americans, including Gwendolyn Brooks herself, are buried.

QUESTIONS

1. What view of its subject does this poem take? Through what words is it conveyed?
2. Is there more than one relevant meaning of *fortune* in line 8?

Timothy Steele (b. 1948)

Epitaph   1979

Here lies Sir Tact, a diplomatic fellow
Whose silence was not golden, but just yellow.

QUESTIONS

1. To what famous saying does the poet allude?
2. What are the connotations of *golden*? Of *yellow*?

E. E. Cummings (1894–1962)

next to of course god america i   1926

"next to of course god america i
love you land of the pilgrims' and so forth oh
say can you see by the dawn's early my
country 'tis of centuries come and go
and are no more what of it we should worry   5
in every language even deafanddumb
thy sons acclaim your glorious name by gorry
by jingo by gee by gosh by gum
why talk of beauty what could be more beautiful than these heroic happy dead   10
who rushed like lions to the roaring slaughter
they did not stop to think they died instead
then shall the voice of liberty be mute?"

He spoke. And drank rapidly a glass of water

QUESTIONS

1. How many allusions can you identify? What do their sources have in common?
2. Look up the origin of *jingo* (line 8). Is it used here as more than just a mindless exclamation?
3. Beyond what is actually said, what do the rhetoric of the first thirteen lines and the description in the last one suggest about the author's intentions in this poem?

Robert Frost (1874–1963)

Fire and Ice
1923

Some say the world will end in fire,
Some say in ice.
From what I've tasted of desire
I hold with those who favor fire.
But if it had to perish twice,   5
I think I know enough of hate
To say that for destruction ice
Is also great
And would suffice.

QUESTIONS

1. To whom does Frost refer in line 1? In line 2?
2. What connotations of *fire* and *ice* contribute to the richness of Frost's comparison?

Alfred, Lord Tennyson (1809–1892)

Tears, Idle Tears
1847

Tears, idle tears, I know not what they mean,
Tears from the depth of some divine despair
Rise in the heart, and gather to the eyes,
In looking on the happy autumn-fields,
And thinking of the days that are no more.   5

Fresh as the first beam glittering on a sail,
That brings our friends up from the underworld,
Sad as the last which reddens over one
That sinks with all we love below the verge;
So sad, so fresh, the days that are no more.   10

Ah, sad and strange as in dark summer dawns
The earliest pipe of half-awakened birds
To dying ears, when unto dying eyes
The casement slowly grows a glimmering square;
So sad, so strange, the days that are no more.   15

Dear as remembered kisses after death,
And sweet as those by hopeless fancy feigned
On lips that are for others; deep as love,
Deep as first love, and wild with all regret;
O Death in Life, the days that are no more!   20

WRITING EFFECTIVELY

WRITING ABOUT DENOTATION AND CONNOTATION

The Ways a Poem Suggests

Poems, like people, often convey their meanings indirectly. If we open the front door and find a friend standing there in hysterical tears, the person does not need to say "I'm miserable." We see that already. Similarly, the imagery, tone, and diction of a poem can suggest a message so clearly that it doesn't need to be stated outright.

Pay careful attention to what a poem suggests. Before beginning your essay, jot down a few key observations both about what the poem says directly and what you might want to know but aren't told. What important details are you left to infer for yourself?

When journalists write a news story, they usually try to cover the "five W's" in the opening paragraph—*who, what, when, where,* and *why*. These questions are worthwhile ones to ask about a poem.

- *Who?* Who is the speaker or central figure of the poem? (In William Blake's "London," for instance, the speaker is also the protagonist who witnesses the hellish horror of the city.) If the poem seems to be addressed not simply to the reader but to a more specific listener, identify that listener as well.
- *What?* What objects or events are being seen or presented? Does the poem ever suddenly change its subject? (In Wallace Stevens's "Disillusionment of Ten O'Clock," for example, there are essentially two scenes—one dull and proper, the other wild and disreputable. What does that obvious shift suggest about Stevens's meaning?)
- *When?* When does the poem take place? If a poet explicitly states a time of day or a season of the year, it is likely that the *when* of the poem is important. (The fact that Stevens's poem takes place at 10 P.M. and not 2 A.M. tells us a great deal about the people it describes.)

- *Where?* Where is the poem set? Sometimes the setting suggests something important, or plays a part in setting a mood, as it does in John Masefield's "Cargoes."
- *Why?* If the poem describes some dramatic action but does not provide an overt reason for the occurrence, perhaps the reader is meant to draw his or her own conclusions on the subject. (Tennyson's "Tears, Idle Tears" becomes more evocative by not being explicit about why the speaker weeps.)

Not all of these questions will be answered in every poem, but even that lack of information can clue you in to the poem's intentions. Remember, it is almost as important to know what a poem does not tell us as what it does.

CHECKLIST

Analyzing What a Poem Says and Suggests

✓ Who speaks the words of the poem? Is it a voice close to the poet's own? A fictional character? A real person, living or dead?

✓ Who is the poem's central figure?

✓ To whom—if anyone—is the poem addressed?

✓ What objects or events are depicted?

✓ Where does the action of the poem take place? What season? Time of day?

✓ When does the poem take place? Is that timing significant in any way?

✓ Why does the action of the poem take place? Is there some significant motivation?

✓ Does the poem leave any of the above information out? If so, what does that lack of information reveal about the poem's intentions?

WRITING ASSIGNMENT ON DENOTATION AND CONNOTATION

Search a poem of your own choosing for the answers to the "five W's"—*who, what, when, where,* and *why.* Indicate, with details, which of the questions are explicitly answered by the poem and which are left unexplained.

MORE TOPICS FOR WRITING

1. To which of the "five W's" does Robert Frost's brief poem "Fire and Ice" provide answers? In a brief essay, suggest why so many of the questions remain unanswered.

2. What do the various images in Tennyson's "Tears, Idle Tears" suggest about the speaker's reasons for weeping? Address each image, and explain what the images add up to.

3. Browse through a newspaper or magazine for an advertisement that tries to surround a product with an aura. A new car, for instance, might be described in terms of some powerful jungle cat ("purring power, ready to spring"). Clip or photocopy the ad and circle words in it that seem especially suggestive. Then, in an accompanying essay, unfold the suggestions in these words and try to explain the ad's appeal. What differences can you see between how poetry and advertising copy use connotative language?

13
Imagery

Ezra Pound (1885–1972)

In a Station of the Metro   1916

The apparition of these faces in the crowd;
Petals on a wet, black bough.

     Pound said he wrote this poem to convey an experience: emerging one
day from a train in the Paris subway (*Métro*), he beheld "suddenly a beautiful
face, and then another and another." Originally he had described his impression in a poem thirty lines long. In this final version, each line contains an
image, which, like a picture, may take the place of a thousand words.

     Though the term **image** suggests a thing seen, when speaking of images in
poetry, we generally mean *a word or sequence of words that refers to any sensory
experience*. Often this experience is a sight (**visual imagery**, as in Pound's
poem), but it may be a sound (**auditory imagery**) or a touch (**tactile imagery**,
as a perception of roughness or smoothness). It may be an odor or a taste or
perhaps a bodily sensation such as pain, the prickling of gooseflesh, the
quenching of thirst, or—as in the following brief poem—the perception of
something cold.

Taniguchi Buson (1716–1783)

The piercing chill I feel   (About 1760)

The piercing chill I feel:
   my dead wife's comb, in our bedroom,
     under my heel . . .
       —*Translated by Harold G. Henderson*

     As in this haiku (in Japanese, a poem of seventeen syllables) an image
can convey a flash of understanding. Had he wished, the poet might have spoken of the dead woman, of the contrast between her death and his memory of
her, of his feelings toward death in general. But such a discussion would be
quite different from the poem he actually wrote. Striking his bare foot against

the comb, now cold and motionless but associated with the living wife (perhaps worn in her hair), the widower feels a shock as if he had touched the woman's corpse. A literal, physical sense of death is conveyed; the abstraction "death" is understood through the senses. To render the abstract in concrete terms is what poets often try to do; in this attempt, an image can be valuable.

An image may occur in a single word, a phrase, a sentence, or, as in this case, an entire short poem. To speak of the **imagery** of a poem—all its images taken together—is often more useful than to speak of separate images. To divide Buson's haiku into five images—*chill, wife, comb, bedroom, heel*—is possible, for any noun that refers to a visible object or a sensation is an image, but this is to draw distinctions that in themselves mean little and to disassemble a single experience.

Does an image cause a reader to experience a sense impression? Not quite. Reading the word *petals*, no one literally sees petals; but the occasion is given for imagining them. The image asks to be seen with the mind's eye. And although "In a Station of the Metro" records what Ezra Pound saw, it is of course not necessary for a poet actually to have lived through a sensory experience in order to write of it. Keats may never have seen a newly discovered planet through a telescope, despite the image in his sonnet on Chapman's Homer.

Some literary critics look for much of the meaning of a poem in its imagery, wherein they expect to see the mind of the poet more truly revealed than in whatever the poet explicitly claims to believe. Though Shakespeare's Theseus (in *A Midsummer Night's Dream*) accuses poets of being concerned with "airy nothings," poets are usually very much concerned with what is in front of them. This concern is of use to us. Perhaps, as Alan Watts has remarked, Americans are not the materialists they are sometimes accused of being. How could anyone taking a look at an American city think that its inhabitants deeply cherish material things? Involved in our personal hopes and apprehensions, anticipating the future so hard that much of the time we see the present through a film of thought across our eyes, perhaps we need a poet occasionally to remind us that even the coffee we absentmindedly sip comes in (as Yeats put it) a "heavy spillable cup."

T. S. **Eliot** (1888–1965)

The winter evening settles down   1917

The winter evening settles down
With smell of steaks in passageways.
Six o'clock.
The burnt-out ends of smoky days.
And now a gusty shower wraps
The grimy scraps
Of withered leaves about your feet
And newspapers from vacant lots;
The showers beat

5

On broken blinds and chimney-pots,   10
And at the corner of the street
A lonely cab-horse steams and stamps.

And then the lighting of the lamps.

QUESTIONS

1. What mood is evoked by the images in Eliot's poem?
2. What kind of city neighborhood has the poet chosen to describe? How can you tell?

Theodore Roethke (1908–1963)

Root Cellar   1948

Nothing would sleep in that cellar, dank as a ditch,
Bulbs broke out of boxes hunting for chinks in the dark,
Shoots dangled and drooped,
Lolling obscenely from mildewed crates,
Hung down long yellow evil necks, like tropical snakes.   5
And what a congress of stinks!—
Roots ripe as old bait,
Pulpy stems, rank, silo-rich,
Leaf-mold, manure, lime, piled against slippery planks.
Nothing would give up life: 10
Even the dirt kept breathing a small breath.

QUESTIONS

1. As a boy growing up in Saginaw, Michigan, Theodore Roethke spent much of his time in a large commercial greenhouse run by his family. What details in his poem show more than a passing acquaintance with growing things?
2. What varieties of image does "Root Cellar" contain? Point out examples.
3. What do you understand to be Roethke's attitude toward the root cellar? Does he view it as a disgusting chamber of horrors? Pay special attention to the last two lines.

Elizabeth Bishop (1911–1979)

The Fish   1946

I caught a tremendous fish
and held him beside the boat
half out of water, with my hook
fast in a corner of his mouth.
He didn't fight.   5
He hadn't fought at all.
He hung a grunting weight,
battered and venerable
and homely. Here and there
his brown skin hung in strips   10
like ancient wall-paper,
and its pattern of darker brown
was like wall-paper:
shapes like full-blown roses
stained and lost through age.   15
He was speckled with barnacles,
fine rosettes of lime,
and infested
with tiny white sea-lice,
and underneath two or three   20
rags of green weed hung down.
While his gills were breathing in
the terrible oxygen
—the frightening gills,
fresh and crisp with blood,   25
that can cut so badly—
I thought of the coarse white flesh
packed in like feathers,
the big bones and the little bones,
the dramatic reds and blacks   30
of his shiny entrails,
and the pink swim-bladder
like a big peony.
I looked into his eyes
which were far larger than mine   35
but shallower, and yellowed,
the irises backed and packed
with tarnished tinfoil
seen through the lenses
of old scratched isinglass.   40

They shifted a little, but not
to return my stare.
—It was more like the tipping
of an object toward the light.
I admired his sullen face,   45
the mechanism of his jaw,
and then I saw
that from his lower lip
—if you could call it a lip—
grim, wet, and weapon-like,   50
hung five old pieces of fish-line,
or four and a wire leader
with the swivel still attached,
with all their five big hooks
grown firmly in his mouth.   55
A green line, frayed at the end
where he broke it, two heavier lines,
and a fine black thread
still crimped from the strain and snap
when it broke and he got away.   60
Like medals with their ribbons
frayed and wavering,
a five-haired beard of wisdom
trailing from his aching jaw.
I stared and stared   65
and victory filled up
the little rented boat,
from the pool of bilge
where oil had spread a rainbow
around the rusted engine   70
to the bailer rusted orange,
the sun-cracked thwarts,
the oarlocks on their strings,
the gunnels—until everything
was rainbow, rainbow, rainbow!   75
And I let the fish go.

QUESTIONS

1. How many abstract words does this poem contain? What proportion of the
   poem is imagery?
2. What is the speaker's attitude toward the fish? Comment in particular on lines
   61–64.

3. What attitude do the images of the rainbow of oil (line 69), the orange bailer (bailing bucket, line 71), the *sun-cracked thwarts* (line 72) convey? Does the poet expect us to feel mournful because the boat is in such sorry condition?

4. What is meant by *rainbow, rainbow, rainbow*?

5. How do these images prepare us for the conclusion? Why does the speaker let the fish go?

Anne Stevenson (b. 1933)

The Victory   1974

I thought you were my victory
though you cut me like a knife
when I brought you out of my body
into your life.

Tiny antagonist, gory,   5
blue as a bruise. The stains
of your cloud of glory
bled from my veins.

How can you dare, blind thing,
blank insect eyes?   10
You barb the air. You sting
with bladed cries.

Snail! Scary knot of desires!
Hungry snarl! Small son.
Why do I have to love you?   15
How have you won?

QUESTIONS

1. Newborn babies are often described as "little angels" or "bundles of joy." How does the speaker of "The Victory" describe her son?

2. Why does the speaker describe the child as an "antagonist" (line 5)?

3. Why is the poem titled "The Victory"?

4. Why is the infant compared to a knife in both lines 2 and 12?

Emily Dickinson (1830–1886)

A Route of Evanescence (1879)

A Route of Evanescence
With a revolving Wheel –
A Resonance of Emerald –
A Rush of Cochineal° –   *red dye*
And every Blossom on the Bush   5
Adjusts its tumbled Head –
The mail from Tunis, probably,
An easy Morning's Ride –

A ROUTE OF EVANESCENCE. Dickinson titled this poem "A Humming-bird" in an 1880
letter to a friend. 1 *Evanescence;* ornithologist's term for the luminous sheen of certain
birds' feathers. 7 *Tunis:* capital city of Tunisia, North Africa.

QUESTIONS

What is the subject of this poem? How can you tell?

Jean Toomer (1894–1967)

Reapers 1923

Black reapers with the sound of steel on stones
Are sharpening scythes. I see them place the hones
In their hip-pockets as a thing that's done,
And start their silent swinging, one by one.
Black horses drive a mower through the weeds,   5
And there, a field rat, startled, squealing bleeds,
His belly close to ground. I see the blade,
Blood-stained, continue cutting weeds and shade.

QUESTIONS

1. Imagine the scene Jean Toomer describes. Which particulars most vividly strike
   the mind's eye?
2. What kind of image is *silent swinging*?
3. Read the poem aloud. Notice especially the effect of the words *sound of steel on
   stones* and *field rat, startled, squealing bleeds*. What interesting sounds are present
   in the very words that contain these images?
4. What feelings do you get from this poem as a whole? Would you agree with someone
   who said, "This poem gives us a sense of happy, carefree life down on the farm, close
   to nature"? Exactly what in "Reapers" makes you feel the way you do? Besides appealing to our auditory and visual imagination, what do the images contribute?

Gerard Manley Hopkins (1844–1889)

Pied Beauty (1877)

Glory be to God for dappled things—
    For skies of couple-color as a brinded° cow;   *streaked*
        For rose-moles all in stipple upon trout that swim;
Fresh-firecoal chestnut-falls; finches' wings;
    Landscape plotted and pieced—fold, fallow, and plow;   5
    And áll trádes, their gear and tackle and trim.°   *equipment*

All things counter, original, spare, strange;
    Whatever is fickle, freckled (who knows how?)
        With swift, slow; sweet, sour; adazzle, dim;
He fathers-forth whose beauty is past change: 10
            Praise him.

QUESTIONS

1. What does the word *pied* mean? (Hint: what does a Pied Piper look like?)
2. According to Hopkins, what do *skies, cow, trout, ripe chestnuts, finches' wings,* and *landscapes* all have in common? What landscapes can the poet have in mind? (Have you ever seen any *dappled* landscape while looking down from an airplane, or from a mountain or high hill?)
3. What do you make of line 6: what can carpenters' saws and ditch-diggers' spades possibly have in common with the dappled things in lines 2–4?
4. Does Hopkins refer only to contrasts that meet the eye? What other kinds of variation interest him?
5. Try to state in your own words the theme of this poem. How essential to our understanding of this theme are Hopkins's images?

About Haiku

Arakida Moritake (1473–1549)

The falling flower

The falling flower
I saw drift back to the branch
Was a butterfly.

      —Translated by Babette Deutsch

Haiku means "beginning-verse" in Japanese—perhaps because the form may have originated in a game. Players, given a haiku, were supposed to extend its three lines into a longer poem. Haiku (the word can also be plural) consist mainly of imagery, but as we saw in Buson's lines about the cold comb, their imagery is not always only pictorial; it can also involve any of the five senses. Haiku are so short that they depend on imagery to trigger associations and responses in the reader. A haiku in Japanese is rimeless; its seventeen syllables are traditionally arranged in three lines, usually following a pattern of five, seven, and five syllables. English haiku frequently ignore such a pattern, being rimed or unrimed as the poet prefers. What English haiku do try to preserve is the powerful way Japanese haiku capture the intensity of a particular moment, usually by linking two concrete images. There is little room for abstract thoughts or general observations. The following attempt, though containing seventeen syllables, is far from haiku in spirit:

> Now that our love is gone
> I feel within my soul
> a nagging distress.

Unlike the author of those lines, haiku poets look out upon a literal world, seldom looking inward to *discuss* their feelings. Japanese haiku tend to be seasonal in subject, but because they are so highly compressed, they usually just *imply* a season: a blossom indicates spring; a crow on a branch, autumn; snow, winter. Not just pretty little sketches of nature (as some Westerners think), haiku assume a view of the universe in which observer and nature are not separated.

Haiku emerged in sixteenth-century Japan and soon developed into a deeply esteemed form. Even today, Japanese soldiers, stockbrokers, scientists, schoolchildren, and even the emperor still find occasion to pen haiku. Soon after the form first captured the attention of Western poets at the end of the nineteenth century, it became immensely influential for modern poets such as Ezra Pound, William Carlos Williams, and H. D., as a model for the kind of verse they wanted to write—concise, direct, and imagistic.

The Japanese consider the poems of the "Three Masters"—Basho, Buson, and Issa—to be the pinnacle of the classical haiku. Each poet had his own personality: Basho, the ascetic seeker of Zen enlightenment; Buson, the worldly artist; Issa, the sensitive master of wit and pathos. Here are free translations of poems from each of the "Three Masters."

Matsuo Basho (1644–1694)

Heat-lightning streak

Heat-lightning streak—
through darkness pierces
the heron's shriek.

—*Translated by X. J. Kennedy*

In the old stone pool

In the old stone pool
a frogjump:
splishhhhh.

—*Translated by X. J. Kennedy*

Taniguchi Buson (1716–1783)

On the one-ton temple bell

On the one-ton temple bell
a moonmoth, folded into sleep,
sits still.

—Translated by X. J. Kennedy

I go

I go,
you stay;
two autumns.

—Translated by Robert Hass

Kobayashi Issa (1763–1827)

only one guy

only one guy and
only one fly trying to
make the guest room do.

—Translated by Cid Corman

Cricket

Cricket, be
careful! I'm rolling
over!

—Translated by Robert Bly

Haiku from Japanese Internment Camps

Japanese immigrants brought the tradition of haiku-writing to the United States, often forming local clubs to pursue their shared literary interests. During World War II, when Japanese Americans were unjustly considered "enemy aliens" and confined to federal internment camps, these poets continued to write in their bleak new surroundings. Today these haiku provide a vivid picture of the deprivations suffered by the poets, their families, and their fellow internees.

Suiko Matsushita

Rain shower from mountain

Rain shower from mountain
quietly soaking
barbed wire fence

—Translated by Violet Kazue de Cristoro

Neiji Ozawa

War forced us from California

War forced us from California
No ripples this day
on desert lake

—Translated by Violet Kazue de Cristoro

Contemporary Haiku

Here are four more recent haiku written in English. (Don't expect them all to observe a strict arrangement of seventeen syllables, however.) Haiku, in any language, is an art of few words, many suggestions. A haiku starts us thinking and telling. "So the reader," Raymond Roseliep wrote, "keeps getting on where the poet got off."

Etheridge Knight (1931–1991)

Making jazz swing in

Making jazz swing in
Seventeen syllables AIN'T
No square poet's job.

John Ridland (b. 1933)

The Lazy Man's Haiku

out in the night
a wheelbarrowful
of moonlight.

Lee Gurga (b. 1949)

Visitor's Room

Visitor's Room—
everything bolted down
except my brother.

Connie Bensley (b. 1929)

Last Haiku

No, wait a minute,
I can't be old already:
I'm just about to

For Review and Further Study

John Keats (1795–1821)

Bright Star! would I were steadfast as thou art   (1819)

Bright star! would I were steadfast as thou art—
    Not in lone splendor hung aloft the night,
And watching, with eternal lids apart,
    Like Nature's patient, sleepless Eremite,°   *hermit*
The moving waters at their priest-like task   5
    Of pure ablution round earth's human shores,
Or gazing on the new soft-fallen mask
    Of snow upon the mountains and the moors—
No—yet still steadfast, still unchangeable,
    Pillowed upon my fair love's ripening breast,   10
To feel for ever its soft fall and swell,
    Awake for ever in a sweet unrest,
Still, still to hear her tender-taken breath,
And so live ever—or else swoon to death.

QUESTIONS

1. Stars are conventional symbols for love and a loved one. (Love, Shakespeare tells us in a sonnet, "is the star to every wandering bark.") In this sonnet, why is it not possible for the star to have this meaning? How does Keats use it?

2. What seems concrete and particular in the speaker's observations?

3. Suppose Keats had said *slow and easy* instead of *tender-taken* in line 13. What would have been lost?

EXPERIMENT: Writing with Images

Taking the following poems as examples from which to start rather than as models to be slavishly copied, try to compose a brief poem that consists largely of imagery.

Walt Whitman (1819–1892)

The Runner   1867

On a flat road runs the well-train'd runner;
He is lean and sinewy, with muscular legs;
He is thinly clothed—he leans forward as he runs,
With lightly closed fists, and arms partially rais'd.

T. E. Hulme (1883–1917)

Image   (About 1910)

Old houses were scaffolding once
                              and workmen whistling.

William Carlos Williams (1883–1963)

El Hombre   1917

It's a strange courage
You give me ancient star:

Shine alone in the sunrise
Toward which you lend no part!

Robert Bly (b. 1926)

Driving to Town Late to Mail a Letter   1962

It is a cold and snowy night. The main street is deserted.
The only things moving are swirls of snow.
As I lift the mailbox door, I feel its cold iron.
There is a privacy I love in this snowy night.
Driving around, I will waste more time.

Rita Dove (b. 1952)

Silos   1989

Like martial swans in spring paraded against the city sky's
shabby blue, they were always too white and
suddenly there.

They were never fingers, never xylophones, although once
a stranger said they put him in mind of Pan's pipes   5
and all the lost songs of Greece. But to the townspeople
they were like cigarettes, the smell chewy and bitter
like a field shorn of milkweed, or beer brewing, or
a fingernail scorched over a flame.

No, no, exclaimed the children. They're a fresh packet of chalk,   10
dreading math work.

They were masculine toys. They were tall wishes. They
were the ribs of the modern world.

Stevie Smith (1902–1971)

Not Waving but Drowning   1957

Nobody heard him, the dead man,
But still he lay moaning:
I was much further out than you thought
And not waving but drowning.

Poor chap, he always loved larking
And now he's dead   5
It must have been too cold for him his heart gave way,
They said.

Oh, no no no, it was too cold always
(Still the dead one lay moaning)   10
I was much too far out all my life
And not waving but drowning.

WRITING EFFECTIVELY

WRITING ABOUT IMAGERY

Analyzing Images

Images are powerful things—thus the old saw, "A picture is worth a thousand words." A poem, however, must build its pictures from words—no mean feat. By taking note of its imagery, and watching how the nature of those images evolves from start to finish, you can go a long way toward a better understanding of the poem. The following steps can help:

- Make a short list of the poem's key images. Be sure to write down the images in the order they appear, because the sequence can be as important as the images themselves. (For example, a poem whose images move from sunlight to darkness might well signify something different from one that begins with darkness and concludes with sunlight.)

- Don't forget to take the poem's title into account. A title often points the way to important insights.

- Remember: not all images are visual. Images can draw on any or all of the five senses.

- Be sure to jot down key adjectives or other qualifying words. (T. E. Hulme's image of "whistling" workmen on page 395, for instance, implies something happier than "sweating" workmen would.)

- Go back through your list and take notes about what moods or attitudes are suggested by each image, and by the movement from the first image to the last.

Let's try this method on a short poem. An initial list of images in Robert Bly's "Driving to Town Late to Mail a Letter" (page 395) might look like this:

cold and snowy night
deserted main street
mailbox door—cold iron
snowy night (speaker *loves* its privacy)
speaker drives around (to waste time)

Bly's title also contains several crucial images. Let's add them to the top of the list:

driving (to town)
late night
a letter (to be mailed)

Looking over our list, we see how the images provide an outline of the poem's story. We also see how Bly begins the poem without providing an initial sense of how his speaker feels about the situation. Is driving to town late on a snowy evening a positive, negative, or neutral experience? By noting where (in line 4) the speaker reveals a subjective response to an image ("There is a privacy I love in this snowy night"), we may also begin to grasp the poem's overall emotional structure. We might also note on our list how the poem begins and ends with the same image (driving), but uses it for different effects. At the beginning, the speaker is driving for the practical purpose of mailing a letter but at the end purely for pleasure.

Simply by noting the images from start to finish, we have already worked out a rough outline—all on a single sheet of paper or computer screen.

CHECKLIST

Thinking About Imagery

✓ List a poem's key images, in the order in which they appear.

✓ Remember, images can draw on all five senses—not just the visual.

✓ List key adjectives or other qualifying words.

✓ Go through your list. What emotions or attitudes are suggested by each image?

✓ What is suggested by the movement from one image to the next? Remember that the order or sequence of images is almost as important as the images themselves.

✓ Does the mood of the imagery change from start to finish?

✓ What does the poem's title suggest?

WRITING ASSIGNMENT ON IMAGERY

Examining any poem in this chapter, demonstrate how its imagery helps communicate its general theme. Be specific in noting how each key image contributes to the poem's total effect. Feel free to consult criticism on the poem but make sure to credit any observation you borrow exactly from a critical source.

MORE TOPICS FOR WRITING

1. Apply the steps listed above to one of the poems in this chapter. Make a brief list of images, and jot down notes on what the images suggest. Now write a two-page description of this process—what it revealed about the poem itself, and about reading poetry in general.

2. Choose a small, easily overlooked object in your home that has special significance to you. Write a paragraph-long, excruciatingly detailed description of the item, putting at least four senses into play. Without making any direct statements about the item's importance to you, try to let the imagery convey the mood you associate with it. Bring your paragraph to class, exchange it with a partner, and see if he or she can identify the mood you were trying to convey.

14
Figures of Speech

Why Speak Figuratively?

"I will speak daggers to her, but use none," says Hamlet, preparing to confront his mother. His statement makes sense only because we realize that *daggers* is to be taken two ways: literally (denoting sharp, pointed weapons) and nonliterally (referring to something that can be used *like* weapons—namely, words). Reading poetry, we often meet comparisons between two things whose similarity we have never noticed before. When Marianne Moore observes that a fir tree has "an emerald turkey-foot at the top," the result is a pleasure that poetry richly affords: the sudden recognition of likenesses.

A treetop like a turkey-foot, words like daggers—such comparisons are called **figures of speech**. In its broadest definition, a figure of speech may be said to occur whenever a speaker or writer, for the sake of freshness or emphasis, departs from the usual denotations of words. Certainly, when Hamlet says he will speak daggers, no one expects him to release pointed weapons from his lips, for *daggers* is not to be read solely for its denotation. Its connotations—sharp, stabbing, piercing, wounding—also come to mind, and we see ways in which words and daggers work alike. (Words too can hurt: by striking through pretense, possibly, or by wounding their hearer's self-esteem.) In the statement "A razor is sharper than an ax," there is no departure from the usual denotations of *razor* and *ax*, and no figure of speech results. Both objects are of the same class; the comparison is not offensive to logic. But in "How sharper than a serpent's tooth it is to have a thankless child," the objects—snake's tooth (fang) and ungrateful offspring—are so unlike that no reasonable comparison may be made between them. To find similarity, we attend to the connotations of *serpent's tooth*—biting, piercing, venom, pain—rather than to its denotations. If we are aware of the connotations of *red rose* (beauty, softness, freshness, and so forth), then the line "My love is like a red, red rose" need not call to mind a woman with a scarlet face and a thorny neck.

Figures of speech are not devices to state what is demonstrably untrue. Indeed they often state truths that more literal language cannot communicate; they call attention to such truths; they lend them emphasis.

Alfred, Lord Tennyson (1809–1892)

The Eagle   1851

He clasps the crag with crooked hands;
Close to the sun in lonely lands,
Ringed with the azure world, he stands.

The wrinkled sea beneath him crawls;
He watches from his mountain walls,   5
And like a thunderbolt he falls.

This brief poem is rich in figurative language. In the first line, the phrase *crooked hands* may surprise us. An eagle does not have hands, we might protest; but the objection would be a quibble, for evidently Tennyson is indicating exactly how an eagle clasps a crag, in the way that human fingers clasp a thing. By implication, too, the eagle is a person. *Close to the sun*, if taken literally, is an absurd exaggeration, the sun being a mean distance of 93,000,000 miles from the earth. For the eagle to be closer to it by the altitude of a mountain is an approach so small as to be insignificant. But figuratively, Tennyson conveys that the eagle stands above the clouds, perhaps silhouetted against the sun, and for the moment belongs to the heavens rather than to the land and sea. The word *ringed* makes a circle of the whole world's horizons and suggests that we see the world from the eagle's height; the *wrinkled sea* becomes an aged, sluggish animal; *mountain walls*, possibly literal, also suggests a fort or castle; and finally the eagle itself is likened to a thunderbolt in speed and in power, perhaps also in that its beak is—like our abstract conception of a lightning bolt—pointed. How much of the poem can be taken literally? Only *he clasps the crag, he stands, he watches, he falls*. The rest is made of figures of speech. The result is that, reading Tennyson's poem, we gain a bird's-eye view of sun, sea, and land—and even of bird. Like imagery, figurative language refers us to the physical world.

William Shakespeare (1564–1616)

Shall I compare thee to a summer's day?   1609

Shall I compare thee to a summer's day?
Thou art more lovely and more temperate.
Rough winds do shake the darling buds of May,
And summer's lease hath all too short a date.
Sometime too hot the eye of heaven shines,   5
And often is his gold complexion dimmed;
And every fair° from fair sometimes declines,   *fair one*
By chance, or nature's changing course, untrimmed.

But thy eternal summer shall not fade,
Nor lose possession of that fair thou ow'st,°   *ownest, have*   10
Nor shall death brag thou wand'rest in his shade,
When in eternal lines to time thou grow'st.
　So long as men can breathe or eyes can see,
　So long lives this, and this gives life to thee.

Howard Moss (1922–1987)

Shall I Compare Thee to a Summer's Day?   1976

Who says you're like one of the dog days?
You're nicer. And better.
Even in May, the weather can be gray,
And a summer sub-let doesn't last forever.
Sometimes the sun's too hot;   5
Sometimes it is not.
Who can stay young forever?
People break their necks or just drop dead!
But you? Never!
If there's just one condensed reader left   10
Who can figure out the abridged alphabet,
　After you're dead and gone,
　In this poem you'll live on!

SHALL I COMPARE THEE TO A SUMMER'S DAY? (MOSS). *Dog days:* the hottest days of summer.
The ancient Romans believed that the Dog-star, Sirius, added heat to summer months.

QUESTIONS

1. In Howard Moss's streamlined version of Shakespeare, from a series called "Modified
   Sonnets (Dedicated to adapters, abridgers, digesters, and condensers everywhere),"
   to what extent does the poet use figurative language? In Shakespeare's original
   sonnet, how high a proportion of Shakespeare's language is figurative?

2. Compare some of Moss's lines to the corresponding lines in Shakespeare's sonnet.
   Why is *Even in May, the weather can be gray* less interesting than the original? In the
   lines on the sun (5–6 in both versions), what has Moss's modification deliberately
   left out? Why is Shakespeare's seeing death as a braggart memorable? Why aren't
   you greatly impressed by Moss's last two lines?

3. Can you explain Shakespeare's play on the word *untrimmed* (line 8)? Evidently the
   word can mean "divested of trimmings," but what other suggestions do you find in it?

4. How would you answer someone who argued, "Maybe Moss's language isn't as
   good as Shakespeare's, but the meaning is still there. What's wrong with putting
   Shakespeare into up-to-date words that can be understood by everybody?"

Metaphor and Simile

> Life, like a dome of many-colored glass,
> Stains the white radiance of Eternity.

The first of these lines (from Shelley's "Adonais") is a **simile**: a comparison of two things, indicated by some connective, usually *like, as, than,* or a verb such as *resembles*. A simile expresses a similarity. Still, for a simile to exist, the things compared have to be dissimilar in kind. It is no simile to say "Your fingers are like mine"; it is a literal observation. But to say "Your fingers are like sausages" is to use a simile. Omit the connective—say, "Your fingers are sausages"—and the result is a **metaphor**, a statement that one thing *is* something else, which, in a literal sense, it is not. In the second of Shelley's lines, it is *assumed* that Eternity is light or radiance, and we have an **implied metaphor**, one that uses neither a connective nor the verb *to be*. Here are examples:

Oh, my love is like a red, red rose.	*Simile*
Oh, my love resembles a red, red rose.	*Simile*
Oh, my love is redder than a rose.	*Simile*
Oh, my love is a red, red rose.	*Metaphor*
Oh, my love has red petals and sharp thorns.	*Implied metaphor*

Often you can tell a metaphor from a simile by much more than just the presence or absence of a connective. In general, a simile refers to only one characteristic that two things have in common, while a metaphor is not plainly limited in the number of resemblances it may indicate. To use the simile "He eats like a pig" is to compare man and animal in one respect: eating habits. But to say "He's a pig" is to use a metaphor that might involve comparisons of appearance and morality as well.

For scientists as well as poets, the making of metaphors is customary. In 1933 George Lemaitre, the Belgian priest and physicist credited with the Big Bang theory of the origin of the universe, conceived of a primal atom that existed before anything else, which expanded and produced everything. And so, he remarked, making a wonderful metaphor, the evolution of the cosmos as it is today "can be compared to a display of fireworks that has just ended." As astrophysicist and novelist Alan Lightman has noted, we can't help envisioning scientific discoveries in terms of things we know from daily life—spinning balls, waves in water, pendulums, weights on springs. "We have no other choice," Lightman reasons. "We cannot avoid forming mental pictures when we try to grasp the meaning of our equations, and how can we picture what we have not seen?"[1] In science as well as in poetry, it would seem, metaphors are necessary instruments of understanding.

In everyday speech, simile and metaphor occur frequently. We use metaphors ("She's a doll") and similes ("The tickets are selling like hotcakes")

[1]"Physicists' Use of Metaphor," *The American Scholar* (Winter 1989): 99.

without being fully conscious of them. If, however, we are aware that words possess literal meanings as well as figurative ones, we do not write *died in the wool* for *dyed in the wool* or *tow the line* for *toe the line*, nor do we use **mixed metaphors** as did the writer who advised, "Water the spark of knowledge and it will bear fruit," or the speaker who urged, "To get ahead, keep your nose to the grindstone, your shoulder to the wheel, your ear to the ground, and your eye on the ball." Perhaps the unintended humor of these statements comes from our seeing that the writer, busy stringing together stale metaphors, was not aware that they had any physical reference.

A poem may make a series of comparisons, or the whole poem may be one extended comparison:

Emily Dickinson (1830–1886)

My Life had stood – a Loaded Gun   (about 1863)

My Life had stood – a Loaded Gun –
In Corners – till a Day
The Owner passed – identified –
And carried Me away –

And now We roam in Sovreign Woods –   5
And now We hunt the Doe –
And every time I speak for Him –
The Mountains straight reply –

And do I smile, such cordial light
Upon the Valley glow –   10
It is as a Vesuvian face
Had let its pleasure through –

And when at Night – Our good Day done –
I guard My Master's Head –
'Tis better than the Eider-Duck's   15
Deep Pillow – to have shared –

To foe of His – I'm deadly foe –
None stir the second time –
On whom I lay a Yellow Eye –
Or an emphatic Thumb –   20

Though I than He – may longer live
He longer must – than I –
For I have but the power to kill,
Without – the power to die –

How much life metaphors bring to poetry may be seen by comparing two poems by Tennyson and Blake.

Alfred, Lord Tennyson (1809–1892)

Flower in the Crannied Wall   1869

Flower in the crannied wall,
I pluck you out of the crannies,
I hold you here, root and all, in my hand,
Little flower—but *if* I could understand
What you are, root and all, and all in all,   5
I should know what God and man is.

How many metaphors does this poem contain? None. Compare it with a briefer poem on a similar theme: the quatrain that begins Blake's "Auguries of Innocence." (We follow here the opinion of W. B. Yeats, who, in editing Blake's poems, thought the lines ought to be printed separately.)

William Blake (1757–1827)

To see a world in a grain of sand   (about 1803)

To see a world in a grain of sand
And a heaven in a wild flower,
Hold infinity in the palm of your hand
And eternity in an hour.

Set beside Blake's poem, Tennyson's—short though it is—seems lengthy. What contributes to the richness of "To see a world in a grain of sand" is Blake's use of a metaphor in every line. And every metaphor is loaded with suggestion. Our world does indeed resemble a grain of sand: in being round, in being stony, in being one of a myriad (the suggestions go on and on). Like Blake's grain of sand, a metaphor holds much, within a small circumference.

Sylvia Plath (1932–1963)

Metaphors   1960

I'm a riddle in nine syllables,
An elephant, a ponderous house,
A melon strolling on two tendrils.
O red fruit, ivory, fine timbers!
This loaf's big with its yeasty rising.   5
Money's new-minted in this fat purse.
I'm a means, a stage, a cow in calf.
I've eaten a bag of green apples,
Boarded the train there's no getting off.

QUESTIONS

1. To what central fact do all the metaphors in "Metaphors" refer?
2. In the first line, what has the speaker in common with a riddle? Why does she say she has *nine* syllables?

N. Scott Momaday (b. 1934)

Simile   1974

What did we say to each other
that now we are as the deer
who walk in single file
with heads high
with ears forward   5
with eyes watchful
with hooves always placed on firm ground
in whose limbs there is latent flight

QUESTIONS

1. Momaday never tells us what was said. Does this omission keep us from understanding the comparison?
2. The comparison is extended with each detail adding some new twist. Explain the implications of the last line.

EXERCISE: What Is Similar?

Each of these quotations contains a simile or a metaphor. In each of these figures of speech, what two things is the poet comparing? Try to state exactly what you understand the two things to have in common: the most striking similarity or similarities that the poet sees.

1.   All the world's a stage,
    And all the men and women merely players:
    They have their exits and their entrances,
    And one man in his time plays many parts,
    His acts being seven ages.
              —William Shakespeare, *As You Like It*

2. Art is long, and Time is fleeting,
       And our hearts, though strong and brave,
    Still, like muffled drums are beating
       Funeral marches to the grave.
              —Henry Wadsworth Longfellow, "A Psalm of Life"

3. Why should I let the toad *work*
     Squat on my life?
   Can't I use my wit as a pitchfork
     And drive the brute off?
                    —Philip Larkin, "Toads"

4. I wear my patience like a light-green dress
   and wear it thin.
                    —Emily Grosholz, "Remembering the Ardèche"

Other Figures of Speech

When Shakespeare asks, in a sonnet,

> O! how shall summer's honey breath hold out
> Against the wrackful siege of batt'ring days,

it might seem at first that he mixes metaphors. How can a *breath* confront the battering ram of an invading army? But it is summer's breath and, by giving it to summer, Shakespeare makes the season a man or woman. It is as if the fragrance of summer were the breath within a person's body, and winter were the onslaught of old age.

Such is one instance of **personification**: a figure of speech in which a thing, an animal, or an abstract term (*truth, nature*) is made human. A personification extends throughout this short poem in which the wind is a wild man, and evidently it is not just any autumn breeze but a hurricane or at least a stiff gale.

James Stephens (1882–1950)

The Wind   1915

The wind stood up and gave a shout.
He whistled on his fingers and

Kicked the withered leaves about
And thumped the branches with his hand

And said he'd kill and kill and kill,   5
And so he will and so he will.

Hand in hand with personification often goes **apostrophe**: a way of addressing someone or something invisible or not ordinarily spoken to. In an apostrophe, a poet (in these examples Wordsworth) may address an inanimate object ("Spade! with which Wilkinson hath tilled his lands"), some dead or absent person ("Milton! thou shouldst be living at this hour"), an abstract thing ("Return, Delights!"), or a spirit ("Thou Soul that art the eternity of thought"). More often than not, the poet uses apostrophe to announce a lofty and serious tone. An "O" may even be put in front of it ("O moon!") since, according to W. D. Snodgrass, every poet has a right to do so at least once in a lifetime. But apostrophe doesn't have to be highfalutin. It is a means of giving life to the inanimate. It is a way of giving body to the intangible, a way of speaking to it person to person, as in the words of a moving American spiritual: "Death, ain't you got no shame?"

Most of us, from time to time, emphasize a point with a statement containing exaggeration: "Faster than greased lightning," "I've told him a thousand times." We speak, then, not literal truth but use a figure of speech called **overstatement** (or **hyperbole**). Poets too, being fond of emphasis, often exaggerate for effect. Instances are Marvell's profession of a love that should grow "Vaster than empires, and more slow" and John Burgon's description of Petra: "A rose-red city, half as old as Time." Overstatement can be used also for humorous purposes, as in a fat woman's boast (from a blues song): "Every time I shake, some skinny gal loses her home."[2] The opposite is **understatement**, implying more than is said. Mark Twain in *Life on the Mississippi* recalls how, as an apprentice steamboat-pilot asleep when supposed to be on watch, he was roused by the pilot and sent clambering to the pilot house: "Mr. Bixby was close behind, commenting." Another example is Robert Frost's line "One could do worse than be a swinger of birches"—the conclusion of a poem that has suggested that to swing on a birch tree is one of the most deeply satisfying activities in the world.

Asked to tell the difference between men and women, Samuel Johnson replied, "I can't conceive, madam, can you?" The great dictionary-maker was using a figure of speech known to classical rhetoricians as *paronomasia*, better known to us as a **pun** or play on words. How does a pun operate? It reminds us of another word (or other words) of similar or identical sound but of very different denotation. Although puns at their worst can be mere piddling quibbles, at best they can sharply point to surprising but genuine resemblances. The name of a dentist's country estate, Tooth Acres, is accurate: aching teeth paid for the property. In his novel *Moby-Dick,* Herman Melville takes up questions about whales that had puzzled scientists: for instance, are the whale's spoutings water or gaseous vapor? And when Melville speaks pointedly of the great whale "sprinkling and mistifying the gardens of the deep," we catch his pun, and conclude that the creature both mistifies and mystifies at once.

In poetry, a pun may be facetious, as in Thomas Hood's ballad of "Faithless Nelly Gray":

> Ben Battle was a soldier bold,
>   And used to war's alarms;
> But a cannon-ball took off his legs,
>   So he laid down his arms!

Or it may be serious, as in these lines on war by E. E. Cummings:

> the bigness of cannon
> is skillful,

---

[2] Quoted by Amiri Baraka [LeRoi Jones] in *Blues People* (New York: Morrow, 1963).

(*is skillful* becoming *is kill-ful* when read aloud), or perhaps, as in Shakespeare's song in *Cymbeline*, "Fear no more the heat o' th' sun," both facetious and serious at once:

> Golden lads and girls all must,
> As chimney-sweepers, come to dust.

Poets often make puns on images, combining the sensory force of imagery with the verbal pleasure of wordplay, as in the following poem:

Margaret Atwood (b. 1939)

You fit into me   1971

you fit into me
like a hook into an eye

a fish hook
an open eye

Dana Gioia (b. 1950)

Money   1991

> *Money is a kind of poetry.*
> —*Wallace Stevens*

Money, the long green,
cash, stash, rhino, jack
or just plain dough.

Chock it up, fork it over,
shell it out. Watch it   5
burn holes through pockets.

To be made of it! To have it
to burn! Greenbacks, double eagles,
megabucks and Ginnie Maes.

It greases the palm, feathers a nest,   10
holds heads above water,
makes both ends meet.

Money breeds money.
Gathering interest, compounding daily.
Always in circulation.   15

Money. You don't know where it's been,
but you put it where your mouth is.
And it talks.

QUESTION

What figures of speech can you identify in "Money"?

To sum up: even though figures of speech are not to be taken *only* literally, they refer us to a tangible world. By *personifying* an eagle, Tennyson reminds us that the bird and humankind have certain characteristics in common. Through *hyperbole* and *understatement*, a poet can make us see the physical actuality in back of words. *Pun* causes us to realize this actuality, too, and probably surprises us enjoyably at the same time. Through *apostrophe*, the poet animates the inanimate and asks it to listen—speaks directly to an immediate god or to the revivified dead. Put to such uses, figures of speech have power. They are more than just ways of playing with words.

For Review and Further Study

Robert Frost (1874–1963)

The Silken Tent   1942

She is as in a field a silken tent
At midday when a sunny summer breeze
Has dried the dew and all its ropes relent,
So that in guys° it gently sways at ease,   *attachments that steady it*
And its supporting central cedar pole,   5
That is its pinnacle to heavenward
And signifies the sureness of the soul,
Seems to owe naught to any single cord,
But strictly held by none, is loosely bound
By countless silken ties of love and thought   10
To everything on earth the compass round,
And only by one's going slightly taut
In the capriciousness of summer air
Is of the slightest bondage made aware.

QUESTIONS

1. Is Frost's comparison of a woman and tent a simile or a metaphor?
2. What are the ropes or cords?
3. Does the poet convey any sense of this woman's character? What sort of person do you believe her to be?
4. Paraphrase the poem, trying to state its implied meaning. (To be refreshed about paraphrase, turn back to page 312.) Be sure to include the implications of the last three lines.

Jane Kenyon (1947–1995)

The Suitor   1978

We lie back to back. Curtains
lift and fall,
like the chest of someone sleeping.
Wind moves the leaves of the box elder;
they show their light undersides,   5
turning all at once
like a school of fish.
Suddenly I understand that I am happy.
For months this feeling
has been coming closer, stopping   10
for short visits, like a timid suitor.

QUESTION

In each simile you find in "The Suitor," exactly what is the similarity?

EXERCISE: Figures of Speech

Identify the central figure of speech in the following two short poems.

Robert Frost (1874–1963)

The Secret Sits   1936

We dance round in a ring and suppose,
But the Secret sits in the middle and knows.

A. R. Ammons (1926–2001)

Coward   1975

Bravery runs in my family.

Heather McHugh (b. 1950)

Language Lesson, 1976   1981, 1993

When Americans say a man
takes liberties, they mean

he's gone too far. In Philadelphia today I saw
a kid on a leash look mom-ward

and announce his fondest wish: one   5
bicentennial burger, hold

the relish. Hold is forget,
in American.

On the courts of Philadelphia
the rich prepare   10

to serve, to fault. The language is a game as well,
in which love can mean nothing,

doubletalk mean lie. I'm saying
doubletalk with me. I'm saying

go so far the customs are untold.   15
Make nothing without words,

and let me be
the one you never hold.

QUESTION

Does this poem just play with words, or does it have a deeper meaning?

Robert Burns (1759–1796)

Oh, my love is like a red, red rose   (about 1788)

Oh, my love is like a red, red rose
   That's newly sprung in June;
My love is like the melody
   That's sweetly played in tune.

So fair art thou, my bonny lass,   5
   So deep in love am I;
And I will love thee still, my dear,
   Till a' the seas gang° dry.   go

Till a' the seas gang dry, my dear,
   And the rocks melt wi' the sun;   10
And I will love thee still, my dear,
   While the sands o' life shall run.

And fare thee weel, my only love!
   And fare thee weel awhile!
And I will come again, my love   15
   Though it were ten thousand mile.

WRITING ABOUT METAPHORS

How Metaphors Enlarge a Poem's Meaning

Metaphors are more than mere decoration. Sometimes, for example, they help us envision an unfamiliar thing more clearly by comparing it with another, more familiar item. By connecting an object to something else, a metaphor can reveal interesting aspects of both items.

Usually we can see the main point of a good metaphor immediately, but in interpreting a poem, the practical issue sometimes arises of how far to extend a comparison. If at the dinner table a big brother calls his kid brother "a pig," he probably does not mean to imply that the child has a snout and a kinky tail. Most metaphors have a finite set of associations—even insults from a big brother.

To write effectively about a highly metaphorical poem, examine the poem's key comparison or comparisons. You will need to determine the general scope of the metaphor. In what ways, for instance, does the beloved resemble a rose in Robert Burns's "Oh, my love is like a red, red rose"? The speaker's beloved might not have thorns, and she probably doesn't stand around in the dirt. Before you begin to write, clarify which aspects of the comparison are true and which are false.

You may notice obvious connections among all the metaphors or similes in a poem. Perhaps all of them are threatening, or inviting, or nocturnal, or exaggerated. Such similarities, if they occur, will almost certainly be significant.

CHECKLIST

Analyzing Metaphor

✓ Underline a poem's key comparisons. Look for both similes and metaphors.
✓ How are the two things being compared alike?
✓ In what ways are the two things unlike each other?
✓ Do the metaphors or similes in the poem have anything in common?
✓ If so, what does that commonality suggest?

WRITING ASSIGNMENT ON FIGURES OF SPEECH

In a brief essay of approximately 500 words, analyze the figures of speech to be found in any poem in this chapter. To what effect does the poem employ metaphors, similes, hyperbole, overstatement, paradox, or any other figure of speech?

MORE TOPICS FOR WRITING

1. Examine the extended implied metaphor that constitutes John Donne's "The Flea." Paraphrase the poem's argument. In your opinion, does the use of metaphor strengthen the speaker's case?

2. Whip up some similes of your own. Choose someone likely to be unfamiliar to your classmates—your brother or your best friend from home, for example. Write a paragraph in which you use multiple metaphors and similes to communicate a sense of what that person looks, sounds, and acts like. Come up with at least one figure of speech in each sentence.

3. Write a paragraph on any topic, tossing in as many hyperbolic statements as possible. Then write another version, changing all your exaggeration to understatement. In one last paragraph, sum up what this experience taught you about figurative language.

4. Rewrite a short poem rich in figurative language: Sylvia Plath's "Metaphors," for example, or Robert Burns's "Oh, my love is like a red, red rose." Taking for your model Howard Moss's deliberately bepiddling version of "Shall I compare thee to a summer's day?," use language as flat and unsuggestive as possible. Eliminate every figure of speech. (Just ignore any rime or rhythm in the original.) Then, in a paragraph, indicate lines in your revised version that seem glaringly worsened. In conclusion, sum up what your barbaric rewrite tells you about the nature of poetry.

15
Sound

Sound as Meaning

Isak Dinesen, in a memoir of her life on a plantation in East Africa, tells how some Kikuyu tribesmen reacted to their first hearing of rimed verse:

> The Natives, who have a strong sense of rhythm, know nothing of verse, or at least did not know anything before the times of the schools, where they were taught hymns. One evening out in the maize-field, where we had been harvesting maize, breaking off the cobs and throwing them on to the ox-carts, to amuse myself, I spoke to the field laborers, who were mostly quite young, in Swahili verse. There was no sense in the verses, they were made for the sake of rime— "Ngumbe na-penda chumbe, Malaya mbaya. Wakamba na-kula mamba." The oxen like salt—whores are bad—The Wakamba eat snakes. It caught the interest of the boys, they formed a ring round me. They were quick to understand that meaning in poetry is of no consequence, and they did not question the thesis of the verse, but waited eagerly for the rime, and laughed at it when it came. I tried to make them themselves find the rime and finish the poem when I had begun it, but they could not, or would not, do that, and turned away their heads. As they had become used to the idea of poetry, they begged: "Speak again. Speak like rain." Why they should feel verse to be like rain I do not know. It must have been, however, an expression of applause, since in Africa rain is always longed for and welcomed.[1]

What the tribesmen had discovered is that poetry, like music, appeals to the ear. However limited it may be in comparison with the sound of an orchestra—or a tribal drummer—the sound of words in itself gives pleasure. However, we might doubt Isak Dinesen's assumption that "meaning in poetry is of no consequence." "Hey nonny-nonny" and such nonsense has a place in song lyrics and other poems, and we might take pleasure in hearing rimes in Swahili; but most good poetry has meaningful sound as well as musical sound. Certainly the words of a song have an effect different from that of wordless music: they go along with their music and, by making statements, add more meaning. The French poet Isidore Isou, founder of a literary movement called *lettrisme,* maintained

[1] Isak Dinesen, *Out of Africa* (New York: Random, 1972).

414

that poems can be written not only in words but also in letters (sample lines: *xyl, xyl, / prprali dryl / znglo trpylo pwi*). But the sound of letters alone, without denotation and connotation, has not been enough to make Letterist poems memorable. In the response of the Kikuyu tribesmen, there may have been not only the pleasure of hearing sounds but also the agreeable surprise of finding that things not usually associated had been brought together.

More powerful when in the company of meaning, not apart from it, the sounds of consonants and vowels can contribute greatly to a poem's effect. The sound of *s*, which can suggest the swishing of water, has rarely been used more accurately than in Surrey's line "Calm is the sea, the waves work less and less." When, in a poem, the sound of words working together with meaning pleases mind and ear, the effect is **euphony**, as in the following lines from Tennyson's "Come down, O maid":

> Myriads of rivulets hurrying through the lawn,
> The moan of doves in immemorial elms,
> And murmuring of innumerable bees.

Its opposite is **cacophony**: a harsh, discordant effect. It too is chosen for the sake of meaning. We hear it in Milton's scornful reference in "Lycidas" to corrupt clergymen whose songs "Grate on their scrannel pipes of wretched straw." (Read that line and one of Tennyson's aloud and see which requires lips, teeth, and tongue to do more work.) But note that although Milton's line is harsh in sound, the line (when we meet it in his poem) is pleasing because it is artful. In a famous passage from his *Essay on Criticism*, Pope has illustrated both euphony and cacophony. (Given here as Pope printed it, the passage relies heavily on italics and capital letters, for particular emphasis. If you will read these lines aloud, dwelling a little longer or harder on the words italicized, you will find that Pope has given you very good directions for a meaningful reading.)

Alexander Pope (1688–1744)

True Ease in Writing comes from Art, not Chance   1711

True Ease in Writing comes from Art, not Chance,
As those move easiest who have learned to dance.
'Tis not enough no Harshness gives Offence,
The *Sound* must seem an *Echo* to the *Sense*.
Soft is the strain when *Zephyr*° gently blows,   *the west wind*   5
And the *smooth Stream* in *smoother Numbers*° flows;   *metrical rhythm*
But when loud Surges lash the sounding Shore,
The *hoarse, rough Verse* should like the *Torrent* roar.
When *Ajax* strives, some Rock's vast Weight to throw,

The Line too *labors*, and the Words move *slow;*   10
Not so, when swift *Camilla* scours the Plain,
Flies o'er th' unbending Corn, and skims along the Main.°   *expanse (of sea)*
Hear how *Timotheus'* varied Lays surprise,
And bid Alternate Passions fall and rise!
While, at each Change, the Son of *Lybian Jove*   15
Now *burns* with Glory, and then *melts* with Love;
Now his *fierce Eyes* with *sparkling Fury* glow;
Now *Sighs* steal out, and *Tears begin to flow:*
Persians and Greeks like *Turns of Nature* found,
And the *World's Victor* stood subdued by *Sound!*   20
The Pow'rs of Music all our Hearts allow;
And what *Timotheus* was, is *Dryden* now.

TRUE EASE IN WRITING COMES FROM ART, NOT CHANCE (*An Essay on Criticism,* lines
362–383). 9 *Ajax:* Greek hero, almost a superman, who in Homer's account of the siege
of Troy hurls an enormous rock that momentarily flattens Hector, the Trojan prince
(*Iliad* VII, 268–272). 11 *Camilla:* a kind of Amazon or warrior woman of the Volcians,
whose speed and lightness of step are praised by the Roman poet Virgil: "She could have
skimmed across an unmown grainfield / Without so much as bruising one tender blade; /
She could have sped across an ocean's surge / Without so much as wetting her quicksil-
ver soles" (*Aeneid* VII, 808–811). 13 *Timotheus:* favorite musician of Alexander the
Great. In "Alexander's Feast, or The Power of Music," John Dryden imagines him:
"Timotheus, placed on high / Amid the tuneful choir, / With flying fingers touched the
lyre: / The trembling notes ascend the sky, / And heavenly joys inspire." 15 *Lybian Jove:*
name for Alexander. A Libyan oracle had declared the king to be the son of the god
Zeus Ammon.

    Notice the pleasing effect of all the *s* sounds in the lines about the west
wind and the stream, and in another meaningful place, the effect of the consonants in *Ajax strives,* a phrase that makes our lips work almost as hard as
Ajax throwing the rock.

    Is sound identical with meaning in lines such as these? Not quite. In the
passage from Tennyson, for instance, the cooing of doves is not *exactly* a
moan. As John Crowe Ransom pointed out, the sound would be almost the
same but the meaning entirely different in "The murdering of innumerable
beeves." While it is true that the consonant sound *sl-* will often begin a word
that conveys ideas of wetness and smoothness—*slick, slimy, slippery, slush*—we
are so used to hearing it in words that convey nothing of the kind—*slave, slow,
sledgehammer*—that it is doubtful whether, all by itself, the sound communicates
anything definite. The most beautiful phrase in the English language, according
to Dorothy Parker, is *cellar door.* Another wit once nominated, as our most
euphonious word, not *sunrise* or *silvery* but *syphilis.*

    Relating sound more closely to meaning, the device called **onomatopoeia**
is an attempt to represent a thing or action by a word that imitates the sound
associated with it: *zoom, whiz, crash, bang, ding-dong, pitter-patter, yakety-yak.*
Onomatopoeia is often effective in poetry, as in Emily Dickinson's line about

the fly with its "uncertain stumbling Buzz," in which the nasal sounds *n, m, ng* and the sibilants *c, s* help make a droning buzz.

Like the Kikuyu tribesmen, others who care for poetry have discovered in the sound of words something of the refreshment of cool rain. Dylan Thomas, telling how he began to write poetry, said that from early childhood words were to him "as the notes of bells, the sounds of musical instruments, the noises of wind, sea, and rain, the rattle of milkcarts, the clopping of hooves on cobbles, the fingering of branches on the window pane, might be to someone, deaf from birth, who has miraculously found his hearing."[2] For readers, too, the sound of words can have a magical spell, most powerful when it points to meaning.

William Butler Yeats (1865–1939)a

Who Goes with Fergus?   1892

Who will go drive with Fergus now,
And pierce the deep wood's woven shade,
And dance upon the level shore?
Young man, lift up your russet brow,
And lift your tender eyelids, maid,   5
And brood on hopes and fear no more.

And no more turn aside and brood
Upon love's bitter mystery;
For Fergus rules the brazen cars,°   *chariots*
And rules the shadows of the wood,   10
And the white breast of the dim sea
And all dishevelled wandering stars.

WHO GOES WITH FERGUS? *Fergus:* Irish king who gave up his throne to be a wandering poet.

QUESTIONS

1. In what lines do you find euphony?
2. In what line do you find cacophony?
3. How do the sounds of these lines stress what is said in them?

---

[2]"Notes on the Art of Poetry," *Modern Poetics*, ed. James Scully (New York: McGraw-Hill, 1965).

EXERCISE: Listening to Meaning

Read aloud the following brief poem. In the sounds of which particular words are meanings well captured?

John Updike (b. 1932)

Recital   1963

> ROGER BOBO GIVES
> RECITAL ON TUBA
> —*Headline in the Times*

Eskimos in Manitoba,
    Barracuda off Aruba,
Cock an ear when Roger Bobo
    Starts to solo on the tuba.

Men of every station—Pooh-Bah,   5
    Nabob, bozo, toff, and hobo—
Cry in unison, "Indubi-
    Tably, there is simply nobo-

Dy who oompahs on the tubo,
    Solo, quite like Roger Bubo!"   10

Alliteration and Assonance

Listening to a symphony in which themes are repeated throughout each movement, we enjoy both their recurrence and their variation. We take similar pleasure in the repetition of a phrase or a single chord. Something like this pleasure is afforded us frequently in poetry.

Analogies between poetry and wordless music, it is true, tend to break down when carried far, since poetry—to mention a single difference—has denotation. But like musical compositions, poems have patterns of sounds. Among such patterns long popular in English poetry is **alliteration**, which has been defined as a succession of similar sounds. Alliteration occurs in the repetition of the same consonant sound at the beginning of successive words—"round and round the rugged rocks the ragged rascal ran." Or it may occur inside the words, as in Milton's description of the gates of Hell:

> On a sudden open fly
> With impetuous recoil and jarring sound
> The infernal doors, and on their hinges grate
> Harsh thunder, that the lowest bottom shook
> Of Erebus.

The former kind is called **initial alliteration**, the latter **internal alliteration** or **hidden alliteration**. We recognize alliteration by sound, not by spelling: *know* and *nail* alliterate, *know* and *key* do not. In a line by E. E. Cummings, "colossal hoax of clocks and calendars," the sound of *x* within ho*x* alliterates with the *cks* in clo*cks*.

As we have seen, to repeat the sound of a consonant is to produce alliteration, but to repeat the sound of a *vowel* is to produce **assonance**. Like alliteration, assonance may occur either initially—"*all* the *awful auguries*"[3]—or internally—Edmund Spenser's "Her goodly *eyes* like sapphires sh*i*ning br*i*ght, / Her forehead *ivory* wh*i*te . . ." and it can help make common phrases unforgettable: "eager beaver," "holy smoke." Like alliteration, it slows the reader down and focuses attention.

A. E. Housman (1859–1936)

Eight O'Clock   1922

He stood, and heard the steeple
   Sprinkle the quarters on the morning town.
One, two, three, four, to market-place and people
   It tossed them down.

Strapped, noosed, nighing his hour,   5
   He stood and counted them and cursed his luck;
And then the clock collected in the tower
   Its strength, and struck.

QUESTIONS

1. Why does the protagonist in this brief drama curse his luck? What is his situation?
2. For so short a poem, "Eight O'Clock" carries a great weight of alliteration. What patterns of initial alliteration do you find? What patterns of internal alliteration? What effect is created by all this heavy emphasis?

James Joyce (1882–1941)

All day I hear   1907

All day I hear the noise of waters
   Making moan,
Sad as the sea-bird is, when going
   Forth alone,

---

[3]Some prefer to call the repetition of an initial vowel-sound by the name of alliteration: "apt alliteration's artful aid."

He hears the winds cry to the waters'   5
    Monotone.

The grey winds, the cold winds are blowing
    Where I go.
I hear the noise of many waters
    Far below.   10
All day, all night, I hear them flowing
    To and fro.

QUESTIONS

1. Find three instances of alliteration in the first stanza. Do any of them serve to reinforce meaning?
2. There is a great deal of assonance throughout the poem on a single vowel sound. What sound is it, and what effect is achieved by its repetition?

EXPERIMENT: Reading for Assonance

Try reading aloud as rapidly as possible the following poem by Tennyson. From the difficulties you encounter, you may be able to sense the slowing effect of assonance. Then read the poem aloud a second time, with consideration.

Alfred, Lord Tennyson (1809–1892)

The splendor falls on castle walls   1850

The splendor falls on castle walls
    And snowy summits old in story;
The long light shakes across the lakes,
    And the wild cataract leaps in glory.
Blow, bugle, blow, set the wild echoes flying,   5
Blow, bugle; answer, echoes, dying, dying, dying.

O hark, O hear! how thin and clear,
    And thinner, clearer, farther going!
O sweet and far from cliff and scar°   *jutting rock*
    The horns of Elfland faintly blowing!   10
Blow, let us hear the purple glens replying:
Blow, bugle; answer, echoes, dying, dying, dying.

O love, they die in yon rich sky,
    They faint on hill or field or river;
Our echoes roll from soul to soul,   15
    And grow for ever and for ever.
Blow, bugle, blow, set the wild echoes flying,
And answer, echoes, answer, dying, dying, dying.

Rime

Isak Dinesen's tribesmen, to whom rime was a new phenomenon, recognized at once that rimed language is special language. So do we, for, although much English poetry is unrimed, rime is one means to set poetry apart from ordinary conversation and bring it closer to music. A **rime** (or rhyme), defined most narrowly, occurs when two or more words or phrases contain an identical or similar vowel-sound, usually accented, and the consonant-sounds (if any) that follow the vowel-sound are identical: *hay* and *sleigh*, *prairie schooner* and *piano tuner*. From these examples it will be seen that rime depends not on spelling but on sound.

Excellent rimes surprise. It is all very well that a reader may anticipate which vowel-sound is coming next, for patterns of rime give pleasure by satis-fying expectations; but riming becomes dull clunking if, at the end of each line, the reader can predict the word that will end the next. Hearing many a jukebox song for the first time, a listener can do so: *charms* lead to *arms, skies above* to *love*. As Alexander Pope observes of the habits of dull rimesters,

> Where'er you find "the cooling western breeze,"
> In the next line it "whispers through the trees";
> If crystal streams "with pleasing murmurs creep,"
> The reader's threatened (not in vain) with "sleep" . . .

But who—given the opening line of this comic poem—could predict the lines that follow?

William Cole (1919–2000)

On my boat on Lake Cayuga   1985

On my boat on Lake Cayuga
I have a horn that goes "Ay-oogah!"
I'm not the modern kind of creep
Who has a horn that goes "beep beep."

Robert Herrick, in a more subtle poem, made good use of rime to indicate a startling contrast:

> Then while time serves, and we are but decaying,
> Come, my Corinna, come, let's go a-Maying.

Though good rimes seem fresh, not all will startle, and probably few will call to mind things so unlike as *May* and *decay*, *Cayuga* and *Ay-oogah*. Some mas-ters of rime often link words that, taken out of text, might seem common and unevocative. Here are the opening lines of Rachel Hadas's poem, "Three Silences," which describe an infant feeding at a mother's breast:

> Of all the times when not to speak is best,
> mother's and infant's is the easiest,
> the milky mouth still warm against her breast.

Hadas's rime words are not especially memorable in themselves, and yet these lines are—at least in part because they rime so well. The quiet echo of sound at the end of each line reinforces the intimate tone of the mother's moment with her child. Poetic invention may be driven home without rime, but it is rime sometimes that rings the doorbell. Admittedly, some rimes wear thin from too much use. More difficult to use freshly than before the establishment of Tin Pan Alley, rimes such as *moon, June, croon* seem leaden and to ring true would need an extremely powerful context. *Death* and *breath* are a rime that poets have used with wearisome frequency; another is *birth, earth, mirth.* And yet we cannot exclude these from the diction of poetry, for they might be the very words a poet would need in order to say something new and original.

To have an **exact rime**, sounds following the vowel sound have to be the same: *red* and *bread, wealthily* and *stealthily, walk to her* and *talk to her.* If final consonant sounds are the same but the vowel sounds are different, the result is **slant rime**, also called **near rime, off rime**, or **imperfect rime:** *sun* riming with *bone, moon, rain, green, gone, thin.* By not satisfying the reader's expectation of an exact chime, but instead giving a clunk, a slant rime can help a poet say some things in a particular way. It works especially well for disappointed letdowns, negations, and denials, as in Blake's couplet:

> He who the ox to wrath has moved
> Shall never be by woman loved.

Consonance, a kind of slant rime, occurs when the rimed words or phrases have the same beginning and ending consonant sounds but a different vowel, as in *chitter* and *chatter.* Owen rimes *spoiled* and *spilled* in this way. Consonance is used in a traditional nonsense poem, "The Cutty Wren": "'O where are you going?' says *Milder* to *Malder.*" (W. H. Auden wrote a variation on it that begins, "'O where are you going?' said *reader* to *rider,*" thus keeping the consonance.)

End rime, as its name indicates, comes at the ends of lines, **internal rime** within them. Most rime tends to be end rime. Few recent poets have used internal rime so heavily as Wallace Stevens in the beginning of "Bantams in Pine-Woods": "Chieftain Iffucan of Azcan in caftan / Of tan with henna hackles, halt!" (lines also heavy on alliteration). A poet may employ both end rime and internal rime in the same poem, as in Robert Burns's satiric ballad "The Kirk's Alarm":

> Orthodox, Orthodox, wha believe in John Knox,
>   Let me sound an alarm to your conscience:
> There's a heretic blast has been blawn i' the wast,°   *west*
>   "That what is not sense must be nonsense."

Masculine rime is a rime of one-syllable words (*jail*, *bail*) or (in words of more than one syllable) stressed final syllables: *di-VORCE*, *re-MORSE*, or *horse*, *re-MORSE*. **Feminine rime** is a rime of two or more syllables, with stress on a syllable other than the last: *TUR-tle*, *FER-tile*, or (to take an example from Byron) *in-tel-LECT-u-al*, *hen-PECKED you all*. Often it lends itself to comic verse, but can occasionally be valuable to serious poems, as in Wordsworth's "Resolution and Independence":

> We poets in our youth begin in gladness,
> But thereof come in the end despondency and madness.

or as in Anne Sexton's seriously witty "Eighteen Days Without You":

> and of course we're not married, we are a pair of scissors
> who come together to cut, without towels saying His. Hers.

Artfully used, feminine rime can give a poem a heightened musical effect for the simple reason that it offers the listener twice as many riming syllables in each line. In the wrong hands, however, that sonic abundance has the unfortunate ability of making a bad poem twice as painful to endure. Serious poems containing feminine rimes of three syllables have been attempted, notably by Thomas Hood in "The Bridge of Sighs":

> Take her up tenderly,
> Lift her with care;
> Fashioned so slenderly,
> Young, and so fair!

But the pattern is hard to sustain without lapsing into unintended comedy, as in the same poem:

> Still, for all slips of hers,
> One of Eve's family—
> Wipe those poor lips of hers,
> Oozing so clammily.

It works better when comedy is wanted.

Hilaire Belloc (1870–1953)

The Hippopotamus   1896

I shoot the Hippopotamus
   with bullets made of platinum,
Because if I use leaden ones
   his hide is sure to flatten 'em.

Ogden Nash (1902–1971)

The Panther   1940

The panther is like a leopard,
Except it hasn't been peppered.
Should you behold a panther crouch,
Prepare to say Ouch.
Better yet, if called by a panther,   5
Don't anther.

Rime in American poetry suffered a significant fall from favor in the early 1960s. A new generation of poets took for models the open forms of Whitman, Pound, and William Carlos Williams. In the last few decades, however, some poets have been skillfully using rime again in their work. Often called the **New Formalists**, these poets include Julia Alvarez, Annie Finch, R. S. Gwynn, Rachel Hadas, Mark Jarman, Paul Lake, Charles Martin, Marilyn Nelson, A. E. Stallings, and Timothy Steele. Their poems often use rime and meter to present unusual contemporary subjects, but they also sometimes write poems that recollect, converse, and argue with the poetry of the past.

Still, most American poets don't write in rime; some even consider its possibilities exhausted. Such a view may be a reaction against the wearing thin of rimes by overuse or the mechanical and meaningless application of a rime scheme. Yet anyone who listens to children skipping rope in the street, making up rimes to delight themselves as they go along, may doubt that the pleasures of rime are ended; and certainly the practice of Yeats and Emily Dickinson, to name only two, suggests that the possibilities of slant rime may be nearly infinite. If successfully employed, as it has been at times by a majority of English-speaking poets whose work we care to save, rime runs through its poem like a spine: the creature moves by means of it.

Gerard Manley Hopkins (1844–1889)

God's Grandeur   (1877)

The world is charged with the grandeur of God.
    It will flame out, like shining from shook foil;
    It gathers to a greatness, like the ooze of oil
Crushed. Why do men then now not reck his rod?
Generations have trod, have trod, have trod;   5
    And all is seared with trade; bleared, smeared with toil;
    And wears man's smudge and shares man's smell: the soil
Is bare now, nor can foot feel, being shod.

And for all this, nature is never spent;
   There lives the dearest freshness deep down things;
And though the last lights off the black West went
   Oh, morning, at the brown brink eastward, springs—
Because the Holy Ghost over the bent
   World broods with warm breast and with ah! bright wings.

             10

GOD'S GRANDEUR. 1 *charged:* as though with electricity. 3–4 *It gathers . . . Crushed:* The grandeur of God will rise and be manifest, as oil rises and collects from crushed olives or grain. 4 *reck his rod:* heed His law. 10 *deep down things:* Tightly packing the poem, Hopkins omits the preposition *in* or *within* before *things.* 11 *last lights . . . went:* When in 1534 Henry VIII broke ties with the Roman Catholic Church and created the Church of England.

QUESTIONS

1. In a letter Hopkins explained *shook foil* (line 2): "I mean foil in its sense of leaf or tinsel. . . . Shaken goldfoil gives off broad glares like sheet lightning and also, and this is true of nothing else, owing to its zigzag dints and creasings and network of small many cornered facets, a sort of fork lightning too." What do you think he meant by the phrase *ooze of oil* (line 3)? Would you call this phrase an example of alliteration?

2. What instances of internal rime does the poem contain? How would you describe their effects?

3. Point out some of the poet's uses of alliteration and assonance. Do you believe that Hopkins perhaps goes too far in his heavy use of devices of sound, or would you defend his practice?

4. Why do you suppose Hopkins, in the last two lines, says *over the bent / World* instead of (as we might expect) *bent over the world?* How can the world be bent? Can you make any sense out of this wording, or is Hopkins just trying to get his rime scheme to work out?

Reading Poems Aloud

Thomas Moore's "The light that lies in women's eyes"—a line rich in internal rime, alliteration, and assonance—is harder to forget than "The light burning in the gaze of a woman." Effective on the page, Moore's line becomes even more striking when heard aloud. Practice reading poetry aloud—there is no better way to understand a poem than to effectively read it aloud. Developing skill at reading poems aloud will not only deepen your understanding of literature, it will also improve your ability to speak in public.

    Before trying to read a poem aloud to other people, understand its meaning as thoroughly as possible. If you know what the poet is saying and the poet's attitude toward it, you will be able to find an appropriate tone of voice and to give each part of the poem a proper emphasis.

Read more slowly than you would read aloud from a newspaper. Keep in mind that you are saying something to somebody. Don't race through the poem as if you are eager to get it over with.

Don't lapse into singsong. A poem may have a definite swing, but swing should never be exaggerated at the cost of sense. If you understand what the poem is saying and utter the poem as if you do, the temptation to fall into such a mechanical intonation should not occur. Observe the punctuation, making slight pauses for commas, longer pauses for full stops (periods, question marks, exclamation points).

If the poem is rimed, don't raise your voice and make the rimes stand out unnaturally. They should receive no more volume than other words in the poem, though a faint pause at the end of each line will call the listener's attention to them.

Listening to a poem, especially if it is unfamiliar, calls for concentration. Merciful people seldom read poetry uninterruptedly to anyone for more than a few minutes at a time. Robert Frost, always kind to his audiences, used to intersperse poems with many silences and seemingly casual remarks—shrewdly giving his hearers a chance to rest from their labors and giving his poems a chance to settle in.

EXERCISE: Reading for Sound and Meaning

Read this brief poem aloud. What devices of sound do you find? Try to explain what sound contributes to the total effect of the poem and how it reinforces what the poet is saying.

Michael Stillman (b. 1940)

In Memoriam John Coltrane   1972

Listen to the coal
rolling, rolling through the cold
    steady rain, wheel on

    wheel, listen to the
turning of the wheels this night   5
    black as coal dust, steel

    on steel, listen to
these cars carry coal, listen
    to the coal train roll.

IN MEMORIAM JOHN COLTRANE. John Coltrane (1926–1967) was a saxophonist whose originality, passion, and technical wizardry have had a deep influence on the history of modern jazz.

WRITING EFFECTIVELY

WRITING ABOUT SOUND

Listening to the Music

A poem's music—the distinct way it sounds—is an important element of its effect and a large part of what separates it from prose. Describing a poem's sound can be tricky, though. Even professional critics often disagree about the sonic effects of particular poems.

Cataloguing every auditory element of a poem would be a huge, unwieldy job. The easiest way to write about sound is to focus your discussion. Rather than trying to explain every possible auditory element a poem possesses, concentrate on a single, clearly defined aspect that strikes you as especially noteworthy. Simply try to understand how that sonic element helps communicate the poem's main theme.

You might examine, for example, how certain features (such as rime, rhythm, meter, alliteration, and so forth) add force to the literal meaning of each line. Or, for an ironic poem, you might look at how those same elements undercut and change the surface meaning of the poem.

Keep in mind that for a detailed analysis of this sort, it often helps to choose a short poem. If you want to write about a longer poem, focus on a short passage that strikes you as especially rich in sonic effects.

Let your data build up before you force any conclusions about the poem's auditory effects. As your list grows, a pattern should emerge, and ideas will probably occur to you that were not apparent earlier.

CHECKLIST

Writing About a Poem's Sound

- ✓ List the main auditory elements you find in the poem.
- ✓ Look for rime, meter, alliteration, assonance, euphony, cacophony, repetition, onomatopoeia.
- ✓ Is there a pattern in your list? Is the poem particularly heavy in alliteration or repetition, for example?
- ✓ Limit your discussion to one or two clearly defined sonic effects.
- ✓ How do your chosen effects help communicate the poem's main theme?

WRITING ASSIGNMENT ON SOUND

Choose a brief poem from this chapter or the chapter "Poems for Further Reading" and examine how one or two elements of sound work throughout the poem to strengthen its meaning. Before you write, review the elements of sound described in this chapter. Back up your argument with specific quotations from the poem.

MORE TOPICS FOR WRITING

1. Silently read Sylvia Plath's "Daddy" (in the chapter "Poems for Further Reading"). Now read the poem aloud, to yourself or to a friend. Now write briefly. What did you perceive about the poem from reading it aloud that you hadn't noticed before?

2. Consider the verbal music of Michael Stillman's "In Memoriam John Coltrane" (or a selection from the chapter "Poems for Further Reading"). Read the poem both silently and aloud, listening for sonic effects. Describe how the poem's sound underscores its meaning.

16
Rhythm

Stresses and Pauses

Rhythms affect us powerfully. We are lulled by a hammock's sway, awakened by an alarm clock's repeated yammer. Long after we come home from a beach, the rising and falling of waves and tides continue in memory. How powerfully the rhythms of poetry also move us may be felt in folk songs of railroad workers and chain gangs whose words were chanted in time to the lifting and dropping of a sledgehammer, and in verse that marching soldiers shout, putting a stress on every word that coincides with a footfall:

> Your LEFT! TWO! THREE! FOUR!
> Your LEFT! TWO! THREE! FOUR!
> You LEFT your WIFE and TWEN-ty-one KIDS
> And you LEFT! TWO! THREE! FOUR!
> You'll NEV-er get HOME to-NIGHT!

A rhythm is produced by a series of recurrences: the returns and departures of the seasons, the repetitions of an engine's stroke, the beats of the heart. A rhythm may be produced by the recurrence of a sound (the throb of a drum, a telephone's busy signal), but rhythm and sound are not identical. A totally deaf person at a parade can sense rhythm from the motions of the marchers' arms and feet, from the shaking of the pavement as they tramp. Rhythms inhere in the motions of the moon and stars, even though when they move, we hear no sound.

In poetry, several kinds of recurrent *sound* are possible, including (as we saw in the last chapter) rime, alliteration, and assonance. But most often when we speak of the **rhythm** of a poem, we mean the recurrence of stresses and pauses in it. When we hear a poem read aloud, stresses and pauses are, of course, part of its sound. It is possible to be aware of rhythms in poems read silently, too.

A **stress** (or **accent**) is a greater amount of force given to one syllable in speaking than is given to another. We favor a stressed syllable with a little more breath and emphasis, with the result that it comes out slightly louder, higher in pitch, or longer in duration than other syllables. In this manner we place a stress on the first syllable of words such as *eagle*, *impact*, *open*, and *statue*, and on the second syllable in *cigar*, *mystique*, *precise*, and *until*. Each word in English carries at least one stress, except (usually) for the articles *a*, *an*, and *the*, the conjunction *and*, and one-syllable prepositions: *at*, *by*, *for*, *from*, *of*, *to*, *with*.

Even these, however, take a stress once in a while: "Get WITH it!" "You're not THE Dolly Parton?" One word by itself is seldom long enough for us to notice a rhythm in it. Usually a sequence of at least a few words is needed for stresses to establish their pattern: a line, a passage, a whole poem. Strong rhythms may be seen in most Mother Goose rimes, to which children have been responding for hundreds of years. This rime is for an adult to chant while jogging a child up and down on a knee:

> Here goes my lord
> A trot, a trot, a trot, a trot!
> Here goes my lady
> A canter, a canter, a canter, a canter!
> Here goes my young master
> Jockey-hitch, jockey-hitch, jockey-hitch, jockey-hitch!
> Here goes my young miss
> An amble, an amble, an amble, an amble!
> The footman lags behind to tipple ale and wine
> And goes gallop, a gallop, a gallop, to make up his time.

More than one rhythm occurs in these lines, as the make-believe horse changes pace. How do these rhythms differ? From one line to the next, the interval between stresses lengthens or grows shorter. In "a TROT a TROT a TROT a TROT," the stress falls on every other syllable. But in the middle of the line "A CAN-ter a CAN-ter a CAN-ter a CAN-ter," the stress falls on every third syllable. When stresses recur at fixed intervals as in these lines, the result is called a **meter**. The line "A trot a trot a trot a trot" is in **iambic meter**, a succession of alternate unstressed and stressed syllables.[1] Of all rhythms in the English language, this one is most familiar; most of our traditional poetry is written in it and ordinary speech tends to resemble it.

Stresses embody meanings. Whenever two or more fall side by side, words gain in emphasis. Consider these hard-hitting lines from John Donne, in which accent marks have been placed, dictionary-fashion, to indicate the stressed syllables:

> Bat·ter my heart, three-per·soned God, for You
> As yet but knock, breathe, shine, and seek to mend.
> That I may rise and stand, o'er throw me, and bend
> Your force to break, blow, burn, and make me new.

Unstressed (or **slack**) **syllables** also can direct our attention to what the poet means. In a line containing few stresses and a great many unstressed syllables,

---

[1]Another kind of meter is possible, in which the intervals between stresses vary. This is **accentual meter**, not often found in contemporary poetry. It is discussed in the second part of this chapter.

there can be an effect not of power and force but of hesitation and uncertainty. Yeats asks in "Among School Children" what young mother, if she could see her baby grown to be an old man, would think him:

> A com·pen·sa·tion for the pang of his birth
> Or the un·cer·tain·ty of his set·ting forth?

When unstressed syllables recur in pairs, the result is a rhythm that trips and bounces, as in Robert Service's rollicking line:

> A bunch of the boys were whoop·ing it up in the Ma·la·mute
> sa·loon . . .

or in Poe's lines—also light but meant to be serious:

> For the moon nev·er beams with·out bring·ing me dreams
> Of the beau·ti·ful An·na·bel Lee.

Apart from the words that convey it, the rhythm of a poem has no meaning. There are no essentially sad rhythms, nor any essentially happy ones. But some rhythms enforce certain meanings better than others do. The bouncing rhythm of Service's line seems fitting for an account of a merry night in a Klondike saloon; but it may be distracting when encountered in Poe's wistful elegy.

The special power of poetry comes from allowing us to hear simultaneously every level of meaning in language—denotation and connotation, image and idea, abstract content and physical sound. Since sound stress is one of the ways that the English language most clearly communicates meaning, any regular rhythmic pattern will affect the poem's effect. Poets learn to use rhythms that reinforce the meaning and the tone of a poem. As film directors know, any movie scene's effect can change dramatically if different background music accompanies the images. Master of the suspense film Alfred Hitchcock, for instance, could fill an ordinary scene with tension or terror just by playing nervous, grating music underneath it. We also often notice the powerful effect rhythm has on meaning when an author goes awry and tries to create a particular mood in a manner that seems to pull us in an opposing direction. In Eliza Cook's "Song of the Sea-Weed," for instance, the poet depicts her grim and ghoulish scene in a bouncy ballad meter that makes the tone unintentionally comic:

> Many a lip is gaping for drink,
>   And madly calling for rain;
> And some hot brains are beginning to think
>   Of a messmate's opened vein.

E X E R C I S E : Get with the Beat

In each of the following passages the author has established a strong rhythm. Describe
how the rhythm helps establish the tone and meaning of the poem. How does each
poem's beat seem appropriate to the tone and subject?

1. I sprang to the stirrup, and Joris and he;
   I galloped, Dirck galloped, we galloped all three;
   "Good speed," cried the watch as the gatebolts undrew;
   "Speed!" echoed the wall to us galloping through.
   Behind shut the postern, the lights sank to rest,
   And into the midnight we galloped abreast.
       —Robert Browning, from "How They Brought the
       Good News from Ghent to Aix"

2. I couldn't be cooler, I come from Missoula,
   And I rope and I chew and I ride.
   But I'm a heroin dealer, and I drive a four-wheeler
   With stereo speakers inside.
   My ol' lady Phoebe's out rippin' off C.B.'s
   From the rigs at the Wagon Wheel Bar,
   Near a Montana truck stop and a shit-outta-luck stop
   For a trucker who's driven too far.
       —Greg Keeler, from "There Ain't No Such Thing as a
       Montana Cowboy" (a song lyric)

Rhythms in poetry are due not only to stresses but also to pauses. "Every
nice ear," observed Alexander Pope (*nice* meaning "finely tuned"), "must, I believe, have observed that in any smooth English verse of ten syllables, there is
naturally a pause either at the fourth, fifth, or sixth syllable." Such a light but definite pause within a line is called a **cesura** (or **caesura**), "a cutting." More liber-
ally than Pope, we apply the name to any pause in a line of any length, after any
word in the line. In studying a poem, we often indicate a cesura by double lines
(‖). Usually, a cesura will occur at a mark of punctuation, but there can be a
cesura even if no punctuation is present. Sometimes you will find it at the end of
a phrase or clause or, as in these lines by William Blake, after an internal rime:

And priests in black gowns ‖ were walking their rounds
And binding with briars ‖ my joys and desires.

Lines of ten or twelve syllables (as Pope knew) tend to have just one cesura,
though sometimes there are more:

Cover her face: ‖ mine eyes dazzle: ‖ she died young.

Pauses also tend to recur at more prominent places—namely, after each
line. At the end of a verse (from *versus*, "a turning"), the reader's eye, before
turning to go on to the next line, makes a pause, however brief. If a line ends
in a full pause—usually indicated by some mark of punctuation—we call it
end-stopped. All the lines in this passage from Christopher Marlowe's *Doctor*

Faustus (in which Faustus addresses the apparition of Helen of Troy) are end-stopped:

> Was this the face that launch'd a thousand ships,
> And burnt the topless towers of Ilium?
> Sweet Helen, make me immortal with a kiss.
> Her lips suck forth my soul: see, where it flies!
> Come, Helen, come, give me my soul again.
> Here will I dwell, for heaven is in these lips,
> And all is dross that is not Helena.

A line that does not end in punctuation and that therefore is read with only a slight pause after it is called a **run-on line**. Because a run-on line gives us only part of a phrase, clause, or sentence, we have to read on to the line or lines following, in order to complete a thought. All these lines from Robert Browning's "My Last Duchess" are run-on lines:

> Sir, 'twas not
> Her husband's presence only, called that spot
> Of joy into the Duchess' cheek: perhaps
> Frà Pandolf chanced to say "Her mantle laps
> Over my lady's wrist too much," or "Paint
> Must never hope to reproduce the faint
> Half-flush that dies along her throat." Such stuff
> Was courtesy, she thought . . .

A passage in run-on lines has a rhythm different from that of a passage like Marlowe's in end-stopped lines. When emphatic pauses occur in the quotation from Browning, they fall within a line rather than at the end of one. The passage by Marlowe and that by Browning are in lines of the same meter (iambic) and the same length (ten syllables). What makes the big difference in their rhythms is the running on, or lack of it.

To sum up: rhythm is recurrence. In poems, it is made of stresses and pauses. The poet can produce it by doing any of several things: making the intervals between stresses fixed or varied, long or short; indicating pauses (cesuras) within lines; end-stopping lines or running them over; writing in short or long lines. Rhythm in itself cannot convey meaning. And yet if a poet's words have meaning, their rhythm must be one with it.

Gwendolyn Brooks (1917–2000)

We Real Cool   1960

The Pool Players.
Seven at the Golden Shovel.

We real cool. We
Left school. We

Lurk late. We
Strike straight. We

Sing sin. We   5
Thin gin. We

Jazz June. We
Die soon.

QUESTION

Describe the rhythms of this poem. By what techniques are they produced?

Alfred, Lord Tennyson (1809–1892)

Break, Break, Break   (1834)

Break, break, break,
　On thy cold gray stones, O Sea!
And I would that my tongue could utter
　The thoughts that arise in me.

O well for the fisherman's boy,   5
　That he shouts with his sister at play!
O well for the sailor lad,
　That he sings in his boat on the bay!

And the stately ships go on
　To their haven under the hill;   10
But O for the touch of a vanish'd hand,
　And the sound of a voice that is still!

Break, break, break,
　At the foot of thy crags, O Sea!
But the tender grace of a day that is dead   15
　Will never come back to me.

QUESTIONS

1. Read the first line aloud. What effect does it create at the beginning of the poem?
2. Is there a regular rhythmic pattern in this poem? If so, how would you describe it?
3. The speaker claims that his or her thoughts are impossible to utter. Using evidence from the poem, can you describe the speaker's thoughts and feelings?

Ben Jonson (1573–1637)

Slow, slow, fresh fount, keep time with my salt tears   1600

Slow, slow, fresh fount, keep time with my salt tears;
  Yet slower yet, oh faintly, gentle springs;
List to the heavy part the music bears,
  Woe weeps out her division° when she sings.   *a part in a song*
    Droop herbs and flowers,   5
    Fall grief in showers;
    Our beauties are not ours;
      Oh, I could still,
Like melting snow upon some craggy hill,
  Drop, drop, drop, drop,   10
Since nature's pride is now a withered daffodil.

SLOW, SLOW, FRESH FOUNT. The nymph Echo sings this lament over the youth Narcissus in Jonson's play *Cynthia's Revels*. In mythology, Nemesis, goddess of vengeance, to punish Narcissus for loving his own beauty, caused him to pine away and then transformed him into a narcissus (another name for a *daffodil*, line 11).

QUESTIONS

1. Read the first line aloud rapidly. Why is it difficult to do so?
2. Which lines rely most heavily on stressed syllables?
3. In general, how would you describe the rhythm of this poem? How is it appropriate to what is said?

Dorothy Parker (1893–1967)

Résumé   1926

Razors pain you;
Rivers are damp;
Acids stain you;
And drugs cause cramp.
Guns aren't lawful;   5
Nooses give;
Gas smells awful;
You might as well live.

Meter

To enjoy the rhythms of a poem, no special knowledge of meter is necessary. All you need do is pay attention to stresses and where they fall, and you will perceive the basic pattern, if there is any. There is nothing occult about the study of meter. Most people find they can master its essentials in no more time than it takes to learn a game such as chess. If you take the time, you will then have the pleasure of knowing what is happening in the rhythms of many a fine poem, and pleasurable knowledge may even deepen your insight into poetry. The following discussion will be of interest only to those who care to go deeper into **prosody**, the study of metrical structures in poetry.

Far from being artificial constructions found only in the minds of poets, meters occur in everyday speech and prose. As the following example will show, they may need only a poet to recognize them. The English satirist Max Beerbohm, after contemplating the title page of his first book, took his pen and added two more lines.

Max Beerbohm (1872–1956)

On the imprint of the first   (1896)
English edition of
The Works of Max Beerbohm

"London: JOHN LANE, *The Bodley Head*
   New York: Charles Scribner's Sons."
This plain announcement, nicely read,
   Iambically runs.

In everyday life, nobody speaks or writes in perfect iambic rhythm, except at moments: "a HAM on RYE and HIT the MUStard HARD!" (As we have seen, iambic rhythm consists of a series of syllables alternately unstressed and stressed.) Poets rarely speak in it for long, either—at least, not with absolute consistency. Reading Max Beerbohm's lines aloud, you'll hear an iambic rhythm, but not an unvarying one. Yet all of us speak with a rising and falling of stress *somewhat like* iambic meter. As the poet and scholar John Thompson has maintained, "The iambic metrical pattern has dominated English verse because it provides the best symbolic model of our language."[2]

To make ourselves aware of a meter, we need only listen to a poem, or sound its words to ourselves. If we care to work out exactly what a poet is doing, we *scan* a line or a poem by indicating the stresses in it. **Scansion**, the art

---

[2]*The Founding of English Metre* (New York: Columbia UP, 1966) 12.

of so doing, is not just a matter of pointing to syllables; it is also a matter of listening to a poem and making sense of it. To scan a poem is one way to indicate how to read it aloud; in order to see where stresses fall, you have to see the places where the poet wishes to put emphasis. That is why, when scanning a poem, you may find yourself suddenly understanding it.

To scan a poem is to make a diagram of the stresses (and absences of stress) we find in it. Various marks are used in scansion; in this book we use ´ for a stressed syllable and ˘ for an unstressed syllable. There are four common accentual-syllabic meters in English—iambic, anapestic, trochaic, and dactylic. Each is named for its basic **foot** (usually a unit of two or three syllables that contains one strong stress) or building block. Here are some examples of each meter.

1. **Iambic**—a line made up primarily of **iambs**, an unstressed syllable followed by a stressed syllable, ˘ ´. The iambic measure is the most common meter in English poetry. Many writers, such as Robert Frost, feel iambs most easily capture the natural rhythms of our speech.

    > ˘ ´ | ˘ ´ | ˘ ´ | ˘ ´ | ˘ ´
    > But soft, | what light | through yon | der win | dow breaks?
    > —*William Shakespeare*

    > ˘ ´ | ˘ ´ | ˘ ´ | ˘ ´ | ˘ ´
    > When I | have fears | that I | may cease | to be
    > —*John Keats*

2. **Anapestic**—a line made up primarily of **anapests**, two unstressed syllables followed by a stressed syllable, ˘ ˘ ´. Anapestic meter resembles iambic but contains an extra unstressed syllable. Totally anapestic lines often start to gallop, so poets sometimes slow them down by substituting an iambic foot (as Poe does in "Annabel Lee").

    > ˘ ´ | ˘ ˘ ´ | ˘ ˘ ´ | ˘ ˘ ´ | ˘ ˘ ´
    > Now this | is the Law | of the Jun | gle—as old | and as true
    > ˘ ˘ ´
    > | as the sky
    > ˘ ˘ ´ | ˘ ˘ ´ | ˘ ˘ ´ | ˘ ˘
    > And the Wolf | that shall keep | it may pros | per,
    > ˘ ˘ ´ | ˘ ˘ ´ | ˘ ˘ ´
    > | but the wolf | that shall break | it must die.
    > —*Rudyard Kipling*

    > ˘ ˘ ´ | ˘ ˘ ´ | ˘ ˘ ´ | ˘ ´
    > It was ma | ny and ma | ny a year | a go
    > ˘ ˘ ´ | ˘ ´ | ˘ ´
    > In a king | dom by | the sea

˘ ˘ ´ | ˘ ˘ ˘ ´ | ˘ ˘ ´ | ˘ ˘ ´
That a maid | en there lived | whom you | may know
˘ ˘ ´ | ˘ ´ | ˘ ˘ ´
By the name | of An | na·bel Lee.
—*Edgar Allan Poe*

3. **Trochaic**—a line made up primarily of **trochees**, a stressed syllable followed by an unstressed syllable, ´˘. The trochaic meter is often associated with songs, chants, and magic spells in English. Trochees make a strong, emphatic meter that is often very mnemonic. Shakespeare used trochaic meter to exploit its magical associations.

´ ˘ | ´ ˘ | ´ ˘ | ´ ˘
Dou·ble, | dou·ble, | toil and | trou·ble
´ ˘ | ´ ˘ | ´ ˘ | ´ ˘
Fi·re | burn and | caul·dron | bub·ble.
—*Shakespeare*

4. **Dactylic**—a line made up primarily of **dactyls**, one stressed syllable followed by two unstressed syllables, ´˘˘. The dactylic meter is less common in English than in classical languages like Greek or Latin. Used carefully, dactylic meter can sound stately, as in Longfellow's *Evangeline*, but it also easily becomes a prancing, propulsive measure and is often used in comic verse. Poets often drop the unstressed syllables at the end of a dactylic line, the omission usually being noted with a caret sign, ˇ.

´ ˘ ˘ | ´ ˘ ˘ | ´ ˘ ˘ | ´ ˘ ˘
This is the | for·est pri | me·val. The | mur·mur·ing
´ ˘ ˘ | ´ ˘ ˘
| pines and the | hem·lock
—*Henry Wadsworth Longfellow*

´ ˘ ˘ | ´ ˘ ˘ | ´ ˘ ˘ | ´ ˇ
Puss·y·cat, | puss·y·cat, | where have you | been?
—*Mother Goose*

Iambic and anapestic meters are called **rising** meters because their movement rises from an unstressed syllable (or syllables) to stress; trochaic and dactylic meters are called **falling**. In the twentieth century, the bouncing meters—anapestic and dactylic—were used more often for comic verse than for serious poetry. Called feet, though they contain no unaccented syllables, are the **monosyllabic foot** (´) and the **spondee** (´´). Meters are not ordinarily made up of them; if one were, it would be like the steady impact of nails being hammered into a board—no pleasure to hear or to dance to. But inserted now and then, they can lend emphasis and variety to a meter, as Yeats well knew when he broke up the predominantly iambic rhythm of "Who Goes with Fergus?" (page 417) with the line

    ˘   ˘   ´   ´ ˘ ˘ ´ ´
And the white breast of the dim sea,

in which two spondees occur. Meters are classified also by line lengths: *trochaic monometer*, for instance, is a line one trochee long, as in this anonymous brief comment on microbes:

> Adam
> Had 'em.

A frequently heard metrical description is **iambic pentameter**: a line of five iambs, a meter especially familiar because it occurs in all blank verse (such as Shakespeare's plays and Milton's *Paradise Lost*), heroic couplets, and sonnets. The commonly used names for line lengths follow:

monometer	one foot
dimeter	two feet
trimeter	three feet
tetrameter	four feet
pentameter	five feet
hexameter	six feet
heptameter	seven feet
octameter	eight feet

Lines of more than eight feet are possible but are rare. They tend to break up into shorter lengths in the listening ear.

Like a basic dance step, a meter is not to be slavishly adhered to. The fun in reading a metrical poem often comes from watching the poet continually departing from perfect regularity, giving a few heel-kicks to display a bit of joy or ingenuity, then easing back into the basic step again. Because meter is orderly and the rhythms of living speech are unruly, poets can play one against the other, in a sort of counterpoint. Robert Frost, a master at pitting a line of iambs against a very natural-sounding and irregular sentence, declared, "I am never more pleased than when I can get these into strained relation. I like to drag and break the intonation across the meter as waves first comb and then break stumbling on a shingle."[3]

Besides the two rising meters (iambic, anapestic) and the two falling meters (trochaic, dactylic), English poets have another valuable meter. It is **accentual meter**, in which the poet does not write in feet (as in the other meters) but

[3]Letter to John Cournos in 1914, in *Selected Letters of Robert Frost*, ed. Lawrance Thompson (New York: Holt, 1964) 128.

instead counts accents (stresses). The idea is to have the same number of stresses in every line. The poet may place them anywhere in the line and may include practically any number of unstressed syllables, which do not count. In "Christabel," for instance, Coleridge keeps four stresses to a line, though the first line has only eight syllables and the last line has eleven:

> There is not wind e·nough to twirl
> The one red leaf, the last of its clan,
> That dan·ces as of·ten as dance it can,
> Hang·ing so light, and hang·ing so high,
> On the top·most twig that looks up at the sky.

Although less popular among poets today than formerly, meter endures. Major poets from Shakespeare through Yeats have fashioned their work by it, and if we are to read their poems with full enjoyment, we need to be aware of it. To enjoy metrical poetry—even to write it—you do not have to slice lines into feet; you do need to recognize when a meter is present in a line, and when the line departs from it. An argument in favor of meter is that it reminds us of body rhythms such as breathing, walking, the beating of the heart. In an effective metrical poem, these rhythms cannot be separated from what the poet is saying—or, in the words of an old jazz song of Duke Ellington's, "It don't mean a thing if it ain't got that swing." As critic Paul Fussell has put it: "No element of a poem is more basic—and I mean physical—in its effect upon the reader than the metrical element, and perhaps no technical triumphs reveal more readily than the metrical the poet's sympathy with that universal human nature . . . which exists outside his own."[4]

EXERCISE: Recognizing Rhythms

Which of the following poems contain predominant meters? Which poems are not wholly metrical, but are metrical in certain lines? Point out any such lines. What reasons do you see, in such places, for the poet's seeking a metrical effect?

Edna St. Vincent Millay (1892–1950)

Counting-out Rhyme   1928

Silver bark of beech, and sallow
Bark of yellow birch and yellow
    Twig of willow.

---

[4]*Poetic Meter and Poetic Form* (New York: Random, 1965) 110.

Stripe of green in moosewood maple,
Color seen in leaf of apple,
  Bark of popple. 5

Wood of popple pale as moonbeam,
Wood of oak for yoke and barn-beam,
  Wood of hornbeam.

Silver bark of beech, and hollow
Stem of elder, tall and yellow 10
  Twig of willow.

A. E. Housman (1859–1936)

When I was one-and-twenty 1896

When I was one-and-twenty
  I heard a wise man say,
"Give crowns and pounds and guineas
  But not your heart away;
Give pearls away and rubies 5
  But keep your fancy free."
But I was one-and-twenty,
  No use to talk to me.

When I was one-and-twenty
  I heard him say again, 10
"The heart out of the bosom
  Was never given in vain;
'Tis paid with sighs a plenty
  And sold for endless rue."
And I am two-and-twenty, 15
  And oh, 'tis true, 'tis true.

William Carlos Williams (1883–1963)

Smell! 1917

Oh strong-ridged and deeply hollowed
nose of mine! what will you not be smelling?
What tactless asses we are, you and I, boney nose,
always indiscriminate, always unashamed,
and now it is the souring flowers of the bedraggled 5

poplars: a festering pulp on the wet earth
beneath them. With what deep thirst
we quicken our desires
to that rank odor of a passing springtime!
Can you not be decent? Can you not reserve your ardors   10
for something less unlovely? What girl will care
for us, do you think, if we continue in these ways?
Must you taste everything? Must you know everything?
Must you have a part in everything?

Walt Whitman (1819–1892)

Beat! Beat! Drums!   (1861)

Beat! beat! drums!—blow! bugles! blow!
Through the windows—through doors—burst like a ruthless force,
Into the solemn church, and scatter the congregation,
Into the school where the scholar is studying;
Leave not the bridegroom quiet—no happiness must he have now
    with his bride,   5
Nor the peaceful farmer any peace, ploughing his field or gathering
    his grain,
So fierce you whirr and pound you drums—so shrill you bugles blow.

Beat! beat! drums!—blow! bugles! blow!
Over the traffic of cities—over the rumble of wheels in the streets;
Are beds prepared for sleepers at night in the houses? no sleepers
    must sleep in those beds,   10
No bargainer's bargains by day—no brokers or speculators—would
    they continue?
Would the talkers be talking? would the singer attempt to sing?
Would the lawyer rise in the court to state his case before the judge?
Then rattle quicker, heavier drums—you bugles wilder blow.

Beat! beat! drums!—blow! bugles! blow!   15
Make no parley—stop for no expostulation,
Mind not the timid—mind not the weeper or prayer,
Mind not the old man beseeching the young man,
Let not the child's voice be heard, nor the mother's entreaties,
Make even the trestles to shake the dead where they lie awaiting
    the hearses.   20
So strong you thump O terrible drums—so loud you bugles blow.

David Mason (b. 1954)

Song of the Powers 1996

Mine, said the stone,
mine is the hour.
I crush the scissors,
such is my power.
Stronger than wishes,   5
my power, alone.

Mine, said the paper,
mine are the words
that smother the stone
with imagined birds,   10
reams of them, flown
from the mind of the shaper.

Mine, said the scissors,
mine all the knives
gashing through paper's   15
ethereal lives;
nothing's so proper
as tattering wishes.

As stone crushes scissors,
as paper snuffs stone   20
and scissors cut paper,
all end alone.
So heap up your paper
and scissor your wishes
and uproot the stone   25
from the top of the hill.
They all end alone
as you will, you will.

SONG OF THE POWERS. The three key images of this poem are drawn from the children's game of Scissors, Paper, Stone. In this game each object has a specific power: Scissors cuts paper, paper covers stone, and stone crushes scissors.

WRITING EFFECTIVELY

WRITING ABOUT RHYTHM

Freeze-Framing the Sound

A casual reader doesn't need to think very hard about a poem's rhythm. We *feel* it as we read, even if we aren't consciously paying attention to matters like iambs or anapests. When we write about a poem, though, it helps to have a clear sense of how the rhythm works, and the best way to reach that understanding is through scansion. A scansion gives us a freeze-frame of the poem's most important sound patterns, mainly by indicating which syllables are stressed and which are unstressed.

Scanning a poem can seem a bit intimidating at first, but it really isn't all that difficult. It helps to read the poem aloud, marking up the page as you go. If you're having a hard time hearing the stresses, read the line a few different ways and try to detect which way seems most like natural speech.

A simple scansion of the opening of Tennyson's poem "Break, Break, Break" (on page 434) might look like this in your notes:

Break, break, break	(3 syllables)
On thy cold gray stones, o sea	(7 syllables)/rime
And I would that my tongue could utter	(9 syllables)
The thoughts that arise in me.	(7 syllables)/rime

By now some basic organizing principles of the poem have become clear. The lines are rimed *a b c b*, but they contain an irregular number of syllables. The number of strong stresses, however, seems to be constant, at least in the opening stanza.

Now that you have a visual diagram of the poem's sound, the rhythm will be much easier to write about.

CHECKLIST

Scanning a Poem

✓ Copy down the passage you plan to analyze. Leave plenty of space between the lines.

✓ Read the poem aloud.

✓ Mark the syllables on which the main speech stresses fall.

✓ When in doubt, read the line aloud several different ways. Which way seems most natural?

✓ Make notes in the margin about any other sonic effects you notice.

✓ Are there rimes? Indicate where they occur.

✓ How many syllables are there in each line?

✓ Do any other recurring sound patterns strike you?

✓ Does the poem set up a reliable pattern and then diverge from it anywhere? If so, how does that irregularity underscore the line's meaning?

WRITING ASSIGNMENT ON RHYTHM

Scan the rhythm of a passage from any poem in this chapter, following the guidelines listed above. Discuss how the poem uses rhythm to create certain key effects. Be sure that your scansion shows all the elements you've chosen to discuss.

MORE TOPICS FOR WRITING

1. How do rhythm and other kinds of sonic effects (alliteration and consonance, for example) combine to make meaning in Edna St. Vincent Millay's "Counting-out Rhyme"?

2. Scan a stanza of Walt Whitman's "Beat! Beat! Drums!" What do you notice about the poem's rhythms? How do the rhythms underscore the poem's meaning?

3. Scan two poems, one in free verse, and the other in regular meter. (For a free verse poem you might pick William Carlos Williams's "Smell!" or Allen Ginsberg's "A Supermarket in California" (page 516); for a poem in regular meter you could go with A. E. Housman's "When I was one-and-twenty" or David Mason's "Song of the Powers." Now write about the experience. Do you detect any particular strengths offered by regular meter? How about by free verse?

4. Robert Frost once claimed he tried to make poetry out of the "sound of sense." Writing to a friend, Frost discussed his notion that "the simple declarative sentence" in English often contained an abstract sound that helped communicate its meaning. "The best place to get the abstract sound of sense," wrote Frost, "is from voices behind a door that cuts off the words." Ask yourself how these sentences of dialogue would sound without the words in which they are embodied:

   You mean to tell me you can't read?
   I said no such thing.
   Well, read then.
   You're not my teacher.

   Frost went on to say that "The reader must be at no loss to give his voice the posture proper to the sentence." Thinking about Frost's theory, can you see how it throws any light on one of his poems? In two or three paragraphs, discuss how Frost uses the "simple declarative sentence" as a distinctive rhythmic feature in his poetry.

17
Closed Form

Form, as a general idea, is the design of a thing as a whole, the configuration of all its parts. No poem can escape having some kind of form, whether its lines are as various in length as broomstraws or all in hexameter. To put this point in another way: if you were to listen to a poem read aloud in a language unknown to you, or if you saw the poem printed in that foreign language, whatever in the poem you could see or hear would be the form of it.[1]

Writing in **closed form,** a poet follows (or finds) some sort of pattern, such as that of a sonnet with its rime scheme and its fourteen lines of iambic pentameter. On a page, poems in closed form tend to look regular and symmetrical, often falling into stanzas that indicate groups of rimes. Along with William Butler Yeats, who held that a successful poem will "come shut with a click, like a closing box," the poet who writes in closed form apparently strives for a kind of perfection—seeking, perhaps, to lodge words so securely in place that no word can be budged without a worsening. For the sake of meaning, though, a competent poet often will depart from a symmetrical pattern. As Robert Frost observed, there is satisfaction to be found in things not mechanically regular: "We enjoy the straight crookedness of a good walking stick."

The poet who writes in **open form** usually seeks no final click. Often, such a poet views the writing of a poem as a process, rather than a quest for an absolute. Free to use white space for emphasis, able to shorten or lengthen lines as the sense seems to require, the poet lets the poem discover its shape as it goes along, moving as water flows downhill, adjusting to its terrain, engulfing obstacles. (Open form will provide the focus of the next chapter.)

Most poetry of the past is in closed form, exhibiting at least a pattern of rime or meter, but since the early 1960s the majority of American poets have preferred forms that stay open. Lately, the situation has been changing yet again, with closed form reappearing in much recent poetry. Whatever the fashion of the moment, the reader who seeks a wide understanding of poetry of both the present and the past will need to know both the closed and open varieties.

---

[1]For a good summary of the uses of the term *form* in criticism of poetry, see the article "Form" by G. N. G. Orsini in *Princeton Encyclopedia of Poetry and Poetics,* 2nd ed., ed. Preminger, Warnke, and Hardison (Princeton: Princeton UP, 1975).

Closed form gives some poems a valuable advantage: it makes them more easily memorable. The **epic** poems of nations—long narratives tracing the adventures of popular heroes: the Greek *Iliad* and *Odyssey*, the French *Song of Roland*, the Spanish *Cid*—tend to occur in patterns of fairly consistent line length or number of stresses because these works were sometimes transmitted orally. Sung to the music of a lyre or chanted to a drumbeat, they may have been easier to memorize because of their patterns. If a singer forgot something, the song would have a noticeable hole in it, so rime or fixed meter probably helped prevent an epic from deteriorating when passed along from one singer to another. It is no coincidence that so many English playwrights of Shakespeare's day favored iambic pentameter. Companies of actors, often called on to perform a different play each day, could count on a fixed line length to aid their burdened memories.

Some poets complain that closed form is a straitjacket, a limit to free expression. Other poets, however, feel that, like fires held fast in a narrow space, thoughts stated in a tightly binding form may take on a heightened intensity. "Limitation makes for power," according to one contemporary practitioner of closed form, Richard Wilbur; "the strength of the genie comes of his being confined in a bottle." Compelled by some strict pattern to arrange and rearrange words, delete, and exchange them, poets must focus on them the keenest attention. Often they stand a chance of discovering words more meaningful than the ones they started out with. And at times, in obedience to a rime scheme, the poet may be surprised by saying something quite unexpected. With the conscious portion of the mind, the poet may wish to express what seems to be a good idea. But a line ending in *year* must be followed by another ending in *atmosphere, beer, bier, bombardier, cashier, deer, friction-gear, frontier*, or some other rime word that otherwise might not have entered the poem. That is why rime schemes and stanza patterns can be mighty allies and valuable disturbers of the unconscious. As Rolfe Humphries has said about strict form: "It makes you think of better things than you would all by yourself."

Formal Patterns

The best-known one-line pattern for a poem in English is **blank verse**: unrimed iambic pentameter. (This pattern is not a stanza: stanzas have more than one line.) Most portions of Shakespeare's plays are in blank verse, and so are Milton's *Paradise Lost*, Tennyson's "Ulysses," certain dramatic monologues of Browning and Frost, and thousands of other poems. Here is a poem in blank verse that startles us by dropping out of its pattern in the final line. Keats appears to have written it late in his life to his fiancée, Fanny Brawne.

John Keats (1795–1821)

This living hand, now warm and capable (1819?)

This living hand, now warm and capable
Of earnest grasping, would, if it were cold
And in the icy silence of the tomb,
So haunt thy days and chill thy dreaming nights
That thou wouldst wish thine own heart dry of blood   5
So in my veins red life might stream again,
And thou be conscience-calmed—see here it is—
I hold it towards you.

The **couplet** is a two-line stanza, usually rimed. Its lines often tend to be equal in length, whether short or long. Here are two examples:

Blow,
Snow!

As I in hoary winter's night stood shivering in the snow,
Surprised I was with sudden heat which made my heart to glow.

Actually, any pair of rimed lines that contains a complete thought is called a couplet, even if it is not a stanza, such as the couplet that ends a sonnet by Shakespeare. Unlike other stanzas, couplets are often printed solid, one couplet not separated from the next by white space. This practice is usual in printing the **heroic couplet**—or **closed couplet**—two rimed lines of iambic pentameter, the first ending in a light pause, the second more heavily end-stopped. George Crabbe, in *The Parish Register*, described a shotgun wedding:

Next at our altar stood a luckless pair,
Brought by strong passions and a warrant there:
By long rent cloak, hung loosely, strove the bride,
From every eye, what all perceived, to hide;
While the boy bridegroom, shuffling in his place,
Now hid awhile and then exposed his face.
As shame alternately with anger strove
The brain confused with muddy ale to move,
In haste and stammering he performed his part,
And looked the rage that rankled in his heart.

Though employed by Chaucer, the heroic couplet was named from its later use by Dryden and others in poems, translations of classical epics, and verse plays of epic heroes. It continued in favor through most of the eighteenth century. Much of our pleasure in reading good heroic couplets comes from the seemingly easy precision with which a skilled poet unites statements and strict pattern. In doing so, the poet may place a pair of words, phrases, clauses, or sentences side by side in agreement or similarity, forming a **parallel**, or in contrast and opposition, forming an **antithesis**. The effect is neat. For such skill in manipulating parallels and antitheses, John Denham's lines on the river Thames were much admired:

> O could I flow like thee, and make thy stream
> My great example, as it is my theme!
> Though deep, yet clear; though gentle, yet not dull;
> Strong without rage, without o'erflowing full.

These lines were echoed by Pope, ridiculing a poetaster, in two heroic couplets in *The Dunciad*:

> Flow, Welsted, flow! like thine inspirer, Beer:
> Though stale, not ripe; though thin, yet never clear;
> So sweetly mawkish, and so smoothly dull;
> Heady, not strong; o'erflowing, though not full.

Reading long poems in so exact a form, one may feel like a spectator at a Ping-Pong match, unless the poet skillfully keeps varying rhythms. One way of escaping such metronome-like monotony is to keep the cesura (see page 432) shifting about from place to place—now happening early in a line, now happening late—and at times unexpectedly to hurl in a second or third cesura.

A **tercet** is a group of three lines. If rimed, they usually keep to one rime sound, as in this anonymous English children's jingle:

> Julius Caesar,
> The Roman geezer,
> Squashed his wife with a lemon-squeezer.

(That, by the way, is a great demonstration of surprising and unpredictable rimes.) **Terza rima**, the form Dante employs in *The Divine Comedy*, is made of tercets linked together by the rime scheme *a b a, b c b, c d c, d e d, e f e*, and so on. Harder to do in English than in Italian—with its greater resources of riming words—the form nevertheless has been managed by Shelley in "Ode to the West Wind" (with the aid of some slant rimes):

> Make me thy lyre, even as the forest is:
> What if my leaves are falling like its own!
> The tumult of thy mighty harmonies
>
> Will take from both a deep, autumnal tone,
> Sweet though in sadness. Be thou, spirit fierce,
> My spirit! Be thou me, impetuous one!

The workhorse of English poetry is the **quatrain**, a stanza consisting of four lines. Quatrains are used in more rimed poems than any other form.

Robert Graves (1895–1985)

Counting the Beats 1959

You, love, and I,
(He whispers) you and I,
And if no more than only you and I
What care you or I?

Counting the beats,   5
Counting the slow heart beats,
The bleeding to death of time in slow heart beats,
Wakeful they lie.

Cloudless day,
Night, and a cloudless day,   10
Yet the huge storm will burst upon their heads one day
From a bitter sky.

Where shall we be,
(She whispers) where shall we be,
When death strikes home, O where then shall we be   15
Who were you and I?

Not there but here,
(He whispers) only here,
As we are, here, together, now and here,
Always you and I.   20

Counting the beats,
Counting the slow heart beats,
The bleeding to death of time in slow heart beats,
Wakeful they lie.

QUESTIONS

What elements of sound and rhythm are consistent from stanza to stanza? Do any features change unpredictably from stanza to stanza?

Quatrains come in many line lengths, and sometimes contain lines of varying length, as in the ballad stanza. Most often, poets rime the second and fourth lines of quatrains, as in the ballad, but the rimes can occur in any combination the poet chooses. Longer and more complicated stanzas are, of course, possible, but couplet, tercet, and quatrain have been called the building blocks of our poetry because most longer stanzas are made up of them. What short stanzas does John Donne mortar together to make the longer stanza of his "Song"?

John Donne (1572–1631)

Song   1633

Go and catch a falling star,
  Get with child a mandrake root,
Tell me where all past years are,
  Or who cleft the Devil's foot,
Teach me to hear mermaids singing,   5
  Or to keep off envy's stinging,
      And find
      What wind
Serves to advance an honest mind.

If thou be'st borne to strange sights,   10
  Things invisible to see,
Ride ten thousand days and nights,
  Till age snow white hairs on thee,
Thou, when thou return'st, wilt tell me
  All strange wonders that befell thee,   15
      And swear
      Nowhere
Lives a woman true, and fair.

If thou findst one, let me know,
  Such a pilgrimage were sweet—   20
Yet do not, I would not go,
  Though at next door we might meet;
Though she were true, when you met her,
  And last, till you write your letter,
      Yet she   25
      Will be
False, ere I come, to two, or three.

Ballads

Any narrative song may be called a **ballad**. In English, some of the most famous ballads are **folk ballads**, loosely defined as anonymous story-songs transmitted orally before they were ever written down. Sir Walter Scott, a pioneer collector of Scottish folk ballads, drew the ire of an old woman whose songs he had transcribed: "They were made for singing and no' for reading, but ye ha'e broken the charm now and they'll never be sung mair." The old singer had a point. Print freezes songs and tends to hold them fast to a single version.

If Scott and others had not written them down, however, many would have been lost.

Anonymous (traditional Scottish ballad)

Bonny Barbara Allan

It was in and about the Martinmas time,
   When the green leaves were afalling,
That Sir John Graeme, in the West Country,
   Fell in love with Barbara Allan.

He sent his men down through the town,   5
   To the place where she was dwelling;
"O haste and come to my master dear,
   Gin° ye be Barbara Allan."   *if*

O hooly,° hooly rose she up,   *slowly*
   To the place where he was lying,   10
And when she drew the curtain by:
   "Young man, I think you're dying."

"O it's I'm sick, and very, very sick,
   And 'tis a' for Barbara Allan."—
"O the better for me ye's never be,   15
   Tho your heart's blood were aspilling.

"O dinna ye mind,° young man," said she,   *don't you remember*
   "When ye was in the tavern adrinking,
That ye made the health° gae round and round,   *toasts*
   And slighted Barbara Allan?"   20

He turned his face unto the wall,
   And death was with him dealing:
"Adieu, adieu, my dear friends all,
   And be kind to Barbara Allan."

And slowly, slowly raise she up,   25
   And slowly, slowly left him,
And sighing said she could not stay,
   Since death of life had reft him.

She had not gane a mile but twa,
   When she heard the dead-bell ringing,   30
And every jow° that the dead-bell geid,   *stroke*
   It cried, "Woe to Barbara Allan!"

"O mother, mother, make my bed!
  O make it saft and narrow!
Since my love died for me today,   35
  I'll die for him tomorrow."

BONNY BARBARA ALLAN. 1 *Martinmas:* Saint Martin's Day, November 11.

QUESTIONS

1. In any line does the Scottish dialect cause difficulty? If so, try reading the line aloud.
2. Without ever coming out and explicitly calling Barbara hard-hearted, this ballad reveals that she is. In which stanza and by what means is her cruelty demonstrated?
3. At what point does Barbara evidently have a change of heart? Again, how does the poem dramatize this change without explicitly talking about it?
4. Paraphrase lines 9, 15–16, 22, 25–28. By putting these lines into prose, what has been lost?

As you can see from "Bonny Barbara Allan," in a traditional English or Scottish folk ballad the storyteller speaks of the lives and feelings of others. Even if the pronoun "I" occurs, it rarely has much personality. Characters often exchange dialogue, but no one character speaks all the way through. Events move rapidly, perhaps because some of the dull transitional stanzas have been forgotten.

A favorite pattern of ballad-makers is the so-called **ballad stanza,** four lines rimed *a b c b*, tending to fall into 8, 6, 8, and 6 syllables:

> Clerk Saunders and Maid Margaret
>   Walked owre yon garden green,
> And deep and heavy was the love
>   That fell thir twa between.°   *between those two*

Though not the only possible stanza for a ballad, this easily singable quatrain has continued to attract poets since the Middle Ages. Close kin to the ballad stanza is **common meter**, a stanza found in hymns such as "Amazing Grace," by the eighteenth-century English hymnist John Newton:

> Amazing grace! how sweet the sound
>   That saved a wretch like me!
> I once was lost, but now am found,
>   Was blind, but now I see.

Notice that its pattern is that of the ballad stanza except for its *two* pairs of rimes. That all its lines rime is probably a sign of more literate artistry than we usually hear in folk ballads. Another sign of schoolteachers' influence is that Newton's rimes are exact. (Rimes in folk ballads are often rough-and-ready, as if made by ear, rather than polished and exact, as if the riming words had been matched for their similar spellings. In "Barbara Allan," for instance, the hard-hearted lover's name rimes with *afalling, dwelling, aspilling, dealing,* and even with *ringing* and *adrinking.*) That so many hymns were written in common meter may have been due to convenience. If a congregation didn't know the tune to a hymn in common meter, they readily could sing its words to the tune of another such hymn they knew. Besides hymnists, many poets have favored common meter, among them A. E. Housman and Emily Dickinson.

Literary ballads, not meant for singing, are written by sophisticated poets for book-educated readers who enjoy being reminded of folk ballads. Literary ballads imitate certain features of folk ballads: they may tell of dramatic conflicts or of mortals who encounter the supernatural; they may use conventional figures of speech or ballad stanzas. Well-known poems of this kind include Keats's "La Belle Dame sans Merci" (see page 528), Coleridge's "Rime of the Ancient Mariner," and (in our time) Dudley Randall's "Ballad of Birmingham."

Dudley Randall (1914–2000)

Ballad of Birmingham 1966

(On the Bombing of a Church in Birmingham, Alabama, 1963)

"Mother dear, may I go downtown
Instead of out to play,
And march the streets of Birmingham
In a Freedom March today?"

"No, baby, no, you may not go,   5
For the dogs are fierce and wild,
And clubs and hoses, guns and jail
Aren't good for a little child."

"But, mother, I won't be alone.
Other children will go with me,   10
And march the streets of Birmingham
To make our country free."

"No, baby, no, you may not go,
For I fear those guns will fire.
But you may go to church instead   15
And sing in the children's choir."

She has combed and brushed her night-dark hair,
And bathed rose petal sweet,
And drawn white gloves on her small brown hands,
And white shoes on her feet.   20

The mother smiled to know her child
Was in the sacred place,
But that smile was the last smile
To come upon her face.

For when she heard the explosion, 25
Her eyes grew wet and wild.
She raced through the streets of Birmingham
Calling for her child.

She clawed through bits of glass and brick,
Then lifted out a shoe. 30
"O here's the shoe my baby wore,
But, baby, where are you?"

QUESTIONS

1. This poem, about a dynamite blast set off in an African American church by a racial terrorist (later convicted), delivers a message without preaching. How would you sum up this message, its implied theme?
2. What is ironic in the mother's denying her child permission to take part in a protest march?
3. How does this modern poem resemble a traditional ballad?

The Sonnet

When we speak of "traditional verse forms," we usually mean **fixed forms**. If written in a fixed form, a poem inherits from other poems certain familiar elements of structure: an unvarying number of lines, say, or a stanza pattern. In addition, it may display certain **conventions**: expected features such as themes, subjects, attitudes, or figures of speech. In medieval folk ballads a "milk-white steed" is a conventional figure of speech; and if its rider be a cruel and beautiful witch who kidnaps mortals, she is a conventional character. (*Conventional* doesn't necessarily mean uninteresting.)

In the poetry of western Europe and America, the **sonnet** is the fixed form that has attracted for the longest time the largest number of noteworthy practitioners. Originally an Italian form (*sonnetto:* "little song"), the sonnet owes much of its prestige to Petrarch (1304–1374), who wrote in it of his love for the unattainable Laura. So great was the vogue for sonnets in England at the end of the sixteenth century that a gentleman might have been thought a boor if he couldn't turn out a decent one. Not content to adopt merely the sonnet's fourteen-line pattern, English poets also tried on its conventional mask of the tormented lover. They borrowed some of Petrarch's similes (a lover's heart, for instance, is like a storm-tossed boat) and invented others.

Soon after English poets imported the sonnet in the middle of the sixteenth century, they worked out their own rime scheme—one easier for them to follow than Petrarch's, which calls for a greater number of riming words than English can readily provide. (In Italian, according to an exaggerated report, practically everything rimes.) In the following **English sonnet**, sometimes called a **Shakespearean sonnet**, the rimes cohere in four clusters: *a b a b, c d c d, e f e f, g g*. Because a rime scheme tends to shape the poet's statements to it, the English sonnet has three places where the procession of thought is likely to turn in another direction. Within its form, a poet may pursue one idea throughout the three quatrains and then in the couplet end with a surprise.

William Shakespeare (1564–1616)

Let me not to the marriage of true minds

1609

Let me not to the marriage of true minds
Admit impediments; love is not love
Which alters when it alteration finds,
Or bends with the remover to remove.
O, no, it is an ever-fixèd mark   5
That looks on tempests and is never shaken;
It is the star to every wand'ring bark,
Whose worth's unknown, although his height be taken.
Love's not Time's fool, though rosy lips and cheeks
Within his bending sickle's compass° come;   *range*   10
Love alters not with his° brief hours and weeks   *Time's*
But bears° it out even to the edge of doom.   *endures*
     If this be error and upon me proved,
     I never writ, nor no man ever loved.

LET ME NOT TO THE MARRIAGE OF TRUE MINDS. 5 *ever-fixèd mark*: a sea-mark like a beacon or a lighthouse that provides mariners with safe bearings. 7 *the star*: presumably the North Star, which gave sailors the most dependable bearing at sea. 12 *edge of doom*: either the brink of death or—taken more generally—Judgment Day.

Claude McKay (1890–1948)

America

1922

Although she feeds me bread of bitterness,
And sinks into my throat her tiger's tooth,
Stealing my breath of life, I will confess
I love this cultured hell that tests my youth.
Her vigor flows like tides into my blood,   5

Giving me strength erect against her hate,
Her bigness sweeps my being like a flood.
Yet, as a rebel fronts a king in state,
I stand within her walls with not a shred
Of terror, malice, not a word of jeer.   10
Darkly I gaze into the days ahead,
And see her might and granite wonders there,
Beneath the touch of Time's unerring hand,
Like priceless treasures sinking in the sand.

QUESTIONS

1. Is "America" written in a personal or public voice? What specific elements seem personal? What elements seem public?
2. McKay was a black immigrant from Jamaica, but he does not mention either his race or national origin in the poem. Is his personal background important to understanding "America"?
3. How does the sonnet form contribute to the poem's impact?

Less frequently met in English poetry, the **Italian sonnet**, or **Petrarchan sonnet**, follows the rime scheme *a b b a, a b b a* in its first eight lines, the **octave**, and then adds new rime sounds in the last six lines, the **sestet**. The sestet may rime *c d c d c d, c d e c d e, c d c c d c*, or in almost any other variation that doesn't end in a couplet. This organization into two parts sometimes helps arrange the poet's thoughts. In the octave, the poet may state a problem, and then, in the sestet, may offer a resolution. A lover, for example, may lament all octave long that a loved one is neglectful, then in line 9 begin to foresee some outcome: the speaker will die, or accept unhappiness, or trust that the beloved will have a change of heart.

Edna St. Vincent Millay (1892–1950)

What lips my lips have kissed, and where, and why   1923

What lips my lips have kissed, and where, and why,
I have forgotten, and what arms have lain
Under my head till morning; but the rain
Is full of ghosts tonight, that tap and sigh
Upon the glass and listen for reply,   5
And in my heart there sits a quiet pain
For unremembered lads that not again
Will turn to me at midnight with a cry.
Thus in the winter stands the lonely tree,

Nor knows what birds have vanished one by one,   10
Yet knows its boughs more silent than before:
I cannot say what loves have come and gone,
I only know that summer sang in me
A little while, that in me sings no more.

In this Italian sonnet, the turn of thought comes at the traditional point—the beginning of the ninth line. Many English-speaking poets, however, feel free to vary its placement. In John Milton's commanding sonnet on his blindness ("When I consider how my light is spent" on page 536), the turn comes midway through line 8, and no one has ever thought the worse of it for bending the rules.

"The sonnet," quipped Robert Bly, a contemporary poet-critic, "is where old professors go to die." And certainly in the hands of an unskilled practitioner, the form can seem moribund. Considering the impressive number of powerful sonnets by modern poets such as Yeats, Frost, Auden, Millay, Cummings, Kees, and Heaney, however, the form hardly appears to be exhausted. To see some of the surprising shapes contemporary sonnets take, read this selection of three recent examples.

Kim Addonizio (b. 1954)

First Poem for You   1994

I like to touch your tattoos in complete
darkness, when I can't see them. I'm sure of
where they are, know by heart the neat
lines of lightning pulsing just above
your nipple, can find, as if by instinct, the blue   5
swirls of water on your shoulder where a serpent
twists, facing a dragon. When I pull you
to me, taking you until we're spent
and quiet on the sheets, I love to kiss
the pictures in your skin. They'll last until   10
you're seared to ashes; whatever persists
or turns to pain between us, they will still
be there. Such permanence is terrifying.
So I touch them in the dark; but touch them, trying.

A. E. Stallings (b. 1968)

Sine Qua Non   2002

Your absence, father, is nothing. It is nought—
The factor by which nothing will multiply,

The gap of a dropped stitch, the needle's eye
Weeping its black thread. It is the spot
Blindly spreading behind the looking glass.   5
It is the startled silences that come
When the refrigerator stops its hum,
And crickets pause to let the winter pass.

Your absence, father, is nothing—for it is
Omega's long last O, memory's elision,   10
The fraction of impossible division,
The element I move through, emptiness,
The void stars hang in, the interstice of lace,
The zero that still holds the sum in place.

SINE QUA NON. *Sine qua non* is from Latin, meaning literally, "without which not." Used to
describe something that is indispensable, an essential part, a prerequisite.

QUESTIONS

1. "Nothing" is a key concept in this poem. As used here, does it have its customary
   connotations of meaninglessness and unimportance? Explain.
2. A. E. Stallings said that when she was young, she felt "that formal verse could not
   be contemporary, lacked spontaneity, had no room for the intimate." Discuss
   whether "Sine Qua Non" demonstrates the shortsightedness of that view.

R. S. Gwynn (b. 1948)

Shakespearean Sonnet   2002

With a first line taken from the TV listings

A man is haunted by his father's ghost.
Boy meets girl while feuding families fight.
A Scottish king is murdered by his host.
Two couples get lost on a summer night.
A hunchback slaughters all who block his way.   5
A ruler's rivals plot against his life.
A fat man and a prince make rebels pay.
A noble Moor has doubts about his wife.
An English king decides to conquer France.
A duke finds out his best friend is a she.   10
A forest sets the scene for this romance.
An old man and his daughters disagree.
A Roman leader makes a big mistake.
A sexy queen is bitten by a snake.

QUESTIONS

1. Explain the play on words in the title.
2. How many of the texts described in this sonnet can you identify?
3. Does this poem intend merely to amuse, or does it have a larger point?

Other Forms

There are many other verse forms used in English. Some forms, like the villanelle and sestina (discussed below), come from other European literatures. But English has borrowed fixed forms from an astonishing variety of sources. The haiku and tanka, for instance, originated in Japan. Other borrowed forms include the ghazal (Arabic), rubaiyat stanza (Persian), pantoum (Malay), and sapphics (Greek). Even blank verse, which seems as English as the royal family, began as an attempt by Elizabethan poets to copy an Italian eleven-syllable line. To conclude this chapter, here are poems in three widely used closed forms—the villanelle, triolet, and sestina. Their patterns, which are sometimes called "French forms," have been particularly fascinating to English-language poets because they do not merely require the repetition of rime sounds; instead, they demand more elaborate echoing, involving the repetition of either full words or whole lines of verse. Sometimes difficult to master, these forms can create a powerful musical effect unlike ordinary riming.

Dylan Thomas (1914–1953)

Do not go gentle into that good night   1952

Do not go gentle into that good night,
Old age should burn and rave at close of day;
Rage, rage against the dying of the light.

Though wise men at their end know dark is right,
Because their words had forked no lightning they   5
Do not go gentle into that good night.

Good men, the last wave by, crying how bright
Their frail deeds might have danced in a green bay,
Rage, rage against the dying of the light.

Wild men who caught and sang the sun in flight,   10
And learn, too late, they grieved it on its way,
Do not go gentle into that good night.

Grave men, near death, who see with blinding sight
Blind eyes could blaze like meteors and be gay,
Rage, rage against the dying of the light.   15

And you, my father, there on the sad height,
Curse, bless, me now with your fierce tears, I pray,
Do not go gentle into that good night.
Rage, rage against the dying of the light.

QUESTIONS

1. "Do not go gentle into that good night" is a **villanelle**: a fixed form originated by French courtly poets of the Middle Ages. What are its rules?
2. Whom does the poem address? What is the speaker saying?
3. Villanelles are sometimes criticized as elaborate exercises in trivial wordplay. How would you defend Thomas's poem against this charge?

Robert Bridges (1844–1930)

Triolet   1879

When first we met we did not guess
That Love would prove so hard a master;
Of more than common friendliness
When first we met we did not guess.
Who could foretell this sore distress,   5
This irretrievable disaster
When first we met—We did not guess
That Love would prove so hard a master.

TRIOLET. The **triolet** is a short lyric form borrowed from the French; its two opening lines are repeated according to a set pattern, as Bridges's poem illustrates. The triolet is often used for light verse, but Bridges's poem demonstrates how it can carry heavier emotional loads, if used with sufficient skill.

QUESTION

How do the first two lines of "Triolet" change in meaning when they reappear at the end of the poem?

Elizabeth Bishop (1911–1979)

Sestina   1965

September rain falls on the house.
In the failing light, the old grandmother
sits in the kitchen with the child
beside the Little Marvel Stove,
reading the jokes from the almanac,   5
laughing and talking to hide her tears.

She thinks that her equinoctial tears
and the rain that beats on the roof of the house
were both foretold by the almanac,
but only known to a grandmother. 10
The iron kettle sings on the stove.
She cuts some bread and says to the child,

It's time for tea now; but the child
is watching the teakettle's small hard tears
dance like mad on the hot black stove, 15
the way the rain must dance on the house.
Tidying up, the old grandmother
hangs up the clever almanac

on its string. Birdlike, the almanac
hovers half open above the child, 20
hovers above the old grandmother
and her teacup full of dark brown tears.
She shivers and says she thinks the house
feels chilly, and puts more wood in the stove.

It was to be, says the Marvel Stove. 25
I know what I know, says the almanac.
With crayons the child draws a rigid house
and a winding pathway. Then the child
puts in a man with buttons like tears
and shows it proudly to the grandmother. 30

But secretly, while the grandmother
busies herself about the stove,
the little moons fall down like tears
from between the pages of the almanac
into the flower bed the child 35
has carefully placed in the front of the house.

Time to plant tears, says the almanac.
The grandmother sings to the marvellous stove
and the child draws another inscrutable house.

SESTINA. As its title indicates, this poem is written in the trickiest of medieval fixed forms, that of the **sestina** (or "song of sixes"), said to have been invented in Provence in the thirteenth century by the troubadour poet Arnaut Daniel. In six six-line stanzas, the poet repeats six end-words (in a prescribed order), then reintroduces the six repeated words (in any order) in a closing **envoy** of three lines. Elizabeth Bishop strictly follows the troubadour rules for the order in which the end-words recur. (If you care, you can figure out the formula: in the first stanza, the six words are arranged A B C D E F; in the second, F A E B D C; and so on.)

QUESTIONS

1. A perceptive comment from a student: "Something seems to be going on here that the child doesn't understand. Maybe some terrible loss has happened." Test this guess by reading the poem closely.

2. In the "little moons" that fall from the almanac (line 33), does the poem introduce dream or fantasy, or do you take these to be small round pieces of paper?

3. What is the tone of this poem—the speaker's apparent attitude toward the scene described?

WRITING EFFECTIVELY

WRITING ABOUT FORM

Turning Points

A poem's form is closely tied to its meaning. This is true of all poems, but it is especially true of the sonnet, a form whose rules dictate not only the sound of a poem but also, to a certain extent, its sense.

A sonnet traditionally looks at a single theme, but reverses its stance on the subject somewhere along the way. In this way, a sonnet bears some resemblance to a good essay, which advances an argument all the more effectively by reconciling the author's stance with alternative points of view.

One possible definition of the sonnet might be a fourteen-line poem divided into two unequal parts. Italian sonnets divide their parts into an octave (the first eight lines) and a sestet (the last six), while English sonnets are more lopsided, with a final couplet balanced against the first twelve lines. Some sonnets use less traditional arrangements, but generally poets build sonnets in which the unequal sections strongly contrast in tone, mood, theme, or point of view. The moment when a sonnet changes its direction is commonly called "the turn."

Identifying the moment when the poem "turns" can help you better understand both its theme and its structure. In a Shakespearean sonnet, the turn usually—but not always—comes in the final couplet. In modern sonnets, the turn is often less overt.

How do you find the moment when a sonnet turns? Study the poem; latch on to the mood and manner of its opening lines. Is the feeling joyful or sad, loving or angry? Read the poem from this opening perspective until you feel it tug strongly in another direction. Sometimes the second part of a sonnet will directly contradict the opening. More often it explains, augments, or qualifies the opening.

CHECKLIST

Thinking About a Sonnet

✓ Read the poem carefully.

✓ What is the mood of its opening lines?

✓ Keep reading until you feel the mood shift.

✓ Where does that shift take place?

✓ What is the tone after the sonnet's turn away from its opening direction?

✓ What do the two alternative points of view add up to?

✓ How does the poem reconcile its contrasting sections?

WRITING ASSIGNMENT ON A SONNET

Examine a sonnet from anywhere in this book. Explain how its two parts combine to create a total effect neither part could achieve alone. Be sure to identify the turning point. Paraphrase what each of the poem's two sections says and describe how the poem as a whole reconciles the two contrasting parts.

(In addition to the sonnets in this chapter, you might consider any of the following from the chapter "Poems for Further Reading": Elizabeth Barrett Browning's "How Do I Love Thee?"; Gerard Manley Hopkins's "The Windhover"; John Milton's "When I consider how my light is spent"; Wilfred Owen's "Anthem for Doomed Youth"; William Shakespeare's "When in disgrace with Fortune and men's eyes"; or William Wordsworth's "Composed upon Westminster Bridge.")

MORE TOPICS FOR WRITING

1. Select a poem that incorporates rime from the chapter "Poems for Further Reading." Write a paragraph describing how the poem's rime scheme helps to advance its meaning.

2. Write ten lines of blank verse on a topic of your own choice. Then write about the experience. What aspects of writing in regular meter did you find most challenging? What did you learn about reading blank verse from trying your hand at writing it?

3. Discuss the use of form in Robert Bridges's "Triolet." What is the effect of so many repeated lines in so brief a poem?

4. Compare Dylan Thomas's "Do not go gentle into that good night" with Wendy Cope's "Lonely Hearts" (page 366). How can the same form be used to create such different kinds of poems?

18
Open Form

Writing in **open form**, a poet seeks to discover a fresh and individual arrangement for words in every poem. Such a poem, generally speaking, has neither a rime scheme nor a basic meter informing the whole of it. Doing without those powerful (some would say hypnotic) elements, the poet who writes in open form relies on other means to engage and to sustain the reader's attention. Novice poets often think that open form looks easy, not nearly so hard as riming everything; but in truth, formally open poems are easy to write only if written carelessly. To compose lines with keen awareness of open form's demands, and of its infinite possibilities, calls for skill: at least as much as that needed to write in meter and rime, if not more. Should the poet succeed, then the discovered arrangement will seem exactly right for what the poem is saying.

Denise Levertov (1923–1997)

Ancient Stairway   1999

Footsteps like water hollow
the broad curves of stone
ascending, descending
century by century.
Who can say if the last   5
to climb these stairs
will be journeying
downward or upward?

Open form, in this brief poem, affords Denise Levertov certain advantages. Able to break off a line at whatever point she likes (a privilege not available to the poet writing, say, a conventional sonnet, who has to break off each line after its tenth syllable), she selects her pauses artfully. Line breaks lend emphasis: a word or phrase at the end of a line takes a little more stress (and receives a little more attention), because the ending of the line compels the reader to make a slight pause, if only for the brief moment it takes to sling back one's eyes and fix them on the line following. Slight pauses, then, follow the words and phrases *hollow / stone / descending / century / last / stairs / journeying / upward*—all these being elements that apparently the poet wishes to call our attention to. (The pause after a line break also casts a little more weight on the *first* word or phrase of each succeeding line.) Levertov makes the most of white space—another means of calling attention to things, as any good picture-framer knows. She has greater control over the shape of the poem, its look on the page, than would be allowed by the demands of meter; she uses that control to stack on top of one another lines that are (roughly) equivalent in width, like the steps of a staircase. The opening line with its quick stresses might suggest to us the many feet passing over the steps. From there, Levertov slows the rhythm to the heavy beats of lines 3–4, which could communicate a sense of repeated trudging up and down the stairs (in a particularly effective touch, all four of the stressed syllables in these two lines make the same sound), a sense that is reinforced by the poem's last line, which echoes the rhythm of line 3. Note too how, without being restricted by the need of a rime, she can order the terms in that last line according to her intended thematic emphasis. In all likelihood, we perceive these effects instinctively, not consciously (which may also be the way the author created them), but no matter how we apprehend them, they serve to deepen our understanding of and pleasure in the text.

Poetry in open form used to be called **free verse** (from the French *vers libre*), suggesting a kind of verse liberated from the shackles of rime and meter. "Writing free verse," said Robert Frost, who wasn't interested in it, "is like playing tennis with the net down." And yet, as Denise Levertov and many other poets demonstrate, high scores can be made in such an unconventional game, provided it doesn't straggle all over the court. For a successful poem in open form, the term *free verse* seems inaccurate. "Being an art form," said William Carlos Williams, "verse cannot be 'free' in the sense of having *no* limitations or guiding principles."[1] Various substitute names have been suggested: organic poetry, composition by field, raw (as against cooked) poetry, open form poetry. "But what does it matter what you call it?" remark the editors of a 1969 anthology called *Naked Poetry*. "The best poems of the last thirty years don't rhyme (usually) and don't move on feet of more or less equal duration (usually). That nondescription moves toward the only technical principle they all have in common."[2]

To the poet working in open form, no less than to the poet writing a sonnet, line length can be valuable. Walt Whitman, who loved to expand vast sentences for line after line, knew well that an impressive rhythm can accumulate if the poet will keep long lines approximately the same length, causing a pause to recur at about the same interval after every line. Sometimes, too, Whitman repeats the same words at each line's opening. An instance is the

---

[1]"Free Verse," *Princeton Encyclopedia of Poetry and Poetics*, 2nd ed., 1975.

[2]Stephen Berg and Robert Mezey, eds., foreword, *Naked Poetry: Recent American Poetry in Open Forms* (Indianapolis: Bobbs, 1969).

masterly sixth section of "When Lilacs Last in the Dooryard Bloom'd," an elegy for Abraham Lincoln:

> Coffin that passes through lanes and streets,
> Through day and night with the great cloud darkening the land,
> With the pomp of the inloop'd flags with the cities draped in black,
> With the show of the States themselves as of crape-veil'd women
> standing,
> With processions long and winding and the flambeaus of the night,
> With the countless torches lit, with the silent sea of faces and
> the unbared heads,
> With the waiting depot, the arriving coffin, and the somber faces,
> With dirges through the night, with the thousand voices rising
> strong and solemn,
> With all the mournful voices of the dirges pour'd around the coffin,
> The dim-lit churches and the shuddering organs—where amid
> these you journey,
> With the tolling tolling bells' perpetual clang,
> Here, coffin that slowly passes,
> I give you my sprig of lilac.

There is music in such solemn, operatic arias. Whitman's lines echo another model: the Hebrew **psalms**, or sacred songs, as translated in the King James Version of the Bible. In Psalm 150, repetition also occurs inside of lines:

> Praise ye the Lord. Praise God in his sanctuary: praise him in
> the firmament of his power.
> Praise him for his mighty acts: praise him according to his
> excellent greatness.
> Praise him with the sound of the trumpet: praise him with the
> psaltery and harp.
> Praise him with the timbrel and dance: praise him with stringed
> instruments and organs.
> Praise him upon the loud cymbals: praise him upon the high
> sounding cymbals.
> Let every thing that hath breath praise the Lord. Praise ye the
> Lord.

In biblical Psalms, we are in the presence of (as Robert Lowell has said) "supreme poems, written when their translators merely intended prose and were forced by the structure of their originals to write poetry."[3]

---

[3]"On Freedom in Poetry," in Berg and Mezey, *Naked Poetry*.

Whitman was a more deliberate craftsman than he let his readers think, and to anyone interested in writing in open form, his work will repay close study. He knew that repetitions of any kind often make memorable rhythms, as in this passage from "Song of Myself," with every line ending on an -*ing* word (a stressed syllable followed by an unstressed syllable):

> Here and there with dimes on the eyes walking,
> To feed the greed of the belly the brains liberally spooning,
> Tickets buying, taking, selling, but in to the feast never once going,
> Many sweating, ploughing, thrashing, and then the chaff for
>   payment receiving,
> A few idly owning, and they the wheat continually claiming.

Much more than simply repetition, of course, went into the music of those lines—the internal rime *feed, greed,* the use of assonance, the trochees that begin the third and fourth lines, whether or not they were calculated.

In such classics of open form poetry, sound and rhythm are positive forces. When speaking a poem in open form, you often may find that it makes a difference for the better if you pause at the end of each line. Try pausing there, however briefly; but don't allow your voice to drop. Read just as you would normally read a sentence in prose (except for the pauses, of course). Why do the pauses matter? Open form poetry usually has no meter to lend it rhythm. *Some* lines in an open form poem, as we have seen in Whitman's "dimes on the eyes" passage, do fall into metrical feet; sometimes the whole poem does. Usually lacking meter's aid, however, open form, in order to have more and more noticeable rhythms, has need of all the recurring pauses it can get. As we can hear in recordings of them reading their work aloud, open form poets such as Robert Creeley and Allen Ginsberg would often pause very definitely at each line break—and so, for that matter, did Ezra Pound.

Some poems, to be sure, seem more widely open in form than others. A poet may wish to avoid the rigidity and predictability of fixed line lengths and stanzaic forms but still wish to hold a poem together through a strong rhythmic impulse and even a discernible metrical emphasis. A poet may employ rime, but have the rimes recur at various intervals, or perhaps rime lines of varying lengths. In a 1917 essay called "Reflections on *vers libre*" (French for "free verse"), T. S. Eliot famously observed, "No *vers* is *libre* for the man who wants to do a good job." In that same year, Eliot published his first collection of poems, whose title piece was the classic "The Love Song of J. Alfred Prufrock" (see page 509). Is "Prufrock" a closed poem left ajar or an open poem trying to slam itself?

E. E. Cummings (1894–1962)

Buffalo Bill's   1923

Buffalo Bill's
defunct
    who used to
    ride a watersmooth-silver
        stallion   5
and break onetwothreefourfive pigeonsjustlikethat
                  Jesus
he was a handsome man
         and what i want to know is
how do you like your blueeyed boy   10
Mister Death

QUESTION

Cummings's poem would look like this if given conventional punctuation and set in a
solid block like prose:

> Buffalo Bill's defunct, who used to ride a water-smooth silver stallion and
> break one, two, three, four, five pigeons just like that. Jesus, he was a hand-
> some man. And what I want to know is: "How do you like your blue-eyed boy,
> Mister Death?"

If this were done, by what characteristics would it still be recognizable as poetry? But
what would be lost?

Stephen Crane (1871–1900)

The Heart   1895

In the desert
I saw a creature, naked, bestial,
Who, squatting upon the ground,
Held his heart in his hands,
And ate of it.   5

I said, "Is it good, friend?"
"It is bitter—bitter," he answered;
"But I like it
Because it is bitter,
And because it is my heart."   10

Walt Whitman (1819–1892)

Cavalry Crossing a Ford   1865

A line in long array where they wind betwixt green islands,
They take a serpentine course, their arms flash in the sun—hark to
    the musical clank,
Behold the silvery river, in it the splashing horses loitering stop to
    drink,
Behold the brown-faced men, each group, each person a picture, the
    negligent rest on the saddles,
Some emerge on the opposite bank, others are just entering the   5
    ford—while,
Scarlet and blue and snowy white,
The guidon flags flutter gayly in the wind.

QUESTIONS

The following nitpicking questions are intended to help you see exactly what makes these two open form poems by Crane and Whitman so different in their music.

1. What devices of sound occur in Whitman's phrase *silvery river* (line 3)? Where else in his poem do you find these devices?
2. Does Crane use any such devices?
3. In number of syllables, Whitman's poem is almost twice as long as Crane's. Which poem has more pauses in it? (Count pauses at the ends of lines, at marks of punctuation.)
4. Read the two poems aloud. In general, how would you describe the effect of their sounds and rhythms? Is Crane's poem necessarily an inferior poem for having less music?

Ezra Pound (1885–1972)

Salutation   1915

O generation of the thoroughly smug
    and thoroughly uncomfortable,
I have seen fishermen picnicking in the sun,
I have seen them with untidy families,
I have seen their smiles full of teeth   5
    and heard ungainly laughter.
And I am happier than you are,
And they were happier than I am;
And the fish swim in the lake
    and do not even own clothing   10

Wallace Stevens (1879–1955)

Thirteen Ways of Looking at a Blackbird   1923

I

Among twenty snowy mountains,
The only moving thing
Was the eye of the blackbird.

II

I was of three minds,
Like a tree
In which there are three blackbirds.   5

III

The blackbird whirled in the autumn winds.
It was a small part of the pantomime.

IV

A man and a woman
Are one.
A man and a woman and a blackbird   10
Are one.

V

I do not know which to prefer,
The beauty of inflections
Or the beauty of innuendoes,
The blackbird whistling   15
Or just after.

VI

Icicles filled the long window
With barbaric glass.
The shadow of the blackbird
Crossed it, to and fro.   20
The mood
Traced in the shadow
An indecipherable cause.

VII

O thin men of Haddam,   25
Why do you imagine golden birds?
Do you not see how the blackbird
Walks around the feet
Of the women about you?

VIII

I know noble accents   30
And lucid, inescapable rhythms;
But I know, too,
That the blackbird is involved
In what I know.

IX

When the blackbird flew out of sight,   35
It marked the edge
Of one of many circles.

X

At the sight of blackbirds
Flying in a green light,
Even the bawds of euphony   40
Would cry out sharply.

XI

He rode over Connecticut
In a glass coach.
Once, a fear pierced him,
In that he mistook   45
The shadow of his equipage
For blackbirds.

XII

The river is moving.
The blackbird must be flying.

XIII

It was evening all afternoon.
It was snowing
And it was going to snow.
The blackbird sat
In the cedar-limbs.

THIRTEEN WAYS OF LOOKING AT A BLACKBIRD. 25 *Haddam:* This biblical-sounding name is
that of a town in Connecticut.

QUESTIONS

1. What is the speaker's attitude toward the men of Haddam? What attitude toward this world does he suggest they lack? What is implied by calling them *thin* (line 25)?

2. What do the landscapes of winter contribute to the poem's effectiveness? If Stevens had chosen images of summer lawns, what would have been lost?

3. In which sections of the poem does Stevens suggest that a unity exists between human being and blackbird, between blackbird and the entire natural world? Can we say that Stevens "philosophizes"? What role does imagery play in Stevens's statement of his ideas?

4. What sense can you make of Part X? Make an enlightened guess.

5. Consider any one of the thirteen parts. What patterns of sound and rhythm do you find in it? What kind of structure does it have?

6. If the thirteen parts were arranged in some different order, would the poem be just as good? Or can we find a justification for its beginning with Part I and ending with Part XIII?

7. Does the poem seem an arbitrary combination of thirteen separate poems? Or is there any reason to call it a whole?

Prose Poetry

No law requires a poet to split thoughts into verse lines at all. Charles Baudelaire, Rainer Maria Rilke, Jorge Luis Borges, Alexander Solzhenitsyn, T. S. Eliot, and many others have written **prose poems**, in which, without caring that eye appeal and some of the rhythm of a line structure may be lost, the poet prints words in a block like a prose paragraph. To some, the term "prose poetry" is as oxymoronic as "jumbo shrimp" or "plastic glasses," if not a flat-out contradiction in terms. On the other hand, we might recall Samuel Johnson's response when told that Bishop Berkeley's theory that the material world is an illusion, while obviously false, could not be refuted; Johnson kicked a large stone, saying "I refute him *thus.*" Like stones, prose poems exist. To prove it, here is one by a contemporary American poet. As you read it, ask yourself: Is it a prose poem, or a very short piece of prose? If it is poetry, what features distinguish it from prose? If it should be considered prose, what essential features of poetry does it lack?

Charles Simic (b. 1939)

The Magic Study of Happiness

1992

In the smallest theater in the world the bread crumbs speak. It's a mystery play on the subject of a lost paradise. Once there was a kitchen with a table on which a few crumbs were left. Through the window you could see your young mother by the fence talking to a neighbor. She was cold and kept hugging her thin dress tighter and tighter. The clouds in the sky 5 sailed on as she threw her head back to laugh.

Where the words can't go any further—there's the hard table. The crumbs are watching you as you in turn watch them. The unknown in you and the unknown in them attract each other. The two unknowns are like illicit lovers when they're exceedingly and unaccountably happy.

QUESTIONS

1. What is the effect of the phrases "the smallest theater in the world" and "mystery play"?
2. How do you interpret "Where the words can't go any further—there's the hard table"?
3. What is the significance of the simile in the last sentence?

Seeing the Logic of Open Form Verse

Read the following poem in open form silently to yourself, noticing what the poet does with white space, repetitions, line breaks, and indentations. Then read the poem aloud, trying to indicate by slight pauses where lines end and also pausing slightly at any space inside a line. Can you see any reasons for the poet's placing his words in this arrangement rather than in a prose paragraph? Does the poet seem to care also about visual effect?

E. E. Cummings (1894–1962)

in Just-

1923

in Just-
spring   when the world is mud-
luscious the little
lame balloonman

whistles   far   and wee   5

and eddieandbill come
running from marbles and
piracies and it's
spring

when the world is puddle-wonderful   10

the queer
old balloonman whistles
far   and   wee
and bettyandisbel come dancing

from hop-scotch and jump-rope and   15

it's
spring
and
   the
      goat-footed   20

balloonMan   whistles
far
and
wee

Carole Satyamurti (b. 1939)

I Shall Paint My Nails Red   1990

Because a bit of colour is a public service.

Because I am proud of my hands.

Because it will remind me I'm a woman.

Because I will look like a survivor.

Because I can admire them in traffic jams.   5

Because my daughter will say ugh.

Because my lover will be surprised.

Because it is quicker than dyeing my hair.

Because it is a ten-minute moratorium.

Because it is reversible.   10

QUESTION

"I Shall Paint My Nails Red" is written in free verse, but the poem has several organizing principles. How many can you discover?

Langston Hughes (1902–1967)

I, Too   1926

I, too, sing America.

I am the darker brother.
They send me to eat in the kitchen
When company comes,
But I laugh,   5
And eat well,
And grow strong.

Tomorrow,
I'll be at the table
When company comes.   10
Nobody'll dare
Say to me,
"Eat in the kitchen,"
Then.

Besides,   15
They'll see how beautiful I am
And be ashamed—

I, too, am America.

WRITING EFFECTIVELY

WRITING ABOUT FREE VERSE

Lining Up for Free Verse

"That's not poetry! It's just chopped-up prose." So runs one old-fashioned complaint about free verse. Such criticism may be true of inept poems, but in the best free verse the line endings transform language in ways beyond the possibilities of prose. When we consider the effects that line breaks can achieve, we might even begin to see prose as poetry's poor cousin.

A line break implies a slight pause so that the last word of each line receives special emphasis. The last word in a line is meant to linger, however briefly, in the listener's ear. Look at how Wallace Stevens's lineation in "Thirteen Ways of Looking at a Blackbird" allows us not only to see but also to savor the implications of the ideas and images:

I was of three minds,
Like a tree
In which there are three blackbirds.

On a purely semantic level, these lines may mean the same as the prose statement, "I was of three minds like a tree in which there are three blackbirds," but Stevens's choice of line breaks adds decisive emphasis at several points. Each of these three lines isolates and presents a separate image (the speaker, the tree, and the blackbirds). The placement of *three* at the same position in the opening and closing lines helps us feel the similar nature of the two statements. The short middle line allows us to see the image of the tree before we fully understand why it is parallel to the divided mind—thus adding a touch of suspense that the prose version of this statement just can't supply. Ending each line with a key noun and image also gives the poem a concrete feel not altogether evident in the prose.

For a better sense of how a poem's line breaks operate, note whether the breaks tend to come at the end of sentences or phrases, or in the middle of an idea. An abundance of breaks in mid-thought can create a tumbling, headlong effect, forcing your eye to speed down the page. Conversely, lines that tend to break at the end of a full idea can give a more stately rhythm to a poem.

Next, determine whether the lines tend to be all brief, all long, or a mix. A very short line forces us to pay special attention to its every word, no matter how small.

With line breaks as with any other element of verse, always ask yourself how a poet's choices help to reinforce a poem's meaning.

CHECKLIST

Analyzing Line Breaks in Free Verse

✓ Reread a poem, paying attention to where its lines end.

✓ Do the breaks tend to come at the end of the sentences or phrases?

✓ Do they tend to come in the middle of an idea?

✓ Do the lines tend to be long? Short? A mix of both?

✓ What mood is created by the breaks?

✓ How is each line's meaning underscored by its line break?

✓ Is the poem broken into stanzas? Are they long? Short? A mix of both?

✓ How do line breaks and stanza breaks reinforce the poem's meaning as a whole?

WRITING ASSIGNMENT ON OPEN FORM

Retype a free verse poem as prose, adding conventional punctuation and capitalization if necessary. Then compare and contrast the prose version with the poem itself. How do the two texts differ in tone, rhythm, emphasis, and effect? How do they remain similar? Use any poem from this chapter or any of the following from the chapter "Poems for Further Reading": W. H. Auden's "Musée des Beaux Arts"; Robert Lowell's "Skunk Hour"; Ezra Pound's "The River-Merchant's Wife: A Letter."

MORE TOPICS FOR WRITING

1. Write a brief essay (approximately 500 words) on how the line breaks and white space (or lack thereof) in E. E. Cummings's "Buffalo Bill's" contribute to the poem's effect.

2. Imagine Charles Simic's "The Magic Study of Happiness" broken into free-verse lines. What are the benefits of the prose-poem form to this particular text?

3. Compare any poem in this chapter with a poem in rime and meter. Discuss several key features that they have in common despite their apparent differences in style. Features it might be useful to compare include imagery, tone, figures of speech, and word choice.

4. Write an imitation of Wallace Stevens's "Thirteen Ways of Looking at a Blackbird." Come up with thirteen ways of looking at your car, a can opener, a housecat—or any object that intrigues you. Choose your line breaks carefully, to recreate some of the mood of the original.

19
Symbol

The national flag is supposed to stir our patriotic feelings. When a black cat crosses his path, a superstitious man shivers, foreseeing bad luck. To each of these, by custom, our society expects a standard response. A flag, a black cat crossing one's path—each is a **symbol**: a visible object or action that suggests some further meaning in addition to itself. In literature, a symbol might be the word *flag* or the words *a black cat crossed his path* or every description of flag or cat in an entire novel, story, play, or poem.

A flag and the crossing of a black cat may be called **conventional symbols**, since they can have a conventional or customary effect on us. Conventional symbols are also part of the language of poetry, as we know when we meet the red rose, emblem of love, in a lyric, or the Christian cross in the devotional poems of George Herbert. More often, however, symbols in literature have no conventional, long-established meaning, but particular meanings of their own. In Melville's novel *Moby-Dick*, to take a rich example, whatever we associate with the great white whale is *not* attached unmistakably to white whales by custom. Though Melville tells us that men have long regarded whales with awe and relates Moby Dick to the celebrated fish that swallowed Jonah, the reader's response is to one particular whale, the creature of Herman Melville. Only the experience of reading the novel in its entirety can give Moby Dick his particular meaning.

We should say *meanings*, for as Eudora Welty has observed, it is a good thing Melville made Moby Dick a whale, a creature large enough to contain all that critics have found in him. A symbol in literature, if not conventional, has more than just one meaning. In "The Raven," by Edgar Allan Poe, the appearance of a strange black bird in the narrator's study is sinister; and indeed, if we take the poem seriously, we may even respond with a sympathetic shiver of dread. Does the bird mean death, fate, melancholy, the loss of a loved one, knowledge in the service of evil? All these, perhaps. Like any well-chosen symbol, Poe's raven sets off within the reader an unending train of feelings and associations.

We miss the value of a symbol, however, if we think it can mean absolutely anything we wish. If a poet has any control over our reactions, the poem will guide our responses in a certain direction.

T. S. Eliot (1888–1965)

The *Boston Evening Transcript* 1917

The readers of the *Boston Evening Transcript*
Sway in the wind like a field of ripe corn.

When evening quickens faintly in the street,
Wakening the appetites of life in some
And to others bringing the *Boston Evening Transcript*, 5
I mount the steps and ring the bell, turning
Wearily, as one would turn to nod good-bye to La Rochefoucauld,
If the street were time and he at the end of the street,
And I say, "Cousin Harriet, here is the *Boston Evening Transcript*."

The newspaper, whose name Eliot purposely repeats so monotonously, indicates what this poem is about. Now defunct, the *Transcript* covered in detail the slightest activity of Boston's leading families and was noted for the great length of its obituaries. Eliot, then, uses the newspaper as a symbol for an existence of boredom, fatigue (*Wearily*), petty and unvarying routine (since an evening newspaper, like night, arrives on schedule). The *Transcript* evokes a way of life without zest or passion, for, opposed to people who read it, Eliot sets people who do not: those whose desires revive, not expire, when the working day is through. Suggestions abound in the ironic comparison of the *Transcript*'s readers to a cornfield late in summer. To mention only a few: the readers sway because they are sleepy; they vegetate; they are drying up; each makes a rattling sound when turning a page. It is not necessary that we know the remote and similarly disillusioned friend to whom the speaker might nod: La Rochefoucauld, whose cynical *Maxims* entertained Parisian society under Louis XIV (sample: "All of us have enough strength to endure the misfortunes of others"). We understand that the nod is symbolic of an immense weariness of spirit. We know nothing about Cousin Harriet, whom the speaker addresses, but imagine from the greeting she inspires that she is probably a bore.

If Eliot wishes to say that certain Bostonians lead lives of sterile boredom, why does he couch his meaning in symbols? Why doesn't he tell us directly what he means? These questions imply two assumptions not necessarily true: first, that Eliot has a message to impart; second, that he is concealing it. We have reason to think that Eliot did not usually have a message in mind when beginning a poem, for as he once told a critic: "The conscious problems with which one is concerned in the actual writing are more those of a quasi-musical nature . . . than of a conscious exposition of ideas." Poets sometimes discover what they have to say while in the act of saying it. And it may be that in his *Transcript* poem, Eliot is saying exactly what he means. By communicating his meaning through symbols instead of statements, he may be choosing the only kind of language appropriate to an idea of great subtlety and complexity. (The paraphrase "Certain Bostonians are bored" hardly begins to describe the poem in all its possible meaning.) And by his use of symbolism, Eliot affords us the pleasure of finding our own entrances to his poem.

This power of suggestion that a symbol contains is, perhaps, its greatest advantage. Sometimes, as in the following poem by Emily Dickinson, a symbol will lead us from a visible object to something too vast to be perceived.

Emily Dickinson (1830–1886)

The Lightning is a yellow Fork   (about 1870)

The Lightning is a yellow Fork
From Tables in the sky
By inadvertent fingers dropt
The awful Cutlery

Of mansions never quite disclosed   5
And never quite concealed
The Apparatus of the Dark
To ignorance revealed.

If the lightning is a fork, then whose are the fingers that drop it, the table from which it slips, the household to which it belongs? The poem implies this question without giving an answer. An obvious answer is "God," but can we be sure? We wonder, too, about these partially lighted mansions: if our vision were clearer, what would we behold?

"But how am I supposed to know a symbol when I see one?" The best approach is to read poems closely, taking comfort in the likelihood that it is better not to notice symbols at all than to find significance in every literal stone and huge meanings in every thing. In looking for the symbols in a poem, pick out all the references to concrete objects—newspapers, black cats, twisted pins. Consider these with special care. Notice any that the poet emphasizes by detailed description, by repetition, or by placing it at the very beginning or end of the poem. Ask: What is the poem about, what does it add up to? If, when the poem is paraphrased, the paraphrase depends primarily on the meaning of certain concrete objects, these richly suggestive objects may be the symbols.

There are some things a literary symbol usually is *not*. A symbol is not an abstraction. Such terms as *truth*, *death*, *love*, and *justice* cannot work as symbols (unless personified, as in the traditional figure of Justice holding a scale). Most often, a symbol is something we can see in the mind's eye: a newspaper, a lightning bolt, a gesture of nodding good-bye.

In narratives, a well-developed character who speaks much dialogue and is not the least bit mysterious is usually not a symbol. But watch out for an executioner in a black hood; a character, named for a biblical prophet, who does little but utter a prophecy; a trio of old women who resemble the Three Fates. (It has been argued, with good reason, that Milton's fully rounded character of Satan in *Paradise Lost* is a symbol embodying evil and human pride, but a narrower definition of symbol is more frequently useful.) A symbol *may* be a part of a person's body (the baleful eye of the murder victim in Poe's story "The Tell-Tale Heart") or a look, a voice, or a mannerism.

A symbol usually is not the second term of a metaphor. In the line "The Lightning is a yellow Fork," the symbol is the lightning, not the fork.

Sometimes a symbol addresses a sense other than sight: the sound of a mysterious snapping string at the end of Chekhov's play *The Cherry Orchard;* or, in William Faulkner's tale "A Rose for Emily," the odor of decay that surrounds the house of the last survivor of a town's leading family—suggesting not only physical dissolution but also the decay of a social order. A symbol is a special kind of image, for it exceeds the usual image in the richness of its connotations. The dead wife's cold comb in the haiku of Buson (discussed on page 385) works symbolically, suggesting among other things the chill of the grave, the contrast between the living and the dead.

Holding a narrower definition than that used in this book, some readers of poetry prefer to say that a symbol is always a concrete object, never an act. They would deny the label "symbol" to Ahab's breaking his tobacco pipe before setting out to pursue Moby Dick (suggesting, perhaps, his determination to allow no pleasure to distract him from the chase) or to any large motion (as Ahab's whole quest). This distinction, while confining, does have the merit of sparing one from seeing all motion to be possibly symbolic. Some would call Ahab's gesture not a symbol but a **symbolic act**.

To sum up: a symbol radiates hints or casts long shadows (to use Henry James's metaphor). We are unable to say it "stands for" or "represents" a meaning. It evokes, it suggests, it manifests. It demands no single necessary interpretation, such as the interpretation a driver gives to a red traffic light. Rather, like Emily Dickinson's lightning bolt, it points toward an indefinite meaning, which may lie in part beyond the reach of words. In a symbol, as Thomas Carlyle said in *Sartor Resartus,* "the Infinite is made to blend with the Finite, to stand visible, and as it were, attainable there."

Thomas Hardy (1840–1928)

Neutral Tones   1898

We stood by a pond that winter day,
And the sun was white, as though chidden of° God,   *rebuked by*
And a few leaves lay on the starving sod;
    —They had fallen from an ash, and were gray.

Your eyes on me were as eyes that rove   5
Over tedious riddles of years ago;
And some words played between us to and fro
    On which lost the more by our love.

The smile on your mouth was the deadest thing
Alive enough to have strength to die;   10
And a grin of bitterness swept thereby
    Like an ominous bird a-wing. . . .

Since then, keen lessons that love deceives,
And wrings with wrong, have shaped to me
Your face, and the God-curst sun, and a tree,   15
    And a pond edged with grayish leaves.

QUESTIONS

1. Sum up the story told in this poem. In lines 1–12, what is the dramatic situation? What has happened in the interval between the experience related in these lines and the reflection in the last stanza?
2. What meanings do you find in the title?
3. Explain in your own words the metaphor in line 2.
4. What connotations appropriate to this poem does the *ash* (line 4) have that *oak* or *maple* would lack?
5. What visible objects in the poem function symbolically? What actions or gestures?

If we read of a ship, its captain, its sailors, and the rough seas, and we realize we are reading about a commonwealth and how its rulers and workers keep it going even in difficult times, then we are reading an **allegory**. Closely akin to symbolism, allegory is a description—usually narrative—in which persons, places, and things are employed in a continuous and consistent system of equivalents.

Although more strictly limited in its suggestions than symbolism, allegory need not be thought inferior. Few poems continue to interest readers more than Dante's allegorical *Divine Comedy*. Sublime evidence of the appeal of allegory may be found in Christ's use of the **parable**: a brief narrative—usually allegorical but sometimes not—that teaches a moral.

Matthew 13:24–30 (King James Version, 1611)

The Parable of the Good Seed

The kingdom of heaven is likened unto a man which sowed good
    seed in his field:
But while men slept, his enemy came and sowed tares among the
    wheat, and went his way.

But when the blade was sprung up, and brought forth fruit, then
    appeared the tares also.
So the servants of the householder came and said unto him, Sir,
    didst not thou sow good seed in thy field? From whence then
    hath it tares?
He said unto them, An enemy hath done this. The servants said   5
    unto him, Wilt thou then that we go and gather them up?
But he said, Nay; lest while ye gather up the tares, ye root up also
    the wheat with them.
Let both grow together until the harvest: and in the time of harvest I
    will say to the reapers, Gather ye together first the tares, and bind
    them in bundles to burn them: but gather the wheat into my barn.

The sower is the Son of man, the field is the world, the good seed are the children of the Kingdom, the tares are the children of the wicked one, the enemy is
the devil, the harvest is the end of the world, the reapers are angels. "As therefore the tares are gathered and burned in the fire; so shall it be in the end of this
world" (Matthew 13:36–42).

    Usually, as in this parable, the meanings of an allegory are plainly labeled
or thinly disguised. In John Bunyan's allegorical narrative *The Pilgrim's Progress*,
it is clear that the hero Christian, on his journey through places with such
pointed names as Vanity Fair, the Valley of the Shadow of Death, and Doubting
Castle, is the soul, traveling the road of life on the way toward Heaven. An
allegory, when carefully built, is systematic. It makes one principal comparison,
the working out of whose details may lead to further comparisons, then still
further comparisons: Christian, thrown by Giant Despair into the dungeon of
Doubting Castle, escapes by means of a key called Promise.

    An object in allegory is like a bird whose cage is clearly lettered with its
identity—"RAVEN, *Corvus corax*; habitat of specimen, Maine." A symbol, by
contrast, is a bird with piercing eyes that mysteriously appears one evening in
your library. It is there; you can touch it. But what does it mean? You look at it.
It continues to look at you.

Edwin Markham (1852–1940)

Outwitted   1914

He drew a circle that shut me out—
Heretic, rebel, a thing to flout.
But Love and I had the wit to win:
We drew a circle that took him in!

QUESTIONS

What does a circle symbolize in this poem? Does it represent the same thing both
times it is mentioned?

Yusef Komunyakaa (b. 1947)

Facing It   1988

My black face fades,
hiding inside the black granite.
I said I wouldn't,
dammit: No tears.
I'm stone. I'm flesh.   5
My clouded reflection eyes me
like a bird of prey, the profile of night
slanted against morning. I turn
this way—the stone lets me go.
I turn that way—I'm inside   10
the Vietnam Veterans Memorial
again, depending on the light
to make a difference.
I go down the 58,022 names,
half-expecting to find   15
my own in letters like smoke.
I touch the name Andrew Johnson;
I see the booby trap's white flash.
Names shimmer on a woman's blouse
but when she walks away   20
the names stay on the wall.
Brushstrokes flash, a red bird's
wings cutting across my stare.
The sky. A plane in the sky.
A white vet's image floats   25
closer to me, then his pale eyes
look through mine. I'm a window.
He's lost his right arm
inside the stone. In the black mirror
a woman's trying to erase names: 30
No, she's brushing a boy's hair.

QUESTIONS

1. How does the title of "Facing It" relate to the poem? Does it have more than one
   meaning?
2. The narrator describes the people around him by their reflections on the polished
   granite rather than by looking at them directly. What does this indirect way of
   scrutinizing contribute to the poem?

Whether an object in literature is a symbol, part of an allegory, or no such thing at all, it has at least one sure meaning. Moby Dick is first a whale, and the *Boston Evening Transcript* is a newspaper. Besides deriving a multitude of intangible suggestions from the title symbol in Eliot's long poem *The Waste Land*, its readers cannot fail to carry away a sense of the land's physical appearance: a river choked with sandwich papers and cigarette ends, London Bridge "under the brown fog of a winter dawn." A virtue of *The Pilgrim's Progress* is that its walking abstractions are no mere abstractions but are also human: Giant Despair is a henpecked husband. The most vital element of a literary work may pass us by, unless before seeking further depths in a thing, we look to the thing itself.

Robert Frost (1874–1963)

The Road Not Taken   1916

Two roads diverged in a yellow wood,
And sorry I could not travel both
And be one traveler, long I stood
And looked down one as far as I could
To where it bent in the undergrowth;   5

Then took the other, as just as fair,
And having perhaps the better claim,
Because it was grassy and wanted wear;
Though as for that the passing there
Had worn them really about the same,   10

And both that morning equally lay
In leaves no step had trodden black.
Oh, I kept the first for another day!
Yet knowing how way leads on to way,
I doubted if I should ever come back.   15

I shall be telling this with a sigh
Somewhere ages and ages hence:
Two roads diverged in a wood, and I—
I took the one less traveled by,
And that has made all the difference.   20

QUESTION

What symbolism do you find in this poem, if any? Back up your claim with evidence.

For Review and Further Study

EXERCISE: Symbol Hunting

After you have read each of the following poems, decide which description best suits it:

1. The poem has a central symbol.
2. The poem contains no symbolism, but is to be taken literally.

Robert Frost (1874–1963)

Nothing Gold Can Stay   1923

Nature's first green is gold,
Her hardest hue to hold.
Her early leaf's a flower;
But only so an hour.
Then leaf subsides to leaf.   5
So Eden sank to grief,
So dawn goes down to day.
Nothing gold can stay.

Ted Kooser (b. 1939)

Carrie   1979

"There's never an end to dust
and dusting," my aunt would say
as her rag, like a thunderhead,
scudded across the yellow oak
of her little house. There she lived   5
seventy years with a ball
of compulsion closed in her fist,
and an elbow that creaked and popped
like a branch in a storm. Now dust
is her hands and dust her heart.   10
There is never an end to it.

Lorine Niedecker (1903–1970)

Popcorn-can cover (about 1959)

Popcorn-can cover
screwed to the wall
over a hole
    so the cold
can't mouse in   5

Wallace Stevens (1879–1955)

Anecdote of the Jar   1923

I placed a jar in Tennessee,
And round it was, upon a hill.
It made the slovenly wilderness
Surround that hill.

The wilderness rose up to it,
And sprawled around, no longer wild.   5
The jar was round upon the ground
And tall and of a port in air.

It took dominion everywhere.
The jar was gray and bare.   10
It did not give of bird or bush,
Like nothing else in Tennessee.

WRITING EFFECTIVELY

WRITING ABOUT SYMBOLS

Reading a Symbol

A symbol, to use poet John Drury's concise definition, is "an image that radiates meanings." While images in a poem can and should be read as what they literally are, images often do double duty, suggesting deeper meanings. Exactly what those meanings are, however, often differ from poem to poem.

In one poem snow may be a reassuring symbol of sleep and forgetfulness, while in another it becomes a chilling symbol of death. Both meanings easily connect to the natural image of snow, but in each poem the author has nudged that image in a different direction.

Some symbols have been used so often and effectively over time that a traditional reading of them has developed. Sometimes a poet clearly adopts an image's traditional symbolic meaning. In "Go, Lovely Rose" (page 560), Edmund Waller masterfully employs the image of the rose with all its conventional associations as a symbol of the transience of human beauty.

However, some poems deliberately play against a symbol's conventional associations. In her poem "The Victory" (page 389), Anne Stevenson presents a newborn child not as a conventional little bundle of joy, but as a frightening, inhuman antagonist.

To determine the meaning (or meanings) of a symbol, start by asking if it has traditional associations. (Think of a rose, a cross, a reaper, and so on.) If so, consider whether the symbol is being used in the expected way or if the poet is playing with those associations.

Then, consider the symbol's relationship to the rest of the poem. Let context be your guide. The image might have a unique meaning to the poem's speaker. Consider the emotions that the image evokes. If it recurs in the poem, pay attention to how it changes from one mention to the next.

Finally, keep in mind that not everything is a symbol. If an image doesn't appear to radiate meanings above and beyond its literal sense, don't feel you have failed as a critic. As Sigmund Freud once commented about symbol-hunting, "Sometimes a cigar is just a cigar."

CHECKLIST

Analyzing a Symbol

✓ Is the symbol a traditional one?

✓ If so, is it being used in the expected way? Or is the poet playing with its associations?

✓ What does the image seem to mean to the poem's speaker?

✓ What emotions are evoked by the image?

✓ If an image recurs in a poem, how does it change from one mention to the next?

✓ Does the image radiate meaning beyond its literal sense? If not, it might not be intended to be taken as a symbol.

WRITING ASSIGNMENT ON SYMBOLISM

Do an in-depth analysis of the symbolism in a poem of your choice from the chapter "Poems for Further Reading." Some likely choices would be Robert Lowell's "Skunk Hour," Sylvia Plath's "Daddy," and Gerard Manley Hopkins's "The Windhover."

MORE TOPICS FOR WRITING

1. Write an explication of any poem from this chapter, paying careful attention to its symbols. For a further description of poetic explication, see the chapter "Writing About Literature."

2. Take a relatively simple, straightforward poem, such as William Carlos Williams's "This Is Just to Say" (page 353), and write a burlesque critical interpretation of it. Claim to discover symbols that the poem doesn't contain. While running wild with your "reading into" the poem, don't invent anything that you can't somehow support from the text of the poem itself. At the end of your burlesque, sum up in a paragraph what this exercise taught you about how to read poems, or how not to.

20
What Is Poetry?

What is poetry? By now, perhaps, you have formed your own idea, whether or not you can define it. Robert Frost made a try at a definition: "A poem is an idea caught in the act of dawning." Just in case further efforts at definition may be useful, here are a few memorable ones:

things that are true expressed in words that are beautiful.
—*Dante*

the art of uniting pleasure with truth by calling imagination to
the help of reason.
—*Samuel Johnson*

the best words in the best order.
—*Samuel Taylor Coleridge*

a way of taking life by the throat.
—*Robert Frost*

the spontaneous overflow of powerful feelings.
—*William Wordsworth*

musical thought.
—*Thomas Carlyle*

emotion put into measure.
—*Thomas Hardy*

a way of remembering what it would impoverish us to forget.
—*Robert Frost*

a revelation in words by means of the words.
—*Wallace Stevens*

Poetry is prose bewitched.
—*Mina Loy*

not the assertion that something is true, but the making of that
truth more fully real to us.
—*T. S. Eliot*

the clear expression of mixed feelings.
—*W. H. Auden*

hundreds of things coming together at the right moment.
—*Elizabeth Bishop*

> Verse should have two obligations: to communicate a precise
> instance and to touch us physically, as the presence of the
> sea does.
> > —*Jorge Luis Borges*

> Reduced to its simplest and most essential form, the poem is a
> song. Song is neither discourse nor explanation.
> > —*Octavio Paz*

> anything said in such a way, or put on the page in such a way,
> as to invite from the hearer or the reader a certain kind of
> attention.
> > —*William Stafford*

A poem differs from most prose in several ways. For one, both writer and reader tend to regard it differently. The poet's attitude is something like this: I offer this piece of writing to be read not as prose but as a poem—that is, more perceptively, thoughtfully, and considerately, with more attention to sounds and connotations. This is a great deal to expect, but in return, the reader, too, has a right to certain expectations. Approaching the poem in the anticipation of out-of-the-ordinary knowledge and pleasure, the reader assumes that the poem may use certain enjoyable devices not available to prose: rime, alliteration, meter, and rhythms—definite, various, or emphatic. (The poet may not *always* decide to use these things.) The reader expects the poet to make greater use, perhaps, of resources of meaning such as figurative language, allusion, symbol, and imagery. As readers of prose, we might seek no more than meaning: no more than what could be paraphrased without serious loss. Meeting any figurative language or graceful turns of word order, we think them pleasant extras. But in poetry all these "extras" matter as much as the paraphrasable content, if not more. For, when we finish reading a good poem, we cannot explain precisely to ourselves what we have experienced—without repeating, word for word, the language of the poem itself. Archibald MacLeish makes this point memorably in "Ars Poetica":

> A poem should not mean
> But be.

Throughout this book, we have been working on the assumption that the patient and conscious explication of poems will sharpen unconscious perceptions. We can only hope that it will; the final test lies in whether you care to go on by yourself, reading other poems, finding in them pleasure and enlightenment. Pedagogy must have a stop; so too must the viewing of poems as if their elements fell into chapters. For the total experience of reading a poem surpasses the mind's categories. The wind in the grass, says a proverb, cannot be taken into the house.

21
Poems for Further Reading

Anonymous (traditional Scottish ballad)

Lord Randall

"O where ha you been, Lord Randal, my son?
And where ha you been, my handsome young man?"
"I ha been at the greenwood; mother, mak my bed soon,
For I'm wearied wi hunting, and fain wad lie down."

"An wha° met ye there, Lord Randal, my son?   *who*   5
An wha met you there, my handsome young man?"
"O I met wi my true-love; mother, mak my bed soon,
For I'm wearied wi hunting, and fain wad lie down."

"And what did she give you, Lord Randal, my son?
And what did she give you, my handsome young man?"   10
"Eels fried in a pan; mother, mak my bed soon,
For I'm wearied wi hunting, and fain wad lie down."

"And wha gat° your leavins,° Lord Randal, my son?   *got; leftovers*
And wha gat your leavins, my handsome young man?"
"My hawks and my hounds; mother, mak my bed soon,   15
For I'm wearied wi hunting, and fain wad lie down."

"And what becam of them, Lord Randal, my son?
And what becam of them, my handsome young man?"
"They stretched their legs out an died; mother, mak my bed soon,
For I'm wearied wi hunting, and fain wad lie down."   20

"O I fear you are poisoned, Lord Randal, my son!
I fear you are poisoned, my handsome young man!"
"O yes, I am poisoned; mother, mak my bed soon,
For I'm sick at the heart, and I fain wad lie down."

"What d' ye leave to your mother, Lord Randal, my son?   25
What d' ye leave to your mother, my handsome young man?"

"Four and twenty milk kye;° mother, mak my bed soon,   *cows*
For I'm sick at the heart, and I fain wad lie down."

"What d' ye leave to your sister, Lord Randal, my son?
What d' ye leave to your sister, my handsome young man?"   30
"My gold and my silver; mother, mak my bed soon,
For I'm sick at the heart, and I fain wad lie down."

"What d' ye leave to your brother, Lord Randal, my son?
What d' ye leave to your brother, my handsome young man?"
"My house and my lands; mother, mak my bed soon,   35
For I'm sick at the heart, and I fain wad lie down."

"What d' ye leave to your true-love, Lord Randal, my son?
What d' ye leave to your true-love, my handsome young man?"
"I leave her hell and fire; mother, mak my bed soon,
For I'm sick at the heart, and I fain wad lie down."   40

Matthew Arnold (1822–1888)

Dover Beach   1867

The sea is calm tonight.
The tide is full, the moon lies fair
Upon the straits;—on the French coast the light
Gleams and is gone; the cliffs of England stand,
Glimmering and vast, out in the tranquil bay.   5
Come to the window, sweet is the night-air!
Only, from the long line of spray
Where the sea meets the moon-blanched land,
Listen! you hear the grating roar
Of pebbles which the waves draw back, and fling,   10
At their return, up the high strand,
Begin, and cease, and then again begin,
With tremulous cadence slow, and bring
The eternal note of sadness in.

Sophocles long ago   15
Heard it on the Aegean, and it brought
Into his mind the turbid ebb and flow
Of human misery; we
Find also in the sound a thought,
Hearing it by this distant northern sea.   20
The Sea of Faith
Was once, too, at the full, and round earth's shore
Lay like the folds of a bright girdle furled.
But now I only hear

Its melancholy, long, withdrawing roar,   25
Retreating, to the breath
Of the night-wind, down the vast edges drear
And naked shingles° of the world.   *gravel beaches*

Ah, love, let us be true
To one another! for the world, which seems   30
To lie before us like a land of dreams,
So various, so beautiful, so new,
Hath really neither joy, nor love, nor light,
Nor certitude, nor peace, nor help for pain;
And we are here as on a darkling° plain   *darkened or darkening*   35
Swept with confused alarms of struggle and flight,
Where ignorant armies clash by night.

MARGARET ATWOOD

Margaret Atwood (b. 1939)

Siren Song   1974

This is the one song everyone
would like to learn: the song
that is irresistible:

the song that forces men
to leap overboard in squadrons   5
even though they see the beached skulls

the song nobody knows
because anyone who has heard it
is dead, and the others can't remember.

Shall I tell you the secret   10
and if I do, will you get me
out of this bird suit?

I don't enjoy it here
squatting on this island
looking picturesque and mythical 15

with these two feathery maniacs,
I don't enjoy singing
this trio, fatal and valuable.

I will tell the secret to you,
to you, only to you. 20
Come closer. This song

is a cry for help: Help me!
Only you, only you can,
you are unique

at last. Alas 25
it is a boring song
but it works every time.

SIREN SONG. In Greek mythology, sirens were half-woman, half-bird nymphs who lured sailors to their deaths by singing hypnotically beautiful songs.

The Fall of Icarus by Pieter Brueghel the Elder (1520?–1569)

W. H. Auden (1907–1973)

Musée des Beaux Arts   1940

About suffering they were never wrong,
The Old Masters: how well they understood
Its human position; how it takes place
While someone else is eating or opening a window or just walking
    dully along;
How, when the aged are reverently, passionately waiting   5
For the miraculous birth, there always must be
Children who did not specially want it to happen, skating
On a pond at the edge of the wood:
They never forgot
That even the dreadful martyrdom must run its course   10
Anyhow in a corner, some untidy spot
Where the dogs go on with their doggy life and the torturer's horse
Scratches its innocent behind on a tree.

In Brueghel's *Icarus*, for instance: how everything turns away
Quite leisurely from the disaster; the ploughman may   15
Have heard the splash, the forsaken cry,
But for him it was not an important failure; the sun shone
As it had to on the white legs disappearing into the green
Water; and the expensive delicate ship that must have seen
Something amazing, a boy falling out of the sky,   20
Had somewhere to get to and sailed calmly on.

Elizabeth Bishop (1911–1979)

One Art   1976

The art of losing isn't hard to master;
so many things seem filled with the intent
to be lost that their loss is no disaster.

Lose something every day. Accept the fluster
of lost door keys, the hour badly spent.   5
The art of losing isn't hard to master.

Then practice losing farther, losing faster:
places, and names, and where it was you meant
to travel. None of these will bring disaster.

I lost my mother's watch. And look! my last, or 10
next-to-last, of three loved houses went.
The art of losing isn't hard to master.

I lost two cities, lovely ones. And, vaster,
some realms I owned, two rivers, a continent.
I miss them, but it wasn't a disaster. 15

—Even losing you (the joking voice, a gesture
I love) I shan't have lied. It's evident
the art of losing's not too hard to master
though it may look like (*Write* it!) like disaster.

Detail of William Blake's *The Tyger*

William Blake (1757–1827)

The Tyger   1794

Tyger! Tyger! burning bright
In the forests of the night,
What immortal hand or eye
Could frame thy fearful symmetry?

In what distant deeps or skies 5
Burnt the fire of thine eyes?
On what wings dare he aspire?
What the hand dare seize the fire?

And what shoulder, and what art,
Could twist the sinews of thy heart? 10
And when thy heart began to beat,
What dread hand? and what dread feet?

What the hammer? what the chain?
In what furnace was thy brain?
What the anvil? what dread grasp 15
Dare its deadly terrors clasp?

When the stars threw down their spears,
And watered heaven with their tears,
Did he smile his work to see?
Did he who made the Lamb make thee? 20

Tyger! Tyger! burning bright
In the forests of the night,
What immortal hand or eye
Dare frame thy fearful symmetry?

Gwendolyn Brooks (1917–2000)

the preacher: ruminates behind the sermon

1945

I think it must be lonely to be God.
Nobody loves a master. No. Despite
The bright hosannas, bright dear-Lords, and bright
Determined reverence of Sunday eyes.

Picture Jehovah striding through the hall 5
Of His importance, creatures running out
From servant-corners to acclaim, to shout
Appreciation of His merit's glare.

But who walks with Him?—dares to take His arm,
To slap Him on the shoulder, tweak His ear, 10
Buy Him a Coca-Cola or a beer,
Pooh-pooh His politics, call Him a fool?

Perhaps—who knows?—He tires of looking down.
Those eyes are never lifted. Never straight.
Perhaps sometimes He tires of being great 15
In solitude. Without a hand to hold.

Elizabeth Barrett Browning (1806–1861)

How Do I Love Thee?   1850
Let Me Count the Ways

How do I love thee? Let me count the ways.
I love thee to the depth and breadth and height
My soul can reach, when feeling out of sight
For the ends of being and ideal grace.
I love thee to the level of every day's   5
Most quiet need, by sun and candle-light.
I love thee freely, as men strive for right.
I love thee purely, as they turn from praise.
I love thee with the passion put to use
In my old griefs, and with my childhood's faith.   10
I love thee with a love I seemed to lose
With my lost saints. I love thee with the breath,
Smiles, tears, of all my life; and, if God choose,
I shall but love thee better after death.

Judith Ortiz Cofer (b. 1952)

Quinceañera   1987

My dolls have been put away like dead
children in a chest I will carry
with me when I marry.
I reach under my skirt to feel
a satin slip bought for this day. It is soft   5
as the inside of my thighs. My hair
has been nailed back with my mother's
black hairpins to my skull. Her hands
stretched my eyes open as she twisted
braids into a tight circle at the nape   10
of my neck. I am to wash my own clothes
and sheets from this day on, as if
the fluids of my body were poison, as if
the little trickle of blood I believe
travels from my heart to the world were   15
shameful. Is not the blood of saints and
men in battle beautiful? Do Christ's hands
not bleed into your eyes from His cross?

At night I hear myself growing and wake
to find my hands drifting of their own will   20
to soothe skin stretched tight
over my bones.
I am wound like the guts of a clock,
waiting for each hour to release me.

QUINCEAÑERA. The title refers to a fifteen-year-old girl's coming-out party in Latin cultures.

Samuel Taylor Coleridge (1772–1834)

Kubla Khan   (1797–1798)

Or, a Vision in a Dream. A Fragment.

In Xanadu did Kubla Khan
A stately pleasure-dome decree:
Where Alph, the sacred river, ran
Through caverns measureless to man
    Down to a sunless sea.   5
So twice five miles of fertile ground
With walls and towers were girdled round;
And there were gardens bright with sinuous rills,
Where blossomed many an incense-bearing tree;
And here were forests ancient as the hills,   10
Enfolding sunny spots of greenery.

But oh! that deep romantic chasm which slanted
Down the green hill athwart a cedarn cover!
A savage place! as holy and enchanted
As e'er beneath a waning moon was haunted   15
By woman wailing for her demon-lover!
And from this chasm, with ceaseless turmoil seething,
As if this earth in fast thick pants were breathing,
A mighty fountain momently was forced:
Amid whose swift half-intermitted burst   20
Huge fragments vaulted like rebounding hail,
Or chaffy grain beneath the thresher's flail:
And 'mid these dancing rocks at once and ever
It flung up momently the sacred river.
Five miles meandering with a mazy motion   25
Through wood and dale the sacred river ran,
Then reached the caverns measureless to man,

And sank in tumult to a lifeless ocean:
And 'mid this tumult Kubla heard from far
Ancestral voices prophesying war!   30

    The shadow of the dome of pleasure
    Floated midway on the waves;
    Where was heard the mingled measure
    From the fountain and the caves.
It was a miracle of rare device,   35
A sunny pleasure-dome with caves of ice!

    A damsel with a dulcimer
    In a vision once I saw:
    It was an Abyssinian maid,
    And on her dulcimer she played,   40
    Singing of Mount Abora.
    Could I revive within me
    Her symphony and song,
    To such a deep delight 'twould win me,
That with music loud and long,   45
I would build that dome in air,
That sunny dome! those caves of ice!
And all who heard should see them there,
And all should cry, Beware! Beware!
His flashing eyes, his floating hair!   50
Weave a circle round him thrice,
And close your eyes with holy dread,
For he on honey-dew hath fed,
And drunk the milk of Paradise.

KUBLA KHAN. There was an actual Kublai Khan, a thirteenth-century Mongol emperor,
and a Chinese city of Xanadu; but Coleridge's dream vision also borrows from travelers' descriptions of such other exotic places as Abyssinia and America. 51 *circle:* a magic circle
drawn to keep away evil spirits.

Billy Collins (b. 1941)

Care and Feeding   2003

Because I will turn 420 tomorrow
in dog years
I will take myself for a long walk
along the green shore of the lake,

and when I walk in the door,
I will jump up on my chest
and lick my nose and ears and eyelids
while I tell myself again and again to get down.   5

I will fill my metal bowl at the sink
with cold fresh water,
and lift a biscuit from the jar   10
and hold it gingerly with my teeth.

Then I will make three circles
and lie down at my feet on the wood floor
and close my eyes   15
while I type all morning and into the afternoon,

checking every once in a while
to make sure I am still there,
reaching down
to stroke my furry, venerable head.   20

E. E. CUMMINGS

E. E. Cummings (1894–1962)

somewhere i have never travelled, gladly beyond   1931

somewhere i have never travelled,gladly beyond
any experience,your eyes have their silence:
in your most frail gesture are things which enclose me,
or which i cannot touch because they are too near

your slightest look easily will unclose me   5
though i have closed myself as fingers,
you open always petal by petal myself as Spring opens
(touching skilfully,mysteriously)her first rose

or if your wish be to close me,i and
my life will shut very beautifully,suddenly,   10
as when the heart of this flower imagines
the snow carefully everywhere descending;

nothing which we are to perceive in this world equals
the power of your intense fragility:whose texture
compels me with the colour of its countries,   15
rendering death and forever with each breathing

(i do not know what it is about you that closes
and opens;only something in me understands
the voice of your eyes is deeper than all roses)
nobody,not even the rain,has such small hands   20

MARISA DE LOS SANTOS

Marisa de los Santos (b. 1966)

Perfect Dress   2000

It's here in a student's journal, a blue confession
in smudged, erasable ink: "I can't stop hoping
I'll wake up, suddenly beautiful," and isn't it strange
how we want it, despite all we know? To be at last

the girl in the photograph, cobalt-eyed, hair puddling   5
like cognac, or the one stretched at the ocean's edge,
curved and light-drenched, more like a beach than
the beach. I confess I have longed to stalk runways,

leggy, otherworldly as a mantis, to balance a head
like a Fabergé egg on the longest, most elegant neck.   10
Today in the checkout line, I saw a magazine
claiming to know "How to Find the Perfect Dress

for that Perfect Evening," and I felt the old pull, flare
of the pilgrim's twin flames, desire and faith. At fifteen,
I spent weeks at the search. Going from store to store,   15
hands thirsty for shine, I reached for polyester satin,

machine-made lace, petunia- and Easter egg-colored,
brilliant and flammable. Nothing *haute* about this
couture but my hopes for it, as I tugged it on
and waited for my one, true body to emerge.   20

(Picture the angel inside uncut marble, articulation
of wings and robes poised in expectation of release.)
What I wanted was ordinary miracle, the falling away
of everything wrong. Silly maybe or maybe

I was right, that there's no limit to the ways eternity   25
suggests itself, that one day I'll slip into it, say
floor-length plum charmeuse. Someone will murmur,
"She is sublime," will be precisely right, and I will step,

with incandescent shoulders, into my perfect evening.

PERFECT DRESS. 10 *Fabergé*: Peter Carl Fabergé (1846–1920) was a Russian jeweler
renowned for his elaborately decorated, golden, jeweled eggs.

EMILY DICKINSON
(Amherst College Archives and Special Collections)

Emily Dickinson (1830–1886)

I'm Nobody! Who are you?   (about 1861)

I'm Nobody! Who are you?
Are you – Nobody – Too?
Then there's a pair of us!
Don't tell! they'd advertise – you know!

How dreary – to be – Somebody!   5
How public – like a Frog –
To tell one's name – the livelong June –
To an admiring Bog!

Emily Dickinson (1830–1886)

I heard a Fly buzz – when I died   (about 1862)

I heard a Fly buzz – when I died –
The Stillness in the Room
Was like the Stillness in the Air –
Between the Heaves of Storm –

The Eyes around – had wrung them dry –   5
And Breaths were gathering firm
For that last Onset – when the King
Be witnessed – in the Room –

I willed my Keepsakes – Signed away
What portion of me be   10
Assignable – and then it was
There interposed a Fly –

With Blue – uncertain stumbling Buzz –
Between the light – and me –
And then the Windows failed – and then   15
I could not see to see –

Emily Dickinson (1830–1886)

Because I could not stop for Death   (about 1863)

Because I could not stop for Death –
He kindly stopped for me –
The Carriage held but just Ourselves –
And Immortality.

We slowly drove – He knew no haste   5
And I had put away
My labor and my leisure too,
For His Civility –

We passed the School, where Children strove
At Recess – in the Ring –   10
We passed the Fields of Gazing Grain –
We passed the Setting Sun –

Or rather – He passed Us –
The Dews drew quivering and chill –
For only Gossamer, my Gown –   15
My Tippet° – only Tulle –   *cape*

We paused before a House that seemed
A Swelling of the Ground –
The Roof was scarcely visible –
The Cornice – in the Ground –   20

Since then – 'tis Centuries – and yet
Feels shorter than the Day
I first surmised the Horses' Heads
Were toward Eternity –

JOHN DONNE

John Donne (1572–1631)

Death be not proud   (about 1610)

Death be not proud, though some have callèd thee
Mighty and dreadful, for thou art not so;
For those whom thou think'st thou dost overthrow
Die not, poor death, nor yet canst thou kill me.
From rest and sleep, which but thy pictures be,   5
Much pleasure, then from thee much more must flow,
And soonest our best men with thee do go,
Rest of their bones, and soul's delivery.
Thou art slave to fate, chance, kings, and desperate men,
And dost with poison, war, and sickness dwell,   10
And poppy, or charms can make us sleep as well,
And better than thy stroke; why swell'st thou then?
One short sleep past, we wake eternally,
And death shall be no more; death, thou shalt die.

John Donne (1572–1631)

The Flea   1633

Mark but this flea, and mark in this
How little that which thou deny'st me is;
It sucked me first, and now sucks thee,
And in this flea our two bloods mingled be;
Thou know'st that this cannot be said   5
A sin, nor shame, nor loss of maidenhead,
    Yet this enjoys before it woo,
    And pampered swells with one blood made of two,
    And this, alas, is more than we would do.

Oh stay, three lives in one flea spare,   10
Where we almost, yea more than married are.
This flea is you and I, and this
Our marriage bed, and marriage temple is;
Though parents grudge, and you, we're met
And cloistered in these living walls of jet.   15
    Though use° make you apt to kill me,   *custom*
    Let not to that, self-murder added be,
    And sacrilege, three sins in killing three.

Cruel and sudden, hast thou since
Purpled thy nail in blood of innocence?   20
Wherein could this flea guilty be,
Except in that drop which it sucked from thee?
Yet thou triumph'st, and say'st that thou
Find'st not thyself, nor me, the weaker now;
    'Tis true; then learn how false, fears be;   25
    Just so much honor, when thou yield'st to me,
    Will waste, as this flea's death took life from thee.

Paul Laurence Dunbar (1872–1906)

We Wear the Mask   1895

We wear the mask that grins and lies,
It hides our cheeks and shades our eyes,—
This debt we pay to human guile;
With torn and bleeding hearts we smile,
And mouth with myriad subtleties.   5

Why should the world be otherwise,
In counting all our tears and sighs?

Nay, let them only see us, while
  We wear the mask.

We smile, but, O great Christ, our cries   10
To thee from tortured souls arise.
We sing, but oh the clay is vile
Beneath our feet, and long the mile;
But let the world dream otherwise,
  We wear the mask!   15

T. S. ELIOT

T. S. Eliot (1888–1965)

The Love Song of J. Alfred Prufrock   1917

> *S'io credessi che mia risposta fosse*
> *A persona che mai tornasse al mondo,*
> *Questa fiamma staria senza più scosse.*
> *Ma per ciò che giammai di questo fondo*
> *Non tornò vivo alcun, s'i'odo il vero,*
> *Senza tema d'infamia ti rispondo.*

Let us go then, you and I,
When the evening is spread out against the sky
Like a patient etherized upon a table;
Let us go, through certain half-deserted streets,
The muttering retreats   5
Of restless nights in one-night cheap hotels
And sawdust restaurants with oyster-shells:
Streets that follow like a tedious argument
Of insidious intent
To lead you to an overwhelming question . . .   10
Oh, do not ask, "What is it?"
Let us go and make our visit.

In the room the women come and go
Talking of Michelangelo.

The yellow fog that rubs its back upon the window-panes,   15
The yellow smoke that rubs its muzzle on the window-panes,
Licked its tongue into the corners of the evening,
Lingered upon the pools that stand in drains,
Let fall upon its back the soot that falls from chimneys,
Slipped by the terrace, made a sudden leap,   20
And seeing that it was a soft October night,
Curled once about the house, and fell asleep.

And indeed there will be time
For the yellow smoke that slides along the street
Rubbing its back upon the window-panes;   25
There will be time, there will be time
To prepare a face to meet the faces that you meet;
There will be time to murder and create,
And time for all the works and days of hands
That lift and drop a question on your plate;   30
Time for you and time for me,
And time yet for a hundred indecisions,
And for a hundred visions and revisions,
Before the taking of a toast and tea.

In the room the women come and go   35
Talking of Michelangelo.

And indeed there will be time
To wonder, "Do I dare?" and, "Do I dare?"
Time to turn back and descend the stair,
With a bald spot in the middle of my hair—   40
(They will say: "How his hair is growing thin!")
My morning coat, my collar mounting firmly to the chin,
My necktie rich and modest, but asserted by a simple pin—
(They will say: "But how his arms and legs are thin!")
Do I dare   45
Disturb the universe?
In a minute there is time
For decisions and revisions which a minute will reverse.

For I have known them all already, known them all—
Have known the evenings, mornings, afternoons,   50
I have measured out my life with coffee spoons;
I know the voices dying with a dying fall
Beneath the music from a farther room.
So how should I presume?

And I have known the eyes already, known them all—   55
The eyes that fix you in a formulated phrase,
And when I am formulated, sprawling on a pin,
When I am pinned and wriggling on the wall,
Then how should I begin
To spit out all the butt-ends of my days and ways?   60
    And how should I presume?

And I have known the arms already, known them all—
Arms that are braceleted and white and bare
(But in the lamplight, downed with light brown hair!)
Is it perfume from a dress   65
That makes me so digress?
Arms that lie along a table, or wrap about a shawl.
    And should I then presume?
    And how should I begin?

· · ·

Shall I say, I have gone at dusk through narrow streets   70
And watched the smoke that rises from the pipes
Of lonely men in shirt-sleeves, leaning out of windows? . . .

I should have been a pair of ragged claws
Scuttling across the floors of silent seas.

· · ·

And the afternoon, the evening, sleeps so peacefully!   75
Smoothed by long fingers,
Asleep . . . tired . . . or it malingers,
Stretched on the floor, here beside you and me.
Should I, after tea and cakes and ices,
Have the strength to force the moment to its crisis?   80
But though I have wept and fasted, wept and prayed,
Though I have seen my head (grown slightly bald) brought in upon a
    platter,
I am no prophet—and here's no great matter;
I have seen the moment of my greatness flicker,
And I have seen the eternal Footman hold my coat, and snicker,   85
And in short, I was afraid.

And would it have been worth it, after all,
After the cups, the marmalade, the tea,
Among the porcelain, among some talk of you and me,
Would it have been worth while,   90
To have bitten off the matter with a smile,

To have squeezed the universe into a ball
To roll it towards some overwhelming question,
To say: "I am Lazarus, come from the dead,
Come back to tell you all, I shall tell you all"—   95
If one, settling a pillow by her head,
   Should say: "That is not what I meant at all.
   That is not it, at all."

   And would it have been worth it, after all,
Would it have been worth while,   100
After the sunsets and the dooryards and the sprinkled streets,
After the novels, after the teacups, after the skirts that trail along the
    floor—
And this, and so much more?—
It is impossible to say just what I mean!
But as if a magic lantern threw the nerves in patterns on a screen: 105
Would it have been worth while
If one, settling a pillow or throwing off a shawl,
And turning toward the window, should say:
   "That is not it at all,
   That is not what I meant, at all."   110

* * *

No! I am not Prince Hamlet, nor was meant to be;
Am an attendant lord, one that will do
To swell a progress, start a scene or two,
Advise the prince; no doubt, an easy tool,
Deferential, glad to be of use,   115
Politic, cautious, and meticulous;
Full of high sentence, but a bit obtuse;
At times, indeed, almost ridiculous—
Almost, at times, the Fool.

   I grow old . . . I grow old . . .   120
I shall wear the bottoms of my trousers rolled.

   Shall I part my hair behind? Do I dare to eat a peach?
I shall wear white flannel trousers, and walk upon the beach.
I have heard the mermaids singing, each to each.

   I do not think that they will sing to me.   125

   I have seen them riding seaward on the waves
Combing the white hair of the waves blown back
When the wind blows the water white and black.

We have lingered in the chambers of the sea
By sea-girls wreathed with seaweed red and brown
Till human voices wake us, and we drown.

130

THE LOVE SONG OF J. ALFRED PRUFROCK. The epigraph, from Dante's *Inferno*, is the speech of one dead and damned, who thinks that his hearer also is going to remain in Hell. Count Guido da Montefeltro, whose sin has been to give false counsel after a corrupt prelate had offered him prior absolution and whose punishment is to be wrapped in a constantly burning flame, offers to tell Dante his story:

> If I thought my answer were to someone who
>   might see the world again, then there would be
>   no more stirrings of this flame. Since it is true
> that no one leaves these depths of misery
>   alive, from all that I have heard reported,
>   I answer you without fear of infamy.

(Translation by Michael Palma from: Dante Alighieri, *Inferno: A New Verse Translation* [New York: Norton, 2002].)

29 *works and days:* title of a poem by Hesiod (eighth century B.C.), depicting his life as a hard-working Greek farmer and exhorting his brother to be like him. 82 *head . . . platter:* like that of John the Baptist, prophet and praiser of chastity, whom King Herod beheaded at the demand of Herodias, his unlawfully wedded wife (see Mark 6:17–28). 92–93 *squeezed . . . To roll it:* an echo from Marvell's "To His Coy Mistress," lines 41–42. 94 *Lazarus:* probably the Lazarus whom Jesus called forth from the tomb (John 11:1–44), but possibly the beggar seen in Heaven by the rich man in Hell (Luke 16:19–25). 105 *magic lantern:* an early type of projector used to display still pictures from transparent slides.

RHINA ESPAILLAT

Rhina Espaillat (b. 1932)

Bilingual/Bilingüe

1998

My father liked them separate, one there,
one here (allá y aquí), as if aware

that words might cut in two his daughter's heart
(el corazón) and lock the alien part

to what he was—his memory, his name
(su nombre)—with a key he could not claim. 5

"English outside this door, Spanish inside,"
he said, "y basta." But who can divide

the world, the word (mundo y palabra) from
any child? I knew how to be dumb 10

and stubborn (testaruda); late, in bed,
I hoarded secret syllables I read

until my tongue (mi lengua) learned to run
where his stumbled. And still the heart was one.

I like to think he knew that, even when, 15
proud (orgulloso) of his daughter's pen,

he stood outside mis versos, half in fear
of words he loved but wanted not to hear.

ROBERT FROST

Robert Frost (1874–1963)

Mending Wall   1914

Something there is that doesn't love a wall,
That sends the frozen-ground-swell under it,
And spills the upper boulders in the sun;
And makes gaps even two can pass abreast.
The work of hunters is another thing: 5

I have come after them and made repair
Where they have left not one stone on a stone,
But they would have the rabbit out of hiding,
To please the yelping dogs. The gaps I mean,
No one has seen them made or heard them made,   10
But at spring mending-time we find them there.
I let my neighbor know beyond the hill;
And on a day we meet to walk the line
And set the wall between us once again.
We keep the wall between us as we go.   15
To each the boulders that have fallen to each.
And some are loaves and some so nearly balls
We have to use a spell to make them balance:
"Stay where you are until our backs are turned!"
We wear our fingers rough with handling them.   20
Oh, just another kind of outdoor game,
One on a side. It comes to little more:
There where it is we do not need the wall:
He is all pine and I am apple orchard.
My apple trees will never get across   25
And eat the cones under his pines, I tell him.
He only says, "Good fences make good neighbors."
Spring is the mischief in me, and I wonder
If I could put a notion in his head:
"Why do they make good neighbors? Isn't it   30
Where there are cows? But here there are no cows.
Before I built a wall I'd ask to know
What I was walling in or walling out,
And to whom I was like to give offence.
Something there is that doesn't love a wall,   35
That wants it down." I could say "Elves" to him,
But it's not elves exactly, and I'd rather
He said it for himself. I see him there
Bringing a stone grasped firmly by the top
In each hand, like an old-stone savage armed.   40
He moves in darkness as it seems to me,
Not of woods only and the shade of trees.
He will not go behind his father's saying,
And he likes having thought of it so well
He says again, "Good fences make good neighbors."   45

Robert Frost (1874–1963)

Stopping by Woods on a Snowy Evening

1923

Whose woods these are I think I know.
His house is in the village though;
He will not see me stopping here
To watch his woods fill up with snow.

My little horse must think it queer   5
To stop without a farmhouse near
Between the woods and frozen lake
The darkest evening of the year.

He gives his harness bells a shake
To ask if there is some mistake.   10
The only other sound's the sweep
Of easy wind and downy flake.

The woods are lovely, dark and deep,
But I have promises to keep,
And miles to go before I sleep,   15
And miles to go before I sleep.

Allen Ginsberg (1926–1997)

A Supermarket in California

1956

What thoughts I have of you tonight, Walt Whitman, for I
walked down the sidestreets under the trees with a headache self-
conscious looking at the full moon.

In my hungry fatigue, and shopping for images, I went into the
neon fruit supermarket, dreaming of your enumerations!

What peaches and what penumbras! Whole families shopping
at night! Aisles full of husbands! Wives in the avocados, babies in
the tomatoes!—and you, García Lorca, what were you doing down
by the watermelons?

I saw you, Walt Whitman, childless, lonely old grubber, poking
among the meats in the refrigerator and eyeing the grocery boys.

I heard you asking questions of each: Who killed the pork   5
chops? What price bananas? Are you my Angel?

I wandered in and out of the brilliant stacks of cans following
you, and followed in my imagination by the store detective.

We strode down the open corridors together in our solitary
fancy tasting artichokes, possessing every frozen delicacy, and never
passing the cashier.

Where are we going, Walt Whitman? The doors close in an
hour. Which way does your beard point tonight?

(I touch your book and dream of our odyssey in the supermarket
and feel absurd.)

Will we walk all night through solitary streets? The trees add   10
shade to shade, lights out in the houses, we'll both be lonely.

Will we stroll dreaming of the lost America of love past blue
automobiles in driveways, home to our silent cottage?

Ah, dear father, graybeard, lonely old courage-teacher, what
America did you have when Charon quit poling his ferry and you got
out on a smoking bank and stood watching the boat disappear on the
black waters of Lethe?

A SUPERMARKET IN CALIFORNIA. *2 enumerations:* many of Whitman's poems contain lists of
observed details. 3 *García Lorca:* modern Spanish poet who wrote an "Ode to Walt Whitman"
in his book-length sequence *Poet in New York.* 12 *Charon . . . Lethe:* Is the poet confusing
two underworld rivers? Charon, in Greek and Roman mythology, is the boatman who
ferries the souls of the dead across the River Styx. The River Lethe also flows through
Hades, and a drink of its waters makes the dead lose their painful memories of loved ones
they have left behind.

Thomas Hardy (1840–1928)

The Convergence of the Twain   1912

Lines on the Loss of the "Titanic"

I

In a solitude of the sea
Deep from human vanity,
And the Pride of life that planned her, stilly couches she.

II

Steel chambers, late the pyres
Of her salamandrine fires,
Cold currents thrid,° and turn to rhythmic tidal lyres.   *thread*   5

III

Over the mirrors meant
To glass the opulent
The sea-worm crawls—grotesque, slimed, dumb, indifferent.

IV

Jewels In joy designed   10
To ravish the sensuous mind
Lie lightless, all their sparkles bleared and black and blind.

V

Dim moon-eyed fishes near
Gaze at the gilded gear
And query: "What does this vaingloriousness down here?" . . .   15

VI

Well: while was fashioning
This creature of cleaving wing,
The Immanent Will that stirs and urges everything

VII

Prepared a sinister mate
For her—so gaily great—   20
A Shape of Ice, for the time far and dissociate.

VIII

And as the smart ship grew
In stature, grace, and hue,
In shadowy silent distance grew the Iceberg too.

IX

Alien they seemed to be: 25
No mortal eye could see
The intimate welding of their later history,

X

Or sign that they were bent
By paths coincident
On being anon twin halves of one august event,   30

XI

Till the Spinner of the Years
Said "Now!" And each one hears,
And consummation comes, and jars two hemispheres.

THE CONVERGENCE OF THE TWAIN. The luxury liner *Titanic*, supposedly unsinkable, went
down in 1912 after striking an iceberg on its first Atlantic voyage. 5 *salamandrine:* like the
salamander, a lizard that supposedly thrives in fires, or like a spirit of the same name that
inhabits fire (according to alchemists).

Robert Hayden

Robert Hayden (1913–1980)

Those Winter Sundays 1962

Sundays too my father got up early
and put his clothes on in the blueblack cold,
then with cracked hands that ached
from labor in the weekday weather made
banked fires blaze. No one ever thanked him.   5

I'd wake and hear the cold splintering, breaking.
When the rooms were warm, he'd call,
and slowly I would rise and dress,
fearing the chronic angers of that house,

Speaking indifferently to him,   10
who had driven out the cold
and polished my good shoes as well.
What did I know, what did I know
of love's austere and lonely offices?

Seamus Heaney (b. 1939)

Digging 1966

Between my finger and my thumb
The squat pen rests; snug as a gun.

Under my window, a clean rasping sound
When the spade sinks into gravelly ground:
My father, digging. I look down   5

Till his straining rump among the flowerbeds
Bends low, comes up twenty years away
Stooping in rhythm through potato drills
Where he was digging.

The coarse boot nestled on the lug, the shaft   10
Against the inside knee was levered firmly.
He rooted out tall tops, buried the bright edge deep
To scatter new potatoes that we picked
Loving their cool hardness in our hands.

By God, the old man could handle a spade.   15
Just like his old man.

My grandfather cut more turf in a day
Than any other man on Toner's bog.
Once I carried him milk in a bottle
Corked sloppily with paper. He straightened up   20
To drink it, then fell to right away

Nicking and slicing neatly, heaving sods
Over his shoulder, going down and down
For the good turf. Digging.

The cold smell of potato mould, the squelch and slap   25
Of soggy peat, the curt cuts of an edge
Through living roots awaken in my head.
But I've no spade to follow men like them.

Between my finger and my thumb
The squat pen rests.   30
I'll dig with it.

George Herbert (1593–1633)

Easter Wings   1633

Lord, who createdst man in wealth and store,
Though foolishly he lost the same,
Decaying more and more
Till he became
Most poor;
With thee
Oh, let me rise
As larks, harmoniously,
And sing this day thy victories;
Then shall the fall further the flight in me.

My tender age in sorrow did begin;
And still with sicknesses and shame
Thou didst so punish sin,
That I became
Most thin.
With thee
Let me combine,
And feel this day thy victory;
For if I imp my wing on thine,
Affliction shall advance the flight in me.

Robert Herrick (1591–1674)

To the Virgins, to Make Much of Time   1648

Gather ye rose-buds while ye may,
   Old Time is still a-flying;
And this same flower that smiles today,
   Tomorrow will be dying.

The glorious lamp of heaven, the sun,   5
   The higher he's a-getting,
The sooner will his race be run,
   And nearer he's to setting.

That age is best which is the first,
   When youth and blood are warmer;   10
But being spent, the worse, and worst
   Times still succeed the former.

Then be not coy, but use your time,
   And while ye may, go marry;
For having lost but once your prime,   15
   You may for ever tarry.

Gerard Manley Hopkins (1844–1889)

Spring and Fall (1880)

To a young child

Márgarét, áre you grieving
Over Goldengrove unleaving°   *shedding its leaves*
Leáves, líke the things of man, you
With your fresh thoughts care for, can you?
Áh! ás the heart grows older   5
It will come to such sights colder
By and by, nor spare a sigh
Though worlds of wanwood leafmeal lie;
And yet you wíll weep and know why.
Now no matter, child, the name: 10
Sórrow's spríngs áre the same.
Nor mouth had, no nor mind, expressed
What heart heard of, ghost° guessed: *spirit*
It ís the blight man was born for,
It is Márgarét you mourn for.   15

Gerard Manley Hopkins (1844–1889)

The Windhover (1877)

To Christ Our Lord

I caught this morning morning's minion, king-
 dom of daylight's dauphin, dapple-dawn-drawn Falcon, in his
  riding
 Of the rolling level underneath him steady air, and striding
High there, how he rung upon the rein of a wimpling wing
In his ecstasy! then off, off forth on swing,   5
 As a skate's heel sweeps smooth on a bow-bend: the hurl and
  gliding
 Rebuffed the big wind. My heart in hiding
Stirred for a bird, —the achieve of, the mastery of the thing!

Brute beauty and valor and act, oh, air, pride, plume, here
 Buckle! AND the fire that breaks from thee then, a billion 10
Times told lovelier, more dangerous, O my chevalier!

 No wonder of it: shéer plód makes plow down sillion°   *furrow*
Shine, and blue-bleak embers, ah my dear,
 Fall, gall themselves, and gash gold-vermilion.

THE WINDHOVER. A windhover is a kestrel, or small falcon, so called because it can hover upon the wind. 4 *rung . . . wing:* A horse is "rung upon the rein" when its trainer holds the end of a long rein and has the horse circle him. The possible meanings of *wimpling* include: (1) curving; (2) pleated, arranged in many little folds one on top of another; (3) rippling or undulating like the surface of a flowing stream.

A. E. Housman (1859–1936)

To an Athlete Dying Young   1896

The time you won your town the race
We chaired you through the market-place;
Man and boy stood cheering by,
And home we brought you shoulder-high.

Today, the road all runners come,   5
Shoulder-high we bring you home,
And set you at your threshold down,
Townsman of a stiller town.

Smart lad, to slip betimes away
From fields where glory does not stay,   10
And early though the laurel grows
It withers quicker than the rose.

Eyes the shady night has shut
Cannot see the record cut,
And silence sounds no worse than cheers   15
After earth has stopped the ears:

Now you will not swell the rout
Of lads that wore their honors out,
Runners whom renown outran
And the name died before the man.   20

So set, before its echoes fade,
The fleet foot on the sill of shade,
And hold to the low lintel up
The still-defended challenge-cup.

And round that early-laureled head   25
Will flock to gaze the strengthless dead,
And find unwithered on its curls
The garland briefer than a girl's.

A. E. Housman (1859–1936)

Loveliest of trees, the cherry now · 1896

Loveliest of trees, the cherry now
Is hung with bloom along the bough,
And stands about the woodland ride°   *path*
Wearing white for Eastertide.

Now, of my threescore years and ten,   5
Twenty will not come again,
And take from seventy springs a score,
It only leaves me fifty more.

And since to look at things in bloom
Fifty springs are little room,   10
About the woodlands I will go
To see the cherry hung with snow.

LANGSTON HUGHES

Langston Hughes (1902–1967)

The Negro Speaks of Rivers · (1921) 1926

I've known rivers:
I've known rivers ancient as the world and older than the flow of
    human blood in human veins.

My soul has grown deep like the rivers.

I bathed in the Euphrates when dawns were young.
I built my hut near the Congo and it lulled me to sleep.   5
I looked upon the Nile and raised the pyramids above it.
I heard the singing of the Mississippi when Abe Lincoln went down
    to New Orleans, and I've seen its muddy bosom turn all golden
    in the sunset.

I've known rivers:
Ancient, dusky rivers.

My soul has grown deep like the rivers.   10

Langston Hughes (1902–1967)

Harlem [Dream Deferred]   1951

What happens to a dream deferred?

    Does it dry up
    like a raisin in the sun?
    Or fester like a sore—
    And then run?   5
    Does it stink like rotten meat?
    Or crust and sugar over—
    like a syrupy sweet?

    Maybe it just sags
    like a heavy load.   10

    Or does it explode?

HARLEM. This famous poem appeared under two titles in the author's lifetime. Both titles
appear above.

Randall Jarrell (1914–1965)

The Death of the Ball Turret Gunner   1945

From my mother's sleep I fell into the State,
And I hunched in its belly till my wet fur froze.
Six miles from earth, loosed from its dream of life,
I woke to black flak and the nightmare fighters.
When I died they washed me out of the turret with a hose.   5

THE DEATH OF THE BALL TURRET GUNNER. Jarrell has written: "A ball turret was a plexi-
glass sphere set into the belly of a B-17 or B-24, and inhabited by two .50 caliber machine-
guns and one man, a short small man. When this gunner tracked with his machine-guns a
fighter attacking his bomber from below, he revolved with the turret; hunched in his little
sphere, he looked like the fetus in the womb. The fighters which attacked him were armed
with cannon firing explosive shells. The hose was a steam hose."

Robinson Jeffers (1887–1962)

To the Stone-Cutters   1925

Stone-cutters fighting time with marble, you foredefeated
Challengers of oblivion
Eat cynical earnings, knowing rock splits, records fall down,
The square-limbed Roman letters
Scale in the thaws, wear in the rain. The poet as well   5

Builds his monument mockingly;
For man will be blotted out, the blithe earth die, the brave sun
Die blind, his heart blackening:
Yet stones have stood for a thousand years, and pained thoughts found
The honey peace in old poems.   10

Ben Jonson (1573?–1637)

On My First Son   (1603)

Farewell, thou child of my right hand, and joy.
My sin was too much hope of thee, loved boy;
Seven years thou wert lent to me, and I thee pay,
Exacted by thy fate, on the just day.
Oh, could I lose all father° now. For why   *fatherhood*   5
Will man lament the state he should envy̖—
To have so soon 'scaped world's and flesh's rage,
And, if no other misery, yet age?
Rest in soft peace, and asked, say, "Here doth lie
Ben Jonson his best piece of poetry,"   10
For whose sake henceforth all his vows be such
As what he loves may never like° too much.   *thrive*

ON MY FIRST SON. 1 *child of my right hand*: Jonson's son was named Benjamin; this phrase
translates the Hebrew name. 4 *the just day*: the very day. The boy had died on his seventh
birthday. 10 *poetry*: Jonson uses the word *poetry* here reflecting its Greek root *poiesis*, which
means *creation*.

Donald Justice (1925–2004)

On the Death of Friends in Childhood   1960

We shall not ever meet them bearded in heaven,
Nor sunning themselves among the bald of hell;
If anywhere, in the deserted schoolyard at twilight,
Forming a ring, perhaps, or joining hands
In games whose very names we have forgotten.   5
Come, memory, let us seek them there in the shadows.

JOHN KEATS

John Keats (1795–1821)

Ode on a Grecian Urn   1820

Thou still unravished bride of quietness,
　　Thou foster-child of silence and slow time,
Sylvan historian, who canst thus express
　　A flowery tale more sweetly than our rhyme:
What leaf-fringed legend haunts about thy shape   5
　　Of deities or mortals, or of both,
　　　　In Tempe or the dales of Arcady?
What men or gods are these? What maidens loth?
What mad pursuit? What struggle to escape?
　　　　What pipes and timbrels? What wild ecstasy?   10

Heard melodies are sweet, but those unheard
　　Are sweeter; therefore, ye soft pipes, play on;
Not to the sensual° ear, but, more endeared,   *physical*
　　Pipe to the spirit ditties of no tone:
Fair youth, beneath the trees, thou canst not leave   15
　　Thy song, nor ever can those trees be bare;
　　　　Bold Lover, never, never canst thou kiss,
Though winning near the goal—yet, do not grieve;
　　She cannot fade, though thou hast not thy bliss,
　　　　For ever wilt thou love, and she be fair!   20

Ah, happy, happy boughs! that cannot shed
　　Your leaves, nor ever bid the Spring adieu;
And, happy melodist, unwearièd,
　　For ever piping songs for ever new;
More happy love! more happy, happy love!   25
　　For ever warm and still to be enjoyed,
　　　　For ever panting, and for ever young;

All breathing human passion far above,
  That leaves a heart high-sorrowful and cloyed,
    A burning forehead, and a parching tongue.   30

Who are these coming to the sacrifice?
  To what green altar, O mysterious priest,
Lead'st thou that heifer lowing at the skies,
  And all her silken flanks with garlands drest?
What little town by river or sea shore,   35
  Or mountain-built with peaceful citadel,
    Is emptied of this folk, this pious morn?
And, little town, thy streets for evermore
  Will silent be; and not a soul to tell
    Why thou art desolate, can e'er return.   40

O Attic shape! Fair attitude! with brede°   *design*
  Of marble men and maidens overwrought,
With forest branches and the trodden weed;
  Thou, silent form, dost tease us out of thought
As doth Eternity: Cold Pastoral!   45
  When old age shall this generation waste,
    Thou shalt remain, in midst of other woe
Than ours, a friend to man, to whom thou say'st,
Beauty is truth, truth beauty,—that is all
  Ye know on earth, and all ye need to know.   50

ODE ON A GRECIAN URN. *7 Tempe, dales of Arcady*: valleys in Greece. *41 Attic*: Athenian, possessing a classical simplicity and grace. *49–50*: if Keats had put the urn's words in quotation marks, critics might have been spared much ink. Does the urn say just "beauty is truth, truth beauty," or does its statement take in the whole of the last two lines?

John Keats (1795–1821)

La Belle Dame sans Merci   1819

I

O what can ail thee, knight at arms,
  Alone and palely loitering?
The sedge has wither'd from the lake,
  And no birds sing.

II

O what can ail thee, knight at arms,   5
  So haggard and so woe-begone?
The squirrel's granary is full,
  And the harvest's done.

III

I see a lily on thy brow
    With anguish moist and fever dew,   10
And on thy cheeks a fading rose
    Fast withereth too.

IV

I met a lady in the meads,
    Full beautiful—a fairy's child;
Her hair was long, her foot was light,   15
    And her eyes were wild.

V

I made a garland for her head,
    And bracelets too, and fragrant zone;
She look'd at me as she did love,
    And made sweet moan.   20

VI

I set her on my pacing steed,
    And nothing else saw all day long,
For sidelong would she bend, and sing
    A fairy's song.

VII

She found me roots of relish sweet,   25
    And honey wild, and manna dew,
And sure in language strange she said—
    "I love thee true."

VIII

She took me to her elfin grot,
    And there she wept, and sigh'd full sore,   30
And there I shut her wild wild eyes
    With kisses four.

IX

And there she lulled me asleep,
    And there I dream'd—Ah! woe betide!
The latest dream I ever dream'd   35
    On the cold hill's side.

X

I saw pale kings and princes too,
    Pale warriors, death-pale were they all;
They cried—"La belle dame sans merci
    Hath thee in thrall!"   40

XI

I saw their starv'd lips in the gloam,
    With horrid warning gaped wide,
And I awoke and found me here,
    On the cold hill's side.

XII

And this is why I sojourn here,   45
    Alone and palely loitering,
Though the sedge is wither'd from the lake,
    And no birds sing.

LA BELLE DAME SANS MERCI. The title is French for "the beautiful woman without mercy."
Keats borrowed the title from a fifteenth-century French poem.

Ted Kooser (b. 1939)

Abandoned Farmhouse   1969/1974

He was a big man, says the size of his shoes
on a pile of broken dishes by the house;
a tall man too, says the length of the bed
in an upstairs room; and a good, God-fearing man,
says the Bible with a broken back   5
on the floor below the window, dusty with sun;
but not a man for farming, say the fields
cluttered with boulders and the leaky barn.

A woman lived with him, says the bedroom wall
papered with lilacs and the kitchen shelves   10
covered with oilcloth, and they had a child,
says the sandbox made from a tractor tire.
Money was scarce, say the jars of plum preserves
and canned tomatoes sealed in the cellar hole.
And the winters cold, say the rags in the window frames.   15
It was lonely here, says the narrow country road.

Something went wrong, says the empty house
in the weed-choked yard. Stones in the fields
say he was not a farmer; the still-sealed jars
in the cellar say she left in a nervous haste.   20
And the child? Its toys are strewn in the yard
like branches after a storm—a rubber cow,
a rusty tractor with a broken plow,
a doll in overalls. Something went wrong, they say.

PHILIP LARKIN

Philip Larkin (1922–1985)

Home is so Sad   1964

Home is so sad. It stays as it was left,
Shaped to the comfort of the last to go
As if to win them back. Instead, bereft
Of anyone to please, it withers so,
Having no heart to put aside the theft   5

And turn again to what it started as,
A joyous shot at how things ought to be,
Long fallen wide. You can see how it was:
Look at the pictures and the cutlery.
The music in the piano stool. That vase.   10

Emma Lazarus (1849–1887)

The New Colossus   1883

Not like the brazen giant of Greek fame,
With conquering limbs astride from land to land;
Here at our sea-washed, sunset gates shall stand
A mighty woman with a torch, whose flame
Is the imprisoned lightning, and her name   5
Mother of Exiles. From her beacon-hand
Glows world-wide welcome; her mild eyes command
The air-bridged harbor that twin cities frame.
"Keep, ancient lands, your storied pomp!" cries she
With silent lips. "Give me your tired, your poor,   10
Your huddled masses yearning to breathe free,
The wretched refuse of your teeming shore.
Send these, the homeless, tempest-tost to me,
I lift my lamp beside the golden door!"

THE NEW COLOSSUS. In 1883, a committee formed to raise funds to build a pedestal for what would be the largest statue in the world, "Liberty Enlightening the World" by Fréderic-Auguste Bartholdi, which was a gift from the French people to celebrate America's centennial. American authors were asked to donate manuscripts for a fund-raising auction. The young poet Emma Lazarus, whose parents had come to America as immigrants, sent in this sonnet composed for the occasion. When President Grover Cleveland unveiled the Statue of Liberty in October 1886, Lazarus's sonnet was read at the ceremony. In 1903, the poem was carved on the statue's pedestal. The reference in the opening line to "the brazen giant of Greek fame" is to the famous Colossus of Rhodes, a huge bronze statue that once stood in the harbor on the Aegean island of Rhodes. Built to commemorate a military victory, it was one of the so-called Seven Wonders of the World.

Shirley Geok-lin Lim (b. 1944)

Learning to love America   1998

because it has no pure products

because the Pacific Ocean sweeps along the coastline
because the water of the ocean is cold
and because land is better than ocean

because I say we rather than they   5

because I live in California
I have eaten fresh artichokes
and jacarandas bloom in April and May

because my senses have caught up with my body
my breath with the air it swallows   10
my hunger with my mouth

because I walk barefoot in my house

because I have nursed my son at my breast
because he is a strong American boy
because I have seen his eyes redden when he is asked who he is   15
because he answers I don't know

because to have a son is to have a country
because my son will bury me here
because countries are in our blood and we bleed them

because it is late and too late to change my mind   20
because it is time.

LEARNING TO LOVE AMERICA. 1 *pure products:* an allusion to poem XVIII of *Spring and All* (1923)
by William Carlos Williams, which begins: "The pure products of America / go crazy—."

Robert Lowell (1917–1977)

Skunk Hour   1959

For Elizabeth Bishop

Nautilus Island's hermit
heiress still lives through winter in her Spartan cottage;
her sheep still graze above the sea.
Her son's a bishop. Her farmer
is first selectman in our village;   5
she's in her dotage.

Thirsting for
the hierarchic privacy
of Queen Victoria's century,
she buys up all   10
the eyesores facing her shore,
and lets them fall.

The season's ill—
we've lost our summer millionaire,
who seemed to leap from an L. L. Bean   15
catalogue. His nine-knot yawl
was auctioned off to lobstermen.
A red fox stain covers Blue Hill.

And now our fairy
decorator brightens his shop for fall;   20
his fishnet's filled with orange cork,
orange, his cobbler's bench and awl;
there is no money in his work,
he'd rather marry.

One dark night,   25
my Tudor Ford climbed the hill's skull;
I watched for love-cars. Lights turned down,
they lay together, hull to hull,
where the graveyard shelves on the town. . . .
My mind's not right.   30

A car radio bleats,
"Love, O careless Love. . . ." I hear
my ill-spirit sob in each blood cell,
as if my hand were at its throat. . . .
I myself am hell;   35
nobody's here—

only skunks, that search
in the moonlight for a bite to eat.
They march on their soles up Main Street:
white stripes, moonstruck eyes' red fire   40
under the chalk-dry and spar spire
of the Trinitarian Church.

I stand on top
of our back steps and breathe the rich air—
a mother skunk with her column of kittens swills the garbage pail. 45
She jabs her wedge-head in a cup
of sour cream, drops her ostrich tail,
and will not scare.

Andrew Marvell (1621–1678)

To His Coy Mistress   1681

Had we but world enough and time,
This coyness,° lady, were no crime.   *modesty, reluctance*
We would sit down and think which way
To walk, and pass our long love's day.
Thou by the Indian Ganges' side   5
Should'st rubies find; I by the tide
Of Humber would complain.° I would   *sing sad songs*
Love you ten years before the Flood,
And you should, if you please, refuse
Till the conversion of the Jews.   10
My vegetable° love should grow   *vegetative, flourishing*
Vaster than empires, and more slow.
An hundred years should go to praise
Thine eyes, and on thy forehead gaze,
Two hundred to adore each breast,   15
But thirty thousand to the rest.
An age at least to every part,
And the last age should show your heart.
For, lady, you deserve this state,°   *pomp, ceremony*
Nor would I love at lower rate.   20
    But at my back I always hear
Time's wingèd chariot hurrying near,
And yonder all before us lie
Deserts of vast eternity.
Thy beauty shall no more be found,   25
Nor in thy marble vault shall sound
My echoing song; then worms shall try
That long preserved virginity,
And your quaint honor turn to dust,
And into ashes all my lust.   30
The grave's a fine and private place,
But none, I think, do there embrace.
    Now therefore, while the youthful hue
Sits on thy skin like morning glew°   *glow*
And while thy willing soul transpires   35
At every pore with instant° fires,   *eager*
Now let us sport us while we may;
And now, like amorous birds of prey,

Rather at once our time devour
Than languish in his slow-chapped° power.   *slow-jawed*   40
Let us roll all our strength and all
Our sweetness up into one ball
And tear our pleasures with rough strife
Thorough° the iron gates of life.   *through*
Thus, though we cannot make our sun   45
Stand still, yet we will make him run.

To His Coy Mistress. 7 *Humber:* a river that flows by Marvell's town of Hull (on the side of the world opposite from the Ganges). 10 *conversion of the Jews:* an event that, according to St. John the Divine, is to take place just before the end of the world. 35 *transpires:* exudes, as a membrane lets fluid or vapor pass through it.

John Milton (1608–1674)

When I consider how my light is spent   (1655?)

When I consider how my light is spent,
    Ere half my days in this dark world and wide,
    And that one talent which is death to hide
    Lodged with me useless, though my soul more bent
To serve therewith my Maker, and present   5
    My true account, lest He returning chide;
    "Doth God exact day-labor, light denied?"
    I fondly° ask. But Patience, to prevent   *foolishly*
That murmur, soon replies, "God doth not need
    Either man's work or His own gifts. Who best   10
    Bear His mild yoke, they serve Him best. His state
Is kingly: thousands at His bidding speed,
    And post o'er land and ocean without rest;
    They also serve who only stand and wait."

When I consider how my light is spent. 1 *my light is spent:* Milton had become blind. 3 *that one talent:* For Jesus' parable of the talents (measures of money), see Matthew 25:14–30.

MARIANNE MOORE

Marianne Moore (1887–1972)

Poetry   1921

I too, dislike it: there are things that are important beyond all this fiddle.
   Reading it, however, with a perfect contempt for it, one discovers
          that there is in
   it after all, a place for the genuine.
      Hands that can grasp, eyes
      that can dilate, hair that can rise   5
         if it must, these things are important not because a

high sounding interpretation can be put upon them but because they
          are
   useful; when they become so derivative as to become
         unintelligible, the
   same thing may be said for all of us—that we
      do not admire what   10
      we cannot understand. The bat,
         holding on upside down or in quest of something to

eat, elephants pushing, a wild horse taking a roll, a tireless wolf under
   a tree, the immovable critic twinkling his skin like a horse that
         feels a flea, the base-
   ball fan, the statistician—case after case   15
      could be cited did
      one wish it; nor is it valid
         to discriminate against "business documents and

school-books"; all these phenomena are important. One must make a
         distinction
   however: when dragged into prominence by half poets, the result
         is not poetry,   20

nor till the autocrats among us can be
"literalists of
the imagination"—above
insolence and triviality and can present

for inspection, imaginary gardens with real toads in them, shall we
have   25
it. In the meantime, if you demand on one hand, in defiance of
their opinion—
the raw material of poetry in
all its rawness and
that which is, on the other hand,
genuine then you are interested in poetry.   30

MARILYN NELSON

Marilyn Nelson (b. 1946)

A Strange Beautiful Woman   1985

A strange beautiful woman
met me in the mirror
the other night.
Hey,
I said,
What you doing here?   5
She asked me
the same thing.

Pablo Neruda (1904–1973)

We Are Many   1958

Of the many men who I am, who we are,
I can't find a single one;
they disappear among my clothes,
they've left for another city.

When everything seems to be set   5
to show me off as intelligent,
the fool I always keep hidden
takes over all that I say.

At other times, I'm asleep
among distinguished people,   10
and when I look for my brave self,
a coward unknown to me
rushes to cover my skeleton
with a thousand fine excuses.

When a decent house catches fire,   15
instead of the fireman I summon,
an arsonist bursts on the scene,
and that's me. What can I do?
What can I do to distinguish myself?
How can I pull myself together?   20

All the books I read
are full of dazzling heroes,
always sure of themselves.
I die with envy of them;
and in films full of wind and bullets,   25
I goggle at the cowboys,
I even admire the horses.

But when I call for a hero,
out comes my lazy old self;
so I never know who I am,   30
nor how many I am or will be.
I'd love to be able to touch a bell
and summon the real me,
because if I really need myself,
I mustn't disappear.   35

While I am writing, I'm far away;
and when I come back, I've gone.
I would like to know if others
go through the same things that I do,
have as many selves as I have,   40
and see themselves similarly;
and when I've exhausted this problem,
I'm going to study so hard
that when I explain myself,
I'll be talking geography.   45
        —*Translated by Alastair Reid, 1967*

Lorine Niedecker (1903–1970)

Poet's Work   (about 1962)

Grandfather
    advised me:
        Learn a trade

I learned
    to sit at desk
        and condense   5

No layoff
    from this
        condensery

Yone Noguchi (1875–1947)

A Selection of Hokku   1920

Leaves blown,
Birds flown away.

I wander in and out the Hall of Autumn.

                    *

Are the fallen stars
Returning up the sky?—
The dews on the grass.

*

Like a cobweb hung upon the tree,
A prey to wind and sunlight!
Who will say that we are safe and strong?

*

Oh, How cool—
The sound of the bell
That leaves the bell itself.

HOKKU. *hokku* is an alternate form of the word *haiku*.

SHARON OLDS

Sharon Olds (b. 1942)

The One Girl at the Boys' Party   1983

When I take my girl to the swimming party
I set her down among the boys. They tower and
bristle, she stands there smooth and sleek,
her math scores unfolding in the air around her.
They will strip to their suits, her body hard and   5
indivisible as a prime number,
they'll plunge in the deep end, she'll subtract
her height from ten feet, divide it into
hundreds of gallons of water, the numbers
bouncing in her mind like molecules of chlorine   10
in the bright blue pool. When they climb out,
her ponytail will hang its pencil lead
down her back, her narrow silk suit
with hamburgers and french fries printed on it
will glisten in the brilliant air, and they will   15

see her sweet face, solemn and
sealed, a factor of one, and she will
see their eyes, two each,
their legs, two each, and the curves of their sexes,
one each, and in her head she'll be doing her   20
wild multiplying, as the drops
sparkle and fall to the power of a thousand from her body.

WILFRED OWEN

Wilfred Owen (1893–1918)

Anthem for Doomed Youth   (1917)

What passing-bells for these who die as cattle?
 Only the monstrous anger of the guns.
 Only the stuttering rifles' rapid rattle
Can patter out their hasty orisons.

No mockeries now for them; no prayers nor bells,   5
 Nor any voice of mourning save the choirs,—
The shrill, demented choirs of wailing shells;
 And bugles calling for them from sad shires.°   *counties*

What candles may be held to speed them all?
 Not in the hands of boys, but in their eyes   10
 Shall shine the holy glimmers of good-byes.
The pallor of girls' brows shall be their pall;
Their flowers the tenderness of patient minds,
And each slow dusk a drawing-down of blinds.

José Emilio Pacheco (b. 1939)

High Treason   1978

I do not love my country. Its abstract lustre
is beyond my grasp.
But (although it sounds bad) I would give my life
for ten places in it, for certain people,
seaports, pinewoods, fortresses,   5
a run-down city, gray, grotesque,
various figures from its history,
mountains
(and three or four rivers).

—Translated by Alastair Reid

SYLVIA PLATH

Sylvia Plath (1932–1963)

Daddy   (1962) 1965

You do not do, you do not do
Any more, black shoe
In which I have lived like a foot
For thirty years, poor and white,
Barely daring to breathe or Achoo.   5

Daddy, I have had to kill you.
You died before I had time—
Marble-heavy, a bag full of God,
Ghastly statue with one grey toe
Big as a Frisco seal   10

And a head in the freakish Atlantic
Where it pours bean green over blue
In the waters off beautiful Nauset.
I used to pray to recover you.
Ach, du.   15

In the German tongue, in the Polish town
Scraped flat by the roller
Of wars, wars, wars.
But the name of the town is common.
My Polack friend   20

Says there are a dozen or two.
So I never could tell where you
Put your foot, your root,
I never could talk to you.
The tongue stuck in my jaw.   25

It stuck in a barb wire snare.
Ich, ich, ich, ich,
I could hardly speak.
I thought every German was you.
And the language obscene   30

An engine, an engine
Chuffing me off like a Jew.
A Jew to Dachau, Auschwitz, Belsen.
I began to talk like a Jew.
I think I may well be a Jew.   35

The snows of the Tyrol, the clear beer of Vienna
Are not very pure or true.
With my gypsy ancestress and my weird luck
And my Taroc pack and my Taroc pack
I may be a bit of a Jew.   40

I have always been scared of *you*,
With your Luftwaffe, your gobbledygoo.
And your neat moustache
And your Aryan eye, bright blue.
Panzer-man, panzer-man, O You—   45

Not God but a swastika
So black no sky could squeak through.
Every woman adores a Fascist,
The boot in the face, the brute
Brute heart of a brute like you.   50

You stand at the blackboard, daddy,
In the picture I have of you,
A cleft in your chin instead of your foot
But no less a devil for that, no not
Any less the black man who   55

Bit my pretty red heart in two.
I was ten when they buried you.
At twenty I tried to die
And get back, back, back to you.
I thought even the bones would do.   60

But they pulled me out of the sack,
And they stuck me together with glue.
And then I knew what to do.
I made a model of you,
A man in black with a Meinkampf look   65

And a love of the rack and the screw.
And I said I do, I do.
So daddy, I'm finally through.
The black telephone's off at the root,
The voices just can't worm through.   70

If I've killed one man, I've killed two—
The vampire who said he was you
And drank my blood for a year,
Seven years, if you want to know.
Daddy, you can lie back now.   75

There's a stake in your fat black heart
And the villagers never liked you.
They are dancing and stamping on you.
They always *knew* it was you.
Daddy, daddy, you bastard, I'm through.   80

DADDY. Introducing this poem in a reading, Sylvia Plath remarked:

> The poem is spoken by a girl with an Electra complex. Her father died while she
> thought he was God. Her case is complicated by the fact that her father was also a Nazi
> and her mother very possibly part jewish. In the daughter the two strains marry and
> paralyze each other—she has to act out the awful little allegory before she is free of it.

(Quoted by A. Alvarez, *Beyond All This Fiddle* [New York: Random, 1968).

In some details "Daddy" is autobiography: the poet's father, Otto Plath, a German, had
come to the United States from Grabow, Poland. He had died following the amputation of
a gangrened foot and leg when Sylvia was eight years old. Politically, Otto Plath was a Republican, not a Nazi, but was apparently a somewhat domineering head of the household.
(See the recollections of the poet's mother, Aurelia Schober Plath, in her edition of *Letters
Home* by Sylvia Plath [New York: Harper, 1975].)

15 *Ach, du:* Oh, you. 27 *Ich, ich, ich, ich:* I, I, I, I. 51 *blackboard:* Otto Plath had been a professor of biology at Boston University. 65 *Meinkampf:* Adolf Hitler entitled his autobiography *Mein Kampf* ("My Struggle").

Alexander Pope (1688–1744)

A little Learning is a dang'rous Thing (from *An Essay on Criticism*) 1711

A *little Learning* is a dang'rous Thing;
Drink deep, or taste not the *Pierian* Spring:
There *shallow Draughts* intoxicate the Brain,
And drinking *largely* sobers us again.
Fir'd at first Sight with what the *Muse* imparts,   5
In *fearless Youth* we tempt the Heights of Arts,
While from the bounded *Level* of our Mind,
Short Views we take, nor see the *Lengths behind*,
But *more advanc'd*, behold with strange Surprize
New, distant Scenes of *endless* Science rise!   10
So pleas'd at first, the towring *Alps* we try,
Mount o'er the Vales, and seem to tread the Sky;
Th' Eternal Snows appear already past,
And the first *Clouds* and *Mountains* seem the last:
But *those attain'd*, we tremble to survey   15
The growing Labours of the lengthen'd Way,
Th' *increasing* Prospect *tires* our wandring Eyes,
Hills peep o'er Hills, and *Alps* on *Alps* arise!

A LITTLE LEARNING IS A DANG'ROUS THING. 2 *Pierian Spring*: the spring of the Muses.

Ezra Pound (1885–1972)

The River-Merchant's Wife: A Letter 1915

While my hair was still cut straight across my forehead
I played about the front gate, pulling flowers.
You came by on bamboo stilts, playing horse,
You walked about my seat, playing with blue plums.
And we went on living in the village of Chokan: 5
Two small people, without dislike or suspicion.

At fourteen I married My Lord you.
I never laughed, being bashful.
Lowering my head, I looked at the wall.
Called to, a thousand times, I never looked back.   10

At fifteen I stopped scowling,
I desired my dust to be mingled with yours
Forever and forever and forever.
Why should I climb the lookout?

At sixteen you departed,   15
You went into far Ku-to-yen, by the river of swirling eddies,
And you have been gone five months.
The monkeys make sorrowful noise overhead.

You dragged your feet when you went out.
By the gate now, the moss is grown, the different mosses,   20
Too deep to clear them away!
The leaves fall early this autumn, in wind.
The paired butterflies are already yellow with August
Over the grass in the West garden;
They hurt me. I grow older.   25
If you are coming down through the narrows of the river Kiang,
Please let me know beforehand,
And I will come out to meet you
    As far as Cho-fu-sa.

THE RIVER-MERCHANT'S WIFE: A LETTER. A free translation from the Chinese poet Li Po
(eighth century).

DUDLEY RANDALL

Dudley Randall (1914–2000)

A Different Image   1968

The age
requires this task:
create
a different image;
re-animate   5
the mask.

Shatter the icons of slavery and fear.
Replace

the leer
of the minstrel's burnt-cork face   10
with a proud, serene
and classic bronze of Benin.

Henry Reed (1914–1986)

Naming of Parts   1946

Today we have naming of parts. Yesterday,
We had daily cleaning. And tomorrow morning,
We shall have what to do after firing. But today,
Today we have naming of parts. Japonica
Glistens like coral in all of the neighboring gardens,   5
       And today we have naming of parts.

This is the lower sling swivel. And this
Is the upper sling swivel, whose use you will see,
When you are given your slings. And this is the piling swivel,
Which in your case you have not got. The branches   10
Hold in the gardens their silent, eloquent gestures,
       Which in our case we have not got.

This is the safety-catch, which is always released
With an easy flick of the thumb. And please do not let me
See anyone using his finger. You can do it quite easy   15
If you have any strength in your thumb. The blossoms
Are fragile and motionless, never letting anyone see
       Any of them using their finger.

And this you can see is the bolt. The purpose of this
Is to open the breech, as you see. We can slide it   20
Rapidly backwards and forwards: we call this
Easing the spring. And rapidly backwards and forwards
The early bees are assaulting and fumbling the flowers:
       They call it easing the Spring.

They call it easing the Spring: it is perfectly easy   25
If you have any strength in your thumb: like the bolt,
And the breech, and the cocking-piece, and the point of balance,
Which in our case we have not got; and the almond-blossom
Silent in all of the gardens and the bees going backwards and forwards,
       For today we have naming of parts.   30

Adrienne Rich (b. 1929)

Living in Sin   1955

She had thought the studio would keep itself;
no dust upon the furniture of love.
Half heresy, to wish the taps less vocal,
the panes relieved of grime. A plate of pears,
a piano with a Persian shawl, a cat   5
stalking the picturesque amusing mouse
had risen at his urging.
Not that at five each separate stair would writhe
under the milkman's tramp; that morning light
so coldly would delineate the scraps   10
of last night's cheese and three sepulchral bottles;
that on the kitchen shelf among the saucers
a pair of beetle-eyes would fix her own—
envoy from some village in the moldings . . .
Meanwhile, he, with a yawn,   15
sounded a dozen notes upon the keyboard,
declared it out of tune, shrugged at the mirror,
rubbed at his beard, went out for cigarettes;
while she, jeered by the minor demons,
pulled back the sheets and made the bed and found   20
a towel to dust the table-top,
and let the coffee-pot boil over on the stove.
By evening she was back in love again,
though not so wholly but throughout the night
she woke sometimes to feel the daylight coming   25
like a relentless milkman up the stairs.

Edwin Arlington Robinson (1869–1935)

Miniver Cheevy   1910

Miniver Cheevy, child of scorn,
    Grew lean while he assailed the seasons;
He wept that he was ever born,
    And he had reasons.

Miniver loved the days of old   5
    When swords were bright and steeds were prancing;
The vision of a warrior bold
    Would set him dancing.

Miniver sighed for what was not,
    And dreamed, and rested from his labors;   10
He dreamed of Thebes and Camelot,
    And Priam's neighbors.

Miniver mourned the ripe renown
    That made so many a name so fragrant;
He mourned Romance, now on the town,   15
    And Art, a vagrant.

Miniver loved the Medici,
    Albeit he had never seen one;
He would have sinned incessantly
    Could he have been one.   20

Miniver cursed the commonplace
    And eyed a khaki suit with loathing;
He missed the medieval grace
    Of iron clothing.

Miniver scorned the gold he sought,   25
    But sore annoyed was he without it;
Miniver thought, and thought, and thought,
    And thought about it.

Miniver Cheevy, born too late,
    Scratched his head and kept on thinking;   30
Miniver coughed, and called it fate,
    And kept on drinking.

MINIVER CHEEVY. 11 *Thebes:* a city in ancient Greece and the setting of many famous
Greek myths; *Camelot:* the legendary site of King Arthur's Court. 12 *Priam:* the last king of
Troy; his "neighbors" would have included Helen of Troy, Aeneas, and other famous figures.
17 *the Medici:* the ruling family of Florence during the high Renaissance, the Medici were
renowned patrons of the arts.

William Shakespeare (1564–1616)

When, in disgrace with Fortune and men's eyes   1609

When, in disgrace with Fortune and men's eyes,
I all alone beweep my outcast state,
And trouble deaf heaven with my bootless° cries,   *futile*
And look upon myself and curse my fate,

Wishing me like to one more rich in hope,   5
Featured like him, like him with friends possessed,
Desiring this man's art, and that man's scope,
With what I most enjoy contented least,
Yet in these thoughts myself almost despising,
Haply° I think on thee, and then my state,   *luckily*   10
Like to the lark at break of day arising
From sullen earth, sings hymns at heaven's gate;
    For thy sweet love rememb'red such wealth brings
    That then I scorn to change my state with kings.

WILLIAM SHAKESPEARE

William Shakespeare (1564–1616)

My mistress' eyes are nothing like the sun   1609

My mistress' eyes are nothing like the sun;
Coral is far more red than her lips' red;
If snow be white, why then her breasts are dun;
If hairs be wires, black wires grow on her head.
I have seen roses damasked red and white,   5
But no such roses see I in her cheeks;
And in some perfumes is there more delight
Than in the breath that from my mistress reeks.
I love to hear her speak, yet well I know
That music hatch a far more pleasing sound;   10
I grant I never saw a goddess go:
My mistress, when she walks, treads on the ground.
    And yet, by heaven, I think my love as rare
    As any she,° belied with false compare.   *woman*

Percy Bysshe Shelley (1792–1822)

Ozymandias
1818

I met a traveler from an antique land
Who said: Two vast and trunkless legs of stone
Stand in the desert. Near them, on the sand,
Half sunk, a shattered visage lies, whose frown,
And wrinkled lip, and sneer of cold command,   5
Tell that its sculptor well those passions read
Which yet survive, stamped on these lifeless things,
The hand that mocked° them and the heart that fed;   *imitated*
And on the pedestal these words appear:
"My name is Ozymandias, king of kings: 10
Look on my works, ye Mighty, and despair!"
Nothing beside remains. Round the decay
Of that colossal wreck, boundless and bare
The lone and level sands stretch far away.

David R. Slavitt (b. 1935)

Titanic
1983

Who does not love the *Titanic*?
If they sold passage tomorrow for that same crossing,
who would not buy?

To go down . . . We all go down, mostly
alone. But with crowds of people, friends, servants,   5
well fed, with music, with lights! Ah!

And the world, shocked, mourns, as it ought to do
and almost never does. There will be the books and movies
to remind our grandchildren who we were
and how we died, and give them a good cry.   10

Not so bad, after all. The cold
water is anaesthetic and very quick.
The cries on all sides must be a comfort.

We all go: only a few, first-class.

Wallace Stevens (1879–1955)

The Emperor of Ice-Cream   1923

Call the roller of big cigars,
The muscular one, and bid him whip
In kitchen cups concupiscent curds.
Let the wenches dawdle in such dress
As they are used to wear, and let the boys   5
Bring flowers in last month's newspapers.
Let be be finale of seem.
The only emperor is the emperor of ice-cream.

Take from the dresser of deal,
Lacking the three glass knobs, that sheet   10
On which she embroidered fantails once
And spread it so as to cover her face.
If her horny feet protrude, they come
To show how cold she is, and dumb.
Let the lamp affix its beam.   15
The only emperor is the emperor of ice-cream.

THE EMPEROR OF ICE-CREAM. 9 *deal*: fir or pine wood used to make cheap furniture.

LARISSA SZPORLUK

Larissa Szporluk (b. 1967)

Vertigo   2000

Sing now.
Sing from on high, high roof
you're afraid of
losing. Sing yourself into
a tiny blue worm,   5

maybe no eyes,
squeezing its mite
through a tinier
passage, maybe no
outlet, maybe   10
no light, maybe you'll never
ever find light,
and the stars that you think
in a world of height
there should be   15
aren't even stars, only actors
that swing in the dark
like paper lanterns
and don't serve as guides
as you peer from the edge   20
at the people below
without nets;
they don't know who you are,
but they're waiting
in droves   25
for your butterfly nerves
to tuck in their tails
and fold.

Alfred, Lord Tennyson (1809–1892)

Ulysses   (1833)

It little profits that an idle king,
By this still hearth, among these barren crags,
Matched with an agèd wife, I mete and dole
Unequal laws unto a savage race
That hoard, and sleep, and feed, and know not me.   5
I cannot rest from travel; I will drink
Life to the lees. All times I have enjoyed
Greatly, have suffered greatly, both with those
That loved me, and alone; on shore, and when
Through scudding drifts the rainy Hyades   10
Vexed the dim sea. I am become a name;
For always roaming with a hungry heart
Much have I seen and known—cities of men
And manners, climates, councils, governments,
Myself not least, but honored of them all—   15
And drunk delight of battle with my peers,

Far on the ringing plains of windy Troy.
I am a part of all that I have met;
Yet all experience is an arch wherethrough
Gleams that untraveled world whose margin fades 20
Forever and forever when I move.
How dull it is to pause, to make an end,
To rust unburnished, not to shine in use!
As though to breathe were life! Life piled on life
Were all too little, and of one to me 25
Little remains; but every hour is saved
From that eternal silence, something more,
A bringer of new things; and vile it were
For some three suns to store and hoard myself,
And this grey spirit yearning in desire 30
To follow knowledge like a sinking star,
Beyond the utmost bound of human thought.

    This is my son, mine own Telemachus,
To whom I leave the scepter and the isle—
Well-loved of me, discerning to fulfill 35
This labor, by slow prudence to make mild
A rugged people, and through soft degrees
Subdue them to the useful and the good.
Most blameless is he, centered in the sphere
Of common duties, decent not to fail 40
In offices of tenderness, and pay
Meet adoration to my household gods,
When I am gone. He works his work, I mine.

    There lies the port; the vessel puffs her sail;
There gloom the dark, broad seas. My mariners, 45
Souls that have toiled, and wrought, and thought with me—
That ever with a frolic welcome took
The thunder and the sunshine, and opposed
Free hearts, free foreheads—you and I are old;
Old age hath yet his honor and his toil. 50
Death closes all; but something ere the end,
Some work of noble note, may yet be done,
Not unbecoming men that strove with Gods.
The lights begin to twinkle from the rocks;
The long day wanes; the slow moon climbs; the deep 55
Moans round with many voices. Come, my friends,
'Tis not too late to seek a newer world.
Push off, and sitting well in order smite
The sounding furrows; for my purpose holds
To sail beyond the sunset, and the baths 60

Of all the western stars, until I die.
It may be that the gulfs will wash us down;
It may be we shall touch the Happy Isles,
And see the great Achilles, whom we knew.
Though much is taken, much abides; and though   65
We are not now that strength which in old days
Moved earth and heaven, that which we are, we are—
One equal temper of heroic hearts,
Made weak by time and fate, but strong in will
To strive, to seek, to find, and not to yield.   70

ULYSSES. 10 *Hyades:* daughters of Atlas, who were transformed into a group of stars. Their rising with the sun was thought to be a sign of rain. 63 *Happy Isles:* Elysium, a paradise believed to be attainable by sailing west.

DYLAN THOMAS

Dylan Thomas (1914–1953)

Fern Hill   1946

Now as I was young and easy under the apple boughs
About the lilting house and happy as the grass was green,
      The night above the dingle° starry,   *wooded valley*
        Time let me hail and climb
        Golden in the heydays of his eyes,   5
And honored among wagons I was prince of the apple towns
And once below a time I lordly had the trees and leaves
        Trail with daisies and barley
      Down the rivers of the windfall light.

And as I was green and carefree, famous among the barns   10
About the happy yard and singing as the farm was home,
        In the sun that is young once only,

Time let me play and be
Golden in the mercy of his means,
And green and golden I was huntsman and herdsman, the calves   15
Sang to my horn, the foxes on the hills barked clear and cold,
And the sabbath rang slowly
In the pebbles of the holy streams.

All the sun long it was running, it was lovely, the hay
Fields high as the house, the tunes from the chimneys, it was air   20
And playing, lovely and watery
And fire green as grass.
And nightly under the simple stars
As I rode to sleep the owls were bearing the farm away,
All the moon long I heard, blessed among stables, the nightjars   25
Flying with the ricks, and the horses
Flashing into the dark.

And then to awake, and the farm, like a wanderer white
With the dew, come back, the cock on his shoulder: it was all
Shining, it was Adam and maiden,   30
The sky gathered again
And the sun grew round that very day.
So it must have been after the birth of the simple light
In the first, spinning place, the spellbound horses walking warm
Out of the whinnying green stable   35
On to the fields of praise.

And honored among foxes and pheasants by the gay house
Under the new made clouds and happy as the heart was long,
In the sun born over and over,
I ran my heedless ways,   40
My wishes raced through the house high hay
And nothing I cared, at my sky blue trades, that time allows
In all his tuneful turning so few and such morning songs
Before the children green and golden
Follow him out of grace,   45

Nothing I cared, in the lamb white days, that time would take me
Up to the swallow thronged loft by the shadow of my hand,
In the moon that is always rising,
Nor that riding to sleep
I should hear him fly with the high fields   50
And wake to the farm forever fled from the childless land.
Oh as I was young and easy in the mercy of his means,
Time held me green and dying
Though I sang in my chains like the sea.

John Updike (b. 1932)

Ex-Basketball Player 1958

Pearl Avenue runs past the high-school lot,
Bends with the trolley tracks, and stops, cut off
Before it has a chance to go two blocks,
At Colonel McComsky Plaza. Berth's Garage
Is on the corner facing west, and there,   5
Most days, you'll find Flick Webb, who helps Berth out.

Flick stands tall among the idiot pumps—
Five on a side, the old bubble-head style,
Their rubber elbows hanging loose and low.
One's nostrils are two S's, and his eyes   10
An E and O. And one is squat, without
A head at all—more of a football type.

Once Flick played for the high-school team, the Wizards.
He was good: in fact, the best. In '46
He bucketed three hundred ninety points,   15
A county record still. The ball loved Flick.
I saw him rack up thirty-eight or forty
In one home game. His hands were like wild birds.

He never learned a trade, he just sells gas,
Checks oil, and changes flats. Once in a while,   20
As a gag, he dribbles an inner tube,
But most of us remember anyway.
His hands are fine and nervous on the lug wrench.
It makes no difference to the lug wrench, though.

Off work, he hangs around Mae's luncheonette.   25
Grease-gray and kind of coiled, he plays pinball,
Smokes those thin cigars, nurses lemon phosphates.
Flick seldom says a word to Mae, just nods
Beyond her face toward bright applauding tiers
Of Necco Wafers, Nibs, and Juju Beads.   30

DEREK WALCOTT

Derek Walcott (b. 1930)

The Virgins

1976

Down the dead streets of sun-stoned Frederiksted,
the first free port to die for tourism,
strolling at funeral pace, I am reminded
of life not lost to the American dream;
but my small-islander's simplicities   5
can't better our new empire's civilized
exchange of cameras, watches, perfumes, brandies
for the good life, so cheaply underpriced
that only the crime rate is on the rise
in streets blighted with sun, stone arches   10
and plazas blown dry by the hysteria
of rumour. A condominium drowns
in vacancy; its bargains are dusted,
but only a jewelled housefly drones
over the bargains. The roulettes spin   15
rustily to the wind—the vigorous trade
that every morning would begin afresh
by revving up green water round the pierhead
heading for where the banks of silver thresh.

THE VIRGINS. The title of this poem refers to the Virgin Islands, a group of 100 small islands
in the Caribbean. 1 *Frederiksted:* the biggest seaport in St. Croix, the largest of the American
Virgin Islands. 2 *free port:* a port city where goods can be bought and sold without paying
customs taxes. 5 *small-islander's:* Walcott was born on St. Lucia, another island in the West
Indies. 16 *trade:* trade winds.

Edmund Waller (1606–1687)

Go, Lovely Rose   1645

Go, lovely rose,
Tell her that wastes her time and me
   That now she knows,
When I resemble° her to thee,   *compare*
How sweet and fair she seems to be.   5

   Tell her that's young
And shuns to have her graces spied,
   That hadst thou sprung
In deserts where no men abide,
Thou must have uncommended died.   10

   Small is the worth
Of beauty from the light retired:
   Bid her come forth,
Suffer herself to be desired,
And not blush so to be admired.   15

   Then die, that she
The common fate of all things rare
   May read in thee,
How small a part of time they share
That are so wondrous sweet and fair.   20

WALT WHITMAN

Walt Whitman (1819–1892)

from Song of the Open Road   1856, 1881

Allons! the road is before us!
It is safe—I have tried it—my own feet have tried it well—be not
   detain'd!

Let the paper remain on the desk unwritten, and the book on the
    shelf unopen'd!
Let the tools remain in the workshop! let the money remain
    unearn'd!
Let the school stand! mind not the cry of the teacher!   5
Let the preacher preach in his pulpit! let the lawyer plead in the
    court, and the judge expound the law.

Camerado, I give you my hand!
I give you my love more precious than money,
I give you myself before preaching or law;
Will you give me yourself? will you come travel with me?   10
Shall we stick by each other as long as we live?

SONG OF THE OPEN ROAD. This is part 15 of Whitman's long poem. 1 *Allons!*: French for
"Come on!" or "Let's go!"

Richard Wilbur (b. 1921)

The Writer   1976

In her room at the prow of the house
Where light breaks, and the windows are tossed with linden,
My daughter is writing a story.

I pause in the stairwell, hearing
From her shut door a commotion of typewriter-keys   5
Like a chain hauled over a gunwale.

Young as she is, the stuff
Of her life is a great cargo, and some of it heavy:
I wish her a lucky passage.

But now it is she who pauses,   10
As if to reject my thought and its easy figure.
A stillness greatens, in which

The whole house seems to be thinking,
And then she is at it again with a bunched clamor
Of strokes, and again is silent.   15

I remember the dazed starling
Which was trapped in that very room, two years ago;
How we stole in, lifted a sash

And retreated, not to affright it;
And how for a helpless hour, through the crack of the door,   20
We watched the sleek, wild, dark

And iridescent creature
Batter against the brilliance, drop like a glove
To the hard floor, or the desk-top,

And wait then, humped and bloody,   25
For the wits to try it again; and how our spirits
Rose when, suddenly sure,

It lifted off from a chair-back,
Beating a smooth course for the right window
And clearing the sill of the world.   30

It is always a matter, my darling,
Of life or death, as I had forgotten. I wish
What I wished you before, but harder.

WILLIAM CARLOS WILLIAMS

William Carlos Williams (1883–1963)

Spring and All   1923

By the road to the contagious hospital
under the surge of the blue
mottled clouds driven from the
northeast—a cold wind. Beyond, the
waste of broad, muddy fields   5
brown with dried weeds, standing and fallen

patches of standing water
the scattering of tall trees

All along the road the reddish
purplish, forked, upstanding, twiggy   10
stuff of bushes and small trees
with dead, brown leaves under them
leafless vines—

Lifeless in appearance, sluggish
dazed spring approaches—   15

They enter the new world naked,
cold, uncertain of all
save that they enter. All about them
the cold, familiar wind—

Now the grass, tomorrow   20
the stiff curl of wildcarrot leaf

One by one objects are defined—
It quickens: clarity, outline of leaf

But now the stark dignity of
entrance—Still, the profound change   25
has come upon them: rooted, they
grip down and begin to awaken

William Wordsworth (1770–1850)

Composed upon Westminster Bridge   1807

Earth has not anything to show more fair:
Dull would he be of soul who could pass by
A sight so touching in its majesty:
This City now doth, like a garment, wear
The beauty of the morning; silent, bare,   5
Ships, towers, domes, theatres, and temples lie
Open unto the fields, and to the sky;
All bright and glittering in the smokeless air.
Never did sun more beautifully steep
In his first splendor, valley, rock, or hill;   10
Ne'er saw I, never felt, a calm so deep!
The river glideth at his own sweet will:
Dear God! the very houses seem asleep;
And all that mighty heart is lying still!

James Wright (1927–1980)

Autumn Begins in Martins Ferry, Ohio   1963

In the Shreve High football stadium,
I think of Polacks nursing long beers in Tiltonsville,
And gray faces of Negroes in the blast furnace at Benwood,
And the ruptured night watchman of Wheeling Steel,
Dreaming of heroes.   5

All the proud fathers are ashamed to go home.
Their women cluck like starved pullets,
Dying for love.

Therefore,
Their sons grow suicidally beautiful   10
At the beginning of October,
And gallop terribly against each other's bodies.

WILLIAM BUTLER YEATS

William Butler Yeats (1865–1939)

Sailing to Byzantium   1927

That is no country for old men. The young
In one another's arms, birds in the trees
—Those dying generations—at their song,
The salmon-falls, the mackerel-crowded seas,
Fish, flesh, or fowl, commend all summer long   5
Whatever is begotten, born, and dies.
Caught in that sensual music all neglect
Monuments of unaging intellect.

An aged man is but a paltry thing,
A tattered coat upon a stick, unless   10
Soul clap its hands and sing, and louder sing
For every tatter in its mortal dress,
Nor is there singing school but studying
Monuments of its own magnificence;
And therefore I have sailed the seas and come   15
To the holy city of Byzantium.

O sages standing in God's holy fire
As in the gold mosaic of a wall,
Come from the holy fire, perne in a gyre,°   *spin down a spiral*
And be the singing-masters of my soul.   20
Consume my heart away; sick with desire
And fastened to a dying animal
It knows not what it is; and gather me
Into the artifice of eternity.

Once out of nature I shall never take   25
My bodily form from any natural thing,
But such a form as Grecian goldsmiths make
Of hammered gold and gold enameling
To keep a drowsy Emperor awake;
Or set upon a golden bough to sing   30
To lords and ladies of Byzantium
Of what is past, or passing, or to come.

SAILING TO BYZANTIUM. Byzantium was the capital of the Byzantine Empire, the city now
called Istanbul. Yeats means, though, not merely the physical city. Byzantium is also a name
for his conception of paradise.

William Butler Yeats (1865–1939)

When You Are Old   1893

When you are old and grey and full of sleep,
And nodding by the fire, take down this book,
And slowly read, and dream of the soft look
Your eyes had once, and of their shadows deep;

How many loved your moments of glad grace,   5
And loved your beauty with love false or true,
But one man loved the pilgrim soul in you,
And loved the sorrows of your changing face;

And bending down beside the glowing bars,
Murmur, a little sadly, how Love fled   10
And paced upon the mountains overhead
And hid his face amid a crowd of stars.

Bernice Zamora (b. 1938)

Penitents   1976

Once each year *penitentes* in mailshirts
journey through arroyos Seco, Huerfano,
to join *"edmanos"* at the *morada*.

Brothers Carrasco, Ortiz, Abeyta
prepare the Cristo for an unnamed task.   5
Nails, planks and type O blood are set
upon wooden tables facing, it is decreed,
the sacred mountain range to the Southwest.

Within the dark *morada* average
chains rattle and clacking prayer wheels jolt 10
the hissing spine to uncoil wailing tongues
of Nahuatl converts who slowly wreath
rosary whips to flog one another.

From the mountains *alabados* are heard:
"En una columna atado se   15
hallo el Rey de los Cielos,
herido y ensangrentado,
y arrastrado por los suelos."

The irresistible ceremony
beckoned me many times like crater lakes   20
and desecrated groves. I wished to swim
arroyos and know their estuaries
where, for one week, all is sacred in the valley.

PENITENTS. The poem is set in southern Colorado and deals with a ritual of sacrifice performed by secret groups of *penitentes*. 2 *arroyos Seco, Huerfano*: Arroyos are washes or gullies
in the West, and these are named Seco (Dry) and Huerfano (Orphan). 3 *edmanos*: possibly
a mispronunciation of *hermanos*, or *"brothers."* *morada*: a dwelling or abode where the ceremony will be performed—usually flagellation, but sometimes a form of crucifixion. 12
Nahuatl: descendants of Aztecs in Mexico. 14 *alabados*: songs of praise. 15–18 *"En una
columna . . . . por los suelos"*: Translated as "In a bundled formation is met / the King of the
Sky, / wounded and bloodstained, / and poverty-stricken for the low ones."

DRAMA

Arthur Miller, New York, 1987

Drama is life with the dull bits left out.
—ALFRED HITCHCOCK

Unlike a short story or a novel, a **play** is a work of storytelling in which actors represent the characters. In another essential, a play differs from a work of fiction: it is addressed not to readers but to spectators.

To be part of an audience in a theater is an experience far different from reading a story in solitude. Expectant as the house lights dim and the curtain rises, we become members of a community. The responses of people around us affect our own responses. We, too, contribute to the community's response whenever we laugh, sigh, applaud, murmur in surprise, or catch our breath in excitement. A theater of live actors has another advantage: a sensitive give-and-take between actors and audience. Such rapport, of course, depends on the actors being skilled and the audience being perceptive. As veteran playgoers well know, something unique and wonderful can happen when good actors and a good audience respond to each other.

The sense of immediacy we derive from **drama** is suggested by the root of the word. *Drama* means "action" or "deed" (from the Greek *dran,* "to do"). We use *drama* as a synonym for *plays,* but the word has several meanings. Sometimes it refers to one play ("a stirring drama"); or to the work of a playwright, or **dramatist** ("Ibsen's drama"); or perhaps to a body of plays written in a particular time or place ("Elizabethan drama," "French drama of the seventeenth century"). In yet another familiar sense, *drama* often means events that elicit high excitement: "A real-life drama," a news story might begin, "was enacted today before lunchtime crowds in downtown Manhattan as firefighters battled to free two children trapped on the sixteenth floor of a burning building." In this sense, whatever is "dramatic" implies suspense, tension, or conflict. Plays, as we shall see, frequently contain such "dramatic" chains of events; and yet, if we expect all plays to be crackling with suspense or conflict, we may be disappointed. "Good drama," said critic George Jean Nathan, "is anything that interests an intelligently emotional group of persons assembled together in an illuminated hall."

In partaking of the nature of ritual—something to be repeated in front of an audience on a special occasion—drama is akin to a festival (whether a religious festival or a rock festival) or a church service. Twice in the history of Europe, drama has sprung forth as a part of worship: when, in ancient Greece, plays were performed on feast days; and when, in the Christian church of the Middle Ages, a play was introduced as an adjunct to the Easter mass with the enactment of the meeting between the three Marys and the angel at Jesus' empty tomb. Evidently, something in drama remains constant over the years—something as old, perhaps, as the deepest desires and highest aspirations of humanity.

22
Reading a Play

Most plays are written not to be read in books but to be performed. Finding plays in a literature anthology, the student may well ask: Isn't there something wrong with the idea of reading plays on the printed page? Isn't that a perversion of their nature?

True, plays are meant to be seen on stage, but equally true, reading a play may afford advantages. One is that it is better to know some masterpieces by reading them than never to know them at all. Even if you live in a large city with many theaters, even if you attend a college with many theatrical productions, to succeed in your lifetime in witnessing, say, all the plays of Shakespeare might well be impossible. In print, they are as near to hand as a book on a shelf, ready to be enacted (if you like) on the stage of the mind.

After all, a play is literature before it comes alive in a theater, and it might be argued that when we read an unfamiliar play, we meet it in the same form in which it first appears to its actors and its director. If a play is rich and complex or if it dates from the remote past and contains difficulties of language and allusion, to read it on the page enables us to study it at our leisure and return to the parts that demand greater scrutiny.

Let us admit, by the way, that some plays, whatever the intentions of their authors, are destined to be read more often than they are acted. Such a play is sometimes called a **closet drama**—*closet* meaning "a small, private room." Percy Bysshe Shelley's neo-Shakespearean tragedy *The Cenci* (1819) has seldom escaped from its closet, even though Shelley tried without luck to have it performed on the London stage. Perhaps too rich in talk to please an audience or too sparse in opportunities for actors to use their bodies, such works nevertheless may lead long, respectable lives on their own, solely as literature.

But even if a play may be seen in a theater, sometimes to read it in print may be our way of knowing it as the author wrote it in its entirety. Far from regarding Shakespeare's words as holy writ, producers of *Hamlet, King Lear, Othello,* and other masterpieces often leave out whole speeches and scenes, or shorten them. Besides, the nature of the play, as far as you can tell from a stage production, may depend on decisions of the director. Shall Othello dress as a Renaissance Moor or as a modern general? Every actor who plays Iago in *Othello* makes his own interpretation of this knotty character. Some see Iago as a figure of pure evil; others, as a madman; still others, as a suffering human being consumed by hatred, jealousy, and pride. What do you think

Shakespeare meant? You can always read the play and decide for yourself. If every stage production of a play is a fresh interpretation, so, too, is every reader's reading of it.

Some readers, when silently reading a play to themselves, try to visualize a stage, imagining the characters in costume and under lights. If such a reader is an actor or a director and is reading the play with an eye toward staging it, then he or she may try to imagine every detail of a possible production, even shades of makeup and the loudness of sound effects. But the nonprofessional reader, who regards the play as literature, need not attempt such exhaustive imagining. Although some readers find it enjoyable to imagine the play taking place on a stage, others prefer to imagine the people and events that the play brings vividly to mind. Sympathetically following the tangled life of Nora in *A Doll's House* by Henrik Ibsen, we forget that we are reading printed stage directions and instead find ourselves in the presence of human conflict. Thus regarded, a play becomes a form of storytelling, and the playwright's instructions to the actors and the director become a conventional mode of narrative that we accept much as we accept the methods of a novel or short story. If we read *A Doll's House* caring more about Nora's fate than the imagined appearance of an actress portraying her, we speed through an ordinary passage such as this (from a scene in which Nora's husband hears the approach of an unwanted caller, Dr. Rank):

> Helmer (*with quiet irritation*): Oh, what does he want now? (*Aloud.*) Hold on. (*Goes and opens the door.*) Oh, how nice that you didn't just pass us by!

We read the passage, if the story absorbs us, as though we were reading a novel whose author, emplosying the conventional devices for recording speech in fiction, might have written:

> "Oh, what does he want now?" said Helmer under his breath, in annoyance. Aloud, he called, "Hold on." Then he walked to the door and opened it and greeted Rank with all the cheer he could muster— "Oh, how nice that you didn't just pass us by!"

Such is the power of an excellent play to make us ignore the playwright's artistry that it becomes a window through which the reader's gaze, given focus, encompasses more than language and typography and beholds a scene of imagined life.

Most plays, whether seen live or in print, employ *some* **conventions**: customary methods of presenting an action, usual and recognizable devices that an audience is willing to accept. In reading a great play from the past, such as *Oedipus the King* or *Othello*, it will help if we know some of the conventions of the classical Greek theater or the Elizabethan theater. When in *Oedipus the King* we encounter a character called the Chorus, it may be useful to be aware that this is a group of citizens who stand to one side of the action, conversing with the principal character and commenting. In *Othello*, when the sinister Iago, left on stage alone, begins to speak (at the end of Act I, Scene 3), we recognize the conventional device of a **soliloquy**, a dramatic monologue in which we seem to overhear the character's inmost thoughts uttered aloud. Like conventions in poetry, such familiar methods of staging a narrative afford us a happy shock of recognition. Often, as in these examples, they are ways of making clear to us exactly what the playwright would have us know.

A Play in Its Elements

When we read a play on the printed page and find ourselves swept forward by the motion of its story, we need not wonder how—and from what ingredients— the playwright put it together. Still, to analyze the structure of a play is one way to understand and appreciate a playwright's art. Analysis is complicated, however, because in an excellent play the elements (including plot, theme, and characters) do not stand in isolation. Often, deeds clearly follow from the kinds of people the characters are, and from those deeds it is left to the reader to infer the **theme** of the play—the general point or truth about human beings that may be drawn from it. Perhaps the most meaningful way to study the elements of a play (and certainly the most enjoyable) is to consider a play in its entirety.

Here is a short, famous one-act play worth reading for the boldness of its elements—and for its own sake. *Trifles* tells the story of a murder. As you will discover, the "trifles" mentioned in its title are not of trifling stature. In reading the play, you will probably find yourself imagining what you might see on stage if you were in a theater. You may also care to imagine what took place in the lives of the characters before the curtain rose. All this imagining may sound like a tall order, but don't worry. Just read the play for enjoyment the first time through, and then we will consider what makes it effective.

Susan Glaspell

Trifles 1916

Susan Glaspell (1882–1948) grew up in her native Davenport, Iowa, daughter of a grain dealer. After four years at Drake University and a reporting job in Des Moines, she settled in New York's Greenwich Village. In 1915, with her husband, George Cram Cook, a theatrical director, she founded the Province-town Players, the first influential noncommercial the-ater troupe in America. Summers, in a makeshift playhouse on a Cape Cod pier, the Players staged the earliest plays of Eugene O'Neill and works by John

SUSAN GLASPELL

Reed, Edna St. Vincent Millay, and Glaspell herself. (Later transplanting the company to New York, Glaspell and Cook renamed it the Playwrights' Theater.) Glaspell wrote several still-remembered plays, among them a pioneering work of feminist drama, The Verge *(1921), and the Pulitzer Prize-winning* Alison's House *(1930), about the family of a reclusive poet like Emily Dickinson who, after her death, squabble over the right to publish her poems. First widely known for her fiction with an Iowa background, Glaspell wrote ten novels, including* Fidelity *(1915) and* The Morning Is Near Us *(1939). Shortly after writing the play* Trifles, *she rewrote it as a short story, "A Jury of Her Peers."*

CHARACTERS

George Henderson, *county attorney*
Henry Peters, *sheriff*
Lewis Hale, *a neighboring farmer*
Mrs. Peters
Mrs. Hale

SCENE: *The kitchen in the now abandoned farmhouse of John Wright, a gloomy kitchen, and left without having been put in order—unwashed pans under the sink, a loaf of bread outside the breadbox, a dish towel on the table—other signs of incompleted work. At the rear the outer door opens and the Sheriff comes in followed by the County Attorney and Hale. The Sheriff and Hale are men in middle life, the County Attorney is a young man; all are much bundled up and go at once to the stove. They are followed by two women—the Sheriff's wife first; she is a slight wiry woman, a thin nervous face. Mrs. Hale is larger and would ordinarily be called more comfortable looking, but she is disturbed now and looks fearfully about as she enters. The women have come in slowly, and stand close together near the door.*

County Attorney: [*Rubbing his hands.*] This feels good. Come up to the fire, ladies.

Mrs. Peters: [*After taking a step forward.*] I'm not—cold.

Sheriff: [*Unbuttoning his overcoat and stepping away from the stove as if to mark the beginning of official business.*] Now, Mr. Hale, before we move things about, you explain to Mr. Henderson just what you saw when you came here yesterday morning.

County Attorney: By the way, has anything been moved? Are things just as you left them yesterday?

Sheriff: [*Looking about.*] It's just the same. When it dropped below zero last night I thought I'd better send Frank out this morning to make a fire for us—no use getting pneumonia with a big case on, but I told him not to touch anything except the stove—and you know Frank.

County Attorney: Somebody should have been left here yesterday.

Sheriff: Oh—yesterday. When I had to send Frank to Morris Center for
that man who went crazy—I want you to know I had my hands full
yesterday, I knew you could get back from Omaha by today and as
long as I went over everything here myself—

County Attorney: Well, Mr. Hale, tell just what happened when you
came here yesterday morning.

Hale: Harry and I had started to town with a load of potatoes. We came
along the road from my place and as I got here I said, "I'm going to
see if I can't get John Wright to go in with me on a party telephone."
I spoke to Wright about it once before and he put me off, saying
folks talked too much anyway, and all he asked was peace and
quiet—I guess you know about how much he talked himself; but I
thought maybe if I went to the house and talked about it before his
wife, though I said to Harry that I didn't know as what his wife
wanted made much difference to John—

County Attorney: Let's talk about that later, Mr. Hale. I do want to talk
about that, but tell now just what happened when you got to the
house.

Hale: I didn't hear or see anything; I knocked at the door, and still it was
all quiet inside. I knew they must be up, it was past eight o'clock. So
I knocked again, and I thought I heard somebody say, "Come in." I
wasn't sure, I'm not sure yet, but I opened the door—this door
[*Indicating the door by which the two women are still standing*] and there
in that rocker—[*Pointing to it*] sat Mrs. Wright.

[*They all look at the rocker.*]

County Attorney: What—was she doing?

Hale: She was rockin' back and forth. She had her apron in her hand
and was kind of—pleating it.

County Attorney: And how did she—look?

Hale: Well, she looked queer.

County Attorney: How do you mean—queer?

Hale: Well, as if she didn't know what she was going to do next. And
kind of done up.

County Attorney: How did she seem to feel about your coming?

Hale: Why, I don't think she minded—one way or other. She didn't pay
much attention. I said, "How do, Mrs. Wright, it's cold, ain't it?" And
she said, "Is it?"—and went on kind of pleating at her apron. Well, I
was surprised; she didn't ask me to come up to the stove, or to set
down, but just sat there, not even looking at me, so I said, "I want to
see John." And then she—laughed. I guess you would call it a laugh. I
thought of Harry and the team outside, so I said a little sharp: "Can't

I see John?" "No," she says, kind o' dull like. "Ain't he home?" says I. "Yes," says she, "he's home." "Then why can't I see him?" I asked her, out of patience. "'Cause he's dead," says she. "*Dead?*" says I. She just nodded her head, not getting a bit excited, but rockin' back and forth. "Why—where is he?" says I, not knowing what to say. She just pointed upstairs—like that [*Himself pointing to the room above.*] I got up, with the idea of going up there. I walked from there to here— then I says, "Why, what did he die of?" "He died of a rope round his neck," says she, and just went on pleatin' at her apron. Well, I went out and called Harry. I thought I might—need help. We went upstairs and there he was lyin'—

County Attorney: I think I'd rather have you go into that upstairs, where you can point it all out. Just go on now with the rest of the story.

Hale: Well, my first thought was to get that rope off. It looked . . . [*Stops, his face twitches*] . . . but Harry, he went up to him, and he said, "No, he's dead all right, and we'd better not touch anything." So we went back down stairs. She was still sitting that same way. "Has anybody been notified?" I asked. "No," says she, unconcerned. "Who did this, Mrs. Wright?" said Harry. He said it businesslike—and she stopped pleatin' of her apron. "I don't know," she says. "You don't *know?*" says Harry. "No," says she. "Weren't you sleepin' in the bed with him?" says Harry. "Yes," says she, "but I was on the inside." "Somebody slipped a rope round his neck and strangled him and you didn't wake up?" says Harry. "I didn't wake up," she said after him. We must 'a looked as if we didn't see how that could be, for after a minute she said, "I sleep sound." Harry was going to ask her more questions but I said maybe we ought to let her tell her story first to the coroner, or the sheriff, so Harry went fast as he could to Rivers' place, where there's a telephone.

County Attorney: And what did Mrs. Wright do when she knew that you had gone for the coroner?

Hale: She moved from that chair to this one over here [*Pointing to a small chair in the corner*] and just sat there with her hands held together and looking down. I got a feeling that I ought to make some conversation, so I said I had come in to see if John wanted to put in a telephone, and at that she started to laugh, and then she stopped and looked at me— scared. [*The County Attorney, who has had his notebook out, makes a note.*] I dunno, maybe it wasn't scared. I wouldn't like to say it was. Soon Harry got back, and then Dr. Lloyd came, and you, Mr. Peters, and so I guess that's all I know that you don't.

County Attorney: [*Looking around.*] I guess we'll go upstairs first—and then out to the barn and around there. [*To the Sheriff*] You're convinced that there was nothing important here—nothing that would point to any motive.

Sheriff: Nothing here but kitchen things.

[*The County Attorney, after again looking around the kitchen, opens the door of a cupboard closet. He gets up on a chair and looks on a shelf. Pulls his hand away, sticky.*]

County Attorney: Here's a nice mess.

[*The women draw nearer.*]

Mrs. Peters: [*To the other woman.*] Oh, her fruit; it did freeze. [*To the County Attorney*] She worried about that when it turned so cold. She said the fire'd go out and her jars would break.

Sheriff: Well, can you beat the women! Held for murder and worryin' about her preserves.

County Attorney: I guess before we're through she may have something more serious than preserves to worry about.

Hale: Well, women are used to worrying over trifles.

[*The two women move a little closer together.*]

County Attorney: [*With the gallantry of a young politician.*] And yet, for all their worries, what would we do without the ladies? [*The women do not unbend. He goes to the sink, takes a dipperful of water from the pail and pouring it into a basin, washes his hands. Starts to wipe them on the roller towel, turns it for a cleaner place.*] Dirty towels! [*Kicks his foot against the pans under the sink.*] Not much of a housekeeper, would you say, ladies?

Mrs. Hale: [*Stiffly.*] There's a great deal of work to be done on a farm.

County Attorney: To be sure. And yet [*With a little bow to her*] I know there are some Dickson County farmhouses which do not have such roller towels.

[*He gives it a pull to expose its full length again.*]

Mrs. Hale: Those towels get dirty awful quick. Men's hands aren't always as clean as they might be.

County Attorney: Ah, loyal to your sex, I see. But you and Mrs. Wright were neighbors. I suppose you were friends, too.

Mrs. Hale: [*Shaking her head.*] I've not seen much of her of late years. I've not been in this house—it's more than a year.

County Attorney: And why was that? You didn't like her?

Mrs. Hale: I liked her all well enough. Farmers' wives have their hands full, Mr. Henderson. And then—

County Attorney: Yes—?

Mrs. Hale: [*Looking about.*] It never seemed a very cheerful place.

County Attorney: No—it's not cheerful. I shouldn't say she had the home-making instinct.

Mrs. Hale: Well, I don't know as Wright had, either.

County Attorney: You mean that they didn't get on very well?

Mrs. Hale: No, I don't mean anything. But I don't think a place'd be any cheerfuller for John Wright's being in it.

County Attorney: I'd like to talk more of that a little later. I want to get the lay of things upstairs now.

[*He goes to the left, where three steps lead to a stair door.*]

Sheriff: I suppose anything Mrs. Peters does'll be all right. She was to take in some clothes for her, you know, and a few little things. We left in such a hurry yesterday.

County Attorney: Yes, but I would like to see what you take, Mrs. Peters, and keep an eye out for anything that might be of use to us.

Mrs. Peters: Yes, Mr. Henderson.

[*The women listen to the men's steps on the stairs, then look about the kitchen.*]

Mrs. Hale: I'd hate to have men coming into my kitchen, snooping around and criticizing.

[*She arranges the pans under sink which the County Attorney had shoved out of place.*]

Mrs. Peters: Of course it's no more than their duty.

Mrs. Hale: Duty's all right, but I guess that deputy sheriff that came out to make the fire might have got a little of this on. [*Gives the roller towel a pull.*] Wish I'd thought of that sooner. Seems mean to talk about her for not having things slicked up when she had to come away in such a hurry.

Mrs. Peters: [*Who has gone to a small table in the left rear corner of the room, and lifted one end of a towel that covers a pan.*] She had bread set.

[*Stands still.*]

Mrs. Hale: [*Eyes fixed on a loaf of bread beside the breadbox, which is on a low shelf at the other side of the room. Moves slowly toward it.*] She was going to put this in there. [*Picks up loaf, then abruptly drops it. In a manner of returning to familiar things.*] It's a shame about her fruit. I wonder if it's all gone. [*Gets up on the chair and looks.*] I think there's some here that's all right, Mrs. Peters. Yes—here; [*Holding it toward the window*] this is cherries, too. [*Looking again.*] I declare I believe that's the only one. [*Gets down, bottle in her hand. Goes to the sink and wipes it off on the outside.*] She'll feel awful bad after all her hard work in the hot weather. I remember the afternoon I put up my cherries last summer.

[*She puts the bottle on the big kitchen table, center of the room. With a sigh, is about to sit down in the rocking-chair. Before she is seated realizes what chair it is; with a slow look at it, steps back. The chair which she has touched rocks back and forth.*]

Mrs. Peters: Well, I must get those things from the front room closet. [*She goes to the door at the right, but after looking into the other room, steps back.*] You coming with me, Mrs. Hale? You could help me carry them.

[*They go in the other room; reappear, Mrs. Peters carrying a dress and skirt, Mrs. Hale following with a pair of shoes.*]

Mrs. Peters: My, it's cold in there.

[*She puts the clothes on the big table, and hurries to the stove.*]

Mrs. Hale: [*Examining her skirt.*] Wright was close. I think maybe that's why she kept so much to herself. She didn't even belong to the Ladies Aid. I suppose she felt she couldn't do her part, and then you don't enjoy things when you feel shabby. She used to wear pretty clothes and be lively, when she was Minnie Foster, one of the town girls singing in the choir. But that—oh, that was thirty years ago. This all you was to take in?

Mrs. Peters: She said she wanted an apron. Funny thing to want, for there isn't much to get you dirty in jail, goodness knows. But I suppose just to make her feel more natural. She said they was in the top drawer in this cupboard. Yes, here. And then her little shawl that always hung behind the door. [*Opens stair door and looks.*] Yes, here it is.

[*Quickly shuts door leading upstairs.*]

Mrs. Hale: [*Abruptly moving toward her.*] Mrs. Peters?
Mrs. Peters: Yes, Mrs. Hale?
Mrs. Hale: Do you think she did it?
Mrs. Peters: [*In a frightened voice.*] Oh, I don't know.
Mrs. Hale: Well, I don't think she did. Asking for an apron and her little shawl. Worrying about her fruit.
Mrs. Peters: [*Starts to speak, glances up, where footsteps are heard in the room above. In a low voice.*] Mr. Peters says it looks bad for her. Mr. Henderson

is awful sarcastic in a speech and he'll make fun of her sayin' she
didn't wake up.

Mrs. Hale: Well, I guess John Wright didn't wake when they was slipping that rope under his neck.

Mrs. Peters: No, it's strange. It must have been done awful crafty and
still. They say it was such a—funny way to kill a man, rigging it all
up like that.

Mrs. Hale: That's just what Mr. Hale said. There was a gun in the house.
He says that's what he can't understand.

Mrs. Peters: Mr. Henderson said coming out that what was needed for
the case was a motive; something to show anger, or—sudden feeling.

Mrs. Hale: [Who is standing by the table.] Well, I don't see any signs of
anger around here. [She puts her hand on the dish towel which lies on the
table, stands looking down at table, one half of which is clean, the other half
messy.] It's wiped to here. [Makes a move as if to finish work, then turns
and looks at loaf of bread outside the breadbox. Drops towel. In that voice
of coming back to familiar things.] Wonder how they are finding things
upstairs. I hope she had it a little more red-up° there. You know, it
seems kind of sneaking. Locking her up in town and then coming out
here and trying to get her own house to turn against her!

Mrs. Peters: But Mrs. Hale, the law is the law.

Mrs. Hale: I s'pose 'tis. [Unbuttoning her coat.] Better loosen up your
things, Mrs. Peters. You won't feel them when you go out.

[Mrs. Peters takes off her fur tippet, goes to hang it on hook at back of
room, stands looking at the under part of the small corner table.]

Mrs. Peters: She was piecing a quilt.

[She brings the large sewing basket and they look at the bright pieces.]

Mrs. Hale: It's a log cabin pattern. Pretty, isn't it? I wonder if she was
goin' to quilt it or just knot it?

[Footsteps have been heard coming down the stairs. The Sheriff enters followed by Hale and the County Attorney.]

Sheriff: They wonder if she was going to quilt it or just knot it!

[The men laugh; the women look abashed.]

County Attorney: [Rubbing his hands over the stove.] Frank's fire didn't do
much up there, did it? Well, let's go out to the barn and get that
cleared up.

[The men go outside.]

---

red-up: (slang) readied up, ready to be seen.

Mrs. Hale: [*Resentfully.*] I don't know as there's anything so strange, our takin' up our time with little things while we're waiting for them to get the evidence. [*She sits down at the big table smoothing out a block with decision.*] I don't see as it's anything to laugh about.

Mrs. Peters: [*Apologetically.*] Of course they've got awful important things on their minds.

[*Pulls up a chair and joins Mrs. Hale at the table.*]

Mrs. Hale: [*Examining another block.*] Mrs. Peters, look at this one. Here, this is the one she was working on, and look at the sewing! All the rest of it has been so nice and even. And look at this! It's all over the place! Why, it looks as if she didn't know what she was about!

[*After she has said this they look at each, then start to glance back at the door. After an instant Mrs. Hale has pulled at a knot and ripped the sewing.*]

Mrs. Peters: Oh, what are you doing, Mrs. Hale?

Mrs. Hale: [*Mildly.*] Just pulling out a stitch or two that's not sewed very good. [*Threading a needle.*] Bad sewing always made me fidgety.

Mrs. Peters: [*Nervously.*] I don't think we ought to touch things.

Mrs. Hale: I'll just finish up this end. [*Suddenly stopping and leaning forward.*] Mrs. Peters?

Mrs. Peters: Yes, Mrs. Hale?

Mrs. Hale: What do you suppose she was so nervous about?

Mrs. Peters: Oh—I don't know. I don't know as she was nervous. I sometimes sew awful queer when I'm just tired. [*Mrs. Hale starts to say something, looks at Mrs. Peters, then goes on sewing.*] Well, I must get these things wrapped up. They may be through sooner than we think. [*Putting apron and other things together.*] I wonder where I can find a piece of paper, and string.

Mrs. Hale: In that cupboard, maybe.

Mrs. Peters: [*Looking in cupboard.*] Why, here's a birdcage. [*Holds it up.*] Did she have a bird, Mrs. Hale?

Mrs. Hale: Why, I don't know whether she did or not—I've not been here for so long. There was a man around last year selling canaries cheap, but I don't know as she took one; maybe she did. She used to sing real pretty herself.

Mrs. Peters: [*Glancing around.*] Seems funny to think of a bird here. But she must have had one, or why would she have a cage? I wonder what happened to it.

Mrs. Hale: I s'pose maybe the cat got it.

Mrs. Peters: No, she didn't have a cat. She's got that feeling some people have about cats—being afraid of them. My cat got in her room and she was real upset and asked me to take it out.

Mrs. Hale: My sister Bessie was like that. Queer, ain't it?

Mrs. Peters: [*Examining the cage.*] Why, look at this door. It's broke. One hinge is pulled apart.

Mrs. Hale: [*Looking too.*] Looks as if someone must have been rough with it.

Mrs. Peters: Why, yes.

[*She brings the cage forward and puts it on the table.*]

Mrs. Hale: I wish if they're going to find any evidence they'd be about it. I don't like this place.

Mrs. Peters: But I'm awful glad you came with me, Mrs. Hale. It would be lonesome for me sitting here alone.

Mrs. Hale: It would, wouldn't it? [*Dropping her sewing.*] But I tell you what I do wish, Mrs. Peters. I wish I had come over sometimes when *she* was here. I—[*Looking around the room.*]—wish I had.

Mrs. Peters: But of course you were awful busy, Mrs. Hale—your house and your children.

Mrs. Hale: I could've come. I stayed away because it weren't cheerful—and that's why I ought to have come. I—I've never liked this place. Maybe because it's down in a hollow and you don't see the road. I dunno what it is but it's a lonesome place and always was. I wish I had come over to see Minnie Foster sometimes. I can see now—

[*Shakes her head.*]

Mrs. Peters: Well, you mustn't reproach yourself, Mrs. Hale. Somehow we just don't see how it is with other folks until—something comes up.

Mrs. Hale: Not having children makes less work—but it makes a quiet house, and Wright out to work all day, and no company when he did come in. Did you know John Wright, Mrs. Peters?

Mrs. Peters: Not to know him; I've seen him in town. They say he was a good man.

Mrs. Hale: Yes—good; he didn't drink, and kept his word as well as most, I guess, and paid his debts. But he was a hard man, Mrs. Peters. Just to pass the time of day with him—[*Shivers.*] Like a raw wind that gets to the bone. [*Pauses, her eye falling on the cage.*] I should think she would'a wanted a bird. But what do you suppose went with it?

Mrs. Peters: I don't know, unless it got sick and died.

[*She reaches over and swings the broken door, swings it again. Both women watch it.*]

Mrs. Hale: You weren't raised round here, were you? [*Mrs. Peters shakes her head.*] You didn't know—her?

Mrs. Peters: Not till they brought her yesterday.

2000 production of *Trifles,* by Echo Theatre of Dallas

Mrs. Hale: She—come to think of it, she was kind of like a bird herself—real sweet and pretty, but kind of timid and—fluttery. How—she—did—change. [*Silence; then as if struck by a happy thought and relieved to get back to everyday things.*] Tell you what, Mrs. Peters, why don't you take the quilt in with you? It might take up her mind.

Mrs. Peters: Why, I think that's a real nice idea, Mrs. Hale. There couldn't possibly be any objection to it, could there? Now, just what would I take? I wonder if her patches are in here—and her things.

[*They look in the sewing basket.*]

Mrs. Hale: Here's some red. I expect this has got sewing things in it. [*Brings out a fancy box.*] What a pretty box. Looks like something somebody would give you. Maybe her scissors are in here. [*Opens box. Suddenly puts her hand to her nose.*] Why—[*Mrs. Peters bends nearer, then turns her face away.*] There's something wrapped up in this piece of silk.

Mrs. Peters: Why, this isn't her scissors.

Mrs. Hale: [*Lifting the silk.*] Oh, Mrs. Peters—it's—

[*Mrs. Peters bends closer.*]

Mrs. Peters: It's the bird.

Mrs. Hale: [Jumping up.] But, Mrs. Peters—look at it! Its neck! Look at its neck! It's all—other side too.

Mrs. Peters: Somebody—wrung—its—neck.

[Their eyes meet. A look of growing comprehension, of horror. Steps are heard outside. Mrs. Hale slips box under quilt pieces, and sinks into her chair. Enter Sheriff and County Attorney. Mrs. Peters rises.]

County Attorney: [As one turning from serious things to little pleasantries.] Well, ladies, have you decided whether she was going to quilt it or knot it?

Mrs. Peters: We think she was going to—knot it.

County Attorney: Well, that's interesting, I'm sure. [Seeing the birdcage.] Has the bird flown?

Mrs. Hale: [Putting more quilt pieces over the box.] We think the—cat got it.

County Attorney: [Preoccupied.] Is there a cat?

[Mrs. Hale glances in a quick covert way at Mrs. Peters.]

Mrs. Peters: Well, not now. They're superstitious, you know. They leave.

County Attorney: [To Sheriff Peters, continuing an interrupted conversation.] No sign at all of anyone having come from the outside. Their own rope. Now let's go up again and go over it piece by piece. [They start upstairs.] It would have to have been someone who knew just the—

[Mrs. Peters sits down. The two women sit there not looking at one another, but as if peering into something and at the same time holding back. When they talk now it is in the manner of feeling their way over strange ground, as if afraid of what they are saying, but as if they cannot help saying it.]

Mrs. Hale: She liked the bird. She was going to bury it in that pretty box.

Mrs. Peters: [In a whisper.] When I was a girl—my kitten—there was a boy took a hatchet, and before my eyes—and before I could get there—[Covers her face an instant.] If they hadn't held me back I would have—[Catches herself, looks upstairs where steps are heard, falters weakly]—hurt him.

Mrs. Hale: [With a slow look around her.] I wonder how it would seem never to have had any children around. [Pause.] No, Wright wouldn't like the bird—a thing that sang. She used to sing. He killed that, too.

Mrs. Peters: [Moving uneasily.] We don't know who killed the bird.

Mrs. Hale: I knew John Wright.

Mrs. Peters: It was an awful thing was done in this house that night, Mrs. Hale. Killing a man while he slept, slipping a rope around his neck that choked the life out of him.

Mrs. Hale: His neck. Choked the life out of him.

[*Her hand goes out and rests on the birdcage.*]

Mrs. Peters: [*With rising voice.*] We don't know who killed him. We don't know.

Mrs. Hale: [*Her own feeling not interrupted.*] If there'd been years and years of nothing, then a bird to sing to you, it would be awful—still, after the bird was still.

Mrs. Peters: [*Something within her speaking.*] I know what stillness is. When we homesteaded in Dakota, and my first baby died—after he was two years old, and me with no other then—

Mrs. Hale: [*Moving.*] How soon do you suppose they'll be through looking for the evidence?

Mrs. Peters: I know what stillness is. [*Pulling herself back.*] The law has got to punish crime, Mrs. Hale.

Mrs. Hale: [*Not as if answering that.*] I wish you'd seen Minnie Foster when she wore a white dress with blue ribbons and stood up there in the choir and sang. [*A look around the room.*] Oh, I *wish* I'd come over here once in a while! That was a crime! That was a crime! Who's going to punish that?

Mrs. Peters: [*Looking upstairs.*] We mustn't—take on.

Mrs. Hale: I might have known she needed help! I know how things can be—for women. I tell you, it's queer, Mrs. Peters. We live close together and we live far apart. We all go through the same things—it's all just a different kind of the same thing. [*Brushes her eyes; noticing the bottle of fruit, reaches out for it.*] If I was you I wouldn't tell her her fruit was gone. Tell her it *ain't.* Tell her it's all right. Take this in to prove it to her. She—she may never know whether it was broke or not.

Mrs. Peters: [*Takes the bottle, looks about for something to wrap it in; takes petticoat from the clothes brought from the other room, very nervously begins winding this around the bottle. In a false voice.*] My, it's a good thing the men couldn't hear us. Wouldn't they just laugh! Getting all stirred up over a little thing like a—dead canary. As if that could have anything to do with—with—wouldn't they *laugh!*

[*The men are heard coming down stairs.*]

Mrs. Hale: [*Under her breath.*] Maybe they would—maybe they wouldn't.

County Attorney: No, Peters, it's all perfectly clear except a reason for doing it. But you know juries when it comes to women. If there was some definite thing. Something to show—something to make a story about—a thing that would connect up with this strange way of doing it—

[*The women's eyes meet for an instant. Enter Hale from outer door.*]

Hale: Well, I've got the team around. Pretty cold out there.

County Attorney: I'm going to stay here a while by myself. [*To the Sheriff.*] You can send Frank out for me, can't you? I want to go over everything. I'm not satisfied that we can't do better.

Sheriff: Do you want to see what Mrs. Peters is going to take in?

[*The County Attorney goes to the table, picks up the apron, laughs.*]

County Attorney: Oh, I guess they're not very dangerous things the ladies have picked out. [*Moves a few things about, disturbing the quilt pieces which cover the box. Steps back.*] No, Mrs. Peters doesn't need supervising. For that matter, a sheriff's wife is married to the law. Ever think of it that way, Mrs. Peters?

Mrs. Peters: Not—just that way.

Sheriff: [*Chuckling.*] Married to the law. [*Moves toward the other room.*] I just want you to come in here a minute, George. We ought to take a look at these windows.

County Attorney: [*Scoffingly.*] Oh, windows!

Sheriff: We'll be right out, Mr. Hale.

[*Hale goes outside. The Sheriff follows the County Attorney into the other room. Then Mrs. Hale rises, hands tight together, looking intensely at Mrs. Peters, whose eyes make a slow turn, finally meeting Mrs. Hale's. A moment Mrs. Hale holds her, then her own eyes point the way to where the box is concealed. Suddenly Mrs. Peters throws back quilt pieces and tries to put the box in the bag she is wearing. It is too big. She opens box, starts to take bird out, cannot touch it, goes to pieces, stands there helpless. Sound of a knob turning in the other room. Mrs. Hale snatches the box and puts it in the pocket of her big coat. Enter County Attorney and Sheriff.*]

County Attorney: [*Facetiously.*] Well, Henry, at least we found out that she was not going to quilt it. She was going to—what is it you call it, ladies?

Mrs. Hale: [*Her hand against her pocket.*] We call it—knot it, Mr. Henderson.

CURTAIN

QUESTIONS

1. What attitudes toward women do the Sheriff and the County Attorney express? How do Mrs. Hale and Mrs. Peters react to these sentiments?

2. Why does the County Attorney care so much about discovering a motive for the killing?

3. What does Glaspell show us about the position of women in this early twentieth-century community?

4. What do we learn about the married life of the Wrights? By what means is this knowledge revealed to us?
5. What is the setting of this play, and how does it help us to understand Mrs. Wright's deed?
6. What do you infer from the wildly stitched block in Minnie's quilt? Why does Mrs. Hale rip out the crazy stitches?
7. What is so suggestive in the ruined birdcage and the dead canary wrapped in silk? What do these objects have to do with Minnie Foster Wright? What similarity do you notice between the way the canary died and John Wright's own death?
8. What thoughts and memories confirm Mrs. Peters and Mrs. Hale in their decision to help Minnie beat the murder rap?
9. In what places does Mrs. Peters show that she is trying to be a loyal, law-abiding sheriff's wife? How do she and Mrs. Hale differ in background and temperament?
10. What ironies does the play contain? Comment on Mrs. Hale's closing speech: "We call it—knot it, Mr. Henderson." Why is that little hesitation before "knot it" such a meaningful pause?
11. Point out some moments in the play when the playwright conveys much to the audience without needing dialogue.
12. How would you sum up the play's major theme?
13. How does this play, first produced in 1916, show its age? In what ways does it seem still remarkably new?
14. "*Trifles* is a lousy mystery. All the action took place before the curtain went up. Almost in the beginning, on the third page, we find out 'who done it.' So there isn't really much reason for us to sit through the rest of the play." Discuss this view.

Some plays endure, perhaps because (among other reasons) actors take pleasure in performing them. *Trifles* is such a play, a showcase for the skills of its two principals. While the men importantly bumble about, trying to discover a motive, Mrs. Peters and Mrs. Hale solve the case right under their dull noses. The two players in these leading roles face a challenging task: to show both characters growing onstage before us. Discovering a secret that binds them, the two must realize painful truths in their own lives, become aware of all they have in common with Minnie Wright, and gradually resolve to side with the accused against the men. That *Trifles* has enjoyed a revival of attention may reflect its evident feminist views, its convincing portrait of two women forced reluctantly to arrive at a moral judgment and to make a defiant move.

Some critics say that the essence of drama is conflict. Evidently, Glaspell's play is rich in this essential, even though its most violent conflict—the war between John and Minnie Wright—takes place earlier, off scene. Right away, when the menfolk barge through the door into the warm room, letting the women trail in after them; right away, when the sheriff makes fun of Minnie for worrying about "trifles" and the county attorney (that slick politician) starts crudely trying to flatter the "ladies," we sense a conflict between officious, self-important men and the women they expect to wait on them. What is the play's *theme*? Surely the title points to it: women, who men say worry over trifles, can find in those little things large meanings.

Like a carefully constructed traditional short story, *Trifles* has a **plot**, a term sometimes taken to mean whatever happens in a story, but more exactly referring to the unique arrangement of events that the author has made. (For more about plot in a story, see Chapter 1.) If Glaspell had elected to tell the story of John and Minnie Wright in chronological order, the sequence in which events took place in time, she might have written a much longer play, opening perhaps with a scene of Minnie's buying her canary and John's cold complaint, "That damned bird keeps twittering all day long!" She might have included scenes showing John strangling the canary and swearing when it beaks him; the Wrights in their loveless bed while Minnie knots her noose; and farmer Hale's entrance after the murder, with Minnie rocking. Only at the end would she have shown us what happened after the crime. That arrangement of events would have made for a quite different play than the short, tight one Glaspell wrote. By telling of events in retrospect, by having the women detectives piece together what happened, Glaspell leads us to focus not only on the murder but, more importantly, on the developing bond between the two women and their growing compassion for the accused.

If *Trifles* may be said to have a **protagonist**, a leading character—a word we usually save for the primary figure of a larger and more eventful play such as *Othello* or *Death of a Salesman*—then you would call the two women dual protagonists. They act in unison to make the plot unfold. Or you could argue that Mrs. Hale—because she destroys the wild stitching in the quilt; because she finds the dead canary; because she invents a cat to catch the bird (thus deceiving the county attorney); and because in the end when Mrs. Peters helplessly "goes to pieces," it is she who takes the initiative and seizes the evidence—deserves to be called the protagonist. More than anyone else in the play, you could claim, the more decisive Mrs. Hale makes things happen.

A vital part in most plays is an **exposition**, the part in which we first meet the characters, learn what happened before the curtain rose, and find out what is happening now. For a one-act play, *Trifles* has a fairly long exposition, extending from the opening of the kitchen door through the end of farmer Hale's story. Clearly, this substantial exposition is necessary to set the situation and to fill in the facts of the crime. By comparison, Shakespeare's far longer *Tragedy of Richard III* begins almost abruptly, with its protagonist, a duke who yearns to be king, summing up history in an opening speech and revealing his evil character: "And therefore, since I cannot prove a lover . . . I am determined to prove a villain." But Glaspell, too, knows her craft. In the exposition, we are given a **foreshadowing** (or hint of what is to come) in Hale's dry remark, "I didn't know as what his wife wanted made much difference to John." The remark announces the play's theme that men often ignore women's feelings, and it hints at Minnie Wright's motive, later to be revealed. The county attorney, failing to pick up a valuable clue, tables the discussion. (Still another foreshadowing occurs in Mrs. Hale's ripping out the wild, panicky stitches in Minnie's quilt. In the end, Mrs. Hale will make a similar final move to conceal the evidence.)

With the county attorney's speech to the sheriff, "You're convinced that there was nothing important here—nothing that would point to any motive," we begin to understand what he seeks. As he will make even clearer later, the attorney needs a motive in order to convict the accused wife of murder in the first degree. Will Minnie's motive in killing her husband be discovered? Through the first two-thirds of *Trifles*, this is the play's **dramatic question**. Whether or not we state such a question in our minds (and it is doubtful that we do), our interest quickens as we sense that here is a problem to be solved, an uncertainty to be dissipated. When Mrs. Hale and Mrs. Peters find the dead canary with the twisted neck, the question is answered. We know that Minnie killed John to repay him for his act of gross cruelty. The playwright, however, now raises a *new* dramatic question. Having discovered Minnie's motive, will the women reveal it to the lawmen? Alternatively (if you care to phrase the new question differently), what will they do with the incriminating evidence? We keep reading, or stay clamped to our theater seats, because we want that question answered. We share the women's secret now, and we want to see what they will do with it.

Tightly packed, the one-act *Trifles* contains but one plot: the story of how two women discover evidence that might hang another woman and then hide it. Some plays, usually longer ones, may be more complicated. They may contain a **double plot** (or **subplot**), a secondary arrangement of incidents, involving not the protagonist but someone less important. In Henrik Ibsen's *A Doll's House*, the main plot involves a woman and her husband; they are joined by a second couple, whose fortunes we also follow with interest and whose futures pose another dramatic question.

Step by step, *Trifles* builds to a **climax**: a moment, usually coming late in a play, when tension reaches its greatest height. At such a moment, we sense that the play's dramatic question (or its final dramatic question, if the writer has posed more than one) is about to be answered. In *Trifles* this climax occurs when Mrs. Peters finds herself torn between her desire to save Minnie and her duty to the law. "It was an awful thing was done in this house that night," she reminds herself in one speech, suggesting that Minnie deserves to be punished; then in the next speech she insists, "We don't know who killed him. We don't *know*." Shortly after that, in one speech she voices two warring attitudes. Remembering the loss of her first child, she sympathizes with Minnie: "I know what stillness is." But in her next breath she recalls once more her duty to be a loyal sheriff's wife: "The law has got to punish crime, Mrs. Hale." For a moment, she is placed in conflict with Mrs. Hale, who knew

Minnie personally. The two now stand on the edge of a fateful brink. Which way will they decide?[1]

From this moment of climax, the play, like its protagonist (or if you like, protagonists), will make a final move. Mrs. Peters takes her stand. Mrs. Hale, too, decides. She owes Minnie something to make up for her own "crime"— her failure to visit the desperate woman. The plot now charges ahead to its outcome or **resolution**, also called the **conclusion** or **dénouement** (French for "untying of a knot"). The two women act: they scoop up the damaging evidence. Seconds before the very end, Glaspell heightens the **suspense**, our enjoyable anxiety, by making Mrs. Peters fumble with the incriminating box as the sheriff and the county attorney draw near. Mrs. Hale's swift grab for the evidence saves the day and presumably saves Minnie's life. The sound of the doorknob turning in the next room, as the lawmen return, is a small but effective bit of **stage business**—any nonverbal action that engages the attention of an audience. Earlier, when Mrs. Hale almost sits down in Minnie's place, the empty chair that ominously starts rocking is another brilliant piece of stage business. Not only does it give us something interesting to watch, but it also gives us something to think about.

Some critics maintain that events in a plot can be arranged in the outline of a pyramid.[2] In this view, a play begins with a **rising action**, that part of the story (including the exposition) in which events start moving toward a climax. After the climax, the story tapers off in a **falling action**, that is, the subsequent events, including a resolution. In a tragedy, this falling action usually is recognizable: the protagonist's fortunes proceed downhill to an inexorable end.

Some plays indeed have demonstrable pyramids. In *Trifles*, we might claim that in the first two-thirds of the play a rising action builds in intensity. It proceeds through each main incident: the finding of the crazily stitched quilt, Mrs. Hale's ripping out the evidence, the discovery of the bird cage, then the bird itself, and Mrs. Hale's concealing it. At the climax, the peak of the pyramid, the two women seem about to clash as Mrs. Peters wavers uncertainly. The action then falls to a swift resolution. If you outlined that pyramid on paper, however, it would look lopsided—a long rise and a short, steep fall. The pyramid metaphor seems more meaningfully to fit longer plays, among them some classic tragedies. Try it on *Oedipus the King* or, for an even neater fit, on Shakespeare's *Julius Caesar*—an unusual play in that its climax, the

---

[1]You will sometimes hear *climax* used in a different sense to mean any **crisis**—that is, a moment of tension when one or another outcome is possible. What *crisis* means will be easy to remember if you think of a crisis in medicine: the turning point in a disease when it becomes clear that a patient will either die or recover. In talking about plays, you will probably find both *crisis* and *climax* useful. You can say that a play has more than one crisis, perhaps several. In such a play, the last and most decisive crisis is the climax. A play has only one climax.

[2]The metaphor of a play as a pyramid was invented by German critic Gustav Freytag, in his *Techniques of the Drama*, 1904, reprint ed. (New York: Arno, 1968).

assassination of Caesar, occurs exactly in the middle (Act III, Scene i), right where a good pyramid's point ought to be. Nevertheless, in most other plays, it is hard to find a symmetrical pyramid.

Because its action occurs all at one time and in one place, *Trifles* happens to observe the **unities**, certain principles of good drama laid down by Italian literary critics in the sixteenth century. Interpreting the theories of Aristotle as binding laws, these critics set down three basic principles: a good play, they maintained, should display unity of *action*, unity of *time*, and unity of *place*. In practical terms, this theory maintained that a play must represent a single series of interrelated actions that take place within twenty-four hours in a single location. Furthermore, they insisted, to have true unity of action, a play had to be entirely serious or entirely funny. Mixing tragic and comic elements was not allowed. That Glaspell consciously strove to obey those critics is doubtful, and certainly many great plays, such as Shakespeare's *Othello*, defy such arbitrary rules. Still, it is at least arguable that some of the power of *Trifles* (or Sophocles' *Oedipus the King*) comes from the intensity of the playwright's concentration on what happens in one place, in one short expanse of time.

Brief though it is, *Trifles* has main elements you will find in much longer, more complicated plays. It even has **symbols**, things that hint at large meanings—for example, the broken bird cage and the dead canary, both suggesting the music and the joy that John Wright stifled in Minnie and the terrible stillness that followed his killing the one thing she loved. Perhaps the lone remaining jar of cherries, too, radiates suggestions: it is the one bright, cheerful thing poor Minnie has to show for a whole summer of toil. Symbols in drama may be as big as a house—the home in Ibsen's A *Doll's House*, for instance—or they may appear to be trifles. In Glaspell's rich art, such trifles aren't trifling at all.

WRITING EFFECTIVELY

WRITING ABOUT CONFLICT

Conflict Resolution

A good play almost always presents a **conflict**. Conflict creates suspense and keeps an audience from meandering out to the lobby water fountain. Without it, a play would be static and, most likely, dull. When a character intensely desires something but some obstacle—perhaps another character—stands in the way, the result is dramatic tension. The central action of the play generally grows out of how these two opposing forces deal with—and ultimately resolve—conflict.

To better understand a play, begin by identifying the central dramatic conflict. If you can determine which character is the play's protagonist, what that character wants, and who or what opposes the protagonist, you will have a sense of the plot's overall design. Identify the play's three or four main characters and what each character wants most at the beginning of the play. A single compelling motive might not be clear to you right away, but it will be helpful to take note of all of the protagonist's longings. Keep in mind that sometimes what a character wants most is to avoid something unpleasant or dangerous; also remember that what stands in the protagonist's way might even be some aspect of his or her personality.

By determining which character is the play's protagonist, or hero, what he or she wants, and what or who opposes that ambition, you will have defined the play's central conflict. As for the other main characters and their desires, these may turn out to constitute a double plot or subplot, often present in longer plays and films.

CHECKLIST

Analyzing Conflict

- ✓ List the play's three or four main characters.
- ✓ Jot down what each character wants most at the play's beginning. If the main motive isn't clear yet, list more than one motive per character.
- ✓ Which of these characters is the protagonist?
- ✓ What stands in the way of the protagonist achieving his or her goal?
- ✓ How do the other characters' motivations fit into the central conflict? Identify any double plots or subplots.
- ✓ What are the play's main events? How does each relate to the protagonist's struggle?
- ✓ Where do you find the play's climax, or crisis?
- ✓ How is the conflict resolved?
- ✓ Does the protagonist achieve his or her goal?
- ✓ What qualities in the protagonist's character bring about the play's outcome?
- ✓ How does success or failure affect the protagonist?
- ✓ How are the other main characters' conflicts resolved?

WRITING ASSIGNMENT ON CONFLICT

Select any short play, and write a brief essay identifying the protagonist, central conflict, and dramatic question.

MORE TOPICS FOR WRITING

1. Write a brief essay on the role gender differences play in Susan Glaspell's *Trifles*.
2. Write an analysis of the exposition—how the scene is set, characters introduced, and background information communicated—in *Trifles*.
3. Describe the significance of setting in *Trifles*.
4. Imagine you are a lawyer hired to defend Minnie Wright. Present your closing argument to the jury.
5. Watch any hour-long television drama. Write about the main conflict that drives the story. What motivates the protagonist? What stands in his or her way? How do each of the drama's main events relate to the protagonist's struggle? How is the conflict resolved? Is the show's outcome connected to the protagonist's character, or do events just happen to him or her? Do you believe the script is well written? Why or why not?

23
Modes of Drama: Tragedy and Comedy

"The world," wrote Horace Walpole in 1770, "is a comedy to those that think, a tragedy to those that feel." All of us, of course, both think and feel, and all of us have moments when we stand back and laugh, whether ruefully or with glee, at life's absurdities, just as we all have times when our hearts are broken by its pains and losses. Thus, the modes of tragedy and comedy, diametrically opposed to one another though they are, do not demand that we choose between them: both of them speak to something deep and real within us, and each of them has its own truth to tell about the infinitely complex experience of living in this world.

Tragedy

By **tragedy** we mean a play that portrays a serious conflict between human beings and some superior, overwhelming force. It ends sorrowfully and disastrously, and this outcome seems inevitable. Few spectators of *Oedipus the King* wonder how the play will turn out or wish for a happy ending. "In a tragedy," French playwright Jean Anouilh has remarked, "nothing is in doubt and everyone's destiny is known. . . . Tragedy is restful, and the reason is that hope, that foul, deceitful thing, has no part in it. There isn't any hope. You're trapped. The whole sky has fallen on you, and all you can do about it is shout."[1]

Many of our ideas of tragedy (from the Greek *tragoidia*, "goat song," referring to the goatskin dress of the performers), go back to ancient Athens; the plays of the Greek dramatists Sophocles, Aeschylus, and Euripides exemplify the art of tragedy. In the fourth century B.C., the philosopher Aristotle described Sophocles' *Oedipus the King* and other tragedies he had seen, analyzing their elements and trying to account for their power over our emotions. Aristotle's observations will make more sense after you read *Oedipus the King,* so we will save our principal discussion of them for the next chapter. But for now, to understand something of the nature of tragedy, let us take a brief overview of the subject.

One of the oldest and most durable of literary genres, tragedy is also one of the simplest—the protagonist undergoes a reversal of fortune, from good to

[1]Preface to *Antigonê,* translated by Louis Galantière (New York: Random, 1946).

bad, ending in catastrophe. However simple, though, tragedy can be one of the most complex genres to explain satisfactorily, with almost every principal point of its definition open to differing and often hotly debated interpretations. It is a fluid and adaptive genre, and for every one of its defining points, we can cite a tragic masterpiece that fails to observe that particular convention. Its fluidity and adaptability can also be shown by the way in which the classical tragic pattern is played out in pure form in such unlikely places as Orson Welles's *Citizen Kane* (1941) and Chinua Achebe's great novel *Things Fall Apart* (1958): in each of these works, a man of high position and character—one a multimillionaire newspaper publisher, the other a late nineteenth-century African warrior—moves inexorably to destruction, impelled by his rigidity and self-righteousness. Even a film such as *King Kong*—despite its oversized and hirsute protagonist—exemplifies some of the principles of tragedy.

To gain a clearer understanding of what tragedy is, let us first take a moment to talk about what it is not. Consider the kinds of events that customarily bring the term "tragedy" to mind: the death of a child, a fire that destroys a family's home and possessions, the killing of a bystander caught in the crossfire of a shootout between criminals, and so on. What all of these unfortunate instances have in common, obviously, is that they involve the infliction of great and irreversible suffering. But what they also share is the sense that the sufferers are innocent, that they have done nothing to cause or to deserve their fate. This is what we usually describe as a tragedy in real life, but tragedy in a literary or dramatic context has a different meaning: most theorists take their lead from Aristotle (see the next chapter for a fuller discussion of several of the points raised here) in maintaining that the protagonist's reversal of fortune is brought about through some error or weakness on his part, generally referred to as his **tragic flaw**.

Despite this weakness, the hero is traditionally a person of nobility, of both social rank and personality. Just as the suffering of totally innocent people stirs us to sympathetic sorrow rather than a tragic response, so too the destruction of a purely evil figure, a tyrant or a murderer with no redeeming qualities, would inspire only feelings of relief and satisfaction—hardly the emotions that tragedy seeks to stimulate. In most tragedies, the catastrophe entails not only the loss of outward fortune—things such as reputation, power, and life itself, which even the basest villain may possess and then be deprived of—but also the erosion of the protagonist's moral character and greatness of spirit.

In keeping with this emphasis on nobility of spirit, tragedies are customarily written in an elevated style, one characterized by dignity and seriousness. In the Middle Ages, just as *tragedy* meant a work written in a high style in which the central character went from good fortune to bad, *comedy* indicated just the opposite, a work written in a low or common style, in which the protagonist moved from adverse circumstances to happy ones—hence Dante's great triptych of hell, purgatory, and heaven, written in everyday Italian rather than scholarly Latin, is known as *The Divine Comedy*, despite the relative absence of humor, let alone hilarity, in its pages. The tragic view of life, clearly, presupposes that in the end we will prove unequal to the challenges we must face, while the comic outlook asserts a sense of human possibility in which our common sense and resilience—or pure dumb luck—will enable us to win out.

Tragedy's complexity can be seen also in the response that, according to Aristotle, it seeks to arouse in the viewer: pity and fear. By its very nature, pity distances the one who pities from the object of that pity, since we can feel sorry only for those whom we perceive to be worse off than ourselves. When we watch or read a tragedy, moved as we may be, we observe the downfall of the protagonist with a certain detachment; "better him than me" may be a rather crude way of putting it, but perhaps not an entirely incorrect one. Fear, on the other hand, usually involves an immediate anxiety about our own well-being. Even as we regard the hero's destruction from the safety of a better place, we are made to feel our own vulnerability in the face of life's dangers and instability, because we see that neither position nor virtue can protect even the great from ruin.

The following is a scene from Christopher Marlowe's classic Elizabethan tragedy *Doctor Faustus*. Based on an anonymous pamphlet published in Germany in 1587 and translated into English shortly thereafter, this celebrated play tells the story of an elderly professor who feels that he has wasted his life in fruitless inquiry. Chafing at the limits of human understanding, he makes a pact with the devil to gain forbidden knowledge and power. The scene presented here is the decisive turning point of the play, in which Faustus seals the satanic bargain that will damn him. Stimulated by his thirst for knowledge and experience, spurred on by his pride to assume that the divinely ordained limits of human experience no longer apply to him, he rushes to embrace his own undoing. Marlowe dramatizes Faustus's situation by bringing a good angel and a fallen angel (i.e., a demon) to whisper conflicting advice in this pivotal scene. (This good angel versus bad angel device has proved popular for centuries. One still sees it today in everything from TV commercials to cartoons such as *The Simpsons*.) Notice the dignified and often gorgeous language Marlowe employs to create the serious mood necessary for tragedy.

Christopher Marlowe

Scene from Doctor Faustus[2]   about 1588

EDITED BY SYLVAN BARNET

Christopher Marlowe was born in Canterbury, England, in February 1564, about ten weeks before William Shakespeare. Marlowe, the son of a prosperous

---

[2]This scene is from the 1616 text, or "B-Text," published as *The Tragicall History of the Life and Death of Doctor Faustus*. Modernizations have been made in spelling and punctuation.

shoemaker, received a B.A. from Cambridge University in 1584 and an M.A. in 1587, after which he settled in London. The rest of his short life was marked by rumor, secrecy, and violence, including suspicions that he was a secret agent for Queen Elizabeth's government and allegations against him of blasphemy and atheism—no small matter in light of the political instability and religious controversies of the times. Peripherally implicated in several violent deaths, he met his own end in May 1593 when he was stabbed above the right eye during a tavern brawl, under circumstances that have never been fully explained. Brief and crowded as his life was, he wrote a number of intense, powerful, and highly influential tragedies—Tamburlaine the Great, Parts 1 and 2 (1587), Doctor Faustus (1588), The Jew of Malta (1589), Edward the Second (c. 1592), The Massacre at Paris (1593), and Dido, Queen of Carthage (c. 1593, with Thomas Nashe). He is also the author of the lyric poem "The Passionate Shepherd to His Love," with its universally known first line: "Come live with me and be my love."

DRAMATIS PERSONAE

Doctor Faustus
Good Angel
Bad Angel
Mephistophilis, a devil

Doctor Faustus with the Bad Angel and the Good Angel, from the Utah Shakespearean Festival's 2005 production

ACT II

SCENE I

(*Enter Faustus in his study.*)

Faustus: Now, Faustus, must thou needs be damned;
    Canst thou not be saved!
    What boots° it then to think on God or heaven?
    Away with such vain fancies, and despair—
    Despair in God and trust in Belzebub!   5
    Now go not backward Faustus; be resolute!
    Why waver'st thou? O something soundeth in mine ear,
    "Abjure this magic, turn to God again."

    Ay, and Faustus will turn to God again.
    To God? He loves thee not.   10
    The god thou serv'st is thine own appetite
    Wherein is fixed the love of Belzebub!
    To him I'll build an altar and a church,
    And offer lukewarm blood of newborn babes!

(*Enter the two Angels.*)

Bad Angel: Go forward, Faustus, in that famous art.   15
Good Angel: Sweet Faustus, leave that execrable art.
Faustus: Contrition, prayer, repentance? What of these?
Good Angel: O, they are means to bring thee unto heaven.
Bad Angel: Rather illusions, fruits of lunacy,
    That make men foolish that do use them most.   20
Good Angel: Sweet Faustus, think of heaven and heavenly things.
Bad Angel: No, Faustus, think of honor and of wealth.
                          (*Exeunt Angels.*)

Faustus: Wealth!
    Why, the signory of Emden° shall be mine!
    When Mephistophilis shall stand by me   25
    What power can hurt me? Faustus, thou art safe.
    Cast no more doubts! Mephistophilis, come,
    And bring glad tidings from great Lucifer.
    Is't not midnight? Come Mephistophilis,
    Veni, veni, Mephostophile!°   30

(*Enter Mephistophilis.*)

    Now tell me, what saith Lucifer thy lord?

---

3 *boots* avails   24 *signory of Emden* lordship of the rich German port at the mouth of
the Ems   30 *Veni, veni, Mephostophile!* Come, come, Mephistophilis (Latin)

Mephistophilis: That I shall wait on Faustus whilst he lives,
 So he will buy my service with his soul.
Faustus: Already Faustus hath hazarded that for thee.
Mephistophilis: But now thou must bequeath it solemnly   35
 And write a deed of gift with thine own blood,
 For that security craves Lucifer.
 If thou deny it I must back to hell.
Faustus: Stay Mephistophilis and tell me,
 What good will my soul do thy lord?   40
Mephistophilis: Enlarge his kingdom.
Faustus: Is that the reason why he tempts us thus?
Mephistophilis: Solamen miseris socios habuisse doloris.°
Faustus: Why, have you any pain that torture other?°
Mephistophilis: As great as have the human souls of men.   45
 But tell me, Faustus, shall I have thy soul—
 And I will be thy slave and wait on thee
 And give thee more than thou hast wit to ask?
Faustus: Ay Mephistophilis, I'll give it him.°
Mephistophilis: Then, Faustus, stab thy arm courageously,   50
 And bind thy soul, that at some certain day
 Great Lucifer may claim it as his own.
 And then be thou as great as Lucifer!
Faustus: Lo, Mephistophilis: for love of thee
 Faustus hath cut his arm, and with his proper° blood   55
 Assures° his soul to be great Lucifer's,
 Chief Lord and Regent of perpetual night.
 View here this blood that trickles from mine arm,
 And let it be propitious for my wish.
Mephistophilis: But, Faustus,   60
 Write it in manner of a deed of gift.
Faustus: Ay, so I do—But Mephistophilis,
 My blood congeals and I can write no more.
Mephistophilis: I'll fetch thee fire to dissolve it straight.

           (*Exit.*)

Faustus: What might the staying of my blood portend?
 Is it unwilling I should write this bill?°   65
 Why streams it not that I may write afresh:
 "Faustus gives to thee his soul"? O there it stayed.
 Why should'st thou not? Is not thy soul thine own?
 Then write again: "Faustus gives to thee his soul."   70

---

43 *Solamen . . . doloris* Misery loves company (Latin) 44 *other* others 49 *him* i.e., to
Lucifer 55 *proper* own 56 *Assures* conveys by contract 66 *bill* contract

(*Enter Mephistophilis, with the chafer° of fire.*)

Mephistophilis: See, Faustus, here is fire. Set it° on.
Faustus: So, now the blood begins to clear again.
    Now will I make an end immediately.
Mephistophilis (aside): What will not I do to obtain his soul!
Faustus: Consummatum est!° This bill is ended: 75
    And Faustus hath bequeathed his soul to Lucifer.
    —But what is this inscription on mine arm?
    Homo fuge!° Whither should I fly?
    If unto God, He'll throw me down to hell.
    My senses are deceived; here's nothing writ.   80
    O yes, I see it plain! Even here is writ
    Homo fuge! Yet shall not Faustus fly!
Mephistophilis (aside.): I'll fetch him somewhat° to delight his mind.
                    (*Exit Mephistophilis*)

(*Enter Devils, giving crowns and rich apparel to Faustus. They dance and then depart.*)

(*Enter Mephistophilis.*)

Faustus: What means this show? Speak, Mephistophilis.
Mephistophilis: Nothing, Faustus, but to delight thy mind,   85
    And let thee see what magic can perform.
Faustus: But may I raise such spirits when I please?
Mephistophilis: Ay, Faustus, and do greater things than these.
Faustus: Then, Mephistophilis, receive this scroll,
    A deed of gift of body and of soul: 90
    But yet conditionally that thou perform
    All covenants and articles between us both.
Mephistophilis: Faustus, I swear by hell and Lucifer
    To effect all promises between us both.
Faustus: Then hear me read it, Mephistophilis: 95

"On these conditions following:

First, that Faustus may be a spirit° in form and substance.

Secondly, that Mephistophilis shall be his servant, and be by him commanded.

---

70 s.d. *chafer* portable grate   71 *it* i.e., the receptacle containing the congealed blood   75 *Consummatum est* It is finished. (Latin: a blasphemous repetition of Christ's words on the Cross; see John 19:30.)   78 *Homo fuge* fly, man (Latin)   83 *somewhat* something   97 *spirit* evil spirit, devil. (But to see Faustus as transformed now into a devil deprived of freedom to repent is to deprive the remainder of the play of much of its meaning.)

Thirdly, that Mephistophilis shall do for him and bring him whatsoever.

Fourthly, that he shall be in his chamber or house invisible.

Lastly, that he shall appear to the said John Faustus, at all times, in what shape and form soever he please.

I, John Faustus of Wittenberg, Doctor, by these presents, do give both body and soul to Lucifer, Prince of the East, and his minister Mephistophilis, and furthermore grant unto them that, four and twenty years being expired, and these articles written being inviolate°, full power to fetch or carry the said John Faustus, body and soul, flesh, blood, into their habitation wheresoever.

By me John Faustus."

Mephistophilis: Speak, Faustus, do you deliver this as your deed?
Faustus: Ay, take it, and the devil give thee good of it!
Mephistophilis: So, now Faustus, ask me what thou wilt.
Faustus: First, I will question with thee about hell.
    Tell me, where is the place that men call hell?
Mephistophilis: Under the heavens.
Faustus: Ay, so are all things else, but whereabouts?
Mephistophilis: Within the bowels of these elements,
    Where we are tortured, and remain forever.
    Hell hath no limits, nor is circumscribed,
    In one self place, but where we are is hell,
    And where hell is there must we ever be.
    And to be short, when all the world dissolves,
    And every creature shall be purified,
    All places shall be hell that is not heaven!
Faustus: I think hell's a fable.
Mephistophilis: Ay, think so still—till experience change thy mind.
Faustus: Why, dost thou think that Faustus shall be damned?
Mephistophilis: Ay, of necessity, for here's the scroll
    In which thou hast given thy soul to Lucifer.
Faustus: Ay, and body too; but what of that?
    Think'st thou that Faustus is so fond° to imagine,
    That after this life there is any pain?
    No, these are trifles, and mere old wives' tales.
Mephistophilis: But I am an instance to prove the contrary,
    For I tell thee I am damned, and now in hell!
Faustus: Nay, and this be hell, I'll willingly be damned—
    What, sleeping, eating, walking, and disputing?

100

105

110

115

120

125

130

135

109 *inviolate* unviolated   133 *fond* foolish

But leaving this, let me have a wife,   140
The fairest maid in Germany,
For I am wanton and lascivious,
And cannot live without a wife.
Mephistophilis: Well, Faustus, thou shalt have a wife.

(*He fetches in a woman Devil.*)

Faustus: What sight is this?   145
Mephistophilis: Now, Faustus, wilt thou have a wife?
Faustus: Here's a hot whore indeed! No, I'll no wife.
Mephistophilis: Marriage is but a ceremonial toy,°

(*Exit she-devil.*)

And if thou lov'st me, think no more of it.
I'll cull thee out° the fairest courtesans   150
And bring them every morning to thy bed.
She whom thine eye shall like, thy heart shall have,
Were she as chaste as was Penelope,°
As wise as Saba,° or as beautiful
As was bright Lucifer before his fall.   155
Here, take this book and peruse it well.
The iterating° of these lines brings gold;
The framing° of this circle on the ground
Brings thunder, whirlwinds, storm, and lightning;
Pronounce this thrice devoutly to thyself,   160
And men in harness° shall appear to thee,
Ready to execute what thou command'st.
Faustus: Thanks, Mephistophilis, for this sweet book.
This will I keep as chary as my life.

(*Exeunt.*)

QUESTIONS

1. What specifically motivates Faustus to make his satanic compact? Cite the text to back up your response.
2. How does his behavior constitute a compromise of his nobility?
3. "Is not thy soul thine own?" Faustus asks rhetorically (line 69). Discuss the implications of this statement in terms of the larger thematic concerns of the work.
4. Does Faustus inspire your pity and fear in this scene? Why or why not?

148 *toy* trifle   150 *cull thee out* select for you   153 *Penelope* wife of Ulysses, famed for her fidelity   154 *Saba* the Queen of Sheba   157 *iterating* repetition   158 *framing* drawing   161 *harness* armor

Traditional masks of Comedy and Tragedy

Comedy

The best-known traditional emblem of drama—a pair of masks, one sorrowful (representing tragedy) and one smiling (representing comedy)—suggests that tragedy and comedy, although opposites, are close relatives. Often, comedy shows people getting into trouble through error or weakness; in this respect it is akin to tragedy. An important difference between comedy and tragedy lies in the attitude toward human failing that is expected of us. When a main character in a comedy suffers from overweening pride, as does Oedipus, or if he fails to recognize that his bride-to-be is actually his mother, we laugh—something we would never do in watching a competent performance of *Oedipus the King.*

Comedy, from the Greek *komos*, "a revel," is thought to have originated in festivities to celebrate spring, ritual performances in praise of Dionysus, god of fertility and wine. In drama, comedy may be broadly defined as whatever makes us laugh. A comedy may be a name for one entire play, or we may say that there is comedy in only part of a play—as in a comic character or a comic situation.

Many theories have been propounded to explain why we laugh; most of these notions fall into a few familiar types. One school, exemplified by French philosopher Henri Bergson, sees laughter as a form of ridicule, implying a feeling of disinterested superiority; all jokes are *on* somebody. Bergson suggests that laughter springs from situations in which we sense a conflict between some mechanical or rigid pattern of behavior and our sense of a more natural or "organic" kind of behavior that is possible.[3] An example occurs in Buster Keaton's comic film *The Boat.* Having launched a little boat that springs a leak, Keaton rigidly goes down with it, with frozen face. (The more natural and organic thing to do would be to swim for shore.) Other thinkers view

[3]See Bergson's essay "Le Rire" (1990), translated as "Laughter" in *Comedy*, ed. Wylie Sypher (New York: Anchor, 1956).

laughter as our response to expectations fulfilled or to expectations set up but then suddenly frustrated. Some hold it to be the expression of our delight in seeing our suppressed urges acted out (as when a comedian hurls an egg at a pompous stuffed shirt); some, to be our defensive reaction to a painful and disturbing truth.

Derisive humor is basic to **satiric comedy**, in which human weakness or folly is ridiculed from a vantage point of supposedly enlightened superiority. Satiric comedy may be coolly malicious and gently biting, but it tends to be critical of people, their manners, and their morals. It is at least as old as the comedies of Aristophanes, who thrived in the fifth century B.C. In *Lysistrata*, the satirist shows how the women of two warring cities speedily halt a war by agreeing to deny themselves to their husbands. (The satirist's target is men so proud that they go to war rather than make the slightest concession.)

Comedy is often divided into two varieties—"high" and "low." **High comedy** relies more on wit and wordplay than on physical action for its humor. It tries to address the audience's intelligence by pointing out the pretension and hypocrisy of human behavior. High comedy also generally avoids derisive humor. Jokes about physical appearance would, for example, be avoided. One technique it employs to appeal to a sophisticated, verbal audience is use of the **epigram**, a brief and witty statement that memorably expresses some truth, large or small. Oscar Wilde's plays such as *The Importance of Being Earnest* (1895) and *Lady Windermere's Fan* (1892) sparkle with such brilliant epigrams as: "I can resist everything except temptation"; "Experience is simply the name we give our mistakes"; "There is only one thing in the world worse than being talked about, and that is not being talked about."

Low comedy explores the opposite extreme of humor. It places greater emphasis on physical action and visual gags, and its verbal jokes do not require much intellect to appreciate (as in Groucho Marx's pithy put-down to his brother Chico, "You have the brain of a five-year-old, and I bet he was glad to get rid of it!"). Low comedy does not avoid derisive humor; rather, it revels in making fun of whatever will get a good laugh. Drunkenness, stupidity, lust, senility, trickery, insult, and clumsiness are inexhaustible staples of this style of comedy. Although it is all too easy for critics to dismiss low comedy, like high comedy it also serves a valuable purpose in satirizing human failings. Shakespeare indulged in coarse humor in some of his noblest plays. Low comedy is usually the preferred style of popular culture, and it has inspired many incisive satires on modern life—from the classic films of W. C. Fields and the Marx Brothers to the weekly TV antics of *Monty Python's Flying Circus* and Matt Groening's *The Simpsons*.

Low comedy includes several distinct types. One is the **burlesque**, a broadly humorous parody or travesty of another play or kind of play. (In the United States, *burlesque* is something else: a once-popular form of show business featuring stripteases interspersed with bits of ribald low comedy.) Another valuable type of low comedy is the **farce**, a broadly humorous play whose action is usually fast-moving and improbable. **Slapstick comedy** (such as that of the Three Stooges) is a kind of farce. Featuring pratfalls, pie-throwing, fisticuffs, and other violent action, it takes its name from a circus clown's device—a bat with two boards that loudly clap together when one clown swats another.

Romantic comedy, another traditional sort of comedy, is subtler. Its main characters are generally lovers, and its plot unfolds their ultimately successful strivings to be united. Unlike satiric comedy, romantic comedy portrays its characters not with withering contempt but with kindly indulgence. It may take place in the everyday world, or perhaps in some never-never land, such as the forest of Arden in Shakespeare's *As You Like It*. Romantic comedy is also a popular staple of Hollywood, which depicts two people undergoing humorous mishaps on their way to falling in love. The characters often suffer humiliation and discomfort along the way, but these moments are funny rather than sad, and the characters are rewarded in the end by true love.

Here is a short contemporary comedy by one of America's most ingenious playwrights.

David Ives

Sure Thing   1988

David Ives (b. 1950) grew up on the South Side of Chicago. He attended Catholic schools before enter-ing Northwestern University. Later Ives studied at the Yale Drama School—"a blissful time for me," he recalls, "in spite of the fact that there is slush on the ground in New Haven 238 days a year." Ives re-ceived his first professional production in Los Angeles at the age of twenty-one "at America's smallest, and possibly worst theater, in a storefront that had a pillar dead center in the middle of the stage." He continued writing for the theater while working as an editor at Foreign Affairs, and gradually achieved a reputation

DAVID IVES

in theatrical circles for his wildly original and brilliantly written short comic plays. His public breakthrough came in 1993 with the New York staging of All in the Timing, *which presented six short comedies, including* Sure Thing. *This produc-tion earned ecstatic reviews and a busy box office. In the 1995–1996 season,* All in the Timing *was the most widely performed play in America (except for the works of Shakespeare). In 1997 a second group of one-act comedies,* Mere Mortals, *was produced with great success in New York City; it was published with* Lives of the Saints, *another cycle of his one-act plays, in the volume* Time Flies (2001). *His full-length plays are* Don Juan in Chicago (1995), Ancient History (1996), The Red Address (1997), *and* Polish Joke (2000); *they are collected in the*

Original 1993 Off-Broadway production of *Sure Thing* by Primary Stages

volume Polish Joke and Other Plays *(2004). Ives also writes short stories and screenplays for both motion pictures and television. He lives in New York City.*

CHARACTERS

Betty
Bill

SCENE: *A café. Betty, a woman in her late twenties, is reading at a café table. An empty chair is opposite her. Bill, same age, enters.*

Bill: Excuse me. Is this chair taken?
Betty: Excuse me?
Bill: Is this taken?
Betty: Yes it is.
Bill: Oh. Sorry.
Betty: Sure thing.

   (*A bell rings softly.*)

Bill: Excuse me. Is this chair taken?
Betty: Excuse me?
Bill: Is this taken?

Betty: No, but I'm expecting somebody in a minute.

Bill: Oh. Thanks anyway.

Betty: Sure thing.

(*A bell rings softly.*)

Bill: Excuse me. Is this chair taken?

Betty: No, but I'm expecting somebody very shortly.

Bill: Would you mind if I sit here till he or she or it comes?

Betty (glances at her watch): They do seem to be pretty late. . . .

Bill: You never know who you might be turning down.

Betty: Sorry. Nice try, though.

Bill: Sure thing.

(*Bell.*)

Is this seat taken?

Betty: No it's not.

Bill: Would you mind if I sit here?

Betty: Yes I would.

Bill: Oh.

(*Bell.*)

Is this chair taken?

Betty: No it's not.

Bill: Would you mind if I sit here?

Betty: No. Go ahead.

Bill: Thanks. (*He sits. She continues reading.*) Everyplace else seems to be taken.

Betty: Mm-hm.

Bill: Great place.

Betty: Mm-hm.

Bill: What's the book?

Betty: I just wanted to read in quiet, if you don't mind.

Bill: No. Sure thing.

(*Bell.*)

Everyplace else seems to be taken.

Betty: Mm-hm.

Bill: Great place for reading.

Betty: Yes, I like it.

Bill: What's the book?

Betty: *The Sound and the Fury.*

Bill: Oh. Hemingway.

(*Bell.*)

What's the book?

Betty: *The Sound and the Fury.*

Bill: Oh. Faulkner.

Betty: Have you read it?

Bill: Not . . . actually. I've sure read *about* it, though. It's supposed to be great.

Betty: It is great.

Bill: I hear it's great. (*Small pause.*) Waiter?

(*Bell.*)

What's the book?

Betty: *The Sound and the Fury.*

Bill: Oh. Faulkner.

Betty: Have you read it?

Bill: I'm a Mets fan, myself.

(*Bell.*)

Betty: Have you read it?

Bill: Yeah, I read it in college.

Betty: Where was college?

Bill: I went to Oral Roberts University.

(*Bell.*)

Betty: Where was college?

Bill: I was lying. I never really went to college. I just like to party.

(*Bell.*)

Betty: Where was college?

Bill: Harvard.

Betty: Do you like Faulkner?

Bill: I love Faulkner. I spent a whole winter reading him once.

Betty: I've just started.

Bill: I was so excited after ten pages that I went out and bought everything else he wrote. One of the greatest reading experiences of my life. I mean, all that incredible psychological understanding. Page after page of gorgeous prose. His profound grasp of the mystery of time and human existence. The smells of the earth . . . What do you think?

Betty: I think it's pretty boring.

(*Bell.*)

Bill: What's the book?

Betty: *The Sound and the Fury.*

Bill: Oh! Faulkner!

Betty: Do you like Faulkner?

Bill: I love Faulkner.

Betty: He's incredible.

Bill: I spent a whole winter reading him once.

Betty: I was so excited after ten pages that I went out and bought everything else he wrote.

Bill: All that incredible psychological understanding.

Betty: And the prose is so gorgeous.

Bill: And the way he's grasped the mystery of time—

Betty: —and human existence. I can't believe I've waited this long to read him.

Bill: You never know. You might not have liked him before.

Betty: That's true.

Bill: You might not have been ready for him. You have to hit these things at the right moment or it's no good.

Betty: That's happened to me.

Bill: It's all in the timing. (*Small pause.*) My name's Bill, by the way.

Betty: I'm Betty.

Bill: Hi.

Betty: Hi. (*Small pause.*)

Bill: Yes I thought reading Faulkner was . . . a great experience.

Betty: Yes. (*Small pause.*)

Bill: *The Sound and the Fury.* . . . (*Another small pause.*)

Betty: Well. Onwards and upwards. (*She goes back to her book.*)

Bill: Waiter—?

   (*Bell.*)

   You have to hit these things at the right moment or it's no good.

Betty: That's happened to me.

Bill: It's all in the timing. My name's Bill, by the way.

Betty: I'm Betty.

Bill: Hi.

Betty: Hi.

Bill: Do you come in here a lot?

Betty: Actually I'm just in town for two days from Pakistan.

Bill: Oh. Pakistan.

   (*Bell.*)

   My name's Bill, by the way.

Betty: I'm Betty.

Bill: Hi.

Betty: Hi.

Bill: Do you come in here a lot?

Betty: Every once in a while. Do you?

Bill: Not so much anymore. Not as much as I used to. Before my nervous breakdown.

(*Bell.*)

Do you come in here a lot?

Betty: Why are you asking?

Bill: Just interested.

Betty: Are you really interested, or do you just want to pick me up?

Bill: No, I'm really interested.

Betty: Why would you be interested in whether I come in here a lot?

Bill: I'm just . . . getting acquainted.

Betty: Maybe you're only interested for the sake of making small talk long enough to ask me back to your place to listen to some music, or because you've just rented this great tape for your VCR, or because you've got some terrific unknown Django Reinhardt record, only all you really want to do is fuck—which you won't do very well—after which you'll go into the bathroom and pee very loudly, then pad into the kitchen and get yourself a beer from the refrigerator without asking me whether I'd like anything, and then you'll proceed to lie back down beside me and confess that you've got a girlfriend named Stephanie who's away at medical school in Belgium for a year, and that you've been involved with her—*off and on*—in what you'll call a very "intricate" relationship, for the past *seven YEARS*. None of which *interests* me, mister!

Bill: Okay.

(*Bell.*)

Do you come in here a lot?

Betty: Every other day, I think.

Bill: I come in here quite a lot and I don't remember seeing you.

Betty: I guess we must be on different schedules.

Bill: Missed connections.

Betty: Yes. Different time zones.

Bill: Amazing how you can live right next door to somebody in this town and never even know it.

Betty: I know.

Bill: City life.

Betty: It's crazy.

Bill: We probably pass each other in the street every day. Right in front of this place, probably.

Betty: Yep.

Bill (*looks around*): Well the waiters here sure seem to be in some different time zone. I can't seem to locate one anywhere. . . . . Waiter! (*He looks back.*) So what do you—(*He sees that she's gone back to her book.*)

Betty: I beg pardon?

Bill: Nothing. Sorry.

(*Bell.*)

Betty: I guess we must be on different schedules.

Bill: Missed connections.

Betty: Yes. Different time zones.

Bill: Amazing how you can live right next door to somebody in this town and never even know it.

Betty: I know.

Bill: City life.

Betty: It's crazy.

Bill: You weren't waiting for somebody when I came in, were you?

Betty: Actually I was.

Bill: Oh. Boyfriend?

Betty: Sort of.

Bill: What's a sort-of boyfriend?

Betty: My husband.

Bill: Ah-ha.

(*Bell.*)

You weren't waiting for somebody when I came in, were you?

Betty: Actually I was.

Bill: Oh. Boyfriend?

Betty: Sort of.

Bill: What's a sort-of boyfriend?

Betty: We were meeting here to break up.

Bill: Mm-hm . . .

(*Bell.*)

What's a sort-of boyfriend?

Betty: My lover. Here she comes right now!

(*Bell.*)

Bill: You weren't waiting for somebody when I came in, were you?

Betty: No, just reading.

Bill: Sort of a sad occupation for a Friday night, isn't it? Reading here, all by yourself?

Betty: Do you think so?

Bill: Well sure. I mean, what's a good-looking woman like you doing out alone on a Friday night?

Betty: Trying to keep away from lines like that.

Bill: No, listen—

(*Bell.*)

You weren't waiting for somebody when I came in, were you?

Betty: No, just reading.

Bill: Sort of a sad occupation for a Friday night, isn't it? Reading here all by yourself?

Betty: I guess it is, in a way.

Bill: What's a good-looking woman like you doing out alone on a Friday night anyway? No offense, but . . .

Betty: I'm out alone on a Friday night for the first time in a very long time.

Bill: Oh.

Betty: You see, I just recently ended a relationship.

Bill: Oh.

Betty: Of rather long standing.

Bill: I'm sorry. (*Small pause.*) Well listen, since reading by yourself *is* such a sad occupation for a Friday night, would you like to go elsewhere?

Betty: No . . .

Bill: Do something else?

Betty: No thanks.

Bill: I was headed out to the movies in a while anyway.

Betty: I don't think so.

Bill: Big chance to let Faulkner catch his breath. All those long sentences get him pretty tired.

Betty: Thanks anyway.

Bill: Okay.

Betty: I appreciate the invitation.

Bill: Sure thing.

(*Bell.*)

You weren't waiting for somebody when I came in, were you?

Betty: No, just reading.

Bill: Sort of a sad occupation for a Friday night, isn't it? Reading here all by yourself?

Betty: I guess I was trying to think of it as existentially romantic. You know—cappuccino, great literature, rainy night . . .

Bill: That only works in Paris. We *could* hop the late plane to Paris. Get on a Concorde. Find a café . . .

Betty: I'm a little short on plane fare tonight.

Bill: Darn it, so am I.

Betty: To tell you the truth, I was headed to the movies after I finished this section. Would you like to come along? Since you can't locate a waiter?

Bill: That's a very nice offer, but . . .

Betty: Uh-huh. Girlfriend?

Bill: Two, actually. One of them's pregnant, and Stephanie—

(*Bell.*)

Betty: Girlfriend?

Bill: No, I don't have a girlfriend. Not if you mean the castrating bitch I dumped last night.

(*Bell.*)

Betty: Girlfriend?

Bill: Sort of. Sort of.

Betty: What's a sort-of girlfriend?

Bill: My mother.

(*Bell.*)

I just ended a relationship, actually.

Betty: Oh.

Bill: Of rather long standing.

Betty: I'm sorry to hear it.

Bill: This is my first night out alone in a long time. I feel a little bit at sea, to tell you the truth.

Betty: So you didn't stop to talk because you're a Moonie, or you have some weird political affiliation—?

Bill: Nope. Straight-down-the-ticket Republican.

(*Bell.*)

Straight-down-the-ticket Democrat.

(*Bell.*)

Can I tell you something about politics?

(*Bell.*)

I like to think of myself as a citizen of the universe.

(*Bell.*)

I'm unaffiliated.

Betty: That's a relief. So am I.

Bill: I vote my beliefs.

Betty: Labels are not important.

Bill: Labels are not important, exactly. Take me, for example. I mean, what does it matter if I had a two-point at—

(*Bell.*)

three-point at—

(*Bell.*)

four-point at college? Or if I did come from Pittsburgh—

(*Bell.*)

Cleveland—

(*Bell.*)

Westchester County?

Betty: Sure.

Bill: I believe that a man is what he is.

(*Bell.*)

A person is what he is.

(*Bell.*)

A person is . . . what they are.

Betty: I think so too.

Bill: So what if I admire Trotsky?

(*Bell.*)

So what if I once had a total-body liposuction?

(*Bell.*)

So what if I don't have a penis?

(*Bell.*)

So what if I spent a year in the Peace Corps? I was acting on my convictions.

Betty: Sure.

Bill: You just can't hang a sign on a person.

Betty: Absolutely. I'll bet you're a Scorpio.

(*Many bells ring.*)

Listen, I was headed to the movies after I finished this section. Would you like to come along?

Bill: That sounds like fun. What's playing?

Betty: A couple of the really early Woody Allen movies.

Bill: Oh.

Betty: You don't like Woody Allen?

Bill: Sure. I like Woody Allen.

Betty: But you're not crazy about Woody Allen.

Bill: Those early ones kind of get on my nerves.

Betty: Uh-huh.

(*Bell.*)

Bill: Y'know I was headed to the—

Betty (*simultaneously*): I was thinking about—

Bill: I'm sorry.

Betty: No, go ahead.

Bill: I was going to say that I was headed to the movies in a little while, and . . .

Betty: So was I.

Bill: The Woody Allen festival?

Betty: Just up the street.

Bill: Do you like the early ones?

Betty: I think anybody who doesn't ought to be run off the planet.

Bill: How many times have you seen *Bananas*?

Betty: Eight times.

Bill: Twelve. So are you still interested? (*Long pause.*)

Betty: Do you like Entenmann's crumb cake. . . .

Bill: Last night I went out at two in the morning to get one. Did you have an Etch-a-Sketch as a child?

Betty: Yes! And do you like Brussels sprouts? (*Pause.*)

Bill: No, I think they're disgusting.

Betty: They *are* disgusting!

Bill: Do you still believe in marriage in spite of current sentiments against it?

Betty: Yes.

Bill: And children?

Betty: Three of them.

Bill: Two girls and a boy.

Betty: Harvard, Vassar, and Brown.

Bill: And will you love me?

Betty: Yes.

Bill: And cherish me forever?

Betty: Yes.

Bill: Do you still want to go to the movies?

Betty: Sure thing.

Bill and Betty (*together*): Waiter!

BLACKOUT

QUESTIONS

1. Ives originally planned to set *Sure Thing* at a bus stop. What does its current setting in a café suggest about the characters?
2. What happens on stage when the bell rings?
3. Who is the protagonist? What does the protagonist want?
4. Does the play have a dramatic question?
5. When does the climax of the play occur?
6. Is *Sure Thing* a romantic comedy or a farce? (See pages 602–603 for a discussion of these types of comedy.)
7. "*Sure Thing* was not a funny play because it isn't realistic. Conversations just don't happen this way." Discuss that opinion. Do you agree or disagree?

WRITING EFFECTIVELY

WRITING ABOUT COMEDY

Getting Serious About Comedy

If you have ever tried to explain a punchline to an uncomprehending friend, you know how hard it can be to convey the essence of humor. Too much explanation makes any joke fizzle out fast. We don't often stop to analyze why a joke strikes us as funny. It simply make us laugh. For this reason, writing about comedy can be challenging.

In analyzing a stage comedy, however, it can be enlightening to have a sense of what makes the play amusing. You may find it helpful to pin down the sort of comedy with which you are dealing. Perhaps it is a romantic comedy, featuring protagonists you root for and identify with, even as you laugh at their exploits. Maybe it is a satire, in which human folly is ridiculed. Or it may be a black comedy, mingling the comic with the tragic.

Consider, also, the flavor of the humor itself. Does low comedy (slapstick, visual gags, and unsophisticated verbal humor) prevail? Or does the humor tend toward the sophistication and wit associated with high comedy? Is the humor primarily verbal or mostly physical? Keep in mind that a play may mix different kinds of comedy. If this is the case, what is the effect of the mixture? Finally, when trying to account for why a particular bit of dialogue or a piece of dramatic action is funny, don't overlook the importance of character.

Even when comedy arises out of a situation, character is likely to play an important role. In *A Midsummer Night's Dream*, for example, a spell is cast, causing the fairy queen Titania to fall in love with the weaver Bottom, whose head has been transformed into that of an ass. Though the situation is funny in its own right, the humor is intensified by the personalities involved, the proud fairy queen chasing after the lowly and foolish tradesman.

The unlikelihood of Titania's romance with Bottom is, in large part, what makes it funny. Humor often may be found in the unexpected, a twist on the normal and the logical.

CHECKLIST

Writing About a Comedy

- ✓ Is the play a romantic comedy? A slapstick comedy? A satire?
- ✓ How can you tell?
- ✓ Identify moments of high comedy in the play. Now look for low comedy. Which style of comedy prevails?
- ✓ Look for verbal humor. Look for physical comedy. Does one type prevail?
- ✓ Focus on a key comic moment. Does the comedy grow out of situation? Character? A mix of both?
- ✓ How does the play end? In a wedding or romance? A reconciliation? Mutual understanding?

WRITING ASSIGNMENT ON COMEDY

Write a brief analysis of what makes *Sure Thing* amusing or humorous. Provide details to back up your argument. See pages 601 to 603 for more information on specific types of humor.

TOPICS FOR WRITING ON TRAGEDY

1. According to Oscar Wilde, "In this world there are only two tragedies: one is not getting what one wants, and the other is getting it." Write an essay in which you discuss this statement in its application to the scene from *Doctor Faustus*.

2. Imagine that Faustus, after his death, has sought forgiveness and salvation with the claim, "The Devil tricked me. I didn't know what I was doing." Write a "judicial opinion" setting forth the grounds for the denial of his plea.

TOPICS FOR WRITING ON COMEDY

1. Consider *Sure Thing*. What or who is being satirized? How true or incisive do you find this satire? Why?

2. "*Sure Thing* isn't good drama because it doesn't have a plot or conflict." Write a two-page response to that complaint.

3. Write about a recent romantic comedy film. How does its plot fulfill the notion of comedy?

4. Write about a movie you've seen lately that was meant to be funny but fell short. What was lacking?

24
The Theater of Sophocles

The Theater of Sophocles

For the citizens of Athens in the fifth century B.C. theater was both a religious and a civic occasion. Plays were presented only twice a year at religious festivals—both associated with Dionysus, the god of wine and crops. In January there was the Lenaea, the festival of the winepress, when plays, especially comedies, were performed. But the major theatrical event of the year came in March at the Great Dionysia, a citywide celebration that included sacrifices, prize ceremonies, and spectacular processions as well as three days of drama.

Each day at dawn a different author presented a trilogy of tragic plays—three interrelated dramas that portrayed an important mythic or legendary event. Each intense tragic trilogy was followed by a **satyr play**, an obscene parody of a mythic story, performed with the chorus dressed as satyrs, unruly mythic attendants of Dionysus who were half goat or horse and half human.

The Greeks loved competition and believed it fostered excellence. Even theater was a competitive event—not unlike the Olympic games. A panel of five judges voted each year at the Great Dionysia for the best dramatic presentation, and a substantial cash prize was given to the winning poet-playwright (all plays were written in verse). Any aspiring writer who has ever lost a literary contest may be comforted to learn that Sophocles, who triumphed in the competition twenty-four times, seems not to have won the annual prize for *Oedipus the King*. Although this play ultimately proved to be the most celebrated Greek tragedy ever written, it lost the award to a revival of a popular trilogy by Aeschylus, who had recently died.

Staging

Seated in the open air in a hillside amphitheater, as many as 17,000 spectators could watch a performance that must have somewhat resembled an opera or musical. The audience was arranged in rows, with the Athenian governing council and young military cadets seated in the middle sections. Priests, priestesses, and foreign dignitaries were given special places of honor in the front rows. The performance space they watched was divided into two parts—the **orchestra**, a level circular "dancing space" (at the base of the amphitheater), and a slightly raised stage built in front of the *skene* or stage house, originally a canvas or wooden hut for costume changes.

The actors spoke and performed primarily on the stage, and the chorus sang and danced in the orchestra. The *skene* served as a general set or backdrop—the exterior of a palace, a temple, a cave, or a military tent, depending on the action of the play. The *skene* had a large door at its center that served as the major entrance for principal characters. When opened wide, the door could be used to frame a striking tableau, as when the body of Eurydicê is displayed at the end of Sophocles' play *Antigonê*.

By Sophocles' time, the tragedy had a conventional structure understood by most of the citizens sitting in the audience. No more than three actors were allowed on stage at any one time, along with a chorus of fifteen (the number was fixed by Sophocles himself). The actors' spoken monologue and dialogue alternated with the chorus' singing and dancing. Each tragedy began with a **prologue**, a preparatory scene. In *Oedipus the King,* for example, the play begins with Oedipus asking the suppliants why they have come and the priest telling him about the plague ravaging Thebes. Next came the *párados*, the song for the entrance of the chorus. Then the action was enacted in **episodes**, like the acts or scenes in modern plays; the episodes were separated by danced choral songs or odes. Finally, there was a closing *éxodos*, the last scene, in which the characters and chorus concluded the action and departed.

What did the actors look like? They wore **masks** (*personae*, the source of our word *person*, "a thing through which sound comes"): some of these masks had exaggerated mouthpieces, possibly designed to project speech across the open air. Certainly, the masks, each of which covered an actor's entire head, helped spectators far away recognize the chief characters. The masks often represented certain conventional types of characters: the old king, the young soldier, the shepherd, the beautiful girl (women's parts were played by male actors). Perhaps in order to gain in both increased dignity and visibility, actors in the Greek theater eventually came to wear **cothurni**, high, thick-soled elevator shoes that made them appear taller than ordinary men. All this equipment must have given the actors a slightly inhuman yet very imposing appearance, but we may infer that the spectators accepted such conventions as easily as opera lovers accept an opera's special artifice. Today's football fans, for instance, hardly think twice about the elaborate helmets, shoulderpads, kneepads, and garishly colored uniforms worn by their favorite teams.

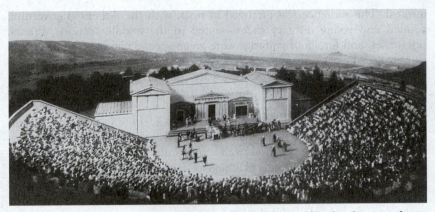

A modern reconstruction of a classical Athenian theater. Note that the chorus performs in the circular orchestra while the actors stand on the raised stage behind.

The Civic Role of Greek Drama

Athenian drama was supported and financed by the state. Administration of the Great Dionysia fell to the head civil magistrate. He annually appointed three wealthy citizens to serve as *choregoi,* or producers, for the competing plays. Each producer had to equip the chorus and rent the rehearsal space in which the poet-playwright would prepare the new work for the festival. The state covered the expenses of the theater, actors, and prizes (which went to author, actors, and *choregos* alike). Theater tickets were distributed free to citizens, which meant that every registered Athenian, even the poorest, could participate. The playwrights therefore addressed themselves to every element of the Athenian democracy. Only the size of the amphitheater limited the attendance. Holding between 14,000 and 17,000 spectators, it could hold slightly less than half of Athens' 40,000 citizens.

Greek theater was directed at the moral and political education of the community. The poet's role was the improvement of the *polis* or city-state (made up of a town and its surrounding countryside). Greek city-states traditionally sponsored public contests between *rhapsodes* (professional poetry performers) reciting stories from Homer's epics, the *Iliad* and *Odyssey.* As Greek society developed and urbanized, however, the competitive and individualized heroism of the Homeric epics had to be tempered with the values of cooperation and compromise necessary to a democracy. Civic theater provided the ideal medium to address these cultural needs.

As a public art form, tragedy was not simply a stage for political propaganda to promote the status quo. Nor was it exclusively a celebration of idealized heroes nobly enduring the blows of harsh circumstance and misfortune.

Tragedy often enabled its audience to reflect on personal values that might be in conflict with civic ideals, on the claims of minorities that it neglected or excluded from public life, or on its own irrational prejudices toward the foreign or the unknown.

Aristotle's Concept of Tragedy

> *Tragedy is an imitation of an action of high importance,*
> *complete and of some amplitude; in language enhanced by*
> *distinct and varying beauties; acted not narrated; by means*
> *of pity and fear effecting its purgation of these emotions.*
>
> —ARISTOTLE, *POETICS*, CHAPTER VI

Aristotle's famous definition of tragedy, constructed in the fourth century B.C., is the testimony of one who probably saw many classical tragedies performed. In making his observations, Aristotle does not seem to be laying down laws for what a tragedy ought to be. More likely, he is drawing—from tragedies he has seen or read—a general description of them.

Aristotle observes that the protagonist, the hero or chief character of a tragedy, is a person of "high estate," apparently a king or queen or other member of a royal family. In thus being as keenly interested as contemporary dramatists in the private lives of the powerful, Greek dramatists need not be accused of snobbery. It is the nature of tragedy that the protagonist must fall from power and from happiness; his high estate gives him a place of dignity to fall from and perhaps makes his fall seem all the more a calamity in that it involves an entire nation or people. Nor is the protagonist extraordinary merely in his position in society. Oedipus is not only a king but also a noble soul who suffers profoundly and who employs splendid speech to express his suffering.

The tragic hero, however, is not a superman; he is fallible. The hero's downfall is the result, as Aristotle said, of his *hamartia*: his error or transgression or (as some translators would have it) his flaw or weakness of character. The notion that a tragic hero has such a **tragic flaw** has often been attributed to Aristotle, but it is by no means clear that Aristotle meant just that. According to this interpretation, every tragic hero has some fatal weakness, some moral Achilles' heel, that brings him to a bad end. In some classical tragedies, his transgression is a weakness the Greeks called **hubris**—extreme pride, leading to overconfidence.

Whatever Aristotle had in mind, however, many later critics find value in the idea of the tragic flaw. In this view, the downfall of a hero follows from his very nature. Whatever view we take—whether we find the hero's sufferings due to a flaw of character or to an error of judgment—we will probably find that his downfall results from acts for which he himself is responsible. In a Greek tragedy, the hero is a character amply capable of making choices—capable, too, of accepting the consequences.

It may be useful to take another look at Aristotle's definition of *tragedy*, with which we began. By **purgation** (or *katharsis*), did the ancient theorist mean that after witnessing a tragedy we feel relief, having released our pent-up emotions? Or did he mean that our feelings are purified, refined into something more ennobling? Scholars continue to argue. Whatever his exact meaning, clearly Aristotle implies that after witnessing a tragedy we feel better, not worse—not depressed, but somehow elated. We take a kind of pleasure in the spectacle of a noble man being abased, but surely this pleasure is a legitimate one. Part of that catharsis may also be based in our feeling of the "rightness" or accuracy of what we have just witnessed. The terrible but undeniable truth of the tragic vision of life is that blind overreaching and the destruction of hopes and dreams are very much a part of what really happens in the world. For tragedy, Edith Hamilton wrote, affects us as "pain transmuted into exaltation by the alchemy of poetry."[1]

Aristotle, in describing the workings of this inexorable force in *Oedipus the King*, uses terms that later critics have found valuable. One is **recognition**, or discovery (*anagnorisis*): the revelation of some fact not known before or some person's true identity. Oedipus makes such a discovery: he recognizes that he himself was the child whom his mother had given over to be destroyed. Such a recognition also occurs in Shakespeare's *Macbeth* when Macduff reveals himself to have been "from his mother's womb / Untimely ripped," thus disclosing a double meaning in the witches' prophecy that Macbeth could be harmed by "none of woman born," and sweeping aside Macbeth's last shred of belief that he is infallible. Modern critics have taken the term to mean also the terrible enlightenment that accompanies such a recognition. "To see things plain—that is *anagnorisis*," Clifford Leech observes, "and it is the ultimate experience we shall have if we have leisure at the point of death . . . It is what tragedy ultimately is about: the realization of the unthinkable."[2]

Having made his discovery, Oedipus suffers a reversal in his fortunes; he goes off into exile, blinded and dethroned. Such a fall from happiness seems intrinsic to tragedy, but we should know that Aristotle has a more particular meaning for his term **reversal** (*peripeteia*, anglicized as **peripety**). He means an action that turns out to have the opposite effect from the one its doer had intended. One of his illustrations of such an ironic reversal is from *Oedipus the King*. The first messenger intends to cheer Oedipus with

---

[1]"The Idea of Tragedy," *The Greek Way to Western Civilization* (New York: Norton, 1942).

[2]*Tragedy* (London: Methuen, 1969) 65.

the partially good news that, contrary to the prophecy that Oedipus would kill his father, his father has died of old age. The reversal is in the fact that, when the messenger further reveals that old Polybus was Oedipus' father only by adoption, the king, instead of having his fears allayed, is stirred to new dread.

We are not altogether sorry, perhaps, to see an arrogant man such as Oedipus humbled, and yet it is difficult not to feel that the punishment of Oedipus is greater than he deserves. Possibly this feeling is what Aristotle meant in his observation that a tragedy arouses our pity and our fear—our compassion for Oedipus and our terror as we sense the remorselessness of a universe in which a man is doomed. Notice, however, that at the end of the play Oedipus does not curse God and die. Although such a complex play is open to many interpretations, it is probably safe to say that the play is not a bitter complaint against the universe. At last, Oedipus accepts the divine will, prays for blessings upon his children, and prepares to endure his exile—fallen from high estate but uplifted in moral dignity.

Sophocles

Sophocles (496?–406 B.C.)—tragic dramatist, priest, for a time one of ten Athenian generals—was one of the three great ancient Greek writers of tragedy. (The other two were his contemporaries: Aeschylus, his senior, and Euripides, his junior.) Sophocles won his first victory in the Athenian spring drama competition in 468 B.C., when a tragedy he had written defeated one by Aeschylus. He went on to win many prizes, writing more than 120 plays, of which only seven have survived in their entirety—Ajax, Antigonê, Oedipus the King, Electra, Philoctetes, The Trachinian Women, and Oedipus at Colonus. (Of the lost

SOPHOCLES

plays, about a thousand fragments remain.) In his long life, Sophocles saw Greece rise to supremacy over the Persian Empire. He enjoyed the favor of the statesman Pericles, who, making peace with enemy Sparta, ruled Athens during a Golden Age (461–429 B.C.), during which the Parthenon was built and music, art, drama, and philosophy flourished. The playwright lived on to see his native city-state in decline, its strength drained by the disastrous Peloponnesian War. His last play, Oedipus at Colonus, set twenty years after the events of Oedipus the King, shows the former king in old age, ragged and blind, cast into exile by his sons, but still accompanied by his faithful daughter Antigonê. It was written when Sophocles was nearly ninety.

Oedipus the King *is believed to have been first produced in 425* B.C.*, five years after the plague had broken out in Athens.*

The Origins of *Oedipus the King*

On a Great Dionysia feast day within several years after Athens had survived a devastating plague, the audience turned out to watch a tragedy by Sophocles, set in the city of Thebes at the moment of another terrible plague. This timely play was *Oedipus,* later given the name (in Greek) *Oedipus Tyrannos* to distinguish it from Sophocles' last Oedipus play, *Oedipus at Colonus,* written many years later when the author was ninety. A folktale figure, Oedipus gets his name through a complex pun. *Oida* means "to know" (from the root *vid-,* "see"), pointing to the tale's contrasting themes of sight and blindness, wisdom and ignorance. *Oedipus* also means "swollen foot" or "clubfoot," pointing to the injury sustained in the title character's infancy, when his ankles were pinioned together like a goat's. Oedipus is the man who comes to knowledge of his true parentage through the evidence of his feet and his old injury. The term *tyrannos,* in the context of the play, simply means a man who comes to rule through his own intelligence and merit, though not related to the ruling family. The traditional Greek title might be translated, therefore, as *Clubfoot the Ruler.* (*Oedipus Rex,* which means "Oedipus the King," is the conventional Latin title for the play.)

Presumably the audience already knew this old tale referred to in Homer's *Odyssey.* They would have known that because a prophecy had foretold that Oedipus would grow up to slay his father, he had been taken out as a newborn to perish in the wilderness of Mount Cithaeron outside Thebes. (Exposure was the common fate of unwanted children in ancient Greece, though only in the most extraordinary circumstance would a royal heir be exposed.) The audience would also have known that before he was left to die, the baby's feet had been pinned together. And they would also have known that later, adopted by King Polybus and Queen Merope of Corinth and grown to maturity, Oedipus won both the throne and the recently widowed queen of Thebes as a reward for ridding the city of the Sphinx, a winged, woman-headed lion. All who approached the Sphinx were asked a riddle, and failure to solve it meant death. Her lethal riddle was: "What goes on four legs in the morning, two at noon, and three at evening?" Oedipus correctly answered, "Man." (As a baby he crawls on all fours, then as a man he walks erect, then as an old man he uses a cane.) Chagrined and outwitted, the Sphinx leaped from her rocky perch and dashed herself to death. Familiarity with all these events is necessary to understand *Oedipus the King,* which begins years later, after the title character has long been established as ruler of Thebes.

Laurence Olivier in *Oedipus Rex*

Oedipus the King   425 B.C.?

TRANSLATED BY DUDLEY FITTS AND ROBERT FITZGERALD

CHARACTERS°

Oedipus	Messenger
A Priest	Shepherd of Laïos
Creon	Second Messenger
Teiresias	Chorus of Theban Elders
Iocastê	

SCENE: *Before the palace of Oedipus, King of Thebes. A central door and two lateral doors open onto a platform which runs the length of the façade. On the platform, right and left, are altars; and three steps lead down into the "orchestra," or chorus-ground. At the beginning of the action these steps are crowded by suppliants° who have brought branches and chaplets of olive leaves and who lie in various attitudes of despair. Oedipus enters.*

Characters: Some of these names are usually anglicized: Jocasta, Laius. In this version, the translators prefer spelling names more like the Greek originals.   *suppliants:* persons who come to ask some favor of the king.

PROLOGUE°

Oedipus: My children, generations of the living
    In the line of Kadmos,° nursed at his ancient hearth:
    Why have you strewn yourself before these altars
    In supplication, with your boughs and garlands?
    The breath of incense rises from the city   5
    With a sound of prayer and lamentation.
                                      Children,
    I would not have you speak through messengers,
    And therefore I have come myself to hear you—
    I, Oedipus, who bear the famous name.
    (*To a Priest.*) You, there, since you are eldest in the company,   10
    Speak for them all, tell me what preys upon you,
    Whether you come in dread, or crave some blessing:
    Tell me, and never doubt that I will help you
    In every way I can; I should be heartless
    Were I not moved to find you suppliant here.   15
Priest: Great Oedipus, O powerful King of Thebes!
    You see how all the ages of our people
    Cling to your altar steps: here are boys
    Who can barely stand alone, and here are priests
    By weight of age, as I am a priest of God,   20
    And young men chosen from those yet unmarried;
    As for the others, all that multitude,
    They wait with olive chaplets in the squares,
    At the two shrines of Pallas,° and where Apollo°
    Speaks in the glowing embers.
                        Your own eyes   25
    Must tell you: Thebes is tossed on a murdering sea
    And can not lift her head from the death surge.
    A rust consumes the buds and fruits of the earth;
    The herds are sick; children die unborn,
    And labor is vain. The god of plague and pyre   30
    Raids like detestable lightning through the city,
    And all the house of Kadmos is laid waste,
    All emptied, and all darkened: Death alone
    Battens upon the misery of Thebes.

Prologue: portion of the play containing the exposition. 2 *line of Kadmos:* according to legend the city of Thebes, where the play takes place, had been founded by the hero Cadmus. 24 *Pallas:* title for Athena, goddess of wisdom. *Apollo:* god of music, poetry, and prophecy. At his shrine near Thebes, the ashes of fires were used to divine the future.

You are not one of the immortal gods, we know;   35
Yet we have come to you to make our prayer
As to the man surest in mortal ways
And wisest in the ways of God. You saved us
From the Sphinx, that flinty singer, and the tribute
We paid to her so long; yet you were never   40
Better informed than we, nor could we teach you:
It was some god breathed in you to set us free.

Therefore, O mighty King, we turn to you:
Find us our safety, find us a remedy,
Whether by counsel of the gods or men.   45
A king of wisdom tested in the past
Can act in a time of troubles, and act well.
Noblest of men, restore
Life to your city! Think how all men call you
Liberator for your triumph long ago;   50
Ah, when your years of kingship are remembered,
Let them not say *We rose, but later fell*—
Keep the State from going down in the storm!
Once, years ago, with happy augury,
You brought us fortune; be the same again!   55
No man questions your power to rule the land:
But rule over men, not over a dead city!
Ships are only hulls, citadels are nothing,
When no life moves in the empty passageways.
Oedipus: Poor children! You may be sure I know   60
All that you longed for in your coming here.
I know that you are deathly sick; and yet,
Sick as you are, not one is as sick as I.
Each of you suffers in himself alone
His anguish, not another's; but my spirit   65
Groans for the city, for myself, for you.

I was not sleeping, you are not waking me.
No, I have been in tears for a long while
And in my restless thought walked many ways.
In all my search, I found one helpful course,   70
And that I have taken: I have sent Creon,
Son of Menoikeus, brother of the Queen,
To Delphi, Apollo's place of revelation,°

---

73 *Delphi . . . revelation:* In the temple of Delphi at the foot of Mount Parnassus, a priestess of Dionysos, while in an ecstatic trance, would speak the wine god's words. Such a priestess was called an *oracle;* the word can also mean "a message from the god."

To learn there, if he can,
What act or pledge of mine may save the city.   75
I have counted the days, and now, this very day,
I am troubled, for he has overstayed his time.
What is he doing? He has been gone too long.
Yet whenever he comes back, I should do ill
To scant whatever duty God reveals.   80

Priest: It is a timely promise. At this instant
    They tell me Creon is here.

Oedipus: O Lord Apollo!
    May his news be fair as his face is radiant!

Priest: It could not be otherwise: he is crowned with bay,
    The chaplet is thick with berries.

Oedipus: We shall soon know;   85
    He is near enough to hear us now.

    Enter Creon.

                    O Prince:
    Brother: son of Menoikeus:
    What answer do you bring us from the god?

Creon: A strong one. I can tell you, great afflictions
    Will turn out well, if they are taken well.   90

Oedipus: What was the oracle? These vague words
    Leave me still hanging between hope and fear.

Creon: Is it your pleasure to hear me with all these
    Gathered around us? I am prepared to speak,
    But should we not go in?

Oedipus: Let them all hear it   95
    It is for them I suffer, more than for myself.

Creon: Then I will tell you what I heard at Delphi.

    In plain words
    The god commands us to expel from the land of Thebes
    An old defilement we are sheltering.   100
    It is a deathly thing, beyond cure.
    We must not let it feed upon us longer.

Oedipus: What defilement? How shall we rid ourselves of it?

Creon: By exile or death, blood for blood. It was
    Murder that brought the plague-wind on the city.   105

Oedipus: Murder of whom? Surely the god has named him?

Creon: My lord: long ago Laïos was our king,
    Before you came to govern us.

Oedipus: I know;
    I learned of him from others; I never saw him.

Creon: He was murdered; and Apollo commands us now   110
    To take revenge upon whoever killed him.
Oedipus: Upon whom? Where are they? Where shall we find a clue
    To solve that crime, after so many years?
Creon: Here in this land, he said.
                       If we make enquiry,
    We may touch things that otherwise escape us.   115
Oedipus: Tell me: Was Laïos murdered in his house,
    Or in the fields, or in some foreign country?
Creon: He said he planned to make a pilgrimage.
    He did not come home again.
Oedipus: And was there no one,
    No witness, no companion, to tell what happened?   120
Creon: They were all killed but one, and he got away
    So frightened that he could remember one thing only.
Oedipus: What was that one thing? One may be the key
    To everything, if we resolve to use it.
Creon: He said that a band of highwaymen attacked them,   125
    Outnumbered them, and overwhelmed the King.
Oedipus: Strange, that a highwayman should be so daring—
    Unless some faction here bribed him to do it.
Creon: We thought of that. But after Laïos' death
    New troubles arose and we had no avenger.   130
Oedipus: What troubles could prevent your hunting down the killers?
Creon: The riddling Sphinx's song
    Made us deaf to all mysteries but her own.
Oedipus: Then once more I must bring what is dark to light.
    It is most fitting that Apollo shows,   135
    As you do, this compunction for the dead.
    You shall see how I stand by you, as I should,
    To avenge the city and the city's god,
    And not as though it were for some distant friend,
    But for my own sake, to be rid of evil.   140
    Whoever killed King Laïos might—who knows?—
    Decide at any moment to kill me as well.
    By avenging the murdered king I protect myself.

    Come, then, my children: leave the altar steps,
    Lift up your olive boughs!
                    One of you go   145
    And summon the people of Kadmos to gather here.
    I will do all that I can; you may tell them that.

    Exit a Page.

So, with the help of God,
We shall be saved—or else indeed we are lost.
Priest: Let us rise, children. It was for this we came, 150
And now the King has promised it himself.
Phoibos° has sent us an oracle; may he descend
Himself to save us and drive out the plague.

Exeunt Oedipus and Creon into the palace by the central door. The Priest and the Suppliants disperse right and left. After a short pause the Chorus enters the orchestra.

PÁRODOS°

Strophe° 1

Chorus: What is God singing in his profound
Delphi of gold and shadow?
What oracle for Thebes, the sunwhipped city?

Fear unjoints me, the roots of my heart tremble.

Now I remember, O Healer, your power, and wonder: 5
Will you send doom like a sudden cloud, or weave it
Like nightfall of the past?

Speak, speak to us, issue of holy sound:
Dearest to our expectancy: be tender!

Antistrophe° 1

Let me pray to Athenê, the immortal daughter of Zeus, 10
And to Artemis her sister
Who keeps her famous throne in the market ring,
And to Apollo, bowman at the far butts of heaven—

O gods, descend! Like three streams leap against
The fires of our grief, the fires of darkness; 15
Be swift to bring us rest!

As in the old time from the brilliant house
Of air you stepped to save us, come again!

Strophe 2

Now our afflictions have no end,
Now all our stricken host lies down 20
And no man fights off death with his mind;

---

152 *Phoibos:* the sun god Phoebus Apollo. *Párodos:* part to be sung by the chorus on first entering. A *strophe* (according to theory) was sung while the chorus danced from stage right to stage left. An *antistrophe* was sung while the chorus danced back again across the stage, from left to right.

The noble plowland bears no grain,
And groaning mothers can not bear—

See, how our lives like birds take wing,
Like sparks that fly when a fire soars,   25
To the shore of the god of evening.

Antistrophe 2

The plague burns on, it is pitiless,
Though pallid children laden with death
Lie unwept in the stony ways,

And old gray women by every path   30
Flock to the strand about the altars

There to strike their breasts and cry
Worship of Phoibos in wailing prayers:
Be kind, God's golden child!

Strophe 3

There are no swords in this attack by fire,   35
No shields, but we are ringed with cries.

Send the besieger plunging from our homes
Into the vast sea-room of the Atlantic
Or into the waves that foam eastward of Thrace—

For the day ravages what the night spares—   40

Destroy our enemy, lord of the thunder!
Let him be riven by lightning from heaven!

Antistrophe 3

Phoibos Apollo, stretch the sun's bowstring,
That golden cord, until it sing for us,
Flashing arrows in heaven!
                               Artemis, Huntress,   45
Race with flaring lights upon our mountains!

O scarlet god, O golden-banded brow,
O Theban Bacchos in a storm of Maenads,°

Enter Oedipus, center.

Whirl upon Death, that all the Undying hate!
Come with blinding torches, come in joy!   50

48 *Bacchos . . . Maenads:* god of wine with his attendant girl revelers.

SCENE I

Oedipus: Is this your prayer? It may be answered. Come,
    Listen to me, act as the crisis demands,
    And you shall have relief from all these evils.

    Until now I was a stranger to this tale,
    As I had been a stranger to the crime.   5
    Could I track down the murderer without a clue?
    But now, friends,
    As one who became a citizen after the murder,
    I make this proclamation to all Thebans:

    If any man knows by whose hand Laïos, son of Labdakos,   10
    Met his death, I direct that man to tell me everything,
    No matter what he fears for having so long withheld it.
    Let it stand as promised that no further trouble
    Will come to him, but he may leave the land in safety.

    Moreover: If anyone knows the murderer to be foreign,   15
    Let him not keep silent: he shall have his reward from me.
    However, if he does conceal it; if any man
    Fearing for his friend or for himself disobeys this edict,
    Hear what I propose to do:

    I solemnly forbid the people of this country,   20
    Where power and throne are mine, ever to receive that man
    Or speak to him, no matter who he is, or let him
    Join in sacrifice, lustration,° or in prayer.
    I decree that he be driven from every house,
    Being, as he is, corruption itself to us: the Delphic   25
    Voice of Zeus has pronounced this revelation.
    Thus I associate myself with the oracle
    And take the side of the murdered king.

    As for the criminal, I pray to God—
    Whether it be a lurking thief, or one of a number—   30
    I pray that that man's life be consumed in evil and wretchedness.
    And as for me, this curse applies no less
    If it should turn out that the culprit is my guest here,
    Sharing my hearth.
                You have heard the penalty.
    I lay it on you now to attend to this   35
    For my sake, for Apollo's, for the sick
    Sterile city that heaven has abandoned.
    Suppose the oracle had given you no command:

23 *lustration:* propitiatory sacrifice.

Should this defilement go uncleansed for ever?
You should have found the murderer: your king,   40
A noble king, had been destroyed!
                         Now I,
Having the power that he held before me,
Having his bed, begetting children there
Upon his wife, as he would have, had he lived—
Their son would have been my children's brother,   45
If Laïos had had luck in fatherhood!
(But surely ill luck rushed upon his reign)—
I say I take the son's part, just as though
I were his son, to press the fight for him
And see it won! I'll find the hand that brought   50
Death to Labdakos' and Polydoros' child,
Heir of Kadmos' and Agenor's line.
And as for those who fail me,
May the gods deny them the fruit of the earth,
Fruit of the womb, and may they rot utterly!   55
Let them be wretched as we are wretched, and worse!

For you, for loyal Thebans, and for all
Who find my actions right, I pray the favor
Of justice, and of all the immortal gods.
Choragos:° Since I am under oath, my lord, I swear   60
    I did not do the murder, I can not name
    The murderer. Might not the oracle
    That has ordained the search tell where to find him?
Oedipus: An honest question. But no man in the world
    Can make the gods do more than the gods will.   65
Choragos: There is one last expedient—
Oedipus: Tell me what it is.
    Though it seem slight, you must not hold it back.
Choragos: A lord clairvoyant to the lord Apollo,
    As we all know, is the skilled Teiresias.
    One might learn much about this from him, Oedipus.   70
Oedipus: I am not wasting time:
    Creon spoke of this, and I have sent for him—
    Twice, in fact; it is strange that he is not here.
Choragos: The other matter—that old report—seems useless.
Oedipus: Tell me. I am interested in all reports.   75
Choragos: The King was said to have been killed by highwaymen.
Oedipus: I know. But we have no witnesses to that.

60 *Choragos:* spokesperson for the chorus.

Choragos: If the killer can feel a particle of dread,
    Your curse will bring him out of hiding!
Oedipus: No.
    The man who dared that act will fear no curse.   80

    Enter the blind seer Teiresias, led by a Page.

Choragos: But there is one man who may detect the criminal.
    This is Teiresias, this is the holy prophet
    In whom, alone of all men, truth was born.
Oedipus: Teiresias: seer: student of mysteries,
    Of all that's taught and all that no man tells,   85
    Secrets of Heaven and secrets of the earth:
    Blind though you are, you know the city lies
    Sick with plague; and from this plague, my lord,
    We find that you alone can guard or save us.

    Possibly you did not hear the messengers?   90
    Apollo, when we sent to him,
    Sent us back word that this great pestilence
    Would lift, but only if we established clearly
    The identity of those who murdered Laïos.
    They must be killed or exiled.
                              Can you use   95
    Birdflight or any art of divination
    To purify yourself, and Thebes, and me
    From this contagion? We are in your hands.
    There is no fairer duty
    Than that of helping others in distress.   100
Teiresias: How dreadful knowledge of the truth can be
    When there's no help in truth! I knew this well,
    But made myself forget. I should not have come.
Oedipus: What is troubling you? Why are your eyes so cold?
Teiresias: Let me go home. Bear your own fate, and I'll   105
    Bear mine. It is better so: trust what I say.
Oedipus: What you say is ungracious and unhelpful
    To your native country. Do not refuse to speak.
Teiresias: When it comes to speech, your own is neither temperate
    Nor opportune. I wish to be more prudent.   110
Oedipus: In God's name, we all beg you—
Teiresias: You are all ignorant.
    No; I will never tell you what I know.
    Now it is my misery; then, it would be yours.
Oedipus: What! You do know something, and will not tell us?
    You would betray us all and wreck the State?

Teiresias: I do not intend to torture myself, or you.   115
    Why persist in asking? You will not persuade me.
Oedipus: What a wicked old man you are! You'd try a stone's
    Patience! Out with it! Have you no feeling at all?
Teiresias: You call me unfeeling. If you could only see   120
    The nature of your own feelings . . .
Oedipus: Why,
    Who would not feel as I do? Who could endure
    Your arrogance toward the city?
Teiresias: What does it matter!
    Whether I speak or not; it is bound to come.
Oedipus: Then, if "it" is bound to come, you are bound to tell me.   125
Teiresias: No, I will not go on. Rage as you please.
Oedipus: Rage? Why not!
                    And I'll tell you what I think:
    You planned it, you had it done, you all but
    Killed him with your own hands: if you had eyes,
    I'd say the crime was yours, and yours alone.   130
Teiresias: So? I charge you, then,
    Abide by the proclamation you have made:
    From this day forth
    Never speak again to these men or to me;
    You yourself are the pollution of this country.   135
Oedipus: You dare say that! Can you possibly think you have
    Some way of going free, after such insolence?
Teiresias: I have gone free. It is the truth sustains me.
Oedipus: Who taught you shamelessness? It was not your craft.
Teiresias: You did. You made me speak. I did not want to.   140
Oedipus: Speak what? Let me hear it again more clearly.
Teiresias: Was it not clear before? Are you tempting me?
Oedipus: I did not understand it. Say it again.
Teiresias: I say that you are the murderer whom you seek.
Oedipus: Now twice you have spat out infamy. You'll pay for it!   145
Teiresias: Would you care for more? Do you wish to be really angry?
Oedipus: Say what you will. Whatever you say is worthless.
Teiresias: I say you live in hideous shame with those
    Most dear to you. You can not see the evil.
Oedipus: It seems you can go on mouthing like this for ever.   150
Teiresias: I can, if there is power in truth.
Oedipus: There is:
    But not for you, not for you,
    You sightless, witless, senseless, mad old man!
Teiresias: You are the madman. There is no one here
    Who will not curse you soon, as you curse me.   155

Oedipus: You child of endless night! You can not hurt me
　　Or any other man who sees the sun.
Teiresias: True: it is not from me your fate will come.
　　That lies within Apollo's competence,
　　As it is his concern.
Oedipus:　　　　　　Tell me:　　　　　　　　　　　　　　　160
　　Are you speaking for Creon, or for yourself?
Teiresias: Creon is no threat. You weave your own doom.
Oedipus: Wealth, power, craft of statesmanship!
　　Kingly position, everywhere admired!
　　What savage envy is stored up against these,　　　　　165
　　If Creon, whom I trusted, Creon my friend,
　　For this great office which the city once
　　Put in my hands unsought—if for this power
　　Creon desires in secret to destroy me!

　　He has brought this decrepit fortune-teller, this　　　170
　　Collector of dirty pennies, this prophet fraud—
　　Why, he is no more clairvoyant than I am!
　　　　　　　　　　　　　　　　　　Tell us:
　　Has your mystic mummery ever approached the truth?
　　When that hellcat the Sphinx was performing here,
　　What help were you to these people?　　　　　　　175
　　Her magic was not for the first man who came along:
　　It demanded a real exorcist. Your birds—
　　What good were they? or the gods, for the matter of that?
　　But I came by,
　　Oedipus, the simple man, who knows nothing—　　180
　　I thought it out for myself, no birds helped me!
　　And this is the man you think you can destroy,
　　That you may be close to Creon when he's king!
　　Well, you and your friend Creon, it seems to me,
　　Will suffer most. If you were not an old man,　　　185
　　You would have paid already for your plot.
Choragos: We can not see that his words or yours
　　Have been spoken except in anger, Oedipus,
　　And of anger we have no need. How can God's will
　　Be accomplished best? That is what most concerns us.　190
Teiresias: You are a king. But where argument's concerned
　　I am your man, as much a king as you.
　　I am not your servant, but Apollo's.
　　I have no need of Creon to speak for me.

　　Listen to me. You mock my blindness, do you?　　195
　　But I say that you, with both your eyes, are blind:

You can not see the wretchedness of your life,
Nor in whose house you live, no, nor with whom.
Who are your father and mother? Can you tell me?
You do not even know the blind wrongs   200
That you have done them, on earth and in the world below.
But the double lash of your parents' curse will whip you
Out of this land some day, with only night
Upon your precious eyes.
Your cries then—where will they not be heard?   205
What fastness of Kithairon will not echo them?
And that bridal-descant of yours—you'll know it then,
The song they sang when you came here to Thebes
And found your misguided berthing.
All this, and more, that you can not guess at now,   210
Will bring you to yourself among your children.

Be angry, then. Curse Creon. Curse my words.
I tell you, no man that walks upon the earth
Shall be rooted out more horribly than you.
Oedipus: Am I to bear this from him?—Damnation   215
   Take you! Out of this place! Out of my sight!
Teiresias: I would not have come at all if you had not asked me.
Oedipus: Could I have told that you'd talk nonsense, that
   You'd come here to make a fool of yourself, and of me?
Teiresias: A fool? Your parents thought me sane enough.   220
Oedipus: My parents again!—Wait: who were my parents?
Teiresias: This day will give you a father, and break your heart.
Oedipus: Your infantile riddles! Your damned abracadabra!
Teiresias: You were a great man once at solving riddles.
Oedipus: Mock me with that if you like; you will find it true.   225
Teiresias: It was true enough. It brought about your ruin.
Oedipus: But if it saved this town?
Teiresias (to the Page):   Boy, give me your hand.
Oedipus: Yes, boy; lead him away.
                              —While you are here
   We can do nothing. Go; leave us in peace.
Teiresias: I will go when I have said what I have to say.   230
   How can you hurt me? And I tell you again:
   The man you have been looking for all this time,
   The damned man, the murderer of Laïos,
   That man is in Thebes. To your mind he is foreign-born,
   But it will soon be shown that he is a Theban,   235
   A revelation that will fail to please.
                        A blind man,

Who has his eyes now; a penniless man, who is rich now;
And he will go tapping the strange earth with his staff;
To the children with whom he lives now he will be
Brother and father—the very same; to her   240
Who bore him, son and husband—the very same
Who came to his father's bed, wet with his father's blood.

Enough. Go think that over.
If later you find error in what I have said,
You may say that I have no skill in prophecy.   245

Exit Teiresias, led by his Page. Oedipus goes into the palace.

ODE° I

Strophe 1

Chorus: The Delphic stone of prophecies
       Remembers ancient regicide
       And a still bloody hand.
       That killer's hour of flight has come.
       He must be stronger than riderless   5
       Coursers of untiring wind,
       For the son of Zeus° armed with his father's thunder
       Leaps in lightning after him;
       And the Furies° follow him, the sad Furies.

Antistrophe 1

Holy Parnassos' peak of snow   10
Flashes and blinds that secret man,
That all shall hunt him down:
Though he may roam the forest shade
Like a bull gone wild from pasture
To rage through glooms of stone.   15
Doom comes down on him; flight will not avail him;
For the world's heart calls him desolate,
And the immortal Furies follow, for ever follow.

Strophe 2

But now a wilder thing is heard
From the old man skilled at hearing Fate in the wingbeat of a bird. 20
Bewildered as a blown bird, my soul hovers and can not find

Ode: a choral song. Here again (as in the *párodos*), *strophe* and *antistrophe* probably indicate the
movements of a dance.   7 *son of Zeus:* Apollo.   9 *Furies:* three horrific female spirits whose
task was to seek out and punish evildoers.

Foothold in this debate, or any reason or rest of mind.
But no man ever brought—none can bring
Proof of strife between Thebes' royal house,
Labdakos' line,° and the son of Polybos;°   25
And never until now has any man brought word
Of Laïos' dark death staining Oedipus the King.

Antistrophe 2

Divine Zeus and Apollo hold
Perfect intelligence alone of all tales ever told;
And well though this diviner works, he works in his own night;   30
No man can judge that rough unknown or trust in second sight,
For wisdom changes hands among the wise.
Shall I believe my great lord criminal
At a raging word that a blind old man let fall?
I saw him, when the carrion woman faced him of old,   35
Prove his heroic mind! These evil words are lies.

SCENE II

Creon: Men of Thebes:
    I am told that heavy accusations
    Have been brought against me by King Oedipus.

I am not the kind of man to bear this tamely.

If in these present difficulties   5
He holds me accountable for any harm to him
Through anything I have said or done—why, then,
I do not value life in this dishonor.

It is not as though this rumor touched upon
Some private indiscretion. The matter is grave.   10
The fact is that I am being called disloyal
To the State, to my fellow citizens, to my friends.
Choragos: He may have spoken in anger, not from his mind.
Creon: But did you not hear him say I was the one
    Who seduced the old prophet into lying?   15
Choragos: The thing was said; I do not know how seriously.
Creon: But you were watching him! Were his eyes steady?
    Did he look like a man in his right mind?
Choragos: I do not know.

---

25 *Labdakos' line:* descendants of Laïos (true father of Oedipus, although the chorus does not know it).   *Polybos:* king who adopted the child Oedipus.

I can not judge the behavior of great men.
But here is the King himself.

Enter Oedipus.

Oedipus: So you dared come back.   20
Why? How brazen of you to come to my house,
You murderer!
                    Do you think I do not know
That you plotted to kill me, plotted to steal my throne?
Tell me, in God's name: am I coward, a fool,
That you should dream you could accomplish this?   25
A fool who could not see your slippery game?
A coward, not to fight back when I saw it?
You are the fool, Creon, are you not? hoping
Without support or friends to get a throne?
Thrones may be won or bought: you could do neither.   30
Creon: Now listen to me. You have talked; let me talk, too.
    You can not judge unless you know the facts.
Oedipus: You speak well: there is one fact; but I find it hard
    To learn from the deadliest enemy I have.
Creon: That above all I must dispute with you.   35
Oedipus: That above all I will not hear you deny.
Creon: If you think there is anything good in being stubborn
    Against all reason, then I say you are wrong.
Oedipus: If you think a man can sin against his own kind
    And not be punished for it, I say you are mad.   40
Creon: I agree. But tell me: what have I done to you?
Oedipus: You advised me to send for that wizard, did you not?
Creon: I did. I should do it again.
Oedipus: Very well. Now tell me:
    How long has it been since Laïos—
Creon: What of Laïos?
Oedipus: Since he vanished in that onset by the road?   45
Creon: It was long ago, a long time.
Oedipus: And this prophet,
    Was he practicing here then?
Creon: He was; and with honor, as now.
Oedipus: Did he speak of me at that time?
Creon: He never did;
    At least, not when I was present.
Oedipus: But . . . the enquiry?
    I suppose you held one?
Creon: We did, but we learned nothing.   50
Oedipus: Why did the prophet not speak against me then?

Creon: I do not know; and I am the kind of man
    Who holds his tongue when he has no facts to go on.
Oedipus: There's one fact that you know, and you could tell it.
Creon: What fact is that? If I know it, you shall have it.   55
Oedipus: If he were not involved with you, he could not say
    That it was I who murdered Laïos.
Creon: If he says that, you are the one that knows it!—
    But now it is my turn to question you.
Oedipus: Put your questions. I am no murderer.   60
Creon: First then: You married my sister?
Oedipus: I married your sister.
Creon: And you rule the kingdom equally with her?
Oedipus: Everything that she wants she has from me.
Creon: And I am the third, equal to both of you?
Oedipus: That is why I call you a bad friend.   65
Creon: No. Reason it out, as I have done.
    Think of this first: Would any sane man prefer
    Power, with all a king's anxieties,
    To that same power and the grace of sleep?
    Certainly not I.   70
    I have never longed for the king's power—only his rights.
    Would any wise man differ from me in this?
    As matters stand, I have my way in everything
    With your consent, and no responsibilities.
    If I were king, I should be a slave to policy.   75

    How could I desire a scepter more
    Than what is now mine—untroubled influence?
    No, I have not gone mad; I need no honors,
    Except those with the perquisites I have now.
    I am welcome everywhere; every man salutes me,   80
    And those who want your favor seek my ear,
    Since I know how to manage what they ask.
    Should I exchange this ease for that anxiety?
    Besides, no sober mind is treasonable.
    I hate anarchy   85
    And never would deal with any man who likes it.

    Test what I have said. Go to the priestess
    At Delphi, ask if I quoted her correctly.
    And as for this other thing: if I am found
    Guilty of treason with Teiresias,   90
    Then sentence me to death! You have my word
    It is a sentence I should cast my vote for—
    But not without evidence!
                You do wrong

When you take good men for bad, bad men for good.
A true friend thrown aside—why, life itself   95
Is not more precious!

                     In time you will know this well:
For time, and time alone, will show the just man,
Though scoundrels are discovered in a day.
Choragos: This is well said, and a prudent man would ponder it.
    Judgments too quickly formed are dangerous.   100
Oedipus: But is he not quick in his duplicity?
    And shall I not be quick to parry him?
    Would you have me stand still, hold my peace, and let
    This man win everything, through my inaction?
Creon: And you want—what is it, then? To banish me?   105
Oedipus: No, not exile. It is your death I want,
    So that all the world may see what treason means.
Creon: You will persist, then? You will not believe me?
Oedipus: How can I believe you?
Creon: Then you are a fool.
Oedipus: To save myself?
Creon: In justice, think of me.   110
Oedipus: You are evil incarnate.
Creon: But suppose that you are wrong?
Oedipus: Still I must rule.
Creon: But not if you rule badly.
Oedipus: O city, city!
Creon: It is my city, too!
Choragos: Now, my lords, be still. I see the Queen,
    Iocastê, coming from her palace chambers;   115
    And it is time she came, for the sake of you both.
    This dreadful quarrel can be resolved through her.

Enter Iocastê.

Iocastê: Poor foolish men, what wicked din is this?
    With Thebes sick to death, is it not shameful
    That you should rake some private quarrel up?   120
    (*To Oedipus.*) Come into the house.
                       —And you, Creon, go now:
    Let us have no more of this tumult over nothing.
Creon: Nothing? No, sister: what your husband plans for me
    Is one of two great evils: exile or death.
Oedipus: He is right.

                Why, woman, I have caught him squarely   125
Plotting against my life.
Creon: No! Let me die
    Accurst if ever I have wished you harm!
Iocastê: Ah, believe it, Oedipus!
    In the name of the gods, respect this oath of his
    For my sake, for the sake of these people here!   130

                                      Strophe 1

Choragos: Open your mind to her, my lord. Be ruled by her, I beg you!
Oedipus: What would you have me do?
Choragos: Respect Creon's word. He has never spoken like a fool,
    And now he has sworn an oath.
Oedipus: You know what you ask?
Choragos: I do.
Oedipus: Speak on, then.
Choragos: A friend so sworn should not be baited so,   135
    In blind malice, and without final proof.
Oedipus: You are aware, I hope, that what you say
    Means death for me, or exile at the least.

                                      Strophe 2

Choragos: No, I swear by Helios, first in Heaven!
    May I die friendless and accurst,   140
    The worst of deaths, if ever I meant that!
        It is the withering fields
            That hurt my sick heart:
        Must we bear all these ills,
            And now your bad blood as well?   145
Oedipus: Then let him go. And let me die, if I must,
    Or be driven by him in shame from the land of Thebes.
    It is your unhappiness, and not his talk,
    That touches me.
                As for him—
    Wherever he goes, hatred will follow him.   150
Creon: Ugly in yielding, as you were ugly in rage!
    Natures like yours chiefly torment themselves.
Oedipus: Can you not go? Can you not leave me?
Creon: I can.
    You do not know me; but the city knows me,
    And in its eyes I am just, if not in yours.   155

    Exit Creon.

                                    Antistrophe 1

Choragos: Lady Iocastê, did you not ask the King to go to his chambers?
Iocastê: First tell me what has happened.
Choragos: There was suspicion without evidence; yet it rankled
    As even false charges will.
Iocastê: On both sides?
Choragos: On both.
Iocastê: But what was said?
Choragos: Oh let it rest, let it be done with!   160
    Have we not suffered enough?
Oedipus: You see to what your decency has brought you:
    You have made difficulties where my heart saw none.

                                      Antistrophe 2

Choragos: Oedipus, it is not once only I have told you—
    You must know I should count myself unwise   165
    To the point of madness, should I now forsake you—
        You, under whose hand,
            In the storm of another time,
        Our dear land sailed out free.
            But now stand fast at the helm!   170
Iocastê: In God's name, Oedipus, inform your wife as well:
    Why are you so set in this hard anger?
Oedipus: I will tell you, for none of these men deserves
    My confidence as you do. It is Creon's work,
    His treachery, his plotting against me.   175
Iocastê: Go on, if you can make this clear to me.
Oedipus: He charges me with the murder of Laïos.
Iocastê: Has he some knowledge? Or does he speak from hearsay?
Oedipus: He would not commit himself to such a charge,
    But he has brought in that damnable soothsayer   180
    To tell his story.
Iocastê: Set your mind at rest.
    If it is a question of soothsayers, I tell you
    That you will find no man whose craft gives knowledge
    Of the unknowable.
                Here is my proof:

An oracle was reported to Laïos once   185
(I will not say from Phoibos himself, but from
His appointed ministers, at any rate)
That his doom would be death at the hands of his own son—
His son, born of his flesh and of mine!

Now, you remember the story: Laïos was killed   190
By marauding strangers where three highways meet;
But his child had not been three days in this world

Before the King had pierced the baby's ankles
And left him to die on a lonely mountainside.

Thus, Apollo never caused that child   195
To kill his father, and it was not Laïos' fate
To die at the hands of his son, as he had feared.
This is what prophets and prophecies are worth!
Have no dread of them.
                              It is God himself
Who can show us what he wills, in his own way.   200
Oedipus: How strange a shadowy memory crossed my mind,
    Just now while you were speaking; it chilled my heart.
Iocastê: What do you mean? What memory do you speak of?
Oedipus: If I understand you, Laïos was killed
    At a place where three roads meet.
Iocastê: So it was said;   205
    We have no later story.
Oedipus: Where did it happen?
Iocastê: Phokis, it is called: at a place where the Theban Way
    Divides into the roads toward Delphi and Daulia.
Oedipus: When?
Iocastê: We had the news not long before you came
    And proved the right to your succession here.   210
Oedipus: Ah, what net has God been weaving for me?
Iocastê: Oedipus! Why does this trouble you?
Oedipus: Do not ask me yet.
    First, tell me how Laïos looked, and tell me
    How old he was.
Iocastê: He was tall, his hair just touched
    With white; his form was not unlike your own.   215
Oedipus: I think that I myself may be accurst
    By my own ignorant edict.
Iocastê: You speak strangely.
    It makes me tremble to look at you, my King.
Oedipus: I am not sure that the blind man can not see.
    But I should know better if you were to tell me—   220
Iocastê: Anything—though I dread to hear you ask it.
Oedipus: Was the King lightly escorted, or did he ride
    With a large company, as a ruler should?
Iocastê: There were five men with him in all: one was a herald,
    And a single chariot, which he was driving.   225
Oedipus: Alas, that makes it plain enough!
                              But who—
Who told you how it happened?

Iocastê: A household servant,
  The only one to escape.
Oedipus: And is he still
  A servant of ours?
Iocastê: No; for when he came back at last
  And found you enthroned in the place of the dead king,   230
  He came to me, touched my hand with his, and begged
  That I would send him away to the frontier district
  Where only the shepherds go—
  As far away from the city as I could send him.
  I granted his prayer; for although the man was a slave,   235
  He had earned more than this favor at my hands.
Oedipus: Can he be called back quickly?
Iocastê: Easily.
  But why?
Oedipus: I have taken too much upon myself
  Without enquiry; therefore I wish to consult him.
Iocastê: Then he shall come.
                      But am I not one also   240
  To whom you might confide these fears of yours?
Oedipus: That is your right; it will not be denied you,
  Now least of all; for I have reached a pitch
  Of wild foreboding. Is there anyone
  To whom I should sooner speak?   245

  Polybos of Corinth is my father.
  My mother is a Dorian: Meropê.
  I grew up chief among the men of Corinth
  Until a strange thing happened—
  Not worth my passion, it may be, but strange.   250

  At a feast, a drunken man maundering in his cups
  Cries out that I am not my father's son!

  I contained myself that night, though I felt anger
  And a sinking heart. The next day I visited
  My father and mother, and questioned them. They stormed,   255
  Calling it all the slanderous rant of a fool;
  And this relieved me. Yet the suspicion
  Remained always aching in my mind;
  I knew there was talk; I could not rest;
  And finally, saying nothing to my parents,   260
  I went to the shrine at Delphi.
  The god dismissed my question without reply;
  He spoke of other things.
                      Some were clear,

Full of wretchedness, dreadful, unbearable:
As, that I should lie with my own mother, breed   265
Children from whom all men would turn their eyes;
And that I should be my father's murderer.

I heard all this, and fled. And from that day
Corinth to me was only in the stars
Descending in that quarter of the sky,   270
As I wandered farther and farther on my way
To a land where I should never see the evil
Sung by the oracle. And I came to this country
Where, so you say, King Laïos was killed.

I will tell you all that happened there, my lady.   275

There were three highways
Coming together at a place I passed;
And there a herald came towards me, and a chariot
Drawn by horses, with a man such as you describe
Seated in it. The groom leading the horses   280
Forced me off the road at his lord's command;
But as this charioteer lurched over towards me
I struck him in my rage. The old man saw me
And brought his double goad down upon my head
As I came abreast.

                He was paid back, and more!   285
Swinging my club in this right hand I knocked him
Out of his car, and he rolled on the ground.

                              I killed him.

I killed them all.
Now if that stranger and Laïos were—kin,
Where is a man more miserable than I?   290
More hated by the gods? Citizen and alien alike
Must never shelter me or speak to me—
I must be shunned by all.

                And I myself
Pronounced this malediction upon myself!

Think of it: I have touched you with these hands,   295
These hands that killed your husband. What defilement!

Am I all evil, then? It must be so,
Since I must flee from Thebes, yet never again
See my own countrymen, my own country,

For fear of joining my mother in marriage 300
And killing Polybos, my father.
                    Ah,
If I was created so, born to this fate,
Who could deny the savagery of God?

O holy majesty of heavenly powers!
May I never see that day! Never! 305
Rather let me vanish from the race of men
Than know the abomination destined me!
Choragos: We too, my lord, have felt dismay at this.
    But there is hope: you have yet to hear the shepherd.
Oedipus: Indeed, I fear no other hope is left me. 310
Iocastê: What do you hope from him when he comes?
Oedipus: This much:
If his account of the murder tallies with yours,
    Then I am cleared.
Iocastê: What was it that I said
    Of such importance?
Oedipus: Why, "marauders," you said,
    Killed the King, according to this man's story. 315
    If he maintains that still, if there were several,
    Clearly the guilt is not mine: I was alone.
    But if he says one man, singlehanded, did it,
    Then the evidence all points to me.
Iocastê: You may be sure that he said there were several; 320
    And can he call back that story now? He can not.
    The whole city heard it as plainly as I.
    But suppose he alters some detail of it:
    He can not ever show that Laïos' death
    Fulfilled the oracle: for Apollo said 325
    My child was doomed to kill him; and my child—
    Poor baby!—it was my child that died first.

    No. From now on, where oracles are concerned,
    I would not waste a second thought on any.
Oedipus: You may be right.
                    But come: let someone go 330
    For the shepherd at once. This matter must be settled.
Iocastê: I will send for him.
    I would not wish to cross you in anything,
    And surely not in this.—Let us go in.

Exeunt into the palace.

ODE II

Chorus: Let me be reverent in the ways of right,   *Strophe 1*
    Lowly the paths I journey on;
    Let all my words and actions keep
    The laws of the pure universe
    From highest Heaven handed down.   5
    For Heaven is their bright nurse,
    Those generations of the realms of light;
    Ah, never of mortal kind were they begot,
    Nor are they slaves of memory, lost in sleep:
    Their Father is greater than Time, and ages not.   10

                                       Antistrophe 1

    The tyrant is a child of Pride
    Who drinks from his great sickening cup
    Recklessness and vanity,
    Until from his high crest headlong
    He plummets to the dust of hope.   15
    That strong man is not strong.
    But let no fair ambition be denied;
    May God protect the wrestler for the State
    In government, in comely policy,
    Who will fear God, and on His ordinance wait.   20

                                       Strophe 2

    Haughtiness and the high hand of disdain
    Tempt and outrage God's holy law;
    And any mortal who dares hold
    No immortal Power in awe
    Will be caught up in a net of pain: 25
    The price for which his levity is sold.
    Let each man take due earnings, then,
    And keep his hands from holy things,
    And from blasphemy stand apart—
    Else the crackling blast of heaven   30
    Blows on his head, and on his desperate heart;
    Though fools will honor impious men,
    In their cities no tragic poet sings.

                                     Antistrophe 2

    Shall we lose faith in Delphi's obscurities,
    We who have heard the world's core   35
    Discredited, and the sacred wood
    Of Zeus at Elis praised no more?
    The deeds and the strange prophecies
    Must make a pattern yet to be understood.

Zeus, if indeed you are lord of all, 40
Throned in light over night and day,
Mirror this in your endless mind:
Our masters call the oracle
Words on the wind, and the Delphic vision blind!
Their hearts no longer know Apollo, 45
And reverence for the gods has died away.

SCENE III

Enter Iocastê.

Iocastê: Princes of Thebes, it has occurred to me
    To visit the altars of the gods, bearing
    These branches as a suppliant, and this incense.
    Our King is not himself: his noble soul
    Is overwrought with fantasies of dread, 5
    Else he would consider
    The new prophecies in the light of the old.
    He will listen to any voice that speaks disaster,
    And my advice goes for nothing.

She approaches the altar, right.

                          To you, then, Apollo,
    Lycean lord, since you are nearest, I turn in prayer. 10
    Receive these offerings, and grant us deliverance
    From defilement. Our hearts are heavy with fear
    When we see our leader distracted, as helpless sailors
    Are terrified by the confusion of their helmsman.

Enter Messenger.

Messenger: Friends, no doubt you can direct me: 15
    Where shall I find the house of Oedipus,
    Or, better still, where is the King himself?
Choragos: It is this very place, stranger; he is inside.
    This is his wife and mother of his children.
Messenger: I wish her happiness in a happy house, 20
    Blest in all the fulfillment of her marriage.
Iocastê: I wish as much for you: your courtesy
    Deserves a like good fortune. But now, tell me:
    Why have you come? What have you to say to us?
Messenger: Good news, my lady, for your house and your husband. 25
Iocastê: What news? Who sent you here?
Messenger: I am from Corinth.

The news I bring ought to mean joy for you,
Though it may be you will find some grief in it.
Iocastê: What is it? How can it touch us in both ways?
Messenger: The word is that the people of the Isthmus   30
Intend to call Oedipus to be their king.
Iocastê: But old King Polybos—is he not reigning still?
Messenger: No. Death holds him in his sepulchre.
Iocastê: What are you saying? Polybos is dead?
Messenger: If I am not telling the truth, may I die myself.   35
Iocastê (*to a Maidservant*): Go in, go quickly; tell this to your master.

O riddlers of God's will, where are you now!
This was the man whom Oedipus, long ago,
Feared so, fled so, in dread of destroying him—
But it was another fate by which he died.   40

Enter Oedipus, center.

Oedipus: Dearest Iocastê, why have you sent for me?
Iocastê: Listen to what this man says, and then tell me
What has become of the solemn prophecies.
Oedipus: Who is this man? What is his news for me?
Iocastê: He has come from Corinth to announce your father's death!   45
Oedipus: Is it true, stranger? Tell me in your own words.
Messenger: I can not say it more clearly: the King is dead.
Oedipus: Was it by treason? Or by an attack of illness?
Messenger: A little thing brings old men to their rest.
Oedipus: It was sickness, then?
Messenger: Yes, and his many years.   50
Oedipus: Ah!
Why should a man respect the Pythian hearth,° or
Give heed to the birds that jangle above his head?
They prophesied that I should kill Polybos,
Kill my own father; but he is dead and buried,   55
And I am here—I never touched him, never,
Unless he died of grief for my departure,
And thus, in a sense, through me. No. Polybos
Has packed the oracles off with him underground.
They are empty words.
Iocastê: Had I not told you so?   60
Oedipus: You had; it was my faint heart that betrayed me.
Iocastê: From now on never think of those things again.
Oedipus: And yet—must I not fear my mother's bed?

---

52 *Pythian hearth:* the shrine at Delphi, whose priestess was famous for her prophecies.

Iocastê: Why should anyone in this world be afraid,
    Since Fate rules us and nothing can be foreseen?   65
    A man should live only for the present day.

    Have no more fear of sleeping with your mother:
    How many men, in dreams, have lain with their mothers!
    No reasonable man is troubled by such things.
Oedipus: That is true; only—   70
    If only my mother were not still alive!
    But she is alive. I can not help my dread.
Iocastê: Yet this news of your father's death is wonderful.
Oedipus: Wonderful. But I fear the living woman.
Messenger: Tell me, who is this woman that you fear?   75
Oedipus: It is Meropê, man; the wife of King Polybos.
Messenger: Meropê? Why should you be afraid of her?
Oedipus: An oracle of the gods, a dreadful saying.
Messenger: Can you tell me about it or are you sworn to silence?
Oedipus: I can tell you, and I will.   80
    Apollo said through his prophet that I was the man
    Who should marry his own mother, shed his father's blood
    With his own hands. And so, for all these years
    I have kept clear of Corinth, and no harm has come—
    Though it would have been sweet to see my parents again.   85
Messenger: And is this the fear that drove you out of Corinth?
Oedipus: Would you have me kill my father?
Messenger: As for that
    You must be reassured by the news I gave you.
Oedipus: If you could reassure me, I would reward you.
Messenger: I had that in mind, I will confess: I thought   90
    I could count on you when you returned to Corinth.
Oedipus: No: I will never go near my parents again.
Messenger: Ah, son, you still do not know what you are doing—
Oedipus: What do you mean? In the name of God tell me!
Messenger: —If these are your reasons for not going home.   95
Oedipus: I tell you, I fear the oracle may come true.
Messenger: And guilt may come upon you through your parents?
Oedipus: That is the dread that is always in my heart.
Messenger: Can you not see that all your fears are groundless?
Oedipus: How can you say that? They are my parents, surely?   100
Messenger: Polybos was not your father.
Oedipus: Not my father?
Messenger: No more your father than the man speaking to you.
Oedipus: But you are nothing to me!
Messenger: Neither was he.

Oedipus: Then why did he call me son?
Messenger: I will tell you:
    Long ago he had you from my hands, as a gift.   105
Oedipus: Then how could he love me so, if I was not his?
Messenger: He had no children, and his heart turned to you.
Oedipus: What of you? Did you buy me? Did you find me by chance?
Messenger: I came upon you in the crooked pass of Kithairon.
Oedipus: And what were you doing there?
Messenger: Tending my flocks.   110
Oedipus: A wandering shepherd?
Messenger: But your savior, son, that day.
Oedipus: From what did you save me?
Messenger: Your ankles should tell you that.
Oedipus: Ah, stranger, why do you speak of that childhood pain?
Messenger: I cut the bonds that tied your ankles together.
Oedipus: I have had the mark as long as I can remember.   115
Messenger: That was why you were given the name you bear.
Oedipus: God! Was it my father or my mother who did it?
    Tell me!
Messenger: I do not know. The man who gave you to me
    Can tell you better than I.   120
Oedipus: It was not you that found me, but another?
Messenger: It was another shepherd gave you to me.
Oedipus: Who was he? Can you tell me who he was?
Messenger: I think he was said to be one of Laïos' people.
Oedipus: You mean the Laïos who was king here years ago?   125
Messenger: Yes; King Laïos; and the man was one of his herdsmen.
Oedipus: Is he still alive? Can I see him?
Messenger: These men here
    Know best about such things.
Oedipus: Does anyone here
    Know this shepherd that he is talking about?
    Have you seen him in the fields, or in the town?   130
    If you have, tell me. It is time things were made plain.
Choragos: I think the man he means is that same shepherd
    You have already asked to see. Iocastê perhaps
    Could tell you something.
Oedipus: Do you know anything
    About him, Lady? Is he the man we have summoned?   135
    Is that the man this shepherd means?
Iocastê: Why think of him?
    Forget this herdsman. Forget it all.
    This talk is a waste of time.
Oedipus: How can you say that,

When the clues to my true birth are in my hands?

Iocastê: For God's love, let us have no more questioning!   140
Is your life nothing to you?
My own is pain enough for me to bear.

Oedipus: You need not worry. Suppose my mother a slave,
And born of slaves: no baseness can touch you.

Iocastê: Listen to me, I beg you: do not do this thing!   145

Oedipus: I will not listen; the truth must be made known.

Iocastê: Everything that I say is for your own good!

Oedipus: My own good
Snaps my patience, then; I want none of it.

Iocastê: You are fatally wrong! May you never learn who you are!

Oedipus: Go, one of you, and bring the shepherd here.   150
Let us leave this woman to brag of her royal name.

Iocastê: Ah, miserable!
That is the only word I have for you now.
That is the only word I can ever have.

Exit into the palace.

Choragos: Why has she left us, Oedipus? Why has she gone   155
In such a passion of sorrow? I fear this silence:
Something dreadful may come of it.

Oedipus: Let it come!
However base my birth, I must know about it.
The Queen, like a woman, is perhaps ashamed
To think of my low origin. But I   160
Am a child of Luck; I can not be dishonored.
Luck is my mother; the passing months, my brothers,
Have seen me rich and poor.
                              If this is so,
How could I wish that I were someone else?
How could I not be glad to know my birth?   165

ODE III

Chorus: If ever the coming time were known
To my heart's pondering,
Kithairon, now by Heaven I see the torches
At the festival of the next full moon,
And see the dance, and hear the choir sing   5
A grace to your gentle shade:
Mountain where Oedipus was found,
O mountain guard of a noble race!

May the god who heals us lend his aid,
And let that glory come to pass   10
For our king's cradling-ground.

Antistrophe

Of the nymphs that flower beyond the years,
Who bore you, royal child,
To Pan of the hills or the timberline Apollo,
Cold in delight where the upland clears,   15
Or Hermês for whom Kyllenê's° heights are piled?
Or flushed as evening cloud,
Great Dionysos, roamer of mountains,
He—was it he who found you there,
And caught you up in his own proud   20
Arms from the sweet god-ravisher
Who laughed by the Muses' fountains?

SCENE IV

Oedipus: Sirs: though I do not know the man,
   I think I see him coming, this shepherd we want:
   He is old, like our friend here, and the men
   Bringing him seem to be servants of my house.
   But you can tell, if you have ever seen him.   5

   Enter Shepherd escorted by servants.

Choragos: I know him, he was Laïos' man. You can trust him.
Oedipus: Tell me first, you from Corinth: is this the shepherd
   We were discussing?
Messenger: This is the very man.
Oedipus (to Shepherd): Come here. No, look at me. You must answer
   Everything I ask.—You belonged to Laïos?   10
Shepherd: Yes: born his slave, brought up in his house.
Oedipus: Tell me: what kind of work did you do for him?
Shepherd: I was a shepherd of his, most of my life.
Oedipus: Where mainly did you go for pasturage?
Shepherd: Sometimes Kithairon, sometimes the hills near-by.   15
Oedipus: Do you remember ever seeing this man out there?
Shepherd: What would he be doing there? This man?
Oedipus: This man standing here. Have you ever seen him before?

---

16 *Kyllenê*: a sacred mountain, birthplace of Hermês, the deities' messenger. The chorus assumes
that the mountain was created in order to afford him birth.

Shepherd: No. At least, not to my recollection.

Messenger: And that is not strange, my lord. But I'll refresh   20
His memory: he must remember when we two
Spent three whole seasons together, March to September,
On Kithairon or thereabouts. He had two flocks;
I had one. Each autumn I'd drive mine home
And he would go back with his to Laïos' sheepfold.—   25
Is this not true, just as I have described it?

Shepherd: True, yes; but it was all so long ago.

Messenger: Well, then: do you remember, back in those days
That you gave me a baby boy to bring up as my own?

Shepherd: What if I did? What are you trying to say?   30

Messenger: King Oedipus was once that little child.

Shepherd: Damn you, hold your tongue!

Oedipus: No more of that!
It is your tongue needs watching, not this man's.

Shepherd: My King, my Master, what is it I have done wrong?

Oedipus: You have not answered his question about the boy.   35

Shepherd: He does not know . . . He is only making trouble . . .

Oedipus: Come, speak plainly, or it will go hard with you.

Shepherd: In God's name, do not torture an old man!

Oedipus: Come here, one of you; bind his arms behind him.

Shepherd: Unhappy king! What more do you wish to learn?   40

Oedipus: Did you give this man the child he speaks of?

Shepherd: I did.
And I would to God I had died that very day.

Oedipus: You will die now unless you speak the truth.

Shepherd: Yet if I speak the truth, I am worse than dead.

Oedipus: Very well; since you insist upon delaying—   45

Shepherd: No! I have told you already that I gave him the boy.

Oedipus: Where did you get him? From your house? From somewhere else?

Shepherd: Not from mine, no. A man gave him to me.

Oedipus: Is that man here? Do you know whose slave he was?

Shepherd: For God's love, my King, do not ask me any more!   50

Oedipus: You are a dead man if I have to ask you again.

Shepherd: Then . . . Then the child was from the palace of Laïos.

Oedipus: A slave child? or a child of his own line?

Shepherd: Ah, I am on the brink of dreadful speech!

Oedipus: And I of dreadful hearing. Yet I must hear.   55

Shepherd: If you must be told, then . . .
                    They said it was Laïos' child;
But it is your wife who can tell you about that.

Oedipus: My wife!—Did she give it to you?

Shepherd: My lord, she did.

Oedipus: Do you know why?
Shepherd: I was told to get rid of it.
Oedipus: An unspeakable mother!
Shepherd: There had been prophecies . . .   60
Oedipus: Tell me.
Shepherd: It was said that the boy would kill his own father.
Oedipus: Then why did you give him over to this old man?
Shepherd: I pitied the baby, my King,
    And I thought that this man would take him far away   65
    To his own country.
                    He saved him—but for what a fate!
    For if you are what this man says you are,
    No man living is more wretched than Oedipus.
Oedipus: Ah God!
    It was true!
        All the prophecies!
                    —Now,   70
    O Light, may I look on you for the last time!
    I, Oedipus,
    Oedipus, damned in his birth, in his marriage damned,
    Damned in the blood he shed with his own hand!

He rushes into the palace.

ODE IV

Strophe 1

Chorus: Alas for the seed of men.

    What measure shall I give these generations
    That breathe on the void and are void
    And exist and do not exist?

    Who bears more weight of joy   5
    Than mass of sunlight shifting in images,
    Or who shall make his thought stay on
    That down time drifts away?

    Your splendor is all fallen.

    O naked brow of wrath and tears,   10
    O change of Oedipus!
    I who saw your days call no man blest—
    Your great days like ghosts gone.

Antistrophe 1

    That mind was a strong bow.

Deep, how deep you drew it then, hard archer,   15
At a dim fearful range,
And brought dear glory down!

You overcame the stranger—
The virgin with her hooking lion claws—
And though death sang, stood like a tower   20
To make pale Thebes take heart.

Fortress against our sorrow!

True king, giver of laws,
Majestic Oedipus!
No prince in Thebes had ever such renown,   25
No prince won such grace of power.

Strophe 2

And now of all men ever known
Most pitiful is this man's story:
His fortunes are most changed, his state
Fallen to a low slave's   30
Ground under bitter fate.

O Oedipus, most royal one!
The great door that expelled you to the light
Gave at night—ah, gave night to your glory:
As to the father, to the fathering son.   35

All understood too late.

How could that queen whom Laïos won,
The garden that he harrowed at his height,
Be silent when that act was done?

Antistrophe 2

But all eyes fail before time's eye,   40
All actions come to justice there.
Though never willed, though far down the deep past,
Your bed, your dread sirings,
Are brought to book at last.

Child by Laïos doomed to die,   45
Then doomed to lose that fortunate little death,
Would God you never took breath in this air
That with my wailing lips I take to cry:

For I weep the world's outcast.

I was blind, and now I can tell why: 50
Asleep, for you had given ease of breath
To Thebes, while the false years went by.

ÉXODOS°

Enter, from the palace, Second Messenger.

Second Messenger: Elders of Thebes, most honored in this land,
What horrors are yours to see and hear, what weight
Of sorrow to be endured, if, true to your birth,
You venerate the line of Labdakos!
I think neither Istros nor Phasis, those great rivers,   5
Could purify this place of the corruption
It shelters now, or soon must bring to light—
Evil not done unconsciously, but willed.

The greatest griefs are those we cause ourselves.
Choragos: Surely, friend, we have grief enough already;   10
What new sorrow do you mean?
Second Messenger: The Queen is dead.
Choragos: Iocastê? Dead? But at whose hand?
Second Messenger: Her own.
The full horror of what happened, you can not know,
For you did not see it; but I, who did, will tell you
As clearly as I can how she met her death.   15

When she had left us,
In passionate silence, passing through the court,
She ran to her apartment in the house,
Her hair clutched by the fingers of both hands.
She closed the doors behind her; then, by that bed   20
Where long ago the fatal son was conceived—
That son who should bring about his father's death—
We heard her call upon Laïos, dead so many years,
And heard her wail for the double fruit of her marriage,
A husband by her husband, children by her child.   25

Exactly how she died I do not know:
For Oedipus burst in moaning and would not let us
Keep vigil to the end: it was by him
As he stormed about the room that our eyes were caught.
From one to another of us he went, begging a sword,   30
Cursing the wife who was not his wife, the mother
Whose womb had carried his own children and himself.
I do not know: it was none of us aided him,
But surely one of the gods was in control!
For with a dreadful cry   35

Éxodos: final scene, containing the resolution.

He hurled his weight, as though wrenched out of himself,
At the twin doors: the bolts gave, and he rushed in.
And there we saw her hanging, her body swaying
From the cruel cord she had noosed about her neck.
A great sob broke from him, heartbreaking to hear,   40
As he loosed the rope and lowered her to the ground.

I would blot out from my mind what happened next!
For the King ripped from her gown the golden brooches
That were her ornament, and raised them, and plunged them down
Straight into his own eyeballs, crying, "No more,   45
No more shall you look on the misery about me,
The horrors of my own doing! Too long you have known
The faces of those whom I should never have seen,
Too long been blind to those for whom I was searching!
From this hour, go in darkness!" And as he spoke,   50
He struck at his eyes—not once, but many times;
And the blood spattered his beard,
Bursting from his ruined sockets like red hail.

So from the unhappiness of two this evil has sprung,
A curse on the man and woman alike. The old   55
Happiness of the house of Labdakos
Was happiness enough: where is it today?
It is all wailing and ruin, disgrace, death—all
The misery of mankind that has a name—
And it is wholly and for ever theirs.   60
Choragos: Is he in agony still? Is there no rest for him?
Second Messenger: He is calling for someone to lead him to the gates
So that all the children of Kadmos may look upon
His father's murderer, his mother's—no,
I can not say it!
               And then he will leave Thebes,   65
Self-exiled, in order that the curse
Which he himself pronounced may depart from the house.
He is weak, and there is none to lead him,
So terrible is his suffering.
              But you will see:
Look, the doors are opening; in a moment   70
You will see a thing that would crush a heart of stone.

The central door is opened; Oedipus, blinded, is led in.

Choragos: Dreadful indeed for men to see.
    Never have my own eyes
Looked on a sight so full of fear.

Oedipus!   75
What madness came upon you, what daemon
Leaped on your life with heavier
Punishment than a mortal man can bear?
No: I can not even
Look at you, poor ruined one.   80
And I would speak, question, ponder,
If I were able. No.
You make me shudder.
Oedipus: God. God.
    Is there a sorrow greater?   85
    Where shall I find harbor in this world?
    My voice is hurled far on a dark wind.
    What has God done to me?
Choragos: Too terrible to think of, or to see.

                                                              Strophe 1

Oedipus: O cloud of night,   90
    Never to be turned away: night coming on,
    I can not tell how: night like a shroud!

    My fair winds brought me here.
                                        Oh God. Again
    The pain of the spikes where I had sight,
    The flooding pain   95
    Of memory, never to be gouged out.
Choragos: This is not strange.
    You suffer it all twice over, remorse in pain,
    Pain in remorse.

                                                           Antistrophe 1

Oedipus: Ah dear friend   100
    Are you faithful even yet, you alone?
    Are you still standing near me, will you stay here,
    Patient, to care for the blind?
                                      The blind man!
    Yet even blind I know who it is attends me,
    By the voice's tone—   105
    Though my new darkness hide the comforter.
Choragos: Oh fearful act!
    What god was it drove you to rake black
    Night across your eyes?

                                                              Strophe 2

Oedipus: Apollo. Apollo. Dear   110
    Children, the god was Apollo.

He brought my sick, sick fate upon me.
But the blinding hand was my own!
How could I bear to see
When all my sight was horror everywhere?   115
Choragos: Everywhere; that is true.
Oedipus: And now what is left?
   Images? Love? A greeting even,
   Sweet to the senses? Is there anything?
   Ah, no, friends: lead me away.   120
   Lead me away from Thebes.
                        Lead the great wreck
   And hell of Oedipus, whom the gods hate.
Choragos: Your fate is clear, you are not blind to that.
   Would God you had never found it out!

                                                      Antistrophe 2

Oedipus: Death take the man who unbound   125
   My feet on that hillside
   And delivered me from death to life! What life?
   If only I had died,
   This weight of monstrous doom
   Could not have dragged me and my darlings down.   130
Choragos: I would have wished the same.
Oedipus: Oh never to have come here
   With my father's blood upon me! Never
   To have been the man they call his mother's husband!
   Oh accurst! Oh child of evil,   135
   To have entered that wretched bed—
                        the selfsame one!
   More primal than sin itself, this fell to me.
Choragos: I do not know how I can answer you.
   You were better dead than alive and blind.
Oedipus: Do not counsel me any more. This punishment   140
   That I have laid upon myself is just.
   If I had eyes,
   I do not know how I could bear the sight
   Of my father, when I came to the house of Death,
   Or my mother: for I have sinned against them both   145
   So vilely that I could not make my peace
   By strangling my own life.
                        Or do you think my children,
   Born as they were born, would be sweet to my eyes?
   Ah never, never! Nor this town with its high walls,
   Nor the holy images of the gods.
                        For I,   145

Thrice miserable!—Oedipus, noblest of all the line
Of Kadmos, have condemned myself to enjoy
These things no more, by my own malediction
Expelling that man whom the gods declared
To be a defilement in the house of Laïos.   155
After exposing the rankness of my own guilt,
How could I look men frankly in the eyes?
No, I swear it,
If I could have stifled my hearing at its source,
I would have done it and made all this body   160
A tight cell of misery, blank to light and sound:
So I should have been safe in a dark agony
Beyond all recollection.
                                  Ah Kithairon!
Why did you shelter me? When I was cast upon you,
Why did I not die? Then I should never   165
Have shown the world my execrable birth.

Ah Polybos! Corinth, city that I believed
The ancient seat of my ancestors: how fair
I seemed, your child! And all the while this evil
Was cancerous within me!
                            For I am sick   170
In my daily life, sick in my origin.

O three roads, dark ravine, woodland and way
Where three roads met: you, drinking my father's blood,
My own blood, spilled by my own hand: can you remember
The unspeakable things I did there, and the things   175
I went on from there to do?
                            O marriage, marriage!
The act that engendered me, and again the act
Performed by the son in the same bed—
                                  Ah, the net
Of incest, mingling fathers, brothers, sons,
With brides, wives, mothers: the last evil   180
That can be known by men: no tongue can say
How evil!
          No. For the love of God, conceal me
Somewhere far from Thebes; or kill me; or hurl me
Into the sea, away from men's eyes for ever.

Come, lead me. You need not fear to touch me.   185
Of all men, I alone can bear this guilt.

Enter Creon.

Choragos: We are not the ones to decide; but Creon here
    May fitly judge of what you ask. He only
    Is left to protect the city in your place.
Oedipus: Alas, how can I speak to him? What right have I   190
    To beg his courtesy whom I have deeply wronged?
Creon: I have not come to mock you, Oedipus,
    Or to reproach you, either.
    (*To Attendants.*)   —You, standing there:
    If you have lost all respect for man's dignity,
    At least respect the flame of Lord Helios: 195
    Do not allow this pollution to show itself
    Openly here, an affront to the earth
    And Heaven's rain and the light of day. No, take him
    Into the house as quickly as you can.
    For it is proper   200
    That only the close kindred see his grief.
Oedipus: I pray you in God's name, since your courtesy
    Ignores my dark expectation, visiting
    With mercy this man of all men most execrable:
    Give me what I ask—for your good, not for mine.   205
Creon: And what is it that you would have me do?
Oedipus: Drive me out of this country as quickly as may be
    To a place where no human voice can ever greet me.
Creon: I should have done that before now—only,
    God's will had not been wholly revealed to me.   210
Oedipus: But his command is plain: the parricide
    Must be destroyed. I am that evil man.
Creon: That is the sense of it, yes; but as things are,
    We had best discover clearly what is to be done.
Oedipus: You would learn more about a man like me?   215
Creon: You are ready now to listen to the god.
Oedipus: I will listen. But it is to you
    That I must turn for help. I beg you, hear me.

    The woman in there—
    Give her whatever funeral you think proper: 220
    She is your sister.
                —But let me go, Creon!
    Let me purge my father's Thebes of the pollution
    Of my living here, and go out to the wild hills,
    To Kithairon, that has won such fame with me,
    The tomb my mother and father appointed for me,   225

And let me die there, as they willed I should.
And yet I know
Death will not ever come to me through sickness
Or in any natural way: I have been preserved
For some unthinkable fate. But let that be.   230

As for my sons, you need not care for them.
They are men, they will find some way to live.
But my poor daughters, who have shared my table,
Who never before have been parted from their father—
Take care of them, Creon; do this for me.   235
And will you let me touch them with my hands
A last time, and let us weep together?
Be kind, my lord,
Great prince, be kind!
                              Could I but touch them,
They would be mine again, as when I had my eyes.   240

Enter Antigonê and Ismene, attended.

Ah, God!
Is it my dearest children I hear weeping?
Has Creon pitied me and sent my daughters?
Creon: Yes, Oedipus: I knew that they were dear to you
In the old days, and know you must love them still.   245
Oedipus: May God bless you for this—and be a friendlier
Guardian to you than he has been to me!

Children, where are you?
Come quickly to my hands: they are your brother's—
Hands that have brought your father's once clear eyes   250
To this way of seeing—
                              Ah dearest ones,
I had neither sight nor knowledge then, your father
By the woman who was the source of his own life!
And I weep for you—having no strength to see you—,
I weep for you when I think of the bitterness   255
That men will visit upon you all your lives.
What homes, what festivals can you attend
Without being forced to depart again in tears?
And when you come to marriageable age,
Where is the man, my daughters, who would dare   260
Risk the bane that lies on all my children?
Is there any evil wanting? Your father killed

His father; sowed the womb of her who bore him;
Engendered you at the fount of his own existence!
That is what they will say of you.
Then, whom   265
Can you ever marry? There are no bridegrooms for you,
And your lives must wither away in sterile dreaming.

O Creon, son of Menoikeus!
You are the only father my daughters have,
Since we, their parents, are both of us gone for ever. 270
They are your own blood: you will not let them
Fall into beggary and loneliness;
You will keep them from the miseries that are mine!
Take pity on them; see, they are only children,
Friendless except for you. Promise me this, 275
Great Prince, and give me your hand in token of it.

Creon clasps his right hand.

Children:
I could say much, if you could understand me,
But as it is, I have only this prayer for you:
Live where you can, be as happy as you can— 280
Happier, please God, than God has made your father!
Creon: Enough. You have wept enough. Now go within.
Oedipus: I must; but it is hard.
Creon: Time eases all things.
Oedipus: But you must promise—
Creon: Say what you desire.
Oedipus: Send me from Thebes!
Creon: God grant that I may! 285
Oedipus: But since God hates me . . .
Creon: No, he will grant your wish.
Oedipus: You promise?
Creon: I can not speak beyond my knowledge.
Oedipus: Then lead me in.
Creon: Come now, and leave your children.
Oedipus: No! Do not take them from me!
Creon: Think no longer
That you are in command here, but rather think 290
How, when you were, you served your own destruction.

Exeunt into the house all but the Chorus; the Choragos chants directly to the audience.

Choragos: Men of Thebes: look upon Oedipus.

This is the king who solved the famous riddle
And towered up, most powerful of men.
No mortal eyes but looked on him with envy,   295
Yet in the end ruin swept over him.

Let every man in mankind's frailty
Consider his last day; and let none
Presume on his good fortune until he find
Life, at his death, a memory without pain.   300

QUESTIONS

1. How explicitly does the prophet Teiresias reveal the guilt of Oedipus? Does it seem to you stupidity on the part of Oedipus or a defect in Sophocles' play that the king takes so long to recognize his guilt and to admit to it?

2. How does Oedipus exhibit weakness of character? Point to lines that reveal him as imperfectly noble in his words, deeds, or treatment of others.

3. "Oedipus is punished not for any fault in himself, but for his ignorance. Not knowing his family history, unable to recognize his parents on sight, he is blameless; and in slaying his father and marrying his mother, he behaves as any sensible person might behave in the same circumstances." Do you agree with this interpretation?

4. Besides the predictions of Teiresias, what other foreshadowings of the shepherd's revelation does the play contain?

5. Consider the character of Iocastê. Is she a "flat" character—a generalized queen figure—or an individual with distinctive traits of personality? Point to speeches or details in the play to back up your opinion.

6. What is dramatic irony? Besides the example given on page 343, what other instances of dramatic irony do you find in *Oedipus the King*? What do they contribute to the effectiveness of the play?

7. In the drama of Sophocles, violence and bloodshed take place offstage; thus, the suicide of Iocastê is only reported to us. Nor do we witness Oedipus' removal of his eyes; this horror is only given in the report by the second messenger. Of what advantage or disadvantage to the play is this limitation?

8. For what reason does Oedipus blind himself? What meaning, if any, do you find in his choice of a surgical instrument?

9. What are your feelings toward him as the play ends?

10. With what attitude toward the gods does the play leave you? By inflicting a plague on Thebes, by causing barrenness, by cursing both the people and their king, do the gods seem cruel, unjust, or tyrannical? Does the play show any reverence toward them?

11. Does this play end in total gloom?

WRITING EFFECTIVELY

Some Things Change, Some Things Don't

Reading an ancient work of literature, such as Sophocles' *Oedipus the King*, you might have two contradictory reactions. On the one hand, you are likely to note how differently people thought, spoke, and conducted themselves in the ancient world from the way they do now. On the other hand, you might notice how many facets of human nature remain constant across the ages. Though Sophocles' characters are mythic, they also are recognizably human.

Writing about a classical tragedy, you should stay alert to both impulses. Be open to the play's universal appeal, but never forget its foreignness. Take note of the basic beliefs and values that the characters hold that are different from your own. How do those elements influence their actions and motivations?

In making notes for your paper, jot down something about each major character that seems odd or exotic to you. Don't worry about being too basic. The notes don't represent your finished essay, just a starting place. You might observe, for example, that Oedipus and Iocastê both believe in the power of prophecy. They also believe that Apollo and the other gods would punish the city with a plague because of an unsolved crime committed twenty years earlier. These are certainly not mainstream modern beliefs.

You do not need to understand the historical origins or cultural context of the differences you note. You can safely leave those things to scholars. What you need to observe are the differences themselves—at least a few important ones—so that you don't automatically make inaccurate modern assumptions about the characters. Keeping those differences in mind will give you greater insight into the characters.

CHECKLIST

Analyzing Greek Tragedy

- ✓ Identify the play's major characters.
- ✓ In what ways do they seem alien to you?
- ✓ What do you notice about a character's beliefs? About his or her values?
- ✓ How do these differ from your own?
- ✓ How do a character's beliefs influence his or her actions and motivations?
- ✓ In what ways are the play's characters like the people you know?
- ✓ How do these familiar qualities influence the character's actions and motivations?

WRITING ASSIGNMENT ON SOPHOCLES

Write a brief personality profile (two or three pages) of any major character in *Oedipus the King*. Describe the character's age, social position, family background, personality, and beliefs. What is his or her major motivation in the play? In what ways does the character resemble his or her modern equivalent? In what ways do they differ?

MORE TOPICS FOR WRITING

1. Suppose you face the task of directing and producing a new stage production of *Oedipus the King*. Decide how you would go about it. Would you use masks? How would you render the chorus? Would you set the play in contemporary North America? Justify your decisions by referring to the play itself.

2. Compare the version of *Oedipus the King* given in this book with a different English translation of the play. You might use, for instance, any of the versions by Robert Fagles; Gilbert Murray, J. T. Sheppard, and H. D. F. Kitto; by Paul Roche (in a Signet paperback); by William Butler Yeats (in his *Collected Plays*); by David Grene (University of Chicago Press, 1942); or by Stephen Berg and Diskin Clay (Oxford UP, 1978). Point to significant differences between the two texts. What decisions did the translators have to make? Which version do you prefer? Why?

3. Write an essay explaining how Oedipus exemplifies or refutes Aristotle's definition of a tragic hero.

25
The Theater of Shakespeare

The Theater of Shakespeare

Compared with the technical resources of a theater of today, those of a London public theater in the time of Queen Elizabeth I seem hopelessly limited. Plays had to be performed by daylight, and scenery had to be kept simple: a table, a chair, a throne, perhaps an artificial tree or two to suggest a forest. But these limitations were, in a sense, advantages. What the theater of today can spell out for us realistically, with massive scenery and electric lighting, Elizabethan playgoers had to imagine and the playwright had to make vivid for them by means of language. Not having a lighting technician to work a panel, Shakespeare had to indicate the dawn by having Horatio, in *Hamlet*, say in a speech rich in metaphor and descriptive detail:

> But look, the morn in russet mantle clad
> Walks o'er the dew of yon high eastward hill.

And yet the theater of Shakespeare was not bare, for the playwright did have *some* valuable technical resources. Costumes could be elaborate, and apparently some costumes conveyed recognized meanings: one theater manager's inventory included "a robe for to go invisible in." There could be musical accompaniment and sound effects such as gunpowder explosions and the beating of a pan to simulate thunder.

The stage itself was remarkably versatile. At its back were doors for exits and entrances and a curtained booth or alcove useful for hiding inside. Above the stage was a higher acting area—perhaps a porch or balcony—useful for a Juliet to stand upon and for a Romeo to raise his eyes to. In the stage floor was a trapdoor leading to a "hell" or cellar, especially useful for ghosts or devils who had to appear or disappear. The stage itself was a rectangular platform that projected into a yard enclosed by three-storied galleries.

The building was round or octagonal. In *Henry V*, Shakespeare calls it a "wooden O." The audience sat in these galleries or else stood in the yard in front of the stage and at its sides. A roof or awning protected the stage and the high-priced gallery seats, but in a sudden rain, the *groundlings*, who paid a penny to stand in the yard, must have been dampened.

The newly reconstructed Globe Theatre in today's London—built as an exact replica of the original

Built by the theatrical company to which Shakespeare belonged, the Globe, most celebrated of Elizabethan theaters, was not in the city of London itself but on the south bank of the Thames River. This location had been chosen because earlier, in 1574, public plays had been banished from the city by an ordinance that blamed them for "corruptions of youth and other enormities" (such as providing opportunities for prostitutes and pickpockets).

A playwright had to please all members of the audience, not only the mannered and educated. This obligation may help to explain the wide range of matter and tone in an Elizabethan play: passages of subtle poetry, of deep philosophy, of coarse bawdry; scenes of sensational violence and of quiet psychological conflict (not that most members of the audience did not enjoy all these elements). Because he was an actor as well as a playwright, Shakespeare well knew what his company could do and what his audience wanted. In devising a play, he could write a part to take advantage of some actor's specific skills, or he could avoid straining the company's resources (some of his plays have few female parts, perhaps because of a shortage of competent boy actors). The company might offer as many as thirty plays in a season, customarily changing the program daily. The actors thus had to hold many parts in their heads, which may account for Elizabethan playwrights' fondness for blank verse. Lines of fixed length were easier for actors to commit to memory.

William Shakespeare

William Shakespeare (1564–1616), the supreme writer of English, was born, baptized, and buried in the market town of Stratford-on-Avon, eighty miles from London. Son of a glove maker and merchant who was high bailiff (or mayor) of the town, he probably attended grammar school and learned to read Latin authors in the original. At eighteen, he married Anne Hathaway, twenty-six, by whom he had three children, including twins. By 1592 he had become well-known and envied as an actor and playwright in London. From 1594 until he retired, he belonged to the same theatrical company, the Lord Chamberlain's Men

WILLIAM SHAKESPEARE

(later renamed the King's Men in honor of their patron, James I), for whom he wrote thirty-six plays—some of them, such as Hamlet *and* King Lear, *profound reworkings of old plays. As an actor, Shakespeare is believed to have played supporting roles, such as the ghost of Hamlet's father. The company prospered, moved into the Globe in 1599, and in 1608 bought the fashionable Blackfriars as well; Shakespeare owned an interest in both theaters. When plagues shut down the theaters from 1592 to 1594, Shakespeare turned to story poems; his great Sonnets (published only in 1609) probably also date from the 1590s. Plays were regarded as entertainments of little literary merit, like comic books today, and Shakespeare did not bother to supervise their publication. After writing* The Tempest *(1611), the last play entirely from his hand, he retired to Stratford, where since 1597 he had owned the second-largest house in town. Most critics agree that when he wrote* Othello, *about 1604, Shakespeare was at the height of his powers.*

A Note on *Othello*

Othello, the Moor of Venice, here offered for study, may be (if you are fortunate) new to you. It is seldom taught in high school, for it is ablaze with passion and violence. Even if you already know the play, we trust that you (like your instructor and your editors) still have much more to learn from it. Following his usual practice, Shakespeare based the play on a story he had appropriated—from a tale, "Of the Unfaithfulness of Husbands and Wives," by a sixteenth-century Italian writer, Giraldi Cinthio. As he could not help but do, Shakespeare freely transformed his source material. In the original

James Earl Jones as Othello

tale, the heroine Disdemona (whose name Shakespeare so hugely improved) is beaten to death with a stocking full of sand—a shoddier death than the bard imagined for her.

Surely no character in literature can touch us more than Desdemona; no character can shock and disgust us more than Iago. Between these two extremes stands Othello, a black man of courage and dignity—and yet insecure, capable of being fooled, a pushover for bad advice. Besides breathing life into these characters and a host of others, Shakespeare—as brilliant a writer as any the world has known—enables them to speak poetry. Sometimes this poetry seems splendid and rich in imagery; at other times quiet and understated. Always, it seems to grow naturally from the nature of Shakespeare's characters and from their situations. *Othello, the Moor of Venice* has never ceased to grip readers and beholders alike. It is a safe bet that it will triumphantly live as long as fathers dislike whomever their daughters marry, as long as husbands suspect their wives of cheating, as long as blacks remember slavery, and as long as the ambitious court favor and the jealous practice deceit. The play may well make sense as long as public officials connive behind smiling faces, and it may even endure as long as the world makes room for the kind, the true, the beautiful—the blessed pure in heart.

Kenneth Branagh as Iago, Laurence Fishburne as Othello, and Nathaniel Parker as Cassio in Oliver Parker's 1995 film version of *Othello*

Othello, the Moor of Venice   1604?

EDITED BY DAVID BEVINGTON

THE NAMES OF THE ACTORS

Othello, the Moor
Brabantio, [a senator,] father to Desdemona
Cassio, an honorable lieutenant [to Othello]
Iago, [Othello's ancient,] a villain
Roderigo, a gulled gentleman
Duke of Venice
Senators [of Venice]

NOTE ON THE TEXT: This text of *Othello* is based on that of the First Folio, or large collection, of Shakespeare's plays (1623). But there are many differences between the Folio text and that of the play's first printing in the Quarto, or small volume, of 1621 (eighteen or nineteen years after the play's first performance). Some readings from the Quarto are included. For the reader's convenience, some material has been added by the editor, David Bevington (some indications of scene, some stage directions). Such additions are enclosed in brackets. Mr. Bevington's text and notes were prepared for his book, *The Complete Works of Shakespeare*, updated 4th ed. (New York: Longman, 1997).

NOTE ON PRODUCTION PHOTOS: The photos included are from the 2003 production of *Othello* by the Guthrie Theater of Minneapolis, with Larry Purry (Othello), Bill McCallum (Iago), Cheyenne Casebier (Desdemona), Robert O. Berdahl (Cassio), Virginia S. Burke (Emilia), Nathaniel Fuller (Brabantio), and Shawn Hamilton (Montano).

Montano, governor of Cyprus
Gentlemen of Cyprus
Lodovico and Gratiano, [kinsmen to Brabantio,] two noble Venetians
Sailors
Clown
Desdemona, [daughter to Brabantio and] wife to Othello
Emilia, wife to Iago
Bianca, a courtesan [and mistress to Cassio]
[A Messenger
A Herald
A Musician
Servants, Attendants, Officers, Senators, Musicians, Gentlemen

Scene. *Venice; a seaport in Cyprus*]

ACT I

SCENE I [VENICE. A STREET.]

Enter Roderigo and Iago.

Roderigo: Tush, never tell me!° I take it much unkindly
  That thou, Iago, who hast had my purse
  As if the strings were thine, shouldst know of this.°
Iago: 'Sblood,° but you'll not hear me.
  If ever I did dream of such a matter,   5
  Abhor me.
Roderigo: Thou toldst me thou didst hold him in thy hate.
Iago: Despise me
  If I do not. Three great ones of the city,
  In personal suit to make me his lieutenant,
  Off-capped to him;° and by the faith of man,   10
  I know my price, I am worth no worse a place.
  But he, as loving his own pride and purposes,
  Evades them with a bombast circumstance°
  Horribly stuffed with epithets of war,°   15
  And, in conclusion,
  Nonsuits° my mediators. For, "Certes,"° says he,
  "I have already chose my officer."

---

1 *never tell me* (An expression of incredulity, like "tell me another one.")   3 *this* i.e., Desdemona's elopement   4 *'Sblood* by His (Christ's) blood   11 *him* i.e., Othello   14 *bombast circumstance* wordy evasion. (Bombast is cotton padding.)   15 *epithets of war* military expressions   17 *Nonsuits* rejects the petition of.   *Certes* certainly

And what was he?
Forsooth, a great arithmetician,°   20
One Michael Cassio, a Florentine,
A fellow almost damned in a fair wife,°
That never set a squadron in the field
Nor the division of a battle° knows
More than a spinster°—unless the bookish theoric,°   25
Wherein the togaed° consuls° can propose°
As masterly as he. Mere prattle without practice
Is all his soldiership. But he, sir, had th' election;
And I, of whom his° eyes had seen the proof
At Rhodes, at Cyprus, and on other grounds   30
Christened° and heathen, must be beeled and calmed°
By debitor and creditor.° This countercaster,°
He, in good time,° must his lieutenant be,
And I—God bless the mark!°—his Moorship's ancient.°
Roderigo: By heaven, I rather would have been his hangman.°   35
Iago: Why, there's no remedy. 'Tis the curse of service;
Preferment° goes by letter and affection,°
And not by old gradation,° where each second
Stood heir to th' first. Now, sir, be judge yourself
Whether I in any just term° am affined°   40
To love the Moor.
Roderigo: I would not follow him then.
Iago: O sir, content you.°
I follow him to serve my turn upon him.
We cannot all be masters, nor all masters   45

---

20 *arithmetician* i.e., a man whose military knowledge is merely theoretical, based on books of tactics   22 *A . . . wife* (Cassio does not seem to be married, but his counterpart in Shakespeare's source does have a woman in his house. See also Act IV, Scene i, line 127.) 24 *division of a battle* disposition of a military unit   25 *a spinster* i.e., a housewife, one whose regular occupation is spinning.   *theoric* theory   26 *togaed* wearing the toga. *consuls* counselors, senators. *propose* discuss   29 *his* i.e., Othello's   31 *Christened* Christian. *beeled and calmed* left to leeward without wind, becalmed. (A sailing metaphor.)   32 *debitor and creditor* (A name for a system of bookkeeping, here used as a contemptuous nickname for Cassio.)   *countercaster* i.e., bookkeeper, one who tallies with *counters*, or "metal disks." (Said contemptuously.)   33 *in good time* opportunely, i.e., forsooth   34 *God bless the mark* (Perhaps originally a formula to ward off evil; here an expression of impatience.)   *ancient* standard-bearer, ensign   35 *his hangman* the executioner of him   37 *Preferment* promotion.   *letter and affection* personal influence and favoritism   38 *old gradation* step-by-step seniority, the traditional way   40 *term* respect.   *affined* bound   43 *content you* don't you worry about that

Cannot be truly° followed. You shall mark
Many a duteous and knee-crooking knave
That, doting on his own obsequious bondage,
Wears out his time, much like his master's ass,
For naught but provender, and when he's old, cashiered.°   50
Whip me° such honest knaves. Others there are
Who, trimmed in forms and visages of duty,°
Keep yet their hearts attending on themselves,
And, throwing but shows of service on their lords,
Do well thrive by them, and when they have lined their coats,°   55
Do themselves homage.° These fellows have some soul,
And such a one do I profess myself. For, sir,
It is as sure as you are Roderigo,
Were I the Moor I would not be Iago.°
In following him, I follow but myself—   60
Heaven is my judge, not I for love and duty,
But seeming so for my peculiar° end.
For when my outward action doth demonstrate
The native° act and figure° of my heart
In compliment extern,° 'tis not long after   65
But I will wear my heart upon my sleeve
For daws° to peck at. I am not what I am.°
Roderigo: What a full° fortune does the thick-lips° owe°
        If he can carry 't thus!°
Iago: Call up her father.
        Rouse him, make after him, poison his delight,   70
        Proclaim him in the streets; incense her kinsmen,
        And, though he in a fertile climate dwell,
        Plague him with flies.° Though that his joy be joy,°

---

46 *truly* faithfully   50 *cashiered* dismissed from service   51 *Whip me* whip, as far as I'm concerned   52 *trimmed . . . duty* dressed up in the mere form and show of dutifulness   55 *lined their coats* i.e., stuffed their purses   56 *Do themselves homage* i.e., attend to self-interest solely   59 *Were . . . Iago* i.e., if I were able to assume command, I certainly would not choose to remain a subordinate, or, I would keep a suspicious eye on a flattering subordinate   62 *peculiar* particular, personal   64 *native* innate. *figure* shape, intent   65 *compliment extern* outward show. (Conforming in this case to the inner workings and intention of the heart.)   67 *daws* small crowlike birds, proverbially stupid and avaricious.   *I am not what I am* i.e., I am not one who wears his heart on his sleeve   68 *full* swelling. *thick-lips* (Elizabethans often applied the term "Moor" to Negroes.)   *owe* own   69 *carry 't thus* carry this off   72–73 *though . . . flies* though he seems prosperous and happy now, vex him with misery   73 *Though . . . be joy* although he seems fortunate and happy. (Repeats the idea of line 72.)

Yet throw such changes of vexation° on 't
As it may° lose some color.°   75
Roderigo: Here is her father's house. I'll call aloud.
Iago: Do, with like timorous° accent and dire yell
    As when, by night and negligence,° the fire
    Is spied in populous cities.
Roderigo: What ho, Brabantio! Signor Brabantio, ho!   80
Iago: Awake! What ho, Brabantio! Thieves, thieves, thieves!
    Look to your house, your daughter, and your bags!
    Thieves, thieves!

Brabantio [enters] above [at a window].°

Brabantio: What is the reason of this terrible summons?
    What is the matter° there?   85
Roderigo: Signor, is all your family within?
Iago: Are your doors locked?
Brabantio: Why, wherefore ask you this?
Iago: Zounds,° sir, you're robbed. For shame, put on your gown!
    Your heart is burst; you have lost half your soul.
    Even now, now, very now, an old black ram   90
    Is tupping° your white ewe. Arise, arise!
    Awake the snorting° citizens with the bell,
    Or else the devil° will make a grandsire of you.
    Arise, I say!
Brabantio: What, have you lost your wits?
Roderigo: Most reverend signor, do you know my voice?   95
Brabantio: Not I. What are you?
Roderigo: My name is Roderigo.
Brabantio: The worser welcome.
    I have charged thee not to haunt about my doors.
    In honest plainness thou hast heard me say   100
    My daughter is not for thee; and now, in madness,
    Being full of supper and distempering° drafts,
    Upon malicious bravery° dost thou come
    To start° my quiet.

---

74 *changes of vexation* vexing changes   75 *As it may* that may cause it to.   *some color* some
of its fresh gloss   77 *timorous* frightening   78 *and negligence* i.e., by negligence   83 s.d. *at a
window* (This stage direction, from the Quarto, probably calls for an appearance on the
gallery above and rearstage.)   85 *the matter* your business   88 *Zounds* by His (Christ's)
wounds   91 *tupping* covering, copulating with. (Said of sheep.)   92 *snorting* snoring   93
the devil (The devil was conventionally pictured as black.)   102 *distempering* intoxicating
103 *Upon malicious bravery* with hostile intent to defy me   104 *start* startle, disrupt

Roderigo: Sir, sir, sir—

Brabantio: But thou must needs be sure   105
   My spirits and my place° have in° their power
   To make this bitter to thee.

Roderigo: Patience, good sir.

Brabantio: What tell'st thou me of robbing? This is Venice;
   My house is not a grange.°

Roderigo: Most grave Brabantio,
   In simple° and pure soul I come to you.   110

Iago: Zounds, sir, you are one of those that will not serve God if the devil
   bid you. Because we come to do you service and you think we are
   ruffians, you'll have your daughter covered with a Barbary° horse;
   you'll have your nephews° neigh to you; you'll have coursers° for
   cousins° and jennets° for germans.°   115

Brabantio: What profane wretch art thou?

Iago: I am one, sir, that comes to tell you your daughter and the Moor
   are now making the beast with two backs.

Brabantio: Thou art a villain.

Iago: You are—a senator.°

Brabantio: This thou shalt answer.° I know thee, Roderigo.   120

Roderigo: Sir, I will answer anything. But I beseech you,
   If't be your pleasure and most wise° consent—
   As partly I find it is—that your fair daughter,
   At this odd-even° and dull watch o' the night,
   Transported with° no worse nor better guard   125
   But with a knave° of common hire, a gondolier,
   To the gross clasps of a lascivious Moor—
   If this be known to you and your allowance°
   We then have done you bold and saucy° wrongs.
   But if you know not this, my manners tell me   130
   We have your wrong rebuke. Do not believe
   That, from° the sense of all civility,°

---

106 *My spirits and my place* my temperament and my authority of office. *have in* have it in
109 *grange* isolated country house   110 *simple* sincere   113 *Barbary* from northern Africa
(and hence associated with Othello)   114 *nephews* i.e., grandsons. *coursers* powerful
horses. *cousins* kinsmen.   115 *jennets* small Spanish horses. *germans* near relatives   119 *a
senator* (Said with mock politeness, as though the word itself were an insult.)   120 *answer*
be held accountable for   122 *wise* well-informed   124 *odd-even* between one day and the
next, i.e., about midnight   125 *with* by   126 *But with a knave* than by a low fellow, a servant   128 *allowance* permission   129 *saucy* insolent   132 *from* contrary to. *civility* good
manners, decency

I thus would play and trifle with your reverence.°
Your daughter, if you have not given her leave,
I say again, hath made a gross revolt,   135
Tying her duty, beauty, wit,° and fortunes
In an extravagant° and wheeling° stranger°
Of here and everywhere. Straight° satisfy yourself.
If she be in her chamber or your house,
Let loose on me the justice of the state   140
For thus deluding you.

Brabantio: Strike on the tinder,° ho!
Give me a taper! Call up all my people!
This accident° is not unlike my dream.
Belief of it oppresses me already.   145
Light, I say, light!   *Exit [above].*

Iago: Farewell, for I must leave you.
It seems not meet° nor wholesome to my place°
To be produced°—as, if I stay, I shall—
Against the Moor. For I do know the state,
However this may gall° him with some check,°   150
Cannot with safety cast° him, for he's embarked°
With such loud reason° to the Cyprus wars,
Which even now stands in act,° that, for their souls,°
Another of his fathom° they have none
To lead their business; in which regard,°   155
Though I do hate him as I do hell pains,
Yet for necessity of present life°
I must show out a flag and sign of love,
Which is indeed but sign. That you shall surely find him,
Lead to the Sagittary° the raisèd search,°   160
And there will I be with him. So farewell.   *Exit.*

Enter [below] Brabantio [in his nightgown°] with servants and torches.

---

133 *your reverence* the respect due to you   136 *wit* intelligence   137 *extravagant* expatriate,
wandering far from home. *wheeling* roving about, vagabond. *stranger* foreigner   138 *Straight*
straightway   142 *tinder* charred linen ignited by a spark from flint and steel, used to light
torches or *tapers* (lines 143, 168)   144 *accident* occurrence, event   147 *meet* fitting. *place* position (as ensign)   148 *produced* produced (as a witness)   150 *gall* rub; oppress. *check* rebuke
151 *cast* dismiss. *embarked* engaged   152 *loud reason* unanimous shout of confirmation (in the
Senate)   153 *stands in act* are going on.   *for their souls* to save themselves   154 *fathom* i.e.,
ability, depth of experience   155 *in which regard* out of regard for which   157 *life* liveli-
hood   160 *Sagittary* (An inn or house where Othello and Desdemona are staying, named
for its sign of Sagittarius, or Centaur.)   *raisèd search* search party roused out of sleep   161
s.d. *nightgown* dressing gown. (This costuming is specified in the Quarto text.)

Roused from sleep, Desdemona's father, Brabantio, rushes to the street to search out his daughter (I, i, 161–185).

Brabantio: It is too true an evil. Gone she is;
　　And what's to come of my despisèd time°
　　Is naught but bitterness. Now, Roderigo,
　　Where didst thou see her?—O unhappy girl!—　　　　　　165
　　With the Moor, sayst thou?—Who would be a father!—
　　How didst thou know 'twas she?—O, she deceives me

163 *time* i.e., remainder of life

Past thought!—What said she to you?—Get more tapers.
Raise all my kindred.—Are they married, think you?
Roderigo: Truly, I think they are.   170
Brabantio: O heaven! How got she out? O treason of the blood!
    Fathers, from hence trust not your daughters' minds
    By what you see them act. Is there not charms°
    By which the property° of youth and maidhood
    May be abused?° Have you not read, Roderigo,   175
    Of some such thing?
Roderigo: Yes, sir, I have indeed.
Brabantio: Call up my brother.—O, would you had had her!—
    Some one way, some another.—Do you know
    Where we may apprehend her and the Moor?
Roderigo: I think I can discover° him, if you please   180
    To get good guard and go along with me.
Brabantio: Pray you, lead on. At every house I'll call;
    I may command° at most.—Get weapons, ho!
    And raise some special officers of night.—
    On, good Roderigo. I will deserve° your pains.   185

Exeunt.

SCENE II [VENICE. ANOTHER STREET, BEFORE OTHELLO'S LODGINGS.]

Enter Othello, Iago, attendants with torches.

Iago: Though in the trade of war I have slain men,
    Yet do I hold it very stuff° o' the conscience
    To do no contrived° murder. I lack iniquity
    Sometimes to do me service. Nine or ten times
    I had thought t' have yerked° him° here under the ribs.   5
Othello: 'Tis better as it is.
Iago: Nay, but he prated,
    And spoke such scurvy and provoking terms
    Against your honor
    That, with the little godliness I have,

173 *charms* spells   174 *property* special quality, nature   175 *abused* deceived   180
discover reveal, uncover   183 *command* demand assistance   185 *deserve* show gratitude
for   2 *very stuff* essence, basic material (continuing the metaphor of *trade* from line 1)
3 *contrived* premeditated   5 *yerked* stabbed.   *him* i.e., Roderigo

I did full hard forbear him.° But, I pray you, sir,   10
Are you fast married? Be assured of this,
That the magnifico° is much beloved,
And hath in his effect° a voice potential°
As double as the Duke's. He will divorce you,
Or put upon you what restraint or grievance   15
The law, with all his might to enforce it on,
Will give him cable.°

Othello: Let him do his spite.
My services which I have done the seigniory°
Shall out-tongue his complaints. 'Tis yet to know°—
Which, when I know that boasting is an honor,   20
I shall promulgate—I fetch my life and being
From men of royal siege,° and my demerits°
May speak unbonneted° to as proud a fortune
As this that I have reached. For know, Iago,
But that I love the gentle Desdemona,   25
I would not my unhousèd° free condition
Put into circumscription and confine°
For the sea's worth.° But look, what lights come yond?

Enter Cassio [and certain officers°] with torches.

Iago: Those are the raisèd father and his friends.
You were best go in.

Othello: Not I. I must be found.   30
My parts, my title, and my perfect soul°
Shall manifest me rightly. Is it they?

Iago: By Janus,° I think no.

Othello: The servants of the Duke? And my lieutenant?
The goodness of the night upon you, friends!   35
What is the news?

---

10 *I . . . him* I restrained myself with great difficulty from assaulting him   12 *magnifico*
Venetian grandee, i.e., Brabantio   13 *in his effect* at his command. *potential* powerful   17
cable i.e., scope   18 *seigniory* Venetian government   19 *yet to know* not yet widely known
22 *siege* i.e., rank. (Literally, a seat used by a person of distinction.)   *demerits* deserts   23
unbonneted without removing the hat, i.e., on equal terms (?) (Or "with hat off," "in all due
modesty.")   26 *unhousèd* unconfined, undomesticated   27 *circumscription and confine* re-
striction and confinement   28 *the sea's worth* all the riches at the bottom of the sea.   s.d.
officers (The Quarto text calls for "Cassio with lights, officers with torches.")   31 *My . . .
soul* my natural gifts, my position or reputation, and my unflawed conscience   33 *Janus*
Roman two-faced god of beginnings

Cassio: The Duke does greet you, General,
        And he requires your haste-post-haste appearance
        Even on the instant.
Othello: What is the matter,° think you?
Cassio: Something from Cyprus, as I may divine.°
        It is a business of some heat.° The galleys   40
        Have sent a dozen sequent° messengers
        This very night at one another's heels,
        And many of the consuls,° raised and met,
        Are at the Duke's already. You have been hotly called for;
        When, being not at your lodging to be found,   45
        The Senate hath sent about° three several° quests
        To search you out.
Othello: 'Tis well I am found by you.
        I will but spend a word here in the house
        And go with you.
                                                          [*Exit.*]

Cassio: Ancient, what makes° he here?
Iago: Faith, he tonight hath boarded° a land carrack.°   50
        If it prove lawful prize,° he's made forever.
Cassio: I do not understand.
Iago: He's married.
Cassio: To who?

        [*Enter Othello.*]

Iago: Marry,° to—Come, Captain, will you go?
Othello: Have with you.°
Cassio: Here comes another troop to seek for you.   55

        Enter Brabantio, Roderigo, with officers and torches.°

Iago: It is Brabantio. General, be advised.°
        He comes to bad intent.

---

38 *matter* business   39 *divine* guess   40 *heat* urgency   41 *sequent* successive   43 *consuls*
senators   46 *about* all over the city.   *several* separate   49 *makes* does   50 *boarded* gone
aboard and seized as an act of piracy (with sexual suggestion).   *carrack* large merchant ship
51 *prize* booty   53 *Marry* (An oath, originally "by the Virgin Mary"; here used with wordplay on *married.*)   54 *Have with you* i.e., let's go   55 s.d.   *officers and torches* (The Quarto
text calls for "others with lights and weapons.")   56 *be advised* be on your guard

Othello: Holla! Stand there!
Roderigo: Signor, it is the Moor.
Brabantio: Down with him, thief!

    [*They draw on both sides.*]

Iago: You, Roderigo! Come, sir, I am for you.
Othello: Keep up° your bright swords, for the dew will rust them.   60
    Good signor, you shall more command with years
    Than with your weapons.
Brabantio: O thou foul thief, where hast thou stowed my daughter?
    Damned as thou art, thou hast enchanted her!
    For I'll refer me° to all things of sense,°   65
    If she in chains of magic were not bound
    Whether a maid so tender, fair, and happy,
    So opposite to marriage that she shunned
    The wealthy curlèd darlings of our nation,
    Would ever have, t' incur a general mock,   70
    Run from her guardage° to the sooty bosom
    Of such a thing as thou—to fear, not to delight.
    Judge me the world if 'tis not gross in sense°
    That thou hast practiced on her with foul charms,
    Abused her delicate youth with drugs or minerals°   75
    That weakens motion.° I'll have 't disputed on;°
    'Tis probable and palpable to thinking.
    I therefore apprehend and do attach° thee
    For an abuser of the world, a practicer
    Of arts inhibited° and out of warrant.°—   80
    Lay hold upon him! If he do resist,
    Subdue him at his peril.
Othello: Hold your hands,
    Both you of my inclining° and the rest.
    Were it my cue to fight, I should have known it
    Without a prompter.—Whither will you that I go   85
    To answer this your charge?

---

60 *Keep up* keep in the sheath   65 *refer me* submit my case.   *things of sense* commonsense understandings, or, creatures possessing common sense   71 *her guardage* my guardianship of her   73 *gross in sense* obvious   75 *minerals* i.e., poisons   76 *weakens motion* impair the vital faculties.   *disputed on* argued in court by professional counsel, debated by experts   78 *attach* arrest   80 *arts inhibited* prohibited arts, black magic.   *out of warrant* illegal   83 *inclining* following, party

Brabantio: To prison, till fit time
    Of law and course of direct session°
    Call thee to answer.
Othello: What if I do obey?
    How may the Duke be therewith satisfied,   90
    Whose messengers are here about my side
    Upon some present business of the state
    To bring me to him?
Officer: 'Tis true, most worthy signor.
    The Duke's in council, and your noble self,
    I am sure, is sent for.
Brabantio: How? The Duke in council?   95
    In this time of the night? Bring him away.°
    Mine's not an idle° cause. The Duke himself,
    Or any of my brothers of the state,
    Cannot but feel this wrong as 'twere their own;
    For if such actions may have passage free,°   100
    Bondslaves and pagans shall our statesmen be.

    Exeunt.

SCENE III [VENICE. A COUNCIL CHAMBER.]

Enter Duke [and] Senators [and sit at a table, with lights], and Officers.°
[The Duke and Senators are reading dispatches.]

Duke: There is no composition° in these news
    That gives them credit.
First Senator: Indeed, they are disproportioned.°
    My letters say a hundred and seven galleys.
Duke: And mine, a hundred forty.
Second Senator: And mine, two hundred.   5
    But though they jump° not on a just° account—
    As in these cases, where the aim° reports
    'Tis oft with difference—yet do they all confirm
    A Turkish fleet, and bearing up to Cyprus.
Duke: Nay, it is possible enough to judgment.   10
    I do not so secure me in the error

---

88 *course of direct session* regular or specially convened legal proceedings   96 *away* right
along   97 *idle* trifling   100 *have passage free* are allowed to go unchecked
s.d. *Enter . . . Officers* (The Quarto text calls for the Duke and senators to "sit at a table
with lights and attendants.")   1 *composition* consistency   3 *disproportioned* inconsistent   6
jump agree.   *just* exact   7 *the aim* conjecture

But the main article I do approve°
In fearful sense.

Sailor (*within*):　　　What ho, what ho, what ho!

Enter Sailor.

Officer: A messenger from the galleys.
Duke: Now, what's the business?　　　　　　　　　　　　　　15
Sailor: The Turkish preparation° makes for Rhodes.
　　So was I bid report here to the state
　　By Signor Angelo.
Duke: How say you by° this change?
First Senator:　　　　　　　　　　This cannot be
　　By no assay° of reason. 'Tis a pageant°　　　　　　　　20
　　To keep us in false gaze.° When we consider
　　Th' importancy of Cyprus to the Turk,
　　And let ourselves again but understand
　　That, as it more concerns the Turk than Rhodes,
　　So may he with more facile question bear it,°　　　　　　25
　　For that° it stands not in such warlike brace,°
　　But altogether lacks th' abilities°
　　That Rhodes is dressed in°—if we make thought of this,
　　We must not think the Turk is so unskillful°
　　To leave that latest° which concerns him first,　　　　　30
　　Neglecting an attempt of ease and gain
　　To wake° and wage° a danger profitless.
Duke: Nay, in all confidence, he's not for Rhodes.
Officer: Here is more news.

Enter a Messenger.

Messenger: The Ottomites, reverend and gracious,　　　　　35
　　Steering with due course toward the isle of Rhodes,
　　Have there injointed them° with an after° fleet.
First Senator: Ay, so I thought. How many, as you guess?

11–12 *I do not . . . approve* I do not take such (false) comfort in the discrepancies that I fail to perceive the main point, i.e., that the Turkish fleet is threatening　16 *preparation* fleet prepared for battle　19 *by* about　20 *assay* test.　*pageant* mere show　21 *in false gaze* looking the wrong way　25 *So may . . . it* so also he (the Turk) can more easily capture it (Cyprus)　26 *For that* since.　*brace* state of defense　27 *abilities* means of self-defense　28 *dressed in* equipped with　29 *unskillful* deficient in judgment　30 *latest* last　32 *wake* stir up.　*wage* risk　37 *injointed them* joined themselves.　*after* second, following

Messenger: Of thirty sail; and now they do restem
    Their backward course,° bearing with frank appearance°   40
    Their purposes toward Cyprus. Signor Montano,
    Your trusty and most valiant servitor,°
    With his free duty° recommends° you thus,
    And prays you to believe him.
Duke: 'Tis certain then for Cyprus.   45
    Marcus Luccicos, is not he in town?
First Senator: He's now in Florence.
Duke: Write from us to him, post-post-haste. Dispatch.
First Senator: Here comes Brabantio and the valiant Moor.

    Enter Brabantio, Othello, Cassio, Iago, Roderigo, and officers.

Duke: Valiant Othello, we must straight° employ you   50
    Against the general enemy° Ottoman.
    [*To Brabantio.*] I did not see you; welcome, gentle° signor.
    We lacked your counsel and your help tonight.
Brabantio: So did I yours. Good Your Grace, pardon me;
    Neither my place° nor aught I heard of business   55
    Hath raised me from my bed, nor doth the general care
    Take hold on me, for my particular° grief
    Is of so floodgate° and o'erbearing nature
    That it engluts° and swallows other sorrows
    And it is still itself.°
Duke: Why, what's the matter?   60
Brabantio: My daughter! O, my daughter!
Duke and Senators: Dead?
Brabantio: Ay, to me.
    She is abused,° stol'n from me, and corrupted
    By spells and medicines bought of mountebanks;
    For nature so preposterously to err,
    Being not deficient,° blind, or lame of sense,°   65
    Sans° witchcraft could not.
Duke: Whoe'er he be that in this foul proceeding
    Hath thus beguiled your daughter of herself,

39–40 *restem . . . course* retrace their original course   40 *frank appearance* undisguised intent
42 *servitor* officer under your command   43 *free duty* freely given and loyal service. *recom-
mends* commends himself and reports to   50 *straight* straightway   51 *general enemy* universal
enemy to all Christendom   52 *gentle* noble   55 *place* official position   57 *particular* personal   58 *floodgate* i.e., overwhelming (as when floodgates are opened)   59 *engluts* engulfs
60 *is still itself* remains undiminished   62 *abused* deceived   65 *deficient* defective. *lame of
sense* deficient in sensory perception   66 *Sans* without

Othello answers Brabantio's charges before the Duke (I, iii, 78–172).

And you of her, the bloody book of law
You shall yourself read in the bitter letter
After your own sense°—yea, though our proper° son   70
Stood in your action.°
Brabantio: Humbly I thank Your Grace.
Here is the man, this Moor, whom now it seems
Your special mandate for the state affairs
Hath hither brought.
All: We are very sorry for 't.   75
Duke [*to Othello*]: What, in your own part, can you say to this?
Brabantio: Nothing, but this is so.
Othello: Most potent, grave, and reverend signors,
My very noble and approved° good masters:
That I have ta'en away this old man's daughter,   80
It is most true; true, I have married her.
The very head and front° of my offending
Hath this extent, no more. Rude° am I in my speech,
And little blessed with the soft phrase of peace;

71 *After . . . sense* according to your own interpretation.   *our proper* my own   72 *Stood . . . action* were under your accusation   79 *approved* proved, esteemed   82 *head and front* height and breadth, entire extent   83 *Rude* unpolished

For since these arms of mine had seven years' pith,°   85
Till now some nine moons wasted,° they have used
Their dearest° action in the tented field;
And little of this great world can I speak
More than pertains to feats of broils and battle,
And therefore little shall I grace my cause   90
In speaking for myself. Yet, by your gracious patience,
I will a round° unvarnished tale deliver
Of my whole course of love—what drugs, what charms,
What conjuration, and what mighty magic,
For such proceeding I am charged withal,°   95
I won his daughter.
Brabantio: A maiden never bold;
Of spirit so still and quiet that her motion
Blushed at herself;° and she, in spite of nature,
Of years,° of country, credit,° everything,
To fall in love with what she feared to look on!   100
It is a judgment maimed and most imperfect
That will confess° perfection so could err
Against all rules of nature, and must be driven
To find out practices° of cunning hell
Why this should be. I therefore vouch° again   105
That with some mixtures powerful o'er the blood,°
Or with some dram conjured to this effect,°
He wrought upon her.
Duke: To vouch this is no proof,
Without more wider° and more overt test°
Than these thin habits° and poor likelihoods°   110
Of modern seeming° do prefer° against him.
First Senator: But Othello, speak.
Did you by indirect and forcèd courses°
Subdue and poison this young maid's affections?

---

85 *since . . . pith* i.e., since I was seven. *pith* strength, vigor 86 *Till . . . wasted* until some
nine months ago (since when Othello has evidently not been on active duty, but in
Venice) 87 *dearest* most valuable 92 *round* plain 95 *withal* with 97–98 *her . . . herself*
i.e., she blushed easily at herself. (*Motion* can suggest the impulse of the soul or of the emotions, or physical movement.) 99 *years* i.e., difference in age. *credit* virtuous reputation
102 *confess* concede (that) 104 *practices* plots 105 *vouch* assert 106 *blood* passions
107 *dram . . . effect* dose made by magical spells to have this effect 109 *more wider* fuller.
test testimony 110 *habits* garments, i.e., appearances. *poor likelihoods* weak inferences
111 *modern seeming* commonplace assumption. *prefer* bring forth 113 *forcèd courses*
means used against her will

Or came it by request and such fair question° 115
As soul to soul affordeth?

Othello: I do beseech you,
Send for the lady to the Sagittary
And let her speak of me before her father.
If you do find me foul in her report,
The trust, the office I do hold of you 120
Not only take away, but let your sentence
Even fall upon my life.

Duke: Fetch Desdemona hither.

Othello: Ancient, conduct them. You best know the place.

[*Exeunt Iago and attendants.*]

And, till she come, as truly as to heaven
I do confess the vices of my blood,° 125
So justly° to your grave ears I'll present
How I did thrive in this fair lady's love,
And she in mine.

Duke: Say it, Othello.

Othello: Her father loved me, oft invited me, 130
Still° questioned me the story of my life
From year to year—the battles, sieges, fortunes
That I have passed.
I ran it through, even from my boyish days
To th' very moment that he bade me tell it, 135
Wherein I spoke of most disastrous chances,
Of moving accidents° by flood and field,
Of hairbreadth scapes i' th' imminent deadly breach,°
Of being taken by the insolent foe
And sold to slavery, of my redemption thence, 140
And portance° in my travels' history,
Wherein of antres° vast and deserts idle,°
Rough quarries,° rocks, and hills whose heads touch heaven,
It was my hint° to speak—such was my process—
And of the Cannibals that each other eat, 145
The Anthropophagi,° and men whose heads

---

115 *question* conversation   125 *blood* passions, human nature   126 *justly* truthfully, accurately   131 *Still* continually   137 *moving accidents* stirring happenings   138 *imminent . . . breach* death-threatening gaps made in a fortification   141 *portance* conduct   142 *antres* caverns.   *idle* barren, desolate   143 *Rough quarries* rugged rock formations   144 *hint* occasion, opportunity   146 *Anthropophagi* man-eaters. (A term from Pliny's *Natural History*.)

Do grow beneath their shoulders. These things to hear
Would Desdemona seriously incline;
But still the house affairs would draw her thence,
Which ever as she could with haste dispatch   150
She'd come again, and with a greedy ear
Devour up my discourse. Which I, observing,
Took once a pliant° hour, and found good means
To draw from her a prayer of earnest heart
That I would all my pilgrimage dilate,°   155
Whereof by parcels° she had something heard,
But not intentively.° I did consent,
And often did beguile her of her tears,
When I did speak of some distressful stroke
That my youth suffered. My story being done,   160
She gave me for my pains a world of sighs.
She swore, in faith, 'twas strange, 'twas passing° strange,
'Twas pitiful, 'twas wondrous pitiful.
She wished she had not heard it, yet she wished
That heaven had made her° such a man. She thanked me,   165
And bade me, if I had a friend that loved her,
I should but teach him how to tell my story,
And that would woo her. Upon this hint° I spake.
She loved me for the dangers I had passed,
And I loved her that she did pity them.   170
This only is the witchcraft I have used.
Here comes the lady. Let her witness it.

Enter Desdemona, Iago, [and] attendants.

Duke: I think this tale would win my daughter too.
     Good Brabantio,
     Take up this mangled matter at the best.°   175
     Men do their broken weapons rather use
     Than their bare hands.
Brabantio: I pray you, hear her speak.
     If she confess that she was half the wooer,
     Destruction on my head if my bad blame
     Light on the man!—Come hither, gentle mistress.   180

---

153 *pliant* well-suiting 155 *dilate* relate in detail 156 *by parcels* piecemeal 157 *intentively* with full attention, continuously 162 *passing* exceedingly 165 *made her* created her to be 168 *hint* opportunity. (Othello does not mean that she was dropping hints.) 175 *Take . . . best* make the best of a bad bargain

Do you perceive in all this noble company
Where most you owe obedience?
Desdemona: My noble Father,
  I do perceive here a divided duty.
  To you I am bound for life and education;°
  My life and education both do learn° me   185
  How to respect you. You are the lord of duty;°
  I am hitherto your daughter. But here's my husband,
  And so much duty as my mother showed
  To you, preferring you before her father,
  So much I challenge° that I may profess   190
  Due to the Moor my lord.
Brabantio: God be with you! I have done.
  Please it Your Grace, on to the state affairs.
  I had rather to adopt a child than get° it.
  Come hither, Moor.   [*He joins the hands of Othello and Desdemona.*] 195
  I here do give thee that with all my heart°
  Which, but thou hast already, with all my heart°
  I would keep from thee.—For your sake,° jewel,
  I am glad at soul I have no other child,
  For thy escape° would teach me tyranny,   200
  To hang clogs° on them.—I have done, my lord.
Duke: Let me speak like yourself,° and lay a sentence°
  Which, as a grece° or step, may help these lovers
  Into your favor.
  When remedies° are past, the griefs are ended   205
  By seeing the worst, which late on hopes depended.°
  To mourn a mischief° that is past and gone
  Is the next° way to draw new mischief on.
  What° cannot be preserved when fortune takes,
  Patience her injury a mockery makes.°   210
  The robbed that smiles steals something from the thief;
  He robs himself that spends a bootless grief.°

---

184 *education* upbringing 185 *learn* teach 186 *of duty* to whom duty is due 190
challenge claim 194 *get* beget 196 *with all my heart* wherein my whole affection has been
engaged 197 *with all my heart* willingly, gladly 198 *For your sake* on your account 200
escape elopement 201 *clogs* (Literally, blocks of wood fastened to the legs of criminals or
convicts to inhibit escape.) 202 *like yourself* i.e., as you would, in your proper temper. *lay
a sentence* apply a maxim 203 *grece* step 205 *remedies* hopes of remedy 206 *which . . .
depended* which griefs were sustained until recently by hopeful anticipation 207 *mischief*
misfortune, injury 208 *next* nearest 209 *What* whatever 210 *Patience . . . makes* patience laughs at the injury inflicted by fortune (and thus eases the pain) 212 *spends a bootless grief* indulges in unavailing grief

Brabantio: So let the Turk of Cyprus us beguile,
We lose it not, so long as we can smile.
He bears the sentence well that nothing bears° 215
But the free comfort which from thence he hears,
But he bears both the sentence and the sorrow
That, to pay grief, must of poor patience borrow.°
These sentences, to sugar or to gall,
Being strong on both sides, are equivocal.° 220
But words are words. I never yet did hear
That the bruisèd heart was piercèd through the ear.°
I humbly beseech you, proceed to th' affairs of state.

Duke: The Turk with a most mighty preparation makes for Cyprus. Othello,
the fortitude° of the place is best known to you; and though we have 225
there a substitute° of most allowed° sufficiency, yet opinion, a sover-
eign mistress of effects, throws a more safer voice on you.° You must
therefore be content to slubber° the gloss of your new fortunes with
this more stubborn° and boisterous expedition.

Othello: The tyrant custom, most grave senators, 230
Hath made the flinty and steel couch of war
My thrice-driven° bed of down. I do agnize°
A natural and prompt alacrity
I find in hardness,° and do undertake
These present wars against the Ottomites. 235
Most humbly therefore bending to your state,°
I crave fit disposition for my wife,
Due reference of place and exhibition,°
With such accommodation° and besort°
As levels° with her breeding.° 240

215–218 *He bears . . . borrow* a person well bears out your maxim who can enjoy its plati-
tudinous comfort, free of all genuine sorrow, but anyone whose grief bankrupts his poor
patience is left with your saying and his sorrow, too. (*Bears the sentence* also plays on the
meaning, "receives judicial sentence.") 219–220 *These . . . equivocal* these fine maxims
are equivocal, either sweet or bitter in their application 222 *piercèd . . . ear* i.e., surgi-
cally lanced and cured by mere words of advice 225 *fortitude* strength 226 *substitute*
deputy. *allowed* acknowledged 226–227 *opinion . . . on you* general opinion, an important determiner of affairs, chooses you as the best man 228 *slubber* soil, sully 229
stubborn harsh, rough 232 *thrice-driven* thrice sifted, winnowed. *agnize* know in myself,
acknowledge 234 *hardness* hardship 236 *bending . . . state* bowing or kneeling to your
authority 238 *reference . . . exhibition* provision of appropriate place to live and allowance of money 239 *accommodation* suitable provision. *besort* attendance 240 *levels*
equals, suits. *breeding* social position, upbringing

Duke: Why, at her father's.

Brabantio: I will not have it so.

Othello: Nor I.

Desdemona: Nor I. I would not there reside,
    To put my father in impatient thoughts
    By being in his eye. Most gracious Duke,
    To my unfolding° lend your prosperous° ear,   245
    And let me find a charter° in your voice,
    T' assist my simpleness.

Duke: What would you, Desdemona?

Desdemona: That I did love the Moor to live with him,
    My downright violence and storm of fortunes°   250
    May trumpet to the world. My heart's subdued
    Even to the very quality of my lord.°
    I saw Othello's visage in his mind,
    And to his honors and his valiant parts°
    Did I my soul and fortunes consecrate.   255
    So that, dear lords, if I be left behind
    A moth° of peace, and he go to the war,
    The rites° for why I love him are bereft me,
    And I a heavy interim shall support
    By his dear° absence. Let me go with him.   260

Othello: Let her have your voice.°
    Vouch with me, heaven, I therefor beg it not
    To please the palate of my appetite,
    Nor to comply with heat°—the young affects°
    In me defunct—and proper° satisfaction,   265
    But to be free° and bounteous to her mind.
    And heaven defend° your good souls that you think°
    I will your serious and great business scant
    When she is with me. No, when light-winged toys
    Of feathered Cupid seel° with wanton dullness   270

---

245 *unfolding* explanation, proposal. *prosperous* propitious   246 *charter* privilege, authorization   250 *My . . . fortunes* my plain and total breach of social custom, taking my future by storm and disrupting my whole life   251–252 *My heart's . . . lord* my heart is brought wholly into accord with Othello's virtues; I love him for his virtues   254 *parts* qualities   257 *moth* i.e., one who consumes merely   258 *rites* rites of love (with a suggestion, too, of "rights," sharing)   260 *dear* (1) heartfelt (2) costly   261 *voice* consent   264 *heat* sexual passion. *young affects* passions of youth, desires   265 *proper* personal   266 *free* generous   267 *defend* forbid. *think* should think   270 *seel* i.e., make blind (as in falconry, by sewing up the eyes of the hawk during training)

My speculative and officed instruments,°
That° my disports° corrupt and taint° my business,
Let huswives make a skillet of my helm,
And all indign° and base adversities
Make head° against my estimation!°   275

Duke: Be it as you shall privately determine,
Either for her stay or going. Th' affair cries haste,
And speed must answer it.

A Senator: You must away tonight.

Desdemona: Tonight, my lord?

Duke: This night.

Othello: With all my heart.

Duke: At nine i' the morning here we'll meet again.   280
Othello, leave some officer behind,
And he shall our commission bring to you,
With such things else of quality and respect°
As doth import° you.

Othello: So please Your Grace, my ancient;
A man he is of honesty and trust.   285
To his conveyance I assign my wife,
With what else needful Your Good Grace shall think
To be sent after me.

Duke: Let it be so.
Good night to everyone. [*To Brabantio.*] And, noble signor,
If virtue no delighted° beauty lack,   290
Your son-in-law is far more fair than black.

First Senator: Adieu, brave Moor. Use Desdemona well.

Brabantio: Look to her, Moor, if thou hast eyes to see.
She has deceived her father, and may thee.

            Exeunt [Duke, Brabantio, Cassio, Senators, and officers].

Othello: My life upon her faith! Honest Iago,   295
My Desdemona must I leave to thee.
I prithee, let thy wife attend on her,
And bring them after in the best advantage.°
Come, Desdemona. I have but an hour
Of love, of worldly matters and direction,°   300
To spend with thee. We must obey the time.°

---

271 *speculative . . . instruments* eyes and other faculties used in the performance of duty   272
That so that.   *disports* sexual pastimes.   *taint* impair   274 *indign* unworthy, shameful   275
Make head raise an army.   *estimation* reputation   283 *of quality and respect* of importance and
relevance   284 *import* concern   290 *delighted* capable of delighting   298 *in . . . advantage* at
the most favorable opportunity   300 *direction* instructions   301 *the time* the urgency of the
present crisis

Exit [*with Desdemona*].

Roderigo: Iago—

Iago: What sayst thou, noble heart?

Roderigo: What will I do, think'st thou?

Iago: Why, go to bed and sleep.   305

Roderigo: I will incontinently° drown myself.

Iago: If thou dost, I shall never love thee after. Why, thou silly gentleman?

Roderigo: It is silliness to live when to live is torment; and then have we
    a prescription° to die when death is our physician.

Iago: O villainous!° I have looked upon the world for four times seven   310
    years, and, since I could distinguish betwixt a benefit and an injury, I
    never found man that knew how to love himself. Ere I would say I
    would drown myself for the love of a guinea hen,° I would change
    my humanity with a baboon.

Roderigo: What should I do? I confess it is my shame to be so fond,° but   315
    it is not in my virtue° to amend it.

Iago: Virtue? A fig!° 'Tis in ourselves that we are thus or thus. Our bodies
    are our gardens, to the which our wills are gardeners; so that if we
    will plant nettles or sow lettuce, set hyssop° and weed up thyme,
    supply it with one gender° of herbs or distract it with° many, either   320
    to have it sterile with idleness° or manured with industry—why, the
    power and corrigible authority° of this lies in our wills. If the beam°
    of our lives had not one scale of reason to poise° another of sensual-
    ity, the blood° and baseness of our natures would conduct us to most
    preposterous conclusions. But we have reason to cool our raging   325
    motions,° our carnal stings, our unbitted° lusts, whereof I take this
    that you call love to be a sect or scion.°

Roderigo: It cannot be.

Iago: It is merely a lust of the blood and a permission of the will. Come,
    be a man. Drown thyself? Drown cats and blind puppies. I have pro-   330
    fessed me thy friend, and I confess me knit to thy deserving with ca-
    bles of perdurable° toughness. I could never better stead° thee than

---

306 *incontinently* immediately, without self-restraint   309 *prescription* (1) right based on
long-established custom (2) doctor's prescription   310 *villainous* i.e., what perfect nonsense   313 *guinea hen* (A slang term for a prostitute.)   315 *fond* infatuated   316 *virtue*
strength, nature   317 *fig* (To give a fig is to thrust the thumb between the first and second
fingers in a vulgar and insulting gesture.)   319 *hyssop* an herb of the mint family   320
gender kind. *distract it with* divide it among   321 *idleness* want of cultivation   322
corrigible authority power to correct. *beam* balance   323 *poise* counterbalance   324 *blood*
natural passions   326 *motions* appetites. *unbitted* unbridled, uncontrolled   327 *sect or
scion* cutting or offshoot   332 *perdurable* very durable. *stead* assist

now. Put money in thy purse. Follow thou the wars; defeat thy favor°
with an usurped° beard. I say, put money in thy purse. It cannot be
long that Desdemona should continue her love to the Moor—put   335
money in thy purse—nor he his to her. It was a violent commence-
ment in her, and thou shalt see an answerable sequestration°—put
but money in thy purse. These Moors are changeable in their
wills°—fill thy purse with money. The food that to him now is as luscious as locusts° shall be to him shortly as bitter as coloquintida.°   340
She must change for youth; when she is sated with his body, she will
find the error of her choice. She must have change, she must. Therefore put money in thy purse. If thou wilt needs damn thyself, do it a
more delicate way than drowning. Make° all the money thou canst.
If sanctimony° and a frail vow betwixt an erring° barbarian and a su-   345
persubtle Venetian be not too hard for my wits and all the tribe
of hell, thou shalt enjoy her. Therefore make money. A pox of
drowning thyself! It is clean out of the way.° Seek thou rather to be
hanged in compassing° thy joy than to be drowned and go without
her.   350
Roderigo: Wilt thou be fast° to my hopes if I depend on the issue?°
Iago: Thou art sure of me. Go, make money. I have told thee often, and I
retell thee again and again, I hate the Moor. My cause is hearted;°
thine hath no less reason. Let us be conjunctive° in our revenge against
him. If thou canst cuckold him, thou dost thyself a pleasure, me a   355
sport. There are many events in the womb of time which will be
delivered. Traverse,° go, provide thy money. We will have more of
this tomorrow. Adieu.
Roderigo: Where shall we meet i' the morning?
Iago: At my lodging.   360
Roderigo: I'll be with thee betimes.°   [*He starts to leave.*]
Iago: Go to, farewell.—Do you hear, Roderigo?
Roderigo: What say you?
Iago: No more of drowning, do you hear?
Roderigo: I am changed.   365

---

333 *defeat thy favor* disguise your face   334 *usurped* (The suggestion is that Roderigo is not
man enough to have a beard of his own.)   337 *an answerable sequestration* a corresponding
separation or estrangement   339 *wills* carnal appetites   340 *locusts* fruit of the carob tree
(see Matthew 3:4), or perhaps honeysuckle.   *coloquintida* colocynth or bitter apple, a
purgative   344 *Make* raise, collect   345 *sanctimony* sacred ceremony.   *erring* wandering,
vagabond, unsteady   348 *clean . . . way* entirely unsuitable as a course of action   349
compassing encompassing, embracing   351 *fast* true.   *issue* (successful) outcome   353
hearted fixed in the heart, heartfelt   354 *conjunctive* united   357 *Traverse* (A military
marching term.)   361 *betimes* early

Iago: Go to, farewell. Put money enough in your purse.
Roderigo: I'll sell all my land.   *Exit.*
Iago: Thus do I ever make my fool my purse;
    For I mine own gained knowledge should profane
    If I would time expend with such a snipe°   370
    But for my sport and profit. I hate the Moor;
    And it is thought abroad° that twixt my sheets
    He's done my office.° I know not if 't be true;
    But I, for mere suspicion in that kind,
    Will do as if for surety.° He holds me well;°   375
    The better shall my purpose work on him.
    Cassio's a proper° man. Let me see now:
    To get his place and to plume up° my will
    In double knavery—How, how?—Let's see:
    After some time, to abuse° Othello's ear   380
    That he° is too familiar with his wife.
    He hath a person and a smooth dispose°
    To be suspected, framed to make women false.
    The Moor is of a free° and open° nature,
    That thinks men honest that but seem to be so,   385
    And will as tenderly° be led by the nose
    As asses are.
    I have 't. It is engendered. Hell and night
    Must bring this monstrous birth to the world's light.

    [*Exit.*]

ACT II

SCENE I [A SEAPORT IN CYPRUS. AN OPEN PLACE NEAR THE QUAY.]

    Enter Montano and two Gentlemen.

Montano: What from the cape can you discern at sea?
First Gentleman: Nothing at all. It is a high-wrought flood.°
    I cannot, twixt the heaven and the main,°
    Descry a sail.

---

370 *snipe* woodcock, i.e., fool   372 *it is thought abroad* it is rumored   373 *my office* i.e., my
sexual function as husband   375 *do . . . surety* act as if on certain knowledge. *holds me well*
regards me favorably   377 *proper* handsome   378 *plume up* put a feather in the cap of, i.e.,
glorify, gratify   380 *abuse* deceive   381 *he* i.e., Cassio   382 *dispose* disposition   384 *free*
frank, generous.   *open* unsuspicious   386 *tenderly* readily   2 *high-wrought flood* very agitated sea   3 *main* ocean (also at line 41)

Montano: Methinks the wind hath spoke aloud at land;   5
   A fuller blast ne'er shook our battlements.
   If it hath ruffianed° so upon the sea,
   What ribs of oak, when mountains° melt on them,
   Can hold the mortise?° What shall we hear of this?
Second Gentleman: A segregation° of the Turkish fleet.   10
   For do but stand upon the foaming shore,
   The chidden° billow seems to pelt the clouds;
   The wind-shaked surge, with high and monstrous mane,°
   Seems to cast water on the burning Bear°
   And quench the guards of th' ever-fixèd pole.   15
   I never did like molestation° view
   On the enchafèd° flood.
Montano: If that° the Turkish fleet
   Be not ensheltered and embayed,° they are drowned;
   It is impossible to bear it out.°   20

Enter a [Third] Gentleman.

Third Gentleman: News, lads! Our wars are done.
   The desperate tempest hath so banged the Turks
   That their designment° halts.° A noble ship of Venice
   Hath seen a grievous wreck° and sufferance°
   On most part of their fleet.   25
Montano: How? Is this true?
Third Gentleman: The ship is here put in,
   A Veronesa;° Michael Cassio,
   Lieutenant to the warlike Moor Othello,
   Is come on shore; the Moor himself at sea,   30
   And is in full commission here for Cyprus.

---

7 *ruffianed* raged   8 *mountains* i.e., of water   9 *hold the mortise* hold their joints together. (A *mortise* is the socket hollowed out in fitting timbers.)   10 *segregation* dispersal   12 *chidden* i.e., rebuked, repelled (by the shore), and thus shot into the air   13 *monstrous mane* (The surf is like the mane of a wild beast.)   14 *the burning Bear* i.e., the constellation Ursa Minor or the Little Bear, which includes the polestar (and hence regarded as the *guards of th' ever-fixèd pole* in the next line; sometimes the term *guards* is applied to the two "pointers" of the Big Bear or Dipper, which may be intended here).   16 *like molestation* comparable disturbance   17 *enchafèd* angry   18 *If that* if   19 *embayed* sheltered by a bay   20 *bear it out* survive, weather the storm   23 *designment* design, enterprise. *halts* is lame   24 *wreck* shipwreck. *sufferance* damage, disaster   28 *Veronesa* i.e., fitted out in Verona for Venetian service, or possibly *Verennessa* (the Folio spelling), i.e., *verrinessa*, a cutter (from *verrinare*, "to cut through")

Montano: I am glad on 't. 'Tis a worthy governor.
Third Gentleman: But this same Cassio, though he speak of comfort
    Touching the Turkish loss, yet he looks sadly°
    And prays the Moor be safe, for they were parted   35
    With foul and violent tempest.
Montano: Pray heaven he be,
    For I have served him, and the man commands
    Like a full° soldier. Let's to the seaside, ho!
    As well to see the vessel that's come in
    As to throw out our eyes for brave Othello,   40
    Even till we make the main and th' aerial blue°
    An indistinct regard.°
Third Gentleman: Come, let's do so,
    For every minute is expectancy°
    Of more arrivance.°

    Enter Cassio.

Cassio: Thanks, you the valiant of this warlike isle,   45
    That so approve° the Moor! O, let the heavens
    Give him defense against the elements,
    For I have lost him on a dangerous sea.
Montano: Is he well shipped?
Cassio: His bark is stoutly timbered, and his pilot   50
    Of very expert and approved allowance;°
    Therefore my hopes, not surfeited to death,°
    Stand in bold cure.°
    [*A cry*] *within:*   "A sail, a sail, a sail!"
Cassio: What noise?
A Gentleman: The town is empty. On the brow o' the sea°   55
    Stand ranks of people, and they cry "A sail!"
Cassio: My hopes do shape him for° the governor.

    [*A shot within.*]

Second Gentleman: They do discharge their shot of courtesy;°
    Our friends at least.

---

34 *sadly* gravely   38 *full* perfect   41 *the main . . . blue* the sea and the sky   42 *An indistinct regard* indistinguishable in our view   43 *is expectancy* gives expectation   44 *arrivance* arrival   46 *approve* admire, honor   51 *approved allowance* tested reputation   52 *surfeited to death* i.e., overextended, worn thin through repeated application or delayed fulfillment   53 *in bold cure* in strong hopes of fulfillment   55 *brow o' the sea* cliff-edge   57 *My . . . for* I hope it is   58 *discharge . . . courtesy* fire a salute in token of respect and courtesy

Cassio: I pray you, sir, go forth,
   And give us truth who 'tis that is arrived.   60
Second Gentleman: I shall.   *Exit.*
Montano: But, good Lieutenant, is your general wived?
Cassio: Most fortunately. He hath achieved a maid
   That paragons° description and wild fame,°
   One that excels the quirks° of blazoning° pens,   65
   And in th' essential vesture of creation
   Does tire the enginer.°

   Enter [Second] Gentleman.°

                How now? Who has put in?°
Second Gentleman: 'Tis one Iago, ancient to the General.
Cassio: He's had most favorable and happy speed.
   Tempests themselves, high seas, and howling winds,   70
   The guttered° rocks and congregated sands—
   Traitors ensteeped° to clog the guiltless keel—
   As° having sense of beauty, do omit°
   Their mortal° natures, letting go safely by
   The divine Desdemona.
Montano: What is she?   75
Cassio: She that I spake of, our great captain's captain,
   Left in the conduct of the bold Iago,
   Whose footing° here anticipates our thoughts
   A sennight's° speed. Great Jove, Othello guard,
   And swell his sail with thine own powerful breath,   80
   That he may bless this bay with his tall° ship,
   Make love's quick pants in Desdemona's arms,
   Give renewed fire to our extincted spirits,
   And bring all Cyprus comfort!

   Enter Desdemona, Iago, Roderigo, and Emilia.

                O, behold,
   The riches of the ship is come on shore!   85

---

64 *paragons* surpasses. *wild fame* extravagant report   65 *quirks* witty conceits. *blazoning* setting forth as though in heraldic language   66–67 *in . . . enginer* in her real, God-given, beauty, (she) defeats any attempt to praise her. *enginer* engineer, i.e., poet, one who devises. s.d. *[Second] Gentleman* (So identified in the Quarto text here and in lines 58, 61, 68, and 96; the Folio calls him a gentleman.) 67 *put in* i.e., to harbor   71 *guttered* jagged, trenched   72 *ensteeped* lying under water   73 *As* as if. *omit* forbear to exercise   74 *mortal* deadly   78 *footing* landing   79 *sennight's* week's   81 *tall* splendid, gallant

You men of Cyprus, let her have your knees.

[*The gentlemen make curtsy to Desdemona.*]

Hail to thee, lady! And the grace of heaven
Before, behind thee, and on every hand
Enwheel thee round!
Desdemona: I thank you, valiant Cassio.
What tidings can you tell me of my lord?   90
Cassio: He is not yet arrived, nor know I aught
But that he's well and will be shortly here.
Desdemona: O, but I fear—How lost you company?
Cassio: The great contention of the sea and skies
Parted our fellowship.

(*Within*)   "A sail, a sail!" [*A shot.*]
                                        But hark. A sail!   95
Second Gentleman: They give their greeting to the citadel.
This likewise is a friend.
Cassio: See for the news.

[*Exit Second Gentleman.*]

Good Ancient, you are welcome. [*Kissing Emilia.*] Welcome, mistress.
Let it not gall your patience, good Iago,
That I extend° my manners; 'tis my breeding°   100
That gives me this bold show of courtesy.
Iago: Sir, would she give you so much of her lips
As of her tongue she oft bestows on me,
You would have enough.
Desdemona: Alas, she has no speech!°   105
Iago: In faith, too much.
I find it still,° when I have list° to sleep.
Marry, before your ladyship, I grant,
She puts her tongue a little in her heart
And chides with thinking.°
Emilia: You have little cause to say so.   110
Iago: Come on, come on. You are pictures out of doors,°
Bells° in your parlors, wildcats in your kitchens,°

---

100 *extend* give scope to. *breeding* training in the niceties of etiquette   105 *she has no speech* i.e., she's not a chatterbox, as you allege   107 *still* always. *list* desire   110 *with thinking* i.e., in her thoughts only   111 *pictures out of doors* i.e., silent and well-behaved in public   112 *Bells* i.e., jangling, noisy, and brazen. *in your kitchens* i.e., in domestic affairs. (Ladies would not do the cooking.)

Saints° in your injuries, devils being offended,
Players° in your huswifery,° and huswives° in your beds.

Desdemona: O, fie upon thee, slanderer! 115

Iago: Nay, it is true, or else I am a Turk.°
You rise to play, and go to bed to work.

Emilia: You shall not write my praise.

Iago: No, let me not.

Desdemona: What wouldst write of me, if thou shouldst praise me?

Iago: O gentle lady, do not put me to 't, 120
For I am nothing if not critical.°

Desdemona: Come on, essay.°—There's one gone to the harbor?

Iago: Ay, madam.

Desdemona: I am not merry, but I do beguile
The thing I am° by seeming otherwise. 125
Come, how wouldst thou praise me?

Iago: I am about it, but indeed my invention
Comes from my pate as birdlime° does from frieze°—
It plucks out brains and all. But my Muse labors,°
And thus she is delivered: 130
If she be fair and wise, fairness and wit,
The one's for use, the other useth it.°

Desdemona: Well praised! How if she be black° and witty?

Iago: If she be black, and thereto have a wit,
She'll find a white° that shall her blackness fit.° 135

Desdemona: Worse and worse.

Emilia: How if fair and foolish?

Iago: She never yet was foolish that was fair,
For even her folly° helped her to an heir.°

Desdemona: These are old fond° paradoxes to make fools laugh i' th' alehouse.
What miserable praise hast thou for her that's foul and foolish? 140

Iago: There's none so foul° and foolish thereunto,°
But does foul° pranks which fair and wise ones do.

---

113 _Saints_ martyrs   114 _Players_ idlers, triflers, or deceivers. _huswifery_ housekeeping.
huswives hussies (i.e., women are "busy" in bed, or unduly thrifty in dispensing sexual favors)
116 _a Turk_ an infidel, not to be believed   121 _critical_ censorious   122 _essay_ try   125 _The
thing I am_ i.e., my anxious self   128 _birdlime_ sticky substance used to catch small birds.   _frieze_
coarse woolen cloth   129 _labors_ (1) exerts herself (2) prepares to deliver a child (with a following pun on _delivered_ in line 130)   132 _The one's . . . it_ i.e., her cleverness will make use of
her beauty   133 _black_ dark-complexioned, brunette   135 _a white_ a fair person (with wordplay on "wight," a person).   _fit_ (with sexual suggestion of mating)   138 _folly_ (with added
meaning of "lechery, wantonness").   _to an heir_ i.e., to bear a child   139 _fond_ foolish   141
foul ugly.   _thereunto_ in addition   142 _foul_ sluttish

Desdemona: O heavy ignorance! Thou praisest the worst best. But what
    praise couldst thou bestow on a deserving woman indeed, one that,
    in the authority of her merit, did justly put on the vouch° of very 145
    malice itself?

Iago: She that was ever fair, and never proud,
    Had tongue at will, and yet was never loud,
    Never lacked gold and yet went never gay,°
    Fled from her wish, and yet said, "Now I may,"° 150
    She that being angered, her revenge being nigh,
    Bade her wrong stay° and her displeasure fly,
    She that in wisdom never was so frail
    To change the cod's head for the salmon's tail,°
    She that could think and ne'er disclose her mind, 155
    See suitors following and not look behind,
    She was a wight, if ever such wight were—

Desdemona: To do what?

Iago: To suckle fools° and chronicle small beer.°

Desdemona: O most lame and impotent conclusion! Do not learn of him, 160
    Emilia, though he be thy husband. How say you, Cassio? Is he not a
    most profane° and liberal° counselor?

Cassio: He speaks home,° madam. You may relish° him more in° the
    soldier than in the scholar.

[Cassio and Desdemona stand together, conversing intimately.]

Iago [aside]: He takes her by the palm. Ay, well said,° whisper. With as 165
    little a web as this will I ensnare as great a fly as Cassio. Ay, smile
    upon her, do; I will gyve° thee in thine own courtship.° You say
    true;° 'tis so, indeed. If such tricks as these strip you out of your lieu-
    tenantry, it had been better you had not kissed your three fingers so
    oft, which now again you are most apt to play the sir° in. Very good; 170
    well kissed! An excellent courtesy! 'Tis so, indeed. Yet again your
    fingers to your lips? Would they were clyster pipes° for your sake!
    [Trumpet within.] The Moor! I know his trumpet.

---

145 *put . . . vouch* compel the approval   149 *gay* extravagantly clothed   150 *Fled . . . may*
avoided temptation where the choice was hers   152 *Bade . . . stay* i.e., resolved to put up
with her injury patiently   154 *To . . . tail* i.e., to exchange a lackluster husband for a sexy
lover (?) (*Cod's head* is slang for "penis," and *tail*, for "pudendum.")   159 *suckle fools* breast-
feed babies. *chronicle small beer* i.e., keep petty household accounts, keep track of trivial
matters   162 *profane* irreverent, ribald. *liberal* licentious, free-spoken   163 *home* right to
the target. (A term from fencing.) *relish* appreciate *in* in the character of   165 *well said*
well done   167 *gyve* fetter, shackle. *courtship* courtesy, show of courtly manners   167–168
You say true i.e., that's right, go ahead   170 *the sir* i.e., the fine gentleman   172 *clyster pipes*
tubes used for enemas and douches

Othello and Desdemona happily reunite in Cyprus. "They kiss" (II, i, 194 s.d.).

Cassio: 'Tis truly so.
Desdemona: Let's meet him and receive him.   175
Cassio: Lo, where he comes!

  Enter Othello and attendants.

Othello: O my fair warrior!
Desdemona: My dear Othello!
Othello: It gives me wonder great as my content
  To see you here before me. O my soul's joy,
  If after every tempest come such calms,   180
  May the winds blow till they have wakened death,

And let the laboring bark climb hills of seas
Olympus-high, and duck again as low
As hell's from heaven! If it were now to die,
'Twere now to be most happy, for I fear   185
My soul hath her content so absolute
That not another comfort like to this
Succeeds in unknown fate.°
Desdemona: The heavens forbid
But that our loves and comforts should increase
Even as our days do grow!   190
Othello: Amen to that, sweet powers!
I cannot speak enough of this content.
It stops me here; it is too much of joy.
And this, and this, the greatest discords be

[*They kiss.*]°

That e'er our hearts shall make!   195
Iago [*aside*]: O, you are well tuned now!
But I'll set down° the pegs that make this music,
As honest as I am.°
Othello: Come, let us to the castle.
News, friends! Our wars are done, the Turks are drowned. 200
How does my old acquaintance of this isle?—
Honey, you shall be well desired° in Cyprus;
I have found great love amongst them. O my sweet,
I prattle out of fashion,° and I dote
In mine own comforts.—I prithee, good Iago,   205
Go to the bay and disembark my coffers.°
Bring thou the master° to the citadel;
He is a good one, and his worthiness
Does challenge° much respect.—Come, Desdemona.—
Once more, well met at Cyprus!   210

Exeunt Othello and Desdemona [*and all but Iago and Roderigo*].

Iago [*to an attendant*]: Do thou meet me presently at the harbor. [To
Roderigo.] Come hither. If thou be'st valiant—as, they say, base men°

188 *Succeeds . . . fate* i.e., can follow in the unknown future   194 s.d. *They kiss* (The direction is from the Quarto.)   197 *set down* loosen (and hence untune the instrument)
198 *As . . . I am* for all my supposed honesty   202 *desired* welcomed   204 *out of fashion*
irrelevantly, incoherently (?)   206 *coffers* chests, baggage   207 *master* ship's captain
209 *challenge* lay claim to, deserve   212 *base men* even lowly born men

being in love have then a nobility in their natures more than is native to them—list° me. The Lieutenant tonight watches on the court of guard.° First, I must tell thee this: Desdemona is directly in love with him. 215

Roderigo: With him? Why, 'tis not possible.

Iago: Lay thy finger thus,° and let thy soul be instructed. Mark me with what violence she first loved the Moor, but° for bragging and telling her fantastical lies. To love him still for prating? Let not thy discreet 220 heart think it. Her eye must be fed; and what delight shall she have to look on the devil? When the blood is made dull with the act of sport,° there should be, again to inflame it and to give satiety a fresh appetite, loveliness in favor,° sympathy° in years, manners, and beauties—all which the Moor is defective in. Now, for want of these 225 required conveniences,° her delicate tenderness will find itself abused,° begin to heave the gorge,° disrelish and abhor the Moor. Very nature° will instruct her in it and compel her to some second choice. Now, sir, this granted—as it is a most pregnant° and unforced position—who stands so eminent in the degree of° this 230 fortune as Cassio does? A knave very voluble,° no further conscionable° than in putting on the mere form of civil and humane° seeming for the better compassing of his salt° and most hidden loose affection.° Why, none, why, none. A slipper° and subtle knave, a finder out of occasions, that has an eye can stamp° and counterfeit 235 advantages,° though true advantage never present itself; a devilish knave. Besides, the knave is handsome, young, and hath all those requisites in him that folly° and green° minds look after. A pestilent complete knave, and the woman hath found him° already.

Roderigo: I cannot believe that in her. She's full of most blessed condition.° 240

Iago: Blessed fig's end!° The wine she drinks is made of grapes. If she had been blessed, she would never have loved the Moor. Blessed pudding!° Didst thou not see her paddle with the palm of his hand? Didst not mark that?

---

214 *list* listen to   215 *court of guard* guardhouse. (Cassio is in charge of the watch.)   218 *thus* i.e., on your lips   219 *but* only   222–223 *the act of sport* sex   224 *favor* appearance. *sympathy* correspondence, similarity   226 *required conveniences* things conducive to sexual compatibility   227 *abused* cheated, revolted.   *heave the gorge* experience nausea   228 *Very nature* her very instincts   229 *pregnant* evident, cogent   230 *in . . . of* as next in line for   231 *voluble* facile, glib   231–232 *conscionable* conscientious, conscience-bound   232 *humane* polite, courteous.   233 *salt* licentious   234 *affection* passion.   *slipper* slippery   235 *an eye can stamp* an eye that can coin, create   236 *advantages* favorable opportunities   238 *folly* wantonness.   *green* immature   239 *found him* sized him up, perceived his intent   240 *condition* disposition   241 *fig's end* (See Act I, Scene iii, line   317 for the vulgar gesture of the fig.)   243 *pudding* sausage

Roderigo: Yes, that I did; but that was but courtesy. 245

Iago: Lechery, by this hand. An index° and obscure° prologue to the history of lust and foul thoughts. They met so near with their lips that their breaths embraced together. Villainous thoughts, Roderigo! When these mutualities° so marshal the way, hard at hand° comes the master and main exercise, th' incorporate° conclusion. Pish! But, 250 sir, be you ruled by me. I have brought you from Venice. Watch you° tonight; for the command, I'll lay 't upon you.° Cassio knows you not. I'll not be far from you. Do you find some occasion to anger Cassio, either by speaking too loud, or tainting° his discipline, or from what other course you please, which the time shall more favorably 255 minister.°

Roderigo: Well.

Iago: Sir, he's rash and very sudden in choler,° and haply° may strike at you. Provoke him that he may, for even out of that will I cause these of Cyprus to mutiny,° whose qualification° shall come into no true 260 taste° again but by the displanting of Cassio. So shall you have a shorter journey to your desires by the means I shall then have to prefer° them, and the impediment most profitably removed, without the which there were no expectation of our prosperity.

Roderigo: I will do this, if you can bring it to any opportunity. 265

Iago: I warrant° thee. Meet me by and by° at the citadel. I must fetch his necessaries ashore. Farewell.

Roderigo: Adieu.   *Exit.*

Iago: That Cassio loves her, I do well believe 't;
That she loves him, 'tis apt° and of great credit.° 270
The Moor, howbeit that I endure him not,
Is of a constant, loving, noble nature,
And I dare think he'll prove to Desdemona
A most dear husband. Now, I do love her too,
Not out of absolute lust—though peradventure 275
I stand accountant° for as great a sin—
But partly led to diet° my revenge
For that I do suspect the lusty Moor

---

246 *index* table of contents.   *obscure* (i.e., the *lust and foul thoughts* in line 247 are secret, hidden from view)   249 *mutualities* exchanges, intimacies.   *hard at hand* closely following   250 *incorporate* carnal   251 *Watch you* stand watch   252 *for the command . . . you* I'll arrange for you to be appointed, given orders   254 *tainting* disparaging   256 *minister* provide   258 *choler* wrath.   *haply* perhaps   260 *mutiny* riot.   *qualification* appeasement   260–261 *true taste* i.e., acceptable state   262 *prefer* advance   266 *warrant* assure.   *by and by* immediately   270 *apt* probable.   *credit* credibility   276 *accountant* accountable   277 *diet* feed

Hath leaped into my seat, the thought whereof
Doth, like a poisonous mineral, gnaw my innards; 280
And nothing can or shall content my soul
Till I am evened with him, wife for wife,
Or failing so, yet that I put the Moor
At least into a jealousy so strong
That judgment cannot cure. Which thing to do, 285
If this poor trash of Venice, whom I trace°
For° his quick hunting, stand the putting on,°
I'll have our Michael Cassio on the hip,°
Abuse° him to the Moor in the rank garb°—
For I fear Cassio with my nightcap° too— 290
Make the Moor thank me, love me, and reward me
For making him egregiously an ass
And practicing upon° his peace and quiet
Even to madness. 'Tis here, but yet confused.
Knavery's plain face is never seen till used.   *Exit.* 295

SCENE II [CYPRUS. A STREET.]

Enter Othello's Herald with a proclamation.

Herald: It is Othello's pleasure, our noble and valiant general, that, upon
certain tidings now arrived, importing the mere perdition° of the
Turkish fleet, every man put himself into triumph:° some to dance,
some to make bonfires, each man to what sport and revels his addiction°
leads him. For, besides these beneficial news, it is the celebration of   5
his nuptial. So much was his pleasure should be proclaimed. All
offices° are open, and there is full liberty of feasting from this present
hour of five till the bell have told eleven. Heaven bless the isle of
Cyprus and our noble general Othello!

Exit.

---

286 *trace* i.e., train, or follow (?), or perhaps *trash*, a hunting term, meaning to put weights
on a hunting dog in order to slow him down   287 *For* to make more eager.   *stand . . . on* respond properly when I incite him to quarrel   288 *on the hip* at my mercy, where I can throw
him. (A wrestling term.)   289 *Abuse* slander.   *rank garb* coarse manner, gross fashion   290
with my nightcap i.e., as a rival in my bed, as one who gives me cuckold's horns   293
practicing upon plotting against   2 *mere perdition* complete destruction   3 *triumph* public
celebration   4 *addiction* inclination   7 *offices* rooms where food and drink are kept

SCENE III [CYPRUS. THE CITADEL.]

Enter Othello, Desdemona, Cassio, and attendants.

Othello: Good Michael, look you to the guard tonight.
　　Let's teach ourselves that honorable stop°
　　Not to outsport° discretion.
Cassio: Iago hath direction what to do,
　　But notwithstanding, with my personal eye　　　　　　　　5
　　Will I look to 't.
Othello:　　　　　Iago is most honest.
　　Michael, good night. Tomorrow with your earliest°
　　Let me have speech with you. [*To Desdemona.*]
　　　　　　　　　Come, my dear love,
　　The purchase made, the fruits are to ensue;
　　That profit's yet to come 'tween me and you.°—　　　　　10
　　Good night.

　　Exit [Othello, with Desdemona and attendants].

　　Enter Iago.

Cassio: Welcome, Iago. We must to the watch.
Iago: Not this hour,° Lieutenant; 'tis not yet ten o' the clock. Our
　　general cast° us thus early for the love of his Desdemona; who° let us
　　not therefore blame. He hath not yet made wanton the night with　　15
　　her, and she is sport for Jove.
Cassio: She's a most exquisite lady.
Iago: And, I'll warrant her, full of game.
Cassio: Indeed, she's a most fresh and delicate creature.
Iago: What an eye she has! Methinks it sounds a parley° to provocation.　20
Cassio: An inviting eye, and yet methinks right modest.
Iago: And when she speaks, is it not an alarum° to love?
Cassio: She is indeed perfection.
Iago: Well, happiness to their sheets! Come, Lieutenant, I have a stoup°
　　of wine, and here without° are a brace° of Cyprus gallants that would　25
　　fain have a measure° to the health of black Othello.

---

2 *stop* restraint　3 *outsport* celebrate beyond the bounds of　7 *with your earliest* at your earliest convenience　9–10 *The purchase . . . you* i.e., though married, we haven't yet consum-
mated our love　13 *Not this hour* not for an hour yet　14 *cast* dismissed.　*who* i.e., Othello
20 *sounds a parley* calls for a conference, issues an invitation　22 *alarum* signal calling men to
arms (continuing the military metaphor of *parley*, line 20)　24 *stoup* measure of liquor, two
quarts　25 *without* outside. *brace* pair　26 *fain have a measure* gladly drink a toast

Cassio: Not tonight, good Iago. I have very poor and unhappy brains for drinking. I could well wish courtesy would invent some other custom of entertainment.

Iago: O, they are our friends. But one cup! I'll drink for you.° 30

Cassio: I have drunk but one cup tonight, and that was craftily qualified° too, and behold what innovation° it makes here.° I am unfortunate in the infirmity and dare not task my weakness with any more.

Iago: What, man? 'Tis a night of revels. The gallants desire it.

Cassio: Where are they? 35

Iago: Here at the door. I pray you, call them in.

Cassio: I'll do 't, but it dislikes me.° *Exit.*

Iago: If I can fasten but one cup upon him,
With that which he hath drunk tonight already,
He'll be as full of quarrel and offense° 40
As my young mistress' dog. Now, my sick fool Roderigo,
Whom love hath turned almost the wrong side out,
To Desdemona hath tonight caroused°
Potations pottle-deep;° and he's to watch.°
Three lads of Cyprus—noble swelling° spirits, 45
That hold their honors in a wary distance,°
The very elements° of this warlike isle—
Have I tonight flustered with flowing cups,
And they watch° too. Now, 'mongst this flock of drunkards
Am I to put our Cassio in some action 50
That may offend the isle.—But here they come.

Enter Cassio, Montano, and gentlemen; [servants following with wine].

If consequence do but approve my dream,°
My boat sails freely both with wind and stream.°

Cassio: 'Fore God, they have given me a rouse° already.

Montano: Good faith, a little one; not past a pint, as I am a soldier. 55

Iago: Some wine, ho! [He sings.]

"And let me the cannikin° clink, clink,
And let me the cannikin clink.

---

30 *for you* in your place. (Iago will do the steady drinking to keep the gallants company while Cassio has only one cup.) 31 *qualified* diluted 32 *innovation* disturbance, insurrection. *here* i.e., in my head 37 *it dislikes me* i.e., I'm reluctant 40 *offense* readiness to take offense 43 *caroused* drunk off 44 *pottle-deep* to the bottom of the tankard. *watch* stand watch 45 *swelling* proud 46 *hold . . . distance* i.e., are extremely sensitive of their honor 47 *very elements* typical sort 49 *watch* are members of the guard 52 *If . . . dream* if subsequent events will only substantiate my scheme 53 *stream* current 54 *rouse* full draft of liquor 57 *cannikin* small drinking vessel

> A soldier's a man,
> O, man's life's but a span;° 60
> Why, then, let a soldier drink."

Some wine, boys!

Cassio: 'Fore God, an excellent song.

Iago: I learned it in England, where indeed they are most potent in potting.° Your Dane, your German, and your swag-bellied Hollander— 65
drink, ho!—are nothing to your English.

Cassio: Is your Englishman so exquisite in his drinking?

Iago: Why, he drinks you,° with facility, your Dane° dead drunk; he
sweats not° to overthrow your Almain;° he gives your Hollander a
vomit ere the next pottle can be filled. 70

Cassio: To the health of our general!

Montano: I am for it, Lieutenant, and I'll do you justice.°

Iago: O sweet England! [*He sings.*]

> "King Stephen was and-a worthy peer,
> His breeches cost him but a crown; 75
> He held them sixpence all too dear,
> With that he called the tailor lown.°
>
> He was a wight of high renown,
> And thou art but of low degree.
> 'Tis pride° that pulls the country down; 80
> Then take thy auld° cloak about thee."

Some wine, ho!

Cassio: 'Fore God, this is a more exquisite song than the other.

Iago: Will you hear 't again?

Cassio: No, for I hold him to be unworthy of his place that does those 85
things. Well, God's above all; and there be souls must be saved, and
there be souls must not be saved.

Iago: It's true, good Lieutenant.

Cassio: For mine own part—no offense to the General, nor any man of
quality°—I hope to be saved. 90

Iago: And so do I too, Lieutenant.

---

60 *span* brief span of time. (Compare Psalm 39:6 as rendered in the 1928 Book of Common
Prayer: "Thou hast made my days as it were a span long.") 64–65 *potting* drinking 68
drinks you drinks. *your Dane* your typical Dane. 69 *sweats not* i.e., need not exert himself
Almain German 72 *I'll . . . justice* i.e., I'll drink as much as you 77 *lown* lout, rascal 80
pride i.e., extravagance in dress 81 *auld* old 90 *quality* rank

Cassio: Ay, but, by your leave, not before me; the lieutenant is to be
saved before the ancient. Let's have no more of this; let's to our
affairs.—God forgive us our sins!—Gentlemen, let's look to our business.
Do not think, gentlemen, I am drunk. This is my ancient; this is my   95
right hand, and this is my left. I am not drunk now. I can stand well
enough, and speak well enough.

Gentlemen: Excellent well.

Cassio: Why, very well then; you must not think then that I am drunk.
                                                                Exit.

Montano: To th' platform, masters. Come, let's set the watch.°   100

[*Exeunt Gentlemen.*]

Iago: You see this fellow that is gone before.
    He's a soldier fit to stand by Caesar
    And give direction; and do but see his vice.
    'Tis to his virtue a just equinox,°
    The one as long as th' other. 'Tis pity of him.   105
    I fear the trust Othello puts him in,
    On some odd time of his infirmity,
    Will shake this island.

Montano: But is he often thus?

Iago: 'Tis evermore the prologue to his sleep.
    He'll watch the horologe a double set,°   110
    If drink rock not his cradle.

Montano: It were well
    The General were put in mind of it.
    Perhaps he sees it not, or his good nature
    Prizes the virtue that appears in Cassio
    And looks not on his evils. Is not this true?   115

Enter Roderigo.

Iago [*aside to him*]: How now, Roderigo?
    I pray you, after the Lieutenant; go.   [*Exit Roderigo.*]

Montano: And 'tis great pity that the noble Moor
    Should hazard such a place as his own second
    With° one of an engraffed° infirmity.   120
    It were an honest action to say so
    To the Moor.

---

100 *set the watch* mount the guard   104 *just equinox* exact counterpart. (*Equinox* is an equal
length of days and nights.)   110 *watch . . . set* stay awake twice around the clock or
horologe   119–120 *hazard . . . With* risk giving such an important position as his second in
command to   120 *engraffed* engrafted, inveterate

Iago: Not I, for this fair island.
  I do love Cassio well and would do much
  To cure him of this evil.   [*Cry within:* "*Help! Help!*"]
                       But, hark! What noise?

  Enter Cassio, pursuing° *Roderigo.*

Cassio: Zounds, you rogue! You rascal!
Montano: What's the matter, Lieutenant?   125
Cassio: A knave teach me my duty? I'll beat the knave into a twiggen°
  bottle.
Roderigo: Beat me?
Cassio: Dost thou prate, rogue?   [*He strikes Roderigo.*]
Montano: Nay, good Lieutenant. [*Restraining him.*] I pray you, sir, hold   130
  your hand.
Cassio: Let me go, sir, or I'll knock you o'er the mazard.°
Montano: Come, come, you're drunk.
Cassio: Drunk?   [*They fight.*]
Iago [*aside to Roderigo*]: Away, I say. Go out and cry a mutiny.°   135

  [*Exit Roderigo.*]

  Nay, good Lieutenant—God's will, gentlemen—
  Help, ho!—Lieutenant—sir—Montano—sir—
  Help, masters!°—Here's a goodly watch indeed!

  [*A bell rings.*]°

  Who's that which rings the bell?—Diablo,° ho!
  The town will rise.° God's will, Lieutenant, hold!   140
  You'll be ashamed forever.

  Enter Othello and attendants [*with weapons*].

Othello: What is the matter here?
Montano: Zounds, I bleed still.
  I am hurt to th' death. He dies!   [*He thrusts at Cassio.*]
Othello: Hold, for your lives!
Iago: Hold, ho! Lieutenant—sir—Montano—gentlemen—

---

124 s.d. *pursuing* (The Quarto text reads, "driving in.")   126 *twiggen* wicker-covered. (Cassio vows to assail Roderigo until his skin resembles wickerwork or until he has driven
Roderigo through the holes in a wickerwork.)   132 *mazard* i.e., head. (Literally, a drinking
vessel.)   135 *mutiny* riot   138 *masters* sirs.   s.d. *A bell rings* (This direction is from the
Quarto, as are *Exit Roderigo* at line 117, *They fight* at line 134, and *with weapons* at line 141.)
139 *Diablo* the devil   140 *rise* grow riotous

Cassio, encouraged to drink by Iago, starts a fight with Montano (II, iii, 134).

    Have you forgot all sense of place and duty?   145
    Hold! The General speaks to you. Hold, for shame!
Othello: Why, how now, ho! From whence ariseth this?
    Are we turned Turks, and to ourselves do that
    Which heaven hath forbid the Ottomites?°
    For Christian shame, put by this barbarous brawl!   150
    He that stirs next to carve for° his own rage
    Holds his soul light;° he dies upon his motion.°
    Silence that dreadful bell. It frights the isle
    From her propriety.° What is the matter, masters?
    Honest Iago, that looks dead with grieving,   155
    Speak. Who began this? On thy love, I charge thee.

148–149 *to ourselves . . . Ottomites* inflict on ourselves the harm that heaven has prevented the Turks from doing (by destroying their fleet)   151 *carve for* i.e., indulge, satisfy with his sword   152 *Holds . . . light* i.e., places little value on his life. *upon his motion* if he moves 154 *propriety* proper state or condition

Iago: I do not know. Friends all but now, even now,
    In quarter° and in terms° like bride and groom
    Devesting them° for bed; and then, but now—
    As if some planet had unwitted men—   160
    Swords out, and tilting one at others' breasts
    In opposition bloody. I cannot speak°
    Any beginning to this peevish odds;°
    And would in action glorious I had lost
    Those legs that brought me to a part of it!   165
Othello: How comes it, Michael, you are thus forgot?°
Cassio: I pray you, pardon me. I cannot speak.
Othello: Worthy Montano, you were wont be° civil;
    The gravity and stillness° of your youth
    The world hath noted, and your name is great   170
    In mouths of wisest censure.° What's the matter
    That you unlace° your reputation thus
    And spend your rich opinion° for the name
    Of a night-brawler? Give me answer to it.
Montano: Worthy Othello, I am hurt to danger.   175
    Your officer, Iago, can inform you—
    While I spare speech, which something° now offends° me—
    Of all that I do know; nor know I aught
    By me that's said or done amiss this night,
    Unless self-charity be sometimes a vice,   180
    And to defend ourselves it be a sin
    When violence assails us.
Othello: Now, by heaven,
    My blood° begins my safer guides° to rule,
    And passion, having my best judgment collied,°
    Essays° to lead the way. Zounds, if I stir,   185
    Or do but lift this arm, the best of you
    Shall sink in my rebuke. Give me to know
    How this foul rout° began, who set it on;
    And he that is approved in° this offense,
    Though he had twinned with me, both at a birth,   190

---

158 *In quarter* in friendly conduct, within bounds. *in terms* on good terms 159 *Devesting them*
undressing themselves 162 *speak* explain 163 *peevish odds* childish quarrel 166 *are thus forgot* have forgotten yourself thus 168 *wont be* accustomed to be 169 *stillness* sobriety 171
censure judgment 172 *unlace* undo, lay open (as one might loose the strings of a purse containing reputation) 173 *opinion* reputation 177 *something* somewhat. *offends* pains 183 *blood*
passion (of anger). *guides* i.e., reason 184 *collied* darkened 185 *Essays* undertakes 188 *rout*
riot 189 *approved in* found guilty of

Shall lose me. What? In a town of° war
Yet wild, the people's hearts brim full of fear,
To manage° private and domestic quarrel?
In night, and on the court and guard of safety?°
'Tis monstrous. Iago, who began 't?   195

Montano [*to Iago*]: If partially affined,° or leagued in office,°
Thou dost deliver more or less than truth,
Thou art no soldier.

Iago: Touch me not so near.
I had rather have this tongue cut from my mouth
Than it should do offense to Michael Cassio;   200
Yet, I persuade myself, to speak the truth
Shall nothing wrong him. Thus it is, General.
Montano and myself being in speech,
There comes a fellow crying out for help,
And Cassio following him with determined sword   205
To execute° upon him. Sir, this gentleman

[*indicating Montano*]

Steps in to Cassio and entreats his pause.°
Myself the crying fellow did pursue,
Lest by his clamor—as it so fell out—
The town might fall in fright. He, swift of foot,   210
Outran my purpose, and I returned, the rather°
For that I heard the clink and fall of swords
And Cassio high in oath, which till tonight
I ne'er might say before. When I came back—
For this was brief—I found them close together   215
At blow and thrust, even as again they were
When you yourself did part them.
More of this matter cannot I report.
But men are men; the best sometimes forget.°
Though Cassio did some little wrong to him,   220
As men in rage strike those that wish them best,°
Yet surely Cassio, I believe, received
From him that fled some strange indignity,
Which patience could not pass.°

---

191 *town of* town garrisoned for   193 *manage* undertake   194 *on . . . safety* at the main guardhouse or headquarters and on watch   196 *partially affined* made partial by some personal relationship.   *leagued in office* in league as fellow officers   206 *execute* give effect to (his anger)
207 *his pause* him to stop   211 *rather* sooner   219 *forget* forget themselves   221 *those . . . best*
i.e., even those who are well disposed   224 *pass* pass over, overlook

Othello: I know, Iago,
    Thy honesty and love doth mince this matter,   225
    Making it light to Cassio. Cassio, I love thee,
    But nevermore be officer of mine.

Enter Desdemona, attended.

    Look if my gentle love be not raised up.
    I'll make thee an example.
Desdemona: What is the matter, dear?
Othello: All's well now, sweeting;   230
    Come away to bed. [*To Montano.*] Sir, for your hurts,
    Myself will be your surgeon.°—Lead him off.

[*Montano is led off.*]

    Iago, look with care about the town
    And silence those whom this vile brawl distracted.
    Come, Desdemona. 'Tis the soldiers' life   235
    To have their balmy slumbers waked with strife.

Exit [with all but Iago and Cassio].

Iago: What, are you hurt, Lieutenant?
Cassio: Ay, past all surgery.
Iago: Marry, God forbid!
Cassio: Reputation, reputation, reputation! O, I have lost my reputa-   240
tion! I have lost the immortal part of myself, and what remains is
bestial. My reputation, Iago, my reputation!
Iago: As I am an honest man, I thought you had received some bodily
wound; there is more sense in that than in reputation. Reputation is
an idle and most false imposition,° oft got without merit and lost   245
without deserving. You have lost no reputation at all, unless you
repute yourself such a loser. What, man, there are more ways to
recover° the General again. You are but now cast in his mood°—a
punishment more in policy° than in malice, even so as one would beat
his offenseless dog to affright an imperious lion.° Sue° to him again   250
and he's yours.

---

232 *be your surgeon* i.e., make sure you receive medical attention   245 *false imposition* thing
artificially imposed and of no real value   248 *recover* regain favor with.   *cast in his mood*
dismissed in a moment of anger.   249 *in policy* done for expediency's sake and as a public
gesture   249–250 *would . . . lion* i.e., would make an example of a minor offender in order
to deter more important and dangerous offenders   250 *Sue* petition

Iago advises Cassio to ask Desdemona to plea his cause with Othello (II, iii, 237–297).

Cassio: I will rather sue to be despised than to deceive so good a commander with so slight,° so drunken, and so indiscreet an officer.
Drunk? And speak parrot?° And squabble? Swagger? Swear? And discourse fustian with one's own shadow? O thou invisible spirit of   255
wine, if thou hast no name to be known by, let us call thee devil!

Iago: What was he that you followed with your sword? What had he
done to you?

Cassio: I know not.

Iago: Is 't possible?   260

Cassio: I remember a mass of things, but nothing distinctly; a quarrel,
but nothing wherefore.° O God, that men should put an enemy in
their mouths to steal away their brains! That we should, with joy,
pleasance, revel, and applause° transform ourselves into beasts!

Iago: Why, but you are now well enough. How came you thus recovered?   265

Cassio: It hath pleased the devil drunkenness to give place to the devil
wrath. One unperfectness shows me another, to make me frankly
despise myself.

253 *slight* worthless   254 *speak parrot* talk nonsense, rant   262 *wherefore* why   264 *applause*
desire for applause

Iago: Come, you are too severe a moraler.° As the time, the place, and
the condition of this country stands, I could heartily wish this had   270
not befallen; but since it is as it is, mend it for your own good.

Cassio: I will ask him for my place again; he shall tell me I am a drunkard. Had I as many mouths as Hydra,° such an answer would stop
them all. To be now a sensible man, by and by a fool, and presently
a beast! O, strange! Every inordinate cup is unblessed, and the ingre-   275
dient is a devil.

Iago: Come, come, good wine is a good familiar creature, if it be well
used. Exclaim no more against it. And, good Lieutenant, I think you
think I love you.

Cassio: I have well approved° it, sir. I drunk!   280

Iago: You or any man living may be drunk at a time,° man. I'll tell you
what you shall do. Our general's wife is now the general—I may say
so in this respect, for that° he hath devoted and given up himself to
the contemplation, mark, and denotement° of her parts° and graces.
Confess yourself freely to her; importune her help to put you in your   285
place again. She is of so free,° so kind, so apt, so blessed a disposition, she holds it a vice in her goodness not to do more than she is
requested. This broken joint between you and her husband entreat
her to splinter;° and, my fortunes against any lay° worth naming, this
crack of your love shall grow stronger than it was before.   290

Cassio: You advise me well.

Iago: I protest,° in the sincerity of love and honest kindness.

Cassio: I think it freely;° and betimes in the morning I will beseech the
virtuous Desdemona to undertake for me. I am desperate of my fortunes
if they check° me here.   295

Iago: You are in the right. Good night, Lieutenant. I must to the watch.

Cassio: Good night, honest Iago.   *Exit Cassio.*

Iago: And what's he then that says I play the villain,
    When this advice is free° I give, and honest,
    Probal° to thinking, and indeed the course   300
    To win the Moor again? For 'tis most easy
    Th' inclining° Desdemona to subdue°

---

269 *moraler* moralizer   273 *Hydra* the Lernaean Hydra, a monster with many heads and the
ability to grow two heads when one was cut off, slain by Hercules as the second of his twelve
labors   280 *approved* proved   281 *at a time* at one time or another   283 *in . . . that* in view of
this fact, that   284 *mark, and denotement* (Both words mean "observation.")   *parts* qualities
286 *free* generous   289 *splinter* bind with splints.   *lay* stake, wager   292 *protest* insist, declare
293 *freely* unreservedly   295 *check* repulse   299 *free* (1) free from guile (2) freely given
300 *Probal* probable, reasonable   302 *inclining* favorably disposed.   *subdue* persuade

In any honest suit; she's framed as fruitful°
As the free elements.° And then for her
To win the Moor—were 't to renounce his baptism,   305
All seals and symbols of redeemèd sin—
His soul is so enfettered to her love
That she may make, unmake, do what she list,
Even as her appetite° shall play the god
With his weak function.° How am I then a villain,   310
To counsel Cassio to this parallel° course
Directly to his good? Divinity of hell!°
When devils will the blackest sins put on,°
They do suggest° at first with heavenly shows,
As I do now. For whiles this honest fool   315
Plies Desdemona to repair his fortune,
And she for him pleads strongly to the Moor,
I'll pour this pestilence into his ear,
That she repeals him° for her body's lust;
And by how much she strives to do him good,   320
She shall undo her credit with the Moor.
So will I turn her virtue into pitch,°
And out of her own goodness make the net
That shall enmesh them all.

Enter Roderigo.

                       How now, Roderigo?

Roderigo: I do follow here in the chase, not like a hound that hunts, but   325
    one that fills up the cry.° My money is almost spent; I have been
    tonight exceedingly well cudgeled; and I think the issue will be I
    shall have so much° experience for my pains, and so, with no money
    at all and a little more wit, return again to Venice.

Iago: How poor are they that have not patience!   330
    What wound did ever heal but by degrees?

---

303 *framed as fruitful* created as generous   304 *free elements* i.e., earth, air, fire, and water,
unrestrained and spontaneous   309 *her appetite* her desire, or, perhaps, his desire for her
310 *function* exercise of faculties (weakened by his fondness for her)   311 *parallel* corresponding to these facts and to his best interests   312 *Divinity of hell* inverted theology of
hell (which seduces the soul to its damnation)   313 *put on* further, instigate   314 *suggest*
tempt   319 *repeals him* attempts to get him restored   322 *pitch* i.e., (1) foul blackness (2) a
snaring substance   326 *fills up the cry* merely takes part as one of the pack   328 *so much*
just so much and no more

Thou know'st we work by wit, and not by witchcraft,
And wit depends on dilatory time.
Does 't not go well? Cassio hath beaten thee,
And thou, by that small hurt, hast cashiered° Cassio.   335
Though other things grow fair against the sun,
Yet fruits that blossom first will first be ripe.°
Content thyself awhile. By the Mass, 'tis morning!
Pleasure and action make the hours seem short.
Retire thee; go where thou art billeted.   340
Away, I say! Thou shalt know more hereafter.
Nay, get thee gone.   *Exit Roderigo.*
                    Two things are to be done.
My wife must move° for Cassio to her mistress;
I'll set her on;
Myself the while to draw the Moor apart   345
And bring him jump° when he may Cassio find
Soliciting his wife. Ay, that's the way.
Dull not device° by coldness° and delay.   *Exit.*

ACT III

SCENE I [BEFORE THE CHAMBER OF OTHELLO AND DESDEMONA.]

Enter Cassio [and] Musicians.

Cassio: Masters, play here—I will content your pains°—
    Something that's brief, and bid "Good morrow, General." [*They play.*]

[*Enter*] *Clown.*

Clown: Why, masters, have your instruments been in Naples, that they
    speak i' the nose° thus?
A Musician: How, sir, how?   5
Clown: Are these, I pray you, wind instruments?

---

335 *cashiered* dismissed from service   336–337 *Though . . . ripe* i.e., plans that are well prepared and set expeditiously in motion will soonest ripen into success   343 *move* plead
346 *jump* precisely   348 *device* plot.   *coldness* lack of zeal   1 *content your pains* reward your
efforts   4 *speak i' the nose* (1) sound nasal (2) sound like one whose nose has been attacked
by syphilis. (Naples was popularly supposed to have a high incidence of venereal disease.)

A Musician: Ay, marry, are they, sir.

Clown: O, thereby hangs a tail.

A Musician: Whereby hangs a tale, sir?

Clown: Marry, sir, by many a wind instrument° that I know. But, 10
masters, here's money for you. [*He gives money.*] And the General so
likes your music that he desires you, for love's sake,° to make no
more noise with it.

A Musician: Well, sir, we will not.

Clown: If you have any music that may not° be heard, to 't again; but, as 15
they say, to hear music the General does not greatly care.

A Musician: We have none such, sir.

Clown: Then put up your pipes in your bag, for I'll away.° Go, vanish
into air, away! *Exeunt Musicians.*

Cassio: Dost thou hear, mine honest friend? 20

Clown: No, I hear not your honest friend; I hear you.

Cassio: Prithee, keep up° thy quillets.° There's a poor piece of gold for
thee. [*He gives money.*] If the gentle-woman that attends the General's wife be stirring, tell her there's one Cassio entreats her a little
favor of speech.° Wilt thou do this? 25

Clown: She is stirring, sir. If she will stir° hither, I shall seem° to notify
unto her.

Cassio: Do, good my friend. *Exit Clown.*

Enter Iago.

In happy time,° Iago.

Iago: You have not been abed, then?

Cassio: Why, no. The day had broke 30
Before we parted. I have made bold, Iago,
To send in to your wife. My suit to her
Is that she will to virtuous Desdemona
Procure me some access.

Iago: I'll send her to you presently; 35
And I'll devise a means to draw the Moor

---

10 *wind instrument* (With a joke on flatulence.   The *tail,* line 8, that hangs nearby the *wind instrument* suggests the penis.)   12 *for love's sake* (1) out of friendship and affection (2) for the sake of lovemaking in Othello's marriage   15 *may not* cannot   18 *I'll away* (Possibly a misprint, or a snatch of song?)   22 *keep up* do not bring out, do not use.   *quillets* quibbles, puns   24–25 *a little . . . speech* the favor of a brief talk   26 *stir* bestir herself (with a play on stirring, "rousing herself from rest")   *seem* deem it good, think fit   28 *In happy time* i.e., well met

Out of the way, that your converse and business
May be more free.
Cassio: I humbly thank you for 't.   *Exit* [*Iago*].
                       I never knew
A Florentine° more kind and honest.   40

Enter Emilia.

Emilia: Good morrow, good Lieutenant. I am sorry
For your displeasure;° but all will sure be well.
The General and his wife are talking of it,
And she speaks for you stoutly.° The Moor replies
That he you hurt is of great fame° in Cyprus   45
And great affinity,° and that in wholesome wisdom
He might not but refuse you; but he protests° he loves you
And needs no other suitor but his likings
To take the safest occasion by the front°
To bring you in again.
Cassio: Yet I beseech you,   50
If you think fit, or that it may be done,
Give me advantage of some brief discourse
With Desdemona alone.
Emilia: Pray you, come in.
                   I will bestow you where you shall have time
To speak your bosom° freely.   55
Cassio: I am much bound to you.   [*Exeunt.*]

SCENE II [THE CITADEL.]

Enter Othello, Iago, and Gentlemen.

Othello [*giving letters*]: These letters give, Iago, to the pilot,
And by him do my duties° to the Senate.
That done, I will be walking on the works;°
Repair° there to me.

---

40 *Florentine* i.e., even a fellow Florentine. (Iago is a Venetian; Cassio is a Florentine.)   42
displeasure fall from favor   44 *stoutly* spiritedly   45 *fame* reputation, importance   46
affinity kindred, family connection   47 *protests* insists   49 *occasion . . . front* opportunity
by the forelock   55 *bosom* inmost thoughts   2 *do my duties* convey my respects   3 *works*
breastworks, fortifications   4 *Repair* return, come

Iago:　　　　　　　　　　　Well, my good lord, I'll do 't.
Othello:　This fortification, gentlemen, shall we see 't?　　　　　　5
Gentlemen:　We'll wait upon° your lordship.　　　　　　*Exeunt.*

SCENE III [THE GARDEN OF THE CITADEL.]

　Enter Desdemona, Cassio, and Emilia.

Desdemona:　Be thou assured, good Cassio, I will do
　All my abilities in thy behalf.
Emilia:　Good madam, do. I warrant it grieves my husband
　As if the cause were his.
Desdemona:　O, that's an honest fellow. Do not doubt, Cassio,　　5
　But I will have my lord and you again
　As friendly as you were.
Cassio:　　　　　　　　　　Bounteous madam,
　Whatever shall become of Michael Cassio,
　He's never anything but your true servant.
Desdemona:　I know 't. I thank you. You do love my lord;　　　10
　You have known him long, and be you well assured
　He shall in strangeness° stand no farther off
　Than in a politic° distance.
Cassio:　　　　　　　　　　Ay, but, lady,
　That policy may either last so long,
　Or feed upon such nice and waterish diet,°　　　　　　15
　Or breed itself so out of circumstance,°
　That, I being absent and my place supplied,°
　My general will forget my love and service.
Desdemona:　Do not doubt° that. Before Emilia here
　I give thee warrant° of thy place. Assure thee,　　　　　20
　If I do vow a friendship I'll perform it
　To the last article. My lord shall never rest.
　I'll watch him tame° and talk him out of patience;°
　His bed shall seem a school, his board° a shrift;°
　I'll intermingle everything he does　　　　　　　　25

6 *wait upon* attend　　12 *strangeness* aloofness　　13 *politic* required by wise policy　　15 *Or . . . diet* or sustain itself at length upon such trivial and meager technicalities　　16 *breed . . . circumstance* continually renew itself so out of chance events, or yield so few chances for my being pardoned　　17 *supplied* filled by another person　　19 *doubt* fear　　20 *warrant* guarantee　　23 *watch him tame* tame him by keeping him from sleeping. (A term from falconry.)　*out of patience* past his endurance　　24 *board* dining table.　*shrift* confessional

With Cassio's suit. Therefore be merry, Cassio,
For thy solicitor° shall rather die
Than give thy cause away.°

Enter Othello and Iago [at a distance].

Emilia: Madam, here comes my lord.
Cassio: Madam, I'll take my leave.
Desdemona: Why, stay, and hear me speak.   30
Cassio: Madam, not now. I am very ill at ease,
    Unfit for mine own purposes.
Desdemona: Well, do your discretion.°   *Exit Cassio.*
Iago: Ha? I like not that.   35
Othello: What dost thou say?
Iago: Nothing, my lord; or if—I know not what.
Othello: Was not that Cassio parted from my wife?
Iago: Cassio, my lord? No, sure, I cannot think it,
    That he would steal away so guiltylike,   40
    Seeing you coming.
Othello: I do believe 'twas he.
Desdemona: How now, my lord?
    I have been talking with a suitor here,
    A man that languishes in your displeasure.   45
Othello: Who is 't you mean?
Desdemona: Why, your lieutenant, Cassio. Good my lord,
    If I have any grace or power to move you,
    His present reconciliation take;°
    For if he be not one that truly loves you,   50
    That errs in ignorance and not in cunning,°
    I have no judgment in an honest face.
    I prithee, call him back.
Othello: Went he hence now?
Desdemona: Yes, faith, so humbled   55
    That he hath left part of his grief with me
    To suffer with him. Good love, call him back.
Othello: Not now, sweet Desdemon. Some other time.
Desdemona: But shall 't be shortly?
Othello: The sooner, sweet, for you.   60

27 *solicitor* advocate   28 *away* up   34 *do your discretion* act according to your own
discretion   49 *His . . . take* let him be reconciled to you right away   51 *in cunning* wit-
tingly

Desdemona: Shall 't be tonight at supper?
Othello: No, not tonight.
Desdemona: Tomorrow dinner,° then?
Othello: I shall not dine at home.
    I meet the captains at the citadel. 65
Desdemona: Why, then, tomorrow night, or Tuesday morn,
    On Tuesday noon, or night, on Wednesday morn.
    I prithee, name the time, but let it not
    Exceed three days. In faith, he's penitent;
    And yet his trespass, in our common reason°— 70
    Save that, they say, the wars must make example
    Out of her best°—is not almost° a fault
    T' incur a private check.° When shall he come?
    Tell me, Othello. I wonder in my soul
    What you would ask me that I should deny, 75
    Or stand so mammering on.° What? Michael Cassio,
    That came a-wooing with you, and so many a time,
    When I have spoke of you dispraisingly,
    Hath ta'en your part—to have so much to do
    To bring him in!° By 'r Lady, I could do much— 80
Othello: Prithee, no more. Let him come when he will;
    I will deny thee nothing.
Desdemona: Why, this is not a boon.
    'Tis as I should entreat you wear your gloves,
    Or feed on nourishing dishes, or keep you warm, 85
    Or sue to you to do a peculiar° profit
    To your own person. Nay, when I have a suit
    Wherein I mean to touch° your love indeed,
    It shall be full of poise° and difficult weight,
    And fearful to be granted. 90
Othello: I will deny thee nothing.
    Whereon,° I do beseech thee, grant me this,
    To leave me but a little to myself.
Desdemona: Shall I deny you? No. Farewell, my lord.
Othello: Farewell, my Desdemona. I'll come to thee straight.° 95

---

63 *dinner* (The noontime meal.)   70 *common reason* everyday judgments   71–72 *Save . . . best* were it not that, as the saying goes, military discipline requires making an example of the very best men. (Her refers to *wars* as a singular concept.)   72 *not almost* scarcely   73 *private check* even a private reprimand   76 *mammering on* wavering about   80 *bring him in* restore him to favor   86 *peculiar* particular, personal   88 *touch* test   89 *poise* weight, heaviness; or equipoise, delicate balance involving hard choice   92 *Whereon* in return for which   95 *straight* straightway

Desdemona: Emilia, come.—Be as your fancies° teach you;
    Whate'er you be, I am obedient.   *Exit [with Emilia].*
Othello: Excellent wretch!° Perdition catch my soul
    But I do love thee! And when I love thee not,
    Chaos is come again.°   100
Iago: My noble lord—
Othello: What dost thou say, Iago?
Iago: Did Michael Cassio, when you wooed my lady,
    Know of your love?
Othello: He did, from first to last. Why dost thou ask?   105
Iago: But for a satisfaction of my thought;
    No further harm.
Othello: Why of thy thought, Iago?
Iago: I did not think he had been acquainted with her.
Othello: O, yes, and went between us very oft.
Iago: Indeed?   110
Othello: Indeed? Ay, indeed. Discern'st thou aught in that?
    Is he not honest?
Iago: Honest, my lord?
Othello: Honest. Ay, honest.
Iago: My lord, for aught I know.   115
Othello: What dost thou think?
Iago: Think, my lord?
Othello: "Think, my lord?" By heaven, thou echo'st me,
    As if there were some monster in thy thought
    Too hideous to be shown. Thou dost mean something.   120
    I heard thee say even now, thou lik'st not that,
    When Cassio left my wife. What didst not like?
    And when I told thee he was of my counsel°
    In my whole course of wooing, thou criedst "Indeed?"
    And didst contract and purse° thy brow together   125
    As if thou then hadst shut up in thy brain
    Some horrible conceit.° If thou dost love me,
    Show me thy thought.
Iago: My lord, you know I love you.
Othello: I think thou dost;   130
    And, for° I know thou'rt full of love and honesty,

---

96 *fancies* inclinations   98 *wretch* (A term of affectionate endearment.)   99–100 *And . . .*
again i.e., my love for you will last forever, until the end of time when chaos will return.
(But with an unconscious, ironic suggestion that, if anything should induce Othello to
cease loving Desdemona, the result would be chaos.)   123 *of my counsel* in my confidence
125 *purse* knit   127 *conceit* fancy   131 *for* because

And weigh'st thy words before thou giv'st them breath,
Therefore these stops° of thine fright me the more;
For such things in a false disloyal knave
Are tricks of custom,° but in a man that's just   135
They're close dilations,° working from the heart
That passion cannot rule.°

Iago: For° Michael Cassio,
I dare be sworn I think that he is honest.

Othello: I think so too.

Iago: Men should be what they seem;
Or those that be not, would they might seem none!°   140

Othello: Certain, men should be what they seem.

Iago: Why, then, I think Cassio's an honest man.

Othello: Nay, yet there's more in this.
I prithee, speak to me as to thy thinkings,
As thou dost ruminate, and give thy worst of thoughts   145
The worst of words.

Iago: Good my lord, pardon me.
Though I am bound to every act of duty,
I am not bound to that° all slaves are free to.°
Utter my thoughts? Why, say they are vile and false,
As where's the palace whereinto foul things   150
Sometimes intrude not? Who has that breast so pure
But some uncleanly apprehensions
Keep leets and law days,° and in sessions sit
With° meditations lawful?°

Othello: Thou dost conspire against thy friend,° Iago,   155
If thou but think'st him wronged and mak'st his ear
A stranger to thy thoughts.

Iago: I do beseech you,
Though I perchance am vicious° in my guess—
As I confess it is my nature's plague
To spy into abuses, and oft my jealousy°   160

---

133 *stops* pauses   135 *of custom* customary   136 *close dilations* secret or involuntary expressions or delays   137 *That passion cannot rule* i.e., that are too passionately strong to be restrained (referring to the workings), or that cannot rule its own passions (referring to the heart).   *For* as for   140 *none* i.e., not to be men, or not seem to be honest   148 *that* that which.   *free to* free with respect to   153 *Keep leets and law days* i.e., hold court, set up their authority in one's heart. (*Leets* are a kind of manor court; *law days* are the days courts sit in session, or those sessions.)   154 *With* along with.   *lawful* innocent   155 *thy friend* i.e., Othello.   158 *vicious* wrong   160 *jealousy* suspicious nature

Shapes faults that are not—that your wisdom then,°
From one° that so imperfectly conceits,°
Would take no notice, nor build yourself a trouble
Out of his scattering° and unsure observance.
It were not for your quiet nor your good,   165
Nor for my manhood, honesty, and wisdom,
To let you know my thoughts.

Othello: What dost thou mean?

Iago: Good name in man and woman, dear my lord,
    Is the immediate° jewel of their souls.
    Who steals my purse steals trash; 'tis something, nothing;   170
    'Twas mine, 'tis his, and has been slave to thousands;
    But he that filches from me my good name
    Robs me of that which not enriches him
    And makes me poor indeed.

Othello: By heaven, I'll know thy thoughts.   175

Iago: You cannot, if° my heart were in your hand,
    Nor shall not, whilst 'tis in my custody.

Othello: Ha?

Iago: O, beware, my lord, of jealousy.
    It is the green-eyed monster which doth mock
    The meat it feeds on.° That cuckold lives in bliss   180
    Who, certain of his fate, loves not his wronger;°
    But O, what damnèd minutes tells° he o'er
    Who dotes, yet doubts, suspects, yet fondly loves!

Othello: O misery!

Iago: Poor and content is rich, and rich enough,°   185
    But riches fineless° is as poor as winter
    To him that ever fears he shall be poor.
    Good God, the souls of all my tribe defend
    From jealousy!

Othello: Why, why is this?   190
    Think'st thou I'd make a life of jealousy,
    To follow still the changes of the moon

---

161 *then* on that account   162 *one* i.e., myself, Iago. *conceits* judges, conjectures   164
scattering random   169 *immediate* essential, most precious   176 *if* even if   179–180 *doth
mock . . . on* mocks and torments the heart of its victim, the man who suffers jealousy   181
his wronger i.e., his faithless wife. (The unsuspecting cuckold is spared the misery of loving
his wife only to discover she is cheating on him.)   182 *tells* counts   185 *Poor . . . enough*
to be content with what little one has is the greatest wealth of all. (Proverbial.)   186
fineless boundless

With fresh suspicions?° No! To be once in doubt
Is once° to be resolved.° Exchange me for a goat
When I shall turn the business of my soul   195
To such exsufflicate and blown° surmises
Matching thy inference.° 'Tis not to make me jealous
To say my wife is fair, feeds well, loves company,
Is free of speech, sings, plays, and dances well;
Where virtue is, these are more virtuous.   200
Nor from mine own weak merits will I draw
The smallest fear or doubt of her revolt,°
For she had eyes, and chose me. No, Iago,
I'll see before I doubt; when I doubt, prove;
And on the proof, there is no more but this—   205
Away at once with love or jealousy.

Iago: I am glad of this, for now I shall have reason
To show the love and duty that I bear you
With franker spirit. Therefore, as I am bound,
Receive it from me. I speak not yet of proof.   210
Look to your wife; observe her well with Cassio.
Wear your eyes thus, not° jealous nor secure.°
I would not have your free and noble nature,
Out of self-bounty,° be abused.° Look to 't.
I know our country disposition well;   215
In Venice they do let God see the pranks
They dare not show their husbands; their best conscience
Is not to leave 't undone, but keep 't unknown.

Othello: Dost thou say so?

Iago: She did deceive her father, marrying you;   220
And when she seemed to shake and fear your looks,
She loved them most.

Othello: And so she did.

Iago: Why, go to,° then!
She that, so young, could give out such a seeming,°
To seel° her father's eyes up close as oak,°

192–193 *To follow . . . suspicions* to be constantly imagining new causes for suspicion, changing incessantly like the moon   194 *once* once and for all.   *resolved* free of doubt, having settled the matter   196 *exsufflicate and blown* inflated and blown up, rumored about, or, spat out and flyblown, hence, loathsome, disgusting   197 *inference* description or allegation   202 *doubt . . . revolt* fear of her unfaithfulness   212 *not* neither.   *secure* free from uncertainty   214 *self-bounty* inherent or natural goodness and generosity.   *abused* deceived   222 *go to* (An expression of impatience.)   223 *seeming* false appearance   224 *seel* blind. (A term from falconry.)   *oak* (A close-grained wood.)

He thought 'twas witchcraft! But I am much to blame.   225
I humbly do beseech you of your pardon
For too much loving you.
Othello: I am bound° to thee forever.
Iago: I see this hath a little dashed your spirits.
Othello: Not a jot, not a jot.
Iago: I' faith, I fear it has.   230
I hope you will consider what is spoke
Comes from my love. But I do see you're moved.
I am to pray you not to strain my speech
To grosser issues° nor to larger reach°
Than to suspicion.   235
Othello: I will not.
Iago: Should you do so, my lord,
My speech should fall into such vile success°
Which my thoughts aimed not. Cassio's my worthy friend.
My lord, I see you're moved.
Othello: No, not much moved.   240
I do not think but Desdemona's honest.°
Iago: Long live she so! And long live you to think so!
Othello: And yet, how nature erring from itself—
Iago: Ay, there's the point! As—to be bold with you—
Not to affect° many proposèd matches   245
Of her own clime, complexion, and degree,°
Whereto we see in all things nature tends—
Foh! One may smell in such a will° most rank,
Foul disproportion,° thoughts unnatural.
But pardon me. I do not in position°   250
Distinctly speak of her, though I may fear
Her will, recoiling° to her better° judgment,
May fall to match you with her country forms°
And happily° repent.
Othello: Farewell, farewell!
If more thou dost perceive, let me know more.   255
Set on thy wife to observe. Leave me, Iago.

228 *bound* indebted (but perhaps with ironic sense of "tied")   234 *issues* significances.
reach meaning, scope   238 *success* effect, result   241 *honest* chaste   245 *affect* prefer, desire
246 *clime . . . degree* country, color, and social position   248 *will* sensuality,
appetite   249 *disproportion* abnormality   250 *position* argument, proposition
252 *recoiling* reverting.   *better* i.e., more natural and reconsidered   253 *fall . . . forms* undertake to compare you with Venetian norms of handsomeness   254 *happily repent* haply repent
her marriage

Iago [going]: My lord, I take my leave.
Othello: Why did I marry? This honest creature doubtless
    Sees and knows more, much more, than he unfolds.
Iago [returning]: My Lord, I would I might entreat your honor   260
    To scan° this thing no farther. Leave it to time.
    Although 'tis fit that Cassio have his place—
    For, sure, he fills it up with great ability—
    Yet, if you please to hold him off awhile,
    You shall by that perceive him and his means.°   265
    Note if your lady strain his entertainment°
    With any strong or vehement importunity;
    Much will be seen in that. In the meantime,
    Let me be thought too busy° in my fears—
    As worthy cause I have to fear I am—   270
    And hold her free,° I do beseech your honor.
Othello: Fear not my government.°
Iago: I once more take my leave.   *Exit.*
Othello: This fellow's of exceeding honesty,
    And knows all qualities,° with a learnèd spirit,   275
    Of human dealings. If I do prove her haggard,°
    Though that her jesses° were my dear heartstrings,
    I'd whistle her off and let her down the wind°
    To prey at fortune.° Haply, for° I am black
    And have not those soft parts of conversation°   280
    That chamberers° have, or for I am declined
    Into the vale of years—yet that's not much—
    She's gone. I am abused,° and my relief
    Must be to loathe her. O curse of marriage,
    That we can call these delicate creatures ours   285
    And not their appetites! I had rather be a toad
    And live upon the vapor of a dungeon
    Than keep a corner in the thing I love
    For others' uses. Yet, 'tis the plague of great ones;

---

261 *scan* scrutinize   265 *his means* the method he uses (to regain his post)   266 *strain his entertainment* urge his reinstatement   269 *busy* interfering   271 *hold her free* regard her as innocent   272 *government* self-control, conduct   275 *qualities* natures, types   276 *haggard* wild (like a wild female hawk)   277 *jesses* straps fastened around the legs of a trained hawk   278 *I'd . . . wind* i.e., I'd let her go forever. (To release a hawk downwind was to invite it not to return.)   279 *prey at fortune* fend for herself in the wild.   *Haply, for* perhaps because   280 *soft . . . conversation* pleasing graces of social behavior   281 *chamberers* gallants   283 *abused* deceived

Desdemona offers Othello her handkerchief to ease his headache (III, iii, 301–304).

Prerogatived° are they less than the base.°   290
'Tis destiny unshunnable, like death.
Even then this forkèd° plague is fated to us
When we do quicken.° Look where she comes.

Enter Desdemona and Emilia.

If she be false, O, then heaven mocks itself!
I'll not believe 't.
Desdemona: How now, my dear Othello?   295
Your dinner, and the generous° islanders
By you invited, do attend° your presence.
Othello: I am to blame.
Desdemona: Why do you speak so faintly?
Are you not well?

290 *Prerogatived* privileged (to have honest wives).   *the base* ordinary citizens. (Socially prominent men are especially prone to the unavoidable destiny of being cuckolded and to the public
shame that goes with it.)   292 *forkèd* (An allusion to the horns of the cuckold.)   293 *quicken*
receive life. (Quicken may also mean to swarm with maggots as the body festers, as in Act IV,
Scene ii, line 69, in which case lines 292–293 suggest that *even then*, in death, we are cuckolded
by *forkèd* worms.)   296 *generous* noble   297 *attend* await

Othello: I have a pain upon my forehead here. 300
Desdemona: Faith, that's with watching.° 'Twill away again.

> [*She offers her handkerchief.*]

Let me but bind it hard, within this hour
It will be well.
Othello: Your napkin° is too little.
Let it alone.° Come, I'll go in with you.

> [*He puts the handkerchief from him, and it drops.*]

Desdemona: I am very sorry that you are not well. 305

> *Exit* [*with Othello*].

Emilia [*picking up the handkerchief*]: I am glad I have found this napkin.
This was her first remembrance from the Moor.
My wayward° husband hath a hundred times
Wooed me to steal it, but she so loves the token—
For he conjured her she should ever keep it— 310
That she reserves it evermore about her
To kiss and talk to. I'll have the work ta'en out,°
And give 't Iago. What he will do with it
Heaven knows, not I;
I nothing but to please his fantasy.° 315

> *Enter Iago.*

Iago: How now? What do you here alone?
Emilia: Do not you chide. I have a thing for you.
Iago: You have a thing for me? It is a common thing°—
Emilia: Ha?
Iago: To have a foolish wife. 320
Emilia: O, is that all? What will you give me now
For that same handkerchief?
Iago: What handkerchief?
Emilia: What handkerchief?
Why, that the Moor first gave to Desdemona; 325
That which so often you did bid me steal.
Iago: Hast stolen it from her?
Emilia: No, faith. She let it drop by negligence,
And to th' advantage° I, being here, took 't up.
Look, here 'tis.

---

301 *watching* too little sleep   303 *napkin* handkerchief   304 *Let it alone* i.e., never mind   308
wayward capricious   312 *work ta'en out* design of the embroidery copied   315 *fantasy* whim
318 *common thing* (With bawdy suggestion; *common* suggests coarseness and availability to all
comers, and *thing* is a slang term for the pudendum.)   329 *to th' advantage* taking the opportunity

IAGO: "I have use for it. Go, leave me. / I will in Cassio's lodging lose this napkin" (III, iii, 336–337).

Iago:	A good wench! Give it me.	330
Emilia:	What will you do with 't, that you have been so earnest
	To have me filch it?
Iago [*snatching it*]:	Why, what is that to you?
Emilia:	If it be not for some purpose of import,
	Give 't me again. Poor lady, she'll run mad
	When she shall lack° it.
Iago:	Be not acknown on 't.°	335
	I have use for it. Go, leave me.	*Exit Emilia.*

335 *lack* miss.   *Be . . . on 't* do not confess knowledge of it

I will in Cassio's lodging lose° this napkin
And let him find it. Trifles light as air
Are to the jealous confirmations strong
As proofs of Holy Writ. This may do something.   340
The Moor already changes with my poison.
Dangerous conceits° are in their natures poisons,
Which at the first are scarce found to distaste,°
But with a little act° upon the blood
Burn like the mines of sulfur.

Enter Othello.

                                 I did say so.   345
Look where he comes! Not poppy nor mandragora°
Nor all the drowsy syrups of the world
Shall ever medicine thee to that sweet sleep
Which thou owedst° yesterday.
Othello: Ha, ha, false to me?
Iago: Why, how now, General? No more of that.   350
Othello: Avaunt! Begone! Thou hast set me on the rack.
I swear 'tis better to be much abused
Than but to know 't a little.
Iago: How now, my lord?
Othello: What sense had I of her stolen hours of lust?
I saw 't not, thought it not, it harmed not me.   355
I slept the next night well, fed well, was free° and merry;
I found not Cassio's kisses on her lips.
He that is robbed, not wanting° what is stolen,
Let him not know 't and he's not robbed at all.
Iago: I am sorry to hear this.   360
Othello: I had been happy if the general camp,
Pioners° and all, had tasted her sweet body,
So° I had nothing known. O, now, forever
Farewell the tranquil mind! Farewell content!
Farewell the plumèd troops and the big° wars   365
That makes ambition virtue! O, farewell!

---

337 *lose* (The Folio spelling, *loose,* is a normal spelling for "lose," but it may also contain the idea of "let go," "release.")   342 *conceits* fancies, ideas   343 *distaste* be distasteful   344 *act* action, working   346 *mandragora* an opiate made of the mandrake root   349 *thou owedst* you did own   356 *free* carefree   358 *wanting* missing   362 *Pioners* diggers of mines, the lowest grade of soldiers   363 *So* provided   365 *big* stately

Farewell the neighing steed and the shrill trump,
The spirit-stirring drum, th' ear-piercing fife,
The royal banner, and all quality,°
Pride,° pomp, and circumstance° of glorious war! 370
And O, you mortal engines,° whose rude throats
Th' immortal Jove's dread clamors° counterfeit,
Farewell! Othello's occupation's gone.

Iago: Is 't possible, my lord?

Othello: Villain, be sure thou prove my love a whore! 375
Be sure of it. Give me the ocular proof,
Or, by the worth of mine eternal soul,
Thou hadst been better have been born a dog
Than answer my waked wrath!

Iago: Is 't come to this?

Othello: Make me to see 't, or at the least so prove it 380
That the probation° bear no hinge nor loop
To hang a doubt on, or woe upon thy life!

Iago: My noble lord—

Othello: If thou dost slander her and torture me,
Never pray more; abandon all remorse;° 385
On horror's head horrors accumulate;°
Do deeds to make heaven weep, all earth amazed;°
For nothing canst thou to damnation add
Greater than that.

Iago: O grace! O heaven forgive me!
Are you a man? Have you a soul or sense? 390
God b' wi' you; take mine office. O wretched fool,°
That lov'st to make thine honesty a vice!°
O monstrous world! Take note, take note, O world,
To be direct and honest is not safe.
I thank you for this profit,° and from hence° 395
I'll love no friend, sith° love breeds such offense.°

Othello: Nay, stay. Thou shouldst be° honest.

---

369 *quality* character, essential nature   370 *Pride* rich display. *circumstance* pageantry   371 *mortal engines* i.e., cannon. (*Mortal* means "deadly.")   372 *Jove's dread clamors* i.e., thunder   381 *probation* proof   385 *remorse* pity, penitent hope for salvation   386 *horrors accumulate* add still more horrors   387 *amazed* confounded with horror   391 *O wretched fool* (Iago addresses himself as a fool for having carried honesty too far.)   392 *vice* failing, something overdone   395 *profit* profitable instruction. *hence* henceforth   396 *sith* since. *offense* i.e., harm to the one who offers help and friendship   397 *Thou shouldst be* it appears that you are. (But Iago replies in the sense of "ought to be.")

Iago: I should be wise, for honesty's a fool
And loses that° it works for.

Othello: By the world,
I think my wife be honest and think she is not;   400
I think that thou art just and think thou art not.
I'll have some proof. My name, that was as fresh
As Dian's° visage, is now begrimed and black
As mine own face. If there be cords, or knives,
Poison, or fire, or suffocating streams,   405
I'll not endure it. Would I were satisfied!

Iago: I see, sir, you are eaten up with passion.
I do repent me that I put it to you.
You would be satisfied?

Othello: Would? Nay, and I will.

Iago: And may; but how? How satisfied, my lord?   410
Would you, the supervisor,° grossly gape on?
Behold her topped?

Othello: Death and damnation! O!

Iago: It were a tedious difficulty, I think,
To bring them to that prospect. Damn them then,°
If ever mortal eyes do see them bolster°   415
More° than their own.° What then? How then?
What shall I say? Where's satisfaction?
It is impossible you should see this,
Were they as prime° as goats, as hot as monkeys,
As salt° as wolves in pride,° and fools as gross   420
As ignorance made drunk. But yet I say,
If imputation and strong circumstances°
Which lead directly to the door of truth
Will give you satisfaction, you might have 't.

Othello: Give me a living reason she's disloyal.   425

Iago: I do not like the office.
But sith° I am entered in this cause so far,
Pricked° to 't by foolish honesty and love,
I will go on. I lay with Cassio lately,
And being troubled with a raging tooth   430
I could not sleep. There are a kind of men

---

399 *that* what   403 *Dian* Diana, goddess of the moon and of chastity   411 *supervisor* on-looker   414 *Damn them then* i.e., they would have to be really incorrigible   415 *bolster* go to bed together, share a bolster   416 *More* other.   *own* own eyes   419 *prime* lustful   420 *salt* wanton, sensual.   *pride* heat   422 *imputation . . . . circumstances* strong circumstantial evidence   427 *sith* since   428 *Pricked* spurred

So loose of soul that in their sleeps will mutter
Their affairs. One of this kind is Cassio.
In sleep I heard him say, "Sweet Desdemona,
Let us be wary, let us hide our loves!"   435
And then, sir, would he grip and wring my hand,
Cry "O sweet creature!", then kiss me hard,
As if he plucked up kisses by the roots
That grew upon my lips; then laid his leg
Over my thigh, and sighed, and kissed, and then   440
Cried, "Cursèd fate that gave thee to the Moor!"
Othello: O monstrous! Monstrous!
Iago: Nay, this was but his dream.
Othello: But this denoted a foregone conclusion.°
'Tis a shrewd doubt,° though it be but a dream.
Iago: And this may help to thicken other proofs   445
That do demonstrate thinly.
Othello: I'll tear her all to pieces.
Iago: Nay, but be wise. Yet we see nothing done;
She may be honest yet. Tell me but this:
Have you not sometimes seen a handkerchief
Spotted with strawberries° in your wife's hand?   450
Othello: I gave her such a one. 'Twas my first gift.
Iago: I know not that; but such a handkerchief—
I am sure it was your wife's—did I today
See Cassio wipe his beard with.
Othello: If it be that—
Iago: If it be that, or any that was hers,   455
It speaks against her with the other proofs.
Othello: O, that the slave° had forty thousand lives!
One is too poor, too weak for my revenge.
Now do I see 'tis true. Look here, Iago,
All my fond° love thus do I blow to heaven.   460
'Tis gone.
Arise, black vengeance, from the hollow hell!
Yield up, O love, thy crown and hearted° throne
To tyrannous hate! Swell, bosom, with thy freight,°
For 'tis of aspics'° tongues!   465

---

443 *foregone conclusion* concluded experience or action   444 *shrewd doubt* suspicious circumstance   450 *Spotted with strawberries* embroidered with a strawberry pattern   457 *the
slave* i.e., Cassio   460 *fond* foolish (but also suggesting "affectionate")   463 *hearted* fixed
in the heart   464 *freight* burden   465 *aspics'* venomous serpents'

Iago: Yet be content.°
Othello: O, blood, blood, blood!
Iago: Patience, I say. Your mind perhaps may change.
Othello: Never, Iago. Like to the Pontic Sea,°
    Whose icy current and compulsive course   470
    Ne'er feels retiring ebb, but keeps due on
    To the Propontic° and the Hellespont,°
    Even so my bloody thoughts with violent pace
    Shall ne'er look back, ne'er ebb to humble love,
    Till that a capable° and wide revenge   475
    Swallow them up. Now, by yond marble° heaven,
    [*Kneeling*] In the due reverence of a sacred vow
    I here engage my words.
Iago: Do not rise yet.
    [*He kneels.*]° Witness, you ever-burning lights above,
    You elements that clip° us round about,   480
    Witness that here Iago doth give up
    The execution° of his wit,° hands, heart,
    To wronged Othello's service. Let him command,
    And to obey shall be in me remorse,°
    What bloody business ever.°   [*They rise.*]
Othello: I greet thy love,   485
    Not with vain thanks, but with acceptance bounteous,
    And will upon the instant put thee to 't.°
    Within these three days let me hear thee say
    That Cassio's not alive.
Iago: My friend is dead;
    'Tis done at your request. But let her live.   490
Othello: Damn her, lewd minx!° O, damn her, damn her!
    Come, go with me apart. I will withdraw
    To furnish me with some swift means of death
    For the fair devil. Now art thou my lieutenant.
Iago: I am your own forever.   *Exeunt.* 495

---

466 *content* calm   469 *Pontic Sea* Black Sea   472 *Propontic* Sea of Marmara, between the
Black Sea and the Aegean. *Hellespont* Dardanelles, straits where the Sea of Marmara
joins with the Aegean   475 *capable* ample, comprehensive   476 *marble* i.e., gleaming like
marble and unrelenting   479 s.d. *He kneels* (In the Quarto text, Iago kneels here after Othello has knelt at line 477.)   480 *clip* encompass   482 *execution* exercise, action. *wit* mind
484 *remorse* pity (for Othello's wrongs)   485 *ever* soever   487 *to 't* to the proof   491 *minx*
wanton

SCENE IV [BEFORE THE CITADEL.]

    Enter Desdemona, Emilia, and Clown.

Desdemona: Do you know, sirrah,° where Lieutenant Cassio lies?°
Clown: I dare not say he lies anywhere.
Desdemona: Why, man?
Clown: He's a soldier, and for me to say a soldier lies, 'tis stabbing.
Desdemona: Go to. Where lodges he?   5
Clown: To tell you where he lodges is to tell you where I lie.
Desdemona: Can anything be made of this?
Clown: I know not where he lodges, and for me to devise a lodging and
    say he lies here, or he lies there, were to lie in mine own throat.°
Desdemona: Can you inquire him out, and be edified by report?   10
Clown: I will catechize the world for him; that is, make questions, and by
    them answer.
Desdemona: Seek him, bid him come hither. Tell him I have moved° my
    lord on his behalf and hope all will be well.
Clown: To do this is within the compass of man's wit, and therefore I   15
    will attempt the doing it.   *Exit Clown.*
Desdemona: Where should I lose that handkerchief, Emilia?
Emilia: I know not, madam.
Desdemona: Believe me, I had rather have lost my purse
    Full of crusadoes;° and but my noble Moor   20
    Is true of mind and made of no such baseness
    As jealous creatures are, it were enough
    To put him to ill thinking.
Emilia: Is he not jealous?
Desdemona: Who, he? I think the sun where he was born
    Drew all such humors° from him.
Emilia: Look where he comes.   25

    Enter Othello.

Desdemona: I will not leave him now till Cassio
    Be called to him.—How is 't with you, my lord?
Othello: Well, my good lady. [*Aside.*] O, hardness to dissemble!—
    How do you, Desdemona?
Desdemona: Well, my good lord.
Othello: Give me your hand. [*She gives her hand.*] This hand is moist, my lady.   30

---

1 *sirrah* (A form of address to an inferior.)   *lies* lodges. (But the Clown makes the obvious pun.)   9 *lie . . . throat* (1) lie egregiously and deliberately (2) use the windpipe to speak a lie   13 *moved* petitioned   20 *crusadoes* Portuguese gold coins   25 *humors* (Refers to the four bodily fluids thought to determine temperament.)

Desdemona: It yet hath felt no age nor known no sorrow.
Othello: This argues° fruitfulness° and liberal° heart.
  Hot, hot, and moist. This hand of yours requires
  A sequester° from liberty, fasting and prayer,
  Much castigation,° exercise devout;°   35
  For here's a young and sweating devil here
  That commonly rebels. 'Tis a good hand,
  A frank° one.
Desdemona: You may indeed say so,
  For 'twas that hand that gave away my heart.
Othello: A liberal hand. The hearts of old gave hands,°   40
  But our new heraldry is hands, not hearts.°
Desdemona: I cannot speak of this. Come now, your promise.
Othello: What promise, chuck?°
Desdemona: I have sent to bid Cassio come speak with you.
Othello: I have a salt and sorry rheum° offends me;   45
  Lend me thy handkerchief.
Desdemona: Here, my lord.   [*She offers a handkerchief.*]
Othello: That which I gave you.
Desdemona: I have it not about me.
Othello: Not?
Desdemona: No, faith, my lord.   50
Othello: That's a fault. That handkerchief
  Did an Egyptian to my mother give.
  She was a charmer,° and could almost read
  The thoughts of people. She told her, while she kept it
  'Twould make her amiable° and subdue my father   55
  Entirely to her love, but if she lost it
  Or made a gift of it, my father's eye
  Should hold her loathèd and his spirits should hunt
  After new fancies.° She, dying, gave it me,
  And bid me, when my fate would have me wived,   60
  To give it her.° I did so; and take heed on 't;

---

32 *argues* gives evidence of. *fruitfulness* generosity, amorousness, and fecundity. *liberal* generous and sexually free   34 *sequester* separation, sequestration   35 *castigation* corrective discipline. *exercise devout* i.e., prayer, religious meditation, etc.   38 *frank* generous, open (with sexual suggestion)   40 *The hearts . . . hands* i.e., in former times, people would give their hearts when they gave their hands to something   41 *But . . . hearts* i.e., in our decadent times, the joining of hands is no longer a badge to signify the giving of hearts   43 *chuck* (A term of endearment.)   45 *salt . . . rheum* distressful head cold or watering of the eyes   53 *charmer* sorceress   55 *amiable* desirable   59 *fancies* loves   61 *her* i.e., to my wife

Make it a darling like your precious eye.
To lose 't or give 't away were such perdition°
As nothing else could match.

Desdemona: Is 't possible?

Othello: 'Tis true. There's magic in the web° of it.   65
A sibyl, that had numbered in the world
The sun to course two hundred compasses,°
In her prophetic fury° sewed the work;°
The worms were hallowed that did breed the silk,
And it was dyed in mummy° which the skillful   70
Conserved of° maidens' hearts.

Desdemona: I' faith! Is 't true?

Othello: Most veritable. Therefore look to 't well.

Desdemona: Then would to God that I had never seen 't!

Othello: Ha? Wherefore?

Desdemona: Why do you speak so startingly and rash?°   75

Othello: Is 't lost? Is 't gone? Speak, is 't out o' the way?°

Desdemona: Heaven bless us!

Othello: Say you?

Desdemona: It is not lost; but what an if° it were?

Othello: How?   80

Desdemona: I say it is not lost.

Othello: Fetch 't, let me see 't.

Desdemona: Why, so I can, sir, but I will not now.
This is a trick to put me from my suit.
Pray you, let Cassio be received again.

Othello: Fetch me the handkerchief! My mind misgives.   85

Desdemona: Come, come,
You'll never meet a more sufficient° man.

Othello: The handkerchief!

Desdemona: I pray, talk° me of Cassio.

Othello: The handkerchief!

Desdemona: A man that all his time°
Hath founded his good fortunes on your love,   90
Shared dangers with you—

---

63 *perdition* loss   65 *web* fabric, weaving   67 *compasses* annual circlings. (The *sibyl*, or
prophetess, was two hundred years old.)   68 *prophetic fury* frenzy of prophetic inspiration.
work embroidered pattern   70 *mummy* medicinal or magical preparation drained from mummified bodies   71 *Conserved of* prepared or preserved out of   75 *startingly and rash* disjoint-
edly and impetuously, excitedly   76 *out o' the way* lost, misplaced   79 *an if* if   87 *sufficient*
able, complete   88 *talk* talk to   89 *all his time* throughout his career

Othello: The handkerchief!
Desdemona: I' faith, you are to blame.
Othello: Zounds!   *Exit Othello.*
Emilia: Is not this man jealous?   95
Desdemona: I ne'er saw this before.
    Sure, there's some wonder in this handkerchief.
    I am most unhappy in the loss of it.
Emilia: 'Tis not a year or two shows us a man.°
    They are all but stomachs, and we all but° food;
    They eat us hungerly,° and when they are full   100
    They belch us.

    Enter Iago and Cassio.

                  Look you, Cassio and my husband.
Iago [to Cassio]: There is no other way; 'tis she must do 't.
    And, lo, the happiness!° Go and importune her.
Desdemona: How now, good Cassio? What's the news with you?   105
Cassio: Madam, my former suit. I do beseech you
    That by your virtuous° means I may again
    Exist and be a member of his love
    Whom I, with all the office° of my heart,
    Entirely honor. I would not be delayed.   110
    If my offense be of such mortal° kind
    That nor my service past, nor° present sorrows,
    Nor purposed merit in futurity
    Can ransom me into his love again,
    But to know so must be my benefit;°   115
    So shall I clothe me in a forced content,
    And shut myself up in° some other course,
    To fortune's alms.°
Desdemona: Alas, thrice-gentle Cassio,
    My advocation° is not now in tune.
    My lord is not my lord; nor should I know him,   120
    Were he in favor° as in humor° altered.
    So help me every spirit sanctified

---

99 *'Tis . . . man* i.e., you can't really know a man even in a year or two of experience (?), or, real men come along seldom (?)   100 *but* nothing but   101 *hungerly* hungrily   104 *the happiness* in happy time, fortunately met   107 *virtuous* efficacious   109 *office* loyal service   111 *mortal* fatal   112 *nor . . . nor* neither . . . nor   115 *But . . . benefit* merely to know that my case is hopeless will have to content me (and will be better than uncertainty)   117 *shut . . . in* confine myself to   118 *To fortune's alms* throwing myself on the mercy of fortune   119 *advocation* advocacy   121 *favor* appearance. *humor* mood

As I have spoken for you all my best
And stood within the blank° of his displeasure
For my free speech! You must awhile be patient.   125
What I can do I will, and more I will
Than for myself I dare. Let that suffice you.

Iago: Is my lord angry?

Emilia: He went hence but now,
And certainly in strange unquietness.

Iago: Can he be angry? I have seen the cannon   130
When it hath blown his ranks into the air,
And like the devil from his very arm
Puffed his own brother—and is he angry?
Something of moment° then. I will go meet him.
There's matter in 't indeed, if he be angry.   135

Desdemona: I prithee, do so.   *Exit [Iago].*
                         Something, sure, of state,°
Either from Venice, or some unhatched practice°
Made demonstrable here in Cyprus to him,
Hath puddled° his clear spirit; and in such cases
Men's natures wrangle with inferior things,   140
Though great ones are their object. 'Tis even so;
For let our finger ache, and it indues°
Our other, healthful members even to a sense
Of pain. Nay, we must think men are not gods,
Nor of them look for such observancy°   145
As fits the bridal.° Beshrew me° much, Emilia,
I was, unhandsome° warrior as I am,
Arraigning his unkindness with° my soul;
But now I find I had suborned the witness,°
And he's indicted falsely.

Emilia: Pray heaven it be   150
State matters, as you think, and no conception
Nor no jealous toy° concerning you.

Desdemona: Alas the day! I never gave him cause.

---

124 *within the blank* within point-blank range. (The *blank* is the center of the target.)   134 *of moment* of immediate importance, momentous   136 *of state* concerning state affairs   137 *unhatched practice* as yet unexecuted or undiscovered plot   139 *puddled* muddied   142 *indues* brings to the same condition   145 *observancy* attentiveness   146 *bridal* wedding (when a bridegroom is newly attentive to his bride). *Beshrew me* (A mild oath.)   147 *unhandsome* insufficient, unskillful   148 *with* before the bar of   149 *suborned the witness* induced the witness to give false testimony   152 *toy* fancy

Emilia: But jealous souls will not be answered so;
    They are not ever jealous for the cause,   155
    But jealous for° they're jealous. It is a monster
    Begot upon itself,° born on itself.
Desdemona: Heaven keep that monster from Othello's mind!
Emilia: Lady, amen.
Desdemona: I will go seek him. Cassio, walk hereabout.   160
    If I do find him fit, I'll move your suit
    And seek to effect it to my uttermost.
Cassio: I humbly thank your ladyship.

    Exit [Desdemona with Emilia].

    Enter Bianca.

Bianca: Save° you, friend Cassio!
Cassio: What make° you from home?
    How is 't with you, my most fair Bianca?   165
    I' faith, sweet love, I was coming to your house.
Bianca: And I was going to your lodging, Cassio.
    What, keep a week away? Seven days and nights?
    Eightscore-eight° hours? And lovers' absent hours
    More tedious than the dial° eightscore times?   170
    O weary reckoning!
Cassio: Pardon me, Bianca.
    I have this while with leaden thoughts been pressed;
    But I shall, in a more continuate° time,
    Strike off this score° of absence. Sweet Bianca,

    [giving her Desdemona's handkerchief]

    Take me this work out.°
Bianca: O Cassio, whence came this?   175
    This is some token from a newer friend.°
    To the felt absence now I feel a cause.
    Is 't come to this? Well, well.
Cassio: Go to, woman!
    Throw your vile guesses in the devil's teeth,
    From whence you have them. You are jealous now   180

---

156 *for* because   157 *Begot upon itself* generated solely from itself   164 *Save* God save.
make do   169 *Eightscore-eight* one hundred sixty-eight, the number of hours in a week
170 *the dial* a complete revolution of the clock   173 *continuate* uninterrupted   174 *Strike*
. . . *score* settle this account   175 *Take . . . out* copy this embroidery for me   176 *friend*
mistress

Cassio explains to Bianca that he does not know how the handkerchief appeared in his room (III, iv, 175–195).

That this is from some mistress, some remembrance.
No, by my faith, Bianca.
Bianca: Why, whose is it?
Cassio: I know not, neither. I found it in my chamber.
I like the work well. Ere it be demanded°—
As like° enough it will—I would have it copied.   185
Take it and do 't, and leave me for this time.
Bianca: Leave you? Wherefore?
Cassio: I do attend here on the General,

184 *demanded* inquired for   185 *like* likely

And think it no addition,° nor my wish,
To have him see me womaned.   190
Bianca: Why, I pray you?
Cassio: Not that I love you not.
Bianca: But that you do not love me.
  I pray you, bring° me on the way a little,
  And say if I shall see you soon at night.   195
Cassio: 'Tis but a little way that I can bring you,
  For I attend here; but I'll see you soon.
Bianca: 'Tis very good. I must be circumstanced.°

  Exeunt omnes.

ACT IV

SCENE I [BEFORE THE CITADEL.]

  Enter Othello and Iago.

Iago: Will you think so?
Othello: Think so, Iago?
Iago: What,
  To kiss in private?
Othello: An unauthorized kiss!
Iago: Or to be naked with her friend in bed
  An hour or more, not meaning any harm?
Othello: Naked in bed, Iago, and not mean harm?   5
  It is hypocrisy against the devil.
  They that mean virtuously and yet do so,
  The devil their virtue tempts, and they tempt heaven.
Iago: If they do nothing, 'tis a venial° slip.
  But if I give my wife a handkerchief—   10
Othello: What then?
Iago: Why then, 'tis hers, my lord, and being hers,
  She may, I think, bestow 't on any man.
Othello: She is protectress of her honor too.
  May she give that?   15
Iago: Her honor is an essence that's not seen;
  They have it° very oft that have it not.
  But, for the handkerchief—

189 *addition* i.e., addition to my reputation   194 *bring* accompany   198 *be circumstanced* be
governed by circumstance, yield to your conditions   9 *venial* pardonable   17 *They have it*
i.e., they enjoy a reputation for it

Othello: By heaven, I would most gladly have forgot it.
　　Thou saidst—O, it comes o'er my memory　　　　　　　　20
　　As doth the raven o'er the infectious house,°
　　Boding to all—he had my handkerchief.
Iago: Ay, what of that?
Othello:　　　　　　　　That's not so good now.
Iago:　　　　　　　　　　　　　　What
　　If I had said I had seen him do you wrong?
　　Or heard him say—as knaves be such abroad,°　　　　　　25
　　Who having, by their own importunate suit,
　　Or voluntary dotage° of some mistress,
　　Convincèd or supplied° them, cannot choose
　　But they must blab—
Othello:　　　　　　　　Hath he said anything?
Iago: He hath, my lord; but, be you well assured,　　　　　30
　　No more than he'll unswear.
Othello:　　　　　　　What hath he said?
Iago: Faith, that he did—I know not what he did.
Othello: What? What?
Iago: Lie—
Othello:　　With her?
Iago:　　　　　　　　With her, on her; what you will.
Othello: Lie with her? Lie on her? We say "lie on her" when they belie°　　35
　　her. Lie with her? Zounds, that's fulsome.°—Handkerchief—confes-
　　sions—handkerchief!—To confess and be hanged for his labor—first
　　to be hanged and then to confess.°—I tremble at it. Nature would
　　not invest herself in such shadowing passion without some instruc-
　　tion.° It is not words° that shakes me thus. Pish! Noses, ears, and　　40
　　lips.—Is 't possible?—Confess—handkerchief!—O devil!

Falls in a trance.

Iago: Work on,
　　My medicine, work! Thus credulous fools are caught,
　　And many worthy and chaste dames even thus,

---

21 *raven . . . house* (Allusion to the belief that the raven hovered over a house of sickness or in-
fection, such as one visited by the plague.)　25 *abroad* around about　27 *voluntary dotage* willing
infatuation　28 *Convincèd or supplied* seduced or sexually gratified　35 *belie* slander　36 *fulsome*
foul　37–38 *first . . . to confess* (Othello reverses the proverbial *confess* and *be hanged*; Cassio is to
be given no time to confess before he dies.)　38–40 *Nature . . . instruction* i.e., without some
foundation in fact, nature would not have dressed herself in such an overwhelming passion that
comes over me now and fills my mind with images, or in such a lifelike fantasy as Cassio had in
his dream of lying with Desdemona　40 *words* mere words

Iago lies to Cassio that Othello has "fall'n into an epilepsy" (IV, i, 48).

All guiltless, meet reproach.—What, ho! My lord!   45
My lord, I say! Othello!

Enter Cassio.

                              How now, Cassio?
Cassio: What's the matter?
Iago: My lord is fall'n into an epilepsy.
This is his second fit. He had one yesterday.
Cassio: Rub him about the temples.
Iago: No, forbear.   50
The lethargy° must have his° quiet course.
If not, he foams at mouth, and by and by
Breaks out to savage madness. Look, he stirs.
Do you withdraw yourself a little while.

51 *lethargy* coma.   *his* its

He will recover straight. When he is gone,   55
I would on great occasion° speak with you.

[*Exit Cassio.*]

How is it, General? Have you not hurt your head?
Othello: Dost thou mock me?°
Iago: I mock you not, by heaven.
Would you would bear your fortune like a man!
Othello: A hornèd man's a monster and a beast.   60
Iago: There's many a beast then in a populous city,
And many a civil° monster.
Othello: Did he confess it?
Iago: Good sir, be a man.
Think every bearded fellow that's but yoked°   65
May draw with you.° There's millions now alive
That nightly lie in those unproper° beds
Which they dare swear peculiar.° Your case is better.°
O, 'tis the spite of hell, the fiend's arch-mock,
To lip° a wanton in a secure° couch   70
And to suppose her chaste! No, let me know,
And knowing what I am,° I know what she shall be.°
Othello: O, thou art wise. 'Tis certain.
Iago: Stand you awhile apart;
Confine yourself but in a patient list.°   75
Whilst you were here o'erwhelmèd with your grief—
A passion most unsuiting such a man—
Cassio came hither. I shifted him away,°
And laid good 'scuse upon your ecstasy,°
Bade him anon return and here speak with me,   80
The which he promised. Do but encave° yourself
And mark the fleers,° the gibes, and notable° scorns
That dwell in every region of his face;
For I will make him tell the tale anew,

---

56 *on great occasion* on a matter of great importance   58 *mock me* (Othello takes Iago's
question about hurting his head to be a mocking reference to the cuckold's horns.)   62
civil i.e., dwelling in a city   65 *yoked* (1) married (2) put into the yoke of infamy and cuck-
oldry   66 *draw with you* pull as you do, like oxen who are yoked, i.e., share your fate as
cuckold   67 *unproper* not exclusively their own   68 *peculiar* private, their own. *better* i.e.,
because you know the truth   70 *lip* kiss.   *secure* free from suspicion   72 *what I am* i.e., a
cuckold.   *she shall be* will happen to her   75 *in . . . list* within the bounds of patience   78
shifted him away used a dodge to get rid of him   79 *ecstasy* trance   81 *encave* conceal   82
fleers sneers.   *notable* obvious

Where, how, how oft, how long ago, and when 85
He hath and is again to cope° your wife.
I say, but mark his gesture. Marry, patience!
Or I shall say you're all-in-all in spleen,°
And nothing of a man.
Othello: Dost thou hear, Iago?
I will be found most cunning in my patience; 90
But—dost thou hear?—most bloody.
Iago: That's not amiss;
But yet keep time° in all. Will you withdraw?

[Othello stands apart.]

Now will I question Cassio of Bianca,
A huswife° that by selling her desires
Buys herself bread and clothes. It is a creature 95
That dotes on Cassio—as 'tis the strumpet's plague
To beguile many and be beguiled by one.
He, when he hears of her, cannot restrain°
From the excess of laughter. Here he comes.

Enter Cassio.

As he shall smile, Othello shall go mad; 100
And his unbookish° jealousy must conster°
Poor Cassio's smiles, gestures, and light behaviors
Quite in the wrong.—How do you now, Lieutenant?
Cassio: The worser that you give me the addition°
Whose want° even kills me. 105
Iago: Ply Desdemona well and you are sure on 't.
[Speaking lower.] Now, if this suit lay in Bianca's power,
How quickly should you speed!
Cassio [laughing]: Alas, poor caitiff!°
Othello [aside]: Look how he laughs already! 110
Iago: I never knew a woman love man so.
Cassio: Alas, poor rogue! I think, i' faith, she loves me.
Othello: Now he denies it faintly, and laughs it out.
Iago: Do you hear, Cassio?
Othello: Now he importunes him
To tell it o'er. Go to!° Well said,° well said. 115

86 *cope* encounter with, have sex with   88 *all-in-all in spleen* utterly governed by passionate impulses   92 *keep time* keep yourself steady (as in music)   94 *huswife* hussy   98 *restrain* refrain   101 *unbookish* uninstructed.   *conster* construe   104 *addition* title   105 *Whose want* the lack of which   109 *caitiff* wretch   115 *Go to* (An expression of remonstrance.)   *Well said* well done

Iago: She gives it out that you shall marry her.
    Do you intend it?
Cassio: Ha, ha, ha!
Othello: Do you triumph, Roman?° Do you triumph?
Cassio: I marry her? What? A customer?° Prithee, bear some charity to   120
    my wit;° do not think it so unwholesome. Ha, ha, ha!
Othello: So, so, so, so! They laugh that win.°
Iago: Faith, the cry° goes that you shall marry her.
Cassio: Prithee, say true.
Iago: I am a very villain else.°   125
Othello: Have you scored me?° Well.
Cassio: This is the monkey's own giving out. She is persuaded I will
    marry her out of her own love and flattery,° not out of my promise.
Othello: Iago beckons me.° Now he begins the story.
Cassio: She was here even now; she haunts me in every place. I was the   130
    other day talking on the seabank° with certain Venetians, and
    thither comes the bauble,° and, by this hand,° she falls me thus
    about my neck—

    [*He embraces Iago.*]

Othello: Crying, "O dear Cassio!" as it were; his gesture imports it.
Cassio: So hangs and lolls and weep upon me, so shakes and pulls me.   135
    Ha, ha, ha!
Othello: Now he tells how she plucked him to my chamber. O, I see that
    nose of yours, but not that dog I shall throw it to.°
Cassio: Well, I must leave her company.
Iago: Before me,° look where she comes.   140

    Enter Bianca [with Othello's handkerchief].

Cassio: 'Tis such another fitchew!° Marry, a perfumed one.—What do
    you mean by this haunting of me?
Bianca: Let the devil and his dam° haunt you! What did you mean by
    that same handkerchief you gave me even now? I was a fine fool to

---

119 *Roman* (The Romans were noted for their *triumphs* or triumphal processions.)   120
customer i.e., prostitute   120–121 *bear . . . wit* be more charitable to my judgment   122
They . . . win i.e., they that laugh last laugh best   123 *cry* rumor   125 *I . . . else* call me a
complete rogue if I'm not telling the truth   126 *scored me* scored off
me, beaten me, made up my reckoning, branded me   128 *flattery* self-flattery, self-
deception   129 *beckons* signals   131 *seabank* seashore   132 *bauble* plaything. *by this
hand* I make my vow   138 *not . . . to* (Othello imagines himself cutting off Cassio's
nose and throwing it to a dog.)   140 *Before me* i.e., on my soul   141 *'Tis . . . fitchew* what
a polecat she is! Just like all the others. (Polecats were often compared with prostitutes because of their rank smell and presumed lechery.)   143 *dam* mother

take it. I must take out the work? A likely piece of work,° that you 145
should find it in your chamber and know not who left it there! This
is some minx's token, and I must take out the work? There; give it
your hobbyhorse.° *[She gives him the handkerchief.]* Wheresoever you
had it, I'll take out no work on 't.

Cassio: How now, my sweet Bianca? How now? How now? 150

Othello: By heaven, that should be° my handkerchief!

Bianca: If you'll come to supper tonight, you may; if you will not, come
when you are next prepared for.° *Exit.*

Iago: After her, after her.

Cassio: Faith, I must. She'll rail in the streets else. 155

Iago: Will you sup there?

Cassio: Faith, I intend so.

Iago: Well, I may chance to see you, for I would very fain speak with you.

Cassio: Prithee, come. Will you?

Iago: Go to.° Say no more. *[Exit Cassio.]* 160

Othello [advancing]: How shall I murder him, Iago?

Iago: Did you perceive how he laughed at his vice?

Othello: O, Iago!

Iago: And did you see the handkerchief?

Othello: Was that mine? 165

Iago: Yours, by this hand. And to see how he prizes the foolish woman
your wife! She gave it him, and he hath given it his whore.

Othello: I would have him nine years a-killing. A fine woman! A fair
woman! A sweet woman!

Iago: Nay, you must forget that. 170

Othello: Ay, let her rot and perish, and be damned tonight, for she shall
not live. No, my heart is turned to stone; I strike it, and it hurts my
hand. O, the world hath not a sweeter creature! She might lie by an
emperor's side and command him tasks.

Iago: Nay, that's not your way.° 175

Othello: Hang her! I do but say what she is. So delicate with her needle!
An admirable musician! O, she will sing the savageness out of a bear.
Of so high and plenteous wit and invention!°

Iago: She's the worse for all this.

Othello: O, a thousand, a thousand times! And then, of so gentle a 180
condition!°

---

145 *A likely . . . . work* a fine story   148 *hobbyhorse* harlot   151 *should be* must be   153
when . . . for when I'm ready for you (i.e., never)   160 *Go to* (An expression of remonstrance.)   175 *your way* i.e., the way you should think of her   178 *invention* imagination
180–181 *gentle a condition* wellborn and well-bred

Iago: Ay, too gentle.°

Othello: Nay, that's certain. But yet the pity of it, Iago! O, Iago, the pity of it, Iago!

Iago: If you are so fond° over her iniquity, give her patent° to offend, for   185
if it touch not you it comes near nobody.

Othello: I will chop her into messes.° Cuckold me?

Iago: O, 'tis foul in her.

Othello: With mine officer?

Iago: That's fouler.   190

Othello: Get me some poison, Iago, this night. I'll not expostulate with
her, lest her body and beauty unprovide° my mind again. This night,
Iago.

Iago: Do it not with poison. Strangle her in her bed, even the bed she
hath contaminated.   195

Othello: Good, good! The justice of it pleases. Very good.

Iago: And for Cassio, let me be his undertaker.° You shall hear more by
midnight.

Othello: Excellent good. [*A trumpet within.*] What trumpet is that same?

Iago: I warrant, something from Venice.   200

> *Enter Lodovico, Desdemona, and attendants.*

'Tis Lodovico. This comes from the Duke.
See, your wife's with him.

Lodovico: God save you, worthy General!

Othello: With all my heart,° sir.

Lodovico [*giving him a letter*]: The Duke and the senators of Venice
greet you.   205

Othello: I kiss the instrument of their pleasures.

> [*He opens the letter, and reads.*]

Desdemona: And what's the news, good cousin Lodovico?

Iago: I am very glad to see you, signor.
Welcome to Cyprus.

Lodovico: I thank you. How does Lieutenant Cassio?   210

Iago: Lives, sir.

Desdemona: Cousin, there's fall'n between him and my lord
An unkind° breach; but you shall make all well.

---

182 *gentle* generous, yielding (to other men)   185 *fond* foolish.   *patent* license   187 *messes*
portions of meat, i.e., bits   192 *unprovide* weaken, render unfit   197 *be his undertaker* undertake to dispatch him   203 *With all my heart* i.e., I thank you most heartily   213 *unkind* unnatural, contrary to their natures; hurtful

Othello: Are you sure of that?

Desdemona: My lord? 215

Othello [*reads*]: "This fail you not to do, as you will—"

Lodovico: He did not call; he's busy in the paper.
    Is there division twixt my lord and Cassio?

Desdemona: A most unhappy one. I would do much
    T' atone° them, for the love I bear to Cassio. 220

Othello: Fire and brimstone!

Desdemona: My lord?

Othello: Are you wise?

Desdemona: What, is he angry?

Lodovico: Maybe the letter moved him;
    For, as I think, they do command him home, 225
    Deputing Cassio in his government.°

Desdemona: By my troth, I am glad on 't.°

Othello: Indeed?

Desdemona: My lord?

Othello: I am glad to see you mad.° 230

Desdemona: Why, sweet Othello—

Othello [*striking her*]: Devil!

Desdemona: I have not deserved this.

Lodovico: My lord, this would not be believed in Venice,
    Though I should swear I saw 't. 'Tis very much.° 235
    Make her amends; she weeps.

Othello: O devil, devil!
    If that the earth could teem° with woman's tears,
    Each drop she falls would prove a crocodile.°
    Out of my sight!

Desdemona: I will not stay to offend you. [*Going.*]

Lodovico: Truly, an obedient lady. 240
    I do beseech your lordship, call her back.

Othello: Mistress!

Desdemona [*returning*]: My lord?

Othello: What would you with her, sir?°

Lodovico: Who, I, my lord? 245

Othello: Ay, you did wish that I would make her turn.
    Sir, she can turn, and turn, and yet go on

---

220 *atone* reconcile   226 *government* office   227 *on 't* of it   230 *I am . . . mad* i.e., I am glad to see that you are insane enough to rejoice in Cassio's promotion (?) (Othello bitterly plays on Desdemona's *I am glad.*)   235 *very much* too much, outrageous   237 *teem* breed, be impregnated   238 *falls . . . crocodile* (Crocodiles were supposed to weep hypocritical tears for their victims.)   244 *What . . . sir* (Othello implies that Desdemona is pliant and will do a *turn,* lines 246–248, for any man.)

And turn again; and she can weep, sir, weep;
And she's obedient,° as you say, obedient,
Very obedient.—Proceed you in your tears.—
Concerning this, sir—O well-painted passion!°—   250
I am commanded home.—Get you away;
I'll send for you anon.—Sir, I obey the mandate
And will return to Venice.—Hence, avaunt!

[*Exit Desdemona.*]

Cassio shall have my place. And, sir, tonight   255
I do entreat that we may sup together.
You are welcome, sir, to Cyprus.—Goats and monkeys!°   *Exit.*
Lodovico: Is this the noble Moor whom our full Senate
    Call all in all sufficient? Is this the nature
    Whom passion could not shake? Whose solid virtue   260
    The shot of accident nor dart of chance
    Could neither graze nor pierce?
Iago: He is much changed.
Lodovico: Are his wits safe? Is he not light of brain?
Iago: He's that he is. I may not breathe my censure
    What he might be. If what he might he is not,   265
    I would to heaven he were!°
Lodovico: What, strike his wife?
Iago: Faith, that was not so well; yet would I knew
    That stroke would prove the worst!
Lodovico: Is it his use?°
    Or did the letters work upon his blood°
    And new-create his fault?
Iago: Alas, alas!   270
    It is not honesty in me to speak
    What I have seen and known. You shall observe him,
    And his own courses will denote° him so
    That I may save my speech. Do but go after,
    And mark how he continues.   275
Lodovico: I am sorry that I am deceived in him.   *Exeunt.*

---

249 *obedient* (With much the same sexual connotation as *turn* in lines 246–248.)   251
passion i.e., grief   257 *Goats and monkeys* (See Act III, Scene iii, line 419.)   264–266 *I may
. . . were* i.e., I dare not venture an opinion as to whether he's of unsound mind, as you suggest, but, if he isn't, then it might be better to wish he were in fact insane, since only that
could excuse his wild behavior   268 *use* custom   269 *blood* passions   273 *courses will denote* actions will reveal

SCENE II [THE CITADEL.]

    Enter Othello and Emilia.

Othello: You have seen nothing then?
Emilia: Nor ever heard, nor ever did suspect.
Othello: Yes, you have seen Cassio and she together.
Emilia: But then I saw no harm, and then I heard
    Each syllable that breath made up between them.   5
Othello: What, did they never whisper?
Emilia: Never, my lord.
Othello: Nor send you out o' the way?
Emilia: Never.
Othello: To fetch her fan, her gloves, her mask, nor nothing?   10
Emilia: Never, my lord.
Othello: That's strange.
Emilia: I durst, my lord, to wager she is honest,
    Lay down my soul at stake.° If you think other,
    Remove your thought; it doth abuse your bosom.°   15
    If any wretch have put this in your head,
    Let heaven requite it with the serpent's curse!°
    For if she be not honest, chaste, and true,
    There's no man happy; the purest of their wives
    Is foul as slander.
Othello: Bid her come hither. Go.   20

    Exit Emilia.

    She says enough; yet she's a simple bawd
    That cannot say as much.° This° is a subtle whore,
    A closet lock and key° of villainous secrets.
    And yet she'll kneel and pray; I have seen her do 't.

    Enter Desdemona and Emilia.

Desdemona: My lord, what is your will?   25
Othello: Pray you, chuck, come hither.
Desdemona: What is your pleasure?
Othello: Let me see your eyes.
    Look in my face.
Desdemona: What horrible fancy's this?

---

14 *at stake* as the wager   15 *abuse your bosom* deceive you   17 *the serpent's curse* the curse
pronounced by God on the serpent for deceiving Eve, just as some man has done to Othello
and Desdemona. (See Genesis 3:14.)   21–22 *she's . . . much* i.e., any procuress or go-be-
tween who couldn't make up as plausible a story as Emilia's would have to be pretty stupid
22 *This* i.e., Desdemona   23 *closet lock and key* i.e., concealer

Othello [*to Emilia*]: Some of your function,° mistress.
    Leave procreants° alone and shut the door;   30
    Cough or cry "hem" if anybody come.
    Your mystery, your mystery!° Nay, dispatch.

    Exit Emilia.

Desdemona [*kneeling*]: Upon my knees, what doth your speech import?
    I understand a fury in your words,
    But not the words.   35
Othello: Why, what art thou?
Desdemona: Your wife, my lord, your true
    And loyal wife.
Othello: Come, swear it, damn thyself,
    Lest, being like one of heaven,° the devils themselves
    Should fear to seize thee. Therefore be double damned:
    Swear thou art honest.
Desdemona: Heaven doth truly know it.   40
Othello: Heaven truly knows that thou art false as hell.
Desdemona: To whom, my lord? With whom? How am I false?
Othello [*weeping*]: Ah, Desdemon! Away, away, away!
Desdemona: Alas the heavy day! Why do you weep?
    Am I the motive° of these tears, my lord?   45
    If haply you my father do suspect
    An instrument of this your calling back,
    Lay not your blame on me. If you have lost him,
    I have lost him too.
Othello: Had it pleased heaven
    To try me with affliction, had they° rained   50
    All kinds of sores and shames on my bare head,
    Steeped me in poverty to the very lips,
    Given to captivity me and my utmost hopes,
    I should have found in some place of my soul
    A drop of patience. But, alas, to make me   55
    A fixèd figure for the time of scorn°
    To point his° slow and moving finger° at!
    Yet could I bear that too, well, very well.

---

29 *Some . . . function* i.e., practice your chosen profession, that of bawd (by guarding the door)
30 *procreants* mating couples   32 *mystery* trade, occupation   38 *being . . . heaven* looking like
an angel   45 *motive* cause   50 *they* i.e., heavenly powers   56 *time of scorn* i.e., scornful world
57 *his* its. *slow and moving finger* i.e., hour hand of the clock, moving so slowly it seems hardly to
move at all. (Othello envisages himself as being eternally pointed at by the scornful world as the
numbers on a clock are pointed at by the hour hand.)

"Ah, Desdemon! Away, away, away!" (IV, ii, 43).

But there where I have garnered° up my heart,
Where either I must live or bear no life,   60
The fountain° from the which my current runs
Or else dries up—to be discarded thence!
Or keep it as a cistern° for foul toads
To knot° and gender° in! Turn thy complexion there,°
Patience, thou young and rose-lipped cherubin—   65
Ay, there look grim as hell!°
Desdemona: I hope my noble lord esteems me honest.°
Othello: O, ay, as summer flies are in the shambles,°

59 *garnered* stored   61 *fountain* spring   63 *cistern* cesspool   64 *knot* couple.   *gender* engender.   *Turn . . . there* change your color, grow pale, at such a sight   65–66 *Patience . . . hell* (Even Patience, that rose-lipped cherub, will look grim and pale at this spectacle.)   67 *honest* chaste
68 *shambles* slaughterhouse

That quicken° even with blowing.° O thou weed,
Who art so lovely fair and smell'st so sweet   70
That the sense aches at thee, would thou hadst ne'er been born!
Desdemona: Alas, what ignorant° sin have I committed?
Othello: Was this fair paper, this most goodly book,
Made to write "whore" upon? What committed?
Committed? O thou public commoner!°   75
I should make very forges of my cheeks,
That would to cinders burn up modesty,
Did I but speak thy deeds. What committed?
Heaven stops the nose at it and the moon winks;°
The bawdy° wind, that kisses all it meets,   80
Is hushed within the hollow mine° of earth
And will not hear 't. What committed?
Impudent strumpet!
Desdemona: By heaven, you do me wrong.
Othello: Are not you a strumpet?
Desdemona: No, as I am a Christian.   85
If to preserve this vessel° for my lord
From any other foul unlawful touch
Be not to be a strumpet, I am none.
Othello: What, not a whore?
Desdemona: No, as I shall be saved.   90
Othello: Is 't possible?
Desdemona: O, heaven forgive us!
Othello: I cry you mercy,° then.
I took you for that cunning whore of Venice
That married with Othello. [*Calling out.*] You, mistress,
That have the office opposite to Saint Peter   95
And keep the gate of hell!

Enter Emilia.

                        You, you, ay, you!
We have done our course.° There's money for your pains. [*He gives
money.*]
I pray you, turn the key and keep our counsel.
Exit.

---

69 *quicken* come to life.   *with blowing* i.e., with the puffing up of something rotten in which
maggots are breeding   72 *ignorant sin* sin in ignorance   75 *commoner* prostitute   79 *winks*
closes her eyes. (The moon symbolizes chastity.)   80 *bawdy* kissing one and all   81 *mine* cave
(where the winds were thought to dwell)   86 *vessel* body   92 *cry you mercy* beg your pardon   97 *course* business (with an indecent suggestion of "trick," turn at sex)

Emilia: Alas, what does this gentleman conceive?°
    How do you, madam? How do you, my good lady?   100
Desdemona: Faith, half asleep.°
Emilia: Good madam, what's the matter with my lord?
Desdemona: With who?
Emilia: Why, with my lord, madam.
Desdemona: Who is thy lord?
Emilia: He that is yours, sweet lady.   105
Desdemona: I have none. Do not talk to me, Emilia.
    I cannot weep, nor answers have I none
    But what should go by water.° Prithee, tonight
    Lay on my bed my wedding sheets, remember;
    And call thy husband hither.   110
Emilia: Here's a change indeed!   *Exit.*
Desdemona: 'Tis meet I should be used so, very meet.°
    How have I been behaved, that he might stick°
    The small'st opinion° on my least misuse?°

    Enter Iago.

Iago: What is your pleasure, madam? How is 't with you?   115
Desdemona: I cannot tell. Those that do teach young babes
    Do it with gentle means and easy tasks.
    He might have chid me so, for, in good faith,
    I am a child to chiding.
Iago: What is the matter, lady?   120
Emilia: Alas, Iago, my lord hath so bewhored her,
    Thrown such despite and heavy terms upon her,
    That true hearts cannot bear it.
Desdemona: Am I that name, Iago?
Iago: What name, fair lady?   125
Desdemona: Such as she said my lord did say I was.
Emilia: He called her whore. A beggar in his drink
    Could not have laid such terms upon his callet.°
Iago: Why did he so?
Desdemona [*weeping*]:
    I do not know. I am sure I am none such.   130
Iago: Do not weep, do not weep. Alas the day!
Emilia: Hath she forsook so many noble matches,

---

99 *conceive* suppose, think   101 *half asleep* i.e., dazed   108 *go by water* be expressed by tears
112 *meet* fitting   113 *stick* attach   114 *opinion* censure.   *least misuse* slightest misconduct
128 *callet* whore

Iago comforts Desdemona about Othello's accusations (IV, ii, 115–171).

Her father and her country and her friends,
To be called whore? Would it not make one weep?
Desdemona: It is my wretched fortune.
Iago: Beshrew° him for 't!   135
How comes this trick° upon him?
Desdemona: Nay, heaven doth know.
Emilia: I will be hanged if some eternal° villain,
Some busy and insinuating° rogue,
Some cogging,° cozening° slave, to get some office,
Have not devised this slander. I will be hanged else.   140
Iago: Fie, there is no such man. It is impossible.
Desdemona: If any such there be, heaven pardon him!
Emilia: A halter° pardon him! And hell gnaw his bones!
Why should he call her whore? Who keeps her company?
What place? What time? What form?° What likelihood?   145
The Moor's abused by some most villainous knave,
Some base notorious knave, some scurvy fellow.
O heaven, that° such companions° thou'dst unfold,°

135 *Beshrew* curse   136 *trick* strange behavior, delusion   137 *eternal* inveterate   138 *insinuating* ingratiating, fawning, wheedling   139 *cogging* cheating. *cozening* defrauding   143 *halter* hangman's noose   145 *form* appearance, circumstance   148 *that* would that. *companions* fellows.   *unfold* expose

And put in every honest hand a whip
To lash the rascals naked through the world   150
Even from the east to th' west!

Iago: Speak within door.°

Emilia: O, fie upon them! Some such squire° he was
That turned your wit the seamy side without°
And made you to suspect me with the Moor.

Iago: You are a fool. Go to.°

Desdemona: Alas, Iago,   155
What shall I do to win my lord again?
Good friend, go to him; for, by this light of heaven,
I know not how I lost him. Here I kneel. [*She kneels.*]
If e'er my will did trespass 'gainst his love,
Either in discourse of thought° or actual deed,   160
Or that° mine eyes, mine ears, or any sense
Delighted them° in any other form;
Or that I do not yet,° and ever did,
And ever will—though he do shake me off
To beggarly divorcement—love him dearly,   165
Comfort forswear° me! Unkindness may do much,
And his unkindness may defeat° my life,
But never taint my love. I cannot say "whore."
It does abhor° me now I speak the word;
To do the act that might the addition° earn   170
Not the world's mass of vanity° could make me.

[*She rises.*]

Iago: I pray you, be content. 'Tis but his humor.°
The business of the state does him offense,
And he does chide with you.

Desdemona: If 'twere no other—   175

Iago: It is but so, I warrant.   [*Trumpets within.*]
Hark, how these instruments summon you to supper!
The messengers of Venice stays the meat.°
Go in, and weep not. All things shall be well.

Exeunt Desdemona and Emilia.

---

151 *within door* i.e., not so loud   152 *squire* fellow   153 *seamy side without* wrong side out
155 *Go to* i.e., that's enough   160 *discourse of thought* process of thinking   161 *that* if.
(Also in line 163.)   162 *Delighted them* took delight   163 *yet* still   166 *Comfort forswear*
may heavenly comfort forsake   167 *defeat* destroy   169 *abhor* (1) fill me with abhorrence
(2) make me whorelike   170 *addition* title   171 *vanity* showy splendor   172 *humor* mood
178 *stays the meat* are waiting to dine

Enter Roderigo.

How now, Roderigo?   180

Roderigo: I do not find that thou deal'st justly with me.

Iago: What in the contrary?

Roderigo: Every day thou daff'st me° with some device,° Iago, and rather,
as it seems to me now, keep'st from me all conveniency° than sup-
pliest me with the least advantage° of hope. I will indeed no longer   185
endure it, nor am I yet persuaded to put up° in peace what already I
have foolishly suffered.

Iago: Will you hear me, Roderigo?

Roderigo: Faith, I have heard too much, for your words and performances
are no kin together.   190

Iago: You charge me most unjustly.

Roderigo: With naught but truth. I have wasted myself out of my means.
The jewels you have had from me to deliver° Desdemona would half
have corrupted a votarist.° You have told me she hath received them
and returned me expectations and comforts of sudden respect° and   195
acquaintance, but I find none.

Iago: Well, go to, very well.

Roderigo: "Very well"! "Go to"! I cannot go to,° man, nor 'tis not very
well. By this hand, I think it is scurvy, and begin to find myself fopped°
in it.   200

Iago: Very well.

Roderigo: I tell you 'tis not very well.° I will make myself known to
Desdemona. If she will return me my jewels, I will give over my suit
and repent my unlawful solicitation; if not, assure yourself I will seek
satisfaction° of you.   205

Iago: You have said now?°

Roderigo: Ay, and said nothing but what I protest intendment° of doing.

Iago: Why, now I see there's mettle in thee, and even from this instant
do build on thee a better opinion than ever before. Give me thy hand,
Roderigo. Thou hast taken against me a most just exception; but yet   210
I protest I have dealt most directly in thy affair.

---

183 *thou daff'st me* you put me off. *device* excuse, trick   184 *conveniency* advantage, opportunity   185 *advantage* increase   186 *put up* submit to, tolerate   193 *deliver* deliver to
194 *votarist* nun   195 *sudden respect* immediate consideration   198 *I cannot go to*
(Roderigo changes Iago's *go to*, an expression urging patience, to *I cannot go to*, "I have no
opportunity for success in wooing.")   199 *fopped* fooled, duped   202 *not very well*
(Roderigo changes Iago's *very well*, "all right, then," to *not very well*, "not at all good.")
205 *satisfaction* repayment. (The term normally means settling of accounts in a duel.)   206
You . . . now have you finished?   207 *intendment* intention

Roderigo: It hath not appeared.

Iago: I grant indeed it hath not appeared, and your suspicion is not without wit and judgment. But, Roderigo, if thou hast that in thee indeed which I have greater reason to believe now than ever—I mean 215 purpose, courage, and valor—this night show it. If thou the next night following enjoy not Desdemona, take me from this world with treachery and devise engines for° my life.

Roderigo: Well, what is it? Is it within reason and compass?

Iago: Sir, there is especial commission come from Venice to depute 220 Cassio in Othello's place.

Roderigo: Is that true? Why, then Othello and Desdemona return again to Venice.

Iago: O, no; he goes into Mauritania and takes away with him the fair Desdemona, unless his abode be lingered here by some accident; 225 wherein none can be so determinate° as the removing of Cassio.

Roderigo: How do you mean, removing of him?

Iago: Why, by making him uncapable of Othello's place—knocking out his brains.

Roderigo: And that you would have me to do? 230

Iago: Ay, if you dare do yourself a profit and a right. He sups tonight with a harlotry,° and thither will I go to him. He knows not yet of his honorable fortune. If you will watch his going thence, which I will fashion to fall out° between twelve and one, you may take him at your pleasure. I will be near to second your attempt, and he shall fall bet- 235 ween us. Come, stand not amazed at it, but go along with me. I will show you such a necessity in his death that you shall think yourself bound to put it on him. It is now high° suppertime, and the night grows to waste.° About it.

Roderigo: I will hear further reason for this. 240

Iago: And you shall be satisfied. *Exeunt.*

SCENE III [THE CITADEL.]

Enter Othello, Lodovico, Desdemona, Emilia, and attendants.

Lodovico: I do beseech you, sir, trouble yourself no further.

Othello: O, pardon me; 'twill do me good to walk.

Lodovico: Madam, good night. I humbly thank your ladyship.

Desdemona: Your honor is most welcome.

Othello: Will you walk, sir?

O, Desdemona! 5

218 *engines for* plots against   226 *determinate* conclusive   232 *harlotry* slut   234 *fall out* occur   238 *high* fully   239 *grows to waste* wastes away

Desdemona: My lord?

Othello: Get you to bed on th' instant.
 I will be returned forthwith. Dismiss your attendant there. Look
 't be done.

Desdemona: I will, my lord.   10

    Exit [Othello, with Lodovico and attendants].

Emilia: How goes it now? He looks gentler than he did.

Desdemona: He says he will return incontinent,°
 And hath commanded me to go to bed,
 And bid me to dismiss you.

Emilia: Dismiss me?   15

Desdemona: It was his bidding. Therefore, good Emilia,
 Give me my nightly wearing, and adieu.
 We must not now displease him.

Emilia: I would you had never seen him!

Desdemona: So would not I. My love doth so approve him   20
 That even his stubbornness,° his checks,° his frowns—
 Prithee, unpin me—have grace and favor in them.

    [Emilia prepares Desdemona for bed.]

Emilia: I have laid those sheets you bade me on the bed.

Desdemona: All's one.° Good faith, how foolish are our minds!
 If I do die before thee, prithee shroud me   25
 In one of these same sheets.

Emilia: Come, come, you talk.°

Desdemona: My mother had a maid called Barbary.
 She was in love, and he she loved proved mad°
 And did forsake her. She had a song of "Willow."
 An old thing 'twas, but it expressed her fortune,   30
 And she died singing it. That song tonight
 Will not go from my mind; I have much to do
 But to go hang° my head all at one side
 And sing it like poor Barbary. Prithee, dispatch.

Emilia: Shall I go fetch your nightgown?°   35

Desdemona: No, unpin me here.
 This Lodovico is a proper° man.

Emilia: A very handsome man.

---

12 *incontinent* immediately   21 *stubbornness* roughness.   *checks* rebukes   24 *All's one* all right. It doesn't really matter   26 *talk* i.e., prattle   28 *mad* wild, i.e., faithless   32–33 *I . . . hang* I can scarcely keep myself from hanging   35 *nightgown* dressing gown   37 *proper* handsome

Desdemona: He speaks well.

Emilia: I know a lady in Venice would have walked barefoot to Palestine 40
for a touch of his nether lip.

Desdemona [singing]:

        "The poor soul sat sighing by a sycamore tree,

        Sing all a green willow;°

        Her hand on her bosom, her head on her knee,

        Sing willow, willow, willow. 45

        The fresh streams ran by her and murmured her moans;

        Sing willow, willow, willow;

        Her salt tears fell from her, and softened the stones—"

Lay by these.

        [*Singing.*] "Sing willow, willow, willow—" 50

Prithee, hie thee.° He'll come anon.°

        [*Singing.*] "Sing all a green willow must be my garland.

        Let nobody blame him; his scorn I approve—"

Nay, that's not next.—Hark! Who is 't that knocks?

Emilia: It's the wind. 55

Desdemona [singing]:

        "I called my love false love; but what said he then?

        Sing willow, willow, willow;

        If I court more women, you'll couch with more men."

So, get thee gone. Good night. Mine eyes do itch;

Doth that bode weeping?

Emilia: 'Tis neither here nor there. 60

Desdemona: I have heard it said so. O, these men, these men!

Dost thou in conscience think—tell me, Emilia—

That there be women do abuse° their husbands

In such gross kind?

Emilia: There be some such, no question.

Desdemona: Wouldst thou do such a deed for all the world? 65

Emilia: Why, would not you?

Desdemona: No, by this heavenly light!

Emilia: Nor I neither by this heavenly light;

I might do 't as well i' the dark.

Desdemona: Wouldst thou do such a deed for all the world?

Emilia: The world's a huge thing. It is a great price 70

For a small vice.

---

43 *willow* (A conventional emblem of disappointed love.) 51 *hie thee* hurry. *anon* right
away 63 *abuse* deceive

Desdemona: Good troth, I think thou wouldst not.

Emilia: By my troth, I think I should, and undo 't when I had done.
Marry, I would not do such a thing for a joint ring,° nor for measures
of lawn,° nor for gowns, petticoats, nor caps, nor any petty   75
exhibition.° But for all the whole world! Uds° pity, who would not
make her husband a cuckold to make him a monarch? I should venture
purgatory for 't.

Desdemona: Beshrew me if I would do such a wrong
For the whole world.   80

Emilia: Why, the wrong is but a wrong i' the world, and having the
world for your labor, 'tis a wrong in your own world, and you might
quickly make it right.

Desdemona: I do not think there is any such woman.

Emilia: Yes, a dozen, and as many   85
To th' vantage° as would store° the world they played° for.
But I do think it is their husbands' faults
If wives do fall. Say that they slack their duties°
And pour our treasures into foreign laps,°
Or else break out in peevish jealousies,   90
Throwing restraint upon us? Or say they strike us,°
Or scant our former having in despite?°
Why, we have galls,° and though we have some grace,
Yet have we some revenge. Let husbands know
Their wives have sense° like them. They see, and smell,   95
And have their palates both for sweet and sour,
As husbands have. What is it that they do
When they change us for others? Is it sport?°
I think it is. And doth affection° breed it?
I think it doth. Is 't frailty that thus errs?   100
It is so, too. And have not we affections,
Desires for sport, and frailty, as men have?
Then let them use us well; else let them know,
The ills we do, their ills instruct us so.

---

74 *joint ring* a ring made in separate halves   75 *lawn* fine linen   76 *exhibition* gift.   *Uds*
God's   86 *To th' vantage* in addition, to boot.   *store* populate.   *played* (1) gambled (2)
sported sexually   88 *duties* marital duties   89 *pour . . . laps* i.e., are unfaithful, give what is
rightfully ours (semen) to other women   91 *Throwing . . . us* i.e., jealously restricting our
freedom to see other men   92 *scant . . . despite* reduce our allowance to spite us   93 *have
galls* i.e., are capable of resenting injury and insult   95 *sense* physical sense   98 *sport* sexual
pastime   99 *affection* passion

Desdemona: Good night, good night. God me such uses° send   105
    Not to pick bad from bad, but by bad mend!°

Exeunt.

ACT V

SCENE I [A STREET IN CYPRUS.]

Enter Iago and Roderigo.

Iago: Here stand behind this bulk.° Straight will he come.
    Wear thy good rapier bare,° and put it home.
    Quick, quick! Fear nothing. I'll be at thy elbow.
    It makes us or it mars us. Think on that,
    And fix most firm thy resolution.   5
Roderigo: Be near at hand. I may miscarry in 't.
Iago: Here, at thy hand. Be bold, and take thy stand.

    [*Iago stands aside. Roderigo conceals himself.*]

Roderigo: I have no great devotion to the deed;
    And yet he hath given me satisfying reasons.
    'Tis but a man gone. Forth, my sword! He dies.   10

    [*He draws.*]

Iago: I have rubbed this young quat° almost to the sense,°
    And he grows angry. Now, whether he kill Cassio
    Or Cassio him, or each do kill the other,
    Every way makes my gain. Live Roderigo,°
    He calls me to a restitution large   15
    Of gold and jewels that I bobbed° from him
    As gifts to Desdemona.
    It must not be. If Cassio do remain,
    He hath a daily beauty in his life
    That makes me ugly; and besides, the Moor   20
    May unfold° me to him; there stand I in much peril.
    No, he must die. Be 't so. I hear him coming.

---

105 *uses* habit, practice   106 *Not . . . mend* i.e., not to learn bad conduct from others' badness (as Emilia has suggested women learn from men), but to mend my ways by perceiving
what badness is, making spiritual benefit out of evil and adversity   1 *bulk* framework pro-
jecting from the front of a shop   2 *bare* unsheathed   11 *quat* pimple, pustule.   *to the sense*
to the quick   14 *Live Roderigo* if Roderigo lives   16 *bobbed* swindled   21 *unfold* expose

Enter Cassio.

Roderigo [*coming forth*]: I know his gait, 'tis he.—Villain, thou diest!

　　[*He attacks Cassio.*]

Cassio: That thrust had been mine enemy indeed,
　　But that my coat° is better than thou know'st.　　　　　　25
　　I will make proof° of thine.

　　[*He draws, and wounds Roderigo.*]

Roderigo:　　　　　　　　O, I am slain!　　　　　　　　[*He falls.*]

　　[*Iago, from behind, wounds Cassio in the leg, and exits.*]

Cassio: I am maimed forever. Help, ho! Murder! Murder!

　　Enter Othello.

Othello: The voice of Cassio! Iago keeps his word.
Roderigo: O, villain that I am!
Othello: It is even so.　　　　　　　　　　　　　　　　　　30
Cassio: O, help, ho! Light! A surgeon!
Othello: 'Tis he. O brave Iago, honest and just,
　　That hast such noble sense of thy friend's wrong!
　　Thou teachest me. Minion,° your dear lies dead,
　　And your unblest fate hies.° Strumpet, I come.　　　　　35
　　Forth of° my heart those charms, thine eyes, are blotted;
　　Thy bed, lust-stained, shall with lust's blood be spotted.

　　Exit Othello.

　　Enter Lodovico and Gratiano.

Cassio: What ho! No watch? No passage?° Murder! Murder!
Gratiano: 'Tis some mischance. The voice is very direful.
Cassio: O, help!
Lodovico: Hark!　　　　　　　　　　　　　　　　　　　　40
Roderigo: O wretched villain!
Lodovico: Two or three groan. 'Tis heavy° night;
　　These may be counterfeits. Let's think 't unsafe
　　To come in to° the cry without more help.　　　　　　　45

　　[*They remain near the entrance.*]

25 *coat* (Possibly a garment of mail under the outer clothing, or simply a tougher coat than
Roderigo expected.)　　26 *proof* a test　　34 *Minion* hussy (i.e., Desdemona)　　35 *hies* hastens
on　　36 *Forth of* from out　　38 *passage* people passing by　　43 *heavy* thick, dark　　45 *come in
to* approach

Roderigo: Nobody come? Then shall I bleed to death.

    Enter Iago [in his shirtsleeves, with a light].

Lodovico: Hark!
Gratiano: Here's one comes in his shirt, with light and weapons.
Iago: Who's there? Whose noise is this that cries on° murder?
Lodovico: We do not know.
Iago: Did not you hear a cry?   50
Cassio: Here, here! For heaven's sake, help me!
Iago: What's the matter?

    [He moves toward Cassio.]

Gratiano [to Lodovico]: This is Othello's ancient, as I take it.
Lodovico [to Gratiano]: The same indeed, a very valiant fellow.
Iago [to Cassio]: What° are you here that cry so grievously?
Cassio: Iago? O, I am spoiled,° undone by villains!   55
     Give me some help.
Iago: O me, Lieutenant! What villains have done this?
Cassio: I think that one of them is hereabout,
     And cannot make° away.
Iago: O treacherous villains!

    [To Lodovico and Gratiano.]

     What are you there? Come in, and give some help.   *[They advance.]*   60
Roderigo: O, help me there!
Cassio: That's one of them.
Iago: O murderous slave! O villain!

    [He stabs Roderigo.]

Roderigo: O damned Iago! O inhuman dog!
Iago: Kill men i' the dark?—Where be these bloody thieves?—
     How silent is this town!—Ho! Murder, murder!—   65
     [To Lodovico and Gratiano.] What may you be? Are you of good or evil?
Lodovico: As you shall prove us, praise° us.
Iago: Signor Lodovico?
Lodovico: He, sir.
Iago: I cry you mercy.° Here's Cassio hurt by villains.   70

---

49 *cries on* cries out   54 *What* who (also at lines 60 and 66)   55 *spoiled* ruined, done for
59 *make* get   67 *praise* appraise   70 *I cry you mercy* I beg your pardon

Gratiano: Cassio?
Iago: How is 't, brother?
Cassio: My leg is cut in two.
Iago: Marry, heaven forbid!
    Light, gentlemen! I'll bind it with my shirt.   75

    [*He hands them the light, and tends to Cassio's wound.*]

    Enter Bianca.

Bianca: What is the matter, ho? Who is 't that cried?
Iago: Who is 't that cried?
Bianca: O my dear Cassio!
    My sweet Cassio! O Cassio, Cassio, Cassio!
Iago: O notable strumpet! Cassio, may you suspect
    Who they should be that have thus mangled you?   80
Cassio: No.
Gratiano: I am sorry to find you thus. I have been to seek you.
Iago: Lend me a garter. [*He applies a tourniquet.*] So.—O, for a chair,°
    To bear him easily hence!
Bianca: Alas, he faints! O Cassio, Cassio, Cassio!   85
Iago: Gentlemen all, I do suspect this trash
    To be a party in this injury.—
    Patience awhile, good Cassio.—Come, come;
    Lend me a light.   [*He shines the light on Roderigo.*]
        Know we this face or no?
    Alas, my friend and my dear countryman   90
    Roderigo! No.—Yes, sure.—O heaven! Roderigo!
Gratiano: What, of Venice?
Iago: Even he, sir. Did you know him?
Gratiano: Know him? Ay.
Iago: Signor Gratiano? I cry your gentle° pardon.   95
    These bloody accidents° must excuse my manners
    That so neglected you.
Gratiano: I am glad to see you.
Iago: How do you, Cassio? O, a chair, a chair!
Gratiano: Roderigo!
Iago: He, he, 'tis he. [*A litter is brought in.*] O, that's well said;° the chair.   100
    Some good man bear him carefully from hence;
    I'll fetch the General's surgeon. [*To Bianca.*] For you, mistress,

---

83 *chair* litter   95 *gentle* noble   96 *accidents* sudden events   100 *well said* well done

Save you your labor.°—He that lies slain here, Cassio,
Was my dear friend. What malice° was between you?
Cassio: None in the world, nor do I know the man.   105
Iago [*to Bianca*]: What, look you pale?—O, bear him out o' th' air.°

[*Cassio and Roderigo are borne off.*]

Stay you,° good gentlemen.—Look you pale, mistress?—
Do you perceive the gastness° of her eye?—
Nay, if you stare,° we shall hear more anon.—
Behold her well; I pray you, look upon her.   110
Do you see, gentlemen? Nay, guiltiness
Will speak, though tongues were out of use.

[*Enter Emilia.*]

Emilia: 'Las, what's the matter? What's the matter, husband?
Iago: Cassio hath here been set on in the dark
      By Roderigo and fellows that are scaped.   115
      He's almost slain, and Roderigo dead.
Emilia: Alas, good gentleman! Alas, good Cassio!
Iago: This is the fruits of whoring. Prithee, Emilia,
      Go know° of Cassio where he supped tonight.
      [*To Bianca.*] What, do you shake at that?   120
Bianca: He supped at my house, but I therefore shake not.
Iago: O, did he so? I charge you go with me.
Emilia: O, fie upon thee, strumpet!
Bianca: I am no strumpet, but of life as honest°
      As you that thus abuse me.   125
Emilia: As I? Faugh! Fie upon thee!
Iago: Kind gentlemen, let's go see poor Cassio dressed.°—
      Come, mistress, you must tell's another tale.
      Emilia, run you to the citadel
      And tell my lord and lady what hath happed.—   130
      Will you go on afore? [*Aside.*] This is the night
      That either makes me or fordoes° me quite.   *Exeunt.*

---

103 *Save . . . labor* i.e., never you mind tending Cassio   104 *malice* enmity   106 *bear . . . air*
(Fresh air was thought to be dangerous for a wound.)   107 *Stay you* (Lodovico and Gratiano are evidently about to leave.)   108 *gastness* terror   109 *stare* (Iago pretends to interpret Bianca's wild looks as an involuntary confession of guilt.)   119 *know* learn   124
honest chaste   127 *Cassio dressed* Cassio's wounds dressed   132 *fordoes* undoes, ruins

"Enter Othello, and Desdemona in her bed" (V, ii, s.d.).

SCENE II [A BEDCHAMBER IN THE CITADEL.]

> *Enter Othello [with a light], and Desdemona in her bed.°*

Othello: It is the cause,° it is the cause, my soul.
　　Let me not name it to you, you chaste stars!
　　It is the cause. Yet I'll not shed her blood,
　　Nor scar that whiter skin of hers than snow,
　　And smooth as monumental° alabaster.　　　　　　　　　5
　　Yet she must die, else she'll betray more men.
　　Put out the light, and then put out the light.°
　　If I quench thee, thou flaming minister,°
　　I can again thy former light restore,
　　Should I repent me;° once put out thy light,　　　　　10
　　Thou cunning'st pattern° of excelling nature,

---

s.d. *in her bed* (Either the curtains are drawn back to reveal the bed in a recessed area back-stage, or the bed is "thrust out" onstage as the scene begins.)　1 *cause* i.e., cause of justice, the offense itself, which Othello must correct as an agent of justice　5 *monumental* i.e., used in making tombs and funeral monuments　7 *the light . . . light* the torch or lamp . . . Desdemona's life　8 *flaming minister* torch or lamp that serves me　10 *repent me* change my mind　11 *Thou . . . pattern* you skillfully wrought perfect example

I know not where is that Promethean heat°
That can thy light relume.° When I have plucked thy rose,
I cannot give it vital growth again;
It needs must wither. I'll smell thee on the tree.   15

[*He kisses her.*]

O balmy breath, that dost almost persuade
Justice to break her sword! One more, one more.
Be thus when thou art dead, and I will kill thee,
And love thee after. One more, and that's the last.

[*He kisses her.*]

So sweet was ne'er so fatal. I must weep,   20
But they are cruel° tears. This sorrow's heavenly;
It strikes where it doth love.° She wakes.
Desdemona: Who's there? Othello?
Othello: Ay, Desdemona.
Desdemona: Will you come to bed, my lord?   25
Othello: Have you prayed tonight, Desdemon?
Desdemona: Ay, my lord.
Othello: If you bethink yourself of any crime°
       Unreconciled as yet to heaven and grace,
       Solicit° for it straight.°   30
Desdemona: Alack, my lord, what may you mean by that?
Othello: Well, do it, and be brief. I will walk by.
       I would not kill thy unprepared spirit.
       No, heaven forfend!° I would not kill thy soul.
Desdemona: Talk you of killing?
Othello: Ay, I do.
Desdemona: Then heaven   35
       Have mercy on me!
Othello: Amen, with all my heart!
Desdemona: If you say so, I hope you will not kill me.
Othello: Humh!
Desdemona: And yet I fear you; for you're fatal then
       When your eyes roll so. Why I should fear I know not,   40
       Since guiltiness I know not; but yet I feel I fear.

12 *Promethean heat* divine fire. (Alluding to the theft of fire from heaven by Prometheus.)
13 *relume* rekindle   21 *cruel* unrelenting   22 *It . . . love* (Compare Hebrews 12:6: "For
whom the Lord loveth he chasteneth.")   28 *crime* sin   30 *Solicit* petition, pray.   *straight*
immediately   34 *forfend* forbid

Othello: Think on thy sins.
Desdemona: They are loves I bear to you.°
Othello: Ay, and for that thou diest.
Desdemona: That death's unnatural that kills for loving.
　　Alas, why gnaw you so your nether lip?   45
　　Some bloody passion shakes your very frame.
　　These are portents; but yet I hope, I hope,
　　They do not point on° me.
Othello: Peace, and be still!
Desdemona: I will so. What's the matter?   50
Othello: That handkerchief which I so loved and gave thee
　　Thou gav'st to Cassio.
Desdemona: No, by my life and soul!
　　Send for the man and ask him.
Othello: Sweet soul, take heed, take heed of perjury.
　　Thou art on thy deathbed.   55
Desdemona: Ay, but not yet to die.
Othello: Yes, presently.°
　　Therefore confess thee freely of thy sin;
　　For to deny each article with oath
　　Cannot remove nor choke the strong conception°
　　That I do groan withal.° Thou art to die.   60
Desdemona: Then Lord have mercy on me!
Othello: I say, amen.
Desdemona: And have you mercy too! I never did
　　Offend° you in my life; never loved Cassio
　　But with such general warranty° of heaven
　　As I might love. I never gave him token.   65
Othello: By heaven, I saw my handkerchief in 's hand.
　　O perjured woman! Thou dost stone° my heart,
　　And makes me call what I intend to do
　　A murder, which I thought a sacrifice.
　　I saw the handkerchief.
Desdemona: He found it, then.   70
　　I never gave it him. Send for him hither;
　　Let him confess a truth.

42 *They are . . . you* i.e., if I sinned, it was in loving you more than my father or more than God   48 *point on* point at, predict what is to happen to   56 *presently* immediately   59 *conception* (1) belief in your guilt (2) plan in my mind   60 *groan withal* (1) groan at in sorrow (2) as in giving birth   63 *Offend* wrong   64 *warranty* sanction   67 *stone* turn to stone, harden

Othello: He hath confessed.
Desdemona: What, my lord?
Othello: That he hath used thee.
Desdemona: How? Unlawfully?
Othello: Ay.
Desdemona: He will not say so.
Othello: No, his mouth is stopped;   75
     Honest Iago hath ta'en order° for 't.
Desdemona: O, my fear interprets. What, is he dead?
Othello: Had all his hairs been lives, my great revenge
     Had stomach for them all.
Desdemona: Alas, he is betrayed and I undone!   [*She weeps.*]   80
Othello: Out, strumpet! Weep'st thou for him to my face?
Desdemona: O, banish me, my lord, but kill me not!
Othello: Down, strumpet!
Desdemona: Kill me tomorrow; let me live tonight!
Othello: Nay, if you strive—   85
Desdemona: But half an hour!
Othello: Being done,° there is no pause.
Desdemona: But while I say one prayer!
Othello: It is too late.

     Smothers her.

Emilia [at the door]: My lord, my lord! What, ho! My lord, my lord!
Othello: What noise is this? Not dead? Not yet quite dead?
     I that am cruel am yet merciful;   90
     I would not have thee linger in thy pain.

     [*He dispatches her.*]

                                             So, so.
Emilia [within]: What, ho! My lord, my lord!
Othello: Who's there?
Emilia [within]: O, good my lord, I would speak a word with you!
Othello: Yes, 'tis Emilia.—By and by.—She's dead.
     'Tis like° she comes to speak of Cassio's death.—   95
     The noise was here.° Ha! No more moving?
     Still as the grave. Shall she come in? Were 't good?—
     I think she stirs again. No. What's best to do?

---

76 *ta'en order* taken measures   86 *Being done* i.e., since justice has begun its relentless course   95 *like* likely that   96 *here* (The Folio's *high* is possible, suggesting that the commotion of the attack on Cassio was loud.)

Othello with his murdered Desdemona (V, ii)

If she come in, she'll sure speak to my wife.
My wife! My wife! What wife? I have no wife.   100
O, insupportable! O heavy hour!
Methinks it should be now a huge eclipse
Of sun and moon, and that th' affrighted globe
Should yawn° at alteration.°
Emilia [*within*]:   I do beseech you
That I may speak with you, O, good my lord!   105
Othello: I had forgot thee. O, come in, Emilia.—
    Soft,° by and by. Let me the curtains draw.—

---

104 *yawn* gape in amazement, i.e., move in an earthquake. (According to Pliny, earthquakes often happen during eclipses.) *at alteration* at these cataclysmic events in nature, well suited to express the horror of Desdemona's death   107 *Soft* wait a minute

[*He closes the bed-curtains and opens the door.*]

Where art thou?

Enter Emilia.

                              What's the matter with thee now?

Emilia: O, my good lord, yonder's foul murders done!

Othello: What, now?   110

Emilia: But now, my lord.

Othello: It is the very error° of the moon;
    She comes more nearer earth than she was wont,
    And makes men mad.

Emilia: Cassio, my lord, hath killed a young Venetian   115
    Called Roderigo.

Othello: Roderigo killed?
    And Cassio killed?

Emilia: No, Cassio is not killed.

Othello: Not Cassio killed? Then murder's out of tune,
    And sweet revenge grows harsh.

Desdemona: O, falsely, falsely murdered!   120

Emilia: O Lord, what cry is that?

Othello: That? What?

Emilia: Out° and alas, that was my lady's voice.

[*She opens the bed-curtains.*]

    Help, help, ho, help! O lady, speak again!
    Sweet Desdemona! O sweet mistress, speak!   125

Desdemona: A guiltless death I die.

Emilia: O, who hath done this deed?

Desdemona: Nobody; I myself. Farewell.
    Commend me to my kind lord. O, farewell!   [*She dies.*]

Othello: Why, how should she be murdered?

Emilia: Alas, who knows?   130

Othello: You heard her say herself it was not I.

Emilia: She said so. I must needs report the truth.

Othello: She's like a liar gone to burning hell!
    'Twas I that killed her.

Emilia: O, the more angel she,
    And you the blacker devil!   135

Othello: She turned to folly,° and she was a whore.

---

112 *error* aberration, irregularity   123 *Out* (A cry of dismay, intensifying *alas.*)   136 *folly* i.e.,
wantonness, fleshly sin

Emilia: Thou dost belie° her, and thou art a devil.

Othello: She was false as water.

Emilia: Thou art rash as fire to say

That she was false. O, she was heavenly true! 140

Othello: Cassio did top her. Ask thy husband else.°

O, I were damned beneath all depth in hell

But that I did proceed upon just grounds

To this extremity. Thy husband knew it all.

Emilia: My husband? 145

Othello: Thy husband.

Emilia: That she was false to wedlock?

Othello: Ay, with Cassio. Nay, had she been true,

If heaven would make me such another world

Of one entire and perfect chrysolite,° 150

I'd not have sold her for it.

Emilia: My husband?

Othello: Ay, 'twas he that told me on her first.

An honest man he is, and hates the slime

That sticks on filthy deeds. 155

Emilia: My husband?

Othello: What needs this iterance,° woman? I say thy husband.

Emilia: O mistress, villainy hath made mocks with° love!

My husband say she was false?

Othello: He, woman;

I say thy husband. Dost understand the word? 160

My friend, thy husband, honest, honest Iago.

Emilia: If he say so, may his pernicious soul

Rot half a grain a day! He lies to th' heart.

She was too fond of her most filthy bargain.

Othello: Ha?   [*He draws.*] 165

Emilia: Do thy worst!

This deed of thine is no more worthy heaven

Than thou wast worthy her.

Othello: Peace, you were best.°

Emilia: Thou hast not half that power to do me harm

As I have to be hurt.° O gull!° O dolt! 170

As ignorant as dirt! Thou hast done a deed—

I care not for thy sword; I'll make thee known,

---

137 *belie* slander   141 *else* i.e., if you don't believe me   150 *chrysolite* precious topaz   157
iterance iteration, repetition   158 *made mocks with* derided, made sport of   168 *you were*
best it would be best for you   170 *to be hurt* i.e., to endure hurt.   *gull* dupe

Though I lost twenty lives.—Help! Help, ho, help!
The Moor hath killed my mistress! Murder, murder!

Enter Montano, Gratiano, and Iago.

Montano: What is the matter? How now, General?   175
Emilia: O, are you come, Iago? You have done well,
That men must lay their murders on your neck.
Gratiano: What is the matter?
Emilia [to Iago]: Disprove this villain, if thou be'st a man.
He says thou toldst him that his wife was false.   180
I know thou didst not; thou'rt not such a villain.
Speak, for my heart is full.
Iago: I told him what I thought, and told no more
Than what he found himself was apt° and true.
Emilia: But did you ever tell him she was false?   185
Iago: I did.
Emilia: You told a lie, an odious, damnèd lie!
Upon my soul, a lie, a wicked lie.
She false with Cassio? Did you say with Cassio?
Iago: With Cassio, mistress. Go to, charm° your tongue.   190
Emilia: I will not charm my tongue; I am bound to speak.
My mistress here lies murdered in her bed—
All: O heavens forfend!
Emilia: And your reports have set the murder on.
Othello: Nay, stare not, masters. It is true indeed.   195
Gratiano: 'Tis a strange truth.
Montano: O monstrous act!
Emilia: Villainy, villainy, villainy!
I think upon 't—I think I smell 't! O villainy!
I thought so then°—I'll kill myself for grief—
O villainy, villainy!   200
Iago: What, are you mad? I charge you, get you home.
Emilia: Good gentlemen, let me have leave to speak.
'Tis proper I obey him, but not now.
Perchance, Iago, I will ne'er go home.
Othello: O! O! O!   [*Othello falls on the bed.*°]
Emilia: Nay, lay thee down and roar,   205

---

184 *apt* plausible   190 *charm* keep silent (as though by a magic spell)   199 *then* (Perhaps
at Act III, Scene iii, lines 331–332 and Act IV, Scene ii, lines 137–154.)   205 s.d. *Othello
. . . bed* (This direction is from the Quarto, as also *He kisses her* at line 19 and *She dies* at line
129.)

For thou hast killed the sweetest innocent
That e'er did lift up eye.°
Othello [*rising*]:   O, she was foul!
I scarce did know you, uncle. There lies your niece,
Whose breath indeed these hands have newly stopped.
I know this act shows° horrible and grim.   210
Gratiano: Poor Desdemon! I am glad thy father's dead.
Thy match was mortal to him, and pure grief
Shore his old thread° in twain. Did he live now,
This sight would make him do a desperate turn,°
Yea, curse his better angel from his side,   215
And fall to reprobance.°
Othello: 'Tis pitiful. But yet Iago knows
That she with Cassio hath the act of shame
A thousand times committed. Cassio confessed it;
And she did gratify° his amorous works   220
With that recognizance° and pledge of love
Which I first gave her. I saw it in his hand;
It was a handkerchief, an antique token
My father gave my mother.
Emilia: O God! O heavenly God!   225
Iago: Zounds, hold your peace.
Emilia: 'Twill out, 'twill out! I peace?
No, I will speak as liberal as the north.°
Let heaven and men and devils, let them all,
All, all, cry shame against me, yet I'll speak.
Iago: Be wise, and get you home.
Emilia: I will not.

[*Iago threatens Emilia.*]

Gratiano: Fie   230
Your sword upon a woman?
Emilia: O thou dull Moor! That handkerchief thou speak'st of
I found by fortune and did give my husband;
For often, with a solemn earnestness,
More than indeed belonged° to such a trifle,   235
He begged of me to steal 't.

207 *lift up eye* i.e., lift her eyes to heaven   210 *shows* looks   213 *Shore . . . thread* sheared the thread of his old age (as Atropos, one of the three Fates, was thought to do)   214 *turn* deed   216 *reprobance* damnation, i.e., suicide   220 *gratify* reward   221 *recognizance* token   227 *liberal as the north* freely as the north wind (blows)   235 *belonged* was appropriate

Iago: Villainous whore!

Emilia: She give it Cassio? No, alas! I found it,
     And I did give 't my husband.

Iago: Filth, thou liest!

Emilia: By heaven, I do not, I do not, gentlemen.
     O murderous coxcomb!° What should such a fool   240
     Do with so good a wife?

Othello: Are there no stones° in heaven
     But what serves for the thunder?—Precious° villain!

[*He runs at Iago; Montano disarms Othello. Iago, from behind, stabs Emilia.*°]

Gratiano: The woman falls! Sure he hath killed his wife.

Emilia: Ay, ay. O, lay me by my mistress' side.   245

     Exit [*Iago.*]

Gratiano: He's gone, but his wife's killed.

Montano: 'Tis a notorious villain. Take you this weapon,
     Which I have here recovered from the Moor.
     Come, guard the door without. Let him not pass,
     But kill him rather. I'll after that same villain,   250
     For 'tis a damnèd slave.

     Exit [*with all but Othello and Emilia, who has been laid by Desdemona's side*].

Othello: I am not valiant neither,
     But every puny whipster° gets my sword.
     But why should honor° outlive honesty?°
     Let it go all.

Emilia: What did thy song bode, lady?   255
     Hark, canst thou hear me? I will play the swan,
     And die in music. [*She sings.*] "Willow, willow, willow."
     Moor, she was chaste. She loved thee, cruel Moor.
     So come my soul to bliss as I speak true.
     So speaking as I think, alas, I die.   260

[*She dies.*]

240 *coxcomb* fool. (Addressed to Othello.)   242 *stones* bolts, such as those used for thunderbolts   243 *Precious* i.e., arrant, utter.   243 s.d. *He . . . Emilia* (The Quarto text reads, "The Moor runs at Iago. Iago kills his wife." The Quarto also specifies the exit of Iago at line 245 and the death of Emilia at line 260.)   253 *whipster* contemptible fellow (one who is always ready to whip out his sword)   254 *honor* i.e., the bravery for which one enjoys a soldier's reputation.   *honesty* true integrity

Othello: I have another weapon in this chamber;
      It was a sword of Spain, the ice-brook's temper°—
      O, here it is. [*He finds a sword.*] Uncle, I must come forth.
Gratiano [*within*]: If thou attempt it, it will cost thee dear.
      Thou hast no weapon, and perforce must suffer.   265
Othello: Look in upon me then and speak with me,
      Or, naked° as I am, I will assault thee.

      [*Enter Gratiano.*]

Gratiano: What is the matter?
Othello: Behold, I have a weapon;
      A better never did itself sustain
      Upon a soldier's thigh. I have seen the day   270
      That, with this little arm and this good sword,
      I have made my way through more impediments
      Than twenty times your stop.° But O, vain boast!
      Who can control his fate? 'Tis not so now.
      Be not afraid, though you do see me weaponed;   275
      Here is my journey's end, here is my butt°
      And very seamark° of my utmost sail.

      [*Gratiano steps back.*]

      Do you go back dismayed? 'Tis a lost° fear;
      Man but a rush° against Othello's breast
      And he retires. Where should Othello go?   280

      [*He turns to Desdemona.*]

      Now, how dost thou look now? O ill-starred wench!
      Pale as thy smock! When we shall meet at compt,°
      This look of thine will hurl my soul from heaven,
      And fiends will snatch at it. Cold, cold, my girl?
      Even like thy chastity. O cursèd, cursèd slave!°   285
      Whip me, ye devils,
      From the possession of this heavenly sight!
      Blow me about in winds! Roast me in sulfur!
      Wash me in steep-down gulfs of liquid fire!
      O Desdemon! Dead, Desdemon! Dead! O! O!   290

---

262 *the ice-brook's temper* tempered in ice-cold water   267 *naked* unarmed   273 *stop* power
(to stop)   276 *butt* goal, limit. (An archery term.)   277 *seamark* beacon (marking his destination or limit)   278 *lost* wasted, unneeded   279 *Man . . . rush* wield no more than a
reed   282 *compt* account, judgment day   285 *slave* i.e., Othello himself

Enter Lodovico, Cassio [carried in a litter°], Montano, and Iago [prisoner], with officers.

Lodovico: Where is this rash and most unfortunate man?
Othello: That's he that was Othello. Here I am.
Lodovico: Where is that viper? Bring the villain forth.

[Iago is led forward.]

Othello: I look down towards his feet;° but that's a fable.
    If that thou be'st a devil, I cannot kill thee.   295

[He wounds Iago.]

Lodovico: Wrench his sword from him.   *[Othello is disarmed.]*
Iago: I bleed, sir, but not killed.
Othello: I am not sorry neither. I'd have thee live,
    For in my sense° 'tis happiness to die.
Lodovico: O thou Othello, that was once so good,
    Fall'n in the practice° of a cursèd slave,°   300
    What shall be said to thee?
Othello: Why, anything.
    An honorable murderer, if you will,
    For naught I did in hate, but all in honor.
Lodovico: This wretch hath part confessed his villainy.
    Did you and he consent° in Cassio's death?   305
Othello: Ay.
Cassio: Dear General, I never gave you cause.
Othello: I do believe it, and I ask your pardon.
    Will you, I pray, demand that demi-devil
    Why he hath thus ensnared my soul and body?   310
Iago: Demand me nothing. What you know, you know.
    From this time forth I never will speak word.
Lodovico: What, not to pray?
Gratiano: Torments° will ope your lips.
Othello: Well, thou dost best.   315
Lodovico: Sir, you shall understand what hath befall'n,
    Which, as I think, you know not. Here is a letter
    Found in the pocket of the slain Roderigo;
    And here another. *[He produces letters.]* The one of them imports
    The death of Cassio, to be undertook   320
    By Roderigo.

290 s.d. *in a litter* (The Quarto specifies that Cassio is "in a chair.") 294 *towards his feet* i.e., to see if they are cloven, as the devil's are fabled to be 298 *in my sense* to one who feels as I do 300 *in the practice* through the plotting, into the snare. *slave* villain 305 *consent* agree 314 *Torments* torture

Othello: O villain!
Cassio: Most heathenish and most gross!°
Lodovico [*showing another paper*]: Now here's another discontented° paper
   Found in his pocket too. And this, it seems,
   Roderigo meant t' have sent this damnèd villain;   325
   But that belike° Iago in the interim
   Came in and satisfied him.°
Othello: O thou pernicious caitiff!—
   How came you, Cassio, by that handkerchief
   That was my wife's?
Cassio: I found it in my chamber;   330
   And he himself confessed but even now
   That there he dropped it for a special purpose
   Which wrought to his desire.°
Othello: O fool, fool, fool!
Cassio: There is besides in Roderigo's letter
   How he upbraids Iago, that he made him   335
   Brave° me upon the watch, whereon it came°
   That I was cast;° and even but now he spake,
   After long seeming dead, Iago hurt him,
   Iago set him on.
Lodovico [*to Othello*]: You must forsake this room and go with us. 340
   Your power and your command is taken off,°
   And Cassio rules in Cyprus. For this slave,
   If there be any cunning cruelty
   That can torment him much and hold him long,°
   It shall be his. You shall close prisoner rest°   345
   Till that the nature of your fault be known
   To the Venetian state.—Come, bring away.
Othello: Soft you;° a word or two before you go.
   I have done the state some service, and they know 't.
   No more of that. I pray you, in your letters,   350
   When you shall these unlucky° deeds relate,
   Speak of me as I am; nothing extenuate,
   Nor set down aught in malice. Then must you speak
   Of one that loved not wisely but too well;
   Of one not easily jealous but, being wrought,°   355

322 *gross* monstrous   323 *discontented* full of discontent   326 *belike* most likely   327 *Came
. . . him* interposed and gave him satisfactory explanation   333 *wrought . . . desire* worked out
as he wished, fitted in with his plan   336 *Brave* defy.   *whereon it came* whereof it came about
337 *cast* dismissed   341 *taken off* taken away   344 *hold him long* keep him alive a long time
(during his torture)   345 *rest* remain   348 *Soft you* one moment   351 *unlucky* unfortunate
355 *wrought* worked upon, worked into a frenzy

Perplexed° in the extreme; of one whose hand,
Like the base Indian,° threw a pearl away
Richer than all his tribe; of one whose subdued° eyes,
Albeit unusèd to the melting mood,
Drops tears as fast as the Arabian trees   360
Their medicinable gum.° Set you down this;
And say besides that in Aleppo once,
Where a malignant and a turbaned Turk
Beat a Venetian and traduced the state,
I took by th' throat the circumcisèd dog   365
And smote him, thus.   [*He stabs himself.°*]
Lodovico: O bloody period!°
Gratiano: All that is spoke is marred.
Othello: I kissed thee ere I killed thee. No way but this,
Killing myself, to die upon a kiss.   370

[*He kisses Desdemona and dies.*]

Cassio: This did I fear, but thought he had no weapon;
For he was great of heart.
Lodovico [*to Iago*]:   O Spartan dog,°
More fell° than anguish, hunger, or the sea!
Look on the tragic loading of this bed.
This is thy work. The object poisons sight;   375
Let it be hid.° Gratiano, keep° the house,

[*The bed curtains are drawn*]

And seize upon° the fortunes of the Moor,
For they succeed on° you. [*To Cassio.*] To you, Lord Governor,
Remains the censure° of this hellish villain,
The time, the place, the torture. O, enforce it!   380
Myself will straight aboard, and to the state
This heavy act with heavy heart relate.

                                                          Exeunt.

---

356 *Perplexed* distraught   357 *Indian* (This reading from the Quarto pictures an ignorant
savage who cannot recognize the value of a precious jewel. The Folio reading, *Iudean* or
Judean, i.e., infidel or disbeliever, may refer to Herod, who slew Miriamne in a fit of jealousy, or to Judas Iscariot, the betrayer of Christ.)   358 *subdued* i.e., overcome by grief
361 *gum* i.e., myrrh   366 s.d. *He stabs himself* (This direction is in the Quarto text.)   367
period termination, conclusion   372 *Spartan dog* (Spartan dogs were noted for their savagery and silence.)   373 *fell* cruel   376 *Let it be hid* i.e., draw the bed curtains. (No stage
direction specifies that the dead are to be carried offstage at the end of the play.)   *keep* remain in   377 *seize upon* take legal possession of   378 *succeed on* pass as though by inheri-
tance to   379 *censure* sentencing

QUESTIONS

ACT I

1. What is Othello's position in society? How is he regarded by those who know him? By his own words, when we first meet him in Scene ii, what traits of character does he manifest?

2. How do you account for Brabantio's dismay on learning of his daughter's marriage, despite the fact that Desdemona has married a man so generally honored and admired?

3. What is Iago's view of human nature? In his fondness for likening men to animals (as in I, i, 49–50; I, i, 90–91; and I, iii, 386–387), what does he tell us about himself?

4. What reasons does Iago give for his hatred of Othello?

5. In Othello's defense before the senators (Scene iii), how does he explain Desdemona's gradual falling in love with him?

6. Is Brabantio's warning to Othello (I, iii, 293–294) an accurate or an inaccurate prophecy?

7. By what strategy does Iago enlist Roderigo in his plot against the Moor? In what lines do we learn Iago's true feelings toward Roderigo?

ACT II

1. What do the Cypriots think of Othello? Do their words (in Scene i) make him seem to us a lesser man or a larger one?

2. What cruelty does Iago display toward Emilia? How well founded is his distrust of his wife's fidelity?

3. In II, iii, 225, Othello speaks of Iago's "honesty and love." How do you account for Othello's being so totally deceived?

4. For what major events does the merrymaking (proclaimed in Scene ii) give opportunity?

ACT III

1. Trace the steps by which Iago rouses Othello to suspicion. Is there anything in Othello's character or circumstances that renders him particularly susceptible to Iago's wiles?

2. In III, iv, 49–98, Emilia knows of Desdemona's distress over the lost handkerchief. At this moment, how do you explain her failure to relieve Desdemona's mind? Is Emilia aware of her husband's villainy?

ACT IV

1. In this act, what circumstantial evidence is added to Othello's case against Desdemona?

2. How plausible do you find Bianca's flinging the handkerchief at Cassio just when Othello is looking on? How important is the handkerchief in this play? What does it represent? What suggestions or hints do you find in it?

3. What prevents Othello from being moved by Desdemona's appeal (IV, ii, 33–92)?

4. When Roderigo grows impatient with Iago (IV, ii, 181–205), how does Iago make use of his fellow plotter's discontent?

5. What does the conversation between Emilia and Desdemona (Scene iii) tell us about the nature of each?
6. In this act, what scenes (or speeches) contain memorable dramatic irony?

ACT V

1. Summarize the events that lead to Iago's unmasking.
2. How does Othello's mistaken belief that Cassio is slain (V, i, 27–34) affect the outcome of the play?
3. What is Iago's motive in stabbing Roderigo?
4. In your interpretation of the play, exactly what impels Othello to kill Desdemona? Jealousy? Desire for revenge? Excess idealism? A wish to be a public avenger who punishes, "else she'll betray more men"?
5. What do you understand by Othello's calling himself "one that loved not wisely but too well" (V, ii, 354)?
6. In your view, does Othello's long speech in V, ii, 348–366 succeed in restoring his original dignity and nobility? Do you agree with Cassio (V, ii, 372) that Othello was "great of heart"?

GENERAL QUESTIONS

1. What motivates Iago to carry out his schemes? Do you find him a devil incarnate, a madman, or a rational human being?
2. Whom besides Othello does Iago deceive? What is Desdemona's opinion of him? Emilia's? Cassio's (before Iago is found out)? To what do you attribute Iago's success as a deceiver?
3. How essential to the play is the fact that Othello is a black man, a Moor, and not a native of Venice?
4. In the introduction to his edition of the play in *The Complete Signet Classic Shakespeare*, Alvin Kernan remarks:

> Othello is probably the most neatly, the most formally constructed of Shakespeare's plays. Every character is, for example, balanced by another similar or contrasting character. Desdemona is balanced by her opposite, Iago; love and concern for others at one end of the scale, hatred and concern for self at the other.

Besides Desdemona and Iago, what other pairs of characters strike balances?
5. Consider any passage of the play in which there is a shift from verse to prose, or from prose to verse. What is the effect of this shift?
6. Indicate a passage that you consider memorable for its poetry. Does the passage seem introduced for its own sake? Does it in any way advance the action of the play, express theme, or demonstrate character?
7. Does the play contain any tragic *recognition*—as discussed on page 620, a moment of terrible enlightenment, a "realization of the unthinkable"?
8. Does the downfall of Othello proceed from any flaw in his nature, or is his downfall entirely the work of Iago?

WRITING EFFECTIVELY

WRITING ABOUT SHAKESPEARE

Breaking the Language Barrier

The basic problem a modern reader faces with Shakespeare is language. Shakespeare's English is now four hundred years old, and it differs in innumerable small ways from contemporary American English.

Although Shakespeare's idiom may at first seem daunting, it is easily mastered if you make the effort. To grow comfortable with his language, you must immerse yourself in it. Fortunately, doing so isn't all that hard; you might even find it pleasurable.

There is no substitute for hearing Shakespeare's words in performance. After all, the plays were written to be viewed, not to be read silently on the page. Let your ears do the work. After reading the play, listen to or watch a recording of it. It sometimes helps to read along as you listen or watch, hitting the pause button as needed. If you can attend a live performance of any Shakespearean play, do so.

Remember, though, that watching a production is never a substitute for reading an assigned play. Many productions abridge the play, leaving passages out. Even more important, directors and actors choose a particular interpretation of a play, and their choices might skew your understanding of events and motivations if you are unfamiliar with the original itself.

Before you write about any Shakespearean play, read the text more than once. The first time through an Elizabethan-era text, you will almost certainly miss many things. As you grow more familiar with Shakespeare's language, you will be able to read it with more complete comprehension. If you choose to write about a particular episode or character, carefully study the speeches and dialogue in question (and pay special attention to the footnotes) so that you understand each word. In your paper, don't hesitate to bring in what you have learned. Discuss how key words you quote had different meanings in Shakespeare's day.

Enjoy yourself. From Peking to Berlin, Buenos Aires to Oslo, Shakespeare is almost universally acknowledged as the world's greatest playwright, a master entertainer as well as a consummate artist.

Reading a Shakespearean Play

✓ Read closely, working through passages with difficult language.

✓ Pay special attention to footnotes.

✓ Read the play more than once if necessary.

✓ After reading a play, view a DVD or listen to an audiotape. Immerse yourself in Shakespeare's language until it becomes familiar.

✓ As you view or listen to a play, read along, or revisit the text afterward.

✓ If you choose to write about a particular episode or character, carefully study the speeches and dialogue in question.

✓ Understand each word of any passage you decide to discuss or quote.

WRITING ASSIGNMENT ON TRAGEDY

Select any tragedy, and analyze it using Aristotle's definition of the form. Does the play measure up to Aristotle's requirements for a tragedy? In what ways does it meet the definition? In what ways does it depart from it? (Be sure to state clearly the Aristotelian rules by which drama is to be judged.)

MORE TOPICS FOR WRITING

1. Write a defense of Iago.

2. Suppose yourself a casting director assigned to a film version of *Othello*. What well-known actors would you cast in the principal roles? Write a report justifying your choices. Don't merely discuss the stars and their qualifications; discuss (with specific reference to the play) what Shakespeare appears to call for.

3. Emilia's long speech at the end of Act IV (iii, 85–104) has been called a Renaissance plea for women's rights. Do you agree? Write a brief, close analysis of this speech. How timely is it?

4. "The downfall of Oedipus is the work of the gods; the downfall of Othello is self-inflicted." Test this comment with reference to the two plays, and report your findings.

26
The Modern Theater

Realism and Naturalism

As the twentieth century began, realism in the theaters of Western Europe, England, and America appeared to have won a resounding victory. (**Realism** in drama, like realism in fiction, may be broadly defined as an attempt to reproduce faithfully the surface appearance of life, especially that of ordinary people in everyday situations.) The theater had been slow to admit controversial or unpleasant themes and reluctant to shed its traditional conventions. From Italian playhouses of the sixteenth century, it had inherited the **picture-frame stage**: one that holds the action within a **proscenium arch**, a gateway standing (as the word *proscenium* indicates) "in front of the scenery." This manner of constructing a playhouse in effect divided the actors from their audience; most commercial theaters even today are so constructed. But as the new century began, actors less often declaimed their passions in oratorical style in front of backdrops painted with waterfalls and volcanoes, while stationed exactly at the center of the stage as if to sing "duets meant to bring forth applause" (as Swedish playwright August Strindberg complained). By 1891 even Victorian London had witnessed a production of a play that frankly portrayed a man dying of venereal disease—Henrik Ibsen's *Ghosts*.

In the theater of realism, a room was represented by a **box set**—three walls that joined in two corners and a ceiling that tilted as if seen in perspective—replacing drapery walls that had billowed and doors that had flapped, not slammed. Instead of posing at stage center to deliver key speeches, actors were instructed to speak from wherever the dramatic situation placed them and now and then turn their backs upon the audience. They were to behave as if they were in a room with the fourth wall sliced away, unaware that they had an audience.

This realistic convention is familiar to us today, not only from realistic plays but also from the typical television soap opera or situation comedy that takes place in such a three-walled room, with every cup and spoon revealed by the camera. However, such realism went against a long tradition. Watching a play by Sophocles, the spectators, we may safely assume, had to exert their imaginations. We do not expect an ancient Greek tragedy literally to represent the lives of ordinary people in everyday situations. On the contrary, a tragedy, according to Aristotle, its leading ancient theorist, represents an "action of supreme importance," an extraordinary moment in the life of a king or queen or other person of high estate. An open-air stage, though Sophocles adorned it with painted scenery, could hardly change day into night as lighting technicians commonly do today or aspire to reproduce in detail a whole palace. Such limitations prevailed upon the theater of Shakespeare as well, encouraging the Bard to flesh out his scene with vivid language, making the spectator willing to imagine that the simple stage—the "wooden O"—is a forest, a storm-swept landscape, or a battlefield.

In the realistic three-walled room, actors could hardly rant (or, Hamlet said, "tear a passion to tatters") without seeming foolish. Another effect of more lifelike direction was to discourage use of such devices as the soliloquy and the **aside** (villain to audience: "Heh! heh! Now she's in my power!"). To encourage actors further to imitate reality, the influential director Constantin Stanislavsky of the Moscow Art Theater developed his famous system to help actors feel at home inside a playwright's characters. One of Stanislavsky's exercises was to have actors search their memories for personal experiences like those of the characters in the play; another was to have them act out things a character did *not* do in the play but might do in life. The system enabled Stanislavsky to bring authenticity to his productions of Chekhov's plays and of Maxim Gorky's *The Lower Depths* (1902), a play that showed the tenants of a sordid lodging house drinking themselves to death (and hanging themselves) in surroundings of realistic squalor.

Gorky's play is a masterpiece of **naturalism**, a kind of realism in fiction and drama dealing with the more brutal or unpleasant aspects of reality. As codified by French novelist and playwright Émile Zola, who influenced Ibsen, naturalism viewed a person as a creature whose acts are determined by heredity and environment; Zola urged writers to study their characters' behavior with the detachment of zoologists studying animals.

One of the pioneering works of realism is Henrik Ibsen's *A Doll's House*. The play derives a good deal of its power from our ability to identify with its characters and the lives they live, an identification that Ibsen achieves in part by framing the action with the details of daily existence.

Henrik Ibsen

A Doll's House

1879

TRANSLATED BY R. FARQUHARSON SHARP

REVISED BY VIKTORIA MICHELSEN

Henrik Ibsen (1828–1906) was born in Skien, a seaport in Norway. When he was six, his father's business losses suddenly reduced his wealthy family to poverty. After a brief attempt to study medicine, young Ibsen worked as a stage manager in provincial Bergen; then, becoming known as a playwright, he moved to Oslo as artistic director of the National Theater—practical experiences that gained him firm grounding in his craft. Discouraged when his theater failed and the king turned down his plea for a grant to enable him to write, Ibsen left Norway and for twenty-seven years lived in Italy and Germany. There, in his middle

HENRIK IBSEN

years (1879–1891), he wrote most of his famed plays about small-town life, among them A Doll's House, Ghosts, An Enemy of the People, The Wild Duck, *and* Hedda Gabler. *Introducing social problems to the stage, these plays aroused storms of controversy. Although best known as a Realist, Ibsen early in his career wrote poetic dramas based on Norwegian history and folklore: the tragedy* Brand *(1866) and the powerful, wildly fantastic* Peer Gynt *(1867). He ended as a Symbolist in* John Gabriel Borkman *(1896) and* When We Dead Awaken *(1899), both encompassing huge mountains that heaven-assaulting heroes try to climb. Late in life Ibsen returned to Oslo, honored at last both at home and abroad.*

CHARACTERS

Torvald Helmer, a lawyer
Nora, his wife
Doctor Rank
Mrs. Kristine Linde
Nils Krogstad
The Helmers' three young children
Anne Marie, their nursemaid
Helene, the maid
A Porter

The action takes place in the Helmers' apartment.

ACT I

The scene is a room furnished comfortably and tastefully, but not extravagantly. At the back wall, a door to the right leads to the entrance hall. Another to the left leads to Helmer's study. Between the doors there is a piano. In the middle of the left-hand wall is a door, and beyond it a window. Near the window are a round table, armchairs, and a small sofa. In the right-hand wall, at the farther end, is another door, and on the same side, nearer the footlights, a stove, two easy chairs and a rocking chair. Between the stove and the door there is a small table. There are engravings on the walls, a cabinet with china and other small objects, and a small bookcase with expensively bound books. The floors are carpeted, and a fire burns in the stove. It is winter.

A bell rings in the hall. A moment later, we hear the door being opened. Enter Nora, humming a tune and in high spirits. She is wearing a hat and coat and carries a number of packages, which she puts down on the table to the right. She leaves the outer door open behind her. Through the door we see a porter who is carrying a Christmas tree and a basket, which he gives to the maid, who has opened the door.

Nora: Hide the Christmas tree carefully, Helene. Make sure the children don't see it till it's decorated this evening. (*To the Porter, taking out her purse.*) How much?

Porter: Fifty ore.

Nora: Here's a krone. No, keep the change.

(*The Porter thanks her and goes out. Nora shuts the door. She is laughing to herself as she takes off her hat and coat. She takes a bag of macaroons from her pocket and eats one or two, then goes cautiously to the door of her husband's study and listens.*)

Yes, he's there. (*Still humming, she goes to the table on the right.*)

Helmer (calls out from his study): Is that my little lark twittering out there?

Nora (busy opening some of the packages): Yes, it is!

Helmer: Is it my little squirrel bustling around?

Nora: Yes!

Helmer: When did my squirrel come home?

Nora: Just now. (*Puts the bag of macaroons into her pocket and wipes her mouth.*) Come in here, Torvald, and see what I bought.

Helmer: I'm very busy right now. (*A little later, he opens the door and looks into the room, pen in hand.*) Bought, did you say? All these things? Has my little spendthrift been wasting money again?

Nora: Yes, but, Torvald, this year we really can let ourselves go a little. This is the first Christmas that we don't have to watch every penny.

1896 production of *A Doll's House* at the Empire Theatre in New York

Helmer: Still, you know, we can't spend money recklessly.

Nora: Yes, Torvald, but we can be a little more reckless now, can't we? Just a tiny little bit! You're going to have a big salary and you'll be making lots and lots of money.

Helmer: Yes, after the New Year. But it'll still be a whole three months before the money starts coming in.

Nora: Pooh! We can borrow till then.

Helmer: Nora! (*Goes up to her and takes her playfully by the ear.*) The same little featherbrain! Just suppose that I borrowed a thousand kroner today, and you spent it all on Christmas, and then on New Year's Eve a roof tile fell on my head and killed me, and—

Nora (*putting her hand over his mouth*): Oh! Don't say such horrible things.

Helmer: Still, suppose that happened. What then?

Nora: If that happened, I don't suppose I'd care whether I owed anyone money or not.

Helmer: Yes, but what about the people who'd lent it to us?

Nora: Them? Who'd care about them? I wouldn't even know who they were.

Helmer: That's just like a woman! But seriously, Nora, you know how I feel about that. No debt, no borrowing. There can't be any freedom or beauty in a home life that depends on borrowing and debt. We two have managed to stay on the straight road so far, and we'll go on the same way for the short time that we still have to be careful.

Nora (*moving towards the stove*): As you wish, Torvald.

Helmer (*following her*): Now, now, my little skylark mustn't let her wings droop. What's the matter? Is my little squirrel sulking? (*Taking out his purse.*) Nora, what do you think I've got here?

Nora (*turning round quickly*): Money!

Helmer: There you are. (*Gives her some money.*) Do you think I don't know how much you need for the house at Christmastime?

Nora (*counting*): Ten, twenty, thirty, forty! Thank you, thank you, Torvald. That'll keep me going for a long time.

Helmer: It's going to have to.

Nora: Yes, yes, it will. But come here and let me show you what I bought. And all so cheap! Look, here's a new suit for Ivar, and a sword. And a horse and a trumpet for Bob. And a doll and doll's bed for Emmy. They're not the best, but she'll break them soon enough anyway. And here's dress material and handkerchiefs for the maids. Old Anne Marie really should have something nicer.

Helmer: And what's in this package?

Nora (*crying out*): No, no! You can't see that till this evening.

Helmer: If you say so. But now tell me, you extravagant little thing, what would you like for yourself?

Nora: For myself? Oh, I'm sure I don't want anything.

Helmer: But you must. Tell me something that you'd especially like to have—within reasonable limits.

Nora: No, I really can't think of anything. Unless, Torvald . . .

Helmer: Well?

Nora (*playing with his coat buttons, and without raising her eyes to his*): If you really want to give me something, you might . . . you might . . .

Helmer: Well, out with it!

Nora (*speaking quickly*): You might give me money, Torvald. Only just as much as you can afford. And then one of these days I'll buy something with it.

Helmer: But, Nora—

Nora: Oh, do! Dear Torvald, please, please do! Then I'll wrap it up in beautiful gold paper and hang it on the Christmas tree. Wouldn't that be fun?

Helmer: What do they call those little creatures that are always wasting money?

Nora: Spendthrifts. I know. Let's do as I suggest, Torvald, and then I'll have time to think about what I need most. That's a very sensible plan, isn't it?

Helmer (*smiling*): Yes, it is. That is, if you really did save some of the money I give you, and then really buy something for yourself. But if you spend it all on the housekeeping and all kinds of unnecessary things, then I just have to open my wallet all over again.

Nora: Oh, but, Torvald—

Helmer: You can't deny it, my dear little Nora. (*Puts his arm around her waist.*) She's a sweet little spendthrift, but she uses up a lot of money. One would hardly believe how expensive such little creatures are!

Nora: That's a terrible thing to say. I really do save all I can.

Helmer (*laughing*): That's true. All you can. But you can't save anything!

Nora (*smiling quietly and happily*): You have no idea how many bills skylarks and squirrels have, Torvald.

Helmer: You're an odd little soul. Just like your father. You always find some new way of wheedling money out of me, and, as soon as you've got it, it seems to melt in your hands. You never know where it's gone. Still, one has to take you as you are. It's in the blood. Because, you know, it's true that you can inherit these things, Nora.

Nora: Ah, I wish I'd inherited a lot of Papa's traits.

Helmer: And I wouldn't want you to be anything but just what you are, my sweet little skylark. But, you know, it seems to me that you look rather—how can I put it—rather uneasy today.

Nora: Do I?

Helmer: You do, really. Look straight at me.

Nora (*looks at him*): Well?

Helmer (*wagging his finger at her*): Has little Miss Sweet Tooth been breaking our rules in town today?

Nora: No, what makes you think that?

Helmer: Has she paid a visit to the bakery?

Nora: No, I assure you, Torvald—

Helmer: Not been nibbling pastries?

Nora: No, certainly not.

Helmer: Not even taken a bite of a macaroon or two?

Nora: No, Torvald, I assure you, really—

Helmer: Come on, you know I was only kidding.

Nora (*going to the table on the right*): I wouldn't dream of going against your wishes.

Helmer: No, I'm sure of that. Besides, you gave me your word. (*Going up to her.*) Keep your little Christmas secrets to yourself, my darling. They'll all be revealed tonight when the Christmas tree is lit, no doubt.

Nora: Did you remember to invite Doctor Rank?

Helmer: No. But there's no need. It goes without saying that he'll have dinner with us. All the same, I'll ask him when he comes over this morning. I've ordered some good wine. Nora, you have no idea how much I'm looking forward to this evening.

Nora: So am I! And how the children will enjoy themselves, Torvald!

Helmer: It's great to feel that you have a completely secure position and a big enough income. It's a delightful thought, isn't it?

Nora: It's wonderful!

Helmer: Do you remember last Christmas? For three whole weeks you hid yourself away every evening until long after midnight, making ornaments for the Christmas tree and all the other fine things that were going to be a surprise for us. It was the most boring three weeks I ever spent!

Nora: I wasn't bored.

Helmer (smiling): But there was precious little to show for it, Nora.

Nora: Oh, you're not going to tease me about that again. How could I help it that the cat went in and tore everything to pieces?

Helmer: Of course you couldn't, poor little girl. You had the best of intentions to make us all happy, and that's the main thing. But it's a good thing that our hard times are over.

Nora: Yes, it really is wonderful.

Helmer: This time I don't have to sit here and be bored all by myself, and you don't have to ruin your dear eyes and your pretty little hands—

Nora (clapping her hands): No, Torvald, I don't have to any more, do I! It's wonderfully lovely to hear you say so! (*Taking his arm.*) Now let me tell you how I've been thinking we should arrange things, Torvald. As soon as Christmas is over— (*A bell rings in the hall.*) There's the bell. (*She tidies the room a little.*) There's somebody at the door. What a nuisance!

Helmer: If someone's visiting, remember I'm not home.

Maid (in the doorway): A lady to see you, ma'am. A stranger.

Nora: Ask her to come in.

Maid (to Helmer): The doctor's here too, sir.

Helmer: Did he go straight into my study?

Maid: Yes, sir.

(*Helmer goes into his study. The maid ushers in Mrs. Linde, who is in traveling clothes, and shuts the door.*)

Mrs. Linde (in a dejected and timid voice): Hello, Nora.

Nora (doubtfully): Hello.

Mrs. Linde: You don't recognize me, I suppose.

Nora: No, I don't know . . . Yes, of course, I think so— (*Suddenly.*) Yes! Kristine! Is it really you?

Mrs. Linde: Yes, it is.

Nora: Kristine! Imagine my not recognizing you! And yet how could I— (*In a gentle voice.*) You've changed, Kristine!

Mrs. Linde: Yes, I certainly have. In nine, ten long years—

Nora: Is it that long since we've seen each other? I suppose it is. The last eight years have been a happy time for me, you know. And so now you've come to town, and you've taken this long trip in the winter. That was brave of you.

Mrs. Linde: I arrived by steamer this morning.

Nora: To have some fun at Christmastime, of course. How delightful! We'll have such fun together! But take off your things. You're not cold, I hope. (*Helps her.*) Now we'll sit down by the stove and be cozy. No, take this armchair. I'll sit here in the rocking chair. (*Takes her hands.*) Now you look like your old self again. It was only that first moment. You are a little paler, Kristine, and maybe a little thinner.

Mrs. Linde: And much, much older, Nora.

Nora: Maybe a little older. Very, very little. Surely not very much. (*Stops suddenly and speaks seriously.*) What a thoughtless thing I am, chattering away like this. My poor, dear Kristine, please forgive me.

Mrs. Linde: What do you mean, Nora?

Nora (*gently*): Poor Kristine, you're a widow.

Mrs. Linde: Yes. For three years now.

Nora: Yes, I knew. I saw it in the papers. I swear to you, Kristine, I kept meaning to write to you at the time, but I always put it off and something always came up.

Mrs. Linde: I understand completely, dear.

Nora: It was very bad of me, Kristine. Poor thing, how you must have suffered. And he left you nothing?

Mrs. Linde: No.

Nora: And no children?

Mrs. Linde: No.

Nora: Nothing at all, then?

Mrs. Linde: Not even any sorrow or grief to live on.

Nora (*looking at her in disbelief*): But, Kristine, is that possible?

Mrs. Linde (*smiles sadly and strokes Nora's hair*): It happens sometimes, Nora.

Nora: So you're completely alone. How terribly sad that must be. I have three beautiful children. You can't see them just now, because they're out with their nursemaid. But now you must tell me all about it.

Mrs. Linde: No, no, I want to hear about you.

Nora: No, you go first. I mustn't be selfish today. Today I should think only about you. But there is one thing I have to tell you. Do you know we've just had a fabulous piece of good luck?

Mrs. Linde: No, what is it?

Nora: Just imagine, my husband's been appointed manager of the bank!

Mrs. Linde: Your husband? That is good luck!

Nora: Yes, it's tremendous! A lawyer's life is so uncertain, especially if he won't take any cases that are the slightest bit shady, and of course Torvald has never been willing to do that, and I completely agree with him. You can imagine how delighted we are! He starts his job in the bank at New Year's, and then he'll have a big salary and lots of commissions. From now on we can live very differently. We can do just what we want. I feel so relieved and so happy, Kristine! It'll be wonderful to have heaps of money and not have to worry about anything, won't it?

Mrs. Linde: Yes. Anyway, I think it would be delightful to have what you need.

Nora: No, not only what you need, but heaps and heaps of money.

Mrs. Linde (smiling): Nora, Nora, haven't you learned any sense yet? Back in school you were a terrible spendthrift.

Nora (laughing): Yes, that's what Torvald says now. (*Wags her finger at her.*) But "Nora, Nora" isn't as silly as you think. We haven't been in a position for me to waste money. We've both had to work.

Mrs. Linde: You too?

Nora: Oh, yes, odds and ends, needlework, crocheting, embroidery, and that kind of thing. (*Dropping her voice.*) And other things too. You know Torvald left his government job when we got married? There was no chance of promotion, and he had to try to earn more money than he was making there. But in that first year he overworked himself terribly. You see, he had to make money any way he could, and he worked all hours, but he couldn't take it, and he got very sick, and the doctors said he had to go south, to a warmer climate.

Mrs. Linde: You spent a whole year in Italy, didn't you?

Nora: Yes. It wasn't easy to get away, I can tell you that. It was just after Ivar was born, but obviously we had to go. It was a wonderful, beautiful trip, and it saved Torvald's life. But it cost a tremendous amount of money, Kristine.

Mrs. Linde: I would imagine so.

Nora: It cost about four thousand, eight hundred kroner. That's a lot, isn't it?

Mrs. Linde: Yes, it is, and when you have an emergency like that it's lucky to have the money.

Nora: Well, the fact is, we got it from Papa.

Mrs. Linde: Oh, I see. It was just about that time that he died, wasn't it?

Nora: Yes, and, just think of it, I couldn't even go and take care of him. I was expecting little Ivar any day and I had my poor sick Torvald to look after. My dear, kind father. I never saw him again, Kristine. That was the worst experience I've gone through since we got married.

Mrs. Linde: I know how fond of him you were. And then you went off to Italy?

Nora: Yes. You see, we had money then, and the doctors insisted that we go, so we left a month later.

Mrs. Linde: And your husband came back completely recovered?

Nora: The picture of health!

Mrs. Linde: But . . . the doctor?

Nora: What doctor?

Mrs. Linde: Didn't your maid say that the gentleman who arrived here with me was the doctor?

Nora: Yes, that was Doctor Rank, but he doesn't come here professionally. He's our dearest friend, and he drops in at least once every day. No, Torvald hasn't been sick for an hour since then, and our children are strong and healthy, and so am I. (*Jumps up and claps her hands.*) Kristine! Kristine! It's good to be alive and happy! But how awful of me. I'm talking about nothing but myself. (*Sits on a nearby stool and rests her arms on her knees.*) Please don't be mad at me. Tell me, is it really true that you didn't love your husband? Why did you marry him?

Mrs. Linde: My mother was still alive then, and she was bedridden and helpless, and I had to provide for my two younger brothers, so I didn't think I had any right to turn him down.

Nora: No, maybe you did the right thing. So he was rich then?

Mrs. Linde: I believe he was quite well off. But his business wasn't very solid, and when he died, it all went to pieces and there was nothing left.

Nora: And then?

Mrs. Linde: Well, I had to turn my hand to anything I could find. First a small shop, then a small school, and so on. The last three years have seemed like one long workday, with no rest. Now it's over, Nora. My poor mother's gone and doesn't need me any more, and the boys don't need me, either. They've got jobs now and can manage for themselves.

Nora: What a relief it must be if—

Mrs. Linde: No, not at all. All I feel is an unbearable emptiness. No one to live for anymore. (*Gets up restlessly.*) That's why I couldn't stand it any longer in my little backwater. I hope it'll be easier to find something here that'll keep me busy and occupy my mind. If I could be lucky enough to find some regular work, office work of some kind—

Nora: But, Kristine, that's so awfully tiring, and you look tired out now. It'd be much better for you if you could get away to a resort.

Mrs. Linde (*walking to the window*): I don't have a father to give me money for a trip, Nora.

Nora (*rising*): Oh, don't be mad at me!

Mrs. Linde (*going up to her*): It's you who mustn't be mad at me, dear. The worst thing about a situation like mine is that it makes you so bitter. No one to work for, and yet you have to always be on the lookout for opportunities. You have to live, and so you grow selfish. When you told me about your good luck—you'll find this hard to believe—I was delighted less for you than for myself.

Nora: What do you mean? Oh, I understand. You mean that maybe Torvald could find you a job.

Mrs. Linde: Yes, that's what I was thinking.

Nora: He must, Kristine. Just leave it to me. I'll broach the subject very cleverly. I'll think of something that'll put him in a really good mood. It'll make me so happy to be of some use to you.

Mrs. Linde: How kind you are, Nora, to be so eager to help me! It's doubly kind of you, since you know so little of the burdens and troubles of life.

Nora: Me? I know so little of them?

Mrs. Linde (*smiling*): My dear! Small household cares and that sort of thing! You're a child, Nora.

Nora (*tosses her head and crosses the stage*): You shouldn't act so superior.

Mrs. Linde: No?

Nora: You're just like the others. They all think I'm incapable of anything really serious—

Mrs. Linde: Come on—

Nora: —that I haven't had to deal with any real problems in my life.

Mrs. Linde: But, my dear Nora, you've just told me all your troubles.

Nora: Pooh! That was nothing. (*Lowering her voice.*) I haven't told you the important thing.

Mrs. Linde: The important thing? What do you mean?

Nora: You really look down on me, Kristine, but you shouldn't. Aren't you proud of having worked so hard and so long for your mother?

Mrs. Linde: Believe me, I don't look down on anyone. But it's true, I'm proud and I'm glad that I had the privilege of making my mother's last days almost worry-free.

Nora: And you're proud of what you did for your brothers?

Mrs. Linde: I think I have the right to be.

Nora: I think so, too. But now, listen to this. I have something to be proud of and happy about too.

Mrs. Linde: I'm sure you do. But what do you mean?

Nora: Keep your voice down. If Torvald were to overhear! He can't find out, not under any circumstances. No one in the world must know, Kristine, except you.

Mrs. Linde: But what is it?

Nora: Come here. (*Pulls her down on the sofa beside her.*) Now I'll show you that I too have something to be proud and happy about. I'm the one who saved Torvald's life.

Mrs. Linde: Saved? How?

Nora: I told you about our trip to Italy. Torvald would never have recovered if he hadn't gone there—

Mrs. Linde: Yes, but your father gave you the money you needed.

Nora (*smiling*): Yes, that's what Torvald thinks, along with everybody else, but—

Mrs. Linde: But—

Nora: Papa didn't give us a penny. I was the one who raised the money.

Mrs. Linde: You? That huge amount?

Nora: That's right, four thousand, eight hundred kroner. What do you think of that?

Mrs. Linde: But, Nora, how could you possibly? Did you win the lottery?

Nora (*disdainfully*): The lottery? That wouldn't have been any accomplishment.

Mrs. Linde: But where did you get it from, then?

Nora (*humming and smiling with an air of mystery*): Hm, hm! Ha!

Mrs. Linde: Because you couldn't have borrowed it.

Nora: Couldn't I? Why not?

Mrs. Linde: No, a wife can't borrow money without her husband's consent.

Nora (*tossing her head*): Oh, if it's a wife with a head for business, a wife who has the brains to be a little clever—

Mrs. Linde: I don't understand this at all, Nora.

Nora: There's no reason why you should. I never said I'd borrowed the money. Maybe I got it some other way. (*Lies back on the sofa.*) Maybe I got it from an admirer. When a woman's as pretty as I am—

Mrs. Linde: You're crazy.

Nora: Now, you know you're dying of curiosity, Kristine.

Mrs. Linde: Listen to me, Nora dear. Have you done something rash?

Nora (*sits up straight*): Is it rash to save your husband's life?

Mrs. Linde: I think it's rash, without his knowledge, to—

Nora: But it was absolutely necessary that he not know! My goodness, can't you understand that? It was necessary he have no idea how sick he was. The doctors came to *me* and said his life was in danger and the only thing that could save him was to live in the south. Don't you think I tried first to get him to do it as if it was for me? I told him how much I would love to travel abroad like other young wives. I tried tears and pleading with him. I told him he should remember the condition I was in, and that he should be kind and indulgent to me. I even hinted that he might take out a loan. That almost made him mad, Kristine. He said I was thoughtless, and that it was his duty as my husband not to indulge me in my "whims and caprices," as I believe he called them. All right, I thought, you need to be saved. And that was how I came to think up a way out of the mess—

Mrs. Linde: And your husband never found out from your father that the money hadn't come from him?

Nora: No, never. Papa died just then. I'd meant to let him in on the secret and beg him never to reveal it. But he was so sick. Unfortunately, there never was any need to tell him.

Mrs. Linde: And since then you've never told your secret to your husband?

Nora: Good heavens, no! How could you think I would? A man with such strong opinions about these things! Besides, how painful and humiliating it would be for Torvald, with his masculine pride, to know that he owed me anything! It would completely upset the balance of our relationship. Our beautiful happy home would never be the same.

Mrs. Linde: Are you never going to tell him about it?

Nora (*meditatively, and with a half smile*): Yes, someday, maybe, in many years, when I'm not as pretty as I am now. Don't laugh at me! I mean, of course, when Torvald is no longer as devoted to me as he is now, when he's grown tired of my dancing and dressing up and reciting. Then it may be a good thing to have something in reserve— (*Breaking off.*) What nonsense! That time will never come. Now, what do you think of my great secret, Kristine? Do you still think I'm useless? And the fact is, this whole situation has caused me a lot of worry. It hasn't been easy for me to make my payments on time. I can tell you that there's something in business that's called quarterly interest, and something else called installment payments, and it's always so terribly difficult to keep up with them. I've had to save a little here and there, wherever I could, you understand. I haven't been able to put much aside from my housekeeping money, because Torvald has to live well. And I couldn't let my children be shabbily dressed. I feel I have to spend everything he gives me for them, the sweet little darlings!

Mrs. Linde: So it's all had to come out of your own allowance, poor Nora?

Nora: Of course. Besides, I was the one responsible for it. Whenever Torvald has given me money for new dresses and things like that, I've never spent more than half of it. I've always bought the simplest and cheapest things. Thank heaven, any clothes look good on me, and so Torvald's never noticed anything. But it was often very hard on me, Kristine, because it is delightful to be really well dressed, isn't it?

Mrs. Linde: I suppose so.

Nora: Well, then I've found other ways of earning money. Last winter I was lucky enough to get a lot of copying to do, so I locked myself up and sat writing every evening until late into the night. A lot of the time I was desperately tired, but all the same it was a tremendous pleasure to sit there working and earning money. It was like being a man.

Mrs. Linde: How much have you been able to pay off that way?

Nora: I can't tell you exactly. You see, it's very hard to keep a strict account of a business matter like that. I only know that I've paid out every penny I could scrape together. Many a time I was at my wits' end. (*Smiles.*) Then I used to sit here and imagine that a rich old gentleman had fallen in love with me—

Mrs. Linde: What! Who was it?

Nora: Oh, be quiet! That he had died, and that when his will was opened it said, in great big letters: "The lovely Mrs. Nora Helmer is to have everything I own paid over to her immediately in cash."

Mrs. Linde: But, my dear Nora, who could the man be?

Nora: Good gracious, can't you understand? There wasn't any old gentleman. It was only something that I used to sit here and imagine, when I couldn't think of any way of getting money. But it's all right now. The tiresome old gent can stay right where he is, as far as I'm concerned. I don't care about him or his will either, because now I'm worry-free. (*Jumps up.*) My goodness, it's delightful to think of, Kristine! Worry-free! To be able to have no worries, no worries at all! To be able to play and romp with the children! To be able to keep the house beautifully and have everything just the way Torvald likes it! And, just think of it, soon the spring will come and the big blue sky! Maybe we can take a little trip. Maybe I can see the sea again! Oh, it's a wonderful thing to be alive and happy.

(*A bell rings in the hall.*)

Mrs. Linde (*rising*): There's the bell. Perhaps I should be going.

Nora: No, don't go. No one will come in here. It's sure to be for Torvald.

Servant (*at the hall door*): Excuse me, ma'am. There's a gentleman to see the master, and as the doctor is still with him—

Nora: Who is it?

Krogstad (at the door): It's me, Mrs. Helmer.

(*Mrs. Linde starts, trembles, and turns toward the window.*)

Nora (takes a step toward him, and speaks in a strained, low voice): You? What is it? What do you want to see my husband for?

Krogstad: Bank business, in a way. I have a small position in the bank, and I hear your husband is going to be our boss now—

Nora: Then it's—

Krogstad: Nothing but dry business matters, Mrs. Helmer, that's all.

Nora: Then please go into the study.

(*She bows indifferently to him and shuts the door into the hall, then comes back and makes up the fire in the stove.*)

Mrs. Linde: Nora, who was that man?

Nora: A lawyer. His name is Krogstad.

Mrs. Linde: Then it really was him.

Nora: Do you know the man?

Mrs. Linde: I used to, many years ago. At one time he was a law clerk in our town.

Nora: That's right, he was.

Mrs. Linde: How much he's changed.

Nora: He had a very unhappy marriage.

Mrs. Linde: He's a widower now, isn't he?

Nora: With several children. There, now it's really caught. (*Shuts the door of the stove and moves the rocking chair aside.*)

Mrs. Linde: They say he's mixed up in a lot of questionable business.

Nora: Really? Maybe he is. I don't know anything about it. But let's not talk about business. It's so tiresome.

Doctor Rank (comes out of Helmer's study. Before he shuts the door he calls to Helmer): No, my dear fellow, I won't disturb you. I'd rather go in and talk to your wife for a little while.

(*Shuts the door and sees Mrs. Linde.*)

I beg your pardon. I'm afraid I'm in the way here too.

Nora: No, not at all. (*Introducing him*): Doctor Rank, Mrs. Linde.

Rank: I've often heard that name in this house. I think I passed you on the stairs when I arrived, Mrs. Linde?

Mrs. Linde: Yes, I take stairs very slowly. I can't manage them very well.

Rank: Oh, some small internal problem?

Mrs. Linde: No, it's just that I've been overworking myself.

Rank: Is that all? Then I suppose you've come to town to get some rest by sampling our social life.

Mrs. Linde: I've come to look for work.

Rank: Is that a good cure for overwork?

Mrs. Linde: One has to live, Doctor Rank.

Rank: Yes, that seems to be the general opinion.

Nora: Now, now, Doctor Rank, you know you want to live.

Rank: Of course I do. However miserable I may feel, I want to prolong the agony for as long as possible. All my patients are the same way. And so are those who are morally sick. In fact, one of them, and a bad case too, is at this very moment inside with Helmer—

Mrs. Linde (sadly): Ah!

Nora: Who are you talking about?

Rank: A lawyer by the name of Krogstad, a fellow you don't know at all. He's a completely worthless creature, Mrs. Helmer. But even he started out by saying, as if it were a matter of the utmost importance, that he has to live.

Nora: Did he? What did he want to talk to Torvald about?

Rank: I have no idea. All I heard was that it was something about the bank.

Nora: I didn't know this—what's his name—Krogstad had anything to do with the bank.

Rank: Yes, he has some kind of a position there. (*To Mrs. Linde.*) I don't know whether you find the same thing in your part of the world, that there are certain people who go around zealously looking to sniff out moral corruption, and, as soon as they find some, they put the person involved in some cushy job where they can keep an eye on him. Meanwhile, the morally healthy ones are left out in the cold.

Mrs. Linde: Still, I think it's the sick who are most in need of being taken care of.

Rank (shrugging his shoulders): Well, there you have it. That's the attitude that's turning society into a hospital.

(*Nora, who has been absorbed in her thoughts, breaks out into smothered laughter and claps her hands.*)

Rank: Why are you laughing at that? Do you have any idea what society really is?

Nora: What do I care about your boring society? I'm laughing at something else, something very funny. Tell me, Doctor Rank, are all the people who work in the bank dependent on Torvald now?

Rank: That's what's so funny?

Nora (*smiling and humming*): That's my business! (*Walking around the room.*) It's just wonderful to think that we have—that Torvald has—so much power over so many people. (*Takes the bag out of her pocket.*) Doctor Rank, what do you say to a macaroon?

Rank: Macaroons? I thought they were forbidden here.

Nora: Yes, but these are some Kristine gave me.

Mrs. Linde: What! Me?

Nora: Oh, well, don't be upset! How could you know that Torvald had forbidden them? I have to tell you, he's afraid they'll ruin my teeth. But so what? Once in a while, that's all right, isn't it, Doctor Rank? With your permission! (*Puts a macaroon into his mouth.*) You have to have one too, Kristine. And I'll have one, just a little one—or no more than two. (*Walking around.*) I am tremendously happy. There's just one thing in the world now that I would dearly love to do.

Rank: Well, what is it?

Nora: It's something I would dearly love to say, if Torvald could hear me.

Rank: Well, why can't you say it?

Nora: No, I don't dare. It's too shocking.

Mrs. Linde: Shocking?

Rank: Well then, I'd advise you not to say it. Still, in front of us you might risk it. What is it you'd so much like to say if Torvald could hear you?

Nora: I would just love to say—"Well, I'll be damned!"

Rank: Are you crazy?

Mrs. Linde: Nora, dear!

Rank: Here he is. Say it!

Nora (*hiding the bag*): Shh, shh, shh!

(*Helmer comes out of his room, with his coat over his arm and his hat in his hand.*)

Nora: Well, Torvald dear, did you get rid of him?

Helmer: Yes, he just left.

Nora: Let me introduce you. This is Kristine. She's just arrived in town.

Helmer: Kristine? I'm sorry, but I don't know any—

Nora: Mrs. Linde, dear, Kristine Linde.

Helmer: Oh, of course. A school friend of my wife's, I believe?

Mrs. Linde: Yes, we knew each other back then.

Nora: And just think, she's come all this way in order to see you.

Helmer: What do you mean?

Mrs. Linde: No, really, I—

Nora: Kristine is extremely good at bookkeeping, and she's very eager to work for some talented man, so she can perfect her skills—

Helmer: Very sensible, Mrs. Linde.

Nora: And when she heard that you'd been named manager of the bank—the news was sent by telegraph, you know—she traveled here as quickly as she could. Torvald, I'm sure you'll be able to do something for Kristine, for my sake, won't you?

Helmer: Well, it's not completely out of the question. I expect that you're a widow, Mrs. Linde?

Mrs. Linde: Yes.

Helmer: And you've had some bookkeeping experience?

Mrs. Linde: Yes, a fair amount.

Helmer: Ah! Well, there's a very good chance that I'll be able to find something for you—

Nora (clapping her hands): What did I tell you? What did I tell you?

Helmer: You've just come at a lucky moment, Mrs. Linde.

Mrs. Linde: How can I thank you?

Helmer: There's no need. (*Puts on his coat.*) But now you must excuse me—

Rank: Wait a minute. I'll come with you. (*Brings his fur coat from the hall and warms it at the fire.*)

Nora: Don't be long, Torvald dear.

Helmer: About an hour, that's all.

Nora: Are you leaving too, Kristine?

Mrs. Linde (putting on her cloak): Yes, I have to go and look for a place to stay.

Helmer: Oh, well then, we can walk down the street together.

Nora (helping her): It's too bad we're so short of space here. I'm afraid it's impossible for us—

Mrs. Linde: Please don't even think of it! Goodbye, Nora dear, and many thanks.

Nora: Goodbye for now. Of course you'll come back this evening. And you too, Dr. Rank. What do you say? If you're feeling up to it? Oh, you have to be! Wrap yourself up warmly.

(*They go to the door all talking together. Children's voices are heard on the staircase.*)

Nora: There they are! There they are!

(*She runs to open the door. The nursemaid comes in with the children.*)

Come in! Come in! (*Stoops and kisses them.*) Oh, you sweet blessings! Look at them, Kristine! Aren't they darlings?

Rank: Let's not stand here in the draft.

Helmer: Come along, Mrs. Linde. Only a mother will be able to stand it in here now!

(*Rank, Helmer, and Mrs. Linde go downstairs. The Nursemaid comes forward with the children. Nora shuts the hall door.*)

Nora: How fresh and healthy you look! Cheeks as red as apples and roses. (*The children all talk at once while she speaks to them.*) Did you have a lot of fun? That's wonderful! What, you pulled Emmy and Bob on the sled? Both at once? That was really something. You *are* a clever boy, Ivar. Let me take her for a little, Anne Marie. My sweet little baby doll! (*Takes the baby from the maid and dances her up and down.*) Yes, yes, mother will dance with Bob too. What! Have you been throwing snowballs? I wish I'd been there too! No, no, I'll take their things off, Anne Marie, please let me do it, it's such fun. Go inside now, you look half frozen. There's some hot coffee for you on the stove.

(*The Nursemaid goes into the room on the left. Nora takes off the children's things and throws them around, while they all talk to her at once.*)

Nora: Really! Did a big dog run after you? But it didn't bite you? No, dogs don't bite nice little dolly children. You mustn't look at the packages, Ivar. What are they? Oh, I'll bet you'd like to know. No, no, it's something boring! Come on, let's play a game! What should we play? Hide and seek? Yes, we'll play hide and seek. Bob will hide first. You want me to hide? All right, I'll hide first.

(*She and the children laugh and shout, and romp in and out of the room. At last Nora hides under the table. The children rush in and out looking for her, but they don't see her. They hear her smothered laughter, run to the table, lift up the cloth and find her. Shouts of laughter. She crawls forward and pretends to scare them. More laughter. Meanwhile there has been a knock at the hall door, but none of them has noticed it. The door is opened halfway and Krogstad appears. He waits for a little while. The game goes on.*)

Krogstad: Excuse me, Mrs. Helmer.

Nora (*with a stifled cry, turns round and gets up onto her knees*): Oh! What do you want?

Krogstad: Excuse me, the outside door was open. I suppose someone forgot to shut it.

Nora (*rising*): My husband is out, Mr. Krogstad.

Krogstad: I know that.

Nora: What do you want here, then?

Krogstad: A word with you.

Nora: With me? (*To the children, gently.*) Go inside to Anne Marie. What? No, the strange man won't hurt Mother. When he's gone we'll play another game. (*She takes the children into the room on the left, and shuts the door after them.*) You want to speak to me?

Krogstad: Yes, I do.

Nora: Today? It isn't the first of the month yet.

Krogstad: No, it's Christmas Eve, and it's up to you what kind of Christmas you're going to have.

Nora: What do you mean? Today it's absolutely impossible for me—

Krogstad: We won't talk about that until later on. This is something else. I presume you can spare me a moment?

Nora: Yes, yes, I can. Although . . .

Krogstad: Good. I was in Olsen's restaurant and I saw your husband going down the street—

Nora: Yes?

Krogstad: With a lady.

Nora: So?

Krogstad: May I be so bold as to ask if it was a Mrs. Linde?

Nora: It was.

Krogstad: Just arrived in town?

Nora: Yes, today.

Krogstad: She's a very good friend of yours, isn't she?

Nora: She is. But I don't see—

Krogstad: I knew her too, once upon a time.

Nora: I'm aware of that.

Krogstad: Are you? So you know all about it. I thought so. Then I can ask you, without beating around the bush. Is Mrs. Linde going to work in the bank?

Nora: What right do you have to question me, Mr. Krogstad? You're one of my husband's employees. But since you ask, I'll tell you. Yes, Mrs. Linde is going to work in the bank. And I'm the one who spoke up for her, Mr. Krogstad. So now you know.

Krogstad: So I was right, then.

Nora (*walking up and down the stage*): Sometimes one has a tiny little bit of influence, I should hope. Just because I'm a woman, it doesn't necessarily follow that— You know, when somebody's in a subordinate position, Mr. Krogstad, they should really be careful to avoid offending anyone who—who—

Krogstad: Who has influence?

Nora: Exactly.

Krogstad (changing his tone): Mrs. Helmer, may I ask you to use *your* influence on my behalf?

Nora: What? What do you mean?

Krogstad: Will you be kind enough to see to it that I'm allowed to keep my subordinate position in the bank?

Nora: What do you mean by that? Who's threatening to take your job away from you?

Krogstad: Oh, there's no need to keep up the pretence of ignorance. I can understand that your friend isn't very anxious to expose herself to the chance of rubbing shoulders with me. And now I realize exactly who I have to thank for pushing me out.

Nora: But I swear to you—

Krogstad: Yes, yes. But, to get right to the point, there's still time to prevent it, and I would advise you to use your influence to do so.

Nora: But, Mr. Krogstad, I have no influence.

Krogstad: Oh no? Didn't you yourself just say—

Nora: Well, obviously, I didn't mean for you to take it that way. Me? What would make you think I have that kind of influence with my husband?

Krogstad: Oh, I've known your husband since our school days. I don't suppose he's any more unpersuadable than other husbands.

Nora: If you're going talk disrespectfully about my husband, I'll have to ask you to leave my house.

Krogstad: Bold talk, Mrs. Helmer.

Nora: I'm not afraid of you anymore. When the New Year comes, I'll soon be free of the whole thing.

Krogstad (controlling himself): Listen to me, Mrs. Helmer. If I have to, I'm ready to fight for my little job in the bank as if I were fighting for my life.

Nora: So it seems.

Krogstad: It's not just for the sake of the money. In fact, that matters the least to me. There's another reason. Well, I might as well tell you. Here's my situation. I suppose, like everybody else, you know that many years ago I did something pretty foolish.

Nora: I think I heard something about it.

Krogstad: It never got as far as the courtroom, but every door seemed closed to me after that. So I got involved in the business that you know about. I had to do something, and, honestly, I think there are many worse than me. But now I have to get myself free of all that. My sons are growing up. For their sake I have to try to win back as much respect as I can in this town. The job in the bank was like the first step up for me, and now your husband is going to kick me downstairs back into the mud.

Nora: But you have to believe me, Mr. Krogstad, it's not in my power to help you at all.

Krogstad: Then it's because you don't want to. But I have ways of making you.

Nora: You don't mean you'll tell my husband I owe you money?

Krogstad: Hm! And what if I did tell him?

Nora: That would be a terrible thing for you to do. (*Sobbing.*) To think he would learn my secret, which has been my pride and joy, in such an ugly, clumsy way—that he would learn it from you! And it would put me in a horribly uncomfortable position—

Krogstad: Just uncomfortable?

Nora (*impetuously*): Well, go ahead and do it, then! And it'll be so much the worse for you. My husband will see for himself how vile you are, and then you'll lose your job for sure.

Krogstad: I asked you if it's just an uncomfortable situation at home that you're afraid of.

Nora: If my husband does find out about it, of course he'll immediately pay you what I still owe, and then we'll be through with you once and for all.

Krogstad (*coming a step closer*): Listen to me, Mrs. Helmer. Either you have a very bad memory or you don't know much about business. I can see I'm going to have to remind you of a few details.

Nora: What do you mean?

Krogstad: When your husband was sick, you came to me to borrow four thousand, eight hundred kroner.

Nora: I didn't know anyone else to go to.

Krogstad: I promised to get you that amount—

Nora: Yes, and you did so.

Krogstad: I promised to get you that amount, on certain conditions. You were so preoccupied with your husband's illness, and you were so anxious to get the money for your trip, that you seem to have paid no attention to the conditions of our bargain. So it won't be out of place for me to remind you of them. Now, I promised to get the money on the security of a note which I drew up.

Nora: Yes, and which I signed.

Krogstad: Good. But underneath your signature there were a few lines naming your father as a co-signer who guaranteed the repayment of the loan. Your father was supposed to sign that part.

Nora: Supposed to? He did sign it.

Krogstad: I had left the date blank. That was because your father was supposed to fill in the date when he signed the paper. Do you remember that?

Nora: Yes, I think I remember. . . .

Krogstad: Then I gave you the note to mail to your father. Isn't that so?

Nora: Yes.

Krogstad: And obviously you mailed it right away, because five or six days later you brought me the note with your father's signature. And then I gave you the money.

Nora: Well, haven't I been paying it back regularly?

Krogstad: Fairly regularly, yes. But, to get back to the point, that must have been a very difficult time for you, Mrs. Helmer.

Nora: Yes, it was.

Krogstad: Your father was very sick, wasn't he?

Nora: He was very near the end.

Krogstad: And he died soon after?

Nora: Yes.

Krogstad: Tell me, Mrs. Helmer, can you by any chance remember what day your father died? On what day of the month, I mean.

Nora: Papa died on the 29th of September.

Krogstad: That's right. I looked it up myself. And, since that is the case, there's something extremely peculiar (*taking a piece of paper from his pocket*) that I can't account for.

Nora: Peculiar in what way? I don't know—

Krogstad: The peculiar thing, Mrs. Helmer, is the fact that your father signed this note three days after he died.

Nora: What do you mean? I don't understand—

Krogstad: Your father died on the 29th of September. But, look here. Your father dated his signature the 2nd of October. It is mighty peculiar, isn't it? (*Nora is silent.*) Can you explain it to me? (*Nora is still silent.*) And what's just as peculiar is that the words "October 2," as well as the year, are not in your father's handwriting, but in someone else's, which I think I recognize. Well, of course it can all be explained. Your father might have forgotten to date his signature, and someone else might have filled in the date before they knew that he had died. There's no harm in that. It all depends on the signature, and that's genuine, isn't it, Mrs. Helmer? It was your father himself who signed his name here?

Nora (*after a short pause, lifts her head up and looks defiantly at him*): No, it wasn't. I'm the one who wrote Papa's name.

Krogstad: Are you aware that you're making a very serious confession?

Nora: How so? You'll get your money soon.

Krogstad: Let me ask you something. Why didn't you send the paper to your father?

Nora: It was out of the question. Papa was too sick. If I had asked him to sign something, I'd have had to tell him what the money was for, and when he was so sick himself I couldn't tell him that my husband's life was in danger. It was out of the question.

Krogstad: It would have been better for you if you'd given up your trip abroad.

Nora: No, that was impossible. That trip was to save my husband's life. I couldn't give that up.

Krogstad: But didn't it ever occur to you that you were committing a fraud against me?

Nora: I couldn't take that into account. I didn't trouble myself about you at all. I couldn't stand you, because you put so many heartless difficulties in my way, even though you knew how seriously ill my husband was.

Krogstad: Mrs. Helmer, you evidently don't realize clearly what you're guilty of. But, believe me, my one mistake, which cost me my whole reputation, was nothing more and nothing worse than what you did.

Nora: You? You expect me to believe that you were brave enough to take a risk to save your wife's life?

Krogstad: The law doesn't care about motives.

Nora: Then the law must be very stupid.

Krogstad: Stupid or not, it's the law that's going to judge you, if I produce this paper in court.

Nora: I don't believe it. Isn't a daughter allowed to spare her dying father anxiety and concern? Isn't a wife allowed to save her husband's life? I don't know much about the law, but I'm sure there must be provisions for things like that. Don't you know anything about such provisions? You seem like a very poor excuse for a lawyer, Mr. Krogstad.

Krogstad: That's as may be. But business, the kind of business you and I have done together—do you think I don't know about that? Fine. Do what you want. But I can assure you of this. If I lose everything all over again, this time you're going down with me. (*He bows, and goes out through the hall.*)

Nora (*appears buried in thought for a short time, then tosses her head*): Nonsense! He's just trying to scare me! I'm not as naive as he thinks I am. (*Begins to busy herself putting the children's things in order.*) And yet . . . ? No, it's impossible! I did it for love.

Children (*in the doorway on the left*): Mother, the strange man is gone. He went out through the gate.

Nora: Yes, dears, I know. But don't tell anyone about the strange man. Do you hear me? Not even Papa.

Children: No, Mother. But will you come and play with us again?

Nora: No, no, not just now.

Children: But, Mother, you promised us.

Nora: Yes, but I can't right now. Go inside. I have too much to do. Go inside, my sweet little darlings.

(*She gets them into the room bit by bit and shuts the door on them. Then she sits down on the sofa, takes up a piece of needlework and sews a few stitches, but soon stops.*)

No! (*Throws down the work, gets up, goes to the hall door and calls out.*) Helene! Bring the tree in. (*Goes to the table on the left, opens a drawer, and stops again.*) No, no! It's completely impossible!

Maid (*coming in with the tree*): Where should I put it, ma'am?

Nora: Here, in the middle of the floor.

Maid: Do you need anything else?

Nora: No, thank you. I have everything I want.

(*Exit Maid.*)

Nora (*begins decorating the tree*): A candle here, and flowers here. That horrible man! It's all nonsense, there's nothing wrong. The tree is going to be magnificent! I'll do everything I can think of to make you happy, Torvald! I'll sing for you, dance for you—

(*Helmer comes in with some papers under his arm.*)

Oh! You're back already?

Helmer: Yes. Has anyone been here?

Nora: Here? No.

Helmer: That's strange. I saw Krogstad going out the gate.

Nora: You did? Oh yes, I forgot, Krogstad was here for a moment.

Helmer: Nora, I can tell from the way you're acting that he was here begging you to put in a good word for him.

Nora: Yes, he was.

Helmer: And you were supposed to pretend it was all your idea and not tell me that he'd been here to see you. Didn't he beg you to do that too?

Nora: Yes, Torvald, but—

Helmer: Nora, Nora, to think that you'd be a party to that sort of thing! To have any kind of conversation with a man like that, and promise him anything at all? And to lie to me in the bargain?

Nora: Lie?

Helmer: Didn't you tell me no one had been here? (*Shakes his finger at her.*) My little songbird must never do that again. A songbird must have a clean beak to chirp with. No false notes! (*Puts his arm round her waist.*) That's true, isn't it? Yes, I'm sure it is. (*Lets her go.*) We won't mention this again. (*Sits down by the stove.*) How warm and cozy it is here! (*Turns over his papers.*)

Nora (*after a short pause, during which she busies herself with the Christmas tree.*): Torvald!

Helmer: Yes?

Nora: I'm really looking forward to the masquerade ball at the Stenborgs' the day after tomorrow.

Helmer: And I'm really curious to see what you're going to surprise me with.

Nora: Oh, it was very silly of me to want to do that.

Helmer: What do you mean?

Nora: I can't come up with anything good. Everything I think of seems so stupid and pointless.

Helmer: So my little Nora finally admits that?

Nora (*standing behind his chair with her arms on the back of it*): Are you very busy, Torvald?

Helmer: Well . . .

Nora: What are all those papers?

Helmer: Bank business.

Nora: Already?

Helmer: I've gotten the authority from the retiring manager to reorganize the work procedures and make the necessary personnel changes. I need to take care of it during Christmas week, so as to have everything in place for the new year.

Nora: Then that was why this poor Krogstad—

Helmer: Hm!

Nora (*leans against the back of his chair and strokes his hair*): If you weren't so busy, I would have asked you for a huge favor, Torvald.

Helmer: What favor? Tell me.

Nora: No one has such good taste as you. And I really want to look nice at the fancy-dress ball. Torvald, couldn't you take me in hand and decide what I should go as and what kind of costume I should wear?

Helmer: Aha! So my obstinate little woman has to get someone to come to her rescue?

Nora: Yes, Torvald, I can't get along at all without your help.

Helmer: All right, I'll think it over. I'm sure we'll come up with something.

Nora: That's so nice of you. (*Goes to the Christmas tree. A short pause.*) How pretty the red flowers look. But, tell me, was it really something very bad that this Krogstad was guilty of?

Helmer: He forged someone's name. Do you have any idea what that means?

Nora: Isn't it possible that he was forced to do it by necessity?

Helmer: Yes. Or, the way it is in so many cases, by foolishness. I'm not so heartless that I'd absolutely condemn a man because of one mistake like that.

Nora: No, you wouldn't, would you, Torvald?

Helmer: Many a man has been able to rehabilitate himself, if he's openly admitted his guilt and taken his punishment.

Nora: Punishment?

Helmer: But Krogstad didn't do that. He wriggled out of it with lies and trickery, and that's what completely undermined his moral character.

Nora: But do you think that that would—

Helmer: Just think how a guilty man like that has to lie and act like a hypocrite with everyone, how he has to wear a mask in front of the people closest to him, even with his own wife and children. And the children. That's the most terrible part of it all, Nora.

Nora: How so?

Helmer: Because an atmosphere of lies infects and poisons the whole life of a home. Every breath the children take in a house like that is full of the germs of moral corruption.

Nora (coming closer to him): Are you sure of that?

Helmer: My dear, I've seen it many times in my legal career. Almost everyone who's gone wrong at a young age had a dishonest mother.

Nora: Why only the mother?

Helmer: It usually seems to be the mother's influence, though naturally a bad father would have the same result. Every lawyer knows this. This Krogstad, now, has been systematically poisoning his own children with lies and deceit. That's why I say he's lost all moral character. (*Holds out his hands to her.*) And that's why my sweet little Nora must promise me not to plead his cause. Give me your hand on it. Come now, what's this? Give me your hand. There, that's settled. Believe me, it would be impossible for me to work with him. It literally makes me feel physically ill to be around people like that.

Nora (takes her hand out of his and goes to the opposite side of the Christmas tree): How hot it is in here! And I have so much to do.

Helmer (getting up and putting his papers in order): Yes, and I have to try to read through some of these before dinner. And I have to think about your costume, too. And it's just possible I'll have something wrapped in gold paper to hang up on the tree. (*Puts his hand on her head.*) My precious little songbird! (*He goes into his study and closes the door behind him.*)

Nora (after a pause, whispers): No, no, it's not true. It's impossible. It has to be impossible.

(*The nursemaid opens the door on the left.*)

Nursemaid: The little ones are begging so hard to be allowed to come in to see Mama.

Nora: No, no, no! Don't let them come in to me! You stay with them, Anne Marie.

Nursemaid: Very well, ma'am. (*Shuts the door.*)

Nora (*pale with terror*): Corrupt my little children? Poison my home? (*A short pause. Then she tosses her head.*) It's not true. It can't possibly be true.

ACT II

The same scene. The Christmas tree is in the corner by the piano, stripped of its ornaments and with burnt-down candle-ends on its disheveled branches. Nora's coat and hat are lying on the sofa. She is alone in the room, walking around uneasily. She stops by the sofa and picks up her coat.

Nora (*drops her coat*): Someone's coming! (*Goes to the door and listens.*) No, there's no one there. Of course, no one will come today. It's Christmas Day. And not tomorrow either. But maybe . . . (*opens the door and looks out*) No, nothing in the mailbox. It's empty. (*Comes forward.*) What nonsense! Of course he can't be serious about it. A thing like that couldn't happen. It's impossible. I have three little children.

(Enter the nursemaid Anne Marie from the room on the left, carrying a big cardboard box.)

Nursemaid: I finally found the box with the costume.

Nora: Thank you. Put it on the table.

Nursemaid (*doing so*): But it really needs to be mended.

Nora: I'd like to tear it into a hundred thousand pieces.

Nursemaid: What an idea! It can easily be fixed up. All you need is a little patience.

Nora: Yes, I'll go get Mrs. Linde to come and help me with it.

Nursemaid: What, going out again? In this horrible weather? You'll catch cold, Miss Nora, and make yourself sick.

Nora: Well, worse things than that might happen. How are the children?

Nursemaid: The poor little ones are playing with their Christmas presents, but—

Nora: Do they ask for me much?

Nursemaid: You see, they're so used to having their Mama with them.

Nora: Yes, but, Anne Marie, I won't be able to spend as much time with them now as I did before.

Nursemaid: Oh well, young children quickly get used to anything.

Nora: Do you think so? Do you think they'd forget their mother if she went away for good?

Nursemaid: Good heavens! Went away for good?

Nora: Anne Marie, I want you to tell me something I've often wondered about. How could you have the heart to let your own child be raised by strangers?

Nursemaid: I had to, if I wanted to be little Nora's nursemaid.

Nora: Yes, but how could you agree to it?

Nursemaid: What, when I was going to get such a good situation out of it? A poor girl who's gotten herself in trouble should be glad to. Besides, that worthless man didn't do a single thing for me.

Nora: But I suppose your daughter has completely forgotten you.

Nursemaid: No, she hasn't, not at all. She wrote to me when she was confirmed, and again when she got married.

Nora (putting her arms round her neck): Dear old Anne Marie, you were such a good mother to me when I was little.

Nursemaid: Poor little Nora, you had no other mother but me.

Nora: And if my little ones had no other mother, I'm sure that you would— What nonsense I'm talking! (*Opens the box.*) Go in and see to them. Now I have to . . . You'll see how lovely I'll look tomorrow.

Nursemaid: I'm sure there'll be no one at the ball as lovely as you, Miss Nora.

(*Goes into the room on the left.*)

Nora (begins to unpack the box, but soon pushes it away from her): If only I dared to go out. If only no one would come. If only I could be sure nothing would happen here in the meantime. What nonsense! No one's going to come. I just have to stop thinking about it. This muff needs to be brushed. What beautiful, beautiful gloves! Stop thinking about it, stop thinking about it! One, two, three, four, five, six— (*Screams.*) Aaah! Somebody is coming— (*Makes a movement towards the door, but stands in hesitation.*)

(*Enter Mrs. Linde from the hall, where she has taken off her coat and hat.*)

Nora: Oh, it's you, Kristine. There's no one else out in the hall, is there? How good of you to come!

Mrs. Linde: I heard you came by asking for me.

Nora: Yes, I was passing by. As a matter of fact, it's something you could help me with. Let's sit down here on the sofa. Listen, tomorrow evening there's going to be a fancy-dress ball at the Stenborgs'—they live upstairs from us—and Torvald wants me to go as a Neapolitan fisher-girl and dance the tarantella. I learned it when we were at Capri.

Mrs. Linde: I see. You're going to give them the whole show.

Nora: Yes, Torvald wants me to. Look, here's the dress. Torvald had it made for me there, but now it's all so torn, and I don't have any idea—

Mrs. Linde: We can easily fix that. Some of the trim has just come loose here and there. Do you have a needle and thread? That's all we need.

Nora: This is so nice of you.

Mrs. Linde (*sewing*): So you're going to be dressed up tomorrow, Nora. I'll tell you what. I'll stop by for a moment so I can see you in your finery. Oh, meanwhile I've completely forgotten to thank you for a delightful evening last night.

Nora (*gets up, and crosses the stage*): Well, I didn't think last night was as pleasant as usual. You should have come to town a little earlier, Kristine. Torvald really knows how to make a home pleasant and attractive.

Mrs. Linde: And so do you, if you ask me. You're not your father's daughter for nothing. But tell me, is Doctor Rank always as depressed as he was yesterday?

Nora: No, yesterday it was especially noticeable. But you have to understand that he has a very serious disease. He has tuberculosis of the spine, poor creature. His father was a horrible man who always had mistresses, and that's why his son has been sickly since childhood, if you know what I mean.

Mrs. Linde (*dropping her sewing*): But, my dear Nora, how do you know anything about such things?

Nora (*walking around the room*): Pooh! When you have three children, you get visits now and then from—from married women, who know something about medical matters, and they talk about one thing and another.

Mrs. Linde (*goes on sewing. A short silence*): Does Doctor Rank come here every day?

Nora: Every day, like clockwork. He's Torvald's best friend, and a great friend of mine too. He's just like one of the family.

Mrs. Linde: But tell me, is he really sincere? I mean, isn't he the kind of man who tends to play up to people?

Nora: No, not at all. What makes you think that?

Mrs. Linde: When you introduced him to me yesterday, he told me he'd often heard my name mentioned in this house, but later I could see that your husband didn't have the slightest idea who I was. So how could Doctor Rank—?

Nora: That's true, Kristine. Torvald is so ridiculously fond of me that he wants me completely to himself, as he says. At first he used to seem almost jealous if I even mentioned any of my friends back home, so naturally I stopped talking about them to him. But I often talk about things like that with Doctor Rank, because he likes hearing about them.

Mrs. Linde: Listen to me, Nora. You're still like a child in a lot of ways, and I'm older than you and more experienced. So pay attention. You'd better stop all this with Doctor Rank.

Nora: Stop all what?

Mrs. Linde: Two things, I think. Yesterday you talked some nonsense about a rich admirer who was going to leave you his money—

Nora: An admirer who doesn't exist, unfortunately! But so what?

Mrs. Linde: Is Doctor Rank a wealthy man?

Nora: Yes, he is.

Mrs. Linde: And he has no dependents?

Nora: No, no one. But—

Mrs. Linde: And he comes here every day?

Nora: Yes, I told you he does.

Mrs. Linde: But how can such a well-bred man be so tactless?

Nora: I don't understand what you mean.

Mrs. Linde: Don't try to play dumb, Nora. Do you think I didn't guess who lent you the four thousand, eight hundred kroner?

Nora: Are you out of your mind? How can you even think that? A friend of ours, who comes here every day! Don't you realize what an incredibly awkward position that would put me in?

Mrs. Linde: Then he's really not the one?

Nora: Absolutely not. It would never have come into my head for one second. Besides, he had nothing to lend back then. He inherited his money later on.

Mrs. Linde: Well, I think that was lucky for you, my dear Nora.

Nora: No, it would never have crossed my mind to ask Doctor Rank. Although I'm sure that if I had asked him—

Mrs. Linde: But of course you won't.

Nora: Of course not. I have no reason to think I could possibly need to. But I'm absolutely certain that if I told Doctor Rank—

Mrs. Linde: Behind your husband's back?

Nora: I have to finish up with the other one, and that'll be behind his back too. I've got to wash my hands of him.

Mrs. Linde: Yes, that's what I told you yesterday, but—

Nora (walking up and down): A man can take care of these things so much more easily than a woman.

Mrs. Linde: If he's your husband, yes.

Nora: Nonsense! (*Standing still.*) When you pay off a debt you get your note back, don't you?

Mrs. Linde: Yes, of course.

Nora: And you can tear it into a hundred thousand pieces and burn up the filthy, nasty piece of paper!

Mrs. Linde (*stares at her, puts down her sewing and gets up slowly*): Nora, you're hiding something from me.

Nora: You can tell by looking at me?

Mrs. Linde: Something's happened to you since yesterday morning. Nora, what is it?

Nora (*going nearer to her*): Kristine! (*Listens.*) Shh! I hear Torvald. He's come home. Would you mind going in to the children's room for a little while? Torvald can't stand to see all this sewing going on. You can get Anne Marie to help you.

Mrs. Linde (*gathering some of the things together*): All right, but I'm not leaving this house until we've talked this thing through.

(*She goes into the room on the left, as Helmer comes in from the hall.*)

Nora (*going up to Helmer*): I've missed you so much, Torvald dear.

Helmer: Was that the seamstress?

Nora: No, it was Kristine. She's helping me fix up my dress. You'll see how nice I'm going to look.

Helmer: Wasn't that a good idea of mine, now?

Nora: Wonderful! But don't you think it's nice of me, too, to do what you said?

Helmer: Nice, because you do what your husband tells you to? Go on, you silly little thing, I am sure you didn't mean it like that. But I'll stay out of your way. I imagine you'll be trying on your dress.

Nora: I suppose you're going to do some work.

Helmer: Yes. (*Shows her a stack of papers.*) Look at that. I've just been at the bank. (*Turns to go into his room.*)

Nora: Torvald.

Helmer: Yes?

Nora: If your little squirrel were to ask you for something in a very, very charming way——

Helmer: Well?

Nora: Would you do it?

Helmer: I'd have to know what it is, first.

Nora: Your squirrel would run around and do all her tricks if you would be really nice and do what she wants.

Helmer: Speak plainly.

Nora: Your skylark would chirp her beautiful song in every room—

Helmer: Well, my skylark does that anyhow.

Nora: I'd be a little elf and dance in the moonlight for you, Torvald.

Helmer: Nora, you can't be referring to what you talked about this morning.

Nora (moving close to him): Yes, Torvald, I'm really begging you—

Helmer: You really have the nerve to bring that up again?

Nora: Yes, dear, you have to do this for me. You have to let Krogstad keep his job in the bank.

Helmer: My dear Nora, his job is the one that I'm giving to Mrs. Linde.

Nora: Yes, you've been awfully sweet about that. But you could just as easily get rid of somebody else instead of Krogstad.

Helmer: This is just unbelievable stubbornness! Because you decided to foolishly promise that you'd speak up for him, you expect me to—

Nora: That's not the reason, Torvald. It's for your own sake. This man writes for the trashiest newspapers, you've told me so yourself. He can do you an incredible amount of harm. I'm scared to death of him—

Helmer: Oh, I see, it's bad memories that are making you afraid.

Nora: What do you mean?

Helmer: Obviously you're thinking about your father.

Nora: Yes. Yes, of course. You remember what those hateful creatures wrote in the papers about Papa, and how horribly they slandered him. I believe they'd have gotten him fired if the department hadn't sent you over to look into it, and if you hadn't been so kind and helpful to him.

Helmer: My little Nora, there's an important difference between your father and me. His reputation as a public official was not above suspicion. Mine is, and I hope it will continue to be for as long as I hold my office.

Nora: You never can tell what trouble these men might cause. We could be so well off, so snug and happy here in our peaceful home, without a care in the world, you and I and the children, Torvald! That's why I'm begging you to—

Helmer: And the more you plead for him, the more you make it impossible for me to keep him. They already know at the bank that I'm going to fire Krogstad. Do you think I'm going to let them all say that the new manager has changed his mind because his wife said to—

Nora: And what if they did?

Helmer: Right! What does it matter, as long as this stubborn little creature gets her own way! Do you think I'm going to make myself look ridiculous in front of my whole staff, and let people think that I can be pushed around by all sorts of outside influence? That would soon come back to haunt me, you can be sure! And besides, there's one thing that makes it totally impossible for me to have Krogstad working in the bank as long as I'm the manager.

Nora: What's that?

Helmer: I might have been able to overlook his moral failings, if need be—

Nora: Yes, you could do that, couldn't you?

Helmer: And I hear he's a good worker, too. But I knew him when we were boys. It was one of those rash friendships that so often turn out to be a millstone around the neck later on. I might as well tell you straight out, we were very close friends at one time. But he has no tact and no self-restraint, especially when other people are around. He thinks he has the right to still call me by my first name, and every minute it's Torvald this and Torvald that. I don't mind telling you, I find it extremely annoying. He would make my position at the bank intolerable.

Nora: Torvald, I can't believe you're serious.

Helmer: Oh no? Why not?

Nora: Because it's so petty.

Helmer: What do you mean, petty? You think I'm petty?

Nora: No, just the opposite, dear, and that's why I can't—

Helmer: It's the same thing. You say my attitude's petty, so I must be petty too! Petty! Fine! Well, I'll put a stop to this once and for all. (*Goes to the hall door and calls.*) Helene!

Nora: What are you going to do?

Helmer (*looking among his papers*): Settle it.

(*Enter Maid.*)

Here, take this letter downstairs right now. Find a messenger and tell him to deliver it, and to be quick about it. The address is on it, and here's the money.

Maid: Yes, sir. (*Exits with the letter.*)

Helmer (*putting his papers together*): There, Little Pigheaded Miss.

Nora (*breathlessly*): Torvald, what was that letter?

Helmer: Krogstad's notice.

Nora: Call her back, Torvald! There's still time. Oh, Torvald, call her back! Do it for my sake—for your own sake—for the children's sake! Do you hear me, Torvald? Call her back! You don't know what that letter can do to us.

Helmer: It's too late.

Nora: Yes, it's too late.

Helmer: My dear Nora, I can forgive this anxiety of yours, even though it's insulting to me. It really is. Don't you think it's insulting to suggest that I should be afraid of retaliation from a grubby pen-pusher? But I forgive you anyway, because it's such a beautiful demonstration of how much you love me. (*Takes her in his arms.*) And that is as it should be, my own darling Nora. Come what may, you can rest assured that I'll have both courage and strength if necessary. You'll see that I'm man enough to take everything on myself.

Nora (*in a horror-stricken voice*): What do you mean by that?

Helmer: Everything, I say.

Nora (*recovering herself*): You'll never have to do that.

Helmer: That's right, we'll take it on together, Nora, as man and wife. That's just how it should be. (*Caressing her.*) Are you satisfied now? There, there! Don't look at me that way, like a frightened dove! This whole thing is just your imagination running away with you. Now you should go and run through the tarantella and practice your tambourine. I'll go into my study and shut the door so I can't hear anything. You can make all the noise you want. (*Turns back at the door.*) And when Rank comes, tell him where I am.

(*Nods to her, takes his papers and goes into his room, and shuts the door behind him.*)

Nora (*bewildered with anxiety, stands as if rooted to the spot and whispers*): He's capable of doing it. He's going to do it. He'll do it in spite of everything. No, not that! Never, never! Anything but that! Oh, for somebody to help me find some way out of this! (*The doorbell rings.*) Doctor Rank! Anything but that—anything, whatever it is!

(*She puts her hands over her face, pulls herself together, goes to the door and opens it. Rank is standing in the hall, hanging up his coat. During the following dialogue it starts to grow dark.*)

Nora: Hello, Doctor Rank. I recognized your ring. But you'd better not go in and see Torvald just now. I think he's busy with something.

Rank: And you?

Nora (*brings him in and shuts the door behind him*): Oh, you know perfectly well I always have time for you.

Rank: Thank you. I'll make use of it for as long as I can.

Nora: What does that mean, for as long as you can?

Rank: Why, does that frighten you?

Nora: It was such a strange way of putting it. Is something going to happen?

Rank: Nothing but what I've been expecting for a long time. But I never thought it would happen so soon.

Nora (*gripping him by the arm*): What have you found out? Doctor Rank, you must tell me.

Rank (*sitting down by the stove*): I'm done for. And there's nothing I can do about it.

Nora (*with a sigh of relief*): Oh—you're talking about yourself?

Rank: Who else? And there's no use lying to myself. I'm the sickest patient I have, Mrs. Helmer. Lately I've been adding up my internal account. Bankrupt! In a month I'll probably be rotting in the ground.

Nora: What a horrible thing to say!

Rank: The thing itself is horrible, and the worst of it is all the horrible things I'll have to go through before it's over. I'm going to examine myself just once more. When that's done, I'll be pretty sure when I'm going to start breaking down. There's something I want to say to you. Helmer's sensitive nature makes him completely unable to deal with anything ugly. I don't want him in my sickroom.

Nora: Oh, but, Doctor Rank—

Rank: I won't have him there, period. I'll lock the door to keep him out. As soon as I'm quite sure that the worst has come, I'll send you my card with a black cross on it, and that way you'll know that the final stage of the horror has started.

Nora: You're being really absurd today. And I so much wanted you to be in a good mood.

Rank: With death stalking me? Having to pay this price for another man's sins? Where's the justice in that? In every single family, in one way or another, some such unavoidable retribution is being imposed.

Nora (*putting her hands over her ears*): Nonsense! Can't you talk about something cheerful?

Rank: Oh, this *is* something cheerful. In fact, it's hilarious. My poor innocent spine has to suffer for my father's youthful self-indulgence.

Nora (*sitting at the table on the left*): Yes, he did love asparagus and *pâté de foie gras*, didn't he?

Rank: Yes, and truffles.

Nora: Truffles, yes. And oysters too, I suppose?

Rank: Oysters, of course. That goes without saying.

Nora: And oceans of port and champagne. Isn't it sad that all those delightful things should take their revenge on our bones?

Rank: Especially that they should take their revenge on the unlucky bones of people who haven't even had the satisfaction of enjoying them.

Nora: Yes, that's the saddest part of all.

Rank (*with a searching look at her*): Hm!

Nora (*after a short pause*): Why did you smile?

Rank: No, it was you who laughed.

Nora: No, it was you who smiled, Doctor Rank!

Rank (*rising*): You're even more of a tease than I thought you were.

Nora: I am in a crazy mood today.

Rank: Apparently so.

Nora (*putting her hands on his shoulders*): Dear, dear Doctor Rank, we can't let death take you away from Torvald and me.

Rank: It's a loss that you'll easily recover from. Those who are gone are soon forgotten.

Nora (*looking at him anxiously*): Do you really believe that?

Rank: People make new friends, and then—

Nora: Who'll make new friends?

Rank: Both you and Helmer, when I'm gone. You yourself are already well on the way to it, I think. What was that Mrs. Linde doing here last night?

Nora: Oho! You're not telling me that you're jealous of poor Kristine, are you?

Rank: Yes, I am. She'll be my successor in this house. When I'm six feet under, this woman will—

Nora: Shh! Don't talk so loud. She's in that room.

Rank: Again today. There, you see.

Nora: She's just come to sew my dress for me. Goodness, how unreasonable you are! (*Sits down on the sofa.*) Be nice now, Doctor Rank, and tomorrow you'll see how beautifully I'll dance, and you can pretend that I'm doing it just for you—and for Torvald too, of course. (*Takes various things out of the box.*) Doctor Rank, come and sit down here, and I'll show you something.

Rank (*sitting down*): What is it?

Nora: Just look at these!

Rank: Silk stockings.

Nora: Flesh-colored. Aren't they lovely? It's so dark here now, but tomorrow— No, no, no! You're only supposed to look at the feet. Oh well, you have my permission to look at the legs too.

Rank: Hm!

Nora: Why do you look so critical? Don't you think they'll fit me?

Rank: I have no basis for forming an opinion on that subject.

Nora (*looks at him for a moment*): Shame on you! (*Hits him lightly on the ear with the stockings.*) That's your punishment. (*Folds them up again.*)

Rank: And what other pretty things do I have your permission to look at?

Nora: Not one single thing. That's what you get for being so naughty. (*She looks among the things, humming to herself.*)

Rank (*after a short silence*): When I'm sitting here, talking to you so intimately this way, I can't imagine for a moment what would have become of me if I'd never come into this house.

Nora (*smiling*): I believe you really do feel completely at home with us.

Rank (*in a lower voice, looking straight in front of him*): And to have to leave it all—

Nora: Nonsense, you're not going to leave it.

Rank (*as before*): And not to be able to leave behind the slightest token of my gratitude, hardly even a fleeting regret. Nothing but an empty place to be filled by the first person who comes along.

Nora: And if I were to ask you now for a— No, never mind!

Rank: For a what?

Nora: For a great proof of your friendship—

Rank: Yes, yes!

Nora: I mean a tremendously huge favor—

Rank: Would you really make me so happy, just this once?

Nora: But you don't know what it is yet.

Rank: No, but tell me.

Nora: I really can't, Doctor Rank. It's too much to ask. It involves advice, and help, and a favor—

Rank: So much the better. I can't imagine what you mean. Tell me what it is. You do trust me, don't you?

Nora: More than anyone. I know that you're my best and truest friend, so I'll tell you what it is. Well, Doctor Rank, it's something you have to help me prevent. You know how devoted Torvald is to me, how deeply he loves me. He wouldn't hesitate for a second to give his life for me.

Rank (*leaning towards her*): Nora, do you think that he's the only one—

Nora (*with a slight start*): The only one?

Rank: Who would gladly give his life for you.

Nora (*sadly*): Oh, is that it?

Rank: I'd made up my mind to tell you before I—I go away, and there'll never be a better opportunity than this. Now you know it, Nora. And now you know that you can trust me more than you can trust anyone else.

Nora (*rises, deliberately and quietly*): Let me by.

Rank (*makes room for her to pass him, but sits still*): Nora!

Nora (*at the hall door*): Helene, bring in the lamp. (*Goes over to the stove.*) Dear Doctor Rank, that was really horrible of you.

Rank: To love you just as much as somebody else does? Is that so horrible?

Nora: No, but to go and tell me like that. There was really no need—

Rank: What do you mean? Did you know—

(*Maid enters with lamp, puts it down on the table, and goes out.*)

Nora—Mrs. Helmer—tell me, did you have any idea I felt this way?

Nora: Oh, how do I know whether I did or I didn't? I really can't answer that. How could you be so clumsy, Doctor Rank? When we were getting along so nicely.

Rank: Well, at any rate, now you know that I'm yours to command, body and soul. So won't you tell me what it is?

Nora (*looking at him*): After what just happened?

Rank: I beg you to let me know what it is.

Nora: I can't tell you anything now.

Rank: Yes, yes. Please don't punish me that way. Give me permission to do anything for you that a man can do.

Nora: You can't do anything for me now. Besides, I really don't need any help at all. The whole thing is just my imagination. It really is. It has to be! (*Sits down in the rocking chair, and smiles at him.*) You're a nice man, Doctor Rank. Don't you feel ashamed of yourself, now that the lamp is lit?

Rank: Not a bit. But maybe it would be better if I left—and never came back?

Nora: No, no, you can't do that. You must keep coming here just as you always did. You know very well Torvald can't do without you.

Rank: But what about you?

Nora: Oh, I'm always extremely pleased to see you.

Rank: And that's just what gave me the wrong idea. You're a puzzle to me. I've often felt that you'd almost just as soon be in my company as in Helmer's.

Nora: Yes, you see, there are the people you love the most, and then there are the people whose company you enjoy the most.

Rank: Yes, there's something to that.

Nora: When I lived at home, of course I loved Papa best. But I always thought it was great fun to sneak down to the maids' room, because they never preached at me, and I loved listening to the way they talked to each other.

Rank: I see. So I'm their replacement.

Nora (*jumping up and going to him*): Oh, dear, sweet Doctor Rank, I didn't mean it that way. But surely you can understand that being with Torvald is a little like being with Papa—

(*Enter Maid from the hall.*)

Maid: Excuse me, ma'am. (*Whispers and hands her a card.*)

Nora (*glancing at the card*): Oh! (*Puts it in her pocket.*)

Rank: Is something wrong?

Nora: No, no, not at all. It's just—it's my new dress—

Rank: What? Your dress is lying right there.

Nora: Oh, yes, that one. But this is another one, one that I ordered. I don't want Torvald to find out about it—

Rank: Oh! So that was the big secret.

Nora: Yes, that's it. Why don't you just go inside and see him? He's in his study. Stay with him for as long as—

Rank: Put your mind at ease. I won't let him escape. (*Goes into Helmer's study.*)

Nora (to the maid): And he's waiting in the kitchen?

Maid: Yes, ma'am. He came up the back stairs.

Nora: Didn't you tell him no one was home?

Maid: Yes, but it didn't do any good.

Nora: He won't go away?

Maid: No, he says he won't leave until he sees you, ma'am.

Nora: Well, show him in, but quietly. Helene, I don't want you to say anything about this to anyone. It's a surprise for my husband.

Maid: Yes, ma'am. I understand. (*Exit.*)

Nora: This horrible thing is really going to happen! It's going to happen in spite of me! No, no, no, it can't happen! I can't let it happen!

(*She bolts the door of Helmer's study. The maid opens the hall door for Krogstad and closes it behind him. He is wearing a fur coat, high boots, and a fur cap.*)

Nora (advancing towards him): Speak quietly. My husband's home.

Krogstad: What do I care about that?

Nora: What do you want from me?

Krogstad: An explanation of something.

Nora: Be quick, then. What is it?

Krogstad: I suppose you're aware that I've been let go.

Nora: I couldn't prevent it, Mr. Krogstad. I fought for you as hard as I could, but it was no use.

Krogstad: Does your husband love you so little, then? He knows what I can expose you to, and he still goes ahead and—

Nora: How can you think that he knows any such thing?

Krogstad: I didn't think so for a moment. It wouldn't be at all like dear old Torvald Helmer to show that kind of courage—

Nora: Mr. Krogstad, a little respect for my husband, please.

Krogstad: Certainly—all the respect he deserves. But since you've kept everything so carefully to yourself, may I be bold enough to assume that you see a little more clearly than you did yesterday just what it is that you've done?

Nora: More than you could ever teach me.

Krogstad: Yes, such a poor excuse for a lawyer as I am.

Nora: What is it you want from me?

Krogstad: Only to see how you're doing, Mrs. Helmer. I've been thinking about you all day. A mere bill collector, a pen-pusher, a—well, a man like me—even he has a little of what people call feelings, you know.

Nora: Why don't you show some, then? Think about my little children.

Krogstad: Have you and your husband thought about mine? But never mind about that. I just wanted to tell you not to take this business too seriously. I won't make any accusations against you. Not for now, anyway.

Nora: No, of course not. I was sure you wouldn't.

Krogstad: The whole thing can be settled amicably. There's no need for anyone to know anything about it. It'll be our little secret, just the three of us.

Nora: My husband must never know anything about it.

Krogstad: How are you going to keep him from finding out? Are you telling me that you can pay off the whole balance?

Nora: No, not just yet.

Krogstad: Or that you have some other way of raising the money soon?

Nora: No way that I plan to make use of.

Krogstad: Well, in any case, it wouldn't be any use to you now even if you did. If you stood in front of me with a stack of bills in each hand, I still wouldn't give you back your note.

Nora: What are you planning to do with it?

Krogstad: I just want to hold onto it, just keep it in my possession. No one who isn't involved in the matter will ever know anything about it. So, if you've been thinking about doing something desperate—

Nora: I have.

Krogstad: If you've been thinking about running away—

Nora: I have.

Krogstad: Or doing something even worse—

Nora: How could you know that?

Krogstad: Stop thinking about it.

Nora: How did you know I'd thought of that?

Krogstad: Most of us think about that at first. I did, too. But I didn't have the courage.

Nora (faintly): Neither do I.

Krogstad (in a tone of relief): No, that's true, isn't it? You don't have the courage either?

Nora: No, I don't. I don't.

Krogstad: Besides, it would have been an incredibly stupid thing to do. Once the first storm at home blows over . . . I have a letter for your husband in my pocket.

Nora: Telling him everything?

Krogstad: As gently as possible.

Nora (quickly): He can't see that letter. Tear it up. I'll find some way of getting money.

Krogstad: Excuse me, Mrs. Helmer, but didn't I just tell you—

Nora: I'm not talking about what I owe you. Tell me how much you want from my husband, and I'll get the money.

Krogstad: I don't want any money from your husband.

Nora: Then what do you want?

Krogstad: I'll tell you what I want. I want a fresh start, Mrs. Helmer, and I want to move up in the world. And your husband's going to help me do it. I've steered clear of anything questionable for the last year and a half. In all that time I've been struggling along, pinching every penny. I was content to work my way up step by step. But now I've been fired, and it's not going to be enough just to get my job back, as if you people were doing me some huge favor. I want to move up, I tell you. I want to get back into the bank again, but with a promotion. Your husband's going to have find me a position—

Nora: He'll never do it!

Krogstad: Oh yes, he will. I know him. He won't dare object. And as soon as I'm back there with him, then you'll see! Inside of a year I'll be the manager's right-hand man. It'll be Nils Krogstad, not Torvald Helmer, who's running the bank.

Nora: That's never going to happen!

Krogstad: Do you mean that you'll—

Nora: I have enough courage for it now.

Krogstad: Oh, you can't scare me. An elegant, spoiled lady like you—

Nora: You'll see, you'll see.

Krogstad: Under the ice, maybe? Down in the cold, coal-black water? And then floating up to the surface in the spring, all horrible and unrecognizable, with your hair fallen out—

Nora: You can't scare me.

Krogstad: And you can't scare me. People don't do that kind of thing, Mrs. Helmer. Besides, what good would it do? I'd still have him completely in my power.

Nora: Even then? When I'm no longer—

Krogstad: Have you forgotten that your reputation is completely in my hands? (*Nora stands speechless, looking at him.*) Well, now I've warned you. Don't do anything foolish. I'll be expecting an answer from Helmer after he reads my letter. And remember, it's your husband himself who's forced me to act this way again. I'll never forgive him for that. Goodbye, Mrs. Helmer. (*Exits through the hall.*)

Nora (*goes to the hall door, opens it slightly and listens.*): He's leaving. He isn't putting the letter in the box. Oh no, no! He couldn't! (*Opens the door little by little.*) What? He's standing out there. He's not going downstairs. He's hesitating? Is he?

(*A letter drops into the box. Then Krogstad's footsteps are heard, until they die away as he goes downstairs. Nora utters a stifled cry, and runs across the room to the table by the sofa. A short pause.*)

Nora: In the mailbox. (*Steals across to the hall door.*) It's there! Torvald, Torvald, there's no hope for us now!

(*Mrs. Linde comes in from the room on the left, carrying the dress.*)

Mrs. Linde: There, I can't find anything more to mend. Would you like to try it on?

Nora (*in a hoarse whisper*): Kristine, come here.

Mrs. Linde (*throwing the dress down on the sofa*): What's the matter with you? You look so agitated!

Nora: Come here. Do you see that letter? There, look. You can see it through the glass in the mailbox.

Mrs. Linde: Yes, I see it.

Nora: That letter is from Krogstad.

Mrs. Linde: Nora! It was Krogstad who lent you the money!

Nora: Yes, and now Torvald will know all about it.

Mrs. Linde: Believe me, Nora, that's the best thing for both of you.

Nora: You don't know the whole story. I forged a name.

Mrs. Linde: My God!

Nora: There's something I want to say to you, Kristine. I need you to be my witness.

Mrs. Linde: Your witness? What do you mean? What am I supposed to—

Nora: If I should go out of my mind—and it could easily happen—

Mrs. Linde: Nora!

Nora: Or if anything else should happen to me—anything, for instance, that might keep me from being here—

Mrs. Linde: Nora! Nora! What's the matter with you?

Nora: And if it turned out that somebody wanted to take all the responsibility, all the blame, you understand what I mean—

Mrs. Linde: Yes, yes, but how can you imagine—

Nora: Then you must be my witness that it's not true, Kristine. I'm not out of my mind at all. I'm perfectly rational right now, and I'm telling you that no one else ever knew anything about it. I did the whole thing all by myself. Remember that.

Mrs. Linde: I will. But I don't understand all this.

Nora: How could you understand it? Or the miracle that's going to happen!

Mrs. Linde: A miracle?

Nora: Yes, a miracle! But it's so terrible, Kristine. I can't let it happen, not for the whole world.

Mrs. Linde: I'll go and see Krogstad right this minute.

Nora: No, don't. He'll do something to hurt you too.

Mrs. Linde: There was a time when he would have gladly done anything for my sake.

Nora: What?

Mrs. Linde: Where does he live?

Nora: How should I know? Yes (*feeling in her pocket*), here's his card. But the letter, the letter—

Helmer (*calls from his room, knocking at the door*): Nora!

Nora (*cries out anxiously*): What is it? What do you want?

Helmer: Don't be so afraid. We're not coming in. You've locked the door. Are you trying on your dress?

Nora: Yes, that's it. Oh, it's going to look so nice, Torvald.

Mrs. Linde (*who has read the card*): Look, he lives right around the corner.

Nora: But it's no use. It's all over. The letter's lying right there in the box.

Mrs. Linde: And your husband has the key?

Nora: Yes, always.

Mrs. Linde: Krogstad can ask for his letter back unread. He'll have to make up some reason—

Nora: But now is just about the time that Torvald usually—

Mrs. Linde: You have to prevent him. Go in and talk to him. I'll be back as soon as I can.

(*She hurries out through the hall door.*)

Nora (*goes to Helmer's door, opens it and peeps in*): Torvald!

Helmer (*from the inner room*): Well? May I finally come back into my own room? Come along, Rank, now you'll see— (*Stopping in the doorway.*) But what's this?

Nora: What's what, dear?

Helmer: Rank led me to expect an amazing transformation.

Rank (*in the doorway*): So I understood, but apparently I was mistaken.

Nora: Yes, nobody gets to admire me in my dress until tomorrow.

Helmer: But, my dear Nora, you look exhausted. Have you been practicing too much?

Nora: No, I haven't been practicing at all.

Helmer: But you'll have to—

Nora: Yes, of course I will, Torvald. But I can't get anywhere without you helping me. I've completely forgotten the whole thing.

Helmer: Oh, we'll soon get you back up to form again.

Nora: Yes, help me, Torvald. Promise that you will! I'm so nervous about it—all those people. I need you to devote yourself completely to me this evening. Not even the tiniest little bit of business. You can't even pick up a pen. Do you promise, Torvald dear?

Helmer: I promise. This evening I will be wholly and absolutely at your service, you helpless little creature. But first I'm just going to— (*Goes towards the hall door.*)

Nora: Just going to what?

Helmer: To see if there's any mail.

Nora: No, no! Don't do that, Torvald!

Helmer: Why not?

Nora: Torvald, please don't. There's nothing there.

Helmer: Well, let me look. (*Turns to go to the mailbox. Nora, at the piano, plays the first bars of the tarantella. Helmer stops in the doorway.*) Aha!

Nora: I can't dance tomorrow if I don't practice with you.

Helmer (*going up to her*): Are you really so worried about it, dear?

Nora: Yes, terribly worried about it. Let me practice right now. We have time before dinner. Sit down and play for me, Torvald dear. Criticize me and correct me, the way you always do.

Helmer: With great pleasure, if you want me to. (*Sits down at the piano.*)

Nora (*takes a tambourine and a long multicolored shawl out of the box. She hastily drapes the shawl around her. Then she bounds to the front of the stage and calls out*): Now play for me! I'm going to dance!

(*Helmer plays and Nora dances. Rank stands by the piano behind Helmer and watches.*)

Helmer (*as he plays*): Slower, slower!

Nora: I can't do it any other way.

Helmer: Not so violently, Nora!

Nora: This is the way.

Helmer (*stops playing*): No, no, that's not right at all.

Nora (*laughing and swinging the tambourine*): Didn't I tell you so?

Rank: Let me play for her.

Helmer (*getting up*): Good idea. I can correct her better that way.

(*Rank sits down at the piano and plays. Nora dances more and more wildly. Helmer has taken up a position beside the stove, and as she dances, he gives her frequent instructions. She doesn't seem to hear him. Her hair comes undone and falls over her shoulders. She pays no attention to it, but goes on dancing. Enter Mrs. Linde.*)

Mrs. Linde (*standing as if spellbound in the doorway*): Oh!

Nora (*as she dances*): What fun, Kristine!

Helmer: My dear darling Nora, you're dancing as if your life depended on it.

Nora: It does.

Helmer: Stop, Rank. This is insane! I said stop!

(*Rank stops playing, and Nora suddenly stands still. Helmer goes up to her.*)

I never would have believed it. You've forgotten everything I taught you.

Nora (*throwing the tambourine aside*): There, you see.

Helmer: You're going to need a lot of coaching.

Nora: Yes, you see how much I need it. You have to coach me right up to the last minute. Promise me you will, Torvald!

Helmer: You can depend on me.

Nora: You can't think about anything but me, today or tomorrow. Don't open a single letter. Don't even open the mailbox—

Helmer: You're still afraid of that man—

Nora: Yes, yes, I am.

Helmer: Nora, I can tell from your face that there's a letter from him in the box.

Nora: I don't know. I think there is. But you can't read anything like that now. Nothing nasty must come between us until this is all over.

Rank (*whispers to Helmer*): Don't contradict her.

Helmer (*taking her in his arms*): The child shall have her way. But tomorrow night, after you've danced—

Nora: Then you'll be free. (*The Maid appears in the doorway to the right.*)

Maid: Dinner is served, ma'am.

Nora: We'll have champagne, Helene.

Maid: Yes, ma'am. (*Exit.*)

Helmer: Oh, are we having a banquet?

Nora: Yes, a banquet. Champagne till dawn! (*Calls out.*) And a few macaroons, Helene. Lots of them, just this once!

Helmer: Come on, stop acting so wild and nervous. Be my own little skylark again.

Nora: Yes, dear, I will. But go inside now, and you too, Doctor Rank. Kristine, please help me do up my hair.

Rank (*whispers to Helmer as they go out*): There isn't anything—she's not expecting—?

Helmer: No, nothing like that. It's just this childish nervousness I was telling you about. (*They go into the right-hand room.*)

Nora: Well?

Mrs. Linde: Out of town.

Nora: I could tell from your face.

Mrs. Linde: He'll be back tomorrow evening. I wrote him a note.

Nora: You should have left it alone. Don't try to prevent anything. After all, it's exciting to be waiting for a miracle to happen.

Mrs. Linde: What is it that you're waiting for?

Nora: Oh, you wouldn't understand. Go inside with them, I'll be there in a moment.

(Mrs. Linde goes into the dining room. Nora stands still for a little while, as if to compose herself. Then she looks at her watch.)

Five o'clock. Seven hours till midnight, and another twenty-four hours till the next midnight. And then the tarantella will be over. Twenty-four plus seven? Thirty-one hours to live.

Helmer (from the doorway on the right): Where's my little skylark?

Nora (going to him with her arms outstretched): Here she is!

ACT III

The same scene. The table has been placed in the middle of the stage, with chairs around it. A lamp is burning on the table. The door into the hall stands open. Dance music is heard in the room above. Mrs. Linde is sitting at the table idly turning over the pages of a book. She tries to read, but she seems unable to concentrate. Every now and then she listens intently for a sound at the outer door.

Mrs. Linde (looking at her watch): Not yet—and the time's nearly up. If only he doesn't— *(Listens again.)* Ah, there he is. *(Goes into the hall and opens the outer door carefully. Light footsteps are heard on the stairs. She whispers.)* Come in. There's no one else here.

Krogstad (in the doorway): I found a note from you at home. What does this mean?

Mrs. Linde: It's absolutely necessary that I have a talk with you.

Krogstad: Really? And is it absolutely necessary that we have it here?

Mrs. Linde: It's impossible where I live. There's no private entrance to my apartment. Come in. We're all alone. The maid's asleep, and the Helmers are upstairs at a dance.

Krogstad (coming into the room): Are the Helmers really at a dance tonight?

Mrs. Linde: Yes. Why shouldn't they be?

Krogstad: Certainly—why not?

Mrs. Linde: Now, Nils, let's have a talk.

Krogstad: What can we two have to talk about?

Mrs. Linde: Quite a lot.

Krogstad: I wouldn't have thought so.

Mrs. Linde: Of course not. You've never really understood me.

Krogstad: What was there to understand, except what the whole world could see—a heartless woman drops a man when a better catch comes along?

Mrs. Linde: Do you think I'm really that heartless? And that I broke it off with you so lightly?

Krogstad: Didn't you?

Mrs. Linde: Nils, did you really think that?

Krogstad: If not, why did you write what you did to me?

Mrs. Linde: What else could I do? Since I had to break it off with you, I had an obligation to stamp out your feelings for me.

Krogstad (*wringing his hands*): So that was it. And all this just for the sake of money!

Mrs. Linde: Don't forget that I had an invalid mother and two little brothers. We couldn't wait for you, Nils. Success seemed a long way off for you back then.

Krogstad: That may be so, but you had no right to cast me aside for anyone else's sake.

Mrs. Linde: I don't know if I did or not. Many times I've asked myself if I had the right.

Krogstad (*more gently*): When I lost you, it was as if the earth crumbled under my feet. Look at me now—a shipwrecked man clinging to a bit of wreckage.

Mrs. Linde: But help may be on the way.

Krogstad: It *was* on the way, till you came along and blocked it.

Mrs. Linde: Without knowing it, Nils. It wasn't till today that I found out I'd be taking your job.

Krogstad: I believe you, if you say so. But now that you know it, are you going to step aside?

Mrs. Linde: No, because it wouldn't do you any good.

Krogstad: Good? *I* would quit whether it did any good or not.

Mrs. Linde: I've learned to be practical. Life and hard, bitter necessity have taught me that.

Krogstad: And life has taught me not to believe in fine speeches.

Mrs. Linde: Then life has taught you something very sensible. But surely you believe in actions?

Krogstad: What do you mean by that?

Mrs. Linde: You said you were like a shipwrecked man clinging to a piece of wreckage.

Krogstad: I had good reason to say so.

Mrs. Linde: Well, I'm like a shipwrecked woman clinging to a piece of wreckage, with no one to mourn for and no one to care for.

Krogstad: That was your own choice.

Mrs. Linde: I had no other choice—then.

Krogstad: Well, what about now?

Mrs. Linde: Nils, how would it be if we two shipwrecked people could reach out to each other?

Krogstad: What are you saying?

Mrs. Linde: Two people on the same piece of wreckage would stand a better chance than each one on their own.

Krogstad: Kristine, I . . .

Mrs. Linde: Why do you think I came to town?

Krogstad: You can't mean that you were thinking about me?

Mrs. Linde: Life is unendurable without work. I've worked all my life, for as long as I can remember, and it's been my greatest and my only pleasure. But now that I'm completely alone in the world, my life is so terribly empty and I feel so abandoned. There isn't the slightest pleasure in working only for yourself. Nils, give me someone and something to work for.

Krogstad: I don't trust this. It's just some romantic female impulse, a high-minded urge for self-sacrifice.

Mrs. Linde: Have you ever known me to be like that?

Krogstad: Could you really do it? Tell me, do you know all about my past?

Mrs. Linde: Yes.

Krogstad: And you know what they think of me around here?

Mrs. Linde: Didn't you imply that with me you might have been a very different person?

Krogstad: I'm sure I would have.

Mrs. Linde: Is it too late now?

Krogstad: Kristine, are you serious about all this? Yes, I'm sure you are. I can see it in your face. Do you really have the courage, then—

Mrs. Linde: I want to be a mother to someone, and your children need a mother. We two need each other. Nils, I have faith in your true nature. I can face anything together with you.

Krogstad (grasps her hands): Thank you, thank you, Kristine! Now I can find a way to clear myself in the eyes of the world. Ah, but I forgot—

Mrs. Linde (listening): Shh! The tarantella! You have to go!

Krogstad: Why? What's the matter?

Mrs. Linde: Do you hear them up there? They'll probably come home as soon as this dance is over.

Krogstad: Yes, yes, I'll go. But it won't make any difference. You don't know what I've done about my situation with the Helmers.

Mrs. Linde: Yes, I know all about that.

Krogstad: And in spite of that you still have the courage to—

Mrs. Linde: I understand completely what despair can drive a man like you to do.

Krogstad: If only I could undo it!

Mrs. Linde: You can't. Your letter's lying in the mailbox now.

Krogstad: Are you sure?

Mrs. Linde: Quite sure, but—

Krogstad (with a searching look at her): Is that what this is all about? That you want to save your friend, no matter what you have to do? Tell me the truth. Is that it?

Mrs. Linde: Nils, when a woman has sold herself for someone else's sake, she doesn't do it a second time.

Krogstad: I'll ask for my letter back.

Mrs. Linde: No, no.

Krogstad: Yes, of course I will. I'll wait here until Helmer comes home. I'll tell him he has to give me back my letter, that it's only about my being fired, that I don't want him to read it—

Mrs. Linde: No, Nils, don't ask for it back.

Krogstad: But wasn't that the reason why you asked me to meet you here?

Mrs. Linde: In my first moment of panic, it was. But twenty-four hours have gone by since then, and in the meantime I've seen some incredible things in this house. Helmer has to know all about it. This terrible secret has to come out. They have to have a complete understanding between them. It's time for all this lying and pretending to stop.

Krogstad: All right then, if you think it's worth the risk. But there's at least one thing I can do, and do right away—

Mrs. Linde (listening): You have to leave this instant! The dance is over. They could walk in here any minute.

Krogstad: I'll wait for you downstairs.

Mrs. Linde: Yes, please do. I want you to walk me home.

Krogstad: I've never been so happy in my entire life!

(*Goes out through the outer door. The door between the room and the hall remains open.*)

Mrs. Linde (straightening up the room and getting her hat and coat ready): How different things will be! Someone to work for and live for, a home to bring happiness into. I'm certainly going to try. I wish they'd hurry up and come home—(*Listens.*) Ah, here they are now. I'd better put on my things.

(*Picks up her hat and coat. Helmer's and Nora's voices are heard outside. A key is turned, and Helmer brings Nora into the hall almost by force. She is in an Italian peasant costume with a large black shawl wrapped around her. He is in formal wear and a black domino—a hooded cloak with an eye-mask—which is open.*)

Nora (*hanging back in the doorway and struggling with him*): No, no, no! Don't bring me inside. I want to go back upstairs. I don't want to leave so early.

Helmer: But, my dearest Nora—

Nora: Please, Torvald dear, please, please, only one more hour.

Helmer: Not one more minute, my sweet Nora. You know this is what we agreed on. Come inside. You'll catch cold standing out there.

(*He brings her gently into the room, in spite of her resistance.*)

Mrs. Linde: Good evening.

Nora: Kristine!

Helmer: What are you doing here so late, Mrs. Linde?

Mrs. Linde: You must excuse me. I was so anxious to see Nora in her dress.

Nora: Have you been sitting here waiting for me?

Mrs. Linde: Yes, unfortunately I came too late, you'd already gone upstairs. And I didn't want to go away again without seeing you.

Helmer (*taking off Nora's shawl*): Yes, take a good look at her. I think she's worth looking at. Isn't she charming, Mrs. Linde?

Mrs. Linde: Yes, indeed she is.

Helmer: Doesn't she look especially pretty? Everyone thought so at the dance. But this sweet little person is extremely stubborn. What are we going to do with her? Believe it or not, I almost had to drag her away by force.

Nora: Torvald, you'll be sorry you didn't let me stay, even if only for half an hour.

Helmer: Listen to her, Mrs. Linde! She danced her tarantella and it was a huge success, as it deserved to be, though maybe her performance was a tiny bit too realistic, a little more so than it might have been by strict artistic standards. But never mind about that! The main thing is, she was a success, a tremendous success. Do you think I was going to let her stay there after that, and spoil the effect? Not a chance! I took my charming little Capri girl—my capricious little Capri girl, I should say—I took her by the arm, one quick circle around the room, a curtsey to one and all, and, as they say in novels, the beautiful vision vanished. An exit should always make an effect, Mrs. Linde, but I can't make Nora understand that. Whew, this room is hot!

(*Throws his domino on a chair and opens the door to his study.*)

Why is it so dark in here? Oh, of course. Excuse me.

(*He goes in and lights some candles.*)

Nora (*in a hurried, breathless whisper*): Well?
Mrs. Linde (*in a low voice*): I talked to him.
Nora: And?
Mrs. Linde: Nora, you have to tell your husband the whole story.
Nora (*in an expressionless voice*): I knew it.
Mrs. Linde: You have nothing to fear from Krogstad, but you still have to tell him.
Nora: I'm not going to.
Mrs. Linde: Then the letter will.
Nora: Thank you, Kristine. Now I know what I have to do. Shh!
Helmer (*coming in again*): Well, Mrs. Linde, have you been admiring her?
Mrs. Linde: Yes, I have, and now I'll say goodnight.
Helmer: What, already? Is this your knitting?
Mrs. Linde (*taking it*): Yes, thank you, I'd almost forgotten it.
Helmer: So you knit?
Mrs. Linde: Yes, of course.
Helmer: You know, you ought to embroider.
Mrs. Linde: Really? Why?
Helmer: It's much more graceful-looking. Here, let me show you. You hold the embroidery this way in your left hand, and use the needle with your right, like this, with a long, easy sweep. Do you see?
Mrs. Linde: Yes, I suppose—
Helmer: But knitting, that can never be anything but awkward. Here, look. The arms close together, the knitting needles going up and down. It's sort of Chinese looking. That was really excellent champagne they gave us.
Mrs. Linde: Well, good night, Nora, and don't be stubborn anymore.
Helmer: That's right, Mrs. Linde.
Mrs. Linde: Good night, Mr. Helmer.
Helmer (*seeing her to the door*): Good night, good night. I hope you get home safely. I'd be very happy to—but you only have a short way to go. Good night, good night.

(*She goes out. He closes the door behind her, and comes in again.*)

Ah, rid of her at last! What a bore that woman is.

Nora: Aren't you tired, Torvald?

Helmer: No, not at all.

Nora: You're not sleepy?

Helmer: Not a bit. As a matter of fact, I feel very lively. And what about you? You really look tired *and* sleepy.

Nora: Yes, I am very tired. I want to go to sleep right away.

Helmer: So, you see how right I was not to let you stay there any longer.

Nora: You're always right, Torvald.

Helmer (kissing her on the forehead): Now my little skylark is talking sense. Did you notice what a good mood Rank was in this evening?

Nora: Really? Was he? I didn't talk to him at all.

Helmer: And I only talked to him for a little while, but it's a long time since I've seen him so cheerful. (*Looks at her for a while and then moves closer to her.*) It's delightful to be home again by ourselves, to be alone with you, you fascinating, charming little darling!

Nora: Don't look at me like that, Torvald.

Helmer: Why shouldn't I look at my dearest treasure? At all the beauty that is mine, all my very own?

Nora (going to the other side of the table): I wish you wouldn't talk that way to me tonight.

Helmer (following her): You've still got the tarantella in your blood, I see. And it makes you more captivating than ever. Listen, the guests are starting to leave now. (*In a lower voice.*) Nora, soon the whole house will be quiet.

Nora: Yes, I hope so.

Helmer: Yes, my own darling Nora. Do you know why, when we're out at a party like this, why I hardly talk to you, and keep away from you, and only steal a glance at you now and then? Do you know why I do that? It's because I'm pretending to myself that we're secretly in love, and we're secretly engaged, and no one suspects that there's anything between us.

Nora: Yes, yes, I know you're thinking about me every moment.

Helmer: And when we're leaving, and I'm putting the shawl over your beautiful young shoulders, on your lovely neck, then I imagine that you're my young bride and that we've just come from our wedding and I'm bringing you home for the first time, to be alone with you for the first time, all alone with my shy little darling! This whole night I've been longing for you alone. My blood was on fire watching you move when you danced the tarantella. I couldn't stand it any longer, and that's why I brought you home so early—

Nora: Stop it, Torvald! Let me go. I won't—

Helmer: What? You're not serious, Nora! You won't? You won't? I'm your husband—

(*There is a knock at the outer door.*)

Nora (*starting*): Did you hear—
Helmer (*going into the hall*): Who is it?
Rank (*outside*): It's me. May I come in for a moment?
Helmer (*in an irritated whisper*): What does he want now? (*Aloud.*) Wait a minute! (*Unlocks the door.*) Come in. It's good of you not to pass by our door without saying hello.
Rank: I thought I heard your voice, and I felt like dropping by. (*With a quick look around.*) Ah, yes, these dear familiar rooms. You two are very happy and cozy in here.
Helmer: You seemed to be making yourself pretty happy upstairs too.
Rank: Very much so. Why shouldn't I? Why shouldn't we enjoy everything in this world? At least as much as we can, for as long as we can. The wine was first-rate—
Helmer: Especially the champagne.
Rank: So you noticed that too? It's almost unbelievable how much of it I managed to put away!
Nora: Torvald drank a lot of champagne tonight too.
Rank: Did he?
Nora: Yes, and it always makes him so merry.
Rank: Well, why shouldn't a person have a merry evening after a well-spent day?
Helmer: Well-spent? I'm afraid I can't take credit for that.
Rank (*clapping him on the back*): But I can, you know!
Nora: Doctor Rank, you must have been busy with some scientific investigation today.
Rank: Exactly.
Helmer: Listen to this! Little Nora talking about scientific investigations!
Nora: And may I congratulate you on the result?
Rank: Indeed you may.
Nora: Was it favorable, then?
Rank: The best possible result, for both doctor and patient—certainty.
Nora (*quickly and searchingly*): Certainty?
Rank: Absolute certainty. So wasn't I entitled to make a merry evening of it after that?
Nora: Yes, you certainly were, Doctor Rank.
Helmer: I think so too, as long as you don't have to pay for it in the morning.
Rank: Oh well, you can't have anything in this life without paying for it.

Nora: Doctor Rank, are you fond of fancy-dress balls?

Rank: Yes, if there are a lot of pretty costumes.

Nora: Tell me, what should the two of us wear to the next one?

Helmer: Little featherbrain! You're thinking of the next one already?

Rank: The two of us? Yes, I can tell you. You'll go as a good-luck charm—

Helmer: Yes, but what would be the costume for that?

Rank: She just needs to dress the way she always does.

Helmer: That was very nicely put. But aren't you going to tell us what you'll be?

Rank: Yes, my dear friend, I've already made up my mind about that.

Helmer: Well?

Rank: At the next fancy-dress ball I'm going to be invisible.

Helmer: That's a good one!

Rank: There's a big black cap . . . Haven't you ever heard of the cap that makes you invisible? Once you put it on, no one can see you anymore.

Helmer (*suppressing a smile*): Yes, that's right.

Rank: But I'm clean forgetting what I came for. Helmer, give me a cigar. One of the dark Havanas.

Helmer: With the greatest pleasure. (*Offers him his case.*)

Rank (*takes a cigar and cuts off the end*): Thanks.

Nora (*striking a match*): Let me give you a light.

Rank: Thank you. (*She holds the match for him to light his cigar.*) And now goodbye!

Helmer: Goodbye, goodbye, my dear old friend.

Nora: Sleep well, Doctor Rank.

Rank: Thank you for that wish.

Nora: Wish me the same.

Rank: You? Well, if you want me to. Sleep well! And thanks for the light. (*He nods to them both and goes out.*)

Helmer (*in a subdued voice*): He's had too much to drink.

Nora (*absently*): Maybe.

(*Helmer takes a bunch of keys out of his pocket and goes into the hall.*)

Torvald! What are you going to do out there?

Helmer: Empty the mailbox. It's quite full. There won't be any room for the newspaper in the morning.

Nora: Are you going to work tonight?

Helmer: You know I'm not. What's this? Someone's been at the lock.

Nora: At the lock?

Helmer: Yes, it's been tampered with. What does this mean? I never would have thought the maid— Look, here's a broken hairpin. It's one of yours, Nora.

Nora (*quickly*): Then it must have been the children—

Helmer: Then you'd better break them of those habits. There, I've finally got it open.

(*Empties the mailbox and calls out to the kitchen.*)

Helene! Helene, put out the light over the front door.

(*Comes back into the room and shuts the door into the hall. He holds out his hand full of letters.*)

Look at that. Look what a pile of them there are. (*Turning them over.*) What's this?

Nora (*at the window*): The letter! No! Torvald, no!

Helmer: Two calling cards of Rank's.

Nora: Of Doctor Rank's?

Helmer (*looking at them*): Yes, Doctor Rank. They were on top. He must have put them in there when he left just now.

Nora: Is there anything written on them?

Helmer: There's a black cross over the name. Look. What a morbid thing to do! It looks as if he's announcing his own death.

Nora: That's exactly what he's doing.

Helmer: What? Do you know anything about it? Has he said anything to you?

Nora: Yes. He told me that when the cards came it would be his farewell to us. He means to close himself off and die.

Helmer: My poor old friend! Of course I knew we wouldn't have him for very long. But this soon! And he goes and hides himself away like a wounded animal.

Nora: If it has to happen, it's better that it be done without a word. Don't you think so, Torvald?

Helmer (*walking up and down*): He's become so much a part of our lives, I can't imagine him not being with us anymore. With his poor health and his loneliness, he was like a cloudy background to our sunlit happiness. Well, maybe it's all for the best. For him, anyway. (*Standing still.*) And maybe for us too, Nora. Now we have only each other to rely on. (*Puts his arms around her.*) My darling wife, I feel as though I can't possibly hold you tight enough. You know, Nora, I've often wished you were in some kind of serious danger, so that I could risk everything, even my own life, to save you.

Nora (*disengages herself from him, and says firmly and decidedly*): Now you must go and read your letters, Torvald.

Helmer: No, no, not tonight. I want to be with you, my darling wife.

Nora: With the thought of your friend's death—

Helmer: You're right, it has affected us both. Something ugly has come between us, the thought of the horrors of death. We have to try to put it out of our minds. Until we do, we'll each go to our own room.

Nora (with her arms around his neck): Good night, Torvald. Good night!

Helmer (kissing her on the forehead): Good night, my little songbird. Sleep well, Nora. Now I'll go read all my mail. (*He takes his letters and goes into his room, shutting the door behind him.*)

Nora (gropes distractedly about, picks up Helmer's domino and wraps it around her, while she says in quick, hoarse, spasmodic whispers): Never to see him again. Never! Never! (*Puts her shawl over her head.*) Never to see my children again either, never again. Never! Never! Oh, the icy, black water, the bottomless depths! If only it were over! He's got it now, now he's reading it. Goodbye, Torvald ... children!

(*She is about to rush out through the hall when Helmer opens his door hurriedly and stands with an open letter in his hand.*)

Helmer: Nora!

Nora: Ah!

Helmer: What is this? Do you know what's in this letter?

Nora: Yes, I know. Let me go! Let me get out!

Helmer (holding her back): Where are you going?

Nora (trying to get free): You're not going to save me, Torvald!

Helmer (reeling): It's true? Is this true, what it says here? This is horrible! No, no, it can't possibly be true.

Nora: It is true. I've loved you more than anything else in the world.

Helmer: Don't start with your ridiculous excuses.

Nora (taking a step towards him): Torvald!

Helmer: You little fool, do you know what you've done?

Nora: Let me go. I won't let you suffer for my sake. You're not going to take it on yourself.

Helmer: Stop play-acting. (*Locks the hall door.*) You're going to stay right here and give me an explanation. Do you understand what you've done? Answer me! Do you understand what you've done?

Nora (looks steadily at him and says with a growing look of coldness in her face): Yes, I'm beginning to understand everything now.

Helmer (walking around the room): What a horrible awakening! The woman who was my pride and joy for eight years, a hypocrite, a liar, worse than that, much worse—a criminal! The unspeakable ugliness of it all! The shame of it! The shame!

(*Nora is silent and looks steadily at him. He stops in front of her.*)

I should have realized that something like this was bound to happen. I should have seen it coming. Your father's shifty nature—be quiet!—your father's shifty nature has come out in you. No religion, no morality, no sense of duty. This is my punishment for closing my eyes to what he did! I did it for your sake, and this is how you pay me back.

Nora: Yes, that's right.

Helmer: Now you've destroyed all my happiness. You've ruined my whole future. It's horrible to think about! I'm in the power of an unscrupulous man. He can do what he wants with me, ask me for anything he wants, give me any orders he wants, and I don't dare say no. And I have to sink to such miserable depths, all because of a feather-brained woman!

Nora: When I'm out of the way, you'll be free.

Helmer: Spare me the speeches. Your father had always plenty of those on hand, too. What good would it do me if you were out of the way, as you say? Not the slightest. He can tell everybody the whole story. And if he does, I could be wrongly suspected of having been in on it with you. People will probably think I was behind it all, that I put you up to it! And I have you to thank for all this, after I've cherished you the whole time we've been married. Do you understand what you've done to me?

Nora (coldly and quietly): Yes.

Helmer: It's so incredible that I can't take it all in. But we have to come to some understanding. Take off that shawl. Take it off, I said. I have to try to appease him some way or another. It has to be hushed up, no matter what it costs. And as for you and me, we have to make it look as if everything is just as it always was, but only for the sake of appearances, obviously. You'll stay here in my house, of course. But I won't let you bring up the children. I can't trust them to you. To think that I have to say these things to someone I've loved so dearly, and that I still—No, that's all over. From this moment on happiness is out of the question. All that matters now is to save the bits and pieces, to keep up the appearance—

(The front doorbell rings.)

Helmer (with a start): What's that? At this hour! Can the worst—Can he—Go and hide yourself, Nora. Say you don't feel well. (*Nora stands motionless. Helmer goes and unlocks the hall door.*)

Maid (half-dressed, comes to the door): A letter for Mrs. Helmer.

Helmer: Give it to me. (*Takes the letter, and shuts the door.*) Yes, it's from him. I'm not giving it to you. I'll read it myself.

Nora: Go ahead, read it.

Helmer (*standing by the lamp*): I barely have the courage to. It could mean ruin for both of us. No, I have to know. (*Tears open the letter, runs his eye over a few lines, looks at a piece of paper enclosed with it, and gives a shout of joy.*) Nora! (*She looks at him questioningly.*) Nora! No, I'd better read it again. Yes, it's true! I'm saved! Nora, I'm saved!

Nora: And what about me?

Helmer: You too, of course. We're both saved, you and I. Look, he's returned your note. He says he's sorry and he apologizes—that a happy change in his life—what difference does it make what he says! We're saved, Nora! Nobody can hurt you. Oh, Nora, Nora! No, first I have to destroy these horrible things. Let me see. . . . (*Glances at the note.*) No, no, I don't want to look at it. This whole business will be nothing but a bad dream to me.

(*Tears up the note and both letters, throws them all into the stove, and watches them burn.*)

There, now it doesn't exist anymore. He says that you've known since Christmas Eve. These must have been a horrible three days for you, Nora.

Nora: I fought a hard fight these three days.

Helmer: And suffered agonies, and saw no way out but— No, we won't dwell on any of those horrors. We'll just shout for joy and keep saying, "It's all over! It's all over!" Listen to me, Nora. You don't seem to realize that it's all over. What's this? Such a cold, hard face! My poor little Nora, I understand. You find it hard to believe that I've really forgiven you. But I swear that it's true, Nora. I forgive you for everything. I know that you did it all out of love for me.

Nora: That's true.

Helmer: You've loved me the way a wife ought to love her husband. You just didn't have the awareness to see what was wrong with the means you used. But do you think I love you any less because you don't understand how to deal with these things? No, of course not. I want you to lean on me. I'll advise you and guide you. I wouldn't be a man if this womanly helplessness didn't make you twice as attractive to me. Don't think anymore about the hard things I said when I was so upset at first, when I thought everything was going to crush me. I forgive you, Nora. I swear to you that I forgive you.

Nora: Thank you for your forgiveness. (*She goes out through the door to the right.*)

Helmer: No, don't go—(*Looks in.*) What are you doing in there?

Nora (*from within*): Taking off my costume.

Helmer (*standing at the open door*): Yes, do. Try to calm yourself, and ease your mind again, my frightened little songbird. I want you to rest and feel secure. I have wide wings for you to take shelter underneath. (*Walks up and down by the door.*) What a warm and cozy home we have, Nora: Here's a safe haven for you, and I'll protect you like a hunted dove that I've rescued from a hawk's claws. I'll calm your poor pounding heart. It will happen, little by little, Nora, believe me. In the morning you'll see it in a very different light. Soon everything will be exactly the way it was before. Before you know it, you won't need my reassurances that I've forgiven you. You'll know for certain that I have. You can't imagine that I'd ever consider rejecting you, or even blaming you? You have no idea what a man feels in his heart, Nora. A man finds it indescribably sweet and satisfying to know that he's forgiven his wife, freely and with all his heart. It's as if he's made her his own all over again. He's given her a new life, in a way, and she's become both wife and child to him. And from this moment on that's what you'll be to me, my little scared, helpless darling. Don't worry about anything, Nora. Just be honest and open with me, and I'll be your will and your conscience. What's this? You haven't gone to bed yet? Have you changed?

Nora (*in everyday dress*): Yes, Torvald, I've changed.

Helmer: But why—It's so late.

Nora: I'm not going to sleep tonight.

Helmer: But, my dear Nora—

Nora (*looking at her watch*): It's not that late. Sit down here, Torvald. You and I have a lot to talk about. (*She sits down at one side of the table.*)

Helmer: Nora, what is this? Why this cold, hard face?

Nora: Sit down. This is going to take a while. I have a lot to say to you.

Helmer (*sits down at the opposite side of the table*): You're making me nervous, Nora. And I don't understand you.

Nora: No, that's it exactly. You don't understand me, and I've never understood you either, until tonight. No, don't interrupt me. I want you to listen to what I have to say. Torvald, I'm settling accounts with you.

Helmer: What do you mean by that?

Nora (*after a short silence*): Doesn't anything strike you as odd about the way we're sitting here like this?

Helmer: No, what?

Nora: We've been married for eight years. Doesn't it occur to you that this is the first time the two of us, you and I, husband and wife, have had a serious conversation?

Helmer: What do you mean by serious?

Nora: In the whole eight years—longer than that, for the whole time we've known each other—we've never exchanged one word on any serious subject.

Helmer: Did you expect me to be constantly worrying you with problems that you weren't capable of helping me deal with?

Nora: I'm not talking about business. I mean we've never sat down together seriously to try to get to the bottom of anything.

Helmer: But, dearest Nora, what good would that have done you?

Nora: That's just it. You've never understood me. I've been treated badly, Torvald, first by Papa and then by you.

Helmer: What? The two people who've loved you more than anyone else?

Nora (shaking her head): You've never loved me. You just thought it was pleasant to be in love with me.

Helmer: Nora, what are you saying?

Nora: It's true, Torvald. When I lived at home with Papa, he gave me his opinion about everything, and so I had all the same opinions, and if I didn't, I kept my mouth shut, because he wouldn't have liked it. He used to call me his doll-child, and he played with me the way I played with my dolls. And when I came to live in your house—

Helmer: What kind of way is that to talk about our marriage?

Nora (undisturbed): I mean that I was just passed from Papa's hands to yours. You arranged everything according to your own taste, and so I had all the same tastes as you. Or else I pretended to, I'm not really sure which. Sometimes I think it's one way and sometimes the other. When I look back, it's as if I've been living here like a beggar, from hand to mouth. I've supported myself by performing tricks for you, Torvald. But that's the way you wanted it. You and Papa have committed a terrible sin against me. It's your fault that I've done nothing with my life.

Helmer: This is so unfair and ungrateful of you, Nora! Haven't you been happy here?

Nora: No, I've never really been happy. I thought I was, but it wasn't true.

Helmer: Not—not happy!

Nora: No, just cheerful. You've always been very kind to me. But our home's been nothing but a playroom. I've been your doll-wife, the same way that I was papa's doll-child. And the children have been my dolls. I thought it was great fun when you played with me, the way they thought it was when I played with them. That's what our marriage has been, Torvald.

Helmer: There's some truth in what you're saying, even though your view of it is exaggerated and overwrought. But things will be different from now on. Playtime is over, and now it's lesson-time.

Nora: Whose lessons? Mine, or the children's?

Helmer: Both yours and the children's, my darling Nora.

Nora: I'm sorry, Torvald, but you're not the man to give me lessons on how to be a proper wife to you.

Helmer: How can you say that?

Nora: And as for me, who am I to be allowed to bring up the children?

Helmer: Nora!

Nora: Didn't you say so yourself a little while ago, that you don't dare trust them to me?

Helmer: That was in a moment of anger! Why can't you let it go?

Nora: Because you were absolutely right. I'm not fit for the job. There's another job I have to take on first. I have to try to educate myself. You're not the man to help me with that. I have to do that for myself. And that's why I'm going to leave you now.

Helmer (jumping up): What are you saying?

Nora: I have to stand completely on my own, if I'm going to understand myself and everything around me. That's why I can't stay here with you any longer.

Helmer: Nora, Nora!

Nora: I'm leaving right now. I'm sure Kristine will put me up for the night—

Helmer: You're out of your mind! I won't let you go! I forbid it!

Nora: It's no use forbidding me anything anymore. I'm taking only what belongs to me. I won't take anything from you, now or later.

Helmer: This is insanity!

Nora: Tomorrow I'm going home. Back to where I came from, I mean. It'll be easier for me to find something to do there.

Helmer: You're a blind, senseless woman!

Nora: Then I'd better try to get some sense, Torvald.

Helmer: But to desert your home, your husband, and your children! And aren't you concerned about what people will say?

Nora: I can't concern myself with that. I only know that this is what I have to do.

Helmer: This is outrageous! You're just going to walk away from your most sacred duties?

Nora: What do you consider to be my most sacred duties?

Helmer: Do you need me to tell you that? Aren't they your duties to your husband and your children?

Nora: I have other duties just as sacred.

Helmer: No, you do not. What could they be?

Nora: Duties to myself.

Helmer: First and foremost, you're a wife and a mother.

Nora: I don't believe that anymore. I believe that first and foremost I'm a human being, just as you are—or, at least, that I have to try to become one. I know very well, Torvald, that most people would agree with you, and that opinions like yours are in books, but I can't be satisfied anymore with what most people say, or with what's in books. I have to think things through for myself and come to understand them.

Helmer: Why can't you understand your place in your own home? Don't you have an infallible guide in matters like that? What about your religion?

Nora: Torvald, I'm afraid I'm not sure what religion is.

Helmer: What are you saying?

Nora: All I know is what Pastor Hansen said when I was confirmed. He told us that religion was this, that, and the other thing. When I'm away from all this and on my own, I'll look into that subject too. I'll see if what he said is true or not, or at least whether it's true for me.

Helmer: This is unheard of, coming from a young woman like you! But if religion doesn't guide you, let me appeal to your conscience. I assume you have some moral sense. Or do you have none? Answer me.

Nora: Torvald, that's not an easy question to answer. I really don't know. It's very confusing to me. I only know that you and I look at it in very different ways. I'm learning too that the law isn't at all what I thought it was, and I can't convince myself that the law is right. A woman has no right to spare her old dying father or to save her husband's life? I can't believe that.

Helmer: You talk like a child. You don't understand anything about the world you live in.

Nora: No, I don't. But I'm going to try. I'm going to see if I can figure out who's right, me or the world.

Helmer: You're sick, Nora. You're delirious. I'm half convinced that you're out of your mind.

Nora: I've never felt so clearheaded and sure of myself as I do tonight.

Helmer: Clearheaded and sure of yourself—and that's the spirit in which you forsake your husband and your children?

Nora: Yes, it is.

Helmer: Then there's only one possible explanation.

Nora: Which is?

Helmer: You don't love me anymore.

Nora: Exactly.

Helmer: Nora! How can you say that?

Nora: It's very painful for me to say it, Torvald, because you've always been so good to me, but I can't help it. I don't love you anymore.

Helmer (*regaining his composure*): Are you clearheaded and sure of your-self when you say that too?

Nora: Yes, totally clearheaded and sure of myself. That's why I can't stay here.

Helmer: Can you tell me what I did to make you stop loving me?

Nora: Yes, I can. It was tonight, when the miracle didn't happen. That's when I realized you're not the man I thought you were.

Helmer: Can you explain that more clearly? I don't understand you.

Nora: I've been waiting so patiently for the last eight years. Of course I knew that miracles don't happen every day. Then when I found my-self in this horrible situation, I was sure that the miracle was about to happen at last. When Krogstad's letter was lying out there, never for a moment did I imagine that you would agree to his conditions. I was absolutely certain that you'd say to him: Go ahead, tell the whole world. And when he had—

Helmer: Yes, what then? After I'd exposed my wife to shame and dis-grace?

Nora: When he had, I was absolutely certain you'd come forward and take the whole thing on yourself, and say: I'm the guilty one.

Helmer: Nora—!

Nora: You mean that I would never have let you make such a sacrifice for me? Of course I wouldn't. But who would have believed my word against yours? That was the miracle that I hoped for and dreaded. And it was to keep it from happening that made me want to kill myself.

Helmer: I'd gladly work night and day for you, Nora, and endure sorrow and poverty for your sake. But no man would sacrifice his honor for the one he loves.

Nora: Hundreds of thousands of women have done it.

Helmer: Oh, you think and talk like a thoughtless child.

Nora: Maybe so. But you don't think or talk like the man I want to be with for the rest of my life. As soon as your fear had passed—and it wasn't fear for what threatened me, but for what might happen to you—when the whole thing was past, as far as you were concerned it was just as if nothing at all had happened. I was still your little sky-lark, your doll, but now you'd handle me twice as gently and care-fully as before, because I was so delicate and fragile. (*Getting up.*) Torvald, that's when it dawned on me that for eight years I'd been living here with a stranger and had borne him three children. Oh, I can't bear to think about it! I could tear myself into little pieces!

Helmer (*sadly*): I see, I see. An abyss has opened up between us. There's no denying it. But, Nora, can't we find some way to close it?

Nora: The way I am now, I'm no wife for you.

Helmer: I can find it in myself to become a different man.

Nora: Maybe so—if your doll is taken away from you.

Helmer: But to be apart!—to be apart from you! No, no, Nora, I can't conceive of it.

Nora (going out to the right): All the more reason why it has to be done.

(*She comes back with her coat and hat and a small suitcase which she puts on a chair by the table.*)

Helmer: Nora, Nora, not now! Wait till tomorrow.

Nora (putting on her cloak): I can't spend the night in a strange man's room.

Helmer: But couldn't we live here together like brother and sister?

Nora (putting on her hat): You know how long that would last. (*Puts the shawl around her.*) Goodbye, Torvald. I won't look in on the children. I know they're in better hands than mine. The way I am now, I'm no use to them.

Helmer: But someday, Nora, someday?

Nora: How can I tell? I have no idea what's going to become of me.

Helmer: But you're my wife, whatever becomes of you.

Nora: Listen, Torvald. I've heard that when a wife deserts her husband's house, the way I'm doing now, he's free of all legal obligations to her. In any event, I set you free from all your obligations. I don't want you to feel bound in the slightest, any more than I will. There has to be complete freedom on both sides. Look, here's your ring back. Give me mine.

Helmer: That too?

Nora: That too.

Helmer: Here it is.

Nora: Good. Now it's all over. I've left the keys here. The maids know all about how to run the house, much better than I do. Kristine will come by tomorrow after I leave her place and pack up my own things, the ones I brought with me from home. I'd like to have them sent to me.

Helmer: All over! All over! Nora, will you ever think about me again?

Nora: I know I'll often think about you, and the children, and this house.

Helmer: May I write to you, Nora?

Nora: No, never. You mustn't do that.

Helmer: But at least let me send you—

Nora: Nothing, nothing.

Helmer: Let me help you if you're in need.

Nora: No. I can't accept anything from a stranger.

Helmer: Nora . . . can't I ever be anything more than a stranger to you?

Nora (*picking up her bag*): Ah, Torvald, for that, the most wonderful miracle of all would have to happen.

Helmer: Tell me what that would be!

Nora: We'd both have to change so much that— Oh, Torvald, I've stopped believing in miracles.

Helmer: But I'll believe. Tell me! Change so much that . . . ?

Nora: That our life together would be a true marriage. Goodbye.

(*She goes out through the hall.*)

Helmer (*sinks down into a chair at the door and buries his face in his hands*): Nora! Nora! (*Looks around, and stands up.*) Empty. She's gone. (*A hope flashes across his mind.*) The most wonderful miracle of all . . . ?

(*The heavy sound of a closing door is heard from below.*)

QUESTIONS

ACT I

1. From the opening conversation between Helmer and Nora, what are your impressions of him? Of her? Of their marriage?

2. At what moment in the play do you understand why it is called *A Doll's House*?

3. In what ways does Mrs. Linde provide a contrast for Nora?

4. What in Krogstad's first appearance on stage, and in Dr. Rank's remarks about him, indicates that the bank clerk is a menace?

5. Of what illegal deed is Nora guilty? How does she justify it?

6. When the curtain falls on Act I, what problems now confront Nora?

ACT II

1. As Act II opens, what are your feelings on seeing the stripped, ragged Christmas tree? How is it suggestive?

2. What events that soon occur make Nora's situation even more difficult?

3. How does she try to save herself?

4. Why does Nora fling herself into the wild tarantella?

ACT III

1. For what possible reasons does Mrs. Linde pledge herself to Krogstad?

2. How does Dr. Rank's announcement of his impending death affect Nora and Helmer?

3. What is Helmer's reaction to learning the truth about Nora's misdeed? Why does he blame Nora's father? What is revealing (of Helmer's own character) in his

remark, "From now on, there can be no question of happiness. All we can do is save the bits and pieces from the wreck, preserve appearances . . ."?

4. When Helmer finds that Krogstad has sent back the note, what is his response? How do you feel toward him?
5. How does the character of Nora develop in this act?
6. How do you interpret her final slamming of the door?

GENERAL QUESTIONS

1. In what ways do you find Nora a victim? In what ways at fault?
2. Try to state the theme of the play. Does it involve women's rights? Self-fulfillment?
3. What dramatic question does the play embody? At what moment can this question first be stated?
4. What is the crisis? In what way is this moment or event a "turning point"? (In what new direction does the action turn?)
5. Eric Bentley, in an essay titled "Ibsen, Pro and Con" (*In Search of Theater* [New York: Knopf, 1953]), criticizes the character of Krogstad, calling him "a mere pawn of the plot." He then adds, "When convenient to Ibsen, he is a blackmailer. When inconvenient, he is converted." Do you agree or disagree?
6. Why is the play considered a work of realism? Is there anything in it that does not seem realistic?
7. In what respects does *A Doll's House* seem to apply to life today? Is it in any way dated? Could there be a Nora in North America today?

Tragicomedy

One of the more prominent developments in mid-twentieth-century drama was the rise of **tragicomedies**, plays that stir us not only to pity and fear (echoing Aristotle's description of the effect of tragedy) but also to laughter. Although tragicomedy is a kind of drama we think distinctively modern, it is by no means a new invention. The term was used (although jokingly) by the Roman writer of comedy Plautus in about 185 B.C.

Since ancient times, playwrights have mingled laughter and tears, defying the neoclassical doctrine that required strict unity of action and tone (discussed on page 589) and decreed that a play must be entirely comic or entirely tragic. Shakespeare is fond of tragicomic mingling. For example, in *Hamlet* the prince jokes with a grave-digger, and in *Antony and Cleopatra* the queen commits suicide with a poisonous asp brought to her by a wise-cracking clown. Likewise, Shakespeare's darker comedies such as *Measure for Measure* and *The Merchant of Venice* deal so forcefully with such stark themes as lust, greed, racism, revenge, and cruelty, that they often seem like tragedies until their happy endings. In the tragedies of Shakespeare and others, passages of clownish humor are sometimes called **comic relief**, meaning that the section of comedy introduces a sharp contrast in mood. But such passages can do more than provide relief. In *Othello* (III, iv, 1–22) the clown's banter with

Desdemona for a moment makes the surrounding tragedy seem, by comparison, more poignant and intense.

No one doubts that *Othello* is a tragedy, but some twentieth-century plays leave us both bemused and confused: should we laugh or cry? One of the most talked-about plays after World War II, Samuel Beckett's *Waiting for Godot*, portrays two clownish tramps who mark time in a wasteland, wistfully looking for a savior who never arrives. We cannot help laughing at the tramps' painful situation; but, turning the idea around, we also feel deeply moved by their ridiculous plight. Perhaps a modern tragicomedy like *Godot* does not show us great souls suffering greatly—as Edith Hamilton has said we observe in a classical tragedy—but Beckett's play nonetheless touches mysteriously on the universal sorrows of human existence.

Perhaps the full effect of such a play takes time to sink in. Contemporary playwright Edward Albee suggests that sometimes the spectator's sense of relief after experiencing pity and fear (Aristotle calls it *katharsis*) may be a delayed reaction: "I don't feel that catharsis in a play necessarily takes place during the course of a play. Often it should take place afterwards."[1] If Albee is right, we may be amused while watching a tragicomedy and then go home and feel deeply stirred by it.

The following contemporary play, Milcha Sanchez-Scott's *The Cuban Swimmer*, deftly assimilates several dramatic styles to create a brilliant original work. The play is simultaneously a family drama, a Latin comedy, a religious parable, and a critique of a media-obsessed American culture.

Milcha Sanchez-Scott

The Cuban Swimmer   1984

Milcha Sanchez-Scott was born in 1955 on the island of Bali. Her father was Colombian. Her mother was Chinese, Indonesian, and Dutch. Her father's work as an agronomist required constant travel, so when the young Sanchez-Scott reached school age, she was sent to a convent boarding school near London where she first learned English. Colombia, however, remained the family's one permanent home. Every Christmas and summer vacation was spent on a ranch in San Marta, Colombia, where four generations of family lived together. When she was fourteen, Sanchez-Scott's family moved to California. After attending the University of San Diego, where she

MILCHA SANCHEZ-SCOTT

---

[1]"The Art of the Theater," interview, *Paris Review* 39 (1996).

majored in literature and philosophy, she worked at the San Diego Zoo and later at an employment agency in Los Angeles. Her first play, Latina, premiered in 1980 and won seven Drama-Logue awards. Dog Lady and The Cuban Swimmer followed in 1984. Sanchez-Scott then went to New York for a year to work with playwright Irene Fornes, in whose theater workshop she developed Roosters (1988). A feature-film version of Roosters, starring Edward James Olmos, was released in 1995. Her other plays include Evening Star (1989), El Dorado (1990), and The Old Matador (1995). Sanchez-Scott lives in Los Angeles.

CHARACTERS

Margarita Suárez, the swimmer
Eduardo Suárez, her father, the coach
Simón Suárez, her brother
Aída Suárez, her mother
Abuela, her grandmother
Voice of Mel Munson
Voice of Mary Beth White
Voice of Radio Operator

SETTING: The Pacific Ocean between San Pedro and Catalina Island.

TIME. Summer.

Live conga drums can be used to punctuate the action of the play.

SCENE I

Pacific Ocean. Midday. On the horizon, in perspective, a small boat enters upstage left, crosses to upstage right, and exits. Pause. Lower on the horizon, the same boat, in larger perspective, enters upstage right, crosses and exits upstage left. Blackout.

SCENE II

Pacific Ocean. Midday. The swimmer, Margarita Suárez, is swimming. On the boat following behind her are her father, Eduardo Suárez, holding a megaphone, and Simón, her brother, sitting on top of the cabin with his shirt off, punk sunglasses on, binoculars hanging on his chest.

Eduardo (Leaning forward, shouting in time to Margarita's swimming.):
     Uno, dos, uno, dos. Y uno, dos° . . . keep your shoulders parallel to
     the water.

Uno, dos, uno, dos. Y uno, dos: One, two, one, two. And one, two.

Simón: I'm gonna take these glasses off and look straight into the sun.

Eduardo (*Through megaphone.*): *Muy bien, muy bien*° . . . but punch those arms in, baby.

Simón (*Looking directly at the sun through binoculars.*): Come on, come on, zap me. Show me something. (*He looks behind at the shoreline and ahead at the sea.*) Stop! Stop, *Papi!* Stop!

(*Aída Suárez and Abuela, the swimmer's mother and grandmother, enter running from the back of the boat.*)

Aída and Abuela: *Qué? Qué es?*°

Aída: Es un shark?°

Eduardo: Eh?

Abuela: *Que es un shark dicen?*°

(*Eduardo blows whistle. Margarita looks up at the boat.*)

Simón: No, *Papi*, no shark, no shark. We've reached the halfway mark.

Abuela (*Looking into the water.*): *A dónde está?*°

Aída: It's not in the water.

Abuela: Oh, no? Oh, no?

Aída: No! *A poco* do you think they're gonna have signs in the water to say you are halfway to Santa Catalina? No. It's done very scientific. *A ver, hijo,*° explain it to your grandma.

Simón: Well, you see, Abuela—(*He points behind.*) There's San Pedro. (*He points ahead.*) And there's Santa Catalina. Looks halfway to me.

(*Abuela shakes her head and is looking back and forth, trying to make the decision, when suddenly the sound of a helicopter is heard.*)

Abuela (*Looking up.*): *Virgencita de la Caridad del Cobre. Qué es eso?*°

(*Sound of helicopter gets closer. Margarita looks up.*)

Margarita: *Papi, Papi!*

(*A small commotion on the boat, with everybody pointing at the helicopter above. Shadows of the helicopter fall on the boat. Simón looks up at it through binoculars.*)

Papi—qué es? What is it?

Muy bien, muy bien: Very good, very good.   *Qué? Qué es?:* What? What is it?   *Es un shark?:* Is it a shark?   *Que es un shark dicen?:* Did they say a shark?   *A dónde está?:* Where is it?   *A ver, hijo:* Look here, son.   *Virgencita de la Caridad del Cobre. Qué es eso?:* Virgin of Charity! What is that?

Scene from the University of Colorado's production of *The Cuban Swimmer*

Eduardo (*Through megaphone.*): Uh . . . uh . . . uh, *un momentico . . . mi hija.*° . . . Your *papi*'s got everything under control, understand? Uh . . . you just keep stroking. And stay . . . uh . . . close to the boat.

Simón: Wow, *Papi!* We're on TV, man! Holy Christ, we're all over the fucking U.S.A.! It's Mel Munson and Mary Beth White!

Aída: *Por Dios!*° Simón, don't swear. And put on your shirt.

(*Aída fluffs her hair, puts on her sunglasses and waves to the helicopter. Simón leans over the side of the boat and yells to Margarita.*)

Simón: Yo, Margo! You're on TV, man.

---

un momentico . . . mi hija: Just a second, my daughter.   *Por Dios!:* For God's Sake!

Eduardo: Leave your sister alone. Turn on the radio.

Margarita: Papi! *Qué está pasando?*°

Abuela: *Que es la televisión dicen?* (*She shakes her head.*) *Porque como yo no puedo ver nada sin mis espejuelos.*°

(*Abuela rummages through the boat, looking for her glasses. Voices of Mel Munson and Mary Beth White are heard over the boat's radio.*)

Mel's Voice: As we take a closer look at the gallant crew of *La Havana* . . . and there . . . yes, there she is . . . the little Cuban swimmer from Long Beach, California, nineteen-year-old Margarita Suárez. The unknown swimmer is our Cinderella entry . . . a bundle of tenacity, battling her way through the choppy, murky waters of the cold Pacific to reach the Island of Romance . . . Santa Catalina . . . where should she be the first to arrive, two thousand dollars and a gold cup will be waiting for her.

Aída: Doesn't even cover our expenses.

Abuela: *Qué dice?*

Eduardo: Shhhh!

Mary Beth's Voice: This is really a family effort, Mel, and—

Mel's Voice: Indeed it is. Her trainer, her coach, her mentor, is her father, Eduardo Suárez. Not a swimmer himself, it says here, Mr. Suárez is head usher of the Holy Name Society and the owner-operator of Suárez Treasures of the Sea and Salvage Yard. I guess it's one of those places—

Mary Beth's Voice: If I might interject a fact here, Mel, assisting in this swim is Mrs. Suárez, who is a former Miss Cuba.

Mel's Voice: And a beautiful woman in her own right. Let's try and get a closer look.

(*Helicopter sound gets louder. Margarita, frightened, looks up again.*)

Margarita: Papi!

Eduardo (*Through megaphone.*): Mi hija, don't get nervous . . . it's the press. I'm handling it.

Aída: I see how you're handling it.

Eduardo (*Through megaphone.*): Do you hear? Everything is under control. Get back into your rhythm. Keep your elbows high and kick and kick and kick and kick . . .

Papi! Qué está pasando?: Dad. What's happening? *Que es la televisión dicen? Porque como yo no puedo ver nada sin mis espejuelos:* Did they say television? Because I can't see without my glasses.

Abuela (Finds her glasses and puts them on.): Ay sí, es la televisión . . . *(She points to helicopter.)* Qué lindo mira . . . *(She fluffs her hair, gives a big wave.)* Aló América! Viva mi Margarita, viva todo los Cubanos en los Estados Unidos!°

Aída: Ay por Dios, Cecilia, the man didn't come all this way in his helicopter to look at you jumping up and down, making a fool of yourself.

Abuela: I don't care. I'm proud.

Aída: He can't understand you anyway.

Abuela: Viva . . . *(She stops.)* Simón, cómo se dice viva?°

Simón: Hurray.

Abuela: Hurray for mi Margarita y for all the Cubans living en the United States, y un abrazo . . . Simón, abrazo . . .

Simón: A big hug.

Abuela: Sí, a big hug to all my friends in Miami, Long Beach, Union City, except for my son Carlos, who lives in New York in sin! He lives . . . *(She crosses herself.)* in Brooklyn with a Puerto Rican woman in sin! No decente . . .

Simón: Decent.

Abuela: Carlos, no decente. This family, decente.

Aída: Cecilia, por Dios.

Mel's Voice: Look at that enthusiasm. The whole family has turned out to cheer little Margarita on to victory! I hope they won't be too disappointed.

Mary Beth's Voice: She seems to be making good time, Mel.

Mel's Voice: Yes, it takes all kinds to make a race. And it's a testimonial to the all-encompassing fairness . . . the greatness of this, the Wrigley Invitational Women's Swim to Catalina, where among all the professionals there is still room for the amateurs . . . like these, the simple people we see below us on the ragtag La Havana, taking their long-shot chance to victory. Vaya con Dios!°

(Helicopter sound fading as family, including Margarita, watch silently. Static as Simón turns radio off. Eduardo walks to bow of boat, looks out on the horizon.)

Eduardo (To himself.): Amateurs.

Aída: Eduardo, that person insulted us. Did you hear, Eduardo? That he called us a simple people in a ragtag boat? Did you hear . . . ?

Aló América! Viva mi Margarita, viva todo los Cubanos en los Estados Unidos!: Hello America! Hurray for my Margarita, hurray for all the Cubans in the United States! *cómo se dice viva?:* How do you say "viva" [in English]? *Vaya con Dios!:* Go with God. [God bless you.]

Abuela (*Clenching her fist at departing helicopter.*): Mal-Rayo los parta!°
Simón (*Same gesture.*): Asshole!

(*Aída follows Eduardo as he goes to side of boat and stares at Margarita.*)

Aída: This person comes in his helicopter to insult your wife, your family,
   your daughter . . .
Margarita (*Pops her head out of the water.*): Papi?
Aída: Do you hear me, Eduardo? I am not simple.
Abuela: Sí.
Aída: I am complicated.
Abuela: Sí, demasiada complicada.
Aída: Me and my family are not so simple.
Simón: Mom, the guy's an asshole.
Abuela (*Shaking her fist at helicopter.*): Asshole!
Aída: If my daughter was simple, she would not be in that water
   swimming.
Margarita: Simple? Papi . . . ?
Aída: Ahora, Eduardo, this is what I want you to do. When we get to
   Santa Catalina, I want you to call the TV station and demand an
   apology.
Eduardo: Cállete mujer! Aquí mando yo.° I will decide what is to be done.
Margarita: Papi, tell me what's going on.
Eduardo: Do you understand what I am saying to you, Aída?
Simón (*Leaning over side of boat, to Margarita.*): Yo Margo! You know
   that Mel Munson guy on TV? He called you a simple amateur and
   said you didn't have a chance.
Abuela (*Leaning directly behind Simón.*): Mi hija, insultó a la familia. Des-
   graciado!
Aída (*Leaning in behind Abuela.*): He called us peasants! And your father
   is not doing anything about it. He just knows how to yell at me.
Eduardo (*Through megaphone.*): Shut up! All of you! Do you want to
   break her concentration? Is that what you are after? Eh?

(*Abuela, Aída and Simón shrink back. Eduardo paces before them.*)

 Swimming is rhythm and concentration. You win a race *aquí*.
(*Pointing to his head.*) Now . . . (*To Simón.*) you, take care of the boat,
Aída y Mama . . . do something. Anything. Something practical.

(*Abuela and Aída get on knees and pray in Spanish.*)

Mal-Rayo los parta!: To hell with you!   *Cállete mujer! Aquí mando yo*: Quiet! I'm in
charge here.

Hija, give it everything, eh? . . . *por la familia. Uno . . . dos.* . . . You must win.

(*Simón goes into cabin. The prayers continue as lights change to indicate bright sunlight, later in the afternoon.*)

SCENE III

Tableau for a couple of beats. Eduardo on bow with timer in one hand as he counts strokes per minute. Simón is in the cabin steering, wearing his sunglasses, baseball cap on backward. Abuela and Aída are at the side of the boat, heads down, hands folded, still muttering prayers in Spanish.

Aída and Abuela (*Crossing themselves.*): En el nombre del Padre, del Hijo y del Espíritu Santo amén.°
Eduardo (*Through megaphone.*): You're stroking seventy-two!
Simón (*Singing.*): Mama's stroking, Mama's stroking seventy-two. . . .
Eduardo (*Through megaphone.*): You comfortable with it?
Simón (*Singing.*): Seventy-two, seventy-two, seventy-two for you.
Aída (*Looking at the heavens.*): Ay, Eduardo, *ven acá,°* we should be grateful that *Nuestro Señor°* gave us such a beautiful day.
Abuela (*Crosses herself.*): *Sí, gracias a Dios.°*
Eduardo: She's stroking seventy-two, with no problem (*He throws a kiss to the sky.*) It's a beautiful day to win.
Aída: *Qué hermoso!°* So clear and bright. Not a cloud in the sky. *Mira! Mira!°* Even rainbows on the water . . . a sign from God.
Simón (*Singing.*): Rainbows on the water . . . you in my arms . . .
Abuela and Eduardo (*Looking the wrong way.*): *Dónde?*
Aída (*Pointing toward Margarita.*): There, dancing in front of Margarita, leading her on . . .
Eduardo: Rainbows on . . . Ay *coño!* It's an oil slick! You . . . you . . . (*To Simón.*) Stop the boat. (*Runs to bow, yelling.*) Margarita! Margarita!

(*On the next stroke, Margarita comes up all covered in black oil.*)

Margarita: Papi! Papi . . . !

(*Everybody goes to the side and stares at Margarita, who stares back. Eduardo freezes.*)

En el nombre del Padre, del Hijo y del Espíritu Santo amén: In the name of the Father, the Son, and the Holy Ghost, Amen.   *ven acá:* Look here.   *Nuestro Señor:* Our Father [God]. *Sí, gracias a Dios:* Yes, thanks be to God.   *Qué hermoso!:* How beautiful!   *Mira!:* look.

Aída: *Apúrate,* Eduardo, move . . . what's wrong with you . . . *no me oíste,°* get my daughter out of the water.

Eduardo (*Softly.*): We can't touch her. If we touch her, she's disqualified.

Aída: But I'm her mother.

Eduardo: Not even by her own mother. Especially by her own mother. . . . You always want the rules to be different for you, you always want to be the exception. (*To Simón.*) And you . . . you didn't see it, eh? You were playing again?

Simón: *Papi,* I was watching . . .

Aída (*Interrupting.*): *Pues,* do something Eduardo. You are the big coach, the monitor.

Simón: Mentor! Mentor!

Eduardo: How can a person think around you? (*He walks off to bow, puts head in hands.*)

Abuela (*Looking over side.*): *Mira como todos los* little birds are dead. (*She crosses herself.*)

Aída: Their little wings are glued to their sides.

Simón: Christ, this is like the La Brea tar pits.

Aída: They can't move their little wings.

Abuela: *Esa niña tiene que moverse.°*

Simón: Yeah, Margo, you gotta move, man.

(*Abuela and Simón gesture for Margarita to move. Aída gestures for her to swim.*)

Abuela: *Anda niña, muévete.°*

Aída: Swim, *hija,* swim or the *aceite°* will stick to your wings.

Margarita: *Papi?*

Abuela (*Taking megaphone.*): Your *papi* say "move it!"

(*Margarita with difficulty starts moving.*)

Abuela, Aída and Simón (*Laboriously counting.*): *Uno, dos . . . uno, dos . . . anda . . . uno, dos.*

Eduardo (*Running to take megaphone from Abuela.*): *Uno, dos . . .*

(*Simón races into cabin and starts the engine. Abuela, Aída and Eduardo count together.*)

Simón (*Looking ahead.*): *Papi,* it's over there!

Eduardo: Eh?

Apúrate . . . no me oíste: Finish this! . . . didn't you hear me?   *Esa niña tiene que moverse:* That girl has to move.   *Anda niña, muévete:* Come on, girl, Move!   *aceite:* oil.

Simón (Pointing ahead and to the right.): It's getting clearer over there.
Eduardo (Through megaphone.): Now pay attention to me. Go to the right.

(*Simón, Abuela, Aída and Eduardo all lean over side. They point ahead and to the right, except Abuela, who points to the left.*)

Family (Shouting together.): Para yá!° Para yá!

(*Lights go down on boat. A special light on Margarita, swimming through the oil, and on Abuela, watching her.*)

Abuela: Sangre de mi sangre,° you will be another to save us. En Bolondron, where your great-grandmother Luz Suárez was born, they say one day it rained blood. All the people, they run into their houses. They cry, they pray, *pero* your great-grandmother Luz she had *cojones* like a man. She run outside. She look straight at the sky. She shake her fist. And she say to the evil one, "Mira . . . (*Beating her chest.*) coño, Diablo, aquí estoy si me quieres."° And she open her mouth, and she drunk the blood.

BLACKOUT

SCENE IV

Lights up on boat. Aída and Eduardo are on deck watching Margarita swim. We hear the gentle, rhythmic lap, lap, lap of the water, then the sound of inhaling and exhaling as Margarita's breathing becomes louder. Then Margarita's heartbeat is heard, with the lapping of the water and the breathing under it. These sounds continue beneath the dialogue to the end of the scene.

Aída: Dios mío. Look how she moves through the water. . . .
Eduardo: You see, it's very simple. It is a matter of concentration.
Aída: The first time I put her in water she came to life, she grew before my eyes. She moved, she smiled, she loved it more than me. She didn't want my breast any longer. She wanted the water.
Eduardo: And of course, the rhythm. The rhythm takes away the pain and helps the concentration.

(*Pause. Aída and Eduardo watch Margarita.*)

Aída: Is that my child or a seal. . . .

Para yá: over there.   Sangre de mi sangre: blood of my blood.   Mira . . . coño, Diablo, aquí estoy si me quieres: Look . . . damn it Devil, here I am if you want me.

Eduardo: Ah, a seal, the reason for that is that she's keeping her arms very close to her body. She cups her hands, and then she reaches and digs, reaches and digs.

Aída: To think that a daughter of mine. . . .

Eduardo: It's the training, the hours in the water. I used to tie weights around her little wrists and ankles.

Aída: A spirit, an ocean spirit, must have entered my body when I was carrying her.

Eduardo (To Margarita.): Your stroke is slowing down.

(Pause. We hear Margarita's heartbeat with the breathing under, faster now.)

Aída: Eduardo, that night, the night on the boat . . .

Eduardo: Ah, the night on the boat again . . . the moon was . . .

Aída: The moon was full. We were coming to America. . . . *Qué romantico.*

(Heartbeat and breathing continue.)

Eduardo: We were cold, afraid, with no money, and on top of everything, you were hysterical, yelling at me, tearing at me with your nails. *(Opens his shirt, points to the base of his neck.)* Look, I still bear the scars . . . telling me that I didn't know what I was doing . . . saying that we were going to die. . . .

Aída: You took me, you stole me from my home . . . you didn't give me a chance to prepare. You just said we have to go now, now! Now, you said. You didn't let me take anything. I left everything behind. . . . I left everything behind.

Eduardo: Saying that I wasn't good enough, that your father didn't raise you so that I could drown you in the sea.

Aída: You didn't let me say even a good-bye. You took me, you stole me, you tore me from my home.

Eduardo: I took you so we could be married.

Aída: That was in Miami. But that night on the boat, Eduardo. . . . We were not married, that night on the boat.

Eduardo: No pasó nada!° Once and for all get it out of your head, it was cold, you hated me, and we were afraid. . . .

Aída: Mentiroso!°

Eduardo: A man can't do it when he is afraid.

Aída: Liar! You did it very well.

No pasó nada!: Nothing happened. *Mentiroso!*: Liar!

Eduardo: I did?

Aída: Sí. Gentle. You were so gentle and then strong . . . my passion for you so deep. Standing next to you . . . I would ache . . . looking at your hands I would forget to breathe, you were irresistible.

Eduardo: I was?

Aída: You took me into your arms, you touched my face with your finger-tips . . . you kissed my eyes . . . *la esquina de la boca y* . . .

Eduardo: Sí, Sí, and then . . .

Aída: I look at your face on top of mine, and I see the lights of Havana in your eyes. That's when you seduced me.

Eduardo: Shhh, they're gonna hear you.

(*Lights go down. Special on Aída.*)

Aída: That was the night. A woman doesn't forget those things . . . and later that night was the dream . . . the dream of a big country with fields of fertile land and big, giant things growing. And there by a green, slimy pond I found a giant pea pod and when I opened it, it was full of little, tiny baby frogs.

(*Aída crosses herself as she watches Margarita. We hear louder breathing and heartbeat.*)

Margarita: Santa Teresa. Little Flower of God, pray for me. San Martín de Porres, pray for me. Santa Rosa de Lima, *Virgencita de la Caridad del Cobre*, pray for me. . . . Mother pray for me.

SCENE V

Loud howling of wind is heard, as lights change to indicate unstable weather, fog and mist. Family on deck, braced and huddled against the wind. Simón is at the helm.

Aída: Ay Dios mío, qué viento.°

Eduardo (*Through megaphone.*): Don't drift out . . . that wind is pushing you out. (*To Simón.*) You! Slow down. Can't you see your sister is drifting out?

Simón: It's the wind, *Papi*.

Aída: Baby, don't go so far. . . .

Abuela (*To heaven.*): Ay Gran Poder de Dios, quita este maldito viento.°

Simón: Margo! Margo! Stay close to the boat.

Eduardo: Dig in. Dig in hard . . . . Reach down from your guts and dig in.

Ay Dios mío, qué viento: Oh my God, what wind!   *Ay Gran Poder de Dios, quita este maldito viento:* By the great power of God, keep the cursed winds away!

Abuela (*To heaven.*): Ay *Virgen de la Caridad del Cobre, por lo más tú quieres a pararla.*

Aída (*Putting her hand out, reaching for Margarita.*): Baby, don't go far.

(*Abuela crosses herself. Action freezes. Lights get dimmer, special on Margarita. She keeps swimming, stops, starts again, stops, then, finally exhausted, stops altogether. The boat stops moving.*)

Eduardo: What's going on here? Why are we stopping?

Simón: Papi, she's not moving! Yo Margo!

(*The family all run to the side.*)

Eduardo: Hija! . . . Hijita! You're tired, eh?

Aída: Por supuesto she's tired. I like to see you get in the water, waving your arms and legs from San Pedro to Santa Catalina. A person isn't a machine, a person has to rest.

Simón: Yo, Mama! Cool out, it ain't fucking brain surgery.

Eduardo (*To Simón.*): Shut up, you. (*Louder to Margarita.*) I guess your mother's right for once, huh? . . . I guess you had to stop, eh? . . . Give your brother, the idiot . . . a chance to catch up with you.

Simón (*Clowning like Mortimer Snerd.*): Dum dee dum dee dum ooops, ah shucks . . .

Eduardo: I don't think he's Cuban.

Simón (*Like Ricky Ricardo.*): *Oye,* Lucy! I'm home! Ba ba lu!

Eduardo (*Joins in clowning, grabbing Simón in a headlock.*): What am I gonna do with this idiot, eh? I don't understand this idiot. He's not like us, Margarita. (*Laughing.*) You think if we put him into your bathing suit with a cap on his head . . . (*He laughs hysterically.*) You think anyone would know . . . huh? Do you think anyone would know? (*Laughs.*)

Simón (*Vamping.*): Ay, *mi amor.* Anybody looking for tits would know.

(*Eduardo slaps Simón across the face, knocking him down. Aída runs to Simón's aid. Abuela holds Eduardo back.*)

Margarita: Mía culpa!° Mía culpa!

Abuela: Qué dices hija?

Margarita: Papi, it's my fault, it's all my fault. . . . I'm so cold, I can't move. . . . I put my face in the water . . . and I hear them whispering . . . laughing at me. . . .

Aída: Who is laughing at you?

Mía culpa!: It's my fault.

Margarita: The fish are all biting me . . . they hate me . . . they whisper about me. She can't swim, they say. She can't glide. She has no grace. . . . Yellowtails, bonita, tuna, man-o'-war, snub-nose sharks, *los baracudas* . . . they all hate me . . . only the dolphins care . . . and sometimes I hear the whales crying . . . she is lost, she is dead. I'm so numb, I can't feel. *Papi! Papi!* Am I dead?

Eduardo: *Vamos,* baby, punch those arms in. Come on . . . do you hear me?

Margarita: *Papi* . . . *Papi* . . . forgive me. . . .

(*All is silent on the boat. Eduardo drops his megaphone, his head bent down in dejection. Abuela, Aída, Simón, all leaning over the side of the boat. Simón slowly walks away.*)

Aída: *Mi hija, qué tienes?*

Simón: Oh, Christ, don't make her say it. Please don't make her say it.

Abuela: Say what? *Qué cosa?*

Simón: She wants to quit, can't you see she's had enough?

Abuela: *Mira, para eso. Esta niña* is turning blue.

Aída: *Oyeme, mi hija.* Do you want to come out of the water?

Margarita: *Papi?*

Simón (*To Eduardo.*): She won't come out until *you* tell her.

Aída: Eduardo . . . answer your daughter.

Eduardo: *Le dije* to concentrate . . . concentrate on your rhythm. Then the rhythm would carry her . . . ay, it's a beautiful thing, Aída. It's like yoga, like meditation, the mind over matter . . . the mind controlling the body . . . that's how the great things in the world have been done. I wish you . . . I wish my wife could understand.

Margarita: *Papi?*

Simón (*To Margarita.*): Forget him.

Aída (*Imploring.*): Eduardo, *por favor.*

Eduardo (*Walking in circles.*): Why didn't you let her concentrate? Don't you understand, the concentration, the rhythm is everything. But no, you wouldn't listen. (*Screaming to the ocean.*) Goddamn Cubans, why, God, why do you make us go everywhere with our families? (*He goes to back of boat.*)

Aída (*Opening her arms.*): *Mi hija, ven,* come to Mami. (*Rocking.*) Your *mami* knows.

(*Abuela has taken the training bottle, puts it in a net. She and Simón lower it to Margarita.*)

Simón: Take this. Drink it. (*As Margarita drinks, Abuela crosses herself.*)

Abuela: *Sangre de mi sangre.*

(*Music comes up softly. Margarita drinks, gives the bottle back, stretches out her arms, as if on a cross. Floats on her back. She begins a graceful backstroke. Lights fade on boat as special lights come up on Margarita. She stops. Slowly turns over and starts to swim, gradually picking up speed. Suddenly as if in pain she stops, tries again, then stops in pain again. She becomes disoriented and falls to the bottom of the sea. Special on Margarita at the bottom of the sea.*)

Margarita: *Ya no puedo* . . . I can't. . . . A person isn't a machine . . . *es mi culpa* . . . Father forgive me . . . *Papi! Papi!* One, two. *Uno, dos.* (*Pause.*) *Papi! A dónde estás?* (*Pause.*) One, two, one, two. *Papi!* Ay, *Papi!* Where are you . . . ? Don't leave me. . . . Why don't you answer me? (*Pause. She starts to swim, slowly.*) *Uno, dos, uno, dos.* Dig in, dig in. (*Stops swimming.*) *Por favor, Papi!* (*Starts to swim again.*) One, two, one, two. Kick from your hip, kick from your hip. (*Stops swimming. Starts to cry.*) Oh God, please. . . . (*Pause.*) Hail Mary, full of grace . . . dig in, dig in . . . the Lord is with thee. . . . (*She swims to the rhythm of her Hail Mary.*) Hail Mary, full of grace . . . dig in, dig in . . . the Lord is with thee . . . dig in, dig in. . . . Blessed art thou among women. . . . *Mami*, it hurts. You let go of my hand. I'm lost. . . . And blessed is the fruit of thy womb, now and at the hour of our death. Amen. I don't want to die, I don't want to die.

(*Margarita is still swimming. Blackout. She is gone.*)

SCENE VI

Lights up on boat, we hear radio static. There is a heavy mist. On deck we see only black outline of Abuela with shawl over her head. We hear the voices of Eduardo, Aída, and Radio Operator.

Eduardo's Voice: La Havana! Coming from San Pedro. Over.

Radio Operator's Voice: Right, DT6-6, you say you've lost a swimmer.

Aída's Voice: Our child, our only daughter . . . listen to me. Her name is Margarita Inez Suárez, she is wearing a black one-piece bathing suit cut high in the legs with a white racing stripe down the sides, a white bathing cap with goggles and her whole body covered with a . . . with a . . .

Eduardo's Voice: With lanolin and paraffin.

Aída's Voice: Sí . . . *con lanolin and paraffin.*

(*More radio static. Special on Simón, on the edge of the boat.*)

Simón: Margo! Yo Margo! (*Pause.*) Man don't do this. (*Pause.*) Come on. . . . Come on. . . . (*Pause.*) God, why does everything have to be

so hard? (*Pause.*) Stupid. You know you're not supposed to die for
this. Stupid. It's his dream and he can't even swim. (*Pause.*) Punch
those arms in. Come home. Come home. I'm your little brother.
Don't forget what Mama said. You're not supposed to leave me behind. *Vamos*, Margarita, take your little brother, hold his hand tight
when you cross the street. He's so little. (*Pause.*) Oh Christ, give us
a sign. . . . I know! I know! Margo, I'll send you a message . . . like
mental telepathy. I'll hold my breath, close my eyes, and I'll bring
you home. (*He takes a deep breath; a few beats.*) This time I'll beep . . .
I'll send out sonar signals like a dolphin. (*He imitates dolphin
sounds.*)

(*The sound of real dolphins takes over from Simón, then fades into sound
of Abuela saying the Hail Mary in Spanish, as full lights come up slowly.*)

SCENE VII

*Eduardo coming out of cabin, sobbing, Aída holding him. Simón anxiously
scanning the horizon. Abuela looking calmly ahead.*

Eduardo: Es mi culpa, sí, es mi culpa.° (*He hits his chest.*)
Aída: Ya, ya viejo.° . . . it was my sin . . . I left my home.
Eduardo: Forgive me, forgive me. I've lost our daughter, our sister, our
  granddaughter, *mi carne, mi sangre, mis ilusiones.*° (*To heaven.*) *Dios
  mío*, take me . . . take me, I say . . . Goddammit, take me!
Simón: I'm going in.
Aída and Eduardo: No!
Eduardo (*Grabbing and holding Simón, speaking to heaven.*): God, take
  me, not my children. They are my dreams, my illusions . . . and not
  this one, this one is my mystery . . . he has my secret dreams. In him
  are the parts of me I cannot see.

(*Eduardo embraces Simón. Radio static becomes louder.*)

Aída: I . . . I think I see her.
Simón: No, it's just a seal.
Abuela (*Looking out with binoculars.*): Mi nietacita, dónde estás? (*She feels her
  heart.*) I don't feel the knife in my heart . . . my little fish is not lost.

(*Radio crackles with static. As lights dim on boat, Voices of Mel and
Mary Beth are heard over the radio.*)

Es mi culpa, sí, es mi culpa: It's my fault, yes, it's my fault.   *Ya, ya viejo:* Yes, yes, old man.
mi carne, mi sangre, mis ilusiones: My flesh, my blood, my dreams.

Mel's Voice: Tragedy has marred the face of the Wrigley Invitational Women's Race to Catalina. The Cuban swimmer, little Margarita Suárez, has reportedly been lost at sea. Coast Guard and divers are looking for her as we speak. Yet in spite of this tragedy the race must go on because . . .

Mary Beth's Voice (*Interrupting loudly.*): Mel!

Mel's Voice (*Startled.*): What!

Mary Beth's Voice: Ah . . . excuse me, Mel . . . we have a winner. We've just received word from Catalina that one of the swimmers is just fifty yards from the breakers . . . it's, oh, it's . . . Margarita Suárez!

(*Special on family in cabin listening to radio.*)

Mel's Voice: What? I thought she died!

(*Special on Margarita, taking off bathing cap, trophy in hand, walking on the water.*)

Mary Beth's Voice: Ahh . . . unless . . . unless this is a tragic . . . No . . . there she is, Mel. Margarita Suárez! The only one in the race wearing a black bathing suit cut high in the legs with a racing stripe down the side.

(*Family cheering, embracing.*)

Simón (*Screaming.*): Way to go, Margo!

Mel's Voice: This is indeed a miracle! It's a resurrection! Margarita Suárez, with a flotilla of boats to meet her, is now walking on the waters, through the breakers . . . onto the beach, with crowds of people cheering her on. What a jubilation! This is a miracle!

(*Sound of crowds cheering. Lights and cheering sounds fade.*)

BLACKOUT

WRITING EFFECTIVELY

WRITING ABOUT DRAMATIC REALISM

What's So Realistic About Realism?

When critics use the word *realism* in relation to a play, are they claiming it is true to life? Not necessarily. Realism generally refers to certain dramatic conventions that emerged during the nineteenth century. A realistic play is not necessarily any truer to life than an experimental one, though it's true that the conventions of realist drama have become so familiar to us that other kinds of drama—though no more artificial—can seem mannered and even bizarre to the casual viewer. Remember, though, that all drama is artifice—even realism.

To understand realism's conventions, it might help to contrast a play by Henrik Ibsen with one by Sophocles. Ibsen's characters speak in prose, not verse. His settings are drawn from contemporary life, not a legendary past. His characters are ordinary middle-class citizens, not kings, queens, and aristocrats.

These external characteristics are easy to spot, but you should also notice some less obvious ways in which plays of the Realist movement often differ from earlier drama. Ibsen, like other Realist playwrights, also seeks to portray the complexity of human psychology—especially motivation—in detailed, subtle ways. A character's inner life, memories, and motivations take on a crucial role in a Realist play.

In Shakespeare's *Othello*, the villain Iago announces that he wants revenge on the title character who has reportedly cuckolded him. This far-fetched assertion is never proved—the facts of the play seem to contradict it everywhere else—and Iago never mentions the motivation again. Shakespeare appears less interested in the reason for Iago's villainy than its consequences.

Did Iago have an unhappy childhood or a troubled adolescence? These questions do not greatly matter in Renaissance drama, but to Ibsen they become central. In *A Doll's House*, for example, we can infer that Nora's self-absorption and naiveté result from her father's overprotection. The inner lives, memories, and motivations of the characters now play a crucial role in the dramatic action.

Realist drama does not necessarily come any closer than other dramatic styles to getting at the truths of human existence. *A Doll's House*, for example, does not provide a more profound picture of psychological struggle than *Oedipus the King*. But Ibsen does offer a more detailed view of his protagonist's inner life and her daily routine.

CHECKLIST

Writing About a Realist Play

- ✓ List every detail the play gives about the protagonist's past. How does each detail affect the character's current behavior?
- ✓ Do the play's other characters understand the protagonist's deeper motivations?
- ✓ How much of the plot arises from misunderstandings among characters?
- ✓ Do major plot events grow from characters' interactions or do they occur at random?

✓ If an occurrence seems random, how does the protagonist's psychology determine his or her reactions to that event?

✓ What is the protagonist's primary motivation?

✓ What are the origins of that motivation?

WRITING ASSIGNMENT ON REALISM

Al Capovilla of Folsom Lake Center College has developed an ingenious assignment based on Ibsen's *A Doll's House* that asks you to combine the skills of a literary critic with those of a lawyer. Here is Professor Capovilla's assignment:

> You are the family lawyer for Torvald and Nora Helmer. The couple comes to you with a request. They want you to listen to an account of their domestic problems and recommend whether they should pursue a divorce or try to reconcile.
>
> You listen to both sides of the argument. (You also know everything that is said by every character.)
>
> Now, it is your task to write a short decision. In stating your opinion, provide a clear and organized explanation of your reasoning. Show both sides of the argument. You may employ as evidence anything said or done in the play.
>
> Conclude your paper with your recommendation. What do you advise under the circumstances—divorce or an attempt at reconciliation?

MORE TOPICS FOR WRITING

1. How relevant is *A Doll's House* today? Do women like Nora still exist? How about men like Torvald? Build an argument, either that the concerns of *A Doll's House* are timeless and universal or that the issues addressed by the play are historical, not contemporary.

2. Placing yourself in the character of Ibsen's Torvald Helmer, write a defense of him and his attitudes as he himself might write it.

3. Choose a character from Milcha Sanchez-Scott's *The Cuban Swimmer* and examine his or her motivations. What makes your character act as he or she does? Present evidence from the play to back up your argument.

4. Imagine you're a casting director. Choose a play from this chapter and cast it with well-known television and movie stars. Explain, in depth, what qualities in the characters you hope to emphasize by your casting choices.

5. Describe some of the difficulties of staging *The Cuban Swimmer* as a play. What would be lost or gained by remaking it as a movie?

27
Plays for Further Reading

Jane Martin

Beauty

The identity of Jane Martin is a closely guarded secret. No biographical details, public statements, or photographs of this Kentucky-based playwright have been published, nor has she given any interviews or made any public appearances. Martin first came to public notice in 1981 for Talking With, *a collection of monologues that received a number of productions worldwide and won a Best Foreign Play of the Year award in Germany. Of Martin's many plays, others include* What Mama Don't Know *(1988),* Cementville *(1991),* Keely and Du *(which was a finalist for the 1993 Pulitzer Prize),* Middle-Aged White Guys *(1995),* Jack and Jill *(1996),* Mr. Bundy *(1998),* Anton in Show Business *(2000),* Flaming Guns of the Purple Sage *(2001), and* Good Boys *(2002). Her most recent work is a contribution to* Bill of (W)rights *(2004), a program of short plays based on the first ten amendments to the United States Constitution.**

CHARACTERS

Carla
Bethany

SCENE: *An apartment. Minimalist set. A young woman, Carla, on the phone.*

Carla: In love with me? You're in love with me? Could you describe yourself again? Uh-huh. Uh-huh. And you spoke to me? (*A knock at the door.*) Listen, I always hate to interrupt a marriage proposal, but . . . could you possibly hold that thought? (*Puts phone down and goes to door. Bethany, the same age as Carla and a friend, is there. She carries the sort of mid-eastern lamp we know of from Aladdin.*)
Bethany: Thank God you were home. I mean, you're not going to believe this!

*Please see the Caution Notice in the Acknowledgments, page A-7, which gives important information about using this play in performance.

Carla: Somebody on the phone. (*Goes back to it.*)

Bethany: I mean, I just had a beach urge, so I told them at work my uncle was dying . . .

Carla (*Motions to Bethany for quiet.*): And you were the one in the leather jacket with the tattoo? What was the tattoo? (*Carla again asks Bethany, who is gesturing wildly that she should hang up, to cool it.*) Look, a screaming eagle from shoulder to shoulder, maybe. There were a lot of people in the bar.

Bethany (*Gesturing and mouthing.*): I have to get back to work.

Carla (*On phone.*): See, the thing is, I'm probably not going to marry someone I can't remember . . . particularly when I don't drink. Sorry. Sorry. Sorry. (*She hangs up.*) Madness.

Bethany: So I ran out to the beach . . .

Carla: This was some guy I never met who apparently offered me a beer . . .

Bethany: . . . low tide and this . . . (*The lamp.*) . . . was just sitting there, lying there . . .

Carla: . . . and he tracks me down . . .

Bethany: . . . on the beach, and I lift this lid thing . . .

Carla: . . . and seriously proposes marriage.

Bethany: . . . and a genie comes out.

Carla: I mean, that's twice in a . . . what?

Bethany: A genie comes out of this thing.

Carla: A genie?

Bethany: I'm not kidding, the whole Disney kind of thing, swirling smoke, and then this twenty-foot-high, see-through guy in like an Arabian outfit.

Carla: Very funny.

Bethany: Yes, funny, but twenty feet high! I look up and down the beach, I'm alone. I don't have my pepper spray or my hand alarm. You know me, when I'm petrified I joke. I say his voice is too high for Robin Williams, and he says he's a castrati. Naturally. Who else would I meet?

Carla: What's a castrati?

Bethany: You know . . .

(*The appropriate gesture.*)

Carla: Bethany, dear one, I have three modeling calls. I am meeting Ralph Lauren!

Bethany: Okay, good. Ralph Lauren. Look, I am not kidding!

Carla: You're not kidding what?!

Bethany: There is a genie in this thingamajig.

Carla: Uh-huh. I'll be back around eight.

Bethany: And he offered me *wishes!*

Carla: Is this some elaborate practical joke because it's my birthday?

Bethany: No, happy birthday, but I'm like crazed because I'm on this deserted beach with a twenty-foot-high, see-through genie, so like sarcastically . . . you know how I need a new car . . . I said fine, gimme
25,000 dollars . . .

Carla: On the beach with the genie?

Bethany: Yeah, right, exactly, and it rains down out of the sky.

Carla: Oh sure.

Bethany (Pulling a wad out of her purse.): Count it, those are thousands. I
lost one in the surf.

*(Carla sees the top bill. Looks at Bethany, who nods encouragement.
Carla thumbs through them.)*

Carla: These look real.

Bethany: Yeah.

Carla: And they rained down out of the sky?

Bethany: Yeah.

Carla: You've been really strange lately, are you dealing?

Bethany: Dealing what, I've even given up chocolate.

Carla: Let me see the genie.

Bethany: Wait, wait.

Carla: Bethany, I don't have time to screw around. Let me see the genie
or let me go on my appointments.

Bethany: Wait! So I pick up the money . . . see, there's sand on the
money . . . and I'm like nuts so I say, you know, "Okay, look, ummm,
big guy, my uncle is in the hospital" . . . because as you know when I
said to the people at work my uncle was dying, I was on one level
telling the truth although it had nothing to do with the beach, but
he was in Intensive Care after the accident, and that's on my mind,
so I say, okay, Genie, heal my uncle . . . which is like impossible
given he was hit by two trucks, and the genie says, "Yes, Master" . . .
like they're supposed to say, and he goes into this like kind of whirlwind, kicking up sand and stuff, and I'm like, "Oh my God!" and the
air clears, and he bows, you know, and says, "It is done, Master," and
I say, "Okay, whatever-you-are, I'm calling on my cell phone," and I
get it out and I get this doctor who is like dumbstruck who says my
uncle came to, walked out of Intensive Care and left the hospital!
I'm not kidding, Carla.

Carla: On your mother's grave?

Bethany: On my mother's grave.

(*They look at each other.*)

Carla: Let me see the genie.

Bethany: No, no, look, that's the whole thing . . . I was just, like, reacting, you know, responding, and that's already two wishes . . . although
I'm really pleased about my uncle, the $25,000 thing, I could have
asked for $10 million, and there is only one wish left.

Carla: So ask for $10 million.

Bethany: I don't think so. I don't think so. I mean, I gotta focus in here.
Do you have a sparkling water?

Carla: No. Bethany, I'm missing Ralph Lauren now. Very possibly my
one chance to go from catalogue model to the very, very big time, so,
if you are joking, stop joking.

Bethany: Not joking. See, see, the thing is, I know what I want. In my guts.
Yes. Underneath my entire bitch of a life is this unspoken, ferocious,
all-consuming urge . . .

Carla (*Trying to get her to move this along.*): Ferocious, all-consuming urge . . .

Bethany: I want to be like you.

Carla: Me?

Bethany: Yes.

Carla: Half the time you don't even like me.

Bethany: Jealous. The ogre of jealousy.

Carla: You're the one with the $40,000 job straight out of school. You're
the one who has published short stories. I'm the one hanging on by
her fingernails in modeling. The one who has creeps calling her on
the phone. The one who had to have a nose job.

Bethany: I want to be beautiful.

Carla: You are beautiful.

Bethany: Carla, I'm not beautiful.

Carla: You have charm. You have personality. You know perfectly well
you're pretty.

Bethany: "Pretty," see, that's it. Pretty is the minor leagues of beautiful.
Pretty is what people discover about you after they know you. Beautiful is what knocks them out across the room. Pretty, you get called
a couple of times a year; *beautiful* is 24 hours a day.

Carla: Yeah? So?

Bethany: So?! We're talking *beauty* here. Don't say "So?" Beauty is the
real deal. You are the center of any moment of your life. People
stare. Men flock. I've seen you get offered discounts on makeup for

no reason. Parents treat beautiful children better. Studies show your income goes up. You can have sex anytime you want it. Men have to know me. That takes up to a year. I'm continually horny.

Carla: Bethany, I don't even like sex. I can't have a conversation without men coming on to me. I have no privacy. I get hassled on the street. They start pressuring me from the beginning. Half the time, it never occurs to them to start with a conversation. Smart guys like you. You've had three long-term relationships, and you're only twenty-three. I haven't had one. The good guys, the smart guys are scared to death of me. I'm surrounded by male bimbos who think a preposition is when you go to school away from home. I have no woman friends except you. I don't even want to talk about this!

Bethany: I knew you'd say something like this. See, you're "in the club" so you can say this. It's the way beauty functions as an elite. You're trying to keep it all for yourself.

Carla: I'm trying to tell you it's no picnic.

Bethany: But it's what everybody wants. It's the nasty secret at large in the world. It's the unspoken tidal desire in every room and on every street. It's the unspoken, the soundless whisper . . . millions upon millions of people longing hopelessly and forever to stop being whatever they are and be beautiful, but the difference between those ardent multitudes and me is that I have a goddamn genie and one more wish!

Carla: Well, it's not what I want. This is me, Carla. I have never read a whole book. Page 6, I can't remember page 4. The last thing I read was "The Complete Idiot's Guide to WordPerfect." I leave dinner parties right after the dessert because I'm out of conversation. You know the dumb blond joke about on the application where it says, "Sign here," she put Sagittarius? I've done that. Only beautiful guys approach me, and that's because they want to borrow my eye shadow. I barely exist outside a mirror! You don't want to *be me.*

Bethany: None of you tell the truth. That's why you have no friends. We can all see you're just trying to make us feel better because we aren't in your league. This only proves to me it should be my third wish. Money can only buy things. Beauty makes you the center of the universe.

(*Bethany picks up the lamp.*)

Carla: Don't do it. Bethany, don't wish it! I am telling you you'll regret it.

(*Bethany lifts the lid. There is a tremendous crash, and the lights go out. Then they flicker and come back up, revealing Bethany and Carla on the floor where they have been thrown by the explosion. We don't realize it at first, but they have exchanged places.)*

Carla/Bethany: Oh God.

Bethany/Carla: Oh God.

Carla/Bethany: Am I bleeding? Am I dying?

Bethany/Carla: I'm so dizzy. You're not bleeding.

Carla/Bethany: Neither are you.

Bethany/Carla: I feel so weird.

Carla/Bethany: Me too. I feel . . . (*Looking at her hands.*) Oh, my God, I'm wearing your jewelry. I'm wearing your nail polish.

Bethany/Carla: I know I'm over here, but I can see myself over there.

Carla/Bethany: I'm wearing your dress. I have your legs!!

Bethany/Carla: These aren't my shoes. I can't meet Ralph Lauren wearing these shoes!

Carla/Bethany: I wanted to be beautiful, but I didn't want to be you.

Bethany/Carla: Thanks a lot!!

Carla/Bethany: I've got to go. I want to pick someone out and get laid.

Bethany/Carla: You can't just walk out of here in my body!

Carla/Bethany: Wait a minute. Wait a minute. What's eleven eighteenths of 1,726?

Bethany/Carla: Why?

Carla/Bethany: I'm a public accountant. I want to know if you have my brain.

Bethany/Carla: One hundred thirty-two and a half.

Carla/Bethany: You have my brain.

Bethany/Carla: What shade of Rubenstein lipstick does Cindy Crawford wear with teal blue?

Carla/Bethany: Raging Storm.

Bethany/Carla: You have my brain. You poor bastard.

Carla/Bethany: I don't care. Don't you see?

Bethany/Carla: See what?

Carla/Bethany: We both have the one thing, the one and only thing everybody wants.

Bethany/Carla: What is that?

Carla/Bethany: It's better than beauty for me; it's better than brains for you.

Bethany/Carla: What? What?!

Carla/Bethany: Different problems.

BLACKOUT

Arthur Miller

Death of a Salesman

1949

CERTAIN PRIVATE CONVERSATIONS IN TWO ACTS AND A REQUIEM

ARTHUR MILLER

Arthur Miller (1915–2005) was born in 1915 into a lower-income Jewish family in New York City's Harlem but grew up in Brooklyn. He studied play-writing at the University of Michigan, later wrote radio scripts, and during World War II worked as a steamfitter. When the New York Drama Critics named his All My Sons *best play of 1947, Miller told an interviewer, "I don't see how you can write anything decent without using as your basis the question of right and wrong." (The play is about a guilty manufacturer of defective aircraft parts.)* Death of a Salesman *(1949, Pulitzer Prize for Drama) made* Miller famous. The Crucible *(1953), a dramatic indictment of the Salem witch trials, gained him further attention at a time when Senator Joseph McCarthy was conducting loyalty investigations; in 1996,* The Crucible *was made into a film staring Daniel Day-Lewis and Winona Ryder. For a while (1956–1961), Miller was the husband of actress Marilyn Monroe, whom the main character of his* After the Fall *(1964) resembles. Among Miller's other plays are* A View from the Bridge *(1955);* The Price *(1968);* The Creation of the World and Other Business *(1972);* Playing for Time *(1980), written for television;* Broken Glass *(1994);* Mr. Peters' Connections *(1999);* Resurrection Blues *(2002); and Finishing the Picture *(2004). He published an autobiography, several volumes of essays, two collections of short stories, and two novels,* Focus *(1945) and* The Misfits *(1960), drawn from his screenplay for the film starring Monroe.*

A new production of Death of a Salesman, *starring Brian Dennehy as Willy Loman, opened on Broadway on February 10, 1999, fifty years to the day after its original premiere. Although Miller made a number of memorable contributions to the American theater, this work is unquestionably the pinnacle of his achievement. In Willy Loman, he has given us a figure who is at once both representative and unique, whose desperate plight is conveyed through memorable dialogue and scenes of almost unbearable painfulness and intensity.*

CAST

Willy Loman
Linda
Biff
Charley

Brian Dennehy with Ron Eldard and Ted Koch in a 2000 TV production of *Death of a Salesman*

Uncle Ben
Howard Wagner
Jenny
Happy
Bernard
The Woman
Stanley
Miss Forsythe
Letta

SCENE. *The action takes place in Willy Loman's house and yard and in various places he visits in the New York and Boston of today. Throughout the play, in the stage directions, left and right mean stage left and stage right.*

ACT I

A melody is heard, played upon a flute. It is small and fine, telling of grass and trees and the horizon. The curtain rises.

Before us is the Salesman's house. We are aware of towering, angular shapes behind it, surrounding it on all sides. Only the blue light of the sky falls upon the house and forestage; the surrounding area shows an angry glow of orange. As more light appears, we see a solid vault of apartment houses around the small, fragile-seeming home. An air of the dream clings to the place, a dream rising out of reality. The kitchen at center seems actual enough, for there is a kitchen table with three chairs, and a refrigerator. But no other fixtures are seen. At the back of the kitchen there is a draped entrance, which leads to the living room. To the right of the kitchen, on a level raised two feet, is a bedroom furnished only with a brass bedstead and a straight chair. On a shelf over the bed a silver athletic trophy stands. A window opens onto the apartment house at the side.

Behind the kitchen, on a level raised six and a half feet, is the boys' bedroom, at present barely visible. Two beds are dimly seen, and at the back of the room a dormer window. (This bedroom is above the unseen living room.) At the left a stairway curves up to it from the kitchen.

The entire setting is wholly or, in some places, partially transparent. The roof-line of the house is one-dimensional; under and over it we see the apartment buildings. Before the house lies an apron, curving beyond the forestage into the orchestra. This forward area serves as the backyard as well as the locale of all Willy's imaginings and of his city scenes. Whenever the action is in the present the actors observe the imaginary wall-lines, entering the house only through the door at the left. But in the scenes of the past these boundaries are broken, and characters enter or leave a room by stepping "through" a wall onto the forestage.

From the right, Willy Loman, the Salesman, enters, carrying two large sample cases. The flute plays on. He hears but is not aware of it. He is past sixty years of age, dressed quietly. Even as he crosses the stage to the doorway of the house, his exhaustion is apparent. He unlocks the door, comes into the kitchen, and thankfully lets his burden down, feeling the soreness of his palms. A word-sigh escapes his lips—it might be, "Oh, boy, oh, boy." He closes the door, then carries his cases out into the living room, through the draped kitchen doorway.

Linda, his wife, has stirred in her bed at the right. She gets out and puts on a robe, listening. Most often jovial, she has developed an iron repression of her exceptions to Willy's behavior—she more than loves him, she admires him, as though his mercurial nature, his temper, his massive dreams and little cruelties, served her only as sharp reminders of the turbulent longings within him, longings which she shares but lacks the temperament to utter and follow to their end.

Linda (hearing Willy outside the bedroom, calls with some trepidation): Willy!

Willy: It's all right. I came back.

Linda: Why? What happened? (*Slight pause.*) Did something happen, Willy?

Willy: No, nothing happened.

Linda: You didn't smash the car, did you?

Willy (*with casual irritation*): I said nothing happened. Didn't you hear me?

Linda: Don't you feel well?

Willy: I am tired to the death. (*The flute has faded away. He sits on the bed beside her, a little numb.*) I couldn't make it. I just couldn't make it, Linda.

Linda (*very carefully, delicately*): Where were you all day? You look terrible.

Willy: I got as far as a little above Yonkers. I stopped for a cup of coffee. Maybe it was the coffee.

Linda: What?

Willy (*after a pause*): I suddenly couldn't drive any more. The car kept going onto the shoulder, y'know?

Linda (*helpfully*): Oh. Maybe it was the steering again. I don't think Angelo knows the Studebaker.

Willy: No, it's me, it's me. Suddenly I realize I'm goin' sixty miles an hour and I don't remember the last five minutes. I'm—I can't seem to—keep my mind to it.

Linda: Maybe it's your glasses. You never went for your new glasses.

Willy: No, I see everything. I came back ten miles an hour. It took me nearly four hours from Yonkers.

Linda (*resigned*): Well, you'll just have to take a rest. Willy, you can't continue this way.

Willy: I just got back from Florida.

Linda: But you didn't rest your mind. Your mind is overactive, and the mind is what counts, dear.

Willy: I'll start out in the morning. Maybe I'll feel better in the morning. (*She is taking off his shoes.*) These goddam arch supports are killing me.

Linda: Take an aspirin. Should I get you an aspirin? It'll soothe you.

Willy (*with wonder*): I was driving along, you understand? And I was fine. I was even observing the scenery. You can imagine, me looking at scenery, on the road every week of my life. But it's so beautiful up there, Linda, the trees are so thick, and the sun is warm. I opened the windshield and just let the warm air bathe over me. And then all of a sudden I'm goin' off the road! I'm tellin' ya, I absolutely forgot I was driving. If I'd've gone the other way over the white line I might've killed somebody. So I went on again—and five minutes later I'm dreamin' again, and I nearly—(*He presses two fingers against his eyes.*) I have such thoughts, I have such strange thoughts.

Linda: Willy, dear. Talk to them again. There's no reason why you can't work in New York.

Willy: They don't need me in New York. I'm the New England man. I'm vital in New England.

Linda: But you're sixty years old. They can't expect you to keep traveling every week.

Willy: I'll have to send a wire to Portland. I'm supposed to see Brown and Morrison tomorrow morning at ten o'clock to show the line. Goddammit, I could sell them! (*He starts putting on his jacket.*)

Linda (*taking the jacket from him*): Why don't you go down to the place tomorrow and tell Howard you've simply got to work in New York? You're too accommodating, dear.

Willy: If old man Wagner was alive I'd a been in charge of New York now! That man was a prince, he was a masterful man. But that boy of his, that Howard, he don't appreciate. When I went north the first time, the Wagner Company didn't know where New England was!

Linda: Why don't you tell those things to Howard, dear?

Willy (*encouraged*): I will, I definitely will. Is there any cheese?

Linda: I'll make you a sandwich.

Willy: No, go to sleep. I'll take some milk. I'll be up right away. The boys in?

Linda: They're sleeping. Happy took Biff on a date tonight.

Willy (*interested*): That so?

Linda: It was so nice to see them shaving together, one behind the other, in the bathroom. And going out together. You notice? The whole house smells of shaving lotion.

Willy: Figure it out. Work a lifetime to pay off a house. You finally own it, and there's nobody to live in it.

Linda: Well, dear, life is a casting off. It's always that way.

Willy: No, no, some people—some people accomplish something. Did Biff say anything after I went this morning?

Linda: You shouldn't have criticized him, Willy, especially after he just got off the train. You mustn't lose your temper with him.

Willy: When the hell did I lose my temper? I simply asked him if he was making any money. Is that a criticism?

Linda: But, dear, how could he make any money?

Willy (*worried and angered*): There's such an undercurrent in him. He became a moody man. Did he apologize when I left this morning?

Linda: He was crestfallen, Willy. You know how he admires you. I think if he finds himself, then you'll both be happier and not fight any more.

Willy: How can he find himself on a farm? Is that a life? A farmhand? In the beginning, when he was young, I thought, well, a young man, it's good for him to tramp around, take a lot of different jobs. But it's more than ten years now and he has yet to make thirty-five dollars a week!

Linda: He's finding himself, Willy.
Willy: Not finding yourself at the age of thirty-four is a disgrace!
Linda: Shh!
Willy: The trouble is he's lazy, goddammit!
Linda: Willy, please!
Willy: Biff is a lazy bum.
Linda: They're sleeping. Get something to eat. Go on down.
Willy: Why did he come home? I would like to know what brought
   him home.
Linda: I don't know. I think he's still lost, Willy. I think he's very lost.
Willy: Biff Loman is lost. In the greatest country in the world a young
   man with such—personal attractiveness, gets lost. And such a hard
   worker. There's one thing about Biff—he's not lazy.
Linda: Never.
Willy (*with pity and resolve*): I'll see him in the morning. I'll have a nice
   talk with him. I'll get him a job selling. He could be big in no time.
   My God! Remember how they used to follow him around in high
   school? When he smiled at one of them their faces lit up. When he
   walked down the street . . . (*He loses himself in reminiscences.*)
Linda (*trying to bring him out of it*): Willy, dear, I got a new kind of American-
   type cheese today. It's whipped.
Willy: Why do you get American when I like Swiss?
Linda: I just thought you'd like a change—
Willy: I don't want a change! I want Swiss cheese. Why am I always being
   contradicted?
Linda (*with a covering laugh*): I thought it would be a surprise.
Willy: Why don't you open a window in here, for God's sake?
Linda (*with infinite patience*): They're all open, dear.
Willy: The way they boxed us in here. Bricks and windows, windows and
   bricks.
Linda: We should've bought the land next door.
Willy: The street is lined with cars. There's not a breath of fresh air in
   the neighborhood. The grass don't grow any more, you can't raise a
   carrot in the back yard. They should've had a law against apartment
   houses. Remember those two beautiful elm trees out there? When I
   and Biff hung the swing between them?
Linda: Yeah, like being a million miles from the city.
Willy: They should've arrested the builder for cutting those down. They
   massacred the neighborhood. (*Lost.*) More and more I think of those
   days, Linda. This time of year it was lilac and wisteria. And then the pe-
   onies would come out, and the daffodils. What fragrance in this room!
Linda: Well, after all, people had to move somewhere.

Willy: No, there's more people now.

Linda: I don't think there's more people. I think—

Willy: There's more people! That's what's ruining this country! Population is getting out of control. The competition is maddening! Smell the stink from that apartment house! And another on the other side . . . How can they whip cheese?

On Willy's last line, Biff and Happy raise themselves up in their beds, listening.

Linda: Go down, try it. And be quiet.

Willy (*turning to Linda, guiltily*): You're not worried about me, are you, sweetheart?

Biff: What's the matter?

Happy: Listen!

Linda: You've got too much on the ball to worry about.

Willy: You're my foundation and my support, Linda.

Linda: Just try to relax, dear. You make mountains out of molehills.

Willy: I won't fight with him any more. If he wants to go back to Texas, let him go.

Linda: He'll find his way.

Willy: Sure. Certain men just don't get started till later in life. Like Thomas Edison, I think. Or B. F. Goodrich. One of them was deaf. (*He starts for the bedroom doorway.*) I'll put my money on Biff.

Linda: And Willy—if it's warm Sunday we'll drive in the country. And we'll open the windshield, and take lunch.

Willy: No, the windshields don't open on the new cars.

Linda: But you opened it today.

Willy: Me? I didn't. (*He stops.*) Now isn't that peculiar! Isn't that a remarkable—(*He breaks off in amazement and fright as the flute is heard distantly.*)

Linda: What, darling?

Willy: That is the most remarkable thing.

Linda: What, dear?

Willy: I was thinking of the Chevvy. (*Slight pause.*) Nineteen twenty-eight . . . when I had that red Chevvy—(*Breaks off.*) That funny? I coulda sworn I was driving that Chevvy today.

Linda: Well, that's nothing. Something must've reminded you.

Willy: Remarkable. Ts. Remember those days? The way Biff used to simonize that car? The dealer refused to believe there was eighty thousand miles on it. (*He shakes his head.*) Heh! (*To Linda.*) Close your eyes, I'll be right up. (*He walks out of the bedroom.*)

Happy (*to Biff*): Jesus, maybe he smashed up the car again!

Linda (*calling after Willy*): Be careful on the stairs, dear! The cheese is on the middle shelf! (*She turns, goes over to the bed, takes his jacket, and goes out of the bedroom.*)

Light has risen on the boys' room. Unseen, Willy is heard talking to himself, "Eighty thousand miles," and a little laugh. Biff gets out of bed, comes downstage a bit, and stands attentively. Biff is two years older than his brother Happy, well built, but in these days bears a worn air and seems less self-assured. He has succeeded less, and his dreams are stronger and less acceptable than Happy's. Happy is tall, powerfully made. Sexuality is like a visible color on him, or a scent that many women have discovered. He, like his brother, is lost, but in a different way, for he has never allowed himself to turn his face toward defeat and is thus more confused and hardskinned, although seemingly more content.

Happy (*getting out of bed*): He's going to get his license taken away if he keeps that up. I'm getting nervous about him, y'know, Biff?

Biff: His eyes are going.

Happy: No, I've driven with him. He sees all right. He just doesn't keep his mind on it. I drove into the city with him last week. He stops at a green light and then it turns red and he goes. (*He laughs.*)

Biff: Maybe he's color-blind.

Happy: Pop? Why he's got the finest eye for color in the business. You know that.

Biff (*sitting down on his bed*): I'm going to sleep.

Happy: You're not still sour on Dad, are you, Biff?

Biff: He's all right, I guess.

Willy (*underneath them, in the living room*): Yes, sir, eighty thousand miles—eighty-two thousand!

Biff: You smoking?

Happy (*holding out a pack of cigarettes*): Want one?

Biff (*taking a cigarette*): I can never sleep when I smell it.

Willy: What a simonizing job, heh!

Happy (*with deep sentiment*): Funny, Biff, y'know? Us sleeping in here again? The old beds. (*He pats his bed affectionately.*) All the talk that went across those two beds, huh? Our whole lives.

Biff: Yeah. Lotta dreams and plans.

Happy (*with a deep and masculine laugh*): About five hundred women would like to know what was said in this room.

They share a soft laugh.

Biff: Remember that big Betsy something—what the hell was her name—over on Bushwick Avenue?

Happy (*combing his hair*): With the collie dog!

Biff: That's the one. I got you in there, remember?

Happy: Yeah, that was my first time—I think. Boy, there was a pig! (*They laugh, almost crudely.*) You taught me everything I know about women. Don't forget that.

Biff: I bet you forgot how bashful you used to be. Especially with girls.

Happy: Oh, I still am, Biff.

Biff: Oh, go on.

Happy: I just control it, that's all. I think I got less bashful and you got more so. What happened, Biff? Where's the old humor, the old confidence? (*He shakes Biff's knee. Biff gets up and moves restlessly about the room.*) What's the matter?

Biff: Why does Dad mock me all the time?

Happy: He's not mocking you, he—

Biff: Everything I say there's a twist of mockery on his face. I can't get near him.

Happy: He just wants you to make good, that's all. I wanted to talk to you about Dad for a long time, Biff. Something's—happening to him. He—talks to himself.

Biff: I noticed that this morning. But he always mumbled.

Happy: But not so noticeable. It got so embarrassing I sent him to Florida. And you know something? Most of the time he's talking to you.

Biff: What's he say about me?

Happy: I can't make it out.

Biff: What's he say about me?

Happy: I think the fact that you're not settled, that you're still kind of up in the air . . .

Biff: There's one or two other things depressing him, Happy.

Happy: What do you mean?

Biff: Never mind. Just don't lay it all on me.

Happy: But I think if you just got started—I mean—is there any future for you out there?

Biff: I tell ya, Hap, I don't know what the future is. I don't know—what I'm supposed to want.

Happy: What do you mean?

Biff: Well, I spent six or seven years after high school trying to work myself up. Shipping clerk, salesman, business of one kind or another. And it's a measly manner of existence. To get on that subway on the hot mornings in summer. To devote your whole life to keeping stock, or making phone calls, or selling or buying. To suffer fifty weeks of the year for the sake of a two-week vacation, when all you really desire is to be outdoors, with your shirt off. And always to have to get ahead of the next fella. And still—that's how you build a future.

Happy: Well, you really enjoy it on a farm? Are you content out there?

Biff (with rising agitation): Hap, I've had twenty or thirty different kinds of jobs since I left home before the war, and it always turns out the same. I just realized it lately. In Nebraska when I herded cattle, and the Dakotas, and Arizona, and now in Texas. It's why I came home now, I guess, because I realized it. This farm I work on, it's spring there now, see? And they've got about fifteen new colts. There's nothing more inspiring or—beautiful than the sight of a mare and a new colt. And it's cool there now, see? Texas is cool now, and it's spring. And whenever spring comes to where I am, I suddenly get the feeling, my God, I'm not gettin' anywhere! What the hell am I doing, playing around with horses, twenty-eight dollars a week! I'm thirty-four years old, I oughta be makin' my future. That's when I come running home. And now, I get here, and I don't know what to do with myself. *(After a pause.)* I've always made a point of not wasting my life, and everytime I come back here I know that all I've done is to waste my life.

Happy: You're a poet, you know that, Biff? You're a—you're an idealist!

Biff: No, I'm mixed up very bad. Maybe I oughta get married. Maybe I oughta get stuck into something. Maybe that's my trouble. I'm like a boy. I'm not married, I'm not in business, I just—I'm like a boy. Are you content, Hap? You're a success, aren't you? Are you content?

Happy: Hell, no!

Biff: Why? You're making money, aren't you?

Happy (moving about with energy, expressiveness): All I can do now is wait for the merchandise manager to die. And suppose I get to be merchandise manager? He's a good friend of mine, and he just built a terrific estate on Long Island. And he lived there about two months and sold it, and now he's building another one. He can't enjoy it once it's finished. And I know that's just what I would do. I don't know what the hell I'm workin' for. Sometimes I sit in my apartment—all alone. And I think of the rent I'm paying. And it's crazy. But then, it's what I always wanted. My own apartment, a car, and plenty of women. And still, goddammit, I'm lonely.

Biff (with enthusiasm): Listen, why don't you come out West with me?

Happy: You and I, heh?

Biff: Sure, maybe we could buy a ranch. Raise cattle, use our muscles. Men built like we are should be working out in the open.

Happy (avidly): The Loman Brothers, heh?

Biff (with vast affection): Sure, we'd be known all over the counties!

Happy (*enthralled*): That's what I dream about, Biff. Sometimes I want to just rip my clothes off in the middle of the store and outbox that goddam merchandise manager. I mean I can outbox, outrun, and outlift anybody in that store, and I have to take orders from those common, petty sons-of-bitches till I can't stand it any more.

Biff: I'm tellin' you, kid, if you were with me I'd be happy out there.

Happy (*enthused*): See, Biff, everybody around me is so false that I'm constantly lowering my ideals . . .

Biff: Baby, together we'd stand up for one another, we'd have someone to trust.

Happy: If I were around you—

Biff: Hap, the trouble is we weren't brought up to grub for money. I don't know how to do it.

Happy: Neither can I!

Biff: Then let's go!

Happy: The only thing is—what can you make out there?

Biff: But look at your friend. Builds an estate and then hasn't the peace of mind to live in it.

Happy: Yeah, but when he walks into the store the waves part in front of him. That's fifty-two thousand dollars a year coming through the revolving door, and I got more in my pinky finger than he's got in his head.

Biff: Yeah, but you just said—

Happy: I gotta show some of those pompous, self-important executives over there that Hap Loman can make the grade. I want to walk into the store the way he walks in. Then I'll go with you, Biff. We'll be together yet, I swear. But take those two we had tonight. Now weren't they gorgeous creatures?

Biff: Yeah, yeah, most gorgeous I've had in years.

Happy: I get that any time I want, Biff. Whenever I feel disgusted. The only trouble is, it gets like bowling or something. I just keep knockin' them over and it doesn't mean anything. You still run around a lot?

Biff: Naa. I'd like to find a girl—steady, somebody with substance.

Happy: That's what I long for.

Biff: Go on! You'd never come home.

Happy: I would! Somebody with character, with resistance! Like Mom, y'know? You're gonna call me a bastard when I tell you this. That girl Charlotte I was with tonight is engaged to be married in five weeks. (*He tries on his new hat.*)

Biff: No kiddin'!

Happy: Sure, the guy's in line for the vice-presidency of the store. I don't know what gets into me, maybe I just have an overdeveloped sense

of competition or something, but I went and ruined her, and furthermore I can't get rid of her. And he's the third executive I've done that
to. Isn't that a crummy characteristic? And to top it all, I go to their
weddings! (*Indignantly, but laughing.*) Like I'm not supposed to take
bribes. Manufacturers offer me a hundred-dollar bill now and then to
throw an order their way. You know how honest I am, but it's like
this girl, see. I hate myself for it. Because I don't want the girl, and,
still, I take it and—I love it!

Biff: Let's go to sleep.

Happy: I guess we didn't settle anything, heh?

Biff: I just got one idea that I think I'm going to try.

Happy: What's that?

Biff: Remember Bill Oliver?

Happy: Sure, Oliver is very big now. You want to work for him again?

Biff: No, but when I quit he said something to me. He put his arm on my
shoulder, and he said, "Biff, if you ever need anything, come to me."

Happy: I remember that. That sounds good.

Biff: I think I'll go to see him. If I could get ten thousand or even seven
or eight thousand dollars I could buy a beautiful ranch.

Happy: I bet he'd back you. 'Cause he thought highly of you, Biff. I mean,
they all do. You're well liked, Biff. That's why I say to come back
here, and we both have the apartment. And I'm tellin' you, Biff, any
babe you want . . .

Biff: No, with a ranch I could do the work I like and still be something. I
just wonder though. I wonder if Oliver still thinks I stole that carton
of basketballs.

Happy: Oh, he probably forgot that long ago. It's almost ten years.
You're too sensitive. Anyway, he didn't really fire you.

Biff: Well, I think he was going to. I think that's why I quit. I was never
sure whether he knew or not. I know he thought the world of me,
though. I was the only one he'd let lock up the place.

Willy (below): You gonna wash the engine, Biff?

Happy: Shh!

*Biff looks at Happy, who is gazing down, listening. Willy is mumbling in
the parlor.*

Happy: You hear that?

They listen. Willy laughs warmly.

Biff (growing angry): Doesn't he know Mom can hear that?

Willy: Don't get your sweater dirty, Biff!

A look of pain crosses Biff's face.

Happy: Isn't that terrible? Don't leave again, will you? You'll find a job here. You gotta stick around. I don't know what to do about him, it's getting embarrassing.

Willy: What a simonizing job!

Biff: Mom's hearing that!

Willy: No kiddin', Biff, you got a date? Wonderful!

Happy: Go on to sleep. But talk to him in the morning, will you?

Biff (reluctantly getting into bed): With her in the house. Brother!

Happy (getting into bed): I wish you'd have a good talk with him.

The light on their room begins to fade.

Biff (to himself in bed): That selfish, stupid . . .

Happy: Sh . . . Sleep, Biff.

Their light is out. Well before they have finished speaking, Willy's form is dimly seen below in the darkened kitchen. He opens the refrigerator, searches in there, and takes out a bottle of milk. The apartment houses are fading out, and the entire house and surroundings become covered with leaves. Music insinuates itself as the leaves appear.

Willy: Just wanna be careful with those girls, Biff, that's all. Don't make any promises. No promises of any kind. Because a girl, y'know, they always believe what you tell 'em, and you're very young, Biff, you're too young to be talking seriously to girls.

Light rises on the kitchen. Willy, talking, shuts the refrigerator door and comes downstage to the kitchen table. He pours milk into a glass. He is totally immersed in himself, smiling faintly.

Willy: Too young entirely, Biff. You want to watch your schooling first. Then when you're all set, there'll be plenty of girls for a boy like you. (*He smiles broadly at a kitchen chair.*) That so? The girls pay for you? (*He laughs.*) Boy, you must really be makin' a hit.

Willy is gradually addressing—physically—a point offstage, speaking through the wall of the kitchen, and his voice has been rising in volume to that of a normal conversation.

Willy: I been wondering why you polish the car so careful. Ha! Don't leave the hubcaps, boys. Get the chamois to the hubcaps. Happy, use newspaper on the windows, it's the easiest thing. Show him how to do it, Biff! You see, Happy? Pad it up, use it like a pad. That's it, that's it, good work. You're doin' all right, Hap. (*He pauses, then nods in approbation for a few seconds, then looks upward.*) Biff, first thing we gotta do when we get time is clip that big branch over the house. Afraid it's gonna fall in a storm and hit the roof. Tell you what. We get a rope and sling her around, and then we climb up there with a couple of saws and take her down. Soon as you finish the car, boys, I wanna see ya. I got a surprise for you, boys.

Biff (*offstage*): Whatta ya got, Dad?

Willy: No, you finish first. Never leave a job till you're finished—remember that. (*Looking toward the "big trees."*) Biff, up in Albany I saw a beautiful hammock. I think I'll buy it next trip, and we'll hang it right between those two elms. Wouldn't that be something? Just swingin' there under those branches. Boy, that would be . . .

Young Biff and Young Happy appear from the direction Willy was addressing. Happy carries rags and a pail of water. Biff, wearing a sweater with a block "S," carries a football.

Biff (*pointing in the direction of the car offstage*): How's that, Pop, professional?

Willy: Terrific. Terrific job, boys. Good work, Biff.

Happy: Where's the surprise, Pop?

Willy: In the back seat of the car.

Happy: Boy! (*He runs off.*)

Biff: What is it, Dad? Tell me, what'd you buy?

Willy (*laughing, cuffs him*): Never mind, something I want you to have.

Biff (*turns and starts off*): What is it, Hap?

Happy (*offstage*): It's a punching bag!

Biff: Oh, Pop!

Willy: It's got Gene Tunney's signature on it.

Happy runs onstage with a punching bag.

Biff: Gee, how'd you know we wanted a punching bag?

Willy: Well, it's the finest thing for the timing.

Happy (*lies down on his back and pedals with his feet*): I'm losing weight, you notice, Pop?

Willy (*to Happy*): Jumping rope is good too.

Biff: Did you see the new football I got?

Willy (*examining the ball*): Where'd you get a new ball?

Biff: The coach told me to practice my passing.

Willy: That so? And he gave you the ball, heh?

Biff: Well, I borrowed it from the locker room. (*He laughs confidentially.*)

Willy (*laughing with him at the theft*): I want you to return that.

Happy: I told you he wouldn't like it!

Biff (*angrily*): Well, I'm bringing it back!

Willy (*stopping the incipient argument, to Happy*): Sure, he's gotta practice with a regulation ball, doesn't he? (*To Biff.*) Coach'll probably congratulate you on your initiative.

Biff: Oh, he keeps congratulating my initiative all the time, Pop.

Willy: That's because he likes you. If somebody else took that ball there'd be an uproar. So what's the report, boys, what's the report?

Biff: Where'd you go this time, Dad? Gee we were lonesome for you.

Willy (*pleased, puts an arm around each boy and they come down to the apron*): Lonesome, heh?

Biff: Missed you every minute.

Willy: Don't say? Tell you a secret, boys. Don't breathe it to a soul. Someday I'll have my own business, and I'll never have to leave home any more.

Happy: Like Uncle Charley, heh?

Willy: Bigger than Uncle Charley! Because Charley is not—liked. He's liked, but he's not—well liked.

Biff: Where'd you go this time, Dad?

Willy: Well, I got on the road, and I went north to Providence. Met the Mayor.

Biff: The Mayor of Providence!

Willy: He was sitting in the hotel lobby.

Biff: What'd he say?

Willy: He said, "Morning!" And I said, "You've got a fine city here, Mayor." And then he had coffee with me. And then I went to Waterbury. Waterbury is a fine city. Big clock city, the famous Waterbury clock. Sold a nice bill there. And then Boston—Boston is the cradle of the Revolution. A fine city. And a couple of other towns in Mass., and on to Portland and Bangor and straight home!

Biff: Gee, I'd love to go with you sometime, Dad.

Willy: Soon as summer comes.

Happy: Promise?

Willy: You and Hap and I, and I'll show you all the towns. America is full of beautiful towns and fine, upstanding people. And they know me, boys, they know me up and down New England. The finest people. And when I bring you fellas up, there'll be open sesame for all of us, 'cause one thing, boys: I have friends. I can park my car in any street in New England, and the cops protect it like their own. This summer, heh?

Biff and Happy(*together*): Yeah! You bet!

Willy: We'll take our bathing suits.

Happy: We'll carry your bags, Pop!

Willy: Oh, won't that be something! Me comin' into the Boston stores with you boys carryin' my bags. What a sensation!

Biff is prancing around, practicing passing the ball.

Willy: You nervous, Biff, about the game?

Biff: Not if you're gonna be there.

Willy: What do they say about you in school, now that they made you captain?

Happy: There's a crowd of girls behind him everytime the classes change.

Biff (taking Willy's hand): This Saturday, Pop, this Saturday—just for you, I'm going to break through for a touchdown.

Happy: You're supposed to pass.

Biff: I'm takin' one play for Pop. You watch me, Pop, and when I take off my helmet, that means I'm breakin' out. Then you watch me crash through that line!

Willy (kisses Biff): Oh, wait'll I tell this in Boston!

> *Bernard enters in knickers. He is younger than Biff, earnest and loyal, a worried boy.*

Bernard: Biff, where are you? You're supposed to study with me today.

Willy: Hey, looka Bernard. What're you lookin' so anemic about, Bernard?

Bernard: He's gotta study, Uncle Willy. He's got Regents next week.

Happy (tauntingly, spinning Bernard around): Let's box, Bernard!

Bernard: Biff! (*He gets away from Happy.*) Listen, Biff, I heard Mr. Birnbaum say that if you don't start studyin' math he's gonna flunk you, and you won't graduate. I heard him!

Willy: You better study with him, Biff. Go ahead now.

Bernard: I heard him!

Biff: Oh, Pop, you didn't see my sneakers! (*He holds up a foot for Willy to look at.*)

Willy: Hey, that's a beautiful job of printing!

Bernard (wiping his glasses): Just because he printed University of Virginia on his sneakers doesn't mean they've got to graduate him, Uncle Willy!

Willy (angrily): What're you talking about? With scholarships to three universities they're gonna flunk him?

Bernard: But I heard Mr. Birnbaum say—

Willy: Don't be a pest, Bernard! (*To his boys.*) What an anemic!

Bernard: Okay, I'm waiting for you in my house, Biff.

> *Bernard goes off. The Lomans laugh.*

Willy: Bernard is not well liked, is he?

Biff: He's liked, but he's not well liked.

Happy: That's right, Pop.

Willy: That's just what I mean. Bernard can get the best marks in school, y'understand, but when he gets out in the business world, y'understand, you are going to be five times ahead of him. That's why I thank Almighty God you're both built like Adonises. Because the man who makes an appearance in the business world, the man who creates personal interest, is the man who gets ahead. Be liked and you will never want. You take me, for instance. I never have to wait in line to see a buyer. "Willy Loman is here!" That's all they have to know, and I go right through.

Biff: Did you knock them dead, Pop?

Willy: Knocked 'em cold in Providence, slaughtered 'em in Boston.

Happy (on his back, pedaling again): I'm losing weight, you notice, Pop?

Linda enters, as of old, a ribbon in her hair, carrying a basket of washing.

Linda (with youthful energy): Hello, dear!

Willy: Sweetheart!

Linda: How'd the Chevvy run?

Willy: Chevrolet, Linda, is the greatest car every built. (*To the boys.*) Since when do you let your mother carry wash up the stairs?

Biff: Grab hold there, boy!

Happy: Where to, Mom?

Linda: Hang them up on the line. And you better go down to your friends, Biff. The cellar is full of boys. They don't know what to do with themselves.

Biff: Ah, when Pop comes home they can wait!

Willy (laughs appreciatively): You better go down and tell them what to do, Biff.

Biff: I think I'll have them sweep out the furnace room.

Willy: Good work, Biff.

Biff (goes through wall-line of kitchen to doorway at back and calls down): Fellas! Everybody sweep out the furnace room! I'll be right down!

Voices: All right! Okay, Biff.

Biff: George and Sam and Frank, come out back! We're hangin' up the wash! Come on, Hap, on the double! (*He and Happy carry out the basket.*)

Linda: The way they obey him!

Willy: Well, that's training, the training. I'm tellin' you, I was sellin' thousands and thousands, but I had to come home.

Linda: Oh, the whole block'll be at that game. Did you sell anything?

Willy: I did five hundred gross in Providence and seven hundred gross in Boston.

Linda: No! Wait a minute, I've got a pencil. (*She pulls pencil and paper out of her apron pocket.*) That makes your commission . . . Two hundred— my God! Two hundred and twelve dollars!

Willy: Well, I didn't figure it yet, but . . .

Linda: How much did you do?

Willy: Well, I—I did—about a hundred and eighty gross in Providence. Well, no—it came to—roughly two hundred gross on the whole trip.

Linda (without hesitation): Two hundred gross. That's . . . (*She figures.*)

Willy: The trouble was that three of the stores were half closed for inventory in Boston. Otherwise I woulda broke records.

Linda: Well, it makes seventy dollars and some pennies. That's very good.

Willy: What do we owe?

Linda: Well, on the first there's sixteen dollars on the refrigerator—

Willy: Why sixteen?

Linda: Well, the fan belt broke, so it was a dollar eighty.

Willy: But it's brand new.

Linda: Well, the man said that's the way it is. Till they work themselves in, y'know.

They move through the wall-line into the kitchen.

Willy: I hope we didn't get stuck on that machine.

Linda: They got the biggest ads of any of them.

Willy: I know, it's a fine machine. What else?

Linda: Well, there's nine-sixty for the washing machine. And for the vacuum cleaner there's three and a half due on the fifteenth. Then the roof, you got twenty-one dollars remaining.

Willy: It don't leak, does it?

Linda: No, they did a wonderful job. Then you owe Frank for the carburetor.

Willy: I'm not going to pay that man! That goddam Chevrolet, they ought to prohibit the manufacture of that car!

Linda: Well, you owe him three and a half. And odds and ends, comes to around a hundred and twenty dollars by the fifteenth.

Willy: A hundred and twenty dollars! My God, if business don't pick up I don't know what I'm gonna do!

Linda: Well, next week you'll do better.

Willy: Oh, I'll knock 'em dead next week. I'll go to Hartford. I'm very well liked in Hartford. You know, the trouble is, Linda, people don't seem to take to me.

They move on the forestage.

Linda: Oh, don't be foolish.

Willy: I know it when I walk in. They seem to laugh at me.

Linda: Why? Why would they laugh at you? Don't talk that way, Willy.

Willy moves to the edge of the stage. Linda goes into the kitchen and starts to darn stockings.

Willy: I don't know the reason for it, but they just pass me by. I'm not noticed.

Linda: But you're doing wonderful, dear. You're making seventy to a hundred dollars a week.

Willy: But I gotta be at it ten, twelve hours a day. Other men—I don't know—they do it easier. I don't know why—I can't stop myself—I talk too much. A man oughta come in with a few words. One thing about Charley. He's a man of few words, and they respect him.

Linda: You don't talk too much, you're just lively.

Willy (*smiling*): Well, I figure, what the hell, life is short, a couple of jokes. (*To himself.*) I joke too much! (*The smile goes.*)

Linda: Why? You're—

Willy: I'm fat. I'm very—foolish to look at, Linda. I didn't tell you, but Christmas time I happened to be calling on F. H. Stewarts, and a salesman I know, as I was going in to see the buyer I heard him say something about walrus. And I—I cracked him right across the face. I won't take that. I simply will not take that. But they do laugh at me. I know that.

Linda: Darling . . .

Willy: I gotta overcome it. I know I gotta overcome it. I'm not dressing to advantage, maybe.

Linda: Willy, darling, you're the handsomest man in the world—

Willy: Oh, no, Linda.

Linda: To me you are. (*Slight pause.*) The handsomest.

From the darkness is heard the laughter of a woman. Willy doesn't turn to it, but it continues through Linda's lines.

Linda: And the boys, Willy. Few men are idolized by their children the way you are.

Music is heard as behind a scrim, to the left of the house, The Woman, dimly seen, is dressing.

Willy (*with great feeling*): You're the best there is, Linda, you're a pal, you know that? On the road—on the road I want to grab you sometimes and just kiss the life outa you.

The laughter is loud now, and he moves into a brightening area at the left, where The Woman has come from behind the scrim and is standing, putting on her hat, looking into a "mirror" and laughing.

Willy: 'Cause I get so lonely—especially when business is bad and there's nobody to talk to. I get the feeling that I'll never sell anything again, that I won't make a living for you, or a business, a business for the boys. (*He talks through The Woman's subsiding laughter; The Woman primps at the "mirror."*) There's so much I want to make for—

The Woman: Me? You didn't make me, Willy. I picked you.

Willy (pleased): You picked me?

The Woman (who is quite proper-looking, Willy's age): I did. I've been sitting at that desk watching all the salesmen go by, day in, day out. But you've got such a sense of humor, and we do have such a good time together, don't we?

Willy: Sure, sure. (*He takes her in his arms.*) Why do you have to go now?

The Woman: It's two o'clock . . .

Willy: No, come on in! (*He pulls her.*)

The Woman: . . . my sisters'll be scandalized. When'll you be back?

Willy: Oh, two weeks about. Will you come up again?

The Woman: Sure thing. You do make me laugh. It's good for me. (*She squeezes his arm, kisses him.*) And I think you're a wonderful man.

Willy: You picked me, heh?

The Woman: Sure. Because you're so sweet. And such a kidder.

Willy: Well, I'll see you next time I'm in Boston.

The Woman: I'll put you right through to the buyers.

Willy (slapping her bottom): Right. Well, bottoms up!

The Woman (slaps him gently and laughs): You just kill me, Willy. (*He suddenly grabs her and kisses her roughly.*) You kill me. And thanks for the stockings. I love a lot of stockings. Well, good night.

Willy: Good night. And keep your pores open!

The Woman: Oh, Willy!

> *The Woman bursts out laughing, and Linda's laughter blends in. The Woman disappears into the dark. Now the area at the kitchen table brightens. Linda is sitting where she was at the kitchen table, but now is mending a pair of silk stockings.*

Linda: You are, Willy. The handsomest man. You've got no reason to feel that—

Willy (coming out of The Woman's dimming area and going over to Linda): I'll make it all up to you, Linda, I'll—

Linda: There's nothing to make up, dear. You're doing fine, better than—

Willy (noticing her mending): What's that?

Linda: Just mending my stockings. They're so expensive—

Willy (*angrily, taking them from her*): I won't have you mending stockings in this house! Now throw them out!

Linda puts the stockings in her pocket.

Bernard (*entering on the run*): Where is he? If he doesn't study!
Willy (*moving to the forestage, with great agitation*): You'll give him the answers!
Bernard: I do, but I can't on a Regents! That's a state exam! They're liable to arrest me!
Willy: Where is he? I'll whip him, I'll whip him!
Linda: And he'd better give back that football, Willy, it's not nice.
Willy: Biff! Where is he? Why is he taking everything?
Linda: He's too rough with the girls, Willy. All the mothers are afraid of him!
Willy: I'll whip him!
Bernard: He's driving the car without a license!

The Woman's laugh is heard.

Willy: Shut up!
Linda: All the mothers—
Willy: Shut up!
Bernard (*backing quietly away and out*): Mr. Birnbaum says he's stuck up.
Willy: Get outa here!
Bernard: If he doesn't buckle down he'll flunk math! (*He goes off.*)
Linda: He's right, Willy, you've gotta—
Willy (*exploding at her*): There's nothing the matter with him! You want him to be a worm like Bernard? He's got spirit, personality . . .

As he speaks, Linda, almost in tears, exits into the living room. Willy is alone in the kitchen, wilting and staring. The leaves are gone. It is night again, and the apartment houses look down from behind.

Willy: Loaded with it. Loaded! What is he stealing? He's giving it back, isn't he? Why is he stealing? What did I tell him? I never in my life told him anything but decent things.

Happy in pajamas has come down the stairs; Willy suddenly becomes aware of Happy's presence.

Happy: Let's go now, come on.
Willy (*sitting down at the kitchen table*): Huh! Why did she have to wax the floors herself? Everytime she waxes the floors she keels over. She knows that!
Happy: Shh! Take it easy. What brought you back tonight?

Willy: I got an awful scare. Nearly hit a kid in Yonkers. God! Why didn't I go to Alaska with my brother Ben that time! Ben! That man was a genius, that man was success incarnate! What a mistake! He begged me to go.

Happy: Well, there's no use in—

Willy: You guys! There was a man started with the clothes on his back and ended up with diamond mines!

Happy: Boy, someday I'd like to know how he did it.

Willy: What's the mystery? The man knew what he wanted and went out and got it! Walked into a jungle, and comes out, the age of twenty-one, and he's rich! The world is an oyster, but you don't crack it open on a mattress!

Happy: Pop, I told you I'm gonna retire you for life.

Willy: You'll retire me for life on seventy goddam dollars a week? And your women and your car and your apartment, and you'll retire me for life! Christ's sake, I couldn't get past Yonkers today! Where are you guys, where are you? The woods are burning! I can't drive a car!

Charley has appeared in the doorway. He is a large man, slow of speech, laconic, immovable. In all he says, despite what he says, there is pity, and, now, trepidation. He has a robe over his pajamas, slippers on his feet. He enters the kitchen.

Charley: Everything all right?

Happy: Yeah, Charley, everything's . . .

Willy: What's the matter?

Charley: I heard some noise. I thought something happened. Can't we do something about the walls? You sneeze in here, and in my house hats blow off.

Happy: Let's go to bed, Dad. Come on.

Charley signals to Happy to go.

Willy: You go ahead, I'm not tired at the moment.

Happy (to Willy): Take it easy, huh? (*He exits.*)

Willy: What're you doin' up?

Charley (sitting down at the kitchen table opposite Willy): Couldn't sleep good. I had a heartburn.

Willy: Well, you don't know how to eat.

Charley: I eat with my mouth.

Willy: No, you're ignorant. You gotta know about vitamins and things like that.

Charley: Come on, let's shoot. Tire you out a little.

Willy (hesitantly): All right. You got cards?

Charley (taking a deck from his pocket): Yeah, I got them. Someplace. What is it with those vitamins?

Willy (dealing): They build up your bones. Chemistry.

Charley: Yeah, but there's no bones in a heartburn.

Willy: What are you talkin' about? Do you know the first thing about it?

Charley: Don't get insulted.

Willy: Don't talk about something you don't know anything about.

> *They are playing. Pause.*

Charley: What're you doin' home?

Willy: A little trouble with the car.

Charley: Oh. (*Pause.*) I'd like to take a trip to California.

Willy: Don't say.

Charley: You want a job?

Willy: I got a job, I told you that. (*After a slight pause.*) What the hell are you offering me a job for?

Charley: Don't get insulted.

Willy: Don't insult me.

Charley: I don't see no sense in it. You don't have to go on this way.

Willy: I got a good job. (*Slight pause.*) What do you keep comin' in here for?

Charley: You want me to go?

Willy (after a pause, withering): I can't understand it. He's going back to Texas again. What the hell is that?

Charley: Let him go.

Willy: I got nothin' to give him, Charley, I'm clean, I'm clean.

Charley: He won't starve. None a them starve. Forget about him.

Willy: Then what have I got to remember?

Charley: You take it too hard. To hell with it. When a deposit bottle is broken you don't get your nickel back.

Willy: That's easy enough for you to say.

Charley: That ain't easy for me to say.

Willy: Did you see the ceiling I put up in the living room?

Charley: Yeah, that's a piece of work. To put up a ceiling is a mystery to me. How do you do it?

Willy: What's the difference?

Charley: Well, talk about it.

Willy: You gonna put up a ceiling?

Charley: How could I put up a ceiling?

Willy: Then what the hell are you bothering me for?

Charley: You're insulted again.

Willy: A man who can't handle tools is not a man. You're disgusting.

Charley: Don't call me disgusting, Willy.

> *Uncle Ben, carrying a valise and an umbrella, enters the forestage from around the right corner of the house. He is a stolid man, in his sixties, with a mustache and an authoritative air. He is utterly certain of his destiny, and there is an aura of far places about him. He enters exactly as Willy speaks.*

Willy: I'm getting awfully tired, Ben.

> *Ben's music is heard. Ben looks around at everything.*

Charley: Good, keep playing; you'll sleep better. Did you call me Ben?

> *Ben looks at his watch.*

Willy: That's funny. For a second there you reminded me of my brother Ben.

Ben: I have only a few minutes. (*He strolls, inspecting the place. Willy and Charley continue playing.*)

Charley: You never heard from him again, heh? Since that time?

Willy: Didn't Linda tell you? Couple of weeks ago we got a letter from his wife in Africa. He died.

Charley: That so.

Ben (*chuckling*): So this is Brooklyn, eh?

Charley: Maybe you're in for some of his money.

Willy: Naa, he had seven sons. There's just one opportunity I had with that man . . .

Ben: I must make a train, William. There are several properties I'm looking at in Alaska.

Willy: Sure, sure! If I'd gone with him to Alaska that time, everything would've been totally different.

Charley: Go on, you'd froze to death up there.

Willy: What're you talking about?

Ben: Opportunity is tremendous in Alaska, William. Surprised you're not up there.

Willy: Sure, tremendous.

Charley: Heh?

Willy: There was the only man I ever met who knew the answers.

Charley: Who?

Ben: How are you all?

Willy (*taking a pot, smiling*): Fine, fine.

Charley: Pretty sharp tonight.

Ben: Is Mother living with you?

Willy: No, she died a long time ago.

Charley: Who?

Ben: That's too bad. Fine specimen of a lady, Mother.

Willy (to Charley): Heh?

Ben: I'd hoped to see the old girl.

Charley: Who died?

Ben: Heard anything from Father, have you?

Willy (unnerved): What do you mean, who died?

Charley (taking a pot): What're you talkin' about?

Ben (looking at his watch): William, it's half-past eight!

Willy (as though to dispel his confusion he angrily stops Charley's hand): That's my build!

Charley: I put the ace—

Willy: If you don't know how to play the game I'm not gonna throw my money away on you!

Charley (rising): It was my ace, for God's sake!

Willy: I'm through, I'm through!

Ben: When did Mother die?

Willy: Long ago. Since the beginning you never knew how to play cards.

Charley (picks up the cards and goes to the door): All right! Next time I'll bring a deck with five aces.

Willy: I don't play that kind of game!

Charley (turning to him): You ought to be ashamed of yourself!

Willy: Yeah?

Charley: Yeah! (He goes out.)

Willy (slamming the door after him): Ignoramus!

Ben (as Willy comes toward him through the wall-line of the kitchen): So you're William.

Willy (shaking Ben's hand): Ben! I've been waiting for you so long! What's the answer? How did you do it?

Ben: Oh, there's a story in that.

Linda enters the forestage, as of old, carrying the wash basket.

Linda: Is this Ben?

Ben (gallantly): How do you do, my dear.

Linda: Where've you been all these years? Willy's always wondered why you—

Willy (pulling Ben away from her impatiently): Where is Dad? Didn't you follow him? How did you get started?

Ben: Well, I don't know how much you remember.

Willy: Well, I was just a baby, of course, only three or four years old—

Ben: Three years and eleven months.

Willy: What a memory, Ben!

Ben: I have many enterprises, William, and I have never kept books.

Willy: I remember I was sitting under the wagon in—was it Nebraska?

Ben: It was South Dakota, and I gave you a bunch of wild flowers.

Willy: I remember you walking away down some open road.

Ben (laughing): I was going to find Father in Alaska.

Willy: Where is he?

Ben: At that age I had a very faulty view of geography, William. I discovered after a few days that I was heading due south, so instead of Alaska, I ended up in Africa.

Linda: Africa!

Willy: The Gold Coast!

Ben: Principally, diamond mines.

Linda: Diamond mines!

Ben: Yes, my dear. But I've only a few minutes—

Willy: No! Boys! Boys! (*Young Biff and Happy appear.*) Listen to this. This is your Uncle Ben, a great man! Tell my boys, Ben!

Ben: Why, boys, when I was seventeen I walked into the jungle, and when I was twenty-one I walked out. (*He laughs.*) And by God I was rich.

Willy (to the boys): You see what I been talking about? The greatest things can happen!

Ben (glancing at his watch): I have an appointment in Ketchikan Tuesday week.

Willy: No, Ben! Please tell about Dad. I want my boys to hear. I want them to know the kind of stock they sprang from. All I remember is a man with a big beard, and I was in Mamma's lap, sitting around a fire, and some kind of high music.

Ben: His flute. He played the flute.

Willy: Sure, the flute, that's right!

New music is heard, a high, rollicking tune.

Ben: Father was a very great and a very wild-hearted man. We would start in Boston, and he'd toss the whole family into the wagon, and then he'd drive the team right across the country; through Ohio, and Indiana, Michigan, Illinois, and all the Western states. And we'd stop in the towns and sell the flutes that he'd made on the way. Great inventor, Father. With one gadget he made more in a week than a man like you could make in a lifetime.

Willy: That's just the way I'm bringing them up, Ben—rugged, well-liked, all-around.

Ben: Yeah? (*To Biff.*) Hit that, boy—hard as you can. (*He pounds his stomach.*)

Biff: Oh, no, sir!

Ben (*taking boxing stance*): Come on, get to me! (*He laughs.*)

Willy: Go to it, Biff! Go ahead, show him!

Biff: Okay! (*He cocks his fist and starts in.*)

Linda (*to Willy*): Why must he fight, dear?

Ben (*sparring with Biff*): Good boy! Good boy!

Willy: How's that, Ben, heh?

Happy: Give him the left, Biff!

Linda: Why are you fighting?

Ben: Good boy! (*Suddenly comes in, trips Biff, and stands over him, the point of his umbrella poised over Biff's eye.*)

Linda: Look out, Biff!

Biff: Gee!

Ben (*patting Biff's knee*): Never fight fair with a stranger, boy. You'll never get out of the jungle that way. (*Taking Linda's hand and bowing.*) It was an honor and a pleasure to meet you, Linda.

Linda (*withdrawing her hand coldly, frightened*): Have a nice—trip.

Ben (*to Willy*): And good luck with your—what do you do?

Willy: Selling.

Ben: Yes. Well . . . (*He raises his hand in farewell to all.*)

Willy: No, Ben, I don't want you to think . . . (*He takes Ben's arm to show him.*) It's Brooklyn, I know, but we hunt too.

Ben: Really, now.

Willy: Oh, sure, there's snakes and rabbits and—that's why I moved out here. Why, Biff can fell any one of these trees in no time! Boys! Go right over to where they're building the apartment house and get some sand. We're gonna rebuild the entire front stoop right now! Watch this, Ben!

Biff: Yes, sir! On the double, Hap!

Happy (*as he and Biff run off*): I lost weight, Pop, you notice?

Charley enters in knickers, even before the boys are gone.

Charley: Listen, if they steal any more from that building the watchman'll put the cops on them!

Linda (*to Willy*): Don't let Biff . . .

Ben laughs lustily.

Willy: You shoulda seen the lumber they brought home last week. At least a dozen six-by-tens worth all kinds of money.

Charley: Listen, if that watchman—

Willy: I gave them hell, understand. But I got a couple of fearless characters there.

Charley: Willy, the jails are full of fearless characters.

Ben (clapping Willy on the back, with a laugh at Charley): And the stock exchange, friend!

Willy (joining in Ben's laughter): Where are the rest of your pants?

Charley: My wife bought them.

Willy: Now all you need is a golf club and you can go upstairs and go to sleep. *(To Ben.)* Great athlete! Between him and his son Bernard they can't hammer a nail!

Bernard (rushing in): The watchman's chasing Biff!

Willy (angrily): Shut up! He's not stealing anything!

Linda (alarmed, hurrying off left): Where is he? Biff, dear! *(She exits.)*

Willy (moving toward the left, away from Ben): There's nothing wrong. What's the matter with you?

Ben: Nervy boy. Good!

Willy (laughing): Oh, nerves of iron, that Biff!

Charley: Don't know what it is. My New England man comes back and he's bleedin', they murdered him up there.

Willy: It's contacts, Charley, I got important contacts!

Charley (sarcastically): Glad to hear it, Willy. Come in later, we'll shoot a little casino. I'll take some of your Portland money. *(He laughs at Willy and exits.)*

Willy (turning to Ben): Business is bad, it's murderous. But not for me, of course.

Ben: I'll stop by on my way back to Africa.

Willy (longingly): Can't you stay a few days? You're just what I need, Ben, because I—I have a fine position, but I—well, Dad left when I was such a baby and I never had a chance to talk to him and I still feel— kind of temporary about myself.

Ben: I'll be late for my train.

They are at opposite ends of the stage.

Willy: Ben, my boys—can't we talk? They'd go into the jaws of hell for me, see, but I—

Ben: William, you're being first-rate with your boys. Outstanding, manly chaps!

Willy (hanging on to his words): Oh, Ben, that's good to hear! Because sometimes I'm afraid that I'm not teaching them the right kind of— Ben, how should I teach them?

Ben (giving great weight to each word, and with a certain vicious audacity): William, when I walked into the jungle, I was seventeen. When I walked out I was twenty-one. And, by God, I was rich! (*He goes off into darkness around the right corner of the house.*)

Willy: . . . was rich! That's just the spirit I want to imbue them with! To walk into a jungle! I was right! I was right! I was right!

Ben is gone, but Willy is still speaking to him as Linda, in nightgown and robe, enters the kitchen, glances around for Willy, then goes to the door of the house, looks out and sees him. Comes down to his left. He looks at her.

Linda: Willy, dear? Willy?

Willy: I was right!

Linda: Did you have some cheese? (*He can't answer.*) It's very late, darling. Come to bed, heh?

Willy (*looking straight up*): Gotta break your neck to see a star in this yard.

Linda: You coming in?

Willy: What ever happened to that diamond watch fob? Remember? When Ben came from Africa that time? Didn't he give me a watch fob with a diamond in it?

Linda: You pawned it, dear. Twelve, thirteen years ago. For Biff's radio correspondence course.

Willy: Gee, that was a beautiful thing. I'll take a walk.

Linda: But you're in your slippers.

Willy (*starting to go around the house at the left*): I was right! I was! (*Half to Linda, as he goes, shaking his head.*) What a man! There was a man worth talking to. I was right!

Linda (*calling after Willy*): But in your slippers, Willy!

Willy is almost gone when Biff, in his pajamas, comes down the stairs and enters the kitchen.

Biff: What is he doing out there?

Linda: Sh!

Biff: God Almighty, Mom, how long has he been doing this?

Linda: Don't, he'll hear you.

Biff: What the hell is the matter with him?

Linda: It'll pass by morning.

Biff: Shouldn't we do anything?

Linda: Oh, my dear, you should do a lot of things, but there's nothing to do, so go to sleep.

Happy comes down the stairs and sits on the steps.

Happy: I never heard him so loud, Mom.

Death of a Salesman: Act I **915**

Linda: Well, come around more often; you'll hear him. (*She sits down at the table and mends the lining of Willy's jacket.*)

Biff: Why didn't you ever write me about this, Mom?

Linda: How would I write to you? For over three months you had no address.

Biff: I was on the move. But you know I thought of you all the time. You know that, don't you, pal?

Linda: I know, dear, I know. But he likes to have a letter. Just to know that there's still a possibility for better things.

Biff: He's not like this all the time, is he?

Linda: It's when you come home he's always the worst.

Biff: When I come home?

Linda: When you write you're coming, he's all smiles, and talks about the future, and—he's just wonderful. And then the closer you seem to come, the more shaky he gets, and then, by the time you get here, he's arguing, and he seems angry at you. I think it's just that maybe he can't bring himself to—to open up to you. Why are you so hateful to each other? Why is that?

Biff (*evasively*): I'm not hateful, Mom.

Linda: But you no sooner come in the door than you're fighting!

Biff: I don't know why. I mean to change. I'm tryin', Mom, you understand?

Linda: Are you home to stay now?

Biff: I don't know. I want to look around, see what's doin'.

Linda: Biff, you can't look around all your life, can you?

Biff: I just can't take hold, Mom. I can't take hold of some kind of a life.

Linda: Biff, a man is not a bird, to come and go with the springtime.

Biff: Your hair . . . (*He touches her hair.*) Your hair got so gray.

Linda: Oh, it's been gray since you were in high school. I just stopped dyeing it, that's all.

Biff: Dye it again, will ya? I don't want my pal looking old. (*He smiles.*)

Linda: You're such a boy! You think you can go away for a year and . . . You've got to get it into your head now that one day you'll knock on this door and there'll be strange people here—

Biff: What are you talking about? You're not even sixty, Mom.

Linda: But what about your father?

Biff (*lamely*): Well, I meant him too.

Happy: He admires Pop.

Linda: Biff dear, if you don't have any feeling for him, then you can't have any feeling for me.

Biff: Sure I can, Mom.

Linda: No. You can't just come to see me, because I love him. (*With a threat, but only a threat, of tears.*) He's the dearest man in the world to me, and I won't have anyone making him feel unwanted and low and blue. You've got to make up your mind now, darling, there's no leeway any more. Either he's your father and you pay him that respect, or else you're not to come here. I know he's not easy to get along with—nobody knows that better than me—but . . .

Willy (from the left, with a laugh): Hey, hey, Biffo!

Biff (starting to go out after Willy): What the hell is the matter with him? *(Happy stops him.)*

Linda: Don't—don't go near him!

Biff: Stop making excuses for him! He always, always wiped the floor with you. Never had an ounce of respect for you.

Happy: He's always had respect for—

Biff: What the hell do you know about it?

Happy (surlily): Just don't call him crazy!

Biff: He's got no character—Charley wouldn't do this. Not in his own house—spewing out that vomit from his mind.

Happy: Charley never had to cope with what he's got to.

Biff: People are worse off than Willy Loman. Believe me, I've seen them!

Linda: Then make Charley your father, Biff. You can't do that, can you? I don't say he's a great man. Willy Loman never made a lot of money. His name was never in the paper. He's not the finest character that ever lived. But he's a human being, and a terrible thing is happening to him. So attention must be paid. He's not to be allowed to fall into his grave like an old dog. Attention, attention must be finally paid to such a person. You called him crazy—

Biff: I didn't mean—

Linda: No, a lot of people think he's lost his—balance. But you don't have to be very smart to know what his trouble is. The man is exhausted.

Happy: Sure!

Linda: A small man can be just as exhausted as a great man. He works for a company thirty-six years this March, opens up unheard-of territories to their trademark, and now in his old age they take his salary away.

Happy (indignantly): I didn't know that, Mom!

Linda: You never asked, my dear! Now that you get your spending money someplace else you don't trouble your mind with him.

Happy: But I gave you money last—

Linda: Christmas time, fifty dollars! To fix the hot water it cost ninety-seven fifty! For five weeks he's been on straight commission, like a beginner, an unknown!

Biff: Those ungrateful bastards!

Linda: Are they any worse than his sons? When he brought them business, when he was young, they were glad to see him. But now his old friends, the old buyers that loved him so and always found some order to hand him in a pinch—they're all dead, retired. He used to be able to make six, seven calls a day in Boston. Now he takes his valises out of the car and puts them back and takes them out again and he's exhausted. Instead of walking he talks now. He drives seven hundred miles, and when he gets there no one knows him any more, no one welcomes him. And what goes through a man's mind, driving seven hundred miles home without having earned a cent? Why shouldn't he talk to himself? Why? When he has to go to Charley and borrow fifty dollars a week and pretend to me that it's his pay? How long can that go on? How long? You see what I'm sitting here and waiting for? And you tell me he has no character? The man who never worked a day but for your benefit? When does he get the medal for that? Is this his reward—to turn around at the age of sixty-three and find his sons, who he loved better than his life, one a philandering bum—

Happy: Mom!

Linda: That's all you are, my baby! (*To Biff.*) And you! What happened to the love you had for him? You were such pals! How you used to talk to him on the phone every night! How lonely he was till he could come home to you!

Biff: All right, Mom. I'll live here in my room, and I'll get a job. I'll keep away from him, that's all.

Linda: No, Biff. You can't stay here and fight all the time.

Biff: He threw me out of this house, remember that.

Linda: Why did he do that? I never knew why.

Biff: Because I know he's a fake and he doesn't like anybody around who knows!

Linda: Why a fake? In what way? What do you mean?

Biff: Just don't lay it all at my feet. It's between me and him—that's all I have to say. I'll chip in from now on. He'll settle for half my pay check. He'll be all right. I'm going to bed. (*He starts for the stairs.*)

Linda: He won't be all right.

Biff (*turning on the stairs, furiously*): I hate this city and I'll stay here. Now what do you want?

Linda: He's dying, Biff.

Happy turns quickly to her, shocked.

Biff (*after a pause*): Why is he dying?

Linda: He's been trying to kill himself.

Biff (with great horror): How?

Linda: I live from day to day.

Biff: What're you talking about?

Linda: Remember I wrote you that he smashed up the car again? In February?

Biff: Well?

Linda: The insurance inspector came. He said that they have evidence. That all these accidents in the last year—weren't—weren't—accidents.

Happy: How can they tell that? That's a lie.

Linda: It seems there's a woman . . . *(She takes a breath as—)*

Biff (sharply but contained): What woman?

Linda (simultaneously): . . . and this woman . . .

Linda: What?

Biff: Nothing. Go ahead.

Linda: What did you say?

Biff: Nothing. I just said what woman?

Happy: What about her?

Linda: Well, it seems she was walking down the road and saw his car. She says that he wasn't driving fast at all, and that he didn't skid. She says he came to that little bridge, and then deliberately smashed into the railing, and it was only the shallowness of the water that saved him.

Biff: Oh, no, he probably just fell asleep again.

Linda: I don't think he fell asleep.

Biff: Why not?

Linda: Last month . . . *(With great difficulty.)* Oh, boys, it's so hard to say a thing like this! He's just a big stupid man to you, but I tell you there's more good in him than in many other people. *(She chokes, wipes her eyes.)* I was looking for a fuse. The lights blew out, and I went down the cellar. And behind the fuse box—it happened to fall out—was a length of rubber pipe—just short.

Happy: No kidding?

Linda: There's a little attachment on the end of it. I knew right away. And sure enough, on the bottom of the water heater there's a new little nipple on the gas pipe.

Happy (angrily): That—jerk.

Biff: Did you have it taken off?

Linda: I'm—I'm ashamed to. How can I mention it to him? Every day I go down and take away that little rubber pipe. But, when he comes home, I put it back where it was. How can I insult him that way? I don't know what to do. I live from day to day, boys. I tell you, I know every thought in his mind. It sounds so old-fashioned and silly, but I tell you he put his whole life into you and you've turned your backs on him. (*She is bent over in the chair, weeping, her face in her hands.*) Biff, I swear to God! Biff, his life is in your hands!

Happy (*to Biff*): How do you like that damned fool!

Biff (*kissing her*): All right, pal, all right. It's all settled now. I've been remiss. I know that, Mom. But now I'll stay, and I swear to you, I'll apply myself. (*Kneeling in front of her, in a fever of self-reproach.*) It's just—you see, Mom, I don't fit in business. Not that I won't try. I'll try, and I'll make good.

Happy: Sure you will. The trouble with you in business was you never tried to please people.

Biff: I know, I—

Happy: Like when you worked for Harrison's. Bob Harrison said you were tops, and then you go and do some damn fool thing like whistling whole songs in the elevator like a comedian.

Biff (*against Happy*): So what? I like to whistle sometimes.

Happy: You don't raise a guy to a responsible job who whistles in the elevator!

Linda: Well, don't argue about it now.

Happy: Like when you'd go off and swim in the middle of the day instead of taking the line around.

Biff (*his resentment rising*): Well, don't you run off? You take off sometimes, don't you? On a nice summer day?

Happy: Yeah, but I cover myself!

Linda: Boys!

Happy: If I'm going to take a fade the boss can call any number where I'm supposed to be and they'll swear to him that I just left. I'll tell you something that I hate to say, Biff, but in the business world some of them think you're crazy.

Biff (*Angered*): Screw the business world!

Happy: All right, screw it! Great, but cover yourself!

Linda: Hap! Hap!

Biff: I don't care what they think! They've laughed at Dad for years, and you know why? Because we don't belong in this nut-house of a city! We should be mixing cement on some open plain, or—or carpenters. A carpenter is allowed to whistle!

Willy walks in from the entrance of the house, at left.

Willy: Even your grandfather was better than a carpenter. (*Pause. They watch him.*) You never grew up. Bernard does not whistle in the elevator, I assure you.

Biff (as though to laugh Willy out of it): Yeah, but you do, Pop.

Willy: I never in my life whistled in an elevator! And who in the business world thinks I'm crazy?

Biff: I didn't mean it like that, Pop. Now don't make a whole thing out of it, will ya?

Willy: Go back to the West! Be a carpenter, a cowboy, enjoy yourself!

Linda: Willy, he was just saying—

Willy: I heard what he said!

Happy (trying to quiet Willy): Hey, Pop, come on now . . .

Willy (continuing over Happy's line): They laugh at me, heh? Go to Filene's, go to the Hub, go to Slattery's, Boston. Call out the name Willy Loman and see what happens! Big shot!

Biff: All right, Pop.

Willy: Big!

Biff: All right!

Willy: Why do you always insult me?

Biff: I didn't say a word. *(To Linda.)* Did I say a word?

Linda: He didn't say anything, Willy.

Willy (going to the doorway of the living room): All right, good night, good night.

Linda: Willy, dear, he just decided . . .

Willy (to Biff): If you get tired hanging around tomorrow, paint the ceiling I put up in the living room.

Biff: I'm leaving early tomorrow.

Happy: He's going to see Bill Oliver, Pop.

Willy (interestedly): Oliver? For what?

Biff (with reserve, but trying, trying): He always said he'd stake me. I'd like to go into business, so maybe I can take him up on it.

Linda: Isn't that wonderful?

Willy: Don't interrupt. What's wonderful about it? There's fifty men in the City of New York who'd stake him. *(To Biff.)* Sporting goods?

Biff: I guess so. I know something about it and—

Willy: He knows something about it! You know sporting goods better than Spalding, for God's sake! How much is he giving you?

Biff: I don't know, I didn't even see him yet, but—

Willy: Then what're you talkin' about?

Biff (getting angry): Well, all I said was I'm gonna see him, that's all!

Willy (turning away): Ah, you're counting your chickens again.

Biff (starting left for the stairs): Oh, Jesus, I'm going to sleep!

Willy (calling after him): Don't curse in this house!

Biff (turning): Since when did you get so clean!

Happy (trying to stop them): Wait a . . .

Willy: Don't use that language to me! I won't have it!

Happy (*grabbing Biff, shouts*): Wait a minute! I got an idea. I got a feasi-
ble idea. Come here, Biff, let's talk this over now, let's talk some
sense here. When I was down in Florida last time, I thought of a
great idea to sell sporting goods. It just came back to me. You and I,
Biff—we have a line, the Loman Line. We train a couple of weeks,
and put on a couple of exhibitions, see?

Willy: That's an idea!

Happy: Wait! We form two basketball teams, see? Two water-polo
teams. We play each other. It's a million dollars' worth of publicity.
Two brothers, see? The Loman Brothers. Displays in the Royal
Palms—all the hotels. And banners over the ring and the basketball
court: "Loman Brothers." Baby, we could sell sporting goods!

Willy: That is a one-million-dollar idea.

Linda: Marvelous!

Biff: I'm in great shape as far as that's concerned.

Happy: And the beauty of it is, Biff, it wouldn't be like a business. We'd
be out playin' ball again . . .

Biff (*enthused*): Yeah, that's . . .

Willy: Million-dollar . . .

Happy: And you wouldn't get fed up with it, Biff. It'd be the family again.
There'd be the old honor, and comradeship, and if you wanted to go
off for a swim or somethin'—well, you'd do it! Without some smart
cooky gettin' up ahead of you!

Willy: Lick the world! You guys together could absolutely lick the civilized world.

Biff: I'll see Oliver tomorrow. Hap, if we could work that out . . .

Linda: Maybe things are beginning to—

Willy (*wildly enthused, to Linda*): Stop interrupting! (*To Biff.*) But don't
wear sport jacket and slacks when you see Oliver.

Biff: No, I'll—

Willy: A business suit, and talk as little as possible, and don't crack any
jokes.

Biff: He did like me. Always liked me.

Linda: He loved you!

Willy (*to Linda*): Will you stop! (*To Biff.*) Walk in very serious. You are
not applying for a boy's job. Money is to pass. Be quiet, fine, and serious. Everybody likes a kidder, but nobody lends him money.

Happy: I'll try to get some myself, Biff. I'm sure I can.

Willy: I can see great things for you, kids, I think your troubles are over.
But remember, start big and you'll end big. Ask for fifteen. How
much you gonna ask for?

Biff: Gee, I don't know—

Willy: And don't say "Gee." "Gee" is a boy's word. A man walking in for fifteen thousand dollars does not say "Gee!"

Biff: Ten, I think, would be top though.

Willy: Don't be so modest. You always started too low. Walk in with a big laugh. Don't look worried. Start off with a couple of your good stories to lighten things up. It's not what you say, it's how you say it—because personality always wins the day.

Linda: Oliver always thought the highest of him—

Willy: Will you let me talk?

Biff: Don't yell at her, Pop, will ya?

Willy (angrily): I was talking, wasn't I?

Biff: I don't like you yelling at her all the time, and I'm tellin' you, that's all.

Willy: What're you, takin' over the house?

Linda: Willy—

Willy (turning on her): Don't take his side all the time, goddammit!

Biff (furiously): Stop yelling at her!

Willy (suddenly pulling on his cheek, beaten down, guilt ridden): Give my best to Bill Oliver—he may remember me. (*He exits through the living room doorway.*)

Linda (her voice subdued): What'd you have to start that for? (*Biff turns away.*) You see how sweet he was as soon as you talked hopefully? (*She goes over to Biff.*) Come up and say good night to him. Don't let him go to bed that way.

Happy: Come on, Biff, let's buck him up.

Linda: Please, dear. Just say good night. It takes so little to make him happy. Come. (*She goes through the living room doorway, calling upstairs from within the living room.*) Your pajamas are hanging in the bathroom. Willy!

Happy (looking toward where Linda went out): What a woman! They broke the mold when they made her. You know that, Biff?

Biff: He's off salary. My God, working on commission!

Happy: Well, let's face it: he's no hot-shot selling man. Except that sometimes, you have to admit, he's a sweet personality.

Biff (deciding): Lend me ten bucks, will ya? I want to buy some new ties.

Happy: I'll take you to a place I know. Beautiful stuff. Wear one of my striped shirts tomorrow.

Biff: She got gray. Mom got awful old. Gee, I'm gonna go in to Oliver tomorrow and knock him for a—

Happy: Come on up. Tell that to Dad. Let's give him a whirl. Come on.

Biff (*steamed up*): You know, with ten thousand bucks, boy!

Happy (*as they go into the living room*): That's the talk, Biff, that's the first time I've heard the old confidence out of you! (*From within the living room, fading off.*) You're gonna live with me, kid, and any babe you want you just say the word . . . (*The last lines are hardly heard. They are mounting the stairs to their parents' bedroom.*)

Linda (*entering her bedroom and addressing Willy, who is in the bathroom. She is straightening the bed for him*): Can you do anything about the shower? It drips.

Willy (*from the bathroom*): All of a sudden everything falls to pieces! Goddam plumbing, oughta be sued, those people. I hardly finished putting it in and the thing . . . (*His words rumble off.*)

Linda: I'm just wondering if Oliver will remember him. You think he might?

Willy (*coming out of the bathroom in his pajamas*): Remember him? What's the matter with you, you crazy? If he'd've stayed with Oliver he'd be on top by now! Wait'll Oliver gets a look at him. You don't know the average caliber any more. The average young man today—(*he is getting into bed*)—is got a caliber of zero. Greatest thing in the world for him was to bum around.

Biff and Happy enter the bedroom. Slight pause.

Willy (*stops short, looking at Biff*): Glad to hear it, boy.

Happy: He wanted to say good night to you, sport.

Willy (*to Biff*): Yeah. Knock him dead, boy. What'd you want to tell me?

Biff: Just take it easy, Pop. Good night. (*He turns to go.*)

Willy (*unable to resist*): And if anything falls off the desk while you're talking to him—like a package or something—don't you pick it up. They have office boys for that.

Linda: I'll make a big breakfast—

Willy: Will you let me finish? (*To Biff.*) Tell him you were in the business in the West. Not farm work.

Biff: All right, Dad.

Linda: I think everything—

Willy (*going right through her speech*): And don't undersell yourself. No less than fifteen thousand dollars.

Biff (*unable to bear him*): Okay. Good night, Mom. (*He starts moving.*)

Willy: Because you got a greatness in you, Biff, remember that. You got all kinds a greatness . . . (*He lies back, exhausted. Biff walks out.*)

Linda (*calling after Biff*): Sleep well, darling!

Happy: I'm gonna get married, Mom. I wanted to tell you.

Linda: Go to sleep, dear.

Happy (going): I just wanted to tell you.

Willy: Keep up the good work. (*Happy exits.*) God . . . remember that Ebbets Field game? The championship of the city?

Linda: Just rest. Should I sing to you?

Willy: Yeah. Sing to me. (*Linda hums a soft lullaby.*) When that team came out—he was the tallest, remember?

Linda: Oh, yes. And in gold.

> *Biff enters the darkened kitchen, takes a cigarette, and leaves the house. He comes downstage into a golden pool of light. He smokes, staring at the night.*

Willy: Like a young god. Hercules—something like that. And the sun, the sun all around him. Remember how he waved to me? Right up from the field, with the representatives of three colleges standing by? And the buyers I brought, and the cheers when he came out—Loman, Loman, Loman! God Almighty, he'll be great yet. A star like that, magnificent, can never really fade away!

> *The light on Willy is fading. The gas heater begins to glow through the kitchen wall, near the stairs, a blue flame beneath red coils.*

Linda (timidly): Willy, dear, what has he got against you?

Willy: I'm so tired. Don't talk any more.

> *Biff slowly returns to the kitchen. He stops, stares toward the heater.*

Linda: Will you ask Howard to let you work in New York?

Willy: First thing in the morning. Everything'll be all right.

> *Biff reaches behind the heater and draws out a length of rubber tubing. He is horrified and turns his head toward Willy's room, still dimly lit, from which the strains of Linda's desperate but monotonous humming rise.*

Willy (staring through the window into the moonlight): Gee, look at the moon moving between the buildings!

> *Biff wraps the tubing around his hand and quickly goes up the stairs. Curtain.*

ACT II

Music is heard, gay and bright. The curtain rises as the music fades away. Willy, in shirt sleeves, is sitting at the kitchen table, sipping coffee, his hat in his lap. Linda is filling his cup when she can.

Willy: Wonderful coffee. Meal in itself.

Linda: Can I make you some eggs?

Willy: No. Take a breath.

Linda: You look so rested, dear.

Willy: I slept like a dead one. First time in months. Imagine, sleeping till ten on a Tuesday morning. Boys left nice and early, heh?

Linda: They were out of here by eight o'clock.

Willy: Good work!

Linda: It was so thrilling to see them leaving together. I can't get over the shaving lotion in this house.

Willy (smiling): Mmm—

Linda: Biff was very changed this morning. His whole attitude seemed to be hopeful. He couldn't wait to get downtown to see Oliver.

Willy: He's heading for a change. There's no question, there simply are certain men that take longer to get—solidified. How did he dress?

Linda: His blue suit. He's so handsome in that suit. He could be a—anything in that suit!

Willy gets up from the table. Linda holds his jacket for him.

Willy: There's no question, no question at all. Gee, on the way home tonight I'd like to buy some seeds.

Linda (laughing): That'd be wonderful. But not enough sun gets back there. Nothing'll grow any more.

Willy: You wait, kid, before it's all over we're gonna get a little place out in the country, and I'll raise some vegetables, a couple of chickens . . .

Linda: You'll do it yet, dear.

Willy walks out of his jacket. Linda follows him.

Willy: And they'll get married, and come for a weekend. I'd build a little guest house. 'Cause I got so many fine tools, all I'd need would be a little lumber and some peace of mind.

Linda (Joyfully): I sewed the lining . . .

Willy: I could build two guest houses, so they'd both come. Did he decide how much he's going to ask Oliver for?

Linda (getting him into the jacket): He didn't mention it, but I imagine ten or fifteen thousand. You going to talk to Howard today?

Willy: Yeah. I'll put it to him straight and simple. He'll just have to take me off the road.

Linda: And Willy, don't forget to ask for a little advance, because we've got the insurance premium. It's the grace period now.

Willy: That's a hundred . . . ?

Linda: A hundred and eight, sixty-eight. Because we're a little short again.

Willy: Why are we short?

Linda: Well, you had the motor job on the car . . .

Willy: That goddam Studebaker!

Linda: And you got one more payment on the refrigerator . . .

Willy: But it just broke again!

Linda: Well, it's old, dear.

Willy: I told you we should've bought a well-advertised machine. Charley bought a General Electric and it's twenty years old and it's still good, that son-of-a-bitch.

Linda: But, Willy—

Willy: Whoever heard of a Hastings refrigerator? Once in my life I would like to own something outright before it's broken! I'm always in a race with the junkyard! I just finished paying for the car and it's on its last legs. The refrigerator consumes belts like a goddam maniac. They time those things. They time them so when you finally paid for them, they're used up.

Linda (buttoning up his jacket as he unbuttons it): All told, about two hundred dollars would carry us, dear. But that includes the last payment on the mortgage. After this payment, Willy, the house belongs to us.

Willy: It's twenty-five years!

Linda: Biff was nine years old when we bought it.

Willy: Well, that's a great thing. To weather a twenty-five year mortgage is—

Linda: It's an accomplishment.

Willy: All the cement, the lumber, the reconstruction I put in this house! There ain't a crack to be found in it any more.

Linda: Well, it served its purpose.

Willy: What purpose? Some stranger'll come along, move in, and that's that. If only Biff would take this house, and raise a family . . . . (*He starts to go.*) Good-by, I'm late.

Linda (suddenly remembering): Oh, I forgot! You're supposed to meet them for dinner.

Willy: Me?

Linda: At Frank's Chop House on Forty-eighth near Sixth Avenue.

Willy: Is that so! How about you?

Linda: No, just the three of you. They're gonna blow you to a big meal!

Willy: Don't say! Who thought of that?

Linda: Biff came to me this morning, Willy, and he said, "Tell Dad, we want to blow him to a big meal." Be there six o'clock. You and your two boys are going to have dinner.

Willy: Gee whiz! That's really somethin'. I'm gonna knock Howard for a loop, kid. I'll get an advance, and I'll come home with a New York job. Goddammit, now I'm gonna do it!

Linda: Oh, that's the spirit, Willy!

Willy: I will never get behind a wheel the rest of my life!

Linda: It's changing, Willy, I can feel it changing!

Willy: Beyond a question. G'by, I'm late. (*He starts to go again.*)

Linda (*calling after him as she runs to the kitchen table for a handkerchief*): You got your glasses?

Willy (*feels for them, then comes back in*): Yeah, yeah, got my glasses.

Linda (*giving him the handkerchief*): And a handkerchief.

Willy: Yeah, handkerchief.

Linda: And your saccharine?

Willy: Yeah, my saccharine.

Linda: Be careful on the subway stairs.

> *She kisses him, and a silk stocking is seen hanging from her hand. Willy notices it.*

Willy: Will you stop mending stockings? At least while I'm in the house. It gets me nervous. I can't tell you. Please.

> *Linda hides the stocking in her hand as she follows Willy across the forestage in front of the house.*

Linda: Remember, Frank's Chop House.

Willy (*passing the apron*): Maybe beets would grow out there.

Linda (*laughing*): But you tried so many times.

Willy: Yeah. Well, don't work hard today. (*He disappears around the right corner of the house.*)

Linda: Be careful!

> *As Willy vanishes, Linda waves to him. Suddenly the phone rings. She runs across the stage and into the kitchen and lifts it.*

Linda: Hello? Oh, Biff! I'm so glad you called, I just . . . Yes, sure, I just told him. Yes, he'll be there for dinner at six o'clock, I didn't forget. Listen, I was just dying to tell you. You know that little rubber pipe I told you about? That he connected to the gas heater? I finally decided to go down the cellar this morning and take it away and destroy it. But it's gone! Imagine? He took it away himself, it isn't there! (*She listens.*) When? Oh, then you took it. Oh—nothing, it's just that I'd hoped he'd taken it away himself. Oh, I'm not worried, darling, because this morning he left in such high spirits, it was like the old days! I'm not afraid any more. Did Mr. Oliver see you? . . . Well, you wait there then. And make a nice impression on him, darling. Just don't perspire too much before you see him. And have a nice time with Dad. He may have big news too! . . . That's right, a New York job. And be sweet to him tonight, dear. Be loving to him.

Because he's only a little boat looking for a harbor. (*She is trembling with sorrow and joy.*) Oh, that's wonderful, Biff, you'll save his life. Thanks, darling. Just put your arm around him when he comes into the restaurant. Give him a smile. That's the boy . . . Good-by, dear. . . . You got your comb? . . . That's fine. Good-by, Biff dear.

In the middle of her speech, Howard Wagner, thirty-six, wheels in a small typewriter table on which is a wire-recording machine and proceeds to plug it in. This is on the left forestage. Light slowly fades on Linda as it rises on Howard. Howard is intent on threading the machine and only glances over his shoulder as Willy appears.

Willy: Pst! Pst!
Howard: Hello, Willy, come in.
Willy: Like to have a little talk with you, Howard.
Howard: Sorry to keep you waiting. I'll be with you in a minute.
Willy: What's that, Howard?
Howard: Didn't you ever see one of these? Wire recorder.
Willy: Oh. Can we talk a minute?
Howard: Records things. Just got delivery yesterday. Been driving me crazy, the most terrific machine I ever saw in my life. I was up all night with it.
Willy: What do you do with it?
Howard: I bought it for dictation, but you can do anything with it. Listen to this. I had it home last night. Listen to what I picked up. The first one is my daughter. Get this. (*He flicks the switch and "Roll out the Barrel" is heard being whistled.*) Listen to that kid whistle.
Willy: That is lifelike, isn't it?
Howard: Seven years old. Get that tone.
Willy: Ts, ts. Like to ask a little favor if you . . .

The whistling breaks off, and the voice of Howard's Daughter is heard.

His Daughter: "Now you, Daddy."
Howard: She's crazy for me! (*Again the same song is whistled.*) That's me! Ha! (*He winks.*)
Willy: You're very good!

The whistling breaks off again. The machine runs silent for a moment.

Howard: Sh! Get this now, this is my son.
His Son: "The capital of Alabama is Montgomery; the capital of Arizona is Phoenix; the capital of Arkansas is Little Rock; the capital of California is Sacramento . . ." (*And on, and on.*)
Howard (*holding up five fingers*): Five years old, Willy!

Willy: He'll make an announcer some day!

His Son (*continuing*): "The capital . . . "

Howard: Get that—alphabetical order! (*The machine breaks off suddenly.*) Wait a minute. The maid kicked the plug out.

Willy: It certainly is a—

Howard: Sh, for God's sake!

His son: "It's nine o'clock, Bulova watch time. So I have to go to sleep."

Willy: That really is—

Howard: Wait a minute! The next is my wife.

They wait.

Howard's Voice: "Go on, say something." (*Pause.*) "Well, you gonna talk?"

His Wife: "I can't think of anything."

Howard's Voice: "Well, talk—it's turning."

His Wife (*shyly, beaten*): "Hello." (*Silence.*) "Oh, Howard, I can't talk into this . . . "

Howard (*snapping the machine off*): That was my wife.

Willy: That is a wonderful machine. Can we—

Howard: I tell you, Willy, I'm gonna take my camera, and my bandsaw, and all my hobbies, and out they go. This is the most fascinating relaxation I ever found.

Willy: I think I'll get one myself.

Howard: Sure, they're only a hundred and a half. You can't do without it. Supposing you wanna hear Jack Benny, see? But you can't be at home at that hour. So you tell the maid to turn the radio on when Jack Benny comes on, and this automatically goes on with the radio . . .

Willy: And when you come home you . . .

Howard: You can come home twelve o'clock, one o'clock, any time you like, and you get yourself a Coke and sit yourself down, throw the switch, and there's Jack Benny's program in the middle of the night!

Willy: I'm definitely going to get one. Because lots of times I'm on the road, and I think to myself, what I must be missing on the radio!

Howard: Don't you have a radio in the car?

Willy: Well, yeah, but who ever thinks of turning it on?

Howard: Say, aren't you supposed to be in Boston?

Willy: That's what I want to talk to you about, Howard. You got a minute?

(*He draws a chair in from the wing.*)

Howard: What happened? What're you doing here?

Willy: Well . . .

Howard: You didn't crack up again, did you?

Willy: Oh, no. No . . .

Howard: Geez, you had me worried there for a minute. What's the trouble?

Willy: Well, to tell you the truth, Howard, I've come to the decision that I'd rather not travel any more.

Howard: Not travel! Well, what'll you do?

Willy: Remember, Christmas time, when you had the party here? You said you'd try to think of some spot for me here in town.

Howard: With us?

Willy: Well, sure.

Howard: Oh, yeah, yeah. I remember. Well, I couldn't think of anything for you, Willy.

Willy: I tell ya, Howard. The kids are all grown up, y'know. I don't need much any more. If I could take home—well, sixty-five dollars a week, I could swing it.

Howard: Yeah, but Willy, see I—

Willy: I tell ya why, Howard. Speaking frankly and between the two of us, y'know—I'm just a little tired.

Howard: Oh, I could understand that, Willy. But you're a road man, Willy, and we do a road business. We've only got a half-dozen salesmen on the floor here.

Willy: God knows, Howard, I never asked a favor of any man. But I was with the firm when your father used to carry you in here in his arms.

Howard: I know that, Willy, but—

Willy: Your father came to me the day you were born and asked me what I thought of the name of Howard, may he rest in peace.

Howard: I appreciate that, Willy, but there just is no spot here for you. If I had a spot I'd slam you right in, but I just don't have a single, solitary spot.

He looks for his lighter. Willy has picked it up and gives it to him. Pause.

Willy (with increasing anger): Howard, all I need to set my table is fifty dollars a week.

Howard: But where am I going to put you, kid?

Willy: Look, it isn't a question of whether I can sell merchandise, is it?

Howard: No, but it's a business, kid, and everybody's gotta pull his own weight.

Willy (desperately): Just let me tell you a story, Howard—

Howard: 'Cause you gotta admit, business is business.

Willy (angrily): Business is definitely business, but just listen for a minute. You don't understand this. When I was a boy—eighteen, nineteen—

I was already on the road. And there was a question in my mind as to whether selling had a future for me. Because in those days I had a yearning to go to Alaska. See, there were three gold strikes in one month in Alaska, and I felt like going out. Just for the ride, you might say.

Howard (*barely interested*): Don't say.

Willy: Oh, yeah, my father lived many years in Alaska. He was an adventurous man. We've got quite a little streak of self-reliance in our family. I thought I'd go out with my older brother and try to locate him, and maybe settle in the North with the old man. And I was almost decided to go, when I met a salesman in the Parker House. His name was Dave Singleman. And he was eighty-four years old, and he'd drummed merchandise in thirty-one states. And old Dave, he'd go up to his room, y'understand, put on his green velvet slippers—I'll never forget—and pick up his phone and call the buyers, and without ever leaving his room, at the age of eighty-four, he made his living. And when I saw that, I realized that selling was the greatest career a man could want. 'Cause what could be more satisfying than to be able to go, at the age of eighty-four, into twenty or thirty different cities, and pick up a phone, and be remembered and loved and helped by so many different people? Do you know? When he died—and by the way he died the death of a salesman, in his green velvet slippers in the smoker of the New York, New Haven and Hartford, going into Boston—when he died, hundreds of salesmen and buyers were at his funeral. Things were sad on a lotta trains for months after that. (*He stands up. Howard has not looked at him.*) In those days there was personality in it, Howard. There was respect, and comradeship, and gratitude in it. Today, it's all cut and dried, and there's no chance for bringing friendship to bear—or personality. You see what I mean? They don't know me any more.

Howard (*moving away, to the right*): That's just the thing, Willy.

Willy: If I had forty dollars a week—that's all I'd need. Forty dollars, Howard.

Howard: Kid, I can't take blood from a stone, I—

Willy (*desperation is on him now*): Howard, the year Al Smith was nominated, your father came to me and—

Howard (*starting to go off*): I've got to see some people, kid.

Willy (*stopping him*): I'm talking about your father! There were promises made across this desk! You mustn't tell me you've got people to see—I put thirty-four years into this firm, Howard, and now I can't pay my insurance! You can't eat the orange and throw the peel away—a man is not a piece of fruit! (*After a pause.*) Now pay attention.

Your father—in 1928 I had a big year. I averaged a hundred and seventy dollars a week in commissions.

Howard (*impatiently*): Now, Willy, you never averaged—

Willy (*banging his hand on the desk*): I averaged a hundred and seventy dollars a week in the year of 1928! And your father came to me—or rather, I was in the office here—it was right over this desk—and he put his hand on my shoulder—

Howard (*getting up*): You'll have to excuse me, Willy, I gotta see some people. Pull yourself together. (*Going out.*) I'll be back in a little while.

On Howard's exit, the light on his chair grows very bright and strange.

Willy: Pull yourself together! What the hell did I say to him? My God, I was yelling at him! How could I! (*Willy breaks off, staring at the light, which occupies the chair, animating it. He approaches this chair, standing across the desk from it.*) Frank, Frank, don't you remember what you told me that time? How you put your hand on my shoulder, and Frank . . . (*He leans on the desk and as he speaks the dead man's name he accidentally switches on the recorder, and instantly—*)

Howard's Son: ". . . of New York is Albany. The capital of Ohio is Cincinnati, the capital of Rhode Island is . . ." (*The recitation continues.*)

Willy (*leaping away with fright, shouting*): Ha! Howard! Howard! Howard!

Howard (*rushing in*): What happened?

Willy (*pointing at the machine, which continues nasally, childishly, with the capital cities*): Shut it off! Shut it off!

Howard (*pulling the plug out*): Look, Willy . . .

Willy (*pressing his hands to his eyes*): I gotta get myself some coffee. I'll get some coffee . . .

Willy starts to walk out. Howard stops him.

Howard (*rolling up the cord*): Willy, look . . .

Willy: I'll go to Boston.

Howard: Willy, you can't go to Boston for us.

Willy: Why can't I go?

Howard: I don't want you to represent us. I've been meaning to tell you for a long time now.

Willy: Howard, are you firing me?

Howard: I think you need a good long rest, Willy.

Willy: Howard—

Howard: And when you feel better, come back, and we'll see if we can work something out.

Willy: But I gotta earn money, Howard. I'm in no position—

Howard: Where are your sons? Why don't your sons give you a hand?

Willy: They're working on a very big deal.

Howard: This is no time for false pride, Willy. You go to your sons and tell them that you're tired. You've got two great boys, haven't you?

Willy: Oh, no question, no question, but in the meantime . . .

Howard: Then that's that, heh?

Willy: All right, I'll go to Boston tomorrow.

Howard: No, no.

Willy: I can't throw myself on my sons. I'm not a cripple!

Howard: Look, kid, I'm busy this morning.

Willy (grasping Howard's arm): Howard, you've got to let me go to Boston!

Howard (hard, keeping himself under control): I've got a line of people to see this morning. Sit down, take five minutes, and pull yourself together, and then go home, will ya? I need the office, Willy. (*He starts to go, turns, remembering the recorder, starts to push off the table holding the recorder.*) Oh, yeah. Whenever you can this week, stop by and drop off the samples. You'll feel better, Willy, and then come back and we'll talk. Pull yourself together, kid, there's people outside.

Howard exits, pushing the table off left. Willy stares into space, exhausted. Now the music is heard—Ben's music—first distantly, then closer, closer. As Willy speaks, Ben enters from the right. He carries valise and umbrella.

Willy: Oh, Ben, how did you do it? What is the answer? Did you wind up the Alaska deal already?

Ben: Doesn't take much time if you know what you're doing. Just a short business trip. Boarding ship in an hour. Wanted to say good-by.

Willy: Ben, I've got to talk to you.

Ben (glancing at his watch): Haven't the time, William.

Willy (crossing the apron to Ben): Ben, nothing's working out. I don't know what to do.

Ben: Now, look here, William. I've bought timberland in Alaska and I need a man to look after things for me.

Willy: God, timberland! Me and my boys in those grand outdoors!

Ben: You've a new continent at your doorstep, William. Get out of these cities, they're full of talk and time payments and courts of law. Screw on your fists and you can fight for a fortune up there.

Willy: Yes, yes! Linda! Linda!

Linda enters as of old, with the wash.

Linda: Oh, you're back?

Ben: I haven't much time.

Willy: No, wait! Linda, he's got a proposition for me in Alaska.

Linda: But you've got—(*To Ben.*) He's got a beautiful job here.

Willy: But in Alaska, kid, I could—

Linda: You're doing well enough, Willy!

Ben (*to Linda*): Enough for what, my dear?

Linda (*frightened of Ben and angry at him*): Don't say those things to him! Enough to be happy right here, right now. (*To Willy, while Ben laughs.*) Why must everybody conquer the world? You're well liked, and the boys love you, and someday—(*to Ben*)—why, old man Wagner told him just the other day that if he keeps it up he'll be a member of the firm, didn't he, Willy?

Willy: Sure, sure. I am building something with this firm, Ben, and if a man is building something he must be on the right track, mustn't he?

Ben: What are you building? Lay your hand on it. Where is it?

Willy (*hesitantly*): That's true, Linda, there's nothing.

Linda: Why? (*To Ben.*) There's a man eighty-four years old—

Willy: That's right, Ben, that's right. When I look at that man I say, what is there to worry about?

Ben: Bah!

Willy: It's true, Ben. All he has to do is go into any city, pick up the phone, and he's making his living and you know why?

Ben (*picking up his valise*): I've got to go.

Willy (*holding Ben back*): Look at this boy!

Biff, in his high school sweater, enters carrying suitcase. Happy carries Biff's shoulder guards, gold helmet, and football pants.

Willy: Without a penny to his name, three great universities are begging for him, and from there the sky's the limit, because it's not what you do, Ben. It's who you know and the smile on your face! It's contacts, Ben, contacts! The whole wealth of Alaska passes over the lunch table at the Commodore Hotel, and that's the wonder, the wonder of this country, that a man can end with diamonds here on the basis of being liked! (*He turns to Biff.*) And that's why when you get out on that field today it's important. Because thousands of people will be rooting for you and loving you. (*To Ben, who has again begun to leave.*) And Ben! when he walks into a business office his name will sound out like a bell and all the doors will open to him! I've seen it, Ben, I've seen it a thousand times! You can't feel it with your hand like timber, but it's there!

Ben: Good-by, William.

Willy: Ben, am I right? Don't you think I'm right? I value your advice.

Ben: There's a new continent at your doorstep, William. You could walk out rich. Rich. (*He is gone.*)

Willy: We'll do it here, Ben! You hear me? We're gonna do it here!

Young Bernard rushes in. The gay music of the boys is heard.

Bernard: Oh, gee, I was afraid you left already!

Willy: Why? What time is it?

Bernard: It's half-past one!

Willy: Well, come on, everybody! Ebbets Field next stop! Where's the pennants? (*He rushes through the wall-line of the kitchen and out into the living room.*)

Linda (*to Biff*): Did you pack fresh underwear?

Biff (*who has been limbering up*): I want to go!

Bernard: Biff, I'm carrying your helmet, ain't I?

Happy: No, I'm carrying the helmet.

Bernard: Oh, Biff, you promised me.

Happy: I'm carrying the helmet.

Bernard: How am I going to get in the locker room?

Linda: Let him carry the shoulder guards. (*She puts her coat and hat on in the kitchen.*)

Bernard: Can I, Biff? 'Cause I told everybody I'm going to be in the locker room.

Happy: In Ebbets Field it's the clubhouse.

Bernard: I meant the clubhouse. Biff!

Happy: Biff!

Biff (*grandly, after a slight pause*): Let him carry the shoulder guards.

Happy (*as he gives Bernard the shoulder guards*): Stay close to us now.

Willy rushes in with the pennants.

Willy (*handing them out*): Everybody wave when Biff comes out on the field. (*Happy and Bernard run off.*) You set now, boy?

The music has died away.

Biff: Ready to go, Pop. Every muscle is ready.

Willy (*at the edge of the apron*): You realize what this means?

Biff: That's right, Pop.

Willy (*feeling Biff's muscles*): You're comin' home this afternoon captain of the All-Scholastic Championship Team of the City of New York.

Biff: I got it, Pop. And remember, pal, when I take off my helmet, that touchdown is for you.

Willy: Let's go! (*He is starting out, with his arm around Biff, when Charley enters, as of old, in knickers.*) I got no room for you, Charley.

Charley: Room? For what?

Willy: In the car.

Charley: You goin' for a ride? I wanted to shoot some casino.

Willy (furiously): Casino! (*Incredulously.*) Don't you realize what today is?

Linda: Oh, he knows, Willy. He's just kidding you.

Willy: That's nothing to kid about!

Charley: No, Linda, what's goin' on?

Linda: He's playing in Ebbets Field.

Charley: Baseball in this weather?

Willy: Don't talk to him. Come on, come on! (*He is pushing them out.*)

Charley: Wait a minute, didn't you hear the news?

Willy: What?

Charley: Don't you listen to the radio? Ebbets Field just blew up.

Willy: You go to hell! (*Charley laughs. Pushing them out.*) Come on, come on! We're late.

Charley (as they go): Knock a homer, Biff, knock a homer!

Willy (the last to leave, turning to Charley): I don't think that was funny, Charley. This is the greatest day of his life.

Charley: Willy, when are you going to grow up?

Willy: Yeah, heh? When this game is over, Charley, you'll be laughing out of the other side of your face. They'll be calling him another Red Grange. Twenty-five thousand a year.

Charley (kidding): Is that so?

Willy: Yeah, that's so.

Charley: Well, then, I'm sorry, Willy. But tell me something.

Willy: What?

Charley: Who is Red Grange?

Willy: Put up your hands. Goddam you, put up your hands!

Charley, chuckling, shakes his head and walks away, around the left corner of the stage. Willy follows him. The music rises to a mocking frenzy.

Willy: Who the hell do you think you are, better than everybody else? You don't know everything, you big, ignorant, stupid . . . Put up your hands!

Light rises, on the right side of the forestage, on a small table in the reception room of Charley's office. Traffic sounds are heard. Bernard, now mature, sits whistling to himself. A pair of tennis rackets and an overnight bag are on the floor beside him.

Willy (offstage): What are you walking away for? Don't walk away! If you're going to say something say it to my face! I know you laugh at me behind my back. You'll laugh out of the other side of your god-dam face after this game. Touchdown! Touchdown! Eighty thousand people! Touchdown! Right between the goal posts.

Bernard is a quiet, earnest, but self-assured young man. Willy's voice is coming from right upstage now. Bernard lowers his feet off the table and listens. Jenny, his father's secretary, enters.

Jenny (*distressed*): Say, Bernard, will you go out in the hall?

Bernard: What is that noise? Who is it?

Jenny: Mr. Loman. He just got off the elevator.

Bernard (*getting up*): Who's he arguing with?

Jenny: Nobody. There's nobody with him. I can't deal with him any more, and your father gets all upset everytime he comes. I've got a lot of typing to do, and your father's waiting to sign it. Will you see him?

Willy (*entering*): Touchdown! Touch—(*He sees Jenny.*) Jenny, Jenny, good to see you. How're ya? Workin'? Or still honest?

Jenny: Fine. How've you been feeling?

Willy: Not much any more, Jenny. Ha, ha! (*He is surprised to see the rackets.*)

Bernard: Hello, Uncle Willy.

Willy (*almost shocked*): Bernard! Well, look who's here! (*He comes quickly, guiltily, to Bernard and warmly shakes his hand.*)

Bernard: How are you? Good to see you.

Willy: What are you doing here?

Bernard: Oh, just stopped by to see Pop. Get off my feet till my train leaves. I'm going to Washington in a few minutes.

Willy: Is he in?

Bernard: Yes, he's in his office with the accountant. Sit down.

Willy (*sitting down*): What're you going to do in Washington?

Bernard: Oh, just a case I've got there, Willy.

Willy: That so? (*indicating the rackets.*) You going to play tennis there?

Bernard: I'm staying with a friend who's got a court.

Willy: Don't say. His own tennis court. Must be fine people, I bet.

Bernard: They are, very nice. Dad tells me Biff's in town.

Willy (*with a big smile*): Yeah, Biff's in. Working on a very big deal, Bernard.

Bernard: What's Biff doing?

Willy: Well, he's been doing very big things in the West. But he decided to establish himself here. Very big. We're having dinner. Did I hear your wife had a boy?

Bernard: That's right. Our second.

Willy: Two boys! What do you know!

Bernard: What kind of deal has Biff got?

Willy: Well, Bill Oliver—very big sporting-goods man—he wants Biff very badly. Called him in from the West. Long distance, carte blanche, special deliveries. Your friends have their own private tennis court?

Bernard: You still with the old firm, Willy?

Willy (after a pause): I'm—I'm overjoyed to see how you made the grade, Bernard, overjoyed. It's an encouraging thing to see a young man really—really—Looks very good for Biff—very—(*He breaks off, then.*) Bernard—(*He is so full of emotion, he breaks off again.*)

Bernard: What is it, Willy?

Willy (small and alone): What—what's the secret?

Bernard: What secret?

Willy: How—how did you? Why didn't he ever catch on?

Bernard: I wouldn't know that, Willy.

Willy (confidentially, desperately): You were his friend, his boyhood friend. There's something I don't understand about it. His life ended after that Ebbets Field game. From the age of seventeen nothing good ever happened to him.

Bernard: He never trained himself for anything.

Willy: But he did, he did. After high school he took so many correspondence courses. Radio mechanics; television; God knows what, and never made the slightest mark.

Bernard (taking off his glasses): Willy, do you want to talk candidly?

Willy (rising, faces Bernard): I regard you as a very brilliant man, Bernard. I value your advice.

Bernard: Oh, the hell with the advice, Willy. I couldn't advise you. There's just one thing I've always wanted to ask you. When he was supposed to graduate, and the math teacher flunked him—

Willy: Oh, that son-of-a-bitch ruined his life.

Bernard: Yeah, but, Willy, all he had to do was go to summer school and make up that subject.

Willy: That's right, that's right.

Bernard: Did you tell him not to go to summer school?

Willy: Me? I begged him to go. I ordered him to go!

Bernard: Then why wouldn't he go?

Willy: Why? Why! Bernard, that question has been trailing me like a ghost for the last fifteen years. He flunked the subject, and laid down and died like a hammer hit him!

Bernard: Take it easy, kid.

Willy: Let me talk to you—I got nobody to talk to. Bernard, Bernard, was it my fault? Y'see? It keeps going around in my mind, maybe I did something to him. I got nothing to give him.

Bernard: Don't take it so hard.

Willy: Why did he lay down? What is the story there? You were his friend!

Bernard: Willy, I remember, it was June, and our grades came out. And he'd flunked math.

Willy: That son-of-a-bitch!

Bernard: No, it wasn't right then. Biff just got very angry, I remember, and he was ready to enroll in summer school.

Willy (*surprised*): He was?

Bernard: He wasn't beaten by it at all. But then, Willy, he disappeared from the block for almost a month. And I got the idea that he'd gone up to New England to see you. Did he have a talk with you then?

Willy stares in silence.

Bernard: Willy?

Willy (*with a strong edge of resentment in his voice*): Yeah, he came to Boston. What about it?

Bernard: Well, just that when he came back—I'll never forget this, it always mystifies me. Because I'd thought so well of Biff, even though he'd always taken advantage of me. I loved him, Willy, y'know? And he came back after that month and took his sneakers—remember those sneakers with "University of Virginia" printed on them? He was so proud of those, wore them every day. And he took them down in the cellar, and burned them up in the furnace. We had a fist fight. It lasted at least half an hour. Just the two of us, punching each other down the cellar, and crying right through it. I've often thought of how strange it was that I knew he'd given up his life. What happened in Boston, Willy?

Willy looks at him as at an intruder.

Bernard: I just bring it up because you asked me.

Willy (*angrily*): Nothing. What do you mean, "What happened?" What's that got to do with anything?

Bernard: Well, don't get sore.

Willy: What are you trying to do, blame it on me? If a boy lays down is that my fault?

Bernard: Now, Willy, don't get—

Willy: Well, don't—don't talk to me that way! What does that mean, "What happened?"

Charley enters. He is in his vest, and he carries a bottle of bourbon.

Charley: Hey, you're going to miss that train. (*He waves the bottle.*)

Bernard: Yeah, I'm going. (*He takes the bottle.*) Thanks, Pop. (*He picks up his rackets and bag.*) Good-by, Willy, and don't worry about it. You know, "If at first you don't succeed . . ."

Willy: Yes, I believe in that.

Bernard: But sometimes, Willy, it's better for a man just to walk away.

Willy: Walk away?

Bernard: That's right.

Willy: But if you can't walk away?

Bernard (after a slight pause): I guess that's when it's tough. (*Extending his hand.*) Good-by, Willy.

Willy (shaking Bernard's hand): Good-by, boy.

Charley (an arm on Bernard's shoulder): How do you like this kid? Gonna argue a case in front of the Supreme Court.

Bernard (protesting): Pop!

Willy (genuinely shocked, pained, and happy): No! The Supreme Court!

Bernard: I gotta run. 'By, Dad!

Charley: Knock 'em dead, Bernard!

Bernard goes off.

Willy (as Charley takes out his wallet): The Supreme Court! And he didn't even mention it!

Charley (counting out money on the desk): He don't have to—he's gonna do it.

Willy: And you never told him what to do, did you? You never took any interest in him.

Charley: My salvation is that I never took any interest in anything. There's some money—fifty dollars. I got an accountant inside.

Willy: Charley, look . . . (*With difficulty.*) I got my insurance to pay. If you can manage it—I need a hundred and ten dollars.

Charley doesn't reply for a moment; merely stops moving.

Willy: I'd draw it from my bank but Linda would know, and I . . .

Charley: Sit down, Willy.

Willy (moving toward the chair): I'm keeping an account of everything, re-member. I'll pay every penny back. (*He sits.*)

Charley: Now listen to me, Willy.

Willy: I want you to know I appreciate . . .

Charley (sitting down on the table): Willy, what're you doin'? What the hell is goin' on in your head?

Willy: Why? I'm simply . . .

Charley: I offered you a job. You can make fifty dollars a week. And I won't send you on the road.

Willy: I've got a job.

Charley: Without pay? What kind of a job is a job without pay? (*He rises.*) Now, look, kid, enough is enough. I'm no genius but I know when I'm being insulted.

Willy: Insulted!

Charley: Why don't you want to work for me?

Willy: What's the matter with you? I've got a job.

Charley: Then what're you walkin' in here every week for?

Willy (*getting up*): Well, if you don't want me to walk in here—

Charley: I am offering you a job.

Willy: I don't want your goddam job!

Charley: When the hell are you going to grow up?

Willy (*furiously*): You big ignoramus, if you say that to me again I'll rap you one! I don't care how big you are! (*He's ready to fight.*)

Pause.

Charley (*kindly, going to him*): How much do you need, Willy?

Willy: Charley, I'm strapped. I'm strapped. I don't know what to do. I was just fired.

Charley: Howard fired you?

Willy: That snotnose. Imagine that? I named him. I named him Howard.

Charley: Willy, when're you gonna realize that them things don't mean anything? You named him Howard, but you can't sell that. The only thing you got in this world is what you can sell. And the funny thing is that you're a salesman, and you don't know that.

Willy: I've always tried to think otherwise, I guess. I always felt that if a man was impressive, and well liked, that nothing—

Charley: Why must everybody like you? Who liked J. P. Morgan? Was he impressive? In a Turkish bath he'd look like a butcher. But with his pockets on he was very well liked. Now listen, Willy, I know you don't like me, and nobody can say I'm in love with you, but I'll give you a job because—just for the hell of it, put it that way. Now what do you say?

Willy: I—I just can't work for you, Charley.

Charley: What're you, jealous of me?

Willy: I can't work for you, that's all, don't ask me why.

Charley (*angered, takes out more bills*): You been jealous of me all your life, you damned fool! Here, pay your insurance. (*He puts the money in Willy's hand.*)

Willy: I'm keeping strict accounts.

Charley: I've got some work to do. Take care of yourself. And pay your insurance.

Willy (*moving to the right*): Funny, y'know? After all the highways, and the trains, and the appointments, and the years, you end up worth more dead than alive.

Charley: Willy, nobody's worth nothin' dead. (*After a slight pause.*) Did you hear what I said?

Willy stands still, dreaming.

Charley: Willy!

Willy: Apologize to Bernard for me when you see him. I didn't mean to argue with him. He's a fine boy. They're all fine boys, and they'll end up big—all of them. Someday they'll all play tennis together. Wish me luck, Charley. He saw Bill Oliver today.

Charley: Good luck.

Willy (*on the verge of tears*): Charley, you're the only friend I got. Isn't that a remarkable thing? (*He goes out.*)

Charley: Jesus!

Charley stares after him a moment and follows. All light blacks out. Suddenly raucous music is heard, and a red glow rises behind the screen at right. Stanley, a young waiter, appears, carrying a table, followed by Happy, who is carrying two chairs.

Stanley (*putting the table down*): That's all right, Mr. Loman, I can handle it myself. (*He turns and takes the chairs from Happy and places them at the table.*)

Happy (*glancing around*): Oh, this is better.

Stanley: Sure, in the front there you're in the middle of all kinds a noise. Whenever you got a party, Mr. Loman, you just tell me and I'll put you back here. Y'know, there's a lotta people they don't like it private, because when they go out they like to see a lotta action around them because they're sick and tired to stay in the house by theirself. But I know you, you ain't from Hackensack. You know what I mean?

Happy (*sitting down*): So how's it coming, Stanley?

Stanley: Ah, it's a dog's life. I only wish during the war they'd a took me in the Army. I coulda been dead by now.

Happy: My brother's back, Stanley.

Stanley: Oh, he come back, heh? From the Far West.

Happy: Yeah, big cattle man, my brother, so treat him right. And my father's coming too.

Stanley: Oh, your father too!

Happy: You got a couple of nice lobsters?

Stanley: Hundred per cent, big.

Happy: I want them with the claws.

Stanley: Don't worry, I don't give you no mice. (*Happy laughs.*) How about some wine? It'll put a head on the meal.

Happy: No. You remember, Stanley, that recipe I brought you from overseas? With the champagne in it?

Stanley: Oh, yeah, sure. I still got it tacked up yet in the kitchen. But that'll have to cost a buck apiece anyways.

Happy: That's all right.

Stanley: What'd you, hit a number or somethin'?

Happy: No, it's a little celebration. My brother is—I think he pulled off a big deal today. I think we're going into business together.

Stanley: Great! That's the best for you. Because a family business, you know what I mean?—that's the best.

Happy: That's what I think.

Stanley: 'Cause what's the difference? Somebody steals? It's in the family. Know what I mean? (*Sotto voce.*) Like this bartender here. The boss is goin' crazy what kinda leak he's got in the cash register. You put it in but it don't come out.

Happy (raising his head): Sh!

Stanley: What?

Happy: You notice I wasn't lookin' right or left, was I?

Stanley: No.

Happy: And my eyes are closed.

Stanley: So what's the—?

Happy: Strudel's comin'.

Stanley (catching on, looks around): Ah, no, there's no—

> He breaks off as a furred, lavishly dressed Girl enters and sits at the next table. Both follow her with their eyes.

Stanley: Geez, how'd ya know?

Happy: I got radar or something. (*Staring directly at her profile.*) Ooooooooo . . . Stanley.

Stanley: I think that's for you, Mr. Loman.

Happy: Look at that mouth. Oh, God. And the binoculars.

Stanley: Geez, you got a life, Mr. Loman.

Happy: Wait on her.

Stanley (going to The Girl's table): Would you like a menu, ma'am?

Girl: I'm expecting someone, but I'd like a—

Happy: Why don't you bring her—excuse me, miss, do you mind? I sell champagne, and I'd like you to try my brand. Bring her a champagne, Stanley.

Girl: That's awfully nice of you.

Happy: Don't mention it. It's all company money. (*He laughs.*)

Girl: That's a charming product to be selling, isn't it?

Happy: Oh, gets to be like everything else. Selling is selling, y'know.

Girl: I suppose.

Happy: You don't happen to sell, do you?

Girl: No, I don't sell.

Happy: Would you object to a compliment from a stranger? You ought to be on a magazine cover.

Girl (looking at him a little archly): I have been.

Stanley comes in with a glass of champagne.

Happy: What'd I say before, Stanley? You see? She's a cover girl.

Stanley: Oh, I could see, I could see.

Happy (to The Girl): What magazine?

Girl: Oh, a lot of them. (*She takes the drink.*) Thank you.

Happy: You know what they say in France, don't you? "Champagne is the drink of the complexion"—Hya, Biff!

Biff has entered and sits with Happy.

Biff: Hello, kid. Sorry I'm late.

Happy: I just got here. Uh, Miss—?

Girl: Forsythe.

Happy: Miss Forsythe, this is my brother.

Biff: Is Dad here?

Happy: His name is Biff. You might've heard of him. Great football player.

Girl: Really? What team?

Happy: Are you familiar with football?

Girl: No, I'm afraid I'm not.

Happy: Biff is quarterback with the New York Giants.

Girl: Well, that is nice, isn't it? (*She drinks.*)

Happy: Good health.

Girl: I'm happy to meet you.

Happy: That's my name. Hap. It's really Harold, but at West Point they called me Happy.

Girl (now really impressed): Oh, I see. How do you do? (*She turns her profile.*)

Biff: Isn't Dad coming?

Happy: You want her?

Biff: Oh, I could never make that.

Happy: I remember the time that idea would never come into your head. Where's the old confidence, Biff?

Biff: I just saw Oliver—

Happy: Wait a minute. I've got to see that old confidence again. Do you want her? She's on call.

Biff: Oh, no. (*He turns to look at The Girl.*)

Happy: I'm telling you. Watch this. (*Turning to The Girl.*) Honey? (*She turns to him.*) Are you busy?

Girl: Well, I am . . . but I could make a phone call.

Happy: Do that, will you, honey? And see if you can get a friend. We'll be here for a while. Biff is one of the greatest football players in the country.

Girl (*standing up*): Well, I'm certainly happy to meet you.

Happy: Come back soon.

Girl: I'll try.

Happy: Don't try, honey, try hard.

The Girl exits. Stanley follows, shaking his head in bewildered admiration.

Happy: Isn't that a shame now? A beautiful girl like that? That's why I can't get married. There's not a good woman in a thousand. New York is loaded with them, kid!

Biff: Hap, look—

Happy: I told you she was on call!

Biff (*strangely unnerved*): Cut it out, will ya? I want to say something to you.

Happy: Did you see Oliver?

Biff: I saw him all right. Now look, I want to tell Dad a couple of things and I want you to help me.

Happy: What? Is he going to back you?

Biff: Are you crazy? You're out of your goddam head, you know that?

Happy: Why? What happened?

Biff (*breathlessly*): I did a terrible thing today, Hap. It's been the strangest day I ever went through. I'm all numb, I swear.

Happy: You mean he wouldn't see you?

Biff: Well, I waited six hours for him, see? All day. Kept sending my name in. Even tried to date his secretary so she'd get me to him, but no soap.

Happy: Because you're not showin' the old confidence, Biff. He remembered you, didn't he?

Biff (*stopping Happy with a gesture*): Finally, about five o'clock, he comes out. Didn't remember who I was or anything. I felt like such an idiot, Hap.

Happy: Did you tell him my Florida idea?

Biff: He walked away. I saw him for one minute. I got so mad I could've torn the walls down! How the hell did I ever get the idea I was a salesman there? I even believed myself that I'd been a salesman for him! And then he gave me one look and—I realized what a ridiculous lie my whole life has been! We've been talking in a dream for fifteen years. I was a shipping clerk.

Happy: What'd you do?

Biff (with great tension and wonder): Well, he left, see. And the secretary went out. I was all alone in the waiting-room. I don't know what came over me, Hap. The next thing I know I'm in his office—paneled walls, everything. I can't explain it. I—Hap, I took his fountain pen.

Happy: Geez, did he catch you?

Biff: I ran out. I ran down all eleven flights. I ran and ran and ran.

Happy: That was an awful dumb—what'd you do that for?

Biff (agonized): I don't know, I just—wanted to take something, I don't know. You gotta help me, Hap. I'm gonna tell Pop.

Happy: You crazy? What for?

Biff: Hap, he's got to understand that I'm not the man somebody lends that kind of money to. He thinks I've been spiting him all these years and it's eating him up.

Happy: That's just it. You tell him something nice.

Biff: I can't.

Happy: Say you got a lunch date with Oliver tomorrow.

Biff: So what do I do tomorrow?

Happy: You leave the house tomorrow and come back at night and say Oliver is thinking it over. And he thinks it over for a couple of weeks, and gradually it fades away and nobody's the worse.

Biff: But it'll go on forever!

Happy: Dad is never so happy as when he's looking forward to something!

Willy enters.

Happy: Hello, scout!

Willy: Gee, I haven't been here in years!

Stanley has followed Willy in and sets a chair for him. Stanley starts off but Happy stops him.

Happy: Stanley!

Stanley stands by, waiting for an order.

Biff (going to Willy with guilt, as to an invalid): Sit down, Pop. You want a drink?

Willy: Sure, I don't mind.

Biff: Let's get a load on.

Willy: You look worried.

Biff: N-no. (*To Stanley.*) Scotch all around. Make it doubles.

Stanley: Doubles, right. (*He goes.*)

Willy: You had a couple already, didn't you?

Biff: Just a couple, yeah.

Willy: Well, what happened, boy? (*Nodding affirmatively, with a smile.*)
Everything go all right?

Biff (*takes a breath, then reaches out and grasps Willy's hand*): Pal . . . (*He is
smiling bravely, and Willy is smiling too.*) I had an experience today.

Happy: Terrific, Pop.

Willy: That so? What happened?

Biff (*high, slightly alcoholic, above the earth*): I'm going to tell you everything from first to last. It's been a strange day. (*Silence. He looks
around, composes himself as best he can, but his breath keeps breaking the
rhythm of his voice.*) I had to wait quite a while for him, and—

Willy: Oliver?

Biff: Yeah, Oliver. All day, as a matter of cold fact. And a lot of—instances—facts, Pop, facts about my life came back to me. Who was
it, Pop? Who ever said I was a salesman with Oliver?

Willy: Well, you were.

Biff: No, Dad, I was a shipping clerk.

Willy: But you were practically—

Biff (*with determination*): Dad, I don't know who said it first, but I was
never a salesman for Bill Oliver.

Willy: What're you talking about?

Biff: Let's hold on to the facts tonight, Pop. We're not going to get anywhere bullin' around. I was a shipping clerk.

Willy (*angrily*): All right, now listen to me—

Biff: Why don't you let me finish?

Willy: I'm not interested in stories about the past or any crap of that
kind because the woods are burning, boys, you understand? There's a
big blaze going on all around. I was fired today.

Biff (*shocked*): How could you be?

Willy: I was fired, and I'm looking for a little good news to tell your
mother, because the woman has waited and the woman has suffered.
The gist of it is that I haven't got a story left in my head, Biff. So don't
give me a lecture about facts and aspects. I am not interested. Now
what've you got to say to me?

Stanley enters with three drinks. They wait until he leaves.

Willy: Did you see Oliver?

Biff: Jesus, Dad!

Willy: You mean you didn't go up there?

Happy: Sure he went up there.

Biff: I did. I—saw him. How could they fire you?

Willy (on the edge of his chair): What kind of a welcome did he give you?

Biff: He won't even let you work on commission?

Willy: I'm out! (*Driving.*) So tell me, he gave you a warm welcome?

Happy: Sure, Pop, sure!

Biff (driven): Well, it was kind of—

Willy: I was wondering if he'd remember you. (*To Happy.*) Imagine, man doesn't see him for ten, twelve years and gives him that kind of welcome!

Happy: Damn right!

Biff (trying to return to the offensive): Pop, look—

Willy: You know why he remembered you, don't you? Because you impressed him in those days.

Biff: Let's talk quietly and get this down to the facts, huh?

Willy (as though Biff had been interrupting): Well, what happened? It's great news, Biff. Did he take you into his office or'd you talk in the waiting-room?

Biff: Well, he came in, see, and—

Willy (with a big smile): What'd he say? Betcha he threw his arm around you.

Biff: Well, he kinda—

Willy: He's a fine man. (*To Happy.*) Very hard man to see, y'know.

Happy (agreeing): Oh, I know.

Willy (to Biff): Is that where you had the drinks?

Biff: Yeah, he gave me a couple of—no, no!

Happy (cutting in): He told him my Florida idea.

Willy: Don't interrupt. (*To Biff.*) How'd he react to the Florida idea?

Biff: Dad, will you give me a minute to explain?

Willy: I've been waiting for you to explain since I sat down here! What happened? He took you into his office and what?

Biff: Well—I talked. And—and he listened, see.

Willy: Famous for the way he listens, y'know. What was his answer?

Biff: His answer was—(*He breaks off, suddenly angry.*) Dad, you're not letting me tell you what I want to tell you!

Willy (accusing, angered): You didn't see him, did you?

Biff: I did see him!

Willy: What'd you insult him or something? You insulted him, didn't you?

Biff: Listen, will you let me out of it, will you just let me out of it!

Happy: What the hell!

Willy: Tell me what happened!
Biff (to Happy): I can't talk to him!

> *A single trumpet note jars the ear. The light of green leaves stains the house, which holds the air of night and a dream. Young Bernard enters and knocks on the door of the house.*

Young Bernard (frantically): Mrs. Loman, Mrs. Loman!
Happy: Tell him what happened!
Biff (to Happy): Shut up and leave me alone!
Willy: No, no! You had to go and flunk math!
Biff: What math? What're you talking about?
Young Bernard: Mrs. Loman, Mrs. Loman!

> *Linda appears in the house, as of old.*

Willy (wildly): Math, math, math!
Biff: Take it easy, Pop.
Young Bernard: Mrs. Loman!
Willy (furiously): If you hadn't flunked you'd've been set by now!
Biff: Now, look, I'm gonna tell you what happened, and you're going to
     listen to me.
Young Bernard: Mrs. Loman!
Biff: I waited six hours—
Happy: What the hell are you saying?
Biff: I kept sending in my name but he wouldn't see me. So finally he . . .
     (*He continues unheard as light fades low on the restaurant.*)
Young Bernard: Biff flunked math!
Linda: No!
Young Bernard: Birnbaum flunked him! They won't graduate him!
Linda: But they have to. He's gotta go to the university. Where is he?
     Biff! Biff!
Young Bernard: No, he left. He went to Grand Central.
Linda: Grand—You mean he went to Boston?
Young Bernard: Is Uncle Willy in Boston?
Linda: Oh, maybe Willy can talk to the teacher. Oh, the poor, poor boy!

> *Light on house area snaps out.*

Biff (at the table, now audible, holding up a gold fountain pen): . . . so I'm
     washed up with Oliver, you understand? Are you listening to me?
Willy (at a loss): Yeah, sure. If you hadn't flunked—
Biff: Flunked what? What're you talking about?
Willy: Don't blame everything on me! I didn't flunk math—you did!
     What pen?

Happy: That was awful dumb, Biff, a pen like that is worth—
Willy (*seeing the pen for the first time*): You took Oliver's pen?
Biff (*weakening*): Dad, I just explained it to you.
Willy: You stole Bill Oliver's fountain pen!
Biff: I didn't exactly steal it! That's just what I've been explaining to you!
Happy: He had it in his hand and just then Oliver walked in, so he got nervous and stuck it in his pocket!
Willy: My God, Biff!
Biff: I never intended to do it, Dad!
Operator's voice: Standish Arms, good evening!
Willy (*shouting*): I'm not in my room!
Biff (*frightened*): Dad, what's the matter? (*He and Happy stand up.*)
Operator: Ringing Mr. Loman for you!
Willy: I'm not there, stop it!
Biff (*horrified, gets down on one knee before Willy*): Dad, I'll make good, I'll make good. (*Willy tries to get to his feet. Biff holds him down.*) Sit down now.
Willy: No, you're no good, you're no good for anything.
Biff: I am, Dad, I'll find something else, you understand? Now don't worry about anything. (*He holds up Willy's face.*) Talk to me, Dad.
Operator: Mr. Loman does not answer. Shall I page him?
Willy (*attempting to stand, as though to rush and silence the Operator*): No, no, no!
Happy: He'll strike something, Pop.
Willy: No, no . . .
Biff (*desperately, standing over Willy*): Pop, listen! Listen to me! I'm telling you something good. Oliver talked to his partner about the Florida idea. You listening? He—he talked to his partner, and he came to me . . . I'm to be all right, you hear? Dad, listen to me, he said it was just a question of the amount!
Willy: Then you . . . got it?
Happy: He's gonna be terrific, Pop!
Willy (*trying to stand*): Then you got it, haven't you? You got it! You got it!
Biff (*agonized, holds Willy down*): No, no. Look, Pop. I'm supposed to have lunch with them tomorrow. I'm just telling you this so you'll know that I can still make an impression, Pop. And I'll make good somewhere, but I can't go tomorrow, see?
Willy: Why not? You simply—
Biff: But the pen, Pop!
Willy: You give it to him and tell him it was an oversight!
Happy: Sure, have lunch tomorrow!
Biff: I can't say that—

Willy: You were doing a crossword puzzle and accidentally used his pen!

Biff: Listen, kid, I took those balls years ago, now I walk in with his fountain pen? That clinches it, don't you see? I can't face him like that! I'll try elsewhere.

Page's voice: Paging Mr. Loman!

Willy: Don't you want to be anything?

Biff: Pop, how can I go back?

Willy: You don't want to be anything, is that what's behind it?

Biff (now angry at Willy for not crediting his sympathy): Don't take it that way! You think it was easy walking into that office after what I'd done to him? A team of horses couldn't have dragged me back to Bill Oliver!

Willy: Then why'd you go?

Biff: Why did I go? Why did I go? Look at you! Look at what's become of you!

Off left, The Woman laughs.

Willy: Biff, you're going to go to that lunch tomorrow, or—

Biff: I can't go. I've got no appointment!

Happy: Biff, for . . . !

Willy: Are you spiting me?

Biff: Don't take it that way! Goddammit!

Willy (strikes Biff and falters away from the table): You rotten little louse! Are you spiting me?

The Woman: Someone's at the door, Willy!

Biff: I'm no good, can't you see what I am?

Happy (separating them): Hey, you're in a restaurant! Now cut it out, both of you! (*The Girls enter.*) Hello, girls, sit down.

The Woman laughs, off left.

Miss Forsythe: I guess we might as well. This is Letta.

The Woman: Willy, are you going to wake up?

Biff (ignoring Willy): How're ya, miss, sit down. What do you drink?

Miss Forsythe: Letta might not be able to stay long.

Letta: I gotta get up very early tomorrow. I got jury duty. I'm so excited! Were you fellows ever on a jury?

Biff: No, but I been in front of them! (*The Girls laugh.*) This is my father.

Letta: Isn't he cute? Sit down with us, Pop.

Happy: Sit him down, Biff!

Biff (going to him): Come on, slugger, drink us under the table. To hell with it! Come on, sit down, pal.

On Biff's last insistence, Willy is about to sit.

The Woman (now urgently): Willy, are you going to answer the door!

> *The Woman's call pulls Willy back. He starts right, befuddled.*

Biff: Hey, where are you going?
Willy: Open the door.
Biff: The door?
Willy: The washroom . . . the door . . . where's the door?
Biff (leading Willy to the left): Just go straight down.

> *Willy moves left.*

The Woman: Willy, Willy, are you going to get up, get up, get up, get up?

> *Willy exits left.*

Letta: I think it's sweet you bring your daddy along.
Miss Forsythe: Oh, he isn't really your father!
Biff (at left, turning to her resentfully): Miss Forsythe, you've just seen a prince walk by. A fine, troubled prince. A hard-working, unappreciated prince. A pal, you understand? A good companion. Always for his boys.
Letta: That's so sweet.
Happy: Well, girls, what's the program? We're wasting time. Come on, Biff. Gather round. Where would you like to go?
Biff: Why don't you do something for him?
Happy: Me!
Biff: Don't you give a damn for him, Hap?
Happy: What're you talking about? I'm the one who—
Biff: I sense it, you don't give a good goddam about him. (*He takes the rolled-up hose from his pocket and puts it on the table in front of Happy.*) Look what I found in the cellar, for Christ's sake. How can you bear to let it go on?
Happy: Me? Who goes away? Who runs off and—
Biff: Yeah, but he doesn't mean anything to you. You could help him—I can't! Don't you understand what I'm talking about? He's going to kill himself, don't you know that?
Happy: Don't I know it! Me!
Biff: Hap, help him! Jesus . . . Help him . . . Help me, help me, I can't bear to look at his face! (*Ready to weep, he hurries out, up right.*)
Happy (starting after him): Where are you going?
Miss Forsythe: What's he so mad about?
Happy: Come on, girls, we'll catch up with him.
Miss Forsythe (as Happy pushes her out): Say, I don't like that temper of his!

Happy: He's just a little overstrung, he'll be all right!

Willy (*off left, as The Woman laughs*): Don't answer! Don't answer!

Letta: Don't you want to tell your father—

Happy: No, that's not my father. He's just a guy. Come on, we'll catch Biff, and, honey, we're going to paint this town! Stanley, where's the check? Hey, Stanley!

They exit. Stanley looks toward left.

Stanley (*calling to Happy indignantly*): Mr. Loman! Mr. Loman!

Stanley picks up a chair and follows them off. Knocking is heard off left. The Woman enters, laughing. Willy follows her. She is in a black slip; he is buttoning his shirt. Raw, sensuous music accompanies their speech.

Willy: Will you stop laughing? Will you stop?

The Woman: Aren't you going to answer the door? He'll wake the whole hotel.

Willy: I'm not expecting anybody.

The Woman: Whyn't you have another drink, honey, and stop being so damn self-centered?

Willy: I'm so lonely.

The Woman: You know you ruined me, Willy? From now on, whenever you come to the office, I'll see that you go right through to the buyers. No waiting at my desk any more, Willy. You ruined me.

Willy: That's nice of you to say that.

The Woman: Gee, you are self-centered! Why so sad? You are the saddest self-centeredest soul I ever did see-saw. (*She laughs. He kisses her.*) Come on inside, drummer boy. It's silly to be dressing in the middle of the night. (*As knocking is heard.*) Aren't you going to answer the door?

Willy: They're knocking on the wrong door.

The Woman: But I felt the knocking. And he heard us talking in here. Maybe the hotel's on fire!

Willy (*his terror rising*): It's a mistake.

The Woman: Then tell him to go away!

Willy: There's nobody there.

The Woman: It's getting on my nerves, Willy. There's somebody standing out there and it's getting on my nerves!

Willy (*pushing her away from him*): All right, stay in the bathroom here, and don't come out. I think there's a law in Massachusetts about it, so don't come out. It may be that new room clerk. He looked very mean. So don't come out. It's a mistake, there's no fire.

The knocking is heard again. He takes a few steps away from her, and she vanishes into the wing. The light follows him, and now he is facing Young Biff, who carries a suitcase. Biff steps toward him. The music is gone.

Biff: Why didn't you answer?

Willy: Biff! What are you doing in Boston?

Biff: Why didn't you answer? I've been knocking for five minutes, I called you on the phone—

Willy: I just heard you. I was in the bathroom and had the door shut. Did anything happen at home?

Biff: Dad—I let you down.

Willy: What do you mean?

Biff: Dad . . .

Willy: Biffo, what's this about? (*Putting his arm around Biff.*) Come on, let's go downstairs and get you a malted.

Biff: Dad, I flunked math.

Willy: Not for the term?

Biff: The term. I haven't got enough credits to graduate.

Willy: You mean to say Bernard wouldn't give you the answers?

Biff: He did, he tried, but I only got a sixty-one.

Willy: And they wouldn't give you four points?

Biff: Birnbaum refused absolutely. I begged him, Pop, but he won't give me those points. You gotta talk to him before they close the school. Because if he saw the kind of man you are, and you just talked to him in your way, I'm sure he'd come through for me. The class came right before practice, see, and I didn't go enough. Would you talk to him? He'd like you, Pop. You know the way you could talk.

Willy: You're on. We'll drive right back.

Biff: Oh, Dad, good work! I'm sure he'll change it for you!

Willy: Go downstairs and tell the clerk I'm checkin' out. Go right down.

Biff: Yes, Sir! See, the reason he hates me, Pop—one day he was late for class so I got up at the blackboard and imitated him. I crossed my eyes and talked with a lithp.

Willy (laughing): You did? The kids like it?

Biff: They nearly died laughing!

Willy: Yeah? What'd you do?

Biff: The thquare root of thixthy twee is . . . (*Willy bursts out laughing; Biff joins him.*) And in the middle of it he walked in!

Willy laughs and The Woman joins in offstage.

Willy (without hesitating): Hurry downstairs and—

Biff: Somebody in there?

Willy: No, that was next door.

> *The Woman laughs offstage.*

Biff: Somebody got in your bathroom!

Willy: No, it's the next room, there's a party—

The Woman (enters, laughing. She lisps this): Can I come in? There's something in the bathtub, Willy, and it's moving!

> *Willy looks at Biff, who is staring open-mouthed and horrified at The Woman.*

Willy: Ah—you better go back to your room. They must be finished painting by now. They're painting her room so I let her take a shower here. Go back, go back . . . (*He pushes her.*)

The Woman (resisting): But I've got to get dressed, Willy, I can't—

Willy: Get out of here! Go back, go back . . . (*Suddenly striving for the ordinary.*) This is Miss Francis, Biff, she's a buyer. They're painting her room. Go back, Miss Francis, go back . . .

The Woman: But my clothes, I can't go out naked in the hall!

Willy (pushing her offstage): Get outa here! Go back, go back!

> *Biff slowly sits down on his suitcase as the argument continues offstage.*

The Woman: Where's my stockings? You promised me stockings, Willy!

Willy: I have no stockings here!

The Woman: You had two boxes of size nine sheers for me, and I want them!

Willy: Here, for God's sake, will you get outa here!

The Woman (enters holding a box of stockings): I just hope there's nobody in the hall. That's all I hope. (*To Biff.*) Are you football or baseball?

Biff: Football.

The Woman (angry, humiliated): That's me too. G'night. (*She snatches her clothes from Willy, and walks out.*)

Willy (after a pause): Well, better get going. I want to get to the school first thing in the morning. Get my suits out of the closet. I'll get my valise. (*Biff doesn't move.*) What's the matter? (*Biff remains motionless, tears falling.*) She's a buyer. Buys for J. H. Simmons. She lives down the hall—they're painting. You don't imagine—(*He breaks off. After a pause.*) Now listen, pal, she's just a buyer. She sees merchandise in her room and they have to keep it looking just so . . . (*Pause. Assuming command.*) All right, get my suits. (*Biff doesn't move.*) Now stop crying and do as I say. I gave you an order. Biff, I gave you an order! Is that what you do when I give you an order? How dare you cry! (*Putting his arm around Biff.*) Now look, Biff,

when you grow up you'll understand about these things. You mustn't—
you mustn't overemphasize a thing like this. I'll see Birnbaum first
thing in the morning.

Biff: Never mind.

Willy (getting down beside Biff): Never mind! He's going to give you those
points. I'll see to it.

Biff: He wouldn't listen to you.

Willy: He certainly will listen to me. You need those points for the U. of
Virginia.

Biff: I'm not going there.

Willy: Heh? If I can't get him to change that mark you'll make it up in
summer school. You've got all summer to—

Biff (his weeping breaking from him): Dad . . .

Willy (infected by it): Oh, my boy . . .

Biff: Dad . . .

Willy: She's nothing to me, Biff. I was lonely, I was terribly lonely.

Biff: You—you gave her Mama's stockings! (*His tears break through and
he rises to go.*)

Willy (grabbing for Biff): I gave you an order!

Biff: Don't touch me, you—liar!

Willy: Apologize for that!

Biff: You fake! You phony little fake! (*Overcome, he turns quickly and
weeping fully goes out with his suitcase. Willy is left on the floor on his
knees.*)

Willy: I gave you an order! Biff, come back here or I'll beat you! Come
back here! I'll whip you!

Stanley comes quickly in from the right and stands in front of Willy.

Willy (shouts at Stanley): I gave you an order . . .

Stanley: Hey, let's pick it up, pick it up, Mr. Loman. (*He helps Willy to his
feet.*) Your boys left with the chippies. They said they'll see you at
home.

A second waiter watches some distance away.

Willy: But we were supposed to have dinner together.

Music is heard, Willy's theme.

Stanley: Can you make it?

Willy: I'll—sure, I can make it. (*Suddenly concerned about his clothes.*) Do
I—I look all right?

Stanley: Sure, you look all right. (*He flicks a speck off Willy's lapel.*)

Willy: Here—here's a dollar.

Stanley: Oh, your son paid me. It's all right.

Willy (putting it in Stanley's hand): No, take it. You're a good boy.

Stanley: Oh, no, you don't have to . . .

Willy: Here—here's some more, I don't need it any more. (*After a slight pause.*) Tell me—is there a seed store in the neighborhood?

Stanley: Seeds? You mean like to plant?

As Willy turns, Stanley slips the money back into his jacket pocket.

Willy: Yes. Carrots, peas . . .

Stanley: Well, there's hardware stores on Sixth Avenue, but it may be too late now.

Willy (anxiously): Oh, I'd better hurry. I've got to get some seeds. (*He starts off to the right.*) I've got to get some seeds, right away. Nothing's planted. I don't have a thing in the ground.

Willy hurries out as the light goes down. Stanley moves over to the right after him, watches him off. The other waiter has been staring at Willy.

Stanley (to the waiter): Well, whatta you looking at?

The waiter picks up the chairs and moves off right. Stanley takes the table and follows him. The light fades on this area. There is a long pause, the sound of the flute coming over. The light gradually rises on the kitchen, which is empty. Happy appears at the door of the house, followed by Biff. Happy is carrying a large bunch of long-stemmed roses. He enters the kitchen, looks around for Linda. Not seeing her, he turns to Biff, who is just outside the house door, and makes a gesture with his hands, indicating "Not here, I guess." He looks into the living room and freezes. Inside, Linda, unseen, is seated, Willy's coat on her lap. She rises ominously and quietly and moves toward Happy, who backs up into the kitchen, afraid.

Happy: Hey, what're you doing up? (*Linda says nothing but moves toward him implacably.*) Where's Pop? (*He keeps backing to the right, and now Linda is in full view in the doorway to the living room.*) Is he sleeping?

Linda: Where were you?

Happy (trying to laugh it off): We met two girls, Mom, very fine types. Here, we brought you some flowers. (*Offering them to her.*) Put them in your room, Ma.

She knocks them to the floor at Biff's feet. He has now come inside and closed the door behind him. She stares at Biff, silent.

Happy: Now what'd you do that for? Mom, I want you to have some flowers—

Linda (cutting Happy off, violently to Biff): Don't you care whether he lives or dies?

Happy (going to the stairs): Come upstairs, Biff.

Biff (with a flare of disgust, to Happy): Go away from me! (*To Linda.*) What do you mean, lives or dies? Nobody's dying around here, pal.

Linda: Get out of my sight! Get out of here!

Biff: I wanna see the boss.

Linda: You're not going near him!

Biff: Where is he? (*He moves into the living room and Linda follows.*)

Linda (shouting after Biff): You invite him for dinner. He looks forward to it all day—(*Biff appears in his parents' bedroom, looks around, and exits*)—and then you desert him there. There's no stranger you'd do that to!

Happy: Why? He had a swell time with us. Listen, when I—(*Linda comes back into the kitchen*)—desert him I hope I don't outlive the day!

Linda: Get out of here!

Happy: Now look, Mom . . .

Linda: Did you have to go to women tonight? You and your lousy rotten whores!

Biff re-enters the kitchen.

Happy: Mom, all we did was follow Biff around trying to cheer him up! (*To Biff.*) Boy, what a night you gave me!

Linda: Get out of here, both of you, and don't come back! I don't want you tormenting him anymore. Go on now, get your things together! (*To Biff.*) You can sleep in his apartment. (*She starts to pick up the flowers and stops herself.*) Pick up this stuff, I'm not your maid any more. Pick it up, you bum, you!

Happy turns his back to her in refusal. Biff slowly moves over and gets down on his knees, picking up the flowers.

Linda: You're a pair of animals! Not one, not another living soul would have had the cruelty to walk out on that man in a restaurant!

Biff (not looking at her): Is that what he said?

Linda: He didn't have to say anything. He was so humiliated he nearly limped when he came in.

Happy: But, Mom he had a great time with us—

Biff (cutting him off violently): Shut up!

Without another word, Happy goes upstairs.

Linda: You! You didn't even go in to see if he was all right!

Biff (*still on the floor in front of Linda, the flowers in his hand; with self-loathing*): No. Didn't. Didn't do a damned thing. How do you like that, heh? Left him babbling in a toilet.

Linda: You louse. You . . .

Biff: Now you hit it on the nose! (*He gets up, throws the flowers in the wastebasket.*) The scum of the earth, and you're looking at him!

Linda: Get out of here!

Biff: I gotta talk to the boss, Mom. Where is he?

Linda: You're not going near him. Get out of this house!

Biff (*with absolute assurance, determination*): No. We're gonna have an abrupt conversation, him and me.

Linda: You're not talking to him!

Hammering is heard from outside the house, off right. Biff turns toward the noise.

Linda (*suddenly pleading*): Will you please leave him alone?

Biff: What's he doing out there?

Linda: He's planting the garden!

Biff (*quietly*): Now? Oh, my God!

Biff moves outside, Linda following. The light dies down on them and comes up on the center of the apron as Willy walks into it. He is carrying a flashlight, a hoe and a handful of seed packets. He raps the top of the hoe sharply to fix it firmly, and then moves to the left, measuring off the distance with his foot. He holds the flashlight to look at the seed packets, reading off the instructions. He is in the blue of night.

Willy: Carrots . . . quarter-inch apart. Rows . . . one-foot rows. (*He measures it off.*) One foot. (*He puts down a package and measures off.*) Beets. (*He puts down another package and measures again.*) Lettuce. (*He reads the package, puts it down.*) One foot—(*He breaks off as Ben appears at the right and moves slowly down to him.*) What a proposition, ts, ts. Terrific, terrific. 'Cause she's suffered, Ben, the woman has suffered. You understand me? A man can't go out the way he came in, Ben, a man has got to add up to something. You can't, you can't—(*Ben moves toward him as though to interrupt.*) You gotta consider, now. Don't answer so quick. Remember, it's a guaranteed twenty-thousand-dollar proposition. Now look, Ben, I want you to go through the ins and outs of this thing with me. I've got nobody to talk to, Ben, and the woman has suffered, you hear me?

Ben (*standing still, considering*): What's the proposition?

Willy: It's twenty thousand dollars on the barrelhead. Guaranteed, gilt-edged, you understand?

Ben: You don't want to make a fool of yourself. They might not honor the policy.

Willy: How can they dare refuse? Didn't I work like a coolie to meet every premium on the nose? And now they don't pay off? Impossible!

Ben: It's called a cowardly thing, William.

Willy: Why? Does it take more guts to stand here the rest of my life ringing up a zero?

Ben (yielding): That's a point, William. (*He moves, thinking, turns.*) And twenty thousand—that is something one can feel with the hand, it is there.

Willy (now assured, with rising power): Oh, Ben, that's the whole beauty of it! I see it like a diamond, shining in the dark, hard and rough, that I can pick up and touch in my hand. Not like—like an appointment! This would not be another damned-fool appointment, Ben, and it changes all the aspects. Because he thinks I'm nothing, see, and so he spites me. But the funeral—(*Straightening up.*) Ben, that funeral will be massive! They'll come from Maine, Massachusetts, Vermont, New Hampshire! All the old-timers with the strange license plates—that boy will be thunder-struck, Ben, because he never realized—I am known! Rhode Island, New York, New Jersey—I am known, Ben, and he'll see it with his eyes once and for all. He'll see what I am, Ben! He's in for a shock, that boy!

Ben (coming down to the edge of the garden): He'll call you a coward.

Willy (suddenly fearful): No, that would be terrible.

Ben: Yes. And a damned fool.

Willy: No, no, he mustn't, I won't have that! (*He is broken and desperate.*)

Ben: He'll hate you, William.

The gay music of the boys is heard.

Willy: Oh, Ben, how do we get back to all the great times? Used to be so full of light, and comradeship, the sleigh-riding in winter, and the ruddiness on his cheeks. And always some kind of good news coming up, always something nice coming up ahead. And never even let me carry the valises in the house, and simonizing, simonizing that little red car! Why, why can't I give him something and not have him hate me?

Ben: Let me think about it. (*He glances at his watch.*) I still have a little time. Remarkable proposition, but you've got to be sure you're not making a fool of yourself.

Ben drifts off upstage and goes out of sight. Biff comes down from the left.

Willy (*suddenly conscious of Biff, turns and looks up at him, then begins picking up the packages of seeds in confusion*): Where the hell is that seed? (*Indignantly.*) You can't see nothing out here! They boxed in the whole goddam neighborhood!

Biff: There are people all around here. Don't you realize that?

Willy: I'm busy. Don't bother me.

Biff (*taking the hoe from Willy*): I'm saying good-by to you, Pop. (*Willy looks at him, silent, unable to move.*) I'm not coming back any more.

Willy: You're not going to see Oliver tomorrow?

Biff: I've got no appointment, Dad.

Willy: He put his arm around you, and you've got no appointment?

Biff: Pop, get this now, will you? Everytime I've left it's been a fight that sent me out of here. Today I realized something about myself and I tried to explain it to you and I—I think I'm just not smart enough to make any sense out of it for you. To hell with whose fault it is or anything like that. (*He takes Willy's arm.*) Let's just wrap it up, heh? Come on in, we'll tell Mom. (*He gently tries to pull Willy to the left.*)

Willy (*frozen, immobile, with guilt in his voice*): No, I don't want to see her.

Biff: Come on! (*He pulls again, and Willy tries to pull away.*)

Willy (*highly nervous*): No, no, I don't want to see her.

Biff (*tries to look into Willy's face, as if to find the answer there*): Why don't you want to see her?

Willy (*more harshly now*): Don't bother me, will you?

Biff: What do you mean, you don't want to see her? You don't want them calling you yellow, do you? This isn't your fault; it's me, I'm a bum. Now come inside! (*Willy strains to get away.*) Did you hear what I said to you?

Willy pulls away and quickly goes by himself into the house. Biff follows.

Linda (*to Willy*): Did you plant, dear?

Biff (*at the door, to Linda*): All right, we had it out. I'm going and I'm not writing any more.

Linda (*going to Willy in the kitchen*): I think that's the best way, dear. 'Cause there's no use drawing it out, you'll just never get along.

Willy doesn't respond.

Biff: People ask where I am and what I'm doing, you don't know, and you don't care. That way it'll be off your mind and you can start brightening up again. All right? That clears it, doesn't it? (*Willy is silent, and Biff goes to him.*) You gonna wish me luck, scout? (*He extends his hand.*) What do you say?

Linda: Shake his hand, Willy.

Willy (*turning to her, seething with hurt*): There's no necessity to mention the pen at all, y'know.

Biff (*gently*): I've got no appointment, Dad.

Willy (*erupting fiercely*): He put his arm around . . . ?

Biff: Dad, you're never going to see what I am, so what's the use of arguing? If I strike oil I'll send you a check. Meantime forget I'm alive.

Willy (*to Linda*): Spite, see?

Biff: Shake hands, Dad.

Willy: Not my hand.

Biff: I was hoping not to go this way.

Willy: Well, this is the way you're going. Good-by.

> *Biff looks at him a moment, then turns sharply and goes to the stairs.*

Willy (*stops him with*): May you rot in hell if you leave this house!

Biff (*turning*): Exactly what is it that you want from me?

Willy: I want you to know, on the train, in the mountains, in the valleys, wherever you go, that you cut down your life for spite!

Biff: No, no.

Willy: Spite, spite, is the word of your undoing! And when you're down and out, remember what did it. When you're rotting somewhere beside the railroad tracks, remember, and don't you dare blame it on me!

Biff: I'm not blaming it on you!

Willy: I won't take the rap for this, you hear?

> *Happy comes down the stairs and stands on the bottom step, watching.*

Biff: That's just what I'm telling you!

Willy (*sinking into a chair at the table, with full accusation*): You're trying to put a knife in me—don't think I don't know what you're doing!

Biff: All right, phony! Then let's lay it on the line. (*He whips the rubber tube out of his pocket and puts it on the table.*)

Happy: You crazy—

Linda: Biff! (*She moves to grab the hose, but Biff holds it down with his hand.*)

Biff: Leave it there! Don't move it!

Willy (*not looking at it*): What is that?

Biff: You know goddam well what that is.

Willy (*caged, wanting to escape*): I never saw that.

Biff: You saw it. The mice didn't bring it into the cellar! What is this supposed to do, make a hero out of you? This supposed to make me sorry for you?

Willy: Never heard of it.

Biff: There'll be no pity for you, you hear? No pity!

Willy (to Linda): You hear the spite!

Biff: No, you're going to hear the truth—what you are and what I am!

Linda: Stop it!

Willy: Spite!

Happy (coming down toward Biff): You cut it now!

Biff (to Happy): The man don't know who we are! The man is gonna
   know! (*To Willy.*) We never told the truth for ten minutes in this
   house!

Happy: We always told the truth!

Biff (turning on him): You big blow, are you the assistant buyer? You're
   one of the two assistants to the assistant, aren't you?

Happy: Well, I'm practically—

Biff: You're practically full of it! We all are! And I'm through with it.
   (*To Willy.*) Now hear this, Willy, this is me.

Willy: I know you!

Biff: You know why I had no address for three months? I stole a suit in
   Kansas City and I was in jail. (*To Linda, who is sobbing.*) Stop crying.
   I'm through with it.

Linda turns away from them, her hands covering her face.

Willy: I suppose that's my fault!

Biff: I stole myself out of every good job since high school!

Willy: And whose fault is that?

Biff: And I never got anywhere because you blew me so full of hot air
   I could never stand taking orders from anybody! That's whose
   fault it is!

Willy: I hear that!

Linda: Don't, Biff!

Biff: It's goddam time you heard that! I had to be boss big shot in two
   weeks, and I'm through with it!

Willy: Then hang yourself! For spite, hang yourself!

Biff: No! Nobody's hanging himself, Willy! I ran down eleven flights
   with a pen in my hand today. And suddenly I stopped, you hear
   me? And in the middle of that office building, do you hear this? I
   stopped in the middle of that building and I saw—the sky. I saw
   the things that I love in this world. The work and the food and
   time to sit and smoke. And I looked at the pen and said to myself,
   what the hell am I grabbing this for? Why am I trying to become
   what I don't want to be? What am I doing in an office, making a

contemptuous, begging fool of myself, when all I want is out there, waiting for me the minute I say I know who I am! Why can't I say that, Willy? (*He tries to make Willy face him, but Willy pulls away and moves to the left.*)

Willy (*with hatred, threateningly*): The door of your life is wide open!

Biff: Pop! I'm a dime a dozen, and so are you!

Willy (*turning on him now in an uncontrolled outburst*): I am not a dime a dozen! I am Willy Loman, and you are Biff Loman!

Biff starts for Willy, but is blocked by Happy. In his fury, Biff seems on the verge of attacking his father.

Biff: I am not a leader of men, Willy, and neither are you. You were never anything but a hard-working drummer who landed in the ash can like all the rest of them! I'm one dollar an hour, Willy! I tried seven states and couldn't raise it. A buck an hour! Do you gather my meaning? I'm not bringing home any prizes any more, and you're going to stop waiting for me to bring them home!

Willy (*directly to Biff*): You vengeful, spiteful mutt!

Biff breaks from Happy. Willy, in fright, starts up the stairs. Biff grabs him.

Biff (*at the peak of his fury*): Pop, I'm nothing! I'm nothing, Pop. Can't you understand that? There's no spite in it any more. I'm just what I am, that's all.

Biff's fury has spent itself, and he breaks down, sobbing, holding on to Willy, who dumbly fumbles for Biff's face.

Willy (*astonished*): What're you doing? What're you doing? (*To Linda.*) Why is he crying?

Biff (*crying, broken*): Will you let me go, for Christ sake? Will you take that phony dream and burn it before something happens? (*Struggling to contain himself, he pulls away and moves to the stairs.*) I'll go in the morning. Put him—put him to bed. (*Exhausted, Biff moves up the stairs to his room.*)

Willy (*after a long pause, astonished, elevated*): Isn't that remarkable? Biff—he likes me!

Linda: He loves you, Willy!

Happy (*deeply moved*): Always did, Pop.

Willy: Oh, Biff! (*Staring wildly.*) He cried! Cried to me. (*He is choking with his love, and now cries out his promise.*) That boy—that boy is going to be magnificent!

Ben appears in the light just outside the kitchen.

Ben: Yes, outstanding, with twenty thousand behind him.

Linda (sensing the racing of his mind, fearfully, carefully): Now come to bed, Willy. It's all settled now.

Willy (finding it difficult not to rush out of the house): Yes, we'll sleep. Come on. Go to sleep, Hap.

Ben: And it does take a great kind of man to crack the jungle.

In accents of dread, Ben's idyllic music starts up.

Happy (his arm around Linda): I'm getting married, Pop, don't forget it. I'm changing everything. I'm gonna run that department before the year is up. You'll see, Mom. (*He kisses her.*)

Ben: The jungle is dark but full of diamonds, Willy.

Willy turns, moves, listening to Ben.

Linda: Be good. You're both good boys, just act that way, that's all.

Happy: 'Night, Pop. (*He goes upstairs.*)

Linda (to Willy): Come, dear.

Ben (with greater force): One must go in to fetch a diamond out.

Willy (to Linda, as he moves slowly along the edge of the kitchen, toward the door): I just want to get settled down, Linda. Let me sit alone for a little.

Linda (almost uttering her fear): I want you upstairs.

Willy (taking her in his arms): In a few minutes, Linda. I couldn't sleep right now. Go on, you look awful tired. (*He kisses her.*)

Ben: Not like an appointment at all. A diamond is rough and hard to the touch.

Willy: Go on now, I'll be right up.

Linda: I think this is the only way, Willy.

Willy: Sure, it's the best thing.

Ben: Best thing!

Willy: The only way. Everything is gonna be—go on, kid, get to bed. You look so tired.

Linda: Come right up.

Willy: Two minutes.

Linda goes into the living room, then reappears in her bedroom. Willy moves just outside the kitchen door.

Willy: Loves me. (*Wonderingly.*) Always loved me. Isn't that a remarkable thing? Ben, he'll worship me for it!

Ben (with promise): It's dark there, but full of diamonds.

Willy: Can you imagine that magnificence with twenty thousand dollars in his pocket?

Linda (*calling from her room*): Willy! Come up!

Willy (*calling from the kitchen*): Yes! Yes! Coming! It's very smart, you realize that, don't you, sweetheart? Even Ben sees it. I gotta go, baby. 'By! 'By! (*Going over to Ben, almost dancing.*) Imagine? When the mail comes he'll be ahead of Bernard again!

Ben: A perfect proposition all around.

Willy: Did you see how he cried to me? Oh, if I could kiss him, Ben!

Ben: Time, William, time!

Willy: Oh, Ben, I always knew one way or another we were gonna make it, Biff and I!

Ben (*looking at his watch*): The boat. We'll be late. (*He moves slowly off into the darkness.*)

Willy (*elegiacally, turning to the house*): Now when you kick off, boy, I want a seventy-yard boot, and get right down the field under the ball, and when you hit, hit low and hit hard, because it's important, boy. (*He swings around and faces the audience.*) There's all kinds of important people in the stands, and the first thing you know . . . (*Suddenly realizing he is alone.*) Ben! Ben, where do I . . . ? (*He makes a sudden movement of search.*) Ben, how do I . . . ?

Linda (*calling*): Willy, you coming up?

Willy (*uttering a gasp of fear, whirling about as if to quiet her*): Sh! (*He turns around as if to find his way; sounds, faces, voices, seem to be swarming in upon him and he flicks at them, crying.*) Sh! Sh! (*Suddenly music, faint and high, stops him. It rises in intensity, almost to an unbearable scream. He goes up and down on his toes, and rushes off around the house.*) Shhh!

Linda: Willy?

There is no answer. Linda waits. Biff gets up off his bed. He is still in his clothes. Happy sits up. Biff stands listening.

Linda (*with real fear*): Willy, answer me! Willy!

There is the sound of a car starting and moving away at full speed.

Linda: No!

Biff (*rushing down the stairs*): Pop!

As the car speeds off, the music crashes down in a frenzy of sound, which becomes the soft pulsation of a single cello string. Biff slowly returns to his bedroom. He and Happy gravely don their jackets. Linda slowly walks out of her room. The music has developed into a dead march. The leaves of day are appearing over everything. Charley and Bernard, somberly dressed, appear and knock on the kitchen door. Biff and Happy slowly descend the stairs to the kitchen as Charley and Bernard enter. All stop a moment when Linda, in clothes of mourning, bearing a little bunch of roses, comes through the draped doorway into the kitchen. She goes to Charley and takes his arm. Now all move toward the audience, through the wall-line of the kitchen. At the limit of the apron, Linda lays down the flowers, kneels, and sits back on her heels. All stare down at the grave.

REQUIEM

Charley: It's getting dark, Linda.

Linda doesn't react. She stares at the grave.

Biff: How about it, Mom? Better get some rest, heh? They'll be closing the gate soon.

Linda makes no move. Pause.

Happy (deeply angered): He had no right to do that! There was no necessity for it. We would've helped him.

Charley (grunting): Hmmm.

Biff: Come along, Mom.

Linda: Why didn't anybody come?

Charley: It was a very nice funeral.

Linda: But where are all the people he knew? Maybe they blame him.

Charley: Naa. It's a rough world, Linda. They wouldn't blame him.

Linda: I can't understand it. At this time especially. First time in thirty-five years we were just about free and clear. He only needed a little salary. He was even finished with the dentist.

Charley: No man only needs a little salary.

Linda: I can't understand it.

Biff: There were a lot of nice days. When he'd come home from a trip; or on Sundays, making the stoop; finishing the cellar; putting on the new porch; when he built the extra bathroom; and put up the garage. You know something, Charley, there's more of him in that front stoop than in all the sales he ever made.

Charley: Yeah. He was a happy man with a batch of cement.

Linda: He was so wonderful with his hands.

Biff: He had the wrong dreams. All, all, wrong.

Happy (almost ready to fight Biff): Don't say that!

Biff: He never knew who he was.

Charley (stopping Happy's movement and reply. To Biff.): Nobody dast blame this man. You don't understand: Willy was a salesman. And for a salesman, there is no rock bottom to the life. He don't put a bolt to a nut, he don't tell you the law or give you medicine. He's a man out there in the blue, riding on a smile and a shoeshine. And when they start not smiling back—that's an earthquake. And then you get yourself a couple of spots on your hat, and you're finished. Nobody dast blame this man. A salesman is got to dream, boy. It comes with the territory.

Biff: Charley, the man didn't know who he was.

Happy (infuriated): Don't say that!

Biff: Why don't you come with me, Happy?

Happy: I'm not licked that easily. I'm staying right in this city, and I'm gonna beat this racket! (*He looks at Biff, his chin set.*) The Loman Brothers!

Biff: I know who I am, kid.

Happy: All right, boy. I'm gonna show you and everybody else that Willy Loman did not die in vain. He had a good dream. It's the only dream you can have—to come out number-one man. He fought it out here, and this is where I'm gonna win it for him.

Biff (with a hopeless glance at Happy, bends toward his mother): Let's go, Mom.

Linda: I'll be with you in a minute. Go on, Charley. (*He hesitates.*) I want to, just for a minute. I never had a chance to say good-by.

Charley moves away, followed by Happy. Biff remains a slight distance up and left of Linda. She sits there, summoning herself. The flute begins, not far away, playing behind her speech.

Linda: Forgive me, dear. I can't cry. I don't know what it is, but I can't cry. I don't understand it. Why did you ever do that? Help me, Willy, I can't cry. It seems to me that you're just on another trip. I keep expecting you. Willy, dear, I can't cry. Why did you do it? I search and search and search, and I can't understand it, Willy. I made the last payment on the house today. Today, dear. And there'll be nobody home. (*A sob rises in her throat.*) We're free and clear. (*Sobbing more fully, released.*) We're free. (*Biff comes slowly toward her.*) We're free . . . We're free . . .

Biff lifts her to her feet and moves out up right with her in his arms. Linda sobs quietly. Bernard and Charley come together and follow them, followed by Happy. Only the music of the flute is left on the darkening stage as over the house the hard towers of the apartment buildings rise into sharp focus, and—

THE CURTAIN FALLS

Tennessee Williams

The Glass Menagerie 1945

Tennessee Williams (1914–1983) was born Thomas Lanier Williams in Columbus, Mississippi, went to high school in St. Louis, and graduated from the University of Iowa. As an undergraduate, he saw a performance of Ibsen's Ghosts and decided to become a playwright himself. His family bore a close resemblance to the Wingfields in The Glass Menagerie: *his mother came from a line of Southern blue bloods (Tennessee pioneers); his sister Rose suffered from incapacitating shyness; and as a young man, Williams himself, like Tom, worked at a job he disliked (in a shoe factory where his father worked), wrote poetry,*

TENNESSEE WILLIAMS

sought refuge in moviegoing, and finally left home to wander and hold odd jobs. He worked as a bellhop in a New Orleans hotel; a teletype operator in Jacksonville, Florida; an usher and a waiter in New York. In 1945 The Glass Menagerie *scored a success on Broadway, winning a Drama Critics Circle award. Two years later Williams received a Pulitzer Prize for* A Streetcar Named Desire, *a grim, powerful study of a woman's illusions and frustrations, set in New Orleans. In 1955 Williams was awarded another Pulitzer Prize for* Cat on a Hot Tin Roof. *Besides other plays, including* Summer and Smoke *(1948),* Sweet Bird of Youth *(1959),* The Night of the Iguana *(1961),* Small Craft Warnings *(1973),* Clothes for a Summer Hotel *(1980), and* A House Not Meant to Stand *(1981), Williams wrote two novels, poetry, essays, short stories, and* Memoirs *(1975).*

> Nobody, not even the rain, has such small hands.
>
> —E. E. CUMMINGS

CHARACTERS

Amanda Wingfield, the mother. A little woman of great but confused vitality clinging frantically to another time and place. Her characterization must be carefully created, not copied from type. She is not paranoiac, but her life is paranoia. There is much to admire in Amanda, and as much to love and pity as there is to laugh at. Certainly she has endurance and a kind of heroism, and though her foolishness makes her unwittingly cruel at times, there is tenderness in her slight person.

Laura Wingfield, her daughter. Amanda, having failed to establish contact with reality, continues to live vitally in her illusions, but Laura's situation is even graver. A childhood illness has left her crippled, one leg slightly shorter than the other, and held in a brace. This defect need not be more than suggested on the stage. Stemming from this, Laura's separation increases till she is like a piece of her own glass collection, too exquisitely fragile to move from the shelf.

Tom Wingfield, her son. And the narrator of the play. A poet with a job in a warehouse. His nature is not remorseless, but to escape from a trap he has to act without pity.

Jim O'Connor, the gentleman caller. A nice, ordinary, young man.

SCENE. *An alley in St. Louis.*

PART I. *Preparation for a Gentleman Caller.*

PART II. *The Gentleman Calls.*

TIME. *Now and the Past.*

SCENE I

The Wingfield apartment is in the rear of the building, one of those vast hive-like conglomerations of cellular living-units that flower as warty growths in overcrowded urban centers of lower middle-class population and are symptomatic

The 1945 original production of *The Glass Menagerie,* The Playhouse, New York. Left to right: Anthony Ross (Jim), Laurette Taylor (Amanda), Eddie Dowling (Tom), and Julie Hayden (Laura).

of the impulse of this largest and fundamentally enslaved section of American society to avoid fluidity and differentiation and to exist and function as one interfused mass of automatism.

The apartment faces an alley and is entered by a fire-escape, a structure whose name is a touch of accidental poetic truth, for all of these huge buildings are always burning with the slow and implacable fires of human desperation. The fire-escape is included in the set—that is, the landing of it and steps descending from it.

The scene is memory and is therefore unrealistic. Memory takes a lot of poetic license. It omits some details; others are exaggerated, according to the emotional value of the articles it touches, for memory is seated predominantly in the heart. The interior is therefore rather dim and poetic.

At the rise of the curtain, the audience is faced with the dark, grim rear wall of the Wingfield tenement. This building, which runs parallel to the footlights, is flanked on both sides by dark, narrow alleys which run into murky canyons of tangled clotheslines, garbage cans, and the sinister latticework of neighboring fire-escapes. It is up and down these side alleys that exterior entrances and exits are made, during the play. At the end of Tom's opening commentary, the dark tenement wall slowly reveals (by means of a transparency) the interior of the ground floor Wingfield apartment.

Downstage is the living room, which also serves as a sleeping room for Laura, the sofa unfolding to make her bed. Upstage, center, and divided by a wide arch or second proscenium with transparent faded portieres (or second curtain), is the dining room. In an old-fashioned what-not in the living room are seen scores of transparent glass animals. A blown-up photograph of the father hangs on the wall of the living room, facing the audience, to the left of the archway. It is the face of a very handsome young man in a doughboy's First World War cap. He is gallantly smiling, ineluctably smiling, as if to say, "I will be smiling forever."

The audience hears and sees the opening scene in the dining room through both the transparent fourth wall of the building and the transparent gauze portieres of the dining room arch. It is during this revealing scene that the fourth wall slowly ascends, out of sight. This transparent exterior wall is not brought down again until the very end of the play, during Tom's final speech.

The narrator is an undisguised convention of the play. He takes whatever license with dramatic convention as is convenient to his purposes.

Tom enters dressed as a merchant sailor from the alley, stage left, and strolls across the front of the stage to the fire-escape. There he stops and lights a cigarette. He addresses the audience.

Tom: Yes, I have tricks in my pocket, I have things up my sleeve. But I am the opposite of a stage magician. He gives you illusion that has the appearance of truth. I give you truth in the pleasant disguise of illusion. To begin with, I turn back time. I reverse it to that quaint period, the thirties, when the huge middle class of America was matriculating in a school for the blind. Their eyes had failed them, or they had failed their eyes, and so they were having their fingers pressed forcibly down on the fiery Braille alphabet of a dissolving economy. In Spain there was revolution. Here there was only shouting and confusion. In Spain there was Guernica. Here there were disturbances of labor, sometimes pretty violent, in otherwise peaceful cities such as Chicago, Cleveland, St. Louis. . . . This is the social background of the play.

(Music.)

The play is memory. Being a memory play, it is dimly lighted, it is sentimental, it is not realistic. In memory everything seems to happen to music. That explains the fiddle in the wings. I am the narrator of the play, and also a character in it. The other characters are my mother, Amanda, my sister, Laura, and a gentleman caller who appears in the final scenes. He is the most realistic character in the play, being an emissary from a world of reality that we were somehow set apart from. But since I have a poet's weakness for symbols, I am using this character also as a symbol; he is the long delayed but always expected something that we live for. There is a fifth character in the play who doesn't appear except in this larger-than-life photograph over the mantel. This is our father who left us a long time ago. He was a telephone man who fell in love with long distances; he gave up his job with the telephone company and skipped the light fantastic out of town. . . . The last we heard of him was a picture post-card from Mazatlan, on the Pacific coast of Mexico, containing a message of two words—"Hello—Good-bye!" and an address. I think the rest of the play will explain itself. . . .

Amanda's voice becomes audible through the portieres.

(Screen Legend: "Où Sont Les Neiges.")°

He divides the portieres and enters the upstage area.

Amanda and Laura are seated at a drop-leaf table. Eating is indicated by gestures without food or utensils. Amanda faces the audience. Tom and Laura are seated in profile.

(*Screen Legend . . . Neiges."*): "Where are the snows (of yesteryear)?" A slide bearing this line by the French poet François Villon is to be projected on a stage wall.

The interior has lit up softly and through the scrim we see Amanda and Laura seated at the table in the upstage area.

Amanda (*calling*): Tom?

Tom: Yes, Mother.

Amanda: We can't say grace until you come to the table!

Tom: Coming, Mother. (*He bows slightly and withdraws, reappearing a few moments later in his place at the table.*)

Amanda (*to her son*): Honey, don't *push* with your *fingers*. If you have to push with something, the thing to push with is a crust of bread. And chew—chew! Animals have sections in their stomachs which enable them to digest food without mastication, but human beings are supposed to chew their food before they swallow it down. Eat food leisurely, son, and really enjoy it. A well-cooked meal has lots of delicate flavors that have to be held in the mouth for appreciation. So chew your food and give your salivary glands a chance to function!

Tom deliberately lays his imaginary fork down and pushes his chair back from the table.

Tom: I haven't enjoyed one bite of this dinner because of your constant directions on how to eat it. It's you that makes me rush through meals with your hawk-like attention to every bite I take. Sickening— spoils my appetite—all this discussion of animals' secretion—salivary glands—mastication!

Amanda (*lightly*): Temperament like a Metropolitan star! (*He rises and crosses downstage.*) You're not excused from the table.

Tom: I am getting a cigarette.

Amanda: You smoke too much.

Laura rises.

Laura: I'll bring in the blanc mange.

He remains standing with his cigarette by the portieres during the following.

Amanda (*rising*): No, sister, no, sister—you be the lady this time and I'll be the darky.

Laura: I'm already up.

Amanda: Resume your seat, little sister—I want you to stay fresh and pretty—for gentlemen callers!

Laura: I'm not expecting any gentlemen callers.

Amanda (*crossing out to kitchenette. Airily*): Sometimes they come when they are least expected! Why, I remember one Sunday afternoon in Blue Mountain—(*Enters kitchenette.*)

Tom: I know what's coming!

Laura: Yes. But let her tell it.

Tom: Again?

Laura: She loves to tell it.

Amanda returns with bowl of dessert.

Amanda: One Sunday afternoon in Blue Mountain—your mother received—*seventeen!*—gentlemen callers! Why, sometimes there weren't chairs enough to accommodate them all. We had to send the nigger over to bring in folding chairs from the parish house.

Tom (remaining at portieres): How did you entertain those gentlemen callers?

Amanda: I understood the art of conversation!

Tom: I bet you could talk.

Amanda: Girls in those days *knew* how to talk, I can tell you.

Tom: Yes?

(Image: Amanda As A Girl On A Porch Greeting Callers.)

Amanda: They knew how to entertain their gentlemen callers. It wasn't enough for a girl to be possessed of a pretty face and a graceful figure—although I wasn't slighted in either respect. She also needed to have a nimble wit and a tongue to meet all occasions.

Tom: What did you talk about?

Amanda: Things of importance going on in the world! Never anything coarse or common or vulgar. (*She addresses Tom as though he were seated in the vacant chair at the table though he remains by portieres. He plays this scene as though he held the book.*) My callers were gentlemen—all! Among my callers were some of the most prominent young planters of the Mississippi Delta—planters and sons of planters!

Tom motions for music and a spot of light on Amanda. Her eyes lift, her face glows, her voice becomes rich and elegiac.

(Screen Legend: "Où Sont Les Neiges.")

There was young Champ Laughlin who later became vice-president of the Delta Planters Bank. Hadley Stevenson who was drowned in Moon Lake and left his widow one hundred and fifty thousand in Government bonds. There were the Cutrere brothers, Wesley and Bates. Bates was one of my bright particular beaux! He got in a quarrel with that wild Wainright boy. They shot it out on the floor of Moon Lake Casino. Bates was shot through the stomach. Died in the ambulance on his way to Memphis. His widow was also well-provided for, came into eight or ten thousand acres, that's all. She married him on the rebound—never loved her—carried my picture on him the night he died! And there was that boy that every girl in the Delta had set her cap for! That beautiful, brilliant young Fitzhugh boy from Green County!

Tom: What did he leave his widow?

Amanda: He never married! Gracious, you talk as though all of my old admirers had turned up their toes to the daisies!

Tom: Isn't this the first you mentioned that still survives?

Amanda: That Fitzhugh boy went North and made a fortune—came to be known as the Wolf of Wall Street! He had the Midas touch, whatever he touched turned to gold! And I could have been Mrs. Duncan J. Fitzhugh, mind you! But—I picked your *father!*

Laura (*rising*): Mother, let me clear the table.

Amanda: No dear, you go in front and study your typewriter chart. Or practice your shorthand a little. Stay fresh and pretty!—It's almost time for our gentlemen callers to start arriving. (*She flounces girlishly toward the kitchenette.*) How many do you suppose we're going to entertain this afternoon?

Tom throws down the paper and jumps up with a groan.

Laura (*alone in the dining room*): I don't believe we're going to receive any, Mother.

Amanda (*reappearing, airily*): What? No one—not one? You must be joking! (*Laura nervously echoes her laugh. She slips in a fugitive manner through the half-open portieres and draws them gently behind her. A shaft of very clear light is thrown on her face against the jaded tapestry of the curtains.*) (**Music: "The Glass Menagerie" Under Faintly.**) (*Lightly.*) Not one gentleman caller? It can't be true! There must be a flood, there must have been a tornado!

Laura: It isn't a flood, it's not a tornado, Mother. I'm just not popular like you were in Blue Mountain. . . . (*Tom utters another groan. Laura glances at him with a faint, apologetic smile. Her voice catching a little.*) Mother's afraid I'm going to be an old maid.

(The Scene Dims Out With "Glass Menagerie" Music.)

SCENE II

"Laura, Haven't You Ever Liked Some Boy?"

On the dark stage the screen is lighted with the image of blue roses.

Gradually Laura's figure becomes apparent and the screen goes out.

The music subsides.

Laura is seated in the delicate ivory chair at the small clawfoot table.

She wears a dress of soft violet material for a kimono—her hair tied back from her forehead with a ribbon.

She is washing and polishing her collection of glass.

Amanda appears on the fire-escape steps. At the sound of her ascent, Laura catches her breath, thrusts the bowl of ornaments away and seats herself stiffly before the diagram of the typewriter keyboard as though it held her spellbound. Something has happened to Amanda. It is written in her face as she climbs to the landing: a look that is grim and hopeless and a little absurd.

She has on one of those cheap or imitation velvety-looking cloth coats with imitation fur collar. Her hat is five or six years old, one of those dreadful cloche hats that were worn in the late twenties, and she is clasping an enormous black patent-leather pocketbook with nickel clasp and initials. This is her full-dress outfit, the one she usually wears to the D.A.R.

Before entering she looks through the door.

She purses her lips, opens her eyes wide, rolls them upward and shakes her head.

Then she slowly lets herself in the door. Seeing her mother's expression Laura touches her lips with a nervous gesture.

Laura: Hello, Mother, I was—(*She makes a nervous gesture toward the chart on the wall. Amanda leans against the shut door and stares at Laura with a martyred look.*)

Amanda: Deception? Deception? (*She slowly removes her hat and gloves, continuing the swift suffering stare. She lets the hat and gloves fall on the floor—a bit of acting.*)

Laura (*shakily*): How was the D.A.R. meeting? (*Amanda slowly opens her purse and removes a dainty white handkerchief which she shakes out delicately and delicately touches to her lips and nostrils.*) Didn't you go to the D.A.R. meeting, Mother?

Amanda (*faintly, almost inaudibly*): —No.—No. (*Then more forcibly.*) I did not have the strength—to go to the D.A.R. In fact, I did not have the courage! I wanted to find a hole in the ground and hide myself in it forever! (*She crosses slowly to the wall and removes the diagram of the typewriter keyboard. She holds it in front of her for a second, staring at it sweetly and sorrowfully—then bites her lips and tears it in two pieces.*)

Laura (*faintly*): Why did you do that, Mother? (*Amanda repeats the same procedure with the chart of the Gregg Alphabet.*) Why are you—

Amanda: Why? Why? How old are you, Laura?

Laura: Mother, you know my age.

Amanda: I thought that you were an adult; it seems that I was mistaken. (*She crosses slowly to the sofa and sinks down and stares at Laura.*)

Laura: Please don't stare at me, Mother.

Amanda closes her eyes and lowers her head. Count ten.

Amanda: What are we going to do, what is going to become of us, what is the future?

Count ten.

Laura: Has something happened, Mother? (*Amanda draws a long breath and takes out the handkerchief again. Dabbing process.*) Mother, has—something happened?

Amanda: I'll be all right in a minute. I'm just bewildered—(*count five*)—by life . . .

Laura: Mother, I wish that you would tell me what's happened.

Amanda: As you know, I was supposed to be inducted into my office at the D.A.R. this afternoon. (**Image: A Swarm of Typewriters.**) But I stopped off at Rubicam's Business College to speak to your teachers about your having a cold and ask them what progress they thought you were making down there.

Laura: Oh . . .

Amanda: I went to the typing instructor and introduced myself as your mother. She didn't know who you were. Wingfield, she said. We don't have any such student enrolled at the school! I assured her she did, that you had been going to classes since early in January. "I wonder," she said, "if you could be talking about that terribly shy little girl who dropped out of school after only a few days' attendance?" "No," I said, "Laura, my daughter, has been going to school every day for the past six weeks!" "Excuse me," she said. She took the attendance book out and there was your name, unmistakably printed, and all the dates you were absent until they decided that you had dropped out of school. I still said, "No, there must have been some mistake! There must have been some mix-up in the records!" And she said, "No—I remember her perfectly now. Her hand shook so that she couldn't hit the right keys! The first time we gave a speedtest, she broke down completely—was sick at the stomach and almost had to be carried into the wash-room! After that morning she never showed up any more. We phoned the house but never got any answer"—while I was working at Famous and Barr, I suppose, demonstrating those—Oh! I felt so weak I could barely keep on my feet. I had to sit down while they got me a glass of water! Fifty dollars' tuition, all of our plans—my hopes and ambitions for you—just gone up the spout, just gone up the spout like that. (*Laura draws a long breath and gets awkwardly to her feet. She crosses to the victrola and winds it up.*) What are you doing?

Laura: Oh! (*She releases the handle and returns to her seat.*)

Amanda: Laura, where have you been going when you've gone out pretending that you were going to business college?

Laura: I've just been going out walking.

Amanda: That's not true.

Laura: It is. I just went walking.

Amanda: Walking? Walking? In winter? Deliberately courting pneumonia in that light coat? Where did you walk to, Laura?

Laura: It was the lesser of two evils, Mother. (**Image: Winter Scene In Park.**) I couldn't go back. I—threw up—on the floor!

Amanda: From half past seven till after five every day you mean to tell me you walked around in the park, because you wanted to make me think that you were still going to Rubicam's Business College?

Laura: It wasn't as bad as it sounds. I went inside places to get warmed up.

Amanda: Inside where?

Laura: I went in the art museum and the bird-houses at the Zoo. I visited the penguins every day! Sometimes I did without lunch and went to the movies. Lately I've been spending most of my afternoons in the Jewel-box, that big glass house where they raise the tropical flowers.

Amanda: You did all this to deceive me, just for the deception? (*Laura looks down.*) Why?

Laura: Mother, when you're disappointed, you get that awful suffering look on your face, like the picture of Jesus' mother in the museum!

Amanda: Hush!

Laura: I couldn't face it.

Pause. A whisper of strings.

(**Legend: "The Crust Of Humility."**)

Amanda (*hopelessly fingering the huge pocketbook*): So what are we going to do the rest of our lives? Stay home and watch the parades go by? Amuse ourselves with the glass menagerie, darling? Eternally play those worn-out phonograph records your father left as a painful reminder of him? We won't have a business career—we've given that up because it gave us nervous indigestion! (*Laughs wearily.*) What is there left but dependence all our lives? I know so well what becomes of unmarried women who aren't prepared to occupy a position. I've seen such pitiful cases in the South—barely tolerated spinsters living upon the grudging patronage of sister's husband or brother's wife!—stuck away in some little mouse-trap of a room—encouraged by one in-law to visit another—little birdlike women without any nest—eating the crust of humility all their life! Is that the future that we've mapped out for ourselves? I swear it's the only alternative I can think of! It isn't a very pleasant alternative, is it? Of course—some girls *do* marry. (*Laura twists her hands nervously.*) Haven't you ever liked some boy?

Laura: Yes I liked one once. (*Rises.*) I came across his picture a while ago.

Amanda (*with some interest*): He gave you his picture?

Laura: No, it's in the year-book.

Amanda (*disappointed*): Oh—a high-school boy.

(Screen Image: Jim As A High-School Hero Bearing A Silver Cup.)

Laura: Yes. His name was Jim. (*Laura lifts the heavy annual from the claw-foot table.*) Here he is in *The Pirates of Penzance*.

Amanda (*absently*): The what?

Laura: The operetta the senior class put on. He had a wonderful voice and we sat across the aisle from each other Mondays, Wednesdays, and Fridays in the Aud. Here he is with the silver cup for debating! See his grin?

Amanda (*absently*): He must have had a jolly disposition.

Laura: He used to call me—Blue Roses.

(Image: Blue Roses.)

Amanda: Why did he call you such a name as that?

Laura: When I had that attack of pleurosis—he asked me what was the matter when I came back. I said pleurosis—he thought that I said Blue Roses! So that's what he always called me after that. Whenever he saw me, he'd holler, "Hello, Blue Roses!" I didn't care for the girl he went out with. Emily Meisenbach. Emily was the best-dressed girl at Soldan. She never struck me, though, as being sincere . . . It says in the Personal Section—they're engaged. That's—six years ago! They must be married by now.

Amanda: Girls that aren't cut out for business careers usually wind up married to some nice man. (*Gets up with a spark of revival.*) Sister, that's what you'll do!

Laura utters a startled, doubtful laugh. She reaches quickly for a piece of glass.

Laura: But, Mother—
Amanda: Yes? (*Crossing to phonograph.*)
Laura (*in a tone of frightened apology*): I'm—crippled!

(**Image: Screen.**)

Amanda: Nonsense! Laura, I've told you never, never to use that word. Why, you're not crippled, you just have a little defect—hardly noticeable, even! When people have some slight disadvantage like that, they cultivate other things to make up for it—develop charm— and vivacity—and—*charm!* That's all you have to do! (*She turns again to the phonograph.*) One thing your father had *plenty of*—was charm!

Tom motions to the fiddle in the wings.

(**The Scene Fades Out With Music.**)

SCENE III

(**Legend On The Screen: "After The Fiasco—"**)

Tom speaks from the fire-escape landing.

Tom: After the fiasco at Rubicam's Business College, the idea of getting a gentleman caller for Laura began to play a more important part in Mother's calculations. It became an obsession. Like some archetype of the universal unconscious, the image of the gentleman caller haunted our small apartment. . . . (**Image: Young Man At Door With Flowers.**) An evening at home rarely passed without some allusion to this image, this spectre, this hope. . . . Even when he wasn't mentioned, his presence hung in Mother's preoccupied look and in my sister's frightened, apologetic manner—hung like a sentence passed upon the Wingfields! Mother was a woman of action as well as words. She began to take logical steps in the planned direction. Late that winter and in the early spring—realizing that extra money would be needed to properly feather the nest and plume the bird— she conducted a vigorous campaign on the telephone, roping in subscribers to one of those magazines for matrons called *The Homemaker's Companion,* the type of journal that features the serialized sublimations of ladies of letters who think in terms of delicate cup-like breasts, slim, tapering waists, rich, creamy thighs, eyes like woodsmoke in autumn, fingers that soothe and caress like strains of music, bodies as powerful as Etruscan sculpture.

(Screen Image: Glamor Magazine Cover.)

Amanda enters with phone on long extension cord. She is spotted in the dim stage.

Amanda: Ida Scott? This is Amanda Wingfield! We *missed* you at the D.A.R. last Monday! I said to myself: She's probably suffering with that sinus condition! How is that sinus condition? Horrors! Heaven have mercy!—You're a Christian martyr, yes, that's what you are, a Christian martyr! Well, I just now happened to notice that your subscription to the *Companion's* about to expire! Yes, it expires with the next issue, honey!—just when that wonderful new serial by Bessie Mae Hopper is getting off to such an exciting start. Oh, honey, it's something that you can't miss! You remember how *Gone With the Wind* took everybody by storm? You simply couldn't go out if you hadn't read it. All everybody *talked* was Scarlett O'Hara. Well, this is a book that critics already compare to *Gone With the Wind*. It's the *Gone With the Wind* of the post-World War generation!—What?—Burning?—Oh, honey, don't let them burn, go take a look in the oven and I'll hold the wire! Heavens—I think she's hung up!

(Dim Out.)

(Legend On Screen: "You Think I'm In Love With Continental Shoemakers?")

Before the stage is lighted, the violent voices of Tom and Amanda are heard. They are quarreling behind the portieres. In front of them stands Laura with clenched hands and panicky expression.

A clear pool of light on her figure throughout this scene.

Tom: What in Christ's name am I—
Amanda (shrilly): Don't you use that—
Tom: Supposed to do!
Amanda: Expression! Not in my—
Tom: Ohhh!
Amanda: Presence! Have you gone out of your senses?
Tom: I have, that's true, *driven* out!
Amanda: What is the matter with you, you—big—big—IDIOT!
Tom: Look—I've got *no thing,* no single thing—
Amanda: Lower your voice!
Tom: In my life here that I can call my OWN! Everything is—
Amanda: Stop that shouting!
Tom: Yesterday you confiscated my books! You had the nerve to—

Amanda: I took that horrible novel back to the library—yes! That hideous book by that insane Mr. Lawrence. (*Tom laughs wildly.*) I cannot control the output of diseased minds or people who cater to them—(*Tom laughs still more wildly.*) BUT I WON'T ALLOW SUCH FILTH BROUGHT INTO MY HOUSE! No, no, no, no, no!

Tom: House, house! Who pays rent on it, who makes a slave of himself to—

Amanda (*fairly screeching*): Don't you DARE to—

Tom: No, no, I mustn't say things! *I've* got to just—

Amanda: Let me tell you—

Tom: I don't want to hear any more! (*He tears the portieres open. The upstage area is lit with a turgid smoky red glow.*)

Amanda's hair is in metal curlers and she wears a very old bathrobe, much too large for her slight figure, a relic of the faithless Mr. Wingfield.

An upright typewriter and a wild disarray of manuscripts are on the dropleaf table. The quarrel was probably precipitated by Amanda's interruption of his creative labor. A chair lying overthrown on the floor.

Their gesticulating shadows are cast on the ceiling by the fiery glow.

Amanda: You *will* hear more, you—

Tom: No, I won't hear more, I'm going out!

Amanda: You come right back in—

Tom: Out, out out! Because I'm—

Amanda: Come back here, Tom Wingfield! I'm not through talking to you!

Tom: Oh, go—

Laura (*desperately*): Tom!

Amanda: You're going to listen, and no more insolence from you! I'm at the end of my patience! (*He comes back toward her.*)

Tom: What do you think I'm at? Aren't I supposed to have any patience to reach the end of, Mother? I know, I know. It seems unimportant to you, what I'm *doing*—what *I want* to do—having a little *difference* between them! You don't think that—

Amanda: I think you've been doing things that you're ashamed of. That's why you act like this. I don't believe that you go every night to the movies. Nobody goes to the movies night after night. Nobody in their right minds goes to the movies as often as you pretend to. People don't go to the movies at nearly midnight, and movies don't let out at two A.M. Come in stumbling. Muttering to yourself like a maniac! You get three hours' sleep and then go to work. Oh, I can picture the way you're doing down there. Moping, doping, because you're in no condition.

Tom (*wildly*): No, I'm in no condition!

Amanda: What right have you got to jeopardize your job? Jeopardize the security of us all? How do you think we'd manage if you were—

Tom: Listen! You think I'm crazy *about* the *warehouse*? (*He bends fiercely toward her slight figure.*) You think I'm in love with the Continental Shoemakers? You think I want to spend fifty-five *years* down there in that—*celotex interior!* with—*fluorescent—tubes!* Look! I'd rather somebody picked up a crowbar and battered out my brains—than go back mornings! I *go!* Every time you come in yelling that God damn *"Rise and Shine!" "Rise and Shine!"* I say to myself "How *lucky dead* people are!" But I get up. I *go!* For sixty-five dollars a month I give up all that I dream of doing and being *ever!* And you say self—*self's* all I ever think of. Why, listen, if self is what I thought of, Mother, I'd be where he is—GONE! (*Pointing to father's picture.*) As far as the system of transportation reaches! (*He starts past her. She grabs his arm.*) Don't grab at me, Mother!

Amanda: Where are you going?

Tom: I'm going to the *movies!*

Amanda: I don't believe that lie!

Tom (*crouching toward her, overtowering her tiny figure. She backs away, gasping*): I'm going to opium dens! Yes, opium dens, dens of vice and criminals' hangouts, Mother. I've joined the Hogan gang, I'm a hired assassin, I carry a tommy-gun in a violin case! I run a string of cat-houses in the Valley! They call me Killer, Killer Wingfield, I'm leading a double-life, a simple, honest warehouse worker by day, by night a dynamic *czar* of the *underworld*, Mother. I go to gambling casinos, I spin away fortunes on the roulette table! I wear a patch over one eye and a false mustache, sometimes I put on green whiskers. On those occasions they call me—*El Diablo!* Oh, I could tell you things to make you sleepless! My enemies plan to dynamite this place. They're going to blow us all sky-high some night! I'll be glad, very happy, and so will you! You'll go up, up on a broomstick, over Blue Mountain with seventeen gentlemen callers! You ugly—babbling old—*witch*. . . . (*He goes through a series of violent, clumsy movements, seizing his overcoat, lunging to the door, pulling it fiercely open. The women watch him, aghast. His arm catches in the sleeve of the coat as he struggles to pull it on. For a moment he is pinioned by the bulky garment. With an outraged groan he tears the coat off again, splitting the shoulders of it, and hurls it across the room. It strikes against the shelf of Laura's glass collection, there is a tinkle of shattering glass. Laura cries out as if wounded.*)

(**Music Legend: "The Glass Menagerie."**)

Laura (shrilly): My glass!—menagerie. . . . *(She covers her face and turns away.)*

But Amanda is still stunned and stupefied by the "ugly witch" so that she barely notices this occurrence. Now she recovers her speech.

Amanda (in an awful voice): I won't speak to you—until you apologize! *(She crosses through portieres and draws them together behind her. Tom is left with Laura. Laura clings weakly to the mantel with her face averted. Tom stares at her stupidly for a moment. Then he crosses to shelf. Drops awkwardly to his knees to collect the fallen glass, glancing at Laura as if he would speak but couldn't.)*

("The Glass Menagerie" steals in as the Scene Dims Out.)

SCENE IV

The interior is dark. Faint in the alley.

A deep-voiced bell in a church is tolling the hour of five as the scene commences.

Tom appears at the top of the alley. After each solemn boom of the bell in the tower, he shakes a little noise-maker or rattle as if to express the tiny spasm of man in contrast to the sustained power and dignity of the Almighty. This and the unsteadiness of his advance make it evident that he has been drinking.

As he climbs the few steps to the fire-escape landing light steals up inside. Laura appears in night-dress, observing Tom's empty bed in the front room.

Tom fishes in his pockets for the door-key, removing a motley assortment of articles in the search, including a perfect shower of movie-ticket stubs and an empty bottle. At last he finds the key, but just as he is about to insert it, it slips from his fingers. He strikes a match and crouches below the door.

Tom (bitterly): One crack—and it falls through!

Laura opens the door.

Laura: Tom! Tom, what are you doing?
Tom: Looking for a door-key.
Laura: Where have you been all this time?
Tom: I have been to the movies.
Laura: All this time at the movies?

Tom: There was a very long program. There was a Garbo picture and a Mickey Mouse and a travelogue and a newsreel and a preview of coming attractions. And there was an organ solo and a collection for the milk-fund—simultaneously—which ended up in a terrible fight between a fat lady and an usher!

Laura (*innocently*): Did you have to stay through everything?

Tom: Of course! And, oh, I forgot! There was a big stage show! The headliner on this stage show was Malvolio the Magician. He performed wonderful tricks, many of them, such as pouring water back and forth between pitchers. First it turned to wine and then it turned to beer and then it turned to whiskey. I know it was whiskey it finally turned into because he needed somebody to come up out of the audience to help him, and I came up—both shows! It was Kentucky Straight Bourbon. A very generous fellow, he gave souvenirs. (*He pulls from his back pocket a shimmering rainbow-colored scarf.*) He gave me this. This is his magic scarf. You can have it, Laura. You wave it over a canary cage and you get a bowl of gold-fish. You wave it over the gold-fish bowl and they fly away canaries. . . . But the wonderfullest trick of all was the coffin trick. We nailed him into a coffin and he got out of the coffin without removing one nail. (*He has come inside.*) There is a trick that would come in handy for me— get me out of this 2 by 4 situation! (*Flops onto bed and starts removing shoes.*)

Laura: Tom—Shhh!

Tom: What're you shushing me for?

Laura: You'll wake up Mother.

Tom: Goody, goody! Pay'er back for all those "Rise an' Shines." (*Lies down, groaning.*) You know it don't take much intelligence to get yourself into a nailed-up coffin, Laura. But who in hell ever got himself out of one without removing one nail?

As if in answer, the father's grinning photograph lights up.

(Scene Dims Out.)

Immediately following: The church bell is heard striking six. At the sixth stroke the alarm clock goes off in Amanda's room, and after a few moments we hear her calling: "Rise and Shine! Rise and Shine! Laura, go tell your brother to rise and shine!"

Tom (*sitting up slowly*): I'll rise—but I won't shine.

The light increases.

Amanda: Laura, tell your brother his coffee is ready.

Laura slips into front room.

Laura: Tom! it's nearly seven. Don't make Mother nervous. (*He stares at her stupidly. Beseechingly.*) Tom, speak to Mother this morning. Make up with her, apologize, speak to her!

Tom: She won't to me. It's her that started not speaking.

Laura: If you just say you're sorry she'll start speaking.

Tom: Her not speaking—is that such a tragedy?

Laura: Please—please!

Amanda (*calling from kitchenette*): Laura, are you going to do what I asked you to do, or do I have to get dressed and go out myself?

Laura: Going, going—soon as I get on my coat! (*She pulls on a shapeless felt hat with nervous, jerky movements, pleadingly glancing at Tom. Rushes awkwardly for coat. The coat is one of Amanda's inaccurately made-over, the sleeves too short for Laura.*) Butter and what else?

Amanda (*entering upstage*): Just butter. Tell them to charge it.

Laura: Mother, they make such faces when I do that.

Amanda: Sticks and stones may break my bones, but the expression on Mr. Garfinkel's face won't harm us! Tell your brother his coffee is getting cold.

Laura (*at door*): Do what I asked you, will you, will you, Tom?

He looks sullenly away.

Amanda: Laura, go now or just don't go at all!

Laura (*rushing out*): Going—going! (*A second later she cries out. Tom springs up and crosses to the door. Amanda rushes anxiously in. Tom opens the door.*)

Tom: Laura?

Laura: I'm all right. I slipped, but I'm all right.

Amanda (*peering anxiously after her*): If anyone breaks a leg on those fire-escape steps, the landlord ought to be sued for every cent he possesses! (*She shuts door. Remembers she isn't speaking and returns to other room.*)

As Tom enters listlessly for his coffee, she turns her back to him and stands rigidly facing the window on the gloomy gray vault of the areaway. Its light on her face with its aged but childish features is cruelly sharp, satirical as a Daumier print.

(Music Under: "Ave Maria.")

Tom glances sheepishly but sullenly at her averted figure and slumps at the table. The coffee is scalding hot; he sips it and gasps and spits it back in the cup. At his gasp, Amanda catches her breath and half turns. Then catches herself and turns back to window.

Tom blows on his coffee, glancing sidewise at his mother. She clears her throat. Tom clears his. He starts to rise. Sinks back down again, scratches his head, clears his throat again. Amanda coughs. Tom raises his cup in both hands to blow on it, his eyes staring over the rim of it at his mother for several moments. Then he slowly sets the cup down and awkwardly and hesitantly rises from the chair.

Tom (*hoarsely*): Mother. I—I apologize. Mother. (*Amanda draws a quick, shuddering breath. Her face works grotesquely. She breaks into childlike tears.*) I'm sorry for what I said, for everything that I said, I didn't mean it.

Amanda (*sobbingly*): My devotion has made me a witch and so I make myself hateful to my children!

Tom: No, you *don't*.

Amanda: I worry so much, don't sleep, it makes me nervous!

Tom (*gently*): I understand that.

Amanda: I've had to put up a solitary battle all these years. But you're my right-hand bower! Don't fall down, don't fail!

Tom (*gently*): I try, Mother.

Amanda (*with great enthusiasm*): Try and you will SUCCEED! (*The notion makes her breathless.*) Why, you—you're just *full* of natural endowments! Both of my children—they're *unusual* children! Don't you think I know it? I'm so—*proud*! Happy and—feel I've—so much to be thankful for but—Promise me one thing, son!

Tom: What, Mother?

Amanda: Promise, son you'll—never be a drunkard!

Tom (*turns to her grinning*): I will never be a drunkard, Mother.

Amanda: That's what frightened me so, that you'd be drinking! Eat a bowl of Purina!

Tom: Just coffee, Mother.

Amanda: Shredded wheat biscuit?

Tom: No. No, Mother, just coffee.

Amanda: You can't put in a day's work on an empty stomach. You've got ten minutes—don't gulp! Drinking too-hot liquids makes cancer of the stomach. . . . Put cream in.

Tom: No, thank you.

Amanda: To cool it.

Tom: No! No, thank you, I want it black.

Amanda: I know, but it's not good for you. We have to do all that we can to build ourselves up. In these trying times we live in, all that we

have to cling to is—each other. . . . That's why it's so important to—
Tom, I—I sent out your sister so I could discuss something with you.
If you hadn't spoken I would have spoken to you. (*Sits down.*)

Tom (*gently*): What is it, Mother, that you want to discuss?

Amanda: Laura!

Tom puts his cup down slowly.

(Legend On Screen: "Laura.")

(Music: "The Glass Menagerie.")

Tom: —Oh.—Laura . . .

Amanda (*touching his sleeve*): You know how Laura is. So quiet but—still
water runs deep! She notices things and I think she—broods about
them. (*Tom looks up.*) A few days ago I came in and she was crying.

Tom: What about?

Amanda: You.

Tom: Me?

Amanda: She has an idea that you're not happy here.

Tom: What gave her that idea?

Amanda: What gives her any idea? However, you do act strangely. I—
I'm not criticizing, understand *that!* I know your ambitions do not lie
in the warehouse, that like everybody in the whole wide world—
you've had to—make sacrifices, but—Tom—Tom—life's not easy, it
calls for—Spartan endurance! There's so many things in my heart
that I cannot describe to you! I've never told you but I—*loved* your
father. . . .

Tom (*gently*): I know that, Mother.

Amanda: And you—when I see you taking after his ways! Staying out
late—and—well, you had been drinking the night you were in
that—terrifying condition! Laura says that you hate the apartment
and that you go out nights to get away from it! Is that true, Tom?

Tom: No. You say there's so much in your heart that you can't describe
to me. That's true of me, too. There's so much in my heart that I
can't describe to you! So let's respect each other's—

Amanda: But, why—*why*, Tom—are you always so *restless?* Where do
you go to, nights?

Tom: I—go to the movies.

Amanda: Why do you go to the movies so much, Tom?

Tom: I go to the movies because—I like adventure. Adventure is something I don't have much of at work, so I go to the movies.

Amanda: But, Tom, you go to the movies *entirely* too *much!*

Tom: I like a lot of adventure.

Amanda looks baffled, then hurt. As the familiar inquisition resumes he becomes hard and impatient again. Amanda slips back into her querulous attitude toward him.

(Image On Screen: Sailing Vessel With Jolly Roger.)

Amanda: Most young men find adventure in their careers.

Tom: Then most young men are not employed in a warehouse.

Amanda: The world is full of young men employed in warehouses and offices and factories.

Tom: Do all of them find adventure in their careers?

Amanda: They do or they do without it! Not everybody has a craze for adventure.

Tom: Man is by instinct a lover, a hunter, a fighter, and none of those instincts are given much play at the warehouse!

Amanda: Man is by instinct! Don't quote instinct to me! Instinct is something that people have got away from! It belongs to animals! Christian adults don't want it!

Tom: What do Christian adults want, then, Mother?

Amanda: Superior things! Things of the mind and the spirit! Only animals have to satisfy instincts! Surely your aims are somewhat higher than theirs! Than monkeys—pigs—

Tom: I reckon they're not.

Amanda: You're joking. However, that isn't what I wanted to discuss.

Tom (rising): I haven't much time.

Amanda (pushing his shoulder): Sit down.

Tom: You want me to punch in red at the warehouse, Mother?

Amanda: You have five minutes. I want to talk about Laura.

(Legend: "Plans And Provisions.")

Tom: All right! What about Laura?

Amanda: We have to be making plans and provisions for her. She's older than you, two years, and nothing has happened. She just drifts along doing nothing. It frightens me terribly how she just drifts along.

Tom: I guess she's the type that people call home girls.

Amanda: There's no such type, and if there is, it's a pity! That is unless the home is hers, with a husband!

Tom: What?

Amanda: Oh, I can see the handwriting on the wall as plain as I see the nose in front of my face! It's terrifying! More and more you remind me of your father! He was out all hours without explanation—Then *left! Goodbye!* And me with the bag to hold. I saw that letter you got from the Merchant Marine. I know what you're dreaming of.

I'm not standing here blindfolded. Very well, then. Then *do* it! But not till there's somebody to take your place.

Tom: What do you mean?

Amanda: I mean that as soon as Laura has got somebody to take care of her, married, a home of her own, independent—why, then you'll be free to go wherever you please, on land, on sea, whichever way the wind blows! But until that time you've got to look out for your sister. I don't say me because I'm old and don't matter! I say for your sister because she's young and dependent. I put her in business college—a dismal failure! Frightened her so it made her sick to her stomach. I took her over to the Young People's League at the church. Another fiasco. She spoke to nobody, nobody spoke to her. Now all she does is fool with those pieces of glass and play those worn-out records. What kind of a life is that for a girl to lead!

Tom: What can I do about it?

Amanda: Overcome selfishness! Self, self, self is all that you ever think of! (*Tom springs up and crosses to get his coat. It is ugly and bulky. He pulls on a cap with earmuffs.*) Where is your muffler? Put your wool muffler on! (*He snatches it angrily from the closet and tosses it around his neck and pulls both ends tight.*) Tom! I haven't said what I had in mind to ask you.

Tom: I'm too late to—

Amanda (*catching his arms—very importunately. Then shyly*): Down at the warehouse, aren't there some—nice young men?

Tom: No!

Amanda: There *must* be—some . . .

Tom: Mother—

Gesture.

Amanda: Find one that's clean-living—doesn't drink and—ask him out for sister!

Tom: What?

Amanda: For *Sister!* To meet! Get *acquainted!*

Tom (*stamping to door*): Oh, my go-osh!

Amanda: Will you? (*He opens door. Imploringly.*) Will you? (*He starts down.*) Will you? Will, you, dear?

Tom (*calling back*): YES!

Amanda closes the door hesitantly and with a troubled but faintly hopeful expression.

(Screen Image: Glamor Magazine Cover.)

Spot Amanda at phone.

Amanda: Ella Cartwright? This is Amanda Wingfield! How are you, honey? How is that kidney condition? (*Count five.*) Horrors! (*Count five.*) You're a Christian martyr, yes, honey, that's what you are, a Christian martyr! Well, I just happened to notice in my little red book that your subscription to the *Companion* has just run out! I knew that you wouldn't want to miss out on the wonderful serial starting in this new issue. It's by Bessie Mae Hopper, the first thing she's written since *Honeymoon for Three.* Wasn't that a strange and interesting story? Well, this one is even lovelier, I believe. It has a sophisticated society background. It's all about the horsey set on Long Island!

(Fade Out.)

SCENE V

(Legend On Screen: "Annunciation.") *Fade with music.*

It is early dusk of a spring evening. Supper has just been finished in the Wingfield apartment. Amanda and Laura in light colored dresses are removing dishes from the table, in the upstage area, which is shadowy, their movements formalized almost as a dance or ritual, their moving forms as pale and silent as moths.

Tom, in white shirt and trousers, rises from the table and crosses toward the fire-escape.

Amanda (as he passes her): Son, will you do me a favor?

Tom: What?

Amanda: Comb your hair! You look so pretty when your hair is combed! (*Tom slouches on sofa with evening paper. Enormous caption "Franco Triumphs."*) There is only one respect in which I would like you to emulate your father.

Tom: What respect is that?

Amanda: The care he always took of his appearance. He never allowed himself to look untidy. (*He throws down the paper and crosses to fire-escape.*) Where are you going?

Tom: I'm going out to smoke.

Amanda: You smoke too much. A pack a day at fifteen cents a pack. How much would that amount to in a month? Thirty times fifteen is how much, Tom? Figure it out and you will be astounded at what you could save. Enough to give you a night-school course in accounting at Washington U! Just think what a wonderful thing that would be for you, son!

Tom is unmoved by the thought.

Tom: I'd rather smoke. (*He steps out on landing, letting the screen door slam.*)

Amanda (*sharply*): I know! That's the tragedy of it. . . . (*Alone, she turns to look at her husband's picture.*)

(Dance Music: "All The World Is Waiting For The Sunrise.")

Tom (*to the audience*): Across the alley from us was the Paradise Dance Hall. On evenings in spring the windows and doors were open and the music came outdoors. Sometimes the lights were turned out except for a large glass sphere that hung from the ceiling. It would turn slowly about and filter the dusk with delicate rainbow colors. Then the orchestra played a waltz or a tango, something that had a slow and sensuous rhythm. Couples would come outside, to the relative privacy of the alley. You could see them kissing behind ash-pits and telephone poles. This was the compensation for lives that passed like mine, without any change or adventure. Adventure and change were imminent in this year. They were waiting around the corner for all these kids. Suspended in the mist over Berchtesgaden, caught in the folds of Chamberlain's umbrella—In Spain there was Guernica! But here there was only hot swing music and liquor, dance halls, bars, and movies, and sex that hung in the gloom like a chandelier and flooded the world with brief, deceptive rainbows. . . . All the world was waiting for bombardments!

Amanda turns from the picture and comes outside.

Amanda (*sighing*): A fire-escape landing's a poor excuse for a porch. (*She spreads a newspaper on a step and sits down, gracefully and demurely as if she were settling into a swing on a Mississippi veranda.*) What are you looking at?

Tom: The moon.

Amanda: Is there a moon this evening?

Tom: It's rising over Garfinkel's Delicatessen.

Amanda: So it is! A little silver slipper of a moon. Have you made a wish on it yet?

Tom: Um-hum.

Amanda: What did you wish for?

Tom: That's a secret.

Amanda: A secret, huh? Well, I won't tell mine either. I will be just as mysterious as you.

Tom: I bet I can guess what yours is.

Amanda: Is my head so transparent?

Tom: You're not a sphinx.

Amanda: No, I don't have secrets. I'll tell you what I wished for on the
    moon. Success and happiness for my precious children! I wish for
    that whenever there's a moon, and when there isn't a moon, I wish
    for it, too.

Tom: I thought perhaps you wished for a gentleman caller.

Amanda: Why do you say that?

Tom: Don't you remember asking me to fetch one?

Amanda: I remember suggesting that it would be nice for your sister if
    you brought home some nice young man from the warehouse. I
    think I've made that suggestion more than once.

Tom: Yes, you have made it repeatedly.

Amanda: Well?

Tom: We are going to have one.

Amanda: What?

Tom: A gentleman caller!

(The Annunciation Is Celebrated With Music.)

Amanda rises.

(Image On Screen: Caller With Bouquet.)

Amanda: You mean you have asked some nice young man to come over?

Tom: Yep. I've asked him to dinner.

Amanda: You really did?

Tom: I did!

Amanda: You did, and did he—*accept?*

Tom: He did!

Amanda: Well, well—well, well! That's—lovely!

Tom: I thought that you would be pleased.

Amanda: It's definite, then?

Tom: Very definite.

Amanda: Soon?

Tom: Very soon.

Amanda: For heaven's sake, stop putting on and tell me some things,
    will you?

Tom: What things do you want me to tell you?

Amanda: Naturally I would like to know when he's *coming!*

Tom: He's coming tomorrow.

Amanda: *Tomorrow?*

Tom: Yep. Tomorrow.

Amanda: But, Tom!

Tom: Yes, Mother?

Amanda: Tomorrow gives me no time!

Tom: Time for what?

Amanda: Preparations! Why didn't you phone me at once, as soon as you asked him, the minute that he accepted? Then, don't you see, I could have been getting ready!

Tom: You don't have to make any fuss.

Amanda: Oh, Tom, Tom, Tom, of course I have to make a fuss! I want things nice, not sloppy! Not thrown together. I'll certainly have to do some fast thinking, won't I?

Tom: I don't see why you have to think at all.

Amanda: You just don't know. We can't have a gentleman caller in a pig-sty! All my wedding silver has to be polished, the mono-grammed table linen ought to be laundered! The windows have to be washed and fresh curtains put up. And how about clothes? We have to *wear* something, don't we?

Tom: Mother, this boy is no one to make a fuss over!

Amanda: Do you realize he's the first young man we've introduced to your sister? It's terrible, dreadful, disgraceful that poor little sister has never received a single gentleman caller! Tom, come inside! (*She opens the screen door.*)

Tom: What for?

Amanda: I want to ask you some things.

Tom: If you're going to make such a fuss, I'll call it off, I'll tell him not to come.

Amanda: You certainly won't do anything of the kind. Nothing offends people worse than broken engagements. It simply means I'll have to work like a Turk! We won't be brilliant, but we'll pass inspection. Come on inside. (*Tom follows, groaning.*) Sit down.

Tom: Any particular place you would like me to sit?

Amanda: Thank heavens I've got that new sofa! I'm also making pay-ments on a floor lamp I'll have sent out! And put the chintz covers on, they'll brighten things up! Of course I'd hoped to have these walls re-papered. . . . What is the young man's name?

Tom: His name is O'Connor.

Amanda: That, of course, means fish—tomorrow is Friday! I'll have that salmon loaf—with Durkee's dressing! What does he do? He works at the warehouse?

Tom: Of course! How else would I—

Amanda: Tom, he—doesn't drink?

Tom: Why do you ask me that?

Amanda: Your father *did*!

Tom: Don't get started on that!

Amanda: He *does* drink, then?

Tom: Not that I know of!

Amanda: Make sure, be certain! The last thing I want for my daughter's a boy who drinks!

Tom: Aren't you being a little premature? Mr. O'Connor has not yet appeared on the scene!

Amanda: But will tomorrow. To meet your sister, and what do I know about his character? Nothing! Old maids are better off than wives of drunkards!

Tom: Oh, my God!

Amanda: Be still!

Tom (leaning forward to whisper): Lots of fellows meet girls whom they don't marry!

Amanda: Oh, talk sensibly, Tom—and don't be sarcastic! *(She has gotten a hairbrush.)*

Tom: What are you doing?

Amanda: I'm brushing that cow-lick down! What is this young man's position at the warehouse?

Tom (submitting grimly to the brush and the interrogation): This young man's position is that of a shipping clerk, Mother.

Amanda: Sounds to me like a fairly responsible job, the sort of a job *you* would be in if you just had more *get-up.* What is his salary? Have you got any idea?

Tom: I would judge it to be approximately eighty-five dollars a month.

Amanda: Well—not princely, but—

Tom: Twenty more than I make.

Amanda: Yes, how well I know! But for a family man, eighty-five dollars a month is not much more than you can just get by on. . . .

Tom: Yes, but Mr. O'Connor is not a family man.

Amanda: He might be, mightn't he? Some time in the future?

Tom: I see. Plans and provisions.

Amanda: You are the only young man that I know of who ignores the fact that the future becomes the present, the present the past, and the past turns into everlasting regret if you don't plan for it!

Tom: I will think that over and see what I can make of it!

Amanda: Don't be supercilious with your mother! Tell me some more about this—what do you call him?

Tom: James D. O'Connor. The D. is for Delaney.

Amanda: Irish on *both* sides! *Gracious!* And doesn't drink?

Tom: Shall I call him up and ask him right this minute?

Amanda: The only way to find out about those things is to make discreet inquiries at the proper moment. When I was a girl in Blue Mountain and it was suspected that a young man drank, the girl whose attentions he had been receiving, if any girl *was*, would sometimes speak to the minister of his church, or rather her father would if her father was living, and sort of feel him out on the young man's character. That is the way such things are discreetly handled to keep a young woman from making a tragic mistake!

Tom: Then how did you happen to make a tragic mistake?

Amanda: That innocent look of your father's had everyone fooled! He *smiled*—the world was *enchanted!* No girl can do worse than put herself at the mercy of a handsome appearance! I hope that Mr. O'Connor is not too good-looking.

Tom: No, he's not too good-looking. He's covered with freckles and hasn't too much of a nose.

Amanda: He's not right-down homely, though?

Tom: Not right-down homely. Just medium homely, I'd say.

Amanda: Character's what to look for in a man.

Tom: That's what I've always said, Mother.

Amanda: You've never said anything of the kind and I suspect you would never give it a thought.

Tom: Don't be suspicious of me.

Amanda: At least I hope he's the type that's up and coming.

Tom: I think he really goes in for self-improvement.

Amanda: What reason have you to think so?

Tom: He goes to night school.

Amanda (beaming): Splendid! What does he do, I mean study?

Tom: Radio engineering and public speaking!

Amanda: Then he has visions of being advanced in the world! Any young man who studies public speaking is aiming to have an executive job some day! And radio engineering? A thing for the future! Both of these facts are very illuminating. Those are the sort of things that a mother should know concerning any young man who comes to call on her daughter. Seriously or—not.

Tom: One little warning. He doesn't know about Laura. I didn't let on that we had dark ulterior motives. I just said, why don't you come have dinner with us? He said okay and that was the whole conversation.

Amanda: I bet it was! You're eloquent as an oyster. However, he'll know about Laura when he gets here. When he sees how lovely and sweet and pretty she is, he'll thank his lucky stars he was asked to dinner.

Tom: Mother, you mustn't expect too much of Laura.

Amanda: What do you mean?

Tom: Laura seems all those things to you and me because she's ours and we love her. We don't even notice she's crippled any more.

Amanda: Don't say crippled! You know that I never allow that word to be used!

Tom: But face facts, Mother. She is and—that not's all—

Amanda: What do you mean "not all"?

Tom: Laura is very different from other girls.

Amanda: I think the difference is all to her advantage.

Tom: Not quite all—in the eyes of others—strangers—she's terribly shy and lives in a world of her own and those things make her seem a little peculiar to people outside the house.

Amanda: Don't say peculiar.

Tom: Face the facts. She is.

(The Dance-Hall Music Changes To A Tango That Has A Minor And Somewhat Ominous Tone.)

Amanda: In what way is she peculiar—may I ask?

Tom (gently): She lives in a world of her own—a world of—little glass ornaments, Mother. . . . (*Gets up. Amanda remains holding brush, looking at him, troubled.*) She plays old phonograph records and—that's about all—(*He glances at himself in the mirror and crosses to door.*)

Amanda (sharply): Where are you going?

Tom: I'm going to the movies. (*Out screen door.*)

Amanda: Not to the movies, every night to the movies! (*Follows quickly to screen door.*) I don't believe you always go to the movies! (*He is gone. Amanda looks worriedly after him for a moment. Then vitality and optimism return and she turns from the door. Crossing to portieres.*) Laura! Laura! (*Laura answers from kitchenette.*)

Laura: Yes, Mother.

Amanda: Let those dishes go and come in front! (*Laura appears with dish towel. Gaily.*) Laura, come here and make a wish on the moon!

Laura (entering): Moon—moon?

Amanda: A little silver slipper of a moon. Look over your left shoulder, Laura, and make a wish! (*Laura looks faintly puzzled as if called out of sleep. Amanda seizes her shoulders and turns her at an angle by the door.*) Now! Now, darling, wish!

Laura: What shall I wish for, Mother?

Amanda (her voice trembling and her eyes suddenly filling with tears): Happiness! Good Fortune!

The violin rises and the stage dims out.

SCENE VI

(**Image: High-School Hero.**)

Tom: And so the following evening I brought him home to dinner. I had known Jim slightly in high school. In high school Jim was a hero. He had tremendous Irish good nature and vitality with the scrubbed and polished look of white chinaware. He seemed to move in a continual spotlight. He was a star in basketball, captain of the debating club, president of the senior class and the glee club and he sang the male lead in the annual light operas. He was always running or bounding, never just walking. He seemed always at the point of defeating the law of gravity. He was shooting with such velocity through his ado-lescence that you would logically expect him to arrive at nothing short of the White House by the time he was thirty. But Jim appar-ently ran into more interference after his graduation from Soldan. His speed had definitely slowed. Six years after he left high school he was holding a job that wasn't much better than mine.

(**Image: Clerk.**)

He was the only one at the warehouse with whom I was on friendly terms. I was valuable to him as someone who could remem-ber his former glory, who had seen him win basketball games and the silver cup in debating. He knew of my secret practice of retiring to a cabinet of the washroom to work on my poems when business was slack in the warehouse. He called me Shakespeare. And while the other boys in the warehouse regarded me with suspicious hostility, Jim took a humorous attitude toward me. Gradually his attitude af-fected the others, their hostility wore off and they also began to smile at me as people smile at an oddly fashioned dog who trots across their path at some distance.

I knew that Jim and Laura had known each other at Soldan, and I had heard Laura speak admiringly of his voice. I didn't know if Jim remembered her or not. In high school Laura had been as unobtru-sive as Jim had been astonishing. If he did remember Laura, it was not as my sister, for when I asked him to dinner, he grinned and said, "You know, Shakespeare, I never thought of you as having folks!"

He was about to discover that I did. . . .

(**Light Up Stage.**)

(**Legend On Screen: "The Accent Of A Coming Foot."**)

Friday evening. It is about five o'clock of a late spring evening which comes "scattering poems in the sky."

A delicate lemony light is in the Wingfield apartment.

Amanda has worked like a Turk in preparation for the gentleman caller. The results are astonishing. The new floor lamp with its rose-silk shade is in place, a colored paper lantern conceals the broken light fixture in the ceiling, new billowing white curtains are at the windows, chintz covers are on chairs and sofa, a pair of new sofa pillows make their initial appearance.

Open boxes and tissue paper are scattered on the floor.

Laura stands in the middle with lifted arms while Amanda crouches before her, adjusting the hem of the new dress, devout and ritualistic. The dress is colored and designed by memory. The arrangement of Laura's hair is changed; it is softer and more becoming. A fragile, unearthly prettiness has come out in Laura: she is like a piece of translucent glass touched by light, given a momentary radiance, not actual, not lasting.

Amanda (impatiently): Why are you trembling?
Laura: Mother, you've made me so nervous!
Amanda: How have I made you nervous?
Laura: By all this fuss! You make it seem so important!
Amanda: I don't understand you, Laura. You couldn't be satisfied with just sitting home, and yet whenever I try to arrange something for you, you seem to resist it. (*She gets up.*) Now take a look at yourself. No, wait! Wait just a moment—I have an idea!
Laura: What is it now?

Amanda produces two powder puffs which she wraps in handkerchiefs and stuffs in Laura's bosom.

Laura: Mother, what are you doing?
Amanda: They call them "Gay Deceivers"!
Laura: I won't wear them!
Amanda: You will!
Laura: Why should I?
Amanda: Because, to be painfully honest, your chest is flat.
Laura: You make it seem like we were setting a trap.
Amanda: All pretty girls are a trap, a pretty trap, and men expect them to be. (**Legend: "A Pretty Trap."**) Now look at yourself, young lady. This is the prettiest you will ever be! I've got to fix myself now! You're going to be surprised by your mother's appearance! (*She crosses through the portieres, humming gaily.*)

Laura moves slowly to the long mirror and stares solemnly at herself.

A wind blows the white curtains inward in a slow, graceful motion and with a faint, sorrowful sighing.

Amanda (*offstage*): It isn't dark enough yet. (*She turns slowly before the mirror with a troubled look.*)

(**Legend On Screen: "This Is My Sister: Celebrate Her With Strings!" Music.**)

Amanda (*laughing, off*): I'm going to show you something. I'm going to make a spectacular appearance!

Laura: What is it, Mother?

Amanda: Possess your soul in patience—you will see! Something I've resurrected from that old trunk! Styles haven't changed so terribly much after all. . . . (*She parts the portieres.*) Now just look at your mother! (*She wears a girlish frock of yellowed voile with a blue silk sash. She carries a bunch of jonquils—the legend of her youth is nearly revived. Feverishly.*) This is the dress in which I led the cotillion. Won the cakewalk twice at Sunset Hill, wore one spring to the Governor's ball in Jackson! See how I sashayed around the ballroom, Laura? (*She raises her skirt and does a mincing step around the room.*) I wore it on Sundays for my gentlemen callers! I had it on the day I met your father—I had malaria fever all that spring. The change of climate from East Tennessee to the Delta—weakened resistance—I had a little temperature all the time—not enough to be serious—just enough to make me restless and giddy! Invitations poured in—parties all over the Delta!—"Stay in bed," said Mother, "you have fever!"—but I just wouldn't.—I took quinine but kept on going, going!—Evenings, dances!—Afternoons, long, long rides! Picnics—lovely!—So lovely, that country in May.— All lacy with dogwood, literally flooded with jonquils!—That was the spring I had the craze for jonquils. Jonquils became an absolute obsession. Mother said, "Honey, there's no more room for jonquils." And still I kept bringing in more jonquils. Whenever, wherever I saw them, I'd say, "Stop! Stop! I see jonquils!" I made the young men help me gather the jonquils! It was a joke, Amanda and her jonquils! Finally there were no more vases to hold them, every available space was filled with jonquils. No vases to hold them? All right, I'll hold them myself! And then I—(*She stops in front of the picture.*) (**Music.**) met your father! Malaria fever and jonquils and then—this—boy. . . . (*She switches on the rose-colored lamp.*) I hope they get here before it starts to rain. (*She crosses upstage and places the jonquils in bowl on table.*) I gave your brother a little extra change so he and Mr. O'Connor could take the service car home.

Laura (*with altered look*): What did you say his name was?

Amanda: O'Connor.

Laura: What is his first name?

Amanda: I don't remember. Oh, yes, I do. It was—Jim!

> *Laura sways slightly and catches hold of a chair.*

(Legend On Screen. "Not Jim!")

Laura (*faintly*): Not—Jim!

Amanda: Yes, that was it, it was Jim! I've never known a Jim that wasn't nice!

(Music: Ominous.)

Laura: Are you sure his name is Jim O'Connor?

Amanda: Yes. Why?

Laura: Is he the one that Tom used to know in high school?

Amanda: He didn't say so. I think he just got to know him at the warehouse.

Laura: There was a Jim O'Connor we both knew in high school—(*Then, with effort.*) If that is the one that Tom is bringing to dinner—you'll have to excuse me, I won't come to the table.

Amanda: What sort of nonsense is this?

Laura: You asked me once if I'd ever liked a boy. Don't you remember I showed you this boy's picture?

Amanda: You mean the boy you showed me in the year-book?

Laura: Yes, that boy.

Amanda: Laura, Laura, were you in love with that boy?

Laura: I don't know, Mother. All I know is I couldn't sit at the table if it was him!

Amanda: It won't be him! It isn't the least bit likely. But whether it is or not, you will come to the table. You will not be excused.

Laura: I'll have to be, Mother.

Amanda: I don't intend to humor your silliness, Laura. I've had too much from you and your brother, both! So just sit down and compose yourself till they come. Tom has forgotten his key so you'll have to let them in, when they arrive.

Laura (*panicky*): Oh, Mother—*you* answer the door!

Amanda (*lightly*): I'll be in the kitchen—busy!

Laura: Oh, Mother, please answer the door, don't make me do it!

Amanda (*crossing into kitchenette*): I've got to fix the dressing for the salmon. Fuss, fuss—silliness!—over a gentleman caller!

> *Door swings shut. Laura is left alone.*

(Legend: "Terror!")

> *She utters a low moan and turns off the lamp—sits stiffly on the edge of the sofa, knotting her fingers together.*

(**Legend On Screen: "The Opening Of A Door!"**)

Tom and Jim appear on the fire-escape steps and climb to landing. Hearing their approach, Laura rises with a panicky gesture. She retreats to the portieres.

The doorbell. Laura catches her breath and touches her throat. Low drums.

Amanda (*calling*): Laura, sweetheart! The door!

Laura stares at it without moving.

Jim: I think we just beat the rain.

Tom: Uh-huh. (*He rings again, nervously. Jim whistles and fishes for a cigarette.*)

Amanda (*very, very gaily*): Laura, that is your brother and Mr. O'Connor! Will you let them in, darling?

Laura crosses toward kitchenette door.

Laura (*breathlessly*): Mother—you go to the door!

Amanda steps out of kitchenette and stares furiously at Laura. She points imperiously at the door.

Laura: Please, please!

Amanda (*in a fierce whisper*): What is the matter with you, you silly thing?

Laura (*desperately*): Please, you answer it, *please!*

Amanda: I told you I wasn't going to humor you, Laura. Why have you chosen this moment to lose your mind?

Laura: Please, please, please, you go!

Amanda: You'll have to go to the door because I can't!

Laura (*despairingly*): I can't either!

Amanda: Why?

Laura: I'm sick!

Amanda: I'm sick, too—of your nonsense! Why can't you and your brother be normal people? Fantastic whims and behavior! (*Tom gives a long ring.*) Preposterous goings on! Can you give me one reason— (*Calls out lyrically.*) COMING! JUST ONE SECOND!—why should you be afraid to open a door? Now you answer it, Laura!

Laura: Oh, oh, oh . . . (*She returns through the portieres. Darts to the victrola and winds it frantically and turns it on.*)

Amanda: Laura Wingfield, you march right to that door!

Laura: Yes—yes, Mother!

A faraway, scratchy rendition of "Dardanella" softens the air and gives her strength to move through it. She slips to the door and draws it cautiously open. Tom enters with the caller, Jim O'Connor.

Tom: Laura, this is Jim. Jim, this is my sister, Laura.
Jim (stepping inside): I didn't know that Shakespeare had a sister!
Laura (retreating stiff and trembling from the door): How—how do you do?
Jim (heartily extending his hand): Okay!

Laura touches it hesitantly with hers.

Jim: Your hand's *cold,* Laura!
Laura: Yes, well—I've been playing the victrola. . . .
Jim: Must have been playing classical music on it! You ought to play a little hot swing music to warm you up!
Laura: Excuse me—I haven't finished playing the victrola. . . .

She turns awkwardly and hurries into the front room. She pauses a second by the victrola. Then catches her breath and darts through the portieres like a frightened deer.

Jim (grinning): What was the matter?
Tom: Oh—with Laura? Laura is—terribly shy.
Jim: Shy, huh? It's unusual to meet a shy girl nowadays. I don't believe you ever mentioned you had a sister.
Tom: Well, now you know. I have one. Here is the *Post Dispatch.* You want a piece of it?
Jim: Uh-huh.
Tom: What piece? The comics?
Jim: Sports! (*Glances at it.*) Ole Dizzy Dean is on his bad behavior.
Tom (disinterest): Yeah? (*Lights cigarette and crosses back to fire-escape door.*)
Jim: Where are you going?
Tom: I'm going out on the terrace.
Jim (goes after him): You know, Shakespeare—I'm going to sell you a bill of goods!
Tom: What goods?
Jim: A course I'm taking.
Tom: Huh?
Jim: In public speaking! You and me, we're not the warehouse type.
Tom: Thanks—that's good news. But what has public speaking got to do with it?
Jim: It fits you for—executive positions!
Tom: Awww.

Jim: I tell you it's done a helluva lot for me.

(Image: Executive At Desk.)

Tom: In what respect?

Jim: In every! Ask yourself what is the difference between you an' me and men in the office down front? Brains?—No!—Ability?—No! Then what? Just one little thing—

Tom: What is that one little thing?

Jim: Primarily it amounts to—social poise! Being able to square up to people and hold your own on any social level!

Amanda (offstage): Tom?

Tom: Yes, Mother?

Amanda: Is that you and Mr. O'Connor?

Tom: Yes, Mother.

Amanda: Well, you just make yourselves comfortable in there.

Tom: Yes, Mother.

Amanda: Ask Mr. O'Connor if he would like to wash his hands.

Jim: Aw—no—thank you—I took care of that at the warehouse. Tom—

Tom: Yes?

Jim: Mr. Mendoza was speaking to me about you.

Tom: Favorably?

Jim: What do you think?

Tom: Well—

Jim: You're going to be out of a job if you don't wake up.

Tom: I am waking up—

Jim: You show no signs.

Tom: The signs are interior.

(Image On Screen: The Sailing Vessel With Jolly Roger Again.)

Tom: I'm planning to change. (*He leans over the rail speaking with quiet exhilaration. The incandescent marquees and signs of the first-run movie houses light his face from across the alley. He looks like a voyager.*) I'm right at the point of committing myself to a future that doesn't include the warehouse and Mr. Mendoza or even a night-school course in public speaking.

Jim: What are you gassing about?

Tom: I'm tired of the movies.

Jim: Movies!

Tom: Yes, movies! Look at them—(*A wave toward the marvels of Grand Avenue.*) All of those glamorous people—having adventures—hogging it all, gobbling the whole thing up! You know what happens?

People go to the *movies* instead of *moving!* Hollywood characters are supposed to have all the adventures for everybody in America, while everybody in America sits in a dark room and watches them have them! Yes, until there's a war. That's when adventure becomes available to the masses! *Everyone's* dish, not only Gable's! Then the people in the dark room come out of the dark room to have some adventures themselves—Goody, goody—It's our turn now, to go to the South Sea Island—to make a safari—to be exotic, far-off—But I'm not patient. I don't want to wait till then. I'm tired of the *movies* and I am *about* to *move!*

Jim (incredulously): Move?

Tom: Yes!

Jim: When?

Tom: Soon!

Jim: Where? Where?

> *Theme three music seems to answer the question, while Tom thinks it over. He searches among his pockets.*

Tom: I'm starting to boil inside. I know I seem dreamy, but inside—well, I'm boiling! Whenever I pick up a shoe, I shudder a little thinking how short life is and what I am doing!—Whatever that means. I know it doesn't mean shoes—except as something to wear on a traveler's feet! (*Finds paper.*) Look—

Jim: What?

Tom: I'm a member.

Jim (reading): The Union of Merchant Seamen.

Tom: I paid my dues this month, instead of the light bill.

Jim: You will regret it when they turn the lights off.

Tom: I won't be here.

Jim: How about your mother?

Tom: I'm like my father. The bastard son of a bastard! See how he grins? And he's been absent going on sixteen years!

Jim: You're just talking, you drip. How does your mother feel about it?

Tom: Shhh—Here comes Mother! Mother is not acquainted with my plans!

Amanda (enters portieres): Where are you all?

Tom: On the terrace, Mother.

> *They start inside. She advances to them. Tom is distinctly shocked at her appearance. Even Jim blinks a little. He is making his first contact with girlish Southern vivacity and in spite of the night-school course in public speaking is somewhat thrown off the beam by the unexpected outlay of social charm.*

Certain responses are attempted by Jim but are swept aside by Amanda's gay laughter and chatter. Tom is embarrassed but after the first shock Jim reacts very warmly. Grins and chuckles, is altogether won over.

(Image: Amanda As A Girl.)

Amanda (coyly smiling, shaking her girlish ringlets): Well, well, well, so this is Mr. O'Connor. Introductions entirely unnecessary. I've heard so much about you from my boy. I finally said to him, Tom—good gracious!—why don't you bring this paragon to supper? I'd like to meet this nice young man at the warehouse!—Instead of just hearing him sing your praises so much! I don't know why my son is so stand-offish—that's not Southern behavior! Let's sit down and—I think we could stand a little more air in here! Tom, leave the door open. I felt a nice fresh breeze a moment ago. Where has it gone? Mmm, so warm already! And not quite summer, even. We're going to burn up when summer really gets started. However, we're having—we're having a very light supper. I think light things are better fo' this time of year. The same as light clothes are. Light clothes an' light food are what warm weather calls fo'. You know our blood gets so thick during th' winter—it takes a while fo' us to *adjust* ou'selves!—when the season changes . . . It's come so quick this year. I wasn't prepared. All of a sudden—heavens! Already summer!—I ran to the trunk an' pulled out this light dress—Terribly old! Historical almost! But feels so good—so good an' co-ol, y'know. . . .

Tom: Mother—

Amanda: Yes, honey?

Tom: How about—supper?

Amanda: Honey, you go ask Sister if supper is ready! You know that Sister is in full charge of supper! Tell her you hungry boys are waiting for it. *(To Jim.)* Have you met Laura?

Jim: She—

Amanda: Let you in? Oh, good, you've met already! It's rare for a girl as sweet an' pretty as Laura to be domestic! But Laura is, thank heavens, not only pretty but also very domestic. I'm not at all. I never was a bit. I never could make a thing but angel-food cake. Well, in the South we had so many servants. Gone, gone, gone. All vestiges of gracious living! Gone completely! I wasn't prepared for what the future brought me. All of my gentlemen callers were sons of planters and so of course I assumed that I would be married to one and raise my family on a large piece of land with plenty of servants. But man proposes—and woman accepts the proposal!—To vary that old, old saying a little bit—I married no planter! I married a man who worked for the telephone company!—that gallantly smiling gentleman over there! (*Points to the picture.*) A telephone man who—fell in love with long-distance!—Now he travels and I don't even know where!—But what am I going on for about my—tribulations? Tell me yours—I hope you don't have any! Tom?

Tom (*returning*): Yes, Mother?

Amanda: Is supper nearly ready?

Tom: It looks to me like supper is on the table.

Amanda: Let me look—(*She rises prettily and looks through portieres.*) Oh, lovely—But where is Sister?

Tom: Laura is not feeling well and she says that she thinks she'd better not come to the table.

Amanda: What?—Nonsense!—Laura? Oh, Laura!

Laura (*offstage, faintly*): Yes, Mother.

Amanda: You really must come to the table. We won't be seated until you come to the table! Come in, Mr. O'Connor. You sit over there and I'll—Laura? Laura Wingfield! You're keeping us waiting, honey! We can't say grace until you come to the table!

The back door is pushed weakly open and Laura comes in. She is obviously quite faint, her lips trembling, her eyes wide and staring. She moves unsteadily toward the table.

(Legend: "Terror!")

Outside a summer storm is coming abruptly. The white curtains billow inward at the windows and there is a sorrowful murmur and deep blue dusk.

Laura suddenly stumbles—She catches at a chair with a faint moan.

Tom: Laura!

Amanda: Laura! (*There is a clap of thunder.*) **(Legend: "Ah!")** (*Despairingly.*) Why, Laura, you *are* sick, darling! Tom, help your sister into the living room, dear! Sit in the living room, Laura—rest on the sofa. Well! (*To the gentleman caller.*) Standing over the hot stove made her ill!—I told her that it was just too warm this evening, but—(*Tom comes back in. Laura is on the sofa.*) Is Laura all right now?

Tom: Yes.

Amanda: What *is* that? Rain? A nice cool rain has come up! (*She gives the gentleman caller a frightened look.*) I think we may—have grace—now . . . (*Tom looks at her stupidly.*) Tom, honey—you say grace!

Tom: Oh . . . "For these and all thy mercies—" (*They bow their heads, Amanda stealing a nervous glance at Jim. In the living room Laura,*

*stretched on the sofa, clenches her hand to her lips, to hold back a shudder-
ing sob.)* God's Holy Name be praised—

(The Scene Dims Out.)

SCENE VII

A Souvenir.

*Half an hour later. Dinner is just being finished in the upstage area which is
concealed by the drawn portieres.*

*As the curtain rises Laura is still huddled upon the sofa, her feet drawn under
her, her head resting on a pale blue pillow, her eyes wide and mysteriously
watchful. The new floor lamp with its shade of rose-colored silk gives a soft, becoming light to her face, bringing out the fragile, unearthly prettiness which
usually escapes attention. There is a steady murmur of rain, but it is slackening
and stops soon after the scene begins; the air outside becomes pale and luminous as the moon breaks out.*

A moment after the curtain rises, the lights in both rooms flicker and go out.

Jim: Hey, there, Mr. Light Bulb!

Amanda laughs nervously.

(Legend: "Suspension Of A Public Service.")

Amanda: Where was Moses when the lights went out? Ha-ha. Do you
know the answer to that one, Mr. O'Connor?
Jim: No, Ma'am, what's the answer?
Amanda: In the dark! (*Jim laughs appreciatively.*) Everybody sit still. I'll
light the candles. Isn't it lucky we have them on the table? Where's
a match? Which of you gentlemen can provide a match?
Jim: Here.
Amanda: Thank you, sir.
Jim: Not at all, Ma'am!
Amanda: I guess the fuse has burnt out. Mr. O'Connor, can you tell a
burnt-out fuse? I know I can't and Tom is a total loss when it comes
to mechanics. (**Sound: Getting Up: Voices Recede A Little To
Kitchenette.**) Oh, be careful you don't bump into something. We
don't want our gentleman caller to break his neck. Now wouldn't
that be a fine howdy-do?
Jim: Ha-ha! Where is the fuse-box?
Amanda: Right here next to the stove. Can you see anything?
Jim: Just a minute.

Amanda: Isn't electricity a mysterious thing? Wasn't it Benjamin
  Franklin who tied a key to a kite? We live in such a mysterious universe, don't we? Some people say that science clears up all the mysteries for us. In my opinion it only creates more! Have you found it
  yet?

Jim: No, Ma'am. All these fuses look okay to me.

Amanda: Tom!

Tom: Yes, Mother?

Amanda: That light bill I gave you several days ago. The one I told you
  we got the notices about?

Tom: Oh.—Yeah.

  (Legend: "Ha!")

Amanda: You didn't neglect to pay it by any chance?

Tom: Why, I—

Amanda: Didn't! I might have known it!

Jim: Shakespeare probably wrote a poem on that light bill, Mrs. Wingfield.

Amanda: I might have known better than to trust him with it! There's
  such a high price for negligence in this world!

Jim: Maybe the poem will win a ten-dollar prize.

Amanda: We'll just have to spend the remainder of the evening in the
  nineteenth century, before Mr. Edison made the Mazda lamp!

Jim: Candlelight is my favorite kind of light.

Amanda: That shows you're romantic! But that's no excuse for Tom.
  Well, we got through dinner. Very considerate of them to let us get
  through dinner before they plunged us into everlasting darkness,
  wasn't it, Mr. O'Connor?

Jim: Ha-ha!

Amanda: Tom, as a penalty for your carelessness you can help me with the
  dishes.

Jim: Let me give you a hand.

Amanda: Indeed you will not!

Jim: I ought to be good for something.

Amanda: Good for something? (*Her tone is rhapsodic.*) *You?* Why, Mr.
  O'Connor, nobody, *nobody's* given me this much entertainment in
  years—as you have!

Jim: Aw, now, Mrs. Wingfield!

Amanda: I'm not exaggerating, not one bit! But Sister is all by her lonesome. You go keep her company in the parlor! I'll give you this lovely
  old candelabrum that used to be on the altar at the church of the
  Heavenly Rest. It was melted a little out of shape when the church
  burnt down. Lightning struck it one spring. Gypsy Jones was holding

a revival at the time and he intimated that the church was destroyed because the Episcopalians gave card parties.

Jim: Ha-ha.

Amanda: And how about coaxing Sister to drink a little wine? I think it would be good for her! Can you carry both at once?

Jim: Sure. I'm Superman!

Amanda: Now, Thomas, get into this apron!

The door of kitchenette swings closed on Amanda's gay laughter; the flickering light approaches the portieres.

Laura sits up nervously as he enters. Her speech at first is low and breathless from the almost intolerable strain of being alone with a stranger.

(The Legend: "I Don't Suppose You Remember Me At All!")

In her first speeches in this scene, before Jim's warmth overcomes her paralyzing shyness, Laura's voice is thin and breathless as though she has run up a steep flight of stairs.

Jim's attitude is gently humorous. In playing this scene it should be stressed that while the incident is apparently unimportant, it is to Laura the climax of her secret life.

Jim: Hello, there, Laura.

Laura (faintly): Hello. (*She clears her throat.*)

Jim: How are you feeling now? Better?

Laura: Yes. Yes, thank you.

Jim: This is for you. A little dandelion wine. (*He extends it toward her with extravagant gallantry.*)

Laura: Thank you.

Jim: Drink it—but don't get drunk! (*He laughs heartily. Laura takes the glass uncertainly; laughs shyly.*) Where shall I set the candles?

Laura: Oh—oh, anywhere . . .

Jim: How about here on the floor? Any objections?

Laura: No.

Jim: I'll spread a newspaper under to catch the drippings. I like to sit on the floor. Mind if I do?

Laura: Oh, no.

Jim: Give me a pillow?

Laura: What?

Jim: A pillow!

Laura: Oh . . . (*Hands him one quickly.*)

Jim: How about you? Don't you like to sit on the floor?

Laura: Oh—yes.

Jim: Why don't you, then?

Laura: I—will.

Jim: Take a pillow! (*Laura does. Sits on the other side of the candelabrum. Jim crosses his legs and smiles engagingly at her.*) I can't hardly see you sitting way over there.

Laura: I can—see you.

Jim: I know, but that's not fair, I'm in the limelight. (*Laura moves her pillow closer.*) Good! Now I can see you! Comfortable?

Laura: Yes.

Jim: So am I. Comfortable as a cow. Will you have some gum?

Laura: No, thank you.

Jim: I think that I will indulge, with your permission. (*Musingly unwraps it and holds it up.*) Think of the fortune made by the guy that invented the first piece of chewing gum. Amazing, huh? The Wrigley Building is one of the sights of Chicago.—I saw it summer before last when I went up to the Century of Progress. Did you take in the Century of Progress?

Laura: No, I didn't.

Jim: Well, it was quite a wonderful exposition. What impressed me most was the Hall of Science. Gives you an idea of what the future will be in America, even more wonderful than the present time is! (*Pause. Smiling at her.*) Your brother tells me you're shy. Is that right, Laura?

Laura: I—don't know.

Jim: I judge you to be an old-fashioned type of girl. Well, I think that's pretty good type to be. Hope you don't think I'm being too personal—do you?

Laura (*hastily, out of embarrassment*): I believe I *will* take a piece of gum, if you—don't mind. (*Clearing her throat.*) Mr. O'Connor, have you—kept up with your singing?

Jim: Singing? Me?

Laura: Yes. I remember what a beautiful voice you had.

Jim: When did you hear me sing?

(Voice Offstage In The Pause.)

Voice (*offstage*):

> O blow, ye winds, heigh-ho,
> A-roving I will go!
> I'm off to my love
> With a boxing glove—
> Ten thousand miles away!

Jim: You say you've heard me sing?

Laura: Oh, yes! Yes, very often . . . I—don't suppose you remember me—at all?

Jim (*smiling doubtfully*): You know I have an idea I've seen you before. I had that idea soon as you opened the door. It seemed almost like I was about to remember your name. But the name that I started to call you—wasn't a name! And so I stopped myself before I said it.

Laura: Wasn't it—Blue Roses?

Jim (*springs up, grinning*): Blue Roses! My gosh, yes—Blue Roses! That's what I had on my tongue when you opened the door! Isn't it funny what tricks your memory plays? I didn't connect you with the high school somehow or other. But that's where it was; it was high school. I didn't even know you were Shakespeare's sister! Gosh, I'm sorry.

Laura: I didn't expect you to. You—barely knew me!

Jim: But we did have a speaking acquaintance, huh?

Laura: Yes, we—spoke to each other.

Jim: When did you recognize me?

Laura: Oh, right away!

Jim: Soon as I came in the door?

Laura: When I heard your name I thought it was probably you. I knew that Tom used to know you a little in high school. So when you came in the door—Well, then I was—sure.

Jim: Why didn't you say something, then?

Laura (*breathlessly*): I didn't know what to say, I was—too surprised!

Jim: For goodness sakes! You know, this sure is funny!

Laura: Yes! Yes, isn't it, though . . .

Jim: Didn't we have a class in something together?

Laura: Yes, we did.

Jim: What class was that?

Laura: It was—singing—Chorus!

Jim: Aw!

Laura: I sat across the aisle from you in the Aud.

Jim: Aw.

Laura: Mondays, Wednesdays and Fridays.

Jim: Now I remember—you always came in late.

Laura: Yes, it was so hard for me, getting upstairs. I had that brace on my leg—it clumped so loud!

Jim: I never heard any clumping.

Laura (*wincing at the recollection*): To me it sounded like thunder!

Jim: Well, well, well. I never even noticed.

Laura: And everybody was seated before I came in. I had to walk in front of all those people. My seat was in the back row. I had to go clumping all the way up the aisle with everyone watching!

Jim: You shouldn't have been self-conscious.

Laura: I know, but I was. It was always such a relief when the singing started.

Jim: Aw, yes, I've placed you now! I used to call you Blue Roses. How was it that I got started calling you that?

Laura: I was out of school a little while with pleurosis. When I came back you asked me what was the matter. I said I had pleurosis—you thought I said Blue Roses. That's what you always called me after that!

Jim: I hope you didn't mind.

Laura: Oh, no—I liked it. You see, I wasn't acquainted with many—people. . . .

Jim: As I remember you sort of stuck by yourself.

Laura: I—I—never had much luck at—making friends.

Jim: I don't see why you wouldn't.

Laura: Well, I—started out badly.

Jim: You mean being—

Laura: Yes, it sort of—stood between me——

Jim: You shouldn't have let it!

Laura: I know, but it did, and—

Jim: You were shy with people!

Laura: I tried not to be but never could—

Jim: Overcome it?

Laura: No, I—I never could!

Jim: I guess being shy is something you have to work out of kind of gradually.

Laura (sorrowfully): Yes—I guess it—

Jim: Takes time!

Laura: Yes—

Jim: People are not so dreadful when you know them. That's what you have to remember! And everybody has problems, not just you, but practically everybody has got some problems. You think of yourself as having the only problems, as being the only one who is disappointed. But just look around you and you will see lots of people as disappointed as you are. For instance, I hoped when I was going to high school that I would be further along at this time, six years later, than I am now—You remember that wonderful write-up I had in *The Torch?*

Laura: Yes! (*She rises and crosses to table.*)

Jim: It said I was bound to succeed in anything I went into! (*Laura returns with the annual.*) Holy Jeez! *The Torch!* (*He accepts it reverently. They smile across it with mutual wonder. Laura crouches beside him and they begin to turn through it. Laura's shyness is dissolving in his warmth.*)

Laura: Here you are in *Pirates of Penzance!*

Jim (wistfully): I sang the baritone lead in that operetta.

Laura (rapidly): So—beautifully!

Jim (*protesting*): Aw—
Laura: Yes, yes—beautifully—beautifully!
Jim: You heard me?
Laura: All three times!
Jim: No!
Laura: Yes!
Jim: All three performances?
Laura (*looking down*): Yes.
Jim: Why?
Laura: I—wanted to ask you to—autograph my program.
Jim: Why didn't you ask me to?
Laura: You were always surrounded by your own friends so much that I
    never had a chance to.
Jim: You should have just—
Laura: Well, I—thought you might think I was—
Jim: Thought I might think you was—what?
Laura: Oh—
Jim (*with reflective relish*): I was beleaguered by females in those days.
Laura: You were terribly popular!
Jim: Yeah—
Laura: You had such a—friendly way—
Jim: I was spoiled in high school.
Laura: Everybody—liked you!
Jim: Including you?
Laura: I—yes, I—did, too—(*She gently closes the book in her lap.*)
Jim: Well, well, well!—Give me that program, Laura. (*She hands it to
    him. He signs it with a flourish.*) There you are—better late than
    never!
Laura: Oh, I—what a—surprise!
Jim: My signature isn't worth very much right now. But some day—
    maybe—it will increase in value! Being disappointed is one thing
    and being discouraged is something else. I am disappointed but I'm
    not discouraged. I'm twenty-three years old. How old are you?
Laura: I'll be twenty-four in June.
Jim: That's not old age!
Laura: No, but—
Jim: You finished high school?
Laura (*with difficulty*): I didn't go back.
Jim: You mean you dropped out?
Laura: I made bad grades in my final examinations. (*She rises and replaces
    the book and the program. Her voice strained.*) How is—Emily Meisen-
    bach getting along?

Jim: Oh, that kraut-head!

Laura: Why do you call her that?

Jim: That's what she was.

Laura: You're not still—going with her?

Jim: I never see her.

Laura: It said in the Personal Section that you were—engaged!

Jim: I know, but I wasn't impressed by that—propaganda!

Laura: It wasn't—the truth?

Jim: Only in Emily's optimistic opinion!

Laura: Oh—

(Legend: "What Have You Done Since High School?")

Jim lights a cigarette and leans indolently back on his elbows smiling at Laura with a warmth and charm which light her inwardly with altar candles. She remains by the table and turns in her hands a piece of glass to cover her tumult.

Jim (after several reflective puffs on a cigarette): What have you done since high school? (*She seems not to hear him.*) Huh? (*Laura looks up.*) I said what have you done since high school, Laura?

Laura: Nothing much.

Jim: You must have been doing something these six long years.

Laura: Yes.

Jim: Well, then, such as what?

Laura: I took a business course at business college—

Jim: How did that work out?

Laura: Well, not very—well—I had to drop out, it gave me—indigestion—

Jim laughs gently.

Jim: What are you doing now?

Laura: I don't do anything—much. Oh, please don't think I sit around doing nothing! My glass collection takes up a good deal of my time. Glass is something you have to take good care of.

Jim: What did you say—about glass?

Laura: Collection I said—I have one—(*She clears her throat and turns away again, acutely shy.*)

Jim (abruptly): You know what I judge to be the trouble with you? Inferiority complex! Know what that is? That's what they call it when someone low-rates himself! I understand it because I had it, too. Although my case was not so aggravated as yours seems to be. I had it until I took up public speaking, developed my voice, and learned that I had an aptitude for science. Before that time I never thought of myself as being outstanding in any way whatsoever! Now I've never made a regular study of it, but I have a friend who says I can analyze people better than doctors that make a profession of it. I don't claim that to be necessarily true, but I can sure guess a person's psychology, Laura! (*Takes out his gum.*) Excuse me, Laura. I always take it out when the flavor is gone. I'll use this scrap of paper to wrap it in. I know how it is to get it stuck on a shoe. Yep—that's what I judge to be your principal trouble. A lack of confidence in yourself as a person. You don't have the proper amount of faith in yourself. I'm basing that fact on a number of your remarks and also on certain observations I've made. For instance that clumping you thought was so awful in high school. You say that you even dreaded to walk into class. You see what you did? You dropped out of school, you gave up an education because of a clump, which as far as I know was practically non-existent! A little physical defect is what you have. Hardly noticeable even! Magnified thousands of times by imagination! You know what my strong advice to you is? Think of yourself as *superior* in some way!

Laura: In what way would I think?

Jim: Why, man alive, Laura! Just look about you a little. What do you see? A world full of common people! All of 'em born and all of 'em going to die! Which of them has one-tenth of your good points! Or mine! Or anyone else's, as far as that goes—Gosh! Everybody excels in some one thing. Some in many! (*Unconsciously glances at himself in the mirror.*) All you've got to do is discover in *what!* Take me, for instance. (*He adjusts his tie at the mirror.*) My interest happens to lie in electrodynamics. I'm taking a course in radio engineering at night school, Laura, on top of a fairly responsible job at the warehouse. I'm taking that course and studying public speaking.

Laura: Ohhhh.

Jim: Because I believe in the future of television! (*Turning back to her.*) I wish to be ready to go up right along with it. Therefore I'm planning to get in on the ground floor. In fact, I've already made the right connections and all that remains is for the industry itself to get under way! Full steam—(*His eyes are starry.*) Knowledge—Zzzzzp! Money—Zzzzzp!—Power! That's the cycle democracy is built on! (*His attitude is convincingly dynamic. Laura stares at him, even her shyness eclipsed in her absolute wonder. He suddenly grins.*) I guess you think I think a lot of myself!

Laura: No—o-o-o, I—

Jim: Now how about you? Isn't there something you take more interest in than anything else?

Laura: Well, I do—as I said—have my—glass collection—

   A peal of girlish laughter from the kitchen.

Jim: I'm not right sure I know what you're talking about. What kind of glass is it?

Laura: Little articles of it, they're ornaments mostly! Most of them are little animals made out of glass, the tiniest little animals in the world. Mother calls them a glass menagerie! Here's an example of one, if you'd like to see it! This one is one of the oldest. It's nearly thirteen. (*He stretches out his hand.*) (**Music: "The Glass Menagerie."**) Oh, be careful—if you breathe, it breaks!

Jim: I'd better not take it. I'm pretty clumsy with things.

Laura: Go on, I trust you with him! (*Places it in his palm.*) There now— you're holding him gently! Hold him over the light, he loves the light! You see how the light shines through him?

Jim: It sure does shine!

Laura: I shouldn't be partial, but he is my favorite one.

Jim: What kind of a thing is this one supposed to be?

Laura: Haven't you noticed the single horn on his forehead?

Jim: A unicorn, huh?

Laura: Mmm-hmmm!

Jim: Unicorns, aren't they extinct in the modern world?

Laura: I know!

Jim: Poor little fellow, he must feel sort of lonesome.

Laura (smiling): Well, if he does he doesn't complain about it. He stays on a shelf with some horses that don't have horns and all of them seem to get along nicely together.

Jim: How do you know?

Laura (lightly): I haven't heard any arguments among them!

Jim (grinning): No arguments, huh? Well, that's a pretty good sign! Where shall I set him?

Laura: Put him on the table. They all like a change of scenery once in a while!

Jim (stretching): Well, well, well, well—Look how big my shadow is when I stretch!

Laura: Oh, oh, yes—it stretches across the ceiling!

Jim (crossing to door): I think it's stopped raining. (*Opens fire-escape door.*) Where does the music come from?

Laura: From the Paradise Dance Hall across the alley.

Jim: How about cutting the rug a little, Miss Wingfield?

Laura: Oh, I—

Jim: Or is your program filled up? Let me have a look at it. (*Grasps imaginary card.*) Why, every dance is taken! I'll just have to scratch some out. (**Waltz Music: "La Golondrina."**) Ahhh, a waltz! (*He executes some sweeping turns by himself, then holds his arms toward Laura.*)

Laura (*breathlessly*): I—can't dance!

Jim: There you go, that inferiority stuff!

Laura: I've never danced in my life!

Jim: Come on, try!

Laura: Oh, but I'd step on you!

Jim: I'm not made out of glass.

Laura: How—how—how do we start?

Jim: Just leave it to me. You hold your arms out a little.

Laura: Like this?

Jim: A little bit higher. Right. Now don't tighten up, that's the main thing about it—relax.

Laura (*laughing breathlessly*): It's hard not to.

Jim: Okay.

Laura: I'm afraid you can't budge me.

Jim: What do you bet I can't? (*He swings her into motion.*)

Laura: Goodness, yes, you can!

Jim: Let yourself go, now, Laura, just let yourself go.

Laura: I'm—

Jim: Come on!

Laura: Trying!

Jim: Not so stiff—Easy does it!

Laura: I know but I'm—

Jim: Loosen th' backbone! There now, that's a lot better.

Laura: Am I?

Jim: Lots, lots better! (*He moves her about the room in a clumsy waltz.*)

Laura: Oh, my!

Jim: Ha-ha!

Laura: Goodness, yes you can!

Jim: Ha-ha-ha! (*They suddenly bump into the table, Jim stops.*) What did we hit on?

Laura: Table.

Jim: Did something fall off it? I think—

Laura: Yes.

Jim: I hope that it wasn't the little glass horse with the horn!

Laura: Yes.

Jim: Aw, aw, aw. Is it broken?

Laura: Now it is just like all the other horses.

Jim: It's lost its—

Laura: Horn! It doesn't matter. Maybe it's a blessing in disguise.

Jim: You'll never forgive me. I bet that that was your favorite piece of glass.

Laura: I don't have favorites much. It's no tragedy, Freckles. Glass breaks so easily. No matter how careful you are. The traffic jars the shelves and things fall off them.

Jim: Still I'm awfully sorry that I was the cause.

Laura (smiling): I'll just imagine he had an operation. The horn was removed to make him feel less—freakish! (*They both laugh.*) Now he will feel more at home with the other horses, the ones that don't have horns . . .

Jim: Ha-ha, that's very funny! (*Suddenly serious.*) I'm glad to see that you have a sense of humor. You know—you're—well—very different! Surprisingly different from anyone else I know! (*His voice becomes soft and hesitant with a genuine feeling.*) Do you mind me telling you that? (*Laura is abashed beyond speech.*) You make me feel sort of—I don't know how to put it! I'm usually pretty good at expressing things, but—This is something that I don't know how to say! (*Laura touches her throat and clears it—turns the broken unicorn in her hands.*) (*Even softer.*) Has anyone ever told you that you were pretty? **(Pause: Music.)** (*Laura looks up slowly, with wonder, and shakes her head.*) Well, you are! In a very different way from anyone else. And all the nicer because of the difference, too. (*His voice becomes low and husky. Laura turns away, nearly faint with the novelty of her emotions.*) I wish you were my sister. I'd teach you to have some confidence in yourself. The different people are not like other people, but being different is nothing to be ashamed of. Because other people are not such wonderful people. They're one hundred times one thousand. You're one times one! They walk all over the earth. You just stay here. They're common as—weeds, but—you—well, you're—*Blue Roses!*

(Image On Screen: Blue Roses.)

(Music Changes.)

Laura: But blue is wrong for—roses . . .

Jim: It's right for you—You're—pretty!

Laura: In what respect am I pretty?

Jim: In all respects—believe me! Your eyes—your hair—are pretty! Your hands are pretty! (*He catches hold of her hand.*) You think I'm making this up because I'm invited to dinner and have to be nice. Oh, I could do that! I could put on an act for you, Laura, and say lots of things without being very sincere. But this time I am. I'm talking to you sincerely. I happened to notice you had this inferiority complex that keeps you from feeling comfortable with people. Somebody needs to build your confidence up and make you proud instead of shy and turning away and—blushing—Somebody ought to—ought to—kiss you, Laura! (*His hand slips slowly up her arm to her shoulder.*) **(Music Swells Tumultuously.)** (*He suddenly turns her about and kisses her on the lips. When he releases her Laura sinks on the sofa with a bright, dazed look. Jim backs away and fishes in his pocket for a cigarette.*) **(Legend On Screen: "Souvenir.")** Stumble-john! (*He lights the cigarette, avoiding her look. There is a peal of girlish laughter from Amanda in the kitchen. Laura slowly raises and opens her hand. It still contains the little broken glass animal. She looks at it with a tender, bewildered expression.*) Stumble-john! I shouldn't have done that—That was way off the beam. You don't smoke, do you? (*She looks up, smiling, not hearing the question. He sits beside her a little gingerly. She looks at him speechlessly—waiting. He coughs decorously and moves a little farther aside as he considers the situation and senses her feelings, dimly, with perturbation. Gently.*) Would you—care for a—mint? (*She doesn't seem to hear him but her look grows brighter even.*) Peppermint—Life Saver? My pocket's a regular drug store—wherever I go . . . (*He pops a mint in his mouth. Then gulps and decides to make a clean breast of it. He speaks slowly and gingerly.*) Laura, you know, if I had a sister like you, I'd do the same thing as Tom, I'd bring out fellows—introduce her to them. The right type of boys of a type to—appreciate her. Only—well—he made a mistake about me. Maybe I've got no call to be saying this. That may not have been the idea in having me over. But what if it was? There's nothing wrong about that. The only trouble is that in my case—I'm not in a situation to—do the right thing. I can't take down your number and say I'll phone. I can't call up next week and—ask for a date. I thought I had better explain the situation in case you misunderstood it and—hurt your feelings. . . . (*Pause. Slowly, very slowly, Laura's look changes, her eyes returning slowly from his to the ornament in her palm.*)

Amanda utters another gay laugh in the kitchen.

Laura (*faintly*): You—won't—call again?

Jim: No, Laura, I can't. (*He rises from the sofa.*) As I was just explaining, I've—got strings on me, Laura, I've—been going steady! I go out all the time with a girl named Betty. She's a home-girl like you, and Catholic, and Irish, and in a great many ways we—get along fine. I met her last summer on a moonlight boat trip up the river to Alton, on the *Majestic*. Well—right away from the start it was—love! **(Legend: Love!)** (*Laura sways slightly forward and grips the arm of the sofa. He fails to notice, now enrapt in his own comfortable being.*) Being in love has made a new man of me! (*Leaning stiffly forward, clutching the arm of the sofa, Laura struggles visibly with her storm. But Jim is oblivious, she is a long way off.*) The power of love is really pretty tremendous! Love is something that—changes the whole world, Laura! (*The storm abates a little and Laura leans back. He notices her again.*) It happened that Betty's aunt took sick, she got a wire and had to go to Centralia. So Tom—when he asked me to dinner—I naturally just accepted the invitation, not knowing that you—that he—that I—(*He stops awkwardly.*) Huh—I'm a stumble-john! (*He flops back on the sofa. The holy candles in the altar of Laura's face have been snuffed out! There is a look of almost infinite desolation. Jim glances at her uneasily.*) I wish that you would—say something. (*She bites her lip which was trembling and then bravely smiles. She opens her hand again on the broken glass ornament. Then she gently takes his hand and raises it level with her own. She carefully places the unicorn in the palm of his hand, then pushes his fingers closed upon it.*) What are you—doing that for? You want me to have him?— Laura? (*She nods.*) What for?

Laura: A—souvenir . . .

She rises unsteadily and crouches beside the victrola to wind it up.

(Legend On Screen: "Things Have A Way Of Turning Out So Badly.")

(Or Image: "Gentleman Caller Waving Good-bye! Gaily.")

At this moment Amanda rushes brightly back in the front room. She bears a pitcher of fruit punch in an old-fashioned cut-glass pitcher and a plate of macaroons. The plate has a gold border and poppies painted on it.

Amanda: Well, well, well! Isn't the air delightful after the shower? I've made you children a little liquid refreshment. (*Turns gaily to the gentleman caller.*) Jim, do you know that song about lemonade?

> "Lemonade, lemonade
> Made in the shade and stirred with a spade—
> Good enough for any old maid!"

Jim (*uneasily*): Ha-ha! No—I never heard it.
Amanda: Why, Laura! You look so serious!
Jim: We were having a serious conversation.

Amanda: Good! Now you're better acquainted!

Jim (*uncertainly*): Ha-ha! Yes.

Amanda: You modern young people are much more serious-minded than my generation. I was so gay as a girl!

Jim: You haven't changed, Mrs. Wingfield.

Amanda: Tonight I'm rejuvenated! The gaiety of the occasion, Mr. O'Connor! (*She tosses her head with a peal of laughter. Spills lemonade.*) Oooo! I'm baptizing myself!

Jim: Here—let me—

Amanda (*setting the pitcher down*): There now. I discovered we had some maraschino cherries. I dumped them in, juice and all!

Jim: You shouldn't have gone to that trouble, Mrs. Wingfield.

Amanda: Trouble, trouble? Why it was loads of fun! Didn't you hear me cutting up in the kitchen? I bet your ears were burning! I told Tom how outdone with him I was for keeping you to himself so long a time! He should have brought you over much, much sooner! Well, now that you've found your way, I want you to be a very frequent caller! Not just occasional but all the time. Oh, we're going to have a lot of gay times together! I see them coming! Mmm, just breathe that air! So fresh, and the moon's so pretty! I'll skip back out—I know where my place is when young folks are having a—serious conversation!

Jim: Oh, don't go out, Mrs. Wingfield. The fact of the matter is I've got to be going.

Amanda: Going, now? You're joking! Why, it's only the shank of the evening, Mr. O'Connor!

Jim: Well, you know how it is.

Amanda: You mean you're a young workingman and have to keep workingmen's hours. We'll let you off early tonight. But only on the condition that next time you stay later. What's the best night for you? Isn't Saturday night the best night for you workingmen?

Jim: I have a couple of time-clocks to punch, Mrs. Wingfield. One at morning, another one at night!

Amanda: My, but you *are* ambitious! You work at night, too?

Jim: No, Ma'am, not work but—Betty! (*He crosses deliberately to pick up his hat. The band at the Paradise Dance Hall goes into a tender waltz.*)

Amanda: Betty? Betty? Who's—Betty? (*There is an ominous cracking sound in the sky.*)

Jim: Oh, just a girl. The girl I go steady with! (*He smiles charmingly. The sky falls.*)

(Legend: "The Sky Falls.")

Amanda (*a long-drawn exhalation*): Ohhhh . . . Is it a serious romance, Mr. O'Connor?

Jim: We're going to be married the second Sunday in June.

Amanda: Ohhhh—how nice! Tom didn't mention that you were engaged to be married.

Jim: The cat's not out of the bag at the warehouse yet. You know how they are. They call you Romeo and stuff like that. (*He stops at the oval mirror to put on his hat. He carefully shapes the brim and the crown to give a discreetly dashing effect.*) It's been a wonderful evening, Mrs. Wingfield. I guess this is what they mean by Southern hospitality.

Amanda: It really wasn't anything at all.

Jim: I hope it don't seem like I'm rushing off. But I promised Betty I'd pick her up at the Wabash depot, an' by the time I get my jalopy down there her train'll be in. Some women are pretty upset if you keep 'em waiting.

Amanda: Yes, I know—The tyranny of women! (*Extends her hand.*) Goodbye, Mr. O'Connor. I wish you luck—and happiness—and success! All three of them, and so does Laura!—Don't you, Laura?

Laura: Yes!

Jim (*taking her hand*): Goodbye, Laura. I'm certainly going to treasure that souvenir. And don't you forget the good advice I gave you. (*Raises his voice to a cheery shout.*) So long, Shakespeare! Thanks again, ladies—Good night!

He grins and ducks jauntily out.

Still bravely grimacing, Amanda closes the door on the gentleman caller. Then she turns back to the room with a puzzled expression. She and Laura don't dare to face each other. Laura crouches beside the victrola to wind it.

Amanda (*faintly*): Things have a way of turning out so badly. I don't believe that I would play the victrola. Well, well—well—Our gentleman caller was engaged to be married! Tom!

Tom (*from back*): Yes, Mother?

Amanda: Come in here a minute. I want to tell you something awfully funny.

Tom (*enters with macaroon and a glass of the lemonade*): Has the gentleman caller gotten away already?

Amanda: The gentleman caller has made an early departure. What a wonderful joke you played on us!

Tom: How do you mean?

Amanda: You didn't mention that he was engaged to be married.

Tom: Jim? Engaged?

Amanda: That's what he just informed us.

Tom: I'll be jiggered! I didn't know about that.

Amanda: That seems very peculiar.

Tom: What's peculiar about it?

Amanda: Didn't you call him your best friend down at the warehouse?

Tom: He is, but how did I know?

Amanda: It seems extremely peculiar that you wouldn't know your best friend was going to be married!

Tom: The warehouse is where I work, not where I know things about people!

Amanda: You don't know things anywhere! You live in a dream; you manufacture illusions! (*He crosses to door.*) Where are you going?

Tom: I'm going to the movies.

Amanda: That's right, now that you've had us make such fools of ourselves. The effort, the preparations, all the expense! The new floor lamp, the rug, the clothes for Laura! All for what? To entertain some other girl's fiancé! Go to the movies, go! Don't think about us, a mother deserted, an unmarried sister who's crippled and has no job! Don't let anything interfere with your selfish pleasure! Just go, go, go—to the movies!

Tom: All right, I will! The more you shout about my selfishness to me the quicker I'll go, and I won't go to the movies!

Amanda: Go, then! Then go to the moon—you selfish dreamer!

Tom smashes his glass on the floor. He plunges out on the fire-escape, slamming the door. Laura screams—cut by door.

Dance-hall music up. Tom goes to the rail and grips it desperately, lifting his face in the chill white moonlight penetrating the narrow abyss of the alley.

(Legend On Screen: "And So Good-bye . . . ")

Tom's closing speech is timed with the interior pantomime. The interior scene is played as though viewed through sound-proof glass. Amanda appears to be making a comforting speech to Laura who is huddled upon the sofa. Now that we cannot hear the mother's speech, her silliness is gone and she has dignity and tragic beauty. Laura's dark hair hides her face until at the end of the speech she lifts it to smile at her mother. Amanda's gestures are slow and graceful, almost dance-like, as she comforts the daughter. At the end of her speech she glances a moment at the father's picture—then withdraws through the portieres. At close of Tom's speech, Laura blows out the candles, ending the play.

Tom: I didn't go to the movies, I went much further—for time is the longest distance between two places—Not long after that I was fired for writing a poem on the lid of a shoe-box. I left Saint Louis. I descended the steps of this fire-escape for a last time and followed, from then on, in my father's footsteps, attempting to find in motion what was lost in space—I traveled around a great deal. The cities swept about me like dead leaves, leaves that were brightly colored but torn away from the branches. I would have stopped, but was pursued by something. It always came upon me unawares, taking me altogether by surprise. Perhaps it was a familiar bit of music. Perhaps it was only a piece of transparent glass. Perhaps I am walking along a street at night, in some strange city, before I have found companions. I pass the lighted window of a shop where perfume is sold. The window is filled with pieces of colored glass, tiny transparent bottles in delicate colors, like bits of a shattered rainbow. Then all at once my sister touches my shoulder. I turn around and look into her eyes. . . Oh, Laura, Laura, I tried to leave you behind me, but I am more faithful than I intended to be! I reach for a cigarette, I cross the street, I run into the movies or a bar, I buy a drink, I speak to the nearest stranger—anything that can blow your candles out! (*Laura bends over the candles.*)—for nowadays the world is lit by lightning! Blow out your candles, Laura—and so good-bye. . . .

She blows the candles out.

(The Scene Dissolves.)

August Wilson

Fences

1983, 1987

*August Wilson was born in Pittsburgh in 1945, one of
six children of a German American father and an
African American mother. His parents separated early,
and the young Wilson was raised on the Hill, a Pittsburgh ghetto neighborhood. Although he quit school
in the ninth grade when a teacher wrongly accused
him of submitting a ghost-written paper, Wilson
continued his education in local libraries, supporting
himself by working as a cook and stock clerk. In
1968 he co-founded a community troupe, the Black
Horizons Theater, staging plays by LeRoi Jones and
other militants; later he moved from Pittsburgh to*

AUGUST WILSON

*Saint Paul, Minnesota, where at last he saw a play of his own performed. Jitney,
his first important work, won him entry to a 1982 playwrights' conference at the
Eugene O'Neill Theater Center. There, Lloyd Richards, dean of Yale University
School of Drama, took an interest in Wilson's work and offered to produce his plays
at Yale. Ma Rainey's Black Bottom was the first to reach Broadway (in 1985),
where it ran for ten months and received an award from the New York Drama
Critics Circle. In 1987 Fences, starring Mary Alice and James Earl Jones, won
another Critics Circle Award, as well as a Tony Award and the Pulitzer Prize for best
American play of its year. It set a box office record for a Broadway nonmusical. Joe
Turner's Come and Gone (1988) also received high acclaim, and The Piano Lesson
(1990) won Wilson a second Pulitzer Prize. His subsequent plays were Two Trains
Running (1992), Seven Guitars (1995), King Hedley II (2000), Gem of the
Ocean (2003), and Radio Golf (2005).*

*Wilson's ten plays, each one set in a different decade of the 1900s, constitute a cy-
cle that traces the black experience in America throughout the twentieth century. Seam-
lessly interweaving realistic and mythic approaches, filled with vivid characters, pungent
dialogue, and strong dramatic scenes, it is one of the most ambitious projects in the history of the American theater and an epic achievement in our literature. Wilson died of
liver cancer in October 2005, a few months after completing the final play in his cycle.
Two weeks after his death the Virginia Theater on Broadway was renamed the August
Wilson Theater in his honor. A published poet as well as a dramatist, Wilson once told
an interviewer, "After writing poetry for twenty-one years, I approach a play the same
way. The mental process is poetic: you use metaphor and condense."*

FOR LLOYD RICHARDS, WHO ADDS TO WHATEVER HE TOUCHES

> *When the sins of our fathers visit us*
> *We do not have to play host.*
> *We can banish them with forgiveness*
> *As God, in His Largeness and Laws.*
>
> —AUGUST WILSON

LIST OF CHARACTERS

Troy Maxson
Jim Bono, Troy's friend
Rose, Troy's wife
Lyons, Troy's oldest son by previous marriage
Gabriel, Troy's brother
Cory, Troy and Rose's son
Raynell, Troy's daughter

SETTING. *The setting is the yard which fronts the only entrance to the Maxson household, an ancient two-story brick house set back off a small alley in a big-city neighborhood. The entrance to the house is gained by two or three steps leading to a wooden porch badly in need of paint.*

A relatively recent addition to the house and running its full width, the porch lacks congruence. It is a sturdy porch with a flat roof. One or two chairs of dubious value sit at one end where the kitchen window opens onto the porch. An old-fashioned icebox stands silent guard at the opposite end.

The yard is a small dirt yard, partially fenced, except for the last scene, with a wooden saw horse, a pile of lumber, and other fence-building equipment set off to the side. Opposite is a tree from which hangs a ball made of rags. A baseball bat leans against the tree. Two oil drums serve as garbage receptacles and sit near the house at right to complete the setting.

THE PLAY. *Near the turn of the century, the destitute of Europe sprang on the city with tenacious claws and an honest and solid dream. The city devoured them. They swelled its belly until it burst into a thousand furnaces and sewing machines, a thousand butcher shops and bakers' ovens, a thousand churches and hospitals and funeral parlors and money-lenders. The city grew. It nourished itself and offered each man a partnership limited only by his talent, his guile, and his willingness and capacity for hard work. For the immigrants of Europe, a dream dared and won true.*

The descendants of African slaves were offered no such welcome or participation. They came from places called the Carolinas and the Virginias, Georgia, Alabama, Mississippi, and Tennessee. They came strong, eager, searching. The city rejected them and they fled and settled along the riverbanks and under bridges in shallow, ramshackle houses made of sticks and tarpaper. They collected rags and wood. They sold the use of their muscles and their bodies. They

Mary Alice and James Earl Jones in Yale Repertory Theater's world premiere of *Fences*

cleaned houses and washed clothes, they shined shoes, and in quiet desperation and vengeful pride, they stole, and lived in pursuit of their own dream. That they could breathe free, finally, and stand to meet life with the force of dignity and whatever eloquence the heart could call upon.

By 1957, the hard-won victories of the European immigrants had solidified the industrial might of America. War had been confronted and won with new energies that used loyalty and patriotism as its fuel. Life was rich, full, and flourishing. The Milwaukee Braves won the World Series, and the hot winds of change that would make the sixties a turbulent, racing, dangerous, and provocative decade had not yet begun to blow full.

ACT I
SCENE I

It is 1957. Troy and Bono enter the yard, engaged in conversation. Troy is fifty-three years old, a large man with thick, heavy hands; it is this largeness that he strives to fill out and make an accommodation with. Together with his blackness, his largeness informs his sensibilities and the choices he has made in his life.

Of the two men, Bono is obviously the follower. His commitment to their friendship of thirty-odd years is rooted in his admiration of Troy's honesty, capacity for hard work, and his strength, which Bono seeks to emulate.

It is Friday night, payday, and the one night of the week the two men engage in a ritual of talk and drink. Troy is usually the most talkative and at times he can be crude and almost vulgar, though he is capable of rising to profound heights of expression. The men carry lunch buckets and wear or carry burlap aprons and are dressed in clothes suitable to their jobs as garbage collectors.

Bono: Troy, you ought to stop that lying!

Troy: I ain't lying! The nigger had a watermelon this big. (*He indicates with his hands.*) Talking about . . . "What watermelon, Mr. Rand?" I liked to fell out! "What watermelon, Mr. Rand?" . . . And it sitting there big as life.

Bono: What did Mr. Rand say?

Troy: Ain't said nothing. Figure if the nigger too dumb to know he carrying a watermelon, he wasn't gonna get much sense out of him. Trying to hide that great big old watermelon under his coat. Afraid to let the white man see him carry it home.

Bono: I'm like you . . . I ain't got no time for them kind of people.

Troy: Now what he look like getting mad cause he see the man from the union talking to Mr. Rand?

Bono: He come to me talking about . . . "Maxson gonna get us fired." I told him to get away from me with that. He walked away from me calling you a troublemaker. What Mr. Rand say?

Troy: Ain't said nothing. He told me to go down the Commissioner's office next Friday. They called me down there to see them.

Bono: Well, as long as you got your complaint filed, they can't fire you. That's what one of them white fellows tell me.

Troy: I ain't worried about them firing me. They gonna fire me cause I asked a question? That's all I did. I went to Mr. Rand and asked him, "Why? Why you got the white mens driving and the colored lifting?" Told him, "what's the matter, don't I count? You think only white fellows got sense enough to drive a truck. That ain't no paper job! Hell, anybody can drive a truck. How come you got all whites driving and the colored lifting?" He told me "take it to the union." Well, hell, that's what I done! Now they wanna come up with this pack of lies.

Bono: I told Brownie if the man come and ask him any questions . . . just tell the truth! It ain't nothing but something they done trumped up on you cause you filed a complaint on them.

Troy: Brownie don't understand nothing. All I want them to do is change the job description. Give everybody a chance to drive the truck. Brownie can't see that. He ain't got that much sense.

Bono: How you figure he be making out with that gal be up at Taylors' all the time . . . that Alberta gal?

Troy: Same as you and me. Getting just as much as we is. Which is to say nothing.

Bono: It is, huh? I figure you doing a little better than me . . . and I ain't saying what I'm doing.

Troy: Aw, nigger, look here . . . I know you. If you had got anywhere near that gal, twenty minutes later you be looking to tell somebody. And the first one you gonna tell . . . that you gonna want to brag to . . . is gonna be me.

Bono: I ain't saying that. I see where you be eyeing her.

Troy: I eye all the women. I don't miss nothing. Don't never let nobody tell you Troy Maxson don't eye the women.

Bono: You been doing more than eyeing her. You done bought her a drink or two.

Troy: Hell yeah, I bought her a drink! What that mean? I bought you one, too. What that mean cause I buy her a drink? I'm just being polite.

Bono: It's alright to buy her one drink. That's what you call being polite. But when you wanna be buying two or three . . . that's what you call eyeing her.

Troy: Look here, as long as you known me . . . you ever known me to chase after women?

Bono: Hell yeah! Long as I done known you. You forgetting I knew you when.

Troy: Naw, I'm talking about since I been married to Rose?

Bono: Oh, not since you been married to Rose. Now, that's the truth, there. I can say that.

Troy: Alright then! Case closed.

Bono: I see you be walking up around Alberta's house. You supposed to be at Taylors' and you be walking up around there.

Troy: What you watching where I'm walking for? I ain't watching after you.

Bono: I seen you walking around there more than once.

Troy: Hell, you liable to see me walking anywhere! That don't mean nothing cause you see me walking around there.

Bono: Where she come from anyway? She just kinda showed up one day.

Troy: Tallahassee. You can look at her and tell she one of them Florida gals. They got some big healthy women down there. Grow them right up out the ground. Got a little bit of Indian in her. Most of them niggers down in Florida got some Indian in them.

Bono: I don't know about that Indian part. But she damn sure big and healthy. Woman wear some big stockings. Got them great big old legs and hips as wide as the Mississippi River.

Troy: Legs don't mean nothing. You don't do nothing but push them out of the way. But them hips cushion the ride!

Bono: Troy, you ain't got no sense.

Troy: It's the truth! Like you riding on Goodyears!

(*Rose enters from the house. She is ten years younger than Troy, her devotion to him stems from her recognition of the possibilities of her life without him: a succession of abusive men and their babies, a life of partying and running the streets, the Church, or aloneness with its attendant pain and frustration. She recognizes Troy's spirit as a fine and illuminating one and she either ignores or forgives his faults, only some of which she recognizes. Though she doesn't drink, her presence is an integral part of the Friday night rituals. She alternates between the porch and the kitchen, where supper preparations are under way.*)

Rose: What you all out here getting into?

Troy: What you worried about what we getting into for? This is men talk, woman.

Rose: What I care what you all talking about? Bono, you gonna stay for supper?

Bono: No, I thank you, Rose. But Lucille say she cooking up a pot of pigfeet.

Troy: Pigfeet! Hell, I'm going home with you! Might even stay the night if you got some pigfeet. You got something in there to top them pigfeet, Rose?

Rose: I'm cooking up some chicken. I got some chicken and collard greens.

Troy: Well, go on back in the house and let me and Bono finish what we was talking about. This is men talk. I got some talk for you later. You know what kind of talk I mean. You go on and powder it up.

Rose: Troy Maxson, don't you start that now!

Troy (*Puts his arm around her.*): Aw, woman . . . come here. Look here, Bono . . . when I met this woman . . . I got out that place, say, "Hitch up my pony, saddle up my mare . . . there's a woman out there for me somewhere. I looked here. Looked there. Saw Rose and latched on to her." I latched on to her and told her—I'm gonna tell you the truth—I told her, "Baby, I don't wanna marry, I just wanna be your man." Rose told me . . . tell him what you told me, Rose.

Rose: I told him if he wasn't the marrying kind, then move out the way so the marrying kind could find me.

Troy: That's what she told me. "Nigger, you in my way. You blocking the view! Move out the way so I can find me a husband." I thought it over two or three days. Come back—

Rose: Ain't no two or three days nothing. You was back the same night.

Troy: Come back, told her . . . "Okay, baby . . . but I'm gonna buy me a banty rooster and put him out there in the backyard . . . and when he see a stranger come, he'll flap his wings and crow . . . " Look here, Bono, I could watch the front door by myself . . . it was that back door I was worried about.

Rose: Troy, you ought not talk like that. Troy ain't doing nothing but telling a lie.

Troy: Only thing is . . . when we first got married . . . forget the rooster . . . we ain't had no yard!

Bono: I hear you tell it. Me and Lucille was staying down there on Logan Street. Had two rooms with the outhouse in the back. I ain't mind the outhouse none. But when that goddamn wind blow through there in the winter . . . that's what I'm talking about! To this day I wonder why in the hell I ever stayed down there for six long years. But see, I didn't know I could do no better. I thought only white folks had inside toilets and things.

Rose: There's a lot of people don't know they can do no better than they doing now. That's just something you got to learn. A lot of folks still shop at Bella's.

Troy: Ain't nothing wrong with shopping at Bella's. She got fresh food.

Rose: I ain't said nothing about if she got fresh food. I'm talking about what she charge. She charge ten cents more than the A&P.

Troy: The A&P ain't never done nothing for me. I spends my money where I'm treated right. I go down to Bella, say, "I need a loaf of bread, I'll pay you Friday." She give it to me. What sense that make when I got money to go and spend it somewhere else and ignore the person who done right by me? That ain't in the Bible.

Rose: We ain't talking about what's in the Bible. What sense it make to shop there when she overcharge?

Troy: You shop where you want to. I'll do my shopping where the people been good to me.

Rose: Well, I don't think it's right for her to overcharge. That's all I was saying.

Bono: Look here . . . I got to get on. Lucille going be raising all kind of hell.

Troy: Where you going, nigger? We ain't finished this pint. Come here, finish this pint.

Bono: Well, hell, I am . . . if you ever turn the bottle loose.

Troy (*Hands him the bottle.*): The only thing I say about the A&P is I'm glad Cory got that job down there. Help him take care of his school clothes and things. Gabe done moved out and things getting tight around here. He got that job . . . He can start to look out for himself.

Rose: Cory done went and got recruited by a college football team.

Troy: I told that boy about that football stuff. The white man ain't gonna let him get nowhere with that football. I told him when he first come to me with it. Now you come telling me he done went and got more tied up in it. He ought to go and get recruited in how to fix cars or something where he can make a living.

Rose: He ain't talking about making no living playing football. It's just something the boys in school do. They gonna send a recruiter by to talk to you. He'll tell you he ain't talking about making no living playing football. It's a honor to be recruited.

Troy: It ain't gonna get him nowhere. Bono'll tell you that.

Bono: If he be like you in the sports . . . he's gonna be alright. Ain't but two men ever played baseball as good as you. That's Babe Ruth and Josh Gibson.° Them's the only two men ever hit more home runs than you.

Troy: What it ever get me? Ain't got a pot to piss in or a window to throw it out of.

Rose: Times have changed since you was playing baseball, Troy. That was before the war. Times have changed a lot since then.

Troy: How in hell they done changed?

Rose: They got lots of colored boys playing ball now. Baseball and football.

Bono: You right about that, Rose. Times have changed, Troy. You just come along too early.

Troy: There ought not never have been no time called too early! Now you take that fellow . . . what's that fellow they had playing right field for the Yankees back then? You know who I'm talking about, Bono. Used to play right field for the Yankees.

Josh Gibson: legendary catcher in the Negro Leagues whose batting average and home-run totals far outstripped Major League records; he died of a stroke at age 35 in January 1947, three months before Jackie Robinson's debut with the Brooklyn Dodgers.

Rose: Selkirk?

Troy: Selkirk!° That's it! Man batting .269, understand? .269. What kind of sense that make? I was hitting .432 with thirty-seven home runs! Man batting .269 and playing right field for the Yankees! I saw Josh Gibson's daughter yesterday. She walking around with raggedy shoes on her feet. Now I bet you Selkirk's daughter ain't walking around with raggedy shoes on her feet! I bet you that!

Rose: They got a lot of colored baseball players now. Jackie Robinson° was the first. Folks had to wait for Jackie Robinson.

Troy: I done seen a hundred niggers play baseball better than Jackie Robinson. Hell, I know some teams Jackie Robinson couldn't even make! What you talking about Jackie Robinson. Jackie Robinson wasn't nobody. I'm talking about if you could play ball then they ought to have let you play. Don't care what color you were. Come telling me I come along too early. If you could play . . . then they ought to have let you play.

(Troy takes a long drink from the bottle.)

Rose: You gonna drink yourself to death. You don't need to be drinking like that.

Troy: Death ain't nothing. I done seen him. Done wrassled with him. You can't tell me nothing about death. Death ain't nothing but a fastball on the outside corner. And you know what I'll do to that! Lookee here, Bono . . . am I lying? You get one of them fastballs, about waist high, over the outside corner of the plate where you can get the meat of the bat on it . . . and good god! You can kiss it good-bye. Now, am I lying?

Bono: Naw, you telling the truth there. I seen you do it.

Troy: If I'm lying . . . that 450 feet worth of lying! (Pause.) That's all death is to me. A fastball on the outside corner.

Rose: I don't know why you want to get on talking about death.

Troy: Ain't nothing wrong with talking about death. That's part of life. Everybody gonna die. You gonna die, I'm gonna die. Bono's gonna die. Hell, we all gonna die.

Rose: But you ain't got to talk about it. I don't like to talk about it.

Troy: You the one brought it up. Me and Bono was talking about baseball . . . you tell me I'm gonna drink myself to death. Ain't that right, Bono? You know I don't drink this but one night out of the

---

Selkirk: Andy Selkirk, Yankee outfielder who hit .269 in 118 games in 1940. *Jackie Robinson:* the first African American to play in major league baseball, joined the Brooklyn Dodgers in 1947.

week. That's Friday night. I'm gonna drink just enough to where I can handle it. Then I cuts it loose. I leave it alone. So don't you worry about me drinking myself to death. 'Cause I ain't worried about Death. I done seen him. I done wrestled with him.

Look here, Bono . . . I looked up one day and Death was marching straight at me. Like Soldiers on Parade! The Army of Death was marching straight at me. The middle of July, 1941. It got real cold just like it be winter. It seem like Death himself reached out and touched me on the shoulder. He touch me just like I touch you. I got cold as ice and Death standing there grinning at me.

Rose: Troy, why don't you hush that talk.

Troy: I say . . . what you want, Mr. Death? You be wanting me? You done brought your army to be getting me? I looked him dead in the eye. I wasn't fearing nothing. I was ready to tangle. Just like I'm ready to tangle now. The Bible say be ever vigilant. That's why I don't get but so drunk. I got to keep watch.

Rose: Troy was right down there in Mercy Hospital. You remember he had pneumonia? Laying there with a fever talking plumb out of his head.

Troy: Death standing there staring at me . . . carrying that sickle in his hand. Finally he say, "You want bound over for another year?" See, just like that . . . "You want bound over for another year?" I told him, "Bound over hell! Let's settle this now!"

It seem like he kinda fell back when I said that, and all the cold went out of me. I reached down and grabbed that sickle and threw it just as far as I could throw it . . . and me and him commenced to wrestling.

We wrestled for three days and three nights. I can't say where I found the strength from. Everytime it seemed like he was gonna get the best of me, I'd reach way down deep inside myself and find the strength to do him one better.

Rose: Everytime Troy tell that story he find different ways to tell it. Different things to make up about it.

Troy: I ain't making up nothing. I'm telling you the facts of what happened. I wrestled with Death for three days and three nights and I'm standing here to tell you about it. (*Pause.*) Alright. At the end of the third night we done weakened each other to where we can't hardly move. Death stood up, throwed on his robe . . . had him a white robe with a hood on it. He throwed on that robe and went off to look for his sickle. Say, "I'll be back." Just like that. "I'll be back." I told him, say, "Yeah, but . . . you gonna have to find me!" I wasn't no fool. I wasn't going looking for him. Death ain't nothing to play with. And I know he's gonna get me. I know I got to join his army . . . his camp followers. But as long as I keep my strength and see him coming . . . as long as I keep up my vigilance . . . he's gonna have to fight to get me. I ain't going easy.

Bono: Well, look here, since you got to keep up your vigilance . . . let me have the bottle.

Troy: Aw hell, I shouldn't have told you that part. I should have left out that part.

Rose: Troy be talking that stuff and half the time don't even know what he be talking about.

Troy: Bono know me better than that.

Bono: That's right. I know you. I know you got some Uncle Remus in your blood. You got more stories than the devil got sinners.

Troy: Aw hell, I done seen him too! Done talked with the devil.

Rose: Troy, don't nobody wanna be hearing all that stuff.

(*Lyons enters the yard from the street. Thirty-four years old, Troy's son by a previous marriage, he sports a neatly trimmed goatee, sport coat, white shirt, tieless and buttoned at the collar. Though he fancies himself a musician, he is more caught up in the rituals and "idea" of being a musician than in the actual practice of the music. He has come to borrow money from Troy, and while he knows he will be successful, he is uncertain as to what extent his lifestyle will be held up to scrutiny and ridicule.*)

Lyons: Hey, Pop.

Troy: What you come "Hey, Popping" me for?

Lyons: How you doing, Rose? (*He kisses her.*) Mr. Bono. How you doing?

Bono: Hey, Lyons . . . how you been?

Troy: He must have been doing alright. I ain't seen him around here last week.

Rose: Troy, leave your boy alone. He come by to see you and you wanna start all that nonsense.

Troy: I ain't bothering Lyons. (*Offers him the bottle.*) Here . . . get you a drink. We got an understanding. I know why he come by to see me and he know I know.

Lyons: Come on, Pop . . . I just stopped by to say hi . . . see how you was doing.

Troy: You ain't stopped by yesterday.

Rose: You gonna stay for supper, Lyons? I got some chicken cooking in the oven.

Lyons: No, Rose . . . thanks. I was just in the neighborhood and thought I'd stop by for a minute.

Troy: You was in the neighborhood alright, nigger. You telling the truth there. You was in the neighborhood cause it's my payday.

Lyons: Well, hell, since you mentioned it . . . let me have ten dollars.

Troy: I'll be damned! I'll die and go to hell and play blackjack with the devil before I give you ten dollars.

Bono: That's what I wanna know about . . . that devil you done seen.

Lyons: What . . . Pop done seen the devil? You too much, Pops.

Troy: Yeah, I done seen him. Talked to him too!

Rose: You ain't seen no devil. I done told you that man ain't had nothing to do with the devil. Anything you can't understand, you want to call it the devil.

Troy: Look here, Bono . . . I went down to see Hertzberger about some furniture. Got three rooms for two-ninety-eight. That what it say on the radio. "Three rooms . . . two-ninety-eight." Even made up a little song about it. Go down there . . . man tell me I can't get no credit. I'm working every day and can't get no credit. What to do? I got an empty house with some raggedy furniture in it. Cory ain't got no bed. He's sleeping on a pile of rags on the floor. Working every day and can't get no credit. Come back here—Rose'll tell you—madder than hell. Sit down . . . try to figure what I'm gonna do. Come a knock on the door. Ain't been living here but three days. Who know I'm here? Open the door . . . devil standing there bigger than life. White fellow . . . got on good clothes and everything. Standing there with a clipboard in his hand. I ain't had to say nothing. First words come out of his mouth was . . . "I understand you need some furniture and can't get no credit." I liked to fell over. He say "I'll give you all the credit you want, but you got to pay the interest on it." I told him, "Give me three rooms worth and charge whatever you want." Next day a truck pulled up here and two men unloaded them three rooms. Man what drove the truck give me a book. Say send ten dollars, first of every month to the address in the book and every thing will be alright. Say if I miss a payment the devil was coming back and it'll be hell to pay. That was fifteen years ago. To this day . . . the first of the month I send my ten dollars, Rose'll tell you.

Rose: Troy lying.

Troy: I ain't never seen that man since. Now you tell me who else that could have been but the devil? I ain't sold my soul or nothing like that, you understand. Naw, I wouldn't have truck with the devil about nothing like that. I got my furniture and pays my ten dollars the first of the month just like clockwork.

Bono: How long you say you been paying this ten dollars a month?

Troy: Fifteen years!

Bono: Hell, ain't you finished paying for it yet? How much the man done charged you?

Troy: Aw hell, I done paid for it. I done paid for it ten times over! The fact is I'm scared to stop paying it.

Rose: Troy lying. We got that furniture from Mr. Glickman. He ain't paying no ten dollars a month to nobody.

Troy: Aw hell, woman. Bono know I ain't that big a fool.

Lyons: I was just getting ready to say . . . I know where there's a bridge for sale.

Troy: Look here, I'll tell you this . . . it don't matter to me if he was the devil. It don't matter if the devil give credit. Somebody has got to give it.

Rose: It ought to matter. You going around talking about having truck with the devil . . . God's the one you gonna have to answer to. He's the one gonna be at the Judgment.

Lyons: Yeah, well, look here, Pop . . . Let me have that ten dollars. I'll give it back to you. Bonnie got a job working at the hospital.

Troy: What I tell you, Bono? The only time I see this nigger is when he wants something. That's the only time I see him.

Lyons: Come on, Pop, Mr. Bono don't want to hear all that. Let me have the ten dollars. I told you Bonnie working.

Troy: What that mean to me? "Bonnie working." I don't care if she working. Go ask her for the ten dollars if she working. Talking about "Bonnie working." Why ain't you working?

Lyons: Aw, Pop, you know I can't find no decent job. Where am I gonna get a job at? You know I can't get no job.

Troy: I told you I know some people down there. I can get you on the rubbish if you want to work. I told you that the last time you came by here asking me for something.

Lyons: Naw, Pop . . . thanks. That ain't for me. I don't wanna be carry-ing nobody's rubbish. I don't wanna be punching nobody's time clock.

Troy: What's the matter, you too good to carry people's rubbish? Where you think that ten dollars you talking about come from? I'm just sup-posed to haul people's rubbish and give my money to you cause you too lazy to work. You too lazy to work and wanna know why you ain't got what I got.

Rose: What hospital Bonnie working at? Mercy?

Lyons: She's down at Passavant working in the laundry.

Troy: I ain't got nothing as it is. I give you that ten dollars and I got to eat beans the rest of the week. Naw . . . you ain't getting no ten dollars here.

Lyons: You ain't got to be eating no beans. I don't know why you wanna say that.

Troy: I ain't got no extra money. Gabe done moved over to Miss Pearl's paying her the rent and things done got tight around here. I can't afford to be giving you every payday.

Lyons: I ain't asked you to give me nothing. I asked you to loan me ten dollars. I know you got ten dollars.

Troy: Yeah, I got it. You know why I got it? Cause I don't throw my money away out there in the streets. You living the fast life . . . wanna be a musician . . . running around in them clubs and things . . . then, you learn to take care of yourself. You ain't gonna find me going and asking nobody for nothing. I done spent too many years without.

Lyons: You and me is two different people, Pop.

Troy: I done learned my mistake and learned to do what's right by it. You still trying to get something for nothing. Life don't owe you nothing. You owe it to yourself. Ask Bono. He'll tell you I'm right.

Lyons: You got your way of dealing with the world . . . I got mine. The only thing that matters to me is the music.

Troy: Yeah, I can see that! It don't matter how you gonna eat . . . where your next dollar is coming from. You telling the truth there.

Lyons: I know I got to eat. But I got to live too. I need something that gonna help me to get out of the bed in the morning. Make me feel like I belong in the world. I don't bother nobody. I just stay with my music cause that's the only way I can find to live in the world. Otherwise there ain't no telling what I might do. Now I don't come criticizing you and how you live. I just come by to ask you for ten dollars. I don't wanna hear all that about how I live.

Troy: Boy, your mama did a hell of a job raising you.

Lyons: You can't change me, Pop. I'm thirty-four years old. If you wanted to change me, you should have been there when I was growing up. I come by to see you . . . ask for ten dollars and you want to talk about how I was raised. You don't know nothing about how I was raised.

Rose: Let the boy have ten dollars, Troy.

Troy (To Lyons.): What the hell you looking at me for? I ain't got no ten dollars. You know what I do with my money. (*To Rose.*) Give him ten dollars if you want him to have it.

Rose: I will. Just as soon as you turn it loose.

Troy (Handing Rose the money.): There it is. Seventy-six dollars and forty-two cents. You see this, Bono? Now, I ain't gonna get but six of that back.

Rose: You ought to stop telling that lie. Here, Lyons. (*She hands him the money.*)

Lyons: Thanks, Rose. Look . . . I got to run . . . I'll see you later.

Troy: Wait a minute. You gonna say, "thanks, Rose" and ain't gonna look to see where she got that ten dollars from? See how they do me, Bono?

Lyons: I know she got it from you, Pop. Thanks. I'll give it back to you.

Troy: There he go telling another lie. Time I see that ten dollars . . . he'll be owing me thirty more.

Lyons: See you, Mr. Bono.

Bono: Take care, Lyons!

Lyons: Thanks, Pop. I'll see you again.

(*Lyons exits the yard.*)

Troy: I don't know why he don't go and get him a decent job and take care of that woman he got.

Bono: He'll be alright, Troy. The boy is still young.

Troy: The boy is thirty-four years old.

Rose: Let's not get off into all that.

Bono: Look here . . . I got to be going. I got to be getting on. Lucille gonna be waiting.

Troy (Puts his arm around Rose.): See this woman, Bono? I love this woman. I love this woman so much it hurts. I love her so much . . . I done run out of ways of loving her. So I got to go back to basics. Don't you come by my house Monday morning talking about time to go to work . . . 'cause I'm still gonna be stroking!

Rose: Troy! Stop it now!

Bono: I ain't paying him no mind, Rose. That ain't nothing but gin-talk. Go on, Troy. I'll see you Monday.

Troy: Don't you come by my house, nigger! I done told you what I'm gonna be doing.

(*The lights go down to black.*)

SCENE II

The lights come up on Rose hanging up clothes. She hums and sings softly to herself. It is the following morning.

Rose (Sings.):

> Jesus, be a fence all around me every day
> Jesus, I want you to protect me as I travel on my way.
> Jesus, be a fence all around me every day.

(*Troy enters from the house.*)

      Jesus, I want you to protect me
      As I travel on my way.
(*To Troy.*) 'Morning. You ready for breakfast? I can fix it soon as I finish hanging up these clothes.

Troy: I got the coffee on. That'll be alright. I'll just drink some of that this morning.

Rose: That 651 hit yesterday. That's the second time this month. Miss Pearl hit for a dollar . . . seem like those that need the least always get lucky. Poor folks can't get nothing.

Troy: Them numbers don't know nobody. I don't know why you fool with them. You and Lyons both.

Rose: It's something to do.

Troy: You ain't doing nothing but throwing your money away.

Rose: Troy, you know I don't play foolishly. I just play a nickel here and a nickel there.

Troy: That's two nickels you done thrown away.

Rose: Now I hit sometimes . . . that makes up for it. It always comes in handy when I do hit. I don't hear you complaining then.

Troy: I ain't complaining now. I just say it's foolish. Trying to guess out of six hundred ways which way the number gonna come. If I had all the money niggers, these Negroes, throw away on numbers for one week—just one week—I'd be a rich man.

Rose: Well, you wishing and calling it foolish ain't gonna stop folks from playing numbers. That's one thing for sure. Besides . . . some good things come from playing numbers. Look where Pope done bought him that restaurant off of numbers.

Troy: I can't stand niggers like that. Man ain't had two dimes to rub together. He walking around with his shoes all run over bumming money for cigarettes. Alright. Got lucky there and hit the numbers . . .

Rose: Troy, I know all about it.

Troy: Had good sense, I'll say that for him. He ain't throwed his money away. I seen niggers hit the numbers and go through two thousand dollars in four days. Man bought him that restaurant down there . . . fixed it up real nice . . . . and then didn't want nobody to come in it! A Negro go in there and can't get no kind of service. I seen a white fellow come in there and order a bowl of stew. Pope picked all the meat out of the pot for him. Man ain't had nothing but a bowl of meat! Negro come behind him and ain't got nothing but the potatoes and carrots. Talking about what numbers do for people, you picked a wrong example. Ain't done nothing but make a worser fool out of him than he was before.

Rose: Troy, you ought to stop worrying about what happened at work yesterday.

Troy: I ain't worried. Just told me to be down there at the Commissioner's office on Friday. Everybody think they gonna fire me. I ain't worried about them firing me. You ain't got to worry about that. (*Pause.*) Where's Cory? Cory in the house? (*Calls.*) Cory?

Rose: He gone out.

Troy: Out, huh? He gone out 'cause he know I want him to help me with this fence. I know how he is. That boy scared of work.

(*Gabriel enters. He comes halfway down the alley and, hearing Troy's voice, stops.*)

Troy (*Continues.*): He ain't done a lick of work in his life.

Rose: He had to go to football practice. Coach wanted them to get in a little extra practice before the season start.

Troy: I got his practice . . . running out of here before he get his chores done.

Rose: Troy, what is wrong with you this morning? Don't nothing set right with you. Go on back in there and go to bed . . . get up on the other side.

Troy: Why something got to be wrong with me? I ain't said nothing wrong with me.

Rose: You got something to say about everything. First it's the numbers . . . then it's the way the man runs his restaurant . . . then you done got on Cory. What's it gonna be next? Take a look up there and see if the weather suits you . . . or is it gonna be how you gonna put up the fence with the clothes hanging in the yard?

Troy: You hit the nail on the head then.

Rose: I know you like I know the back of my hand. Go on in there and get you some coffee . . . see if that straighten you up. 'Cause you ain't right this morning.

(*Troy starts into the house and sees Gabriel. Gabriel starts singing. Troy's brother, he is seven years younger than Troy. Injured in World War II, he has a metal plate in his head. He carries an old trumpet tied around his waist and believes with every fiber of his being that he is the Archangel Gabriel. He carries a chipped basket with an assortment of discarded fruits and vegetables he has picked up in the strip district and which he attempts to sell.*)

Gabriel (*Singing.*):
        Yes, ma'am, I got plums
        You ask me how I sell them
        Oh ten cents apiece

> Three for a quarter
> Come and buy now
> 'Cause I'm here today
> And tomorrow I'll be gone

(*Gabriel enters.*)

Hey, Rose!

Rose: How you doing, Gabe?

Gabriel: There's Troy . . . Hey, Troy!

Troy: Hey, Gabe.

(*Exit into kitchen.*)

Rose (*To Gabriel.*): What you got there?

Gabriel: You know what I got, Rose. I got fruits and vegetables.

Rose (*Looking in basket.*): Where's all these plums you talking about?

Gabriel: I ain't got no plums today, Rose. I was just singing that. Have some tomorrow. Put me in a big order for plums. Have enough plums tomorrow for St. Peter and everybody.

(*Troy reenters from kitchen, crosses to steps.*)

(*To Rose.*) Troy's mad at me.

Troy: I ain't mad at you. What I got to be mad at you about? You ain't done nothing to me.

Gabriel: I just moved over to Miss Pearl's to keep out from in your way. I ain't mean no harm by it.

Troy: Who said anything about that? I ain't said anything about that.

Gabriel: You ain't mad at me, is you?

Troy: Naw . . . I ain't mad at you, Gabe. If I was mad at you I'd tell you about it.

Gabriel: Got me two rooms. In the basement. Got my own door too. Wanna see my key? (*He holds up a key.*) That's my own key! Ain't nobody else got a key like that. That's my key! My two rooms!

Troy: Well, that's good, Gabe. You got your own key . . . that's good.

Rose: You hungry, Gabe? I was just fixing to cook Troy his breakfast.

Gabriel: I'll take some biscuits. You got some biscuits? Did you know when I was in heaven . . . every morning me and St. Peter would sit down by the gate and eat some big fat biscuits? Oh, yeah! We had us a good time. We'd sit there and eat us them biscuits and then St. Peter would go off to sleep and tell me to wake him up when it's time to open the gates for the judgment.

Rose: Well, come on . . . I'll make up a batch of biscuits.

(*Rose exits into the house.*)

Gabriel: Troy . . . St. Peter got your name in the book. I seen it. It say . . .
Troy Maxson. I say . . . I know him! He got the same name like what
I got. That's my brother!

Troy: How many times you gonna tell me that, Gabe?

Gabriel: Ain't got my name in the book. Don't have to have my name. I
done died and went to heaven. He got your name though. One
morning St. Peter was looking at his book . . . marking it up for the
judgment . . . and he let me see your name. Got it in there under
M. Got Rose's name . . . I ain't seen it like I seen yours . . . but I know
it's in there. He got a great big book. Got everybody's name what
was ever been born. That's what he told me. But I seen your name.
Seen it with my own eyes.

Troy: Go on in the house there. Rose going to fix you something to eat.

Gabriel: Oh, I ain't hungry. I done had breakfast with Aunt Jemimah.
She come by and cooked me up a whole mess of flapjacks. Remember how we used to eat them flapjacks?

Troy: Go on in the house and get you something to eat now.

Gabriel: I got to sell my plums. I done sold some tomatoes. Got me two
quarters. Wanna see? (*He shows Troy his quarters.*) I'm gonna save
them and buy me a new horn so St. Peter can hear me when it's time
to open the gates. (*Gabriel stops suddenly. Listens.*) Hear that? That's
the hellhounds. I got to chase them out of here. Go on get out of
here! Get out!

(*Gabriel exits singing.*)

> Better get ready for the judgment
> Better get ready for the judgment
> My Lord is coming down

(*Rose enters from the house.*)

Troy: He gone off somewhere.

Gabriel (Offstage.):
> Better get ready for the judgment
> Better get ready for the judgment morning
> Better get ready for the judgment
> My God is coming down

Rose: He ain't eating right. Miss Pearl say she can't get him to eat
nothing.

Troy: What you want me to do about it, Rose? I done did everything I
can for the man. I can't make him get well. Man got half his head
blown away . . . what you expect?

Rose: Seem like something ought to be done to help him.

Troy: Man don't bother nobody. He just mixed up from that metal plate he got in his head. Ain't no sense for him to go back into the hospital.

Rose: Least he be eating right. They can help him take care of himself.

Troy: Don't nobody wanna be locked up, Rose. What you wanna lock him up for? Man go over there and fight the war . . . messin' around with them Japs, get half his head blown off . . . and they give him a lousy three thousand dollars. And I had to swoop down on that.

Rose: Is you fixing to go into that again?

Troy: That's the only way I got a roof over my head . . . cause of that metal plate.

Rose: Ain't no sense you blaming yourself for nothing. Gabe wasn't in no condition to manage that money. You done what was right by him. Can't nobody say you ain't done what was right by him. Look how long you took care of him . . . till he wanted to have his own place and moved over there with Miss Pearl.

Troy: That ain't what I'm saying, woman! I'm just stating the facts. If my brother didn't have that metal plate in his head . . . I wouldn't have a pot to piss in or a window to throw it out of. And I'm fifty-three years old. Now see if you can understand that!

(Troy gets up from the porch and starts to exit the yard.)

Rose: Where you going off to? You been running out of here every Saturday for weeks. I thought you was gonna work on this fence?

Troy: I'm gonna walk down to Taylors'. Listen to the ball game. I'll be back in a bit. I'll work on it when I get back.

(He exits the yard. The lights go to black.)

SCENE III

The lights come up on the yard. It is four hours later. Rose is taking down the clothes from the line. Cory enters carrying his football equipment.

Rose: Your daddy like to had a fit with you running out of here this morning without doing your chores.

Cory: I told you I had to go to practice.

Rose: He say you were supposed to help him with this fence.

Cory: He been saying that the last four or five Saturdays, and then he don't never do nothing, but go down to Taylors'. Did you tell him about the recruiter?

Rose: Yeah, I told him.

Cory: What he say?

Rose: He ain't said nothing too much. You get in there and get started on your chores before he gets back. Go on and scrub down them steps before he gets back here hollering and carrying on.

Cory: I'm hungry. What you got to eat, Mama?

Rose: Go on and get started on your chores. I got some meat loaf in there. Go on and make you a sandwich . . . and don't leave no mess in there.

(*Cory exits into the house. Rose continues to take down the clothes. Troy enters the yard and sneaks up and grabs her from behind.*)

Troy! Go on, now. You liked to scared me to death. What was the score of the game? Lucille had me on the phone and I couldn't keep up with it.

Troy: What I care about the game? Come here, woman. (*He tries to kiss her.*)

Rose: I thought you went down Taylors' to listen to the game. Go on, Troy! You supposed to be putting up this fence.

Troy (*Attempting to kiss her again.*): I'll put it up when I finish with what is at hand.

Rose: Go on, Troy. I ain't studying you.

Troy (*Chasing after her.*): I'm studying you . . . fixing to do my home-work!

Rose: Troy, you better leave me alone.

Troy: Where's Cory? That boy brought his butt home yet?

Rose: He's in the house doing his chores.

Troy (*Calling.*): Cory! Get your butt out here, boy!

(*Rose exits into the house with the laundry. Troy goes over to the pile of wood, picks up a board, and starts sawing. Cory enters from the house.*)

Troy: You just now coming in here from leaving this morning?

Cory: Yeah, I had to go to football practice.

Troy: Yeah, what?

Cory: Yessir.

Troy: I ain't but two seconds off you noway. The garbage sitting in there overflowing . . . you ain't done none of your chores . . . and you come in here talking about "Yeah."

Cory: I was just getting ready to do my chores now, Pop . . .

Troy: Your first chore is to help me with this fence on Saturday. Every-thing else come after that. Now get that saw and cut them boards.

(*Cory takes the saw and begins cutting the boards. Troy continues work-ing. There is a long pause.*)

Cory: Hey, Pop . . . why don't you buy a TV?

Troy: What I want with a TV? What I want one of them for?

Cory: Everybody got one. Earl, Ba Bra . . . Jesse!

Troy: I ain't asked you who had one. I say what I want with one?

Cory: So you can watch it. They got lots of things on TV. Baseball games and everything. We could watch the World Series.

Troy: Yeah . . . and how much this TV cost?

Cory: I don't know. They got them on sale for around two hundred dollars.

Troy: Two hundred dollars, huh?

Cory: That ain't that much, Pop.

Troy: Naw, it's just two hundred dollars. See that roof you got over your head at night? Let me tell you something about that roof. It's been over ten years since that roof was last tarred. See now . . . the snow come this winter and sit up there on that roof like it is . . . and it's gonna seep inside. It's just gonna be a little bit . . . ain't gonna hardly notice it. Then the next thing you know, it's gonna be leaking all over the house. Then the wood rot from all that water and you gonna need a whole new roof. Now, how much you think it cost to get that roof tarred?

Cory: I don't know.

Troy: Two hundred and sixty-four dollars . . . cash money. While you thinking about a TV, I got to be thinking about the roof . . . and whatever else go wrong here. Now if you had two hundred dollars, what would you do . . . fix the roof or buy a TV?

Cory: I'd buy a TV. Then when the roof started to leak . . . when it needed fixing . . . I'd fix it.

Troy: Where you gonna get the money from? You done spent it for a TV. You gonna sit up and watch the water run all over your brand new TV.

Cory: Aw, Pop. You got money. I know you do.

Troy: Where I got it at, huh?

Cory: You got it in the bank.

Troy: You wanna see my bankbook? You wanna see that seventy-three dollars and twenty-two cents I got sitting up in there?

Cory: You ain't got to pay for it all at one time. You can put a down payment on it and carry it on home with you.

Troy: Not me. I ain't gonna owe nobody nothing if I can help it. Miss a payment and they come and snatch it right out of your house. Then what you got? Now, soon as I get two hundred dollars clear, then I'll buy a TV. Right now, as soon as I get two hundred and sixty-four dollars, I'm gonna have this roof tarred.

Cory: Aw . . . Pop!

Troy: You go on and get you two hundred dollars and buy one if ya want it. I got better things to do with my money.

Cory: I can't get no two hundred dollars. I ain't never seen two hundred dollars.

Troy: I'll tell you what . . . you get you a hundred dollars and I'll put the other hundred with it.

Cory: Alright, I'm gonna show you.

Troy: You gonna show me how you can cut them boards right now.

(*Cory begins to cut the boards. There is a long pause.*)

Cory: The Pirates won today. That makes five in a row.

Troy: I ain't thinking about the Pirates. Got an all-white team. Got that boy . . . that Puerto Rican boy . . . Clemente.° Don't even half-play him. That boy could be something if they give him a chance. Play him one day and sit him on the bench the next.

Cory: He gets a lot of chances to play.

Troy: I'm talking about playing regular. Playing every day so you can get your timing. That's what I'm talking about.

Cory: They got some white guys on the team that don't play every day. You can't play everybody at the same time.

Troy: If they got a white fellow sitting on the bench . . . you can bet your last dollar he can't play! The colored guy got to be twice as good before he get on the team. That's why I don't want you to get all tied up in them sports. Man on the team and what it get him? They got colored on the team and don't use them. Same as not having them. All them teams the same.

Cory: The Braves got Hank Aaron and Wes Covington. Hank Aaron hit two home runs today. That makes forty-three.

Troy: Hank Aaron ain't nobody. That's what you supposed to do. That's how you supposed to play the game. Ain't nothing to it. It's just a matter of timing . . . getting the right follow-through. Hell, I can hit forty-three home runs right now!

Cory: Not off no major-league pitching, you couldn't.

Troy: We had better pitching in the Negro leagues. I hit seven home runs off of Satchel Paige.° You can't get no better than that!

Cory: Sandy Koufax.° He's leading the league in strikeouts.

Troy: I ain't thinking of no Sandy Koufax.

Clemente: Hall of Fame outfielder Roberto Clemente, a dark-skinned Puerto Rican, played 17 seasons with the Pittsburgh Pirates. *Satchel Paige . . . Sandy Koufax . . .*

Cory: You got Warren Spahn° and Lew Burdette.° I bet you couldn't hit no home runs off of Warren Spahn.

Troy: I'm through with it now. You go on and cut them boards. (*Pause.*) Your mama tell me you done got recruited by a college football team? Is that right?

Cory: Yeah. Coach Zellman say the recruiter gonna be coming by to talk to you. Get you to sign the permission papers.

Troy: I thought you supposed to be working down there at the A&P. Ain't you suppose to be working down there after school?

Cory: Mr. Stawicki say he gonna hold my job for me until after the football season. Say starting next week I can work weekends.

Troy: I thought we had an understanding about this football stuff? You suppose to keep up with your chores and hold that job down at the A&P. Ain't been around here all day on a Saturday. Ain't none of your chores done . . . and now you telling me you done quit your job.

Cory: I'm going to be working weekends.

Troy: You damn right you are! And ain't no need for nobody coming around here to talk to me about signing nothing.

Cory: Hey, Pop . . . you can't do that. He's coming all the way from North Carolina.

Troy: I don't care where he coming from. The white man ain't gonna let you get nowhere with that football noway. You go on and get your book-learning so you can work yourself up in that A&P or learn how to fix cars or build houses or something, get you a trade. That way you have something can't nobody take away from you. You go on and learn how to put your hands to some good use. Besides hauling people's garbage.

Cory: I get good grades, Pop. That's why the recruiter wants to talk with you. You got to keep up your grades to get recruited. This way I'll be going to college. I'll get a chance . . .

Troy: First you gonna get your butt down there to the A&P and get your job back.

Cory: Mr. Stawicki done already hired somebody else 'cause I told him I was playing football.

Troy: You a bigger fool than I thought . . . to let somebody take away your job so you can play some football. Where you gonna get your money to take out your girlfriend and whatnot? What kind of fool-ishness is that to let somebody take away your job?

Warren Spahn . . . Lew Burdette: The great Satchel Paige pitched many years in the Negro Leagues; beginning in 1948, when he was in his forties and long past his prime, he appeared in nearly 200 games in the American League. Star pitchers Sandy Koufax of the Dodgers and Warren Spahn and Lew Burdette of the Braves were all white.

Cory: I'm still gonna be working weekends.

Troy: Naw . . . naw. You getting your butt out of here and finding you another job.

Cory: Come on, Pop! I got to practice. I can't work after school and play football too. The team needs me. That's what Coach Zellman say . . .

Troy: I don't care what nobody else say. I'm the boss . . . you understand? I'm the boss around here. I do the only saying what counts.

Cory: Come on, Pop!

Troy: I asked you . . . did you understand?

Cory: Yeah . . .

Troy: What?!

Cory: Yessir.

Troy: You go on down there to that A&P and see if you can get your job back. If you can't do both . . . then you quit the football team. You've got to take the crookeds with the straights.

Cory: Yessir. (*Pause.*) Can I ask you a question?

Troy: What the hell you wanna ask me? Mr. Stawicki the one you got the questions for.

Cory: How come you ain't never liked me?

Troy: Liked you? Who the hell say I got to like you? What law is there say I got to like you? Wanna stand up in my face and ask a damn fool-ass question like that. Talking about liking somebody. Come here, boy, when I talk to you.

(*Cory comes over to where Troy is working. He stands slouched over and Troy shoves him on his shoulder.*)

Straighten up, goddammit! I asked you a question . . . what law is there say I got to like you?

Cory: None.

Troy: Well, alright then! Don't you eat every day? (*Pause.*) Answer me when I talk to you! Don't you eat every day?

Cory: Yeah.

Troy: Nigger, as long as you in my house, you put that sir on the end of it when you talk to me.

Cory: Yes . . . sir.

Troy: You eat every day.

Cory: Yessir!

Troy: Got a roof over your head.

Cory: Yessir!

Troy: Got clothes on your back.

Cory: Yessir.

Troy: Why you think that is?

Cory: Cause of you.

Troy: Aw, hell I know it's 'cause of me . . . but why do you think that is?

Cory (Hesitant.): Cause you like me.

Troy: Like you? I go out of here every morning . . . bust my butt . . . putting up with them crackers every day . . . cause I like you? You about the biggest fool I ever saw. (*Pause.*) It's my job. It's my responsibility! You understand that? A man got to take care of his family. You live in my house . . . sleep you behind on my bedclothes . . . fill you belly up with my food . . . cause you my son. You my flesh and blood. Not 'cause I like you! Cause it's my duty to take care of you. I owe a responsibility to you!

Let's get this straight right here . . . before it go along any further . . . I ain't got to like you. Mr. Rand don't give me my money come payday cause he likes me. He gives me cause he owe me. I done give you everything I had to give you. I gave you your life! Me and your mama worked that out between us. And liking your black ass wasn't part of the bargain. Don't you try and go through life worrying about if somebody like you or not. You best be making sure they doing right by you. You understand what I'm saying, boy?

Cory: Yessir.

Troy: Then get the hell out of my face, and get on down to that A&P.

(*Rose has been standing behind the screen door for much of the scene. She enters as Cory exits.*)

Rose: Why don't you let the boy go ahead and play football, Troy? Ain't no harm in that. He's just trying to be like you with the sports.

Troy: I don't want him to be like me! I want him to move as far away from my life as he can get. You the only decent thing that ever happened to me. I wish him that. But I don't wish him a thing else from my life. I decided seventeen years ago that boy wasn't getting involved in no sports. Not after what they did to me in the sports.

Rose: Troy, why don't you admit you was too old to play in the major leagues? For once . . . why don't you admit that?

Troy: What do you mean too old? Don't come telling me I was too old. I just wasn't the right color. Hell, I'm fifty-three years old and can do better than Selkirk's .269 right now!

Rose: How's was you gonna play ball when you were over forty? Sometimes I can't get no sense out of you.

Troy: I got good sense, woman. I got sense enough not to let my boy get hurt over playing no sports. You been mothering that boy too much. Worried about if people like him.

Rose: Everything that boy do . . . he do for you. He wants you to say "Good job, son." That's all.

Troy: Rose, I ain't got time for that. He's alive. He's healthy. He's got to make his own way. I made mine. Ain't nobody gonna hold his hand when he get out there in that world.

Rose: Times have changed from when you was young, Troy. People change. The world's changing around you and you can't even see it.

Troy (Slow, methodical.): Woman . . . I do the best I can do. I come in here every Friday. I carry a sack of potatoes and a bucket of lard. You all line up at the door with your hands out. I give you the lint from my pockets. I give you my sweat and my blood. I ain't got no tears. I done spent them. We go upstairs in that room at night . . . and I fall down on you and try to blast a hole into forever. I get up Monday morning . . . find my lunch on the table. I go out. Make my way. Find my strength to carry me through to the next Friday. *(Pause.)* That's all I got, Rose. That's all I got to give. I can't give nothing else.

(Troy exits into the house. The lights go down to black.)

SCENE IV

It is Friday. Two weeks later. Cory starts out of the house with his football equipment. The phone rings.

Cory (Calling.): I got it! *(He answers the phone and stands in the screen door talking.)* Hello? Hey, Jesse. Naw . . . I was just getting ready to leave now.

Rose (Calling.): Cory!

Cory: I told you, man, them spikes is all tore up. You can use them if you want, but they ain't no good. Earl got some spikes.

Rose (Calling.): Cory!

Cory (Calling to Rose.): Mam? I'm talking to Jesse. *(Into phone.)* When she say that? *(Pause.)* Aw, you lying, man. I'm gonna tell her you said that.

Rose (Calling.): Cory, don't you go nowhere!

Cory: I got to go to the game, Ma! *(Into the phone.)* Yeah, hey, look, I'll talk to you later. Yeah, I'll meet you over Earl's house. Later. Bye, Ma.

(Cory exits the house and starts out the yard.)

Rose: Cory, where you going off to? You got that stuff all pulled out and thrown all over your room.

Cory (In the yard.): I was looking for my spikes. Jesse wanted to borrow my spikes.

Rose: Get up there and get that cleaned up before your daddy get back in here.

Cory: I got to go to the game! I'll clean it up *when* I get back.

(*Cory exits.*)

Rose: That's all he need to do is see that room all messed up.

(*Rose exits into the house. Troy and Bono enter the yard. Troy is dressed in clothes other than his work clothes.*)

Bono: He told him the same thing he told you. Take it to the union.

Troy: Brownie ain't got that much sense. Man wasn't thinking about nothing. He wait until I confront them on it . . . then he wanna come crying seniority. (*Calls.*) Hey, Rose!

Bono: I wish I could have seen Mr. Rand's face when he told you.

Troy: He couldn't get it out of his mouth! Liked to bit his tongue! When they called me down there to the Commissioner's office . . . he thought they was gonna fire me. Like everybody else.

Bono: I didn't think they was gonna fire you. I thought they was gonna put you on the warning paper.

Troy: Hey, Rose! (*To Bono.*) Yeah, Mr. Rand like to bit his tongue.

(*Troy breaks the seal on the bottle, takes a drink, and hands it to Bono.*)

Bono: I see you run right down to Taylors' and told that Alberta gal.

Troy (*Calling.*): Hey, Rose! (*To Bono.*) I told everybody. Hey, Rose! I went down there to cash my check.

Rose (*Entering from the house.*): Hush all that hollering, man! I know you out here. What they say down there at the Commissioner's office?

Troy: You supposed to come when I call you, woman. Bono'll tell you that. (*To Bono.*) Don't Lucille come when you call her?

Rose: Man, hush your mouth. I ain't no dog . . . talk about "come when you call me."

Troy (*Puts his arm around Rose.*): You hear this, Bono? I had me an old dog used to get uppity like that. You say, "C'mere, Blue!" . . . and he just lay there and look at you. End up getting a stick and chasing him away trying to make him come.

Rose: I ain't studying you and your dog. I remember you used to sing that old song.

Troy (*He sings.*):

       Hear it ring! Hear it ring!
       I had a dog his name was Blue.

Rose: Don't nobody wanna hear you sing that old song.

Troy (*Sings.*):

> You know Blue was mighty true.

Rose: Used to have Cory running around here singing that song.

Bono: Hell, I remember that song myself.

Troy (*Sings.*):

> You know Blue was a good old dog.
> Blue treed a possum in a hollow log.

That was my daddy's song. My daddy made up that song.

Rose: I don't care who made it up. Don't nobody wanna hear you sing it.

Troy (*Makes a song like calling a dog.*): Come here, woman.

Rose: You come in here carrying on, I reckon they ain't fired you. What they say down there at the Commissioner's office?

Troy: Look here, Rose . . . Mr. Rand called me into his office today when I got back from talking to them people down there . . . it come from up top . . . he called me in and told me they was making me a driver.

Rose: Troy, you kidding!

Troy: No I ain't. Ask Bono.

Rose: Well, that's great, Troy. Now you don't have to hassle them people no more.

(*Lyons enters from the street.*)

Troy: Aw hell, I wasn't looking to see you today. I thought you was in jail. Got it all over the front page of the *Courier* about them raiding Sefus's place . . . where you be hanging out with all them thugs.

Lyons: Hey, Pop . . . that ain't got nothing to do with me. I don't go down there gambling. I go down there to sit in with the band. I ain't got nothing to do with the gambling part. They got some good music down there.

Troy: They got some rogues . . . is what they got.

Lyons: How you been, Mr. Bono? Hi, Rose.

Bono: I see where you playing down at the Crawford Grill tonight.

Rose: How come you ain't brought Bonnie like I told you? You should have brought Bonnie with you, she ain't been over in a month of Sundays.

Lyons: I was just in the neighborhood . . . thought I'd stop by.

Troy: Here he come . . .

Bono: Your daddy got a promotion on the rubbish. He's gonna be the first colored driver. Ain't got to do nothing but sit up there and read the paper like them white fellows.

Lyons: Hey, Pop . . . if you knew how to read you'd be alright.

Bono: Naw . . . naw . . . you mean if the nigger knew how to *drive* he'd be alright. Been fighting with them people about driving

and ain't even got a license. Mr. Rand know you ain't got no driver's license?

Troy: Driving ain't nothing. All you do is point the truck where you
want it to go. Driving ain't nothing.

Bono: Do Mr. Rand know you ain't got no driver's license? That's what
I'm talking about. I ain't asked if driving was easy. I asked if Mr.
Rand know you ain't got no driver's license.

Troy: He ain't got to know. The man ain't got to know my business.
Time he find out, I have two or three driver's licenses.

Lyons (*Going into his pocket.*): Say, look here, Pop . . .

Troy: I knew it was coming. Didn't I tell you, Bono? I know what kind of
"Look here, Pop" that was. The nigger fixing to ask me for some
money. It's Friday night. It's my payday. All them rogues down there
on the avenue . . . the ones that ain't in jail . . . and Lyons is hopping
in his shoes to get down there with them.

Lyons: See, Pop . . . if you give somebody else a chance to talk sometime,
you'd see that I was fixing to pay you back your ten dollars like I told
you. Here . . . I told you I'd pay you when Bonnie got paid.

Troy: Naw . . . you go ahead and keep that ten dollars. Put it in the bank.
The next time you feel like you wanna come by here and ask me for
something . . . you go on down there and get that.

Lyons: Here's your ten dollars, Pop. I told you I don't want you to give me
nothing. I just wanted to borrow ten dollars.

Troy: Naw . . . you go on and keep that for the next time you want to ask
me.

Lyons: Come on, Pop . . . here go your ten dollars.

Rose: Why don't you go on and let the boy pay you back, Troy?

Lyons: Here you go, Rose. If you don't take it I'm gonna have to hear
about it for the next six months. (*He hands her the money.*)

Rose: You can hand yours over here too, Troy.

Troy: You see this, Bono. You see how they do me.

Bono: Yeah, Lucille do me the same way.

(*Gabriel is heard singing offstage. He enters.*)

Gabriel: Better get ready for the Judgment! Better get ready for . . . Hey!
. . . Hey! . . . There's Troy's boy!

Lyons: How are you doing, Uncle Gabe?

Gabriel: Lyons . . . The King of the Jungle! Rose . . . hey, Rose. Got a
flower for you. (*He takes a rose from his pocket.*) Picked it myself.
That's the same rose like you is!

Rose: That's right nice of you, Gabe.

Lyons: What you been doing, Uncle Gabe?

Gabriel: Oh, I been chasing hellhounds and waiting on the time to tell St. Peter to open the gates.

Lyons: You been chasing hellhounds, huh? Well . . . . you doing the right thing, Uncle Gabe. Somebody got to chase them.

Gabriel: Oh, yeah . . . I know it. The devil's strong. The devil ain't no pushover. Hellhounds snipping at everybody's heels. But I got my trumpet waiting on the judgment time.

Lyons: Waiting on the Battle of Armageddon, huh?

Gabriel: Ain't gonna be too much of a battle when God get to waving that Judgment sword. But the people's gonna have a hell of a time trying to get into heaven if them gates ain't open.

Lyons (Putting his arm around Gabriel.): You hear this, Pop. Uncle Gabe, you alright!

Gabriel (Laughing with Lyons.): Lyons! King of the Jungle.

Rose: You gonna stay for supper, Gabe? Want me to fix you a plate?

Gabriel: I'll take a sandwich, Rose. Don't want no plate. Just wanna eat with my hands. I'll take a sandwich.

Rose: How about you, Lyons? You staying? Got some short ribs cooking.

Lyons: Naw, I won't eat nothing till after we finished playing. (*Pause.*) You ought to come down and listen to me play, Pop.

Troy: I don't like that Chinese music. All that noise.

Rose: Go on in the house and wash up, Gabe . . . I'll fix you a sandwich.

Gabriel (To Lyons, as he exits.): Troy's mad at me.

Lyons: What you mad at Uncle Gabe for, Pop?

Rose: He thinks Troy's mad at him cause he moved over to Miss Pearl's.

Troy: I ain't mad at the man. He can live where he want to live at.

Lyons: What he move over there for? Miss Pearl don't like nobody.

Rose: She don't mind him none. She treats him real nice. She just don't allow all that singing.

Troy: She don't mind that rent he be paying . . . that's what she don't mind.

Rose: Troy, I ain't going through that with you no more. He's over there cause he want to have his own place. He can come and go as he please.

Troy: Hell, he could come and go as he please here. I wasn't stopping him. I ain't put no rules on him.

Rose: It ain't the same thing, Troy. And you know it.

(*Gabriel comes to the door.*)

Now, that's the last I wanna hear about that. I don't wanna hear nothing else about Gabe and Miss Pearl. And next week . . .

Gabriel: I'm ready for my sandwich, Rose.

Rose: And next week . . . when that recruiter come from that school . . . I want you to sign that paper and go on and let Cory play football. Then that'll be the last I have to hear about that.

Troy (*To Rose as she exits into the house.*): I ain't thinking about Cory nothing.

Lyons: What . . . Cory got recruited? What school he going to?

Troy: That boy walking around here smelling his piss . . . thinking he's grown. Thinking he's gonna do what he want, irrespective of what I say. Look here, Bono . . . I left the Commissioner's office and went down to the A&P . . . that boy ain't working down there. He lying to me. Telling me he got his job back . . . telling me he working weekends . . . telling me he working after school . . . Mr. Stawicki tell me he ain't working down there at all!

Lyons: Cory just growing up. He's just busting at the seams trying to fill out your shoes.

Troy: I don't care what he's doing. When he get to the point where he wanna disobey me . . . then it's time for him to move on. Bono'll tell you that. I bet he ain't never disobeyed his daddy without paying the consequences.

Bono: I ain't never had a chance. My daddy came on through . . . but I ain't never knew him to see him . . . or what he had on his mind or where he went. Just moving on through. Searching out the New Land. That's what the old folks used to call it. See a fellow moving around from place to place . . . woman to woman . . . called it searching out the New Land. I can't say if he ever found it. I come along, didn't want no kids. Didn't know if I was gonna be in one place long enough to fix on them right as their daddy. I figured I was going searching too. As it turned out I been hooked up with Lucille near about as long as your daddy been with Rose. Going on sixteen years.

Troy: Sometimes I wish I hadn't known my daddy. He ain't cared nothing about no kids. A kid to him wasn't nothing. All he wanted was for you to learn how to walk so he could start you to working. When it come time for eating . . . he ate first. If there was anything left over, that's what you got. Man would sit down and eat two chickens and give you the wing.

Lyons: You ought to stop that, Pop. Everybody feed their kids. No matter how hard times is . . . everybody care about their kids. Make sure they have something to eat.

Troy: The only thing my daddy cared about was getting them bales of cotton in to Mr. Lubin. That's the only thing that mattered to him. Sometimes I used to wonder why he was living. Wonder why the devil hadn't come and got him. "Get them bales of cotton in to Mr. Lubin" and find out he owe him money . . .

Lyons: He should have just went on and left when he saw he couldn't get nowhere. That's what I would have done.

Troy: How he gonna leave with eleven kids? And where he gonna go? He ain't knew how to do nothing but farm. No, he was trapped and I think he knew it. But I'll say this for him . . . he felt a responsibility toward us. Maybe he ain't treated us the way I felt he should have . . . but without that responsibility he could have walked off and left us . . . made his own way.

Bono: A lot of them did. Back in those days what you talking about . . . they walk out their front door and just take on down one road or another and keep on walking.

Lyons: There you go! That's what I'm talking about.

Bono: Just keep on walking till you come to something else. Ain't you never heard of nobody having the walking blues? Well, that's what you call it when you just take off like that.

Troy: My daddy ain't had them walking blues! What you talking about? He stayed right there with his family. But he was just as evil as he could be. My mama couldn't stand him. Couldn't stand that evilness. She run off when I was about eight. She sneaked off one night after he had gone to sleep. Told me she was coming back for me. I ain't never seen her no more. All his women run off and left him. He wasn't good for nobody.

When my turn come to head out, I was fourteen and got to sniffing around Joe Canewell's daughter. Had us an old mule we called Greyboy. My daddy sent me out to do some plowing and I tied up Greyboy and went to fooling around with Joe Canewell's daughter. We done found us a nice little spot, got real cozy with each other. She about thirteen and we done figured we was grown anyway . . . so we down there enjoying ourselves . . . ain't thinking about nothing. We didn't know Greyboy had got loose and wandered back to the house and my daddy was looking for me. We down there by the creek enjoying ourselves when my daddy come up on us. Surprised us. He had them leather straps off the mule and commenced to whupping me like there was no tomorrow. I jumped up, mad and embarrassed. I was scared of my daddy. When he commenced to whupping on me . . . quite naturally I run to get out of the way. (*Pause.*) Now I thought he was mad cause I ain't done my work. But I see where he was chasing me off so he could have the gal for himself. When I see what the matter of it was, I lost all fear of my daddy. Right there is where I become a man . . . at fourteen years of age. (*Pause.*) Now it was my turn to run him off. I picked up them same reins that he had used on me. I picked up them reins and commenced to whupping on him. The gal jumped up and run off . . . and when my daddy turned to face me, I could see why the devil had never come to get him . . . cause he was the devil himself. I don't know what happened. When I woke up, I was laying right there by the creek, and Blue . . . this old dog we had . . . was licking my face. I thought I was blind. I couldn't see nothing. Both my eyes were swollen shut. I layed there and cried. I didn't know what I was gonna do. The only thing I knew was the time had come for me to leave my daddy's house. And right there the world suddenly got big. And it was a long time before I could cut it down to where I could handle it.

Part of that cutting down was when I got to the place where I could feel him kicking in my blood and knew that the only thing that separated us was the matter of a few years.

(*Gabriel enters from the house with a sandwich.*)

Lyons: What you got there, Uncle Gabe?

Gabriel: Got me a ham sandwich. Rose gave me a ham sandwich.

Troy: I don't know what happened to him. I done lost touch with everybody except Gabriel. But I hope he's dead. I hope he found some peace.

Lyons: That's a heavy story, Pop. I didn't know you left home when you was fourteen.

Troy: And didn't know nothing. The only part of the world I knew was the forty-two acres of Mr. Lubin's land. That's all I knew about life.

Lyons: Fourteen's kinda young to be out on your own. (*Phone rings.*) I don't even think I was ready to be out on my own at fourteen. I don't know what I would have done.

Troy: I got up from the creek and walked on down to Mobile. I was through with farming. Figured I could do better in the city. So I walked the two hundred miles to Mobile.

Lyons: Wait a minute . . . you ain't walked no two hundred miles, Pop. Ain't nobody gonna walk no two hundred miles. You talking about some walking there.

Bono: That's the only way you got anywhere back in them days.

Lyons: Shhh. Damn if I wouldn't have hitched a ride with somebody!

Troy: Who you gonna hitch it with? They ain't had no cars and things like they got now. We talking about 1918.

Rose (*Entering.*): What you all out here getting into?

Troy (*To Rose.*): I'm telling Lyons how good he got it. He don't know nothing about this I'm talking.

Rose: Lyons, that was Bonnie on the phone. She say you supposed to pick her up.

Lyons: Yeah, okay, Rose.

Troy: I walked on down to Mobile and hitched up with some of them fellows that was heading this way. Got up here and found out . . . not only couldn't you get a job . . . you couldn't find no place to live. I thought I was in freedom. Shhh. Colored folks living down there on the riverbanks in whatever kind of shelter they could find for themselves. Right down there under the Brady Street Bridge. Living in shacks made of sticks and tarpaper. Messed around there and went from bad to worse. Started stealing. First it was food. Then I figured, hell, if I steal money I can buy me some food. Buy me some shoes too! One thing led to another. Met your mama. I was young and anxious to be a man. Met your mama and had you. What I do that for? Now I got to worry about feeding you and her. Got to steal three times as much. Went out one day looking for somebody to rob . . . that's what I was, a robber. I'll tell you the truth. I'm ashamed of it today. But it's the truth. Went to rob this fellow . . . pulled out my knife . . . and he pulled out a gun. Shot me in the chest. It felt just like somebody had taken a hot branding iron and laid it on me. When he shot me I jumped at him with my knife. They told me I killed him and they put me in the penitentiary and locked me up for fifteen years. That's where I met Bono. That's where I learned how to play baseball. Got out that place and your mama had taken you and went on to make life without me. Fifteen years was a long time for her to wait. But that fifteen years cured me of that robbing stuff. Rose'll tell you. She asked me when I met her if I had gotten all that foolishness out of my system. And I told her, "Baby, it's you and baseball all what count with me." You hear me, Bono? I meant it too. She say, "Which one comes first?" I told her, "Baby, ain't no doubt it's baseball . . . but you stick and get old with me and we'll both outlive this baseball." Am I right, Rose? And it's true.

Rose: Man, hush your mouth. You ain't said no such thing. Talking about, "Baby you know you'll always be number one with me." That's what you was talking.

Troy: You hear that, Bono. That's why I love her.

Bono: Rose'll keep you straight. You get off the track, she'll straighten you up.

Rose: Lyons, you better get on up and get Bonnie. She waiting on you.

Lyons (Gets up to go.): Hey, Pop, why don't you come on down to the Grill and hear me play?

Troy: I ain't going down there. I'm too old to be sitting around in them clubs.

Bono: You got to be good to play down at the Grill.

Lyons: Come on, Pop . . .

Troy: I got to get up in the morning.

Lyons: You ain't got to stay long.

Troy: Naw, I'm gonna get my supper and go on to bed.

Lyons: Well, I got to go. I'll see you again.

Troy: Don't you come around my house on my payday.

Rose: Pick up the phone and let somebody know you coming. And bring Bonnie with you. You know I'm always glad to see her.

Lyons: Yeah, I'll do that, Rose. You take care now. See you, Pop. See you, Mr. Bono. See you, Uncle Gabe.

Gabriel: Lyons! King of the Jungle!

(*Lyons exits.*)

Troy: Is supper ready, woman? Me and you got some business to take care of. I'm gonna tear it up too.

Rose: Troy, I done told you now!

Troy (*Puts his arm around Bono.*): Aw hell, woman . . . this is Bono. Bono like family. I done known this nigger since . . . how long I done know you?

Bono: It's been a long time.

Troy: I done know this nigger since Skippy was a pup. Me and him done been through some times.

Bono: You sure right about that.

Troy: Hell, I done know him longer than I known you. And we still standing shoulder to shoulder. Hey, look here, Bono . . . a man can't ask for no more than that. (*Drinks to him.*) I love you, nigger.

Bono: Hell, I love you too . . . but I got to get home see my woman. You got yours in hand. I got to go get mine.

(*Bono starts to exit as Cory enters the yard, dressed in his football uniform. He gives Troy a hard, uncompromising look.*)

Cory: What you do that for, Pop?

(*He throws his helmet down in the direction of Troy.*)

Rose: What's the matter? Cory . . . what's the matter?

Cory: Papa done went up to the school and told Coach Zellman I can't play football no more. Wouldn't even let me play the game. Told him to tell the recruiter not to come.

Rose: Troy . . .

Troy: What you Troying me for. Yeah, I did it. And the boy know why I did it.

Cory: Why you wanna do that to me? That was the one chance I had.

Rose: Ain't nothing wrong with Cory playing football, Troy.

Troy: The boy lied to me. I told the nigger if he wanna play football . . . to keep up his chores and hold down that job at the A&P. That was the conditions. Stopped down there to see Mr. Stawicki . . .

Cory: I can't work after school during the football season, Pop! I tried to tell you that Mr. Stawicki's holding my job for me. You don't never want to listen to nobody. And then you wanna go and do this to me!

Troy: I ain't done nothing to you. You done it to yourself.

Cory: Just cause you didn't have a chance! You just scared I'm gonna be better than you, that's all.

Troy: Come here.

Rose: Troy . . .

(*Cory reluctantly crosses over to Troy.*)

Troy: Alright! See. You done made a mistake.

Cory: I didn't even do nothing!

Troy: I'm gonna tell you what your mistake was. See . . . you swung at the ball and didn't hit it. That's strike one. See, you in the batter's box now. You swung and you missed. That's strike one. Don't you strike out!

(*Lights fade to black.*)

ACT II

SCENE I

The following morning. Cory is at the tree hitting the ball with the bat. He tries to mimic Troy, but his swing is awkward, less sure. Rose enters from the house.

Rose: Cory, I want you to help me with this cupboard.

Cory: I ain't quitting the team. I don't care what Poppa say.

Rose: I'll talk to him when he gets back. He had to go see about your Uncle Gabe. The police done arrested him. Say he was disturbing the peace. He'll be back directly. Come on in here and help me clean out the top of this cupboard.

(*Cory exits into the house. Rose sees Troy and Bono coming down the alley.*)

Troy . . . what they say down there?

Troy: Ain't said nothing. I give them fifty dollars and they let him go. I'll talk to you about it. Where's Cory?

Rose: He's in there helping me clean out these cupboards.

Troy: Tell him to get his butt out here.

(*Troy and Bono go over to the pile of wood. Bono picks up the saw and begins sawing.*)

Troy (*To Bono.*): All they want is the money. That makes six or seven times I done went down there and got him. See me coming they stick out their *hands.*

Bono: Yeah. I know what you mean. That's all they care about . . . that money. They don't care about what's right. (*Pause.*) Nigger, why you got to go and get some hard wood? You ain't doing nothing but building a little old fence. Get you some soft pine wood. That's all you need.

Troy: I know what I'm doing. This is outside wood. You put pine wood inside the house. Pine wood is inside wood. This here is outside wood. Now you tell me where the fence is gonna be?

Bono: You don't need this wood. You can put it up with pine wood and it'll stand as long as you gonna be here looking at it.

Troy: How you know how long I'm gonna be here, nigger? Hell, I might just live forever. Live longer than old man Horsely.

Bono: That's what Magee used to say.

Troy: Magee's a damn fool. Now you tell me who you ever heard of gonna pull their own teeth with a pair of rusty pliers.

Bono: The old folks . . . my granddaddy used to pull his teeth with pliers. They ain't had no dentists for the colored folks back then.

Troy: Get clean pliers! You understand? Clean pliers! Sterilize them! Besides we ain't living back then. All Magee had to do was walk over to Doc Goldblum's.

Bono: I see where you and that Tallahassee gal . . . that Alberta . . . I see where you all done got tight.

Troy: What you mean "got tight"?

Bono: I see where you be laughing and joking with her all the time.

Troy: I laughs and jokes with all of them, Bono. You know me.

Bono: That ain't the kind of laughing and joking I'm talking about.

(*Cory enters from the house.*)

Cory: How you doing, Mr. Bono?

Troy: Cory? Get that saw from Bono and cut some wood. He talking about the wood's too hard to cut. Stand back there, Jim, and let that young boy show you how it's done.

Bono: He's sure welcome to it.

(*Cory takes the saw and begins to cut the wood.*)

Whew-e-e! Look at that. Big old strong boy. Look like Joe Louis. Hell, must be getting old the way I'm watching that boy whip through that wood.

Cory: I don't see why Mama want a fence around the yard noways.

Troy: Damn if I know either. What the hell she keeping out with it? She ain't got nothing nobody want.

Bono: Some people build fences to keep people out . . . and other people build fences to keep people in. Rose wants to hold on to you all. She loves you.

Troy: Hell, nigger, I don't need nobody to tell me my wife loves me. Cory . . . go on in the house and see if you can find that other saw.

Cory: Where's it at?

Troy: I said find it! Look for it till you find it!

(*Cory exits into the house.*)

What's that supposed to mean? Wanna keep us in?

Bono: Troy . . . I done known you seem like damn near my whole life. You and Rose both. I done know both of you all for a long time. I re-member when you met Rose. When you was hitting them baseball out the park. A lot of them old gals was after you then. You had the pick of the litter. When you picked Rose, I was happy for you. That was the first time I knew you had any sense. I said . . . My man Troy knows what he's doing . . . I'm gonna follow this nigger . . . he might take me somewhere. I been following you too. I done learned a whole heap of things about life watching you. I done learned how to tell where the shit lies. How to tell it from the alfalfa. You done learned me a lot of things. You showed me how to not make the same mistakes . . . to take life as it comes along and keep putting one foot in front of the other. (*Pause.*) Rose a good woman, Troy.

Troy: Hell, nigger, I know she a good woman. I been married to her for eighteen years. What you got on your mind, Bono?

Bono: I just say she a good woman. Just like I say anything. I ain't got to have nothing on my mind.

Troy: You just gonna say she a good woman and leave it hanging out there like that? Why you telling me she a good woman?

Bono: She loves you, Troy. Rose loves you.

Troy: You saying I don't measure up. That's what you trying to say. I don't measure up cause I'm seeing this other gal. I know what you trying to say.

Bono: I know what Rose means to you, Troy. I'm just trying to say I don't want to see you mess up.

Troy: Yeah, I appreciate that, Bono. If you was messing around on Lucille I'd be telling you the same thing.

Bono: Well, that's all I got to say. I just say that because I love you both.

Troy: Hell, you know me . . . I wasn't out there looking for nothing. You can't find a better woman than Rose. I know that. But seems like this woman just stuck onto me where I can't shake her loose. I done wrestled with it, tried to throw her off me . . . but she just stuck on tighter. Now she's stuck on for good.

Bono: You's in control . . . that's what you tell me all the time. You responsible for what you do.

Troy: I ain't ducking the responsibility of it. As long as it sets right in my heart . . . then I'm okay. Cause that's all I listen to. It'll tell me right from wrong every time. And I ain't talking about doing Rose no bad turn. I love Rose. She done carried me a long ways and I love and respect her for that.

Bono: I know you do. That's why I don't want to see you hurt her. But what you gonna do when she find out? What you got then? If you try and juggle both of them . . . sooner or later you gonna drop one of them. That's common sense.

Troy: Yeah, I hear what you saying, Bono. I been trying to figure a way to work it out.

Bono: Work it out right, Troy. I don't want to be getting all up between you and Rose's business . . . but work it so it come out right.

Troy: Aw hell, I get all up between you and Lucille's business. When you gonna get that woman that refrigerator she been wanting? Don't tell me you ain't got no money now. I know who your banker is. Mellon° don't need that money bad as Lucille want that refrigerator. I'll tell you that.

Bono: Tell you what I'll do . . . when you finish building this fence for Rose . . . I'll buy Lucille that refrigerator.

Troy: You done stuck your foot in your mouth now!

(*Troy grabs up a board and begins to saw. Bono starts to walk out the yard.*)

Hey, nigger . . . where you going?

Bono: I'm going home. I know you don't expect me to help you now. I'm protecting my money. I wanna see you put that fence up by yourself.

Mellon: banker and industrialist Andrew Mellon (1855–1937), U.S. Treasury Secretary 1921–32, was active in philanthropic enterprises, especially in his native Pittsburgh.

That's what I want to see. You'll be here another six months without me.

Troy: Nigger, you ain't right.

Bono: When it comes to my money . . . I'm right as fireworks on the Fourth of July.

Troy: Alright, we gonna see now. You better get out your bankbook.

(*Bono exits, and Troy continues to work. Rose enters from the house.*)

Rose: What they say down there? What's happening with Gabe?

Troy: I went down there and got him out. Cost me fifty dollars. Say he was disturbing the peace. Judge set up a hearing for him in three weeks. Say to show cause why he shouldn't be re-committed.

Rose: What was he doing that cause them to arrest him?

Troy: Some kids was teasing him and he run them off home. Say he was howling and carrying on. Some folks seen him and called the police. That's all it was.

Rose: Well, what's you say? What'd you tell the judge?

Troy: Told him I'd look after him. It didn't make no sense to recommit the man. He stuck out his big greasy palm and told me to give him fifty dollars and take him on home.

Rose: Where's he at now? Where'd he go off to?

Troy: He's gone on about his business. He don't need nobody to hold his hand.

Rose: Well, I don't know. Seem like that would be the best place for him if they did put him into the hospital. I know what you're gonna say. But that's what I think would be best.

Troy: The man done had his life ruined fighting for what? And they wanna take and lock him up. Let him be free. He don't bother nobody.

Rose: Well, everybody got their own way of looking at it I guess. Come on and get your lunch. I got a bowl of lima beans and some cornbread in the oven. Come on get something to eat. Ain't no sense you fretting over Gabe.

(*Rose turns to go into the house.*)

Troy: Rose . . . got something to tell you.

Rose: Well, come on . . . wait till I get this food on the table.

Troy: Rose!

(*She stops and turns around.*)

I don't know how to say this. (*Pause.*) I can't explain it none. It just sort of grows on you till it gets out of hand. It starts out like a little bush . . . and the next thing you know it's a whole forest.

Rose: Troy . . . what is you talking about?

Troy: I'm talking, woman, let me talk. I'm trying to find a way to tell you . . . I'm gonna be a daddy. I'm gonna be somebody's daddy.

Rose: Troy . . . you're not telling me this? You're gonna be . . . what?

Troy: Rose . . . now . . . see . . .

Rose: You telling me you gonna be somebody's daddy? You telling your *wife* this?

(*Gabriel enters from the street. He carries a rose in his hand.*)

Gabriel: Hey, Troy! Hey, Rose!

Rose: I have to wait eighteen years to hear something like this.

Gabriel: Hey, Rose . . . I got a flower for you. (*He hands it to her.*) That's a rose. Same rose like you is.

Rose: Thanks, Gabe.

Gabriel: Troy, you ain't mad at me is you? Them bad mens come and put me away. You ain't mad at me is you?

Troy: Naw, Gabe, I ain't mad at you.

Rose: Eighteen years and you wanna come with this.

Gabriel (*Takes a quarter out of his pocket.*): See what I got? Got a brand new quarter.

Troy: Rose . . . it's just . . .

Rose: Ain't nothing you can say, Troy. Ain't no way of explaining that.

Gabriel: Fellow that give me this quarter had a whole mess of them. I'm gonna keep this quarter till it stop shining.

Rose: Gabe, go on in the house there. I got some watermelon in the Frigidaire. Go on and get you a piece.

Gabriel: Say, Rose . . . you know I was chasing hellhounds and them bad mens come and get me and take me away. Troy helped me. He come down there and told them they better let me go before he beat them up. Yeah, he did!

Rose: You go on and get you a piece of watermelon, Gabe. Them bad mens is gone now.

Gabriel: Okay, Rose . . . gonna get me some watermelon. The kind with the stripes on it.

(*Gabriel exits into the house.*)

Rose: Why, Troy? Why? After all these years to come dragging this in to me now. It don't make no sense at your age. I could have expected this ten or fifteen years ago, but not now.

Troy: Age ain't got nothing to do with it, Rose.

Rose: I done tried to be everything a wife should be. Everything a wife could be. Been married eighteen years and I got to live to see the day you tell me you been seeing another woman and done fathered a child by her. And you know I ain't never wanted no half nothing in my family. My whole family is half. Everybody got different fathers and mothers . . . my two sisters and my brother. Can't hardly tell who's who. Can't never sit down and talk about Papa and Mama. It's your papa and your mama and my papa and my mama . . .

Troy: Rose . . . stop it now.

Rose: I ain't never wanted that for none of my children. And now you wanna drag your behind in here and tell me something like this.

Troy: You ought to know. It's time for you to know.

Rose: Well, I don't want to know, goddamn it!

Troy: I can't just make it go away. It's done now. I can't wish the circumstance of the thing away.

Rose: And you don't want to either. Maybe you want to wish me and my boy away. Maybe that's what you want? Well, you can't wish us away. I've got eighteen years of my life invested in you. You ought to have stayed upstairs in my bed where you belong.

Troy: Rose . . . now listen to me . . . we can get a handle on this thing. We can talk this out . . . come to an understanding.

Rose: All of a sudden it's "we." Where was "we" at when you was down there rolling around with some godforsaken woman? "We" should have come to an understanding before you started making a damn fool of yourself. You're a day late and a dollar short when it comes to an understanding with me.

Troy: It's just . . . She gives me a different idea . . . a different understanding about myself. I can step out of this house and get away from the pressures and problems . . . be a different man. I ain't got to wonder how I'm gonna pay the bills or get the roof fixed. I can just be a part of myself that I ain't never been.

Rose: What I want to know . . . is do you plan to continue seeing her. That's all you can say to me.

Troy: I can sit up in her house and laugh. Do you understand what I'm saying. I can laugh out loud . . . and it feels good. It reaches all the way down to the bottom of my shoes. (*Pause.*) Rose, I can't give that up.

Rose: Maybe you ought to go on and stay down there with her . . . if she's a better woman than me.

Troy: It ain't about nobody being a better woman or nothing. Rose, you ain't the blame. A man couldn't ask for no woman to be a better wife than you've been. I'm responsible for it. I done locked myself into a pattern trying to take care of you all that I forgot about myself.

Rose: What the hell was I there for? That was my job, not somebody else's.

Troy: Rose, I done tried all my life to live decent . . . to live a clean . . . hard . . . useful life. I tried to be a good husband to you. In every way I knew how. Maybe I come into the world backwards, I don't know. But . . . you born with two strikes on you before you come to the plate. You got to guard it closely . . . always looking for the curve-ball on the inside corner. You can't afford to let none get past you. You can't afford a call strike. If you going down . . . you going down swinging. Everything lined up against you. What you gonna do. I fooled them, Rose. I bunted. When I found you and Cory and a halfway decent job . . . I was safe. Couldn't nothing touch me. I wasn't gonna strike out no more. I wasn't going back to the penitentiary. I wasn't gonna lay in the streets with a bottle of wine. I was safe. I had me a family. A job. I wasn't gonna get that last strike. I was on first looking for one of them boys to knock me in. To get me home.

Rose: You should have stayed in my bed, Troy.

Troy: Then when I saw that gal . . . she firmed up my backbone. And I got to thinking that if I tried . . . I just might be able to steal second. Do you understand after eighteen years I wanted to steal second.

Rose: You should have held me tight. You should have grabbed me and held on.

Troy: I stood on first base for eighteen years and I thought . . . well, goddamn it . . . go on for it!

Rose: We're not talking about baseball! We're talking about you going off to lay in bed with another woman . . . and then bring it home to me. That's what we're talking about. We ain't talking about no base-ball.

Troy: Rose, you're not listening to me. I'm trying the best I can to explain it to you. It's not easy for me to admit that I been standing in the same place for eighteen years.

Rose: I been standing with you! I been right here with you, Troy. I got a life too. I gave eighteen years of my life to stand in the same spot with you. Don't you think I ever wanted other things? Don't you think I had dreams and hopes? What about my life? What about me. Don't you think it ever crossed my mind to want to know other men? That I wanted to lay up somewhere and forget about my responsibilities? That I wanted someone to make me laugh so I could feel good? You not the only one who's got wants and needs. But I held on to you, Troy. I took all my feelings, my wants and needs, my dreams . . . and I buried them inside you. I planted a seed and watched and prayed over it. I planted myself inside you and waited to bloom. And it didn't take me no eighteen years to find out the soil was hard and rocky and it wasn't never gonna bloom.

But I held on to you, Troy. I held you tighter. You was my husband. I owed you everything I had. Every part of me I could find to give you. And upstairs in that room . . . with the darkness falling in on me . . . I gave everything I had to try and erase the doubt that you wasn't the finest man in the world. And wherever you was going . . . I wanted to be there with you. Cause you was my husband. Cause that's the only way I was gonna survive as your wife. You always talking about what you give . . . and what you don't have to give. But you take too. You take . . . and don't even know nobody's giving!

(*Rose turns to exit into the house; Troy grabs her arm.*)

Troy: You say I take and don't give!
Rose: Troy! You're hurting me!
Troy: You say I take and don't give.
Rose: Troy . . . you're hurting my arm! Let go!
Troy: I done give you everything I got. Don't you tell that lie on me.
Rose: Troy!
Troy: Don't you tell that lie on me!

(*Cory enters from the house.*)

Cory: Mama!
Rose: Troy. You're hurting me.
Troy: Don't you tell me about no taking and giving.

(*Cory comes up behind Troy and grabs him. Troy, surprised, is thrown off balance just as Cory throws a glancing blow that catches him on the chest and knocks him down. Troy is stunned, as is Cory.*)

Rose: Troy. Troy. No!

(*Troy gets to his feet and starts at Cory.*)

Troy . . . no. Please! Troy!

(*Rose pulls on Troy to hold him back. Troy stops himself.*)

Troy (*To Cory.*): Alright. That's strike two. You stay away from around me, boy. Don't you strike out. You living with a full count. Don't you strike out.

(*Troy exits out the yard as the lights go down.*)

SCENE II

It is six months later, early afternoon. Troy enters from the house and starts to exit the yard. Rose enters from the house.

Rose: Troy, I want to talk to you.

Troy: All of a sudden, after all this time, you want to talk to me, huh? You ain't wanted to talk to me for months. You ain't wanted to talk to me last night. You ain't wanted no part of me then. What you wanna talk to me about now?

Rose: Tomorrow's Friday.

Troy: I know what day tomorrow is. You think I don't know tomorrow's Friday? My whole life I ain't done nothing but look to see Friday coming and you got to tell me it's Friday.

Rose: I want to know if you're coming home.

Troy: I always come home, Rose. You know that. There ain't never been a night I ain't come home.

Rose: That ain't what I mean . . . and you know it. I want to know if you're coming straight home after work.

Troy: I figure I'd cash my check . . . hang out at Taylors' with the boys . . . maybe play a game of checkers . . .

Rose: Troy, I can't live like this. I won't live like this. You livin' on borrowed time with me. It's been going on six months now you ain't been coming home.

Troy: I be here every night. Every night of the year. That's 365 days.

Rose: I want you to come home tomorrow after work.

Troy: Rose . . . I don't mess up my pay. You know that now. I take my pay and I give it to you. I don't have no money but what you give me back. I just want to have a little time to myself . . . a little time to enjoy life.

Rose: What about me? When's my time to enjoy life?

Troy: I don't know what to tell you, Rose. I'm doing the best I can.

Rose: You ain't been home from work but time enough to change your clothes and run out . . . and you wanna call that the best you can do?

Troy: I'm going over to the hospital to see Alberta. She went into the hospital this afternoon. Look like she might have the baby early. I won't be gone long.

Rose: Well, you ought to know. They went over to Miss Pearl's and got Gabe today. She said you told them to go ahead and lock him up.

Troy: I ain't said no such thing. Whoever told you that is telling a lie. Pearl ain't doing nothing but telling a big fat lie.

Rose: She ain't had to tell me. I read it on the papers.

Troy: I ain't told them nothing of the kind.

Rose: I saw it right there on the papers.

Troy: What it say, huh?

Rose: It said you told them to take him.

Troy: Then they screwed that up, just the way they screw up everything. I ain't worried about what they got on the paper.

Rose: Say the government send part of his check to the hospital and the other part to you.

Troy: I ain't got nothing to do with that if that's the way it works. I ain't made up the rules about how it work.

Rose: You did Gabe just like you did Cory. You wouldn't sign the paper for Cory . . . but you signed for Gabe. You signed that paper.

(*The telephone is heard ringing inside the house.*)

Troy: I told you I ain't signed nothing, woman! The only thing I signed was the release form. Hell, I can't read, I don't know what they had on that paper! I ain't signed nothing about sending Gabe away.

Rose: I said send him to the hospital . . . you said let him be free . . . now you done went down there and signed him to the hospital for half his money. You went back on yourself, Troy. You gonna have to answer for that.

Troy: See now . . . you been over there talking to Miss Pearl. She done got mad cause she ain't getting Gabe's rent money. That's all it is. She's liable to say anything.

Rose: Troy, I seen where you signed the paper.

Troy: You ain't seen nothing I signed. What she doing got papers on my brother anyway? Miss Pearl telling a big fat lie. And I'm gonna tell her about it too! You ain't seen nothing I signed. Say . . . you ain't seen nothing I signed.

(*Rose exits into the house to answer the telephone. Presently she returns.*)

Rose: Troy . . . that was the hospital. Alberta had the baby.

Troy: What she have? What is it?

Rose: It's a girl.

Troy: I better get on down to the hospital to see her.

Rose: Troy . . .

Troy: Rose . . . I got to go see her now. That's only right . . . what's the matter . . . the baby's alright, ain't it?

Rose: Alberta died having the baby.

Troy: Died . . . you say she's dead? Alberta's dead?

Rose: They said they done all they could. They couldn't do nothing for her.

Troy: The baby? How's the baby?

Rose: They say it's healthy. I wonder who's gonna bury her.

Troy: She had family, Rose. She wasn't living in the world by herself.

Rose: I know she wasn't living in the world by herself.

Troy: Next thing you gonna want to know if she had any insurance.

Rose: Troy, you ain't got to talk like that.

Troy: That's the first thing that jumped out your mouth. "Who's gonna bury her?" Like I'm fixing to take on that task for myself.

Rose: I am your wife. Don't push me away.

Troy: I ain't pushing nobody away. Just give me some space. That's all. Just give me some room to breathe.

(Rose exits into the house. Troy walks about the yard.)

Troy (With a quiet rage that threatens to consume him.): Alright . . . Mr. Death. See now . . . I'm gonna tell you what I'm gonna do. I'm gonna take and build me a fence around this yard. See? I'm gonna build me a fence around what belongs to me. And then I want you to stay on the other side. See? You stay over there until you're ready for me. Then you come on. Bring your army. Bring your sickle. Bring your wrestling clothes. I ain't gonna fall down on my vigilance this time. You ain't gonna sneak up on me no more. When you ready for me . . . when the top of your list say Troy Maxson . . . that's when you come around here. You come up and knock on the front door. Ain't nobody else got nothing to do with this. This is between you and me. Man to man. You stay on the other side of that fence until you ready for me. Then you come up and knock on the front door. Anytime you want. I'll be ready for you.

(The lights go down to black.)

SCENE III

The lights come up on the porch. It is late evening three days later. Rose sits listening to the ball game waiting for Troy. The final out of the game is made and Rose switches off the radio. Troy enters the yard carrying an infant wrapped in blankets. He stands back from the house and calls.

Rose enters and stands on the porch. There is a long, awkward silence, the weight of which grows heavier with each passing second.

Troy: Rose . . . I'm standing here with my daughter in my arms. She ain't but a wee bittie little old thing. She don't know nothing about grownups' business. She innocent . . . and she ain't got no mama.

Rose: What you telling me for, Troy?

(She turns and exits into the house.)

Troy: Well . . . I guess we'll just sit out here on the porch.

(He sits down on the porch. There is an awkward indelicateness about the way he handles the baby. His largeness engulfs and seems to swallow it. He speaks loud enough for Rose to hear.)

A man's got to do what's right for him. I ain't sorry for nothing I done. It felt right in my heart. *(To the baby.)* What you smiling at? Your daddy's a big man. Got these great big old hands. But sometimes he's scared. And right now your daddy's scared cause we sitting out here and ain't got no home. Oh, I been homeless before. I ain't had no little baby with me. But I been homeless. You just be out on the road by your lonesome and you see one of them trains coming and you just kinda go like this . . .

(He sings as a lullaby.)

> Please, Mr. Engineer let a man ride the line
> Please, Mr. Engineer let a man ride the line
> I ain't got no ticket please let me ride the blinds

(Rose enters from the house. Troy, hearing her steps behind him, stands and faces her.)

She's my daughter, Rose. My own flesh and blood. I can't deny her no more than I can deny them boys. *(Pause.)* You and them boys is my family. You and them and this child is all I got in the world. So I guess what I'm saying is . . . I'd appreciate it if you'd help me take care of her.

Rose: Okay, Troy . . . you're right. I'll take care of your baby for you . . . cause . . . like you say . . . she's innocent . . . and you can't visit the sins of the father upon the child. A motherless child has got a hard time. *(She takes the baby from him.)* From right now . . . this child got a mother. But you a womanless man.

(Rose turns and exits into the house with the baby. Lights go down to black.)

SCENE IV

It is two months later. Lyons enters the street. He knocks on the door and calls.

Lyons: Hey, Rose! *(Pause.)* Rose!

Rose (From inside the house.): Stop that yelling. You gonna wake up Raynell. I just got her to sleep.

Lyons: I just stopped by to pay Papa this twenty dollars I owe him. Where's Papa at?

Rose: He should be here in a minute. I'm getting ready to go down to the church. Sit down and wait on him.

Lyons: I got to go pick up Bonnie over her mother's house.

Rose: Well, sit it down there on the table. He'll get it.

Lyons (*Enters the house and sets the money on the table.*): Tell Papa I said thanks. I'll see you again.

Rose: Alright, Lyons. We'll see you.

(*Lyons starts to exit as Cory enters.*)

Cory: Hey, Lyons.

Lyons: What's happening, Cory? Say man, I'm sorry I missed your gradu-ation. You know I had a gig and couldn't get away. Otherwise, I would have been there, man. So what you doing?

Cory: I'm trying to find a job.

Lyons: Yeah I know how that go, man. It's rough out here. Jobs are scarce.

Cory: Yeah, I know.

Lyons: Look here, I got to run. Talk to Papa . . . he know some people. He'll be able to help get you a job. Talk to him . . . see what he say.

Cory: Yeah . . . alright, Lyons.

Lyons: You take care. I'll talk to you soon. We'll find some time to talk.

(*Lyons exits the yard. Cory wanders over to the tree, picks up the bat, and assumes a batting stance. He studies an imaginary pitcher and swings. Dissatisfied with the result, he tries again. Troy enters. They eye each other for a beat. Cory puts the bat down and exits the yard. Troy starts into the house as Rose exits with Raynell. She is carrying a cake.*)

Troy: I'm coming in and everybody's going out.

Rose: I'm taking this cake down to the church for the bake sale. Lyons was by to see you. He stopped by to pay you your twenty dollars. It's laying in there on the table.

Troy (*Going into his pocket.*): Well . . . here go this money.

Rose: Put it in there on the table, Troy. I'll get it.

Troy: What time you coming back?

Rose: Ain't no use in you studying me. It don't matter what time I come back.

Troy: I just asked you a question, woman. What's the matter . . . can't I ask you a question?

Rose: Troy, I don't want to go into it. Your dinner's in there on the stove. All you got to do is heat it up. And don't you be eating the rest of them cakes in there. I'm coming back for them. We having a bake sale at the church tomorrow.

(*Rose exits the yard. Troy sits down on the steps, takes a pint bottle from his pocket, opens it and drinks. He begins to sing.*)

Troy:

> Hear it ring! Hear it ring!
> Had an old dog his name was Blue
> You know Blue was mighty true
> You know Blue was a good old dog
> Blue trees a possum in a hollow log
> You know from that he was a good old dog

(*Bono enters the yard.*)

Bono: Hey, Troy.

Troy: Hey, what's happening, Bono?

Bono: I just thought I'd stop by to see you.

Troy: What you stop by and see me for? You ain't stopped by in a month of Sundays. Hell, I must owe you money or something.

Bono: Since you got your promotion I can't keep up with you. Used to see you every day. Now I don't even know what route you working.

Troy: They keep switching me around. Got me out in Greentree now . . . hauling white folks' garbage.

Bono: Greentree, huh? You lucky, at least you ain't got to be lifting them barrels. Damn if they ain't getting heavier. I'm gonna put in my two years and call it quits.

Troy: I'm thinking about retiring myself.

Bono: You got it easy. You can *drive* for another five years.

Troy: It ain't the same, Bono. It ain't like working the back of the truck. Ain't got nobody to talk to . . . feel like you working by yourself. Naw, I'm thinking about retiring. How's Lucille?

Bono: She alright. Her arthritis get to acting up on her sometime. Saw Rose on my way in. She going down to the church, huh?

Troy: Yeah, she took up going down there. All them preachers looking for somebody to fatten their pockets. (*Pause.*) Got some gin here.

Bono: Naw, thanks. I just stopped by to say hello.

Troy: Hell, nigger . . . you can take a drink. I ain't never known you to say no to a drink. You ain't got to work tomorrow.

Bono: I just stopped by. I'm fixing to go over to Skinner's. We got us a domino game going over his house every Friday.

Troy: Nigger, you can't play no dominoes. I used to whup you four games out of five.

Bono: Well, that learned me. I'm getting better.

Troy: Yeah? Well, that's alright.

Bono: Look here . . . I got to be getting on. Stop by sometime, huh?

Troy: Yeah, I'll do that, Bono. Lucille told Rose you bought her a new refrigerator.

Bono: Yeah, Rose told Lucille you had finally built your fence . . . so I figured we'd call it even.

Troy: I knew you would.

Bono: Yeah . . . okay. I'll be talking to you.

Troy: Yeah, take care, Bono. Good to see you. I'm gonna stop over.

Bono: Yeah. Okay, Troy.

(*Bono exits. Troy drinks from the bottle.*)

Troy:

     Old Blue died and I dug his grave
     Let him down with a golden chain
     Every night when I hear old Blue bark
     I know Blue treed a possum in Noah's Ark.
     Hear it ring! Hear it ring!

(*Cory enters the yard. They eye each other for a beat. Troy is sitting in the middle of the steps. Cory walks over.*)

Cory: I got to get by.

Troy: Say what? What's you say?

Cory: You in my way. I got to get by.

Troy: You got to get by where? This is my house. Bought and paid for. In full. Took me fifteen years. And if you wanna go in my house and I'm sitting on the steps . . . you say excuse me. Like your mama taught you.

Cory: Come on, Pop . . . I got to get by.

(*Cory starts to maneuver his way past Troy. Troy grabs his leg and shoves him back.*)

Troy: You just gonna walk over top of me?

Cory: I live here too!

Troy (*Advancing toward him.*): You just gonna walk over top of me in my own house?

Cory: I ain't scared of you.

Troy: I ain't asked if you was scared of me. I asked you if you was fixing to walk over top of me in my own house? That's the question. You ain't gonna say excuse me? You just gonna walk over top of me?

Cory: If you wanna put it like that.

Troy: How else am I gonna put it?

Cory: I was walking by you to go into the house cause you sitting on the steps drunk, singing to yourself. You can put it like that.

Troy: Without saying excuse me???

(*Cory doesn't respond.*)

I asked you a question. Without saying excuse me???

Cory: I ain't got to say excuse me to you. You don't count around here no more.

Troy: Oh, I see . . . I don't count around here no more. You ain't got to say excuse me to your daddy. All of a sudden you done got so grown that your daddy don't count around here no more . . . Around here in his own house and yard that he done paid for with the sweat of his brow. You done got so grown to where you gonna take over. You gonna take over my house. Is that right? You gonna wear my pants. You gonna go in there and stretch out on my bed. You ain't got to say excuse me cause I don't count around here no more. Is that right?

Cory: That's right. You always talking this dumb stuff. Now, why don't you just get out my way?

Troy: I guess you got someplace to sleep and something to put in your belly. You got that, huh? You got that? That's what you need. You got that, huh?

Cory: You don't know what I got. You ain't got to worry about what I got.

Troy: You right! You one hundred percent right! I done spent the last seventeen years worrying about what you got. Now it's your turn, see? I'll tell you what to do. You grown . . . we done established that. You a man. Now, let's see you act like one. Turn your behind around and walk out this yard. And when you get out there in the alley . . . you can forget about this house. See? Cause this is my house. You go on and be a man and get your own house. You can forget about this. Cause this is mine. You go on and get yours cause I'm through with doing for you.

Cory: You talking about what you did for me . . . what'd you ever give me?

Troy: Them feet and bones! That pumping heart, nigger! I give you more than anybody else is ever gonna give you.

Cory: You ain't never gave me nothing! You ain't never done nothing but hold me back. Afraid I was gonna be better than you. All you ever did was try and make me scared of you. I used to tremble every time you called my name. Every time I heard your footsteps in the house. Wondering all the time . . . what's Papa gonna say if I do this? . . . What's he gonna say if I do that? . . . What's Papa gonna say if I turn on the radio? And Mama, too . . . she tries . . . but she's scared of you.

Troy: You leave your mama out of this. She ain't got nothing to do with this.

Cory: I don't know how she stand you . . . after what you did to her.

Troy: I told you to leave your mama out of this!

(*He advances toward Cory.*)

Cory: What you gonna do . . . give me a whupping? You can't whup me no more. You're too old. You just an old man.

Troy (*Shoves him on his shoulder.*): Nigger! That's what you are. You just another nigger on the street to me!

Cory: You crazy! You know that?

Troy: Go on now! You got the devil in you. Get on away from me!

Cory: You just a crazy old man . . . talking about I got the devil in me.

Troy: Yeah, I'm crazy! If you don't get on the other side of that yard . . . I'm gonna show you how crazy I am! Go on . . . get the hell out of my yard.

Cory: It ain't your yard. You took Uncle Gabe's money he got from the army to buy this house and then you put him out.

Troy (*Advances on Cory.*): Get your black ass out of my yard!

(*Troy's advance backs Cory up against the tree. Cory grabs up the bat.*)

Cory: I ain't going nowhere! Come on . . . put me out! I ain't scared of you.

Troy: That's my bat!

Cory: Come on!

Troy: Put my bat down!

Cory: Come on, put me out.

(*Cory swings at Troy, who backs across the yard.*)

What's the matter? You so bad . . . put me out!

(*Troy advances toward Cory.*)

Cory (*Backing up.*): Come on! Come on!

Troy: You're gonna have to use it! You wanna draw that bat back on me . . . you're gonna have to use it.

Cory: Come on! . . . Come on!

(*Cory swings the bat at Troy a second time. He misses. Troy continues to advance toward him.*)

Troy: You're gonna have to kill me! You wanna draw that bat back on me. You're gonna have to kill me.

(*Cory, backed up against the tree, can go no farther. Troy taunts him. He sticks out his head and offers him a target.*)

Come on! Come on!

(*Cory is unable to swing the bat. Troy grabs it.*)

Troy: Then I'll show you.

(*Cory and Troy struggle over the bat. The struggle is fierce and fully engaged. Troy ultimately is the stronger, and takes the bat from Cory and stands over him ready to swing. He stops himself.*)

Go on and get away from around my house.

(*Cory, stung by his defeat, picks himself up, walks slowly out of the yard and up the alley.*)

Cory: Tell Mama I'll be back for my things.
Troy: They'll be on the other side of that fence.

(*Cory exits.*)

Troy: I can't taste nothing. Helluljah! I can't taste nothing no more. (*Troy assumes a batting posture and begins to taunt Death, the fastball on the outside corner.*) Come on! It's between you and me now! Come on! Anytime you want! Come on! I be ready for you . . . but I ain't gonna be easy.

(*The lights go down on the scene.*)

SCENE V

The time is 1965. The lights come up in the yard. It is the morning of Troy's funeral. A funeral plaque with a light hangs beside the door. There is a small garden plot off to the side. There is noise and activity in the house as Rose, Lyons, and Bono have gathered. The door opens and Raynell, seven years old, enters dressed in a flannel nightgown. She crosses to the garden and pokes around with a stick. Rose calls from the house.

Rose: Raynell!
Raynell: Mam?
Rose: What you doing out there?
Raynell: Nothing.

(*Rose comes to the door.*)

Rose: Girl, get in here and get dressed. What you doing?
Raynell: Seeing if my garden growed.
Rose: I told you it ain't gonna grow overnight. You got to wait.
Raynell: It don't look like it never gonna grow. Dag!

Rose: I told you a watched pot never boils. Get in here and get dressed.

Raynell: This ain't even no pot, Mama.

Rose: You just have to give it a chance. It'll grow. Now you come on and do what I told you. We got to be getting ready. This ain't no morning to be playing around. You hear me?

Raynell: Yes, Mam.

(*Rose exits into the house. Raynell continues to poke at her garden with a stick. Cory enters. He is dressed in a Marine corporal's uniform, and carries a duffelbag. His posture is that of a military man, and his speech has a clipped sternness.*)

Cory (*To Raynell.*): Hi. (*Pause.*) I bet your name is Raynell.

Raynell: Uh huh.

Cory: Is your mama home?

(*Raynell runs up on the porch and calls through the screen door.*)

Raynell: Mama . . . there's some man out here. Mama?

(*Rose comes to the door.*)

Rose: Cory? Lord have mercy! Look here, you all!

(*Rose and Cory embrace in a tearful reunion as Bono and Lyons enter from the house dressed in funeral clothes.*)

Bono: Aw, looka here . . .

Rose: Done got all grown up!

Cory: Don't cry, Mama. What you crying about?

Rose: I'm just so glad you made it.

Cory: Hey Lyons. How you doing, Mr. Bono.

(*Lyons goes to embrace Cory.*)

Lyons: Look at you, man. Look at you. Don't he look good, Rose. Got them Corporal stripes.

Rose: What took you so long?

Cory: You know how the Marines are, Mama. They got to get all their paperwork straight before they let you do anything.

Rose: Well, I'm sure glad you made it. They let Lyons come. Your Uncle Gabe's still in the hospital. They don't know if they gonna let him out or not. I just talked to them a little while ago.

Lyons: A Corporal in the United States Marines.

Bono: Your daddy knew you had it in you. He used to tell me all the time.

Lyons: Don't he look good, Mr. Bono?

Bono: Yeah, he remind me of Troy when I first met him. (*Pause.*) Say, Rose, Lucille's down at the church with the choir. I'm gonna go down and get the pallbearers lined up. I'll be back to get you all.

Rose: Thanks, Jim.

Cory: See you, Mr. Bono.

Lyons (*With his arm around Raynell.*): Cory . . . look at Raynell. Ain't she precious? She gonna break a whole lot of hearts.

Rose: Raynell, come and say hello to your brother. This is your brother, Cory. You remember Cory.

Raynell: No, Mam.

Cory: She don't remember me, Mama.

Rose: Well, we talk about you. She heard us talk about you. (*To Raynell.*) This is your brother, Cory. Come on and say hello.

Raynell: Hi.

Cory: Hi. So you're Raynell. Mama told me a lot about you.

Rose: You all come on into the house and let me fix you some breakfast. Keep up your strength.

Cory: I ain't hungry, Mama.

Lyons: You can fix me something, Rose. I'll be in there in a minute.

Rose: Cory, you sure you don't want nothing? I know they ain't feeding you right.

Cory: No, Mama . . . thanks. I don't feel like eating. I'll get something later.

Rose: Raynell . . . get on upstairs and get that dress on like I told you.

(*Rose and Raynell exit into the house.*)

Lyons: So . . . I hear you thinking about getting married.

Cory: Yeah, I done found the right one, Lyons. It's about time.

Lyons: Me and Bonnie been split up about four years now. About the time Papa retired. I guess she just got tired of all them changes I was putting her through. (*Pause.*) I always knew you was gonna make something out yourself. Your head was always in the right direction. So . . . you gonna stay in . . . make it a career . . . put in your twenty years?

Cory: I don't know. I got six already, I think that's enough.

Lyons: Stick with Uncle Sam and retire early. Ain't nothing out here. I guess Rose told you what happened with me. They got me down the workhouse. I thought I was being slick cashing other people's checks.

Cory: How much time you doing?

Lyons: They give me three years. I got that beat now. I ain't got but nine more months. It ain't so bad. You learn to deal with it like anything else. You got to take the crookeds with the straights. That's what Papa used to say. He used to say that when he struck out. I seen him strike out three times in a row . . . and the next time up he hit the ball over the grandstand. Right out there in Homestead Field. He wasn't satisfied hitting in the seats . . . he want to hit it over everything! After the game he had two hundred people standing around waiting to shake his hand. You got to take the crookeds with the straights. Yeah, Papa was something else.

Cory: You still playing?

Lyons: Cory . . . you know I'm gonna do that. There's some fellows down there we got us a band . . . we gonna try and stay together when we get out . . . but yeah, I'm still playing. It still helps me to get out of bed in the morning. As long as it do that I'm gonna be right there playing and trying to make some sense out of it.

Rose (Calling.): Lyons, I got these eggs in the pan.

Lyons: Let me go on and get these eggs, man. Get ready to go bury Papa. *(Pause.)* How you doing? You doing alright?

(Cory nods. Lyons touches him on the shoulder and they share a moment of silent grief. Lyons exits into the house. Cory wanders about the yard. Raynell enters.)

Raynell: Hi.

Cory: Hi.

Raynell: Did you used to sleep in my room?

Cory: Yeah . . . that used to be my room.

Raynell: That's what Papa call it. "Cory's room." It got your football in the closet.

(Rose comes to the door.)

Rose: Raynell, get in there and get them good shoes on.

Raynell: Mama, can't I wear these? Them other one hurt my feet.

Rose: Well, they just gonna have to hurt your feet for a while. You ain't said they hurt your feet when you went down to the store and got them.

Raynell: They didn't hurt then. My feet done got bigger.

Rose: Don't you give me no backtalk now. You get in there and get them shoes on.

(Raynell exits into the house.)

Ain't too much changed. He still got that piece of rag tied to that tree. He was out here swinging that bat. I was just ready to go back in the house. He swung that bat and then he just fell over. Seem like he swung it and stood there with this grin on his face . . . and then he just fell over. They carried him on down to the hospital, but I knew there wasn't no need . . . why don't you come on in the house?

Cory: Mama . . . I got something to tell you. I don't know how to tell you this . . . but I've got to tell you . . . I'm not going to Papa's funeral.

Rose: Boy, hush your mouth. That's your daddy you talking about. I don't want hear that kind of talk this morning. I done raised you to come to this? You standing there all healthy and grown talking about you ain't going to your daddy's funeral?

Cory: Mama . . . listen . . .

Rose: I don't want to hear it, Cory. You just get that thought out of your head.

Cory: I can't drag Papa with me everywhere I go. I've got to say no to him. One time in my life I've got to say no.

Rose: Don't nobody have to listen to nothing like that. I know you and your daddy ain't seen eye to eye, but I ain't got to listen to that kind of talk this morning. Whatever was between you and your daddy . . . the time has come to put it aside. Just take it and set it over there on the shelf and forget about it. Disrespecting your daddy ain't gonna make you a man, Cory. You got to find a way to come to that on your own. Not going to your daddy's funeral ain't gonna make you a man.

Cory: The whole time I was growing up . . . living in his house . . . Papa was like a shadow that followed you everywhere. It weighed on you and sunk into your flesh. It would wrap around you and lay there until you couldn't tell which one was you anymore. That shadow digging in your flesh. Trying to crawl in. Trying to live through you. Everywhere I looked, Troy Maxson was staring back at me . . . hiding under the bed . . . in the closet. I'm just saying I've got to find a way to get rid of that shadow, Mama.

Rose: You just like him. You got him in you good.

Cory: Don't tell me that, Mama.

Rose: You Troy Maxson all over again.

Cory: I don't want to be Troy Maxson. I want to be me.

Rose: You can't be nobody but who you are, Cory. That shadow wasn't nothing but you growing into yourself. You either got to grow into it or cut it down to fit you. But that's all you got to make life with. That's all you got to measure yourself against that world out there. Your daddy wanted you to be everything he wasn't . . . and at the same time he tried to make you into everything he was. I don't know if he was right or wrong . . . but I do know he meant to do more good than he meant to do harm. He wasn't always right. Sometimes when he touched he bruised. And sometimes when he took me in his arms he cut.

When I first met your daddy I thought . . . Here is a man I can lay down with and make a baby. That's the first thing I thought when I seen him. I was thirty years old and had done seen my share of men. But when he walked up to me and said, "I can dance a waltz that'll make you dizzy," I thought, Rose Lee, here is a man that you can open yourself up to and be filled to bursting. Here is a man that can fill all them empty spaces you been tipping around the edges of. One of them empty spaces was being somebody's mother.

I married your daddy and settled down to cooking his supper and keeping clean sheets on the bed. When your daddy walked through the house he was so big he filled it up. That was my first mistake. Not to make him leave some room for me. For my part in the matter. But at that time I wanted that. I wanted a house that I could sing in. And that's what your daddy gave me. I didn't know to keep up his strength I had to give up little pieces of mine. I did that. I took on his life as mine and mixed up the pieces so that you couldn't hardly tell which was which anymore. It was my choice. It was my life and I didn't have to live it like that. But that's what life offered me in the way of being a woman and I took it. I grabbed hold of it with both hands.

By the time Raynell came into the house, me and your daddy had done lost touch with one another. I didn't want to make my blessing off of nobody's misfortune . . . but I took on to Raynell like she was all them babies I had wanted and never had.

(*The phone rings.*)

Like I'd been blessed to relive a part of my life. And if the Lord see fit to keep up my strength . . . I'm gonna do her just like your daddy did you . . . I'm gonna give her the best of what's in me.

Raynell (*Entering, still with her old shoes.*): Mama . . . Reverend Tollivier on the phone.

(*Rose exits into the house.*)

Raynell: Hi.
Cory: Hi.
Raynell: You in the Army or the Marines?
Cory: Marines.
Raynell: Papa said it was the Army. Did you know Blue?
Cory: Blue? Who's Blue?
Raynell: Papa's dog what he sing about all the time.

Cory (*Singing.*):
> Hear it ring! Hear it ring!
> I had a dog his name was Blue
> You know Blue was mighty true
> You know Blue was a good old dog
> Blue treed a possum in a hollow log
> You know from that he was a good old dog.
> Hear it ring! Hear it ring!

(*Raynell joins in singing.*)

Cory and Raynell:
> Blue treed a possum out on a limb
> Blue looked at me and I looked at him
> Grabbed that possum and put him in a sack
> Blue stayed there till I came back
> Old Blue's feets was big and round
> Never allowed a possum to touch the ground.

> Old Blue died and I dug his grave
> I dug his grave with a silver spade
> Let him down with a golden chain
> And every night I call his name
> Go on Blue, you good dog you
> Go on Blue, you good dog you.

Raynell:
> Blue laid down and died like a man
> Blue laid down and died . . .

Both:
> Blue laid down and died like a man
> Now he's treeing possums in the Promised Land
> I'm gonna tell you this to let you know
> Blue's gone where the good dogs go
> When I hear old Blue bark
> When I hear old Blue bark
> Blue treed a possum in Noah's Ark
> Blue treed a possum in Noah's Ark.

(*Rose comes to the screen door.*)

Rose: Cory, we gonna be ready to go in a minute.

Cory (*To Raynell.*): You go on in the house and change them shoes like Mama told you so we can go to Papa's funeral.

Raynell: Okay, I'll be back.

(*Raynell exits into the house. Cory gets up and crosses over to the tree. Rose stands in the screen door watching him. Gabriel enters from the alley.*)

Gabriel (Calling.): Hey, Rose!
Rose: Gabe?
Gabriel: I'm here, Rose. Hey, Rose, I'm here!

(*Rose enters from the house.*)

Rose: Lord . . . Look here, Lyons!
Lyons: See, I told you, Rose . . . I told you they'd let him come.
Cory: How you doing, Uncle Gabe?
Lyons: How you doing, Uncle Gabe?
Gabriel: Hey, Rose. It's time. It's time to tell St. Peter to open the gates. Troy, you ready? You ready, Troy. I'm gonna tell St. Peter to open the gates. You get ready now.

(*Gabriel, with great fanfare, braces himself to blow. The trumpet is without a mouthpiece. He puts the end of it into his mouth and blows with great force, like a man who has been waiting some twenty-odd years for this single moment. No sound comes out of the trumpet. He braces himself and blows again with the same result. A third time he blows. There is a weight of impossible description that falls away and leaves him bare and exposed to a frightful realization. It is a trauma that a sane and normal mind would be unable to withstand. He begins to dance. A slow, strange dance, eerie and life-giving. A dance of atavistic signature and ritual. Lyons attempts to embrace him. Gabriel pushes Lyons away. He begins to howl in what is an attempt at song, or perhaps a song turning back into itself in an attempt at speech. He finishes his dance and the gates of heaven stand open as wide as God's closet.*)

That's the way that go!

BLACKOUT

WRITING

Susan Glaspell at work, around 1913

28
Writing About Literature

Assigned to write an essay on *Hamlet,* a student might well wonder, "What can I say that hasn't been said a thousand times before?" Often the most difficult aspect of writing about a story, poem, or play is feeling that we have nothing of interest to contribute to the ongoing conversation about some celebrated literary work. There's always room, though, for a reader's fresh take on an old standby.

Remember that in the study of literature common sense is never out of place. For most of a class hour, a professor once rhapsodized about the arrangement of the contents of W. H. Auden's *Collected Poems.* Auden, he claimed, was a master of thematic continuity, who had brilliantly placed the poems in the order that they ingeniously complemented each other. Near the end of the hour, his theories were punctured—with a great inaudible pop—when a student, timidly raising a hand, pointed out that Auden had arranged the poems in the book not by theme but in alphabetical order according to the first word of each poem. The professor's jaw dropped: "Why didn't you say that sooner?" The student was apologetic: "I—I was afraid I'd sound too *ordinary.*"

Don't be afraid to state a conviction, though it seems obvious. Does it matter that you may be repeating something that, once upon a time or even just the other day, has been said before? What matters more is that you are actively engaged in thinking about literature. There are excellent old ideas as well as new. You have something to say.

Reading Actively

Most people read in a relaxed, almost passive way. They let a story or poem carry them along without asking too many questions. To write about literature well, however, you need to *read actively,* paying special attention to various aspects of a text. This special sort of attention will not only deepen your enjoyment of a story, poem, or play but will also help generate the information and ideas that will eventually become your final paper. How do you become an active reader? Here are some steps to get you started:

- **Preview the text.** To get acquainted with a work of literature before you settle in for a closer reading, skim it for an overview of its content and organization. Pay attention to the title. Take a quick look at all parts of the reading. Even a book's cover, preface, introduction, footnotes, and biographical notes about the author can provide you with some context for reading the work itself.

- **Read closely. Look up any unfamiliar words, allusions, or references.** Often the very words you may be tempted to skim over will provide the key to a work's meaning. Thomas Hardy's poem "The Ruined Maid" will remain elusive to a reader unfamiliar with the archaic meaning of the word "ruin"— a woman's loss of virginity to a man other than her husband.

- **Take notes. Annotate the text.** Read with a highlighter and pencil at hand, making appropriate annotations to the text. Later, you'll easily be able to review these highlights, and, when you write your paper, quickly refer to supporting evidence.

  - Underline words, phrases, or sentences that seem interesting or important, or that raise questions.
  - Jot down brief notes in the margin (*"key symbol—this foreshadows the ending,"* for example, or *"dramatic irony"*).
  - Use lines or arrows to indicate passages that seem to speak to each other—for instance, all the places in which you find the same theme or related symbols.

(If you prefer not to mark up your book, take notes on a separate sheet of paper, being sure to jot down the appropriate page numbers for future reference. This method will allow a lot of room for note taking.)

Robert Frost

Nothing Gold Can Stay

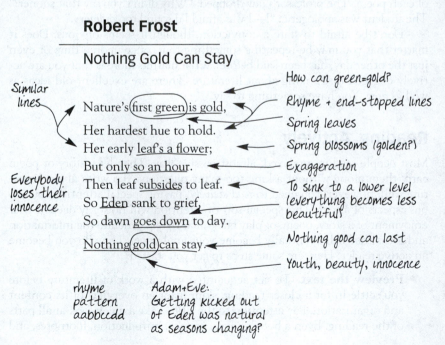

- **Reread as needed.** If a piece is short, read it several times. Often, knowing the ending of a poem or short story will allow you to extract new meaning from its beginning and middle. If the piece is longer, reread the passages you thought important enough to highlight.

- **Read poetry aloud.** There is no better way to understand a poem than to effectively read it aloud. Read slowly, paying attention to punctuation cues. Listen for the audio effects.

- **Read the whole play—not just the dialogue, but also everything in italics, including stage directions and descriptions of settings.** The meaning of a scene, or even of an entire play, may depend on the tone of voice in which an actor is supposed to deliver a significant line or the actions described in the stage directions, as in this passage from Susan Glaspell's *Trifles*.

Mrs. Peters: (*To the other woman.*) Oh, her fruit; it did freeze. (*To the County Attorney.*) She worried about that when it turned so cold. She said the fire'd go out and her jars would break.

Sheriff: Well, can you beat the women! Held for murder and worryin' about her preserves.

County Attorney: I guess before we're through she may have something more serious than preserves to worry about.

Hale: Well, women are used to worrying over trifles.

(The two women move a little closer together.)

County Attorney: (*With the gallantry of a young politician.*) And yet, for all their worries, what would we do without the ladies? (*The women do not unbend.* He goes to the sink, takes a dipperful of water from the pail and pouring it into a basin, washes his hands. Starts to wipe them on the roller towel, turns it for a cleaner place.*) Dirty towels! (*Kicks his foot against the pans under the sink.*) Not much of a housekeeper, would you say, ladies?

Mrs. Hale: (*Stiffly.*) There's a great deal of work to be done on a farm.

[Handwritten margin notes:]

Both men are insulting toward Mrs. Wright.

The women side with each other.

Courtesy toward women, but condescending

The two women aren't buying it.

Small, insignificant things or not? Play's title. Significant word? The men miss the "clues"—too trifling.

She holds back, but she's mad.

I don't like this guy!

Thinking About What You Have Read

Once you have reread a work, you can start to process your ideas about it. Before you begin writing, take some time to collect your thoughts. To get started thinking about fiction or drama, try the following steps:

- **Identify the protagonist and the conflict.** Whose story is being told? What does that character desire more than anything else? What stands in the way of that character's achievement of his or her goal? The answers to these questions can give you a better handle on the plot.

- **Consider a story's point of view.** What does it contribute to the story? How might the tale change if told from another point of view?

- **Think about the setting.** Does it play a significant role in the plot? How does setting affect the tone?

- **Notice key symbols.** If any symbols catch your attention as you go, be sure to highlight each place in which they appear in the text. What do these symbols contribute to the work's meaning? (Remember, not every image is a symbol—only those important recurrent persons, places, or things that seem to suggest more than their literal meaning.)

- **Look for the theme.** Is the work's central meaning stated directly? If not, how does it reveal itself?

- **Think about tone and style.** How would you characterize the style in which the story or play is written? Consider elements such as diction, sentence structure, tone, and organization. How does the work's style contribute to its tone?

You might consider some different approaches when thinking about a poem:

- **Let your emotions guide you into the poem.** Do any images or phrases call up a strong emotional response? If so, try to puzzle out why those passages seem so emotionally loaded. In a word or two, describe the poem's tone.

- **Determine what's literally happening in the poem.** Separating literal language from figurative or symbolic language can be one of the trickiest—and most essential—tasks in poetic interpretation. Begin by working out the literal. Who is speaking the poem? To whom? Under what circumstances? What happens in the poem?

- **Ask what it all adds up to.** Once you've pinned down the literal action of the poem, it's time to take a leap into the figurative. What is the significance of the poem—the "So what?" of it all? Address symbolism, any figures of speech, and any language that means one thing literally but suggests something else. In "My Papa's Waltz," for example, Theodore Roethke tells a simple story of a father dancing his small son around a kitchen. The language of the poem suggests much more, however, implying that while the father is rough to the point of violence, the young boy hungers for his attention.

- **Consider the poem's shape on the page, and the way it sounds.** What patterns of sound do you notice? Are the lines long, short, or a mixture of both? How do these elements contribute to the poem's effect?

- **Pay attention to form.** If a poem makes use of rime or regular meter, ask yourself how those elements contribute to its meaning. If it is in a fixed form, such as a sonnet or villanelle, how do the demands of that form serve to set its tone? If the form calls for repetition—of sounds, words, or entire lines—how does that repetition underscore the poem's message? If, on the other hand, the poem is in free verse—without a consistent pattern of rime or regular meter—how does this choice affect the poem's feel?

- **Take note of line breaks.** If the poem is written in free verse, pay special attention to its line breaks. Poets break their lines with care, conscious that readers pause momentarily over the last word in any line, giving that word special emphasis. Notice whether the lines tend to be broken at the ends of whole phrases and sentences or in the middle of phrases. Then ask yourself what effect is created by the poet's choice of line breaks. How does that effect contribute to the poem's meaning?

Planning Your Essay

If you have actively read the work you plan to write about and have made notes or annotations, you are already well on your way to writing your paper. Your mind has already begun to work through some initial impressions and ideas. Now you need to arrange those early notions into an organized and logical essay. Here is some advice on how to manage the writing process:

- **Leave yourself time.** Good writing involves thought and revision. Anyone who has ever been a student knows what it's like to pull an all-nighter, churning out a term paper hours before it is due. Still, the best writing evolves over time. Your ideas need to marinate. Sometimes, you'll make false starts, and you'll need to salvage what you can and do the rest from scratch. For the sake of your writing—not to mention your health and sanity—it's far better to get the job started well before your deadline.

- **Choose a subject you care about.** If you have been given a choice of literary works to write about, always choose the play, story, or poem that evokes the strongest emotional response. Your writing will be liveliest if you feel engaged by your subject.

▪ **Know your purpose.** As you write, keep the assignment in mind. You may have been asked to write a response, in which you describe your reactions to a literary work. Perhaps your purpose is to interpret a work, analyzing how one or more of its elements contribute to its meaning. You may have been instructed to write an evaluation, in which you judge a work's merits. Whatever the assignment, how you approach your essay will depend, in large part, on your purpose.

▪ **Define your topic narrowly.** Worried about not having enough to say, students sometimes frame their topic so broadly that they can't do justice to it in the allotted number of pages. Your paper will be stronger if you go more deeply into your subject than if you choose a gigantic subject and touch on most aspects of it only superficially. A profound topic ("The Character of Hamlet") might overflow a book, but a more focused one ("Hamlet's View of Acting" or "Hamlet's Puns") could result in a manageable paper.

Prewriting: Discovering Ideas

Topic in hand, you can begin to get your ideas on the page. To generate new ideas and clarify the thoughts you already have, try one or more of the following useful prewriting strategies as one student did preparing a paper on Robert Frost's poem "Nothing Gold Can Stay."

▪ **Brainstorming.** Writing quickly, list everything that comes into your mind about your subject. Set a time limit—ten or fifteen minutes—and force yourself to keep adding items to the list, even when you think you have run out of things to say. Sometimes, if you press onward past the point where you feel you are finished, you will surprise yourself with new and fresh ideas.

```
gold = early leaves/blossoms
Or gold = something precious (both?)
early leaf = flower (yellow blossoms)
spring (lasts an hour)
Leaves subside (sink to lower level)
Eden = paradise = perfection = beauty
Loss of innocence?
What about original sin?
Dawn becomes day (dawn is more precious?)
```

```
Adam and Eve had to fall? Part of natural order.

seasons/days/people's lives

Title = last line: perfection can't last

spring/summer/autumn

dawn/day

Innocence can't last
```

- **Clustering.** This prewriting strategy works especially well for visual thinkers. In clustering, you build a diagram to help you explore the relationships among your ideas. To get started, write your subject at the center of a sheet of paper. Circle it. Then jot down ideas, linking each to the central circle with lines. As you write down each new idea, draw lines to link it to related old ideas. The result will look something like the following web.

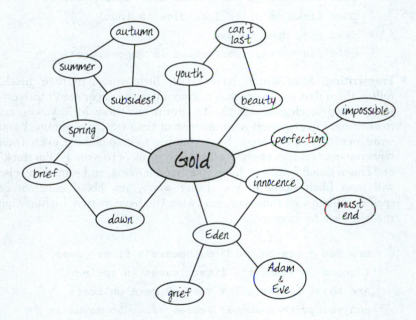

- **Listing.** Look over the notes and annotations that you made in your active reading of the work. You have probably already underlined or noted more information than you can possibly use. One way to sort through your material to find the most useful information is to make a list of the important items. It helps to make several short lists under different headings.

Don't be afraid to add more comments or questions on the lists to help your thought process.

Images	Colors
leaf ("early leaf")	green
flower	gold ("hardest hue to
dawn	hold")
day	
Eden	
gold	

Key Actions

gold is hard to hold

early leaf lasts only an hour

leaf subsides to leaf (what does this mean???)

Eden sinks to grief (paradise is lost)

dawn goes down to day

gold can't stay (perfection is impossible?)

■ **Freewriting.** Most writers have snarky little voices in their heads, telling them that the words they're committing to paper aren't interesting or deep or elegant enough. To drown out those little voices, try freewriting. Give yourself a set amount of time (say, ten minutes) and write, nonstop, on your topic. Force your pen to keep moving, even if you have run out of things to say. If all you can think of to write is "I'm stuck" or "This is dumb," so be it. Keep your hand moving, and something else will most likely occur to you. Don't worry, yet, about grammar or spelling. When your time is up, read what you have written, highlighting the best ideas for later use.

How can green be gold? By nature's first green,

I guess he means the first leaves in spring.

Are those leaves gold? They're more delicate

and yellow than summer leaves . . . so maybe in

a sense they look gold. Or maybe he means

spring blossoms. Sometimes they're yellow. Also

the first line seems to connect with the third

one, where he comes right out and says that

flowers are like early leaves. Still, I think

he also means that the first leaves are the

most precious ones, like gold. I don't think
the poem wants me to take all of these
statements literally. Flowers on trees last
more than an hour, but that really beautiful
moment in spring when blossoms are everywhere
always ends too quickly, so maybe that's what
he means by "only so an hour." I had to look up
"subsides." It means to sink to a lower level
. . . as if the later leaves will be less perfect
than the first ones. I don't know if I agree.
Aren't fall leaves precious? Then he says, "So
Eden sank to grief" which seems to be saying
that Adam and Eve's fall would have happened no
matter what they did, because everything that
seems perfect falls apart . . . nothing gold
can stay. Is he saying Adam and Eve didn't
really have a choice? No matter what,
everything gets older, less beautiful, less
innocent . . . even people.

- **Journal writing.** Your instructor might ask you to keep a journal in which you jot down your ideas, feelings, and impressions before they are fully formulated. Sometimes a journal is meant for your eyes only; in other instances your instructor might read it. Either way, it is meant to be informal and immediate, and to provide raw material that you may later choose to refine into a formal essay. Here are some tips for keeping a useful journal:

  - Get your ideas down as soon as they occur to you.
  - Write quickly.
  - Jot down your feelings about and first impressions of the story, poem, or play you are reading.
  - Don't worry about grammar, spelling, or punctuation.
  - Don't worry about sounding academic.
  - Don't worry about whether your ideas are good or bad ones; you can sort that out later.
  - Try out invention strategies, such as freewriting, clustering, and outlining.
  - Keep writing, even after you think you have run out of things to say. You might surprise yourself.
  - Write about what interests you most.
  - Write in your journal on a regular basis.

- **Outlining.** Some topics by their very nature suggest obvious ways to organize a paper. "An Explication of a Sonnet by Wordsworth" might mean simply working through the poem line by line. If this isn't the case, some kind of outline will probably prove helpful. Your outline needn't be elaborate to be useful. While a long research paper on several literary works might call for a detailed outline, a 500-word analysis of a short story's figures of speech might call for just a simple list of points in the order that makes the most logical sense—not necessarily, of course, the order in which those thoughts first came to mind.

```
1. Passage of time = fall from innocence
     blossoms
     gold
     dawn
     grief
2. Innocence = perfection
     Adam and Eve
     loss of innocence = inevitable
     real original sin = passing of time
     paradise sinks to grief
3. Grief = knowledge
     experience of sin & suffering
     unavoidable as grow older
```

Developing a Literary Argument

Once you have finished a rough outline of your ideas, you need to refine it into a clear and logical shape. You need to state your thesis (or basic idea) clearly and then support it with logical and accurate evidence. Here is a practical approach to this crucial stage of the writing process:

- **Consider your purpose.** As you develop your argument, be sure to refer back to the specific assignment; let it guide you. Your instructor might request one of the following kinds of papers:
  - *Response*, in which you explore your reaction to a work of literature.
  - *Evaluation*, in which you assess the literary merits of a work.
  - *Interpretation*, in which you discuss a work's meaning. If your instructor has assigned an interpretation, he or she may have more specifically asked for an *analysis, explication,* or *comparison/contrast* essay, among other possibilities.

- **Remember your audience.** Practically speaking, your professor (and sometimes your classmates) will be your paper's primary audience. Some assignments, however, specify a particular audience beyond your professor and classmates. Keep your readers in mind. Be sure to adapt your writing to meet their needs and interests. If, for example, the audience has presumably already read a story under discussion, you won't need to relate the plot in its entirety. Instead, you will be free to bring up only those plot points that serve as evidence for your thesis.

- **Narrow down your topic to fit the assignment.** Though you may be tempted to choose a broad topic so that you will have no shortage of things to say, remember that a good paper needs focus. Your choice should be narrow enough for you to do it justice in the space and time allotted.

- **Decide on a thesis.** Just as you need to know your destination before you set out on a trip, you need to decide what point you're traveling toward before you begin your first draft. Start by writing a provisional thesis sentence: a summing up of the main idea or argument your paper will explore. While your thesis doesn't need to be outrageous or deliberately provocative, it does need to take a stand. A clear, decisive statement gives you something to prove and lends vigor to your essay.

  WORKING THESIS

  > The poem argues that like Adam and Eve we all
  > lose our innocence and the passage of time is
  > inevitable.

  This first stab at a thesis sentence gave its author a sense of purpose and direction that allowed him to finish his first draft. Later, as he revised his essay, he found he needed to refine his thesis to make more specific and focused assertions.

- **Build your argument.** Once you've formulated your thesis, your task will be clear: you need to convince your audience that your thesis is sound. To write persuasively, it helps to have an understanding of some key elements of argument:

  - *Claims.* Any time you make a statement you hope will be taken as true, you have made a claim. Some claims are unlikely to be contradicted ("the sky is blue" or "today is Tuesday"), but others are debatable ("every college sophomore dreams of running off to see the world"). Your essay's main claim—your thesis—should not be something entirely obvious. Having to support your point of view will cause you to clarify your ideas about a work of literature.

- *Persuasion.* If the word *argument* makes you think of raised voices and short tempers, it may help to think of your task as the gentler art of persuasion. To convince your audience of your thesis, you will need to present a cogent argument supported by evidence gathered from the text. If the assignment at hand is a research paper, you will also need to cite what others have written on your topic.

- *Evidence.* When you write about a work of literature, the most convincing evidence will generally come from the text itself. Direct quotations from the poem, play, or story under discussion can provide particularly convincing support for your claims. Be sure to introduce any quotation by putting it in the context of the larger work. It is even more important to follow up each quotation with your own analysis of what it shows about the work.

- *Warrants.* Whenever you use a piece of evidence to support a claim, an underlying assumption connects one to the other. For instance, if you were to make the claim that today's weather is absolutely perfect and offer as your evidence the blue sky, your logic would include an unspoken warrant: sunny weather is perfect weather. Not everyone will agree with your warrant, though. Some folks (perhaps farmers) might prefer rain. In making any argument, including one about literature, you may find that you sometimes need to spell out your warrants to demonstrate that they are sound. This is especially true when the evidence you provide can lead to conclusions other than the one you are hoping to prove.

- *Credibility.* When weighing the merits of a claim, you will probably take into account the credibility of the person making the case. Often this happens almost automatically. You are more likely to listen to the opinion that you should take vitamins if it is expressed by your doctor than if it is put forth by a stranger you meet on the street. An expert on any given topic has a certain brand of authority not available to most of us. Fortunately, there are other ways to establish your credibility:

  KEEP YOUR TONE THOUGHTFUL. Your reader will develop a sense of who you are through your words. If you come across as belligerent or disrespectful to those inclined to disagree with your views, you may lose your reader's goodwill. Therefore, express your ideas calmly and thoughtfully. A level tone demonstrates that you are interested in thinking through an issue or idea, not in bullying your reader into submission.

  TAKE OPPOSING ARGUMENTS INTO ACCOUNT. To make an argument more convincing, demonstrate familiarity with other possible points of view. Doing so indicates that you have taken other claims into account before arriving at your thesis; it reveals your fairness as well as your understanding of your subject matter. In laying out other points of view, though, be sure to represent them fairly but also to respectfully make clear why your thesis is the soundest claim; you don't want your reader to doubt where you stand.

DEMONSTRATE YOUR KNOWLEDGE. To gain your reader's trust, it helps to demonstrate a solid understanding of your subject matter. Always check your facts; factual errors can call your knowledge into doubt. It also helps to have a command of the conventions of writing. Rightly or wrongly, errors in punctuation and spelling can undermine a writer's credibility.

- **Organize your argument.** Unless you are writing an explication that works its way line by line through a work of literature, you will need to make crucial decisions about how to shape your essay. Its order should be driven by the logic of your argument, not by the structure of the story, play, or poem you're discussing. In other words, you need not work your way from start to finish through your source material, touching on each major point. Instead, choose only the points needed to prove your thesis, and present them in whatever order best makes your point. A rough outline can help you to determine that order.

- **Make sure your thesis is supported by the evidence.** If you find you can't support certain aspects of your thesis, then refine it so that you can. Remember: until you turn it in, your essay is a work in progress. Anything can and should be changed if it doesn't further the development of the paper's main idea.

CHECKLIST

Developing an Argument

✓ What is your essay's purpose?

✓ Who is your audience?

✓ Is your topic narrow enough?

✓ Is your thesis interesting and thought-provoking?

✓ Does everything in your essay support your thesis?

✓ Have you considered and refuted alternative views?

✓ Is your tone thoughtful?

✓ Is your argument sensibly organized? Are similar ideas grouped together? Does one point lead logically to the next?

Writing a Rough Draft

Seated at last, you prepare to write, only to find yourself besieged with petty distractions. All of a sudden you remember a friend you had promised to call, some double-A batteries you were supposed to pick up, a neglected Coke (in another room) growing warmer and flatter by the minute. If your paper is to be written, you have only one course of action: collar these thoughts and for the moment banish them. Here are a few tips for writing your rough draft:

- **Review your argument.** The shape of your argument, its support, and the evidence you have collected will form the basis of your rough draft.

- **Get your thoughts down.** The best way to draft a paper is to get your ideas down quickly. At this stage, don't fuss over details. The critical, analytical side of your mind can worry about spelling, grammar, and punctuation later. For now, let your creative mind take charge. This part of yourself has the good ideas, insight, and confidence. Forge ahead. Believe in yourself and in your ideas.

- **Write the part you feel most comfortable with first.** There's no need to start at the paper's beginning and work your way methodically through to the end. Instead, plunge right into the parts of the paper you feel most prepared to write. You can always go back later and fill in the blanks.

- **Leave yourself plenty of space.** As you compose, leave plenty of space between lines and set enormous margins. When later thoughts come to you, you will easily be able to go back and squeeze them in.

- **Focus on the argument.** As you jot down your first draft, you might not want to look at the notes you have compiled. When you come to a place where a note will fit, just insert a reminder to yourself such as "See card 19" or "See Aristotle on comedy." Also, whenever you bring up a new point, it's good to tie it back to your thesis. If you can't find a way to connect a point to your thesis, it is probably better to leave it out of your paper and come up with a point that advances your central claim.

- **Does your thesis hold up?** If, as you write, you find that most of the evidence you uncover is not helping you prove your paper's thesis, it may be that the thesis needs honing. Adjust it as needed.

- **Be open to new ideas.** Writing rarely proceeds in a straight line. Even after you outline your paper and begin to write and revise, expect to discover new thoughts—perhaps the best thoughts of all. If you do, be sure to invite them in.

Here is a student's rough draft for an analytical essay on "Nothing Gold Can Stay."

On Frost's "Nothing Gold Can Stay"

Most of the lines in the poem "Nothing Gold Can Stay" by Robert Frost focus on the changing of the seasons. The poem's first line says that the first leaves of spring are actually blossoms, and the actual leaves that follow are less precious. Those first blossoms only last a little while. The reader realizes that nature is a metaphor for a person's state of mind. People start off perfectly innocent, but as time passes, they can't help but lose that innocence. The poem argues that like Adam and Eve we all lose our innocence and the passage of time is inevitable.

The poem's first image is of the color found in nature. The early gold of spring blossoms is nature's "hardest hue to hold." The color gold is associated with the mineral gold, a precious commodity. There's a hint that early spring is nature in its perfect state, and perfection is impossible to hold on to. To the poem's speaker, the colors of early spring seem to last only an hour. If you blink, they are gone. Like early spring, innocence can't last.

The line "leaf subsides to leaf" brings us from early spring through summer and fall. The golden blossoms and delicate leaves of spring subside, or sink to a lower level, meaning they become less special and beautiful. There's nothing more special and beautiful than a baby, so people are the same way. In literature, summer often means the prime of your life, and autumn often means the declining years. These times are less beautiful ones. "So dawn goes down to day" is a similar kind of image. Dawns are unbelievably colorful and beautiful but they don't last very long. Day is nice, but not as special as dawn.

The most surprising line in the poem is the one that isn't about nature. Instead it's about human beings. Eden may have been a garden (a part of nature), but it also represents a state of mind. The traditional religious view is that Adam and Eve chose to disobey God and eat from the tree of knowledge. They could have stayed in paradise forever if they had followed God's orders. So it's surprising that Frost writes "So Eden sank to grief" in a poem that is all about how inevitable change is. It seems like he's saying that no matter what Adam and Eve had done, the Garden of Eden wouldn't stay the paradise it started out being. When Adam and Eve ate the apple, they lost their innocence. The apple is supposed to represent knowledge, so they became wiser but less perfect. But the poem implies that no matter what Adam and Eve had done, they would have grown sadder and wiser. That's true for all people. We can't stay young and innocent.

It's almost as if Frost is defying the Bible, suggesting that there is no such thing as sin. We can't help getting older and wiser. It's a natural process. Suffering happens not because we choose to do bad things but because passing time takes our innocence. The real original sin is that time has to pass and we all have to grow less innocent.

The poem "Nothing Gold Can Stay" makes the point that people can't stay innocent forever. Suffering is the inevitable result of the aging process. Like the first leaves of spring, we are at the best at the very beginning, and it's all downhill from there.

Revising

A writer rarely—if ever—achieves perfection on the first try. For most of us, good writing is largely a matter of revision. Once your first draft is done, you can—and should—turn on your analytical mind. Painstaking revision is more than just tidying up grammar and spelling. It might mean expanding your ideas or sharpening the focus by cutting out any unnecessary thoughts. To achieve effective writing, you must have the courage to be merciless. Tear your rough drafts apart and reassemble their pieces into a stronger order. As you revise, consider the following:

- **Be sure your thesis is clear, decisive, and thought-provoking.** The most basic ingredient in a good essay is a strong thesis—the sentence in which you summarize the claim you are making. Your thesis should say something more than just the obvious; it should be clear and decisive and make a point that requires evidence to persuade your reader to agree. A sharp, bold thesis lends energy to your argument. A revision of the working thesis used in the rough draft above provides a good example.

WORKING THESIS

```
The poem argues that like Adam and Eve we all
lose our innocence and the passage of time is
inevitable.
```

This thesis may not be bold or specific enough to make for an interesting argument. A careful reader would be hard pressed to disagree with the observation that Frost's poem depicts the passage of time or the loss of innocence. In a revision of his thesis, however, the essay's author pushes the claim further, going beyond the obvious to its implications.

REVISED THESIS

```
In "Nothing Gold Can Stay," Frost makes a bold
claim: sin, suffering, and loss are inevitable
because the passage of time causes everyone to
fall from grace.
```

Instead of simply asserting that the poem looks with sorrow on the passage of time, the revised thesis raises the issue of why this is so. It makes a more thought-provoking claim about the poem. An arguable thesis can result in a more energetic, purposeful essay. A thesis that is obvious to everyone, on the other hand, leads to a static, dull paper.

■ **Ascertain whether the evidence you provide supports your theory.**
Does everything within your paper work to support its thesis sentence?
While a solid paper might be written about the poetic form of "Nothing
Gold Can Stay," the student paper above would not be well served by
bringing the subject up unless the author could show how the poem's form
contributes to its message that time causes everyone to lose his or her innocence. If you find yourself including information that doesn't serve your
argument, consider going back into the poem, story, or play for more useful evidence. On the other hand, if you're beginning to have a sneaking
feeling that your thesis itself is shaky, consider reworking *it* so that it more
accurately reflects the evidence in the text.

■ **Check whether your argument is logical.** Does one point lead naturally to the next? Reread the paper, looking for logical fallacies, moments
in which the claims you make are not sufficiently supported by evidence,
or the connection between one thought and the next seems less than rational. Classic logical fallacies include making hasty generalizations, confusing cause and effect, or using a non sequitur, a statement that doesn't
follow from the statement that precedes it. An example of two seemingly
unconnected thoughts may be found in the second paragraph of the draft
above:

> To the poem's speaker, the colors of early
> spring seem to last only an hour. If you blink,
> they are gone. Like early spring, innocence
> can't last.

Though there may well be a logical connection between the first two
sentences and the third one, the paper doesn't spell that connection out.
Asked to clarify the warrant, or assumption, that makes possible the leap
from the subject of spring to the subject of innocence, the author revised
the passage this way:

> To the poem's speaker, the colors of early
> spring seem to last only an hour. When poets
> write of seasons, they often also are
> commenting on the life cycle. To make a
> statement that spring can't last more than an
> hour implies that a person's youth (often
> symbolically associated with spring) is all too
> short. Therefore, the poem implies that
> innocent youth, like spring, lasts for only the
> briefest time.

The revised version spells out the author's thought process, helping the reader to follow the argument.

- **Supply transitional words and phrases.** To ensure that your reader's journey from one idea to the next is a smooth one, insert transitional words and phrases at the start of new paragraphs or sentences. Phrases such as "in contrast" and "however" signal a U-turn in logic, while those such as "in addition" and "similarly" alert the reader that you are continuing in the same direction you have been traveling. Seemingly inconsequential words and phrases such as "also" and "similarly" or "as mentioned above" can smooth the reader's path from one thought to the next, as in the example below.

DRAFT

Though Frost is writing about nature, his real subject is humanity. In literature, spring often represents youth. Summer symbolizes young adulthood, autumn stands for middle age, and winter represents old age. The adult stages of life are, for Frost, less precious than childhood, which passes very quickly. The innocence of childhood is, like those spring leaves, precious as gold.

ADDING TRANSITIONAL WORDS AND PHRASES

Though Frost is writing about nature, his real subject is humanity. <u>As mentioned above</u>, in literature, spring often represents youth. <u>Similarly</u>, summer symbolizes young adulthood, autumn stands for middle age, and winter represents old age. The adult stages of life are, for Frost, less precious than childhood, which passes very quickly. <u>Also</u>, the innocence of childhood is, like those spring leaves, precious as gold.

- **Make sure each paragraph contains a topic sentence.** Each paragraph in your essay should develop a single idea; this idea should be conveyed in a topic sentence. As astute readers often expect to get a sense of a paragraph's purpose from its first few sentences, a topic sentence is often well placed at or near a paragraph's start.

■ **Make a good first impression.** Your introductory paragraph may have seemed just fine as you began the writing process. Be sure to reconsider it in light of the entire paper. Does the introduction draw readers in and prepare them for what follows? If not, be sure to rework it, as the author of the rough draft above did. Look at his first paragraph again:

DRAFT OF OPENING PARAGRAPH

Most of the lines in the poem "Nothing Gold
Can Stay" by Robert Frost focus on the changing
of the seasons. The poem's first line says that
the first leaves of spring are actually
blossoms, and the actual leaves that follow are
less precious. Those first blossoms only last a
little while. The reader realizes that nature
is a metaphor for a person's state of mind.
People start off perfectly innocent, but as
time passes, they can't help but lose that
happy innocence. The poem argues that like Adam
and Eve we all lose our innocence and the
passage of time is inevitable.

While serviceable, this paragraph could be more compelling. Its author improved it by adding specifics to bring his ideas to more vivid life. For example, the rather pedestrian sentence "People start off perfectly innocent, but as time passes, they can't help but lose that innocence," became this livelier one: "As babies we are all perfectly innocent, but as time passes, we can't help but lose that innocence." By adding a specific image—the baby—the author gives the reader a visual picture to illustrate the abstract idea of innocence. He also sharpened his thesis sentence, making it less general and more thought-provoking. By varying the length of his sentences, he made the paragraph less monotonous.

REVISED OPENING PARAGRAPH

Most of the lines in Robert Frost's brief
poem "Nothing Gold Can Stay" focus on nature:
the changing of the seasons and the fading of
dawn into day. The poem's opening line asserts
that the first blossoms of spring are more
precious than the leaves that follow. Likewise,

dawn is more special than day. Though Frost's
subject seems to be nature, the reader soon
realizes that his real subject is human nature.
As babies we are all perfectly innocent, but as
time passes, we can't help but lose that happy
innocence. In "Nothing Gold Can Stay," Frost
makes a bold claim: sin, suffering, and loss
are inevitable because the passage of time
causes everyone to fall from grace.

■ **Remember that last impressions count too.** Your paper's conclusion should give the reader some closure, tying up the paper's loose
ends without simply (and boringly) restating all that has come before.
The author of the rough draft above initially ended his paper with a
paragraph that repeated the paper's main ideas without pushing those
ideas any further:

DRAFT OF CONCLUSION

The poem "Nothing Gold Can Stay" makes the
point that people can't stay innocent forever.
Grief is the inevitable result of the aging
process. Like the first leaves of spring, we
are at the best at the very beginning, and it's
all downhill from there.

While revising his paper, the author realized that the ideas in his next-
to-last paragraph would serve to sum up the paper. The new final paragraph doesn't simply restate the thesis; it pushes the idea further, in its
last two sentences, by exploring the poem's implications.

REVISED CONCLUSION

Some people might view Frost's poem as
sacrilegious, because it seems to say that Adam
and Eve had no choice; everything in life is
doomed to fall. Growing less innocent and more
knowing seems less a choice in Frost's view
than a natural process like the changing of
golden blossoms to green leaves. "Eden sank to

grief" not because we choose to do evil things,
but because time takes away our innocence as we
encounter the suffering and loss of human
existence. Frost suggests that the real
original sin is that time has to pass and we
all must grow wiser and less innocent.

- **Give your paper a compelling title.** Like the introduction, a title should be inviting to readers, giving them a sense of what's coming. Avoid a nontitle such as "A Rose for Emily," which serves as a poor advertisement for your paper. Instead, provide enough specifics to pique your reader's interest. "On Robert Frost's 'Nothing Gold Can Stay'" is a duller, less informative title than "Lost Innocence in Robert Frost's 'Nothing Gold Can Stay,'" which may spark the reader's interest and prepare him or her for what is to come.

CHECKLIST

Revision Steps

✓ Is your thesis clear? Can it be sharpened?

✓ Does all your evidence serve to advance the argument put forth in your thesis?

✓ Is your argument logical?

✓ Do transitional words and phrases signal movement from one idea to the next?

✓ Does each paragraph contain a topic sentence?

✓ Does your introduction draw the reader in? Does it prepare the reader for what follows?

✓ Does your conclusion tie up the paper's loose ends? Does it avoid merely restating what has come before?

✓ Is your title compelling?

Some Final Advice on Rewriting

- **Whenever possible, get feedback from a trusted reader.** In every project, there comes a time when the writer has gotten so close to the work that he or she can't see it clearly. A talented roommate or a tutor in the campus writing center can tell you what isn't yet clear on the page, what questions still need answering, or what line of argument isn't yet as persuasive as it could be.

- **Be willing to refine your thesis.** Once you have fleshed out your whole paper, you may find that your original thesis is not borne out by the rest of your argument. If so, you will need to rewrite your thesis so that it more precisely fits the evidence at hand.

- **Be prepared to question your whole approach to a work of literature.** On occasion, you may even need to entertain the notion of throwing everything you have written into the wastebasket and starting over again. Occasionally having to start from scratch is the lot of any writer.

- **Rework troublesome passages.** Look for skimpy paragraphs of one or two sentences—evidence that your ideas might need more fleshing out. Can you supply more evidence, more explanation, or more examples?

- **Cut out any unnecessary information.** Everything in your paper should serve to further its thesis. Delete any sentences or paragraphs that detract from your focus.

- **Aim for intelligent clarity when you use literary terminology.** Critical terms can help sharpen your thoughts and make them easier to handle. Nothing is less sophisticated or more opaque, however, than too many technical terms thrown together for grandiose effect: "The mythic *symbolism* of this *archetype* is the *antithesis* of the *dramatic situation*." Choose plain words you're already at ease with. When you use specialized terms, do so to smooth the way for your reader—to make your meaning more precise.

- **Set your paper aside for a while.** Even an hour or two away from your essay can help you return to it with fresh eyes. Remember that the literal meaning of "revision" is "seeing again."

- **Finally, carefully read your paper one last time to edit it.** Now it's time to sweat the small stuff. Check any uncertain spellings, scan for run-on sentences and fragments, pull out a weak word and send in a stronger one. Like soup stains on a job interviewee's tie, finicky errors distract from the overall impression and prejudice your reader against your essay.

Here is the revised version of the student paper we have been examining.

Gabriel 1

Noah Gabriel

Professor James

English 2171

7 October 2007

Lost Innocence in

Robert Frost's "Nothing Gold Can Stay"

Most of the lines in Robert Frost's brief poem
"Nothing Gold Can Stay" focus on nature: the
changing of the seasons and the fading of dawn into
day. The poem's opening line asserts that the first
blossoms of spring are more precious than the
leaves that follow. Likewise, dawn is more special
than day. Though Frost's subject seems to be
nature, the reader soon realizes that his real
subject is human nature. As babies we are all
perfectly innocent, but as time passes, we can't
help but lose that happy innocence. In "Nothing
Gold Can Stay," Frost makes a bold claim: sin,
suffering, and loss are inevitable because the
passage of time causes everyone to fall from grace.

The poem begins with a deceptively simple
sentence: "Nature's first green is gold." The subject
seems to be the first, delicate leaves of spring
which are less green and more golden than summer
leaves. However, the poem goes on to say, "Her early
leaf's a flower" (3), indicating that Frost is
describing the first blossoms of spring. In fact,
he's describing both the new leaves and blossoms.
Both are as rare and precious as the mineral gold.
They are precious because they don't last long; the
early gold of spring blossoms is nature's "hardest
hue to hold" (2). Early spring is an example of

Thesis sentence is specific and decisive

Textual evidence to back up thesis

Gabriel 2

nature in its perfect state, and perfection is
impossible to hold on to. To the poem's speaker, in
fact, the colors of early spring seem to last only an
hour. When poets write of seasons, they often also
are commenting on the life cycle. To make a statement
that spring can't last more than an hour implies that
a person's youth (often symbolically associated with
spring) is all too short. Therefore, the poem implies
that innocent youth, like spring, lasts for only the
briefest time.

    While Frost takes four lines to describe the
decline of the spring blossoms, he picks up the
pace when he describes what happens next. The line,
"Then leaf subsides to leaf" (5) brings us from
early spring through summer and fall, compressing
three seasons into a single line. Just as time
seems to pass slowly when we are children, and then
much more quickly when we grow up, the poem moves
quickly once the first golden moment is past. The
word "subsides" feels important. The golden
blossoms and delicate leaves of spring subside, or
sink to a lower level, meaning they become less
special and beautiful.

    Though Frost is writing about nature, his real
subject is humanity. As mentioned above, in
literature, spring often represents youth. Similarly,
summer symbolizes young adulthood, autumn stands for
middle age, and winter represents old age. The adult
stages of life are, for Frost, less precious than
childhood, which passes very quickly, as we later
realize. Also, the innocence of childhood is, like
those spring leaves, precious as gold.

Warrant is spelled out

Claim

Significant word is looked at closely

Claim

Warrant spelled out

Frost shifts his view from the cycle of the
seasons to the cycle of a single day to make a
similar point. Just as spring turns to summer, "So
dawn goes down to day" (7). Like spring, dawn is
unbelievably colorful and beautiful but doesn't
last very long. Like "subsides," the phrase "goes
down" implies that full daylight is actually a
falling off from dawn. As beautiful as daylight is,
it's ordinary, while dawn is special because it is
more fleeting.

**Key phrase is
analyzed
closely**

Among these natural images, one line stands
out: "So Eden sank to grief" (6). This line is the
only one in the poem that deals directly with human
beings. Eden may have been a garden (a part of
nature) but it represents a state of mind--perfect
innocence. In the traditional religious view, Adam
and Eve chose to disobey God by eating an apple
from the tree of knowledge. They were presented
with a choice: to be obedient and remain in
paradise forever, or to disobey God's order. People
often speak of that first choice as "original sin."
In this religious view, "Eden sank to grief"
because the first humans chose to sin.

Claim

Frost, however, takes a different view. He
compares the Fall of Man to the changing of spring
to summer, as though it was as inevitable as the
passage of time. The poem implies that no matter
what Adam and Eve did, they couldn't remain in
paradise. Original sin in Frost's view seems less a
voluntary moral action than a natural, if unhappy
sort of maturation. The innocent perfection of the
garden of Eden couldn't possibly last. The apple
represents knowledge, so in a symbolic sense God

Claim

wanted Adam and Eve to stay unknowing, or innocent. But the poem implies that it was inevitable that Adam and Eve would gain knowledge and lose their innocence, becoming wiser but less perfect. They lost Eden and encountered "grief," the knowledge of suffering and loss associated with the human condition. This is certainly true for the rest of us human beings. As much as we might like to, we can't stay young or innocent forever.

Some people might view Frost's poem as sacrilegious, because it seems to say that Adam and Eve had no choice; everything in life is doomed to fall. Growing less innocent and more knowing seems less a choice in Frost's view than a natural process like the changing of golden blossoms to green leaves. "Eden sank to grief" not because we choose to do evil things but because time takes away our innocence as we encounter the suffering and loss of human existence. Frost suggests that the real original sin is that time has to pass and we all must grow wiser and less innocent.

Restatement of thesis

WORK CITED

Frost, Robert. "Nothing Gold Can Stay." <u>Backpack</u>
   <u>Literature: An Introduction to Fiction, Poetry,</u>
   <u>Drama, and Writing</u>. 2nd ed. Ed. X. J. Kennedy
   and Dana Gioia. New York: Longman, 2008. 487.

What's Your Purpose? Some Common Approaches to Writing About Literature

It is crucial to keep your paper's purpose in mind. When you write an academic paper, you are likely to have been given a specific set of marching orders. Perhaps you have been asked to describe your personal reaction to a literary work. Maybe your purpose is to interpret a work, analyzing how one or more of its elements contribute to its meaning. You may have been instructed to write an evaluation in which you judge a work's merits. Let the assignment dictate your paper's tone and content. Below are several commonly used approaches to writing about literature.

Explication

Explication is the patient unfolding of meanings in a work of literature. An explication proceeds carefully through a story, passage, or poem, usually interpreting it line by line—perhaps even word by word, dwelling on details a casual reader might miss and illustrating how a work's smaller parts contribute to the whole. Alert and willing to take pains, the writer of such an essay notices anything meaningful that isn't obvious, whether it is a colossal theme suggested by a symbol or a little hint contained in a single word.

To write an honest explication of an entire story takes time and space, and is a better assignment for a long-term paper, an honors thesis, or a dissertation than a short essay. A thorough explication of Nathaniel Hawthorne's "Young Goodman Brown," for example, would likely run much longer than the rich and intriguing short story itself. Ordinarily, explication is best suited to a short section of a story: a key scene, a critical conversation, a statement of theme, or an opening or closing paragraph. In drama, explication is best suited for brief passages—a key soliloquy, for example, or a moment of dialogue that lays bare the play's theme. Closely examining a critical moment in a play can shed light on the play in its entirety. To be successful, an explication needs to concentrate on a short passage, probably not much more than 20 lines long.

Storytellers who are especially fond of language invite closer attention to their words than others might. Edgar Allan Poe, for one, is a poet sensitive to the rhythms of his sentences and a symbolist whose stories abound in potent suggestions. Here is a student's explication of a short but essential passage in "The Tell-Tale Heart." The passage occurs in the third paragraph of the story, and to help us follow the explication, the student quotes the passage in full at the paper's beginning. An unusually well-written essay, "By Lantern Light" cost its author two or three careful revisions. Rather than attempting to say something about *everything* in the passage from Poe, she selects only the details that strike her as most meaningful. In her very first sentence, she briefly shows us how the passage functions in the context of Poe's story: how it clinches our suspicions that the narrator is mad. Notice too that the student who wrote the essay doesn't inch through the passage sentence by sentence, but freely takes up its details in an order that seems appropriate to her argument.

Susan Kim

Professor A. M. Lundy

English 100

20 May 2007

By Lantern Light: An Explication

of a Passage in Poe's "The Tell-Tale Heart"

And every night, about midnight, I turned
the latch of his door and opened it--oh,
so gently! And then, when I had made an
opening sufficient for my head, I put in a
dark lantern, all closed, closed, so that
no light shone out, and then I thrust in
my head. Oh, you would have laughed to see
how cunningly I thrust it in! I moved it
slowly--very, very slowly, so that I might
not disturb the old man's sleep. It took
me an hour to place my whole head within
the opening so far that I could see him as
he lay upon his bed. Ha!--would a madman
have been so wise as this? And then, when
my head was well in the room, I undid the
lantern cautiously--oh, so cautiously--
cautiously (for the hinges creaked)--I
undid it just so much that a single thin
ray fell upon the vulture eye. And this I
did for seven long nights--every night
just at midnight--but I found the eye
always closed; and so it was impossible to
do the work; for it was not the old man
who vexed me, but his Evil Eye. (par. 3)

> Passage to be explicated

Although Edgar Allan Poe has suggested in the
first lines of his story "The Tell-Tale Heart" that
the person who addresses us is insane, it is only

> Thesis sentence

when we come to the speaker's account of his
preparations for murdering the old man that we find
his madness fully revealed. Even more convincingly
than his earlier words (for we might possibly think
that someone who claims to hear things in heaven
and hell is a religious mystic), these preparations
reveal him to be mad. What strikes us is that they
are so elaborate and meticulous. A significant
detail is the exactness of his schedule for spying:
"every night just at midnight." The words with
which he describes his motions also convey the most
extreme care (and I will indicate them by
underlining): "how wisely I proceeded--with what
caution," "I turned the latch of his door and
opened it--oh, so gently!" "how cunningly I thrust
it [my head] in! I moved it slowly--very, very
slowly," "I undid the lantern cautiously--oh, so
cautiously--cautiously." Taking a whole hour to
intrude his head into the room, he asks, "Ha!--
would a madman have been so wise as this?" But of
course the word wise is unconsciously ironic, for
clearly it is not wisdom the speaker displays, but
an absurd degree of care, an almost fiendish
ingenuity. Such behavior, I understand, is typical
of certain mental illnesses. All his careful
preparations that he thinks prove him sane only
convince us instead that he is mad.

Obviously his behavior is self-defeating. He
wants to catch the "vulture eye" open, and yet he
takes all these pains not to disturb the old man's
sleep. If he behaved logically, he might go barging
into the bedroom with his lantern ablaze, shouting

Textual evidence supports thesis

Kim 3

at the top of his voice. And yet, if we can see
things his way, there _is_ a strange logic to his
reasoning. He regards the eye as a creature in
itself, quite apart from its possessor. "It was
not," he says, "the old man who vexed me, but his
Evil Eye." Apparently, to be inspired to do his
deed, the madman needs to behold the eye--at least,
this is my understanding of his remark, "I found
the eye always closed; and so it was impossible to
do the work." Poe's choice of the word work, by the
way, is also revealing. Murder is made to seem a
duty or a job; and anyone who so regards murder is
either extremely cold-blooded, like a hired killer
for a gangland assassination, or else deranged.
Besides, the word suggests again the curious sense
of detachment that the speaker feels toward the
owner of the eye.

    In still another of his assumptions, the
speaker shows that he is madly logical, or operating
on the logic of a dream. There seems a dreamlike
relationship between his dark lantern "all closed,
closed, so that no light shone out," and the
sleeping victim. When the madman opens his lantern
so that it emits a single ray, he is hoping that the
eye in the old man's head will be open too, letting
out its corresponding gleam. The latch that he turns
so gently, too, seems like the eye, whose lid needs
to be opened in order for the murderer to go ahead.
It is as though the speaker is trying to get the
eyelid to lift. By taking such great pains and by
going through all this nightly ritual, he is
practicing some kind of magic, whose rules are laid
down not by our logic, but by the logic of dreams.

Topic
sentence on
narrator's
mad logic

Conclusion
pushes thesis
further,
making it
more specific.

```
                                                      Kim 4


                    Work Cited
Poe, Edgar Allan. "The Tell-Tale Heart." Backpack
Literature: An Introduction to Fiction, Poetry,
Drama, and Writing. Ed. X. J. Kennedy and Dana
Gioia. 2nd ed. New York: Longman, 2008. 39.
```

Explication is a particularly useful way to help unravel a poem's complexities. An explication, however, should not be confused with a paraphrase, which puts the poem's literal meaning into plain prose. While an explication might include some paraphrasing, it does more than simply restate. It explains a poem, in great detail, showing how each part contributes to the whole. In writing an explication, keep the following tips in mind:

- **Start with the poem's first line, and keep working straight through to the end.** As needed, though, you can take up points out of order.

- **Read closely, addressing the poem's details.** You may choose to include allusions, the denotations or connotations of words, the possible meanings of symbols, the effects of certain sounds and rhythms and formal elements (rime schemes, for instance), the sense of any statements that contain irony, and other particulars.

- **Show how each part of the poem contributes to the meaning of the whole.** Your explication should go beyond dissecting the pieces of a poem; it should integrate them to cast light on the poem in its entirety.

Here is a famous poem by Robert Frost, followed by a student's concise explication. The assignment was to explain whatever in the poem seemed most essential, in not more than 750 words. This excellent paper finds something worth unfolding in every line in Frost's poem, without seeming mechanical. Although the student proceeds sequentially through the poem from the title to the last line, he takes up some points out of order, when it serves his purpose. In paragraph two, for example, he looks ahead to the poem's ending and briefly states its main theme in order to relate it to the poem's title. In the third paragraph, he explicates the poem's later image of the heal-all, relating it to the first image. He also comments on the poem's form ("Like many other sonnets"), on its similes and puns, and on its denotations and connotations,

Robert Frost (1874–1963)

Design   1936

I found a dimpled spider, fat and white,
On a white heal-all, holding up a moth
Like a white piece of rigid satin cloth—
Assorted characters of death and blight
Mixed ready to begin the morning right,   5
Like the ingredients of a witches' broth—
A snow-drop spider, a flower like a froth,
And dead wings carried like a paper kite.

What had that flower to do with being white,
The wayside blue and innocent heal-all?   10
What brought the kindred spider to that height,
Then steered the white moth thither in the night?
What but design of darkness to appall?—
If design govern in a thing so small.

Jasper 1

Ted Jasper
Professor Hirsch
English 130
21 November 2007

    An Unfolding of Robert Frost's "Design"

    "I always wanted to be very observing," Robert
Frost once told an audience, after reading aloud
his poem "Design." Then he added, "But I have
always been afraid of my own observations" (qtd. in
Cook 126-27). What could Frost have observed that
could scare him? Let's examine the poem in question
and see what we discover.

> Interesting opening. Quotes author

> Central question raised

Jasper 2

Starting with the title, "Design," any reader of this poem will find it full of meaning. As the Merriam-Webster Dictionary defines design, the word can denote among other things a plan, purpose, or intention ("Design"). Some arguments for the existence of God (I remember from Sunday School) are based on the "argument from design": that because the world shows a systematic order, there must be a Designer who made it. But the word design can also mean "a deliberate undercover project or scheme" such as we attribute to a "designing person" ("Design"). As we shall see, Frost's poem incorporates all of these meanings.

His poem raises the old philosophic question of whether there is a Designer, an evil Designer, or no Designer at all.

Like many other sonnets, "Design" is divided into two parts. The first eight lines draw a picture centering on the spider, who at first seems almost jolly. It is dimpled and fat like a baby, or Santa Claus. The spider stands on a

wildflower whose name, heal-all, seems ironic: a heal-all is supposed to cure any disease, but this flower has no power to restore life to the dead moth. (Later, in line ten, we learn that the heal-all used to be blue. Presumably, it has died and become bleached-looking.) In the second line we discover, too, that the spider has hold of another creature, a dead moth. We then see the moth described with an odd simile in line three: "Like a white piece of rigid satin cloth." Suddenly, the moth becomes not a creature but a

Jasper 3

piece of fabric--lifeless and dead--and yet satin

Explores language

has connotations of beauty. Satin is a luxurious
material used in rich formal clothing, such as
coronation gowns and brides' dresses. Additionally,
there is great accuracy in the word: the smooth
and slightly plush surface of satin is like the
powder-smooth surface of moths' wings. But this
"cloth," rigid and white, could be the lining to
Dracula's coffin.

    In the fifth line an invisible hand enters.
The characters are "mixed" like ingredients in an
evil potion. Some force doing the mixing is behind
the scene. The characters in themselves are
innocent enough, but when brought together, their
whiteness and look of rigor mortis are overwhelming.
There is something diabolical in the spider's
feast. The "morning right" echoes the word rite, a

Refers to sound

ritual--in this case apparently a Black Mass or a
Witches' Sabbath. The simile in line seven ("a
flower like a froth") is more ambiguous and harder
to describe. A froth is white, foamy, and
delicate--something found on a brook in the woods
or on a beach after a wave recedes. However, in the
natural world, froth also can be ugly: the foam on
a polluted stream or a rabid dog's mouth. The
dualism in nature--its beauty and its horror--is
there in that one simile.

    So far, the poem has portrayed a small, frozen

Transition words

scene, with the dimpled killer holding its victim
as innocently as a boy holds a kite. Already, Frost
has hinted that Nature may be, as Radcliffe
Squires suggests, "Nothing but an ash-white plain

Quotes secondary source

without love or faith or hope, where ignorant
appetites cross by chance" (87). Now, in the last

Discusses theme

six lines of the sonnet, Frost comes out and
directly states his theme. What else could bring
these deathly pale, stiff things together "but
design of darkness to appall?" The question is
clearly rhetorical; we are meant to answer, "Yes,
there does seem an evil design at work here!" I
take the next-to-last line to mean, "What except a
design so dark and sinister that we're appalled by
it?" "Appall," by the way, is the second pun in the
poem: it sounds like a pall or shroud. (The
derivation of appall, according to Merriam-Webster,
is ultimately from a Latin word meaning "to be

Defines key word

pale"--an interesting word choice for a poem full
of white pale images ["Appall"].) Steered carries
the suggestion of a steering-wheel or rudder that
some pilot had to control. Like the word brought,
it implies that some invisible force charted the
paths of spider, heal-all, and moth, so that they
arrived together.

Having suggested that the universe is in the
hands of that sinister force (an indifferent God?
Fate? the Devil?), Frost adds a note of doubt.
The Bible tells us that "His eye is on the
sparrow," but at the moment the poet doesn't seem
sure. Maybe, he hints, when things in the

Answers question raised in introduction

universe drop below a certain size, they pass
completely out of the Designer's notice. When
creatures are this little, maybe God doesn't
bother to govern them but just lets them run
wild. And possibly the same mindless chance is

Jasper 5

all that governs human lives. And because this is

even more senseless than having an angry God

intent on punishing us, it is, Frost suggests,

the worst suspicion of all.

Conclusion

Jasper 6

Works Cited

"Appall." <u>Merriam-Webster Online</u>. 2006. Merriam-

Webster. 14 Oct. 2006 <http://www.m-w.com/>.

Cook, Reginald. <u>Robert Frost: A Living Voice</u>.

Amherst: U of Massachusetts P, 1974.

"Design." <u>Merriam-Webster Online</u>. 2006. Merriam-

Webster. 14 Oct. 2006 <http://www.m-w.com/>.

Frost, Robert. "Design." <u>Collected Poems, Prose and</u>

<u>Plays</u>. New York: Library of America, 1995. 275.

Squires, Radcliffe. <u>The Major Themes of Robert</u>

<u>Frost</u>. Ann Arbor: U of Michigan P, 1963.

Analysis

Examining a single component of a piece of literature can afford us a better understanding of the entire work. This is perhaps why in most literature classes students are asked to write at least one **analysis** (from the Greek: "breaking up"), an essay that breaks a story, poem, or play into its elements and, usually, studies one part closely. One likely topic for an analysis might be "The Character of Alice Walker's Dee," in which the writer would concentrate on showing us Dee's highly individual features and traits of personality. Other topics for an analysis might be "The Theme of Fragility in Tennessee Williams's *The Glass Menagerie*" or "Imagery of Light and Darkness in Frost's 'Design'." In this book, you probably already have encountered a few brief analyses: the discussion of connotations in John Masefield's "Cargoes" (pages 375–76), for instance, or the examination of symbols in T. S. Eliot's "The *Boston Evening Transcript*" (page 480). In fact, most of the discussions in this book are analyses. To write an analysis, remember two key points:

- **Focus on a single, manageable element.** Some possible choices are tone, irony, literal meaning, imagery, theme, and symbolism. If you are writing about poetry, you could also consider sound, rhythm, rime, or form.

- **Show how the element contributes to the meaning of the whole.** While no element of a work exists apart from all the others, by taking a closer look at one particular aspect, you can see the whole more clearly.

The student papers that follow are examples of brief analyses. The first paper analyzes the imagery of Elizabeth Bishop's poem "The Fish." The second paper analyzes Shakespeare's play *Othello* in light of Aristotle's famous definition of tragedy (discussed on page 619).

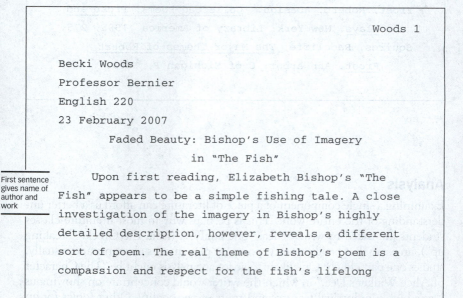

```
                                                              Woods 1

     Becki Woods

     Professor Bernier

     English 220

     23 February 2007

                   Faded Beauty: Bishop's Use of Imagery

                         in "The Fish"

     Upon first reading, Elizabeth Bishop's "The

     Fish" appears to be a simple fishing tale. A close

     investigation of the imagery in Bishop's highly

     detailed description, however, reveals a different

     sort of poem. The real theme of Bishop's poem is a

     compassion and respect for the fish's lifelong
```

First sentence gives name of author and work

Woods 2

struggle to survive. By carefully and effectively
describing the captured fish, his reaction to being
caught, and the symbols of his past struggles to
stay alive, Bishop creates, through her images of
beauty, victory, and survival, something more than
a simple tale.

Thesis
sentence

    The first four lines of the poem are quite
ordinary and factual:

Topic
sentence

        I caught a tremendous fish
        and held him beside the boat
        half out of water, with my hook
        fast in a corner of his mouth. (1-4)

Except for tremendous, Bishop's persona uses no
exaggerations--unlike most fishing stories--to set
up the situation of catching the fish. The
detailed description begins as the speaker
recounts the event further, noticing something
signally important about the captive fish: "He
didn't fight" (5). At this point the poem begins
to seem unusual: most fish stories are about how
ferociously the prey resists being captured. The
speaker also notes that the "battered and
venerable / and homely" fish offered no resistance
to being caught (8-9). The image of the submissive
attitude of the fish is essential to the theme of
the poem. It is his "utter passivity [that] makes
[the persona's] detailed scrutiny possible"
(McNally 192).

Quotation
from
secondary
source

    Once the image of the passive fish has been
established, the speaker begins an examination of
the fish itself, noting that "Here and there /
his brown skin hung in strips / like ancient

Topic
sentence

wall-paper" (9-11). By comparing the fish's skin to
wallpaper, the persona creates, as Sybil Estess
argues, "implicit suggestions of both artistry and
decay" (713). Images of peeling wallpaper are

Essay moves
systematically
through
poem, from
start to finish

instantly brought to mind. The comparison of the
fish's skin and wallpaper, though "helpful in
conveying an accurate notion of the fish's color to
anyone with memories of Victorian parlors and their
yellowed wallpaper . . . is," according to Nancy
McNally, "even more useful in evoking the
associations of deterioration which usually
surround such memories" (192). The fish's faded
beauty has been hinted at in the comparison,
thereby setting up the detailed imagery that soon
follows:

> He was speckled with barnacles,
> fine rosettes of lime,
> and infested
> with tiny white sea-lice,
> and underneath two or three

Textual
evidence,
mix of long
and short
quotations

> rags of green weed hung down. (16-21)

The persona sees the fish as he is; the
infestations and faults are not left out of the
description. Yet, at the same time, the fisher
"express[es] what [he/she] has sensed of the
character of the fish" (Estess 714).

Bishop's persona notices "shapes like full-
blown roses / stained and lost through age" on the
fish's skin (14-15). The persona's perception of
the fish's beauty is revealed along with a
recognition of its faded beauty, which is best
revealed in the description of the fish's being

Woods 4

speckled with barnacles and spotted with lime.
However, the fisher observes these spots and sees
them as rosettes--as objects of beauty, not just
ugly brown spots. These images contribute to the
persona's recognition of beauty's having become
faded beauty.

The poem next turns to a description of the
fish's gills. The imagery in "While his gills were
breathing in / the terrible oxygen" (22-23) leads
"to the very structure of the creature" that is now
dying (Hopkins 201). The descriptions of the fish's
interior beauty--"the coarse white flesh / packed
in like feathers," the colors "of his shiny
entrails," and his "pink swim-bladder / like a big
peony"--are reminders of the life that seems about
to end (27-28, 31-33).

The composite image of the fish's essential
beauty--his being alive--is developed further in
the description of the five fish hooks that the
captive, living fish carries in his lip:

> grim, wet, and weapon-like
> hung five old pieces of fish-line
> . . . .
> with all their five big hooks
> grown firmly in his mouth. (50-51, 54-55)

As if fascinated by them, the persona,
observing how the lines must have been broken
during struggles to escape, sees the hooks as
"medals with their ribbons / frayed and wavering, /
a five-haired beard of wisdom / trailing from his
aching jaw" (61-64), and the fisher becomes
enthralled by re-created images of the fish's

Transitional phrase begins topic sentence

Textual evidence, mix of long and short quotations

Topic sentence

fighting desperately for his life on at least five separate occasions--and winning. Crale Hopkins suggests that "[i]n its capability not only for mere existence, but for action, escaping from previous anglers, the fish shares the speaker's humanity" (202), thus revealing the fisher's deepening understanding of how he must now act. The persona has "all along," notes Estess, "describe[d] the fish not just with great detail but with an imaginative empathy for the aquatic creature. In her more-than-objective description, [the fisher] relates what [he/she] has seen to be both the pride and poverty of the fish" (715). It is at this point that the narrator of this fishing tale has a moment of clarity. Realizing the fish's history and the glory the fish has achieved in escaping previous hookings, the speaker sees everything become "rainbow, rainbow, rainbow!" (75)--and then unexpectedly lets the fish go.

Bishop's "The Fish" begins by describing an event that might easily be a conventional story's climax: "I caught a tremendous fish" (1). The poem, however, develops into a highly detailed account of a fisher noticing both the age and the faded beauty of the captive and his present beauty and past glory as well. The fishing tale is not simply a recounting of a capture; it is a gradually unfolding epiphany in which the speaker sees the fish in an entirely new light. The

Quotations from secondary sources

Conclusion

Woods 6

intensity of this encounter between an apparently
experienced fisher in a rented boat and a battle-
hardened fish is delivered through the poet's
skillful use of imagery. It is through the
description of the capture of an aged fish that
Bishop offers her audience her theme of compassion
derived from a respect for the struggle for
survival.

Restatement
of thesis, in
light of all
that comes
before it.

Woods 7

Works Cited

Bishop, Elizabeth. "The Fish." Backpack Literature:
 An Introduction to Fiction, Poetry, Drama, and
 Writing. Ed. X. J. Kennedy and Dana Gioia. 2nd
 ed. New York: Longman, 2008. 387-88.

Estess, Sybil P. "Elizabeth Bishop: The Delicate
 Art of Map Making." Southern Review 13 (1977):
 713-17.

Hopkins, Crale D. "Inspiration as Theme: Art and
 Nature in the Poetry of Elizabeth Bishop."
 Arizona Quarterly 32 (1976): 200-202.

McNally, Nancy L. "Elizabeth Bishop: The Discipline
 of Description." Twentieth-Century Literature
 11 (1966): 192-94.

Housden 1

Janet Housden

Professor Barth

English 201

3 November 2007

<u>Othello</u>: Tragedy or Soap Opera?

When we hear the word "tragedy," we usually think of either a terrible real-life disaster, or a dark and serious drama filled with pain, suffering, and loss that involves the downfall of a powerful person due to some character flaw or error in judgment. William Shakespeare's <u>Othello</u> is such a drama. Set in Venice and Cyprus during the Renaissance, the play tells the story of Othello, a Moorish general in the Venetian army, who has just married Desdemona, the daughter of a Venetian nobleman. Through the plotting of a jealous villain, Iago, Othello is deceived into believing that Desdemona has been unfaithful to him. He murders her in revenge, only to discover too late how he has been tricked. Overcome by shame and grief, Othello kills himself.

Dealing as it does with jealousy, murder, and suicide, the play is certainly dark, but is <u>Othello</u> a true tragedy? In the fourth century B.C., the Greek philosopher Aristotle proposed a formal definition of tragedy (Kennedy 619), which only partially fits <u>Othello</u>.

The first characteristic of tragedy identified by Aristotle is that the protagonist is a person of outstanding quality and high social position. While Othello is not of royal birth as are many tragic heroes and heroines, he does occupy a sufficiently

First paragraph gives name of author and work

Key plot information avoids excessive retelling

Central question is raised

Thesis statement provides response

Topic sentence on Othello's social position

Housden 2

high position to satisfy this part of Aristotle's definition. Although Othello is a foreigner and a soldier by trade, he has risen to the rank of general and has married into a noble family, which is quite an accomplishment for an outsider. Furthermore, Othello is generally liked and respected by those around him. He is often described by others as being "noble," "brave," and "valiant." By virtue of his high rank and the respect he commands from others, Othello would appear to possess the high stature commonly given to the tragic hero in order to make his eventual fall seem all the more tragic.

While Othello displays the nobility and high status commonly associated with the tragic hero, he also possesses another, less admirable characteristic, the flaw or character defect shared by all heroes of classical tragedy. In Othello's case, it is a stunning gullibility, combined with a violent temper that once awakened overcomes all reason. These flaws permit Othello to be easily deceived and manipulated by the villainous Iago and make him easy prey for the "green-eyed monster" (3.3.179).

It is because of this tragic flaw, according to Aristotle, that the hero is at least partially to blame for his own downfall. While Othello's "free and open nature, / That thinks men honest that but seem to be so" (1.3.384–85) is not a fault in itself, it does allow Iago to convince the Moor of his wife's infidelity without one shred of concrete evidence. Furthermore, once Othello has been convinced of Desdemona's guilt,

Essay systematically applies Aristotle's definition of tragedy to Othello

Topic sentence on Othello's tragic flaw

Quotes from play as evidence to support point

he makes up his mind to take vengeance, and says
that his "bloody thoughts with violent pace /
Shall ne'er look back, ne'er ebb to humble love"
(3.3.473-74). He thereby renders himself deaf to
the voice of reason, and ignoring Desdemona's
protestations of innocence, brutally murders her,
only to discover too late that he has made a
terrible mistake. Although he is goaded into his
crime by Iago, who is a master at manipulating
people, it is Othello's own character flaws that
lead to his horrible misjudgment.

Aristotle's definition also states that the
hero's misfortune is not wholly deserved, that the
punishment he receives exceeds his crime. Although
it is hard to sympathize with a man as cruel as
Othello is to the innocent Desdemona, Othello pays
an extremely high price for his sin of
gullibility. Othello loses everything--his wife,
his position, even his life. Even though it's
partially his fault, Othello is not entirely to
blame, for without Iago's interference it's highly
unlikely that things would turn out as they do.
Though it seems incredibly stupid on Othello's
part, that a man who has travelled the world and
commanded armies should be so easily deceived,
there is little evidence that Othello has had much
experience with civilian society, and although he
is "declined / Into the vale of years" (3.3.281-
82), Othello has apparently never been married
before. By his own admission, "little of this
great world can I speak / More than pertains to
feats of broils and battle" (1.3.88-89).

Topic
sentence
elaborates
on idea raised
in previous
paragraphs

Topic
sentence on
Othello's
misfortune

Furthermore, Othello has no reason to suspect that "honest Iago" is anything but his loyal friend and supporter.

Transitional words signal argument's direction

While it is understandable that Othello could be fooled into believing Desdemona unfaithful, the question remains whether his fate is deserved. In addition to his mistake of believing Iago's lies, Othello commits a more serious error: he lets himself be blinded by anger. Worse yet, in deciding to take vengeance, he also makes up his mind not be swayed from his course, even by his love for Desdemona. In fact, he refuses to listen to her at all, "lest her body and beauty unprovide my mind again" (4.1.192), therefore denying her the right to defend herself. Because of his rage and unfairness, perhaps Othello deserves his fate more than Aristotle's ideal tragic hero. Othello's punishment does exceed his crime, but just barely.

Topic sentence elaborates on Othello's misfortune

According to Aristotle, the tragic hero's fall gives the protagonist deeper understanding and self-awareness. Othello departs from Aristotle's model in that Othello apparently learns nothing from his mistakes. He never realizes that he is partly at fault. He sees himself only as an innocent victim and blames his misfortune on fate rather than accepting responsibility for his actions. To be sure, he realizes he has been tricked and deeply regrets his mistake, but he seems to feel that he was justified under the circumstances, "For naught I did in hate, but all in honor" (5.2.303). Othello sees himself not as someone whose bad judgment and worse temper have resulted in the death of an

Topic sentence on whether Othello learns from his mistakes

innocent party, but as one who has "loved not wisely but too well" (5.2.354). This failure to grasp the true nature of his error indicates that Othello hasn't learned his lesson.

[Topic sentence elaborating further on whether Othello learns from his errors]

Neither accepting responsibility nor learning from his mistakes, Othello fails to fulfill yet another of Aristotle's requirements. Since the protagonist usually gains some understanding along with his defeat, classical tragedy conveys a sense of human greatness and of life's unrealized potentialities--a quality totally absent from Othello. Not only does Othello fail to learn from his mistakes, he never really realizes what those mistakes are, and it apparently never crosses his mind that things could have turned out any differently. "Who can control his fate?" Othello asks (5.2.274), and this defeatist attitude, combined with his failure to salvage any wisdom from his defeat, separates Othello from the tragedy as defined by Aristotle.

[Topic sentence on catharsis]

The last part of Aristotle's definition states that viewing the conclusion of a tragedy should result in catharsis for the audience, and that the audience should be left with a feeling of exaltation rather than depression. Unfortunately, the feeling we are left with after viewing Othello is neither catharsis nor exaltation but rather a feeling of horror, pity, and disgust at the senseless waste of human lives. The deaths of Desdemona and Othello, as well as those of Emilia and Roderigo, serve no purpose whatsoever. They die not in the service of a great cause but because of lies, treachery, jealousy, and spite. Their deaths

Housden 6

don't even benefit Iago, who is directly or
indirectly responsible for all of them. No lesson
is learned, no epiphany is reached, and the
audience, instead of experiencing catharsis, is
left with its negative feeling unresolved.

Since *Othello* only partially fits Aristotle's
definition of tragedy, it is questionable whether
or not it should be classified as one. Though it
does involve a great man undone by a defect in his
own character, the hero gains neither insight nor
understanding from his defeat, and so there can be
no inspiration or catharsis for the audience, as
there would be in a "true" tragedy. *Othello* is
tragic only in the everyday sense of the word, the
way a plane crash or fire is tragic. At least in
terms of Aristotle's classic definition, *Othello*
ultimately comes across as more of a melodrama or
soap opera than a tragedy.

Restatement
of thesis

Conclusion

Housden 7

Works Cited

Kennedy, X. J., and Dana Gioia, eds. Backpack
    Literature: An Introduction to Fiction, Poetry,
    Drama, and Writing. 2nd ed. New York: Longman,
    2008. 619.

Shakespeare, William. Othello, The Moor of Venice.
    Backpack Literature: An Introduction to Fiction,
    Poetry, Drama, and Writing. Ed. X. J. Kennedy
    and Dana Gioia. 2nd ed. New York: Longman,
    2008. 672-788.

Comparison and Contrast

If you were to write on "The Humor of Alice Walker's 'Everyday Use' and John Updike's 'A & P'," you would probably employ one or two methods. You might use **comparison**, placing the two stories side by side and pointing out their similarities, or **contrast**, pointing out their differences. Most of the time, in dealing with works of literature, you will find them similar in some ways and different in others, and you'll use both methods. Keep the following points in mind when writing a comparison-contrast paper:

- **Choose works with something significant in common.** This will simplify your task, and also help ensure that your paper hangs together. Before you start writing, ask yourself if the works you've selected throw some light on each other. If the answer is no, rethink your selection.

- **Choose a focus.** Simply ticking off every similarity and difference between two stories or poems would make for a slack and rambling essay. More compelling writing would result from better-focused topics, such as "The Experience of Coming of Age in James Joyce's 'Araby' and William Faulkner's 'Barn Burning'." Oftentimes a comparison can also involve evaluation—a judgment on the relative quality of the two works.

- **Don't feel you need to spend equal amounts of time on comparing and contrasting.** If your chosen stories are more similar than different, you naturally will spend more space on comparison, and vice versa.

- **Don't devote the first half of your paper to one work and the second half to the other.** This simple structure may weaken your essay if it leads you to keep two works in total isolation from the other. After all, the point is to see what can be learned by comparison. There is nothing wrong in discussing all of poem A first, then discussing poem B—if in discussing B you keep referring back to A. Another strategy is to do a point-by-point comparison of two stories all the way through your paper—dealing first, perhaps, with their themes, then with their central images, and finally, with their respective merits.

- **Before you start writing, draw up a brief list of points you would like to touch on.** Then address each point, first in one story and then in the other. A sample outline follows for a paper on William Faulkner's "A Rose for Emily" and Katherine Mansfield's "Miss Brill." The essay's topic is "Adapting to Change: The Characters of Emily Grierson and Miss Brill."

1. Adapting to change (both women)
   Miss Brill more successful
2. Portrait of women
   Miss Emily--unflattering
   Miss Brill--empathetic
3. Imagery
   Miss Emily--morbid
   Miss Brill--cheerful
4. Plot
   Miss Emily
      - loses sanity
      - refuses to adapt
   Miss Brill
      - finds place in society
      - adapts
5. Summary: Miss Brill is more successful

- **Emphasize the points that interest you the most.** This strategy will help keep you from following your outline in a plodding fashion ("Well, now it's time to whip over to Miss Brill again . . . ").

- **If the assignment allows, consider applying comparison and contrast in an essay on a single story.** You might, for example, analyze the attitudes of the younger and older waiters in Hemingway's "A Clean, Well-Lighted Place." Or you might contrast Willy and Biff's illusions in Arthur Miller's *Death of a Salesman*.

The following student-written paper compares and contrasts the main characters in "A Rose for Emily" and "Miss Brill." Notice how the author focuses the discussion on a single aspect of each woman's personality—the ability to adapt to change and the passage of time. By looking through the lens of three different elements of the short story—diction, imagery, and plot—this clear and systematic essay convincingly argues its thesis.

Ortiz 1

Michelle Ortiz

Professor Gregg

English 200

25 May 2007

Successful Adaptation in

"A Rose for Emily" and "Miss Brill"

In both William Faulkner's "A Rose for Emily"

and Katherine Mansfield's "Miss Brill," the reader

is given a glimpse into the lives of two old women

living in different worlds but sharing many similar

characteristics. Both Miss Emily and Miss Brill

attempt to adapt to a changing environment as they

grow older. Through the authors' use of language,

imagery, and plot, it becomes clear to the reader

Clear
statement
of thesis
that Miss Brill is more successful at adapting to

the world around her and finding happiness.

In "A Rose for Emily," Faulkner's use of

language paints an unflattering picture of Miss

Textual
evidence on
language
supports
thesis.
Emily. His tone evokes pity and disgust rather than

sympathy. The reader identifies with the narrator

of the story and shares the townspeople's opinion

that Miss Emily is somehow "perverse." In "Miss

Brill," however, the reader can identify with the

title character. Mansfield's attitude toward the

young couple at the end makes the reader hate them

for ruining the happiness that Miss Brill has

found, however small it may be.

Imagery in
Faulkner's
story supports
argument.
The imagery in "A Rose for Emily" keeps the

reader from further identifying with Miss Emily by

creating several morbid images of her. For example,

there are several images of decay throughout the

story. The house she lived in is falling apart and

Ortiz 2

described as "filled with dust and shades . . . an eyesore among eyesores." Emily herself is described as being "bloated like a body long submerged in motionless water." Faulkner also uses words like "skeleton," "dank," "decay," and "cold" to reinforce these morbid, deathly images.

In "Miss Brill," however, Mansfield uses more cheerful imagery. The music and the lively action in the park make Miss Brill feel alive inside. She notices the other old people that are in the park are "still as statues," "odd," and "silent." She says they "looked like they'd just come from dark little rooms or even—even cupboards." Her own room is later described as a "cupboard," but during the action of the story she does not include herself among those other old people. She still feels alive.

Contrasting imagery in Mansfield's story supports argument.

Through the plots of both stories the reader can also see that Miss Brill is more successful in adapting to her environment. Miss Emily loses her sanity and ends up committing a crime in order to control her environment. Throughout the story, she refuses to adapt to any of the changes going on in the town, such as the taxes or the mailboxes. Miss Brill is able to find her own special place in society where she can be happy and remain sane.

Characters contrasted with examples drawn from plots.

In "A Rose for Emily" and "Miss Brill" the authors' use of language and the plots of the stories illustrate that Miss Brill is more successful in her story. Instead of hiding herself away she emerges from the "cupboard" to participate in life. She adapts to the world that is changing as she grows older, without losing her sanity or

The final conclusion is stated and the thesis is restated.

Ortiz 3

committing crimes, as Miss Emily does. The language
of "Miss Brill" allows the reader to sympathize with
the main character. The imagery in the story is
lighter and less morbid than in "A Rose for Emily."
The resulting portrait is of an aging woman who has
found creative ways to adjust to her lonely life.

The Form of Your Finished Paper

If your instructor has not specified the form of your finished paper, follow the guidelines in the current edition of the *MLA Handbook for Writers of Research Papers*, which you will find more fully described in the next chapter, "Writing a Research Paper." In brief:

- Choose standard letter-size (8 1/2 × 11) white paper.
- Use standard, easy-to-read type fonts, such as Times New Roman or Courier.
- Give your name, your instructor's name, the course number, and the date at the top left-hand corner of your first page.
- On subsequent pages, give your last name and the page number in the upper right-hand corner, one-half inch from the top.
- Remember to give your paper a title that reflects your thesis.
- Leave an inch or two of margin on all four sides of each page and a few inches of blank paper or an additional sheet after your conclusion, so that your instructor can offer comments.
- If you include a works cited section, it begins on a separate page.
- Double-space your text, including quotations and notes. Don't forget to double-space the works cited page also.
- Put the titles of longer works—books, full-length plays, periodicals, and book-length poems such as *The Odyssey*—in italics or underline them. The titles of shorter works—poems, articles, or short stories—should appear in quotation marks.

What's left to do but hand in your paper? By now, you may be glad to see it go. But a good paper is not only worth submitting; it is also worth keeping. If you return to it after a while, you may find to your surprise that it will preserve and even renew what you have learned.

TOPICS FOR WRITING ON FICTION

TOPICS FOR BRIEF PAPERS (250–500 WORDS)

1. Explicate the opening paragraph or first few lines of a story. Show how the opening prepares the reader for what will follow. In an essay of this length, you will need to limit your discussion to the most important elements of the passage you explicate; there won't be room to deal with everything. Or, as thoroughly as the word count allows, explicate the final paragraph of a story. What does the ending imply about the fates of the story's characters, and about the story's take on its central theme?

2. Select a story that features a first-person narrator. Write a concise yet thorough analysis of how that character's point of view colors the story.

3. Consider a short story in which the central character has to make a decision or must take some decisive step that will alter the rest of his or her life. Faulkner's "Barn Burning" is one such story; another is Updike's "A & P." As concisely and as thoroughly as you can, explain the nature of the character's decision, the reasons for it, and its probable consequences (as suggested by what the author tells us).

4. Choose two stories that might be interesting to compare and contrast. Write a brief defense of your choice. How might these two stories illuminate each other?

5. Choose a key passage from a story you admire. As closely as the word count allows, explicate that passage and explain why it strikes you as an important moment in the story. Concentrate on the aspects of the passage that seem most essential.

6. Write a new ending to a story of your choice. Try to imitate the author's writing style. Add a paragraph explaining how this exercise illuminates the author's choices in the original.

TOPICS FOR MORE EXTENDED PAPERS (600–1,000 WORDS)

1. Write an analysis of a short story, focusing on a single element, such as point of view, theme, symbolism, character, or the author's voice (tone, style, irony).

2. Compare and contrast two stories with protagonists who share an important personality trait. Make character the focus of your essay.

3. Write a thorough explication of a short passage (preferably not more than four sentences) in a story you admire. Pick a crucial moment in the

plot, or a passage that reveals the story's theme. You might look to the paper "By Lantern Light" on page 1119, as a model.

4. Write an analysis of a story in which the protagonist experiences an epiphany or revelation of some sort. Describe the nature of this change of heart. How is the reader prepared for it? What are its repercussions in the character's life? Some possible story choices are Alice Walker's "Everyday Use," William Faulkner's "Barn Burning," and Raymond Carver's "Cathedral."

5. Imagine a reluctant reader, one who would rather play video games than crack a book. Which story in this book would you recommend to him or her? Write an essay to that imagined reader, describing the story's merits.

TOPICS FOR LONG PAPERS (1,500 WORDS OR MORE)

1. Write an analysis of a longer work of fiction. Concentrate on a single element of the story, quoting as necessary to make your point.

2. Read three or four short stories by an author whose work you admire. Concentrating on a single element treated similarly in all of the stories, write an analysis of the author's work as exemplified by your chosen stories.

3. Describe the process of reading a story for the first time and gradually learning to understand and appreciate it. First, choose a story you haven't yet read. As you read it for the first time, take notes on aspects of the story you find difficult or puzzling. Read the story a second time. Now write about the experience. What uncertainties were resolved when you read the story the second time? What, if any, uncertainties remain? What has this experience taught you about reading fiction?

4. Choose two stories that treat a similar theme. Compare and contrast the stance each story takes toward that theme, marshalling quotations and specifics as necessary to back up your argument.

TOPICS FOR WRITING ON POETRY

TOPICS FOR BRIEF PAPERS (250–500 WORDS)

1. Write a concise *explication* of a short poem of your choice. Concentrate on those facets of the poem that you think most need explaining. (For a sample explication, see page 1123).

2. Write an *analysis* of a short poem, focusing on how a single key element shapes its meaning. (A sample analysis appears on page 1128.) Some possible topics are:

   - Imagery in Wallace Stevens's "The Emperor of Ice Cream"
   - Kinds of irony in Thomas Hardy's "The Workbox"
   - Theme in W. H. Auden's "Musée des Beaux Arts"
   - Extended metaphor in Langston Hughes's "The Negro Speaks of Rivers" (Explain the one main comparison that the poem makes and show how the whole poem makes it).

3. Select a poem in which the main speaker is a character who for any reason interests you. You might consider, for instance, T. S. Eliot's "The Love Song of J. Alfred Prufrock" or Rhina Espaillat's "Bilingual/ Bilingüe." Then write a brief profile of this character, drawing only on what the poem tells you (or reveals). What is the character's approximate age? Situation in life? Attitude toward self? Attitude toward others? General personality? Do you find this character admirable?

4. Choose a brief poem that you find difficult. Write an essay in which you begin by listing the points in the poem that strike you as most impenetrable. Next, reread the poem at least twice. In the essay's second half, describe how multiple readings change your experience of the poem.

5. Although each of these poems tells a story, what happens in the poem isn't necessarily obvious: E. E. Cummings's "anyone lived in a pretty how town," T. S. Eliot's "The Love Song of J. Alfred Prufrock," Edwin Arlington Robinson's "Luke Havergal," Anne Stevenson's "The Victory." Choose one of these poems, and in a paragraph sum up what you think happens in it. Then in a second paragraph, ask yourself: what, *besides* the element of story, did you consider in order to understand the poem?

TOPICS FOR MORE EXTENDED PAPERS (600–1,000 WORDS)

1. Perform a line-by-line explication on a brief poem of your choice. Imagine your audience is unfamiliar with the poems and needs your assistance in interpreting it.
2. Explicate a passage from a longer poem. Choose a passage that is, in your opinion, central to the poem's meaning.
3. Compare and contrast any two poems that treat a similar theme. Let your comparison bring you to an evaluation of the poems. Which is the stronger, more satisfying one?
4. Write a comparison and contrast essay on any two or more poems by a single poet. Look for two poems that share a characteristic thematic concern.

   - Mortality in the work of John Keats
   - Nature in the poems of William Wordsworth
   - How Emily Dickinson's lyric poems resemble hymns
   - E. E. Cummings's approach to the free verse line
   - Gerard Manley Hopkins's sonic effects

5. Terry Ehret of Santa Rosa Junior College developed the following assignment:

   > Compose your own answer to the question "What is poetry?" You may want to devise original metaphor(s) to define poetry and then develop your essay with examples and explanations. Select at least one poem from the anthology to illustrate your definition.

TOPICS FOR LONG PAPERS (1,500 WORDS OR MORE)

1. Review an entire poetry collection by a poet featured in this book. You will need to communicate to your reader a sense of the work's style and thematic preoccupations. Finally, make a value judgment about the work's quality.
2. Read five or six poems by a single author. Start with a poet featured in this book, and then find additional poems at the library or on the Internet. Write an analysis of a single element of that poet's work—for example, theme, imagery, diction, or form.
3. Write a line-by-line explication of a poem rich in matters to explain or of a longer poem that offers ample difficulty. Although relatively short, Gerard Manley Hopkins's "The Windhover" is a poem that will take a good bit of time to explicate. Even a short, apparently simple poem such

as Robert Frost's "Stopping by Woods on a Snowy Evening" can provide more than enough material to explicate thoughtfully in a longer paper.

4. Write an analysis of a certain theme (or other element) that you find in the works of two or more poets. It is probable that in your conclusion you will want to set the poets' works side by side, comparing or contrasting them, and perhaps making some evaluation. Here are some sample topics:

- Langston Hughes, Gwendolyn Brooks, and Dudley Randall as Prophets of Social Change
- What It Is to Be a Woman: The Special Knowledge of Sylvia Plath, Anne Sexton, and Adrienne Rich
- Making Up New Words for New Meanings: Neologisms in Lewis Carroll and Kay Ryan

TOPICS FOR WRITING ON DRAMA

TOPICS FOR BRIEF PAPERS (250–500 WORDS)

1. Analyze a key character from any of the plays in this book. Two choices might be Tom in *The Glass Menagerie* or Biff Loman in *Death of a Salesman*. What motivates that character? Point to specific moments in the play to make your case.

2. When the curtain comes down on the conclusion of some plays, the audience is left to decide exactly what finally happened. In a short informal essay, state your interpretation of the conclusion of *The Glass Menagerie*. Don't just give a plot summary; tell what you think the conclusion means.

3. Sum up the main suggestions you find in one of these meaningful objects (or actions): the handkerchief in *Othello*; the Christmas tree in *A Doll's House* (or Nora's doing a wild tarantella); Willy Loman's planting a garden in *Death of a Salesman*; Laura's collection of figurines in *The Glass Menagerie*.

TOPICS FOR MORE EXTENDED PAPERS (600–1,000 WORDS)

1. From a play you have enjoyed, choose a passage that strikes you as difficult, worth reading closely. Try to pick a passage not longer than about 20 lines. Explicate it—give it a close, sentence-by-sentence reading—and explain how this small part of the play relates to the whole. For instance, any of the following passages might be considered memorable (and essential to their plays):

- Othello's soliloquy, beginning "It is the cause, it is the cause, my soul" (*Othello*, 5.2.1–22).
- Oedipus to Teiresias, speech beginning, "Wealth, power, craft of statemanship!" (*Oedipus the King*, l. 163–86).
- Nora to Mrs. Linde, speech beginning "Yes, someday, maybe, in many years when I am not as pretty as I am now . . . " (*A Doll's House*, page 806).

2. Analyze the complexities and contradictions to be found in a well-rounded character from a play of your choice. Some good subjects might be Othello, Nora Helmer (in *A Doll's House*), Willy Loman (in *Death of a Salesman*), or Tom Wingfield (in *The Glass Menagerie*).

3. Take just a single line or sentence from a play—one that stands out for some reason as greatly important. Perhaps it states a theme, reveals a character, or serves as a crisis (or turning point). Write an essay demonstrating its importance—how it functions, why it is necessary. Some possible lines include:

- Iago to Roderigo: "I am not what I am" (*Othello*, 1.1.67).
- Amanda to Tom: "You live in a dream; you manufacture illusions!" (*The Glass Menagerie*, Scene vii).
- Charley to Biff: "A salesman is got to dream, boy. It comes with the territory" (*Death of a Salesman*, the closing Requiem).

4. Write an analysis essay in which you single out an element of a play for examination—character, plot, setting, theme, dramatic irony, tone, language, symbolism, conventions, or any other element. Try to relate this element to the play as a whole. Sample topics: "The Function of Teiresias in *Oedipus the King*," "Imagery of Poison in *Othello*," "Williams's Use of Magic-Lantern Slides in *The Glass Menagerie*," "The Theme of Success in *Death of a Salesman*."

5. How would you stage an updated production of a play by Shakespeare, Sophocles, or Ibsen, transplanting it to our time? Choose a play, and describe the challenges and difficulties of this endeavor. How would you overcome them—or, if they cannot be overcome, why not?

TOPICS FOR LONG PAPERS
(1,500 WORDS OR MORE)

1. Choose a play you have read and admire from this book, and read a second play by the same author. Compare and contrast the two plays with attention to a single element—a common theme, or a particular kind of imagery, for example.

2. Compare and contrast the ways in which *The Glass Menagerie* and *Death of a Salesman* approach the theme of fantasy and wishful thinking.

3. Read *Othello* and view a movie version of the play. You might choose Oliver Parker's 1995 take on the play with Laurence Fishburne and Kenneth Branagh, or even O (2001), an updated version that takes a prep school as its setting and a basketball star as its protagonist. Review the movie. What does it manage to convey of the original? What gets lost in the translation?

4. Choosing any of the works in "Plays for Further Reading" or taking some other modern or contemporary play your instructor suggests, report any difficulties you encountered in reading and responding to it. Explicate any troublesome passages for the benefit of other readers.

29

Writing a Research Paper

Why is it worthwhile to write a research paper? (Apart from the fact that you want a passing grade in the class, that is.) While you can learn much by exploring your own responses to a literary work, there is no substitute for entering into a conversation with others who have studied and thought about your topic. Literary criticism is that conversation. Your reading will expose you to the ideas of others who can shed light on a story, poem, or play. It will introduce you to the wide range of informed opinions that exist about literature, as about almost any subject. Sometimes, too, your research will uncover information about an author's life that leads you to new insights into a literary work. Undertaking a research paper gives you a chance to test your ideas against those of others, and in doing so to clarify your own opinions.

Getting Started

The most daunting aspect of the research paper may well be the mountains of information available on almost any literary subject. It can be hard to know where to begin. Sifting through books and articles is part of the research process. Unfortunately, the first material uncovered in the library or on the Internet is rarely the evidence you need to develop or support your thesis. Keep looking until you uncover helpful sources.

Another common pitfall in the process is the creeping feeling that your idea has already been examined a dozen times over. But take heart: like Odysseus, tie yourself to the mast so that when you hear the siren voices of published professors, you can listen without abandoning your own point of view. Your idea may have been treated, but not yet by you. Your particular take on a topic is bound to be different from someone else's. After all, thousands of books have been written on Shakespeare's plays, but even so there are still new things to say.

Choosing a Topic

- **Find a topic that interests you.** A crucial first step in writing a research paper is coming up with a topic that interests you. Start with a topic that bores you, and the process will be a chore, and will yield dull results. But if you come up with an intriguing research question, seeking the answer will be a more engaging process. The paper that results inevitably will be stronger and more interesting.

- **Find a way to get started.** Browsing through books of literary criticism in the library, or glancing at online journal articles can help to spark an idea or two. Prewriting techniques such as brainstorming, freewriting, listing, and clustering can also help you to generate ideas on a specific work of literature. If you take notes and jot down ideas as they occur to you, when you start the formal writing process, you will discover you have already begun.

- **Keep your purpose and audience in mind.** Refer often to the assignment, and approach your essay accordingly. Think of your audience as well. Is it your professor, your classmates, or some other hypothetical reader? As you plan your essay, keep your audience's expectations and needs in mind.

- **Develop a general thesis that you hope to support with research, and look for material that will help you demonstrate its plausibility.** Remember: the ideal research paper is based on your own observations and interpretations of a literary text.

Finding Research Sources

Finding Print Resources

Writing a research paper on literature calls for two kinds of sources: primary sources, or the literary works that are your subject, and secondary sources, or the books, articles, and Web resources that discuss your primary sources. When you are hunting down secondary sources, the best place to begin is your campus library. Plan to spend some time thumbing through scholarly books and journals, looking for passages that you find particularly interesting or that pertain to your topic. Begin your search with the online catalog to get a sense of where you might find the books and journals you need.

To choose from the many books available on your library's shelves and through interlibrary loan, you might turn to book reviews for a sense of which volumes would best suit your purpose. *Book Review Digest* contains the full texts of many book reviews, and excerpts of others. The *Digest* may be found in printed form in the reference section of your campus library, which may also provide access to the online version. Whether you are using the online or print version, you will need the author's name, title, and date of first publication of any book for which you hope to find a review.

Scholarly journals are another excellent resource for articles on your topic. Indexes to magazines and journals may be found in your library's reference section. You may also find an index to print periodicals on your library's Web site.

Using Online Databases

Most college libraries subscribe to specialized online or CD-ROM database services covering all academic subjects—treasure troves of reliable sources. If you find yourself unsure how to use your library's database system, ask the reference librarian to help you get started. The following databases are particularly useful for literary research:

- The MLA *International Bibliography*, the Modern Language Association's database, is an excellent way to search for books and full-text articles on literary topics.

- *JSTOR*, a not-for-profit organization, indexes articles or abstracts from an archive of journals on language, literature, and African American studies.

- *Literature Resource Center* (Thomson Gale) provides biographies, bibliographies, and critical analyses of more than 120,000 authors and their work. This information is culled from journal articles and reference works.

- *Project MUSE*, a collaboration between publishers and libraries, offers access to more than 300 journals in the humanities, arts, and social sciences.

- *Academic Search Premier* (EBSCO), a multisubject resource, covers literature and the humanities, as well as the social sciences, medical sciences, linguistics, and other fields.

Your library may provide access to some or all of these databases, or it may offer other useful ones. Many college library home pages provide students with access to subscription databases, which means that if you really can't bear to leave your comfy desk at home, you can still pay a virtual visit.

Finding Reliable Web Sources

While online databases are a handy and reliable source for high-quality information, you may find yourself looking to supplement journal articles with information and quotations from the Internet. If so, proceed with care. While the journal articles in online databases have been reviewed for quality by specialists and librarians, Web sites may be written and published by anybody for any purpose, with no oversight. Even the online reference site *Wikipedia*, for example, is an amalgamation of voluntary contributors, and is rife with small factual errors and contributor biases. Carefully analyze the materials you gather online or you may find yourself tangled in the spidery threads of a dubious Web site. To garner the best sources possible, take these steps:

- **Learn to use Internet search engines effectively.** If you enter general terms such as the author's name and story title into an Internet search engine, you may well find yourself bombarded with thousands of hits. Some search engines (*Yahoo!* for example) arrange subject directories in a useful hierarchy, from general topic areas to more specific ones, (from humanities, to literature, to literary criticism, for example). This structure is sometimes—though not always—helpful. For a more efficient approach to navigating the Internet, try using an "advanced" search option, entering keywords to get results that contain those words (LITERARY CRITICISM A DOLL'S HOUSE or SYMBOLISM THE LOTTERY).

■ **Begin your search at a reliable Web site.** Helpful as an advanced search may be, it won't separate valuable sources from useless ones. To weed out sloppy and inaccurate sites, begin your search with one of the following excellent guides through cyberspace:

- *Library of Congress.* Fortunately, you don't have to trek to Washington to visit this venerable institution's annotated collection of Web sites in the Humanities and Social Sciences Division. For your purpose—writing a literary research paper—access the Subject Index <http://www.loc.gov/rr/main/alcove9>, click on "Literatures in English" and then on "Literary Criticism." This will take you to a list of metapages and Web sites with collections of reliable critical and biographical materials on authors and their works. (A metapage provides links to other Web sites.)
- *Internet Public Library.* Created and maintained by the University of Michigan School of Information and Library Studies, this site <http://www.ipl.org> lets you search for literary criticism by author, work, country of origin, or literary period.
- *Library Spot.* Visit <http://www.libraryspot.com> for a portal to over 5,000 libraries around the world, and to periodicals, online texts, reference works, and links to metapages and Web sites on any topic, including literary criticism. This carefully maintained site is published by Start Spot Mediaworks, Inc., in the Northwestern University/Evanston Research Park in Evanston, Illinois.
- *Voice of the Shuttle.* Research links in over 25 categories in the humanities and social sciences, including online texts, libraries, academic Web sites, and metapages may be found at this site. Located at <http://vos.ucsb.edu> it was developed and is maintained by Dr. Alan Liu in the English Department of the University of California.

CHECKLIST

Finding Sources

✓ Begin at your campus library. Ask the reference librarian for advice.
✓ Check the library catalog for books and journals on your topic.
✓ Look into the online databases subscribed to by your library.
✓ Locate reputable Web sites by starting at a reputable Web site designed for that purpose.

Using Visual Images

The Web is an excellent source of visual images. If a picture, chart, or graph will enhance your argument, you may find the perfect one via an image search on *Google*, *Ditto*, or other search engines. The Library of Congress offers a wealth of images documenting American political, social, and cultural history—including portraits, letters, and original manuscripts—at <http://memory .loc.gov>. Remember, though, that not all images are available for use by the general public. Check for a copyright notice to see if its originator allows that image to be reproduced. If so, you may include the photograph, provided you credit your source as you would if you were quoting text.

One note on images: use them carefully. Choose visuals that provide supporting evidence for the point you are trying to make or enhance your reader's understanding of the work. Label your images with captions. Your goal should be to make your argument more convincing. In the example below, a reproduction of Brueghel's painting helps to advance the author's argument and gain insight into Auden's poem.

Fig. 1. Landscape with the Fall of Icarus by
Pieter Brueghel the Elder (c. 1558, Musees Royaux
des Beaux-Arts de Belgique, Brussels)

W. H. Auden's poem "Musée des Beaux Arts" refers
to a specific painting to prove its point that
the most honest depictions of death take into
account the way life simply goes on even after
the most tragic of events. In line 14, Auden
turns specifically to Pieter Brueghel the

Elder's masterwork <u>The Fall of Icarus</u> (see
Fig. 1), pointing to the painting's understated
depiction of tragedy. In this painting, the
death of Icarus does not take place on center
stage. A plowman and his horse take up the
painting's foreground, while the leg of Icarus
falling into the sea takes up a tiny portion of
the painting's lower right corner. A viewer who
fails to take the painting's title into account
might not even notice Icarus at all.

CHECKLIST

Using Visual Images

- ✓ Use images as evidence to support your argument.
- ✓ Use images to enhance communication and understanding.
- ✓ Refer to the images in your text.
- ✓ Label image as "Fig. 1" and provide title or caption.
- ✓ Check copyrights.
- ✓ Include source in works cited list.

Evaluating Sources

Evaluating Print Resources

It's an old saying, but a useful one: don't believe everything you read. The fact
that a book or article is printed and published doesn't necessarily mean it is
accurate or unbiased. Be discriminating about printed resources.

Begin your search in a place that has taken some of the work out of quality
control—your school library. Books and articles you find there are regarded by
librarians as having some obvious merit. If your search takes you beyond the
library, though, you will need to be discerning when choosing print resources.
As you weigh the value of printed matter, take the following into account:

- ■ **Look closely at information provided about the author.** Is he or
  she known for expertise in the field? What are the author's academic or
  association credentials? Is there any reason to believe that the author is
  biased in any way? For example, a biography about an author written by
  that author's child might not be as unbiased as one written by a scholar
  with no personal connections.

- **Determine the publisher's reliability.** Books or articles published by an advocacy group might be expected to take a particular—possibly biased—slant on an issue. Be aware also that some books are published by vanity presses, companies that are paid by an author to publish his or her books. As a result, vanity press-published books generally aren't subject to the same rigorous quality control as those put out by more reputable publishing houses.

- **Always check for a publication date.** If a document lists an edition number, check to see whether you are using the latest edition of the material.

- **For periodicals, decide whether a publication is an academic journal or a popular magazine.** What type of reputation does it have? Obviously, you do not want to use a magazine that periodically reports on Elvis sightings and alien births. And even articles on writers in magazines such as *Time* and *People* are likely to be too brief and superficial for purposes of serious research. Instead, choose scholarly journals designed to enhance the study of literature.

Evaluating Web Resources

As handy and informative as the Internet is, it sometimes serves up some pretty iffy information. A Web site, after all, can be created by anyone with a computer and access to the Internet—no matter how poorly qualified that person might be. Be discerning when it comes to the Internet. Here are some tips on choosing your sources wisely:

- **Check a site's authorship or sponsorship.** Is the site's creator or sponsor known to you or reputable by association? Look closely at information provided about the author. Is he or she known for expertise in the field? What are the author's academic or association credentials? Is the Web entry unsigned and anonymous? If the Web site is sponsored by an organization, is it a reputable one? While government or university-sponsored sites may be considered reliable, think carefully about possible biases in sites sponsored by advocacy or special interest groups.

  A word of warning: individual student pages posted on university sites have not necessarily been reviewed by that university and are not reliable sources of information. Also, postings on the popular encyclopedia Web site *Wikipedia* are not subject to a scholarly review process and recently have been noted to contain a number of inaccuracies. It's safer to use a published encyclopedia.

- **Look at the site's date of publication.** When was it last updated? In some cases you may want to base your essay on the most current information or theories, so you will want to steer toward the most recently published material.

- **Is this an online version of a print publication?** If so, what type of reputation does it have?

- **Make your own assessment of the site.** Does the content seem consistent with demonstrated scholarship? Does it appear balanced in its point of view?

- **Consult experts.** Cornell University has two good documents with guidance for analyzing sources posted at <http://www.library.cornell.edu/services/guides.html>. The titles are "Critically Analyzing Information Sources" and "Distinguishing Scholarly from Non-Scholarly Periodicals." The UCLA College Library also provides useful information: "Thinking Critically About World Wide Web Resources" (<http://www.library.ucla.edu/libraries/college/help/critical/index.htm>) and "Thinking Critically About Discipline-Based World Wide Web Resources" (<http://www.library.ucla.edu/libraries/college/help/critical/discipline.htm>).

CHECKLIST

Evaluating Sources

PRINT

✓ Who wrote it? What are the author's credentials?

✓ Is he or she an expert in the field?

✓ Does he or she appear to be unbiased toward the subject matter?

✓ Is the publisher reputable? Is it an advocacy group or a vanity press?

✓ When was it published? Do later editions exist? If so, would a later edition be more useful?

WEB

✓ Who wrote it? What are the author's credentials?

✓ Is he or she an expert in the field?

✓ Who sponsors the Web site? Is the sponsor reputable?

✓ When was the Web site published? When was it last updated?

✓ Is the Web site an online journal or magazine? Is it scholarly or popular?

✓ Does content seem consistent with demonstrated scholarship?

✓ Can you detect obvious bias?

Organizing Your Research

- **Get your thoughts down on notecards or the equivalent on your laptop.** Once you have amassed your secondary sources, it will be time to begin reading in earnest. As you do so, be sure to take notes on any passages that pertain to your topic. A convenient way to organize your many thoughts is to write them down on index cards, which are easy to shuffle and rearrange. You'll need 3- × 5-inch cards for brief notes and titles and 5- × 8-inch cards for more in-depth notes. Confine your jottings to one side of the card; notes on the back can easily be overlooked. Write a single fact or opinion on each card. This will make it easier for you to shuffle the deck and reenvision the order in which you deliver information to your reader.

- **Keep careful track of the sources of quotations and paraphrases.** As you take notes, make it crystal clear which thoughts and phrases are yours and which derive from others. (Remember, *quotation* means using the exact words of your source and placing the entire quote in quotations marks and citing the author. *Paraphrase* means expressing the ideas of your source in your own words, again citing the author.) Bear in mind the cautionary tale of well-known historian Doris Kearns Goodwin. She was charged with plagiarizing sections of two of her famous books when her words were found to be jarringly similar to those published in other books. Because she had not clearly indicated on her notecards which ideas and passages were hers and which came from other sources, Goodwin was forced to admit to plagiarism. Her enormous reputation suffered from these charges, but you can learn from her mistakes and save your own reputation—and your grades.

- **Keep track of the sources of ideas and concepts.** When an idea is inspired by or directly taken from someone else's writing, be sure to jot down the source on that same card or your computer file. Your deck of cards or computer list will function as a working bibliography, which later will help you put together a works cited list. To save yourself work, keep a separate list of the sources you're using. Then, as you make the note, you need write only the material's author or title and page reference on the card in order to identify your source. It's also helpful to classify the note in a way that will help you to organize your material, making it easy, for example, to separate cards that deal with a story's theme from cards that deal with point of view or symbolism.

- **Make notes of your own thoughts and reactions to your research.** When a critical article sparks your own original idea, be sure to capture that thought in your notes and mark it as your own. As you plan your paper, these notes may form the outline for your arguments.

■ **Make photocopies or printouts to simplify the process and ensure accuracy.** Scholars once had to spend long hours copying out prose passages by hand. Luckily, for a small investment you can simply photocopy your sources to ensure accuracy in quoting and citing your sources. In fact, some instructors will require you to hand in photocopies of your original sources with the final paper, along with printouts of articles downloaded from an Internet database. Even if this is not the case, photocopying your sources and holding onto your printouts can help you to reproduce quotations accurately in your essay—and accuracy is crucial.

Organizing Your Paper

With your thesis in mind and your notes spread before you, draw up an outline—a rough map of how best to argue your thesis and present your material. Determine what main points you need to make, and look for quotations that support those points. Even if you generally prefer to navigate the paper-writing process without a map, you will find that an outline makes the research-paper writing process considerably smoother. When organizing information from many different sources, it pays to plan ahead.

Guarding Academic Integrity

Papers for Sale Are Papers that "F"ail

Do not be seduced by the apparent ease of cheating by computer. Your Internet searches may turn up several sites that offer term papers to download (just as you can find pornography, political propaganda, and questionable get-rich-quick schemes!). Most of these sites charge money for what they offer, but a few do not, happy to strike a blow against the "oppressive" insistence of English teachers that students learn to think and write.

Plagiarized term papers are an old game: the fraternity file and the "research assistance" service have been around far longer than the computer. It may seem easy enough to download a paper, put your name at the head of it, and turn it in for an easy grade. As any writing instructor can tell you, though, such papers usually stick out like a sore thumb. The style will be wrong, the work will not be consistent with other work by the same student in any number of ways, and the teacher will sometimes even have seen the same phony paper before. The ease with which electronic texts are reproduced makes this last possibility increasingly likely.

The odds of being caught and facing the unpleasant consequences are reasonably high. It is far better to take the grade you have earned for your own effort, no matter how mediocre, than to try to pass off someone else's work as your own. Even if, somehow, your instructor does not recognize your submission as a plagiarized paper, you have diminished your character through dishonesty and lost an opportunity to learn something on your own.

A Warning Against Internet Plagiarism

Plagiarism detection services are a professor's newest ally in the battle against academic dishonesty. Questionable research papers can be sent to these services (such as Turnitin.com and EVE2), which perform complex searches of the Internet and of a growing database of purchased term papers. The research paper will be returned to the professor with plagiarized sections annotated and the sources documented. The end result may be a failing grade on the essay, possibly a failing grade for the course, and, depending on the policies of your university, the very real possibility of expulsion.

Acknowledging Sources

The brand of straight-out dishonesty described above is one type of plagiarism. There is, however, another, subtler kind: when students incorporate somebody else's words *or* ideas into their papers without giving proper credit. To avoid this second—sometimes quite accidental—variety of plagiarism, familiarize yourself with the conventions for acknowledging sources. First and foremost, remember to give credit to any writer who supplies you with ideas, information, or specific words and phrases.

Quotations

- **Acknowledge your source when you quote a writer's words or phrases.** When you use someone else's words or phrases, you should reproduce his or her exact words in quotation marks, and be sure to properly credit the source.

      Already, Frost has hinted that Nature may be,
      as Radcliffe Squires suggests, "Nothing but an
      ash-white plain without love or faith or hope,
      where ignorant appetites cross by chance" (87).

- **If you quote more than four lines, set your quotation off from the body of the paper.** Start a new line; indent one inch (or ten spaces), and type the quotation, double-spaced. (You do not need to use quotation marks, as the format already tells the reader the passage is a quotation.)

> Samuel Maio made an astute observation about
> the nature of Weldon Kees's distinctive tone:
>
>> Kees has therefore combined a
>> personal subject matter with an
>> impersonal voice--that is, one that
>> is consistent in its tone evenly
>> recording the speaker's thoughts
>> without showing any emotional
>> intensity which might lie behind
>> those thoughts. (136)

■ **Follow special guidelines for quoting poetry.** If you are quoting fewer than four lines of poetry, transform the passage into prose form, separating each line by a space, diagonal (/), and another space. The diagonal (/) indicates your respect for where the poet's lines begin and end. Do not change the poet's capitalization or punctuation. Be sure to identify the line numbers you are quoting, as follows:

> The color white preoccupies Frost. The spider is
> "fat and white, / On a white heal-all" (1-2),
> and even the victim moth is pale, too.

If you are quoting four or more lines of verse, set them off from your text, and arrange them just as they occur on the page, white space and all. (If you begin the quotation in the middle of a line of verse, position the starting word about where it occurs in the poem—not at the left-hand margin.)

> The poet asks what deity or fate cursed this
> particular mutant flower
>
>   with being white,
>   The wayside blue and innocent heal-all?
>   What brought the kindred spider to that
>   height,
>   Then steered the white moth thither in the
>   night? (9-12)

Citing Ideas

■ **Acknowledge your source when you mention a critic's ideas.**
Even if you are not quoting exact words or phrases, be sure to acknowledge
the source of any original ideas or concepts you have used.

> Another explanation is suggested by Daniel
> Hoffman, a critic who has discussed the story:
> the killer hears the sound of his *own* heart
> (227).

■ **Acknowledge your source when you paraphrase a writer's words.**
To paraphrase a critic, you should do more than just rearrange his or her
words: you should translate them into your own original sentences—again,
always being sure to credit the original source. As an example, suppose you
wish to refer to an insight of Randall Jarrell, who commented as follows on
the images of spider, flower, and moth in Robert Frost's poem "Design":

> RANDALL JARRELL'S ORIGINAL TEXT
>
> Notice how the *heal-all,* because of its name, is the one flower in
> all the world picked to be the altar for this Devil's Mass; notice
> how *holding up* the moth brings something ritual and hieratic, a
> ghostly, ghastly formality, to this priest and its sacrificial victim.[1]

It would be too close to the original to write, without quotation marks,
these sentences:

> PLAGIARISTIC REWORDING
>
> Frost picks the heal-all as the one flower in
> all the world to be the altar for this Devil's
> Mass. There is a ghostly, ghastly formality to
> the spider holding up the moth, like a priest
> holding a sacrificial victim.

This rewording, although not exactly in Jarrell's language, manages to steal
his memorable phrases without giving him credit. Nor is it sufficient just to
include Jarrell's essay in the works cited list at the end of your paper. If you
do, you are still a crook; you merely point to the scene of the crime. Instead,
think through Jarrell's words to the point he is making, so that it can be restated in your own original way. If you want to keep any of his striking phrases
(and why not?), put them exactly as he wrote them in quotations marks:

---

[1]*Poetry and the Age* (New York: Knopf, 1953) 42.

APPROPRIATE PARAPHRASE, ACKNOWLEDGES SOURCE

```
As Randall Jarrell points out, Frost portrays
the spider as a kind of priest in a Mass, or
Black Mass, elevating the moth like an object
for sacrifice, with "a ghostly, ghastly
formality" (42).
```

Note also that this improved passage gives Jarrell the credit not just for his words but for his insight into the poem. Both the idea and the words in which it was originally expressed are the properties of their originator. Finally, notice the page reference that follows the quotation (this system of documenting your sources is detailed in the next section).

Documenting Sources Using MLA Style

You must document everything you take from another source. When you quote from other writers, when you borrow their information, when you summarize or paraphrase their ideas, make sure you give them proper credit. Identify the writer by name and cite the book, magazine, newspaper, pamphlet, Web site, or other source you have used.

The conventions that govern the proper way to document sources are available in the *MLA Handbook for Writers of Research Papers*, 6th ed. (New York: Mod. Lang. Assn., 2003). (Because these conventions grow and change, be sure to use either the most recent edition, or a writer's handbook that reflects the sixth edition of the *MLA Handbook*.) The following brief list of pointers is not meant to take the place of the *MLA Handbook* itself, but to give you a quick sense of the rules for documentation.

List of Sources

Keep a working list of your research sources—all the references from which you might quote, summarize, paraphrase, or take information. When your paper is in finished form, it will end with a neat copy of the works you actually used (once called a "Bibliography," now entitled "Works Cited").

Parenthetical References

In the body of your paper, every time you refer to a source, you only need to provide information to help a reader locate it in your works cited list. You can usually give just the author's name and a page citation in parentheses. For example, if you are writing a paper on Weldon Kees's sonnet "For My Daughter" and want to include an observation you found on page 136 of Samuel Maio's book *Creating Another Self*, write:

```
One critic has observed that the distinctive
tone of "For My Daughter" depends on Kees's
combination of personal subject matter with an
impersonal voice (Maio 136).
```

If you mention the author's name in your sentence, you need give only the page number in your reference:

```
As Samuel Maio has observed, Kees creates a
distinctive tone in this sonnet by combining a
personal subject with an impersonal voice (136).
```

If you have two books or magazine articles by Samuel Maio in your works cited list, how will the reader tell them apart? In your text, refer to the title of each book or article by condensing it into a word or two. Condensed book titles also are underlined or italicized, and condensed article titles are still placed within quotation marks.

```
One critic has observed that the distinctive
tone of "For My Daughter" depends on Kees's
combination of personal subject matter with an
impersonal voice (Maio, Creating 136).
```

Works Cited List

Provide a full citation for each source on your works cited page. At the end of your paper, in your list of works cited, your reader will find a full description of your source—in the above examples, a critical book:

```
Maio, Samuel. Creating Another Self: Voices in
Modern American Personal Poetry. 2nd ed.
Kirksville, MO: Thomas Jefferson UP, 2005.
```

Put your works cited list in proper form. The *MLA Handbook* provides detailed instructions for citing a myriad of different types of sources, from books to online databases. Here is a partial checklist of the *Handbook*'s recommendations for presenting your works cited list.

1. Start a new page for the works cited list, and continue the page numbering from the body of your paper.
2. Center the title, "Works Cited," one inch from the top of the page.

3. Double-space between all lines (including after title and between entries).
4. Type each entry beginning at the left-hand margin. If an entry runs longer than a single line, indent the following lines one-half inch (or five full spaces) from the left-hand margin.
5. Alphabetize each entry according to the author's last name.
6. Include three sections in each entry: author, title, publication or access information. (You will, however, give slightly different information for a book, journal article, online source, or other reference.)

Citing Print Sources in MLA Style

For a book citation

a. **Author's full name** as it appears on the title page, last name first, followed by a period.
b. **Book's full title** (and subtitle, if it has one, separated by a colon) followed by a period. Remember to underline or italicize the title.
c. **Publication information:** city of publication followed by a colon, the name of the publisher followed by a comma, and the year of publication followed by a period.

   (1) **Make your citation of the city of publication brief, but clear.** If the title page lists more than one city, cite only the first. For U.S. cities, you need not provide the state unless the name of the city alone may be confusing or is unfamiliar. For cities outside the United States, add a country abbreviation if the city is unfamiliar. For Canadian cities, use the province abbreviation. (Examples: Rome, GA; Leeds, Eng.; Victoria, BC)

   (2) **Shorten the publisher's name.** Eliminate articles (*A*, *An*, *The*), business abbreviations (*Co.*, *Corp.*, *Inc.*, *Ltd.*), and descriptive words (*Books*, *House*, *Press*, *Publishers*). The exception is a university press, for which you should use the letters *U* (for University) and *P* (for Press). Use only the first listed *surname* of the publisher.

Publisher's Name	Proper Citation
Harvard University Press	Harvard UP
University of Chicago Press	U of Chicago P
Farrar, Straus and Giroux, Inc.	Farrar
Alfred A. Knopf, Inc.	Knopf

The final citation for a book should read:

```
Author's last name, First name. Book Title.
     Publication city: Publisher, Year.
```

For a journal article citation

    a. **Author's name,** last name first, followed by a period.

    b. **Title of the article,** followed by a period, all within quotation marks.

    c. **Publication information:** journal title (underlined or italicized); volume number; year of publication in parentheses, followed by a colon; the inclusive page numbers of the entire article, followed by a period.

The final citation for a journal article should read:

```
Author's last name, First name. "Article
     Title." Journal Volume (Year): Pages.
```

If the journal starts the pagination of *each* issue from page one (in contrast to continuous numbering from the previous issue), then you must give both the volume and issue number, with a period between the two. For example, if the article you cite appears in volume 5, issue 2, of such a journal, cite it as 5.2.

```
Author's last name, First name. "Article Title."
     Journal Volume.Issue (Year): Pages.
```

Citing Internet Sources in MLA Style

Like print sources, Internet sources should be documented with care. Keep in mind, though, that documentation of Internet sources is a bit more complex. Before you begin your Internet search, be aware of the types of information you will want for your works cited list. You can then record the information as you go. Keep track of the following information:

- Author's name
- Title of document
- Full information about publication in print form
- Title of scholarly project, database, periodical, or professional or personal site
- Editor's name of project or database
- Date of electronic publication or last update
- Institution or organization sponsoring the Web site
- Date *you* accessed the source
- Web site address or URL

Although many Web sites provide much of this information at the beginning ending of an article or at the bottom of the home page, you will find that it ˉ always available.

For an Internet citation

a. **Author's name,** last name first, followed by a period.

b. **Title of document,** followed by a period, all within quotation marks.

c. **Print publication information,** if available: title of periodical or book underlined or italicized, volume number and date of publication followed by a period (if page numbers are given, insert a colon followed by the page numbers).

d. **Electronic publication information:** title of the Web site, underlined or italicized, followed by a period; editor's name or version number if provided, followed by a period; date of electronic publication or latest update, followed by a period; name of any organization or institution sponsoring the site, followed by a period.

e. **Access information:** date that you viewed the document online, followed by the URL (uniform resource locator) enclosed in angle brackets.

(1) If the URL is very long and complicated, give the URL for the site's search page. If no specific URL was assigned to the document, give the URL for the site's home page.

(2) If you accessed a document that does not show a specific URL through a series of links from a Web site's home page, insert the word *Path* followed by a colon after the angle bracket enclosing the URL, and give the title of each link, separating each with a semicolon.

In many cases, not all this information is available for an Internet source. However, when available, the final citation for a document obtained on the Web should read:

```
Author's Last Name, First Name. "Document
    Title." Print Periodical Title Volume
    (Date of Print Publication): Page Numbers.
    Title of Internet Site. Site Editor. Date
    of Electronic Publication. Web Site
    Sponsor. Your Access Date <URL>.
```

Sample Works Cited List

For a paper on Weldon Kees's "For My Daughter," a student's works cited list might look as follows:

Works Cited

Grosholz, Emily. "The Poetry of Memory." Weldon
    Kees: A Critical Introduction. Ed. Jim
    Elledge. Metuchen, NJ: Scarecrow, 1985.
    46-47.

Kees, Weldon. The Collected Poems of Weldon
    Kees. Ed. Donald Justice. Lincoln: U of
    Nebraska P, 1975.

Lane, Anthony. "The Disappearing Poet: What
    Ever Happened to Weldon Kees?" New Yorker
    4 July 2005. 22 Aug. 2006 <http://www
    .newyorker.com/critics/atlarge/articles/
    050704crat_atlarge>.

Maio, Samuel. Creating Another Self: Voice in
    Modern American Personal Poetry. 2nd ed.
    Kirksville, MO: Thomas Jefferson UP, 2005.

Reidel, James. Vanished Act: The Life and Art
    of Weldon Kees. Lincoln: U of Nebraska P,
    2003.

Ross, William T. Weldon Kees. Twayne's US
    Authors Ser. 484. Boston: Twayne, 1985.

Weldon Kees. Ed. James Reidel. 2003. Nebraska
    Center for Writers, Creighton University.
    26 Aug. 2006 <http://mockingbird.creighton
    .edu/NCW/kees.htm>.

"Weldon Kees." Poets.org. 2006. Academy of
    American Poets. 20 Sept. 2006 <http://www
    .poets.org/poet.php/prmPID/727>.

See the Reference Guide for Citations at the end of this chapter for additional examples of the types of citations that you are likely to need for your essays or check the sixth edition of the *MLA Handbook*.

Concluding Thoughts

A well-crafted research essay is a wondrous thing—as delightful, in its own way, as a well-crafted poem or short story or play. Good essays prompt thought and add to knowledge. Writing a research paper sharpens your own mind and exposes you to the honed insights of other thinkers. Think of anything you write as a piece that could be published for the benefit of other people interested in your topic. After all, such a goal is not as far-fetched as it seems: this textbook, for example, features a number of papers written by students. Why shouldn't yours number among them? Aim high.

Reference Guide for Citations

Here is a comprehensive summary of the types of citations you are likely to need for most student papers. The format follows the current MLA standards for works cited lists.

Print Publications

Books

No Author Listed

A Keepsake Anthology of the Fiftieth Anniversary
    Celebration of the Consultantship in Poetry.
    Washington: Library of Congress, 1987.

One Author

Middlebrook, Diane Wood. Anne Sexton: A Biography.
    Boston: Houghton, 1991.

Two or Three Authors

Jarman, Mark, and Robert McDowell. The Reaper: Essays.
    Brownsville, OR: Story Line, 1996.

Four or More Authors

Phillips, Rodney, et al. The Hand of the Poet. New York:
    Rizzoli, 1997.

or

Phillips, Rodney, Susan Benesch, Kenneth Benson, and
    Barbara Bergeron. The Hand of the Poet. New York:
    Rizzoli, 1997.

Two Books by Same Author

Bawer, Bruce. The Aspect of Eternity. St. Paul: Graywolf,
    1993.
---. Diminishing Fictions: Essays on the Modern American
    Novel and Its Critics. St. Paul: Graywolf, 1988.

Corporate Author

Poets and Writers. A Writer's Guide to Copyright. New
    York: Poets and Writers, 1979.

Author and Editor

Shakespeare, William. The Sonnets. Ed. G. Blakemore
    Evans. Cambridge, Eng.: Cambridge UP, 1996.

One Editor

Monteiro, George, ed. Conversations with Elizabeth
    Bishop. Jackson: UP of Mississippi, 1996.

Two Editors

Craig, David, and Janet McCann, eds. Odd Angles of Heaven:
    Contemporary Poetry by People of Faith. Wheaton, IL:
    Shaw, 1994.

Translation

Dante Alighieri. Inferno: A New Verse Translation. Trans.
    Michael Palma. New York: Norton, 2002.

Introduction, Preface, Foreword, or Afterword

Thwaite, Anthony, Preface. Contemporary Poets. Ed. Thomas
    Riggs. 6th ed. New York: St. James, 1996. vii-viii.
Lapham, Lewis. Introduction. Understanding Media: The
    Extensions of Man. By Marshall McLuhan. Cambridge:
    MIT P, 1994. vi-x.

Work in an Anthology

Allen, Dick. "The Emperor's New Clothes." Poetry After
    Modernism. Ed. Robert McDowell. Brownsville, OR:
    Story Line, 1991. 71-99.

Translation in an Anthology

Neruda, Pablo. "We Are Many." Trans. Alastair Reid.
 Literature: An Introduction to Fiction, Poetry,
 Drama, and Writing. Ed. X. J. Kennedy and Dana
 Gioia. 5th Compact ed. New York: Longman, 2007. 673.

Multivolume Work

Wellek, René. A History of Modern Criticism, 1750-1950.
 8 vols. New Haven: Yale UP, 1955-92.

One Volume of a Multivolume Work

Wellek René. A History of Modern Criticism, 1750-1950.
 Vol. 7. New Haven: Yale UP, 1991.

Book in a Series

Ross, William T. Weldon Kees. Twayne's US Authors Ser.
 484. Boston: Twayne, 1985.

Republished Book

Ellison, Ralph. Invisible Man. 1952. New York: Vintage,
 1995.

Revised or Subsequent Editions

Janouch, Gustav. Conversations with Kafka. Trans. Goronwy
 Rees. Rev. ed. New York: New Directions, 1971.

Reference Books

Signed Article in Reference Book

Cavoto, Janice E. "Harper Lee's To Kill a Mockingbird." The
 Oxford Encyclopedia of American Literature. Ed. Jay
 Parini. Vol. 2. New York: Oxford UP, 2004. 418-21.

Unsigned Encyclopedia Article—Standard Reference Book

"James Dickey." The New Encyclopaedia Britannica:
 Micropaedia. 15th ed. 1987.

Dictionary Entry

"Design." Merriam-Webster's Collegiate Dictionary. 11th ed.
 2003.

Periodicals

Journal with Continuous Paging

Balée, Susan. "Flannery O'Connor Resurrected." Hudson
Review 47 (1994): 377-93.

Journal That Pages Each Issue Separately

Salter, Mary Jo. "The Heart Is Slow to Learn." New
Criterion 10.8 (1992): 23-29.

Signed Magazine Article

Gioia, Dana. "Studying with Miss Bishop." New Yorker 5
Sept. 1986: 90-101.

Unsigned Magazine Article

"The Real Test." New Republic 5 Feb. 2001: 7.

Newspaper Article

Lyall, Sarah. "In Poetry, Ted Hughes Breaks His Silence
on Sylvia Plath." New York Times 19 Jan. 1998, natl.
ed.: A1+.

Signed Book Review

Harper, John. "Well-Crafted Tales with Tabloid Titles."
Rev. of Tabloid Dreams, by Robert Olen Butler.
Orlando Sentinel 15 Dec. 1996: D4.

Unsigned, Untitled Book Review

Rev. of Otherwise: New and Selected Poems, by Jane
Kenyon. Virginia Quarterly Review 72 (1996): 136.

Electronic Publications

Online Resources

Web Site

Voice of the Shuttle. Ed. Alan Liu. 2003. U of
California, Santa Barbara. 17 Oct. 2003
<http://vos.ucsb.edu/>.

Document on a Web Site

"Wallace Stevens." <u>Poets.org</u>. 31 Jan. 2006. The Academy
    of American Poets. 20 Sept. 2006 <http://www.poets
    .org/poet.php/prmPID/124>.

Document on a Web Site: Citing a Path

"Wallace Stevens." <u>Poets.org</u>. 31 Jan. 2006. The Academy
    of American Poets. 20 Sept. 2006 <http://www.poets
    .org>. Path: Search for a Poet; S; Stevens, Wallace.

Document on a Web Site: Citing a Search Page

"A Hughes Timeline." <u>PBS Online</u>. 2001. Public Broadcasting
    Service. 20 Sept. 2003 <http://www.pbs.org/search>.

An Entire Online Book

Jewett, Sarah Orne. <u>The Country of the Pointed Firs</u>.
    Boston: Houghton, 1910. <u>Bartleby.com: Great Books
    Online</u>. Ed. Steven van Leeuwen. 1999. 10 Oct. 2003
    <http://www.bartleby.com/125/>.

Online Reference Database

<u>Encyclopaedia Britannica Online</u>. 2002. Encyclopaedia
    Britannica. 15 Feb. 2003 <http://www.britannica.com/>.

Article in Online Scholarly Journal

Hoffman, Tyler B. "Emily Dickinson and the Limit of War."
    <u>Emily Dickinson Journal</u> 3.2 (1994). 15 Mar. 2004
    <http://www.colorado.edu/EDIS/journal/articles/
    III.2.Hoffman.html>.

Article from a Scholarly Journal, Part of an Archival Database

Oates, Joyce Carol. "'Soul at the White Heat': The
    Romance of Emily Dickinson's Poetry." <u>Critical
    Inquiry</u> 13.4 (1987). <u>Literary Criticism on the Web</u>.
    Ed. Randy Souther. 7 July 2003
    <http://start.at/literarycriticism>. Path: D;
    Dickinson; Joyce Carol Oates on Emily Dickinson;
    "Soul at the White Heat."

Article in Online Newspaper

Atwood, Margaret. "The Writer: A New Canadian Life-Form."
  New York Times on the Web 18 May 1997. 20 Aug. 2006
  <http://www.nytimes.com/books/97/05/18/bookend/
  bookend.html>.

Article in Online Magazine

Garner, Dwight. "The Salon Interview: Jamaica Kincaid."
  Salon 13 Jan. 1996. 15 Feb. 2006 <http://www
  .salonmagazine.com/05/features/kincaid.html>.

Article Accessed via a Library Subscription Service

Seitler, Dana. "Unnatural Selection: Mothers, Eugenic
  Feminism, and Charlotte Perkins Gilman's Regeneration
  Narratives." American Quarterly 55.1 (2003): 61-87.
  ProQuest. Arcadia U Landman Lib., Glenside, PA. 7
  July 2003 <http://www.il.proquest.com/proquest/>.

Painting or Photograph Accessed Online

Bruegel, Pieter. Landscape with the Fall of Icarus. 1558.
  Musees Royaux des Beaux-Arts de Belgique, Brussels.
  ibiblio. Center for the Public Domain and UNC-CH.
  16 Apr. 2006 <http://www.ibiblio.org/wm/paint/auth/
  bruegel>.

Online Posting

Grossenbacher, Laura. "Comments about the Ending
  Illustration." Online Posting. 4 Sept. 1996. The
  Yellow Wallpaper Site. 14 Mar. 2001
  <http://www.cwrl.utexas.edu/~daniel/amlit/
  wallpaper/readcomments.html>.

CD-ROM Reference Works

CD-ROM Publication

"Appall." The Oxford English Dictionary. 2nd ed. CD-ROM.
  Oxford: Oxford UP, 1992.

Periodically Published Information, Collected on CD-ROM

Kakutani, Michiko. "Slogging Surreally in the Vietnamese
   Jungle." Rev. of <u>The Things They Carried</u>, by Tim
   O'Brien. <u>New York Times Ondisc</u>. CD-ROM. UMI-
   ProQuest. Oct. 1993.

Miscellaneous Sources

Compact Disc (CD)

Shakespeare, William. <u>The Complete Arkangel Shakespeare:
   38 Fully-Dramatized Plays</u>. Narr. Eileen Atkins and
   John Gielgud. Read by Imogen Stubbs, Joseph Fiennes,
   et al. Audio Partners, 2003.

Audiocassette

Roethke, Theodore. <u>Theodore Roethke Reads His Poetry</u>.
   Audiocassette. Caedmon, 1972.

Videocassette

<u>Henry V</u>. By William Shakespeare. Dir. Laurence Olivier.
   Perf. Laurence Olivier. Two Cities Films. 1944.
   Videocassette. Paramount, 1988.

DVD

<u>Hamlet</u>. By William Shakespeare. Perf. Laurence Olivier,
   Eileen Herlie, and Basil Sydney. Two Cities Films.
   1948. DVD. Criterion, 2000.

Film

<u>Hamlet</u>. By William Shakespeare. Dir. Franco Zeffirelli.
   Perf. Mel Gibson, Glenn Close, Helena Bonham Carter,
   Alan Bates, and Paul Scofield. Warner, 1991.

Television or Radio Program

<u>Moby Dick</u>. By Herman Melville. Dir. Franc Roddam. Perf.
   Patrick Stewart and Gregory Peck. 2 episodes. USA
   Network. 16-17 Mar. 1998.

Acknowledgments

Literary Acknowledgments

Fiction

Chinua Achebe: "Dead Men's Path" from *Girls at War and Other Stories* by Chinua Achebe, copyright © 1972, 1973 by Chinua Achebe. Used by permission of Doubleday, a division of Random House, Inc. and The Emma Sweeney Agency.

Margaret Atwood: "Happy Endings" from *Good Bones and Simple Murders* by Margaret Atwood. Copyright © 1983, 1992, 1994 by O. W. Toad Ltd. A Nan A. Talese Book. Used by permission of Doubleday, a division of Random House, Inc. and McClelland & Stewart Ltd.

Bidpai: "The Camel and His Friends" by Bidpai, retold in English by Arundhati Khanwalkar, from *The Panchatantra*. (The Association of Grandparents of Indian Immigrants.)

T. Coraghessan Boyle: "Greasy Lake" from *Greasy Lake and Other Stories* by T. Coraghessan Boyle. Copyright © 1979, 1981, 1982, 1983, 1984, 1985 by T. Coraghessan Boyle. Used by permission of Viking Penguin, a division of Penguin Group (USA) Inc.

Raymond Carver: "Cathedral" from *Cathedral* by Raymond Carver, copyright © 1981, 1982, 1983 by Raymond Carver. Used by permission of Alfred A. Knopf, a division of Random House, Inc.

Sandra Cisneros: "The House on Mango Street" from *The House On Mango Street*. Copyright © 1984 by Sandra Cisneros. Published by Vintage Books, a division of Random House, Inc., and in hardcover by Alfred A. Knopf in 1994. Reprinted by permission of Susan Bergholz Literary Services, New York. All rights reserved.

William Faulkner: "Barn Burning" copyright 1950 by Random House, Inc. Copyright renewed 1977 by Jill Faulkner Summers. "A Rose for Emily" copyright 1930 and renewed 1958 by William Faulkner. Both stories reprinted from *Collected Stories of William Faulkner* by William Faulkner. Used by permission of Random House, Inc.

Ernest Hemingway: "A Clean, Well-Lighted Place" reprinted with permission of Scribner, an imprint of Simon & Schuster Adult Publishing Group, from *The Short Stories of Ernest Hemingway*. Copyright 1933 by Charles Scribner's Sons. Copyright renewed © 1961 by Mary Hemingway.

Zora Neale Hurston: "Sweat" from *Spunk: Selected Short Stories of Zora Neale Hurston*. Copyright © 1985 by Turtle Island Foundation. Reprinted by permission of the author's estate.

Shirley Jackson: "The Lottery" from *The Lottery and Other Stories* by Shirley Jackson. Copyright 1948, 1949 by Shirley Jackson. Renewal copyright 1976, 1977 by Laurence Hyman, Barry Hyman, Mrs. Sarah Webster, and Mrs. Joanne Schnurer. Reprinted by permission of Farrar, Straus & Giroux, LLC.

Ha Jin: "Saboteur" from *The Bridegroom* by Ha Jin, copyright © 2000 by Ha Jin. Used by permission of Pantheon Books, a division of Random House, Inc.

Franz Kafka: "Before the Law" translated by John Siscoe. Reprinted by permission of the translator.

Jamaica Kincaid: "Girl" from *At the Bottom of the River* by Jamaica Kincaid. Copyright © 1978, 1983, by Jamaica Kincaid. Reprinted by permission of Farrar, Straus & Giroux, LLC.

Katherine Mansfield: "Miss Brill" from *The Short Stories of Katherine Mansfield* by Katherine Mansfield, copyright 1923 by Alfred A. Knopf, a division of Random House, Inc. and renewed 1951 by John Middleton Murry. Used by permission of Alfred A. Knopf, a division of Random House, Inc.

W. Somerset Maugham: "The Appointment in Samarra" from *Sheppey* by W. Somerset Maugham, copyright 1933 by W. Somerset Maugham. Used by permission of Doubleday, a division of Random House, Inc. and

Poetry

Used by permission of Doubleday, a division of Random House. "I Go" from *The Essential Haiku: Versions of Basho, Buson & Issa, edited and with an Introduction* by Robert Hass. Introduction and selection copyright © 1994 by Robert Hass. Unless otherwise noted, all translations copyright © 1994 by Robert Hass. Reprinted by permission of HarperCollins Publishers, Inc.

Judith Ortiz Cofer: "Quinceañera" is reprinted with permission from the publisher of *Terms of Survival* by Judith O. Cofer (Houston: Arte Publico Press-University of Houston, 1987).

William Cole: "On my boat on Lake Cayuga" reprinted by permission.

Billy Collins: "Care and Feeding" first appeared in *Five Points*, March 2003. Reprinted by permission of the author.

Wendy Cope: "Lonely Hearts" from *Making Cocoa for Kingsley Amis*. © Wendy Cope 1986. Reprinted by permission of Faber and Faber Ltd.

Robert Creeley: "Oh No" from *The Collected Poems of Robert Creeley, 1945–1975*. Copyright © 1983 by The Regents of the University of California. Reprinted by permission of the University of California Press.

Countee Cullen: "For a Lady I Know" reprinted from *Color* by Countee Cullen. Copyright 1925 by Harper & Brothers; copyright renewed 1953 by Ida M. Cullen. Reprinted by permission of Thompson & Thompson.

E. E. Cummings: "in Just-". Copyright 1923, 1951, © 1991 by the Trustees for the E. E. Cummings Trust. Copyright © 1976 by George James Firmage, "Buffalo Bill 's". Copyright 1923, 1951, © 1991 by the Trustees for the E. E. Cummings Trust. Copyright © 1976 by George James Firmage, "anyone lived in a pretty how town". Copyright 1940, © 1968, 1991 by the Trustees for the E. E. Cummings Trust, "somewhere i have never travelled,gladly beyond". Copyright 1931, © 1959, 1991 by the Trustees for the E. E. Cummings Trust. Copyright © 1979 by George James Firmage, "next to of course god america i". Copyright 1926, 1954, © 1991 by the Trustees for the E. E. Cummings Trust. Copyright © 1985 by George James Firmage, from *Complete Poems: 1904–1962* by E. E. Cummings, edited by George J. Firmage. Used by permission of Liveright Publishing Corporation.

J. V. Cunningham: "Friend, on this scaffold Thomas More lies dead . . ." from *Poems of J. V. Cunningham* (Swallow Press/Ohio University Press, Athens, 1997). Reprinted with the permission of Swallow Press/Ohio University Press, Athens, Ohio.

Maria de los Santos: "Perfect Dress" from *From the Bones Out*. Reprinted by permission of the author.

Emily Dickinson: "I like to see it lap the Miles," "A Route of Evanescence," "My Life had stood – a Loaded Gun," "The Lightning is a yellow fork," "I'm Nobody! Who are you?," "I heard a Fly buzz – when I died," "Because I could not stop for Death" reprinted by permission of the publishers and the Trustees of Amherst College from *The Poems of Emily Dickinson*, Thomas H. Johnson, ed., Cambridge, Mass.: The Belknap Press of Harvard University Press, Copyright © 1951, 1955, 1979, 1983 by the President and Fellows of Harvard College.

Rita Dove: "Silos" from *Grace Notes* by Rita Dove. Copyright © 1989 by Rita Dove. Used by permission of the author and W. W. Norton & Company, Inc.

Richard Eberhart: "The Fury of Aerial Bombardment" from *Collected Poems 1930–1976* by Richard Eberhart. Copyright © 1976 by Richard Eberhart. Used by permission of Oxford University Press, Inc.

T. S. Eliot: "Virginia" from *Collected Poems 1909–1962* by T. S. Eliot, copyright 1936 by Harcourt, Inc., copyright © 1964, 1963 by T. S. Eliot, reprinted by permission of Harcourt, Inc. and Faber and Faber Ltd. "The Love Song of J. Alfred Prufrock" from *Prufrock and Other Observations*. Reprinted by permission of Faber and Faber Ltd.

Rhina P. Espaillat: "Bilingual / Bilingüe" from *Where Horizons Go* by Rhina P. Espaillat, published by Truman State University Press. Copyright © 1998. Reprinted by permission of the author.

Robert Frost: "The Silken Tent," "The Secret Sits," "Fire and Ice," "Design," "Stopping by Woods on a Snowy Evening" from *The Poetry of Robert Frost*, edited by Edward Connery Lathem. © 1964, 1970 by Leslie Frost Ballantine, copyright 1936, 1942, 1956 by Robert Frost, copyright 1928, 1969 by Henry Holt and Company. Reprinted by permission of Henry Holt and Company, LLC.

Shirley Geok-lin Lim: "Learning to love America" from *What the Fortune Teller Didn't*

Say. Copyright © 1998 by Shirley Geok-lin Lim. Reprinted with the permission of West End Press, Albuquerque, NM.

Allen Ginsberg: "A Supermarket in California" from *Collected Poems 1947–1980* by Allen Ginsberg. Copyright © 1955 by Allen Ginsberg. Reprinted by permission of HarperCollins Publishers, Inc.

Dana Gioia: "Money" copyright © 1991 by Dana Gioia. Reprinted from *The Gods of Winter* with the permission of Graywolf Press, Saint Paul, MN.

Robert Graves: "Down, Wanton, Down!" and "Counting the Beats" from *Complete Poems in One* by Robert Graves. Excerpt from *The Crowning Privilege* by Robert Graves copyright © 1955 by Robert Graves, renewed. Reprinted by permission of Carcanet Press Limited.

Lee Gurga: "Visitor's Room" from *Fresh Scent*, edited by Randy M. Brooks. Reprinted by permission of the author and the publisher, Brooks Books.

R. S. Gwynn: "Shakespearean Sonnet" copyright © 2002 by R. S. Gwynn. Reprinted by permission of the author.

Robert Hayden: "Those Winter Sundays" Copyright © 1966 by Robert Hayden from *Collected Poems of Robert Hayden* by Robert Hayden, edited by Frederick Glaysher. Used by permission of Liveright Publishing Company.

Seamus Heaney: "Digging" from *Opened Ground: Selected Poems 1966–1996* by Seamus Heaney. Copyright © 1998 by Seamus Heaney. Reprinted by permission of Farrar, Straus & Giroux, LLC and Faber and Faber Ltd.

Langston Hughes "Theme for English B", copyright © 1994 by The Estate of Langston Hughes, "Harlem (2)", copyright 1951 by Langston Hughes, "The Negro Speaks of Rivers", copyright © 1994 by The Estate of Langston Hughes, "I, Too" from *The Collected Poems of Langston Hughes* by Langston Hughes, edited by Arnold Rampersad with David Roessel, Associate Editor, copyright © 1994 by The Estate of Langston Hughes. Used by permission of Alfred A. Knopf, a division of Random House, Inc.

Ted Hughes: "Hawk Roosting" from *Lupercal* by Ted Hughes, 1960. Reprinted by permission of the publisher, Faber and Faber Ltd.

Kobayashi Issa: "only one guy" translated by Cid Corman from *One Man's Moon: Fifty Haiku* (Gnomon Press, 1984). Reprinted by permission of the publisher and the author. "Cricket" translated by Robert Bly reprinted from *Ten Poems by Issa, English Versions* by Robert Bly, Floating Island, 1992. Copyright © 1972, 1992 by Robert Bly. Reprinted with permission.

Randall Jarrell: "The Death of the Ball Turret Gunner" from *The Complete Poems* by Randall Jarrell. Copyright © 1969 by Mrs. Randall Jarrell. Reprinted by permission of Farrar, Straus & Giroux, LLC.

Robinson Jeffers: "To the Stone-cutters" copyright 1924 & renewed 1952 by Robinson Jeffers from *Selected Poetry of Robinson Jeffers* by Robinson Jeffers. Used by permission of Random House, Inc.

Donald Justice: "On the Death of Friends in Childhood" from *New and Selected Poems* by Donald Justice, copyright © 1995 by Donald Justice. Used by permission of Alfred A. Knopf, a division of Random House, Inc.

Weldon Kees: "For My Daughter" reprinted from *The Collected Poems of Weldon Kees*, edited by Donald Justice, by permission of the University of Nebraska Press. Copyright 1962, 1975, by the University of Nebraska Press.

Jane Kenyon: "The Suitor" from *From Room to Room.* © 1978 by Jane Kenyon. Reprinted courtesy of Alice James Books, 33 Richdale Avenue, Cambridge, MA 02138.

Suji Kwock Kim: "Monologue for an Onion" from *Notes from the Divided Country: Poems* by Suji Kwock Kim. Copyright © 2003 by Suji Kwock Kim. Reprinted by permission of Louisiana State University Press.

Etheridge Knight: "Making jazz swing in" is from *The Essential Etheridge Knight*, by Etheridge Knight, © 1986. Reprinted by permission of the University of Pittsburgh Press.

Yusef Komunyakaa: "Facing It" from *Dien Kai Dau*, in *Pleasure Dome: New and Collected Poems.* © 2001 by Yusef Komunyakaa. Reprinted by permission of Wesleyan University Press.

Ted Kooser: "Carrie" and "Abandoned Farmhouse" are from *Sure Signs: New and Selected Poems*, by Ted Kooser. © 1980 by Ted Kooser. Reprinted by permission of the University of Pittsburgh Press.

Philip Larkin: "Home is so Sad" from *Collected Poems* by Philp Larkin. Copyright © 1988, 2003 by the Estate of Philip Larkin.

Birmingham" from *Cities Burning*, reprinted by permission of the author.

Henry Reed: "Naming of Parts" from *A Map of Verona* by Henry Reed. © 1946 The executor of the Estate of Henry Reed. Reprinted by permission of John Tydeman.

Adrienne Rich: "Aunt Jennifer's Tigers" copyright © 2002, 1951 by Adrienne Rich, "Living in Sin" copyright © 2002, 1955 by Adrienne Rich, from *The Fact of a Doorframe: Selected Poems 1950–2001* by Adrienne Rich. Both used by permission of the author and W. W. Norton & Company, Inc.

John Ridland: "The Lazy Man's Haiku" reprinted by permission of the author.

Theodore Roethke: "My Papa's Waltz" copyright 1942 by Hearst Magazines, Inc., "Root Cellar" copyright 1943 by Modern Poetry Association, Inc. From *The Collected Poems of Theodore Roethke* by Theodore Roethke. Used by permission of Doubleday, a division of Random House, Inc.

Kay Ryan: "Blandeur" from *Say Uncle* by Kay Ryan. Copyright © 2000 by Kay Ryan. (Grove/Atlantic).

Benjamin Alire Saenz: "To the Desert" from *Dark and Perfect Angels* by Benjamin Alire Saenz, 1995. Used by permission of the publisher, Cinco Puntos Press.

Carole Satyamurti: "I Shall Paint My Nails Red" from *Stitching in the Dark: New and Selected Poems* © 2005 by Carole Satyamurti. Reprinted by permission of Bloodaxe Books Ltd.

Anne Sexton: "Her Kind" from *To Bedlam and Part Way Back* by Anne Sexton. Copyright © 1960 by Anne Sexton © renewed 1988 by Linda G. Sexton. Reprinted by permission of Houghton Mifflin Company. All rights reserved.

Charles Simic: "The Magic Study of Happiness" reprinted by permission of the author.

David R. Slavitt: "Titanic" Reprinted by permission of Louisiana State University Press from *Big Nose: Poems* by David R. Slavitt. Copyright © 1983 by David R. Slavitt.

Stevie Smith: "Not Waving But Drowning" by Stevie Smith from *Collected Poems of Stevie Smith*, copyright © 1972 by Stevie Smith. Reprinted by permission of New Directions Publishing Corp.

William Stafford: "Ask Me" copyright © 1962, 1988 by the Estate of William Stafford. Reprinted from *The Way It Is: New & Selected Poems* with the permission of Graywolf Press, Saint Paul, Minnesota.

A. E. Stallings: "Sine Qua Non" first appeared in *Poetry*, October-November 2002. Copyright © 2002 by The Poetry Foundation. Reprinted from *Hapax* by A. E. Stallings (*TriQuarterly*, 2006).

Timothy Steele: "Epitaph" from *Uncertainties and Rest* by Timothy Steele. Copyright © 1979. Reprinted by permission of the author.

Anne Stevenson: "The Victory" from *Poems 1955–2005*, Bloodaxe Books, 2005. Reprinted by permission of Bloodaxe Books.

Michael Stillman: "In Memoriam John Coltrane" from *Occident*, Fall, 1971. Copyright © 1976 by Michael Stillman. Reprinted by permission of the author.

Larissa Szporluk: "Vertigo" reprinted from *Isolato* by permission of the University of Iowa Press.

Dylan Thomas: "Fern Hill" by Dylan Thomas copyright © 1945 by The Trustees for the Copyrights of Dylan Thomas, and "Do Not Go Gentle Into That Good Night" copyright © 1952 by Dylan Thomas. Both from *The Poems of Dylan Thomas*. Reprinted by permission of New Directions Publishing Corp. and David Higham Associates.

Natasha Trethewey: "White Lies" copyright © 2000 by Natasha Trethewey. Reprinted from *Domestic Work* with the permission of Graywolf Press, Saint Paul, Minnesota.

John Updike: "Recital" from *Telephone Poles & Other Poems* by John Updike, coypright © 1959 by John Updike. "Ex-Basketball Player" from *Collected Poems 1953–1993* by John Updike, copyright © 1993 by John Updike. Used by permission of Alfred A. Knopf, a division of Random House, Inc.

Gina Valdés: "English con Salsa" first appeared in *The Americas Review* (Houston, TX 1993) and is reprinted by permission of the author.

Derek Walcott: "The Virgins" from *Sea Grapes* by Derek Walcott. Copyright © 1976 by Derek Walcott. Reprinted by permission of Farrar, Straus and Giroux, LLC.

Richard Wilbur: "The Writer" from *The Mind-Reader*, copyright © 1971 by Richard Wilbur. Reprinted by permission of Harcourt, Inc.

William Carlos Williams: "Spring and All, Section I," "The Red Wheelbarrow," and "This is Just to Say" by William Carlos Williams, from *Collected Poems 1909–1939*, Volume I, copyright © 1938 by New Directions Publishing Corp. All reprinted by permission of New Directions Publishing Corp.

James Wright: "Autumn Begins in Martins Ferry, Ohio" from *The Branch Will Not*

Break. Copyright © 1963 by James Wright. Reprinted by pemission of Wesleyan University Press.

W. B. Yeats: "Sailing to Byzantium" Copyright © 1928 by The Macmillan Company; copyright renewed © 1956 by Georgie Yeats. Reprinted by permission of Scribner, an imprint of Simon & Schuster Adult Publishing Group from *The Collected Works of W. B. Yeats*, Volume I, The Poems, Revised, edited by Richard J. Finneran.

Bernice Zamora: "Penitents" from *Releasing Serpents.* Reprinted by permission of Bilingual Press/Editorial Bilingüe, Arizona State University, Tempe, AZ.

Drama

Henrik Ibsen: "A Doll's House" translated by R. Farquharson Sharp and Eleanor Marx-Aveling. Revised 2008 by Viktoria Michelsen. Copyright © 2008 by Viktoria Michelsen. Reprinted by permission.

David Ives: "Sure Thing" from *All In the Timing* by David Ives, copyright © 1989, 1990, 1992 by David Ives. Used by permission of Vintage Books, a division of Random House, Inc. Excerpt from "The Exploding Rose" by David Ives is reprinted by permission of the author.

Jane Martin: "Beauty." Professionals and amateurs are hereby warned that "Beauty" © 2001 by Alexander Speer, Trustee, is subject to royalty. It is fully protected under the copyright laws of the United States of America, the British Commonwealth, including Canada, and all other countries of the Copyright Union. All rights, including professional, amateur, motion pictures, recitation, lecturing, public reading, radio broadcasting, television, and the rights of translation into foreign languages are strictly reserved. No part of this work may be reproduced, stored in a retrieval system or transmitted in any form, by any means, now known or yet to be invented, including mechanical, electronic, photocopying, recording, videotaping or otherwise, without the prior written permission of the publisher. Particular emphasis is laid on the question of amateur or professional readings, permission and terms for which must be secured in writing from Alexander Speer, Trustee, P.O. Box 66, Goshen, KY 40026.

Arthur Miller: "Death of a Salesman" from *Death of a Salesman* by Arthur Miller. Copyright 1949, renewed © 1977 by Arthur Miller. Used by permission of Viking Penguin, a division of Penguin Group (USA) Inc.

Milcha Sanchez-Scott: "The Cuban Swimmer" copyright © 1984, 1988 by Milcha Sanchez-Scott. Reprinted by permission of William Morris Agency, LLC on behalf of the Author. CAUTION: Professionals and amateurs are hereby warned that "The Cuban Swimmer" is subject to a royalty. It is fully protected under the copyright laws of the United States of America and of all countries covered by the International Copyright Union (including the Dominion of Canada and the rest of the British Commonwealth), the Berne Convention, the Pan-American Copyright Convention and the Universal Copyright Convention as well as all countries with which the United States has reciprocal copyright relations. All rights, including professional/ amateur stage rights, motion picture, recitation, lecturing, public reading, radio broadcasting, television, video or sound recording, all other forms of mechanical or electronic reproduction, such as CD-ROM, CD-I, information storage and retrieval systems and photocopying, and the rights of translation into foreign languages, are strictly reserved. Particular emphasis is laid upon the matter of readings, permission for which must be secured from the Author's agent in writing. Inquiries concerning rights should be addressed to: William Morris Agency, Inc. 1325 Avenue of the Americas, New York, NY 10019, Attn: Eric Lupfer. Originally produced in New York City by INTAR Hispanic American Arts Center.

William Shakespeare: Notes to "Othello" from *The Complete Works of Shakespeare*, 4th edition, by David Bevington. Copyright © 1997 by Addison-Wesley Educational Publishers, Inc. Reprinted by permission of Pearson Education Inc.

Sophocles: "The Oedipus Rex of Sophocles: An English Version" by Dudley Fitts and Robert Fitzgerald, copyright 1949 by Harcourt Inc., and renewed 1977 by Cornelia Fitts and Robert Fitzgerald. Reprinted by permission of the publisher. CAUTION: All rights, including professional, amateur, motion picture, recitation, lecturing, performance, public reading, radio broadcasting, and television are strictly reserved. Inquiries on all rights should be addressed to Harcourt

Inc., Permissions Department, Orlando, FL 32887-6777.
Tennessee Williams: From "The Glass Menagerie" by Tennessee Williams, copyright 1945 by The University of the South. Reprinted by permission of Georges

Borchardt, Inc. for the Tennessee Williams Estate.
August Wilson: "Fences" by August Wilson, copyright © 1986 by August Wilson. Used by permission of Dutton Signet, a division of Penguin Group (USA) Inc.

Photo Acknowledgments

Fiction

1: Robert Capa, © 2001 by Cornell Capa/Magnum Photos, Inc.; 10: Brown Brothers; 16, 31, 39, 68, 119, 141: Bettmann/Corbis; 50: Courtesy Alfred A. Knopf, Inc.; 55: Scott, Foresman and Company; 81: Missouri Historical Society; 86, 96, 165: Nancy Crampton; 146, 265: Jerry Bauer; 160, 247, 280, 294, 298: AP/Wide World Photos; 176: Scott, Foresman and Company; 186: Courtesy Laurence Hyman; 194: The Granger Collection; 211: © Sophie Bassouls/CORBIS SYGMA; 217: Courtesy Peabody Essex Museum (image #14509); 231: © Corbis; 241: Berenice Abbott/Commerce Graphics Ltd., Inc.; 249: Sigrid Estrada; 251: © by Jill Krementz; all rights reserved.

Poetry

307: The Granger Collection; 495: Corbis; 496: Musees Royaux des Beaux-Arts de Belgique/Art Resource, NY; 498: Berg Collection of English and American Literature, New York Public Library; 503, 519: Library of Congress; 504: Luigi Ciufetelli; 505: Amherst College Archives and Special Collections; 507, 509, 537, 543, 559: Bettmann/Corbis; 513: Courtesy of Rhina Espaillat; 514: Brown Brothers; 524: Henri Cartier-Bresson/Magnum Photos, Inc.; 527: By courtesy of the National Portrait Gallery, London; 531: Fay Godwin/ Network Photographers/Corbis Saba; 538: Photo by Doug Anderson; 541: Thomas

Victor, courtesy Poets.org/University of Pennsylvania; 542: The Imperial War Museum, London; 547: Willie Williams; 551: Courtesy National Portrait Gallery, London; 553: Bowling Green State University; 556: Jeff Towns/DBC; 560: Gabriel Harrison/ Library of Congress; 562: Courtesy of New Directions; 564: The Royal Photographic Society.

Drama

567: Inge Morath/Magnum Photos, Inc.; 571: AP/Wide World Photos; 581: Echo Theatre, Dallas, TX; 595: Utah Shakespeare Festival; 601: The Granger Collection; 603: Courtesy Writers and Artists Agency; 604: Andrew Leynse/Primary Stages; 618, 621: Bettmann/Corbis; 623: John Vickers Theatre Collection; 669: Andrea Pistolesi/Getty Images; 670: Courtesy National Portrait Gallery, London; 671: Martha Swope; 672: Photofest; 679, 687, 704, 714, 718, 733, 735, 747, 750, 760, 763, 775, 779: © T. Charles Erickson; 795, 886, 969: Bettmann/Corbis; 797: The Harvard Theatre Collection, The Houghton Library; 861: Courtesy Milcha Sanchez-Scott; 864: Richard Devin; 887: Robbie Jack/Corbis; 970: Private Collection; 1026: Retna; 1028: Yale Repertory Theatre.

Writing

1089: The Berg Collection, New York Public Library; 1156: Musees Royaux des Beaux-Arts de Belgique/Art Resource, NY.

Index of Authors and Titles

Each page number immediately following a writer's name indicates a quotation from or reference to that writer. A number in **bold** refers you to the page on which you will find the author's biography. *n* following a page number indicates an entry in a note.

Index of
Literary Terms

Page numbers indicate discussion of term in anthology. *n* following a page number indicates entry in a note.